Loren Ray Sims
1218 E. Pershing #5
Decatur, Ill. 62526
217·250·2886

THE BIBLE EXPOSITION COMMENTARY

PROPHETS

THE BIBLE EXPOSITION COMMENTARY

PROPHETS

WARREN W.
WIERSBE

Run So That You May Win
ivictor.com

Victor is an imprint of
Cook Communications Ministries, Colorado Springs, Colorado 80918
Cook Communications, Paris, Ontario
Kingsway Communications, Eastbourne, England

THE BIBLE EXPOSITION COMMENTARY/PROPHETS

First printing 2002
Printed in the United States of America.

1 2 3 4 5 6 7 8 9 10 Printing/Year 06 05 04 03 02

Cover Design: Peter Speach Marketing Communications

Library of Congress Cataloging-in-Publication Data
Wiersbe, Warren W.
The Bible exposition commentary / Warren W. Wiersbe.
p. cm.
Contents: 1. The Prophets.
ISBN 0-78143-481-5
1. Bible--Commentaries.

BS491.3. W54 2001
220.7--dc21

00-043561

CONTENTS

FOREWORD

The Bible Exposition Commentary had a modest beginning in 1972 when Victor Books published my commentary on 1 John and called it *Be Real*. Nobody remembers who named the book, but for me it was the beginning of three decades of intensive Bible study as I wrote additional commentaries, all of them with *Be* in the title. It took twenty-three books to cover the New Testament, and they were published in two bound volumes in 1989. Then I started the Old Testament *Be* series, and *Be Obedient*, on the life of Abraham, was published in 1991. Over twenty books are now available in the Old Testament series and, the Lord willing, I hope to complete the Old Testament within a year.

This volume on the Prophets comprises seventeen separate books covering the Major and Minor Prophets, and we plan to issue two more volumes on the rest of the Old Testament: one on the historical books, and one on the wisdom and poetical books. *The Bible Exposition Commentary* will then be complete in six volumes, the joyful work of over thirty years. During this time I have written books for several publishers, but "doing the next *Be* book" was always at the top of the agenda.

Victor Books was purchased by Cook Communications Ministries in 1996 and the *Be* series began to carry the Chariot Victor and now the Cook imprint. I owe a great debt of gratitude to the editorial staff for their encouragement and cooperation these many years, including Mark Sweeney, Jim Adair, Lloyd Cory, Greg Clouse, and Craig Bubeck. These men have been faithful to "shepherd" me through book after book, and I appreciate the friendship and ministry of each more and more. Every author should be as fortunate as I've been to work with such dedicated, skillful people who always take a personal interest in their authors. To the best of my knowledge, during these years we've ministered together, we've never had a cross word or a serious misunderstanding.

I especially want to thank the Lord for His kindness and mercy in allowing me to minister in this way through the printed page. I can think of many of my friends who could have done a far better job than I in this series, bu the Lord graciously gave the privilege to me. He also gave me the widsom and strength to get each book written on time—and sometimes ahead of time—in the midst of a very busy life as a husband and father, a pastor, a radio Bible teacher, a seminary instructor, and a conference speaker.

This leads me to say that I couldn't have done it without the loving care of my wife, Betty. She manages our household affairs so well and takes such good care of me that I've always had the time needed for studying and writing. When I started this series, our four children were all at home. Now they're all married and my wife and I have eight wonderful grandchildren! Time flies when you're checking proofs!

The numerous readers of the *Be* series have been a great source of encouragement to me, even when they have written to disagree with me! I have received letters from many parts of the world, written by people in various walks of life, and they have gladdened my heart. Unless a writer hears from his readers, his writing becomes a one-way street, and he never knows if what he wrote did anybody any good. I want to thank the pastors, missionaries, Sunday school teachers, and other students of the Word who have been kind enough to write. We could compile a book of letters telling what God has done in the lives of people who have studied the *Be* series. To God be the glory!

As I close, there are some other people who ought to be thanked. Dr. Donald Burdick taught me New Testament at Northern Baptist Seminary and showed me how to study the Word of God. Dr. Lloyd Perry and the late Dr. Charles W. Koller both taught me how to "unlock" a Scripture passage and organize an exposition that was understandable and practical. I recommend their books on preaching to any preacher or teacher who wants to organize his or her material better.

For ten happy years, I was privileged to pastor the Calvary Baptist Church in Covington, Kentucky, just across the river from Cincinnati. One of my happy duties was writing Bible study notes for "The Whole Bible Study Course," which was developed by the late Dr. D.B. Eastep, who pastored the church for thirty-five fruitful years. No church I have ever visited or ministered to has a greater love for the Bible or a deeper hunger for spiritual truth than the dear people at Calvary Baptist. The *Be* series is, in many respects, a by-product of Dr. Eastep's kindness in sharing his ministry with me, and the church's love and encouragement while I was their pastor. I honor his memory and thank God for their continued friendship and prayer support.

To you who study God's Word with me, "I commend you to God, and to the word of his grace, which is able to build you up, and to give you an inheritance among all them who are sanctified" (Acts 20:32 KJV).

Warren W. Wiersbe

ISAIAH

OUTLINE

Key theme: The salvation (deliverance) of the Lord.

Key verse: Isaiah 1:18

I. CONDEMNATION. 1–39

1. Sermons against Judah and Israel. 1–12
2. Burdens of Judgment against the Gentiles. 13–23
3. Songs about Future Glory. 24–27
4. Woes of Coming Judgment from Assyria. 28–35
5. Historical Interlude. 36–39
   a. Hezekiah delivered from Assyria. 36–37
   b. Hezekiah deceived by Babylon. 37–38

II. CONSOLATION. 40–66

1. God's Greatness. 40–48 (The Father vs idols)
2. God's Grace. 49–57 (The Son, God's Servant)
3. God's Glory. 58–66 (The Spirit and the kingdom)

CONTENTS

CHAPTER ONE
INTRODUCTION TO ISAIAH
The Lord Is Salvation

Sir Winston Churchill was once asked to give the qualifications a person needed in order to succeed in politics, and he replied: "It is the ability to foretell what is going to happen tomorrow, next week, next month, and next year. And to have the ability afterwards to explain why it didn't happen."

Because God's prophets were correct all of the time, they didn't have to explain away their mistakes. "If what a prophet proclaims in the name of the Lord does not take place or come true," wrote Moses, "that is a message the Lord has not spoken" (Deut. 18:22, NIV). "To the law and to the testimony," wrote Isaiah, "If they speak not according to this word, it is because there is no light in them" (8:20). Isaiah was a man who had God's light, and he was not afraid to let it shine.

Before we examine the text of Isaiah's prophecy, let's get acquainted with the background of the book so that we can better understand the man and his times.

1. The Man

The name "Isaiah" means "salvation of the Lord," and salvation (deliverance) is the key theme of his book. He wrote concerning five different acts of deliverance that God would perform: 1) the deliverance of Judah from Assyrian invasion (chaps. 36–37); 2) the deliverance of the nation from Babylonian captivity (chap. 40); 3) the future deliverance of the Jews from worldwide dispersion among the Gentiles (chaps. 11–12); 4) the deliverance of lost sinners from judgment (chap. 53); and 5) the final deliverance of creation from the bondage of sin when the kingdom is established (chaps. 60; 66:17ff).

There were other Jewish men named Isaiah, so the prophet identified himself seven times as "the son of Amoz," not to be confused with "Amos" (see 1:1; 2:1; 13:1; 20:2; 37:2, 21; 38:1). Isaiah was married, and his wife was called "the prophetess" (8:3), either because she was married to a prophet or because she shared the prophetic gift. He fathered two sons whose names have prophetic significance: Shearjashub ("a remnant shall return," 7:3) and Maher-shalal-hash-baz ("quick to plunder, swift to the spoil," 8:1-4, 18). The two names speak of the nation's judgment and restoration, two important themes in Isaiah's prophecy.

Isaiah was called to his ministry "in the year that King Uzziah died" (6:1), which was 739 B.C. Isaiah ministered through the reigns of Jotham, Ahaz, and Hezekiah, who died in 686. Tradition says that Manasseh, King Hezekiah's successor, killed Isaiah by having him sawn in half (Heb. 11:37), but there is no record of this in Scripture.

What kind of man was Isaiah the prophet? As you read his prophecy, you will discover that he was a man in touch with God. He saw God's Son and God's glory (chap. 6; John 12:41), he heard God's message, and he sought to bring the nation back to God before it was too late.

Isaiah was a man who loved his nation. The phrase "my people" is used at least twenty-six times in his book. He was a patriot with a true love for his country, pleading with Judah to return to God and warning kings when their foreign policy was contrary to God's will. The American political leader Adlai Stevenson called patriotism "not a short and frenzied outburst of emotion, but the tranquil and steady dedication of a life." He was not thinking of Isaiah when he said that, but Stevenson's words perfectly describe the prophet and his work.

He was also a man who hated sin and sham religion. His favorite name for God is "the Holy One of Israel," and he uses it twenty-five times in his book. (It is used only five times in the rest of the Old Testament.) He looked at the crowded courts of the temple and cried out, "They have forsaken the Lord, they have provoked the Holy One of Israel unto anger, they are gone away backward" (1:4). He examined the political policies of the leaders and said, "Woe to those who go down to Egypt for help . . . but they look not to the Holy One of Israel, neither seek the Lord" (31:1). Jehovah was holy, but the nation was sinful, and Isaiah called the people to repent.

Isaiah was certainly a courageous man. Unafraid to denounce kings and priests, and unwavering when public opinion went against him, he boldly declared the Word of God. For three years Isaiah wore only a loincloth to dramatize the victory of Assyria over Egypt (chap. 20). In so doing, he hoped to get the attention of people who were blind to their country's danger.

He was a man skilled in communicating God's truth. Not content with merely declaring facts, Isaiah clothed those facts in striking language that would catch the attention of a people blind and deaf to spiritual truth (6:9-10). He compared the nation to a diseased body (1:5-6), a harlot (v. 21), a useless vineyard (chap. 5), a bulging wall about to fall down (30:13), and a woman in travail (66:8). Assyria, the enemy, would come like a swollen stream (8:7-8), a swarm of bees (7:18), a lion (5:29), and an axe (10:15). Like our Lord Jesus Christ, Isaiah knew how to stir the imagination of his listeners so that he might arouse their interest and teach them God's truth (Matt. 13:10-17).

2. The Monarchs

Isaiah prophesied during the days of "Uzziah, Jotham, Ahaz, and Hezekiah, kings of Judah" (1:1). The nation had divided after the death of Solomon (1 Kings 12), but the priesthood and the Davidic throne belonged to Judah. The ten northern tribes formed the kingdom of Israel (Ephraim), with Samaria as its capital city, and Benjamin and Judah united to form the kingdom of Judah, with Jerusalem as its capital city. Though Isaiah predicted the fall of Israel to Assyria (chap. 28), which occurred in 722 B.C., his major focus was on Judah and Jerusalem (1:1).

Uzziah is also called Azariah. At the age of sixteen, he became co-regent with his father, Amaziah, and was on the throne for fifty-two years (792-740). When his father was assassinated in 767, Uzziah became the sole ruler and brought the nation to its greatest days since David and Solomon (2 Kings 14:17-22; 15:1-7; 2 Chron. 26:1-15). "But when he was strong, his heart was lifted up to his destruction" (v. 16). He tried to intrude into the priest's ministry in the temple, and God judged him by smiting him with leprosy. It was in the year that King Uzziah died that Isaiah was called to minister (Isa. 6:1).

Jotham was co-regent after his father became a leper, and his record as king was a good one (2 Kings 15:32-38; 2 Chron. 27). He reigned for twenty years, and it was during his time that the Assyrian Empire began to emerge as a new and threatening power. During the last twelve years of Jotham's reign, his son Ahaz served as co-regent, but Ahaz was not one of Judah's good kings.

Ahaz forged political alliances that eventually brought Judah into bondage to Assyria (2 Kings 16; 2 Chron. 28). Judah was repeatedly threatened by Egypt from the south and by Syria and Israel from the north, and Ahaz depended on an alliance with Assyria to protect himself. Isaiah warned Ahaz that his alliances with godless Gentiles would not work, and he encouraged the king to put his trust in the Lord (Isa. 7).

Hezekiah reigned forty-two years and was one of Judah's greatest kings (2 Kings 18–20; 2 Chron. 29–32). He not only strengthened the city of Jerusalem and the nation of Judah, but led the people back to the Lord. He built the famous water system that still exists in Jerusalem.

The ministry of Isaiah spans a period of over fifty years, from 739 B.C. (the death of Uzziah) to 686 B.C. (the death of Hezekiah), and it probably extended into the early years of King Manasseh's reign. It was a difficult time of international upheaval, when first one power and then another threatened Judah. But the greatest dangers were not outside the nation: they were within. In spite of the godly leadership of King Hezekiah, Judah had no more godly kings. One by one, Hezekiah's successors led the nation into political and spiritual decay, ending in captivity in Babylon.

The British expositor G. Campbell Morgan said, "The whole story of the prophet Isaiah, as it is revealed to us in this one book, is that of a man who spoke to an inattentive age or to an age which, if attentive, mocked him and refused to obey his message, until, as the prophetic period drew to a close, he inquired in anguish, 'Who hath believed our report? And to whom hath the arm of the Lord been revealed?' " (Westminister Pulpit, vol. 10, p. 10)

3. The Message

Isaiah opens his book with a series of sermons denouncing sin: the personal sins of the people (chaps. 1–6) and the national sins of the leaders (chaps. 7–12). In these messages, he warns of judgment and pleads for repentance. The prophets Amos and Hosea were preaching similar messages to the people of the Northern Kingdom, warning them that time was running out.

But the Gentile nations around Judah and Israel were not innocent! In chapters 13–23, Isaiah denounced those nations for their sins and warned of God's judgment. Israel and Judah had sinned against the Law of God and were even more guilty than their neighbors, but the Gentile nations would not escape God's wrath. In the way they had behaved, these nations had sinned against conscience (Rom. 2:1-16) and against human decency. The prophet Amos was preaching the same message in the Northern Kingdom, but he denounced the Gentiles first and then warned the Jews (Amos 1–2).

As you study the Book of Isaiah, you will discover that the prophet intersperses messages of hope with words of judgment. God remembers His mercy even when declaring His wrath (Hab. 3:2), and He assures His people that they have a "hope and a future" (Jer. 29:11, NIV). Isaiah 24–27 is devoted to "songs of hope" that describe the glory of the future kingdom. Isaiah sees a day when the two kingdoms of Israel and Judah will return to the land, be reunited and redeemed, and enter into the blessings of the promised kingdom.

Chapters 28–35 focus on the impending Assyrian invasion of Israel and Judah. Israel will be destroyed and the ten tribes assimilated into the Assyrian Empire. (This is the origin of the Samaritans, who were part Jewish and part Gentile.) Judah would be invaded and devastated, but Jerusalem would be delivered by the Lord.

At this point in his book, Isaiah moved from prophecy to history and focused on two key events that occurred during the reign of King Hezekiah: God's miraculous deliverance of Jerusalem from the Assyrians (chaps. 36–37), and Hezekiah's foolish cooperation with the Babylonians (chaps. 38–39). This section forms a transition from an emphasis on Assyria to an emphasis on Babylon, for the last twenty-seven chapters look ahead to the return of the Jewish remnant from Babylonian captivity.

The Jewish rabbis call Isaiah 40-66 "The Book of Consolation," and their description is accurate. Addressed originally to the discouraged Jewish exiles returning to an impoverished land and a ruined temple, these chapters have brought comfort and hope to God's people in every age and in every kind of difficult situation. The Hebrew word translated "comfort" also means "to repent." God brings comfort, not to rebellious people but to repentant people.

The arrangement of chapters 40–66 is not accidental. "The Book of Consolation" is divided into three sections; each focuses on a different Person of the Godhead and a different attribute of God. Chapters 40–48 exalt the greatness of God the Father; chapters 49–57, the grace of God the Son, God's Suffering Servant; and chapters 58–66, the glory of the future kingdom when the Spirit is poured out on God's people. Note the references to the Spirit in 59:19 and 21; 61:1; and 63:10-11, 14.

Servant is one of the key words in this second section of the Book of Isaiah. The word is used seventeen times and has three different referents: the nation of Israel (41:8-9; 43:10); Cyrus, king of Persia, whom God raised up to help Israel restore their nation and rebuild their temple (44:28; 45:1; see Ezra 1:1); and Jesus Christ, the Son of God (Isa. 42:1, 19; 52:13; 53:11), the Suffering Servant who died for the sins of the world. While Assyria and Egypt vie for the center stage in chapters 1–39, it is Babylon and Persia that get the attention in chapters 40–66.

In summary, Isaiah had an immediate word of warning to both Israel and Judah that Assyria was on the march and would be used by God to punish them for their sins. Occasionally, Isaiah uses this invasion to picture "the day of the Lord," that future time when the whole world will taste of the wrath of God. The prophets often used immediate circumstances to illustrate future events.

Isaiah had a word of promise to Judah that God would deliver Jerusalem from the enemy for the sake of David's throne. There was also a word of hope for the future Jewish exiles in Babylon, that God would rescue them and help them restore their nation and their temple. But Isaiah's greatest message is his word of salvation, announcing the coming of the Messiah, the Servant of the Lord, who would die for sinners and one day return to earth to establish His glorious kingdom.

4. The Messiah

Isaiah is much more than a prophet. He is an evangelist who presents Jesus Christ and the Good News of the Gospel. Isaiah's "Servant Song" about Jesus (Isa. 52:13–53:12) is quoted or alluded to nearly forty times in the New Testament.

The prophet wrote about the birth of Christ (7:14; 9:6; Matt. 1:18-25); the ministry of John the Baptist (Isa. 40:1-6; Matt. 3:1ff); Christ's anointing by the Spirit (Isa. 61:1-2; Luke 4:17-19); the nation's rejection of their Messiah (Isa. 6:9-11; John 12:38ff); Christ, the "stone of stumbling" (Isa. 8:14; 28:16; Rom. 9:32-33; 10:11; 1 Peter 2:6); Christ's ministry to the Gentiles (Isa. 49:6; Luke 2:32; Acts 13:47); the Savior's suffering and death (Isa. 52:13–53:12; Acts 3:13; 8:32-33; 1 Peter 2:21-25); His resurrection (Isa. 55:3; Acts 13:34); and His return to reign as King (Isa. 9:6-7; 11:1ff; 59:20-21; 63:1-3; Rom. 11:26-27; Rev. 19:13-15). There are many other references in Isaiah to the Messiah, and we will notice them as we study this book.

It is this emphasis on redemption that gives Isaiah a message for the whole world. While it is true he ministered to the little nation of Judah and wrote about nations and empires that for the most part are no longer on the world scene, his focus was on God's plan of salvation for the whole world. Isaiah saw the greatness of God and the vastness of His plan of salvation for Jews and Gentiles alike. Isaiah was a patriot but not a bigot; he saw beyond his own nation to the gracious work God would do among the Gentile nations of the world.

I have a feeling that the Book of Isaiah was a favorite book of the Apostle Paul. He quotes from it or alludes to it at least eighty times in his epistles and in at least three of his recorded messages (Acts 13:34, 47; 17:24-29; 28:26-28). This interest in Isaiah may stem from the fact that Jesus quoted Isaiah 42:7, 16 when He spoke to Paul on the Damascus Road (Acts 26:16-18). When Jesus encouraged Paul during his ministry to Corinth (Acts. 18:9-10), He referred to Isaiah 41:10 and 43:5. Paul's call to evangelize the Gentiles was confirmed by Isaiah 49:6. Like the prophet Isaiah, Paul saw the vastness of God's plan for both Jews and Gentiles; and like Isaiah, Paul magnified Jesus Christ, the Savior of the world. Five times in his letters Paul refers to Isaiah 53.

As you study Isaiah and discover God's prophetic plan for the nations of the world, don't miss his emphasis on the personal message of God's forgiveness. "Though your sins be as scarlet, they shall be as white as snow; though they be red like crimson, they shall be as wool" (1:18, KJV). "I have blotted out, like a thick cloud, your transgressions, and, like a cloud, your sins" (44:22, NKJV). "I, even I, am He, who blots out your transgressions for My own sake; and I will not remember your sins" (43:25, NKJV).

How can "the Holy One of Israel," a just and righteous God, forgive our sins and remember them no more?

"But [Jesus] was wounded for our transgressions, He was bruised for our iniquities; the chastisement for our peace was upon Him, and by His stripes we are healed" (53:5, NKJV).

It was on the basis of this truth that Peter declared, "To [Jesus] all the prophets witness, that through His name, whoever believes in Him shall receive remission of sins" (Acts 10:43).

"Who hath believed our report?" Isaiah asks us (Isa. 53:1).

"If you will not believe, surely you shall not be established," he warns us (7:9, NKJV).

If you have never believed on the Lord Jesus Christ and received Him into your life, then do so now. "Look to Me, and be saved, all you ends of the earth! For I am God, and there is no other" (45:22, NKJV).

"Nor is there salvation in any other, for there is no other name under heaven given among men by which we must be saved" (Acts 4:12, NKJV).

CHAPTER TWO
WANTED: A PROPHET
Isaiah 1–6

The first thing you must know about prophets is that their ministry focuses on the present as well as on the future. They "tell forth" the Word of God as well as "foretell" the works of God. True prophets are like good doctors:

They diagnose the case, prescribe a remedy, and warn the patient what will happen if the prescription is ignored. (See Jer. 6:14 and 8:11). When prophets declare a vision of the future, they do it to encourage people to obey God today. Peter stated this principle when he wrote, "Therefore, since all these things will be dissolved, what manner of persons ought you to be in holy conduct and godliness?" (2 Peter 3:11, NKJV).

Unlike Jeremiah and Ezekiel, Isaiah did not begin his book with an account of his call to ministry. This he gives in chapter 6. Instead, he started with a probing examination of Judah's present situation and gave a passionate plea for God's people to return to the Lord. As you read his analysis, note how closely it parallels our situation in the Western World.

1. What Isaiah Saw (Isa. 1:1-31)

This chapter describes a courtroom scene. God convenes the court and states the charges (vv. 2-4). He presents His case and pronounces the nation guilty (vv. 5-15), but He gives the accused opportunity to repent and be forgiven (vv. 16-31). How did God describe His sinful people?

They were rebellious children (vv. 2-4) who did not have as much devotion to God as animals do to their masters! The word "rebel" carries with it the idea of breaking a contract. At Sinai, Israel had entered into a solemn covenant with Jehovah (Ex. 19–20), but they had broken the contract by their unbelief and idolatry. They did not appreciate what God had done for them and were taking their blessings for granted. They had forsaken the Lord, gone backward, and grown corrupt; therefore, they were guilty and deserved judgment.

From the human point of view, the nation was prospering; but from God's point of view, the nation was like a wretched victim who had been beaten from head to foot and left to die (Isa. 1:5-6). The wounds had become infected, the whole body diseased, and nobody was doing anything to help. The false prophets and hypocritical priests of that day would have challenged Isaiah's autopsy of "the body politic," but the prophet knew that his diagnosis was true. In spite of the optimism of Judah's leaders, the nation was morally and spiritually sick, and judgment was inevitable.

In verses 7-9, God pictures Judah as a ravaged battlefield, a desert that had once been a garden. In using this image, Isaiah may have been looking ahead to the invasion of Sennacherib, when Judah was devastated by the Assyrian army and only Jerusalem was spared (chaps. 36–37). The people would not let God manage the land according to His law, so God turned Judah over to foreigners and permitted His people to suffer (Deut. 28:15ff).

What a humiliating shock the people must have had when they heard Isaiah compare the holy city of Jerusalem to the wicked cities of Sodom and Gomorrah! (Isa. 3:9; Gen. 18–19) And what did the leaders think when Isaiah said only "a very small remnant" would survive? After all, God promised Abraham that the nation would multiply like the dust of the earth and the stars of the heavens (13:16; 15:5). The doctrine of "the remnant" is important in the message of the prophets (Isa. 6:13; 10:20-22; 11:11-13, 16; Jer. 6:9; 23:3; 31:7; Micah 2:12; Zech. 8:12). Paul also referred to it (Rom. 9:27; 11:5). In spite of the apostasy of the nation, a remnant of true believers would be spared so that God's work could be accomplished through the Jewish nation.

The disgusting thing about this rebellious people is that they were also a religious people (Isa. 1:10-15). They attended the temple services and brought a multitude of sacrifices to the Lord, but their hearts were far from God and their worship was hypocritical. Sacrifices alone can never please God, for along with the outward observance, God wants inward obedience (1 Sam. 15:22), a broken heart (Ps. 51:17), and a godly walk (Micah 6:6-8). Judah's worship of Jehovah was iniquity, not piety, and God was sick of it! Instead of lifting up "holy hands" in prayer (1 Tim. 2:8), their hands were stained with blood because of their many sins (Isa. 59:3; Ezek. 7:23).

But before passing judgment on worshipers in a bygone era, perhaps we should confess the sins of the "worshiping church" today. According to researcher George Barna, 93 percent of the households in the United States contain a Bible and more than 60 percent of the people surveyed claim to be religious, but we would never know this from the way people act. One Protestant church exists for every 550 adults in America, but does all this "religion" make much of a difference in our sinful society? Organized religion hasn't affected the nation's crime rate, the divorce rate, or the kind of "entertainment" seen in movies and on TV.

The average church allocates about 5 percent of its budget for reaching others with the Gospel, but 30 percent for buildings and maintenance. At a time when the poor and the aged are pleading for help, churches in America are spending approximately 3 billion dollars a year on new construction. Where churches have life and growth, such construction may be needed, but too often the building becomes "a millstone instead of a milestone," to quote Vance Havner. At least 62 percent of the people Barna surveyed said that the church was not relevant to today's world and is losing its influence on society. It may be that, like the worshipers in the ancient Jewish temple, we are only going through the motions. (See The Frog in the Kettle by George Barna, published by Regal Books.)

Isaiah didn't stop with the diagnosis but also gave the prescription, because he wanted Judah to be a righteous people (Isa. 1:16-31). The word translated "reason" in verse 18 means "to decide a case in court," but instead of pronouncing judgment, the Judge offered pardon! If they would cleanse themselves by repenting and turning from sin (vv. 16-17; see 2 Cor. 7:1), then God would wipe the record clean in response to their faith (Isa. 1:18). God had every reason to punish His people for their sins but in His grace and mercy He offered them His pardon.

What were some of the sins that the nation needed to confess and put away? Isaiah named murder (v. 21), robbery, bribery, and exploiting the helpless (v. 23), and the worship of heathen idols (v. 29). Because of their idolatry, the once-faithful wife was now a harlot, and because of their unjust practices, the pure silver had become dross. The tragedy is that many of the worshipers in the temple participated in these evil practices and thereby encouraged the decay of the nation. The rulers maintained a religious façade to cover up their crimes, and the people let them do it.

What would God do if the people did not repent? He would send a fiery judgment that would purge the dross and burn up those whose rebellion had made them His enemies (vv. 24-31). Isaiah closed this first message with a promise of hope that one day Jerusalem would be a "city of righteousness."

2. What Isaiah Promised (Isa. 2:1–4:6)

Three important phrases sum up Isaiah's second message and its proclamation of God's future work.

The Temple of the Lord (Isa. 2:1-5). The prophet looked ahead to the time when God's righteous kingdom would be established and the temple would become the center for the worldwide worship of the Lord. In Isaiah's day, the Jews were adopting the false gods of the Gentiles, but the day would come when the Gentiles would abandon their idols and worship the true God of Israel. The nations would also lay down their weapons and stop warring. These promises must not be "spiritualized" and applied to the church, for they describe a literal kingdom of righteousness and peace. The Jewish temple will be rebuilt, and the Word of God will go forth from Jerusalem to govern the nations of the world.

In the light of the future glory of God's temple, Isaiah appealed to the people to "walk in the light of the Lord" (v. 5). Christians today have a similar motivation as we await the return of Christ for His church (1 John 2:28-3:3).

The Day of the Lord (Isa. 2:6-3:26). This is that period of time when God will send judgment to the nations and purify Israel in preparation for the coming of His King to reign in Jerusalem. The Day of the Lord is described by John (Rev. 6–19), by the prophets (Isa. 13:6ff; Ezek. 30; Joel 1:15; 2:1ff; Zeph. 1:7ff; Zech. 14:1ff), and by the Lord Jesus (Matt. 24; Mark 13; Luke 21). It will be a time of terrible suffering; the environment will be devastated, and millions of people will die. (Note the repetition of the phrase "in that day": Isa. 2:17, 20; 3:7, 18; 4:1-2.)

To the prophets, "the Day of the Lord" was foreshadowed by events in their own day. In the Book of Isaiah, Assyria's conquest of the Northern Kingdom and invasion of Judah, and the Babylonian captivity of Judah both picture the coming "Day of the Lord."

(1) Why will God judge His people? Because of their idolatry, covetousness, pride, and exploiting of the poor (2:6-22). Instead of holding to the truth of God's Word, they were adopting "superstitions from the East" (v. 6, NIV), not unlike many "religious seekers" today. The growth of Eastern religions in the modern Western world is a phenomenon that is both frightening and challenging. Even nonreligious people are practicing Eastern

forms of meditation and relaxation, following techniques that are being taught in university classes and business seminars.

The prosperity of the nation made leaders proud and covetous. Instead of trusting the Lord, they trusted their wealth and war equipment, not realizing that neither would deliver them in the coming day of judgment. The leaders were exploiting the poor, crushing them like grain in a mill (3:13-15). God will not allow His people to be proud and self-confident, but will humble them and cut them down like trees in the forest. "The Lord alone shall be exalted in that day" (2:11, 17) when men flee from His wrath and discover the worthlessness of their idols and the consequences of their sins (vv. 19-22).

(2) How will God judge His people? By taking away from them everything they were trusting, including food and water, leaders and soldiers, and judges and prophets (3:1-15). The entire support system of the nation would disintegrate, and there would be no remedy. Nobody would want to hold office except women and children. (In Judah's male-dominated society, this would be a humiliating calamity.) The national leaders in Isaiah's day were charting a course that was out of the will of God and would ultimately bring disaster, but the righteous remnant would be protected by God (vv. 10-12).

After denouncing the men in leadership, the prophet zeroed in on the proud women who profited from their husbands' crimes (3:16-4:1). The Prophet Amos had a similar message for the women in the Northern Kingdom (Amos 4:1-3). Everything would be different for these women when the judgment of God came to the land! In that day, nobody would notice their expensive clothes, their jewelry and perfumes, and their elaborate coiffures. They would be prisoners of war, led by a rope, like cattle going to the slaughter. So many men would be killed there wouldn't be enough husbands to go around! (4:1)

God is long-suffering as He watches people viciously exploit one another and selfishly ravage His creation. But there is coming a day when unbelieving sinners will be punished and God's people will share in the glories of His kingdom. Are you ready?

The Branch of the Lord (Isa. 4:2-6). The prophet looks beyond the "Day of the Lord" to that time when the kingdom will be established on earth. "Branch of the Lord" is a messianic title for Jesus Christ, who came as a "shoot" from the seeming dead stump of David's dynasty (11:1; 53:2; see Jer. 23:5; 33:15; Zech. 3:8; 6:12). God will cleanse His people (Isa. 4:4; see Zech. 12:10-13:1), restore the fruitfulness of the land, and dwell with them as He did when He led them through the wilderness (Isa. 4:5-6; Ex. 13:21-22). Not just the temple, but every dwelling will be blessed by the presence of the Lord! Unlike in Isaiah's day, "in that day" the people will be holy (set apart), and the land will be beautiful and glorious.

3. What Isaiah Sang (Isa. 5:1-30)

The preacher become a troubadour and sang a folk song to the Lord ("my beloved"). Perhaps the people who had ignored his sermons would listen to his song. He sang about his own people (v. 7) and pointed out how good God had been to them. God gave them a holy law and a wonderful land, but they broke the law and defiled the land with their sins and failed to produce fruit for God's glory. God had done for them all that He could do. Now all that remained for Him to do was bring judgment on the fruitless vineyard and make it a waste. (Note that Jesus referred to this passage in Matt. 21:33-44).

What were the "wild grapes" that the nation produced instead of the "good grapes" that God sought for? In the six "woes" that follow, Isaiah named the sins that brought judgment on the land.

Covetousness (Isa. 5:8-10). In disobedience to the Law (Lev. 25:23-28; 1 Kings 21:1-3), the rich defrauded the poor and seized the land. These wealthy explorers built large mansions and developed extensive farms, but God warned them that their houses would be empty and their harvests meager. Imagine ten acres of grapevines yielding only six gallons of wine and six bushels of seed producing half a bushel of grain!

Drunkenness (Isa. 5:11-17). In the Old Testament, God did not require total abstinence, but He did warn against drunkenness (Prov. 20:1; 23:29-31; Hab. 2:15). This warning is repeated in the New Testament for believers today (Rom. 13:13; 1 Cor. 6:9-10; Eph. 5:18). Isaiah describes people so addicted to alcohol that they begin their revelries as soon as they wake up in the morning, and they continue their drinking till late at night. They enjoy banquets and music and get involved in drunken brawls (Isa. 5:14, NIV). But when judgment comes, these people will hunger and thirst and become "food" for the grave (v. 14). The "eaters" will themselves be eaten, and the proud drinkers will be brought low.

Carelessness (Isa. 5:18-19). Isaiah describes people who are bound by sin and yet speak frequently of the Lord and His warnings. "They even mock the Holy One of Israel and dare the Lord to punish them" (v. 19, TLB). The name "Holy One of Israel" is used twenty-five times in Isaiah, but these sinners had no respect for that name. We have skeptical scoffers today who speak lightly of the Lord and think they will get away with it.

Deception (Isa. 5:20). Moral standards were destroyed by new definitions of sin (see Amos 5:7), people using God's vocabulary but not His dictionary. Like today's "doublespeak," this kind of language made it easy to deceive people and avoid a guilty conscience. In today's world, increased taxes are "revenue enhancements," and poor people are "fiscal underachievers." Medical malpractice is not the cause of a patient's death; it's a "diagnostic misadventure of high magnitude." (See DoubleSpeak by William Lutz.) The Jerusalem Bible translation of Psalm 12:2 says it perfectly: "All they do is lie to one another, flattering lips, talk from a double heart."

Pride (Isa. 5:21). Instead of listening to God, the leaders consulted with one another and made decisions based on their own wisdom. "Professing themselves to be wise, they became fools" (Rom. 1:22; see 1 Cor. 1:18-25). "Do not be wise in your own eyes; fear the Lord and depart from evil" (Prov. 3:7, NKJV).

Injustice (Isa. 5:22-25). The judges who were supposed to enforce the law used their authority to free the guilty and punish the innocent. They were more interested in cocktail parties than fair trials, and making money (bribes) than promoting justice. Isaiah warned these corrupt politicians that the fire of God's wrath was coming and would burn them up. They were like cut flowers and had no roots, beautiful for a time, but destined to die and turn to dust.

The phrase in verse 25 about God's anger is repeated in 9:12, 17, and 21, and in 10:4. His hand was raised in judgment and would not come down until He had completed His work. He would summon the Assyrian army from afar and use it to chasten His people (5:26-30). The Northern Kingdom of Israel would be destroyed, and Judah, the Southern Kingdom, would be devastated but eventually delivered, only to go in captivity to Babylon a century later. God was serious about the nation's sins. If they would not repent and accept His offer of pardon (1:18), then all He could do was send judgment.

4. What Isaiah Experienced (Isa. 6:1-13)

Anyone reading Isaiah's first two messages might be inclined to ask, "What right does this man have to pronounce judgment on the leaders of our land and the many worshipers in the temple?" The answer is in this chapter: Isaiah's account of his call to ministry. Before he announced any "woes" on others, he first confessed his own sin and said, "Woe is me!" He saw the Holy One of Israel, and he could not keep silent. Note four stages in Isaiah's experience with God.

Sight: He saw the Lord (Isa. 6:1-4). We assume that Isaiah was in the temple when this marvelous event occurred, but we cannot be sure. The temple referred to in verse 1 is the heavenly temple, rather than Solomon's temple. King Uzziah died in 740 B.C. and was one of Judah's greatest leaders, even though in his latter years he was disciplined for disobeying God (2 Chron. 26:16-21). A great king may have left his throne on earth, but the greatest King was still seated on the throne of heaven. According to John 12:41, this was the Lord Jesus Christ.

Only here are the seraphim mentioned in Scripture. The Hebrew word means "to burn" and relates these creatures to the holiness of God. This is why they repeat, "Holy, holy, holy" before the throne of God. Some students think that the seraphim are the "living creatures" described in Revelation 4:6-9.

When I was the radio speaker on "Songs in the Night" from the Moody Church in Chicago, I often received clippings from listeners, items they though might be useful on the weekly broadcast. Most of them I have forgotten, but a few of them still stick in my mind. One of the best was, "When the outlook is bleak, try the uplook!"

For young Isaiah, the outlook was bleak. His beloved King had died, his nation was in peril, and he could do very little about it. The outlook may have been bleak, but the uplook was glorious! God was still on the throne and reigning as the Sovereign of the universe! From heaven's point of view, "the whole earth" was "full of His glory" (Isa. 6:3; see

Num. 14:21-22; Ps. 72:18-19). When your world tumbles in, it is good to look at things from heaven's point of view.

Insight: He saw himself (Isa. 6:5-7). The sight of a holy God and the sound of the holy hymn of worship brought great conviction to Isaiah's heart, and he confessed that he was a sinner. Unclean lips are caused by an unclean heart (Matt. 12:34-35). Isaiah cried out to be cleansed inwardly (Ps. 51:10), and God met his need. If this scene had been on earth, the coals would have come from the brazen altar where sacrificial blood had been shed, or perhaps from the censer of the high priest on the Day of Atonement (Lev. 16:12). Isaiah's cleansing came by blood and fire, and it was verified by the word of the Lord (Isa. 6:7).

Before we can minister to others, we must permit God to minister to us. Before we pronounce "woe" upon others, we must sincerely say, "Woe is me!" Isaiah's conviction led to confession, and confession led to cleansing (1 John 1:9). Like Isaiah, many of the great heroes of faith saw themselves as sinners and humbled themselves before God: Abraham (Gen. 18:27), Jacob (32:10), Job (Job 40:1-5), David (2 Sam. 7:18), Paul (1 Tim. 1:15), and Peter (Luke 5:8-11).

Vision: He saw the need (Isa. 6:8). The nation needed the Lord, and the Lord wanted a servant to minister to the people. Isaiah volunteered to be that servant. He did not discuss his call with the Lord, as did Moses (Ex. 3:11–4:15) and Jeremiah (Jer. 1:4ff), but accepted the appointment and made himself available to his Master.

Never underestimate what God can do with one willing worker. There is an even greater need for laborers today, and we have tremendous opportunities for sharing the Gospel with a lost world. Are you one of God's willing volunteers?

Blindness: The nation could not see (Isa. 6:9-13). The Lord did not give His servant much encouragement! Isaiah's ministry would actually make some people's eyes more blind, their ears more deaf, and their hearts more callused. Verses 9-10 are so important that they are quoted six times in the New Testament (Matt. 13:13-15; Mark 4:12; Luke 8:10; John 12:40; Acts 28:25-28; Rom. 11:8). God does not deliberately make sinners blind, deaf, and hard-hearted; but the more that people resist God's truth, the less able they are to receive God's truth. But the servant is to proclaim the Word no matter how people respond, for the test of ministry is not outward success but faithfulness to the Lord.

God told Isaiah that his ministry would end in seeming failure, with the land ruined and the people taken off to exile (Isa. 6:11-12). But a remnant would survive! It would be like the stump of a fallen tree from which the shoots ("the holy seed") would come, and they would continue the true faith in the land. Isaiah needed a long-range perspective on his ministry or else he would feel like he was accomplishing nothing.

"Go and tell" is still God's command to His people (v. 9; see Matt 28:7; Mark 5:19). He is waiting for us to reply, "Here am I; send me."

CHAPTER THREE
GOD IS WITH US!
ISAIAH 7–12

"Behold, I and the children whom the Lord hath given me are for signs and for wonders in Israel from the Lord of hosts" (8:18).

This statement by the prophet Isaiah is a key to understanding the meaning of the events and prophecies in this section. In his previous messages, Isaiah focused on the spiritual needs of his people, but in this section he deals with the political situation and the failure of the leaders to trust the Lord. Four symbolic names are involved in Isaiah's messages, each of them with a very special meaning: Immanuel, Maher-shalal-hash-baz, Shear-jashub, and Isaiah.

1. Immanuel: A Message of Hope (Isa. 7:1-25)

A promise to King Ahaz (Isa. 7:1-9). These were perilous days for the nation of Judah. Assyria was growing stronger and threatening the smaller nations whose security depended on a very delicate political balance. Syria and Ephraim (the Northern Kingdom) tried to pressure Judah into an alliance against Assyria, but Ahaz refused to join them. Why? Because he had secretly made a treaty with Assyria! (2 Kings 16:5-9) The king was playing "power politics" instead of trusting in the power of God. Syria and Ephraim planned to overthrow Ahaz and put "the son of Tabeel" on the throne, and Ahaz was a frightened man.

The Lord commanded Isaiah to take his son Shear-jashub ("a remnant shall return") and meet Ahaz as the king was inspecting the city's water system. Ahaz's heart had been wavering, and the hearts of his people had been shaking for fear (Isa. 7:2), but Isaiah came with a message of assurance: "Take heed, and be quiet; fear not, neither be fainthearted" (v. 4). How would Ahaz find this inner peace? By believing God's promise that Judah's enemies would be defeated. "If you will not believe, surely you shall not be established" (v. 9, NKJV). Faith in God's promises is the only way to find peace in the midst of trouble. "You will keep him in perfect peace, whose mind is stayed on You, because he trusts in You" (26:3, NKJV).

In God's eyes, the two threatening kings were nothing but "two smoldering stubs of firewood" (7:4, NIV) who would be off the scene very soon, and they both died two years later. Furthermore, within sixty-five years, Ephraim (Israel, the Northern Kingdom) would be gone forever. Isaiah spoke this prophecy in the year 734 B.C. Assyria defeated Syria in 732 B.C. and invaded Israel in 722 B.C. They deported many of the Jews and assimilated the rest by introducing Gentiles into the land. By 669 B.C. (sixty-five years later), the nation no longer existed.

A sign to the house of David (Isa. 7:10-16). If Ahaz had believed God's promise, he would have broken his alliance and called the nation to prayer and praise, but the king continued in his unbelief. Realizing the weakness of the king's faith, Isaiah offered to give a sign to encourage him, but Ahaz put on a "pious front" and refused his offer. Knowing that he was secretly allied with Assyria, how could Ahaz honestly ask the Lord for a special sign? So, instead of speaking only to the king, Isaiah addressed the whole "house of David" and gave the prophecy concerning "Immanuel."

Of course, the ultimate fulfillment of this prophecy is in our Lord Jesus Christ, who is "God with us" (Matt. 1:18-25; Luke 1:31-35). The virgin birth of Christ is a key doctrine; for if Jesus Christ is not God come in sinless human flesh, then we have no Savior. Jesus had to be born of a virgin, apart from human generation, because He existed before His mother. He was not just born in this world; He came down from heaven into the world (John 3:13; 6:33, 38, 41-42, 50-51, 58). Jesus was sent by the Father and therefore came into the world having a human mother but not a human father (4:34; 5:23-24, 30; 9:4).

However, this "sign" had an immediate significance to Ahaz and the people of Judah. A woman who was then a virgin would get married, conceive, and bear a son whose name would be "Immanuel." The son would be a reminder that God was with His people and would care for them. It is likely that this virgin was Isaiah's second wife—his first wife having died after Shear-jasub was born—and that Isaiah's second son was named both "Immanuel" and "Maher-shalal-hash-baz" (8:1-4; note vv. 8 and 10).

Orthodox Jewish boys become "sons of the Law" at the age of twelve. This special son was a reminder that Syria and Ephraim would be out of the picture within the next twelve years. Isaiah delivered his prophecy in 734 B.C. In 732 B.C. Assyria defeated Syria, and in 722 B.C. Assyria invaded the Northern Kingdom. The prophecy was fulfilled.

A warning to Judah (Isa. 7:17-25). Instead of trusting the Lord, Ahaz continued to trust Assyria for help, and Isaiah warned him that Assyria would become Judah's enemy. The Assyrians would invade Judah and so ravage the land that agriculture would cease and the people would have only dairy products to eat (vv. 15, 21-23). The rich farmland would become wasteland, and the people would be forced to hunt wild beasts in order to get food. It would be a time of great humiliation (v. 20; 2 Sam 10:4-5) and suffering that could have been avoided had the leaders trusted in the Lord.

2. Maher-shalal-hash-baz: A Warning of Judgment (Isa. 8:1-22)

Isaiah married the virgin, and the legal documents were duly witnessed and sealed. He even announced that their first child would be a son and his name would be Maher-shalal-hash-baz, which means "quick to plunder, swift to the spoil." Since Isaiah's sons were signs to the nation (8:18), this name was significant. It spoke of future judgment when Assyria would conquer Syria and invade both Israel and Judah, and when Babylon would take Judah into exile. A child would start speaking meaningful sentences about the age of two. In 732 B.C., about two years after Isaiah's son was born, both Pekah and Rezin were dead (7:1), and Assyria had conquered Syria and begun to invade Israel (2 Kings 15:29). The army was "quick to plunder and swift to take the spoil."

In the remainder of this chapter, Isaiah used three vivid contrasts to show the rulers of Judah the mistake they were making by trusting Assyria instead of trusting the Lord.

They chose a flood instead of a peaceful river (Isa. 8:5-10). The pro-Assyrian faction in Judah rejoiced when Assyria defeated Syria and when both Pekah and Rezin died. These victories seemed to prove that an alliance with Assyria was the safest course to follow. Instead of trusting the Lord ("the waters of Shiloah, that go softly" in v. 6), they trusted the great river of Assyria. What they did not realize was that this river would become a flood when Assyria would come and destroy Israel and devastate Judah. God offered His people peace, but in unbelief they opted for war. They were walking by sight and not by faith.

But Isaiah saw no permanent victory for the invading army. After all, they were entering Immanuel's land, and God was with His people and would deliver them for His name's sake. Assyria might plan its strategy, but God would thwart its every move. Sennacherib's army camped around Jerusalem, certain of victory, but God wiped them out with a single blow (chap. 37).

They chose a snare instead of a sanctuary (Isa. 8:11-15). God warned Isaiah not to follow the majority and support the popular pro-Assyrian party. Even though his stand was looked upon as treason, Isaiah opposed all foreign alliances and urged the people to put their faith in the Lord (7:9; 28:16; 30:15). The Jewish political leaders were asking, "Is it popular? Is it safe?" But the prophet was asking, "Is it right? Is it the will of God?"

When you fear the Lord, you don't need to fear people or circumstances. Peter referred to this passage when he wrote, "But even if you should suffer for what is right, you are blessed. 'Do not fear what they fear; do not be frightened.' But in your hearts set apart Christ as Lord" (1 Peter 3:14-15, NIV). Isaiah compared the Lord to a sanctuary, a rock that is a refuge for believers but a snare to those who rebel. The image of Messiah as a rock is found again in Isaiah 28:16 (and see 1 Peter 2:4-7 and Rom. 9:33). "God is our refuge and strength, a very present help in trouble" (Ps. 46:1).

They chose darkness instead of light (Isa. 8:16-22). The nation had rejected Isaiah's message, but that didn't mean that his ministry was a failure. The true disciples of the Lord received God's Word and treasured it in their hearts. By faith, the prophet was willing to wait patiently for God's Word to be fulfilled.

But even if his words fell on deaf ears, Isaiah and his family were themselves a "living prophecy" that the nation could not ignore. Isaiah's name means "Jehovah is salvation," and this would remind the people to trust the Lord to deliver them. His older son's name means "A remnant shall return," and this was a word of promise when it looked as though the nation was destroyed. A believing remnant did return to Jerusalem from Babylon, and they were encouraged by what Isaiah wrote in chapters 40–66. The name of the younger son, Maher-shalal-hash-baz, means "quick to plunder, swift to the spoil," and pointed to the fall of Syria and Ephraim. Verse 18 is quoted in Hebrews 2:13-14 and applied to the Lord Jesus Christ.

In their time of crisis, instead of turning to God for wisdom, the people consulted demons (Isa. 8:19; Deut. 18:10-12), and this only increased their moral and spiritual darkness. The increase of the occult in our own day is evidence that people are deliberately rejecting God's Word and turning to Satan's lies. "If they do not speak according to this word, they have no light of dawn" (Isa. 8:20, NIV). Judah's leaders anxiously looked for the dawning of a new day, but they saw only a deepening darkness. God's Word is our only dependable light in this world's darkness (Ps. 119:105; 2 Peter 1:19-21).

3. Shear-jasub: A Promise of Mercy (Isa. 9:1-11:16)

This name means "A remnant shall return," and the return of the Jewish remnant to their land is a major theme in these chapters (10:20-22; 11:11-12, 16). When Assyria conquered the Northern Kingdom of

Israel (Ephraim), the nation was never restored but became what we know as Samaria. After the Babylonian captivity (606-586 B.C.), the people of Judah were given another chance to establish themselves in the land, and through them the Lord brought the Messiah into the world. Had a remnant not returned, God's plans for redeeming a lost world might have been frustrated. How much depended on that small remnant!

God's mercy to His people is seen in four ministries the Lord performed for them.

The Lord promised them a Redeemer (Isa. 9:1-7). Isaiah continued the theme of light and darkness (8:20-22) by announcing, "There will be no more gloom" (9:1, NIV). The Redeemer will come and bring to the world the dawning of a new day (v. 2; Luke 1:78-79; John 8:12). We know that this prophecy refers to Christ because of the way it is quoted in Matthew 4:13-15. The geographical areas named in Isaiah 9:1 were especially devastated when the Assyrian army moved in, but these areas would be especially honored by the ministry of the Messiah. Jesus was identified with "Galilee of the Gentiles" (Matt. 4:15, NIV), and His loving ministry to the people brought light and joy.

But the prophet looked beyond the first coming of Christ to His second coming and the establishing of His righteous kingdom (Isa. 9:3-7). Instead of protecting a small remnant, God would enlarge the nation. Instead of experiencing sorrow, the people would rejoice like reapers after a great harvest, soldiers after a great victory, or prisoners of war after being released from their yoke of bondage. Of course, some of this occurred when God defeated Assyria and delivered Jerusalem (Isa. 37). But the ultimate fulfillment is still future; all military material will be destroyed (9:5) because the nations will not learn war any more (2:4).

Isaiah 9:6 declared both the humanity ("A Child is born") and the deity ("A Son is given") of the Lord Jesus Christ. The prophet then leaps ahead to the Kingdom Age when Messiah will reign in righteousness and justice from David's throne. God had promised David that his dynasty and throne would be established forever (2 Sam. 7:16), and this is fulfilled literally in Jesus Christ (Luke 1:32-33; Zech. 9:9), who will one day reign from Jerusalem (Isa. 11:1-5; Jer. 23:5-8; 30:8-10). This kingdom is called "the Millennium," which means "one thousand years." The phrase is used six times in Revelation 20.

If His name is "Wonderful," then there will be nothing dull about His reign! As Counselor, He has the wisdom to rule justly and as the Mighty God, He has the power to execute His wise plans. "Everlasting Father" does not suggest that the Son is also the Father, for each Person in the Godhead is distinct. "Father of eternity" is a better translation. Among the Jews, the word "father" means "originator" or "source." For example, Satan is the "father [originator] of lies" (John 8:44, NIV). If you want anything eternal, you must get it from Jesus Christ; He is the "Father of eternity."

The Lord judged Israel for their sins (Isa. 9:8–10:4). This long section describes what will happen to the Northern Kingdom when the Assyrians invade. While Isaiah's ministry was primarily to the people of Judah, he used Israel as an object lesson to warn the Southern Kingdom that God does not take sin lightly. Judah had sinned greatly, but God in His mercy spared them for David's sake (37:35; 1 Kings 11:13; 15:4; 2 Chron. 21:7). However, God's long-suffering would one day end.

The key statement is, "For all this His anger is not turned away, but His hand is stretched out still" (Isa. 9:12, 17, 21; 10:4, and see 5:25). This is the outstretched hand of God's judgment, not His mercy (65:2; Rom. 10:21). God judged them for their pride in thinking that their present difficulties were temporary and the nation could rebuild itself better than before (Isa. 9:8-12). He also judged them for their hardness of heart in their refusal to repent and return to the Lord (vv. 13-17). God's loving purpose in chastening is that we yield to Him, but if we harden our hearts, then chastening becomes judgment (Heb. 12:1-11). Israel was being led astray by false prophets and foolish leaders; the nation would not listen to God's Word.

Ephraim's own wickedness was destroying the nation the way a fire destroys a forest or a field (Isa. 9:18-19). But the sinners would become fuel for the fire God could kindle! In their greed, the people of the Northern Kingdom were devouring one another (v. 20) and battling one another (v. 21), but they would soon be devoured and defeated by Assyria.

In 10:1-4, Isaiah denounced Ephraim for its injustice, especially toward the poor, the widows, and the orphans. Unjust laws and oppressive decrees robbed these people both of their meager possessions and their God-given rights (Deut. 15:7-8; 24:17-18). The prophet's three questions in Isaiah 10:3 ought to be pondered by every person who wants to be ready when the Lord comes.

If God cannot bring us to repentance through His Word, then He must lift His hand and chasten us. If we do not submit to His chastening, then He must stretch out His hand and judge us. God is long-suffering, but we dare not tempt Him by our careless or calloused attitude. "It is a fearful thing to fall into the hands of the living God" (Heb. 10:31).

The Lord will judge the enemy (Isa. 10:5-34). "Woe to the Assyrian!" is the way this section begins (see NIV). Though God used Assyria to chasten Judah, He would not permit His "tool" to exalt itself in pride. Assyria was His rod, club, axe, and saw (10:5, 15, 24), but the Assyrians treated the Jews like mud in the streets (v. 6) and plundered the land like a farmer gathering eggs (v. 14). God's purpose was to discipline, but the Assyrians were out to destroy (v. 7). They boasted of their conquests (vv. 8-14; see 37:10-13) but did not give glory to God.

Because of their arrogant attitude, God would judge Assyria, for the worker certainly has mastery over His tools! Like a wasting disease and a blazing forest fire, God's wrath would come to this proud nation and its army. He would cut them down like trees in the forest (10:33-34). In the days of Hezekiah, God wiped out 185,000 of the Assyrian soldiers (37:36-37), and the great Assyrian Empire ultimately fell to Babylon in 609 B.C.

In spite of Assyria's conquest of the Northern Kingdom and its intention to destroy Judah, God would save a remnant so that "the twelve tribes" would not be annihilated (Acts 26:7; James 1:1; Rev. 21:12). "The remnant shall return" (Isa. 10:21) is the translation of the name of Isaiah's older son, Shear-jashub.

In verses 28-32, Isaiah traces the advance of the Assyrian army as it invaded Judah and marched towards Jersusalem. But God's word to the people was, "O My people that dwell in Zion, be not afraid of the Assyrian!" (v. 24) Isaiah gave the same message to King Hezekiah when the Assyrian army surrounded Jerusalem in 701 B.C. (37:1-7). God used Assyria to discipline His people, but He would not permit this godless nation to go beyond His purposes. God may use unbelievers to accomplish His will in the lives of His people, but He is always in control. We need never fear the disciplining hand of God, for He always disciplines in love (Heb. 12:1-11).

The Lord will restore His people (Isa. 11:1-16). In contrast to the proud trees that God cuts down (10:33-34) is a tender shoot from a seemingly dead stump. Isaiah looks beyond his people's trials to the glorious kingdom that will be established when Messiah comes to reign (11:1-9). David's dynasty was ready to end, but out of his family the Messiah would come (Rom. 1:3; Rev. 5:5). A godly remnant of Jews kept the nation alive so that the Messiah could be born.

His kingdom will involve righteous rule (Isa. 11:1-5) because the Son of God and the Spirit of God will administer its affairs justly. When the Messiah-King speaks the word, it is with power (Ps. 2:9; Rev. 19:15). His kingdom will also mean a restored creation because nature will once again enjoy the harmony it enjoyed before sin entered in (Isa. 11:6-9; Rom. 8:18-25). "The earth shall be full of the knowledge of the Lord, as the waters cover the sea" (Isa. 11:9; see Heb. 2:14).

The nucleus of the kingdom will be a regathered and reunited Jewish nation (Isa. 11:10-16). The "Root" will become a "banner" for the rallying of the people as the Lord reaches out and gathers His people from the nations where they have been exiled (43:5-6). It will be like a "second exodus" as God opens the way for His people to return to their land. In a limited sense, this promise was fulfilled after the Assyrian conquest and when the Jews left Babylonian captivity, but the ultimate fulfillment will be at the end of the age when Messiah regathers His people (27:12-13; 49:22-23; 56:7-8; Matt 24:31; Rom. 11:25-29). The centuries-long division between Israel and Judah will come to an end, and even the Gentiles will walk on "the highway" that leads to Jerusalem.

The "highway" is one of Isaiah's favorite images. Those who obey the Lord have a level and smooth road to walk (Isa. 26:7-8). When God calls His people back to their land, He will prepare the way for them (40:3-4) and lead them safely (42:16). He will remove obstacles so the people can travel easily (49:11; 57:14; 62:10). God's highway will be called "the Way of Holiness" (35:8).

When Isaiah looked at his people, he saw a sinful nation that would one day walk the "highway of holiness" and enter into a righteous kingdom. He saw a suffering people who would one day enjoy a beautiful and peaceful kingdom. He saw a scattered people who would be regathered and reunited under the kingship of Jesus Christ. Jesus taught us to pray, "Thy kingdom come" (Matt. 6:10); for only when His kingdom comes can there be peace on earth.

4. Isaiah: A Song of Salvation (Isa. 12:1-6)

Isaiah's name means "Jehovah is salvation," and "salvation" is a key theme in this song. "In that day" refers to the day of Israel's regathering and reunion and the righteous reign of the Lord Jesus Christ. The Jewish remnant will have come through the time of tribulation on earth ("the time of Jacob's trouble," Jer. 30:7), seen their Messiah, repented, and received Him by faith (Zech. 12:10-13:1; 14:4-11). Cleansed and established in their promised kingdom, the nation will praise the Lord and extol Him among the Gentiles.

The refrain in Isaiah 12:2—"Thy Lord, even Jehovah, is my strength and my son; he also is become my salvation"—was sung at the Exodus (Ex. 15:2) and at the rededication of the temple in Ezra's day (Ps. 118:14). It was sung by the Red Sea after the Jews had been delivered from Egypt by Moses, a prophet. It was sung in Jerusalem when the second temple was dedicated under the leadership of Ezra, a priest. It will be sung again when the Jewish nation accepts Jesus Christ as its King. They will recognize Him as "the Holy One of Israel" and willingly obey His holy law.

This joyful song closes this section of Isaiah in which the prophet has used four significant names to tell the people what God had planned for them. Because of Immanuel, there is a message of hope. Maher-shalal-hash-baz gives a warning of judgment, but his brother Shear-jashub speaks of a promise of mercy. The father's name, Isaiah, brings a song of rejoicing as the people discover that Jehovah is indeed their salvation.

The Lord will never forsake His people. No matter how difficult the days may be, or how long the nights, for the people of God, the best is yet to come.

CHAPTER FOUR
THE BURDENED PROPHET
ISAIAH 13–23

"Whether you like it or not, history is on our side. We will bury you!"

The Premier of the Soviet Union, Nikita Khrushchev, made that statement to a group of Western diplomats on November 18, 1956. But Khrushchev is dead, and the Soviet Union no longer exists. Khrushchev's boastful prophecy was not fulfilled.

Is there a pattern to history? Is anyone in charge? The British historian Edward Gibbon called history "little more than the register of crimes, follies, and misfortunes of mankind." But the American missionary leader Arthur T. Pierson said that "history is His story." Which one is right?

The Prophet Isaiah would stand with Pierson, for these eleven chapters are certainly evidence that God is at work in the nations of the world. In these chapters, the prophet reveals God's plan not only for Judah, but also for ten Gentile nations. President James Garfield called history "the unrolled scroll of prophecy," and Isaiah unrolls the scroll for us to read.

World leaders need to learn the lesson that Nebuchadnezzar learned the hard way, that "the Most High rules in the kingdom of men, and gives it to whomever He chooses" (Dan. 4:25, NKJV). Paul made the same declaration to the Greek philosophers in Athens: "[God] determined the times set for [the nations] and the exact places where they should live" (Acts 17:26, NIV). Indeed, "history is His story."

Isaiah called these prophetic declarations "burdens" (Isa. 13:1; 14:28; 15:1; 17:1; 19:1; 21:1, 11, 13; 22:1; 23:1). The Hebrew word means "to lift up." The prophet was carrying a heavy weight because of the solemn nature of his message (Jer. 23:33). He was announcing judgments that involved the destruction of cities and the slaughter of thousands of people. No wonder he felt burdened!

1. Babylon (Isa. 13:1-14:23; 21:1-10)

The word "Babel" means "gateway to a god" and sounds like the Hebrew word balal, which means "confusion" (Gen. 10:8-10; 11:1-9). In Scripture, Babylon symbolizes the world system man has built in defiance of God. Jerusalem and Babylon are contrasting cities: One is the chosen city of God, the other the wicked city of man. The city of God will last forever, but the rebellious city of man will ultimately be destroyed (Rev. 14:8; 16:19; 17-18).

God musters His army (Isa. 13:1-5, 17-18). God is sovereign. He is able to call any army He desires, to accomplish any task He assigns. He can summon them with a whistle (7:18) or by using leaders to raise a banner, shout, and beckon to the soldiers (13:2). In this case, God is mustering the army of the Medes (v. 17; 21:2), and He calls them "My sanctified ones." Even though they did not believe in Jehovah God, the Medes were set apart by God to do his Holy work.

God punishes His enemies (Isa. 13:6-22). The city of Babylon was completely destroyed in 689 B.C. by Sennacherib and the Assyrian army, but it was rebuilt by Sennacherib's son. In 539 B.C., Darius the Mede captured the city (Dan. 5:31), but he did not destroy it. In the centuries that followed, Babylon had its "shining moments," but after the death of its last great conqueror, Alexander the Great, the city declined and soon was no more. Isaiah's prophecy was fulfilled, for the city was not rebuilt.

But it is clear that Isaiah's prophecy describes something more significant than the ups and downs of an ancient city. The prophets often began a message by focusing on local events, but then enlarged their vision to reveal something greater. Isaiah saw in the fall of Babylon a picture of "the day of the Lord" (Isa. 13:6, 9, 13), that time when God will pour out His wrath on the whole world (v. 11). The image of the woman in travail is used in Scripture to describe a time of judgment (v. 8; 21:3; 26:17; Jer. 6:24; Micah 4:9-10; Matt. 24:8, where "sorrows" is "birthpains"; 1 Thes. 5:3). Isaiah looked beyond that day to the day when the Babylonian world system would be destroyed (Rev. 17-18). Compare Isaiah 13:10 and Matthew 24:29; Joel 2:10; and Revelation 6:12-14; and see Jeremiah 50-51.

God delivers his people (Isa. 14:1-23). Isaiah warned that the kingdom of Judah would be taken into captivity by Babylon (5:13; 6:11-12; 11:11, where "Shinar" is Babylon; 39:6), and this happened in 586 B.C. Jeremiah prophesied that the Captivity would last for seventy years. Then Babylon would be judged and the Jews permitted to go home (Jer. 25:1-14). So, the capture of Babylon by Darius would be good news to the Jews; for it would mean the end of their exile and bondage.

The picture in Isaiah 14:1-23 is that of a mighty monarch whose pride has brought him to destruction. This is what happened to Belshazzar when Darius the Mede captured Babylon in 539 B.C. (Dan. 5). Isaiah described the king's arrival in sheol, the world of the dead, where the king's wealth, glory, and power vanished. The dead kings already in sheol stood in tribute to him (Isa. 14:9), but it was all a mockery. Death is the great leveler; there are no kings in the world of the dead. "Lucifer" (v.12) is Latin for "morning star" and suggests that this king's glory did not last very long. The morning star shines but is soon swallowed up by the light of the sun.

The prophet saw in this event something far deeper than the defeat of an empire. In the fall of the king of Babylon, he saw the defeat of Satan, the "prince of this world," who seeks to energize and motivate the leaders of nations (John 12:31; Eph. 2:1-3). Daniel 10:20 indicates that Satan has assigned "princes" (fallen angels) to the various nations so that he can influence leaders to act contrary to the will of God.

This highest of God's angels tried to usurp the throne of God and capture for himself the worship that belongs only to God (Matt. 4:8-10). The name "Lucifer" ("morning star") indicates that Satan tries to imitate Jesus Christ, who is "the bright and morning star" (Rev. 22:16). "I will be like the Most High" reveals his basic strategy, for he is an imitator (Isa. 14:14; 2 Cor. 11:13-15). Like the king of Babylon, Satan will one day be humiliated and defeated. He will be cast out of heaven (Rev. 12) and finally cast into hell (20:10). Whether God is dealing with kings or angels, Proverbs 16:18 is still true: "Pride goes before destruction, and a haughty spirit before a fall" (NKJV).

God announces the victory (Isa. 21:1-10). "The desert of the sea" is probably the area around the Persian Gulf. Isaiah uses the image of a "desert storm" as he describes the attack of the Assyrians against Babylon, which took place in 689 B.C. At that time, Babylon and Assyria were rival powers (although Assyria was stronger), and the nations in the Fertile Crescent hoped that Babylon would stop the advance of Assyria. Alas, Babylon fell to Assyria, opening the way for Assyria to sweep across the region in conquest.

Realizing the consequences of Babylon's fall, the prophet experienced pain like a woman in travail (vv. 3-4) and felt crushed like grain in a mill (v. 10). Had this announcement referred to the fall of Babylon in 539 B.C., the Jews would have rejoiced; for it would have meant release from captivity. But in 689 B.C., Babylon's defeat meant the destruction of the Northern Kingdom and the devastation of the Southern Kingdom. Note that Jeremiah (Jer. 51:8) and John (Rev. 14:8; 18:2) both adopted Isaiah's words, "Babylon is fallen, is fallen!"

2. Assyria (Isa. 14:24-27)

The key word here is purpose. God is in control of the rise and fall of the nations as He works out His divine purposes in the world. Assyria was His tool to accomplish His purposes (10:5), and the day would come when God would judge Assyria (see vv. 5ff).

The judgment would take place in the land of Judah, and God would be the judge. Assyria invaded Judah during Hezekiah's reign (701 B.C.), and God destroyed the army as it threatened to capture Jerusalem (37:36). God permitted Assyria to discipline Judah, but He would not allow the enemy to destroy His people.

3. Philistia (Isa. 14:28-32)

An Assyrian leader ("rod"; 10:15, 24) died, and the Philistines rejoiced that their enemy had been weakened. (Some scholars think this leader was Shalmaneser V.) But Isaiah warned them that their rejoicing was presumptuous, for the new king would be worse. Isaiah compared the dead Assyrian ruler to a snake that gave birth to an even worse serpent! "Weep, Philistine cities—you are doomed" (14:31, TLB).

Note in this prophecy that God had a special word of assurance for His own people, Judah. Even the poorest of the poor would have food and safety (v. 30) and Zion would be delivered from the enemy (v. 32; 37:36), but the Philistines would be wiped out by war and famine (14:30). The Assyrian army would come from the north like a great cloud of smoke (v. 31), and the gates of the great Philistine cities would not stop them.

The envoys ("messengers" in v. 32, KJV) of the other nations would ask what was happening, but the diplomatic news would focus on Judah and not on Philistia! God's deliverance of Judah was the real news, not Assyria's conquest of Philistia. We wonder if diplomats and news reporters in today's media world would give God credit for a miracle of deliverance.

4. Moab (Isa. 15:1-16:14)

The Moabites were the product of Lot's incestuous union with his daughter (Gen. 19:30-38) and were the avowed enemies of the Jews (Num. 25; 31; Deut. 23:3).

The plight of Moab (Isa. 15:1-9). Within three years (16:14), this prophecy against Moab would be fulfilled with great national lamentation. At least fourteen different references to lamentation occur in this chapter: weeping, wailing, baldness, sackcloth, crying out, etc. The people fled to their temples and prayed to their gods, but to no avail (15:2, NIV). Even a day of national humiliation did not stop Assyria from invading Moab and ravaging the land. Advancing armies often stopped up the springs and watercourses and left the land in desolation (vv. 6-7). Where there was water in Moab, it was stained with blood, so great was the carnage (v. 9). How could the weak Moabites ever hope to defeat the great Assyrian lion?

The plea of Moab (Isa. 16:1-5). The one place the Assyrians could not conquer was Jerusalem (10:24-34). Though the Assyrian army entered the kingdom of Judah and did a great deal of damage to the land, it could not capture Jerusalem (chaps. 36-37). However, instead of fleeing to Mt. Zion, the Moabite fugitives fled south to the fords of the Arnon River and the "rock city" of Sela in Edom.

From Sela, the fugitives sent an appeal to the king of Judah to give them asylum from the enemy. But Isaiah warned them that it would take more than a request: They would need to submit to the king of Judah, which meant acknowledging the God of Judah. In that day, sending animals to a ruler was a form of paying tribute (2 Kings 3:4). Moab begged the leaders of Judah to give them refuge from the enemy, like a protecting rock on a hot day (16:3-4; see 32:1-2).

Isaiah was not impressed with the appeals of the Moabites. He called the Moabites extortioners, spoilers, and oppressors, and announced that the nation was destined to be destroyed (16.4). Why? Because they wanted Judah's help, but they did not want Judah's God. Verse 5 is definitely a messianic promise, pointing to the day when Messiah will reign in righteousness and mercy on David's throne. But Moab would not submit; they wanted deliverance on their own terms.

The pride of Moab (Isa. 16:6-14). We can understand the pride of a city like Babylon (14:12-14), but what did the tiny nation of Moab have to boast about? Their pride kept them from submitting to Judah, and this led to their defeat. Their boasting would turn into wailing and their songs into funeral dirges. Moab would become like a vineyard trampled down and a fruitful field left unharvested. Isaiah 16:9-11 describes the prophet's grief—and the Lord's grief—over the destruction of Moab. "I have no pleasure in the death of the wicked" (Ezek. 33:11). Isaiah could have rejoiced at the destruction of an old enemy, but instead he wept (Prov. 24:17-18).

5. Damascus [Syria] and Ephraim [Israel] (Isa 17:1-14)

These two nations were allied in their opposition to both Assyria and Judah (7:1-2), so the prophet spoke to both in one message. In 17:1-2, he warned Damascus, the capital city of Aram (Syria), that the city would be taken by the enemy. This occurred when the Assyrians conquered Aram in 732 B.C. Following their usual custom, the Assyrians deported many of the citizens, which left the land and cities deserted.

The fall of Damascus was a warning to Israel, the Northern Kingdom that had broken away from Judah and Judah's God (1 Kings 12). The prophet used several images to describe Ephraim's downfall: the destruction of the fortified cities (Isa. 17:3); the setting of the sun (v. 4a; "The glory has departed" [1 Sam. 4:19-22, NKJV]); the wasting away of a sick person (Isa. 17:4b); the gleaning of a small harvest (vv. 5-6); the decaying of a garden into a wasteland (vv. 9-11); the overflowing of a flood (vv. 12-13a); and the blowing away of chaff and tumbleweeds in a storm (v. 13b).

When judgment came, the people of Israel realized that their idols could not save them; so they turned to the Lord for help, but it was too late (Prov. 1:20-33). The nation was sick with sin and beyond recovery. Once the wind began to blow and the floods began to rise, the nation was without hope. In 722 B.C., Assyria conquered, and the kingdom of Israel was no more.

The emphasis in this section is on the God of Israel. He is the Lord of hosts (the Lord almighty), who controls the armies of heaven and earth (Isa. 17:3). He is the Lord God of Israel (v. 6), who called and blessed Israel and warned her of her sins. He is our Maker, the Holy One of Israel (v. 7); He is the God of our salvation and our Rock (v. 10). How foolish of the Israelites to trust their man-made idols instead of trusting the living God (v. 8; 1 Kings 12:25-33). But like Israel of old, people today trust the gods they have made instead of the God who made them; these include the false gods of pleasure, wealth, military might, scientific achievement, and even "religious experience."

6. Ethiopia (Isa. 18:1-7)

The original text has "Cush," a land that covers the area now occupied by Ethiopia, the Sudan, and Somalia. Isaiah called it "a land of whirring wings" (v. 1, NIV), not only because of the insects that infested the land, but also because of the frantic diplomatic activity going on as the nation sought alliances to protect them from Assyria. He pictures the ambassadors in their light, swift boats, going to the African nations for help. But God tells them to go back home (v. 2) because He would deal with Assyria himself, apart from the help of any army.

In contrast to the frantic human activity on earth is the calm patience of God in heaven (v. 4) as He awaits the right time to reap the harvest of judgment. Assyria is pictured as a ripening vine that will never survive, for God will cut it down (v. 5). In verse 6, Isaiah describes the feast that God spreads for the birds and beasts, the corpses of 185,000 Assyrian soldiers (37:36). See Revelation 14:14-20 and 19:17-21, where these same two images are used for end-time judgments.

Instead of rushing here and there with diplomatic plans, the Cushites will go to Jerusalem with gifts for the Lord and for the king of Judah (Isa. 17; 2 Chron. 32:20-23). When the messianic kingdom is established, the Gentile nations will go to Mt. Zion to worship the Lord and bring Him gifts (Isa. 60:1-7).

7. Egypt (Isa. 19:1-20:6)

The late Dr. Wilbur M. Smith, a leading prophetic scholar, wrote that Isaiah 19 "contains the most important prophetic utterance concerning Egypt in all of the Old Testament" (Egypt in Biblical Prophecy, p. 77). It is a remarkable prophecy, for Isaiah declares that the three enemies—Egypt, Israel, and Assyria (modern Iraq)—will one day be united in worshiping the Lord and sharing His blessing!

God will judge Egypt (Isa. 19:1-15; 20:1-6). This prophecy was probably fulfilled in 670 B.C. when Egypt was conquered by Esarhaddon, king of Assyria. The Assyrian conquest proved that the many gods of Egypt were powerless to help (19:1), and that the mediums and wizards were unable to give counsel (v. 3). In the days of Moses, God triumphed over the gods of Egypt (Ex. 12:12; Num. 33:4) and the wisdom of the Egyptian leaders, and He would do it again.

But that is not all. The forty-two provinces of Egypt, called "nomes," would be thrown into disarray and start fighting each other (Isa. 19:2). The Nile River, the source of Egypt's economy, and the streams and canals of the land, would all dry up; this would put farmers, fishermen, and cloth manufacturers out of business (vv. 5-10). For centuries, the Egyptians were respected for their wisdom, but now the princes and counselors would not know what to do (vv. 11-13). Instead of walking a straight path, the nation was led astray by leaders who were as dizzy as a drunken man staggering around in his vomit (vv. 14-15). Not a very pretty picture!

In these days of almost instant communication and of rapid transportation, when in a matter of minutes nations can come to the brink of war, we forget that God is still sovereign and can do whatever He pleases in the affairs of men. God destroyed everything that the Egyptians trusted—their political unity, their economy, religion, wisdom—and made them an easy target for the Assyrians. When the international news is frightening and you wonder where God is, read Psalm 2 and Acts 4:23-32, and take hope.

Isaiah 20 is a footnote to this prophecy and reveals that Isaiah did some unique things to get the attention of the people of Judah. One faction wanted to make an alliance with Egypt and Cush, but Isaiah warned them that such allies were destined to fall. For three years, the prophet dressed like a prisoner of war, wearing only a loincloth, to demonstrate his message. The pro-Egyptian party in Judah gave the prophet as much trouble as the pro-Egyptian people did who journeyed with Moses (30:1-7; 31:1-3; Num. 11; 14).

God will save Egypt (Isa. 19:16-25). The phrase "in that day" is used five times in this passage and refers to the last days when Jesus Christ shall establish His messianic kingdom on earth. Some remarkable changes will take place. Egypt will fear Israel (vv. 16-17) and become converted to the worship of the true God (vv. 18-22). They will trust Him, not their idols, and pray to Him in times of need. This is a promise that vast numbers of Muslims in Egypt will one day turn to the Lord and be saved!

These spiritual changes will bring about a great political change: Israel, Egypt, and Assyria (modern Iraq) will cooperate and enjoy the blessing of the Lord! They will not only receive God's blessing, but they will all be a blessing to the other nations (vv. 23-25). Once again, Isaiah picks up his "highway" theme to emphasize the unity of these three nations (see 11:16). What a wonderful day it will be when there is peace in the Middle East because the nations have bowed before the King of kings! We must continue praying, "Even so, come, Lord Jesus" (Rev. 22:20).

8. Edom (Isa. 21:11-12)

Dumah and Seir are names for Edom (Num. 24:18). Isaiah moved one letter in the Hebrew word Adom and created Dum, which means "stillness, silence." It was his way of saying, "Edom will be silent; it will be no more." The Edomites were descendants of Esau, whose nickname was "red [Edom]" (Gen. 25:21-34). Edom was a rugged land of red sandstone; her people were bitterly hostile to the Jews (Ps. 137:7).

Isaiah was the watchman on the wall (Isa. 21:6; Ezek. 3:16-21; 33:1-11), and he was asked, "What of the night?" What time of night was it? The advance of the Assyrian army had brought fearful darkness to the nations, and Edom wanted to know if there was any hope, any light. The prophet's reply was brief but adequate, with both information and invitation. Morning was coming, because Assyria would be defeated by God in the fields of Judah (Isa. 37:36). But the morning would not last, for Babylon would take Assyria's place and bring further darkness to the nations.

Then Isaiah added an invitation consisting of three simple words: inquire, return, come. "Seek the Lord," urged the prophet. "Turn from sin and return to Him. Come to Him, and He will receive you!" A brief "day of salvation" would dawn, and they had better use the opportunity.

Edom did not heed the invitation. The nation was taken by Babylon, then by the Persians (who changed their name to "Idumea"), and finally by the Romans. The battle between Esau and Jacob was carried on by Herods, who were Idumeans. After the fall of Jerusalem in A.D. 70, Edom vanished from the scene.

9. Arabia (Isa. 21:13-17)

The prophet saw the caravans of the Arabian merchants from Dedan leaving the trade route and hiding in the thickets because of the invasion of the Assyrian army. Food and water were brought to the fugitives by people from Tema, an oasis town. Eventually the caravan had to flee, for how could the merchants' slow animals compete with the Assyrian cavalry or their bows with the invaders' weapons? Like a laborer, God had a "contract" to fulfill (16:14). Within a year, the pomp and glory of the Arabian tribes would be gone.

10. Judah and Jerusalem (Isa. 22:1-25)

The people of Judah were behaving like their pagan neighbors, so it was only right that Isaiah should include them in the list of nations God would judge. Yes, in His mercy, the Lord would deliver Jerusalem from the Assyrian army, but He would not deliver them from Babylon. Isaiah pointed out two particular sins that would cause Judah to decline and ultimately go into captivity in Babylon.

The unbelief of the people (Isa. 22:1-14). While some parts of this description may seem to apply to the Assyrian invasion in Hezekiah's day (chaps. 36-37; 2 Kings 18-19; 2 Chron. 32), the primary reference is to the Babylonian conquest of Jerusalem in 586 B.C. In Isaiah's day, Jerusalem was a "joyous city" as people engaged in all kinds of celebrations (Isa. 5:11-13; 32:12-13). The popular philosophy was, "Let us eat and drink, for tomorrow we shall die" (22:13; 56:12; 1 Cor. 15:32). But the prophet did not participate in the parties, for he saw a day coming when death and destruction would reign in the City of David. The people went up to the housetops, but the prophet went down into one of the three valleys around Jerusalem; there God gave him a vision. Visions and valleys often go together.

He saw people dying, not from battle wounds, but from famine and disease (Isa. 22:2). He saw the nation's rulers fleeing in fear as the enemy army approached (vv. 3-7; 2 Kings 25:1-10). The people would do everything possible to prepare for a long siege (Isa. 22:8-11): collecting armor (1 Kings 7:2; 10:17), fortifying the walls (Isa. 22:9-10), servicing the water supply (v. 9; 2 Chron. 32:1-4, 30; 2 Kings 20:20), and building a reservoir between the walls (Isa. 22:11). But all of this frantic preparation would not deliver them from the enemy. "The defenses of Judah are stripped away (v. 8, NIV). In their false confidence, they said, "Just as the Lord delivered Jerusalem from Assyria, so He will deliver us from Babylon."

The people did everything but trust the Lord (v. 11). Instead of feasting, they should have been fasting, weeping, putting on sackcloth, and pulling out their hair in grief (v. 12; Ezra 9:3; James 4:8-10). God had sent the nation many prophets to warn them, but the people would not listen. Now it was too late; their sins could not be forgiven because their hearts were hard. Judah would go into captivity, and God's word to Isaiah would be fulfilled (Isa. 6:9-13).

The unfaithfulness of the leaders (Isa. 22:15-25). Had the leaders been faithful to the Lord and called the people to repentance, there might have been hope, but too many of the leaders were like Shebna, thinking only of themselves. As treasurer (steward), Shebna was second to King Hezekiah in authority (see chaps. 36-37), but he used his authority (and possibly the king's money) to build himself a monumental tomb (22:16) and to acquire chariots (v. 18; see 2:7). Shebna was not a spiritual man, and he probably sided with the pro-Egypt party in Judah.

God judged Shebna by demoting him (he became "secretary" according to 36:3, NIV), disgracing him, and deporting him. Eventually he was thrown "like a ball" (22:18) into a far country (Assyria?), where he died. He could not have an expensive funeral and be buried in his elaborate tomb.

God chose a new man, Eliakim ("God will raise up"), and called him "My servant." Instead of exploiting the people, he would be a father to them and use his "key" (authority) for the good of the nation. He would be like a dependable peg, hammered into the wall, on which you could hang many burdens. But even a godly leader like Eliakim could not prevent the ultimate fall of Judah, for one day the whole nation would fall (v. 25). Eliakim is a picture of Jesus Christ (Rev. 3:7), the greatest Servant of all.

11. Phoenicia (Isa. 23:1-18)

The Phoenicians were a merchant people whose land approximated what is today known as Lebanon. Their ships plied the Mediterranean coasts, where their many colonies assured them of an abundant supply of the world's wealth. Tyre and Sidon were key cities. Both David and Solomon made use of workers and building materials from Phoenicia (2 Sam. 5:11; 1 Kings 5:8-9). King Ahab married the Phoenician princess Jezebel, who promoted Baal worship in Israel (1 Kings 16:29-33).

Declaration (Isa. 23:1-7). Isaiah addressed ships from Spain (Tarshish) that were docked at Cyprus (Kittim), telling their crews to weep and go home (v. 6) because Tyre was no more. Merchants from Spain, the coastlands, and even Egypt would wail because Tyre's great shipping industry was gone and the Mediterranean economy had been devastated. (See Rev. 17-18 for a parallel, and note that both Babylon and Tyre are compared to prostitutes [Isa. 23:16-17]). The joyful citizens of Tyre would become mourning refugees (v. 7) when Nebuchadnezzar would conquer Phoenicia in 572 B.C. (He did not conquer the island part of Tyre, but Alexander the Great would do it in 332 B.C. See Ezek. 26.)

Explanation (Isa. 23:8-14). "Who planned this against Tyre?" (v. 8, NIV) The Lord Almighty! Just as He purposed to destroy Egypt (19:23) and Babylon (1427), so he purposed to judge Tyre. Just as Assyria had destroyed the city of Babylon in 689 B.C., so Tyre and Sidon would be destroyed by a revived Babylon in 585-572 B.C. (23:13). The pride of Tyre (v. 9) was a sin that God could not ignore.

Anticipation (Isa. 23:15-18). Even before their eventual destruction, Tyre and Sidon would not be involved in business for seventy years. History tells us that the Assyrians restricted Phoenician trade from 700-630 B.C.; but when Assyria began to weaken in power, Tyre and Sidon revived their businesses. The prophet compared the revived city to an old prostitute who had to sing lovely songs in order to get attention. Apparently the shipping business would not be as easy or as lucrative as it once was. In verse 18, Isaiah looked ahead to the messianic kingdom, when the wealth of Tyre would not be hoarded (see Zech. 9:3), but given to the Lord as a holy offering.

Our trek through these eleven chapters has taught us some important lessons. First, God is in control of the nations of the world, and He can do with them what he pleases. "Though the mills of God grind slowly, yet they grind exceeding small" (Friedrich von Logau, translated by Henry Wadsworth Longfellow). Second, God especially hates the sin of pride. (See Isa. 13:11; 16:6; 23:9; and Prov 8:13.) When nations turn from the living God to trust their wealth and their armaments, God must show them that He is the only sure refuge. Third, God judges the nations for the way they treat each other. Judah was the only nation mentioned that had God's law, yet God held the other ten Gentile nations accountable for what they did. "For as many as have sinned without law will also perish without law" (Rom. 2:12, NKJV). Finally, God always gives a word of promise and hope to His people. Babylon will fall, but God will care for Judah (Isa. 14:1-3, 32). Moab will not accept sanctuary from Jerusalem, but God will one day establish Messiah's throne there (16:5). Assyria and Egypt may be avowed enemies of the Jews, but one day the three nations will together glorify God (19:23-25).

Therefore, no matter how frightening the national or international situation may become, God's children can have peace because they know Almighty God is on His throne. The nations may rage and plot against God, but "He who sits in the heaven shall laugh" (Ps. 2:4, NKJV).

When the Lord of heaven and earth is your Father, and you gladly wear Christ's yoke, you have nothing to fear (Matt. 11:25-30). Therefore, be comforted!

CHAPTER FIVE
A REFUGE FROM THE STORM
ISAIAH 24–27

After prophesying concerning eleven different nations, Isaiah enlarged his prophecy and described a judgment that would fall on the whole world. The Hebrew word *erets,* used sixteen times in chapter 24, is translated land, earth, and world in the King James Version. It is not always easy to tell when *erets* refers to one country or to the whole earth, but the context usually guides us. Isaiah 24-27 describes a global judgment that will end with the destruction of God's enemies and the restoration of God's people Israel in their land.

Isaiah warned the Northern Kingdom that the Assyrians would destroy them, and he told Judah that the Babylonians would take them captive, but these local calamities were only forerunners of a vast end-times catastrophe that would engulf the whole world. The prophets call this time of terrible judgment "the Day of the Lord," and in the New Testament it is described in Matthew 24, Mark 13, and Revelation 6-19.

Isaiah makes three declarations that will comfort God's chosen people in that awesome day of judgment. These declarations also encourage us today as we see our world plunging headlong into sin and rebellion against God. Will God ever deal with the wicked? What hope is there for the righteous?

1. The Lord Will Judge His Enemies (Isa. 24:1-23)

The result of God's judgment will be a world that is empty, laid waste, and distorted, and whose inhabitants are scattered. The prophet may have had Genesis 1:2 and 11:9 in mind when he wrote this. Nobody on earth will escape, for "God is no respecter of persons" (Acts 10:34). Position, power, and wealth are no protection against the wrath of God. God merely speaks the word and, like a dying invalid, "the world languishes and fades away" (Isa. 24:3-4, NKJV). People who are proud of their wealth and position will find themselves poor and without power.

Why does God punish the inhabitants of the world? Because they have defiled the world by their sins. When Adam sinned, God cursed the ground as a part of the punishment (Gen. 3:17-19; Rom. 8:20-22), and God warned the people of Israel that their sins polluted the Promised Land (Num. 35:33). Today we see man's greed polluting land, water, and atmosphere, as well as exploiting the earth of its God-given treasures. Sin has consequences in nature as well as in human character and conscience.

For centuries, mankind has polluted the world by disobeying God's laws and violating His statutes. This was the reason for the Flood (Gen. 6:5; 11-13). Long before Moses gave the Law, people knew that it was wrong to lie, steal, and kill (Rom. 1:18-2:16), but they did these evil things anyway. The "everlasting covenant" of Isaiah 24:5 refers to what we generally call the Noahic Covenant (Gen. 8:20-9:17) and deals primarily with our care of God's world and our treatment of fellow humans. Isaiah 24:16 suggests that God will also judge the world because people are treacherous and do not keep their word. The people of the world have abused both the earth and its inhabitants, and they will pay for it.

Verses 6-13 give a vivid picture of what it will be like on the earth during the Day of the Lord. In Israel, the harvest was generally a time for great joy; but there will be no joy because there will be no harvest. God's judgments will destroy the crops as well as the workers who would till the soil. (See Rev. 6:8 and 9:15.) "The city" is mentioned at least eight times in these chapters (Isa. 24:10, 12; 26:5; 27:10) and should be taken generically rather than as a reference to any one particular city. Whether people live in rural areas or in the cities, they will not escape God's wrath. Like a farmer harvesting the last olive or the last grape, God will do a thorough job of judging sinners (24:13). The only singing during His harvest will be done by the believing remnant who trust God and are delivered (vv. 14-16a). The doctrine of "the remnant" is an important part of Isaiah's message (1:9; 10:20-22; 11:11, 16; 14:22, 30); Isaiah's eldest son was named "a remnant shall return" (7:3).

The prophet changed the image in 24:17-18a when he described the futile attempts of frightened animals to avoid the hunters' traps. But apart from faith in the Lord, there will be no place of escape in that great day of judgment. No matter where sinners go, they will not be able to hide from the wrath of God (Rev. 6:15-17).

The opening of the windows of heaven (Isa. 24:18b) reminds us of the Flood (Gen. 7:11). Jesus said that, before the "Day of the Lord," society would be as it was in the days before the Flood (Matt. 24:37-42). In that day, God will shake everything, and anything man has made will stagger like a drunk and collapse like a flimsy hut (Isa. 24:20; see 1:8). The weight of guilt will be too heavy for people to carry.

But the Day of the Lord will affect not only the earth and its people but also Satan and his hosts. God will judge "the powers in the heavens above" as well as "the kings on earth below" (24:21, NIV). These judgments will be part of the spiritual battle that has been waging for centuries between the Lord of Hosts and the armies of the devil (Gen. 3:15; Luke 10:17-24; Eph. 6:10ff; Rev. 12). Isaiah 24:22 parallels Revelation 20:1-3, an event that will take place just before the thousand-year reign of Jesus Christ (Isa. 24:23; Rev. 20:4-10). The word "visited" in Isaiah 24:22 (KJV) means "released" (cf. NIV margin). The climax of the "Day of the Lord" will be "the Lord of hosts shall reign in Mt. Zion" (v. 23).

2. The Lord Will Preserve His People (Isa. 25:1-12)

This chapter is a song of praise to the Lord from the believing remnant that He preserved during "the Day of the Lord." In this song, three striking images stand out.

The ruined city (Isa. 25:1-3). We have met this image before (24:10, 12) and noted that "the city" is a generic term for all cities. Isaiah lived in an agricultural world of towns and villages, and the large cities (or city-states) were places of power and wealth. In times of war, the people fled to the walled cities for protection. But the great cities of the world will offer no protection when God pours His wrath on the nations (2:19; Rev. 16:19). The rebellious cities will be forced to acknowledge the greatness of God and give their homage to Him.

The refuge (Isa. 25:4-5). Isaiah paints two pictures: the buffeting of a storm and the beating down of a burning sun in the desert. Where can travelers go for refuge? They see a huge rock and find refuge in it. God is that Rock (Deut. 32:3-4, 30; 33:27; Pss. 46:1; 61:1-4), and He will be a refuge for His believing people during that terrible "Day of the Lord." The victory shouts of the enemy will disappear the way heat vanishes when a cloud covers the sun.

God cares for His own in times of trial and judgment. He kept Noah and his family alive through the Flood (Gen. 6-8) and guarded Israel when His judgments fell on Egypt (Ex. 8:22-23; 9:4, 6, 26; 10:23; 11:6-7; 12:13). He protected believing Rahab and her family when Jericho fell (Josh. 6:25) and preserved a faithful remnant when Judah was taken into Babylonian captivity (Ezra. 9:8-9). Throughout the centuries, He has kept His church in spite of the attacks of Satan (Matt. 16:18) and will deliver His church from the wrath to come (1 Thes. 1:10; 5:9). When "the Day of the Lord" comes to this godless world, God will see to it that the Jewish remnant will be preserved. "Hide yourselves for a little while until His wrath has passed by. See, the Lord is coming out of his dwelling to punish the people of the earth for their sins" (Isa. 26:20-21, NIV).

The feast (Isa. 25:6-12). For the Old Testament Jew, a feast was a picture of the Kingdom Age when Messiah would reign over Israel and all the nations of the world. Israel would enter into her glory, and the Gentiles would come to Zion to worship the Lord (2:1-5; 55:1-5; 60:1ff). When Jesus used the image of the feast in Matthew 8:11 and Luke 13:28-29, the people knew He was speaking about the promised kingdom.

The food that we eat only sustains life, but at this feast death itself will be conquered. "On this mountain He will destroy the shroud that enfolds all peoples, the sheet that covers all nations; He will swallow up death forever. The Sovereign Lord will wipe away the tears from all faces" (Isa. 25:7-8, NIV). The funeral will turn into a wedding! Verse 8 was quoted by Paul in 1 Corinthians 15:54 and by the Apostle John in Revelation 7:17 and 21:4.

The "covering" and "veil" in Isaiah 25:7 may also suggest the blindness of Israel and the nations to the true God and Savior (2 Cor. 3:12-18; 4:3-4). When the Lord Jesus Christ returns in power and great glory, Israel "shall look upon Me whom they have pierced" (Zech. 12:10) and shall trust in Him for salvation. The veil shall be removed, and they will see their Messiah and their God. Then they will sing the song of Isaiah 25:9 as they enter into the great kingdom feast.

In contrast to the exaltation of Mt. Zion is the humiliation of Moab (vv. 10-12). Isaiah probably selected Moab as an example of how God will humble all of Israel's enemies. The imagery here is quite graphic: The Moabites are compared to straw trampled so deeply into manure that the people have to swim through the manure to get out! (See the NIV.) While the Jews are enjoying a feast of good things, the Moabites are trying to escape from the excrement of the animals the Jews are devouring! Moab was always known for its pride (16:6ff), but God will bring them low along with all the other nations that exalt themselves, exploit others, and refuse to submit to the Lord.

3. The Lord Will Restore the Nation (Isa. 26:1-27:13)

Israel is singing once more (24:14-16; 25:1ff), and this time the emphasis is on righteousness and peace. There can be no true peace apart from righteousness (32:17), and there can be no righteousness apart from God's salvation in Jesus Christ (Rom. 3:21-31). It is at Calvary that "righteousness and peace have kissed each other" (Ps. 85:10). When Jesus Christ reigns on earth, the promise of 72:7 will be fulfilled: "In His days the righteous shall flourish, and abundance of peace, until the moon is no more" (NKJV). Jesus Christ is our true Melchizedek—King of Righteousness and King of Peace (Heb. 7:1-3).

The phrase "in that day" (Isa. 26:1; 27:1-2, 12-13) refers to "the Day of the Lord" and the blessings that will follow when the Lord defeats His enemies. In these two chapters, the prophet encourages God's suffering people by describing in seven pictures the kingdom blessings that await them in the future.

The strong city (Isa. 26:1-6). Samaria fell to the Assyrians and Jerusalem to the Babylonians, but the New Jerusalem would be impregnable. During "the Day of the Lord," God will level the lofty cities of the earth, but Mt. Zion will be exalted to the glory of the Lord (2:1-5). Jerusalem will no longer be the sinful city described in chapter 1; it will be a righteous city for a holy nation whose sins have been washed away (Zech. 13:1). Compare Isaiah 26:2 with Psalms 15 and 24.

Only those who have trusted Jesus Christ will enter into the city, and because they believe, they have peace (Rom. 5:1). The Hebrew word for "peace" *(shalom)* means much more than a cessation of war. It includes blessings such as wholeness, health, quietness of soul, preservation, and completeness. "What is your peace?" is the way Jews often greet one another, and Isaiah's reply would be, "My peace is from the Lord, for I trust wholly in him!" Paul's counsel in Philippians 4:6-9 is based on Isaiah 26:3.

It is worth noting that Augustus Toplady's song "Rock of Ages" is based on the marginal reading of verse 4: "for in the Lord God is the Rock of ages." The New Jerusalem is a city built on a Rock!

The level path (Isa. 26:7-11). We have noted Isaiah's emphasis on the image of the highway (see comments at 11:16). During much of their history, the Jews have traveled a rough road, but when the kingdom is established, God will give them level paths and a smooth way. Because they will be walking in the will of God, their way will be safe and enjoyable. They will wait on the Lord to discern His will. They will yearn for the Lord and worship him even in the night (Ps. 119:55).

According to Isaiah 26:9-11, God wants the world to learn righteousness. He sends his judgments, but the people still will not repent (Rev. 9:20-21; 16:9). He shows them His grace in a thousand ways, but they continue to do evil. His hand is at work, but they will not see it. The prophet prays that God will reveal Himself through His people as He works on their behalf. The reviving and restoring of Israel should help to convince a lost world that God is not dead and that He keeps His promises.

The woman in travail (Isa. 26:12-18). The agony of "the Day of the Lord" is compared to the pain of a woman travailing in birth (13:6-8; 1 Thes. 5:1-3). Isaiah describes the remnant confessing their failures to the Lord. Because of their sins, they had been subjected to many Gentile tyrants, but now these tyrants were dead and could not return to enslave them. God disciplined His people and brought them to the place where all they could do was whisper their prayers (Isa. 26:26, NIV), but He heard them and delivered them. Israel was in pain like a woman giving birth, except that their travail produced nothing! Israel failed to give birth to the blessings God wanted them to bring to the world (v. 18). But during the Kingdom Age, Israel and Mt. Zion will be the source of blessing for the whole world.

What hindered Israel from being the blessing to the world that God wanted them to be? They turned from the sincere worship of the true God and gave their devotion to idols. The Hebrew verb in verse 13 translated "had dominion" (KJV) gives us the noun *baal,* the name of the Canaanite storm god whose cult created so many problems in Israel. But the word *baal* also means "husband," so the suggestion is that Israel was not true to her husband Jehovah, but in her unfaithfulness turned to another god. The same image occurs in James 4:4.

The life-giving dew (Isa. 26:19-21). Just as the dew brings new life to the soil and vegetation, so God will raise the dead out of the earth. The prophet had already announced God's great victory over death (25:7-8), and now he tells us how He will do it: He will raise their bodies from the dust. Resurrection is not reconstruction; God does not reassemble the body and give it life. Paul compared the miracle of resurrection to the harvesting of grain planted in the soil (1 Cor. 15:35-49). The seed is buried and dies, but out of this death comes forth life and fruitfulness. Isaiah had just written about travail (Isa. 26:17-18), so he compares the resurrection to human birth: "The earth will give birth to her dead" (v. 19, NIV).

When Christ returns for His church, believers who "sleep in Jesus" will be raised from the dead (1 Thes. 4:13-18). When He returns with His church to judge His enemies and establish His kingdom, there will also be a resurrection (Rev. 19:11-20:6). These two events are called "the first resurrection" and include only saved people. At the end of the thousand years, when Satan is finally imprisoned, the lost will be raised to face the Great White Throne Judgment (vv. 7-15). While the Old Testament does not give the complete revelation about death and resurrection, it does assure us that there is a future for the human body (Dan. 12:2; Ps. 16:9-10.

The remnant has been praying to God (Isa. 26:11-19), and now God speaks to them and gives them the assurance they need (vv. 20-21). He promises to shelter His people from the terrible attacks of the enemy (Rev. 12). God will punish His enemies who have slain His people, whose blood cries out from the earth for vengeance (Gen. 4:10-11; Ezek. 24:7-8; Rev. 6:9-11). The unjust shedding of blood pollutes the land (Num. 35:29-34; Ps. 106:34-39) and invites the judgment of God.

The conquered beast (Isa. 27:1). The nations around Israel had many myths about sea monsters, one of whom was compared to "leviathan," probably the crocodile (Job 3:8; 41:1ff). To slay leviathan was a great achievement (Ps. 74:14), and the Lord promised to do it. Satan held these nations in bondage through their superstitious religions, but the remnant did not need to fear the false gods of the Gentiles. God's people today are set free from bondage to Satan and the false gods he seduces people to worship (Col. 2:13-15), and we can rejoice in our Lord's great victory (John 12:31). When the battle is over and the Lord has conquered evil, Israel can enter her glorious kingdom without fear.

The fruitful vineyard (Isa. 27:2-11). As in 5:1-7, the vineyard is Israel, but here the prophet sees both the Israel of his day and the Israel of the future day when the kingdom will be established. God was not angry with His people (27:4); He just yearned for them to return to Him and fervently trust Him. He used war (Assyria) to punish the Northern Kingdom and captivity (Babylon) to discipline the Southern Kingdom (v. 8, NIV), but He did this in love and not in anger. Verses 10-11 are a description of Jerusalem after the Babylonian siege. God temporarily took away His mercy until His purposes were fulfilled.

In "the Day of the Lord" God will use suffering to purge His people and prepare them for their kingdom. Verse 9 does not suggest that personal suffering can atone for sin, for only the sacrifice of Jesus Christ can do that. God uses suffering as a discipline to bring us to submission so that we will seek Him and His holiness (Heb. 12:1-11). The Babylonian Captivity cured the Jews of their idolatry once and for all (Isa. 27:9).

In Isaiah's day, the vineyard was producing wild grapes, but in the future kingdom, Israel will be fruitful and flourishing. God will guard His people and give them all that they need to bring glory to His name. The nation will "blossom and bud, and fill the face of the world with fruit" (v. 6). Through Israel, all the nations of the earth will be blessed (Gen. 12:1-3).

The Bible speaks of three vines: the people of Israel (Isa. 5; 27), Christ and His church (John 15), and godless Gentile society, "the vine of the earth" (Rev. 14:18). The vineyard of Israel is not bearing fruit, the "vine of the earth" is filling the world with poisonous fruit, and God's people must be faithful branches in the Vine and produce fruit that glorifies God's name.

The holy and happy feast (Isa. 27:12-13). The camp of Israel was directed by the blowing of trumpets (Num. 10). The Feast of Trumpets took place on the first day of the seventh month and prepared Israel for the annual Day of Atonement (Lev. 23:23-32). But the Day of Atonement prepared them for the Feast of Tabernacles, which is a picture of the joy of the future kingdom (Lev. 23:33-44).

Isaiah envisioned a glorious day when God would repeat the miracle of the Exodus and deliver His people from their bondage to the Gentile nations. The trumpet would summon them to Jerusalem (Matt 24:31) and announce God's victory over their foes, and they would "worship the Lord in the holy mount at Jerusalem." The kingdom will be like an endless feast and a holy day of worship as the people rejoice in the Lord. Of course, God's people today are also awaiting "the sound of the trumpet" (1 Cor. 15:50-58; 1 Thes. 4:13-18) announcing the coming of the Lord for His church. Then we will go with Him to heaven and prepare for the marriage supper of Lamb. We shall return with Him to earth and reign with Him in the kingdom.

Are you praying daily, "Thy kingdom come"?

CHAPTER SIX
STORM CLOUDS OVER JERUSALEM
ISAIAH 28–31

The name "Jerusalem" means "city of peace," but throughout its history it has been associated more with conflict than with peace. Even today, Jerusalem is a focal point for concern in the Middle East. "Pray for the peace of Jerusalem," admonished the psalmist (Ps. 122:6). Why pray for Jerusalem? Why not pray for London or Moscow or Rome? Because when there is true peace in Jerusalem, there will be peace in the whole world (Isa. 52:7; 66:12); so we had better take the psalmist's words to heart.

Chapters 28–31 record a series of five "woes" (28:1; 29:1, 15: 30:1; 31:1) that focus primarily on Jerusalem. A sixth "woe" is found in 33:1, and interspersed with these "woes" of judgment are promises of restoration and glory. Isaiah is attempting to get the rulers of Judah to stop trusting "power politics" and international treaties and start trusting the Lord.

1. The Lord Warns Jerusalem (Isa. 28:1-29)

Like all devout Jews, Isaiah loved Jerusalem, the Holy City, the City of David, the place of God's dwelling (Pss. 122 and 137). But Isaiah saw storm clouds gathering over the city and announced that trouble was coming. It was time for the nation to turn to God in repentance.

He began his message by announcing God's judgment on Ephraim (Isa. 28:1-6). Surely their neighbor's fall would serve as a warning to the people of Judah and Jerusalem! If Assyria conquered Samaria, then Judah was next on the list. The Northern Kingdom was proud of its capital city, Samaria, that sat like a beautiful crown (or wreath) at the head of a fruitful valley. But their arrogance was detestable to God, for they thought their fortress city was impregnable. Samaria reigned in luxury and pleasure and had no fear of her enemies.

The Lord was also appalled by their drunkenness. To the Jews, wine was a gift from God and a source of joy (Jud. 9:13; Ps. 104:15). The Law did not demand total abstinence, but it did warn against drunkenness (Deut. 21:18-21; Prov. 20:1; 23:20-21, 29-35). The prophet Amos denounced the luxurious indulgences of the people in both Judah and Samaria (Amos 6:1-7), and Isaiah also thundered against such godless living (Isa. 5:11-12, 22).

A government official in Washington, D.C. once quipped, "We have three parties in this city: the Democratic Party, the Republican Party, and the cocktail party." Indeed, Washington, D.C. ranks high on the list of cities noted for alcohol consumption. Many people don't realize that alcohol and nicotine, America's favorite legal narcotics, do far more damage than all the illegal drugs combined. According to Dr. Arnold Washton, alcohol and nicotine kill 450,000 people annually, while illegal drugs kill about 6,000 (*Willpower's Not Enough,* Harper & Row, 1989; p. 13). This does not make illegal drugs acceptable, but it does help us put things in perspective. What hope is there for our affluent, pleasure-loving society that gives lip service to religion and ignores the tragic consequences of sin and the judgment that is sure to come?

Samaria was proud of her beauty, but that beauty was fading like a cut flower (28:1, 4) that could never stand before the coming tempest. God was sending a storm across the land, and their proud city would be destroyed by wind, rain, hail, and flood—the Assyrian army! Conquering Samaria would be as easy as plucking a fig from a tree! On that day of judgment, Samaria would learn too late that Jehovah, not Samaria, is the "crown of glory" and "diadem of beauty" (v. 5) and that he is a God of justice (vv. 5-6). The reference here is to God's deliverance of Jerusalem from Assyria, even when the enemy was at the very gates (chaps. 36–37).

Perhaps the people of Judah rejoiced to hear Isaiah announce the fall of their rival kingdom, but their celebration was short-lived; for the prophet announced that Judah was guilty of the same sins as Samaria and therefore was in danger of judgment (28:5-8). The priests and the prophets, who should have been examples to the people, were staggering drunk around the city and carousing at tables covered with vomit. Their counsel to the people did not come from the Spirit of God but from their own drunken delusions (see Eph. 5:18). They not only swallowed wine, but were "swallowed up on wine" (Isa. 28:7). This reminds us of the Japanese proverb: "First the man takes a drink, then the drink takes a drink, and then the drink takes the man."

But pride and drunkeness were not Judah's only sins; they also mocked God's prophet and rejected God's Word (vv. 9-13). Verses 9-10 are the words of the drunken prophets and priests as they ridiculed Isaiah. "He talks to us as though we were little children," they said. "He keeps saying the same things over and over again and uses the vocabulary of a child. There is certainly no need to take anything he says seriously!"

Society today often takes a similar attitude toward God's servants and God's Word. People are so intoxicated by intellectual pride that they laugh at the simple message of the Gospel presented by humble witnesses (1 Cor. 1:18-31). The prophet Amos was ejected from the king's chapel because he was a simple farmer and not a member of the religious elite (Amos 7:10-17). Evangelist D.L. Moody was often laughed at because his speech was not polished, but God used him to bring many thousands to the Savior.

What was Isaiah's answer to this supercritical crowd of religious drunks? "If you will not listen to my simple speech in your own language, God will speak to you with a language you do not understand. He will send the army of Assyria, whose language is foreign to you." This happened to both Ephraim and Judah. The Assyrians completely destroyed the Southern Kingdom in 722 B.C.; and in 701 B.C., after devastating the land of Judah, they came to the very gates of Jerusalem.

This leads to Isaiah's third announcement: God offers His people rest (Isa. 7:4; 8:6-8), but they will not obey (hear) His Word (28:12-20). The prophet had given them a plain message that everybody could understand, but they rejected it. Their faith was in their political alliances and not in God (vv. 15, 18). In the days of King Ahaz, they made a secret treaty with Assyria, and in the days of King Hezekiah, they turned to Egypt for help (30:1-5; 31:1). But these "covenants with death and the grave" were destined to fail because God was not in them. The enemy would come like a flood, a storm, a whip (scourge), and there would be no escape. Ephraim would be destroyed, and Judah would be saved by the skin of her teeth. The bed they had made (their alliances) could not give them rest (see 28:12), and the covering they made (their treaties) would not cover them (see 31:1).

Their only hope was in the tried and true foundation stone (28:16), the "Rock of ages" (26:4; 8:14; 17:10). This is definitely a reference to the Messiah and is so interpreted in the New Testament (1 Peter 2:4-7; Rom. 9:33; Mark 12:10; see Ps. 118:22). If they had faith in Jehovah, they would not be rushing here and there, trying to forge alliances, a practice that only leads to shame and failure (Rom. 10:11). A solid rock is better protection than a flimsy covering of lies!

Isaiah's final announcement was that their confidence that God would not judge them was a delusion (Isa. 28:21-29). "But God defended His people in the past!" they argued. "What about David's victory over the Philistines at Mount Perazim [2 Sam. 5:17-21], or Joshua's victory over the Amorites at Gibeon [John. 10]?" But Joshua and David were godly leaders who trusted Jehovah and obeyed His Word. What Isaiah's scoffing opponents did not realize was that God would do a "strange work": He would use the enemy to fight against His own people! Just as a farmer has different tasks to perform and must adapt himself to each task, whether plowing or threshing, so God must do the work that is necessary to bring about His eternal purposes. He knows just what tool to use and when to use it.

Jerusalem watched the Northern Kingdom fall to the Assyrians, but this judgment did not bring them to repentance. When we start saying to ourselves, "It can never happen to me!"—it is sure to happen!

2. The Lord Humbles Jerusalem (Isa. 29:1-14)

"Ariel" is a code name for Jerusalem and means "lion of God." The lion was a symbol of Assyria, so the prophet may have been saying, "Assyria is now God's lion, and Jerusalem is God's lion in name only." But the Hebrew word also means "an altar hearth," where the burnt offerings were sacrificed (Ezek. 43:13-18). "It [Jerusalem] shall be unto me as Ariel [an altar hearth]" (Isa. 29:2). In other words, it would become a place of slaughter.

God was going to humble the proud city. Instead of roaring and frightening the enemy, the lion would only whisper from the dust (v. 4). Instead of their sacrifices being accepted by God (v.1), the entire city would become an altar, and God would make His people a sacrifice.

When did these things happen? God began to "turn up the heat" in 701 B.C. when Assyria marched triumphantly through Judah and almost took Jerusalem. God defeated Assyria in an instant (37:36), "suddenly" (29:5), like blowing away dust or chaff (v. 6). This discipline should have brought Judah back to the Lord, but after the death of Hezekiah, they returned to their sins. So in 586 B.C. God sent the Babylonians, who conquered Jerusalem and destroyed it, taking thousands of Jews into captivity. God did His "strange work" and permitted His own people to be slain by the enemy. The city indeed was like an altar hearth, and thousands were sacrificed to the wrath of the enemy.

But Isaiah looked far down the highway of history to the end times when Jerusalem would be attacked by the armies of the world (vv. 7-8; Zech. 14:1-3). This is what prophetic students call "the battle of Armageddon," though that title is not used in Scripture (Rev. 14:14-20; 16:13-21). When it looks as though the city is about to fall, and the enemy armies are sure of victory, Jesus Christ will return and deliver His people (19:11-21). The enemy victory will vanish.

Why were the people of Jerusalem so ignorant of what was going on? Their hearts were far from God (Isa. 29:13). They went through the outward forms of worship and faithfully kept the annual feasts (v. 1; 1:10ff), but it was not a true worship of God (Matt. 15:1-9). Going to the temple was the popular thing to do, but most of the people did not take their worship seriously. Therefore, God sent a "spiritual blindness" and stupor on His people so that they could not understand their own Law. Such blindness persists today (Rom. 11:8; 2 Cor. 3:13-18). If people will not accept the truth, then they must become more and more blind and accept lies. (See John 9:39-41 and 2 Thes. 2:1-12.)

3. The Lord Appeals to Jerusalem (Isa. 29:15-24)

This "woe" exposed the devious political tactics of the rulers of Judah, who thought that God would not hold them accountable for what they were doing. They were trying to turn things upside down, the clay telling the potter what to do. (See 45:9; 64:8; Jer. 18; and Rom 9:20.) If only people would seek the counsel of the Lord instead of depending on their own wisdom and the fragile promises of men!

In Isaiah 29:17-24, Isaiah asked the people to look ahead and consider what God had planned for them. In their political strategy, they had turned things upside down, but God would one day turn everything around by establishing His glorious kingdom on earth. The devastated land would become a paradise, the disabled would be healed, and the outcasts would be enriched and rejoice in the Lord. There would be no more scoffers or ruthless people practicing injustice in the courts. The founders of the nation, Abraham and Jacob, would see their many descendants all glorifying the Lord.

In light of this glorious future, why should Judah turn to feeble nations like Egypt for help? God is on their side, and they can trust Him! Abraham went to Egypt for help and got into trouble (Gen. 12:10-20), and Isaac started for Egypt but was stopped by God (26:1-6). God cared for Jacob during all of his years of trial, and surely He could care for Jacob's children. It is tragic when a nation forgets its great spiritual heritage and turns from trusting the Lord to trusting the plans and promises of men.

At the Constitutional Convention in Philadelphia in 1787, Benjamin Franklin said, "I have lived, Sir, a long time, and the longer I live, the more convincing proofs I see of this truth—that God governs in the affairs of men. I therefore beg leave to move that henceforth prayers imploring the assistance of heaven and its blessings on our deliberations be held in this Assembly every morning. . . ."

Isaiah sought that attitude in Jerusalem; but instead he found only scoffing and unbelief.

4. The Lord Rebukes Jerusalem (Isa. 30:1-33)

This fourth "woe" begins with God's rebuke of the nation's rebellion (vv. 1-17). Isaiah opened his prophecy with this accusation (1:2, 20, 23), and he ends it on that same note (63:10; 65:2). After all that God had done for His people, they turned away from Him and sought the help of feeble Egypt. Unlike the leaders of old—Moses (Num. 27:21), Joshua (Josh. 9:14), David (1 Sam. 30:7-8), and Jehoshaphat (1 Kings 22:7ff)— the rulers of Jerusalem did not seek the will of God. Egypt was but a shadow, and what could a shadow do against the great Assyrian army?

Isaiah then uttered an oracle (burden) concerning the caravan that was then traveling from Jerusalem to Egypt with treasures to buy protection against Assyria (Isa. 30:6-7). He saw the burdened animals making their way through the difficult and dangerous terrain of the Negev (the south), and he cried, "It is all to no profit! It is useless! The Egyptians will help in vain!" In verse 7, which should be read in a recent translation, Isaiah gives a nickname to Egypt: "Rahab-hem-shebeth," which means "Rahab the do-nothing." (Rahab is one of the names for Egypt in the Old Testament.)

It was bad enough that Judah rebelled against God by trusting Egypt instead of trusting Jehovah, and depending on money instead of on God's power, but they even went so far as to completely reject the Word of God (vv. 8-11). God told Isaiah to make a placard that said, "This is a rebellious people, lying children, children who will not hear the Law of the Lord" (v. 9). He carried this sign as he walked around Jerusalem, and no doubt most of the people laughed at him. The leaders did not want to hear God's truth; they wanted "pleasant words" from the false prophets, sermons that would not disturb their comfortable way of life. Is this situation much different today? (See Jer. 6:14; 8:11; and 1 Kings 22:1-28.)

Decisions have consequences, and Isaiah told the people what would happen to Judah and Jerusalem because they were trusting their lies: Their wall of protection would suddenly collapse, shattered to pieces like a clay vessel (Isa. 30:12-14). When Assyria invaded the land, Egypt lived up to her nickname and did nothing. It was not till the last minute that God stepped in and rescued His people, and He did it only because of His covenant with David (37:35-36). During Assyria's invasion of Judah, the Jews were not able to flee on their horses imported from Egypt (30:16-17; Deut. 17:16), and one enemy soldier was able to frighten off a thousand Jews! What humiliation! (See Deut. 32:30.)

Their only hope was to repent, return to the Lord, and by faith rest only in Him (Isa. 30:15; 8:6-7; 26:3; 28:12), but they would not listen and obey.

The prophet then turned from the subject of rebellion to the subject of restoration (30:18-26). "Yet the Lord longs to be gracious to you," he told the people; "He rises to show you compassion" (v. 18, NIV). God's grace is His favor toward those who do not deserve it, and it is only because of His grace that we have any blessings at all. Isaiah described that future day when Israel would be restored to her land to enjoy the blessings of the kingdom. They would be like liberated prisoners of war (v. 19). Instead of scoffing, they would listen to God's Word and put away their foolish idols. The land would be restored and become prosperous again, and God would bind up the bruises and heal the wounds of His people v. 26; see 1:5-6). The "great slaughter" of verse 25 is the battle of Armageddon, which will occur just before the return of the Lord to deliver His people and establish His kingdom (Rev. 19:11-21).

His final theme in this "woe" is retribution (Isa. 30:27-33), the announcement that God will defeat the Assyrians. God used Assyria to discipline Judah, but He would not permit the Assyrians to take the city of David. Isaiah used several images to describe God's judgment of Assyria: a storm of fire and hail, a flood, the sifting of grain (see Amos 9:9), and the harnessing of a horse so that the enemy is led off like a farm animal.

Just as Sheol was prepared for the king of Babylon (Isa. 14:9ff), so Topheth was prepared for the king of Assyria. Topheth was a site outside Jerusalem where the worshipers of Molech sacrificed their children (2 Kings 163; 21:6; Jer. 7:31-32; 19:6; 11-14). It was defiled by Josiah (2 Kings 23:10), turned into a garbage dump, and named "Gehenna," which comes from ge-ben-hinnom, meaning "valley of the son of Himmon." That was the location of Topheth. "Gehenna" is the New Testament word for "hell." The funeral pyre for the great king of Assyria would be a garbage dump! How humiliating!

The Jews would rejoice greatly at the defeat of Assyria, not unlike their rejoicing at Passover to commemorate the defeat of Egypt. When the Jews celebrate Passover, they still have "a song in the night" (Matt. 26:30), and the "timbrels and harps" (Isa. 30:32) remind us of the songs of Miriam and the Jewish women at the Red Sea (Ex. 15:20-21).

5. The Lord Defends Jerusalem (Isa. 31:1-9)

This fifth "woe" is a brief summary of what Isaiah had already told the people. Indeed, he was teaching them "line upon line, here a little, and there a little" (28:10), and yet they were not getting the message.

Their faith was in men, not in God. They trusted in the legs of horses and the wheels of chariots, not in the hand of the Lord. God warned the Jewish kings not to go to Egypt for horses and chariots (Deut. 17:14-16), but Solomon ignored this warning (1 Kings 10:28-29). Going to Egypt for help had always been a temptation to the Jews (Ex. 13:17; 14:11-12; Num. 11:5, 18; 14:3ff).

Why should the Lord fear the Assyrians? Does a lion fear a flock of sheep and their shepherds? Do the eagles fear as they hover over their young in the nest? God will pounce on Assyria like a lion and swoop down like an eagle, and that will be the end! In one night, the Assyrian army was wiped out (Isa. 37:36).

Think of the money Judah would have saved and the distress they would have avoided had they only rested in the Lord their God and obeyed His will. All their political negotiations were futile and their treaties worthless. They trusted the words of the Egyptians but not the Word of God!

As God's church today faces enemies and challenges, it is always a temptation to turn to the world or the flesh for help. But our first response must be to examine our hearts to see if there is something we need to confess and make right. Then we just turn to the Lord in faith and obedience and surrender to His will alone. We must trust Him to protect us and fight for us.

A friend of mine kept a card in his office desk that read: Faith Is Living Without Scheming. In one statement, that is what Isaiah was saying to Judah and Jerusalem, and that is what he is saying to us today.

CHAPTER SEVEN
FUTURE SHOCK AND FUTURE GLORY
ISAIAH 32–35

In 1919, American writer Lincoln Steffens visited the Soviet Union to see what the Communist Revolution was accomplishing. In a letter to a friend, he wrote, "I have seen the future, and it works." If he were alive today, he would probably be less optimistic, but in those days, "the Russian experiment" seemed to be dramatically successful.

A university professor posted a sign on his study wall that read, "The future is not what it used to be." Since the advent of atomic energy, many people wonder if there is any future at all. Albert Einstein said that he never thought about the future because it came soon enough!

In the four chapters that conclude the first section of his prophecy, Isaiah invites us to look at four future events to see what God has planned for His people and His world. These chapters are not human speculation;

they are divinely inspired revelation, and they can be trusted.

1. A King Will Reign (Isa. 32:1-20)

At the beginning of its history, the nation of Israel was a theocracy, with God as King; it was not a monarchy led by human rulers. In the days of Samuel, the people asked for a king, and God gave them Saul (1 Sam. 8; see Deut. 17:14-20). God did not establish a dynasty through Saul because Saul did not come from the tribe of Judah (Gen. 49:10). It was David who established both the dynasty for Israel's throne and the ancestry for Israel's Messiah (2 Sam. 7). Every devout Jew knew that the future Messiah-King would be the Son of David (Matt. 22:41-46).

In Isaiah 32:1, Isaiah writes about "a king," but in 33:17, he calls him "the king." By the time you get to verse 22, He is "our king." It is not enough to say that Jesus Christ is "a King" or even "the King." We must confess our faith in Him and say with assurance that He is "our King." Like Nathanael, we must say, "Rabbi, You are the Son of God! You are the King of Israel!" (John 1:49, NKJV)

In contrast to the evil rulers of Isaiah's day (Isa. 1:21-23), Messiah will reign in righteousness and justice (32:1, 16; 33:5; see 9:7; 11:1-5). In addition, the King will be like a rock of refuge for the people (8:14; 17:10; 26:4; 28:16) and like a refreshing river in the desert (8:5-8; 33:21; 41:18; 48:18; 66:12). "He who rules over men must be just," said David, "ruling in the fear of God" (2 Sam. 23:3-4, NKJV).

Isaiah 32:3-4 describes the wonderful transformations that will occur because of Messiah's reign. Isaiah ministered to spiritually blind, deaf, and ignorant people (6:9-10; 29:10-12), but in the kingdom, all will see and hear God's truth as well as understand and obey it. (See 29:18 and 42:7.) This will happen because the nation will have a new heart and enter into a New Covenant with the Lord (Jer. 31:31-34).

The "churl" (Isa. 32:5-8 KJV) is the knave or scoundrel who uses his or her position for personal profit and not for the good of the people. In Isaiah's day, as in our own day, the common people admired "the rich and famous," even though the character and conduct of these "celebrities" deserved no respect. They had money, fame, and influence; and in the eyes of the populace, that made them important. But in the kingdom, there will be no such deception. "Wealthy cheaters will not be spoken of as generous, outstanding men! Everyone will recognize an evil man when he sees him, and hypocrites will fool no one at all" (vv. 5-6, TLB).

Not only will their character and motives be exposed and judged, but so will their ungodly methods (v. 7). No longer will the poor and helpless be cheated by these liars! Instead of knaves, the leaders who rule with Messiah will be noble people who plan noble things.

Behind the selfish rulers of Judah, and influencing them for evil, were the "aristocratic women" of Jerusalem, who were complacent and self-confident in a time of grave national crisis (vv. 9-14; see 3:16-26; Amos 4:1-3; 6:1-6). Isaiah warned them that "in little more than a year [NIV]," the land and the cities would be desolate. This took place in 701 B.C. when Sennacherib's Assyrian army invaded Judah and devastated the land. The Jews confined in Jerusalem were greatly concerned about future harvests, and Isaiah had a word for them (Isa. 37:30-31). But before the siege ended and God delivered Jerusalem, these worldy women in Jerusalem had to sacrifice not only their luxuries, but also their necessities.

In 32:15-20, the prophet returns to his description of the messianic kingdom and emphasizes the restoration of peace and prosperity. None of these changes took place after the deliverance of Jerusalem in 701 B.C. or when the remnant returned to Jerusalem from Babylon, so we must assign these prophecies to the future kingdom. Because of the outpouring of the Holy Spirit, there will be peace and plenty because there will be righteousness in the land (Joel 2:28-32; Zech. 12:10; Ezek. 36:26-27). The land will be so productive that the desert will be like a fruitful field and the fruitful field like a forest. The people will fear no enemies, and their work will be rewarded.

Judah could have enjoyed safety, quietness, and assurance had they trusted wholly in the Lord and not turned to Egypt for help (Isa. 30:15-18; 32:17-18). Righteousness is the key word in verse 17, for there can be no true peace without a right relationship with God (Rom. 5:1; James 3:13-17). When sinners trust Christ and receive the gift of righteousness, then they can have peace in their hearts and peace with one another.

2. Jerusalem Will Be delivered (Isa. 33:1-24)

This is the sixth and final "woe" in this section (28:1; 29:1, 15; 30:1; 31:1), and it is directed against Sennacherib because of his treachery against Judah. In unbelief, King Hezekiah had tried to "buy off" the Assyrians (2 Kings 18:13-15), but Sennacherib had broken the agreement and invaded Judah anyway. He was a thief, a traitor, and a tyrant; and God promised to judge him. He had destroyed others, so he would be destroyed. He had dealt treacherously with nations, so they would deal treacherously with him. God is not mocked; sinners reap what they have sown (Gal. 6:7).

Isaiah 33:2 is the prayer of the godly remnant when Jerusalem was surrounded by the Assyrian army. Isaiah had promised that God would be gracious to them if they would only trust Him (30:18-19), so a few devout people turned His promise into prayer. God spared Jerusalem for David's sake (37:35) and because a believing remnant trusted God and prayed. Never underestimate the power of a praying minority.

Assyria was proud of her power and the spoils she had gathered in battle. The Assyrian army swept through the land like devouring locusts, but that would change. The day would come when Judah would strip the dead Assyrian army and Sennacherib would be assassinated in the temple of the god he claimed was stronger than Jehovah (vv. 36-38).

The Lord was exalted in the defeat of Assyria (33:5), for no human wisdom or power could have done what He did. We must remember that nations and individuals can have stability in uncertain times only when they trust God and seek His wisdom and glory. King Hezekiah did a foolish thing when he took the temple treasures and tried to bribe Sennacherib (2 Kings 18:13-16), but God forgave him and reminded him that "the fear of the Lord is [your] treasure" (Isa. 33:6). Unbelief looks to human resources for help, but faith looks to God.

During the time of the Assyrian invasion, the situation in Judah was grim (vv. 7-9). Judah's bravest soldiers wept when they saw one city after another fall to the enemy. The official Jewish envoys wept because their negotiations accomplished nothing. The roads were dangerous, the fields and orchards were ruined, and there was no way of escape.

Except for—God! " 'Now will I rise,' saith the Lord, 'now will I be exalted, now will I lift up Myself' " (v. 10). In verses 11-12, Isaiah uses several images to describe God's judgment on the Assyrians. The Assyrians were "pregnant" with all sorts of plans to conquer Jerusalem, but they would give birth to chaff and straw, and their plans would amount to nothing. Their army was panting to attack, but their hot breath would only become a fire that would destroy them like dead bones or cut bushes. God is long-suffering with His enemies, but when He decides to judge, He does a thorough job.

The account of the amazing deliverance of Jerusalem was told far and wide, and the Gentile nations had to acknowledge the greatness of Jehovah, the God of the Jews. Some scholars believe that Psalm 126 grew out of this experience and may have been written by Hezekiah. "Then they said among the nations, 'The Lord hath done great things for them' " (v. 2). We witness to a lost world when we trust Him and let Him have His way.

The miracle deliverance of Jerusalem not only brought glory to God among the Gentiles, but it also brought fear and conviction to the Jews (Isa. 33:14-16). God does not deliver us so that we are free to return to our sins. "But there is forgiveness with thee, that thou mayest be feared!" (Ps. 130:4). When Jews in Jerusalem saw 185,000 Assyrian soldiers slain by God in one night, they realized anew that the God of Israel was "a consuming fire" (Isa. 10:17; Heb. 12:29). Were they even safe in Jerusalem?

Isaiah 33:15 describes the kind of person God will accept and bless. (See also Pss. 15 and 24.) By ourselves, we cannot achieve these qualities of character; they come only as we trust Jesus Christ and grow in grace. Many religious people in Jerusalem had hearts far from God because their religion was only a matter of external ceremonies (Isa. 29:13). Isaiah hoped that the miracle deliverance of the city would bring these people to a place of true devotion to the Lord. It is only as we walk with the Lord that we have real security and satisfaction.

In 33:17-24, the prophet lifts his vision to the end times and sees Jerusalem ruled by King Messiah. God's victory over Assyria was but a "dress rehearsal" for His victory over the whole Gentile world system that will one day assemble to destroy the Holy City (Zech. 14:1-9). When our Lord was ministering on earth, the unbelieving Jews said, "There is no beauty that we should desire him" (Isa. 53:2). But when they see Him and believe, then they will perceive His great beauty (Zech. 12:3-13:1; Ps. 45).

In contrast to the ordeal of the Assyrian siege, the Jews in the messianic kingdom will experience no terror, see no arrogant military officers, and hear no foreign speech (Isa. 33:18-19). Jerusalem will be like a tent that will not be moved (see 54:1-3), pitched by a broad river that will never carry the vessels of invading armies. Jerusalem is one of the few great cities of antiquity that was not built near a river, but that will change during the millennial kingdom (Ezek. 47). Of course, the river symbolizes the peace that the Lord gives to His people (Isa. 48:18; 66:12; Ps. 46:4).

Jerusalem was a ship that almost sank (Isa. 33:23), but the Lord brought it through the storm (Ps. 107:23-32), and the weakest of the Jews was able to take spoils from the dead army. "All the functions of government—judicial, legislative, and executive—will be centered in the Messianic King," says the note on Isaiah 33:22 in The New Scofield Reference Bible. No wonder His people can say, "He will save us!"

Both sickness and sin will be absent from the city. Messiah will be their Redeemer and Savior, and the nation "shall be forgiven their iniquity" (v. 24). In Isaiah's day, the Jews were a "sinful nation, a people laden with iniquity" (1:4), just as lost sinners are today, but when they see Him and trust Him, their sins will be washed away. If you have never heeded the gracious invitation of Isaiah 1:18, do so today!

3. The Sinful World Will Be Judged (Isa. 34:1-17)

Israel's ancient enemy Edom is singled out in verses 5-6, but this divine judgment will come upon the whole world. Edom is only one example of God's judgment on the Gentile nations because of what they have done to His people Israel. "For the Lord has a day of vengeance, a year of retribution, to uphold Zion's cause" (v. 8, NIV). In the Day of the Lord, the Gentiles will be repaid for the way they have treated the Jews and exploited their land (Joel 3:1-17). "Zion's cause" may not get much support among the nations today, but God will come to their defense and make their cause succeed.

Isaiah begins this section with a military picture of the armies on earth (Isa. 34:2-3) and in heaven (v. 4). The enemy armies on earth will be slaughtered, the land will be drenched with blood, and the bodies of the slain will be left unburied to rot and to smell. This is a vivid description of the battle of Armageddon (Rev. 19:11-21), the humiliating defeat and destruction of the armies of the world that dare to attack the Son of God. The hosts of heaven will also be affected by vast cosmic disturbances (Isa. 34:4; see Matt. 24:29; Joel 2:10, 30-31; 3:15; Rev. 6:13-14). What a day that will be!

In Isaiah 34:5-8, the prophet moves from the battlefield to the temple and sees the worldwide judgment as a great sacrifice that God offers. (See Jer. 46:10; 50:27; Ezek. 39:17-19.) The practice was for the people to kill the sacrifices and offer them to God, but now it is God who offers the wicked as sacrifices. Bozrah was an important city in Edom; the name means "grape-gathering" (see Isa. 63:1-8). God sees His enemies as animals: rams, goats, lambs, oxen, and bulls to be sacrificed, along with the fat (Lev. 3:9-11). These nations sacrificed the Jews, so God used them for sacrifices.

The picture changes again, and Isaiah compares the Day of the Lord to the judgment of Sodom and Gomorrah (Isa. 34:9-10; Gen. 18-19). This is a significant comparison because, just before the coming of the Lord, society will be "as it was in the days of Lot" (Luke 17:28). Tar running like streams and sulfur like dust will keep the fires of judgment burning (Gen. 14:10; 19:24). The description in Isaiah 34:10 reminds us of the fall of Babylon (Rev. 14:8-11; 19:3). We should also remember that the fires of eternal hell, the lake of fire, will never be quenched (Mark 9:43-48).

While Isaiah focused especially on Edom (Isa. 34:5-6), he was using that proud nation as an example of what God would do to all the Gentile nations during the Day of the Lord. When God finishes His work, the land will be a wilderness, occupied by brambles and thorns, wild beasts, and singular birds (vv. 11-17). God will see to it that each bird will have a mate to reproduce, and no humans will be around to drive them from their nests.

"But the Day of the Lord will come as a thief in the night" (2 Peter 3:10). Why is God waiting? Because God "is long-suffering toward us, not willing that any should perish but that all should come to repentance" (v. 9, NKJV). How much longer God will wait, nobody knows; so it behooves lost sinners to repent today and trust the Savior.

4. The Glorious Kingdom Will Be Established (Isa. 35:1-10)

But the wilderness will not remain a wilderness, for the Lord will transform the earth into a Garden of Eden. All of nature eagerly looks for the coming of the Lord (55:12-13; Rom. 8:19; Pss. 96:11-13; 98:7-9), for nature knows that it will be set free from the curse of sin (Gen. 3:17-19) and share the glory of the kingdom. Lebanon, Carmel, and Sharon were three of the most fruitful and beautiful places in the land, and yet the desert would become more fruitful and beautiful than the three places put together! There will be no more "parched ground" (Isa. 35:7), because the land will become a garden of glory.

Isaiah uses the promise of the coming kingdom to strengthen those in his day who were weak and afraid (vv. 3-4). In the kingdom, there will be no more blind or deaf, lame or dumb; for all will be made whole to enjoy a glorious new world. (In 32:3-4, the prophet wrote about spiritual deficiencies, but here he is describing physical handicaps.) Our Lord referred to these verses when he sent a word of encouragement to John the Baptist (Luke 7:18-23). The King was on earth and sharing with needy people the blessings of the coming kingdom.

Isaiah 35:8 expresses one of Isaiah's favorite themes: the highway (11:16; 19:23; 40:3; 62:10). During the Assyrian invasion, the highways were not safe (33:8), but during the Kingdom Age it will be safe to travel. There will be one special highway: "The Way of Holiness." In ancient cities, there were often special roads that only kings and priests could use, but when Messiah reigns, all of His people will be invited to use this highway. Isaiah pictures God's redeemed, ransomed, and rejoicing Jewish families going up to the yearly feasts in Jerusalem, to praise their Lord.

When Isaiah spoke and wrote these words, it is likely that the Assyrians had ravaged the land, destroyed the crops, and made the highways unsafe for travel. The people were cooped up in Jerusalem, wondering what would happen next. The members of the faithful remnant were trusting God's promises and praying for God's help, and God answered their prayers. If God kept His promises to His people centuries ago and delivered them, will He not keep His promises in the future and establish His glorious kingdom for His chosen people? Of course He will!

The future is your friend when Jesus Christ is your Savior and Lord.

INTERLUDE: KING HEZEKIAH

ISAIAH 36–39

Except for David and Solomon, no king of Judah is given more attention or commendation in Scripture than Hezekiah. Eleven chapters are devoted to him in 2 Kings 18–20; 2 Chronicles 29–32; and Isaiah 36–39. "He trusted in the Lord God of Israel; so that after him was none like him among all the kings of Judah, nor any that were before him" (2 Kings 18:5).

He began his reign about 715 B.C., though he may have been coregent with his father as early as 729 B.C. He restored the temple facilities and services of worship, destroyed the idols and the high places (hill shrines where the people falsely worshiped Jehovah), and sought to bring the people back to vital faith in the Lord. He led the people in a nationwide two-week celebration of Passover and invited Jews from the Northern Kingdom to participate. "And in every work that he began in the service of the house of God, and in the law, and in the commandments, to see His God, he did it with all his heart, and prospered" (2 Chron. 31:21).

After the fall of the Northern Kingdom in 722 B.C., Judah had constant problems with Assyria. Hezekiah finally rebelled against Assyria (2 Kings 18:7), and when Sennacherib threatened to attack, Hezekiah tried to bribe him with tribute (vv. 13-16). It was a lapse of faith on Hezekiah's part that God could not bless. Sennacherib accepted the treasures but broke the treaty (Isa. 33:1) and invaded Judah in 701 B.C. The account of

God's miraculous deliverance of His people is given in Isaiah 36–37.

Bible students generally agree that Hezekiah's sickness (Isa. 38) and foolish reception of the envoys (Isa. 39) took place before the Assyrian invasion, possibly between the time Hezekiah sent the tribute and Sennacherib broke the treaty. Then why are these chapters not arranged chronologically?

The prophet arranged the account as a "bridge" between the two parts of his book. Chapters 36 and 37 end the first part of the book with its emphasis on Assyria, and chapters 38 and 39 introduce the second part of the book, with its emphasis on Babylon. Isaiah mentions Babylon earlier in his book (13:1ff; 31:1ff), but this is the first time he clearly predicts Judah's captivity in Babylon.

Chapters 36–39 teach us some valuable lessons about faith, prayer, and the dangers of pride. Though the setting today may be different, the problems and temptations are still the same; for Hezekiah's history is our history, and Hezekiah's God is our God.

CHAPTER EIGHT
GOD SAVE THE KING!
ISAIAH 36–39

Former U.S. Secretary of State Dr. Henry Kissinger once told the New York Times, "There cannot be a crisis next week. My schedule is already full."

Crises come, whether schedules permit them or not, and sometimes crises seem to pile up. How do we handle them? What life does to us depends on what life finds in us. A crisis does not make a person; it shows what a person is made of.

Hezekiah faced three crises in a short time: an international crisis (the invasion of the Assyrian army), a personal crisis (sickness and near death), and a national crisis (the visit of the Babylonian envoys). He came through the first two victoriously, but the third one tripped him up. Hezekiah was a great and godly man, but he was still a man, and that meant he had all the frailties of human flesh. However, before we find fault with him, we had better examine our own lives to see how successfully we have handled our own tests.

1. The Invasion Crisis (Isa. 36:1–37:38; 2 Kings 18–19; 2 Chron. 32)

Crises often come when circumstances seem to be at their best. Hezekiah had led the nation in a great reformation, and the people were reunited in the fear of the Lord. They had put away their idols, restored the temple services, and sought the blessing of their God. But instead of receiving blessing, they found themselves facing battles! "After all that Hezekiah had so faithfully done, Sennacherib king of Assyria came and invaded Judah" (2 Chron. 32:1, NIV).

Had God turned a blind eye and a deaf ear to all that Hezekiah and his people had done? Of course not! The Assyrian invasion was a part of God's discipline to teach His people to trust Him alone. Even Hezekiah had at first put his trust in treaties and treasures (2 Kings 18:13-16), only to learn that the enemy will keep the wealth but not keep his word. Judah had negotiated to get help from Egypt, an act of unbelief that Isaiah severely rebuked (Isa. 30:1-7; 31:1-3). God's great purpose in the life of faith is to build godly character. Hezekiah and his people needed to learn that faith is living without scheming.

The Assyrians had ravaged Judah and were now at Lachish, about thirty miles southwest of Jerusalem. According to 2 Kings 18:17, Sennacherib sent three of his most important officers to arrange for Hezekiah's surrender of the city: Tartan ("Supreme Commander"), Rabsaris ("Chief Officer"), and Rabshakeh ("Field Commander"). These are military titles, not personal names. The three men were met by three of Judah's leading officials: Eliakim, Shebna (see Isa. 22:15-25), and Joah (36:3).

The place of their meeting is significant, for it is the very place where Isaiah confronted Ahaz, Hezekiah's father, some thirty years before (7:3). Ahaz had refused to trust the Lord but had instead made a treaty with Assyria (2 Kings 16:5-9), and now the Assyrians were ready to take Jerusalem! Isaiah had warned Ahaz what Assyria would do (Isa. 7:17-25), and his words were now fulfilled.

Reproach (Isa. 36:4-21). The field commander's speech is one of the most insolent and blasphemous found anywhere in

Scripture, for he reproached the God of Israel (37:4, 17, 23-24). He emphasized the "greatness" of the king of Assyria (36:4, 13) because he knew the common people were listening and he wanted to frighten them (vv. 11-12). His speech is a masterful piece of psychological warfare in which he discredits everything that the Jews held dear. The key word is trust, used seven times (vv. 4-7, 9, 15). "In what is your confidence?" asked the field commander. "You can have no confidence, for everything you trust in has failed!"

He began with their strategy. They had turned to Egypt for help, but Egypt was only a broken reed. (Isaiah had said the same thing! See 30:1-7 and 31:1-3.) As for trusting the Lord, that was sure to fail. Hezekiah had incurred the Lord's displeasure by removing the high places and altars and requiring everybody to worship at Jerusalem. (What did a heathen soldier know about the worship of the true God?) So, according to the field commander, Judah had no help on earth (Egypt) or in heaven (the Lord). They were already defeated!

What about their military resources? Hezekiah had fortified Jerusalem (2 Chron. 32:2-8), but the field commander laughed at Judah's military might. Judah had neither the men, the horses, nor the chariots to attack the Assyrians. Even if Assyria provided the equipment, the Jewish soldiers were too weak to defeat the least of the enemy's officers. All the chariots and horsemen of Egypt could never defeat Sennacherib's great army. (Isaiah would agree with him again; see Isa. 30:15-17).

The field commander's coup de grace was that everything Assyria had done was according to the will of the Lord (36:10). How could Judah fight against its own God? In one sense, this statement was true; for God is in charge of the nations of the world (10:5-6; Dan. 4:17, 25, 32; 5:21). But no nation can do what it pleases and use God for the excuse, as Sennacherib and his army would soon find out.

According to the field commander, Judah could not trust in its strategy, its military resources, or in its God. Nor could its people trust in their king (Isa. 36:13-20). The king of Assyria was a "great king," but Hezekiah was a nobody who was deceiving the people. Instead of trusting Hezekiah's promise of help from the Lord, the people should trust Sennacherib's promise of a comfortable home in Assyria. The people knew that their farms, orchards, vineyards had been ruined by the Assyrian army, and that Judah was facing a bleak future. If they stayed in Jerusalem, they might starve to death. Perhaps they should surrender and keep themselves and their families alive.

Hezekiah and Isaiah had told the people to trust the Lord, but the field commander reminded the people that the gods of the other nations had not succeeded in protecting or delivering them. (Hezekiah knew why; see 37:18-19.) Even Samaria was defeated, and they worshiped the same God as Judah. To the field commander, Jehovah was just another god, and Sennacherib did not need to worry about Him.

God summons us to walk by faith and not by sight (2 Cor. 5:7). To those Jews in Jerusalem who were living in unbelief, the field commander's arguments must have seemed reasonable, and his evidence compelling. But God had promised to deliver His people from the Assyrian army, and His Word would stand.

Repentance (Isa. 36:22-37:20). By the king's orders, nobody replied to the field commander's speech. Insolence is best answered with silence. Jerusalem's deliverance did not depend on negotiating with the enemy but on trusting the Lord.

Hezekiah and his officers humbled themselves before the Lord and sought His face. As the king went into the temple, perhaps he recalled the promise God had given to Solomon after he had dedicated the temple: "If My people, who are called by My name, shall humble themselves, and pray, and seek My face, and turn from their wicked ways, then will I hear from, and will forgive their sin, and will heal their land" (2 Chron. 7:14).

Even though the Lord had brought Assyria to chasten Judah (Isa. 7:17-25), He had determined that Jerusalem would not be taken by the enemy (10:5-34). Previous to the invasion, when Hezekiah had been deathly ill, Isaiah had assured him of deliverance (38:4-6). God's promises are sure, but God's people must claim them by faith before God can work. So the king sent word to Isaiah, asking him to pray, and the king himself called out to the Lord for help.

In the building up of our faith, the Word of God and prayer go together (Rom. 10:17). That is why Isaiah sent the king a message from the Lord. His word of encouragement had three points: (1) do not be afraid, (2) the Assyrians will depart, and (3) the "great king" will die in Assyria.

When the three Assyrian officers returned to headquarters, they learned that an Egyptian army was on its way to help defend Hezekiah. Sennacherib did not want to fight a war on two fronts, so he started to put more pressure on Jerusalem to surrender immediately. This threatening message came to Hezekiah in the form of a letter, and he took it to the temple and "spread it before the Lord."

Hezekiah's prayer (Isa. 37:15-20) is saturated with biblical theology and is not unlike the prayer of the church in Acts 4:24-31. He affirmed his faith in the one true and living God, and he worshiped Him. Jehovah is "Lord of hosts," that is, "Lord of the armies" (Ps. 46:7, 11). He is the Creator of all things (96:5) and knows what is going on in His creation. His eyes can see our plight, and His ears can hear our plea (see Ps. 115). King Hezekiah did not want deliverance merely for his people's sake, but that God alone might be glorified (Isa. 37:20; Ps. 46-10).

Reply (Isa. 37:21-35). God's response to this prayer was to send King Hezekiah another threefold message of assurance: Jerusalem would not be taken (vv. 22, 31-35); the Assyrians would depart (vv. 23-29); and the Jews would not starve (v. 30).

(1) Jerusalem would be delivered (vv. 22, 31-35). The "daughter of Zion" was still a virgin; she had not been ravaged by the enemy. She could look at the Assyrians and shake her head in scorn, for they could not touch her. God would spare His remnant and plant them once more in the land.

Why did God deliver His people when so many of them were not faithful to Him? First, to glorify His own name (vv. 23, 35), the very thing about which Hezekiah had prayed (v. 20). God defended Jerusalem for His name's sake, because Sennacherib had reproached the Holy One of Israel. The Assyrians had exalted themselves above men and gods, but they could not exalt themselves above Jehovah God, the Holy One of Israel!

God also saved Jerusalem because of His covenant with David (v. 35; 2 Sam. 7). Jerusalem was the City of David, and God had promised that one of David's descendants would reign on the throne forever. This was fulfilled ultimately in Jesus Christ (Luke 1:32-33), but God did keep David's lamp burning in Jerusalem as long as He could (1 Kings 11:13, 36).

The Jewish nation had an important mission to fulfill in bringing the Savior into the world, and no human army could thwart the purposes of Almighty God. Even though only a remnant of Jews might remain, God would use His people to accomplish His divine purposes and fulfill His promise to Abraham that all the world would be blessed through him (Gen. 12:1-3).

(2) The Assyrians would depart (vv. 23-29). God addressed the proud Assyrian king and reminded him of all the boastful words he and his servants had spoken. "I" and "my" occur seven times in this passage. It reminds us of Lucifer's words in 14:12-17 and our Lord's parable in Luke 12:13-21. "Pride goes before destruction, and a haughty spirit before a fall" (Prov. 16:18, NKJV).

Sennacherib boasted of his military might and his great conquests, for no obstacle stood in his way. If he so desired, like a god, he could even dry up the rivers! But the king of Assyria forgot that he was only God's tool for accomplishing His purposes on the earth, and the tool must not boast against the Maker (Isa. 10:5-19). God would humble Sennacherib and his army by treating them like cattle and leading them away from Jerusalem (37:7, 29).

(3) The people would not starve (v. 30). We do not know the month in which these events occurred, but it may have been past the time for sowing a new crop. Before the people could get the land back to its normal productivity, they would have to eat what grew of itself from previous crops, and that would take faith. They would also need to renovate their farms after all the damage the Assyrians had done. But the same God who delivered them would provide for them. It would be like the years before and after the Year of Jubilee (Lev. 25:1-24).

Some Bible scholars believe that Psalm 126 was written to commemorate Jerusalem's deliverance from the Assyrian army. The psalm surely is not referring to the Jews' deliverance from the Babylonian Captivity, because that was not a sudden event that surprised both Jews and Gentiles, nor did the Gentiles praise Jehovah for delivering Israel from Babylon. Psalm 126 fits best with the events described in Isaiah 36 and 37.

The harvest promise in verse 30 parallels

Psalm 126:5-6. The seed would certainly be precious in those days! That grain could be used for making bread for the family, but the father must use it for seed; so it is no wonder he weeps. Yet God promised a harvest, and He kept His promise. The people did not starve.

Retaliation (Isa. 37:36-38). The field commander had joked that one Assyrian junior officer was stronger than 2,000 Jewish charioteers (36:8-9), but it took only one of God's angels to destroy 185,000 Assyrian soldiers! (See Ex. 12:12 and 2 Sam. 24:15-17.) Isaiah had prophesied the destruction of the Assyrian army. God would mow them down like a forest (Isa. 10:33-34), devastate them with a storm (30:27-30), and throw them into the fire like garbage on the city dump (vv. 31-33).

But that was not all. After Sennacherib left Judah a defeated man, he returned to his capital city of Nineveh. Twenty years later, as a result of a power struggle among his sons, Sennacherib was assassinated by two of his sons in fulfillment of Isaiah's prophecy (37:7), and it happened in the temple of his god! The field commander had ridiculed the gods of the nations, but Sennacherib's own god could not protect him.

2. The Illness Crisis (Isa. 38:1-22; 2 Kings 20:1-11)

Peril (Isa. 38:1). As mentioned before, this event took place before the Assyrian invasion, though the invasion was impending (see v. 6). When the president or prime minister of a country is sick or injured, it affects everything from the stock market to the news coverage. Imagine how the people of Judah reacted when they heard that the king was going to die—and Assyria was on the march! If their godly leader died, who would govern them?

But there was even more involved. Apparently, Hezekiah did not have a son and therefore would have to appoint a near relative to take the throne of David. Would God's promise to David fail? (2 Sam. 7:16) And why would it fail at a time of national calamity?

Prayer (Isa. 38:2-3). The king did not turn to the wall in a sulking manner, like Ahab (1 Kings 21:4), but in order to have privacy for his praying. It may be too that he was turning his face toward the temple (8:28-30). Some have criticized Hezekiah for weeping and praying, saying that his prayer was selfish, but most of us would have prayed the same way. It is a natural thing for us to want to live and continue serving God. Furthermore, Hezekiah was burdened for the future of the throne and the nation.

Hezekiah did not ask God to spare him because he had been such a faithful servant (Isa. 38:3). That would be a subtle form of bribery. Rather, he asked God to spare him so he could continue to serve and complete the spiritual restoration of the nation. Certainly he was concerned about his own life, as any of us would be, but he also had a burden for his people.

Promise (Isa. 38:4-8). The request was granted quickly, for Isaiah had not gone very far from the sick room when the Lord gave him the answer (2 Kings 20:4). The prophet became the king's physician and told the attendants what medicine to apply (Isa. 38:21). God can heal by using any means He desires. Isaiah also told the king that his life would be prolonged for fifteen years. The king asked confirmation of the promise (v. 22), and God gave him a sign. The sundial was probably a pillar whose shadow marked the hours on a double set of stairs. In another promise, Isaiah assured the king that the Assyrians would not capture Jerusalem.

Pondering (Isa. 38:9-20). Hezekiah was an author of psalms (v. 20) and supervised a group of scholars who copied the Old Testament Scriptures (Prov. 25:1). In this beautiful meditation, the king tells us how he felt during his experience of illness and recovery. He had some new experiences that transformed him

For one thing, God gave him a new appreciation of life (Isa. 38:9-12). We take life for granted till it is about to be taken from us, and then we cling to it as long as we can. Hezekiah pictured death as the end of the journey (vv. 11-12), a tent taken down (v. 12a; and see 2 Cor. 5:1-8), and a weaving cut from the loom (Isa. 38:12b). Life was hanging by a thread!

He also had a new appreciation of prayer (vv. 13-14). Were it not for prayer, Hezekiah could not have made it. At night the king felt like a frail animal being attacked by a fierce lion, and in the daytime he felt like a helpless bird. During this time of suffering, Hezekiah examined his own heart and confessed his sins, and God forgave him (v. 17). "Undertake for me" means "Be my surety. Stand with me!"

The king ended with a new appreciation of opportunities for service (vv. 15-20). There was a new humility in his walk, a deeper love for the Lord in his heart, and a new song of praise on his lips. He had a new determination to praise God all the days of his life, for now those days were very important to him. "So teach us to number our days, that we may apply our hearts unto wisdom" (Ps. 90:12).

There are some students who feel that Hezekiah was wrong in asking God to spare his life. Three years later, his son Manasseh was born (2 Kings 21:1), and he reigned for fifty-five years, the most wicked king in the entire dynasty! Had Hezekiah died without an heir, this would not have happened. But we have no guarantee that any other successor would have been any better, and Manasseh's grandson was godly King Josiah, who did much to bring the nation back to the Lord. Manasseh did repent after God chastened him, and he ended his years serving the Lord (2 Chron. 33:11-20). It is unwise for us to second-guess God or history.

3. The Investigation Crisis (Isa. 39:1-8)

The news about Hezekiah's sickness and recovery had spread widely so that even people in Babylon knew about it (2 Chron. 32:23). Hezekiah was a famous man, and other nations would be concerned about him and want to court his favor. The stability of Judah was important to the balance of power in that day. At this time, Babylon was not a great world power, and few people would have thought that Assyria would one day collapse and be replaced by Babylon. Of course, God knew, but Hezekiah did not seek His guidance.

The stated reason for the diplomatic mission was to honor Hezekiah and officially rejoice at his recovery. But the real reason was to obtain information about the financial resources of the nation of Judah. After all, Babylon might need some of that wealth in their future negotiations or battles. It is also likely that Hezekiah was seeking Babylon's assistance against Assyria.

When Satan cannot defeat us as the "roaring lion" (1 Peter 5:8-9), he comes as the deceiving serpent (2 Cor. 11:3). What Assyria could not do with weapons, Babylon did with gifts. God permitted the enemy to test Hezekiah so that the proud king might learn what was really in his heart (2 Chron. 32:31).

It was certainly a mistake for Hezekiah to show his visitors all his wealth, but pride made him do it. After a time of severe suffering, sometimes it feels so good just to feel good that we get off guard and fail to watch and pray. The king was basking in fame and wealth and apparently neglecting his spiritual life. Hezekiah was safer as a sick man in bed than as a healthy man on the throne. Had he consulted first with Isaiah, the king would have avoided blundering as he did.

The prophet reminded Hezekiah that, as king, he was only the steward of Judah's wealth and not the owner (Isa. 39:6). Some of that wealth had come from previous kings, and Hezekiah could claim no credit for it. All of us are mere stewards of what God has given to us, and we have no right to boast about anything. "For who makes you differ from another? And what do you have that you did not receive? Now if you did indeed receive it, why do you glory as if you had not received it?" (1 Cor. 4:7, NKJV). "A man can receive nothing unless it has been given to him from heaven" (John 3:27, NKJV).

Isaiah 39:7 is Isaiah's first explicit announcement of the future Babylonian captivity of Judah. In spite of Hezekiah's reforms, the nation decayed spiritually during the next century, and in 586 B.C. Babylon destroyed Jerusalem and took the people captive. Hezekiah's sin was not the cause of this judgment, for the sins of rulers, priests, and false prophets mounted up from year to year till God could take it no longer (2 Chron. 36:13-16).

Is Hezekiah's response in Isaiah 39:8 an expression of relief that he escaped trouble? If so, it would certainly be heartless on his part to rejoice that future generations would suffer what he should have suffered! His statement is more likely an expression of his humble acceptance of God's will, and 2 Chronicles 32:26 bears this out. The king did humble himself before God, and God forgave him.

Even the greatest and most godly of the Lord's servants can become proud and disobey God, so we must pray for Christian leaders that they will stay humble before their Master. But if any of His servants do sin, the Lord is willing to forgive when they sincerely repent and confess to Him (1 John 1:9). "A broken and a contrite heart, O God, thou wilt not despise" (Ps. 51:17).

INTERLUDE
"THE BOOK OF CONSOLATION"
ISAIAH 40–66

The Book of Isaiah can be called "a Bible in miniature." There are sixty-six chapters in Isaiah and sixty-six books in the Bible. The thirty-nine chapters of the first part of Isaiah may be compared to the Old Testament with its thirty-nine books, and both focus primarily on God's judgment of sin. The twenty-seven chapters of the second part may be seen to parallel the twenty-seven books of the New Testament, and both emphasize the grace of God.

The "New Testament" section of Isaiah opens with the ministry of John the Baptist (40:3-5; Mark 1:1-4) and closes with the new heavens and the new earth (Isa. 65:17; 66:22), and in between there are many references to the Lord Jesus Christ as Savior and King. Of course, the chapter divisions in Isaiah are not a part of the original inspired text, but the comparison is still interesting.

In the "New Testament" section of Isaiah, the prophet is particularly addressing a future generation of Jews. In chapters 1–39 his audience was his own generation, and his primary message was that God would defend Jerusalem and defeat the Assyrian invaders. But in chapters 40–66 the prophet looks far ahead and sees Babylon destroying Jerusalem and the Jews going into Captivity. (This happened in 586 B.C.) But he also saw God forgiving His people, delivering them from captivity, and taking them back to Jerusalem to rebuild the temple and restore the nation.

The primary world figure in Isaiah 1–39 is Sennacherib, king of Assyria; but in chapters 40–66 the world leader is Cyrus, king of Persia. It was Cyrus who defeated the Babylonians, and in 541 B.C. issued the decree that permitted the Jews to return to their land to rebuild the city and the temple (Ezra. 1:1-4). When Isaiah wrote these messages, Babylon was not yet a great world power, but the prophet was inspired by God to see the course the international scene would take.

Chapters 40–66 may be divided into three parts (40–48; 49–57; and 58–66), with the same statement separating the first two sections: "There is no peace, saith the Lord, unto the wicked" (48:22; 57:21). Chapters 40–48 emphasize the greatness of God the Father in contrast to the vanity of the heathen idols. Chapters 49–57 extol the graciousness of God the Son, the Suffering Servant; and chapters 58–66 describe the glory of God in the future kingdom, and the emphasis is on the work of the Holy Spirit (59:19, 21; 61:1ff; 63:10-11, 14). Thus, there seems to be a trinitarian structure to these chapters.

The heart of Isaiah 40–66 is chapters 49–57, in which Isaiah exalts the Messiah, God's Suffering Servant. And the heart of chapters 49–57 is 52:13–53:12, the description of the Savior's substitutionary death for the sins of the world. This is the fourth of the "Servant Songs" in Isaiah; the others are 42:1-7; 49:1-6; and 50:1-11. So at the heart of the "New Testament" section of Isaiah's book is our Lord Jesus Christ and His sacrifice on the cross for our sins. No wonder Isaiah has been called "the evangelical prophet."

The Jewish rabbis have called Isaiah 40–66 "The Book of Consolation," and they are right. Isaiah sought to comfort the Jewish remnant in Babylon, after their difficult years of captivity, and to assure them that God was with them and would take them safely home. Along with words of consolation, the prophet also revealed the Messiah, God's Suffering Servant, and described the future regathering of Israel and the promised kingdom. Isaiah saw in Israel's restoration from Babylon a preview of what God would do for them at the end of the age, after the "Day of the Lord" and the destruction of the world's last "Babylon" (Rev. 17–19).

So as you study Isaiah 40–66, keep in mind that it was originally addressed to a group of discouraged Jewish refugees who faced a long journey home and a difficult task when they got there. Note how often God says to them, "Fear not!" and how frequently He assures them of His pardon and His presence. It is no surprise that God's people for centuries have turned to these chapters to find assurance and encouragement in the difficult days of life; for in these messages, God says to all of His people, "Be comforted!"

CHAPTER NINE
HOW GREAT THOU ART!
ISAIAH 40–48

"In your time we have the opportunity to move not only toward the rich society and the powerful society but upward to the Great Society." President Lyndon B. Johnson spoke those words at the University of Michigan on May 22, 1964. Reading them over three decades later, I ask myself, "I wonder how the Jewish captives in Babylon would have responded to what the President said?"

A rich society? They were refugees whose land and holy city were in ruins.

A powerful society? Without king or army, they were weak and helpless before the nations around them.

A great society? They had been guilty of great rebellion against God and had suffered great humiliation and chastening. They faced a great challenge but lacked great human resources.

That is why the prophet told them to get their eyes off themselves and look by faith to the great God who loved them and promised to do great things for them. "Be not afraid!" he admonished them. "Behold your God!" (40:9)

Years ago, one of my radio listeners sent me a motto that has often encouraged me: "Look at others, and be distressed. Look at yourself, and be depressed. Look to God, and you'll be blessed!" This may not be a piece of literature, but it certainly contains great practical theology. When the outlook is bleak, we need the uplook. "Lift up your eyes on high, and behold who hath created these things . . . for He is strong in power" (v. 26).

When, like Israel of old, you face a difficult task and an impossible tomorrow, do what they did and remind yourself of the greatness of God. In these nine chapters, the prophet describes the greatness of God in three different areas of life.

1. God Is Greater than Our Circumstances (Isa. 40:1-31)

The circumstances behind us (Isa. 40:1-11). As the remnant in Babylon looked back, they saw failure and sin, and they needed encouragement. Four voices are heard, each with a special message for these needy people.

(1) The voice of pardon (vv. 1-2). The nation had sinned greatly against the Lord, with their idolatry, injustice, immorality, and insensitivity to His messengers (Jer. 7). But they were still His people, and He loved them. Though He would chasten them, He would not forsake them. "Speak tenderly" means "speak to the heart," and "warfare" means "severe trials." "Double" does not suggest that God's chastenings are unfair, for He is merciful even in His punishments (Ezra 9:13). God chastened them in an equivalent measure to what they had done (Jer. 16:18). We should not sin, but if we do, God is waiting to pardon (1 John 1:5-2:2).

(2) The voice of providence (vv. 3-5). The Jews had a rough road ahead of them as they returned to rebuild Jerusalem and the temple, but the Lord would go before them to open the way. The picture here is of an ambassador repairing the roads and removing obstacles, preparing the way for the coming of a king. The image of the highway is frequent in Isaiah's prophecy (see 11:16). Of course, the ultimate fulfillment here is in the ministry of John the Baptist as he prepared the way for the ministry of Jesus (Matt. 3:1-6). Spiritually speaking, Israel was in the wilderness when Jesus came, but when He came, God's glory came (John 1:14). The way back may not be easy, but if we are trusting God, it will be easier.

(3) The voice of promise (vv. 6-8). "All flesh is grass!" Assyria was gone, and now Babylon was gone. Like the grass, nations and their leaders fulfill their purposes and then fade away, but the Word of God abides forever (Pss. 37:1-2; 90:1-6; 103:15-18; 1 Peter 1:24-25). As they began their long journey home, Israel could depend on God's promises. Perhaps they were especially claiming 2 Chronicles 6:36-39.

(4) The voice of peace (vv. 9-11). Now the nation itself comes out of the valley and climbs the mountaintop to declare God's victory over the enemy. To "bring good tidings" means "to preach the Good News." The good news in that day was the defeat of Babylon and the release of the captive Jews (52:7-9). The Good News today is the defeat of sin and Satan by Jesus Christ and the salvation of all who will trust in Him (61:1-3; Luke 4:18-19). God's arm is a mighty arm for winning the

battle (Isa. 40:10), but it is also a loving arm for carrying His weary lambs (v. 11). "We are coming home!" would certainly be good news to the devastated cities of Judah (1:7; 36:1; 37:26).

The circumstances before us (Isa. 40:12-26). The Jews were few in number, only a remnant, and facing a long and difficult journey. The victories of Assyria, Babylon, and Persia made it look as though the false gods of the Gentiles were stronger than the God of Israel, but Isaiah reminded the people of the greatness of Jehovah. When you behold the greatness of God, then you will see everything else in life in its proper perspective.

God is greater than anything on earth (vv. 12-20) or anything in heaven (vv. 21-26). Creation shows His wisdom, power, and immensity. He is greater than the nations and their gods. He founded the earth and sits on the throne of heaven, and nothing is equal to our God, let alone greater than our God. The next time you are tempted to think that the world is bigger than God, remember the "drop of a bucket" (v. 15) and the "grasshoppers" (v. 22; see Num. 13:33). And if you ever feel so small that you wonder if God really cares about you personally, remember that He knows the name of every star (Isa. 40:26) and your name as well! (See John 10:3, 27.) The same God who numbers and names the stars can heal your broken heart (Ps. 147:3-4).

Someone has defined "circumstances" as "those nasty things you see when you get your eyes off of God." If you look at God through your circumstances, He will seem small and very far away, but if by faith you look at your circumstances through God, He will draw very near and reveal His greatness to you.

The circumstances within us (Isa. 40:27-31). Instead of praising the Lord, the nation was complaining to Him that He acted as though He did not know their situation or have any concern for their problems (v. 27; 49:14). Instead of seeing the open door, the Jews saw only the long road before them, and they complained that they did not have strength for the journey. God was asking them to do the impossible.

But God knows how we feel and how we fear, and He is adequate to meet our every need. We can never obey God in our own strength, but we can always trust Him to provide the strength we need (Phil. 4:13). If we trust ourselves, we will faint and fall, but if we wait on the Lord by faith, we will receive strength for the journey. The word "wait" does not suggest that we sit around and do nothing. It means "to hope," to look to God for all that we need (Isa. 26:3; 30:15). This involves meditating on His character and His promises, praying, and seeking to glorify Him.

The word "renew" means "to exchange," as taking off old clothing and putting on new. We exchange our weakness for His power (2 Cor. 12:1-10). As we wait before Him, God enables us to soar when there is a crisis, to run when the challenges are many, and to walk faithfully in the day-by-day demands of life. It is much harder to walk in the ordinary pressures of life than to fly like the eagle in a time of crisis.

"I can plod," said William Carey, the father of modern missions. "That is my only genius. I can persevere in any definite pursuit. To this I owe everything."

The journey of a thousand miles begins with one step. The greatest heroes of faith are not always those who seem to be soaring; often it is they who are patiently plodding. As we wait on the Lord, He enables us not only to fly higher and run faster, but also to walk longer. Blessed are the plodders, for they eventually arrive at their destination!

2. God Is Greater than Our Fears (Isa. 41:1–44:28)

In this section of the book, the Lord seven times says, "Fear not!" to His people (41:10, 13, 14: 43:1, 5: 44:2, 8), and He says "Fear not!" to us today. As the Jewish remnant faced the challenge of the long journey home and the difficult task of rebuilding, they could think of many causes for fear. But there was one big reason not to be afraid: The Lord was with them and would give them success.

God seeks to calm their fears by assuring them that He is going before them and working on their behalf. The Lord explains a wonderful truth: He has three servants in His employ who will accomplish His will: Cyrus, king of Persia (41:1-7); the nation of Israel (vv. 8-29; 43:1-44:27); and the Messiah (42:1-25).

God's servant Cyrus (Isa. 41:1-7). God convenes the court and asks the nations to present their case against Him, if they can. At least seventeen times in his prophecy,

Isaiah writes about "the islands" (KJV) or "the coastlands" (NIV), referring to the most distant places from the holy land (11:11; 24:15; 41:1, 5; 42:4, 10, 12). "Produce your cause," He challenges these nations (41:21); "present your case" (NIV).

God is not afraid of the nations because He is greater than the nations (40:12-17); He controls their rise and fall. He announced that He would raise up a ruler named Cyrus, who would do His righteous work on earth by defeating other nations for the sake of His people Israel. Cyrus would be a shepherd (44:28) anointed by God (45:1), a ravenous bird that could not be stopped (46:11). "He treads on rulers as if they were mortar, as if he were a potter treading the clay" (41:25, NIV).

Isaiah called Cyrus by name over a century before he was born (590?-529), and while Isaiah nowhere calls Cyrus "God's servant," Cyrus did serve the Lord by fulfilling God's purposes on earth. God handed the nations over to Cyrus and helped him conquer great kings (45:1-4). The enemy was blown away like chaff and dust because the eternal God was leading the army.

As Cyrus moved across the territory east and north of the Holy Land (41:25), the nations were afraid and turned to their idols for help. With keen satire, Isaiah describes various workmen helping each other manufacture a god who cannot help them! After all, when the God of heaven is in charge of the conquest, how can men or gods oppose him?

Cyrus may have thought that he was accomplishing his own plans, but actually he was doing the pleasure of the Lord (44:28). By defeating Babylon, Cyrus made it possible for the Jewish captives to be released and allowed to return to their land to rebuild Jerusalem and the temple (Ezra 1:1-4). "I have raised him up in righteousness, and I will direct all his ways; he shall build my city, and he shall let go my captives" (Isa. 45:13).

Sometimes we forget that God can use even unconverted world leaders for the good of His people and the progress of His work. He raised up Pharaoh in Egypt that He might demonstrate His power (Rom. 9:17), and He even used wicked Herod and cowardly Pontius Pilate to accomplish His plan in the crucifixion of Christ (Acts. 4:24-28). "The king's heart is in the hand of the Lord, like the rivers of water; He turns it wherever He wishes" (Prov. 21:1, NKJV).

God's servant Israel (Isa. 41:8-29; 43:1-44:28) The prophet presents four pictures to encourage the people. In contrast to the fear experienced by the Gentile nations is the confidence shown by Israel, God's chosen servant (41:8-13), because God was working on their behalf. In spite of their past rebellion, Israel was not cast away by the Lord. The Jewish captives did not need to fear either Cyrus or Babylon, because Cyrus was working for God, and Babylon would be no more. As you read their paragraph, you sense God's love for His people and His desire to encourage them to trust Him for the future.

The title "My servant" is an honorable one; it was given to great leaders like Moses (Num. 12:7), David (2 Sam. 3:18), the prophets (Jer. 7:25), and Messiah (Isa. 42:1). But is there any honor in being called a "worm"? (41:14-16) "Servant" defined what they were by God's grace and calling, but "worm" described what they were in themselves. Imagine a worm getting teeth and threshing mountains into dust like chaff! As the nation marched ahead by faith, every mountain and hill would be made low (40:4), and the Lord would turn mountains into molehills!

From the pictures of a servant and a worm, Isaiah turned to the picture of a desert becoming a garden (41:17-20). The image reminds us of Israel's wanderings in the wilderness and God's provision for their every need. Water and trees are important possessions in the East, and God will supply both to His people. Certainly Isaiah was also looking beyond the return from Babylon to the future kingdom when "the desert shall rejoice and blossom like the rose" (35:1).

The final picture is that of the courtroom (41:21-29). "Produce your cause!" means "Present your case!" God challenged the idols of the nations to prove that they were really gods. Did any of their predictions come true? What have they predicted about the future? Did they announce that Cyrus would appear on the scene or that Jerusalem would be restored? "No one told of this, no one foretold it, no one heard any words from you," taunted the Lord (v. 26, NIV). Not only were the idols unable to make any valid predictions, they were not even able to speak! The judgment of the court was correct: "See, they are all false! Their deeds amount to nothing; their images are but wind and confusion" (v. 29, NIV).

The theme of "Israel God's Servant" is continued in Isaiah 43–44 with an emphasis on God the Redeemer of Israel (43:1-7). (Note also v. 14; 44:6, 22-24.) The word translated "redeem" or "Redeemer" is the Hebrew word for "a kinsman redeemer," a near relative who could free family members and their property from bondage by paying their debts for them. (See Lev. 25:23-28 and the Book of Ruth.) God gave Egypt, Ethiopia (Cush), and Seba to Cyrus as a ransom payment to redeem Israel from Babylon, because Israel was so precious to Him. And He gave His own Son as a ransom for lost sinners (Matt. 20:28; 1 Tim. 2:6).

Israel is God's servant in the world and also God's witness to the world (Isa. 43:8-13). This is another courtroom scene where God challenges the idols. "Let them bring in their witnesses!" says the Judge, but of course the idols are helpless and speechless. Twice the Lord says to Israel, "You are My witnesses" (vv. 10, 12, NKJV), for it is in the history of Israel that God has revealed Himself to the world. Frederick the Great asked the Marquis D'Argens, "Can you give me one single irrefutable proof of God?" The Marquis replied, "Yes, your majesty, the Jews."

Along with Israel's new freedom and new witness, Isaiah writes about Israel's new "exodus" (vv. 14-28). Just as God led His people out of Egypt and through the Red Sea (Ex. 12-15), so He will lead them out of Babylon and through the terrible wilderness to their home in the Holy Land. Just as He defeated Pharaoh's army (14:28; 15:4), so He will defeat Israel's enemies and snuff them out "like a wick" (Isa. 43:17, NIV).

When God forgives and restores His people, He wants them to forget the failures of the past, witness for Him in the present, and claim His promises for the future (vv. 18-21). Why should we remember that which God has forgotten? (v. 25) He forgave them, not because they brought Him sacrifices—for they had no altar in Babylon—but purely because of His mercy and grace.

God chose Israel and redeemed them, but He also formed them for Himself (44:1-20). In this chapter, Isaiah contrasts God's forming of Israel (vv. 1-8) and the Gentiles forming their own gods (vv. 9-20). "I have formed thee" is a special theme in chapters 43–44 (43:1, 7, 21; 44:2, 24). Because God formed them, chose them, and redeemed them, they had nothing to fear. He will pour water on the land and His Spirit on the people (59:21; Ezek. 34:26; Joel 2:28-29; John 7:37-39), and both will prosper to the glory of the Lord. The final fulfillment of this will be in the future Kingdom Age when Messiah reigns.

Isaiah 44:9-20 shows the folly of idolatry and should be compared with Psalm 115. Those who defend idols and worship them are just like them: blind and ignorant and nothing. God made people in His own image, and now they are making gods in their own image! Part of the tree becomes a god, and the rest of the tree becomes fuel for the fire. The worshiper is "feeding on ashes" and deriving no benefit at all from the worship experience.

But God formed Israel (Isa. 44:21, 24), forgave His people their sins (v. 22; see 43:25), and is glorified in them (44:23). He speaks to His people and is faithful to keep his Word (v. 26). May we never take for granted the privilege we have of knowing and worshiping the true and living God!

God's Servant Messiah (Isa. 42). Isaiah 42:1-7 is the first of four "Servant Songs" in Isaiah, referring to God's Servant, the Messiah. The others are 49:1-6; 50:1-11; and 52:13–53:12. Contrast "Behold, they [the idols] are all vanity" (41:29) with "Behold My Servant" (42:1). Matthew 12:14-21 applies these words to the earthly ministry of Jesus Christ. He could have destroyed His enemies (the reed and flax), but He was patient and merciful. The Father delights in His Son (Matt. 3:17; 17:5).

It is through the ministry of the Servant that God will accomplish His great plan of salvation for this world. God chose Him, God upheld Him, and God enabled Him to succeed in His mission. Because of the death and resurrection of Jesus Christ, one day there will be a glorious kingdom, and God will "bring justice to the nations" (Isa. 42:1, NIV). Jesus Christ is "the light of the world" (John 8:12), and that includes the Gentiles (Isa. 42:6; Acts 13:47-48; Luke 1:79). Isaiah 42:7 refers to the nation's deliverance from Babylon (29:18; 32:3; 35:5) as well as to the sinner's deliverance from condemnation (61:1-3; Luke 4:18-19).

The closing section (Isa. 42:10-25) describes a singing nation (vv. 10-12), giving praise to the Lord, and a silent God who breaks that silence to become a shouting conqueror (vv. 13-17). God is long-suffering toward sinners, but when He begins to work,

He wastes no time! The "servant" in verses 18-25 is the people of Israel, blind to their own sins and deaf to God's voice (6:9-10); yet the Lord graciously forgave them and led them out of bondage. Now God says to the Babylonians, "Send them back!" (42:22, NIV)

How sad it is when God disciplines us and we do not understand what He is doing or take it to heart (v. 25). Israel's captivity in Babylon cured the nation of their idolatry, but it did not create within them a desire to please God and glorify Him.

3. God Is Greater than Our Enemies (Isa. 45:1-48:22)

These chapters deal with the overthrow of Babylon, and one of the major themes is, "I am the Lord, and there is none else" (45:5-6, 14, 18, 21-22; 46:9). Jehovah again reveals Himself as the true and living God in contrast to the dumb and dead idols.

The conqueror described (Isa. 45:1-25). Just as prophets, priests, and kings were anointed for service, so Cyrus was anointed by God to perform his special service for Israel's sake. In this sense, Cyrus was a "messiah," an "anointed one." God called him by name over a century before he was born! Cyrus was the human instrument for the conquest, but it was Jehovah God who gave the victories. Anyone who opposed Cyrus was arguing with God, and that was like the clay commanding the potter or the child ordering his parents (vv. 9-10). God raised up Cyrus to do His specific will (v. 13), and nothing would prevent him from succeeding. Note the emphasis on salvation. The idols cannot save Babylon (v. 20), but God is the Savior of Israel (vv. 15, 17). He is "a just God and a Savior" (v. 21), and He offers salvation to the whole world (v. 22). It was this verse that brought the light of salvation to the great English pastor Charles Haddon Spurgeon when he was a youth seeking the Lord.

The false gods disgraced (Isa. 46:1-13). Bel was the Babylonian sun god, and Nebo was his son, the god of writing and learning. But both of them together could not stop Cyrus! As the Babylonians fled from the enemy, they had to carry their gods, but their gods went into captivity with the prisoners of war! God assures His people that He will carry them from the womb to the tomb. Verse 4 is the basis for a stanza of the familiar song "How Firm a Foundation" that is usually omitted from our hymnals:

E'en down to old age, all My people shall prove,
My sovereign, eternal unchangeable love,
And then when grey hairs shall their temples adorn,
Like lambs they shall still in My bosom be borne.
(Richard Keen)

How comforting it is to know that our God cares for us before we are born (Ps. 139:13-16), when we get old, and each moment in between!

The city destroyed (Isa. 47:1-15). Babylon, the proud queen, is now a humbled slave. "I will continue forever—the eternal queen!" she boasted (v. 7, NIV). But in a moment, the judgment for her sins caught up with her; and she became a widow. Neither her idols nor her occult practices (vv. 12-14) were able to warn her or prepare her for her destruction. But God knew that Babylon would fall, because He planned it ages ago! He called Cyrus, who swooped down on Babylon like a bird of prey. Babylon showed no mercy to the Jews, and God judged them accordingly.

The Jewish remnant delivered (Isa. 48:1-22). The Jews had become comfortable and complacent in their captivity and did not want to leave. They had followed the counsel of Jeremiah (Jer. 29:4-7) and had houses, gardens, and families, but they had become so attached to those things that it would not be easy for them to pack up and go to the Holy Land. Nevertheless, the Holy Land was where they belonged and where God had a work for them to do. God told them that they were hypocritical in using His name and identifying with His city but not obeying His will (Isa. 48:1-2). They were stubborn (v. 4) and were not excited about the new things God was doing for them.

Had they obeyed the Lord in the first place, they would have experienced peace and not war (vv. 18-19), but it was not too late. He had put them into the furnace to refine them and prepare them for their future work (v. 10). "Go forth from Babylon; flee from the Chaldeans!" was God's command (v. 20; see Jer. 50:8; 51:6; 45; Rev. 18:4). God would go before them and prepare the way, and they had nothing to fear.

One would think that the Jews would have

been eager to leave their "prison" and return to their land to see God do new and great things for them. But they had grown accustomed to the security of bondage and had forgotten the challenges of freedom. The church today can easily grow complacent with its comfort and affluence. God may have to put us into the furnace to remind us that we are here to be servants and not consumers or spectators.

CHAPTER TEN
THIS IS GOD'S SERVANT
ISAIAH 49:1–52:12

A plaque in a friend's office reads: "The world is full of people who want to serve in an advisory capacity."

But Jesus Christ did not come with good advice: He came with good news, the Good News that sinners can be forgiven and life can become excitingly new. The Gospel is good news to us, but it was "bad news" to the Son of God; for it meant that He would need to come to earth in human form and die on a cross as the sacrifice for the sins of the world.

These chapters present God's Servant, Messiah, in three important relationships: to the Gentile nations (49:1-50:3), to His Father (50:4-11), and to His people Israel (51:1-52:12).

1. The Servant and the Gentiles (Isa. 49:1–50:3)

The Servant addresses the nations that did not know Israel's God. The Gentiles were "far off," and only God's Servant could bring them near (Eph. 2:11-22). Christ confirmed God's promises to the Jews and also extended God's grace to the Gentiles (Rom. 15:8-12). In this message, God's Servant explains His ministry as bringing light in the darkness (Isa, 49:1-7), liberty to the captive (vv. 8-13), and love and hope to the discouraged (49:14-50:3).

Light in the darkness (49:1-7). What right did God's Servant have to address the Gentile nations with such authority? From before His birth, He was called by God to His ministry (Jer. 1:5; Gal. 1:15), and God prepared Him like a sharp sword and a polished arrow (Heb. 4:12; Rev. 1:16). Messiah came as both a Servant and a Warrior, serving those who trust Him and ultimately judging those who resist Him.

All of God's servants should be like prepared weapons. "It is not great talents God blesses so much as great likeness to Jesus," wrote Robert Murray McCheyne. "A holy minister [servant] is an awful weapon in the hand of God."

The Jewish nation was called to glorify God and be a light to the Gentiles, but they failed in their mission. This is why Messiah is called "Israel" in Isaiah 49:3: He did the work that Israel was supposed to do. Today, the church is God's light in the dark world (Acts 13:46-49; Matt. 5:14-16), and like Israel, we seem to be failing in our mission to take the Good News to the ends of the earth. We cannot do the job very effectively when only five percent of the average local church budget is devoted to evangelism!

As Jesus Christ ministered on earth, especially to His own people Israel, there were times when His work seemed in vain (Isa. 49:4). The religious leaders opposed Him, the disciples did not always understand Him, and those He helped did not always thank Him. He lived and labored by faith, and God gave Him success.

Our Lord could not minister to the Gentiles until first He ministered to the Jews (vv. 5-6). Read carefully Matthew 10:5-6; 15:24; Luke 24:44-49; Acts 3:25-26; 13:46-47; and Romans 1:16. When our Lord returned to heaven, He left behind a believing remnant of Jews that carried on His work. We must never forget that "salvation is of the Jews" (John 4:22). The Bible is a Jewish book, the first believers and missionaries were Jews, and the Gentiles would not have heard the Gospel had it not been brought to them by Jews. Messiah was despised by both Jews and Gentiles (Isa. 49:7), but He did God's work and was glorified (Phil. 2:1-11).

Liberty to the captives (Isa. 49:8-13). Not only is God's Servant the "new Israel," but He is also the "new Moses" in setting His people free. Jesus Christ is God's covenant (42:6), so we can be sure that God will keep His promises. Moses led the nation out of bondage in Egypt, and God will lead His people out of captivity in Babylon. Joshua led the people into their land so they could claim their inheritance, and God will bring them back to their land "to reassign its desolate inheritances" (49:8, NIV).

How does this apply to the Gentiles? If God had not restored the people, the city, and the temple, He could not have fulfilled His promises concerning the Messiah. Had there been no Bethlehem, where would He have been born? Had there been no Nazareth, where would He have grown up? Had there been no Jerusalem and no temple, where would He have taught, suffered, and died? And He did this for the Gentiles as well as for the Jews.

Verses 10-12 look beyond the deliverance from Babylon in 536 B.C. toward the future glorious kingdom. The Lord will call the Jewish people from the ends of the earth and gather them again in their land (Isa. 14:1-3l; 35:6; 40:11; 43:19).

Love and hope to the discouraged (Isa. 49:14-50:3). "The Lord comforts His people and will have compassion on His afflicted ones" (49:13, NIV). So sing the people of God as they contemplate their future deliverance, but the people of the Captivity and those left in "the desolate inheritances" are not so happy. Instead of singing, they are complaining: "The Lord has forsaken me. And my Lord has forgotten me" (v. 14, NKJV).

The Lord assures them of His love by comparing Himself to a compassionate mother (vv. 14-23), a courageous warrior (vv. 24-26), and a constant lover (50:1-3).

(1) A compassionate mother (vv. 14-23). The Bible emphasizes the fatherhood of God, but there is also a "motherhood" side to God's nature that we must not forget. God is compassionate and comforts us as a mother comforts her children (66:13). Isaiah pictures Israel as a nursing child, totally dependent on the Lord, who will never forget them or forsake them. The high priest bore the names of the tribes of Israel on his shoulders and over his heart (Ex. 28:6-9), engraved on jewels, but God has engraved His children's names on His hands. The word "engraved" means "to cut into," signifying its permanence. God can never forget Zion or Zion's children.

Zion seems like a forsaken and barren mother, but she will be so blessed of God that there will be no room for her children! They will be like beautiful bridal ornaments, not decrepit refugees from captivity. Once again, the prophet looked ahead to the end of the age when the Gentiles will honor Jehovah and Israel, and kings and queens will be babysitters for Israel's children!

(2) A courageous warrior (vv. 24-26). The Babylonians were fierce warriors, but the Lord would snatch Israel from their grasp. In His compassion, He would set the captives free and see to it that Babylon would never afflict them again. The fact that God permitted Babylon to conquer His people did not mean that God was weak or unconcerned. When the right time comes, He will set His people free: ". . . they shall not be ashamed that wait for me" (v. 23).

(3) A constant lover (50:1-3). The image of Israel as the wife of Jehovah is found often in the prophets (54:4-5; 62:1-5; Jer. 2:1-3; 3:1-11; Hosea 2; Ezek. 16). Israel was "married" to Jehovah when they accepted the covenant at Sinai (Ex. 19-20), but they violated that covenant by "playing the harlot" and worshiping idols. But God did not forsake His people even though they had been unfaithful to Him

The Mosaic permission for divorce is found in Deuteronomy 24:1-4 (see Matt. 19:1-12). The "certificate of divorce" declared that the former marriage was broken and that the woman was free to remarry. But it also prevented the woman from returning to her former husband. God had indeed "divorced" the Northern Kingdom and allowed it to be assimilated by the Assyrians (Jer. 3:8), so she could not return. But He had not "divorced" the Southern Kingdom; He had only permitted His unfaithful wife to suffer chastening at the hands of Babylon. He would forgive her and receive her back again.

The second picture in this paragraph is that of a poor family selling their children into servitude (2 Kings 4:1-7; Neh. 5:1-5). God had not sold His people; by their sins, they had sold themselves. God had called to them many times and tried to turn them back from their wicked ways, but they had refused to listen. Judah did not go into exile because of God's weakness, but because of their own sinfulness.

How could the people say they were forgotten and forsaken, when the Lord is a compassionate mother, a courageous warrior, and a constant lover? He is faithful to His Word even when we are unfaithful (2 Tim. 2:11-13).

He is faithful to chasten when we rebel (Heb. 12:1-11), but He is also faithful to forgive when we repent and confess (1 John 1:9).

The Servant's message to the Gentiles was one of hope and blessing. He would deal with His people so that they, in turn, could bring God's blessing to the Gentiles.

2. The Servant and the Lord God (Isa. 50:4-11)

In the first two "Servant Songs" (42:1-7; 49:1-7), you find hints of opposition to Messiah's ministry, but in this third song, His suffering is vividly described. When we get to the fourth song (52:12-53:12), we will be told not only how He suffered, but why His suffering is necessary.

Note that four times in this passage the Servant uses the name "Lord God." "Jehovah Adonai" can be translated "Sovereign Lord," and you will find this title nowhere else in the "Servant Songs." According to Robert B. Girdlestone, the name "Jehovah Adonai" means that "God is the owner of each member of the human family, and that He consequently claims the unrestricted obedience of all" (*Synonyms of the Old Testament,* Eerdmans, 1951; p. 34). So the emphasis here is on the Servant's submission to the Lord God in every area of His life and service.

His mind was submitted to the Lord God so that He could learn His work and His will (50:4). Everything Jesus said and did was taught to Him by His Father (John 5:19, 30; 6:38; 8:28). He prayed to the Father for guidance (John 11:42; Mark 1:35) and meditated on the Word. What God taught the Servant, the Servant shared with those who needed encouragement and help. The Servant sets a good example here for all who know the importance of a daily "quiet time" with the Lord.

The Servant's will was also yielded to the Lord God. An "opened ear" is one that hears and obeys the voice of the master. The people to whom Isaiah ministered were neither "willing" nor "obedient" (Isa. 1:19), but the Servant did gladly the will of the Lord God. This was not easy, for it meant yielding His body to wicked men who mocked Him, whipped Him, spat on Him, and then nailed Him to a cross (Matt. 26:67; 27:26, 30).

The Servant did all of this by faith in the Lord God (Isa. 50:7-11). He was determined to do God's will even if it meant going to a cross (Luke 9:51; John 18:1-11), for He knew that the Lord God would help Him. The Servant was falsely accused, but He knew that God would vindicate Him and eventually put His enemies to shame. Keep in mind that when Jesus Christ was ministering here on earth, He had to live by faith even as we must today. He did not use His divine powers selfishly for Himself but trusted God and depended on the power of the Spirit.

Verses 10-11 are addressed especially to the Jewish remnant, but they have an application to God's people today. His faithful ones were perplexed at what God was doing, but He assured them that their faith would not go unrewarded. Dr. Bob Jones, Sr. often said, "Never doubt in the dark what God has told you in the light." But the unbelieving ones who try to eliminate the darkness by lighting their own fires (i.e., following their own schemes) will end up in sorrow and suffering. In obedience to the Lord, you may find yourself in the darkness, but do not panic, for He will bring you the light you need just at the right time.

3. The Servant and Israel (Isa. 51:1–52:12)

This section contains several admonitions: "hearken to me" (51:1 KJV; also 4, 7); "awake, awake" (vv. 9, 17; 52:1-6); and "depart, depart" (vv. 7-12). Except for 51:9-16, which is a prayer addressed to the Lord, each of these admonitions is from God to His people in Babylon.

"Hearken to Me" (Isa. 51:1-8). These three admonitions are addressed to the faithful remnant in Israel, the people described in 50:10. In the first admonition (51:1-3), the Lord told them to look back and remember Abraham and Sarah, the progenitors of the Jewish nation (Gen. 12-25). God called them "alone," but from these two elderly people came a nation as numerous as the dust of the earth and the stars of the heaven (13:16; 15:5). The remnant leaving Babylon was small and weak, but God was able to increase them into a mighty nation and also turn their ravaged land into a paradise. "Be comforted!" God said to His people. "The best is yet to come!"

In the second command (Isa. 51:4-6), God told them to look ahead and realize that justice would come to the world and they would be vindicated by the Lord. Note the emphasis on the word "My": My people, My nation, My justice, My righteousness, My arms, and My salvation. This is the grace of God, doing for His people what they did not deserve and what they could not do for themselves. The "arm of the Lord" is a key concept in Isaiah's prophecies (30:30; 40:10, 51:5, 9; 52:10; 53:1; 5916; 62:8; 63:5, 12). Heaven and earth will pass away, but God's righteousness and salvation will last forever. That righteousness will be displayed in a special way when Messiah returns and establishes His kingdom on earth.

The third admonition (51:7-8) focuses on looking within, where we find either fear or faith. Why should the nation fear men when God is on its side? "Behold, God is my salvation; I will trust, and not be afraid" (Isa. 12:2 NKJV). "Sanctify the Lord of hosts himself, and let him be your fear, and let him be your dread" (8:13 KJV). To have God's law in your heart means to belong to Him and be saved (Jer. 31:31-34; Heb 10:16). The moth and the worm shall destroy the enemy, but God's salvation will endure. Moths and worms do not do their work conspicuously, but they work efficiently just the same. The seeds of destruction were already in the Babylonian Empire, and the leaders did not know it.

"Awake, awake" (Isa. 51:9–52:6). "Hearken to me" was spoken to admonish the people, but "awake, awake" is for the arousing of the Lord (51:9-16) and of Jerusalem (vv. 17-23; 52:1-6).

The remnant in Babylon prayed as though God were asleep and needed to be awakened (Pss. 7:6; 44:23; 78:65-72). They wanted God to bare His arm as He did when He defeated Pharaoh and redeemed His people from Egyptian bondage. The return from Babylon was looked upon as another "exodus" (Isa. 43:16-17; 49:9-12), with God wholly in charge and the enemy completely defeated.

God replied to their prayer with words of comfort (51:12-16; see vv. 3 and 19). He reminded them again of the frailty of man (see 40:6-8) and the power of God the Creator (51:13). Why should they be afraid of grass when the God of the universe was on their side? Because they are His people, with whom He has deposited His Word, He will release them, protect them, and provide for them. They had an important task to perform and He would enable them to do it.

In the second "wake-up call," the prophet speaks to the ruined city of Jerusalem (vv. 17-23) and pictures her as a mother in a drunken stupor with no children to help her. In the Bible, judgment is sometimes pictured as the drinking of a cup of wine (29:9; 63:6; Ps. 75:8; Jer. 25:15-16; Rev. 14:10). Jerusalem's children had gone into captivity, but now they would return and give their "mother" new hope and a new beginning. God will take the cup of judgment from the Jews and give it to their enemies. To put your foot on the neck of your enemies was a humiliating declaration of their defeat, but instead of Babylon "walking on" the Jews, the Jews would "walk on" the Babylonians!

The third "wake-up call" (Isa. 52:1-6) is also addressed to Jerusalem and is a command not only to wake up but to dress up! It is not enough for her to put off her stupor (51:17-23); she must also put on her glorious garments. Babylon the "queen" would fall to the dust in shame (47:1), but Jerusalem would rise up from the dust and be enthroned as a queen! Egypt had enslaved God's people, Assyria had oppressed them, and Babylon had taken them captive, but now that was ended. Of course, the ultimate fulfillment of this promise will occur when the Messiah returns, delivers Jerusalem from her enemies, and establishes Mt. Zion as the joy of all the earth (61:4-11).

The city of Jerusalem is called "the holy city" eight times in Scripture (Neh. 11:1, 18; Isa. 48:2; 52:1; Dan. 9:24; Matt. 4:5; 27:53; Rev. 11:2). It has been "set apart" by God for His exclusive purposes, but when His people refused to obey Him, He ordered it destroyed, first by the Babylonians and then by the Romans.

During the Captivity, God's name was blasphemed because the enemy taunted the Jews and asked them why their great God did not deliver them (Pss. 115; 137). Paul quoted Isaiah 52:5 in Romans 2:24. But when the remnant is restored, they will know God's name and seek to honor it.

"Depart, depart" (Isa. 52:7-12). The defeat of Babylon by Cyrus was certainly good news to the Jews because it meant freedom for the captives (40:9; 41:27). The Good News we share today is that Jesus Christ can set the prisoners free (Rom. 10:15). For decades, the remnant had suffered in a foreign country, without an altar or a priesthood, but now they would return to their land, rebuild their temple, and restore their God-given ministry.

It has well been said that "good news is for sharing," and that is what happens in

Jerusalem. The leaders (watchmen) take up the message and sing together to the glory of God (Isa. 44:23). But they not only hear what God has done; they also see it happening! The wilderness will join the song because the desolate cities and "waste places" will be transformed (51:3). The remnant prayed for God's holy arm to work, and He answered their prayer (v. 9).

Isaiah likes to use repetition: "Comfort ye, comfort ye" (40:1); "awake, awake" (51:9, 17; 52:1); and now, "depart, depart" (52:11). It seems strange that God would have to urge His people to leave a place of captivity, but some of them had grown accustomed to Babylon and were reluctant to leave. The first group, about 50,000 people, left Babylon in 539-8 B.C.. when Cyrus issued his decree. They were under the leadership of Sheshbazzar, Zerubbabel, and Jeshua the high priest (Ezra 1–2). They carried with them "the vessels of the Lord" (Isa. 52:11), the articles that were needed for the service in the temple. A second group of nearly 1,800 people led by Ezra left in 458 B.C.

God commanded them to depart because Babylon was a condemned city (Jer. 50:8ff; 51:6, 45). He warned them not to linger but to get out quickly while they had the opportunity (Isa. 48:20). They did not have to flee like criminals, but there was no reason to tarry. He also cautioned them not to take any of Babylon's uncleanness with them. "Touch no unclean thing" (52:11) would certainly include the whole Babylonian system of idolatry and occult practices that had helped to ruin the Jewish nation (47:11-15). Paul makes the application to believers today in 2 Corinthians 6:14-7:1.

God had a special word for the priests and Levites who were carrying the vessels of the temple: "Come out from it [Babylon] and be pure" (Isa. 52:11, NIV). This is a good command for all of God's servants to obey. If we defile ourselves, we will also defile the work of the Lord. How tragic for a holy ministry to be a source of defilement to God's people!

The prophet added a final word of encouragement: "The Lord will go before you, and the God of Israel will be your rear guard" (v. 12; see 58:8). This reminds us of Israel's exodus from Egypt when the Lord went before them (Ex. 13:21) and stood between them and the enemy (14:19-20). When God's people obey God's will, they can always count on God's leading and protection.

Isaiah has prepared the way for the "heart" of God's revelation of the Servant Messiah, the fourth Servant Song (52:13-53:12). We must prepare our hearts, for we are walking on holy ground.

CHAPTER ELEVEN
CLIMBING MOUNT EVEREST
ISAIAH 52:13–53:12

These five matchless stanzas of the fourth Servant poem are the Mt. Everest of messianic prophecy." So wrote Old Testament scholar Dr. Kyle M. Yates over fifty years ago, and his words still stand. This passage is at the heart of chapters 49–57, and its message is at the heart of the Gospel. Like Mt. Everest, Isaiah 53 stands out in beauty and grandeur, but only because it reveals Jesus Christ and takes us to Mt. Calvary.

The messianic interpretation of Isaiah 53 was held by Jewish rabbis till the twelfth century. After that, Jewish scholars started interpreting the passage as a description of the sufferings of the nation of Israel. But how could Israel die for the sins of Israel (v. 8)? And who declared that Israel was innocent of sin and therefore had suffered unjustly (v. 9)? No, the prophet wrote about an innocent individual, not a guilty nation. He made it crystal clear that this individual died for the sins of the guilty so that the guilty might go free.

The Servant that Isaiah describes is the Messiah, and the New Testament affirms that this Servant-Messiah is Jesus of Nazareth, the Son of God (Matt. 8:17; Mark 15:28; Luke 22:37; John 12:38; Acts 8:27-40; 1 Peter 2:21-24). Isaiah 53 is quoted or alluded to in the New Testament more frequently than any other Old Testament chapter. The index of quotations in the appendix of my Greek New Testament gives at least forty-one different citations, and this may not be all of them.

The fifteen verses that comprise the fourth Servant Song fall into five stanzas of three verses each, and each of these stanzas reveals an important truth about the Servant and what He accomplished for us.

1. Exaltation: the Shocking Servant (Isa. 52:13-15)

His people did not admire or desire the Servant (52:2-3), and yet when it was all over, He shocked and astonished kings! If we take these verses in their chronological order, we see that people were shocked by His appearance (52:14), His exaltation (v. 13), and His message (v. 15). We have here our Lord's suffering and death, His resurrection and ascension, and the worldwide proclamation of the Gospel.

Startled at the Servant's appearance (Isa. 52:14). "They shall see My Servant beaten and bloodied, so disfigured one would scarcely know it was a person standing there" (TLB). "So disfigured did He look that He seemed no longer human" (JB). When you consider all that Jesus endured physically between the time of His arrest and His crucifixion, it is no wonder He no longer looked like a man. Not only were His legal rights taken away from Him, including the right to a fair trial, but His human rights were taken from Him, so that He was not even treated like a person, let alone a Jewish citizen.

When He was questioned before Annas, Jesus was slapped by an officer (John 18:22). At the hearing before Caiaphas, He was spat upon, slapped, and beaten on the head with fists (Matt. 26:67; Mark 14:65; Luke 22:63). Pilate scourged Him (John 19:1; Matt 27:26; Mark 15:15), and his soldiers beat Him (John 19:3). Scourging was so terrible that prisoners were known to die from the ordeal. "I gave my back to the smiters," said God's Servant, "and my cheeks to them that plucked off the hair; I hid not my face from shame and spitting" (Isa. 50:6 KJV). And they were doing this to the very Son of God!

The graphic account of His suffering that is given in some sermons is not found in Scripture, except perhaps in Psalm 22. The Gospel writers give us the facts but not the details. Suffice it to say that when the sinners were finished with the Savior, He did not look human, and people were so appalled they turned their faces away. What was done to Jesus should have been done to Barabbas—and to us.

Startled at the Servant's exaltation (Isa. 52:13). The Servant suffered and died, but He did not remain dead. He was "exalted and extolled, and [made] very high." The phrase "deal prudently" means "to be successful in one's endeavor." What looked to men like a humiliating defeat was in the eyes of God a great victory (Col. 2:15). "I have glorified thee on the earth," He told His Father; "I have finished the work which thou gavest me to do" (John 17:4 KJV).

Jesus was not only raised from the dead, but His body was glorified. He ascended to heaven, where He sat at the right hand of the Father. He has all authority (Matt. 28:18) because all things have been put under His feet (Eph. 1:20-23). There is no one in the universe higher than Jesus. What an astonishment to those who esteemed Him the lowest of the low! (See. Phil. 2:1-11).

Startled at the servant's message (Isa. 52:15). The people whose mouths dropped open with astonishment at His humiliation and exaltation will shut their mouths in guilt when they hear His proclamation. Paul interprets this as the preaching of the Gospel to the Gentile nations (Rom. 15:20-21). "That every mouth may be stopped, and all the world may become guilty before God" (3:19).

Many people have been tortured and killed in an inhumane way, but knowing about their suffering does not touch our conscience, though it may arouse our sympathy. Our Lord's sufferings and death were different, because they involved everybody in the world. The Gospel message is not "Christ died," for that is only a fact in history, like "Napoleon died." The Gospel message is that "Christ died *for our sins"* (1 Cor. 15:1-4, italics mine). You and I are as guilty of Christ's death as Annas, Caiaphas, Herod Antipas, and Pilate.

Now we see why people are astonished when they understand the message of the Gospel: This Man whom they condemned has declared that they are condemned unless they turn from sin and trust Him. You cannot rejoice in the Good News of salvation until first you face the bad news of condemnation. Jesus did not suffer and die because He was guilty, but because we were guilty. People are astonished at this fact; it shuts their mouths.

The word translated "sprinkle" in Isaiah 52:15 can be translated "startle," but most likely it refers to the ceremonial cleansing that was an important part of the Mosaic sacrificial system (Lev. 14:1-7, 16; 16:14-15; Num. 8:7). While the sprinkling of blood, water, and oil did not take away sins, it did make the recipient ceremonially clean and accepted before God. Because of the sacrifice of Christ, we can tell all the nations that forgiveness and redemption are offered free to all who will receive Him (1 Peter. 1:1-2).

2. Humiliation: the Sorrowing Servant (Isa. 53:1-3)

Isaiah 53 describes the life and ministry of Jesus Christ (vv. 1-4), His death (vv. 5-8) and burial (v. 9), and His resurrection and exaltation (vv. 10-12). The theme that ties the chapter together is that the innocent Servant died in the place of the guilty. When theologians speak about "the vicarious atonement," that is what they mean. We cannot explain everything about the Cross, but this much seems clear: Jesus took the place of guilty sinners and paid the price for their salvation.

There is quite a contrast between "the arm of the Lord," which speaks of mighty power, and "a root out of a dry ground," which is an image of humiliation and weakness. When God made the universe, He used His fingers (Ps. 8:3), and when He delivered Israel from Egypt, it was by His strong hand (Ex. 13:3). But to save lost sinners, He had to bare His mighty arm! Yet people still refuse to believe this great demonstration of God's power (Rom. 1:16; John 12:37-40).

The Servant is God, and yet He becomes human and grows up! The Child is born—that is His humanity; the Son is given—that is His deity (Isa. 9:6). In writing about Israel's future, Isaiah has already used the image of a tree: Messiah is the Branch of the Lord (4:2); the remnant is like the stumps of trees chopped down (6:13); the proud nations will be hewn down like trees, but out of David's seemingly dead stump, the "rod of Jesse" will come (10:33-11:1). Because Jesus Christ is God, He is the "root of David," but because He is man, He is the "offspring of David" (Rev. 22:16).

Israel was not a paradise when Jesus was born; politically and spiritually, it was a wilderness of dry ground. He did not come as a great tree but as a "tender plant." He was born in poverty in Bethlehem and grew up in a carpenter's shop in despised Nazareth (John 1:43-46). Because of His words and works, Jesus attracted great crowds, but nothing about His physical appearance made Him different from any other Jewish man. While few people deliberately try to be unattractive, modern society has made a religion out physical beauty. It is good to remember that Jesus succeeded without it.

Once they understood what He demanded of them, how did most people treat the Servant? The way they treated any other slave: They despised Him, put a cheap price on Him (thirty pieces of silver), and "looked the other way when He went by" (Isa. 53:3, TLB). They were ashamed of Him because He did not represent the things that were important to them: things like wealth (Luke 16:14), social prestige (14:7-14; 15:12), reputation (18:9-14), being served by others (22:24-27), and pampering yourself (Matt. 16:21-28). He is rejected today for the same reasons.

3. Expiation: the Smitten Servant (Isa. 53:4-6)

This is the heart of the passage, and it presents the heart of the Gospel message: the innocent Servant dying as the sacrifice for sin. This message was at the heart of Israel's religious system—the innocent animal sacrifice dying for the guilty sinner (Lev. 16).

Jesus bore our sins on the cross (1 Peter 2:24), but He also identified with the consequences of Adam's sin when He ministered to needy people. Matthew 8:14-17 applies Isaiah 53:4 to our Lord's healing ministry and not to His atoning death. Every blessing we have in the Christian life comes because of the Cross, but this verse does not teach that there is "healing in the atonement" and that every believer therefore has the "right" to be healed. The prophecy was fulfilled during our Lord's life, not His death.

The emphasis in verses 4-6 is on the plural pronouns: our griefs and sorrows, our iniquities, our transgressions. We have gone astray, we have turned to our own way. He did not die because of anything He had done, but because of what we had done.

He was "wounded," which means "pierced through." His hands and feet were pierced by nails (Ps. 22:16; Luke 24:39-40) and His side by a spear (John 19:31-37; Zech. 12:10; Rev. 1:7). He was crucified, which was not a Jewish form of execution (John 12:32-33; 18:31-32). Capital punishment to the Jews meant stoning (Lev. 24:14; Num. 15:35-36). If they wanted to further humiliate the victim, they could publicly expose the corpse (Deut. 21:22-23), a practice that Peter related to the Crucifixion (Acts 5:30; 10:39; 1 Peter 2:24).

On the cross, Jesus Christ was "bruised," which means "crushed under the weight of a burden." What was the burden? "The Lord hath laid on Him the iniquity of us all" (Isa. 53:6; see v. 12; 1:4). Sin is indeed a burden that grows heavier the longer we resist God (Ps. 38:4).

He was "chastised" and given many "stripes," and yet that punishment brought us peace and healing. The only way a law-breaker can be at peace with the law is to suffer the punishment that the law demands. Jesus kept the Law perfectly, yet He suffered the whipping that belonged to us. Because He took our place, we now have peace with God and cannot be condemned by God's law (Rom. 5:1; 8:1). The "healing" in Isaiah 53:5 refers to the forgiveness of sins, not the healing of the body (1 Peter 2:24; Ps. 103:3). Sin is not only like a burden, but it is also like a sickness that only God can cure (Isa. 1:4-6; Jer. 30:12; Nahum 3:19).

Sin is serious. The prophet calls it transgression, which means rebellion against God, daring to cross the line that God has drawn (Isa. 53:5, 8). He also calls it iniquity, which refers to the crookedness of our sinful nature (vv. 5-6). In other words, we are sinners by choice and by nature. Like sheep, we are born with a nature that prompts us to go astray and like sheep we foolishly decide to go our own way. By nature we are born children of wrath (Eph. 2:3) and by choice we become children of disobedience (2:2). Under the Law of Moses, the sheep died for the shepherd; but under grace, the Good Shepherd died for the sheep (John 10:1-18).

4. Resignation: the Silent Servant (Isa. 53:7-9)

A servant is not permitted to talk back; he or she must submit to the will of the master or mistress. Jesus Christ was silent before those who accused Him as well as those who afflicted him. He was silent before Caiaphas (Matt. 26:62-63), the chief priests and elders (27:12), Pilate (27:14; John 19:9) and Herod Antipas (Luke 23:9). He did not speak when the soldiers mocked Him and beat Him (1 Peter 2:21-23). This is what impressed the Ethiopian treasurer as he read this passage in Isaiah (Acts 8:26-40).

Isaiah 53:7 speaks of His silence under suffering and verse 8 of His silence when illegally tried and condemned to death. In today's courts, a person can be found guilty of terrible crimes, but if it can be proved that something in the trial was illegal, the case must be tried again. Everything about His trials was illegal, yet Jesus did not appeal for another trial. "The cup which my Father hath given me. shall I not drink it?" (John 18:11 KJV)

The Servant is compared to a lamb (Isa. 53:7), which is one of the frequent symbols of the Savior in Scripture. A lamb died for each Jewish household at Passover (Ex. 12:1-13), and the Servant died for His people, the nation of Israel (Isa. 53:8). Jesus is "the Lamb of God who takes away the sin of the world" (John 1:29, NKJV), and twenty-eight times in the Book of Revelation, Jesus Christ is referred to as the Lamb.

Since Jesus Christ was crucified with criminals as a criminal, it was logical that His dead body would be left unburied, but God had other plans. The burial of Jesus Christ is as much a part of the Gospel as is His death (1 Cor. 15:1-5), for the burial is proof that He actually died. The Roman authorities would not have released the body to Joseph and Nicodemus if the victim had not been dead (John 19:38-42; Mark 15:42-47). A wealthy man like Joseph would never carve out a tomb for himself so near to a place of execution, particularly when his home was miles away. He prepared it for Jesus and had the spices and graveclothes ready for the burial. How wonderfully God fulfilled Isaiah's prophecy!

5. Vindication: the Satisfied Servant (Isa. 53:10-12)

The prophet now explains the Cross from God's point of view. Even though Jesus was crucified by the hands of wicked men, His death was determined beforehand by God (Act 2:22-23). Jesus was not a martyr, nor was His death an accident. He was God's sacrifice for the sins of the world.

He did not remain dead! "He shall prolong his days" (Isa. 53:10 KJV) means that the Servant was resurrected to live forever. In His resurrection, He triumphed over every enemy and claimed the spoils of victory (Eph. 1:19-23; 4:8). Satan offered Christ a glorious kingdom in return for worship (Matt. 4:8-10), which would have meant bypassing the cross. Jesus was "obedient unto death," and God "highly exalted Him" (Phil. 2:8-10).

Another part of His "reward" is found in the statement, "He shall see his seed [descendants]" (Isa. 53:10). To die childless was a grief and shame to the Jews, but Jesus gave birth to a spiritual family because of His travail on the cross (v. 11). Isaiah's statement about Isaiah's natural family (8:18) is quoted in Hebrews 2:13 and applied to Christ and His spiritual family.

The Servant's work on the cross brought satisfaction (Isa. 53:11). To begin with, the Servant satisfied the heart of the Father. "I do always those things that please him [the Father] (John 8:29). The heavenly Father did not find enjoyment in seeing His beloved Son suffer, for the Father is not pleased with the death of the wicked, let alone the death of the righteous Son of God. But the Father was pleased that His Son's obedience accomplished the redemption that He had planned from eternity (1 Peter 1:20). "It is finished" (John 19:30).

The death of the Servant also satisfied the Law of God. The theological term for this is "propitiation" (Rom. 3:25; 1 John 2:2). In pagan religions, the word meant "to offer a sacrifice to placate an angry god," but the Christian meaning is much richer. God is angry at sin because it offends His holiness and violates His holy Law. In His holiness, He must judge sinners, but in His love, He desires to forgive them. God cannot ignore sin or compromise with it, for that would be contrary to His own nature and Law.

How did God solve the problem? The Judge took the place of the criminals and met the just demands of His own holy Law! "He was numbered with the transgressors" and even prayed for them (Isa. 53:12; Luke 22:37; 23:33-34). The Law has been satisfied, and God can now graciously forgive all who receive His Son.

Grace is love that has paid a price, and sinners are saved by grace (Eph. 2:8-10). Justice can only condemn the wicked and justify the righteous (1 Kings 8:32), but grace justifies the ungodly when they trust Jesus Christ! (See Isa. 53:11; Rom. 4:5.) To justify means "to declare righteous." He took our sins that we might receive the gift of His righteousness (2 Cor. 5:21; Rom. 5:17). Justification means God declares believing sinners righteous in Christ and never again keeps a record of their sins. (See Ps. 32:1-2 and Rom. 4:1-8.)

On the morning of May 29, 1953, Sir Edmund Hillary and Tenzing Norgay conquered Mt. Everest, the highest mountain peak in the world. Nobody has yet "conquered" Isaiah 53, for there are always new heights to reach. The important thing is to know personally God's righteous Servant, Jesus Christ, whose conquest of sin is the subject of this chapter. "By his knowledge [i.e., knowing Him personally by faith] shall My righteous Servant justify many" (v. 11).

"Now this is eternal life; that they may know you, the only true God, and Jesus Christ, whom you have sent" (John 17:3, NIV).

CHAPTER TWELVE
PROMISES AND PUNISHMENTS
ISAIAH 54–59

The Servant obediently finished His work on earth, and today He is at work in heaven, interceding for God's people (Heb. 7:25; Rom. 8:34). But what are the consequences of His sacrifice? What difference does it make that He endured all that suffering? To Israel, it means restoration (Isa. 54:1-17); to the Gentile nations, it means an invitation (55:1-56:8); and to rebellious sinners, it means an accusation (56:9-59:21), a warning from the Lord that they need to repent.

1. Restoration for Israel (Isa. 54:1-17)

The image in this chapter is that of Jehovah, the faithful husband, forgiving Israel, the unfaithful wife, and restoring her to the place of blessing. Isaiah has used the marriage image before (50:1-3) and will use it again (62:4). Jeremiah also used it (Jer. 3:8), and it is an important theme in both Hosea (chap. 2) and Ezekiel (chaps. 16 and 23). The nation was "married" to Jehovah at Mt. Sinai, but she committed adultery by turning to other gods, and the Lord had to abandon her temporarily. However, the prophets promise that Israel will be restored when Messiah comes and establishes His kingdom.

What kind of restoration will it be? For one thing, it is a restoration to joy and therefore an occasion for singing (Isa. 54:1a). Isaiah is certainly the prophet of song; he mentions songs and singing more than thirty times in his book. The immediate occasion for this joy is the nation's deliverance from captivity, but the ultimate fulfillment is when the Redeemer comes to Zion and the nation is born anew (59:20).

It will also be a restoration to fruitfulness when the nation will increase and need more space (54:1b-3). The nation had been diminished because of the Babylonian invasion, but God would help them multiply again. At the end of this age, only a believing remnant will enter into the kingdom, but the Lord will enlarge the nation abundantly. Israel may feel like a barren woman, unable to have children, but she will increase to the glory of God. God will do for her what He did for Sarah and Abraham (49:18-21; 51:1-3). The tents will need to be enlarged, and the desolate cities will be inhabited again!

Paul quoted Isaiah 54:1 in Galatians 4:27 and applied the spiritual principle to the church: Even as God blessed Sarah and the Jewish remnant with children, so He would bless the church, though she is only a small company in the world. Paul was not equating Israel with the church or suggesting that the Old Testament promises to the Jews are not fulfilled in the church. If we claim the Old Testament Jewish prophecies for the church, then we must claim all of them, the judgments as well as the blessings; and most people do not want to do that!

Israel's restoration to her land will also mean confidence (Isa. 54:4-10). Isaiah gives another one of his "fear not" promises (41:10, 13, 14; 43:1, 5: 44:2, 8; 51:7; 54:14) and explains why there was no need for the nation to be afraid. To begin with, their sins were forgiven (v. 4). Why should they fear the future when God had wiped out the sins of the past? (43:25; 44:22) Yes, the people had sinned greatly against their God, but He forgave them, and this meant a new beginning (40:1-5). They could forget the shame of their sins as a young nation, as recorded in Judges and 1 Samuel, as well as the reproach of their "widowhood" in the Babylonian Captivity.

Another reason for confidence is the steadfast love of the Lord (54:5-6). Jehovah is their Maker and would not destroy the people he created for His glory. He is their Redeemer and cannot sell them into the hands of the enemy. He is their Husband and will not break His covenant promises. As an unfaithful wife, Israel had forsaken her Husband, but He had not permanently abandoned her. He only gave her opportunity to see what it was like to live in a land where people worshiped false gods. God would call her back and woo her to Himself (Hosea 2:14-23), and she would no longer be "a wife deserted" (Isa. 54:6, NIV). She felt forsaken (49:14), but God did not give her up.

A third reason for confidence is the dependable promise of God (54:7-10). God had to show His anger at their sin, but now the chastening was over, and they were returning to their land. (On God's anger, see 9:12, 17, and 21.) "With great mercies will I gather thee," He promised. "With everlasting kindness will I have mercy on thee."

Whenever we rebel against God and refuse to listen to His warning, He must chasten us, and He does it in love (Heb. 12:1-11). Our Father cannot permit His children to sin and get away with it. But the purpose of His chastening is to bring us to repentance and enable us to produce "the peaceable fruit of righteousness" (v. 11). When God "spanks" His erring children, He may hurt them, but He never harms them. It is always for our good and His glory.

God kept His promise concerning the Flood (Gen. 9:11-17), and He will keep His promises to His people Israel. They can depend on His love, His covenant, and His mercy.

Not only will the captives be set free and the nation restored, but also the city of Jerusalem will be rebuilt (Isa. 54:11-17). If the language here seems extravagant, keep in mind that the prophet sees both an immediate fulfillment and an ultimate fulfillment (Rev. 21:18-21). The remnant rebuilt the temple and the city under the leadership of Zerubbabel the governor, Joshua the high priest, Ezra the scribe, Nehemiah the wallbuilder, and the prophets Haggai and Zechariah. But the restored Jerusalem was nothing like what Isaiah describes here! For that beautiful city, we must wait till the return of the Lord and the establishing of His kingdom. Then every citizen of Jerusalem will know the Lord (Isa. 54:13), and the city will be free from terror and war (v. 14).

Our Lord quoted the first part of verse 13 in John 6:45. When you read the context, beginning at verse 34, you see that Jesus was speaking about people coming to the Father. "All that the Father gives Me will come to Me" (v. 37, NKJV) does not mean that the Father forces sinners to be saved. People come to Him because they are "taught of God," and the Spirit draws them through the Word. Personal evangelism won't be needed in the New Jerusalem, for all the citizens will know the Lord.

2. Invitation to the Gentiles (Isa. 55:1-56:8)

The Servant died not only for the sins of Israel (53:8), but also for the sins of the whole world (John 1:29; 1 John 4:14). Isaiah makes it clear throughout his book that the Gentiles are included in God's plan. What Isaiah and the other prophets did not know was that believing Jews and Gentiles would one day be united in Jesus Christ in the church (Eph. 3:1-12).

God gives a threefold invitation to the Gentiles: come (Isa. 55:1-5), seek (vv. 6-13), and worship (56:1-8).

Come (Isa. 55:1-5). The invitation is extended to "everyone" and not just to the Jews. Anyone who is thirsting for that which really satisfies (John 4:10-14) is welcome to come. As in Isaiah 25:6, the prophet pictures God's blessings in terms of a great feast, where God is the host.

In the East, water is precious, and an abundance of water is a special blessing (41:17; 44:3). Wine, milk, and bread were staples in their diet. The people were living on substitutes that did not nourish them. They needed "the real thing," which only the Lord could give. In Scripture, both water and wine are pictures of the Holy Spirit (John 7:37-39; Eph. 5:18). Jesus is the "bread of life" (John 6:32-35), and His living Word is like milk (1 Peter 2:2). Our Lord probably had Isaiah 55:2 in mind when He said, "Do not labor for the food which perishes, but for the food which endures to everlasting life" (John 6:27, NKJV).

People have to work hard to dig wells, care for flocks and herds, plant seed, and tend to their vineyards. But the Lord offered to them free everything they were laboring for. If they listen to His Word, they will be inclined to come; for God draws sinners to Himself through the Word (John 5:24). Note the emphasis on hearing in Isaiah 55:2-3.

"The sure mercies of David" involve God's covenant with David (2 Sam. 7) in which He promises that a Descendant would reign on David's throne forever. This, of course, is Jesus Christ (Luke 1:30-33), and the proof that He is God's King is seen in His resurrection from the dead (Acts 13:34-39). Jesus Christ is God's covenant to the Gentiles ("peoples"), and His promises will stand as long as His Son lives, which is forever.

Isaiah 55:5 indicates that God will use Israel to call the Gentiles to salvation, which was certainly true in the early days of the church (Acts 10:1ff; 13:1ff) and will be true during the kingdom (Isa. 2:2-4; 45:14; Zech. 8:22). Jerusalem will be the center for worship in the world, and God will be glorified as the nations meet together with Israel to honor the Lord.

Seek (Isa. 55:6-13). When God delivered His people from Babylon and took them safely back to their own land, it was a witness to the other nations. It also gave Israel another opportunity to be a light to the Gentiles (49:6) and bring them to faith in the true and living God. While it was important for Israel to seek the Lord and be wholly devoted to Him, it was also important that they share this invitation with the nations.

What is involved in "seeking the Lord?" For one thing, it means admitting that we are sinners and that we have offended the holy God. It means repenting (55:7), changing one's mind about sin, and turning away from sin and to the Lord. We must turn to God in faith and believe His promise that in mercy He will abundantly pardon. Repentance and faith go together: "repentance toward God, and faith toward our Lord Jesus Christ" (Acts 20:21).

But no one should delay in doing this! The phrase "while He may be found" suggests that, if we do not take His invitation seriously, the invitation may cease while we are delaying. In the parable of the Great Supper, God closed the door on those who spurned His invitation (Luke 14:16-24; see Prov. 1:20-33). "Behold, now is the accepted time; behold, now is the day of salvation" (2 Cor. 6:2).

It is not a mark of wisdom to try to second-guess God, because His ways and thoughts are far beyond our comprehension (Isa. 55:8-9). We make God after our own image and conclude that He thinks and acts just as we do (Ps. 50:21), and we are wrong! Have you ever tried to explain the grace of God to an unsaved person who thinks that heaven is a "Hall of Fame" for achievers instead of the Father's house for believers? In this world, you work for what you get, and you are suspicious of anything that is free.

How does God go about calling and saving lost sinners? By the power of His Word (Isa. 55:10-11). God's Word is seed (Luke 8:11). Just as the rain and snow are never wasted but accomplish His purposes, so His Word never fails. "The Word of God shall stand forever" (Isa. 40:8). We never know how God will use even a casual word of witness to plant and water the seed in somebody's heart.

Isaiah 55:12-13 describes both the joy of the exiles on their release from captivity and the joy of Israel when they share in that "glorious exodus" in the end of the age and return to their land. When the kingdom is established, all of nature will sing to the Lord (32:13; 35:1-2; 44:23; 52:8-9).

Worship (Isa. 56:1-8). The nation had gone into captivity because she had disobeyed the Law of God, particularly the fourth commandment: "Remember the sabbath day, to keep it holy" (Ex. 20:8 KJV). This commandment was a special "sign" between God and the Jews (31:12-18; Neh. 9:13-14); it was never given to the Gentiles. The Jews were rebuked for the careless way they treated the Sabbath during their wilderness wanderings (Ezek. 20:10-26) and when they lived in the land (Jer. 17:19-27). Even after their return to the Holy Land after the Captivity, the Jews continued to violate the Sabbath (Neh. 13:15-22).

Keep in mind that the Sabbath Day is the seventh day of the week, the day that God sanctified when He completed Creation (Gen. 2:1-3). Sunday is the Lord's Day, the first day of the week, and it commemorates the resurrection of Jesus Christ from the dead. To call Sunday "the Sabbath" or "the Christian Sabbath" is to confuse these two important days. The Sabbath was a sign to the Jews and belongs to the Law: You labor for six days, and then you rest. The Lord's Day speaks of resurrection and belongs to grace. God's people trust in Christ, and then the works follow.

God never before asked the Gentiles to join the Jews in keeping the Sabbath, but here He does so. He calls the very people He prohibited from entering His covenant nation: foreigners and eunuchs (Deut. 23:1-8). This is another picture of the grace of God (see Acts 8:26ff). The invitation is still "Everyone come!" It applies to sinners today, but it will apply in a special way when Israel enters her kingdom, the temple services are restored, and the Sabbath is once again a part of Jewish worship.

God's admonition to the remnant to "keep justice and do righteousness" (Isa. 56:1) was not obeyed. When you read Ezra, Nehemiah, Haggai, and Malachi, you discover that the Jews soon forgot God's goodness and returned to their old ways. Taking special time each week to remember the Lord and worship Him helps us to obey His will.

3. Accusation Against the Sinners (Isa. 56:9-59:21)

The prophet presents in this section a series of indictments against the disobedient in the nation: the leaders (56:9-57:2), the idolaters (57:3-13), the proud and greedy (vv. 14-21), the hypocritical worshipers (58:1-14), and those responsible for injustice in the land (59:1-21). But even in His wrath, God remembers mercy (Hab. 3:2); for along with these indictments, the Lord pleads with people to humble themselves and submit to Him.

The leaders of the nation (Isa. 56:9-57:2). It was the godless conduct of the leaders that caused Judah to fall to Babylon (Lam. 4:13-14). Had the prophets, priests, and rulers turned to God in repentance and faith, He would have intervened on their behalf, but they persisted in their rebellion. With biting sarcasm, Isaiah calls them "blind watchmen" who cannot see the enemy coming, and "sleeping dogs" who could not bark their warning even if they were awake! The leaders were not alert; they loved to sleep, and when they were awake, they loved to eat and drink.

Spiritual leaders are "watchmen" (Ezek. 3:17-21; 33:1-11) who must be awake to the dangers that threaten God's people. They are "shepherds" who must put the care of the flock ahead of their own desires. When the foreign invaders ("beasts of the field") come, the shepherds must protect the flock, no matter what the danger might be. See Acts 20:18-38 for the description of a faithful spiritual ministry.

God permitted the unrighteous leaders to live and suffer the terrible consequences of their sins, but the righteous people died before the judgment fell. The godly found rest and peace, and the ungodly went into captivity, and some of them were killed. Rebellious people do not deserve dedicated spiritual leaders. When His people reject His Word and prefer worldy leaders, God may give them exactly what they desire and let them suffer the consequences.

Idolaters (Isa. 57:3-13). During the last days of Judah and Jerusalem, before Babylon came, the land and the city were polluted with idols. King Hezekiah and King Josiah had led the people in destroying the idols and the high places, but as soon as an ungodly king took the throne, the people went right back to their old ways. Both Isaiah and Jeremiah told the people that God would punish them for breaking His Law, but they persisted in the ways of the godless nations around them.

God sees idolatry as adultery and prostitution (v. 3). The people knew it was wrong, but they arrogantly practiced their sensual worship ("inflaming yourselves with idols") without shame. You would find them everywhere: visiting the shrine prostitutes under the green trees in the groves, offering their children in the fire in the valley, worshiping under the cliffs and by the smooth boulders, sacrificing up in the mountains, and committing fornication behind the doors of their houses. Publicly and privately, the people were devoted to idols and immorality.

But they were also guilty of consorting with pagan leaders and trusting them for protection instead of trusting God (v. 9). To trust a pagan ruler and his army was the same as trusting the false god that he worshiped (see 30:1-7; 31:1-3). They found false strength in their political alliances and refused to admit that these treaties were hopeless (57:10). God would expose their sin and judge it, and when that happened, their collection of idols ("companies" in v. 13, KJV) would not save them.

Anything that we trust other than the Lord becomes our god and therefore is an idol. It may be our training, experience, job, money, friends, or position. One of the best ways to find out whether we have idols in our lives is to ask ourselves, "Where do I instinctively turn when I face a decision or need to solve a problem?" Do we reach for the phone to call a friend? Do we assure ourselves that we can handle the situation ourselves? Or do we turn to God to see His will and receive His help?

When the storm starts blowing, the idols will blow away like chaff (v. 13). They are "vanity," which means "nothingness." The storm does not make a person; it shows what the person is made of and where his or her faith lies. If we make the Lord our refuge, we have nothing to fear.

The proud and greedy (Isa. 57:14-21). God has a word of encouragement for the faithful remnant: The highway will be built and the obstacles removed, so that the exiles might return to the land and serve the Lord. (On the "highway" theme, see 11:16.) God will dwell with them because they are humble in spirit. (See 66:2; Pss. 34:18; 51:17.) Pride is a sin that God hates (Prov. 6:16-17) and that God resists (1 Peter 5:5-6). God was "enraged" by Israel's "sinful greed" and repeatedly chastened them for it, but they would not change (Isa. 57:17). How often He had "taken them to court" and proved them guilty, yet they would not submit. But now that was over. The time had come for God to heal them, guide them, and comfort them.

The hypocrites (Isa. 58:1-14). God told Isaiah to shout aloud with a voice like a trumpet and announce the sins of the nation. The people went to the temple, obeyed God's laws, fasted, and appeared eager to seek the Lord, but their worship was only an outward show. Their hearts were far from God (1:10-15; 29:13; Matt. 15:8-9). When we worship because it is the popular thing to do, not because it is the right thing to do, then our worship becomes hypocritical.

The Jews were commanded to observe only one fast on the annual Day of Atonement (Lev. 16:29-31), but they were permitted to fast personally if they wished. They complained that nobody seemed to notice what they were doing. Perhaps they were trying to "buy God's blessing" by their fasting. Worshiping God involves more than observing an outward ritual; there must be an inward obedience and submission to the Lord (Matt. 6:16-18).

If in my religious duties I am doing what pleases me, and if doing it does not make me a better person, then I am wasting my time, and my worship is only sin. Fasting and fighting do not go together! Yet how many families walk piously out of church at the close of a Sunday worship service, get in the family car, and proceed to argue with each other all the way home!

True fasting will lead to humility before God and ministry to others. We deprive ourselves so that we might share with others and do so to the glory of God. If we fast in order to get something for ourselves from God, instead of to become better people for the sake of others, then we have missed the meaning of worship. It delights the Lord when we delight in the Lord.

The unjust (Isa. 59:1-21). There was a great deal of injustice in the land, with the rich exploiting the poor and the rulers using their authority only to make themselves rich (see 1:17-23; 3:13-15; 5:8-30). The people lifted their hands to worship God, but their hands were stained with blood (1:15, 21). God could not answer their prayers because their sins hid His face from them.

It was a conflict between truth and lies, just as it is today. Isaiah compared the evil rulers to pregnant women giving birth to sin (59:4; Ps. 7:14; Isa. 33:11), to snakes hatching their eggs, and to spiders weaving their webs (Isa. 59:5-6). What they give birth to will only destroy them (James 1:13-15), and their beautiful webs of lies can never protect them.

When people live on lies, they live in a twilight zone and do not know where they are going (Isa. 59:9-11). When trust falls, it creates a "traffic jam," and justice and equity (honesty) cannot make progress (vv. 12-15). God is displeased with injustice, and He wonders that none of His people will intercede or intervene (Prov. 24:11-12). So the Lord Himself intervened and brought the Babylonians to destroy Judah and Jerusalem and to teach His people that they cannot despise His Law and get away with it.

God's judgment on His people was a foreshadowing of that final Day of the Lord when all the nations will be judged. When it is ended, then "the Redeemer shall come to Zion" (Isa. 59:20), and the glorious kingdom will be established. Israel will be not only God's chosen people but God's cleansed people, and the glory of the Lord will radiate from Mt. Zion.

The glory of the Lord in the promised kingdom is the theme of the closing chapters of Isaiah. While we are waiting and praying, "Thy kingdom come," perhaps we should also be interceding and intervening. We are the salt of the earth and the light of the world (Matt. 5:13-16), and God expects us to make a difference.

CHAPTER THIRTEEN
THE KINGDOM AND THE GLORY
ISAIAH 60–66

Grace is but glory begun," said Jonathan Edwards, "and glory is but grace perfected." Whatever begins with God's grace will lead to God's glory (1 Peter 5:10), and that includes the nation of Israel.

Isaiah began his "Book of Consolations" (chaps. 40-66) by promising that "the glory of the Lord shall be revealed" (40:5). Now he concludes by describing that glory for us. In these seven chapters, he used the word "glory" in one form or another at least twenty-three times. When God's glory is on the scene, everything becomes new.

1. The Dawning of a New Day (Isa. 60:1-22)

"Arise and shine!" is God's "wake-up call" to Jerusalem (v. 14), because a new day is dawning for Israel. This light is not from the sun but from the glory of God shining on the city.

God's glory had once dwelt in the tabernacle (Ex. 40:34-38), only to depart because of Israel's sin (1 Sam. 4:21). God's glory then came into the temple (1 Kings 8:11), but it departed when the nation turned to idols (Ezek. 9:3; 10:4, 18; 11:22-23). The glory came to Israel in the person of Jesus Christ (John 1:14), but the nation nailed that glory to a cross. Today, God's glory dwells in His church (Eph. 2:20-22) and in His people individually (1 Cor. 6:19-20); but one day His glory will be revealed to the earth when He answers His people's prayer: "Thy kingdom come."

The Babylonian Captivity had been the nation's darkest hour, but that was not the darkness Isaiah was describing. He was describing the awful darkness that will cover the earth during the Day of the Lord (Amos 5:18), when God punishes the nations of the earth for their sins (Isa. 2:12ff; 13:6ff). But the prophet is also describing the glorious light that will come to Israel when her Messiah returns to reign in Jerusalem. Then "the earth shall be filled with the knowledge of the glory of the Lord, as the waters cover the sea" (Hab. 2:14). Israel's sons and daughters will come home again (Isa. 60:4, 8-9), and all of them will know the Lord.

It will be the dawning of a new day for the nations of the world as well as for Israel (vv. 3, 10-13). The Gentiles will come to Jerusalem to worship the Lord and to share their wealth (2:2-4; 11:9; 27:13; 56:7; 57:13; 65:25; 66:20). Some people "spiritualize" these promises and apply them to the Gentiles coming to Christ and His church today, but that is not the basic interpretation. Isaiah sees ships and caravans bringing people and wealth to Jerusalem (60:5-7), and the nations that refuse to honor the Lord and His city will be judged (v. 12). Even Israel's old enemies will submit and help to serve the Lord (vv. 10, 14).

In verses 15-22, the Lord describes some of the joys and wonders of the glorious kingdom. The nation will no longer be forsaken but will be enriched by the Gentiles and nursed like a beloved child (vv. 4, 16; 49:23; 61:6). As in the days of King Solomon (1 Kings 10:21, 27), precious metals will be plentiful. It will be a time of peace and safety. "I will make peace your governor and righteousness your ruler" (Isa. 60:17, NIV).

John used some of the characteristics of the millennial Jerusalem when he described the Holy City (Rev. 21-22): The sun never sets; there is no sorrow; the gates never close; etc. But the city Isaiah describes is the capital city of the restored Jewish nation, and Jesus Christ shall sit on the throne of David and judge righteously. The Jewish "remnant" will increase and fill the land (Isa. 60:22; 51:2; 54:3).

2. The Beginning of a New Life (Isa. 61:1-11)

The Lord speaks (Isa. 61:1-9). Jesus quoted from this passage when He spoke in the synagogue in Nazareth, and He applied this Scripture to Himself (Luke 4:16-21). (Note that Isa. 61:1 names the Father, the Son, and the Holy Spirit.) However, He did not quote, "And the day of vengeance of our God" from verse 2 because that day is yet to come (34:8; 35:4; 63:4.)

The background of this passage is the "Year of Jubilee" described in Leviticus 25:7ff. Every seven years, the Jews were to observe a "sabbatical year" and allow the land to rest. After seven sabbaticals, or forty-nine years, they were to celebrate the fiftieth year as the "Year of Jubilee." During that year, all debts were canceled, all land was returned to the original owners, the slaves were freed, and everybody was given a fresh new beginning. This was the Lord's way of balancing the economy and keeping the rich from exploiting the poor.

If you have trusted Christ as your Savior, you are living today in a spiritual "Year of Jubilee." You have been set free from bondage; your spiritual debt to the Lord has been paid; you are living in "the acceptable year of the Lord." Instead of the ashes of mourning, you have a crown on your head, for He has made you a king (Rev. 1:6). You have been anointed with the oil of the Holy Spirit, and you wear a garment of righteousness (Isa. 61:3; 10).

In her days of rebellion, Israel was like a fading oak and a waterless garden (1:30), but in the kingdom, she will be like a watered garden (58:11) and a tree (oak) of righteousness (61:3). But all of God's people should be His trees (Ps. 1:1-3), "the planting of the Lord, that He might be glorified" (Isa. 61:3).

In their kingdom "Year of Jubilee," the Jewish people will rebuild, repair, and restore their land, and the Gentiles will shepherd Israel's flocks and herds and tend to their crops. Instead of being farmers and shepherds, the Jews will be priests and ministers! God will acknowledge them as His firstborn (Ex. 4:22) and give them a double portion of His blessing (Isa. 61:7; Deut. 21:17).

The "everlasting covenant" of Isaiah 61:8 is described in Jeremiah 31:31-37 and includes the blessings of the New Covenant that Jesus Christ instituted by His death (Heb. 10:1-18; Matt. 26:28). Note that Isaiah 61:9 speaks of the Jews' "descendants." Those who enter into the millennial kingdom will marry, have families, and enjoy God's blessings on the earth for a thousand years (Rev. 20:1-5). They will study God's Word from generation to generation (Isa. 59:21).

The prophet speaks (Isa. 61:10-11). Isaiah is speaking on behalf of the remnant who are praising God for all He has done. They rejoice that He has cleansed them and clothed them and turned their desert into a fruitful garden (55:10). They have gone from a funeral to a wedding!

3. The Bestowing of a New Name (Isa. 62:1-12)

God will not hold His peace (Isa. 62:1-5). The "I" in verse 6 indicates that the Lord is the speaker. God promises to keep speaking and working till His purposes for Jerusalem are fulfilled. This is not only for the sake of Zion but also for the sake of the nations of the world. There will be no righteousness and peace on this earth till Jerusalem gets her new name and becomes a crown of glory to the Lord.

As an unfaithful wife, Israel was "forsaken" by the Lord, but not "divorced" (50:1-3). Her trials will all be forgotten when she receives the new name, "Hephzibah," which means "my delight is in her." God delights in His people and enjoys giving them His best. The old name "Desolate" will be replaced by "Beulah," which means "married" (see also 54:1). When a bride marries, she receives a new name. In the case of Israel, she is already married to Jehovah, but she will get a new name when she is reconciled to Him.

The watchmen must not hold their peace (Isa. 62:6-12). God gave His people leaders to guide them, but they were not faithful (56:10). Now He gives them faithful watchmen, who constantly remind God of His promises. "Give Him no rest till He establishes Jerusalem and makes her the praise of the earth" (62:7, NIV). What an encouragement to us to "pray for the peace of Jerusalem" (Ps. 122:6).

God promises that the Jews will never again lose their harvests to the enemy but will enjoy the fruit of their labors in the very courts of His sanctuary. What a privilege! According to Ezekiel 40–48, there will be a millennial temple, and the Jews will worship the Lord there. Having received their Messiah, they will now clearly understand the spiritual meaning of their worship. Today, their minds are veiled (2 Cor. 3:14-18), but then, their eyes will be opened.

Isaiah 62:10 is another reference to the "highway" (11:16; 40:3-5), and there is an urgency about these words. The Lord is about to arrive, and the people must get the road ready! When the work is completed, they must lift a banner to signal they are ready.

"See, your Savior comes!" (62:11, NIV). This is a proclamation that goes to the ends of the earth! And when He comes, He shares more new names: Israel is called "the Holy People" and "the Redeemed of the Lord,' and Jerusalem is called "Sought After, the City No Longer Deserted" (v. 12, NIV).

God will have no rest till He accomplishes His purposes for His people, and the world will have no peace till He succeeds. He asks us to "give Him no rest" (v. 7) but to intercede for Israel and Jerusalem, for the prayers of His people are an important part of the program of God.

4. The Announcing of a New Victory (Isa. 63:1-64:12)

The prophet looks ahead in 63:1-6 and sees Jesus Christ returning from the Battle of Armageddon that climaxes the Day of the Lord (Rev. 19:11-21). Edom is named here as a representative of the nations that have oppressed the Jews. Bozrah was one of its main cities, and its name means "grape gathering." This is significant since the image here is that of the winepress (Joel 3:13; Rev. 14:17-20). The name "Edom" means "red" and was a nickname for Esau (Gen. 25:30).

The ancient winepress was a large, hollowed rock into which the grapes were put for the people to tread on them. The juice ran out a hole in the rock and was caught in vessels. As the people crushed the grapes, some of the juice would splash on their garments. Our Lord's garments were dyed with blood as the result of the great victory over His enemies (Rev. 19:13).

When Jesus came to earth the first time, it was to inaugurate "the acceptable year of the Lord" (Isa. 61:2; Luke 4:19). When He comes the second time, it will be to climax "the day of vengeance of our God" (Isa. 63:4; 61:2). The enemy will be crushed like grapes and forced to drink their own blood from the cup of God's wrath (51:17; Jer. 25:15-16). These images may not appeal to sophisticated people today, but the Jews in that day fully understood them.

Then the prophet looks back at what God has done for Israel (Isa. 63:7-14). He praises God for His loving-kindness and goodness, for the pity and love bestowed on Israel. God identified with their sufferings (v. 9; Jud. 10:16; Deut. 32:10-12) as He does with His people today (1 Peter 5:7). The Jews asked, "Where is our God who did wonders for His people? Why is He not working on our behalf?"

The prophet looks up and calls on God to bare His arm and display His power (Isa. 63:15-4:12). For Abraham's sake, for Israel's sake, because God is their Father, he pleads for a demonstration of power just as God did in the ancient days.

He asks God to "look down" (63:15) and to "come down" (64:1). This is one of the greatest "revival prayers" found in Scripture. Just as God came down in fire at Sinai (Ex. 19:16-19), so let Him come down again and reveal His awesome power to the nations. They trust in dead idols, so let them see what the living God of Israel can do!

Why is God not working wonders? They have sinned (Isa. 64:5-6) and must confess their sins and turn from them. If our righteousness is filthy, what must our sins look like in His sight! According to verse 4, God has planned for His people wonderful things beyond their imagination, but their sins prevent Him from sharing His blessings. (See 1 Cor. 2:9 and Eph. 3:20-21). Is there any hope? Yes, because God is a forgiving Father and a patient Potter (Jer. 18). He can cleanse us and make us anew if we will let Him have His way.

This prayer (and the believing remnant) ends with a question: Why is God silent? His temple has been destroyed, His glorious land has been ravaged, and His people are in exile. "After all this, O Lord, will you hold yourself back? Will you keep silent and punish us beyond measure?" (Isa. 64:12, NIV) God's reply is found in the next two chapters.

5. The Blessing of a New Creation (Isa. 65:1-25)

"I will not keep silence, but will recompense, even recompense into their bosom" (65:6). God now replies.

First, He announces that His salvation will go to the Gentiles (v. 1), even though they did not seek the Lord or experience the blessings that He gave to Israel. Paul applies this verse to the Gentiles in Romans 10:19-20. If Israel did not want what God had to offer, then He would give it to others. See Luke 14:16-24 and 21:10 and Acts 28:23-31 for other illustrations of this divine principle.

Then, God describes the sins of His people that kept Him from answering their prayers (Isa. 65:2-7). They resisted His grace and His loving appeals, though He held out His arms to them and spoke to them through His Word (Rom. 10:21). They went their own way (Isa. 53:6) and provoked Him with their evil worship of false gods, getting involved with the occult and demons. They ate food that was unclean and openly worshiped idols in the high places. And yet these rebellious people considered themselves to be better than others! "I am holier than thou!"

God then explains that He had to judge the nation for her sins (65:8-16). He called the Babylonians to be His instrument of punishment to teach His people that they could not sin and get away with it. However, in mercy He preserved a remnant—like a few grapes rescued from the winepress—and that remnant would return to the land and restore the nation. When His people sincerely seek Him (v. 10), then He will bless them (2 Chron. 7:14).

"The Valley of Achor" was the place where Achan was stoned to death because he disobeyed the Lord (Josh. 7). When the Lord restores His estranged wife, Israel, the Valley of Achor will become for them "a door of hope" (Hosea 2:15).

In Isaiah 65:11-16, God sees two kinds of people in the land: those who forsake the Lord and those who serve the Lord. ("My Servant" has now become "My servants.") Those who forsake the Lord ignore His temple and worship false gods, such as fortune and destiny (in v. 11, "that troop" and "that number"). These disobedient Jews will not live but be destroyed, and those who do survive will not enjoy it. In fact, their very names will be used as curses in the years to come!

God saves the best for the last: His description of "the new heavens and new earth" (the millennial kingdom) in 65:17-66:24.

This is not the same as John's "new heaven and new earth" (Rev. 21:1ff), because the characteristics Isaiah gives do not fit the eternal state. As far as we know, in the eternal state people will not get old or die (Isa. 65:20), nor will there be any danger of losing anything to invaders (vv. 21-23).

Jerusalem will be a source of joy, not only to the Lord but to the whole earth. It will be a city of holiness, harmony, and happiness. During the millennial kingdom, people will work, and God will bless their labors. People will pray, and God will answer (v. 24). Nature will be at peace (v. 25) because the curse will be lifted.

6. The Birth of the New Nation (Isa. 66:1-24)

Of course, the remarkable thing will be the "birth of a nation" as Israel takes center stage on the international scene (vv. 7-9). The return of the Jews to their land will be as swift as the birth of a baby. Israel's "travail" will be "the Day of the Lord" or "the time of Jacob's trouble" (Jer. 30:7), when God will purify His people and prepare them for the coming of their messiah. Political Israel was born on May 14, 1948, but "the new Israel" will be "born in a day" when they believe on Jesus Christ. Jerusalem will experience joy, peace, and satisfaction (Isa. 66:10-14). Like a nursing baby, she will find health and peace in the arms of the Lord. "Peace like a river" reminds us of Isaiah's words to Ahaz (85:5-8) and God's promises in 41:18 and 48:18.

There will be a new temple (66:1-6; Ezek. 40-48), but the ceremonies of worship can never take the place of a humble heart. God does not live in buildings; He dwells with those who submit to Him. Stephen quoted Isaiah 66:1-2 in his defense before the Jews (Acts 7:48-50), and Paul referred to these words in his address to the Athenian philosophers (17:24).

In Isaiah's day, were God's people trembling at His Word? No, they were not. Instead, they were going through the motions of worship without having a heart for God. The people were not sacrificing the animals; they were murdering them! Because their hearts were far from God (Isa. 29:13), their offerings were as unclean things to the Lord. It is the heart of the worshiper that determines the value of the offering.

God's hand will bring blessing to His servants but "indignation toward His enemies" (66:14), and Isaiah describes that "indignation" in verses 15-18. The Day of the Lord will be a storm of judgment with fire and whirlwinds, and with the sword of God, "And those slain by the Lord shall be many."

Who will be slain? Those who have disobeyed God's Law in their eating and their worshiping (vv. 17-18). Instead of worshiping the true and living God, they turned to pagan idols and pagan practices. It is not enough to be "religious"; we must serve Him according to what He says in His Word (8:20).

The book closes with a description of messengers going to the ends of the earth to announce what God has done for Israel (66:19). The result will be a flow of people to Jerusalem (see 50:3-14 and 66:12) to bring offerings to the Lord. In the past, Gentile nations came to Jerusalem to attack and destroy, but in the Kingdom Age, they will come to worship and glorify God.

The book ends on a seemingly negative note describing worshipers looking at the desecrated and decayed corpses of the rebels (v. 24). The Valley of Hinnom (Hebrew, ge *hinnom* = *Gehenna* in the Greek) is a picture of judgment (30:33). Jesus used it to picture hell (Mark 9:43-48). The people who come to Jerusalem to worship will also go outside the city to this "garbage dump" and be reminded that God is a consuming fire (Jer. 7:32).

Throughout his book, Isaiah has presented us with alternatives: Trust the Lord and live, or rebel against the Lord and die. He has explained the grace and mercy of God and offered His forgiveness. He has also explained the holiness and wrath of God and warned of His judgment. He has promised glory for those who will believe and judgment for those who scoff. He has explained the foolishness of trusting man's wisdom and the world's resources.

The prophet calls the professing people of God back to spiritual reality. He warns against hypocrisy and empty worship. He pleads for faith, obedience, a heart that delights in God, and a life that glorifies God.

" 'There is no peace,' saith the Lord, 'unto the wicked' " (Isa. 48:22; 57:21); for in order to have peace, you must have righteousness (32:17). The only way to have righteousness is through faith in Jesus Christ (Rom. 3:19-31).

Isaiah's message has been, "Be comforted by the Lord!" (See Isaiah 12:1; 40:1-2; 49:13; 51:3, 19; 52:9; 54:11; 57:18; 61:2; 66:13.) But God cannot comfort rebels! If we are sinning against God and comfortable about it, something is radically wrong. That false comfort will lead to false confidence, and that will lead to the chastening hand of God

"Seek ye the Lord while he may be found" (55:6).

"Though your sins be as scarlet, they shall be as white as snow" (1:18).

"O Lord, I will praise you; though you were angry with me, your anger is turned away, and you comfort me" (12:1 NKJV).

BE COMFORTED!

JEREMIAH

OUTLINE

Key theme: Repent and return to the Lord or He will judge
Key verse: Jeremiah 3:22

I. JEREMIAH'S CALL AND COMMISSION. 1

II. JEREMIAH'S MESSAGES TO HIS PEOPLE JUDAH. 2–33

1. During the time of Josiah's rule. 2–13
   (1) The sins of the nation. 2–6
   (2) The temple messages. 7–10
   (3) The broken covenant. 11–13
2. The coming Babylonian invasion. 14–16
3. The Sabbath message. 17
4. The potter's house sermons. 18–19
5. Messages to the leaders. 20–24
6. Judah's captivity. 25–29
7. National restoration. 30–33

III. JEREMIAH'S MINISTRY AND THE FALL OF JERUSALEM. 34–39

1. Ministry during the siege. 34–38
   (1) To King Zedekiah. 34, 37–38
   (2) To King Jehoiakim. 35–36
2. Jerusalem falls. 39

IV. AFTER THE FALL OF THE CITY. 40–45, 52

V. JEREMIAH'S MESSAGES TO THE NATIONS. 46–51

1. To Egypt. 46
2. To Philistia. 47
3. To Moab. 48
4. To Ammon, Moab, Edom, Syria, Kedar, and Elam. 49
5. To Babylon. 50–51

CONTENTS

PRELUDE

"Power tends to corrupt and absolute power corrupts absolutely." Lord John Acton wrote that in a letter to his friend Mandell Creighton on April 5, 1887. When he ended the letter, the British historian added this postscript: "History provides neither compensation for suffering nor penalties for wrong."

As you study the prophecy of Jeremiah, you'll learn that Lord Acton was right in his first statement; for you will meet in this book some of history's most powerful and corrupt rulers. But Lord Acton was terribly wrong in his postscript. God is still on the throne and history is His story. The German writer Friedrich von Logau said it better:

> Though the mills of God grind slowly,
> yet they grind exceeding small;
> Though with patience He stands waiting, with exactness grinds He all.

God judges the nations and eventually pays them the wages earned from their sin. No nation can despise God's law and defy His rule without suffering for it. The prophecy of Jeremiah teaches that very clearly.

In his familiar poem "The Present Crisis," American poet James Russell Lowell penned words that summarize Jeremiah's life and ministry:

> Once to every man and nation comes
> the moment to decide,
> In the strife of Truth with Falsehood,
> for the good or evil side.

Though at first Jeremiah hesitated when God called him, he surrendered to the Lord and became one of history's most decisive spiritual leaders. Tragically, however, the people who most needed his leadership rejected him and turned their backs on God's Word.

As never before, our homes, churches, cities, and nations need decisive leaders who will obey the Word of God. "If you ever injected truth into politics," quipped Will Rogers, "you have no politics." The politician asks, "Is it popular?" The diplomat asks, "Is it safe?" But the true leader asks, "Is it God's will? Is it right?" To quote James Russell Lowell's "The Present Crisis" again:

> Truth forever on the scaffold, Wrong
> forever on the throne,
> Yet that scaffold sways the future, and,
> behind the dim unknown,
> Standeth God within the shadow, keeping watch above His own.

That's what the Lord told Jeremiah: "I am watching over My word to perform it" (Jer. 1:12, NASB).

CHAPTER ONE
THE RELUCTANT PROPHET
JEREMIAH 1

"For a people to boast in the glory of the past, and to deny the secret that made the past, is to perish."
—G. Campbell Morgan[1]

Jeremiah was perhaps twenty years old when God's call came to him in the thirteenth year of Josiah's reign (626 B.C.). Why did he hesitate to accept God's call? Let me suggest some reasons.

1. The Task Was Demanding (Jer. 1:1)

Jeremiah's father Hilkiah was a priest[2] as was his father before him, and young Jeremiah was also expected to serve at the altar. He may even have been at the age when he would have stepped into his place of ministry when God called him to be a prophet.

Since serving as a prophet was much more demanding than serving as a priest, it's no wonder Jeremiah demurred. If I had my choice, I'd take the priesthood! For one thing, a priest's duties were predictable. Just about everything he had to do was written down in the Law. Thus, all the priest had to do was follow instructions.[3] Day after day, there were sacrifices to offer, lepers to examine, unclean people to exclude from the camp, cleansed people to reinstate, official ceremonies to observe, a sanctuary to care for, and the Law to teach. No wonder some of the priests said,

"Oh, what a weariness!" (Mal. 1:13, NKJV)

The ministry of a prophet, however, was quite another matter, because you never knew from one day to the next what the Lord would call you to say or do. The priest worked primarily to conserve the past by protecting and maintaining the sanctuary ministry, but the prophet labored to change the present so the nation would have a future. When the prophet saw the people going in the wrong direction, he sought to call them back to the right path.

Priests dealt with externals such as determining ritual uncleanness and offering various sacrifices that could never touch the hearts of the people (Heb. 10:1-18), but the prophet tried to reach and change hearts. At least sixty-six times the word "heart" is found in the Book of Jeremiah, for he is preeminently the prophet of the heart.

Priests didn't preach to the crowds very much but ministered primarily to individuals with various ritual needs. Prophets, on the other hand, addressed whole nations, and usually the people they addressed didn't want to hear the message. Priests belonged to a special tribe and therefore had authority and respect, but a prophet could come from any tribe and had to prove his divine call. Priests were supported from the sacrifices and offerings of the people, but prophets had no guaranteed income.

Jeremiah would have had a much easier time serving as priest. Therefore, it's no wonder his first response was to question God's call. Offering sacrifices was one thing, but preaching the Word to hardhearted people was quite something else. When you read his book, you will see a number of pictures of his ministry that reveal how demanding it was to serve the Lord as a faithful prophet. In his ministry, Jeremiah had to be

- a destroyer and a builder (1:9-10)
- a pillar and a wall (l:17-18)
- a watchman (6:17)
- a tester of metals (6:27-30)
- a physician (8:11, 21-22)
- a sacrificial lamb (11:19)
- a long-distance runner (12:5)
- a shepherd (13:17, 20-21; 17:16, 23)
- a troublemaker (15:10, 15-17)

Does this sound like an easy task?

2. The Times Were Difficult (Jer. 1:2-3; 2 Kings 21–25; 2 Chron. 33–36)

I suppose there never is a time when serving God is easy, but some periods in history are especially difficult for spiritual ministry, and Jeremiah lived in such an era. Consider what the history of Judah was like during Jeremiah's lifetime.

Rebellion instead of obedience. To begin with, Jeremiah was born during the reign of King Manasseh, the most evil man who ever reigned over the kingdom of Judah (2 Kings 21:1-18). The son of godly Hezekiah,[4] Manasseh came to the throne when only twelve years old, and the officials around him easily influenced him toward idolatry. "Manasseh seduced them [the people of Judah] to do more evil than the nations whom the Lord had destroyed before the Children of Israel" (v. 9, NKJV). When Manasseh died, his evil son Amon continued his father's evil practices.

Thus, Jeremiah grew up in Anathoth[5] at a time when idolatry flourished in Judah, children were offered in sacrifice to idols, the Law of Moses was disregarded and disobeyed, and it looked as though there was no hope for the nation. Godly priests were not greatly appreciated.

Reformation instead of repentance. In 639 B.C., some of Amon's servants assassinated him. Josiah his son became king, reigning until his untimely death in 609. Josiah was quite young when he began to reign, but he had godly counselors like Hilkiah, and thus he sought the Lord. In the twelfth year of his reign, he began to purge the land of idolatry; six years later, he commanded the priests and workers to repair and cleanse the temple. It was during that time that Hilkiah the priest found the Book of the Law in the temple and had it read to the king. This document may have been the entire five books of Moses or just the Book of Deuteronomy.

When the king heard the Law of God read, he was deeply moved. He tore his robes and sent to Huldah the prophetess for instructions from the Lord (2 Kings 22). Her message was that the people had forsaken God and therefore judgment was coming, but because of Josiah's sincere repentance, judgment would not come during his reign.

Josiah didn't wait for the temple repairs to be completed before calling the whole nation to repentance. He made a covenant with the Lord and led the people in renouncing idolatry and returning to the Law of the Lord. Unfortunately, the obedience of many of the people was only a surface thing. Unlike the king, they displayed no true repentance. Jeremiah knew this and boldly announced God's message: "Judah has not turned to Me with her whole heart, but in pretense" (Jer.3:10, NKJV).

Josiah led the nation in a reformation but not in a heart-changing revival. The idols were removed, the temple was repaired, and the worship of Jehovah was restored, but the people had not turned to the Lord with their whole heart and soul.

Politics instead of principle. No sooner did Josiah die on the battlefield[6] and his son become king than the nation quickly returned to idolatry under the rule of Jehoahaz. But Pharaoh Necho removed Jehoahaz from the throne, exiled him to Egypt where he died, and placed his brother Eliakim on the throne, giving him the name Jehoiakim. Jehoiakim, however, was no better than his brother and "did that which was evil in the sight of the Lord, according to all that his fathers had done" (2 Kings 23:37). He taxed the people heavily in order to pay tribute to Egypt, and then he agreed to pay tribute to Nebuchadnezzar, king of Babylon. After Jehoiakim reneged on that promise, Nebuchadnezzar took him prisoner to Babylon and took the temple vessels with him (597 B.C.).

Jehoiakim's son Jehoiachin reigned only three months; then his uncle Mattaniah, Josiah's third son (1 Chron. 3:15), was made king and renamed Zedekiah. Zedekiah was the last king of Judah, a weak, vacillating man who feared his officials more than he feared the Lord[7] (Jer. 38:19). "And he did that which was evil in the sight of the Lord his God, and humbled not himself before Jeremiah the prophet speaking from the mouth of the Lord" (2 Chron. 36:12). Zedekiah would ask Jeremiah for help while at the same time courting ambassadors from neighboring nations and plotting rebellion against Babylon. He allowed his princes to persecute and even imprison Jeremiah, though he himself had secret meetings with the prophet as if he were seeking God's will.

It's easy for political leaders to invite religious leaders in for consultation and then do exactly what they'd already planned to do. Today, it's good public relations to give people the impression that "religion" is important, but talking to a popular preacher isn't the same as humbling yourself before God.

Jeremiah preached to the nation for forty years, giving them God's promises and warnings; yet he lived to see Jerusalem and his beloved temple destroyed by Nebuchadnezzar's army and his people taken captive to Babylon. Jeremiah ministered in turbulent times and yet remained faithful to the Lord. He exposed the futile foreign policy of the rulers, pleading with them to turn to the Lord with all their hearts and trust God instead of trusting their political allies. Jeremiah is one of Scripture's greatest examples of faithfulness and decisive action in the face of physical danger and national decay.

3. The Servant Was Doubtful (Jer. 1:4-10)

Jeremiah hesitated as he looked at the work before him and the wickedness around him, and when he looked at the weakness within himself, Jeremiah was certain that he wasn't the man for the job.

When it comes to serving the Lord, there's a sense in which nobody is adequate. "And who is sufficient for these things?" (2 Cor. 2:16) asked the great Apostle Paul as he pondered the responsibilities of ministry. Paul then answered his own question. "Not that we are sufficient of ourselves to think any thing as of ourselves; but our sufficiency is of God" (3:5).

When God calls us, however, He isn't making a mistake, and for us to hesitate or refuse to obey is to act on the basis of unbelief and not faith. It's one thing for us to know our own weaknesses, but it's quite something else for us to say that our weaknesses prevent God from getting anything done. Instead of being an evidence of humility, this attitude reeks of pride.[8]

God gave young Jeremiah three wonderful assurances.

God's electing grace (vv. 4-5). One of my seminary professors used to say, "Try to explain divine election and you may lose your mind, but explain it away, and you will lose your soul." God doesn't save us, call us, or use us in His service because we're deserving, but because in His wisdom and grace He chooses to do so. It's grace from start to finish. "But by the grace of God I am what I am," wrote Paul, "and His grace which was bestowed upon me was not in vain; but I laboured more abundantly than they all: yet not I, but the grace of God which was with me" (1 Cor. 15:10).

Each of the phrases in Jeremiah 1:5 is important. To begin with, God *knew* Jeremiah,[9] which refers to His sovereign election of His servant. God chose Jeremiah even before he was conceived or formed in his mother's womb. Then God *formed* Jeremiah and gave him the genetic structure He wanted him to possess. This truth is expressed poetically in Psalm 139:13-16. Jeremiah wasn't too happy about what his birth gave him (Jer. 20:14-18), but the Lord knew what He was doing. What we are is God's gift to us; what we do with it is our gift to Him.

God *sanctified* Jeremiah even before he was born. This means Jeremiah was set apart by the Lord and for the Lord even before he knew the Lord in a personal way. God would later do the same with Paul (Gal. 1:15). The Lord then *ordained* Jeremiah to be His prophet to the nations. God's concern from the beginning is that *all* nations of the earth know His salvation. That's why He called Abraham (Gen. 12:1-3) and set apart the nation of Israel to be His special channel to bring His Word and His Son into the world.

A prophet was a chosen and authorized spokesman for God who declared God's Word to the people. The Hebrew word probably comes from an Arabic root that means "to announce." For example, Moses spoke to Aaron, and Aaron was his spokesman (prophet) before Pharaoh (Ex. 7:1-2). Prophets did more than reveal the future, for their messages had present application to the life of the nation. They were *forth*tellers more than *fore*tellers, exposing the sins of the people and calling them back to their covenant responsibilities before God.

As God's children, we are chosen and set apart *by* Him and *for* Him (Rom. 8:28-30; Eph. 1:3-14). This truth ought to give us great courage as we confront an evil world and seek to serve the Lord. "If God be for us, who can be against us?" (Rom. 8:31)

God's protecting presence (vv. 6-8). God gave young Jeremiah three instructions: Go where I send you, speak what I command you, and don't be afraid of the people. Then He added the great word of promise, "For I am with you to deliver you" (Jer. 1:8, NKJV). He repeated this promise at the end of His call: "'They will fight against you, but they shall not prevail against you. For I am with you,' says the Lord, 'to deliver you'" (v. 19, NKJV).

Please note that there was a condition attached to this encouraging promise: Jeremiah had to go where God sent him and speak what God told him to speak. He also had to believe God's promise and prove it by not fearing the people. We call Jeremiah "the weeping prophet," and he was (9:1), but he was also a courageous man who faced many dangers and trials and remained true to the Lord. He knew that the Lord was with him, just as we should know that the Lord is with us. "For He Himself has said, 'I will never leave you nor forsake you.'[10] So we may boldly say: 'The Lord is my helper; I will not fear. What can man do to me?'" (Heb. 13:5-6, NKJV)

God's effecting Word (vv. 9-10). When the coal from the heavenly altar touched Isaiah's lips, it purified him (Isa. 6:5-7); when God's hand touched Jeremiah's mouth, it gave him power and authority. God put His words into the prophet's mouth and those words were effective to accomplish His will. God not only gave Jeremiah His words, but He also promised "watch over" those words until they were fulfilled (Jer. 1:12).

The Word of God *created* the universe: "By the Word of the Lord the heavens were made, and all the host of them by the breath of His mouth. . . . For He spoke, and it was done; He commanded, and it stood fast" (Ps. 33:6, 9, NKJV). The universe is upheld by the Word of God: "And [Christ] upholding all things by the Word of His power" (Heb. 1:3, NKJV). But God also carries out His purposes on earth by means of His Word: "As the rain and the snow come down from heaven, and do not return to it without watering the earth and making it bud and flourish, so that it yields seed for the sower and bread for the eater, so is my word that goes out from my mouth: It will not return to me empty, but will accomplish what I desire and achieve the purpose for which I sent it" (Isa. 55:10-11, NIV).

In too many churches today, worship has become entertainment and preaching is merely the happy dispensing of good advice. We need to hear and obey Paul's admonition to Timothy: "Preach the Word" (2 Tim. 4:2). The Holy Spirit is the Spirit of truth (John 16:13) and works by means of the Word of truth (Ps. 119:43; 2 Tim. 2:15). Jeremiah didn't accomplish God's will on earth by means of clever speeches, cunning diplomacy, or skillful psychology. He heard God's Word, took it to heart, and then proclaimed it fearlessly to the people. God did the rest.

Jeremiah's ministry was difficult because he had to tear down before he could build, and he had to root up before he could plant. In too many ministries there are organizational "structures" that don't belong there and should be torn down because they're hindering progress. Some "plants" are taking up space but bearing no fruit, and they ought to be pulled up. Jesus said, "Every plant which My Heavenly Father has not planted will be uprooted" (Matt. 15:13, NKJV).

Any servant of God who feels himself or herself too weak to serve needs to consider these three encouragements. Has God called you? Then He will equip you and enable you. Are you obeying His commands by faith? Then He is with you to protect you. Are you sharing the Word? Then He will accomplish His purposes no matter how the people respond. Jeremiah's name means "Jehovah establishes," and God did establish His servant and his ministry and cared for him to the very end. "But the Lord is faithful, who will establish you and guard you from the evil one" (2 Thes. 3:3, NKJV).

4. The Message Was Dangerous (Jer. 1:11-19)

When you study the Old Testament prophets, you discover that three strands of truth wove their messages together: (1) *past sin:* the nation has disobeyed God's Law; (2) *present responsibility:* the people must repent or God will send judgment; and (3) *future hope:* the Lord will come one day and establish His glorious kingdom.

The Lord didn't give Jeremiah a joyful message of deliverance to announce, but rather a tragic message of judgment. So dangerous was this message that people hearing it called Jeremiah a traitor. He would be misunderstood, persecuted, arrested, and imprisoned—and more than once, his life was in danger. The nation didn't want to hear the truth, but Jeremiah told them plainly that they were defying the Lord, disobeying the Law, and destined for judgment.

God gave Jeremiah three promises to prepare him for this dangerous mission. Two of the promises were in visions.

The almond tree: God's Word will be fulfilled (vv. 11-12). In the Holy Land, the almond tree blossoms in January and gives the first indication that spring is coming. The Hebrew word for almond tree is *saqed;* while the word for "watch" or "be awake" is *soqed.* The Lord used this play on words to impress Jeremiah with the fact that He is ever awake to watch over His Word and fulfill it.

Like a husband or wife breaking the marriage vows, the sinful nation had turned from the covenant they had made with the Lord, and now they were giving their love and loyalty to pagan idols. *But that covenant would stand, for the Lord had not forgotten it.* He had promised to bless them if they obeyed and chasten them if they disobeyed, and He was "watching to see that [His] word is fulfilled" (Jer. 1:12, NIV; see Lev. 26; Deut. 28). God had spoken to the nation through the earlier prophets, but the rulers and people wouldn't listen.

> Yet the Lord testified against Israel and against Judah, by all of His prophets, namely every seer, saying, "Turn from your evil ways, and keep My commandments and My statutes, according to all the Law which I commanded your fathers, and which I sent to you by My servants the prophets." Nevertheless they would not hear, but stiffened their necks, like the necks of their fathers, who did not believe in the Lord their God. And they rejected His statutes and His covenant that He had made with their fathers, and His testimonies which He had testified against them; they followed idols, became idolaters, and went after the nations who were all around them, concerning whom the Lord had charged them that they should not do like them (2 Kings 17:13-15, NKJV).

The boiling pot: God's wrath is coming (vv. 13-16). The nations in the East were often in conflict, each trying to gain supremacy. First the Jewish rulers would turn to Egypt for help, then to Assyria (see Isa. 30–31; Jer. 2:18, 36); and all the while, they failed to trust the Lord and seek His help. But this vision reveals that God is in control of the nations of the world and can use them to accomplish His own purposes. The Lord was even then preparing Babylon in the north[11] to be His servant to chasten His people. For

Judah to turn to Egypt for help was futile because Egypt would also fall to Nebuchadnezzar (Jer. 46).

When Jeremiah began his ministry, Assyria, not Babylon, was the dominant power in the Near East, and no doubt many of the political experts thought Jeremiah foolish to worry about Babylon in the north. But the people of Judah lived to see Assyria defeated and Egypt crippled as Babylon rose to power and Jeremiah's words came true. Indeed, the thrones of the conquering Babylonian leaders were set in the gate of Jerusalem (39:1-3), and the holy city was eventually destroyed.

The sin God singled out was idolatry (1:16)—forsaking the true God and worshiping the gods they had made with their own hands. In their hypocrisy, the people of Judah maintained the temple worship, but Jehovah was only one of many gods who claimed their devotion. Some of the foreign idols were even brought into the temple! (See Ezek. 8–9.) The false prophets flourished in a ministry that was shallow and popular because they promised peace and never called for repentance (Jer. 5:12-13; 8:11-12; 14:13-22).

When a nation turns from worshiping the true God, its people begin to exploit one another, and that's what happened in Judah. The rich oppressed the poor and the courts would not defend the rights of the oppressed (2:34-35; 5:26-31; 7:1-11). Yet these evil rulers and judges went to the temple faithfully and pretended to be devoted to Jehovah! All they did was make the temple "a den of robbers" (7:11). It was this kind of sin that God was about to judge.

The city, pillar, and wall: God will protect His servant (vv. 17-19). In order to be able to run or work easily, men in that day had to tie their loose robes together with a belt (1 Kings 18:46; 2 Kings 4:29), so "gird up your loins" (Jer. 1:17) meant "Get ready for action!" It might be paraphrased "Tighten your belt! Roll up your sleeves!" "Gird up the loins of your mind" (1 Peter 1:13) means "Pull your mind together and have the right mental attitude in view of our Lord's return."

God repeated the warning He gave earlier (Jer. 1:8) that Jeremiah must not be afraid of the people who would oppose him, because God would defend him. Surrounded by his enemies, the prophet would become a fortified city they couldn't subdue. Forced to stand alone, Jeremiah would become as strong as an iron pillar. Attacked on all sides by kings, princes, priests, and people, he would be as unyielding as a bronze wall. "I am with you to deliver you" was God's reliable promise (vv. 8, 19, NKJV), and in the battle for truth, one with God is a majority.

In spite of the demands of the task and the difficulties of the times, Jeremiah accepted God's call. He knew his own deficiencies, but he also knew that God was greater and would enable him to do the job. The message God gave him was indeed dangerous, but God was watching over His Word to fulfill it and would protect His faithful servant.

Jeremiah made the right decision and as a result became one of the most unpopular prophets in Jewish history. Measured by human standards, his ministry was a failure, but measured by the will of God, he was a great success. It isn't easy to stand alone, to resist the crowd, and to be out of step with the philosophies and values of the times. Jeremiah, however, lived that kind of a life for over forty years.

In the final chapter of his book *Walden*, Henry David Thoreau writes: "If a man does not keep pace with his companions, perhaps it is because he hears a different drummer. Let him step to the music which he hears, however measured or far away."[12]

"If anyone desires to come after Me," said Jesus, "let him deny himself, and take up his cross, and follow Me. . . . For what is a man profited if he gains the whole world, and loses his own soul?" (Matt. 16:24, 26, NKJV)

In light of that sobering question, what decision will you make? Will you conform to the crowd or carry the cross?

CHAPTER TWO
THE PROPHET PREACHES
JEREMIAH 2–6

"Nations, like individuals, are subjected to punishments and chastisements in this world."

-Abraham Lincoln[1]

In my library is a notebook containing the outlines of messages that I preached when I began my ministry back in 1950. Whenever I read those outlines, I feel very embarrassed and contrite in heart and I marvel that anybody ever listened to those sermons or came back to hear more. A seasoned preacher once said, "When you're young in the ministry, you can't understand why more people don't come to hear you. But when you get older, you're amazed that *anybody* comes to hear you." I agree.

Young Jeremiah, however, started his ministry with messages that were courageous, compassionate, and convicting.[2] Boldly he confronted the people with their sins and pled with them to repent and return to the Lord. Four major themes combine in these messages: rebellion, repentance, righteousness, and retribution.

1. Rebellion: God Sees His People's Sins (Jer. 2:1-37)

Jeremiah had a gift for expressing theological truth in pictorial language. In fact, much of his preaching can be read as poetry.[3] In this chapter, he paints ten pictures that expose the sins of the people.

An unfaithful wife (vv. 1-8). When the Lord gave the Israelites His covenant at Mt. Sinai (Ex. 19–20), He entered into a loving relationship with them that He compared to marriage. "They broke my covenant, though I was a husband to them" (Jer. 31:32, NIV; see 3:14). In the Old Testament, Israel's idolatry is compared to adultery and even prostitution (see Isa. 54:5; Hosea 2:16). At the beginning of this covenant relationship, the Jews were devoted[4] to the Lord and loved Him, but once they conquered the Promised Land, their hearts lusted after the gods of the nations around them and they sank into idolatry (Jud. 1–3). Although God had taken them safely through their wilderness journey and given them a wonderful inheritance in Canaan, they abandoned Him for man-made gods. What kind of loyal love is that?

Broken cisterns (vv. 9-13). "Go from west to east," said the prophet, "and you will not find a nation that changed its gods." But Israel forsook the true God for false gods, which was like abandoning a spring of fresh flowing water for a cracked, muddy cistern that couldn't hold water. In the Holy Land, water is a valuable possession, and nobody would do a foolish thing like that. No wonder the Lord said, "Be appalled at this, O heavens, and shudder with great horror" (Jer. 2:12, NIV). The second phrase literally means "Let your hair stand on end!"

A plundered slave (vv. 14-19). God redeemed the Jews from Egypt and gave them freedom in Canaan, but now their nation had gone back into bondage because of its idolatry. By allying with its pagan neighbors—Egypt and Assyria—instead of trusting the Lord, Judah had become a vassal state and was being plundered and enslaved. Instead of drinking at the pure river that the Lord gave them, the Judahites drank the polluted waters of the Nile and the Euphrates. Memphis and Tahpanhes were Egyptian cities, and Shihor was a branch of the Nile River.[5]

A basic principle is enunciated in verse 19: God punishes us by allowing our own sins to bring pain and discipline to our lives. "Your own conduct and actions have brought this upon you. This is your punishment. How bitter it is!" (4:18, NIV) "Your wrongdoings have kept these [rains] away; your sins have deprived you of good" (5:25, NIV). The greatest judgment God can send to disobedient people is to let them have their own way and reap the sad, painful consequences of their sins.

The word "backsliding" literally means to "turn away" and describes the nation's repeated apostasy.[6] The Book of Judges records at least seven occasions when Israel turned from the Lord and had to be chastened, and there were numerous other times during the period of the monarchy when the Israelites deliberately turned from the Lord. The word "backslide" is not used in the New Testament, but the experience is described in other ways: falling from grace (Gal. 5:4), leaving your first love (Rev. 2:4), loving the world (1 John 2:15-17; 2 Tim. 4:10), and walking in darkness (1 John 1:5-10).

A stubborn animal (v. 20). Jeremiah often used animals to picture the behavior of people, and here he compared the Jews to an unruly animal that won't wear the yoke.[7] One of his recurring phrases is the stubbornness of their evil hearts (3:17; 7:24; 9:14; 11:8; 13:10; 16:12; 18:12; 23:17, NIV).[8] When people, made in the image of God, refuse to obey God, they become like animals (see Ps. 32:9; Prov. 7:21-23; Hosea 4:16).

A degenerate vine (v. 21). Israel as a vine is a familiar image in the Old Testament (Ps. 80:8-16; Isa. 5:1-7; Ezek. 17:1-10; Hosea 10:1-

2). God planted His people in the good land He gave them, but they didn't produce the harvest of righteousness He desired. "So He expected it to bring forth good grapes, but it brought forth wild grapes" (Isa. 5:2, NKJV). Because they worshiped false gods, they became like their degenerate neighbors. How could dead idols ever produce living fruit in their nation?

A defiled body (v. 22). No amount of good works or religious ceremonies could wash away their sins, because the heart of the nation's problem was the problem in their hearts. They had sinful hearts because they had stubborn hearts—hearts that refused to listen to God's servant and obey God's Word. Josiah's reformation was only a cosmetic change in the kingdom of Judah; it never reached the hearts of the people so that they repented and sought forgiveness from the Lord.

Jeremiah is preeminently the prophet of the heart, for he used the word over sixty times. "O Jerusalem, wash the evil from your heart and be saved" (Jer. 4:14, NIV). "The heart is deceitful above all things, and desperately wicked: who can know it?" (17:9) Judah needed to return to the Lord with their *whole* heart, for only then could He bless them.

An animal in the desert (vv. 23-25). Even if the people denied that they were defiled, their actions proved otherwise, for they were like animals: a lost camel looking for an oasis; or a donkey in heat, running here and there looking for a mate. As the Jews pursued the false gods of the pagan nations, their shoes wore out and their throats became dry. How much better had they drunk the refreshing water from the river of God!

But they had given themselves so much to sin that they despaired of being saved. "It's no use!" (2:25, NIV) was their excuse. "It's hopeless!" They sounded like confirmed alcoholics or compulsive gamblers who can't break the habit, or like the invalid at the Pool of Bethesda who had been sick for so long that he'd given up hope (John 5:1-9). *Jesus Christ, however, specializes in hopeless cases.* "He breaks the power of canceled sin/He sets the prisoner free."[9]

A disgraced thief (vv. 26-28). A thief caught in the act may protest his or her innocence, but the evidence is there for all to see. Any visitor to the kingdom of Judah could see what God saw: people turning their backs on God and talking to deaf idols, but then turning desperately to Jehovah for help when they found themselves in trouble. They were caught red-handed!

Incorrigible children (vv. 29-35). God chastened them many times for their sins, but they refused to change their ways, and then they even blamed God! He brought charges against them (Jer. 2:9), but instead of confessing and repenting, they complained and brought charges against Him! None of His discipline seemed to do any good. "You struck them, but they felt no pain; you crushed them, but they refused correction" (5:3, NIV; see 7:28; 17:23; 32:33; 35:13).

God reminded the people how richly He had blessed them. Yet they rebelled against Him (2:29), forgot Him (v. 32), and lied to Him (vv. 33-35), claiming to be innocent. One of the major themes of the Book of Deuteronomy is that the nation should remember the Lord and what He had done for them. Yet the people took their blessings for granted and gave their allegiance to dumb idols. They were so skilled at their harlotry, worshiping false gods, that even the most wicked prostitute could learn new things from them! They exploited the poor and were stained by their blood, and yet they pleaded innocent (see Amos 2:6-8; 5:10-12).

Because the nation at that time was enjoying a measure of political and economic prosperity, they concluded that God's blessing was proof of their innocence! They didn't realize that God can bless the wicked (Pss. 37 and 73; Matt. 5:45) and that the goodness of God should instead lead them to repentance (Luke 15:17-18; Rom. 2:4-5).

Prisoners of war (vv. 36-37). In its attempt to keep peace with its neighbors, Judah had flitted between Egypt and Assyria (Jer. 2:14-19), both of whom would ultimately disappoint Judah. The description in verse 37 is that of prisoners of war, their hands tied above their heads, being led away captive. Any decisions we make that are contrary to God's plan will lead to bondage, because only the truth can set us free (John 8:32). The Babylonian army would eventually overrun the land, take Jerusalem and destroy it, and lead the people away into captivity.

Was there any way Judah could escape the coming wrath? Yes, and that was the theme of the next point in Jeremiah's message.

2. Repentance: God Pleads for His People to Return to Him (Jer. 3:1–4:31)

The two key words in this section are *return* (3:1, 7, 12, 22; 4:1) and *backsliding* (3:6, 8, 11, 12, 14, 22). In the Hebrew, "backsliding" ("faithless," NIV) is actually a form of the word translated "return."

Pictures (3:1-10; 3:21–4:4). The prophet again used four vivid images to picture the sad spiritual condition of the kingdom of Judah.

The unfaithful wife (3:1-10). Jeremiah returned to the metaphor of marriage that he had used in 2:1-2 and 20, but this time he introduced the subject of divorce. The Mosaic Law permitted a man to divorce his wife, but it did not allow him to marry her again (Deut. 24:1-4). God had every right to reject His people, because they had abandoned Him, not in order to marry another "husband," but in order to play the harlot with *many* lovers. The people had gone to the hills and built shrines dedicated to foreign gods. They had acted worse than common prostitutes who at least waited for lovers to come to them, for Judah had *pursued* false gods and repeatedly committed spiritual adultery with them.[10]

Instead of rejecting His people, however, the Lord patiently called for them to return and be restored as His wife. What grace! God had even caused a drought in the land, and the people had called out to Him for help (Jer. 3:4-5), but they had not really repented of their sins. Because of their covenant relationship with God, Judah called Him "Father" and "guide," which were titles Jewish wives sometimes used in addressing their husbands. But how could God give them covenant blessings when they were violating covenant commandments?

When Assyria conquered the Northern Kingdom of Israel in 722 B.C., the Southern Kingdom of Judah witnessed this divine judgment. Nevertheless, the Judahites refused to learn from Israel's destruction and turn from their sins (vv. 6-11). God had "divorced" Israel and put her away; Israel became a part of Assyria, and the Northern Kingdom was never restored. Having seen this judgment, the Judahites persisted in their sins as though it would never happen to them. Because of this arrogant attitude, Judah was even more guilty than Israel. Judah should have been "put away," yet God graciously invited His adulterous wife to return home to Him.

In obedience to the king, the people had cooperated with Josiah's reformation and outwardly put away their idols, but what they did was "only in pretense" (v. 10, NIV). God was "near in their mouth but far from their mind" (12:2, NKJV; see Ezek. 33:31). Even today, when political leaders claim to be born again and are willing to promote evangelical causes, going to church and reading the Bible become the "in" things to do, but you wonder how sincere these people really are. True Christian faith has never been popular, and the road that leads to life is still narrow and lonely (Matt. 7:13-23).

The unhealthy patient (3:21-25). In Scripture, sickness is one of many metaphors for sin (Ps. 41:4; Isa. 1:5-6; Jer. 8:22; 30:12; Mark 2:17). Like an infection entering the bloodstream, sin secretly gets into the system of the "inner man" and goes to work weakening and destroying. It gradually infects the whole system, producing spiritual lassitude and loss of spiritual appetite; and if not cared for, the "sin sickness" can lead to dire consequences. When we hear about believers suddenly falling into open sin, in most cases a gradual slide preceded the sudden fall.

God offers to heal not just the symptoms of their backsliding, but the backsliding itself. The false prophets dealt only with symptoms and announced a false peace that gave the people a false confidence (Jer. 6:14; 7:8; 8:11). But a true physician of souls will tell the truth and seek to lead sinners to genuine spiritual healing that comes from honest confession and repentance.

This reminds me of a story I've often used in sermons. A certain church member was in the habit of closing his public prayers with "And, Lord, take the cobwebs out of my heart!" One of the other members became weary of this litany, so one evening, after hearing it again, he stood and prayed, "And, Lord, while You're at it . . . kill the spider!" Jeremiah was out to kill the spider and cure the patient.

The Jews thought their deliverance would come from the idols they worshiped in the high places—the hill shrines—but their only hope was to repent and trust the Lord.[11] These idols were unable to save them. In fact, they brought nothing but shame. Yet the Jews had sacrificed their God-given produce, flocks, and herds, and even their children to these shameful idols!

The unplowed field (4:1-3). The problem

with the people was their dishonesty; they would use the right language, but they wouldn't mean it from their hearts. They would pray to the true God, but not forsake the false gods. It was easy to say, "As the Lord lives," but they didn't say it in truth, justice, and righteousness. Their hearts were hard and crowded with thorns like a neglected, unplowed field. Hosea used this image (Hosea 10:12) and so did Jesus in His Parable of the Sower (Matt. 13:1-9, 18-23).

The uncircumcised heart (4:4). Jewish boys were circumcised when eight days old, given a name, and made a son of the covenant (Gen. 17:9-14; Lev. 12:3; Luke 1:59). Although no amount of surgery on the body could change the heart, the Jews thought that this ritual was their guarantee of salvation (Matt. 3:7-9; Acts 15:1-5). God, however, wanted them to "operate" on their hearts and put away their callousness and disobedience. "Therefore circumcise the foreskin of your heart, and be stiff-necked no longer" (Deut. 10:16, NKJV; see also 30:6; Rom. 2:28-29; Col. 2:11). They also needed to circumcise their ears (Jer. 6:10) so they could hear the Word of God.

Many people today depend on baptism, the Lord's Supper (Communion, the Eucharist), confirmation, or some other religious ritual for their salvation when what God wants from us is sincere faith from a repentant heart. Salvation is a gift that we receive by faith; it's not a reward that we earn by being religious.

Promises (3:11-13). The Lord even called to the dispersed Israelites to return to Him. This invitation reminds us of God's promises in Leviticus 26:40-45, Deuteronomy 30, and 1 Kings 8:46-53, which assured them that God would forgive if they would repent. In Jeremiah 3:14-19,[12] Jeremiah seemed to be looking far ahead to the Kingdom Age when Israel and Judah would be united, the nation would be purified and multiplied, and God would give them spiritual leaders to care for them. In the darkest days of their history, the Israelites heard their prophets announce this coming messianic kingdom, and the promise gave them hope.

The people must have been shocked when they heard Jeremiah say that the day would come when the ark of the covenant would be gone, forgotten, and never missed (v. 16). They trusted in the ark, the temple, the religious rituals, the covenant, and yet these things were but temporary signs that pointed to something spiritual and eternal.

The day would come when circumcised Jews would be treated like uncircumcised Gentiles (9:25-26), when the temple would no longer be needed (7:1-15; see John 4:20-24), and when there would be a new covenant that would change hearts (11:1-5; 31:31-40). Like Jesus, Jeremiah saw beyond external religion and taught that God was seeking the devotion of the heart. No wonder both of them were accused of being traitors and persecuted for opposing the "true religion," which God had given to Israel.

Punishment (4:5-18). Jeremiah announced the invasion of the Babylonian army from the north (1:14), like a fierce lion (4:7) and a devastating desert storm (vv. 11-13). Dreadful judgment was coming to Judah, and yet the nation was unprepared, because the people believed the deceptive message of peace proclaimed by the false prophets (v. 10).[13] "It can't happen here!" was their slogan. "After all, we have the temple and the ark of the covenant."

God commanded the watchmen to blow the trumpet and alert the people to run to the walled cities for safety. That would have given them time to repent in sackcloth (v. 8) and to wash their hearts by confessing their sins (v. 14). The Babylonian army, however, would come swiftly (v. 13; see Ezek. 38:16) and do their job thoroughly. "Your own conduct and actions have brought this upon you. This is your punishment. How bitter it is! How it pierces to the heart!" (Jer. 4:18, NIV).

Pain (4:19-31). Known as the weeping prophet, Jeremiah here expressed his personal anguish as he contemplated a national tragedy that could have been averted (4:19-21). No other Old Testament prophet revealed his brokenheartedness and sorrow as did Jeremiah (see 6:24; 9:10; 10:19-20). When ministering publicly, he was bold before men; in private, he was heartbroken before God.

God explained to His servant why the judgment was coming: The people were foolish, they did not know God, they were stupid, and they lacked understanding (4:22). If they had been as skillful in holy living as they were in sinning, God would have blessed them instead of judging them.

With prophetic vision, Jeremiah saw what

the Babylonians would do to the land (vv. 23-29), producing chaos such as that described in Genesis 1:2.[14] No matter where he looked, he saw ruin. Even the stable mountains shook! It was only by the mercy of God that everything in Judah wasn't completely devastated (Jer. 4:27; see 5:10, 18; 30:11; 46:28).

But an equally great tragedy was the unbelief of the people who refused to repent and ask God for His help (4:30-31). Jeremiah described them as prostitutes who were trying to seduce other nations to come and help them stop the Babylonians, but their "lovers" wouldn't respond to their pleas. Judah trusted political alliances instead of trusting the Lord. But the prostitutes would become like women in travail—an image of painful judgment that's used often in Jeremiah (6:24; 13:21; 22:23; 30:6; 48:41; 49:22, 24; 50:43).[15]

3. Righteousness: God Searches for the Godly (Jer. 5:1-31)

Since the people would not listen to God's Word, God told Jeremiah to "act out" his message. This is the first of at least ten "action sermons" found in Jeremiah.[16] Meanwhile, this chapter deals with four sins of the people of Jerusalem.

Investigation: they were ungodly (5:1-6). God commanded Jeremiah to conduct a search of all the city of Jerusalem. If even one righteous person were discovered, the Lord would forgive the wicked city and call off the invasion. The background for this "action sermon" is God's agreement with Abraham to spare Sodom if ten righteous men were in the city (Gen. 18:22-33). The test in Jerusalem was, "Does the person practice justice and truth?"

Jeremiah found nobody among the poor who qualified, but he concluded that their lack of religious education would excuse them. The prophet then went to the nobles and the leaders, who he discovered knew God's commandments but threw off the yoke and turned away from the Law (Jer. 5:5; see 2:20; Ps. 2:1-3). When the survey was concluded, not one person was found who was honest and truthful.

One thing was left for God to do: He would allow the invaders to enter the land like marauding animals and destroy the people (see Jer. 2:15; 4:7). The animal had gotten loose from the yoke and run away from the master, only to be met by a lion, a wolf, and a leopard! What kind of freedom was that?

Condemnation: they were ungrateful (5:7-9). God asked two questions: "Why should I forgive you?" (v. 7, NIV) and "Shall I not punish them for these things?" (v. 9, NKJV) "God fed them to the full" (v. 7; "supplied all their needs", NIV), yet they used His gifts in order to commit sin and serve their idols. The goodness of God should have brought them to repentance (Rom. 2:4), but they were ungrateful for His blessings (Hosea 2:4-13). Instead of acting like men and women made in the image of God, they became like animals in heat ("well-fed, lusty stallions," Jer. 5:8, NIV; see 2:24).

The idolatrous nations in Canaan conducted a worship that was unbelievably immoral. In their minds, consorting with the temple prostitutes could guarantee a fruitful harvest. Baal was the storm god who provided the needed rain. Thus, when the Lord held back the rain to warn His people, they turned to pagan idols for help. Josiah had gotten rid of the temple prostitutes, but these prostitutes found other ways to carry on their trade and satisfy the desires they had inflamed in the men of Judah. Not unlike society today, the people worshiped sex and saw nothing wrong with what they were doing.

Devastation: they were unfaithful (5:10-19). This is the heart of the matter: Since the people did not believe God's Word, they turned their backs on God and went their own way. "They have lied about the Lord; they said, 'He will do nothing! No harm will come to us; we will never see sword or famine'" (Jer. 5:12, NIV). They rejected the Word God spoke through the prophets and called it "wind." As a result, God called for devastating judgment to come to His vineyard (vv. 10-11; see 2:21).

God, however, said His Word would be a fire that would consume the people like wood (5:14; see 23:29). Note the repetition of the phrase "eat up" ("devour," NIV) in 5:17, an announcement that the Babylonian invasion would consume the land and the people. This invasion would fulfill the warning given in Deuteronomy 28:49-52, a warning that the people knew. The Jews had forsaken the Lord and served idols in their own land. Now they would be temporarily forsaken by the Lord and taken to Babylon, where they would serve idols in a foreign land.

Yet, this warning opened and closed with the promise that God would not destroy the nation completely (Jer. 5:10, 18; see 4:27;

30:11; 46:28).[17] Even in wrath, He remembers mercy (Hab. 3:2). The Jewish prophets announced judgment, but they also promised that a "remnant" would be spared. Isaiah repeated this promise (Isa. 1:19; 10:20-22; 11:11, 16; 14:22; 46:3) and even named one of his sons "a remnant returns" (Shearjashub, 7:3); Micah echoed the same promise (Micah 2:12; 4:7; 5:3, 7-8; 7:18).

The remnant that returned to Judah from Babylon after the Captivity restored the nation, rebuilt the temple, and maintained the testimony, preparing the way for the coming of the Messiah. God had covenanted with Abraham that through his descendants all the world would be blessed (Gen. 12:1-3), and God kept His promise.

Proclamation: they were unconcerned (5:20-31). Jeremiah was a retiring sort of person. Yet God told him to announce and proclaim boldly to the whole house of Jacob just what the people were like. The prophet's description of the people must have angered them, but it didn't shake them out of their complacency. Jeremiah told them that they were foolish, senseless, blind, and deaf, and that they had no fear of God. They were stubborn and rebellious, having turned away from serving the Lord. The mighty seas obeyed God's rule, but His own people rejected Him. God sent the rains and gave the harvests, but His people refused to thank Him.

Instead of encouraging one another to fear God, they exploited one another like hunters snaring birds. Thus the rich grew richer as the poor languished. The courts were corrupt, the prophets were liars, the priests went right along with them—*and the people approved what was done and enjoyed it!* "My people love to have it so" (Jer. 5:31). When a nation becomes that corrupt, there is no hope.

The sinners thought they were getting away with their crimes, but God asked them, "What will you do in the end?" (5:31, NIV) "There is a way which seems right to a man, but its end is the way of death" (Prov. 14:12, NKJV).

4. Retribution: God Sends His Judgment (Jer. 6:1-30)

This closing section of Jeremiah's sermon focuses on the invading Babylonian army and the devastation they will bring to the kingdom of Judah. In that critical hour, the prophet told the nation what God was doing.

God declares war (vv. 1-5). First, the Lord spoke to His people and warned them that judgment was coming (vv. 1-3). The Jews had three main ways to get military information: from the watchmen on the walls (v. 17), from trumpet signals (v. 1; see Num. 10:1-10), and from signal fires lit on high places (Jer. 6:1). Since Jeremiah's hometown of Anathoth was in Benjamin, he started by warning his own neighbors to get out of Jerusalem. Jerusalem is compared to a "beautiful and delicate woman," but she will end up like a "widow" (Lam. 1:1) with all of her beauty gone (v. 6). Foreign "shepherds" (soldiers) would invade the beautiful pastures and set up their tents only to slaughter the flock.

God then spoke to the Babylonian army over which He had command (Jer. 6:4-5), and He shared His strategy with them: make a surprise attack at noon, the hottest time of the day, when nobody would expect it, and plan to continue the attack through the night when most armies retire. The word translated "prepare" means "to sanctify or consecrate"; the Babylonians considered this war a holy crusade for their gods (see Joel 3:9; Micah 3:5).

God directs the attack (vv. 6-15). The Lord told the Babylonian army *what to do*: chop down trees and build ramps against the walls of the city. Then He told them *why they were doing it*. Jerusalem was like a well that pours out filthy water, and the city must be punished. It was like a dying person with infected wounds that couldn't be healed, and these things must be purged away. Finally, God told them *how to do it*: with precision and thoroughness, the way gleaners go over a vineyard so as not to miss any fruit (Jer. 6:5, 9).

The prophet lamented the fact that, at this critical time in history, *nobody was listening*! (v. 10) Not only were their hearts uncircumcised (4:4), but so were their ears (see Acts 7:51); they refused to hear God's Word. Full of the wrath of the Lord, Jeremiah told them that God's anger will be poured out on young and old, men and women, and even the children. Rulers and priests won't escape; in fact, they were the most guilty because they had given the people false confidence and had refused to repent of their own sins (Jer. 6:13-15; see 7:8; 8:11). "For the sins of her prophets, and the iniquities of her priests" (Lam. 4:13) God would send this judgment.

God delivers the verdict (vv. 16-23). Are

the people guilty? Yes! Do they deserve this punishment? Yes! In fact, God called the Gentiles and the earth to bear witness that He had done all He could to spare them this judgment (Jer. 6:18-19). They would not walk on His path[18] and they would not listen to His prophets. Nevertheless, they continued to bring Him their hypocritical worship! (See Isa. 1:11-14; Amos 5:21; Micah 6:6-8.) God gave them the right way, but they rejected it. There could be no escape. The Babylonian army would be a formidable obstacle to anybody trying to flee the wrath of God. The daughter of Zion could not escape.

God describes the consequences (vv. 24-30). The prophet described the responses of the people as they heard the news—nothing but anguish, fear, and weakness, like a woman in hard labor (Jer. 6:24-26). "Terror on every side" (v. 25, NIV) is a phrase used again in 20:10, 46:5, and 49:29. This was the nickname Jeremiah gave Pashur, the chief officer of the temple (20:1-3).

Sometimes suffering brings out the best in people, but that wouldn't happen in the siege of Jerusalem. When God turned on the furnace, it would reveal the people as rejected silver, nothing but dross to be thrown away. He wasn't purifying them; He was punishing them. They weren't being refined; they were being rejected. They were too cheap to preserve.

"Indeed I tremble for my country when I reflect that God is just, and that His justice cannot sleep forever."

Thomas Jefferson wrote those words in his *Notes on the State of Virginia* over two centuries ago. It is still a sobering thought for us today.

CHAPTER THREE
THE VOICE IN THE TEMPLE
JEREMIAH 7–10

"The more we know about the ancients, the more we find that they were like the moderns."

—Henry David Thoreau[1]

If there had been a newspaper published in Jerusalem in Jeremiah's day, successive editions in the year 609 B.C. might have carried headlines like these:

KING JOSIAH WOUNDED IN BATTLE!
Brave monarch brought to Jerusalem to recover

THE KING IS DEAD!
Jehoahaz succeeds father on throne

EGYPT DETHRONES JEHOAHAZ
Monarch reigned only three months

ELIAKIM IS NEW REGENT
Renamed "Jehoiakim" by Pharaoh

Behind these fictitious headlines were tragic events that hastened the decline and collapse of the kingdom of Judah. Zealous for the Lord, King Josiah had led the nation in a reformation during which he restored the temple buildings and removed the idols from the land. But in 609, he didn't heed God's warning and unwisely meddled in a war involving Egypt, Assyria, and Babylon. He was wounded in battle near Megiddo and taken to Jerusalem, where he died (2 Chron. 35:20-27). Though stunned by Josiah's death, the kingdom of Judah didn't see the loss of their king as God's call to national repentance and confession.

Josiah's son Jehoahaz reigned for three months, but was deposed by the king of Egypt and replaced by his brother Eliakim, whom the Egyptian king named "Jehoiakim." (Because of Josiah's defeat, Judah was now an Egyptian vassal state.) During Jehoiakim's eleven years' reign, he led the nation back into their old idolatrous ways. Although Josiah had removed the idols from the land, he couldn't take idol worship out of the hearts of the people.

The Jews didn't actually abandon the temple ministry; they simply brought their idolatry into the temple courts and made Jehovah one of the many gods they worshiped. If you had watched their worship, you would have thought the people were sincerely honoring the Lord, but their hearts belonged to Baal, Ashtoreth, Chemosh, and the other gods and goddesses of the heathen nations around them. Judah paid lip service to Jehovah but gave heart service to idols.

The Jews knew that idolatry was wrong, but they were confident they had nothing to fear. After all, God would *never* permit anything terrible to happen to the city where His holy temple was located! Didn't Judah possess the Law of Moses, and weren't the Jews the children of Abraham and the sons of the covenant? They were God's chosen people! With a religious heritage like that, no evil could ever fall on their kingdom!

God, however, had quite a different view of the matter. He commanded Jeremiah to go up to the temple and proclaim His message to the hypocritical people gathered there. In this courageous sermon, the prophet exposed the nation's *false worship* (Jer. 7:1–8:3), their *false prophets* (8:4-22), their *false confidence* in the covenant they were disobeying (9:1-26), and the *false gods* they were worshiping (10:1-25). In other words, Jeremiah dealt with their sinful mistreatment of the temple, the Law, the covenant, and the Lord Himself. It wasn't a popular message to deliver, and it almost cost him his life!

1. False Worship: the Temple (Jer. 7:1–8:3)

Three times a year, the Jewish men were required to go up to the temple in Jerusalem to celebrate the feasts (Deut. 16:16), and this may have been one of those occasions. The temple was probably crowded, but there weren't many true worshipers there. The prophet stood at one of the gates that led into the temple courts, and there he preached to the people as they came in. He presented God's four indictments against the people of Judah.

"Their worship does them no good" (vv. 1-15). Because they believed the lies of the false prophets, the people thought they could live in sin and still go to the temple and worship a holy God. According to Jeremiah 7:6 and 9, they were guilty of breaking at least five of the Ten Commandments, but the false prophets assured them that the presence of God's temple in Jerusalem guaranteed the nation God's blessing and protection from every enemy. Of course, this wasn't faith; it was blind superstition[2] and Jeremiah quickly shattered their illusions.

Jesus referred to verse 11 after He cleansed the temple (Matt. 21:13). A den of robbers is the place where thieves go to hide after they've committed their crimes. Thus Jeremiah was declaring that *the Jews were using the temple ceremonies to cover up their secret sins.* Instead of being made holy in the temple, the people were making the temple unholy! A century earlier, Isaiah had preached the same message (Isa. 1), and much later Paul wrote a similar warning to Christians in his day (Eph. 5:1-7; Phil. 3:17-21). *Any theology that minimizes God's holiness and tolerates people's deliberate sinfulness is a false theology.*

The people needed to repent, not only to avoid the awful consequences of their sins in their character and their worship, but also to escape the judgment that was certain to come (Jer. 7:12-15). God's covenant with the Jews included both blessings and judgments—blessings if they obeyed and judgments if they rebelled (Deut. 11:26-30; 27:1-26; Josh. 8:30-35). Although the Jews knew this, they continued in their sins and rejected God's warning.

They also conveniently forgot God's past judgments, including His judgment on the tabernacle when it was located in Shiloh. The evil sons of Eli thought that carrying the ark of the covenant into the battle would defeat the Philistines, but they were slain, and the enemy captured the ark. God then wrote *Ichabod* over the tabernacle, which means in Hebrew the "glory has departed" (1 Sam. 4–6; see especially 4:21-22). Yes, God could protect His holy temple if He desired, *but His temple in Jerusalem was no longer holy.* It was a den of thieves! Better there were no temple at all than that hypocrisy should desecrate God's house.

"Your prayers will do them no good" (vv. 16-20). At least three times, God instructed Jeremiah *not* to pray for the people (Jer. 7:16; 11:4; 14:11)—certainly a terrible indictment against them. God had allowed Abraham to pray for wicked Sodom (Gen. 18:23-33), and He had listened when Moses interceded for sinful Israel (Ex. 32–33; Num. 14), but He wouldn't permit Jeremiah to plead for the kingdom of Judah. The people were too far gone in their sins, and all that remained for them was judgment (see 1 Cor. 11:30; 1 John 5:16).

When a nation decays, it begins in the home, and God saw whole families in Jerusalem working together to worship idols (Jer. 7:17-19). If only the parents had helped their children learn of the Lord and worship Him! The Jews, however, worshiped the "Queen of Heaven," which was a title for Ishtar, the Babylonian goddess of love and fertility, whose worship involved abominable obscenities (44:17-19, 25). This sinful worship certainly grieved God, but the people were hurting themselves more than they were hurting the Lord. This pagan immorality was having a devastating effect on their children, and God would send a judgment that would destroy the land, the city, the temple, and people. Judah was sacrificing the permanent for the immediate, and it was a bad bargain.

"Their sacrifices will do them no good" (vv. 21-26). A superficial reading of this paragraph may give the impression that God was denouncing the whole sacrificial system He had given to His people in Exodus and Leviticus, but such is not the case. In an ironic manner, Jeremiah was only reminding the people that the multitude of their sacrifices meant nothing because their hearts were unfaithful to God. God wants obedience and not sacrifice (1 Sam. 15:22), mercy and not religious rituals (Hosea 6:6). "Will the Lord be pleased with thousands of rams or with ten thousands of rivers of oil?" (Micah 6:7) asked the prophet Micah. Then he answered his own question: "He has shown you, O man, what is good; and what does the Lord require of you but to do justly, to love mercy, and to walk humbly with your God?" (v. 8, NKJV; see Matt. 22:34-40).

God's covenant with Israel at Sinai emphasized the demonstration of His grace to the nation and the importance of their obedience to Him (Ex. 19:1-8). Jehovah was marrying a wife, not buying a slave. When Moses in Deuteronomy rehearsed the Law for the new generation, his emphasis was on loving the Lord and obeying Him from the heart (Deut. 6:1-15; 10:12-22; 11:1, 13, 22). To substitute external ritual for internal devotion would make the sacrifices meaningless and rob the heart of God's blessings. The same principle applies to believers today. How easy it is to be busy for the Lord and yet abandon our first love! (Rev. 2:4)

"My discipline and correction do them no good" (7:27-8:3). "This is the nation that has not obeyed the Lord its God or responded to correction" (Jer. 7:28, NIV). Whom the Lord loves, He chastens (Prov. 3:11-12; Heb. 12:5-13), and if we truly know and love the Lord, His chastening will bring us back to Him in contrite obedience. But God told Jeremiah to lament for the dead nation, because they would not repent.

Topheth is an Aramaic word meaning "fireplace," and it sounds much like the Hebrew word meaning "shameful thing." Topheth was the place in the Valley of the Son of Hinnom where the people sacrificed their children to idols by throwing them into the fire (Isa. 30:33). King Josiah had defiled Topheth and turned it into a garbage dump (2 Kings 23:10), but after his death the gruesome pagan rituals were reinstated. The Greek word *gehenna*, meaning hell, comes from the Hebrew *ge' hinnom*, the valley of Hinnom. Hell is a garbage dump where Christ-rejecting sinners will suffer forever with the devil and his angels (Matt. 25:41).

Jeremiah announced that the day would come when the Valley of Hinnom would become a cemetery too small for all the people who would need burial after the Babylonian invasion. The army would plunder the graves and tombs, and the bones of the great leaders and kings would be desecrated on the altars like so many sacrifices to the gods they worshiped. Gehenna would again become a garbage dump, and the corpses of the Jerusalem citizens would be the garbage! "They will not be gathered up or buried, but will be like refuse lying on the ground" (Jer. 8:2, NIV).[3] Many of the people surviving the siege would be carried off to Babylon, and the land would become desolate.

2. False Prophets: the Law (Jer. 8:4-22)

Having shattered the popular illusions about the temple, Jeremiah then exposed the false prophets who constantly opposed his ministry and led the people astray. He raised a number of questions in this section, but the whole proclamation centers on one major question: "Why did the nation not turn back to God?" In answering the question, Jeremiah dealt with three aspects of the people's stubborn refusal to obey God.

Their refusal was irrational (vv. 4-7). Jeremiah used analogies from human life and nature to illustrate his point. When people fall down, they get up again. That's the sensible thing to do. If they find themselves walking on the wrong path, they retrace their steps and get on the right path. Conclusion: if people can be sensible about these everyday matters, why can't they be sensible about eternal matters, especially since the consequences are much more tragic?

They were like horses rushing into battle,

having no idea of the dangers involved. Horses are trained to obey and may not know any better, but people made in the image of God ought to know where they're going. In fact, the people of Judah weren't as smart as the birds! (See Isa. 1:3.) God gave the birds the instinct to know the seasons and the times of their migrations, but He gave people so much more: a spirit within to hear God's voice and understand His Law. Made in the image of God, men and women ought to be as obedient to divine instruction as birds are to natural instinct.

Their refusal was caused by deception (vv. 8-12). "Lo, they have rejected the word of the Lord; and what wisdom is in them?" (Jer. 8:9) Just as they boasted that they possessed the temple, so they boasted that they had the divine Law (v. 8), *but possessing the Scriptures isn't the same as practicing the Scriptures.* Although the Bible is still a best-seller, its popularity isn't keeping Western society from crumbling morally and spiritually. There appears to be no connection between what people say they believe and the way people act.

The false prophets, who claimed to be writing and speaking in the name of the Lord, deceived the kingdom of Judah. They were men whose personal lives were godless, whose hearts were covetous, and whose remedies for the problems of the nation were useless. Their ministry was popular because they majored on the superficial and marketed whatever good news the people wanted to hear (see 5:12; 14:13-15; 27:8-9; 28:1-17). Jeremiah pictured these men as deceitful physicians (6:14; 8:11), empty wind (5:13), dispensers of chaff (23:28), ruthless, selfish shepherds (23:1-4), and infected people spreading disease (23:15, NIV). God had not sent these so-called prophets (14:14; 23:18, 21; 29:9, 31), nor did they receive their messages from God (23:25-28).

What happens to the Lord's people largely depends on the leaders they follow. Worldly leaders attract and produce worldly people, but you pay a price to follow spiritual leadership. It's much easier to drift with the current and go along with the crowd. Jeremiah had few friends or disciples because his message wasn't popular.

Their refusal would lead to judgment (vv. 13-22). These verses blend three voices: God's voice of judgment, the people's voice of despair, and the prophet's voice of anguish as he contemplated the ruin of a once-great nation. God declared that the fields would be ruined (vv. 13, 17), the cities would be destroyed (v. 17), and the people would be either slain or taken captive (v. 19). It would be like drinking poison (8:14; 9:15; 23:15), experiencing an earthquake (8:16), being attacked by venomous snakes (v. 17), or being crushed and broken (v. 21).

How did the people respond? Instead of turning to the Lord, they fled to their walled cities! (v. 14) Their cry of despair was, "Where is the Lord? Why did He allow this to happen?" (see v. 19). But it happened because they were disobedient and unfaithful to the covenant they had made with the Lord. Their situation was hopeless; nobody would come to save them. Verse 20 was the proverb they quoted: "The harvest is past, the summer has ended, and we are not saved." *They had missed their God-given opportunity, and it would never come again.*

Since Jeremiah was a faithful shepherd, he identified with the hurts of the people: his heart fainted (v. 18), and he mourned in horror as he felt the heavy burden that was crushing the land. "For the hurt of the daughter of my people am I hurt" (v. 21). The false prophets had made a wrong diagnosis and prescribed the wrong remedy, and the wounds of the nation were still open, bleeding, and infected. "To the Law and to the testimony! If they do not speak according to this Word, it is because there is no light in them" (Isa. 8:20, NKJV).

3. False Confidence: the Covenant (Jer. 9:1-26)

The Jews are the only nation in history with whom God has entered into a covenant relationship (Gen. 12:1-3). As the children of Abraham, marked by the seal of circumcision (Gen. 17), they are indeed a special people to the Lord (Ex. 19:4-6). The tragedy is that they trusted the covenant and the ritual to guarantee them acceptance before the Lord. They thought they didn't need to repent or believe; that was for the uncircumcised Gentiles. John the Baptist faced this obstacle in his ministry (Matt. 3:7-10), and so did Jesus (John 8:33ff) and Paul (Rom. 2–4). Jeremiah had to deal with the pride of his people as he pointed out to them three obvious truths.

Being God's covenant people is no excuse for sin (vv. 1-6). Like Jesus (Luke 19:41) and Paul (Rom. 9:1-5), Jeremiah wept over the sad spiritual condition of the people, and this is one reason he's known as the weeping prophet (see Jer. 9:18; 10:19; 13:17; 14:17; Lam. 1:16; 2:11, 18; 3:48). It's unusual today to find tears either in the pulpit or the pews; the emphasis seems to be on enjoyment. Instead of evangelists and revivalists, the church now has "religious comedians" who apparently have never read James 4:9-10, "Lament and mourn and weep! Let your laughter be turned to mourning and your joy to gloom. Humble yourselves in the sight of the Lord, and He will lift you up" (NKJV). Vance Havner was right: "Never in history has there been more ribald hilarity with less to be funny about."[4]

Jeremiah would rather have fled from the people to a place of peace (see Ps. 55:6), but he knew that his calling was to stay and minister God's Word (Jer. 40:6). His soul was grieved at the sins of the people, their immorality, idolatry, deception, and slander. Truth was a precious commodity; you couldn't even trust your friends and relatives!

The people of Judah thought they were "free to sin" because they'd been born children of Abraham and were the people of the covenant. On the contrary, being a part of God's covenant gave them a greater responsibility to live to glorify Him and obey His will! "Shall we continue in sin, that grace may abound? God forbid" (Rom. 6:1-2). As I said before, any theology that minimizes personal holiness and excuses sinfulness is not biblical theology.

Being God's covenant people offers no escape from judgment (vv. 7-16). If anything, their favored relationship with the Lord invited an even greater judgment; for everyone to whom much is given, from him much will be required (Luke 12:48). God said to the Jews, "You only have I chosen of all the families of the earth; therefore I will punish you for all your sins" (Amos 3:2, NIV).

That punishment would be like the heat of a furnace (Jer. 9:7). It would leave the cities in ruins, places for animals to dwell; the fruitful fields would become like deserts because nobody would live there and cultivate them. So terrible would the devastation be that even the birds would flee because there would be no places for them to nest. Why would the land of "milk and honey" become a barren wilderness? Because the people disobeyed God's law and turned to idols. They thought their favored status before the Lord would protect them from judgment.

Being God's covenant people is no assurance of spiritual understanding (vv. 17-26). "Let not the wise man glory in his wisdom, let not the mighty man glory in his might, nor let the rich man glory in his riches; but let him who glories glory in this, that he understands and knows Me" (vv. 23-24, NKJV). No amount of education, power, or wealth—three things the world today depends on and boasts about—can guarantee the blessing of God. God doesn't delight in a nation's learning, political influence, armies, or gross national product. He delights in a people who practice kindness, justice, and righteousness because they know and fear the Lord. God promises covenant blessings to those who obey Him, not to those who only submit to religious ceremonies.

God called the nation to lament because they would soon be going to their own funeral. Death was coming, and the politicians and false prophets wouldn't be able to hinder it. Death is pictured as a thief who comes unhindered through the windows to steal precious lives. Bodies would fall "like cut grain behind the reaper" (v. 22, NIV)[5]

The Jews boasted in the covenant sign of circumcision, but it was only in their flesh; the true spiritual circumcision had never reached their hearts (4:4; Deut. 10:16; Acts 7:51; Rom. 2:25-29). People today who depend on baptism and other church sacraments (ordinances), but who have never repented and trusted Christ, are in the same situation as the Jews in Jeremiah's day; they think they're a part of the divine covenant, but their confidence is a false one. Paul was a good example of this: he had to lose his religious righteousness in order to gain Christ! (Phil. 3:1-11)

4. False Gods: the True and Living God (Jer. 10:1-25)

Before Abraham trusted in the true God, he had been a worshiper of idols (Josh. 24:2-3). During their years in Egypt, the Jews were exposed to the gross idolatry of that land, and some of it stayed in their hearts. While Moses was meeting with God on Mt.

Sinai, the people, aided by Moses' brother Aaron, made a golden calf and worshiped it (Ex. 32). At Sinai, they had seen the glory of God, heard the voice of God, and accepted the Law of God; yet "they changed their glory into the image of an ox that eats grass" (Ps. 106:20, NKJV). Idolatry was in their hearts.

Jeremiah looks around and ridicules the idols (vv. 1-16). Instead of separating themselves from the evil practices of the nations as Moses had instructed (Deut. 7:1-11), Israel gradually imitated those practices and began to worship pagan gods. But these gods were worthless, manufactured by craftsmen, "like a scarecrow in a melon patch" (Jer. 10:5, NIV). They can't speak or walk, and they have to be carried around (see Ps. 115). If only the people would contemplate the glory and majesty of the true and living God—the everlasting God who created the heavens and the earth by the Word of His power!

A.W. Tozer reminds us that "the essence of idolatry is the entertainment of thoughts about God that are unworthy of Him."[6] It means worshiping and serving the creature rather than the Creator (Rom. 1:25), the gifts rather than the Giver. The idols were senseless, and so were the people (Jer. 10:8), because we become like the god we worship (Ps. 115:8).

Our contemporary idols aren't ugly as were the pagan idols in Jeremiah's day, but they capture just as much affection and do just as much damage. Whatever we worship and serve other than the true and living God is an idol, whether it's an expensive house or car, the latest stereo equipment, a boat, a library, a girlfriend or boyfriend, our children, a career, or a bank account. That on which I center my attention and affection and for which I am willing to sacrifice is my god, and if it isn't Jesus Christ, then it's an idol. "Little children, keep yourselves from idols" (1 John 5:21).

The remedy for idolatry is for us to get caught up in the majesty and grandeur of God, the true God, the living God, the everlasting King. An idol is a substitute, and you would never want a substitute once you have experienced the love and power of the Lord God Almighty.

Jeremiah looks ahead and laments the judgment that is coming (vv. 17-22). Jeremiah saw the invasion of the Babylonian army and the distress it would bring. He urged the people to pack their bags and get ready to move, because they would be hurled out of the land like stones from slings. The prophet lamented the ruin of houses and families, the separation of parents and children, the scattering of God's precious flock.

Jeremiah pointed out the reason for this disaster: the shepherds (political and spiritual leaders; KJV "pastors") didn't seek the Lord but instead led the people astray (Jer. 10:21). The judgment came "for the sins of her prophets, and the iniquities of her priests" (Lam. 4:13). A nation went into captivity because its leaders forsook the true and living God.

Jeremiah looks up and prays for mercy (vv. 23-25). God had instructed Jeremiah not to pray for the nation (Jer. 7:16), so he didn't. Instead, he prayed for himself as a representative of the nation. Once again, he identified with the pain of the people (10:19). This prayer presents three arguments to persuade the Lord to be merciful to His people.

First, God must remember that they are only weak humans who don't know how to run their own lives (v. 23). Jeremiah may have been thinking of Psalm 103:13-16.

Second, if God gave them what they deserved, they would be destroyed (Jer. 10:24). Again, Psalm 103:10 comes to mind: "He has not dealt with us according to our sins, nor punished us according to our iniquities" (NKJV). As Ezra expressed it, God punishes us "less [than] our iniquities deserve" (Ezra 9:13).

His third argument was that the nations attacking Judah deserved punishment for seeking to destroy God's chosen people (Jer. 10:25). God called Babylon to be His tool to chasten the Jews, not to wipe them out, but the Babylonians were ruthless in their treatment of Judah. The prophet wasn't giving vent to his own personal wrath; he was pleading for the Lord to keep His promises to Abraham and protect the nation from extinction (Gen. 12:1-3). God answered that prayer and eventually brought an end to the savage rule of Babylon (see Jer. 50–51).7

It was on this note that Jeremiah ended his "temple sermon." The results? According to Jeremiah 26, he was seized and condemned to die! Rather than hear and obey the true Word of God, the priests would rather commit murder! The Lord saved Jeremiah from being killed, but he was banished from the temple (36:5). I wonder how many preachers today would boldly preach a message they knew would result in their being dismissed? And I wonder how many in the congregation would be willing to accept that message and obey it?

God didn't promise Jeremiah an easy ministry, but He did promise to keep him strong (1:7-8, 17-19). He kept His promise to Jeremiah, and He will keep His promises to His servants today.

CHAPTER FOUR
VOTING WITH GOD
JEREMIAH 11–13

Whoso who would be a man must be a nonconformist."

—R.W. Emerson[1]

In his poem "The Need of the Hour", the American poet Edwin Markham wrote:

We need the faith to go a path untrod,
The power to be alone and vote with God.

That's what Jeremiah was doing during the reign of King Josiah—He was walking alone and voting with God. King Josiah was excited when the workmen repairing the temple found the Book of the Law (2 Kings 22), and this discovery led to a movement that temporarily cleansed the kingdom of idolatry (2 Kings 23). This event is commonly called "Josiah's revival," but "reformation" might be a more accurate word. Why? Because the people obeyed the Law only outwardly; in their hearts they still held on to their idols.

Because Jeremiah understood this and knew the shallowness of the unrepentant human heart, he wasn't too vocal during Josiah's reformation.[2] He knew what the people were doing in secret and that they would return to their sins at the first opportunity. In this section of his prophecy, Jeremiah recorded the sins of the nation and pleaded with the people to return to the Lord while there was yet time.

1. Breaking God's Covenant (Jer. 11:1-8)

The king and the people had publicly promised the Lord that they would obey the terms of His covenant (2 Kings 23:3), and there's no question that the king was sincere. With most of the people, however, their obedience was only a matter of going along with the crowd and doing what was popular.

The history of the Jews is the record of covenants: God made them and the people broke them. He made a covenant with Abraham when He called him to leave Ur and go to Canaan (Gen. 12:1-3), and He confirmed this covenant with Isaac (26:1-5) and Jacob (35:1-15). The Abrahamic Covenant is the basis for all the blessings Israel has received from the Lord.

At Sinai, God entered into another covenant with Israel, one that involved obedience to His holy Law (Ex. 19–20). "Now therefore, if you will indeed obey My voice and keep My covenant, then you shall be a special treasure to Me above all people; for all the earth is Mine" (19:5, NKJV). The people agreed to obey the Lord (v. 8), but it didn't take long for them to disobey. While they were still at Sinai, they made an idol and worshiped it (Ex. 32).

Before Israel entered the land of Canaan, Moses reviewed the covenant (the Book of Deuteronomy) and reminded the people of their obligations to the Lord. Their *ownership* of the land depended on God's promise to Abraham, but their *possession* and *enjoyment* of the land depended on their obedience to God's Law. Moses reviewed the blessings and the curses (Deut. 27–28); later, Joshua reaffirmed them in the Promised Land (Josh. 8:30-35). The Jewish people knew that God would bless them if they were true to Him and that He would chasten them if they were disobedient.

The land of Egypt had been an "iron furnace" to Israel (Jer. 11:4), a place of suffering (Deut. 4:20; 1 Kings 8:51; Isa. 48:10); but Canaan was "a land flowing with milk and honey" (Jer. 11:5), a place of prosperity and freedom. God described the Promised Land to Moses in this way (Ex. 3:8, 17; see 33:3), and Moses repeated this description to the people (Lev. 20:24; Deut. 6:3; 11:9; 26:9, 15; 27:3; 31:20). Sad to say, the nation preferred the fleshpots of Egypt to the milk and honey of Canaan (Ex. 16:3; Num. 11:4-5) and repeatedly wanted to go back to Egypt.

During Josiah's reformation when the nation seemed to be turning back to the Lord, God commanded Jeremiah to go through the streets of Jerusalem and declare the terms of His covenant to the people. Both God and Jeremiah knew that the nation's obedience wasn't from the heart. No matter what they were doing in the temple, the people were still visiting the high places and honoring the gods of the nations around them.

The Prophet Ezekiel described their sin perfectly when he wrote, "Son of man, these men have set up their idols in their heart" (Ezek. 14:3). A century earlier, Isaiah had described Judah's empty, hypocritical worship, comparing Jerusalem to Sodom and Gomorrah (Isa. 1:10ff). The people brought abundant sacrifices, but God didn't need them or want them. Their incense was an abomination, their annual feasts were sinful activities, and God hated it all and was tired of it. "If you are willing and obedient, you shall eat the good of the land; but if you refuse and rebel, you shall be devoured by the sword" (Isa. 1:19-20, NIV).

God told Jeremiah to remind the people of both the blessings and the curses written in the covenant. If God's blessings couldn't motivate them to obey His commandments, perhaps the fear of God's judgment might cause them to obey. God had to treat His people like little children who obey either to get a reward or to escape a spanking. How He longed for them to obey because they loved Him and wanted to please Him![3]

Jeremiah answered "So be it!" (Jer. 11:5) to God's words, which is the way Israel was supposed to respond to God's covenant (see Deut. 27:9-26; Josh. 8:30-35). But the prophet was walking alone; the people weren't interested in doing the will of the Lord. Had the nation repented and turned humbly to the Lord, the people could have averted the terrible judgment brought by the armies of Babylon. As it was, their hypocrisy made that judgment only worse.

2. Conspiring against God's Authority (Jer. 11:9–12:6)

The Lord revealed to His servant a twofold conspiracy in the land: a conspiracy of the men of Judah to disobey the covenant and resist the reforms led by King Josiah (11:9-17), and a conspiracy of the people in Jeremiah's hometown to kill the prophet and silence God's Word (11:18–12:6). Both led to a third crisis that threatened Jeremiah's own faith in the Lord.

The conspiracy against the king (vv. 9-17) was actually a hidden rebellion against God's covenant and the reforms that Josiah was bringing to the land. Unless the Word of God is obeyed and worked out practically in our lives, God can't bless us as He desires to do. The people, however, preferred to break the covenant and worship false gods.

But *what* we worship and *the way* we worship are not incidentals in life; they're essentials that determine the character of life itself. "A people's lives are only as good as their worship," writes Eugene Peterson. "Worship defines life. If worship is corrupt, life will be corrupt."[4] God gave His people the covenant so He might bless them and keep the good promises He made to them, but His people preferred to trust the gods of their pagan neighbors.

Worship has consequences, either good or bad, and in the case of Judah, the consequences were bad. The people knew that the curses and judgments were written into the covenant, but they thought God wouldn't send judgment on His own chosen people. Wasn't God's temple in Jerusalem? Wasn't the ark of the covenant there? And didn't the priests have the Law? Would God allow these sacred things to be destroyed? But God always keeps His promises, whether to bless or to chasten, and the greater the privileges we have from Him, the greater the responsibility we have to Him.

Disaster was coming to Judah, and nothing could change it. The people could cry out to their gods, but their gods wouldn't answer them. Even if the people turned back to Jehovah and begged for His help, He wouldn't answer them. Therefore, the Lord commanded Jeremiah a second time not to pray for the people (11:14; see 7:16; 14:11). The people worshiped as many gods as there were cities in Judah, and there were as many altars as streets in Jerusalem. Yet none of these things could rescue the nation from the terrible judgment that was coming.

God presented two pictures of His people that reveal how futile their religious faith really was: a worshiper in the temple (11:15) and a tree in the storm (vv. 17-18). God called the nation "my beloved," reminding them of their marriage contract and how unfaithful they had been to Him. Their worship in the temple should have been an expression of their true love to Him, but instead it was an exercise in futility. Offering sacrifices could never avert God's judgment; the people were merely engaging in wickedness (v. 15, NIV). When worship becomes wickedness, and people rejoice in sinning, then the light has turned into darkness (Matt. 6:22-24), and there is no hope.

In Scripture, trees sometimes symbolize individuals (Jer. 17:8; Pss. 1:3; 52:8; 92:12; Zech. 4:3) and sometimes nations or kingdoms (Isa. 10:33-34; 18:5; Ezek. 17; 31). Israel is compared to an olive tree in Jeremiah 11:16-17, an image Paul used in Romans 11. The olive tree is prized in the Near East because of its fruit and the useful oil made from it. Judah thought of herself as a "thriving olive tree" (Jer. 11:16, NIV) that would never fall, but God saw a storm coming, and the wind would break the branches and the lightning would set the tree on fire. Jerusalem would be broken down and burned like a useless olive tree.

If the greatest sin is the corruption of the highest good, then Judah was guilty of great sin. Their highest good was to know the true God and worship Him, but they perverted that blessing and worshiped idols. They turned His temple into a den of thieves, persecuted His prophets, rejected His covenant, and disgraced His name. "God's name is blasphemed among the Gentiles because of you" (Rom. 2:24, NIV; see Ezek. 36:22). God patiently dealt with His people, seeking to woo them back, but they only hardened their hearts and turned a deaf ear to His warnings.

Before we condemn the people of Judah, however, let's examine our own hearts and churches. Are there idols in our hearts? Do we give wholehearted devotion to the Lord, or is our devotion divided between Christ and another? When unsaved people visit our worship services, are they impressed with the glory and majesty of God? (1 Cor. 14:23-25) Do the worldly lives and questionable activities of professed believers disgrace God's name? Remember, God's "last word" to the church isn't the Great Commission; it's "Repent, or else!" (Rev. 2–3)

The conspiracy against Jeremiah (vv. 18-23) grew out of the people's rejection of God's Word, for if they had accepted the Word of God, they would have honored His prophet and listened to what he had to say. You would think that the priests in Anathoth would have had more discernment than to listen to the false prophets, but holding a religious office is no guarantee that people possess spiritual wisdom.

The men of Anathoth, Jeremiah's hometown, plotted to kill him because his message convicted them. Rather than repent, they decided to destroy the messenger. But they had a second reason: as loyal Jews, they felt that his prophecies were harmful to the welfare of the nation. Jeremiah preached impending judgment from Babylon, while the false prophets were declaring messages of peace (Jer. 6:14; 8:11). Jeremiah insisted that the people obey the Law and bring their sacrifices to the temple and not to the local shrines (high places), some of which were dedicated to idols, and the priests didn't like that. Jeremiah was pro-Babylon while the rulers were pro-Egypt. In other words, Jeremiah was out of step with his times, and because he was decisive, he had to walk alone and "vote with God."

Until God warned him about it, Jeremiah knew nothing about the plot against his life, and when he heard the news, he felt like a helpless lamb being led to the slaughter (11:19, see Isa. 53:7). All he could do was commit himself and his enemies to the Lord and trust God to work. This is the first of several occasions in his life when Jeremiah privately poured out his heart to the Lord and asked Him to right his battles and help him with his depression and fears (Jer. 11:19-20; 12:1-4; 15:10-17; 17:12-18; 18:20-23; 20:7-18). Publicly, Jeremiah was bold before people, but privately he was broken before God. God assured His servant that his enemies would be dealt with when the day of disaster came and the Babylonians captured Jerusalem.

A theological crisis followed (vv. 1-6). No sooner did God take care of the two conspiracies than Jeremiah found himself struggling with a theological crisis (12:1-6). "In the commencement of the spiritual life," wrote the French mystic Madame Guyon, "our hardest task is to bear with our neighbor; in its progress, with ourselves; and in its end, with God." Jeremiah couldn't understand why a holy God would permit the false prophets and the unfaithful priests to prosper in their ministries while he, a faithful servant of God, was treated like a sacrificial lamb.

"Why does the way of the wicked prosper?" (v. 1, NIV) is a question that was asked frequently in Scripture, and it's being asked today. Job wrestled with it (Job 12; 21); the psalmists tried to understand it (Pss. 37; 49; 73); and other prophets besides Jeremiah grappled with the problem (Hab. 1; Mal. 2:17; 3:15). Jewish theologians, pointing to the covenants, taught that God blesses those who obey and judges those who disobey, but the situation in real life seemed just the opposite! How could a holy God of love allow such a thing to happen?[5]

Jeremiah, however, was seeking more than answers to questions; he was also concerned for the welfare of his people. He saw the land distressed because of the sins of the leaders, with many innocent people suffering. God had sent drought to the nation, which was one of the covenant disciplines (Deut. 28:15-24), and the vegetation was withering and the animal life dying. But the evil leaders who were to blame for the drought were not only surviving but also were prospering from the losses of others.

This didn't seem fair, and Jeremiah complained to the Lord. "Why do all the faithless live at ease?" (Jer. 12:1, NIV) "How long will the land lie parched?" (v. 4) "Why?" and "How long?" are questions that are easy to ask but difficult to answer.

Jeremiah's suggested solution was that God judge the wicked and drag them away like cattle to be slaughtered (v. 3). After all, the men of Anathoth were ready to kill him like a sacrificial lamb (11:19). So why shouldn't they receive from God the same fate they had planned for him?

God's reply to Jeremiah, however, wasn't what he expected (12:5-6). *God's focus was not on the wicked; it was on His servant Jeremiah.* As most of us do when we're suffering, Jeremiah was asking, "*How* can I get out of this?" But he should have been asking, "*What* can I get out of this?" God's servants don't live by explanations; they live by promises. Understanding explanations may satisfy our curiosity and make us smarter people, but laying hold of God's promises will build our character and make us better servants.

God's reply revealed three important truths to Jeremiah. First, *the life of godly service isn't easy*; it's like running a race. (Paul used a similar figure in Phil. 3:12-14.) Had he remained a priest, Jeremiah probably would have had a comfortable and secure life, but the life of a prophet was just the opposite. He was like a man running a race and having a hard time keeping up.

Second, *the life of service becomes harder, not easier.* Jeremiah had been running with the foot soldiers and had kept up with them, but now he'd be racing with the horses. In spite of his trials, he'd been living in a land of peace. Now, however, he'd be tackling the thick jungles of the Jordan River, where the wild beasts prowled. His heart had been broken because of the attacks of outsiders, but now *his own family* would start opposing him.

The third truth grows out of the other two: *the life of service gets better as we grow more mature.* Each new challenge (horses, jungles, opposition of relatives) helped Jeremiah develop his faith and grow in his ministry skills. The easy life is ultimately the hard life, because the easy life stifles maturity, but the difficult life challenges us to develop our "spiritual muscles" and accomplish more for the Lord. Phillips Brooks said the purpose of life is the building of character through truth, and you don't build character by being a spectator. You have to run with endurance the race God sets before you *and do it on God's terms* (Heb. 12:1-3).

"It was the answer Jeremiah needed," said Scottish preacher Hugh Black. "He needed to be braced, not pampered."[6] One of my relatives, when a boy, deliberately failed third grade so he wouldn't have to go into fourth grade *and write with ink*! Today, our grandchildren are learning to use simple computer programs in grade school so they'll be prepared to use more difficult programs in high school and college. There's no growth without challenge, and there's no challenge without change. As they get older, many people resist change, forgetting that without the challenge of change, they're in danger of deteriorating physically, mentally, and spiritually. God wanted Jeremiah to grow, and He also wants us to grow.

Gilbert K. Chesterton put it this way: "The fatal metaphor of progress, which means leaving things behind us, has utterly obscured the real idea of growth, which means leaving things inside us."[7] God was concerned about the development within the prophet, not just the difficulties around him. God could handle the problem people in Judah, but God couldn't force His servant to grow. Only Jeremiah could make that choice by staying in the race, accepting new challenges, and thereby maturing in the Lord.

3. Ignoring God's Warnings (Jer. 12:7–13:27)

God used what Jeremiah said and did to speak to the people of Judah and warn them of the terrible judgment that was coming. Comfortable in their false confidence and encouraged by the false prophets, the leaders and people of Judah were living in a fool's paradise, certain that nothing terrible could happen to either the Holy City or the temple. Note the eight vivid images that depict the judgment that was about to fall.

The rejected inheritance (vv. 7-17). The people of Israel were God's special inheritance (Ex. 19:5-6; Deut. 4:20; 32:9), and the land of Canaan was their inheritance from Him (Ex. 15:17; Ps. 78:55). The land belonged to the Lord and was only loaned to the Jews for them to use (Lev. 25:23). The people were to obey the laws that protected the land from abuse and defilement, but they disobeyed those laws and defiled their inheritance (Lev. 18:25, 27; Deut. 21:23). God disciplined them by taking them out of the Promised Land and deporting them to Babylon. This gave the land of Israel opportunity to be healed (Lev. 26:34-43; 2 Chron. 36:21; Jer. 25:9-12).

You can't miss the anguish of God's heart as He spoke concerning His beloved people. Instead of loving Him, they were roaring at Him like an angry lion, and He couldn't express His love to them as He yearned to do.[8] Judah's enemies were like birds of prey and wild beasts, just waiting to attack.

The leaders of those nations ("shepherds," "pastors") and their armies would turn the beautiful vineyard into a wasteland, and the Jewish people would be uprooted from their inheritance. The people of the neighboring nations—Syria, Moab, and Ammon—who had attacked Judah in the past would also be punished by Babylon, and some of them would also be taken captive. The Lord, however, added a word of hope: "I will return, and have compassion on them, and will bring them again, every man to his heritage, and every man to his land" (Jer. 12:15). The people would be in captivity for seventy years (25:11-12; 29:10) and then be permitted to return to their land and restore their temple and nation. God would invite the people of the other nations to worship Him—the true and living God—and they would no longer teach His people how to worship false gods.

The marred waistcloth (vv. 1-11). This was one of Jeremiah's "action sermons."[9] The waistcloth was a thigh-length undergarment worn next to the skin. God had brought the nation close to Himself, but they had defiled themselves with idols and become "good for nothing." When the people saw Jeremiah bury his new garment under a rock in the muddy river, they knew it would ruin the garment, but they didn't realize they were passing judgment on themselves. God would one day take Judah to Babylon, and there He would humble the Judahites and cure them of their idolatry. The city and temple that they were proud of would be ruined, just as the prophet's garment had been ruined.

But something else was involved in this "action sermon." For years, the leaders of Judah had turned to Egypt, Assyria, and Babylon for "help," instead of turning to the Lord, and this help had only defiled them and made them "good for nothing" in God's sight. Jeremiah was showing them that their flirting with the pagan nations was only alienating them further from the Lord and that it would ultimately end in national ruin.

The staggering drunkards (vv. 12-14). Jeremiah used a familiar proverb as his text: "Every [wineskin][10] shall be filled with wine" (13:12). The proverb expresses the assurance that there will be peace and prosperity for the nation, not unlike the American proverb, "A chicken in every pot."[11] With a broken heart, the prophet saw the leaders getting drunk when they should have been soberly seeking the Lord (see Isa. 28:1-8), and he knew that a cup of wrath was about to be poured out on the land (Jer. 25:15ff). The leaders and the people of Jerusalem were filling their jars with wine, preparing for a party, but God would fill them with a drunkenness that would lead to shameful defeat and painful destruction. They would crash into one another and destroy one another like clay pots smashed in a siege. Paul used the image of drunkenness to admonish the church to be ready for the Lord's return (1 Thes. 5:1-11).

The stumbling traveler (vv. 15-16). When Jeremiah called to the people, "Hear ye and give ear [pay attention]!" (Jer. 13:15) he was giving them opportunity to repent and turn to the Lord. He compared them to a traveler on an unfamiliar and dangerous mountain trail, without a map and without light, hoping for the dawn. Instead of the light dawning, however, the darkness only deepens. In centuries past, God had led His people by pillars of cloud and fire. Now He wanted to lead them through the words of His prophet, but the people wouldn't follow. *If we reject God's light, nothing remains but darkness.* The leaders were too proud to admit they were lost, and they wouldn't ask for directions.

The captive flock (vv. 17-20). Jeremiah wept as he saw the Lord's flock being taken captive, defenseless sheep heading for the slaughter. What caused this great tragedy? The shepherds (rulers of Judah) selfishly exploited the sheep and refused to obey the Word of the Lord (23:1ff). Jeremiah spoke to King Jehoiachin and Nehushta, the queen mother (2 Kings 24:8-20), and admonished them to repent and humble themselves, but they refused to listen. Babylon would swoop down from the north and the nation would be ruined. "Pride goes before destruction, a haughty spirit before a fall" (Prov. 16:18, NIV).

The woman in travail (v. 21). This is a familiar biblical image of suffering, and it's usually associated with judgment (Jer. 4:31; 6:24; 22:23; 30:6; 49:24; 50:43; 1 Thes. 5:3). The message of the verse is "The people you sought as allies will come and be your masters. Then what will you say? You'll be so gripped with pain that you won't be able to say anything." Had they looked to Jehovah as their ally, He wouldn't have failed them; but they trusted Babylon, and Babylon turned out to be their enemy.

The disgraced prostitute (vv. 22-23, 26-27). According to the Law of Moses, prostitution was not permitted in the land (Lev. 19:29; 21:7, 14), and public exposure sometimes disgraced the prostitutes. If a prostitute discovers herself stripped, shamed, and abused, why should she be surprised? That's what she asked for! The people of Judah prostituted themselves to heathen idols and turned to godless nations for help. Now they were asking, "Why have all of these things happened to us?" People may live as though sin has no consequences, but those consequences will come just the same. Just as Ethiopians can't change the color of their skin or the leopard remove its spots, so the wicked nation can't naturally do anything good. These people are too accustomed to committing evil. Only God can change the human heart.

The blown chaff (vv. 24-25). God compared the wicked nation to chaff that will be blown away (Ps. 1:4; see Matt. 3:12). Chaff is the useless by-product of the harvesting process. The workers throw the grain into the air, and the desert wind blows the chaff away. Sin had so cheapened the kingdom of Judah that the people were worthless, fit only to be blown away. They forgot their Lord, believed lies, and would not repent of their sins.

How patient the Lord was with His people, and how patient His servant was to minister to them! Jeremiah was willing to walk alone and "vote with God" so his people might have an opportunity to be saved, but they spurned his message.

God is still "long-suffering to us-ward, not willing that any should perish, but that all should come to repentance" (2 Peter 3:9, KJV). Unlike the people of Judah, let us listen to His Word and obey Him; for only then can we escape His discipline and enjoy His blessings.

CHAPTER FIVE
SERMONS, SUPPLICATIONS, AND SOBS
JEREMIAH 14–17

Our modern age is a pushover for the shallow and the shortcut. We want to change everything except the human heart."
—J. Wallace Hamilton[1]

"Preaching that costs nothing accomplishes nothing."[2] The famous British preacher John Henry Jowett made that statement, and it certainly applies to the prophet Jeremiah. Pained by the sins of his people, declaring unpopular messages that majored on judgment, and perplexed by what the Lord was allowing him to suffer, Jeremiah paid a great price to be faithful to his divine calling. If ever an Old Testament servant had to "take up his cross" in order to follow the Lord, it was Jeremiah.

In these chapters, the prophet delivered four messages, and interspersed with these messages were his own prayers to the Lord and the answers he received. Jeremiah was bold before men but broken before God, and yet it was his brokenness that gave him his strength.

1. A Message about the Drought (Jer. 14:1-22)

Unlike the land of Egypt, whose food supply depended on irrigation from the Nile River, the land of Canaan depended on the rains God sent from heaven (Deut. 11:10-12). If His people obeyed His Law, God would send the rains[3] and give them bumper crops (Lev. 26:3-5), but if they disobeyed, the heaven would become like iron and the earth like bronze (Lev. 26:18-20; Deut. 11:13-17; 28:22-24). Over the years, Judah's sins had brought a series of droughts to the land[4] (see Jer. 3:3; 5:24; 12:4; 23:10), and Jeremiah used this painful but timely topic as the basis for a sermon to the people.

The plight of the land (vv. 1-6). Whether in the cities (14:1-3), the farms (v. 4), or the open country (vv. 5-6), no matter where you looked throughout Judah, you found suffering and privation. The land was in mourning and its citizens were lamenting, like people at a funeral. Because of the sins of the people, God was withholding the life-giving rains and thus keeping His covenant promise to Israel. It made no difference how rich you were, there wasn't any water to be found. The rivers were dry, the cisterns were empty, and both the servants in the cities and the farmers in the country covered their heads like people in a funeral procession. Even the animals were suffering because of the sins of the people. The doe, usually faithful to her young, abandoned her newborn fawn to starve to death, and the wild donkeys, their eyes glazed, could only stand on the barren heights and pant hopelessly for water.

It's a serious thing to enter into a covenant relationship with God, because He will always keep His Word, either to bless or to chasten. If we are the recipients of His love, then we can expect to be the recipients of His chastening if we disobey Him (Prov. 3:11-12). God is always faithful.

The plea of the people (vv. 7-12). As people usually do when they're in trouble, the Jews turned to God and prayed, but their prayers were insincere and not linked with repentance. Jeremiah had already confronted these pious hypocrites with their sins when he asked, "Will you steal, murder, commit adultery, swear falsely, burn incense to Baal, and walk after other gods whom you do not know, and then come and stand before Me in this house which is called by My name, and say, 'We are delivered to do all these abominations?'" (Jer. 7:9-10, NKJV)

Because they couldn't plead for help on the basis of their repentance and God's covenant promise (Deut. 30:1-10; 2 Chron. 7:12-15), the people of Judah asked God to help them for His own name's sake. "After all," they argued, "it's Your reputation that's at stake, because we're called by Your name." The Hope and Savior of Israel was like a tourist in the land, unconcerned about either its present condition or its future destruction. The Lord was like a person shocked into paralysis or a warrior completely without strength.

When God disciplines us, it isn't enough that we pray and ask for His help; anybody in trouble can do that. We must repent of our sins, judge and confess them, and sincerely seek the face of God. To weep because of the sufferings that sin causes is to show remorse but not repentance. "Rend your heart and not your garments" (Joel 2:13) was the prophet Joel's counsel to the Jews during another time of great calamity; and David, when he sought God's forgiveness, said, "The sacrifices of God are a broken spirit: a broken and a contrite heart, O God, Thou wilt not despise" (Ps. 51:17).

God responded to the people's words, not by sending rain, but by announcing judgment! (Jer. 14:10) For the third time, He told His servant Jeremiah not to pray for the people (v. 11; see 7:16; 11:14). His long-suffering had run out, and He was determined to punish them for their sins. They could fast, pray, and bring sacrifices, but nothing would change His mind. The nation was destined for the sword, famine, and, pestilence (14:12). The Babylonian army would bring the sword, and the results of its devastating invasion would be famine and pestilence.[5]

The protest of the prophet (vv. 13-16). "But is it really the fault of the people?" Jeremiah asked. "Aren't the people being led astray by the false prophets who are promising them deliverance and peace? *They* are the real culprits" (see 5:12; 6:14; 8:11). God agreed that the prophets were leading the people astray through their false visions and lies, and He assured Jeremiah that these people would suffer for what they had done. The day would come when they and their families would be slain and nobody would bury their corpses—one of the most humiliating things that could happen to a Jew.

The people, however, were responsible for their actions because they should have known that the Lord had not sent these prophets. There were two tests of a true prophet or prophetess in Israel: (1) their predictions were 100 percent accurate (Deut. 18:20-22),[6] and (2) their messages agreed with the Law of God (13:1-18). *Any prophet who permitted the worship of idols, contrary to God's Law, was a false prophet.* "To the law and to the testimony: if they speak not according to this word, it is because there is no light in them" (Isa. 8:20, KJV). Even if a professed prophet performed miracles, he or she was a counterfeit if God's revealed truth in the Word did not support the message. Miracles are no guarantee of a divine call (2 Thes. 2:7-12).

The pain and prayer of the prophet (vv. 17-22). How did Jeremiah feel about his people? The same way God felt: he wept for them (Jer. 9:18; 13:17) the way a father would weep for a virgin daughter who had been violated, beaten, and left to die. In prophetic vision, the prophet saw the land ravaged and the people taken captive to Babylon (14:18), and this led him to turn to God in prayer.

Since Jeremiah had been commanded not to pray *for* the nation (14:11), he identified himself *with* the people and used the pronouns "we" and "us," not "they" and "them" (see Neh. 1:4-10; Ezra 9; Dan. 9; Rom. 9:1-3). In praying for himself, he was praying for them, and he asked God to honor His own name and keep His covenant by sending healing to the land. Although God was certainly willing to keep *His* part of the covenant, the people weren't willing to keep their part. Therefore, the prophet's prayer went unanswered. A faithful God cannot violate His own Word.

Sometimes God permits disasters to occur to bring nations, churches, and individuals to their knees in repentance. The plagues of Egypt should have made Pharaoh a contrite man, but he only hardened his heart even more against the Lord (Ex. 7–12). Israel's treatment of the nations in Canaan was God's judgment because these nations refused to turn from their sins (Gen. 15:16; see Dan. 8:23; Matt. 23:32-35). While we shouldn't interpret every calamity as an expression of divine wrath, we must be sensitive to God and be willing to search our hearts and confess our sins.

2. A Message about the Coming Captivity (Jer. 15:1-21)

Before the Jews even entered the Promised Land, Moses had rehearsed with them the terms of the covenant, warning them that God would remove them from the land if they refused to obey His voice (Deut. 28:63-68). No sooner did Joshua and that generation of spiritual leaders pass from the scene (Jud. 2:7-15) than the nation turned to idolatry and God had to chasten them. First, He punished them *in the land* by allowing other nations to invade and take control. Then, when the people cried out for help, He raised up deliverers (vv. 16-23). By the time of Jeremiah, however, the sins of the people were so great that God had to remove them *from the land* and punish them in distant Babylon.

Two responses are recorded in this chapter: the Lord's response to Jeremiah's prayer (Jer. 15:1-9) and Jeremiah's response to the Lord's answer (vv. 10-21).

The Lord's response to Jeremiah's prayer (vv. 1-9). No matter who sought to intercede for Judah, God's mind was made up, and He would not relent. At critical times in Jewish history, Moses and Samuel had interceded for the people, and God heard and answered (Ex. 32–34; Num. 14; 1 Sam. 7; 12; Ps. 99:6-8). But God's heart would go out to the people no longer. Instead, His people would go out into captivity. "Send them away from my presence! Let them go!" (Jer. 15:1, NIV)

The people faced four possible judgments: death from disease, war, starvation, or, if they survived these calamities, exile in Babylon.[7] The bodies of those slain by the Babylonian army would be desecrated and eaten by dogs, birds, or wild beasts; none would have a decent burial. It wasn't a bright future that God revealed to His people, but it was a future they themselves had chosen by refusing to repent of their sins. You take what you want from life and you pay for it.

God had chosen the Jews to be a blessing to the nations of the world (Gen. 12:1-3), but now they would become "abhorrent to all the kingdoms of the earth" (v. 4, NIV; see 24:9; 29:18; 34:17; Deut. 28:25), an object of scorn, "a byword among the nations" (Ps. 44:14, NIV). Not only that, but Jerusalem and the land itself would bear witness to God's judgment of their sins. "Their land will be laid waste, an object of lasting scorn; all who pass by will be appalled and will shake their heads" (Jer. 18:16, NIV; see 19:8; 25:9, 18; 29:18).

One of the causes for this terrible judgment was King Manasseh, who reigned for fifty-five years (697–642 B.C.) and was the most wicked king in Judah's history (2 Kings 21:1-18; 2 Chron. 33:1-10). He was the son of godly Hezekiah and the grandfather of godly Josiah, and yet he himself was an evil man who encouraged Judah in the sins that brought about the downfall of the kingdom. God wasn't punishing the nation for the sins Manasseh committed but because the nation imitated Manasseh in their sinning.

In fact, the Lord lamented over the suffering that would come to His people because of their disobedience (Jer. 15:5-9). Would anybody pity Jerusalem or even ask about her welfare? Nehemiah did (Neh. 1:1-3), and centuries later, Jesus wept over the city (Matt. 23:37). For God to postpone judgment would have meant encouraging the nation's sins even more, and this He would not do. He was weary with repenting (Jer. 15:6).[8]

The coming judgment would be like separating wheat from the chaff (v. 7; see 51:2). The wives would become widows, and the mothers would be bereaved of their sons. A woman with seven sons would be considered especially blessed, but if all of them were killed in battle, it would be as though the sun went down at noon, cutting the day short. The light of her life would be gone because the future of the family had been destroyed.

We must not think that God enjoyed sending judgment to His people. If He has no pleasure in the death of *the wicked* (Ezek. 18:23, 32), He certainly has no pleasure in the death of *His own people*! God is long-suffering, but when His people resist His gracious call and rebel against His will, He has no alternative but to send chastening.

Jeremiah's response to the Lord's message (vv. 10-21). This is the third of Jeremiah's recorded laments (see 11:18-23). If the mothers of the dead soldiers had reason to weep (Jer. 15:8-9), Jeremiah's mother had even more reason, for the people treated him as though he were the enemy. The soldiers died as heroes, but Jeremiah lived as if he were a traitor to his own people. Jeremiah wasn't a creditor, pressuring his borrowers. Nevertheless, everybody hated him. God promised to deliver him (v. 5), and He kept His promise, but God didn't promise to shield him from persecution. Jeremiah was now running with the horses, and it wasn't easy (12:5).

In resisting Nebuchadnezzar, Judah was fighting a losing battle, for nothing could break the "northern iron" of Babylon. Judah would lose its treasures and become slaves of the Babylonians. This wasn't a popular message to proclaim, and Jeremiah knew it would arouse the opposition of the leaders and the people. Therefore, he asked God for the help he needed to keep going. His requests were "Remember me, care for me, and avenge me of my enemies."

Jeremiah 15:15-18 reveals the turmoil that was in the prophet's heart and mind. One minute he was affirming the Lord's long-suffering and his own faithfulness to the Word,[9] and the next minute he was crying out with pain because of the suffering of his people and the difficulty of his work. He even suggested that God had lied to him when He called him and that God was "like a deceptive brook, like a spring that fails" (v. 18, NIV; see Job 6:15-20).

Jeremiah was human and had his failings, but at least he honestly admitted them to God. Instead of piously covering up his true feelings, he poured out his heart to the Lord, and the Lord answered him. God's answer may have shocked the prophet, for the Lord told him he needed to repent! "If you repent, I will restore you that you may serve me; if you utter worthy, not worthless, words, you will be my spokesman" (Jer. 15:19, NIV). Because of his attitude toward God and his calling, Jeremiah was about to forfeit his ministry! In some ways, he was mirroring the words and attitudes of the people of Judah when they questioned God.

The Lord usually balances rebuke with reassurance. He promised once again to make Jeremiah a fortified wall and give him victory over all his enemies (v. 20; see 1:18-19). Jeremiah had to learn to walk by faith, which meant obeying God's Word no matter how he felt, what he saw, or what others might do to him. God never promised Jeremiah an easy job, but He did promise him all that he needed to do his work faithfully.

Is it unusual for chosen servants of God to become discouraged and endanger their own ministries? No, because every servant of God is human and subject to the weaknesses of human nature. Moses became discouraged and wanted to die (Num. 11:10-15); Joshua was ready to quit and leave the Promised Land (Josh. 7:6-11); Elijah even abandoned his place of duty and hoped to die (1 Kings 19); and Jonah became so angry he refused to help the very people he came to save! (Jonah 4) God doesn't want us to ignore our feelings, because that would make us less than human, but He does want us to trust Him to change our feelings and start walking by faith (see 2 Cor. 1:3-11).

3. A Message about Jeremiah's Strange Conduct (Jer. 16:1-21)

In order to get the attention of the people, God sometimes told the prophets to do unusual things. Isaiah gave two of his sons odd names, which he used as a text for a message (Isa. 8), and he also dressed like a prisoner of war to call attention to a coming conflict (Isa. 20). We've already noted the many "action sermons" of both Jeremiah and Ezekiel.

Jeremiah's prohibitions (vv. 1-9). The Lord forbade Jeremiah from participating in three normal and acceptable activities: getting married, mourning for the dead, and attending feasts. All Jewish men were expected to be married by age twenty. In fact, the rabbis pronounced a curse on any who refused to marry and beget children. Certainly Jeremiah would have appreciated having a loving wife to encourage him, but this blessing was not his to enjoy. When you consider all the trials he endured and the enemies he made, Jeremiah was probably better off a single man. But his refusing marriage was a symbolic act, for the sons and daughters in Jewish families would either die by the sword or starve to death in the coming Babylonian invasion. Whenever anybody asked Jeremiah why he wasn't married, he had opportunity to share God's message of the coming judgment.

The Jewish people in Bible times were experts at mourning and marrying, but Jeremiah was forbidden to attend funerals or weddings and the feasts connected with them. What did this unsociable conduct say to the people? For one thing, God had removed His peace and comfort from the nation. Moreover, the judgment that was coming would be so terrible that the people would be unable to express their grief. There would be so many corpses and so few survivors that nobody would bury the dead, let alone comfort whatever family member remained.

As for wedding feasts, how could people celebrate with such a cloud of destruction hovering over the nation? The days would come when the happy voices of brides and bridegrooms would cease. In fact, all joy and gladness would flee from the land. The exiles would form a funeral march and go to Babylon.

Jeremiah's explanation (vv. 10-13, 16-18). It seems strange that the people would ask why the Lord decreed such a terrible judgment for His people. Surely they knew the terms of His covenant and the extent of their own sins, but they were led astray by the false prophets and comfortable in their sins, and their conscience was dead. Their unbiblical theology gave them a false assurance that God would never abandon His people or allow the Gentiles to desecrate the Holy City and the temple. How wrong they were!

Jeremiah's explanation was simple: They had repeated the sins of their fathers instead of listening to the Law of the Lord and turning from sin. Furthermore, they had not learned from the past judgments that God had sent. This made them even more guilty than their fathers. Had not Assyria taken the Northern Kingdom of Israel captive because of their idolatry? Had not the previous prophets proclaimed the Word of God and warned the people?

Jeremiah used several images to describe the Captivity. The verb "cast you out" (Jer. 16:13) is used for hurling a spear or sending a storm against a ship (Jonah 1:4). God was violently removing His people so the land could be healed and the nation purified (2 Chron. 36:14-21). Jeremiah also used the metaphors of fishing, hunting, and banking (Jer. 16:16-18). The Babylonians would cast out their nets and catch the Jews (Ezek. 12:13), and not one "fish" would escape. If anybody tried to hide in the hills, the fishermen would become hunters and track them down. Why? Because the nation owed a great debt to the Lord for the way they had treated His Law and His land. Now the note was due. "I will repay them double for their wickedness and their sin" (Jer. 16:18, NIV) means that God's judgment would be ample and complete.

Jeremiah's consolation (vv. 14-15). In wrath, God remembers mercy (Hab. 3:2), and Jeremiah gave the people a message of hope: The exiles will one day return to their land. So great will be this deliverance that it will be looked upon as a "second exodus" and far outshine the glory of Israel's exodus from Egypt. Later, Jeremiah would explain that the exiles will be in Babylon for seventy years (Jer. 25), and that a remnant would return to the land, rebuild the temple, and establish the nation (23:3; 31:7-9). They would return as a chastened people who would never again turn to the idols of the Gentile nations.

Jeremiah's affirmation (vv. 19-21). In a burst of faith and prophetic joy, Jeremiah saw not only the gathering of the Jewish remnant but also the coming of the Gentile nations from the ends of the earth to worship the true and living God of Israel. Isaiah had this same vision (Isa. 2:1-5; 11:10-16; 45:14), and so did Zechariah (Zech. 8:20-23). The Gentiles will confess their sin of idolatry and admit that the idols were worthless. Then they will be taught to know the Lord. Meanwhile, it's the task of the church today to spread the message of the Gospel to the ends of the earth so that sinners might abandon their false gods, whatever they may be, and trust in Jesus Christ, the Savior of the world.

4. A Message about Judah's Sins (Jer. 17:1-27)

President Calvin Coolidge came home from church one Sunday, and his wife asked, "What did the preacher preach about?" "Sin," the President said in his usual concise manner. "What did he say about it?" Mrs. Coolidge further inquired, and the President replied, "He was against it."

Jeremiah was against the sins of his people, six of which he named in this chapter.

Idolatry (vv. 1-4). Instead of giving their devotion and obedience to the true and living God, who had blessed them, the Jews adopted the idols of the nations around them and made these false gods more important than Jehovah. At the high places in the hills, they built altars to various gods and planted obscene symbols of the goddess Asherah. This defiled the land—their rich inheritance from Jehovah—and because of their idolatry, their inheritance would be plundered. They would lose everything, and it would be their own fault.

God's holy Law should have been written on their hearts (Prov. 3:3; 7:3; Deut. 6:6, 11:18; 2 Cor. 3:1-3), but instead their sin was engraved there. We may forget our sins, but our sins never forget us. They're inscribed on our hearts until we ask the Lord for forgiveness, and then He cleanses our hearts and makes them new (1 John 1:9; Heb. 10:15-18).

The Apostle John's final admonition to believers in his first epistle is "Little children, keep yourselves from idols" (1 John 5:21). There were many false gods in that day (1 Cor. 8:1-5), but there are false gods in our world today, such as money, possessions, fame, success, power, pleasure, achievement, and many more. Anything that we love and trust more than the true and living God, the God and Father of our Lord Jesus Christ, is an idol and must be torn from our hearts.

Unbelief (vv. 5-10). The leaders of Judah were prone to trust their political allies and lean on the arm of flesh instead of depending on the power of God. To emphasize the difference, Jeremiah contrasted a desert bush with a fruitful tree by the water (see Ps. 1:3-4). Unbelief turns life into a parched wasteland; faith makes it a fruitful orchard. Soon, the Babylonian army would overrun the kingdom of Judah, and the land of milk and honey would become a wasteland.

The heart of every problem is the problem in the heart and the human heart is deceitful (*Jacob* in the Hebrew) and incurable. We often say, "Well, if I know my own heart," *but we don't know our own hearts.* God does. He searches the heart and mind and knows exactly how to reward each person. If we want to know what our hearts are like, we must read the Word and let the Spirit teach us. The hearts of the Jewish leaders were turned away from the Lord and His truth. Consequently, they made unwise decisions and plunged the nation into ruin.

The Jewish people have a record of unbelief. It was unbelief that kept the people of Israel out of the Promised Land (Num. 13–14). It was unbelief that caused them to worship idols and invite the chastening of God during the time of the Judges. During the time of the kingdom, it was unbelief that kept the leaders from repenting and turning to God for help, and they became entangled in the costly politics involving Assyria, Egypt, and Babylon. Would they ever learn?

Greed (v. 11). During those tumultuous days, the rich exploited the poor and became richer, and the courts did nothing about it. "For from the least of them even unto the greatest of them every one is given to covetousness" (Jer. 6:13). Jeremiah quoted a familiar proverb about the partridge, who is supposed to hatch eggs she didn't lay and have the brood desert her—a picture of wealth deserting the rich people who unjustly acquired it. What good would their wealth be when the judgment fell on the land?

Forsaking the Lord (vv. 12-13). The throne of Judah was stained with sin and clouded by shame, but God's throne was glorious and exalted. The Jews considered the ark of the covenant in the holy of holies to be God's throne (Pss. 80:1; 99:1), but even if the temple were destroyed, God's heavenly throne would endure forever (Isa. 6:1). God had never forsaken His people, but they had forsaken Him. This is why Judah was facing terrible judgment. Instead of being written in the Book of Life, those who forsook God were written in the dust where their names perished with them (Ex. 32:32; Ps. 69:28; Phil. 4:3).

Rejecting God's servant (vv. 14-18). This is the fourth of Jeremiah's personal prayers to God for help, and this time the emphasis is on deliverance from his enemies. The people called him a false prophet and kept asking when his dire predictions would come true. They didn't realize that God's delays were opportunities for the nation to repent and be saved from ruin. Except for one episode of unbelief (Jer. 15:15-21), Jeremiah had not tried to run away from his responsibilities nor had he altered the messages God had given him to deliver. But he needed God's help and protection, and the Lord answered his prayers.

Profaning the Sabbath (vv. 19-27). God had given the Sabbath to the Israelites as a special token of their relationship with Him (see Ex. 16:29; 20:8-11; 31:13-17). It was to be a day of rest for the people, their farm animals, and the land. The people, however, repeatedly disregarded the Law and treated the Sabbath like any other day. Their sin was evidence that their hearts were devoted to material gain and not to the Lord.

A mechanical obedience to the Sabbath law wasn't what God wanted, but obedience that came from their hearts because they loved and feared the Lord. If this were the case, then they would obey all His Law, and God could then bless the people, their kings, and their city. If they continued to disobey the Law and desecrate the Sabbath, however, God would have to punish them by destroying their city and their temple.[10]

Jeremiah faithfully and courageously delivered his sermons to the people; he lifted his supplications to the Lord; he poured out his grief over the sins of the nation; and yet the people only hardened their hearts and stubbornly resisted God's truth.

In an age of unconcern and indecision, Jeremiah was burdened and decisive, and God honored him. Humanly speaking, his ministry was a failure, but from the divine perspective, he was an outstanding success. We need men and women of Jeremiah's caliber serving in the church and the nation today. There's a price to pay, but there's also a crown to win.

CHAPTER SIX
THE PROPHET, THE POTTER, AND THE POLICEMAN
JEREMIAH 18–20

The clay is not attractive in itself, but when the hands of the potter touch it, and the thought of the potter is brought to bear upon it, and the plan of the potter is worked out in it and through it, then there is a real transformation."

—J. Wilbur Chapman[1]

The prophet, of course, was Jeremiah. We don't know who the potter was, although he played an important part in the drama. The policeman was Pashur, the priest in charge of temple security, whose job it was to keep peace in the temple and punish troublemakers. Since Pashur considered Jeremiah to be a troublemaker, he punished him by making him spend a night in the stocks. Jeremiah is the chief actor in this three-act drama.

1. Jeremiah, the Threatened Prophet (Jer. 18:1-23)

These events probably occurred during the reign of Jehoiakim, the king who burned Jeremiah's prophetic scrolls (36:21ff). Unlike his father King Josiah, Jehoiakim had no love for either the Lord or His prophet. He wasn't the least bit interested in what Jeremiah had to say about things political or spiritual.

The sovereignty of God (vv. 1-17). Over thirty words in the Hebrew vocabulary relate directly to pottery, because the manufacture of pottery was a major industry in the Near East in that day. No doubt Jeremiah had passed the potter's house many times, but this time God had a special message for him that, after he preached it, would put him in jail. When you follow the Lord, you never know what will happen to you next.

"He did not get his flash of insight while he was praying but while he was watching a potter engaged in his daily work," wrote Charles E. Jefferson. "God reveals Himself in strange places and at unexpected seasons. For instance, He once revealed Himself in a stable."[2]

The potter sat before two parallel stone wheels that were joined by a shaft. He turned the bottom wheel with his feet and worked the clay on the top wheel as the wheel turned. As Jeremiah watched, he saw that the clay resisted the potter's hand so that the vessel was ruined[3] but the potter patiently kneaded the clay and made another vessel.

The *interpretation* of the image was national, relating to the house of Israel (vv. 6-10), but the *application* was individual (vv. 11-17), calling for a response from the people of Judah and Jerusalem. It also calls for a personal response from us today.

Interpretation (vv. 5-10). As the potter has power over the clay, so God has sovereign authority over the nations.[4] This doesn't mean that God is irresponsible and arbitrary in what He does, even though He is free to act as He pleases. His actions are always consistent with His nature, which is holy, just, wise, and loving. God doesn't need any advice from us, nor do we have the right to criticize what He does. "For who has known the mind of the Lord? Or who has become His counselor?" (Rom. 11:34, NKJV, quoted from Isa. 40:13 and Jer. 23:18) "But indeed, O man, who are you to reply against God? Will the thing formed say to him who formed it, 'Why have you made me like this?'" (Rom. 9:20, NKJV)

The Lord presented two scenarios that illustrated His sovereign power over nations (Jer. 18:7-10). If He threatened to *judge* a nation and that nation repented, then He would relent and not send the judgment. He did this with Nineveh when Jonah's preaching brought the city to repentance (Jonah 3). On the other hand, if He promised to *bless* a nation, as He did Israel in His covenants, and that nation did evil in His sight, then He could withhold the blessing and send judgment instead. God neither changes in character nor needs to repent of His actions (Mal. 3:6; Num. 23:19), but He has the sovereign freedom to alter His actions depending on the responses of the people.

To be sure, there's mystery involved in the relationship between divine sovereignty and human responsibility, but we don't have to explain the will of God before we can obey it. We live by divine promises and precepts, not theological explanations, and God isn't obligated to explain anything to us. (If He did, we probably wouldn't be able to grasp it!) "The secret things belong to the Lord our God, but those things which are revealed belong to us and to our children forever, that we may do all the words of this Law" (Deut. 29:29, NKJV). Jesus promised that if we obey what we know, God will reveal more of His truth to us (John 7:17).

Application (Jer. 18:11-17). Nations are made up of individuals, and individuals have the ability to receive God's Word or reject it. Yes, humans are made from the dust (Gen. 2:7) and live in a fragile body (Job 4:19; 10:9; 2 Cor. 4:7). Unlike the clay on the potter's wheel, however, we have the ability to resist. God uses many different hands to mold our lives—parents, siblings, teachers, ministers, authors—and we can fight against them. But if we do, we're fighting against God.

God announced that He was framing evil ("preparing", NIV; "fashioning", NASB; a word related to "potter" in the Hebrew) against the kingdom of Judah. If the people would repent, however, He would deliver them. But the people were so chained to their sins that they chose to follow their own evil plans. They would rather worship dead idols and suffer for it than serve the true and living God and enjoy His blessings! Truly, the heart is deceitful and desperately wicked! (Jer. 17:9)

In rejecting their God and choosing dumb idols, the people of Judah were acting contrary to everything reasonable. God made them for Himself, and they could not succeed apart from Him. The birds obey what God tells them to do (8:7); even the heathen nations don't abandon their gods, false as these gods are. Water in nature is consistent: On the heights, it becomes snow; at lower levels, it flows in the streams. God's people, however, were totally inconsistent, willing to enjoy God's blessings but not willing to obey the laws of God that governed those blessings. If nature acted like that, where would we be?

Instead of walking on God's clear and safe highway of holiness (Isa. 35:8), the people were on a dangerous and painful detour because they abandoned the ancient paths of God's holy Law. Because they wouldn't repent, God had to chasten them; this meant ruin for the land and exile for the people. Instead of His face shining upon them in blessing (Num. 6:24-26), God would turn His back to them and leave them to their own devices.

Like the patient potter, God is willing to mold us again when we resist Him and damage our own lives. The famous Scottish preacher Alexander Whyte used to say that the victorious Christian life was a "series of new beginnings." No failure in our lives need be fatal or final, although we certainly suffer for our sins. God gave new beginnings to Abraham, Moses, David, Jonah, and Peter when they failed, and He can do the same for us today.

The conspiracy of the enemy (v. 18). Proud sinners don't enjoy hearing about God's sovereignty or the threat of impending judgment. They think that by silencing the messenger they will silence the Lord. "He who sits in the heavens shall laugh; the Lord shall have them in derision" (Ps. 2:4, NKJV). Their argument was "We have plenty of priests, prophets, and elders, so we can do without Jeremiah!"

This wasn't the first time Jeremiah had faced a conspiracy that threatened his ministry and his life (Jer. 11:18-23; 12:6; 15:15), and it wouldn't be the last time. His enemies plotted a "smear campaign" consisting of lies about him (see 9:3). The plot probably included quotations from his messages that suggested he was a traitor to the kingdom of Judah. Like the men who plotted against Jesus, Jeremiah's enemies tried to prove he was breaking the law and stirring up the people (Luke 23:1-7).

Faithful servants of God don't enjoy opposition, but they learn to expect it. "In the world you will have tribulation," promised Jesus, "but be of good cheer, I have overcome the world" (John 16:33, NKJV). He also said, "If the world hates you, you know that it hated Me before it hated you" (15:18). And Paul reminded Timothy and us, "Yes, and all who desire to live godly in Christ Jesus will suffer persecution" (2 Tim. 3:12, NKJV).

The agony of the prophet (vv. 19-23). This is the fifth of Jeremiah's private "laments" to the Lord concerning his situation and his ministry (see Jer. 11:18-23; 12:1-5; 15:10-18; 17:14-18; 20:7-18). His words seem terribly harsh to us and unlike the spirit of Jesus, but keep in mind that Jeremiah was a divinely appointed prophet who represented God to the nation. Those who opposed him were opposing God, and Jeremiah asked God to deal with them (Deut. 32:35; see Rom. 12:17-19).

Like Elijah and all the other prophets, Jeremiah was "a man subject to like passions as we are" (James 5:17, "with a nature like ours", NKJV), and he felt deep pain because the leaders rejected the truth. I suppose if you and I were attacked by hateful enemies who lied about us, set traps for us, and dug pits for us, we'd get upset and ask God to deal with them. At least Jeremiah expressed himself honestly to God and left the matter with Him. He needed to remember God's promises when He called him (Jer. 1:7-10, 17-19) and rest in the assurance that the Lord would see him through.

There is a righteous anger against sin that is acceptable to God. "Be angry, and do not sin" (Eph. 4:26, NKJV, quoted from Ps. 4:4). "You who love the Lord, hate evil!" (Ps. 97:10, NKJV; see Rom. 12:9) Jesus was angry at the hardening of the hearts of His critics (Mark 3:5), and Paul was angry because of professed believers who were leading others astray. "Who is led into sin and I do not inwardly burn?" (2 Cor. 11:29, NIV) Unrighteous anger takes matters into its own hands and seeks to destroy the offender, while righteous anger turns the matter over to God and seeks to help the offended. Anguish is anger plus love, and it isn't easy to maintain a holy balance. If Jeremiah seems too angry to us, perhaps some of us today aren't angry enough at the evil in this world. Thanks to the media, we're exposed to so much violence and sin that we tend to accept it as a normal part of life and want to do nothing about it. Crusading has given way to compromising, and it isn't "politically correct" to be dogmatic or critical of ideas that are definitely unbiblical.

2. Jeremiah, the Persecuted Prophet (Jer. 19:1–20:6)

The theme of the potter continues with another action sermon from Jeremiah, a sermon that cost him a beating and a night in the stocks.

Jeremiah preaches the sermon (vv. 1-9). At the command of the Lord, Jeremiah made a second trip to the potter's house, this time as a customer and not a spectator, and he took with him some of the Jewish elders. Knowing their evil plots against him, it's an evidence of his faith that he was willing to walk with them and then do so daring a thing as declare *in their very presence* that disaster was coming to the land because of their sins. Obviously his prayer to the Lord had brought him peace and courage.

The east gate was the Potsherd Gate, where the potters worked and the broken pottery was thrown. It overlooked the Valley of the Son of Hinnom, the Jerusalem garbage dump (Gehenna). But Jeremiah turned the gate into a pulpit and declared impending disaster because of what the kings of Judah had done: forsaken God, worshiped idols, desecrated the temple, murdered the innocent, and offered their children in altar fires dedicated to Baal.

This valley had been a center for idol worship, but Josiah had desecrated it by making it a garbage dump. *Topheth* means a "fire pit, a hearth," because the little children had been put through the fires there. After the Babylonian invasion, however, the new name would be "The Valley of Slaughter." The siege would be so bad that the Jews would have to eat their own children to stay alive!

Jeremiah announces judgment (vv. 10-15). "I will make void[5] the counsel of Judah and Jerusalem in this place" (19:7). To demonstrate this, Jeremiah broke a clay jar and said, "This is what the Lord Almighty says: 'I will smash this nation and this city just as this potter's jar is smashed and cannot be repaired'" (v. 11, NIV). The nation was beyond discipline (2:23), beyond prayer (7:16), and now, beyond repair! They had so hardened themselves against the Lord that all hope was gone.

In the Near East in that day, kings and generals often smashed clay jars in a special ceremony before they went out to battle, symbolic of their total defeat of their enemies. This image is also used of the Messiah in Psalm 2:9: "You shall break them [the enemy nations] with a rod of iron; You shall dash them in pieces like a potter's vessel" (NKJV). But here it was God smashing His own people!

We can only imagine how angry the elders were who had accompanied Jeremiah to the Potsherd Gate. After all, they and the priests (and Jeremiah was a priest) had endorsed the "peace messages" of the false prophets as well as the political schemes of the civil leaders who hoped to get help from Judah's ungodly allies. But what Jeremiah did next made them even more angry, because *he went to the temple and preached the sermon again!* For a man who was broken before God, he certainly had courage before his enemies, but he was trusting God's promise of help (Jer. 1:7-10, 17-19), and the Lord was sustaining him.

Can nations and individuals sin so greatly that even God can't restore them? Yes, they can. As long as the clay is pliable in the hands of the potter, he can make it again if it's marred (18:4), but when the clay becomes hard, it's too late to re-form it. *Judgment is the only response to willful apostasy.* The Northern Kingdom of Israel refused to repent, and the Assyrians took it captive. Now the Southern Kingdom of Judah was resisting God's truth, and Babylon would destroy the land and deport the people. The Jewish people rejected their King when they asked Pilate to crucify Jesus; forty years later, the Romans did to Jerusalem what the Babylonians had done six centuries before. "There is a sin unto death" (1 John 5:16).

Jeremiah experiences pain (20:1-6). What before had been threats now became a reality. Pashur, son of Immer,[6] assistant to the high priest and chief security officer for the temple, didn't like what Jeremiah was saying. Therefore, he had Jeremiah arrested, beaten, and put into the stocks until the next day. The stocks were located at a prominent place in the temple area, in order to add shame to pain. Spending all night with your body bent and twisted wouldn't be at all comfortable, and when you add the pain of the beating, you can imagine how Jeremiah felt.

Being beaten and put into the stocks was the first of several acts of persecution the leaders inflicted on Jeremiah. They threatened to kill him (Jer. 26), they accused him falsely and imprisoned him (37:11-21), and they put him into a pit (38:1-13). He was an official prisoner until Nebuchadnezzar set him free (39:11-18).

God, however, met with Jeremiah that night (see Acts 18:9-11; 23:11; 27:23-24) and gave him a special message and a new name for Pashur: Magor-Missabib, which means "terror on every side" (NIV). Jeremiah had used this phrase before (Jer. 6:25) and would use it again (46:5; 49:5, 29). It described what would happen to Jerusalem when the Babylonian army finally moved in.

For the first time, Jeremiah named the king of Babylon as the invader (20:4).[7] Previously, Jeremiah had announced an invasion from the north (see 1:13-15; 3:12, 18; 4:5-9; 6:1, 22-26; 10:22), but he hadn't named the invading nation. Now the tool of God's discipline was identified as Babylon, and Jeremiah would mention Babylon in one way or another about 200 times in his book.

Pashur's treatment of Jeremiah would receive just recompense, for he and his family would be taken captive to Babylon, and there they would die. For a Jew to be buried outside his own land was considered a judgment, for the Gentile lands were considered unclean. For Pashur and his friends, however, what difference would that make? They'd been preaching lies in the name of the God of truth and had been encouraging idolatry in the temple of the holy God. So why not live in a land of lies and idols and eventually be buried there? They'd be right at home!

If the events described in Jeremiah 18–20 took place during the reign of Jehoiakim (607–597 B.C.), then it didn't take long for Jeremiah's prophecy to be fulfilled. In 605, Nebuchadnezzar plundered the temple and took Jehoiakim and the nobles to Babylon. In 597, he carried off over 10,000 people, and eleven years later, he burned the temple and the city and left it in ruins. Five years later, he deported another group of exiles.

3. Jeremiah, the Discouraged Prophet (Jer. 20:7-18)

This is the last of Jeremiah's recorded laments; it's a human blending of grief and joy, prayer and despair, praise and perplexity. When you call to mind the sensitive nature of this man, you aren't surprised that he's on the mountaintop one minute and in the deepest valley the next. Jeremiah, however, lived above his moods and did the will of God regardless of how he felt. In this honest expression of his deepest emotions, the prophet dealt with three important concerns: God's call (vv. 7-9), his daily peril (vv. 10-13), and his inner despair (vv. 14-18).

His "deceptive" call (vv. 7-9). When the servants of God find themselves in trouble because they've been faithful in ministry, they're often tempted to question their call and reconsider their vocation. Then what do they do? One of the first things they ought to do is *talk to the Lord about it and tell Him the truth.*

The word translated "deceived" carries with it the idea of being enticed or seduced. Of course, God doesn't lie (Titus 1:2), but Jeremiah felt that the Lord had taken advantage of him and lured him into the ministry. "You overpowered me and prevailed" (Jer. 20:7, NIV). Jeremiah felt like a helpless maiden who had been seduced then taken advantage of by a deceptive "lover." This is strong language, but at least Jeremiah said it privately to God and not publicly to others.

When you review the account of Jeremiah's call (Jer. 1), you find no evidence that God had enticed him. The Lord had told him plainly that he would have a difficult time. If he trusted the Lord, however, He would make him a fortified city and a bronze wall before his enemies. God had warned His servant that the demands of ministry would increase and he'd have to grow in order to keep going (12:5). What Jeremiah's ministry was doing for the nation was important, but even more important was what Jeremiah's ministry was doing *for Jeremiah.* As we serve the Lord, our capacity for ministry should increase and enable us to do much more than we ever thought we could do.

After you've told God how you feel, what do you do next? Jeremiah resolved to quit being a prophet! He decided to keep his mouth shut and not even mention the Lord to anybody. But that didn't work, because the message of God was like a burning in his heart and a fire in his bones (see Luke 24:32). Jeremiah didn't preach because he had to say something but because he had something to say, and not saying it would have destroyed him. Paul had the same attitude: "Yet when I preach the gospel, I cannot boast, for I am compelled to preach. Woe to me if I do not preach the gospel!" (1 Cor. 9:16, NIV)

His daily peril (vv. 10-13). Having settled the matter of his call, Jeremiah then looked away from himself to the enemies around him. Faith doesn't ignore problems; it faces them honestly and seeks God's help in solving them. No matter how much he was constrained to preach God's Word, Jeremiah had to deal with the fact that many people wanted him to keep quiet and would take the necessary steps to silence him.

Borrowing the new name God gave Pashur (Jer. 20:3), it's possible that Jeremiah's enemies used "Terror on every side" as a nickname for the prophet. It was another way to ridicule his prophecies before the people. They watched him and took note of what he did and said so they could find something criminal to report to the authorities. David had a similar experience (Ps. 31:13), and this is the way our Lord's enemies treated Him (Matt. 22:15ff).

Jeremiah's mood swings from expressing courage to seeking revenge and then to rejoicing in worship (Jer. 20:11-13). Remembering the promises God gave him at his call, Jeremiah was confident that the Lord was with him and would deal effectively with his enemies. Instead of dishonoring him, his enemies would themselves be dishonored. Since his words in verse 12 are almost identical to his prayer in 11:20, perhaps it's one he prayed often.

His deep despair (vv. 14-18). Having committed his cause to the Lord, Jeremiah had every reason to sing, for now the Lord would have to bear his burdens and help fight his battles. "Trust in Him at all times, you people; pour out your heart before Him, God is a refuge for us" (Ps. 62:8, NKJV).

Jeremiah's euphoria didn't last long, however, because in the next breath he was cursing his birthday (Jer. 15:10; see Job 3). Jewish parents would rejoice at the birth of a son who could wear the family name and be able to sustain his parents in their old age. A priestly family like Jeremiah's would be especially grateful for a son who could carry on the ministry to the Lord.

But Jeremiah's ideas were different. The messenger who announced that a son had been born would bring joy to the family and expect a reward for bringing such good news, but Jeremiah asked that the messenger be treated like Sodom and Gomorrah! He wanted that man to awaken to weeping in the morning and to hear battle cries every noon! "Why didn't my mother's womb become my tomb?" asked the prophet. "My life is nothing but trouble and sorrow and shame! Better that I had never lived!"

"Why came I forth out of the womb?" is an easy question to answer: because God had a special purpose for your life and designed you to fulfill it (Jer. 1:4-5; Ps. 139:13-16). God makes no mistakes when He calls His servants, and we should take care not to question His wisdom. All of us have had times of discouragement when we've felt like quitting, but that's when we must look beyond our feelings and circumstances and see the greatness and wisdom of God. As V. Raymond Edman, former president of Wheaton College (Ill.), often said to the students, "It's always too soon to quit."

And it is!

CHAPTER SEVEN
KINGS ON PARADE
JEREMIAH 21–24

"The tumult and the shouting dies
The captains and the kings depart—
Still stands Thine ancient sacrifice
An humble and a contrite heart.
Lord God of Hosts, be with us yet,
Lest we forget—lest we forget!"
—Rudyard Kipling, "Recessional"

Kipling's "Recessional" was published in 1897 when Queen Victoria's diamond jubilee was celebrated in Great Britain. The poem was a quiet warning to the British people to beware of overconfidence in their hour of imperial glory. Perhaps Kipling had the words of Daniel in mind: "The Most High rules in the kingdom of men, and gives it to whomever He chooses" (Dan. 4:25, NKJV), or he may have been thinking of Proverbs 16:18: "Pride goes before destruction, and a haughty spirit before a fall" (nkjv).

Jeremiah wrote a more pointed "Recessional" for the kingdom of Judah as he described one king after another leaving the scene and marching off to shameful judgment. In the great days of David, Hezekiah, and Josiah, the nation had honored the Lord, but now Judah was rapidly moving toward defeat and disgrace. In these pivotal chapters, Jeremiah delivered four important messages to the leaders and to the people.

1. God opposes the leaders of Judah (Jer. 21:1-14)

These events probably took place in the year 588 when the invincible Babylonian army was camped around the walls of Jerusalem. Hoping to secure help from Egypt, weak King Zedekiah had rebelled against Nebuchadnezzar by refusing to pay tribute (2 Chron. 36:13; see Ezek. 17:11-18); now Judah was suffering the dreadful consequences of his foolish decision. In desperation, he looked to Jeremiah for help by sending Zephaniah the priest and Pashur, one of the court officers, to see whether the prophet could get guidance from the Lord.[1] The king hoped that Jehovah would send a miraculous deliverance to Jerusalem as He had done in the days of godly King Hezekiah (2 Kings 18–19). Jeremiah, however, responded with dire pronouncements to the king (Jer. 21:3-7), the people (vv. 8-10), and the house of David (vv. 11-14).

A pronouncement to King Zedekiah (vv. 3-7). Not only would God refuse to deliver the city from the enemy, but also He would fight with the enemy and bring about Jerusalem's defeat! Judah's military might would be ineffective against the Chaldean army. Whereas in the past, God's mighty "outstretched arm" and "strong hand" had worked *for* His people (Deut. 4:34; 5:15; 26:8), now He would work *against* them, because the nation had turned against God. "To the faithful you show yourself faithful . . . but to the crooked you show yourself shrewd" (Ps. 18:25-26, NIV).

It seems strange that the Lord would use words like "anger," "fury," and "great wrath" (Jer. 21:5) to describe His disposition toward His own people. Yet these words were a part of His covenant with the people, and the nation knew the terms of the covenant (see Deut. 29:23, 28; 32:16-17, 21, 29; Lev. 26:27-28). God had warned the Jews repeatedly that their disobedience would arouse His anger and force Him to bring judgment to the land, but the leaders wouldn't listen. They preferred dead idols to the living God, and power politics to simple faith in His Word.

Jeremiah announced that the people in Jerusalem would die of famine, pestilence, or the sword; many of the survivors would even be taken captive to Babylon. King Zedekiah and his officers would be handed over to Nebuchadnezzar and judged. That's exactly what happened. The siege began January 15, 588, and ended July 18, 586, a period of just over thirty months.[2] After Zedekiah, his sons, and his nobles were captured, his sons were slain before the eyes of the king, who was then blinded and taken to Babylon, where he died (Jer. 39:1-10; 52:8-11, 24-27; 2 Kings 25).

A pronouncement to the people (vv. 8-10). There was no hope for the king, but the Lord did offer hope to the people if they would surrender to Nebuchadnezzar (see Jer. 38:17-23). God set before them two ways—the way of life and the way of death—a choice that must have reminded them of the words of the covenant (Deut. 11:26-32; 30:15-20; see Jer. 27:12-13; 38:2-3, 17-18). With God, we must decide one way or the other (Ps. 1); it's not possible to be neutral (Matt. 7:13-29; 12:22-30).

Of course, to surrender to the enemy was an act of treason, and Jeremiah eventually got into trouble for advocating this plan (Jer. 37:11-21; 38:1-6). The phrase "his life shall be unto him for a prey" (21:9) is literally "his life shall be to him as plunder" (see 38:2; 39:18; 45:5). The Babylonians would treat the deserters like spoils of war, and the Jews, after losing everything in the siege, would be happy to escape with their lives.

Since Nebuchadnezzar was doing the work of God in punishing the kingdom of Judah (50:9, 23; 51:20), and since God was allied with Babylon in fighting Judah, to surrender to Babylon really meant to surrender to the will of God. It meant to confess guilt and submit to the hand of the Lord. Rebellion against the Babylonians was rebellion against the Lord, and that was the way of death.

As God's people today, we need to realize that the only safe and sane response to God's chastening hand is *submission.* "Furthermore, we have had human fathers who corrected us, and we paid them respect. Shall we not much more readily be in subjection to the Father of spirits and live?" (Heb. 12:9, *NKJV*) The implication of the question is that we might not live if we don't submit to the will of God! "There is a sin not unto death" (1 John 5:17).

A pronouncement to the house of David (vv. 11-14). Here the Lord spoke to

David's dynasty—the kings who sat on the throne because of God's covenant with David (2 Sam. 7). If they obeyed God's Law and executed justice in the land, God would keep His promise and maintain David's royal dynasty. If they disobeyed, however, the kings would lose their throne rights. Once again, God was simply reminding them of the terms of the covenant and urging them to obey His Word.[3] The people of Jerusalem were certain that their city was impregnable and that there was no need to be afraid. Surrounded on three sides by valleys—Hinnom on the south and west, and Kidron on the east—the city had to defend itself only on the north. Jerusalem's inhabitants saw themselves enthroned on the rocky plateau, but God would soon dethrone them and cause them to lose their crown. Since the Babylonian army did set fire to the city, God did "kindle a fire in the forest" (Jer. 21:14). The phrase "the forest" probably refers to the structures in the city, especially to the king's palace, the house of the forest of Lebanon (1 Kings 7:2; 10:17, 21). The cedars of Lebanon were used to construct various buildings in the city.

This chapter begins with a king's cry for help and ends with a prophet's pronouncement of doom. What a tragedy!

2. God Discloses the Fate of the Kings (Jer. 22:1–23:8)

Godly King Josiah reigned for thirty-one years and sought to lead the people back to God. But the last four kings of Judah were wicked men, even though three of them were Josiah's sons and one was his grandson (Jehoiachin).

Jehoahaz, or Shallum, succeeded Josiah and reigned only three months (Jer. 22:10-12; 2 Kings 23:30-33). Pharaoh Necho deported him to Egypt, where he died.

Jehoiakim, also called Eliakim, reigned for eleven years (Jer. 22:13-23; 2 Kings 23:34–24:6) and died in Jerusalem. He was followed by his son *Jehoiachin*, also called Jeconiah and Coniah, whose reign lasted only three months (Jer. 22:24-30; 2 Kings 24:6-12). Nebuchadnezzar took him to Babylon, where eventually he died.

The last king of Judah was *Zedekiah*, who reigned eleven years and saw the kingdom and the holy city destroyed by Babylon (Jer. 22:1-9; 2 Kings 24:17–25:21). He was blinded and taken to Babylon to die. As Kipling wrote, "The captains and the kings depart."

Jeremiah disclosed the truth about those four kings, but then he made a promise about Messiah—the Righteous Branch (King) who would one day reign and execute justice in the land.

Zedekiah—callousness (22:1-9). The king had sent messengers to Jeremiah, but the prophet went personally to the palace to deliver God's message. Zedekiah was sitting on David's throne, in David's house of cedar (2 Sam. 5:11; 7:2,7), benefiting from the covenant God had made with David (2 Sam. 7), and yet the king wasn't serving the Lord as David had served Him. Jeremiah repeated what he had preached before (Jer. 21:12), that it was time for the king and his nobles to obey God's Law and execute justice in the land. They were exploiting the poor and needy, shedding innocent blood, and refusing to repent and turn to God.

In 2 Samuel 7, there is a dual meaning to the word "house": a literal building (the temple David wanted to construct for God) and the royal house (dynasty) God established through David by His gracious covenant. These same two meanings are woven into Jeremiah's message: God will destroy both the royal palace and the Davidic dynasty because of the sins of the kings. The royal house of cedar would be cut down and burned as the Chaldean soldiers went through the city like men chopping down a forest in Lebanon.

Meanwhile, Jeremiah appeared to be giving the leaders a small window of opportunity: If they would repent and do justice, God would deliver the city and establish David's throne (Jer. 22:4). Their hearts, however, were hard, and they would not listen. The ruins of Jerusalem would be a monument to their wickedness.

Jehoahaz (Shallum)—hopelessness (22:10-12). The death of godly King Josiah a decade before had brought great sorrow to the people. Even Jeremiah had written a lamentation honoring the dead monarch (2 Chron. 35:25). But there was no hope for the nation in looking back and weeping over a dead past. Nor was there hope in trusting that King Jehoahaz (Shallum) would be released from Egypt, where he was prisoner of Pharaoh Necho (2 Chron. 36:1-4). Apparently there was a pro-Jehoahaz party in Judah that pinned their hopes on his return, and perhaps some of the false prophets encouraged this expectation.

Jeremiah, however, announced that Jehoahaz would never return to Judah but would die in Egypt.

Instead of looking to a dead past or trusting in a deposed leader, the people should have been dealing with the issues of that hour and looking to the Lord for His help. Josiah was dead; Jehoahaz was exiled; it was time for Zedekiah to follow the example of his godly father Josiah and lead the people back to the worship of the true God.

Jehoiakim (Eliakim)—covetousness (22:13-23).[4] During a time of international crisis, Jehoiakim was more concerned about building his own spacious palace than he was about building a righteous kingdom, and he even used unpaid Jewish slave labor to do it! It was against the law to hold back wages or to enslave fellow Jews (Ex. 21:1-11; Lev. 19:13; Deut. 24:14-15; James 5:1-6). The nation was decaying and dying while the king was admiring his palace, the spacious rooms, the large windows, and the decorated cedar paneled walls. Jehoiakim wasn't much different from some modern politicians who profit from dishonest gain while they ignore the cries of the poor and needy.

"Does it make you a king to have more and more cedar?" (Jer. 22:15, NIV) asked the prophet. Then he reminded him that his father King Josiah lived comfortably and still did what was just and right. Josiah defended the cause of the poor, and God blessed him, but Jehoiakim thought only of himself. It didn't worry him that God watched as he robbed the poor, killed the innocent, and oppressed the just in order to satisfy his craving for luxury.

Jeremiah moved from "him" (third person) in verse 13 to "you" (second person) in verse 15, and then he named the king in verse 18. He announced that the king's burial would be quite unlike that given to his beloved father. The nation mourned Josiah's untimely death, but the Jews wouldn't weep when Jehoiakim died, nor would they bury him like a king. Who would pay for an expensive funeral just to bury a donkey? The carcass would be thrown on the garbage dump, where the scavengers and vermin would devour it (Jer. 36:30). Even Jehoiakim's end would be in fulfillment of the covenant curses (Deut. 28:26).[5]

Before going on to discuss the next king, Jeremiah paused to address the people of Jerusalem and describe their terrible plight (Jer. 22:20-23). The advance of the Chaldean army had crushed their allies ("lovers"), who also would be sent into exile. Like the desert wind, the Babylonian soldiers would "round up" Judah's evil leaders and sweep them away. The king and his nobles, living carelessly in the cedar palace ("Lebanon"), would soon suffer terrible pain like a woman in travail. The Lord had warned them, but they felt so secure that they wouldn't listen. The peace promised by the false prophets would never materialize. For the city of Jerusalem, it was the end.

Jehoiachin (Coniah, Jeconiah)—childlessness (22:24-30). The son of Jehoiakim, he reigned only three months and ten days before he was deported with the queen mother to Babylon and replaced by his uncle, Zedekiah (2 Chron. 36:9-10; 2 Kings 24:8-17). Jehoiachin was a wicked man, and Jeremiah 22:26 suggests that his mother was as much to blame as his ungodly father. Jeremiah had warned both the king and the queen mother, but they wouldn't listen (13:18-19).

If the king were the very signet ring on God's right hand God would casually take it off and hand it to the Babylonians (22:24-27). The signet ring was valuable because it was used to prove authority, identify possessions, and "sign" official documents, but Jehoiachin was useless to the Lord, fit only to be thrown away in Babylon.[6]

The question in verse 28 is constructed in such a way that "no" is the answer expected. The people of Judah didn't consider Jehoiachin a broken pot to be tossed away on the trash heap. In fact, one of the false prophets predicted that Jehoiachin would return to Judah, deliver the nation, and reign once again in power (28:1-4). God, however, had another plan for this evil man and his family; the king, his mother, and his sons were all deported to Babylon, where they died.

Jehoiachin had at least seven children (1 Chron. 3:17-18) by several wives (2 Kings 24:15), but none of them would sit on the throne of David. God declared that He would treat Jehoiachin as if the man were childless. Zedekiah, the last king of Judah, saw the Babylonians slay his sons, and it's likely that he himself died before Jehoiachin was freed from prison (Jer. 52:10-11, 31-34). This means that Jehoiachin was the last surviving king in David's line.

Of course, Jesus Christ is the "son of David" (Matt. 1:1; Rom. 1:3) and one day will restore the fortunes of Israel and reign from David's throne (Luke 1:30-33, 67-79). The genealogy in Matthew 1 traces Christ's ancestry through His legal father Joseph. Since Jehoiachin is in that family tree (Matt. 1:11), however, none of his descendants can claim the throne because of the curse pronounced in Jeremiah 22:24-30. Our Lord gets His Davidic throne rights through His mother Mary, whose genealogy is given in Luke 3:21-38. From Abraham to David, the lists are similar, but from David on, they differ. Luke traced the line through David's son Nathan and thus avoided Jehoiachin, a descendant of Solomon. Jesus Christ has every right to David's throne, and His future reign is what Jeremiah dealt with in the next section.

Messiah the King—righteousness (23:1-8). Jeremiah denounced all the leaders ("shepherds") of Judah for the ruthless way they treated the helpless people (vv. 1-4). Instead of *leading* the flock in love, they *drove* it mercilessly and exploited it. The shepherds didn't visit ("care for") the sheep, but God would visit the leaders with punishment. Because the leaders disobeyed the Law and refused to trust God, they destroyed the nation and scattered the flock among the Gentiles. God, however, promised to regather His people and transform the remnant into a nation. (The word "remnant" is used nineteen times in Jeremiah.) A remnant did return to Judah after the Captivity, rebuild the temple, and restore national life.

Jeremiah, however, promised a much greater regathering of the Jews—a greater miracle than their deliverance from Egypt (vv. 7-8; see 16:14-15). God will call His people from the nations of the world, gather them in their land, purge them, and then send them their promised Messiah (Jer. 30; Isa. 2:1-5; 4:1-6; 9:1-7; 11:1–12:6; Zech. 12–14). David's "family tree" might have been cut down, but a "branch" (shoot) would grow from the stump and become Ruler of the nation (Isa. 11:1; 53:2).

In contrast to the unrighteous kings Jeremiah had been describing, this King will be righteous and rule justly. The kingdoms of Israel (northern) and Judah (southern) will be united into one nation; they will experience salvation and they will live in peace and safety. The name of this King is "Jehovah Tsidkenu—The Lord our Righteousness" (see Jer. 33:15-16). According to 1 Corinthians 1:30 and 2 Corinthians 5:21, this exalted name applies only to Jesus Christ. When you put your faith in Jesus Christ, His righteousness is put into your account and you are declared righteous before God. This is called "being justified by faith" (Rom. 3:21–5:11).

No matter how dark the day may be, God sends the light of hope through His promises. The godly remnant in Judah must have been encouraged when they heard Jeremiah's words, and the promises must have sustained them during the difficult days of the Captivity. The return of the Jews to their land after the Captivity was but a foreshadowing of the great worldwide regathering that will occur in the last days when "He shall send His angels with a great sound of a trumpet, and they shall gather together His elect from the four winds, from one end of heaven to the other" (Matt. 24:31).

3. God Exposes the Sins of the False Prophets (Jer. 23:9-40)

What God said, as recorded in Jeremiah 14:14, summarizes this entire section: "The prophets prophesy lies in My name. I have not sent them, commanded them, nor spoken to them; they prophesy to you a false vision, divination, a worthless thing, and the deceit of their heart" (NKJV). Jeremiah focused on three areas in their lives that were especially abhorrent.

Their disgraceful conduct (vv. 9-15). True prophets know how serious it is to be called by God to declare His Word, and they accept the responsibility with fear and trembling. When they see self-styled prophets living like sinners, it grieves them. No wonder Jeremiah had a broken heart and trembled like a drunken man! He realized what the false prophets were doing to the people and the land, and it made him sick. "Horror [indignation][7] hath taken hold upon me because of the wicked that forsake Thy Law" (Ps. 119:53).

The false prophets were committing adultery and thronging the houses of prostitution (Jer. 5:7). Then they would go to the temple and pretend to worship Jehovah (23:11), turning God's house into a den of thieves (7:9-11). But the word "adultery" also includes their worship of idols, turning from the true

God (to whom Israel was "married") and being unfaithful to their covenant promises.

The false prophets had led the Northern Kingdom of Israel astray (23:13), and now they were leading the Southern Kingdom of Judah astray (v. 14). Baal was the Canaanite rain god to whom the Jews were prone to turn for help in times of drought (1 Kings 17–18), and his worship included "sacred prostitution." Jerusalem was becoming like Sodom and Gomorrah—cities so wicked God had to destroy them (Jer. 20:16; Gen. 18–19).

The land was suffering a severe drought (Jer. 23:10; see chap. 14) because the false prophets led the people to violate the terms of their covenant with God. The Lord promised to send the early and latter rains if they obeyed Him (Deut. 11:10-15; 28:12), but He also warned them that He would make the heavens brass and the earth iron if they disobeyed Him (11:16-17; 28:23-24). "Because of the curse the land lies parched" (Jer. 23:10, *NIV*). But the sinners refused to escape, even though God had promised to judge them in due time (vv. 12, 15).

Whenever a nation needs healing, it's usually because God's people aren't obeying and serving Him as they should. We like to blame dishonest politicians and various purveyors of pleasure for a nation's decline in morality, but God blames His own people. "If My people, which are called by My name, shall humble themselves, and pray, and seek My face, and turn from their wicked ways, then will I hear from heaven, and will forgive their sin, and will heal their land" (2 Chron. 7:14).

Their dishonest message (vv. 16-32). To begin with, the false prophets offered the people *a false hope* (Jer. 23:16-20). The Lord says: You will have peace. . . . No harm will come to you (v. 17, NIV; see 6:13-15; 8:10-12). Of course, this was a popular message, and the frightened people grabbed it and held on to it. But the false prophets hadn't heard that message in God's council; they made it up out of their own hearts. Instead of peace, a storm was brewing from the Lord (23:19). God was about to vent His holy anger on His sinful people, and when they finally understood His purposes, it would be too late to stop the whirlwind.

Not only did the false prophets give the people a false hope, but they also ministered under *a false authority* (23:21-24). God hadn't spoken to them, yet they prophesied. God hadn't called them, yet they ran with their message. If they were truly prophets from God, they would have lived godly lives and encouraged the people to turn from their wickedness. Instead, they taught a popular "theology" that made it convenient for people to be religious and still live in sin.

Jehovah wasn't a local deity like the pagan idols, but a transcendent God who reigns above all things and fills heaven and earth (vv. 23-24). Nor was He blind like the idols (Ps. 115:5), unable to see the sins of the people. "Can any hide himself in secret places that I shall not see him?" (Jer. 23:24) Because they listened to the false prophets, the people believed lies about God, and what we believe about God determines how we live.

Finally, the false prophets were speaking *under a false inspiration* (vv. 25-32). They depended on dreams and delusions of the mind, and they even plagiarized messages from one another! Compared to the nourishing wheat of the Word, their messages were only straw; you couldn't eat it, build with it, or even be warmed by it.

The message of the true prophet is like a hammer that can tear down and build up (see 1:10) and even break the hardest rocks (23:29). The Word is like fire that consumes waste and purifies whatever it touches. Jeremiah had the Word burning in his heart (20:9; see Luke 24:32) and on his lips (Jer. 5:14). He was God's assayer, using the fire of the Word to test the lives of the people (6:27).

There are false prophets and teachers in our world today (2 Peter 2:1; 1 John 4:1-6), people who claim to know God's will because of their dreams, their study of astrology, or their special "spiritual" gifts. Some of them have invaded the church (Jude 3-4). Whatever anyone says who claims to be speaking for the Lord must be tested by the Word of God. "To the Law and to the testimony: if they speak not according to this word, it is because there is no light in them" (Isa. 8:20).

Their disrespectful attitude (vv. 33-40). The key Hebrew word in this section is *massa*, which means "a burden." Jeremiah used it to refer to bearing burdens on the Sabbath (Jer. 17:21-27), but in this context it means the burden of the message that the Lord places on His prophets (Nahum 1:1; Hab. 1:1; Mal. 1:1). For this reason, some scholars translate it "oracle," but "burden" is perfectly acceptable (see the NIV and NASB, both of which put "burden" in the margin).

God cautioned Jeremiah not to encourage the careless attitude of the priests, people, and false prophets when they asked him, "What is the burden of the Lord?" The phrase "burden of the Lord" was almost a cliché; it was used to poke fun at God's true prophet. (The phrase "born again" often gets the same kind of treatment.)

Why should the false prophets ask for an oracle from the Lord when Jeremiah had already told them what God wanted them to hear? If they hadn't obeyed what God already commanded, why should He tell them more? Their attitude toward God's message was careless and disrespectful; they weren't taking seriously God's message or God's messenger. The false prophets had distorted the truth to make it mean what they wanted it to mean, and yet they called their messages the "oracles of the Lord."

Jeremiah was to reply, "You are the burden." (v. 33, NIV margin) The Living Bible catches the spirit of the passage:

> When one of the people or one of their "prophets" or priests asks you, "Well, Jeremiah, what is the sad news from the Lord today?" you shall reply, "What sad news? You are the sad news, for the Lord has cast you away!" (Jer. 23:33)

A worldly church puts an emphasis on fun and entertainment and forgets about tears. We now have Christian comedians who generate laughter for thirty minutes and then tack on the Gospel and give an invitation. While there's a proper place for humor in the Christian life, the church today needs to hear the words of James: "Lament and mourn and weep! Let your laughter be turned to mourning and your joy to gloom. Humble yourselves in the sight of the Lord, and He will lift you up" (James 4:9-10, NKJV). The church isn't taking God's Word seriously at an hour when the world is in serious trouble.

4. God Disposes of His Rebellious People (Jer. 24:1-10)

In 597 B.C., the Babylonians deported King Jehoiachin (also called Jeconiah or Coniah) along with many of the nobles and key citizens, leaving only the poorer people to work the land (2 Kings 24:14-16). It was the beginning of the end for Judah, and no doubt Jeremiah was greatly distressed.

Knowing that His servant needed encouragement, the Lord gave him a vision of two baskets of figs sitting before the temple of the Lord. One basket held very good figs, the kind that ripened early in the season, and the other basket contained rotten figs, which nobody could eat. Then the Lord explained that the good figs represented the exiles who had just been taken to Babylon, while the bad figs represented King Zedekiah and his officials as well as the survivors who remained in the land or who had fled to Egypt.

What do you do with rotten figs? You reject them and throw them away! What do you do with tasty, good figs? You preserve them and enjoy them! God promised to care for the exiles, work in their hearts, and one day bring them back to their land. Jeremiah even wrote a letter to the exiles, telling them to live peaceably in the land and seek the Lord with all their hearts (Jer. 29:1-14). There was no future for King Zedekiah, who had succeeded Jehoiachin, or for the nobles that gave him such foolish counsel, but there was a future for a godly remnant that would seek the Lord with all their hearts.

In times of national catastrophe, no matter how discouraging the circumstances may be, God doesn't desert His faithful remnant. Rebels are scattered and destroyed, but true believers find God faithful to meet their needs and accomplish His great plans. The people who returned to the land after the Captivity were by no means perfect, but they had learned to trust the true and living God and not to worship idols. If the Captivity did nothing else, it purged the Jewish people of idolatry.

The destruction of Jerusalem and the fall of Judah were not accidents; they were appointments, for God was in control. Now the land would enjoy its Sabbaths (2 Chron. 36:21; Lev. 25:1-4, and the people exiled in Babylon would have time to repent and seek the Lord. In far off Babylon, God the Potter would remake His people (Jer. 18), and they would return to the land chastened and cleansed.

"No discipline seems pleasant at the time, but painful. Later on, however, it produces a harvest of righteousness and peace for those who have been trained by it" (Heb. 12:11, NIV).

CHAPTER EIGHT
FACING TRUTH AND FIGHTING LIES
JEREMIAH 25–29

An idealist believes the short run doesn't count. A cynic believes the long run doesn't matter. A realist believes that what is done or left undone in the short run determines the long run.

—Sidney J. Harris[1]

In these chapters, we see the prophet involved in four different ministry experiences as he served the Lord and sought to bring the kingdom of Judah back to God.

1. Jeremiah Shares a Secret (Jer. 25:1-38)

Jeremiah had been serving for twenty-three years when he delivered the messages recorded in chapters 25 and 26 (25:3; 26:1). He was called into prophetic service in the year 626 B.C. (1:2) and continued to minister after the fall of Jerusalem in 587 B.C., a period of over forty years. He was now at the midpoint of his career. When you consider the unsympathetic response of the people both to him and to his messages, you marvel that Jeremiah wasn't discouraged and ready to quit, but he continued to be faithful to his calling.

He delivered two messages—one to the Jews (vv. 1-14) and one to the Gentile nations (vv. 15-38).

Chastening for the people of Judah (v. 1-14). Four times in this message, Jeremiah pronounced the solemn indictment, "You have not listened" (vv. 3-4, 7-8, NKJV). The earlier prophets, many of whom are unknown to us, had warned of great judgment if the nation didn't repent and turn to Jehovah, but their ministry went unheeded. Jeremiah had preached to the leaders and common people of Judah for twenty-three years and had received the same response. As they disobeyed the Law, worshiped idols, and rejected God's servants, the people deliberately provoked God to anger, and the day of His wrath was fast approaching.

Once again, Jeremiah announced that Nebuchadnezzar[2] and the armies of Babylon would be God's tool for punishing Judah (21:7, 10), and he dared to call the Babylonian king "My servant" (25:9; 27:6; 43:10). Nebuchadnezzar wasn't a believer in the true God of Israel, but in his conquests he was accomplishing God's will (51:20-23). God's own people wouldn't obey the Lord when they had everything to gain, but pagan rulers like Pharaoh (Rom. 9:17), Cyrus (Isa. 44:28; 45:1), and Nebuchadnezzar were servants of God to fulfill His purposes. The church today needs to remember that the Lord is sovereign and can use whatever tools He deigns to use to accomplish His purposes on earth, even unconverted leaders.

For the first time, Jeremiah shared the "secret" that the Captivity in Babylon would last seventy years (Jer. 25:11-14; 29:10; see Dan. 9:1-2). One reason God determined a period of seventy years was that the land might enjoy the rest that the Jews had denied it (2 Chron. 36:20-21; Lev. 25:3-5). The law of the Sabbatical Year had been ignored for nearly 500 years![3]

Judah, however, wouldn't be the only nation to suffer at the hands of the Babylonians, for "all these nations round about" (Jer. 25:9) would also be punished; among them the nations listed in 25:18-25 and 27:3. In one way or another, these nations were confederate with Judah against Babylon, but God's command was that the nations submit to Nebuchadnezzar. In fact, God would make *even the animals* obey the king of Babylon!

The end of the seventy years would mean not only freedom for the Jewish remnant but also judgment for the Babylonian Empire because of the ruthless way they treated both Jews and Gentiles (25:12-14). It was one thing for Nebuchadnezzar to do God's work, but when his attitude became proud and hateful, he overstepped his bounds. Babylon fell to the armies of the Medes and Persians in 539 B.C. (see Dan. 5).

Judgment for the Gentile nations (vv. 15-38). Jeremiah was called of God to minister not only to Judah but also to the other nations (Jer. 1:5). God had set him over the nations (v. 10) and given him authority to tell the Word of God. Though the Lord had not given His Law to the Gentile nations or entered into a covenant relationship with them, He still held them accountable for their sins (Rom. 1:18ff; Amos 1–2).

In this message, Jeremiah used eight vivid images to describe the judgment God was sending to the Gentiles.[4]

The cup of wrath (vv. 15-29). The psalmists used this familiar image of suffering and judgment (Pss. 60:3; 75:8), as well as the prophets (Isa. 29:9; 51:17, 22; 63:6; Jer. 25:15-16; 49:12; Ezek. 23:32-34; Hab. 2:16). You find the image repeated in the New Testament (Rev. 14:8-10; 16:19; 18:6). "Babylon was a golden cup in the Lord's hand that made all the earth drunk" (Jer. 51:7, NKJV).

Though this message centered mainly on the Gentiles, note that Jeremiah began his list with Jerusalem, and the cities of Judah (25:18); judgment begins with God's people (Ezek. 9:6; 1 Peter 4:17). "See, I am beginning to bring disaster on the city that bears my Name, and will you indeed go unpunished?" (Jer. 25:29, NIV)

How did Jeremiah make the various nations drink the cup of God's wrath? Certainly he didn't travel from nation to nation and meet with their leaders. There wasn't time for such an itinerary, and they wouldn't have welcomed him to their courts anyway. Perhaps he invited representatives of the various nations present in Jerusalem (see 27:3) to have a meal with him, preached his message to them, and then passed the cup around. It could have been another "action sermon" that would have gotten attention in the city, and when the foreign visitors returned to their own nations, they would have reported what the strange prophet in Jerusalem had said and done.

To drink a cup is a symbol of submission to the will of God. "The cup which my Father hath given me, shall I not drink it?" (John 18:11) Jeremiah called the nations to submit to God's will, surrender to Nebuchadnezzar, and be spared destruction. Jeremiah would later illustrate this message by wearing a yoke (Jer. 27). If the nations didn't drink the cup of submission, they would end up drinking the cup of judgment and "get drunk and vomit, and fall, to rise no more" (25:27, NIV).

The roaring lion (vv. 30a, 38). Lions roar to paralyze their prey with fear, and God will roar in judgment when He visits the nations (see Hosea 11:10; Joel 3:16; Amos 1:2; 3:8). God had spoken in love to His people, but they refused to obey. Now He must speak in wrath. In the last days, the Lamb of God will become like the lion and pour out His wrath on a wicked world (Rev. 5:5-7).

The winepress (v. 30b). This is another familiar metaphor for judgment (Isa. 63:3; Joel 3:13; Rev. 14:19-20). As they shared in the joy of the harvest, those treading the grapes shouted and sang to one another (Isa. 16:10), but God would do the shouting as He judged the nations that had resisted His will.

The lawsuit (v. 31). "The Lord will bring charges against the nations" (NIV; see Hosea 4:1; Micah 6:2). The Lord first brought charges against His own people for abandoning Him and turning to idols (Jer. 2:9-13). In this "trial" there would be a Judge but no jury, an indictment but no defense, and a sentence but no appeal. God had given His people plenty of opportunity to admit their guilt and repent, but they refused. Now it was too late.

The storm (vv. 32-33). Like a tornado, Nebuchadnezzar's army would move from nation to nation and city to city and leave only devastation behind. "Behold a whirlwind of the Lord has gone forth in fury—a violent whirlwind! It will fall violently on the head of the wicked" (23:19, NKJV; see 30:23; Isa. 30:30).

The refuse (v. 33). Not to have a proper burial was a disgrace, for then the body was being treated like common rubbish (8:2; 9:22; 16:4; 22:19). The Hebrew word means "dung", which is even worse (see Isa. 25:10-11, NIV).

The broken pottery (v. 34). "You will fall and be shattered like fine pottery" (NIV). This reminds us of Jeremiah's "action sermon" when he publicly broke the clay vessel (Jer. 19:1-13; see also 13:14; 48:38). One day, Jesus Christ shall break the nations like so many clay pots (Ps. 2:9). The Hebrew word translated "pleasant vessel" (Jer. 25:34) refers to fine pottery and not just common pots. God wants His vessels to be clean and yielded. If they aren't, He has the right to smash them.

The slaughtered flock (vv. 34-38). The shepherds were the leaders of the nation—kings and nobles, priests and false prophets—who had exploited God's flock and not compassionately cared for God's people. Now it was time for *them* to be slaughtered, and there would be no place for them to hide! Instead of hearing the cries of the sheep, the shepherds would hear their own wailing as they saw their pasture (Judah) destroyed. Like a fierce lion (v. 38; see v. 30), God would leap out on the shepherds and the sheep, and there would be no escape.

"For the time is come that judgment must begin at the house of God: and if it first begin at us, what shall the end be of them that obey not the Gospel of God?" (1 Peter 4:17)

2. Jeremiah Risks His Life (Jer. 26:1-24)

This chapter should be studied in connection with chapter 7, because they both deal with Jeremiah's courageous sermon given in the temple. The sermon is summarized in verses 3-7, and you will note the emphasis on *hearing the Word of God* (see 25:3-8). Jeremiah preached exactly what God commanded him to preach and didn't alter the message in order to please the people. The false prophets preached what the people *wanted* to hear, but Jeremiah preached what the people *needed* to hear. "Whatever I command thee thou shalt speak" (1:7).

The people in the temple, however, encouraged by the priests and false prophets, rejected Jeremiah's message and treated him like a false prophet who deserved to die. To them, it was blasphemous for Jeremiah to declare that Jehovah would allow the Holy City and His holy temple to fall into the defiling and destructive hands of the heathen the way the ark at Shiloh fell into the hands of the Philistines (1 Sam. 4). Since God's covenant with David protected the city and the temple, Jeremiah was actually denying the covenant! He was leading the people astray and deserved to die (Deut. 18:20).

Receiving a report about a tumult in the temple, the officials left the palace and came to the temple to see what was occurring. (This reminds us of Paul's experience recorded in Acts 21:27-40.) After hearing the people, priests, and prophets charge Jeremiah with blasphemy, they gave the prophet opportunity to speak. Jeremiah then presented three arguments in his defense.

First, what he had spoken was commanded by the Lord because the Lord had sent him (Jer. 26:12, 15). If they killed him, they were killing one of God's prophets, and he would rather be faithful to God and die than unfaithful and live. Second, *they* were the ones in danger; he was the one seeking to rescue them! (v. 13) If they repented and obeyed God's Word, the Lord would relent of His plans to judge the nation and would deliver them. Third, if they killed him, they would shed innocent blood, and that would only make their impending judgment worse.

Three factors led to Jeremiah's release. First, having heard the evidence, the officials decided that the accusations were false and that Jeremiah should not die (v. 16). Second, some of the wise elders of the city argued the case further by citing a precedent: the ministry of the Prophet Micah in the days of King Hezekiah (vv. 18-19; Micah 1:1; 3:12). At that time, the Assyrians were threatening Jerusalem (Isa. 36–37), but Hezekiah obeyed the Lord and led the people in confession and repentance. Third, Ahikam, one of the officials, proved a friend to Jeremiah and effected his release (Jer. 26:24). Ahikam had served King Josiah (2 Kings 22:11-14) and was the father of Gedaliah, the future governor of Judah (Jer. 25:22).[5]

On first reading, the illustration of Uriah (Jer. 26:20-23) seems out of place as a defense of Jeremiah, for the king had executed Uriah the prophet after he had fled to Egypt and been brought back to King Jehoiakim. On the other hand, Jeremiah stayed in the land of Judah and even ministered in the precincts of the temple! Jeremiah gave every evidence of being a loyal citizen, even though he disagreed with the politics of the leaders of the government. Although we can't fault him for trying to save his own life, Uriah had broken the law while trying to prophesy God's truth, and this led to his own death.

3. Jeremiah Wears a Yoke (Jer. 27:1–28:17)[6]

Once again, Jeremiah had to use an "action sermon" to get the attention of the people, and he did it at a time when Zedekiah was conferring with representatives from five neighboring nations. These nations were allies of Judah, and together they were planning a strategy for dealing with Nebuchadnezzar.

The message of the yoke (vv. 1-22). A yoke speaks of submission, and that's the message Jeremiah was trying to get across. First, Jeremiah sent the message to *the envoys of the nations* (vv. 1-11). What these politicians needed was not clever strategy but submission to Babylon. When Jeremiah was asked why he was wearing a yoke,[7] he gave them the message from God: Judah and the other nations must submit to Nebuchadnezzar or else be destroyed. God had given the nations to the king of Babylon, and those nations who rebelled against him were rebelling against God (vv. 7-8, 11-12). He sent this message to the envoys gathered in Jerusalem, who certainly had heard about this peculiar Jewish man who was walking around wearing a yoke (see 28:10).

"And all nations shall serve him [Nebuchadnezzar], and his son, and his son's son" is a proverbial expression that simply means they shall serve him for a long time. Nebuchadnezzar's son Evil-Merodach did succeed him (52:31-34; 2 Kings 25:27), but he was followed by his brother-in-law Nergal-Sharezer (Jer. 39:3), not by Nebuchadnezzar's grandson.

Judah had its false prophets, and the Gentile nations had their diviners (people who read omens), dreamers (those who interpret dreams), and enchanters and sorcerers (those who collaborate with demons in order to discover or control the future), but neither Judah nor the Gentile nations dared to listen to these purveyors of lies. Since dabbling in the occult was forbidden to the Jews (Lev. 19:26; Deut. 18:10-11), why would Zedekiah want to listen to political counsel from the pit of hell? (See 2 Cor. 6:14-18.)

Jeremiah then gave the same message *to King Zedekiah* (Jer. 27:12-15). Since the king had rebelled against Babylon and refused to pay tribute, he was now in serious trouble. When the king saw Jeremiah wearing the yoke, he surely must have gotten the message: "Bring your necks under the yoke of the king of Babylon, and serve him and his people, and live" (v. 12). Jeremiah warned the king not to listen to the deceptive messages of the false prophets, because they were speaking only lies in the name of the Lord.

Jeremiah then delivered the "yoke" message *to the priests and the people* (vv. 16-22). The false prophets were claiming that the valuable articles of gold and bronze that the Babylonians had taken from the temple would soon be returned to Jerusalem, but Jeremiah knew this was a lie.[8] Actually, these treasures weren't brought back until God visited the Jews and the remnant returned to Judah after the decree of Cyrus (Ezra 1–2). The important thing wasn't to rescue the temple furnishings but to save the people from death and the city from destruction. This could be done only if the nation submitted to the king of Babylon.

Jeremiah taunted the false prophets by encouraging them to pray about the matter. After all, if they were true prophets of God, the Lord would surely answer their prayers. He told them to pray, not for the return of the treasures now in Babylon, but for the preservation of the treasures still in the temple. When the Babylonians organized a second deportation in 597 at the beginning of Zedekiah's reign (Jer. 27:1; 28:1), it proved that the false prophets were indeed liars and that their prayers weren't answered.

Jeremiah ended his message to the priests and people with a promise of hope: At the end of the seventy years of captivity, God would visit His people in Babylon and bring them back to their land. Even in wrath, God remembers mercy (Hab. 3:2).

The breaking of the yoke (vv. 1-17). While Jeremiah was wearing the yoke and calling the nation to submit to Babylon, Hananiah, one of the false prophets, confronted him in the temple. About this same time, according to historians, Nebuchadnezzar was putting down a revolt in his own land. Hananiah wrongly interpreted the uprising as the end of Nebuchadnezzar's rule. Hananiah announced that God had broken the yoke of the king of Babylon and that the temple treasures would be returned to Jerusalem within two years. More than that, King Jeconiah and all the exiles would be returned with them.

These messages contradicted what Jeremiah had spoken in the name of the Lord. The Lord had told Jeremiah that the deported people and the temple vessels wouldn't be restored to the land until He visited the exiles at the end of their seventy-year captivity (Jer. 27:16-22). Furthermore, King Jeconiah would never return to Judah but would die in Babylon (22:24-27; 52:31-34).

Jeremiah's response to Hananiah's message was "Amen, so be it! May the Lord fulfill what you have promised!" How are we to interpret this reply? Certainly not as agreement with what the false prophet had said, because Jeremiah knew better. Perhaps we might paraphrase Jeremiah's words, "Oh, that the Lord would do what you have said! This would make me very happy!" But Jeremiah knew that Hananiah's prophecy of peace wouldn't be fulfilled. If it were fulfilled, this would contradict all that the prophets had predicted who had preceded them, for they prophesied judgment.

Hananiah became angry, removed Jeremiah's yoke, and broke it before the people. If Jeremiah could preach "action sermons," so could Hananiah! "Thus saith the Lord," he announced. "Even so will I break the yoke of Nebuchadnezzar king of Babylon from the neck of all nations within the space of two full years" (28:11). Not only would Judah be set free, but also *all nations* would remove the yoke of Babylon. Again, this contradicted the message Jeremiah had preached to the nations.

Jeremiah didn't resist Hananiah when he removed the yoke, nor did he reply to the false prophet's message. "And the prophet Jeremiah went his way" (v. 11). The priests and people witnessing this dramatic scene may have interpreted Jeremiah's silence as agreement, but Jeremiah was only waiting for the right message from the Lord and the right time to deliver it.

The message to Hananiah was both national and personal. As far as the nation was concerned, because they would follow his deceptive counsel, an iron yoke would replace the wooden yoke (see Deut. 28:48). The nations would not escape; Nebuchadnezzar would enslave them. It's always the case that when we reject the light yoke of God's will, we end up wearing a heavier yoke of our own making. The personal message was that the false prophet would die before the year was up, and two months later, he did (Jer. 28:1, 17). But even this striking event didn't awaken the hearts of the people, for they were bent on doing evil.

God doesn't usually strike people dead in such a dramatic fashion, but it did happen to the followers of Korah (Num. 16), to Uzzah (2 Sam. 6), to the Assyrian army (2 Kings 19:35), and to Ananias and Sapphira (Acts 5). "It is a fearful thing to fall into the hands of the living God" (Heb. 10:31).

4. Jeremiah Writes Some Letters (Jer. 29:1-32)

Several different letters are involved in this chapter: a letter from Jeremiah to the exiles (vv. 1-14); a letter concerning Jewish false prophets in Babylon to which Jeremiah replied (vv. 15-23); a letter from Shemaiah to the temple priests concerning Jeremiah, which he read (vv. 24-29); and a letter from Jeremiah to the exiles concerning Shemaiah (vv. 30-32). Correspondence like this wasn't difficult to maintain in those days, for there were regular diplomatic missions between Jerusalem and Babylon (v. 3), and Jeremiah had friends in high places in the government.

Jeremiah's word of encouragement (vv. 1-14).[9] Sometime after the deportation in 597, Jeremiah sent a letter to the exiles in Babylon to tell them how to behave in their new land. A man with the heart of a true shepherd, Jeremiah wanted to enlighten them and encourage them in their life in Babylon. Governed by special laws concerning clean and unclean things, the Jewish people would have a difficult time adjusting to a pagan society. Jeremiah wanted them to be good witnesses to the idolatrous Babylonians, and he also wanted them to be good Jews even though separated from their temple and its services. He addressed himself to the needs of three kinds of people.

Those with no hope (vv. 4-6). The exiles had lost everything but their lives and what few possessions they could carry with them to Babylon. They'd lost their freedom and were now captives. They'd been taken from their homes and had lost their means of making a living. They were separated from relatives and friends, some of whom may have perished in the long march from Jerusalem to Babylon. No matter how they looked at it, the situation seemed hopeless.

How should we handle such a depressing situation? *Accept it from the hand of God (v. 4) and let God have His way.* It does no good to hang our harps on the willow trees and sit around and weep, although this may be a temporary normal reaction to tragedy (Ps. 137:1-4). One of the first steps in turning tragedy into triumph is to accept the situation courageously and put ourselves into the hands of a loving God, who makes no mistakes.

Those with false hopes (Jer. 29:6-9). The false prophets had convinced the people that the stay in Babylon would be a brief one, perhaps two years (vv. 8-9). Thus, there was no need to settle down and try to resume a normal life, but Jeremiah told them just the opposite. Since they would be there as long as seventy years (v. 10), there was plenty of time to build houses and set up homes. It was important that the exiles have families so there would be people available to return to Judea when the Captivity ended. This small

Jewish remnant was holding in its hands the future of God's great plan of salvation, and they must obey Him, be fruitful, and multiply (v. 6).

It would be easy for the Jews to wage constant warfare against their idolatrous Gentile captors, but Jeremiah instructed them to strive to get along with the Babylonians. The exiles were to be peacemakers, not troublemakers, and they were to pray sincerely for their enemies (Matt. 5:43-48; 1 Tim. 2:1-3; Titus 3:1-2). It was possible to be good Jews even in a pagan land. Remember, if we reject the wooden yoke of submission, we end up wearing only an iron yoke of subjugation (Jer. 28:12-14). Thus, the best course is to yield ourselves to the Lord and to those who are over us, no matter how badly they may treat us. (See Peter's counsel to Christian slaves in 1 Peter 2:18-25.) To indulge in false hopes is to miss what God has planned for us.

Those who have true hope (vv. 10-14). True hope is based on the revealed Word of God, not on the "dream messages" of self-appointed prophets (v. 10, NIV). God gave His people a "gracious promise" (v. 10, NIV) to deliver them, and He would keep His promise. God makes His plans for His people, and they are good plans that ultimately bring hope and peace. Therefore, there is no need to be afraid or discouraged.

In every situation, however, God's people have the responsibility to seek the Lord, pray, and ask Him to fulfill His promises, for the Word and prayer go together (Acts 6:4). The purpose of chastening is that we might seek the Lord, confess our sins, and draw near to Him (Heb. 12:3-13). According to Jeremiah 29:14, these promises reach beyond the Jews captive in Babylon and include all of Israel throughout the world. Jeremiah was looking ahead to the end of the age when Israel will be regathered to meet their Messiah and enter their kingdom (Isa. 10:20–12:6).

Jeremiah's word of explanation (vv. 15-23). The false prophets in Babylon were giving false hopes to the people concerning Jerusalem and Judah, and this word got back to Jeremiah. Yes, King Zedekiah was still on the throne and there were Jews still living in Jerusalem, but this was no guarantee that the city and the nation would be delivered. The people still in the land were the "bad figs" that would be thrown out (Jer. 29:17; see chap. 24). The important thing wasn't what happened to the people in the land but what the exiles would do with the Word of God. If they obeyed God, He would work out His purposes and bless them.

Jeremiah named two of the false prophets, Ahab and Zedekiah, who not only preached lies to the people but also lived godless lives. Consequently, he announced their doom in Babylon. Their names would become proverbs in Israel, warning not to rebel against the Word of God.

Jeremiah's word of warning (vv. 24-32). This warning was in response to Shemaiah, another false prophet in Babylon, who had written letters to people in Jerusalem "in the name of the Lord," urging them to imprison Jeremiah because he was a madman. The chief temple officer Zephaniah let Jeremiah read the letter (see 21:1). Because Shemaiah had a following in Babylon, Jeremiah warned the exiles that the man was a rebel against God and that the Lord had neither sent him nor given him a message. Shemaiah would be judged for his sins by dying childless in Babylon, never to see his native land again.

What life does to us depends largely on what life finds in us. If we seek the Lord and want His best, then circumstances will build us and prepare us for what He has planned. If we rebel or if we look for quick and easy shortcuts, then circumstances will destroy us and rob us of the future God wants us to enjoy. The same sun that melts the ice also hardens the clay.

God's thoughts and plans concerning us come from His heart and lead to His peace. Why look for substitutes?

CHAPTER NINE
THE GOD WHO MAKES THINGS NEW
JEREMIAH 30–33

A small man can see when it is growing dark . . . but he cannot see beyond the darkness. He does not know how to put a sunbeam into his picture. A great man pierces the darkness and sees the glory of a hidden dawn."

—Charles E. Jefferson[1]

Bible scholars often call these four chapters "The Book of Consolation." In them, the Lord amplified the wonderful promise He gave to His people in the letter Jeremiah sent the Babylonian exiles:

> "For I know the plans I have for you," declares the Lord, "plans to prosper you and not to harm you, plans to give you hope and a future" (29:11, NIV).

Jeremiah 30–33 describes the glory of the dawning of a new day for the people of Israel, not only for the exiles in Babylon but also for the Jewish people in the latter days before the Lord returns. As you study, you'll discover that Jeremiah had two horizons in view: the nearer horizon of the return of the exiles to Judah and the farther horizon of the regathering of Israel in the end times from the nations of the earth.

1. Redemption: a New Beginning (Jer. 30:1-24)

Jeremiah received the words recorded in 30:1–31:25 while he was asleep (31:26), for God sometimes spoke to His servants through dreams (Dan. 10:9; Zech. 4:1). God instructed Jeremiah to write His words in a book (scroll) so the nation would have a permanent record of the promises God was giving to His people (see Jer. 36:1-4).

In His instructions to Jeremiah, God stated the theme of His message: Israel (the Northern Kingdom, taken by Assyria in 722 B.C.) and Judah (the Southern Kingdom) will eventually return to their land as a united people (30:3). While this promise refers ultimately to the regathering of the Jews at the end of the age, it certainly was an encouragement to the exiles in Babylon, for if God can gather His people from *all* the nations of the world, surely He can deliver Judah from the captivity of *one* nation. (Note His promise in v. 10.)

This "redemption" of His people from bondage is pictured in several ways.

The broken yoke (vv. 4-11). "For it shall come to pass in that day, . . . that I will break his yoke from your neck, and will burst your bonds; foreigners shall no more enslave them" (v. 8, NKJV). When the prophets used the phrase "in that day," they were usually referring to the future time when God will judge the nations of the world and restore the Jews to their land.[2]

Before Israel is delivered, however, all the nations of the earth will experience "the time of Jacob's trouble" (v. 7), a phrase that describes the time of tribulation that will come upon the earth (Matt. 24:21-31; Mark 13:19-27; Rev. 6–19). A frequent biblical symbol of suffering is a woman in travail (Jer. 30:6), and this image is used to describe the Tribulation in the end times (see Isa. 13:8 and context; Micah 4:9-13; 1 Thes. 5:1-3).[3]

The promise in Jeremiah 30:9 applies to the future Kingdom Age, following the Tribulation, when the Messiah shall reign over His people. You find corresponding promises in 23:5 and 33:14-26. When Jesus was here on earth, His people said, "We will not have this man to reign over us" (Luke 19:14), but in that day, they will recognize their Messiah-King and welcome Him (Zech. 12:8–14:21).

The healed wound (vv. 12-17). In Isaiah's day, Judah was a "sick" nation (Isa. 1:5-6), and thanks to the superficial ministry of the false prophets (Jer. 6:14; 8:11), the sickness became worse in Jeremiah's day (10:19; 14:17; 15:18). The wounds on the "body politic" were so bad that there was no medicine that could cure the nation, and the allies ("lovers") that the Jewish leaders trusted abandoned Judah to her fate. The Lord reminded the Jews that it was He who used other nations to wound them because of their disobedience to Him (30:14). He used Assyria to chasten Israel and Babylon to punish Judah, and in the latter days, He will use the Gentile nations to correct Israel and prepare the Jews for the return of their Messiah. However, God will punish the Gentile nations for the way they treat Israel in the last days (v. 16; see Joel 3) just as He punished Assyria and Babylon. "But I will restore you to health and heal your wounds" was God's encouraging promise (Jer. 30:17, NIV).

The calm after the storm (vv. 18-24). Jeremiah then picked up the image of the storm (v. 23) that he had used earlier (23:19-20) to describe the Babylonian assault, but now he related it to the trials of the "latter days" (30:24). God promised that Jerusalem and the cities of Judah will be rebuilt[4] and that the fortunes of the people will be restored. Their mourning will turn to joy and their children will again enjoy a normal life.

Instead of being under despotic Gentile rulers, the Jews will have the Messiah as their ruler—"one of their own" (v. 21, NIV), that is, a Jew. But here's a surprising revelation: Not only will the Messiah be their King, but He will also be their Priest! "Then I will cause him to draw near, and he shall approach Me" (v. 21, NKJV). This is language that applies especially to the Jewish high priest, who alone entered the, Holy of Holies on the annual Day of Atonement (Lev. 16). Only Jesus Christ, who is both King and Priest (Heb. 7–8), can qualify to fulfill this prophecy.

To summarize: The people of Judah and Jerusalem will experience terrible trials at the hands of the Babylonians. They will end up wearing the Gentile yoke, bearing the wounds caused by their sins, and having endured the storm of God's wrath. But God would eventually deliver them, breaking the yoke, healing the wounds, and bringing peace after the storm. All of this will be a foreshadowing of what will happen to the Jews in the end times as they go through the Tribulation, meet their Messiah-King, and enter into their kingdom.

2. Reconciliation: a New People (Jer. 31:1-30)

A nation is more than its land and cities; it's people living together, working together, and worshiping together. In this chapter, Jeremiah described the people of God and the new things the Lord would do for them. He first spoke to a united nation (vv. 1, 27-30), then to Israel (vv. 2-20), and finally to Judah (vv. 21-26).

A united people (vv. 1, 27-30). Because of the sins of Solomon and the foolishness of his son Rehoboam, the Jewish nation divided and became Israel and Judah, the Northern Kingdom and the Southern Kingdom (1 Kings 11–12). But in the last days, the Lord will gather His people, unite them, and be the God of all the families of Israel (Jer. 31:1). In fact, God compared Israel and Judah to seed that will be sown in the land and produce one harvest, not two (v. 27).

Jeremiah's ministry included breaking down and plucking up as well as building and planting (1:10); up to this point, it had been primarily the former. In the future, however, God will build and plant so the people and the land could be restored. There would be no more "blaming the fathers" for what happened (Ezek. 18:1-4, 19-23; Deut. 24:16), for each person will take responsibility for his or her own sins. This principle certainly had application to the remnant that returned to the land after the Captivity, for it was the failure of individuals to obey God that caused the ruin of the nation. If the kings and priests had been like Josiah and Jeremiah, the nation could have been saved.

A restored Israel (vv. 2-20). The names "Ephraim" and "Samaria" are references to the Northern Kingdom of Israel, whose capital was at Samaria (Jer. 31:4-6, 9, 18, 20). The people of the Northern Kingdom were captured in 722 B.C. by the Assyrians, who brought other peoples into the land so as to produce a mixed race (2 Kings 17). When the people of Judah returned to their land from the Captivity, they would have nothing to do with the Samaritans (Ezra 4:1-4; Neh. 2:19-20; 13:28), a practice that persisted into New Testament times (John 4:9).[5] Subsequently, the Samaritans established their own religion, temple, and priesthood, and this alienated the Jews even more.

The promises recorded in Jeremiah 31:2-22 don't apply to Ephraim/Israel after the Captivity, because the Samaritans weren't a part of the rebuilding of the land. These promises apply to the scattered Ten Tribes[6] in the end times when God will call the Jews together and restore them to their land. Then there will be one nation, and the Samaritans will worship, not on Mt. Gerizim, but on Mt. Zion (v. 6; John 4:20-24). Jeremiah pictured God summoning His family and gathering His flock, leading them out of the desert into the fruitful garden. Since none of this happened after the Captivity, we can assume it will occur in the end times when Ephraim repents and turns to the Lord (Jer. 31:18-20). As you read these promises, notice the emphasis on singing, praise, and joy.

Matthew later referred to verses 15-17 (Matt. 2:16-18). Rachel was the mother of Joseph and Benjamin, and Joseph was the father of Ephraim and Manasseh, the two leading tribes in the Northern Kingdom (Gen. 30:22-24). Jeremiah heard Rachel weeping at Ramah, where the Jewish prisoners were assembled for their long journey to Babylon (Jer. 40:1). Her descendants through Joseph had been captured by the Assyrians, and now her descendants through Benjamin (the Southern Kingdom) were going to Babylon. Her labor as a mother had been in vain! (Remember, Rachel died giving birth to Benjamin.) But God assured her that both Ephraim and Judah will be restored (31:16-17), and therefore her sacrifices will not have been in vain.[7]

A restored Judah (vv. 21-26). As the Jews started for Babylon, God instructed them to remember the roads and set up markers along the route, for the people would use those same roads when they return to their land. Jeremiah pictured Judah as a silly girl, flitting from lover to lover, and now summoned to come home. (He used this image before. See 2:1-2, 20; 3:1-11.) According to the Law, a daughter who prostituted herself should have been killed (Lev. 21:9; Deut. 22:21), but God would do a new thing: He would welcome her home and forgive her!

The phrase "a woman shall compass a man" (Jer. 31:22; "surround" in NIV) has been given so many interpretations that to examine them all is to invite confusion. The word translated "compass" also means "to surround with care, to shield"; it's used of God's care for Israel in the wilderness (Deut. 32:10). The word for "man" means "a strong man, a champion," so the "new thing" God does is make the women so strong that they protect the men! (Keep in mind that this was a strongly masculine society.) In other words, the return of the exiles won't be a parade of weak stragglers; it will be the march of warriors, including the women, who were considered too weak to fight in that day.[8]

This is a picture of that future regathering of the people of Israel in the end times. They will enjoy a renewed land, where the citizens will bless their neighbors in the name of the Lord. Farmers and city dwellers will live together in harmony because of the blessing of the Lord.

3. Regeneration: a New Covenant (Jer. 31:31-40)

Any plan for the betterment of human society that ignores the sin problem is destined to failure. It isn't enough to change the environment, for the heart of every problem is the problem of the heart. God must change the hearts of people so that they want to love Him and do His will. That's why He announced a New Covenant to replace the Old Covenant under which the Jews had lived since the days of Moses, a covenant that could direct their conduct but not change their character.

Jewish history is punctuated with a number of "covenant renewals" that brought temporary blessing but didn't change the hearts of the people. The Book of Deuteronomy records a renewal of the covenant under Moses, before the people entered the Promised Land. In addition, before he died, Joshua led the people in reaffirming the covenant (Josh. 23–24). Samuel called the nation to renew their vows to God (1 Sam. 12), and both Hezekiah (2 Chron. 29–31) and Josiah (2 Chron. 34–35) inspired great days of "revival" as they led the people back to God's Law.

The fact that the blessings didn't last is no argument against times of revival and refreshing. When somebody told Billy Sunday that revivals weren't necessary because they didn't last, the evangelist replied, "A bath doesn't last, but it's good to have one occasionally." A nation that is built on spiritual and moral principles must have frequent times of renewal or the foundations will crumble.

But the New Covenant isn't just another renewal of the Old Covenant that God gave at Sinai; it's a covenant that's new in every way. The New Covenant is *inward* so that God's Law is written on the heart and not on stone tablets (2 Cor. 3; Ezek. 11:19-20; 18:31; 36:26-27). The emphasis is *personal* rather than national, with each person putting faith in the Lord and receiving a "new heart" and with it a new disposition toward godliness.

The Old Covenant tried to control conduct, but the New Covenant changes character so that people can love the Lord and one another and want to obey God's will. "By the Law is the knowledge of sin" (Rom. 3:20), but under the New Covenant God promised "I will forgive their iniquity, and I will remember their sin no more" (Jer. 31:34). It is this covenant that the Jews will experience in the last days when they see their Messiah and repent (Zech. 12:10–13:1).

The basis for the New Covenant is the work of Jesus Christ on the cross (Matt. 26:27-28; Mark 14:22-24; Luke 22:19-20). Because the church today partakes in Israel's spiritual riches (Rom. 11:12-32; Eph. 3:1-6), anyone who puts faith in Jesus Christ shares in this New Covenant (Heb. 8:6-13; 10:14-18). It's an experience of regeneration, being born again into the family of God (John 3:1-21).

The Lord also affirmed the permanence of the nation and the faithfulness of His relationship to His people (Jer. 31:35-37). It would be easier for the sun to stop shining and the moon and stars to go out than for God to break His promises to His people Israel. Just as Jerusalem was rebuilt after the Babylonian Captivity, so it will be restored after the time of Jacob's trouble and be holy to the Lord. Because of its ancient associations with Israel, Islam, Jesus, and the church, Jerusalem is called "the holy city," but it will not truly be holy until the Lord restores it and reigns in glory at the end of the age.

4. Restoration: a New Land and Kingdom (Jer. 32:1–33:26)

It wasn't enough for the prophet merely to preach God's promises; he also had to practice them and prove to his hearers that he believed them himself. "Faith without works is dead" (James 2:26). Therefore, God directed Jeremiah to give another "action sermon" and purchase a piece of property at a time when the fortunes of Judah couldn't have been lower. In so doing, Jeremiah got the attention of the people and was able to affirm God's great promises to them. He had to put his money where his mouth was and God blessed him for it.

An "illogical thing" (vv. 1-44). The tenth year of Zedekiah's rule was 587 B.C., one year before Jerusalem fell to the Babylonians, when Jeremiah was confined in the court of the prison (37:21). King Zedekiah didn't like Jeremiah's messages concerning himself and the city (32:3-5), but perhaps his imprisoning the prophet was God's way of protecting Jeremiah from his enemies and providing food for him during the terrible siege. People can imprison God's workers, but God's Word is not bound (2 Tim. 2:9). God's Word came to Jeremiah telling him to do a most illogical thing: Buy a piece of the battlefield!

The transaction (vv. 6-15). God told Jeremiah that his cousin Hanamel was coming with an offer to sell property in their hometown of Anathoth. If Hanamel had suddenly shown up, Jeremiah probably would have refused the offer. After all, the field was in the hands of the Babylonians, Jeremiah was in prison, and the future of the nation was bleak indeed. Of what use would a field be to Jeremiah who couldn't possibly live for another seventy years?

That, however, is what faith is all about: obeying God in spite of what we see, how we feel, and what may happen. It's well been said that faith is not believing in spite of evidence but obeying in spite of consequence, and Jeremiah's actions illustrate that maxim. When word got out that Jeremiah was investing in worthless real estate, many people must have laughed, others shook their heads in disbelief, and some probably thought he was crazy.

The transaction was probably carried out in the court of the prison with all things done legally. Jeremiah signed the deeds, paid the money, and gave the legal documents to his secretary Baruch, who is mentioned here for the first time.[9] The witnesses attested to the signature and the deeds and probably went away wondering whether Jeremiah had lost his mind. The transaction was the talk of the city, you can be sure, with Hanamel the hero. Hanamel may have thought he engineered a shrewd deal, but he only gave evidence of his unbelief.

The reaction (vv. 16-25). As was often the case with Jeremiah, a testing experience of doubt followed a triumphant experience of faith. Having obeyed God's command by faith, Jeremiah was now wondering how God would ever give him his property; he did the right thing by praying about it. The best way to handle doubt is to talk to God, be honest about your feelings, and then wait for Him to give you His message from His Word.

True prayer begins with worship (vv. 17-19) and focuses on the greatness of God. No matter what our problems are, God is greater; and the more we see His greatness, the less threatening our problems will become. True prayer also involves rehearsing what God has done for us in the past and remembering how He kept His promises and met the needs of His people (vv. 20-23). Jeremiah's prayer concluded with the prophet sharing his difficult situation with God and turning it over to Him (vv. 24-25). Outside the city was the besieging Babylonian army; within the city were famine, disease, and disobedience; and in Jeremiah's heart was a nagging doubt that he'd made a fool of himself.

The confirmation (vv. 26-44). God met the needs of His servant and confirmed that his decisions were right. The basic theme of Jeremiah's prayer was "Nothing is too hard for You" (v. 17, NIV), and God reaffirmed that very truth to His servant (v. 27).[10] Good theology always leads to a confident heart if we put our trust in the Word, for "faith comes by hearing, and hearing by the Word of God" (Rom. 10:17, NKJV).

The Lord's reply to Jeremiah affirmed what He had told him in the past: The city was heading for certain destruction because of the repeated sins of the people (Jer. 32:28-35). Their sin of idolatry had provoked the Lord, and the only solution was to put them in the land of Babylon and give them their fill of idols. Because the people had resisted the prophets and refused to obey the Law, they would have to take the consequences.

The Lord then affirmed to Jeremiah that the situation wasn't lost, for He would gather His people and bring them back to their land (vv. 36-44). This promise seems to apply to the end times when Israel will be gathered out of all "countries" (v. 37) and the New Covenant will be in force, for the people will have a changed heart toward the Lord. Next, Jeremiah heard the word that gave him joy: "And fields shall be bought in this land" (v. 43). The day would come when Jeremiah's purchase would be validated and his "action sermon" vindicated!

The application of this Scripture for today's believer is obvious: The world laughs at us for our faith and our investments in the future, but one day God will keep His promises and vindicate us before people and angels. Instead of living for the sinful pleasures of this present world, we seek the joys of the world to come. We refuse to sacrifice the eternal for the temporal. The unbelieving world may ridicule us, but ultimately God will vindicate His people.

"Unsearchable things" (33:1-26). "Call to me and I will answer you and tell you great and unsearchable things you do not know" (v. 3, NIV). The word translated "unsearchable" pictures an impregnable city protected by high walls—an apt image during the siege of Jerusalem. The idea is that God's people don't learn the hidden things of the Lord by "storming the gates" through their own strength but by seeking Him through believing prayer. Because Jeremiah asked the Lord to teach him, God showed him "hidden things" that related to the future of his people. The prophet knew that the city was destined for judgment (vv. 4-5), but the Lord gave him further words of assurance and encouragement—promises that relate to the end times.

The defiled nation would be healed and cleansed (vv. 6-8) and the disgraceful city would bring joy and renown to the Lord and be a testimony to all the nations of the world of the marvelous goodness and grace of God (v. 9). The deserted city would one day be filled with people praising the Lord and expressing their joy to one another (vv. 10-11). The pasture lands, ruined by devastating judgment, would one day be full of flocks and herds, and the little towns would once more enjoy happiness (vv. 12-13). Since these blessings didn't come during the post-exilic period, we have to believe they'll be realized when the Lord returns and restores His people and their land.

The greatest blessing of all will be their promised King reigning in righteousness! (vv. 14-16; see 23:5) Jeremiah already told us that His name is "The Lord our Righteousness" (v. 6), but now God revealed that *Jerusalem will bear the same name*! That certainly didn't happen when the exiles returned to rebuild their temple and their city. Therefore, this promise is for the latter days. Then when people call Jerusalem "the Holy City," the name will be appropriate.

Once again, the Lord used the faithfulness of His creation covenant (Gen. 8:22) to undergird the dependability of His promises and the perpetuity of His people (Jer. 33:19-26; see 31:35-37). But He adds something else: He will multiply the people as the stars of the heaven, which was one of the promises He had made to Abraham (Gen. 15:1-5).[11]

"For I will restore their fortunes and have compassion on them" (Jer. 33:26, NIV). The nation of Israel has a bright and blessed future, and Jeremiah invested in that future.

As God's people, are we putting our money where our mouth is?

CHAPTER TEN
CONTEMPORARY EVENTS AND ETERNAL TRUTHS
JEREMIAH 34–39; 52

A nation that cannot preserve itself ought to die, and it will die—die in the grasp of the evils it is too feeble to overthrow.
—Senator Morris Shepherd[1]

In spite of the long-suffering of God and the faithful ministry of God's prophets, the kingdom of Judah was about to die. It was a nation with a glorious heritage—laws given from heaven by Moses, a land conquered by Joshua, a kingdom established by David and made magnificent by Solomon, a people in whose midst Jehovah dwelt in a splendid temple—and yet that glorious heritage couldn't prevent Judah's shameful ruin at the hands of the idolatrous Babylonians. The end had come.

What caused Judah's slow decay and final collapse? The historian would point to their unwise politics, particularly depending on Egypt for help, and we can't deny that Judah's leaders made some stupid decisions. But behind their "unwise politics" was a more insidious reason: *The leaders really didn't believe the Word of God.* During the dramatic rise and fall of empires in that stormy era, Judah looked *around* for allies instead of looking *up* for divine assistance. Instead of repenting and turning to God, they hardened their hearts against the Word and trusted their own wisdom.

Jeremiah recorded a number of events in Judah's final days that prove we can't treat God's Word any way we please and get away with it.

1. God's Word Dishonored (Jer. 34:1–35:19)

The year was 588 B.C. and Nebuchadnezzar's army was successfully conquering the kingdom of Judah. The last two fortified cities were about to fall: Lachish, twenty-three miles from Jerusalem, and Azekah, eighteen miles from Jerusalem (34:7). Not only did Nebuchadnezzar bring his own invincible Babylonian troops, but also he demanded that the vassal countries he'd conquered send their share of recruits. In a sense, the entire Near East was attacking God's chosen people (see Ps. 74).

The destiny of the king (vv. 1-7). God gave weak King Zedekiah another opportunity to repent and save the city and the temple from ruin, but he refused to listen. Jeremiah warned him that the royal family and the court officials would not escape judgment and that he would be taken captive to Babylon, where he would die in peace. One act of faith and courage would have saved the city from ruin and the people from slaughter, but Zedekiah was afraid of his counselors (38:1-6) and was only a pawn in their hands.

The treachery of the people (vv. 8-22). At one point during the siege, Zedekiah and the people made a covenant with the Lord in the temple (34:15) to free all the Jewish slaves. A calf was slain and then cut in half, and the priests, officers, and people walked between the halves as a sign that they would obey the terms of the covenant (vv. 18-19; Gen. 15:17). In so doing, they were agreeing to free their Jewish slaves or be willing to suffer what the calf had suffered.

According to the Law of Moses, a Jewish master had to free his Jewish slaves at the end of seven years of service (Ex. 21:1-11; Deut. 15:12-18). The Jews hadn't done this for years, and now they decided it was a good thing to do. Why? Perhaps they felt that God would honor their obedience and defeat the enemy in some miraculous way, as He had done for Hezekiah (Isa. 36–37). Instead of believing God's Word and submitting to Babylon, the Jews tried to bargain with the Lord and "bribe" Him into helping their cause.

Of course, there were probably some practical considerations behind this covenant. If the slaves were free, they'd have to care for themselves; their masters wouldn't have to feed them or care for them. Also freemen were more likely to want to fight the enemy and maintain their newfound freedom. Whatever the reason, the effects of the covenant didn't last very long, for when there was a lull in the siege and Nebuchadnezzar went off to confront the Egyptian army (Jer. 34:21-22; 37:5-11), the masters all forced their slaves back into servitude. The solemn covenant made in the temple meant nothing.

Before we condemn these dishonest masters too much, let's admit that God's people often make promises to the Lord when they're in tough times, only to repudiate them when things get better. In my pastoral ministry, I've heard more than one suffering saint on a hospital bed promise to be the best Christian in the church if only God would give healing, and when He granted the request, he or she immediately forgot Him.

Jeremiah took advantage of this event to preach a sermon about Judah's treachery against the Lord (34:12-22). God had set the Israelites free from Egyptian bondage and had made a covenant with them to be their God, but they broke the covenant and returned to idolatry. Now they broke the Law by enslaving their own people unjustly. By what they did in the temple and the way they treated their fellow Jews, they profaned the name of the Lord. They hadn't really proclaimed freedom to their slaves, but God would proclaim "freedom" to the nation—freedom "to fall by the sword, plague, and famine" (v. 17, NIV). The prophet predicted a terrible death for all the treacherous people who had participated in the covenant, and his predictions came true (vv. 19-20).

The integrity of the Rechabites (35:1-19). This event occurred eighteen years earlier, during the reign of Jehoiakim (609–597 B.C.). Jeremiah probably put the account at this point in the book for the sake of contrast: The people of Judah dishonored the Lord by disobeying His Law, while the Rechabites honored their father by obeying his command.

The Rechabites were a clan of nomadic people loyal to their ancestor Jonadab (2 Kings 10:15-23), who commanded them not to live in houses, not to have farms or vineyards, and not to drink wine. They were related to Moses' father-in-law (Jud. 1:16; 4:11) and for over 250 years had composed a small "separatist" clan in the nation. Because of the Babylonian invasion, they had forsaken their tents and moved into Jerusalem.

God didn't ask Jeremiah to serve the Rechabites wine in order to tempt them, because God doesn't tempt us (James 1:13-15). This was another action sermon to give Jeremiah an opportunity to tell the leaders of Judah how unfaithful they had been to God's covenant. It wasn't wrong for the Jewish people to drink wine so long as they didn't get drunk, but it was wrong for the Rechabites to drink wine *because they had made a commitment not to drink it.* God didn't commend these men for their personal standards but for their faithfulness to their father's command.

The message to the nation was clear. If the command of a mere man, Jonadab, was respected and obeyed by his family for over two centuries, why didn't the people of Israel and Judah obey the command of Almighty God—a command that the prophets had repeated over and over again? If a family tradition was preserved with such dedication, why was the very Law of God treated with such disrespect? Obeying Jonadab's words had only a limited and temporal significance, but disobeying God's Word had eternal consequences!

How often God's people are put to shame by the devotion and discipline of people who don't even know the Lord but who are intensely loyal to their family, their religion, or their personal pursuits. Even people who want nothing to do with the Word of God can be loyal to traditions and man-made codes. If Christians were putting into their spiritual walk the kind of discipline that athletes put into their chosen sport, the church would be pulsating with revival life.

2. God's Word Protected (Jer. 36:1-32)

The fourth year of Jehoiakim was 605 B.C., the year of the fateful Battle of Carchemish when Pharaoh Necho defeated King Josiah and made Judah a vassal to Egypt (Jer. 46:2; 2 Chron. 35:20-27). Jehoiakim had gotten his throne only because Egypt had deposed his brother Jehoahaz. Jeremiah had been ministering for twenty-three years, and now God commanded him to write his messages in a scroll so they would be permanent and could be read by others. Note that his messages dealt with Israel, Judah, and all the nations, and when he wrote the second scroll, he added other material (Jer. 36:32). The first forty-five chapters of the Book of Jeremiah focus primarily on Israel and Judah, while chapters 45 to 51 deal with the other nations in the Near East.

God gives His Word (vv. 1-4, 17-18). This is what theologians call *inspiration*—that miraculous working of the Holy Spirit through a human writer so that what was written was the divine Word that God wanted recorded (2 Tim. 3:16; 2 Peter 1:20-21).[2] Inspiration is not some kind of "heavenly dictation," as though God completely bypassed the writer, for the authors of the various books of the Bible have their own distinctive styles and vocabularies. Without making him a robot, God guided Jeremiah in his choice of words; Jeremiah spoke these words to his secretary Baruch; and Baruch wrote them down in the scroll.

God declared His Word (vv. 5-26). Once again, God used human instruments to proclaim His Word to the people. "How shall they hear without a preacher"? (Rom. 10:14) Since Jeremiah wasn't allowed to go to the temple, he sent Baruch in his place. Baruch waited for a day when there would be a good crowd in the temple; when a fast was proclaimed several months later, probably because of the Babylonian menace, he took advantage of it.

It's interesting to see how different people responded to the Word of God. There were three public readings of the book, and the first one was to the people in the temple (Jer. 36:10). There's no record that the crowd responded in any special way. One man, Micaiah, however, became concerned because of what he had heard (v. 11). He was the grandson of Shaphan, the man who read the newly found book of the Law to King Josiah (2 Kings 22), so it's no wonder he had an interest in God's Word.

Micaiah told the princes about the book, and they asked to hear it, so Baruch read it to them (Jer. 36:12-19). Along with Micaiah, the officials trembled when they heard the Word (v. 16), for they knew that the nation was in great danger. They hid the scroll, told Baruch and Jeremiah to hide, and then went to report to the king that he needed to hear what Jeremiah had written.

The third reading of the scroll was before the king (vv. 21-26) and was done by Jehudi, who may have been one of the scribes. The king treated God's Word like fuel for the fire! In spite of the remonstrances of three of his officials, the king continued cutting and burning the scroll until it was completely destroyed. The royal attendants who also heard the reading of the scroll showed no fear and thereby encouraged Jehoiakim in his evil deed.

Over the centuries, God's enemies have tried to destroy the Word of God but have always failed. They forget what Jesus said about the Word: "Heaven and earth shall pass away, but My words shall not pass away" (Matt. 24:35). "The grass withers and the flowers fall, but the word of our God stands forever" (Isa. 40:8, NIV; quoted in 1 Peter 1:24-25). Translators and preachers of the Word have been persecuted and martyred, but the truth of God still stands.

God preserves His Word (vv. 27-32). Any king who thinks he can silence God with a knife and a fire has a very high opinion of himself and a very low opinion of God. The Lord simply told Jeremiah to write another scroll, to which He added more material, including a special judgment on King Jehohkim (Jer. 36:27-32). The same God who gives the Word has the power to protect and preserve the Word. The king had tried to destroy the Word, but the Word destroyed him!

King Jehoiakim and his officials would be punished for the disrespect they showed to the divine Word of God. The king would have no dynasty, nor would he have the burial of a king. His son Jehoiachin succeeded him and ruled for only three months, and then Jehoiakim's brother Zedekiah was made king. If the king and his flattering, servile officers had only feared the Word and obeyed it, they would have saved their nation suffering and ruin, but they preferred to go their own way and ignore God's voice.

3. God's Word Rejected (Jer. 37:1–38:28)

"There's no problem so big or complicated that it can't be run away from." So read a piece of graffito found on a London wall in 1979, probably adapted from the "Peanuts" comic strip drawn by Charles Schulz. Whatever the source, the statement certainly represents King Zedekiah's approach to the terrible problems in Judah when the enemy was at the gates.

Next to Pontius Pilate (John 18–19), no ruler in Scripture reveals such indecision and vacillation as does King Zedekiah. These two chapters record four occasions when Zedekiah made contact with Jeremiah but rejected the Word that the prophet gave him. Listen to his feeble words.

"Pray for us!" (vv. 1-10) Afraid to come personally lest he lose the support of his officials, the king sent Jehucal (Jucal) and Zephaniah to solicit the prayers of Jeremiah for the king and the nation. Jehucal was not Jeremiah's friend, and he eventually urged the king to have the prophet killed (Jer. 38:1, 4). God had told Jeremiah not to pray for the people, but when the Babylonian army departed to deal with the Egyptians, it seemed like prayer wasn't needed (37:5-10). No doubt the false prophets announced that this event was a miracle, like the slaying of the Assyrian army in Hezekiah's day (Isa. 36–37). Once again, they were living on false hopes even though Jeremiah told them that Nebuchadnezzar would return and finish the work God had given him to do.

"Is there any word from the Lord?" (vv. 11-21) Until now, Jeremiah was a free man (v. 4), but his enemies found reason to imprison him. During the lull in the siege, Jeremiah tried to go home to Anathoth to take care of some family business, but the guard at the gate arrested him for defecting to the enemy. Of course, Jeremiah had preached surrender to Babylon (21:9) and would preach it again (38:2, 19; 39:9), but he certainly wasn't a traitor. He loved his nation and gave his life to try to save it, but his first loyalty was to the Lord.

Jeremiah was beaten and put into prison. When Zedekiah heard about it, he recognized it as an opportunity to talk safely to Jeremiah, for the officers would think the king was looking into Jeremiah's case. After bringing him to the palace, the king asked, "Is there any word from the Lord?" The prophet gave him an immediate answer, "Yes . . . you will be handed over to the king of Babylon" (37:17, NIV). Why say more? Jeremiah had already declared God's message many times, only to see the message rejected.

Jeremiah took the opportunity to expose the deceptive, optimistic messages of the false prophets. If they had been speaking the truth, the king should have asked them for a message from the Lord! Meanwhile, Jeremiah asked to be delivered from prison, a request that Zedekiah granted. The prophet was placed in the court of the prison and granted a daily ration of bread as long as the supply lasted. While we appreciate Zedekiah's concern to save Jeremiah, we wonder why the king didn't have a concern to save his people. He was afraid to change his policies because he was afraid of his advisers and officers.

"He is in your hands" (38:1-13). Angry because Jeremiah's words were hurting the war effort, four of Zedekiah's officials banded together to urge the king to kill the prophet. We know nothing about Shephatiah. If Gedaliah was the son of the Pashur who had put Jeremiah in the stocks (20:1-6), he was certainly no friend to Jeremiah or to the truth. Jucal we met before (37:3); he may have been related to the guard who arrested Jeremiah (v. 13).[3] This Pashur must not be confused with the Pashur mentioned in Jeremiah 20. They accused Jeremiah of not seeking the welfare of the people, and yet the welfare of the people was the thing to which he had dedicated his life!

Too weak to oppose his own princes, the king gave in to their request. Instead of simply having Jeremiah slain, which would have been shedding innocent blood, the men had him imprisoned in an old cistern, where he sank in the mire at the bottom. The officers hoped that the prophet would eventually be forgotten there and would die. God, however, raised up a deliverer in the person of Ebed-Melech—a man from Ethiopia, who became an Old Testament "Good Samaritan."

The vacillating, spineless king usually agreed with the last person who spoke to him, and Ebed-Melech took advantage of that fault. Thus, the king gave Ebed-Melech permission to rescue Jeremiah. It wouldn't have taken thirty men to lift the prophet out of the cistern, but the king probably wanted to protect both his officer and the prophet from any attacks by Jeremiah's enemies. (Some commentators suggest that the text should read "three men." Thirty men would certainly call attention to themselves and what they were doing.)

Later, Jeremiah sent a special message of encouragement to Ebed-Melech (39:15-18)—that he would be delivered when the city was taken and that God would spare his life.

"Hide nothing from me" (vv. 14-28). As far as the record is concerned, this was the fourth and last contact King Zedekiah had with Jeremiah before the city fell to the Babylonians. His request presented Jeremiah with a dilemma: If Jeremiah told him the truth, the king might kill him, and he wouldn't obey the Word of God anyway! God gave the king one last chance to repent, but he only made excuses. If he surrendered to Nebuchadnezzar, he might be accused and abused by the Jews who had gone over to the enemy, and what would happen to his family left in the city? Perhaps the men who wanted to kill Jeremiah would kill them.

Jeremiah assured the king that if he obeyed the Word of the Lord, God would protect him and the city. But if he disobeyed, even the women in the palace would taunt him before the Babylonians (38:21-23). We can appreciate the king's concern for his wives and children, but the best way to protect them was to obey the will of God.

Still afraid of his own officers, the king told Jeremiah to keep their conversation confidential. There's no suggestion that Jeremiah lied to the officers who questioned him. To begin with, we may not have a transcript of the complete conversation between Jeremiah and Zedekiah, and Jeremiah may have asked not to be returned to the house of Jonathan. Certainly in their second conversation, Jeremiah had made such a request (37:17-21). He was under no obligation to report everything to the officers, and he didn't have to lie in order to keep the conversation confidential.

Sometimes God judges a sinful nation by sending them weak leaders who are hesitant and vacillating and whose leadership (or lack of it) plunges the nation only deeper into trouble. "I will give children to be their princes, and babes shall rule over them" (Isa. 3:4, NKJV). The late John F. Kennedy put it this way: "We, the people, are the boss, and we get the kind of political leadership, be it good or bad, that we demand and deserve."[4] But Judah wasn't a democracy; the people didn't vote on their king. It was God who gave them what they deserved.

4. God's Word Fulfilled (Jer. 39; 52)

These two chapters, along with 2 Kings 25 and 2 Chronicles 36, describe the tragic fall of Jerusalem, its plunder, and its destruction, as well as the Captivity and deportation of thousands of Jewish people. None of these things would have happened if only one of the kings had sincerely repented, trusted the Lord, and surrendered to the Babylonians.

God's judgment on Zedekiah (39:1-7, 52:1-11). The siege had begun on January 15, 588 (Jer. 52:4); and two and a half years later, on July 18, 586, the Babylonian army penetrated the city walls. The princes of Babylon set up their thrones in the Middle Gate and began to take over the reins of government. The "times of the Gentiles" had begun on God's prophetic calendar (Luke 21:24). When that period ends, the Messiah will return to rescue His people and fulfill the promises made by the prophets.

Zedekiah, his family, and his staff tried to escape (see Jer. 34:3; Ezek. 12:1-12), but the Babylonians caught up with them and delivered them to Nebuchadnezzar at his headquarters at Riblah, some 200 miles north of Jerusalem. There he passed judgment on all of them, and the Babylonians were not known for their tenderness. He slaughtered Zedekiah's sons and then put out Zedekiah's eyes. Thus, the king's last visual memories would haunt him. Ezekiel had prophesied that Zedekiah would not see the land of Babylon (Ezek. 12:13), and his prophecy proved true. The king was bound and taken captive to Babylon, where he died.

God's judgment on the city (39:8-10; 52:12-34). "For this city has been to Me a provocation of My anger and My fury from the day that they built it, even to this day; so I will remove it from before My face" (Jer. 32:31, NKJV). Throughout his ministry, Jeremiah had warned the people that Jerusalem would be captured and destroyed (6:6; 19:8-9, 11-12, 15; 21:10; 26:6, 11; 27:17).

At the same time, the Babylonians pillaged the city and took the precious things out of the temple and carried them to Babylon. The soldiers rounded up the best of the people and took them to Babylon. There had been a previous deportation in 597 B.C. (52:28), and there would be a third deportation in 582 (52:30). The poorer, unskilled people were left to till the land. After all, somebody had to feed the soldiers who were left behind.

God's care for His servant (39:11-14). Since the Lord had promised that Jeremiah would survive all the opposition and persecution against him (1:17-19; 15:20-21), He moved upon Nebuchadnezzar to release the prophet and treat him kindly.[5] He was committed to Gedaliah, who later was named governor of the land (40:7). (This Gedaliah was not the one who wanted to kill Jeremiah, 38:1.)

I close with a solemn word from G. Campbell Morgan: "We in our security need to be reminded that for us also there may come the eleventh year, and the fourth month, and the tenth day of the month, when God will hurl us from our place of privilege, as He surely will, unless we are true to Him."[6]

CHAPTER ELEVEN
TRAGEDY FOLLOWS TRAGEDY
JEREMIAH 40–45

Life only demands from you the strength you possess. Only one feat is possible—not to have run away.

—Dag Hammarskjold[1]

It's been said by more than one scholar that the one thing we learn from history is that we *don't* learn from history. This was certainly true of the destitute Jewish remnant in Judah after the fall of Jerusalem. Instead of seeking the Lord and making a new beginning, the remnant repeated the very sins that had led to the collapse of the nation and the destruction of the city: They wouldn't listen to the Word; they turned to Egypt for help; and they worshiped idols.

The sinful behavior of the people must have broken Jeremiah's heart, but he stayed with them and tried to get them to obey the Word of the Lord. God had punished the nation, but even this severe punishment didn't change their hearts. They were still bent on doing evil.

The drama was a tragic one with a cast of characters that is seen in every age. The script of history may change a bit from time to time, but the characters are still the same.

1. Jeremiah, the Faithful Shepherd (Jer. 40:1-6)

Jeremiah was given his freedom after the Babylonians captured Jerusalem (39:11-14), but somehow he got mixed in with the captives who were being readied at Ramah for their long march to Babylon. He was released and given the choice of going to Babylon and being cared for by the king or remaining in the land to care for the people. Being a man with a shepherd's heart, Jeremiah chose to dwell among the people (v. 14; 40:5-6).

The Babylonian captain of the guard preached a sermon that sounded a great deal like what Jeremiah had been saying for forty years! It must have been embarrassing for the Jews to hear a pagan Babylonian tell them they were sinners, but he was right in what he said. As God's people, we have to bow in shame when the world publicly announces the sins of the saints (Gen. 12:10-20; 20:1ff; 2 Sam. 12:14).

Jeremiah chose to join Gedaliah, whom Nebuchadnezzar had appointed governor of the land. Had the people followed the prophet and the governor, the Jewish remnant could have led safe and fairly comfortable lives even in the midst of ruin, but they chose not to obey. Even a severe chastening like the one Babylon brought to Judah didn't change their hearts, for the human heart can be changed only by the grace of God.

Was Jeremiah violating his own message when he remained with the people in the land? (24:4-10) Why stay with the "bad figs" when the future lay with the "good figs" who had been taken off to Babylon? Certainly Jeremiah knew how to discern the will of God, and the Lord knew how much the prophet loved the land and its people. Ezekiel was taken to Babylon in 597 and would start his ministry five years later (Ezek. 1:1-2), and Daniel had been taken there in 605. There were prophets to minister to the exiles, and Jeremiah was right to remain with the people in the land.

Jeremiah made difficult choices at the beginning and the end of his ministry. It would have been much easier to serve as a priest, but he obeyed God's call to be a prophet, and it would have been much more comfortable in Babylon, but he opted to remain in the land of his fathers. Jeremiah was a true shepherd and not a hireling (see John 10:12-13).

2. Ishmael, a Deceitful Traitor (Jer. 40:7–41:18)

When the good news got out that Gedaliah was in charge of affairs in Judah, the people who had fled and hidden because of the siege began to come back to the land (Jer. 40:7, 11-12). Gedaliah was a good man from a good family, although events proved that he was very naive about practical politics.

The faithful governor (vv. 7-12). Gedaliah told the people exactly what Jeremiah had been telling them for many years: Serve the Babylonians and you will live safely in the land. The people couldn't reap any harvest of grain because the fields hadn't been sown during the siege, but they could gather the produce that had not been destroyed in the war. The remnant in Judah had to follow the same instructions that Jeremiah gave to the exiles in Babylon: Live normal lives, turn to the Lord with all your hearts, and wait for the Lord to deliver you (29:4-14). God had promised a future for the nation because the nation had important work to do.

The concerned captain (vv. 13-16). Johanan started out as a courageous leader, but later he led the people astray. We don't know how he and his associates heard about Ishmael's plot to assassinate Gedaliah, but their information was certainly accurate. Had Gedaliah listened to them, the governor's life would have been spared.

Why did Ishmael want to kill Gedaliah? The fact that the king of the Ammonites had hired him (40:14) suggests that he was making money, but much more was involved. The Ammonites had been a part of the "summit conference" in Jerusalem, where the nations allied with Judah had planned to break the Babylonian yoke (27:1-3). As a friend of Zedekiah and the king of Ammon, Ishmael didn't want to see the Jewish people submit to Nebuchadnezzar even after the war had ended. He was a patriot who used his patriotism to promote his own selfish purposes.

Perhaps the key factor had to do with pride and selfish ambition. Ishmael was a descendant of David through Elishama (41:1; 2 Sam. 5:16), and he no doubt felt that he should have been named ruler of the nation because of his royal blood. Who was Gedaliah that he should take the place of a king? The way the Babylonians had treated Ishmael's relative, King Zedekiah, was no encouragement to submit to their authority.

Johanan wanted to kill Ishmael, but Gedaliah refused the offer. In this, the governor was right, but he was wrong in not assembling a group of loyal men who could guard him day and night. Not only would that have told Ishmael that the governor knew what was going on, but also it would have protected Gedaliah's life from those who wanted to destroy him. The governor should have listened to Johanan and not been so naive about Ishmael. "For lack of guidance a nation falls, but many advisers make victory sure" (Prov. 11:14, NIV).

The deceitful murderer (41:1-18). In the Near East, when people eat together, they're pledging their friendship and loyalty to one another. Ishmael, however, used the meal as a trap to catch Gedaliah and his men so he could kill them. We don't know how many men were with the governor, but ten of Ishmael's men were able to dispatch them quickly.

To his terrible breach of hospitality he added hypocrisy, weeping before the eighty Jewish pilgrims who had come to worship, and then killing seventy of them. His greed was revealed when he spared the other ten in order to find out where their supply of food was hidden. He was a cunning and ruthless man who would stop at nothing to get his own way.

Ishmael climaxed his crimes by kidnapping the helpless Jewish remnant and starting for the land of the Ammonites. At this point, however, Johanan came to the rescue and delivered the remnant from Ishmael's power, but Ishmael escaped. It was a series of tragedies that probably could have been averted had Gedaliah listened to his friends and acted with more caution.

Johanan showed courage in rescuing the Jews, but when he was finally in charge, he revealed his own lack of faith *by wanting to take the remnant to Egypt*! He didn't remember the counsel of Gedaliah (Jer. 40:9) or the messages of Jeremiah, both of whom warned the Jews to stay in the land and not go to Egypt. How easy it is for a good man to go astray simply by turning away from the Word of God!

3. Johanan: a Hypocritical Leader (Jer. 42:1–43:13)

Johanan was once brave enough to want to kill Ishmael, but now he didn't have the courage to stand for what he knew was right. He was afraid to trust the Lord and stay in the land of Judah, perhaps because he feared what the Babylonians might do when they found out that Gedaliah was dead and Ishmael had filled a pit with dead bodies.

The insincere request (vv. 1-6). Their request to Jeremiah sounded sincere and spiritual, but there was deception in the hearts of the leaders, including Johanan (see 42:19-22). They had their minds already made up to go to Egypt, and they were hoping Jeremiah would agree with them. Sometimes God's people take this false approach in discerning the will of God. Instead of honestly seeking God's will, they go from counselor to counselor, asking for advice and hoping they'll find somebody who will agree with their hidden agenda.

The divine answer (vv. 7-22). The Lord kept the people waiting for ten days, possibly to give them time to search their hearts and confess their sins. During those ten days, they could see that the Lord was caring for them and that they had nothing to fear. That should have convinced them that the plan to flee to Egypt was a foolish one.

There were three parts to the answer Jeremiah gave them. First, he gave them *a promise* (vv. 7-12). He told them if they stayed in the land, God would build them and plant them (see 1:10). The prophet encouraged them not to be afraid of the Babylonians because the Lord was with the remnant and would care for them. It was God who was in charge, not the king of Babylon. Indeed, the day would come when this small remnant would be able to reclaim their lost lands and start to enjoy normal lives again.

The second part of Jeremiah's message was *a warning* (42:13-18). Ever since Abraham's lapse of faith in going to Egypt (Gen. 12:10-20), the Jews had a tendency to follow his example. Several times during the wilderness years, whenever they had a trial or testing, the Israelites talked of going back to Egypt. In fact, this was their cry at Kadesh-Barnea when they refused to enter the Promised Land (Num. 13–14). During the final years of the kingdom of Judah, there was a strong pro-Egyptian party in the government, because Egypt seemed to be the closest and strongest ally.

The prophet warned them against going to Egypt, where they thought they would enjoy peace, plenty, and security. The terrors they were trying to avoid in Judah would only follow them to Egypt, and the very judgments that God had sent against Judah during the siege would come upon them in the land of Pharaoh. God knew that Nebuchadnezzar would enter Egypt and punish the land, which he did in 568–567 B.C. (see Jer. 46:13-19).

Jeremiah ended his address with *an exposure of their hearts* (vv. 19-22). He announced publicly that they had tried to deceive him when they promised to obey the Lord's commands (42:5-6). They really didn't want either his prayers or God's plans, they wanted the Lord to approve what they had already decided to do. But this was a fatal decision on their part, for if they carried out their plans, they would die in Egypt.

This event is a warning to us not to be insincere as we seek the will of God. In my itinerant ministry, I've frequently met people who wanted my counsel, and when I asked them if they had talked with their own pastor, the answer was often "Well, no, but he really doesn't know me or understand me."

"But I'm a total stranger to you!" I'd reply.

"Yes, but you seem to understand things better." Flattery!

My conviction is that these people have gone from one speaker to another, looking for somebody who will agree with what they already want to do. When they find him, they'll let their pastor know that a "man of God" gave them wise counsel. It's the Johanan syndrome all over again.

The arrogant rebellion (43:1-7). Convinced that God was wrong and they were right, Johanan and his friends so much as told Jeremiah he was a liar and a false prophet, and that God had neither sent him nor spoken to him. What a heartache it must have been for Jeremiah to hear such false accusations from his own people for whom he had suffered so much. In spite of all he had done for his people, Jeremiah was now accused of being like the false prophets whose lies had led the nation into ruin. Johanan even accused Baruch of influencing Jeremiah, although it's difficult to understand what kind of special power Baruch could possibly have had over this courageous prophet. But they had to blame somebody.

"So they came into the land of Egypt" (43:7). Once again God's people walked by sight and not by faith.

The timely warning (vv. 8-13). This is Jeremiah's final "action sermon." While the Jews were watching, he gathered some large stones and set them in the clay (or mortar) before Pharaoh's house in Tahpanhes. Then he announced that Nebuchadnezzar's throne would one day sit on those stones while the king of Babylon passed judgment on the people. As he did to the temple in Jerusalem, so Nebuchadnezzar would do to the gods and temples in Egypt. His victory would be so easy that it would be like a shepherd wrapping his garment around himself! *And yet these are the very gods that the Jews would worship in Egypt, gods destined to be destroyed!*

4. The Jewish Remnant: Doomed Idolaters (Jer. 44:1-30)

This is Jeremiah's last recorded message to his people, given in Egypt probably in the year 580. If he was called by God in 626, the thirteenth year of Josiah's reign (1:2), then he had been ministering forty-six years. You can't help admiring Jeremiah for his faithfulness in spite of all the discouragements that had come to his life.

A scathing indictment (vv. 1-14). No sooner did the Jewish remnant arrive in Egypt than they began to worship the local gods and goddesses, of which there were many. Jeremiah reminded them of *what they had seen* in the Lord's judgment on Judah (44:2-3). It was because of their idolatry that He had destroyed their land, the city of Jerusalem, and the temple. Then he reminded them of *what they had heard*—the messages of the prophets God had sent to rebuke them time after time (vv. 4-6).

But they hadn't learned their lesson, and now they were jeopardizing their future and inviting the wrath of God by repeating in Egypt the sins they'd committed in Judah. Had they forgotten the past? Were they unconcerned about their future? Didn't they realize that God could judge them in Egypt as easily as He had judged them in their own land? No wonder God called the Jews in the land "bad figs that nobody could eat." The future would rest with the exiles in Babylon who would one day return to their land and carry on the work God had given them to do.

A senseless argument (vv. 15-19). The men and women listening to Jeremiah tried to defend their sins by appealing to experience. They used the pragmatic argument: "If it works, it must be right." When they lived in Judah and secretly worshiped the Queen of Heaven (Astarte or Ishtar, goddess of fertility), everything went well with them. They had plenty of food and enjoyed comfortable circumstances. But when King Josiah made the people give up their idols, things began to get worse for them. Conclusion: They were better off when they disobeyed God and worshiped idols!

It seems that the women led the way in practicing idolatry, and their husbands cooperated with them. The women made vows to worship Astarte, *and their husbands approved of what they did* (vv. 24-26). According to Jewish law, if the husband approved his wife's vow, it was valid (Num. 30). Consequently, the wives blamed their husbands, and the husbands told Jeremiah that they didn't care what he said! They were going to worship Astarte just as they had done in Judah and in that way be sure things would go right for them.

A terrible pronouncement (vv. 20-30). How tragic that twice in a few short years the Lord had to pronounce judgment on His people for the same sins! Jeremiah told them, "Go ahead then, do what you promised! Keep your vows! But hear the Word of the Lord" (Jer. 44:25-26, NIV). The Jews in Egypt would perish, and only a remnant of the remnant would ever return to their own land.

Jeremiah gave them a sign: Pharaoh Hopbra, whom they were trusting to care for them, would be handed over to his enemies just as King Zedekiah was handed over to Nebuchadnezzar. Keep in mind that it was Pharaoh Hopbra who agreed to help Zedekiah against the Babylonians, and his help proved worthless. Historians tell us that a part of the Egyptian army revolted against Hopbra, and the general who stopped the rebellion was proclaimed king. He reigned along with Hopbra, but three years later Hopbra was executed. Nebuchadnezzar then appeared on the scene, and Jeremiah's other prophecy was fulfilled.

It's likely that Jeremiah was dead when all this happened but did the Jews in Egypt remember his words and take them to heart? Did they realize that he had faithfully declared God's Word and that what he had said was true? Did they repent and seek to obey?

5. Baruch: a Faithful Servant (Jer. 45:1-5)

Chronologically, this chapter belongs with Jeremiah 36, but it was placed here to perform several functions.

To begin with, this chapter introduces the prophecies in chapters 46–51, prophecies Baruch had written at Jeremiah's dictation in 605 B.C. Note in Jeremiah 25 the emphasis on Jeremiah's prophecies about the nations, and that this chapter was written at the same time as chapter 45, the fourth year of Jehoiakim. Most of the nations dealt with in chapters 46–51 are named in Jeremiah 25:15-26.

Second, Jeremiah 45 gives us insight into the man Baruch. As we noted earlier, he had a brother on the king's official staff who probably could have secured a good job for him in the palace. Instead, Baruch chose to identify with Jeremiah and do the will of God. We thank God for all that Jeremiah did, but we should also thank God for the assistance Baruch gave Jeremiah so the prophet could do his work. Moses had his seventy elders; David had his mighty men; Jesus had His disciples; Paul had his helpers, such as Timothy, Titus, and Silas; and Jeremiah had his faithful secretary.

Not everybody is called to be a prophet or apostle, but all of us can do the will of God by helping others do their work. Baruch was what we'd today call a "layman." Yet he helped a prophet write the Word of God. In my own ministry, I've appreciated the labors of faithful secretaries and assistants who have helped me in myriads of ways. I may have been on the platform, but without their assistance behind the scenes, I could never have gotten my work done. Baruch was willing to stay in the background and serve God by serving Jeremiah.

A third lesson emerges: Even the most devoted servants occasionally get discouraged. Baruch came to a point in his life where he was so depressed that he wanted to quit. "Woe is me now! For the Lord has added grief to my sorrow. I fainted in my sighing, and I find no rest" (45:3, NKJV). Perhaps the persecution of Jeremiah recorded in chapter 26 was the cause of this anguish. Maybe Baruch was considering leaving Jeremiah and asking his brother for an easier job in the palace.

The Lord, however, had a word of encouragement for His servant. First, He cautioned him not to build his hopes on the future of Judah, because everything would be destroyed in the Babylonian siege. A "soft job" in the government would lead only to death or exile in Babylon. Then God gave him a word of assurance: his life would be spared, so he didn't have to fear the enemy. God was proving to Baruch the reality of a promise that would be written centuries later: "But seek first the kingdom of God and His righteousness, and all these things shall be added to you" (Matt. 6:33, NKJV).

When we're serving the Lord and His people, we never want to seek great things for ourselves. The only important thing is that God's work is accomplished and God's great name is glorified. John the Baptist put it succinctly: "He must increase, but I must decrease" (John 3:30).

A crisis doesn't "make a person"; a crisis reveals what a person is made of. The crisis that followed the destruction of Jerusalem was like a goldsmith's furnace that revealed the dross as well as the pure gold. It's too bad there wasn't more gold.

How will you and I respond when "the fiery trial" comes? (1 Peter 4:12-19) I hope that, like Job, we'll come forth pure gold (Job 23:10).

CHAPTER TWELVE
GOD SPEAKS TO THE NATIONS
JEREMIAH 46–49

I have lived, Sir, a long time, and the longer I live, the more convincing proofs I see of this truth—*that God governs in the affairs of men.*

—Benjamin Franklin[1]

Jeremiah had spoken to his people for over forty years, but they wouldn't listen; now he spoke to the nations related in some way to the Jewish people. As God's spokesman, Jeremiah was "handing the cup" to these nations (25:15ff) and declaring what God had planned for them. He was called to be "a prophet unto the nations" (1:5), and he was fulfilling his ministry.

While these names, places, and events are ancient history to most of us, the lessons behind these events reveal to us the hand of God in the rise and fall of rulers and nations. One of the repeated phrases in these chapters is God's "I will," for "history is His story," as A.T. Pierson used to say. You will also note that God judged *the gods of these nations*, just as He had judged the gods of Egypt before Israel's Exodus (Ex. 12:12).

1. Judgment on Egypt (Jer. 46:1-28)

Pharaoh Necho had defeated Judah and killed King Josiah at Megiddo in 609 (2 Chron. 35:20-27), but then Nebuchadnezar defeated Necho at the famous Battle of Carchemish in 605, the fourth year of Jehoiakim. That defeat broke the power of Egypt and made Babylon supreme in the Near East. Jeremiah described the battle from Egypt's viewpoint (Jer. 46:3-12); then he described Babylon's invasion of Egypt (vv. 13-26), concluding with an application to the people of Israel (vv. 27-28).

Egypt's shameful defeat (vv. 3-12). Jeremiah wrote a graphic description of the famous Battle of Carchemish. He described the officers confidently preparing their troops (vv. 3-4) and then watching the soldiers flee in terror before the Babylonian army (vv. 5-6). Jeremiah doesn't even describe the battle! The phrase "fear was round about" is the familiar "terror on every side" that we've met before (6:25; 20:3) and will meet again (49:29).

When the Egyptian army approached the battlefield, they looked like the Nile in flood season (46:8a). The military leaders were sure of victory (v. 8b), and their mercenaries were eager to fight (v. 9), but the Lord had determined that Egypt would lose the battle. "That day belongs to the Lord, the Lord Almighty" (v. 10, NIV).[2] It was a "holy war" in that God offered Egypt as a sacrifice (v. 10). Egypt's wounds were incurable and her shame was inevitable (vv. 11-12).

Babylon's triumphant invasion (vv. 13-26). Historians tell us that this occurred in 568–67 B.C. and fulfilled not only this prophecy but also the "action sermon" Jeremiah had described earlier (43:8-13). Once again, the Egyptian army stood fast as the Babylonians swept down on them. Before long, however, the men not only fell over but also fell upon one another in their haste to escape (46:13-15). Their mercenaries cried, "Arise, and let us go again to our own people, and to the land of our nativity" (v. 16), and they deserted their posts.

The Babylonian soldiers called Pharaoh Necho a "big noise." We today would probably call him a "loudmouth" or "big mouth," because he was nothing but talk and hot air.[3] While Necho may have been only hot air, Nebuchadnezzar filled the horizon like a huge mountain when he appeared on the scene (v. 18).

Look at the graphic images Jeremiah used. Egypt was like a heifer (v. 20). The mercenaries in Pharaoh's army were like fatted calves that stampeded (v. 21), and the Egyptian soldiers fled like hissing serpents (v. 22) and fell before the Babylonians like trees before woodcutters (v. 23). The invading army was like a swarm of locusts that couldn't be avoided (v. 23). Alas, Egypt was like a young woman being violated and unable to escape (v. 24).

The defeat of Egypt was the defeat of Egypt's gods (v. 25). This didn't mean that the gods of Babylon were stronger than the gods of Egypt, for all of their gods were nothing. It meant that Jehovah had proved Himself stronger than the many gods of Egypt and Babylon by being in control of the entire battle. Nebuchadnezzar won and Pharaoh Necho lost because God decreed it. But God also decreed that Egypt would be restored (v. 26), a promise He also gave to Moab (48:47), Ammon (49:6), and Elam (v. 39).

Israel's assured future (vv. 27-28). They shouldn't have been there, but a band of Jews was in Egypt, and this invasion would affect them terribly. The remnant in Judah and the exiles in Babylon would hear of this victory and wonder whether anything on earth could stop Nebuchadnezzar. God had promised that the exiles would be released from Babylon in seventy years, but Babylon looked stronger than ever.

God's Word will stand no matter what the newspapers report! "I will save you," God promised. "I will wipe out the nations, but I won't wipe you out."[4] Twice the Lord said, "Don't be afraid." No matter how dark the day, God always gives His people the bright light of His promises (2 Peter 1:19-21).

2. Judgment on Philistia (Jer. 47:1-7)

The Philistine people probably came from Crete (Caphtor, v. 4). They built a wealthy nation by developing a merchant marine that sailed the Mediterranean and acquired goods from many lands. But their destiny was destruction. Tyre and Sidon had been confederate with Judah in an attempt to stop Nebuchadnezzar (27:3).

This time Jeremiah used the image of the rising river to describe the Babylonian army as it flooded over the land (47:2). So terrible was the invasion that parents would flee for their lives and leave their children behind (v. 3; see 49:11). The people would act like mourners at a funeral (47:5) and ask the Lord when He would put up the terrible sword of His judgment (v. 6). But this sword would continue to devour the land until God's work of judgment was finished.

3. Judgment on Moab (Jer. 48:1-47)

The Moabites were descendants of Lot (Gen. 19:20-38) and, along with the Ammonites, the enemies of the Jews. During the Babylonian crisis, however, both Moab and Ammon allied themselves with Judah in an ill-fated attempt to defeat Nebuchadnezzar (Jer. 27:3). Over twenty different places are named in this chapter, some of which we can't identify with certainty, but the list shows how detailed God can be when He wants to predict future events.[5]

In 582, Nebuchadnezzar's army invaded Moab, destroyed the people and the cities, and left desolation behind. The reason for this judgment was Moab's pride (48:7, 29-30) and complacency (v. 11). The Moabites were certain that their god Chemosh would protect them (vv. 7, 13, 35, 46) and that no army could scale the heights to reach them on their secure plateau (v. 8).

The image in verses 11-13 pictures Moab as a self-satisfied nation, feeling very secure, like wine aging in a jar and becoming tastier. Because the nation had been comfortable and self-sufficient, they were unprepared for what happened. The Babylonians emptied the wine from jar to jar and then broke the jars! (See v. 38 for another broken jar image.) Instead of sitting on their mountainous throne, the nation had to come down and grovel on the parched earth (vv. 17-18). The horn and the arm are both symbols of strength (v. 25), but Moab's horn was cut off and her arm broken. She had no strength.

The wine image is picked up again in verses 26-27. The nation was drunk from the cup that God gave her (25:15-16, 27-29), and like someone at a drunken party, she was vomiting and wallowing in her own vomit. It isn't a pretty picture. The image then changes to that of a dove hiding in a cave, wondering what will happen next (48:28). The Babylonians are pictured as an eagle swooping down on its prey (v. 40; see Deut. 28:49; Ezek. 17:3); a dove is no match for an eagle.

The remarkable thing is that Jeremiah wept over the fall of Moab (Jer. 48:31) and lamented like a flutist at a funeral (vv. 36-38). Certainly his grief is evidence of the compassion God has for people who are destroyed because of their sins against the Lord. God has "no pleasure in the death of [the wicked]" (Ezek. 18:32; see 18:23; 33:11) and does all He can to call them to repentance before judgment falls.

There is no escape (Jer. 48:44-46; see Amos 5:19). Flee from the army, and you'll fall into a pit. Climb out of the pit, and you'll be caught in a trap. Escape from the trap, and you'll be engulfed by a fire. Escape from the fire, and you'll be captured and taken away to Babylon. Sinners need to face the fact that there is no place to hide when God begins to judge (Rev. 20:11-15). For lost sinners today, their only hope is faith in Jesus Christ, who died for the sins of the world. They need to flee for refuge to Christ (Heb. 6:18)—the only refuge for their souls.

After writing a long chapter on judgment, Jeremiah ended with a promise: "Yet will I bring again the Captivity [restore the fortunes] of Moab in the latter days" (Jer. 48:47). This statement refers to the future Kingdom Age when Jesus Christ will reign.

4. Judgment on Ammon (Jer. 49:1-6)

Like the Moabites, the Ammonites were the product of Lot's incestuous union with one of his daughters (Gen. 19:20-38) and the enemies of the Jews.

Jeremiah's first accusation is that the Ammonites moved into Israel's territory when Assyria took the Northern Kingdom captive in 722 B.C. The Ammonites took Gad and other cities, as though the Jews would never return. The phrase "their king" in Jeremiah 49:1 and 3 can be translated *Molech*, which is the name of the chief god of the Ammonites (1 Kings 11:5, 7, 33). They boasted that their god was stronger than the God of Israel, but one day Israel will "drive" the Ammonites out of the land (Jer. 49:2, NIV).

The Ammonites boasted that their fruitful valley was secure because mountains protected it on three sides (v. 4), but that couldn't stop the invasion. God had decreed judgment for proud Ammon, and nothing they trusted could prevent the invasion.

Once again, however, we see the goodness and mercy of the Lord in promising to restore the fortunes of the Ammonites when He restores the fortunes of Israel and Judah in the future kingdom. God restores them, not because of their own merits, but because they share in the glories that Israel will experience when King Jesus sits on David's throne. "Salvation is of the Jews" (John 4:22).

5. Judgment on Edom (Jer. 49:7-22)

The Edomites had descended from Jacob's elder brother Esau, whom God bypassed for the blessing, giving it to Jacob (Gen. 25:19-34; see Gen. 36). The Edomites weren't friendly to the Jews, but their common enemy, Babylon, caused Edom to join the "Jerusalem summit" in the days of Zedekiah (Jer. 27:3).

You will want to read the prophecy of Obadiah and see how the two prophets agree. Since we don't know when the Book of Obadiah was written, we aren't sure whether Jeremiah borrowed from Obadiah or vice versa. The prophets occasionally quoted one another, an evidence that the same God was the author of their messages. Furthermore, there are a number of parallels between Isaiah and Jeremiah.

Edom's judgment would be like a harvest where nothing would be left for the gleaners (49:9-10; Lev. 19:10; Deut. 24:21). God would do a thorough job the first time. Like the other nations, Edom would have to drink of the cup (Jer. 49:12) because of her pride and rebellion against the Lord (v. 16). With their cities in the rocks, such as Petra, they thought they were impregnable (vv. 16-18), but they would be destroyed like the cities of the plain, Sodom and Gomorrah (Gen. 19).

Nebuchadnezzar would come upon Edom like a lion bounding out of the thick growth around the Jordan River, and he wouldn't spare the flock (Jer. 49:19-21). He would come like an eagle and so frighten the Edomites that they would agonize like women in travail (v. 22; see 48:40-41). The people of Edom were noted for their great wisdom (49:7; Job 2:11), but they wouldn't be able to devise any plan that would save them from the invasion of the Babylonian army.

In the midst of wrath, the Lord remembers mercy (Hab. 3:2) and shows compassion for the widows and orphans (Jer. 49:11; see Ex. 22:21-24; 23:9; Lev. 19:33; Deut. 10:18; 27:19). But Edom's pride would bring her low, as pride always does.

6. Judgment on Syria [Damascus] (Jer. 49:23-27)

The prophet Isaiah condemned Damascus, the capital of Syria (Isa. 17). Amos accused the Syrians of treating the people of Gilead like grain on a threshing floor (Amos 1:3-5). God would judge them for their inhumanity and brutality to His people.

According to Jeremiah, hearing the news of the approaching Babylonian army, the people of Damascus would become as troubled as the restless sea, as weak and shaky as a sick patient, and as full of pain as a woman in travail (Jer. 49:23-24). They would abandon their ancient cities and try to escape, but their best young men would be killed in the streets and their fortress would be burned to the ground.

This message is brief, but it carries power. How much does God have to say to convince people that His wrath is about to fall?

7. Judgment on Kedar and Hazor (Jer. 49:28-33)

These are two desert peoples. Kedar was related to Ishmael (Gen. 25:13). We aren't sure of the origin of Hazor, which is not to be confused with the city of that name in northern Palestine (Josh. 11).

These two nomadic Arab nations lived by raising sheep and camels. When Nebuchadnezzar attacked them in 599–598 B.C., however, they lost everything. Once again, we meet the phrase "fear is on every side" (Jer. 49:29; see 20:3). These two Arab nations were guilty of living at ease, isolating themselves from others, and manifesting pride and arrogant self-confidence (49:31). They didn't need God, and they didn't need the help of any other people! When Nebuchadnezzar arrived on the scene, they learned how foolish they had been.

8. Judgment on Elam (Jer. 49:34-39)

The Elamites were a Semitic people who were neighbors of the Babylonians. (Along with this paragraph, they are mentioned in Gen. 14:1; Isa. 11:11; 21:2; 22:6; Jer. 25:25; Ezek. 32:24; Dan. 8:2.) Their country was located beyond the Tigris River across from Babylon, and it eventually became part of the Medo-Persian Empire. God gave Jeremiah this prophecy about 597 B.C., during the reign of Zedekiah.

Since the Elamite soldiers were known for their archery God promised to break their bows (Jer. 49:35). He compared the Babylonian army to a storm that would not only blow from all directions but also scatter the people in all directions (v. 36). Whenever a nation was defeated, the victors would set up their king's throne in the city gate (1:15; 39:3; 43:8-13), and that's what God promised to do in Elam (49:38). He would let them know that He was King.

The Lord ended this description of judgment with a promise of mercy. Why He chose to restore Egypt, Moab, Ammon, and Elam is not explained, but they will share in the kingdom because of God's grace.

As you studied these chapters, perhaps you became weary of reading the same message: Judgment is coming and there's no escape. There's a sameness about what God said about these nine nations, and if we aren't careful, that sameness can produce "tameness" and cause us to lose a heart sensitive to the Lord's message.

Keep in mind, however, that these prophecies were written about real men, women, and children, and that what Jeremiah wrote actually came true. Whole civilizations were wiped out because of their sins, and eventually Babylon itself was destroyed. This means that multitudes of people died and went into an eternity of darkness.

God sees what the nations do, and He rewards them justly. What King Hezekiah said about the Lord needs to be emphasized today: "O Lord Almighty, God of Israel, enthroned between the cherubim, You alone are God over all the kingdoms of the earth" (Isa. 37:16, NIV). Joshua called Him "the Lord of all the earth" (Josh. 3:11), and both Jesus and Paul called Him "Lord of heaven and earth" (Luke 10:21; Acts 17:24).

God never gave the Law of Moses to any of the nations that Jeremiah addressed, but He still held them accountable for the sins they committed against Him and against humanity. Because of the witness of creation around them and conscience within them, they were without excuse (Rom. 1:17-32, especially v. 20) and guilty before God.

In recent history, the nations haven't acted any better than the ones recorded in Jeremiah 46–49. Innocent blood is shed legally as millions of babies are aborted in their mother's wombs. International terrorism, genocide, exploitation of people and material resources, war, crime, the abuse of children, and a host of other sins have stained the hands of nations with blood. What will they do when the Judge becomes angry and starts to avenge the innocent?

"It is a fearful thing to fall into the hands of the living God" (Heb. 10:31).

CHAPTER THIRTEEN
BABYLON IS FALLEN!
JEREMIAH 50–51

After all, we are not judged so much by how many sins we have committed but by how much light we have rejected.

—Vance Havner[1]

After declaring the destiny of the Gentile nations (Jer. 46–49), the prophet now focused on Judah's hateful enemy, the empire of Babylon. Jeremiah devoted 121 verses to the future of nine nations and 44 verses to the defeat and destruction of Jerusalem. When we count the number of verses in Jeremiah 50 and 51, however, he devoted 110 verses to the fall of Babylon. It is an important subject indeed!

In Scripture, the city of Babylon is contrasted with the city of Jerusalem—the proud city of man versus the Holy City of God. In Hebrew, the name *babel* means "gate of God," but *babel* is so close to the word *balal* ("confusion") that it's associated with the famous tower of Babel and the confusion of human languages (Gen. 11:1-9). The founder of Babylon was Nimrod (10:8-10), "a mighty hunter before the Lord" (v. 9, NIV). Some students interpret this to mean "a mighty rebel against the Lord."[2] Babel/Babylon is a symbol of rebellion against God, the earthly city of human splendor opposing the heavenly city that glorifies God. All of this culminates in the Babylon of Revelation 17:1–19:10, "Babylon the Great" that symbolizes the anti-God system that controls the world in the end times and then is destroyed by the Lord. There are many parallels between Jeremiah 50–51 and Revelation 17–18, and I suggest you read all four chapters carefully.

Jeremiah wrote this prophecy during the fourth year of Zedekiah (594–93) and gave the scroll to Baruch's brother Semiah to read in Babylon and then throw into the Euphrates (Jer. 51:59-64). Since Semiah was an officer in Zedekiah's cabinet, he had access to things officially diplomatic. This would have been the last of Jeremiah's "action sermons," performed without Jeremiah, symbolizing the complete destruction of the great Babylonian Empire.

Jeremiah 50–51 is something like an extended declaration coupled with a conversation. Usually it's the Lord speaking through His prophet, but occasionally we hear the Jewish people speaking and the Lord answering them. God speaks to and about Babylon; He also speaks to the invading army; and He speaks to the exiles of Judah. Three movements are in this declaration: God declares war on Babylon (50:1-28); God assembles the armies against Babylon (50:29–51:26); and God announces victory over Babylon (vv. 27-58).

Jeremiah's prophecy about Babylon has both a near and a far fulfillment. The Medes and Persians captured Babylon in 539 (see Dan. 5), but they didn't destroy the city. Cyrus issued a decree that the Jews could return to their land (Ezra 1:1-4), which many of them did in three stages: in 538 (Ezra 1–6), 458 (Ezra 7–10), and 444 (Book of Nehemiah). It was Alexander the Great who finally destroyed Babylon in 330 and left it a heap of ruins. Since Babylon symbolizes the anti-God world system, however, the ultimate fulfillment is recorded in Revelation 17–18. Remember, the prophets often looked at "two horizons," one near and one far, as they spoke and wrote about the future.

1. God Declares War on Babylon (Jer. 50:1-28)

"Announce and proclaim!" is the commandment. "Raise the signal!" God declared war on Babylon and announced that her great god Bel (also called Marduk) was about to be shamefully defeated.

God declared war on both Babylon and the gods of Babylon. The word translated "idols" means "wooden blocks," and the word translated "images" means "dung pellets." The Lord didn't think much of their gods! The invaders would come from the north just as Nebuchadnezzar came from the north to conquer Judah (1:11-15).

God speaks to and about the Jews (v. 4-10). He saw them as lost sheep without a shepherd, a flock greatly abused both by their leaders and their captors. While the immediate application is to the return of the exiles from Babylon, the ultimate reference includes the gathering of the Jews in the latter days. God warned the people to flee from Babylon so as not to be caught in the judgment that would fall (Isa. 48:20; Rev. 18:4). He would bring the Medes and the Persians against Babylon and give them total victory.

God speaks to Babylon (vv. 11-13). Now we find out why God was destroying this great empire. To begin with, the Babylonians were glad that they could devastate and subjugate Judah. Yes, Babylon was God's tool to chasten His sinful people, but the Babylonians went too far and enjoyed it too much. They acted like a joyful calf threshing the grain and getting his fill! Any nation that cursed the Jews will ultimately be cursed by God (Gen. 12:1-3). As they treated Judah, so God will treat them (see Jer. 51:24, 35, 49).

God speaks to the invading armies (vv. 14-16). Just as Babylon had been God's tool to chasten Judah, so the invaders (Cyrus with the Medes and Persians, and later Alexander with his Greek army) would be God's weapon to defeat Babylon. God spoke to the invading armies and commanded them to get their weapons ready and shout for victory, because they would win the battle. This was no ordinary war; this was the "vengeance of the Lord" (v. 15, NIV).

God speaks about the Jews (vv. 17-20). Once more Jeremiah used the image of the scattered flock. Assyria had ravaged Israel (the Northern Kingdom), and Babylon had ravaged Judah (the Southern Kingdom), but now God would punish Babylon as He had Assyria. (Assyria fell to a Babylonian-Median alliance in 609.) God will bring His people back to their own land, where the flock may graze safely and peacefully. The prophet then looked down to the latter days when God will wipe away the nation's sins and establish His New Covenant with them. We see the "two horizons" of prophecy again.

God speaks to the invaders (vv. 21-27). The Lord was in command of the invasion, and His orders were to be carried out explicitly. Babylon the rod (Isa. 10:5) was itself shattered. Babylon was caught in God's trap and couldn't escape God's weapons. Their fine young men would be slaughtered like cattle, for the day of judgment for Babylon had come.

The Jewish remnant speaks (v. 28). We hear the exiles who had fled the city and arrived in Judah as they report the fall of Babylon. The ultimate sin of the Babylonians was the burning of the temple, and for that sin the ultimate total destruction of their city was their punishment.

2. God Gathers the Armies against Babylon (50:29–51:26)

The first command had been "Declare among the nations!" But now the command was "Call together the archers!" God ordered the armies of the Medes and Persians (and later the Greeks) to shoot to kill and allow no one to escape.

God speaks to Babylon (50:31–51:4). He told them that He was against them because of their pride (50:31-32) and because of the way they had made the Jews suffer unnecessarily (v. 33). The exiles couldn't free themselves, but their Strong Redeemer would free them! The phrase "plead their cause" speaks of a court case. Jehovah was defense attorney, judge, and jury, and He found Babylon guilty.

Now the Lord told Babylon what to expect on the day of their judgment. The first picture is that of a sword going through the land and cutting down the people (vv. 35-38). God's sword will even attack the waters and dry them up (v. 38). Why? Because it is "a land of idols" (v. 38, NIV) and God wanted to reveal that the idols were nothing. Like the overthrow of Sodom and Gomorrah, nothing will be left. Babylon will become a haven for animals and birds, and the city will never be restored.

The Lord directed the Babylonians' attention to the great army that He had called from the north—a cruel army without mercy, whose march sounded like the roaring of the sea (v. 42). This report paralyzed the king of Babylon. Like a hungry lion, looking for prey (see 49:19-21), Cyrus (and then Alexander) will attack Babylon, and nobody will be able to resist. God's chosen servant will always succeed. The Lord's judgment on Babylon will be like the winnowing of the grain: "Great Babylon" will be blown away like chaff along with its idols!

God speaks to the Jews (vv. 5-10). God assured His people that He hadn't forsaken ("widowed") them, and He ordered them a second time (50:8) to get out of Babylon when the opportunity arises. When Cyrus opened the door for them to go home, about 50,000 Jews returned to Judah to restore Jerusalem and the temple. Babylon had been a "winecup" (see 25:15) in God's hands, making the nations act like drunks (Rev. 18:3), but now the cup would be smashed and Babylon's power broken. "Wail over her!" (Jer. 51:8, NIV) finds a fulfillment in Revelation 18:9ff. Anybody who pinned his or her hope on Babylon was doomed to disappointment, but so is anyone today who pins his or her hope on this present world. "The world is passing away" (1 John 2:17, NKJV).

To whom does "we" in Jeremiah 51:9 refer—to the Jews or to Babylon's allies who deserted her? Since the "us" in verse 10 refers clearly to the Jews and their vindication, it is likely that the exiles are speaking in verse 9, because Jeremiah had instructed them to be a blessing while living in Babylon (29:4-14). No doubt many of the Jews did seek the Lord, confess their sins, and trust His promise of deliverance. Some of them certainly prepared their sons and daughters to return to the land. They had the truth about Jehovah God and would have shared it with their captors, but the Babylonians preferred to taunt the Jews instead of listen to them discuss their religion (Ps. 137).

God speaks to Babylon (vv. 11-23). He warned them to get their weapons ready, set up their standards on the walls, and post their watchmen, because the invasion was about to begin. "Your end has come, the time for you to be cut off" (Jer. 51:13, NIV). They had been weaving the luxurious tapestry of their power and wealth on the loom, but now God would cut it off and put an end to their plans (v. 13, NIV).[3]

The enemy soldiers would swoop down on the Babylonians like locusts and prove the utter helplessness of the gods of Babylon. Jeremiah revealed the stupidity of making and worshiping idols (vv. 15-19), and he magnified the greatness of the one true and living God (see 10:12-16; Isa. 40:12-26).

God speaks to His general (vv. 20-24).[4] Just as Assyria had been God's "rod" (Isa. 10:5-19), so His chosen commander (Cyrus, and later Alexander) would be His "hammer" to break the power of Babylon. The word "break" (shatter) is used nine times in this passage. They would pay Babylon back with the same treatment Nebuchadnezzar had given others. There is a law of compensation in God's working in history, and the Lord will enforce it.

God speaks to Babylon (vv. 25-26). The city of Babylon sat on a plain, but in the sight of the nations, it was a huge destroying mountain that loomed on the horizon of history. By the time God was through with it, however, Babylon would be nothing but an extinct volcano ("a burnt mountain," Jer. 51:25). Nobody would even excavate the ruins to find stones to build with; the city would be deserted and desolate forever.

3. God Announces Victory over Babylon (Jer. 51:27-58)

Throughout this prophecy, God has frequently announced the fall of Babylon, but this closing section seems to focus on God's total victory over the enemy.

God describes the victory (vv. 27-33). God's armies were prepared, the commanders were ready, and the battle began; but the Babylonian army was helpless! They lay on the walls exhausted; their courage had failed them. The city was in flames, and the bars of the gates were broken. Nothing kept the enemy from entering the city and doing to it what the Babylonians had done to Jerusalem.[5]

The Babylonians had an effective courier system and could quickly send messages to the various parts of their vast empire. In fact, Jeremiah described the runners meeting and exchanging messages for the king: "The river crossings have been seized!" "The marshes are set on fire!" "The soldiers are terrified!" "The city has been captured!" (see vv. 31-32, NIV) It was God's harvest, and Babylon was on the threshing floor.[6]

God speaks to the Jews (vv. 34-50). First, the Jews reminded the Lord what Nebuchadnezzar had done to them (vv. 34-35). Like a vicious monster, he had picked up Judah as if it were a jar filled with food, swallowed down the food, vomited it up, and then broken the jar! He had chewed them up and spit them out! Now the Jews wanted the Lord to repay the Babylonians for all the suffering they had caused the people of God.

God's reply was encouraging: Like a court advocate, He would take their case, plead their cause, and vindicate them (v. 36). The Lord described vividly what would happen to Babylon: The ruins of the city would become the haunt of animals and birds, a perpetual cemetery for the people slain in the invasion, a slaughterhouse where people would die like so many cattle, sheep, and goats.

Sheshach in verse 41 is a code name for Babylon (25:26) following a system where the last letter of the alphabet is substituted for the first, the next to the last for the second, and so on. Why Jeremiah used a code name for the enemy in one sentence and then the real name in the next sentence isn't easy to understand.

Nevertheless, the enemy army would cover Babylon just as the sea covers the land (51:42), but when "the tide is out," a desert will be left behind. The Babylonian "monster" may have swallowed up God's people, but the Lord would force it to disgorge them (v. 44), and the new king (Cyrus) would permit God's people to return home. "The wall of Babylon shall fall" (v. 44) literally came true under Alexander, but "the wall came down" when Cyrus decreed that the exiles could go back to Judah and rebuild their temple.

For the third time, God ordered His people to get out of Babylon (v. 45; see 50:8; 51:6) and not to linger (51:50; see Gen. 19:16). Neither should they be afraid of the rumors they would hear about, which were about to happen. They didn't need to be afraid of the vain Babylonian idols that could do nothing to hinder them. Heaven and earth will sing songs of praise when Babylon falls (Jer. 51:48; Rev. 18:20ff).

The Jews speak and God replies (vv. 51-58). The exiles felt disgraced before the world because of what the Babylonians had done to the temple in Jerusalem. If the Lord wasn't strong enough to protect His house, how could He ever be strong enough to defeat Babylon? If they left Babylon, they would go home only to ruin and shame. During the years of their captivity, those who had obeyed Jeremiah's instructions (Jer. 29:4-14) probably enjoyed fairly comfortable lives. Thus, they would be exchanging security for danger and plenty for want.[7]

God, however, made it clear that there was no future in Babylon, for He had determined to destroy the city. "For the Lord [is a] God of recompenses" (51:56). If His people remained in Babylon, they would suffer the fate of the city. If they obeyed the Lord and returned home, they would experience a new beginning under the blessing of the Lord.

It's a matter of walking by faith and not by sight, trusting God's Word instead of our own human evaluation. The exiles saw the high walls and huge gates of the city and concluded that such fortifications would repel any enemy, but they were wrong. Those walls and gates would become only "fuel for the flames" when the invaders arrived on the scene (v. 58, NIV).

"Babylon is fallen, is fallen, that great city!" (Rev. 14:8) And Babylon is still fallen!

POSTLUDE

Defeat doesn't finish a man—quitting does. A man is not finished when he's defeated. He's finished when he quits.
—Richard M. Nixon

Jeremiah died an old man, probably in Egypt, and like the grave of Moses, his burial place is a mystery. The brave prophet has long turned to dust, but the words that he wrote are still with us, because God's Word endures forever.

He wrote a long and difficult book, and we haven't been able to deal with everything he wrote. However, you can't help but glean from his life and ministry some clear and important lessons that apply to all of God's people today.

1. In difficult days, we need to hear and heed the Word of God. Since hindsight always has twenty-twenty vision, it's obvious to us that the leaders of Judah did a very stupid thing by resisting what Jeremiah told them to do. Judah had sinned its way into trouble and judgment, and they thought they could negotiate their way out, but it didn't work. What they needed was faith in God's Word and obedience to God's will. Had they confessed their sins, turned to God, and submitted to Nebuchadnezzar, they would have saved their lives, their temple, and their city.

2. True prophets of God are usually (if not always) persecuted. The civil and religious leaders of Judah preferred the pleasant messages of the false prophets to the strong words of God's true servant, because the human heart wants to rest, not repent. It wants peace, but it wants it without having to deal with the basic cause of unrest—unbelief.

The people of Israel resisted God's messengers and challenged their authority from the time of Moses to the days of the apostles. It's difficult to name a prophet or apostle who didn't suffer persecution. If Jeremiah showed up today at the United Nations or some senate or parliament and spoke as he did to the leaders of Judah, he would probably be laughed at and thrown out. But it's a dangerous thing to be a "popular preacher" who has no enemies and pleases everybody. "Prophets are almost extinct in the religious world today," said Vance Havner. "The modern church is a 'non-prophet' organization."[1]

3. True patriotism isn't blind to sin. Charles Jefferson wrote:

> He [Jeremiah] loved his country so passionately he was willing to die for it as a traitor. He loved his country so intensely that he would not leave it even after Jerusalem was in ruins.[2]

Imagine a patriot like Jeremiah being called a traitor! Yet many a courageous leader who has dared to expose lies and call a nation to repentance has been called a traitor and publicly abused.

A true Christian patriot isn't blind to the sins of the nation but seeks to deal with those sins compassionately and realistically. Both Jesus and Jeremiah were true patriots when it came to giving an honest diagnosis of the diseases of the "body politic" and offering the only correct solution. They didn't heal the wounds of the people slightly and say, "Peace, peace." They both recognized that a nation's greatest problem is not unemployment, inflation, or lack of defense; it's sin. The nation that doesn't deal with sin is wasting time and resources trying to solve national problems, which are only symptoms of the deeper problem, which is sin.

4. God's servants occasionally have their doubts and failings. Jeremiah was weak before God but bold before men. He wasn't afraid to tell God just how he felt, and he listened when God told him what he needed to do. Though he once came quite close to resigning his office, he stuck with it and continued to serve the Lord.

Jeremiah was a prophet of the heart. He

wasn't content to give a message that dealt with surface matters; he wanted to penetrate the inner person and see the heart changed. He boldly told the people that the days would come when they wouldn't remember the ark or feel a need for it. In fact, the days would come when they would be part of a New Covenant that would be written on the heart and not on tables of stone. This was radical religion, but it was God's message just the same.

Any servant of God who tries to reach and change hearts is a candidate for sorrow and a sense of failure. But God knows our hearts and sustains us.

5. The important thing isn't success; it's faithfulness. By today's human standards of ministry, Jeremiah was a dismal failure. He preached to the same people for over forty years, and yet few of them believed him or obeyed his message. He had few friends who stood with him and encouraged him. The nation he tried to save from ruin abandoned their God and plunged headlong into disaster. His record wouldn't have impressed the candidate committee of most missions or the pastoral search committee of the average church.

Jeremiah may have thought he had failed, but God saw him as a faithful servant, and that's all that really counts. "Moreover it is required in stewards that one be found faithful" (1 Cor. 4:2, NKJV). He could have quit, but he didn't. As V. Raymond Edman used to say, "It's always too soon to quit."

6. The greatest reward of ministry is to become like Jesus Christ. When Jesus asked His disciples who people said He was, they replied, "Some say John the Baptist, some Elijah, and others say Jeremiah or one of the prophets" (Matt. 16:14, NKJV). What a compliment it would be to have people say, "Jesus Christ is like you!"

The similarities between Jesus and Jeremiah are interesting. Their approaches to teaching and preaching were similar, using "action sermons" and a great deal of imagery from everyday life and from nature. Both spoke out against the commercial "surface" religion practiced in the temple. Both were accused of being traitors to their people, and both suffered physically, even being arrested, beaten, and confined. Both wept over Jerusalem. Both were rejected by their relatives. Both knew what it was to be misunderstood, lonely, and rejected. Both emphasized the need for faith in the heart, and both rejected the mere "furniture" of religion that was external and impotent.

I could go on, but the point is obvious: Jeremiah became like Jesus because he shared "the fellowship of His sufferings" (Phil. 3:10). In the furnaces of life, Jeremiah was "conformed to the image of [God's] Son" (Rom. 8:29). Jeremiah may not have realized that this process was going on in his life, and he might have denied it if it were pointed out to him, but the transformation was going on just the same.

7. God is King, and the nations of the world are under His sovereign control. Nothing catches God by surprise. The nations that defy Him and disobey His Word eventually suffer for it. People who claim to know Him but who refuse to obey also suffer for it. In fact, the greater the light, the greater the responsibility. No nation was blessed the way God blessed the people of Israel, but that blessing brought chastening because they sinned against a flood of light.

It's a solemn responsibility for a people to claim to know God and profess to do His will. It isn't enough for a nation to put "In God We Trust" on its currency, to mention God in its pledge to the flag, or to "tip the hat to God" by quoting the Bible in political campaign speeches. It's righteousness, not religion, that exalts a nation. What pleases the Lord is that we "do justly . . . love mercy . . . and . . . walk humbly with [our] God" (Micah 6:8).

The same Lord who enabled Jeremiah can enable us. The same world that opposed Jeremiah will oppose us. It's time for God's people to be decisive.

ENDNOTES

Chapter 1

1. G. Campbell Morgan, *Studies in the Prophecy of Jeremiah* (Westwood, N.J.: Fleming H. Revell, 1961), 19.

2. It's not likely that Jeremiah's father was the Hilkiah who found the Book of the Law during the repairing of the temple (2 Kings 22). In the Old Testament, there are several other Hilkiahs mentioned. The name was popular, particularly among the priests and Levites. If Jeremiah's father had been that close to the king, some of the prestige might have rubbed off on his son, but that doesn't seem to have happened.

3. I'm not discounting the fact that a priest's ministry was demanding in that he might disobey God and

lose his life. He had to dress properly (Ex. 28:42-43), keep his hands and feet clean while serving (Ex. 30:20-21; Lev. 22:9), do his job carefully (Num. 4:15-20; 18:3), and always seek to glorify God (Lev. 16:13); otherwise, God's judgment could fall on him.

4. The ways of providence are sometimes puzzling. Hezekiah was a godly king, yet his son Manasseh was ungodly. Manasseh's son Amon, who reigned only two years, was as ungodly as his father (2 Kings 21:20-22); but Amon's son Josiah was a godly man. Yet Josiah's son, Jehoahaz, who reigned only three months, was ungodly like his grandfather. I suppose we must take into consideration both the influence of the mothers and of the court officials in charge of educating the princes.

5. The priestly city of Anathoth was located in the tribe of Benjamin (Josh. 21:18) and was about an hour's walk from Jerusalem. The priests would live in their own homes and travel to Jerusalem when their time came to minister in the temple. Contrary to the Law, there were also local shrines at which some of the priests served, making it convenient for the people who didn't want to go all the way to Jerusalem.

6. Josiah made the mistake of rashly getting involved at the Battle of Carchemish, where Pharaoh Necho of Egypt was engaging the army of Assyria. Pharaoh Necho had warned Josiah to mind his own business, but the king persisted and was slain at Megiddo (2 Chron. 35:20-25).

7. Since many of the nobles, key leaders in the land, had already been deported to Babylon, the king was left with a weak staff. But it's doubtful that stronger men would have made any difference in his character or actions.

8. Compare God's call of Moses (Ex. 3–4) and Gideon (Jud. 6), and note how the Lord is patient with His servants and does all He can to encourage their faith. God still likes to use the most unlikely instruments to get His work done in this world, and for good reason: "That no flesh should glory in his presence" (1 Cor. 1:29).

9. God said of the Jews, "You only have I known of all the families of the earth" (Amos 3:2). Certainly God is acquainted with all the nations and knows what they do, but Israel is the only nation in history to have a special covenant relationship with the Lord God, and God chose them wholly by His grace (Deut. 4:32-37; 7:7-8). God said of Abraham, "For I know him" (Gen. 18:19), meaning, "I have chosen him."

10. The promise of His presence was given to Isaac (Gen. 26:1-3, 24); Jacob (Gen. 28:15; 31:3; 46:1-4); Moses (Ex. 3:12; 33:14); Joshua (Deut. 31:7-8; Josh. 1:5; 3:7; 6:27); Gideon (Jud. 6:15-16); Jeremiah (Jer. 1:8, 19; 20:11); and to the church (Matt. 28:19-20; Heb. 13:5-6). See also Isaiah 41:10; 43:5.

11. See Jeremiah 4:6; 6:1, 22; 10:22; 13:20; 15:12; 25:9; 47:2; 50:3, 9, 41; 51:48. The invading Babylonian army is compared to a boiling pot (1:13-14), a marauding lion (4:7), and a flooding river (47:2).

12. Henry David Thoreau, *Walden* (Princeton, N.J.: Princeton University Press, 1971), 326.

Chapter 2

1. National Fast-Day Proclamation, March 30, 1863.

2. The break at Jeremiah 3:6 indicates that two messages are recorded in these chapters, the first from 2:1 to 3:5, and the second from 3:6 to 6:30. Later, Jeremiah's messages were written down by his secretary, Baruch, but King Jehoiakim burned the scroll. So Jeremiah dictated them again and added new messages to the book (Jer. 36).

3. The NIV seeks to convey this thought, and to some extent so does the NASB. Jeremiah was a master of imagery. You can't read his book without seeing pictures. This is a good example for all preachers and teachers of the Word to follow.

4. The word translated "kindness" in the KJV ("devotion," NIV) describes the grace and unfailing love of the Lord toward His people. It involves not just love but also the loyalty and faithfulness that are a part of true love. Israel was unfaithful to her husband and turned to idols. Today, believers who love the world are guilty of spiritual adultery (James 4:4), and local churches must beware of losing their "honeymoon love" for the Lord (2 Cor. 11:1-4; Rev. 2:4-5).

5. The Prophet Isaiah used a similar image in Isaiah 8:5-8, warning King Ahaz that if he trusted Assyria, that nation would overflow like a turbulent river and destroy Judah. The quiet waters of Shiloah (peace) flowed from the Gihon spring to the Pool of Siloam in Jerusalem (2 Chron. 32:30) and represented God's provision for His people (Ps. 46:4).

6. See Jeremiah 2:19; 3:6, 8, 11-12, 14, 22; 5:8; 8:5; 14:7; 21:22; 31:22; 49:4; 50:6; Hosea 11:7; 14:4.

7. According to the KJV and NASB, the "breaking of the yoke" in Jeremiah 2:20 refers to the Exodus when God set the Jews free (Lev. 26:13); but the NIV translates it "you broke off your yoke," referring to the nation's rebellion against God. Jeremiah 5:5 uses "breaking the yoke" to describe rebellion against God's will (see 31:18). The yoke is a recurring image in Jeremiah's writings (see especially 27–28, as well as 30:8; 51:23; Lam. 1:14; 3:27).

8. The KJV reads the "imagination of their evil hearts," based on the view that the Hebrew word comes from a root that means "to observe, to contemplate, hence, to imagine." But the Hebrew word probably comes from a root that means "to be firm, to be hard."

9. Verse 4 of Charles Wesley's "O for a Thousand Tongues."

10. There was also sexual sin, for the pagan rites usually included consorting with prostitutes, both male and female. Idolatry and immorality often go together (Rom. 1:18ff).

11. Some of the hill shrines were devoted to Jehovah, but the Law prohibited the Jews from sacrificing at any place other than in the temple (see Lev. 17:1-7; Deut. 12:1-16).

12. The NIV translates Jeremiah 3:14 "for I am your husband," for the Hebrew word for "husband" is the same as *baal* and means "lord." Baal was the Canaanite rain god that the Jews worshiped so as to have good crops. Therefore, there's a play on words here. "You are worshiping the false god Baal," says the prophet, "when your true *baal*—husband—is the Lord."

13. Jeremiah wasn't accusing God of deceiving the people, because God cannot lie (Num. 23:19; Titus 1:2). He was perplexed that God would even allow

the false prophets to deliver their deceptive messages and lead the people into a false security that would be their undoing. But if people don't want to obey the truth, they will accept lies (2 Thes. 2:10-12). This is the second of fourteen personal prayers recorded in Jeremiah, the first being 1:6 (see 9:1-6; 10:23-25; 12:1-4; 14:7-9, 19-22; 15:15-18; 16:19-20; 17:12-18; 18:18-23; 20:7-18; 32:16-25). Three times, God instructed Jeremiah not to pray for the people (7:16; 11:14; 14:11).

14. In their attempt to prove that between Genesis 1:1 and 1:2 there was a "gap" during which God judged Lucifer and his angels, some scholars have used Jeremiah 4:23ff, building their case mainly on the phrase "without form and void" (KJV). But this passage refers to the invasion of the Babylonian army, not Genesis 1. Furthermore, if this passage does refer to Genesis 1, then we must believe in a pre-Adamic race who lived in cities; and yet Adam is called "the first man" (1 Cor. 15:45).

15. See also Psalm 48:6; Isaiah 13:8; 21:3; 26:17-18; 66:7; Hosea 13:13; Micah 4:9-10; Matthew 24:8; Mark 13:8; Romans 8:22; Galatians 4:19, 27; 1 Thessalonians 5:3.

16. They are: the search (Jer. 5:1-6), the soiled belt (13:1-11), the unwed prophet (16:1-9), the potter (18:1-12), the broken vessel (19:1-15), the yokes (27–28), the purchased field (32:1-15), the wine party (35:1-19), the stones (43:8-13), and the sunken scroll (51:59-64). You also find "action sermons" in the Book of Ezekiel. Whenever people become so spiritually dull that they can't hear and understand God's Word, the Lord graciously stoops to their level and dramatizes the message.

17. For "the remnant" in Jeremiah, see 23:3; 31:7; 39:9; 40:11; 41:16; 42:2, 15, 19; 43:5; 44:12, 14, 28.

18. The phrase "ask for the old paths" (6:16) is a favorite of people who oppose changes in the church and want to maintain a sterile and boring status quo. But the "old ways" refer to God's truth as revealed in His Word, not to methods of ministry. Note that Jeremiah gave two instructions: "stand in the old ways" and "walk in the good way." We stand on His truth in order to make progress in His work. The old Youth for Christ slogan comes to mind: "Geared to the times but anchored to the Rock."

Chapter 3

1. Thoreau wrote this in his journal on September 2, 1851.

2. These false prophets may have based their deceptive message on God's deliverance of Jerusalem in the days of Hezekiah (2 Kings 18–19; Isa. 37). But Hezekiah was a godly king who listened to the Word of God from the Prophet Isaiah, prayed to God for help, and sought to honor the Lord.

3. The Hebrew word translated "refuse" means "dung, manure," and Jeremiah used it again in 9:22, 16:4, and 25:33. What a tragedy that people who could have been children of God ended up manure in a garbage dump (see Mark 9:43-50).

4. Vance Havner, *It Is toward Evening* (Westwood, NJ.: Fleming H. Revell, 1968), 25. Vance Havner was himself a very witty man, and I always enjoyed his fellowship, but he knew how to use humor wisely to get his points across. In that same message, he writes, "Christians are never more ridiculous than when they attempt a religious version of worldly hilarity. It is always an embarrassing imitation that disgusts even the ungodly" (p. 27).

5. Jeremiah 9:22 pictures death as the "grim reaper" with the scythe in his hand, mowing people down like wheat in the field (see also Pss. 90:5; 103:14-16; Isa. 40:7; Job 5:26).

6. A.W. Tozer, *The Knowledge of the Holy* (New York: Harper and Row, 1961), 11.

7. Jeremiah's prayer reminds us of the "imprecatory psalms," such as Psalms 35, 69, 79, 109, 139, and 143. If we keep in mind that these prayers were an expression of *national* concern, not personal vengeance, asking God to keep His covenant promises to the nation (Gen. 12:1-3), then they become expressions of a desire for justice and the vindication of God's holy name. Their spirit is that of Paul's in Galatians 1:6-9 and the saints in heaven in Revelation 6:9-11 and 18:20-24.

Chapter 4

1. Ralph Waldo Emerson, "Self-Reliance," in *Essays*. Of course Emerson used the word "man" generically, referring to either men or women.

2. Jeremiah 11:6 suggests that Jeremiah may have itinerated in Judah and taught the people the Law. This was one of the duties of the priests (2 Chron. 17:8-10; Ezra 7:10; Neh. 8:1-9).

3. Note the emphasis on *love* in the Book of Deuteronomy. The word is used twenty times, and love is presented as the motive for obedience to the Lord (6:4-5; 10:12; 11:1, 13, 22). The word "heart" is used nearly fifty times in Deuteronomy. In this "second edition" of the Law, Moses moved the emphasis from mere outward obedience to inward love and a desire to please God. Why we obey God is a mark of maturity in the Christian life.

4. Eugene Peterson, *Run with the Horses* (Downers Grove, Ill.: InterVarsity, 1983), 61.

5. See my book *Why Us? When Bad Things Happen to God's People* (Old Tappan, NJ.: Fleming H. Revell, 1984) for a discussion of this problem from a biblical/pastoral point of view. Other helpful books are: *In God's Waiting Room* by Lehman Strauss (Radio Bible Class); *The Paradox of Pain* by A.E. Wilder Smith (Harold Shaw); *Through the Fire* by Joseph M. Stowell (Victor); *Where Is God When It Hurts* by Philip Yancey (Zondervan); *The Problem of Pain* by C.S. Lewis (Macmillan); and *Surprised by Suffering* by R.C. Sproul (Tyndale). See also *Be Patient*, my study of the Book of Job (Victor).

The Old Testament system of rewards and punishments was suited to Israel in their "spiritual childhood" (Gal. 4:1-7), but it was never meant to be God's permanent arrangement for believers today. Jesus lived a perfect life and yet He suffered greatly, and nowhere in the New Testament is the church promised immunity from suffering. Quite the contrary is true: "Yes, and all who desire to live godly in Christ Jesus will suffer persecution" (2 Tim. 3:12, NKJV).

6. Hugh Black, *Listening to God* (London: Fleming H. Revell Co., 1906), 282.

7. See his essay "The Romance of Rhyme" in his book *Fancies versus Fads*.

8. The statement in Jeremiah 12:8 that God "hated" His inheritance means that He had to treat them as though they were not His beloved. He withdrew His love by abandoning them to their enemies. God's love for His people is unconditional, but their enjoyment of that love is conditional (see 2 Cor. 6:17-18; John 14:21-24).

9. The big question relating to this "action sermon" is, where did it take place? The Euphrates was 350 miles from Anathoth, and that would mean four journeys of four months each for the prophet (Ezra 7:8-9). Could he make four such trips during such turbulent times? And how significant would his actions be to the people of Judah if he performed them hundreds of miles away? The Hebrew text of Jeremiah 13:4 reads *Perath,* which is the Hebrew word for the Euphrates, but some scholars think it refers to the town of Parah about three miles from Anathoth (Josh. 18:23), or that perhaps it is an abbreviation for Ephrata, the name of Bethlehem, located only five or six miles from Jerusalem. However, if Jeremiah did travel twice to Babylon, it would have made a tremendous impression on the people of Judah when he returned home with his ruined garment. He then could have preached the message that the garment symbolized.

10. The proverb speaks of wineskins, but the Hebrew word means "wine jars." The image in Jeremiah 13:14 is that of jars being dashed together and broken. The prophets used familiar sayings as springboards for teaching God's truth (see Jer. 17:11; 31:9; Ezek. 18:2).

11. Henri IV, King of France, said in his coronation address in 1589, "I hope to make France so prosperous that every peasant will have a chicken in his pot on Sunday." In 1928, the American Republican party used "A chicken in every pot" as a campaign slogan.

Chapter 5

1. J. Wallace Hamilton, *The Thunder of Bare Feet* (Westwood, N.J.: Fleming H. Revell, 1964), 69.

2. John Henry Jowett, *The Preacher, His Life and Work* (New York: Harper & Brothers, 1921), 114.

3. The rainy season was from October to April, with the "early rains" coming in the spring and the "latter rains" in the autumn (Deut. 11:14; Jer. 8:3; 5:24). The "winter rains" began in November/December, the Hebrew month of Kislev.

4. The word "drought" in Jeremiah 14:1 is plural.

5. The three judgments of war, famine, and pestilence are mentioned often in Jeremiah (21:7, 9; 24:10; 27:8, 13; 29:17-18; 32:24, 36; 34:17; 38:2; 42:17, 22; 44:13; see also 5:12; 11:22; 14:13-18; 16:4; 18:21; 42:16; 44:12, 18, 27).

6. Jeremiah had predicted the invasion of the Babylonian army but that invasion didn't occur until many years later. Since his prophecy didn't immediately come to pass, the people didn't take Jeremiah's messages too seriously. But God was watching over Jeremiah's word to perform it (1:12), and the disaster finally occurred.

7. For other references in Jeremiah to the Babylonian Captivity of Judah, see 9:16; 13:24; 16:13; 18:17; 30:11; 46:28.

8. God is holy and never has to repent of sin. The word is used to describe His "change of mind" when He determines not to send judgment. Humanly speaking, God seems to repent. From the divine point of view, however, God's purposes never change, though His providential workings do change.

9. On eating the word (Jer. 15:16); see Ezekiel 3:1-3; Revelation 10:9-10; Job 23:12. Unless the Word becomes a vital part of our inner being, we can't receive nourishment and grow in the spiritual life. This is what Jesus had in mind when He spoke about eating His flesh and drinking His blood (John 6:51-58). As we receive the written Word within, we are also receiving the living Word (1:14) and feeding on Christ.

10. Nine of the Ten Commandments are repeated in the New Testament epistles for believers to obey, but the Sabbath commandment isn't among them. The Sabbath was a special sign given to Israel (Ex. 31:12-18), not to the church. Believers are free to honor special days as they feel convicted by the Lord (Rom. 14:1-23; Col. 2:16-17) and must not judge one another. To make Sabbath-keeping a means of salvation or a mark of special spirituality is to go beyond what the Scriptures teach, and to equate the Sabbath with the New Testament Lord's Day is equally unbiblical. The Sabbath is identified with the Law: You work six days and then you have rest. The Lord's Day is identified with grace: You begin with a resurrected Christ and the works follow.

Chapter 6

1. J. Wilbur Chapman, *Revival Sermons* (New York: Fleming H. Revell, 1911), 231.

2. Charles E. Jefferson, *Cardinal Ideas of Jeremiah* (New York: Macmillan Co., 1928), 102.

3. The word translated "marred" is also used for the ruined girdle in Jeremiah 13:7 and 9. It means to "destroy or corrupt."

4. That God is sovereign over all the nations is proved by such Scriptures as Psalms 115:3; 135:6; Isaiah 46:9-11; Daniel 2:21, 4:17, 34-35; 7:14; Matthew 28:18; Acts 17:22-31; and Ephesians 1:22 to cite but a few.

5. The verb means "to empty" and is similar to the Hebrew word for jar. Perhaps Jeremiah had put water in the clay flask and then poured it out as he spoke these words. God would empty all the nation's plans and then break the nation that conceived them!

6. Three men named Pashur are found in this book: the son of Immer (Jer. 20:1), the son of Malchijah (21:1), and the father of Gedaliah (38:1). All three were enemies of Jeremiah and sought to silence his ministry. Whether the Pashur of 20:1 is the father of Gedaliah, we have no way of knowing for sure.

7. A century and a half before, Isaiah had predicted the Captivity and named Babylon as the aggressor (Isa. 6:11-13; 11:11-12; 39:6). Therefore, any Jew who knew the Word of God would have recognized Jeremiah's witness as true. Jeremiah added the important facts about the seventy years' duration of the Captivity (Jer. 25).

Chapter 7

1. This is not the Pashur who persecuted Jeremiah

(Jer. 20) although this Pashur later assisted in imprisoning Jeremiah and urging the king to kill him (Jer. 38). There's no evidence that Zephaniah the priest was opposed to the prophet. Zephaniah was eventually taken to Babylon and executed (2 Kings 25:18-21).

2. See Charles H. Dyer in *The Bible Knowledge Commentary, Old Testament* (Wheaton, Ill.: Victor Books, 1985), 1185.

3. The phrase "execute judgment in the morning" (Jer. 21:12) reminds us that court was held in the mornings at the city gates when it was still cool outside. But the phrase also suggests that the king needed to make justice the first priority of his day.

4. Obviously this message was delivered to King Jehoiakim before he died in 598 B.C. It's included in this section of Jeremiah's prophecy because it fits with the special messages to the four other kings. We've noted before that the Book of Jeremiah isn't assembled in chronological order. Chapters 21–24 focus especially on the royal house of David.

5. The fact that Jehoiakim "slept [rested] with his fathers" (2 Kings 24:6) is no proof that he had a decent burial. The phrase simply means that he joined his ancestors in death. Second Chronicles 36:6 indicates that Nebuchadnezzar bound Jehoiakim to take him to Babylon, which seems to contradict Jeremiah's prophecy. The easiest explanation is that the Babylonians intended to take Jehoiakim to Babylon, but he died. Therefore, they took Jehoiachin, his son and successor, instead (2 Kings 24:10-12). King Jehoiakim was not given a lavish state funeral and buried with the kings of Judah. His body was disposed of ignominiously somewhere outside the walls of Jerusalem, a shameful way for any man to be buried, especially a Jewish king.

6. Zerubbabel, a grandson of King Jehoiachin, was one of the Jewish leaders who helped the exiles return to the land after the Captivity and reestablish their government and worship. He was a representative of the Davidic line though he didn't reign as a king. The Lord "reversed" the curse and said that Zerubbabel was to Him like a signet ring (Hag. 2:20-23), which meant he was chosen and precious to God.

7. The Hebrew word refers to the hot desert wind that smothers you, leaving you lifeless and ready to give up. In the KJV, the word is translated "terrible" in Lamentations 5:10 ("Our skin was black [hot] like an oven because of the terrible famine") and "horrible" in Psalm 11:6 ("Upon the wicked he shall rain . . . an horrible tempest).

Chapter 8

1. Quoted by Ann Landers in the column "Thoughts at Large" by Sidney J. Harris in *The Washington Post* 12, Nov. 1979, B-7.

2. The name is also spelled Nebuchadrezzar. Famous leaders often had variant spellings to their names. Cf. Tiglath-Pileser (2 Kings 15:29), and Tiglath-Pilneser (1 Chron. 5:26).

3. Bible students don't agree on the dating of the seventy years of Captivity or even on whether the phrase "seventy years" should be considered a round number or be taken literally. From the beginning of the Babylonian invasion (606 B.C. to the return of the Jewish remnant under Zerubbabel (536) is seventy years, but so is the period from the destruction of Jerusalem (587–586) to the completion of the second temple by the returned exiles (516). Daniel 9:1-2 seems to indicate that Daniel took the prophecy to mean seventy actual years.

4. While the main emphasis is on the world of Jeremiah's day there may be a wider application of these words to the nations at the end of the age, for Jeremiah included "all the kingdoms of the world" (Jer. 25:26). In their messages, the prophets often began with a local situation and then used it as a springboard to describe something God would do in the end times.

5. Shaphan, Ahikam's father, is the scribe who delivered the Book of the Law to Josiah after Hilkiah found it in the temple (2 Kings 22). Shaphan had four sons, three of whom were friendly to Jeremiah: Ahikam, who saved his life (Jer. 26:24); Gemariah, who pleaded with King Jehoiakim not to burn Jeremiah's book (36:12, 25); and Elasah, who delivered Jeremiah's letter to the captive Jews in Babylon (29:1-3). The fourth son, Jaazaniah, was unfaithful to the Lord and worshiped idols in the temple (Ezek. 8:11). Ahikam's son Gedaliah became governor of Judah after the destruction of Jerusalem.

6. Don't be puzzled when you read the name "Jehoiakim" in verse 1 and the name "Zedekiah" in verses 3 and 12 (and see 28:1), because this event took place during the reign of Zedekiah. "Jehoiakim" in verse 1 appears to be the error of a copyist whose eyes may have read 26:1, which is almost identical to 27:1. The fact that the rest of the chapter names Zedekiah as king is ample evidence that "Jehoiakim" is a scribal error.

7. Some translations give the impression that the prophet wore more than one yoke and that he sent a yoke to each of the envoys of the five nations (Jer. 27:2-3). The word "yoke" is plural in the Hebrew because the yoke he wore was made of two pieces of wood, one in front of the neck and one at the back, held together by leather straps. "Make a yoke out of straps and crossbars" (NIV) is a good translation of verse 2. He sent word to the five kings that they were to submit to the authority of Nebuchadnezzar, and the yoke that he wore symbolized the prophet's message.

8. There were three deportations—in 605, 597, and 586—during which both people and treasures were taken to Babylon. Since Zedekiah ruled from 597 to 586, the false prophets were referring to the deportation in 605, when Daniel and his friends were taken to Babylon along with some of the temple treasures (Dan. 1:1-2).

9. It's profitable to compare Jeremiah's counsel to the exiles in Babylon with Peter's counsel to the "pilgrims and strangers" in the Roman Empire (1 Peter 2:11-17). Both men told the people to be good citizens and good witnesses and to do good works. Paul agreed with their approach when he wrote, "If it is possible, as much as depends on you, live peaceably with all men" (Rom. 12:18, NKJV).

Chapter 9

1. Charles E. Jefferson, *Cardinal Ideas of Jeremiah* (New York: Macmillan, 1928), 125.

2. Isaiah used the phrase "in that day" at least forty-four times but Jeremiah only seven (4:9; 30:8; 39:16-

17; 49:22, 26; 50:30). In chapters 12 to 14 of Zechariah, "in that day" is used nineteen times with reference to end-time events relating to the restoration of Israel and the return of the Lord.

3. Jesus designated the first part of the Tribulation as "the beginning of sorrows" (Matt. 24:8) which means "the beginning of birthpangs." The Tribulation will bring pain to Israel and the nations of the world, but out of that pain will come the birth of the kingdom.

4. Visitors to the Holy Land visit Tel Aviv and various other "tells" and learn that the Hebrew word *tel* means "a mound of ruins." Cities devastated by war or natural calamities rarely relocated; the survivors simply rebuilt the city on the ruins of the old one, thus giving future archeologists something to do.

5. The ancient breach between Jews and Samaritans was healed when Philip the evangelist took the Gospel to Samaria and the believing Samaritans received the same gift of the Spirit as the Jews (Acts 8:5ff; 2:1-4). Later, the Gentiles would receive the gift (Acts 10:44-48). Thus, believing Jews, Samaritans, and Gentiles made up the body of Christ (Gal. 3:26-29).

6. We sometimes hear about the "ten lost tribes of Israel," and various groups claim the identification, but only God knows where all twelve tribes are in the world (Acts 26:7; James 1:1; Rev. 7).

7. How does this relate to Matthew's quotation? As Rachel died she named her son *Ben-oni*, which means "son of my sorrow," but Jacob named him *Benjamin*, "son of my right hand" (Gen. 35:16-20). In His humiliation and suffering, Jesus Christ is the man of sorrows, but in His exaltation and glory, He is the Son at God's right hand (Acts 2:22-36). Jacob made Bethlehem a burial place, but Jesus made it a birthplace! The Bethlehem mothers, bereft of their sons, wept in despair, but just as God's promises comforted Rachel, so their sacrifice would not be in vain. No matter how many enemies try to destroy Israel, the nation will not perish, for their Messiah reigns and will come one day and deliver His people.

8. To defend this verse as a prediction of the virgin birth of Christ is an exercise in futility. The word for "woman" means "female" without reference to virginity. The nation is the only virgin mentioned in the context (Jer. 31:4, 21). There is no definite article in the text; it simply says "a female" and not "the woman." The Hebrew word translated "surround" (compass) has nothing to do with the conception of a child. It's possible that the statement is a Jewish proverb for an amazing and unthinkable thing.

9. Baruch may have had royal blood in his veins since his brother Semiah was a staff officer in the king's service (Jer. 51:59, NIV), and such officials were usually princes. The fact that Semiah went to Babylon with the king shows how important a man he was in the eyes of the Babylonians. The family of Neriah may have thought that Baruch gave up a bright future in order to serve with Jeremiah, but they were wrong. Many of the royal officers perished, but God protected Jeremiah and Baruch and provided for them (see Jer. 45). No doubt Baruch was an encouragement to the prophet, who was usually friendless and forsaken.

10. The statement goes back to Abraham (Gen. 18:14), and was also used by Moses (Num. 11:23) and Job (Job 42:2). Gabriel echoed it when he said to Mary, "For with God nothing shall be impossible" (Luke 1:37), and Jesus said, "With God all things are possible" (Matt. 19:26). Paul's testimony was "I can do all things through Christ who strengthens me" (Phil. 4:13, NKJV). Jeremiah discovered that God's character is faithful and His promises are true no matter how we feel or what our circumstances may be.

11. Good and godly Bible students disagree as to whether these "kingdom promises" are to be taken literally or interpreted in a "spiritual sense." If these promises are to be applied to the church today, it's difficult to understand what they mean and how they apply. I have therefore taken the approach that these promises will have their real fulfillment in the future kingdom. For further study, see *There Really Is a Difference* by Renald E. Showers (Friends of Israel); *Millennialism: The Two Major Views* by Charles L. Feinberg (Moody Press); *The Millennial Kingdom* by John F. Walvoord (Dunham); and *Continuity and Discontinuity,* edited by John S. Feinberg (Crossway Books).

Chapter 10

1. Senator Shepherd said this during remarks made in the U.S. Senate on Dec. 18, 1914, as recorded in the *Congressional Record*, vol. 52, 338.

2. What was recorded is revelation; the way it was recorded is inspiration. Never confuse divine inspiration with the "human inspiration" of great writers like Shakespeare and Milton.

3. For example, eight men named Shelemiah are found in the Old Testament, so it was a popular name. Because of this, we can never be sure of family relationships.

4. John F. Kennedy, *Profiles in Courage* (New York: Harper & Row, 1955), 245.

5. The contradiction between Jeremiah 39:11-14 and 40:1-6 is only on the surface. When the Babylonians entered the city, they released Jeremiah and took him under their protective custody. He was free to move about and minister to the people. Apparently through some blunder, he was taken captive with the prisoners going to Ramah, but when the mistake was discovered, he was released and allowed to do as he pleased.

6. G. Campbell Morgan, *Studies in the Prophecy of Jeremiah* (Westwood, NJ.: Revell, 1961), 251.

Chapter 11

1. Dag Hammarskjold, *Markings* (New York: Alfred A. Knopf, 1965), 8.

Chapter 12

1. Quoted in *Miracle at Philadelphia,* by Catherine Drinker Bowen (Boston: Lime, Brown and Company, 1966), 126. Italics are in the original.

2. The phrase in the KJV "this is the day of the Lord" (Jer. 46:10) should not be interpreted to mean "the day of the Lord" which will occur in the end times. The battle Jeremiah described took place in 605 and is known as the Battle of Carchemish, named for a town on the Euphrates River.

3. The New English Bible translates it "King Bombast, the man who missed his moment."

4. The phrase "make a full end" is found in Jeremiah 4:27; 5:10, 18; 30:11; and Ezekiel 11:13. The NIV translates it "completely destroy." God knows how much discipline to give His people, and He never makes a mistake. He keeps His eye on the clock and His hand on the thermostat.

5. *Madmen* in Jeremiah 48:2 is the name of a Moabite city. It's not the English word for men who are mad.

Chapter 13

1. Dennis J. Hester, compiler, *The Vance Havner Quotebook* (Grand Rapids: Baker Book House, 1986), 124.

2. Some Hebrew scholars connect the name Nimrod with the word *marad*, which means "to rebel." Certainly the building of the Tower of Babel was an act of rebellion against the Lord. Nimrod chased and conquered other peoples the way a hunter chases and catches game.

3. King Hezekiah used a similar image (Isa. 38:12). Our lives are a weaving that one day will end, and God will cut it off the loom.

4. Some commentators see the hammer as Babylon, but Jeremiah 51:24 seems to require something or someone other than Babylon; otherwise Jeremiah would have used "you" instead of "they."

5. Remember, this didn't happen when Cyrus took Babylon, for his army was in the city before the Babylonians even knew it. He had diverted the waters of the Euphrates and entered under the gates. It was Alexander the Great whose army destroyed Babylon in 330.

6. Before the farmers threshed their grain, they would stamp down the earth to make sure it was hard. This may be the image here: God was stamping down the nation and preparing to cut them down like so much grain in the field.

7. The Jews often wanted to go back to Egypt, because there they had plenty of food and security, even though they were slaves. It's tragic when people sacrifice fulfillment for comfort.

Postlude

1. Dennis J. Hester, compiler, *The Vance Havner Quotebook* (Grand Rapids: Baker, 1986), 179.

2. Charles E. Jefferson, *Cardinal Ideas of Jeremiah* (New York: Macmillan, 1928), 192.

LAMENTATIONS

OUTLINE

Key theme: Suffering sometimes comes from the chastening hand of God.
Key verses: Lamentations 2:17; 3:22-25

I. THE NATION'S DISGRACE. 1:1-22

II. THE CITY'S DESTRUCTION. 2:1-22

III. THE PROPHET'S DISTRESS. 3:1-66

IV. THE LORD'S DISCIPLINE. 4:1-22

V. THE JEWISH REMNANT'S DECLARATION. 5:1-22

Name. The Hebrew title of the book is the first word of the text—*'ekah*—which is translated "how?" (see 2:1 and 4:1). The title in the English Bible comes from the Latin Vulgate *lamentia*, "funeral dirges." The book consists of five laments that Jeremiah wrote after the Babylonians destroyed Jerusalem in 587–86 B.C. Lamentations is found in the third part of the Hebrew Bible, the Megilloth (scrolls), which also includes the Song of Solomon, Ruth, Esther, and Ecclesiastes. In the English Bible, it follows the Book of Jeremiah.

Author. Tradition assigns the book to the prophet Jeremiah, "the weeping prophet." During his forty years of ministry, he sought to persuade the leaders of Judah to turn back to God and avoid national judgment, but they persisted in breaking God's covenant. When Babylon invaded Judah, Jeremiah begged the leaders to surrender and thus spare the people, the city and the temple, and they arrested him as a traitor. But the prophet's words proved true and the Babylonian army took the city, and destroyed it and the temple.

One evidence that Jeremiah wrote the book is the presence of similar phrases in both Lamentations and the prophecy of Jeremiah. Some of them are: "my eyes flow with tears" (1:16; 2:18; 3:48; Jer. 9:1,18; 13:17; 14:17); "laughingstock" (3:14; Jer. 20:7); "terrors on every side" (2:22; Jer. 6:25; 20:4,10; 46:5; 49:5,29); and "destruction" and "wound" (2:11,13; 3:47-48; Jer. 4:6,20; 6:1,14; 8:11,21). Lamentations reads as though it were written by an eyewitness, and Jeremiah certainly qualified.

The basic theme of these five laments is the tragedy of the destruction of Jerusalem, a judgment God sent because His people had rebelled against Him and rejected His warnings (2 Chron. 36:11-21). So critical is this historic event that it's recorded four times in the Old Testament: 2 Kings 25, 2 Chron. 36:11-21, and Jeremiah 39 and 52. Nebuchadnezzar and the Babylonian army first invaded Judah in 605 B.C. to punish King Jehoiakim, who had broken his covenant and revolted against Babylon. At that time Daniel and his three friends, along with many other Jews, were deported to Babylon. The army returned in March of 597 when they looted Jerusalem and deported more people. The actual siege of Jerusalem began on January 15, 588 B.C.; on July 18, 586, the walls were breached, and on August 14, the city was set ablaze.i Each year on this date, the Jews remember the event and read Lamentation aloud in their synagogues.

In writing this book, Jeremiah expressed his own sorrow at the destruction of the Holy City and the beautiful temple of the Lord. It looked to him as though forty years of faithful ministry were wasted, for the people didn't heed his messages. Using numerous similes and metaphors, Jeremiah described the terrible plight of the people, and he prayed to the Lord for assistance and deliverance. At the same time, he wrestled with the Lord over what He had allowed to happen, knowing fully that the sins of the people were to blame (1:5, 8; 5:7, 16). They had violated the terms of the covenant, knowing full well what the consequences would be (Lev. 26; Deut. 28–30; see 2 Kings 17:13-15; 2 Chron. 36:15-16). Jeremiah had warned that if Judah persisted in rebelling, God would send the Babylonians (Jer. 1:13-16; 4:5-9; 5:15; 6:22-26; 10:22; 50:41-43), and Isaiah had preached the same message (Isa. 13-14; 43:14ff; 47:1ff).

But it was reasonable for a sensitive man of God like Jeremiah to raise theological questions as he beheld the ruins of the Holy City. Where was God? Did He no longer love His people, His house, and the city of Jerusalem? At the same time, the Jews exiled in Babylon were expressing similar feelings (Ps. 137). But the people of Judah had held to three false hopes: the Davidic dynasty, the sacred temple, and help of Egypt. God had made a covenant with David that his house would never perish and that one of his descendants would forever sit on his throne (2 Sam. 7). The Jewish people thought this meant that nothing could happen to David's throne (Lam. 4:20; 5:16). This covenant was ultimately fulfilled in Jesus Christ (Luke 1:30-33, 67-75; Acts 2:29-36). David's house (family) didn't come to an end, for Joseph, husband to Mary, was descended from David (Luke 1:26-27).

Judah's second false hope was that the Lord would not permit anything to happen to His holy temple. "Trust . . . not in lying words, saying, The temple of the Lord, . . . the temple of the Lord are these" (Jer. 7:4). The entire message Jeremiah delivered in the temple focused on this false hope of Judah, and Jeremiah repeated part of it in 26:1-11. As for the third false hope—the intervention of Egypt—it was pure illusion. (See Lam. 4:17 and 5:6, as well as Isa. 31, Jer. 37:5-7, and Ezek. 29:16.) Abraham had sought refuge in Egypt and gotten into trouble (Gen. 12), and during their wilderness journey, Israel had repeatedly wanted to go back (Ex. 14:11; 16:1-3; 17:3; Num. 14:1-5). But whenever Israel put faith in Egypt, the nation always proved to be a broken reed.

We must keep in mind that God's chastening is an expression of His love (Heb. 12:1-13), a tool He uses to mature His children. A judge punishes a criminal in order to uphold the law, but a father chastens a child in order to build character into the child and assure the child of his love.

The Covenant

Judah expected the Lord to protect the royal dynasty and keep the covenant He made with David, but they didn't want Him to keep the covenant He made with the nation before they entered the Promised Land (Lev. 26; Deut. 28–30). Israel's title to the land came through the Abrahamic Covenant (Gen. 12:1-3; 13:14-18), but their possessing and enjoying the land depended on their obedience to the covenant in Lev. 26 and Deut. 28–30. The Lord made it very clear that Israel's obedience to this covenant would guarantee protection from their enemies, abundant blessing on their efforts and peace and joy from the Lord. But if they disobeyed, one judgment after another would come to the people, until the Lord would take them off their land drive them to a foreign country. As we study Lamentations, we shall meet the very judgments that were predicted in Lev. 26 and Deut. 28–30. The Lord is always faithful to His covenant, either to bless the obedient or chasten the disobedient. His Word will never fail.

The Laments

Except for chapter 5, these laments are acrostics in which successive verses follow the order of the Hebrew alphabet.[2] Ps. 119 is another example. There are twenty-two letters in the Hebrew alphabet and the twenty-two verses of chapters 1, 2, and 4 follow this alphabetical pattern. In chapter 3, which has sixty-six verses, three lines are assigned to each letter. Even though chapter 5 has twenty-two verses, it is not an acrostic. Jeremiah used the acrostic pattern perhaps as an aid to memorizing these laments. In the Hebrew text, 3:1 is the central verse of the book, and it certainly expresses the theme. Lamentations 3:22-39 is the spiritual heart of the book and records one of the great testimonies of faith found in Scripture. The familiar hymn "Great Is Thy Faithfulness" by Thomas O. Chisholm is based on verse 23. The fall of Jerusalem, the destruction of the temple, and the captivity of the nation were unbearable crises to the Jews and they had every right to express their sorrow. But at the same time, Jeremiah called upon his people to be sorrowful for their sins, confess them, and return to the Lord (3:37-51; ch. 5). Note that chapters 1, 2, and 3 end with prayers and that all of chapter 5 is a prayer.

Jeremiah and Jesus

When Jesus asked His disciples who people said He was, among their answers was "Jeremiah" (Matt. 16:13-14). The ministries of both Jeremiah and Jesus were rejected by the people and both men wept over the city of Jerusalem because they knew that destruction was coming. Both were hated without cause (Lam. 3:52; John 15:25; Ps. 69:4) and both were ridiculed by the leaders (Lam. 3:14; Ps. 69:12). Jeremiah was rejected by his family (Jer. 11:18-23) and Jesus by His family (John 7:1-8). Both Jeremiah and Jesus emphasized a "heart religion" and not just ritual, and both taught by means of visual images and used common objects and activities to instruct the people. The Jewish leaders rejected the messages of both Jeremiah and Jesus, and the prophet ended up in Egypt and Jesus on a Roman cross. In their day, both were considered miserable failures, but history has proved that both were right.

1. The nation's disgrace (1:1-22)

The plight of the city (vv. 1-11). The Jewish people were proud of the city of Jerusalem, for it was their capital city and the home of their holy temple (Pss. 48, 84, 87, 122, 125, 137). The Jebusites originally controlled Zion, but David and Joab wrested it from them (2 Sam. 5:6-10; 1 Chron. 11:4-9). Though it was called "the city of David" (1 Kings 8:1; 2 Chron. 5:2), it was the Lord who was enthroned on Zion (Ps. 9:11; Isa. 8:18). Zion was "the mountain of the Lord" (Isa. 2:3). For this reason, the Jews thought their city was impregnable, particularly because the Lord's house was there. But God would rather His city and temple be destroyed by pagans than to have His name disgraced by the wicked lives of His people.

The image is that of a beautiful princess who has been violated and disgraced and left alone to lament her plight. The city is called "the daughter of Zion" (1:6; 2:1, 4, 8, 10, 13, 18), "the daughter of Judah" (1:15; 2:2), and "the daughter of Jerusalem" 2:13, 15).[3] At one time, she cared for a large family, but now she was a lonely widow for whom nobody seemed to care (Ex. 22:22-24; Deut. 24:19-21; Isa. 1:17). Had God forgotten to protect the widows (Deut. 10:18)? She was desolate (vv. 4, 13), a word used to describe Tamar after she had been raped (2 Sam. 13:20). Once she was a princess who had collected tribute from other nations, but now she was a vassal nation herself and forced to give up her treasures ("pleasant things" KJV; vv. 7, 10-11).

Instead of trusting the Lord, Judah had trusted many "lovers" and "friends"—the heathen nations allied with her—but they had failed her, and now she was forsaken. Judah not only turned to other nations for help but she even worshiped their gods (Jer. 2:36-37; 27:1-11; 37:5-10). The nation had been "married" to Jehovah at Mount Sinai, so the Lord considered her actions the equivalent of adultery. She had rejected the Lord, her allies had abandoned her, and therefore she had no comfort (vv. 2, 9, 16-17, 21). The Lord had set aside the nation of Israel for Himself and she was not "reckoned among the nations" (Num. 23:9), but now she had been taken into captivity and had to dwell with the Babylonians. God had given Israel rest in her own land (Ex. 33:14; Deut. 3:20; Josh. 1:13-15; 21:44), but she would have no rest in Babylon (Deut. 28:65). Year after year, the pilgrims had made their way to the city to celebrate the great feasts (Lev. 23), but now the roads were empty and there was nothing to celebrate. The priests had no temple, the people had no joy, and the virgins wept because there were no men available to marry them.

The people of Judah shouldn't have been surprised at what happened to the nation and the city, because both Isaiah and Jeremiah had announced the coming invasion of the Babylon army. In the terms of the covenant (Deut. 28–30), Moses had warned Israel that God would chasten them if they disobeyed. When she was faithful to God, Israel had been the "head," the chief nation; but now Babylon would be the "head" and Israel the "tail" (v. 5; Deut. 28:44). Israel's army would be defeated (Deut. 28:25) and the people would go into exile (Deut. 28:32). Why did God chasten Judah? Because of "the multitude of her transgressions" (v. 5; see 8-9, 18-20). Two facts stand out in this book: the nation had sinned and deserved chastening, and God was the one who chastened them (1:12-15,17; 2:1-8,17; 3:1,37-38,43-45; 4:11).

When the enemy broke through the walls, the leaders fled like frightened deer, but they were caught and condemned (Jer. 38:14-28; 39:1-7). Had King Zedekiah listened to Jeremiah, the people, the city, and the temple would have been saved, but the king trusted his allies instead of the Lord (2 Chron. 26:2). Jerusalem became unclean (v. 8) and like a harlot was shamefully exposed (v. 17; Jer. 13:20-27). The people kept on sinning and didn't consider that their sins would lead to discipline and destruction (Deut. 32:28-29). "The wages of sin is death" (Rom. 6:23). The enemy entered the temple precincts (Deut. 23:3) and took Israel's sacred treasures, and the people had to use their wealth to buy the bare necessities of life.

The plea of the city for sympathy and help (vv. 12-19). Note the repetition of "the Lord" in this passage. The Lord afflicted Jerusalem (vv. 12-14a); the Lord delivered Jerusalem into enemy hands (v. 14b); the Lord trampled the people under the feet of the enemy (v. 15); the Lord commanded the enemy to attack (v. 17); and "the Lord is righteous" (v. 18). The prophet knew that God was in control of history and that the Babylonian army was serving Him. The enemy showed no mercy as the anger of the Lord was poured out during the invasion (1:12; 2:1, 3, 6, 21; 3:43; 4:11). God's anger is a holy anger, directed against sin. According to the law of Moses, if a priest's daughter was guilty of immorality, she was burned to death (Lev. 21:9). Israel was a kingdom of priests (Ex. 19:6), but she had betrayed the Lord and consorted with idols.

Along with the image of fire, Jeremiah used other pictures to describe the terrible plight of the people. They were caught in a net like animals (v. 13; Ezek. 12:13) and left desolate and faint. The people who had been freed from bondage by the Lord were now under the yoke of a pagan foreign nation (v. 14). Both Jeremiah (Jer. 27–28) and Moses (Deut. 28:48) had warned them about yokes. Sin always promises freedom but brings bondage The people were trodden underfoot and crushed, like grapes in a winepress (v. 15; see Rev. 14:17-20). The nation was drinking the cup of judgment as Jeremiah had warned (Jer. 25:15ff). Their joy was turned into tears (v. 16; 2:11; 3:48), but nobody offered them comfort or dried their tears. Jeremiah had wept copiously because of the sins of his people (Jer. 9:1, 18; 13:17; 14:17), but they wouldn't listen to God's Word.

Once again, the sufferers called out for any passing stranger to show them sympathy and bring them help (v. 18), but nobody could save them. The rulers of Judah had sought help from their Gentile allies, especially Egypt and Assyria, but their friends and lovers had failed them and did not keep their promises. Isaiah had told them not to trust Egypt (Isa. 31), and Jeremiah had echoed that same message (Jer. 2:18, 36). What a tragedy it is when God's people look to the world for help instead of seeking the face of the Lord!

The Babylonian soldiers had no mercy for religious leaders, like the priests, or for older people like the elders (v. 19; 2:10; 4:16; 5:12, 14). The priests were fed from the offerings of the people, but there could be no more offerings; and the elders were cared for by the younger people who had either been slain or deported to Babylon. All this was a fulfillment of the warnings in the covenant (Deut.

28:32, 50). Food became so scarce that mothers killed and ate their own children!

The prayer of the city (vv. 20-22). Each of the first three chapters ends with a prayer (1:20-22; 2:20-22; 3:50-66) and the entire fifth chapter is a prayer. The sufferers had cried out to God, "O Lord, behold my affliction" (v. 9), and to the passersby, "Behold, and see if there be any sorrow like my sorrow" (v. 12), and now they pray, "Behold, O Lord; for I am in distress" (v. 20). They were tormented in their bodies, but even more in their hearts, for they had sinned. If they left the city, they would be slain by the sword; if they remained in the city, they would starve to death. (See Ezek. 7, especially v. 15.) Not only did Judah's allies ("lovers, friends") refuse to help them, but they even rejoiced that the kingdom of Judah and the city of Jerusalem had been taken by the Babylonians. (See Ps. 35:15; Jer. 48:27; 50:11.)

Their prayer was that the Lord would "bring the day that He had announced" through the prophets, the day when Babylon would be defeated (Isa. 13–14; Jer. 50–51). But this prayer may also include God's promise that after seventy years, the Jews would be set free from captivity and allowed to return to their land and rebuild Jerusalem and the temple (Jer. 25:1-14; see Dan. 9:20-27). Now that they were in trouble, the Jews were turning back to God's Word. It's too bad they didn't pay attention to that Word much earlier and keep the trouble from coming! "Do to them as you have done to us!" is not exactly a Christian prayer, but it represented their true feelings (see Ps. 137:7-9).

2. The city's destruction (2:1-22)

That the God of Israel would ever permit the Gentiles, and especially the Babylonians, to enter and destroy Jerusalem and the temple was something inconceivable to the Jewish people (see Hab. 1). By ignoring the covenant and depending on the presence of the temple and its sacred furnishings, especially the ark, the leaders and most of the people had replaced living faith with dead superstition. However, this was not the first time Jerusalem had been invaded. As a warning to His sinful people, the Lord had allowed other enemies to enter the city and plunder it; Egypt (1 Kings 14:25-26 and 2 Kings 23:31-35), Israel, the Northern Kingdom (2 Kings 14:13-14 and 2 Chron. 25:22-24), and the Philistines and Arabs (2 Chron. 21:16-17). Had Israel listened to her prophets and returned to the Lord, she would have been spared the humiliation and suffering of destruction and deportation.

The cloud of anger (vv. 1-9). In the previous chapter, we found the word "anger" only once (v. 12), but in this chapter the word "comfort" is found only one time (v. 13), while "anger" and "wrath" are found eight times (vv. 1 [twice], 2, 3, 4, 6, 21, 22). The nation had once followed a cloud of glory in the wilderness (Ex. 13:21), and the glory of God had filled the tabernacle (Ex. 40:34) and the temple (1 Kings 8:11); but now God had sent them a cloud of His anger. Not only was there a storm cloud of judgment, but Zion was cast down like a falling star, thrown down her buildings and walls and brought down the nation and its leaders (vv. 1-2). "His footstool" refers not only to Zion itself (Ps. 99:5, 9) but also to the temple (Ps. 132:7) and the ark of the covenant, the throne of God that stood in the Holy of Holies (1 Chron. 28:2).

God also put a cloud between Himself and His people so that their prayers would not reach Him (3:44). He had told Jeremiah not to pray for the people because they were so wicked that they were beyond his intercession (Jer. 7:16; 11:14; 14:11). In fact, it was futile for them even to pray for themselves (11:11). God had dishonored ("polluted" KJV) His people and their leaders in a way that couldn't be hidden. All the nations could see what the Lord had done to the people and the city.

"Every horn" in verse 3 means "every strength," that is, everything that Israel trusted: their king, their leaders, their walled city, and even their religion. The "right hand of God" represents His great power (Ex. 15:6,12; Ps. 17:7; 44:3; 74:11), but that power had been withdrawn. Instead of using His right hand to defeat the enemy, God used it to chasten His people (v. 4). God "swallowed up" His people in terrible judgment (vv. 2, 5), although the attacking nations took credit for the victory (v. 16).

Jeremiah described the destruction of the buildings, especially the palaces, strongholds and the temple itself (v. 5). The Babylonians treated the temple like a booth in a garden and not like the dwelling place of the Lord, but the Jews hadn't done much better. They polluted the sanctuary by their sin and hypocrisy (Isa. 1), and this led to the destruction of the temple. The altar and other furnishings were gone, the priests were gone, and there could be no more observance of the high and holy days. The outer and inner walls of the city, and the city gates, were destroyed as well. When the Jews built their temple, they used measuring lines to be sure they were accurately following God's plans, but now the Lord had used a measuring line to be just as accurate in destroying the temple and the city (Isa. 28:17 and Amos 7:7-8).

The summary in verse 9 declares that the Jews had lost everything that was precious to them: the gates and walls, the leaders, the Law, and the prophets. God sent no vision to the people to show them what to do. How gracious God had been to His people in giving them so many blessings (Rom. 9:1-5)! But they had taken these blessings for granted and now had lost them.

The suffering people (vv. 10-17). Both old (elders) and young (virgins), male and female, felt the suffering together. Instead of sitting at the gate in honor and managing the affairs of the city, the elders sat on the ground as in mourning, too overwhelmed to utter a word. The virgins (1:4) walked about in sorrow, with their eyes to the ground, knowing that they would never be married and have children. As Jeremiah beheld the suffering of the little children in the streets, he was consumed with agony and wept copiously. (See 4:3,6, and 10.) If Israel had obeyed the covenant, there would have been no invasion and the people would have enjoyed plenty of food and drink (Deut. 28:1-14; Lev. 26:1-13). But now there was a famine so severe, the mothers even killed and ate their own children (Lam. 4:10; Deut. 28:56-57).

The suffering was so intense that the prophet ran out of things to say and comparisons to make (v. 13). He could neither comfort the people nor himself. God would have buried the nation's sins in the depths of the sea (Micah 7:19), but instead, their wound was as deep as the sea and incurable. What had caused such calamity and tragedy? *The spiritual leaders had given the people a false message and they had believed it (v. 14; 4:13).* For forty years, Jeremiah had openly opposed the false prophets who proclaimed "Peace, peace when there is no peace" (Jer. 6:14; 8:11). They preached a popular message that the people wanted to hear (5:12; 14:13-16; 27:8-9; 28:1-17), while Jeremiah proclaimed the true message of the Lord and was rejected and persecuted. Jeremiah compared the false prophets to deceitful physicians (6:14; 8:11), empty wind (5:13), peddlers of chaff (23:28), selfish shepherds (23:1-4), and toxic people spreading deadly infection (23:15 NIV).

The false prophets refused to expose the sins of the people and call the nation to repentance. The prophet Ezekiel, with the captives in Babylon, compared them to men who whitewashed the wall instead of exposing its weaknesses and repairing it (Ezek. 13:10-16; 22:28). But even today we have religious leaders like these false prophets, people who want to be popular with the crowd instead of pleasing to God. Instead of getting their messages from God's Word, they dream up their own messages and lead people astray. Jesus called them "wolves in sheep's clothing" (Matt. 7:15) and Paul used similar language (Acts 20:28-31).

One of the deepest cuts of all was the mockery of the Gentiles who walked past the devastated city (vv. 16-17). The Jews were proud of Jerusalem and called it "the perfection of beauty" (v. 15; Ps. 48:2; 50:2; Ezek. 16:14), but now it was a heap of rubble. The Gentiles vented their hatred against the Jews. "This is the day we have waited for," they shouted jubilantly, forgetting that God promised to curse all those who cursed His people (Gen. 12:1-3). All that the pious Jews could reply was, "The Lord has done what He purposed; He has fulfilled His word which He commanded in days of old" (v. 17 NKJV). Israel knew the terms of the covenant and had violated them. Now they were paying the price of having their own way and rejecting the messengers of the Lord.

The plea for help (vv. 18-22). But God's people don't live on explanations; they live on promises. The people knew they were guilty of breaking the covenant, so all they could do was turn to the Lord and cry out to Him. The promise of forgiveness and restoration was also a part of God's covenant (Lev. 26:27-29; Deut. 28:53-57; 30:1-10), and seventy years later, God would bring His people back to their land (Jer. 25:1-14; Dan. 9:1ff). Meanwhile, all they could do was cry out for mercy to the God whose Word they had spurned.

The sight of the suffering children broke their hearts, because it's the children who too often suffer most from the sins of the parents.

The priests and prophets had sinned, and many of them were slain; but the children were innocent and deserved no punishment. Israel was suffering in the day of God's anger because they had sinned away the day of God's grace. God was calling various terrors to come to Jerusalem, just as if He were inviting them to a feast. The feast was an image of judgment. (See Jer. 51:39; Ezek. 39:17-20; Rev. 19:17-21.) The people were starving, but God's terrors were feasting on the people.

God's ear is open to the cries of His people, but He doesn't answer until His hand is finished with the discipline He promised (Heb. 12). "The Lord shall judge his people. It is a fearful thing to fall into the hands of the living God" (Heb. 10:30-31).

3. The prophet's distress (3:1-66)[4]

After describing in the first two laments the plight of the city and the people, the prophet now in this central chapter describes his own personal pain and distress. The pronouns "he" and "his" (referring to God) and "I" and "me" (referring to the prophet) are prominent in these sixty-six verses that form the heart of the book. Lamentations 3:1 is the central verse of the book and verses 21-39 comprise the "theological heart" of the chapter and the book. From 1:1 to 3:18, Jeremiah has described "hopelessness," but verses 19-39 focus on the hope that we have in God, no matter how desperate our situation might be. Jeremiah speaks for himself, but as he does, he also reflects the feelings and faith of the godly remnant of Jews who heard God's Word and sought to obey Him.

The prophet's pain (vv. 1-18). Babylon was the rod of God's wrath to the Jewish nation (Isa. 14:3-8), but the sufferings of the people and the destruction of the city and the temple were the great causes of pain in Jeremiah's life. These tragic events would not have occurred if the people had listened to him and obeyed God's will. Jeremiah had faithfully proclaimed God's message for forty years, and yet the nation had turned a deaf ear. Is it any wonder he suffered?

The rod of discipline was bad enough, but the darkness made it even worse (v. 2). In Scripture, darkness is often a picture of defeat and despair (Ps. 107:10, 14; Isa. 9:2) because sitting in darkness is like dwelling with the dead (v. 6). The hand of God was against him (Pss. 32:4; 82:5) and the result of all this suffering was that Jeremiah looked very old (v. 4; see Job 16:8-9). He felt confined, hemmed in by walls and hindered by chains (vv. 5-7).[5] Even worse, when he looked up to pray, Jeremiah felt like God had slammed the door on him (v. 8; see v. 44). God was like a bear and a lion, and Jeremiah felt mangled and dragged away (vv. 10-11). The lion was a symbol of Babylon (Jer. 4:7; 5:6). God was like an enemy and His arrows were aimed at His servant (vv. 12-13; see Job 6:4; 7:20).

Now that Jeremiah's words had been fulfilled, you would think the people would have respected him and listened to him, but they didn't. They ridiculed him and sang disrespectful songs about him (v. 14; see v. 63 and Jer. 20:7-18). Once again, he was like the Lord Jesus who was also ridiculed by the people (Ps. 69:12). We expect the Gentiles to mock the Jews (1:21; 2:15), but we don't expect the Jews to mock their own prophet. Jeremiah compared it to tasting the bitter herbs at the Passover feast or drinking bitter gall (vv. 15, 19; see Job 16:13; 20:25; Ps. 69:21). Myrrh mixed with wine was used as an anesthesia to deaden pain, but what Jeremiah "drank" only made his pain worse. Bitterness and brokenness went together, for he felt like a man with a mouth full of broken teeth and gravel! Most mourners put ashes only on their heads, but he was covered with ashes (v. 16).

A familiar word on the lips of Jewish people is "shalom," which means "peace, prosperity, health, well-being." But the prophet experienced no "shalom," for peace and prosperity were far from him and his people (v. 17). He records the depths of his despair in verse 18 when he cries out, "My splendor is gone! Everything I had hoped for from the Lord is lost!" (NLT). The glory of the city had vanished and along with it, the hope in the heart of God's suffering servant. But this cry of despair is the turning point in Jeremiah's lament, for now he focuses on the Lord and not on himself and he says, "I have hope" (v. 21).[6]

The Lord's promises (vv. 19-39). Jeremiah turned from contemplating his misery to remembering God's mercy. He still experienced pain and sorrow, but he also called to mind the faithfulness of the Lord, and this gave him hope (vv. 19-21). The pessimistic American newspaper editor Henry L. Mencken called hope "a pathological belief in the occurrence of the impossible," but no true child of God could accept that definition. A. W. Tozer said it better when he called hope "the divine alchemy that transmutes the base metal of adversity into gold." (See 1 Peter 1:6-8.) The realization of God's mercy, compassion, and faithfulness generated hope in Jeremiah's soul, and his contemplation of trouble became a confession of faith. Because the Lord loves us, He chastens us (Heb. 12:5-11), but He doesn't consume us; He disciplines, but He doesn't destroy.

Unbelief causes us to look at God through our circumstances, and this creates hopelessness; but faith enables us to look at our circumstances through the reality of God, and this gives us hope. A radio listener once sent me a little rhyme that has encouraged me on more than one occasion.

> Look at yourself and you'll be depressed.
> Look at circumstances and you'll be distressed.
> Look at the Lord and you'll be blessed!

If the Lord is "our portion" (Ps. 73:26; 142:5), then we are strengthened by that which cannot be used up or destroyed. God is our eternal source of strength, hope, and blessing (Ps. 46:1). Our circumstances change, and so do our feelings about them, but God is always good, loving, merciful, and kind, and He never changes. "Jesus Christ is the same yesterday, today, and forever" (Heb. 13:8, NKJV). To build life on that which is always changing is to invite constant unrest and disappointment, but to build on the changeless and the eternal is to have peace and confidence.

As Jeremiah contemplated the character of God, he realized that the best thing he and his people could do was to wait patiently and silently for the Lord to work and accomplish His will in His time (vv. 25-28). God is gracious, God is great in faithfulness, and God is good—no matter how we feel or what we see. But it isn't enough just to sit and wait; we must also seek the Lord and draw closer to Him (vv. 25, 40). As for the children and youths who were suffering, even they could learn from this experience and grow up to be strong men and women (v. 27). Jeremiah was now an old man, but he had suffered in his youth, so he knew what he was talking about (Jer. 1:8, 17-19; 15:10, 15-17). His youthful experiences of trial and opposition helped to prepare him for his present ministry.

The secret of victory in tough times is simply to submit to the Lord and accept the fact that "the Lord has laid it on him" (v. 28 NIV). "It is the Lord. Let Him do what seems good to Him" (1 Sam. 3:18 NKJV). We must bow before the Lord—even putting our faces in the dust—and submit to Him without complaining, knowing that in His time, He will see us through. In that hour of pain and perplexity, Jeremiah laid hold of some wonderful assurances that can encourage us today:

- The Lord doesn't cast off His people and forget them (v. 31)
- In the midst of pain, we know He loves us (v. 32)
- God doesn't enjoy chastening His own and He feels our pain (v. 33)
- God sees the way people treat us (vv. 34-36)
- God is on the throne and in control of all events (vv. 37-38)
- If He chastens us for our sins, we shouldn't complain, for even His chastening is evidence of His love (v. 39)

As I wrote this section of our study, I occasionally glanced at a picture on a nearby bookcase. It's a reproduction of Rembrandt's painting "Jeremiah Lamenting the Destruction of Jerusalem," which Rembrandt painted in 1630. It depicts a sad old man, seated on a rock, a copy of the Scriptures on his left and behind him on his right a scene of people fleeing a burning city. If I weren't a Christian believer, the painting would discourage me, but I see in it the truths Jeremiah shared in verses 19-39. Like the prophet, we must live a day at a time and each morning draw upon a new supply of God's mercy. No matter what the Enemy says to us, we must remind ourselves that "the Lord is good" and He is never closer to us than when He chastens us.

The nation's penitence (vv. 40-51). The phrase "punishment of his sins" in verse 39 naturally brings up the necessity for personal and national repentance. Jeremiah knew that the fall of Jerusalem was an act of chastening on the part of Jehovah (1:8-9, 12-15; 2:1-8; 4:6, 22) and that the purpose of that chastening was to bring the nation to her knees, confessing her sins. This meant searching their hearts, acknowledging their transgressions, and seeking the forgiveness of the Lord. Cleansing and restoration were promised in the covenant (Deut. 30) and also in Solomon's prayer at the dedication of the temple (2 Chron. 6:36-42; 7:11-14). God chastens us that He might be able to cleanse us when we tell Him we're sorry.

In Ezra 9, Nehemiah 9, and Daniel 9, you find prayers of confession on behalf of the people of Israel. You also find similar prayers in the Psalms. Jeremiah's prayer revealed a man with a broken heart who couldn't stop weeping over the sins of the people (see 1:16; 2:11, 18-19). Though the nation was but "scum and refuse" in the eyes of the Gentiles, the prophet knew that Israel was still God's chosen people, bound to Him by the very covenant they had broken. They had forsaken Him, but He would not forsake them, even though He chastened them severely. He had been longsuffering towards them but they had refused to heed His warnings (2 Chron. 36:11ff).

God's call for His people to repent is just as valid today. Are we listening?

The prophet's persecutors (vv. 52-66). These verses summarize much of what you read in Jeremiah's prophecy: his being hunted like a bird and being put into a pit (Jer. 37–38), insults and other verbal abuse, and plots to kill him (Jer. 11:18-23,26-28). Had the people listened to God's servant, their nation, city, and temple would have been saved and their lives spared. Jeremiah found his support and salvation in the Lord, and he called upon Him in times of trouble. "Fear not" was God's message of assurance (see Jer. 1:8). God saw the wrongs that were done to His servant and He heard all the lies that were told about him. But no matter what people may say about us or do to us, the Lord is on our side, even in times of chastening. God didn't desert His servant, nor will He desert us.

We aren't surprised that Jeremiah asked God to treat his persecutors the way they had treated him. Jeremiah was God's servant and spokesman, and their rejection of him meant their rejection of God's Word. You can't reject God's Word and escape eventual judgment. David prayed the same kind of prayer when he was going through persecution (Ps. 28:1-4). As Christians, we're instructed to pray for our persecutors and to do them good, in the name of Jesus (Matt. 5:10-12, 43-48). Our Lord is the greatest example in His treatment of His enemies (1 Peter 2:21-24), for He prayed, "Father, forgive them, for they know not what they do" (Luke 23:34).

4. The Lord's discipline (4:1-22)

In this chapter, Jeremiah brought together a number of vivid images to describe what the people endured in the siege and fall of Jerusalem. These calamities had been announced in the terms of the covenant (Deut. 28–30), so the Jews shouldn't have been surprised when they occurred.

Gold and jewels (vv. 1-2, 7-8). These stand for the people of Israel, precious in the sight of the Lord. The tribes of Israel were represented as jewels set in gold on the breastplate of the high priest and also on his shoulders (Ex. 28:6-30; 39:1-21; see also Zech. 9:16-17 and Mal. 3:6). But their sins had cheapened them and they had lost their beauty. The enemy treated God's precious sons and daughters like pieces of cheap broken pottery that you would throw on the neighborhood trash heap. Nobody was ever made better, more attractive, or more valuable because they sinned.

Animals and birds (vv. 3-5, 10). "Sea monsters" can be translated "whales" or "jackals," and the meaning will not be lost. The mammals feed their young until they're able to care for themselves, but Jerusalem's mothers were heartless toward their young because they had nothing to feed them. In fact, the reverse became true: the babies fed the parents (v. 10; 2:20; and see Lev. 26:29; Deut. 28:53-57; Jer. 19:9). Ostriches were notorious for laying their eggs in the wilderness and then abandoning them (Job 39:13-18), and the Jewish mothers were abandoning their babies. The wealthy people, who were accustomed to eating delicacies, had to rummage in the garbage to find something to eat. God's special people were living like animals because they had turned their backs on their Maker and their God (Rom. 1:18ff).

Enemies (vv. 6, 9). For centuries, the Jewish nation had been the object of God's love and grace. He had delivered them from Egypt, brought them into the Promised Land, given them victory over their enemies, and graciously provided their every need; but now, He was pouring out His wrath upon them and their land. The siege was long and painful, and it would have been better if God had destroyed the city suddenly, as He did Sodom and Gomorrah (Gen. 19). Israel's sins were greater than those of the cities of the plain, because Israel had seen the glory of God, been given His holy law and had entered into covenant with Him. Privileges always bring responsibilities, but the nation refused to obey the Lord and was punished for their rebellion. It would have been better for the people to be slain in battle than to starve to death slowly.

Fire (vv. 11-12). Fire is frequently used in Scripture as a picture of God's wrath, and "the Lord's anger burned" is a familiar image (Ex. 4:14; 15:7; 32:10-12; etc.). The Lord made it clear at Mount Sinai that He was "a consuming fire" (Deut. 4:24; 5:1-5, 23-27; Heb. 12:29) and would not tolerate deliberate sins. The Babylonians looted the city and then burned its walls, gates, and buildings, including the palaces and the temple (2 Chron. 36:19). Jeremiah had warned Israel that God's wrath would "break out like fire" and their city burned down by the Babylonian army, but they refused to listen (Jer. 4:4; 7:20; 21:12; 32:26-29; 34:1-3). God "blazed against Jacob like a flaming fire devouring all around" (2:3, NKJV). The other nations and their rulers were aghast at the destruction of "the impregnable city."

Blood (vv. 13-16). The blood of men and of animals was held in great respect in Israel. The Jews were not allowed to eat the blood with the meat (Lev. 17), and the shedding of innocent blood polluted the land and had to be vindicated (Num. 35:30-34). The Jews were very careful not to be defiled by the dead, but the sins of the false prophets and disobedient priests had defiled the land and its people, and Jeremiah had often cried out against their sins (Jer. 5:31; 6:13-15; 14:14-18; 23:9ff). He was especially grieved because the leaders were ignoring God's law, conducting "fixed" trials and shedding innocent blood (Jer. 2:34-35; 7:6; 19:4; 22:1-5, 17). Some of the wicked rulers were even prepared to shed the innocent blood of the prophet Jeremiah (ch. 26)!

Because they rejected the light of God's law, the people were defiled and unable to see the truth, groping about like blind men in the streets, and crying out like lepers, "Unclean, unclean!" (See Lev. 13:45-46.) Not only would they wander in the city streets but they would become wanderers in the world at large, with no place to call home (Deut. 28:65-66). The sinful people became a scattered people, but the Lord promised that He would bring them back to their land (Deut. 30:1-10; Isa. 11:11-12; Jer. 23:3-8).

Watchmen (vv. 17-19). Unwilling to trust the Lord for help, the leaders made agreements with other nations to secure their aid in fighting against the Babylonians, but their allies failed them. Israel's "lovers and friends" proved unfaithful (1:2; Jer. 2:15-17, 36-37; 37:7; Isa. 30:1-7). The false prophets assured the people that help was coming, but the watchmen on the walls looked in vain. Pharaoh Hophra's army did come to help King Zedekiah, and the siege was interrupted temporarily, but Nebuchadnezzar sent Hophra back to Egypt defeated. (See Jer. 37 and Ezek. 30:20-26.) The brief cessation of the siege brought welcomed relief, but when the Babylonians returned to Jerusalem, things became even worse than before. It was impossible to escape the invaders, whether you walked on the streets or fled to the desert or the mountains. "Swifter than eagles" is a phrase quoted from the covenant (Deut. 28:49-52; see Jer. 4:13 and 48:40). "Our end is near! Our end is come!" was the cry of the people. The prophet Ezekiel in Babylon delivered a message on the same theme (Ezek. 7).

Breath and shadows (v. 20). The false prophets assured the people that the Lord would never break His covenant with David, so there would always be one of his descendants on the throne (2 Sam. 7). They interpreted this to mean that the throne and the nation would always endure, but they were wrong. King Zedekiah, son of godly Josiah, was the last king of the Davidic line until the coming of Jesus Christ (Luke 1:30-33, 68-79). Zedekiah foolishly rebelled against Nebuchadnezzar and then tried to escape, but he was caught, judged, and taken to Babylon, where he died (2 Kings 24–25; Jer. 34, 37–39). The Jews saw their king as the very breath of their lips, the rock in whose shadow they could hide; but he failed on both counts. Because of his unbelief and rebellion, Zedekiah brought death, not life, and proved to be no protection at all.

The cup (vv. 21-22). The Edomites were Judah's neighbors, the descendants of Esau, brother of Jacob who fathered the "fathers" of the twelve tribes of Israel. From before birth, Jacob and Esau fought against each other (Gen. 25:19-34; 27), and the Edomites perpetuated this feud. They rejoiced at the destruction of Jerusalem and encouraged the Babylonians and may even have assisted them in their work (Ps. 83:1-8; 137:7; Ezek. 25:12-14; Obadiah). Israel had drunk the bitter cup of God's wrath, but one day the cup would be handed to Edom and her time of judgment would come (Jer. 25:15ff; 49:7-22; Ezek. 35).

5. The Jewish remnant's declaration (5:1-22)

This chapter has twenty-two verses but it is not an acrostic. It is a prayer; the pronouns are plural, for the prophet prayed for himself and the suffering remnant that had survived the invasion. He asked the Lord to "remember . . . consider . . . behold" (v. 1). This means that he and the people wanted the Lord to act on their behalf and deliver them from their painful and humiliating situation. Jeremiah knew that the Babylonian captivity would not end for seventy years (Jer. 25:1-14; Dan. 9:1ff), but he still asked the Lord to be merciful to the poor people left in the land and to the exiles in Babylon.

God had given His people their land ("inheritance"), their law, the city of Jerusalem, and the temple. They disobeyed the law and defiled the land, the city and the temple because of their sins. Therefore, they lost the land, the city and the temple, just as God had warned in His covenant. People were killed and families destroyed (v. 3); the economy was ruined (vv. 4, 9; see Deut. 29:11); and their freedom was taken from them (vv. 5-6, 8).

It didn't seem fair that God punished the children for the sins of their parents (v. 7; Ex. 20:5 and 34:7; Num. 14:18; see Jer. 31:29 and Ezek. 18:2). But before the prayer ends, the people will confess, "We have sinned" (v. 16). To be sure, the ancestors of that suffering generation had indeed sinned against the Lord, but their sins helped to lead their descendants into sin. God visits His wrath on the fathers and their children *when the children behave like their fathers!*

They remembered that bread was scarce (v. 9) and that the famine caused terrible loss of weight, sickness, and ugliness (v. 10; Deut. 28:48). Their wives and daughters were raped by enemy soldiers (v. 11; Deut. 28:30), so that even if they did survive, they were unacceptable as wives. The leaders of the nation were treated with disrespect (v. 12), and the youths and children were forced to do the work of adults (v. 13). There was no more joy in the city (vv. 14-15). The "crown city" was fallen (v. 16; see 2:15) and the king who wore the crown was in exile (4:20).

What was the cause of all this trouble, loss and pain? The Babylonian army? The wrath of God? No, the sins of the people! Here we see the blinding effects of sin (v. 17 and see 4:14), the binding effects of sin (vv. 5 and 8), and the grinding effects of sin (v. 13). The city of the great King was now a home for wild beasts (v. 18).

But the book doesn't end with this recitation of the tragic losses of the people. It ends with a marvelous confession of faith and a humble confession of sin. Though the throne of Judah was disgraced and destroyed, by faith Jeremiah and the remnant saw the living and unchanging God on His throne in heaven, and this gave them courage (v. 19; Ps. 102:12). Yes, they felt forsaken and forgotten (v. 20; see 2:9; 3:37-39), but they knew God would return to them if they would return to Him. (See Lev. 26:40-45 and Deut. 30:1-10.) "Return to us and renew us" is their final cry. Without God's presence and power, their lives could never be renewed, and they didn't want to go back to the old ways that had caused so much trouble. For a similar prayer, see Jer. 14:19-22.

The final verse seems very pessimistic after such a sincere prayer for redemption and renewal. When the Jews read Lamentations publicly in the synagogue to remember the fall of Jerusalem, they repeat verse 21 so the reading won't end on a negative note. But the verse is still there, and it reminds us of the high cost of sin. God delights in His people and longs to bless them, but if we sin, He will chasten us. If we repent and confess our sins, He will forgive us (1 John 1:9) and give us a new beginning. "It is a fearful thing to fall into the hands of the living God" (Heb. 10:31).

Living lessons

The Book of Lamentations vividly presents to us some important lessons that God's people must learn and never forget.

1. Privilege brings responsibility, and responsibility involves accountability.
2. God is longsuffering, but there comes a time when He must chasten His people.
3. When the blessings He gives are taken for granted and used selfishly, He takes those blessings from us. To enjoy the gifts but ignore the Giver is idolatry.
4. God is always faithful to the terms of His covenant, either to bless because we have obeyed, or to chasten because we have not.

5. When parents sin, the children also suffer.

6. When spiritual leaders refuse to hear and obey God's Word, they lead their followers into sin and judgment.

7. It's possible to declare God's Word faithfully and never see the Lord change the hearts of sinners. Jeremiah was faithful for over forty years, yet the nation became more and more wicked.

8. Jeremiah was a man with a broken heart, a man who suffered much; yet he was rewarded by being identified with Jesus (Matt. 16:13-14). Jeremiah's ministry may not have been "successful" as we measure success, but his character became more and more Christlike, "conformed to the image of his Son" (Rom. 8:29).

Endnotes

1. Jerusalem had been invaded and looted prior to this time, by Egypt in 926 (1 Kings 14:25-26); by Israel, the Northern Kingdom, in 790 (2 Kings 14:13-14); by Egypt again in 609 (2 Kings 23:31-35); by the Arabs and Philistines during the reign of Jehoram, 849–41 (2 Chron. 21:16-17); and again by the Northern Kingdom of Israel in about 784 (2 Chron. 25:22-24).

2. In chapters 2, 3, and 4, the sixteenth and seventeenth Hebrew letters (*ayin* and *pe)* are reversed, but this order has been found in other Hebrew alphabet samples, so the order wasn't unknown. See 2:16-17, 3:46-51, and 4:16-17.

3. How Jeremiah could call the apostate city a "virgin" in 1:15 and 2:13 is a mystery to us. A virgin daughter was a very valuable member of the family and held in high esteem, and the Jews had polluted themselves with foreign alliances and foreign gods. Such is the grace of God! Though He chastened His people, He never forsook them. One day, the nation shall be restored to her Husband, the Lord (Jer. 3; Hosea 2:14-3:5).

4. Keep in mind that in chapter 3, Jeremiah altered the acrostic and gave three verses to each letter of the Hebrew alphabet. As he did in 2:16-17, he reversed the letters *ayin* and *pe* in 3:46-51.

5. The Babylonians were actually very kind to Jeremiah. By mistake, he was chained with the prisoners but them released and given the freedom of the land (Jer. 40:1-6).

6. He names God—"the Lord"—for the first time in this chapter in v. 18. This is Jehovah, the covenant-making God who is faithful to His Word and His people.

EZEKIEL

OUTLINE

Key theme: Showing reverence for the name and glory of God

Key verse: "You will know that I am the Lord" (6:7, NIV) (This statement is found seventy times in the book)

I. THE PROPHET'S CALL (1–3)

1. Seeing God's glory—1
2. Hearing God's Word—2
3. Becoming God's watchman—3

II. THE FALL OF JERUSALEM (4–24)

1. The judgment predicted—4–7
2. God's glory departs—8–11
3. Godless leaders exposed—12–17
4. God's justice defended—18–21
5. The end of the city—22–24

III. THE NATIONS JUDGED (25–32)

1. Ammon—25:1-7
2. Moab— 25:8-11
3. Edom—25:12-14
4. Philistia—25:15-17
5. Tyre—26:1–28:19
6. Sidon—28:20-24
7. Egypt—29–32

IV. THE GLORIOUS FUTURE OF ISRAEL (33–48)

1. The city of Jerusalem restored —33–34
2. The land of Israel renewed—35–36
3. The nation of Israel resurrected and reunited—37–39
4. The temple and the priesthood reestablished—40–48

CONTENTS

CHAPTER ONE
FROM PRIEST TO PROPHET
Ezekiel 1–3

Like Jeremiah (1:2), Zechariah (1:1), and John the Baptist (Luke 1:5ff), Ezekiel ("God strengthens") was called by God from being a priest to serving as a prophet. As God's spokesman to the Jewish exiles in the land of Babylon, he would rebuke them for their sins and expose their idolatry, but he would also reveal the glorious future the Lord had prepared for them. He was thirty years old at the time of his call (Ezek. 1:1), the normal age for a priest to begin his ministry (Num. 4:1-3, 23).[1]

It would have been much easier for Ezekiel to remain a priest, for priests were highly esteemed by the Jews, and a priest could read the Law and learn everything he needed to know to do his work. Prophets were usually despised and persecuted. They received their messages and orders from the Lord as the occasion demanded and could never be sure what would happen next. It was dangerous to be a prophet. Most people resent being told about their sins and prefer to hear messages of cheer, not declarations of judgment.

Jeremiah had been ministering in Jerusalem for four years when Ezekiel was born in 622 B.C., but surely as he grew up, he paid attention to what Jeremiah was saying.[2] It's likely that Daniel and Ezekiel knew each other before the Captivity, though there's no evidence they saw each other in Babylon. Ezekiel's prophetic ministry was greatly needed in Babylon because false prophets abounded and were giving the Jewish people false hopes of a quick deliverance (usually by Egypt) and a triumphant return to their land (Jer. 5:30-31; 27:1-11; 28:1-17). It's possible that King Zedekiah's visit to Babylon (51:59-61) and the arrival of Jeremiah's letter to the exiles (Jer. 29) both occurred the year Ezekiel received his call. Jeremiah's letter told the Jews that they would be in Babylon for seventy years and therefore should settle down, raise families, and pray for their captors. But Jeremiah also announced the ultimate fall of Babylon, a message the exiles were only too eager to hear.

The most difficult task of a prophet is to change people's minds. This means pulling up the weeds of false theology and planting the good seed of the Word of God. It also means tearing down the flimsy thought structures that false prophets build and constructing in their place lasting buildings on solid foundations of truth (Ezek. 1:10; 2 Cor. 10:3-6). To prepare him for his difficult ministry, the Lord caused Ezekiel to participate in three dramatic experiences.

1. Beholding the glory of the Lord (Ezek. 1)

The kingdom of Judah had suffered greatly at the hands of victorious Babylon, and many Jewish people wondered if Jehovah was still the God of Abraham, Isaac, and Jacob (see Ps. 74). Were the Jews not God's chosen people? Had not Jehovah defeated their enemies and given them the Promised Land? Was not Jerusalem His holy city and did He not dwell in their holy temple? Yet now His chosen people were exiles in a pagan land, their Promised Land was devastated, Jerusalem was in enemy hands, and the temple had been robbed of its precious treasures. It was a dark day for Israel, and the first thing Ezekiel needed to understand was that, no matter how discouraging the circumstances, God was still on the throne accomplishing His divine purposes in the world. There are many unexplained mysteries in the vision Ezekiel had, but one message comes through with clarity and power: Jehovah is the sovereign Lord of Israel and of all the nations of the earth.

The storm (Ezek. 1:3-4). The Chebar River (Kebar, NIV) or canal flowed from the Euphrates River, south of the city of Babylon, where the Jewish exiles gathered for prayer (see Acts 16:13). Ezekiel mentions it in Ezekiel 1:1; 3:23; 10:15, 20, 22; and 43:3. Apparently Ezekiel was there interceding with the other captives when the Lord called him to his new ministry. Isaiah was worshiping in the temple when God called him (Isa. 6) and Paul and Barnabas were engaged in worship at Antioch when they received their call (Acts 13:1-3). When Ezekiel went to the prayer meeting, it was just like any other day; but the Lord made it a turning point in his life. We never know what a difference a day will make when we're in the path of duty.

The word of the Lord came to Ezekiel in the form of a vision, and the hand of the Lord laid hold of him and claimed him for special service. The phrase "the word of the Lord came" is used fifty times in his prophecy and speaks of the authority of his message; and "the hand of the Lord" is found also in Ezekiel 3:14, 22; 8:1; 33:22; 37:1; and 40:1. The word of the Lord brings enlightenment and the hand of the Lord enablement (see Eph. 1:15-23). In Scripture, a storm is often an image of divine judgment (Prov. 1:27; Isa. 66:15; Jer. 4:13; 23:19; Nahum 1:3). Since the immense whirlwind cloud Ezekiel beheld was coming from the north, it indicated the invasion of Judah by the Babylonian army and the destruction of the land, the city of Jerusalem, and the temple (Jer. 4:6; 6:1). For forty years, God had graciously led Israel by a fiery cloud; but now a fiery cloud was bringing chastening to His disobedient people. The Prophet Jeremiah saw a similar vision at the beginning of his ministry (Jer. 1:13-16).

Ezekiel saw bright light around the cloud and an enfolding fire, like molten metal, within the cloud. Both are reminders of the holiness of God, for "our God is a consuming fire" (Ex. 19:16, 18; Deut. 4:24; Heb. 12:29). As he describes this vision, Ezekiel uses the words "like" and "likeness" at least twenty-five times, indicating that what he saw was symbolic of realities God wanted to reveal to him. Throughout the Bible, the Lord uses familiar things to illustrate spiritual truths that are beyond human vocabulary and description.

The cherubim (Ezek. 1:5-14). In 10:15 and 20, Ezekiel identified the living creatures as the cherubim, heavenly creatures first mentioned in Genesis 3:24. The tabernacle curtains were embroidered with images of the cherubim (Ex. 26:1), and two cherubim were on the golden covering of the ark, the mercy seat (Ex. 25:18-22). Cherubim were very much in evidence in Solomon's temple (1 Kings 6:23-29; 2 Chron. 3:10-13) and in John's visions in the Book of Revelation (Rev. 4:6-9; 5:6-14; 6:1-11; 14:3; 15:7; 19:4). The creatures had the body of a human, straight feet like that of a calf, four faces and four wings, with human hands under the wings. Their wings were so arranged that the creatures did not have to turn; they could fly straight forward and change directions quickly. Their wings touched so that each creature was at the corner of a square that would be outlined by their wings.

Of special interest are their four faces: a man, a lion, an ox, and an eagle (Ezek. 1:10). Man is the highest of God's creatures, being made in the image of God. The lion is the greatest of the untamed beasts of the forest, while the ox is the strongest of the domesticated beasts of the field. The eagle is the greatest of the birds and is even a picture of God (Deut. 32:11-12). But there is also a connection here with the covenant God made with Noah after the Flood (Gen. 9:8-17). God promised not to destroy the world again with a flood, and He gave this promise to Noah (a man) and his descendants, the birds (the eagle), the livestock (the ox), and the wild animals (the lion). The presence of the cherubim before the throne of God is assurance that God remembers His promise and cares for His creatures. But it also reminds us that all of creation is used by the Lord to bless or to chasten His people. In this vision, they are a part of God's judgment on His sinful people.

The life of these creatures came from the "spirit" (or Spirit)[3] within the cloud (Ezek. 1:12, 20), and this life enabled them to move like lightning; in fact, in their movements, they even looked like flashes of lightning. When Ezekiel first saw these creatures, he compared them to fiery amber or molten metal (v. 4); but as he watched them closely, he compared them to sparkling bronze (v. 7), burning coals of fire, lamps, and lightning (vv. 13-14). Like the Apostle John describing the beauty of the holy city (Rev. 21–22), the prophet ran out of words and had to draw pictures!

The wheels (Ezek. 1:15-21). There were four wheels (v. 16), each with an intersecting wheel and each associated with one of the cherubim. The intersecting wheels enabled the creatures and the cloud to move in any direction instantly without having to turn, moving like a flash of lightning. These wheels looked like chrysolite, a yellow or greenish-yellow precious stone; they were very high, as though reaching from earth to heaven, and their rims were awesome and full of eyes. The spirit (Spirit) of the living creatures was in the wheels, so that the living creatures moved in whatever direction the wheels moved. It was indeed an awesome sight, the huge wheels, the living creatures, the enfolding fire, and the eyes in the rims of the wheels. What an arresting picture of the providence of God, always at work, intricately designed, never wrong, and never late!

The firmament (Ezek. 1:22-25). This awesome expanse looked like sparkling ice (crystal) and stood over the heads of the cherubim. Now we get the total picture: a heavenly chariot with four wheels, moving quickly from place to place at the direction of the Lord. As it moved, the noise of the wings of the cherubim sounded like the noise of great waters coming together, "like the voice of the Almighty," and like the sound of a mighty army (3:13; 10:5; Ps. 46:3; Rev. 1:15; 14:2; 19:6). The wheels symbolize the omnipresence of God, while the eyes on their rims suggest the omniscience of God, seeing and knowing everything. Ezekiel was beholding a representation of the providence of God as He worked in His world. But one more item remained.

The throne (Ezek. 1:26-28). The wheels depicted God's omnipresence and omniscience, and the throne speaks of God's omnipotent authority. The throne was azure blue, with flashes of fire within it (holiness; see Rev. 15:2) and a rainbow around it (covenant grace). Noah saw the rainbow *after the storm* (Gen. 9:13-16), the Apostle John saw it *before the storm* (Rev. 4:3), but Ezekiel saw it *over the storm and in control of the storm.* In His wrath, God remembers mercy (Hab. 3:2). Ezekiel realized that he was beholding the glory of the Lord (Ezek. 1:28), and he fell on his face in awesome fear (3:23; Dan. 8:17; 10:9, 15, 17; Rev. 1:17). The "man" he saw upon the throne was probably a preincarnate appearance of our Lord Jesus Christ. (See Ezek. 8:2 and 40:3.)

The glory of the Lord is one of the key themes in Ezekiel (3:12, 23; 8:4; 9:3; 10:4, 18-19; 11:22-23; 39:21; 43:2, 4-5; 44:4). The prophet will watch God's glory leave the temple and go over the Mount of Olives, and he will also see it return to the kingdom temple. Because of Israel's sins, the glory left the temple; but God's promise is that one day the city of Jerusalem and the temple will be blessed by the glorious presence of the Lord. The city will be called "Jehovah Shammah—the Lord is there" (48:35).

Now we can begin to grasp the message that God was giving His prophet. Though His people were in exile and their nation was about to be destroyed, God was still on the throne and able to handle every situation. In His marvelous providence, He moves in the affairs of nations and works out His hidden plan. Israel wasn't the victim of Babylonian aggression. It was God who enabled the Babylonians to conquer His people and chasten them for their rebellion, but God would also bring the Medes and the Persians to conquer Babylon, and Cyrus, king of Persia, would permit the Jews to return to their land. "Oh, the depth of the riches both of the wisdom and knowledge of God! How unsearchable are His judgments and His ways past finding out!" (Rom. 11:33, NKJV)

No matter what message God gave him to preach, or what opposition arose from the people, Ezekiel would be encouraged and strengthened because he had seen the mighty throne of God in the midst of the fiery trial. He had seen the glory of God.

2. Accepting the burden of the Lord (Ezek. 2:1–3:3)

Ezekiel was now to receive his official commission as a prophet of the Lord God, and the Lord told him he was facing a very difficult task. Whether it's raising a family, teaching a Sunday School class, shepherding a church, or evangelizing in a distant nation, we have to accept people as they are before we can lead them to what God wants them to be. God gave Ezekiel four important commandments to obey.

Stand and listen (Ezek. 2:1-2). As a result of beholding the vision, Ezekiel fell to the ground, completely overwhelmed by the glory of the Lord and the wonder of His providential working in the world. Who but the sovereign Lord could have a throne like a chariot and move as quickly as He pleased? Who but the Lord could travel in the midst of a fiery whirlwind to accomplish His great purposes?

Ezekiel is called "son of man" ninety-three times in his book, a title that the Lord also gave to Daniel (Dan. 8:17). "Son of man" is also a messianic title (Ezek. 7:13) which the Lord Jesus applied to Himself at least eighty-two times when He was ministering on earth. But in the case of Daniel and Ezekiel, the title "son of man" emphasized their humanity and mortality. Ezekiel was facedown in the dust when God spoke to him, reminding him and us of mankind's humble beginning in the dust (Gen. 1:26; 3:19). "For He knows our frame; He remembers that we are dust" (Ps.

103:14, NKJV). God remembers, but sometimes we forget.

There is a time to fall down in humble adoration, and there is a time to stand up and take orders (Josh. 7:6ff). The command of the Word and the power of the Spirit enabled Ezekiel to stand to his feet, and the Spirit entered him and strengthened him. On many occasions, the Spirit would lift him up (Ezek. 2:2, 3:14; 8:3; 11:1, 24; 37:1; 43:5) and give him special power for his tasks (3:24; 11:5). The important thing was that Ezekiel stand obediently before the Lord and listen to His Word.

Go and speak (Ezek. 2:3-5). Prophets weren't people who majored only in foretelling the future, although that was part of their ministry. They were primarily *forth-tellers* who declared God's Word to the people. Sometimes they gave a message of judgment, but it was usually followed by a message of hope and forgiveness. The Jews needed to hear Ezekiel's messages because they were rebellious, stiff-necked, and hard-hearted.[4] At least sixteen times in this book you find the Jews described as "rebellious." They had revolted against the Lord and were obstinate in their refusal to submit to His will. Their refusal to obey the terms of the covenant had led to their defeat and capture by the Babylonian army. Even in their captivity, they were nursing false hopes that Egypt would come to their rescue or the Lord would do a great miracle.

So rebellious were the Jewish people that God called them "a rebellious nation" and used the Hebrew word *goy*, which was usually reserved for the Gentiles! Israel was God's chosen people, a special nation, and yet they were acting like the Gentiles who didn't have all the blessings and privileges God had given the Jews. This wasn't a very encouraging word for the young prophet, but he needed to know in advance that his work would be difficult. God gave the same kind of message to Isaiah when He called him (Isa. 6:8-13). But whether the people listened and obeyed or turned a deaf ear, Ezekiel had to be faithful to his task (1 Cor. 4:2).

Don't be afraid (Ezek. 2:6-7). Three times in verse 6 the Lord admonished the prophet not to be afraid of the people, and He repeated it again (3:9). He had given a similar caution to Jeremiah (Jer. 1:8), and Jesus gave the same warning to His disciples (Matt. 10:26, 28, 31). "Who are you that you should be afraid of a man who will die, and of the son of a man who will be made like grass?" (Isa. 51:12, NKJV) Ezekiel was to declare God's Word boldly no matter how his listeners responded. His own people might act like briars and thorns,[5] and even like painful scorpions, but that must not deter His servant.

Receive the Word within (Ezek. 2:8–3:3). Being a priest, Ezekiel knew that the Hebrew Scriptures pictured God's Word as food to be received within the heart and digested inwardly. Job valued God's Word more than his "necessary food" (Job 23:12), and Moses admonished the Jews to live on God's Word as well as on the bread (manna) that the Lord supplied daily (Deut. 8:3; see Matt. 4:4). The Prophet Jeremiah "ate" the Word of God (Jer. 15:16) and so did the Apostle John (Rev. 10:8-10). God's prophets must speak from within their hearts or their messages will not be authentic.

A hand stretched out and handed Ezekiel a scroll that didn't have any good news written on it, because it was filled on both sides with "words of lament and mourning and woe" (Ezek. 2:10, NIV). Perhaps it contained the messages that are recorded in chapters 4 through 32, God's judgments on Jerusalem and the Gentile nations. (See the suggested outline of the book.) God commanded him to eat the scroll and it tasted sweet like honey (Pss. 19:10; 119:103), although later he tasted bitterness (Ezek. 3:14), not unlike the Apostle John (Rev. 10:8-11). It's a great honor to be a spokesperson for the Lord, but we must be able to handle both the bitter and the sweet.

Had Ezekiel heard the description of the hardness of his people before he saw the vision of God's glory, he might have had a difficult time accepting his call. But having seen the glorious throne of the sovereign Lord, Ezekiel knew that he had all the help he needed to obey the will of God. In his difficult ministry to the Israelites, Moses was encouraged by meeting God on the mountaintop and seeing the display of His glory, and the Prophet Isaiah saw the glory of Christ in the temple before he launched into his ministry (Isa. 6; John 12:37-41). The Prophet Habakkuk was lifted from the valley of despair to the mountain peak of victory by contemplating the glory of God in the history of Israel (Hab. 3). Before Stephen laid down his life for the sake of Jesus Christ, he saw the glory of the Son of God in heaven (Acts 7:55-60). The only motivation that never fails is doing all for the glory of God.

3. Declaring the Word of the Lord (Ezek. 3:4-27)

What the people needed more than anything else was to hear the Word of the Lord. Even before the nation fell, Jeremiah had warned them not to listen to the false prophets, but neither the leaders nor the common people would obey (Jer. 5:30-31; 6:14; 7:8; 8:10). God had spoken loudly in Israel's shameful defeat and captivity, but now the Jews were still clinging to empty hopes and listening to the lying words of false prophets in Babylon (Jer. 29:15-32). The human heart would rather hear lies that bring comfort than truths that bring conviction and cleansing. Ezekiel declared God's Word as a messenger (Ezek. 3:4-10), a sufferer (vv. 10-15), a watchman (vv. 16-21), and a sign (vv. 22-27).

The messenger (Ezek. 3:4-9). Three elements are involved here: speaking, receiving (understanding) the message, and obeying. "Go and speak my word!" (v. 4) was God's commission. Ezekiel was the messenger, the people of Israel were the audience, and the Word of God was the message to be delivered. The prophet wasn't allowed to send a substitute messenger, nor was he permitted to alter the message or go to a different audience. One of the New Testament words for preaching is *kerusso*, which means "to proclaim as a herald." In ancient days, rulers would send out royal heralds to convey their messages to the people, and the herald was obligated to deliver the message just as he received it. If Ezekiel wanted to be a faithful herald, every part of God's commission had to be obeyed to the last detail.

The second element is *receiving* (vv. 5-7). To receive the Word of God means to understand it and take it into the heart and mind (Matt. 13:19). Since Ezekiel was a chosen prophet of the Lord, what he said was important and the people were obligated to receive it. He was speaking their own language, so they couldn't make excuses and say, "We don't understand what you're saying." He understood their speech and they understood his. If God had sent Ezekiel to a nation where he had to use an interpreter, they would have understood his message and received it; but his own people turned a deaf ear to him. Jesus used a similar approach in 11:21-24 when He condemned the Jewish cities for rejecting Him. Had He done those same miracles in heathen cities, they would have repented and turned to the Lord.

The third element is *obeying* (Ezek. 3:7-9). God doesn't send us His messengers to His people to entertain them or give them good advice. He expects us to obey what He commands. Unfortunately, the nation of Israel had a tragic history of disobedience to the law of God and rebellion against the will of God. That was their record during 40 years in the wilderness (Deut. 9:7) as well as during over 800 years in their own land (2 Chron. 36:11-21). No other nation has been blessed by God as Israel has been blessed, for the Jews had God's holy law, the covenants, a wealthy land, the temple, and the prophets to give them warnings and promises as they needed them (Rom. 9:1-5). Like the people of Israel, many people today hear God's Word but won't try to understand, or if they do understand, they refuse to obey.

God assured His prophet that He would give him all he needed to withstand their opposition and disobedience. In Ezekiel 3:8, there is a play on words involving Ezekiel's name which means "God is strong" or "God strengthens." It also means "God hardens." If the people harden their hearts and faces, God will harden His servant and keep him faithful to his mission. He gave a similar promise to Jeremiah (Jer. 1:17).

The sufferer (Ezek. 3:10-15). Ezekiel was by the river Chebar when he saw the vision and heard God's Word (1:3), but now he was commanded to join the other exiles at a place called Tel-Abib. This site hasn't been identified, but it was not at the same location as the modern Tel-Aviv. There were a number of villages along the river (Ezra 2:59; 8:17), and some of the Jewish captives had been settled there by the Babylonians. The Spirit of God lifted the prophet up (Ezek. 3:12, 14)[6] and took him to the place where the captives were gathered together and probably praying. This remarkable experience would be repeated (8:3; 43:5), and Ezekiel would no doubt recall that the Prophet Elijah had been caught away by God (2 Kings 2:11, 16; see 1 Kings 18:12 and Acts 8:39). The prophet had received God's Word, and now he must take it to God's people.

As the Spirit began to work, Ezekiel heard behind him several sounds: the rustling of the cherubim's wings, the whirring of the wheels, and "a loud rumbling sound" (NIV), like an earthquake. He knew that God's glorious throne was moving and that the Lord was working out His purposes. What was the origin of the praise statement, "Blessed be the glory of the Lord from His place"? (Ezek. 3:12) Both the KJV and the NASB translate it as coming from the cherubim, but the NIV suggests that it was Ezekiel himself who spoke it. However, it could also be translated "as the glory of the Lord arose from its place," a description rather than a declaration. As we shall see in chapters 8–11, the movement of God's glory is a key theme in this book.

The Lord brought His servant to Tel-Abib so he could sit with the captives and feel their burden of disappointment and grief. Psalm 137 reveals both their misery and their hatred for the Babylonians. When they should have been repenting and seeking God's face, the Jews were regretting what had happened and praying that one day they might be able to retaliate and defeat their Babylonian captors who taunted them. As Ezekiel sat there with the people, overwhelmed by what the Lord had said to him and done for him, he realized the seriousness of his calling and how great was the responsibility God had placed on his shoulders. It's a good thing for the servant of God to be among his people, to weep with those who weep and rejoice with those who rejoice, for he can better minister to them when he knows their hearts and feels their pain.[7] It isn't enough simply to proclaim the message of God; we must also seek to have the caring heart of God.

The watchman (Ezek. 3:16-21). The watchmen on the walls were important to the safety of the city and the image shows up frequently in the Scriptures (Isa. 21:11-12; 56:10; 62:6; Jer. 6:17; Pss. 127:1; 130:6; Heb. 13:17). The emphasis here is on judgment, while in Ezekiel 33 it is on hope, but the message is the same: the prophet must be faithful to warn the people of judgment, and the people must heed the warning and turn from their sin. Spiritually speaking, the "wall" that protected Israel was their covenant relationship with the Lord. If they obeyed the terms of the covenant declared by Moses, God would care for His people, protect them, and bless them; but if they disobeyed, God would chasten them. But whether He was chastening or blessing, God would always be faithful to His covenant. (See Lev. 26 and Deut. 28.)

Ezekiel is the prophet of human responsibility. Some of the captives were blaming God for their sad plight, while others blamed their ancestors. Ezekiel made it clear that each individual is held responsible and accountable before God (see Ezek. 18). He presented four scenarios. The first is that of *the people dying because the watchman was unfaithful and didn't warn them* (3:18). Their blood would be on the watchman's hands and he would be held accountable (see v. 20; 18:13; 33:4-8). The image of blood on the hands (or the head) goes back to Genesis 9:5 and appears in the Law of Moses (Lev. 20). See also Joshua 2:19; 2 Samuel 1:16 and 3:29; and Isaiah 1:15 and 59:3. Jesus used this image in Matthew 23:35 and Luke 11:50-51; and see Acts 5:28; 18:6; and 20:26. The second scenario is obvious.

A second scenario pictures *the watchman being faithful to warn the wicked but they refuse to listen* (Ezek. 3:19). That was the problem Ezekiel faced as he preached to the hardhearted Jewish captives in Babylon. Jesus wept over Jerusalem because the people would not come to Him (Matt. 23:37-39). The third scenario describes *the righteous dying because they turned from their covenant obedience and the watchman did not warn them* (Ezek. 3:20). The watchman-prophet should not only warn sinners to turn from their sin, but he must also warn those who are obeying the covenant ("the righteous") not to turn from it and disobey God. No matter how much obedience they had practiced, it would mean nothing if they deliberately rebelled against God. However, their blood would be on the watchman's hands if he didn't warn them. By putting a barrier in the way, God seeks to prevent the righteous person from sinning; but that doesn't excuse the watchman from being alert and giving warning.

The final scenario is that of *the righteous heeding the watchman's warning and not being judged* (v. 21). It was a serious thing for the Jewish people to treat lightly the covenant that had been accepted and sealed at Sinai (Ex. 19–20). If the watchman-prophet saw faithful people about to break the covenant, he had to warn them that they would be judged. Sometimes godly people get the idea that their obedience has "earned" them the right to do as they please, but that idea is a great lie. God gives His people many privileges, but He never gives the privilege to sin.

These four examples were given to Jewish people under the Old Covenant and have to do with obedience to the law and the danger of physical death. The righteousness of the law was external, but the righteousness we have through faith in Jesus Christ is internal, and the two must not be confused (Rom. 9:30–10:13). Faith righteousness is God's gift to those who believe in Jesus Christ, and their righteous standing before God doesn't depend on their good works (Rom. 3–4). However, our fellowship with the Father depends on a heart of obedience (2 Cor. 6:14-7:1), and He will discipline those of His children who deliberately oppose His will (Heb. 12:1-11). If they persist in resisting His will, He may take their lives (Heb. 12:9). "There is a sin unto death " (1 John 5:16-17). Personal responsibility is the key here, both of the watchman and of the people. If the Jews under the Old Covenant were held responsible for their actions, how much more responsible are believers today who have the complete Bible, the indwelling Holy Spirit, and the revelation of God through Jesus Christ? See Hebrews 12:12-28.

The sign (Ezek. 3:22-27). Ezekiel not only spoke God's Word to the people, but he also lived before them in such a way that they saw God's message portrayed before their very eyes. God said to him, "I have made you a sign to the house of Israel" (12:6, NIV; see 4:4; 14:8; 24:24, 27). You will find the prophet performing twelve "action sermons" to convey God's truth to people who were becoming more and more deaf to the voice of God.[8] Pharaoh wouldn't listen to God's Word, so the Lord spoke to him through a series of miracles and plagues. The Prophet Jeremiah also tried to reach the people through "action sermons," such as burying a new belt (Jer. 13), refusing to take a wife (Jer. 16), and breaking clay jars (Jer. 19).

It's likely that there is a break between Ezekiel 3:21 and 22. Ezekiel did go to the people and give them God's warning, but they would not listen. God told him to leave the gathering by the river and go out into the plain for a new set of instructions. What do you do when the people close their ears to the Word of God? God certainly could have judged them for their wickedness, but in His grace He gave them further opportunities to hear His saving Word. Jesus took the same approach when He began to teach in parables. He clothed the truth in interesting images and in that way sought to reach the people (Matt. 13:10-17). The careless would hear and brush it aside, but the concerned would ponder the parable and learn God's truth.

The Word of God may not have penetrated the hearts of the people, but the glory of God and the Spirit of God were still with God's servant. If the people wouldn't respond to Ezekiel's public ministry, perhaps he could reach them in his own house. The elders of the people could come to hear his messages (Ezek. 8:1; 14:1; 20:1) and then share them with the people. The prophet shut himself up in his house, although at times he did leave for special reasons (5:2; 12:3), and he never spoke unless he had a message from the Lord. When the news came of the destruction of Jerusalem, this command of silence was removed and he was able to speak as other people (24:25-27; 33:21-22). From the time this command was given to the time it was removed, seven years elapsed (from 593 B.C. to 586 B.C.).

Ezekiel's silence was a sign to the Jews that God's Word is not to be taken for granted or treated lightly like trivial daily conversation. When God speaks, we had better listen and obey! "He that hears, let him hear" (3:27, NIV) is a familiar and important phrase in Scripture because it indicates that we have the responsibility to pay attention to God's Word, cherish what He says, meditate on it, and obey it. At least five times in Deuteronomy Moses said, "Hear, O Israel!" as he repeated the law and reminded them of the great privilege Israel had to hear the very voice of God at Sinai (Deut. 4:1-13). At least eight times in the Gospels Jesus said, "He who has ears to hear, let him hear," (NASB) or similar words (Matt. 11:15, 13:9, 43; Mark 4:9, 23; 7:16; Luke 8:8; 14:35).

What about the "binding" of the prophet? (Ezek. 3:25) This is probably a figurative statement, because there's no evidence that Ezekiel was literally bound and forced to remain in his house. As we have seen, he did leave the house (5:2; 12:3) and nobody prevented him. The Jewish people "bound" Ezekiel in the sense that their sins made it necessary for him to remain home in silence until God gave him a message. The attitude of the people wasn't that of militant opposition but rather passive indifference; hence, the necessity for Ezekiel to use "action sermons" to get their attention.

"I am the Lord!" is repeated fifty-nine times in this book, because it was Ezekiel's task to remind his people who was in charge. The name of God used almost exclusively in the book is "Jehovah Adonai—the Sovereign Lord." A.W. Tozer was right when he wrote, "God being who and what he is, and we being who and what we are, the only thinkable relation between us is one of full lordship on His part and complete submission on ours."[9]

Are we a rebellious people, or, like Ezekiel, are we obedient servants?

CHAPTER TWO THE DEATH OF A GREAT CITY

Ezekiel 4–7

When the sons of Asaph wanted to describe the city of Jerusalem, they wrote, "Beautiful in elevation, the joy of the whole earth, is Mount Zion on the sides of the north, the city of the great King" (Ps. 48:2, NKJV). The Babylonian Talmud says, "Of the ten measures of beauty that came down to the world, Jerusalem took nine" (*Kidushin 49b*), and, "Whoever has not seen Jerusalem in its splendor has never seen a lovely city" (*Succah 51b*). Of modern Jerusalem, Samuel Heilman wrote, "It is a place in which people actually live; it is a place that lives in them."[1] One of the Jewish exiles in Babylonian wrote: "If I forget you, O Jerusalem, let my right hand forget her skill! If I do not remember you, let my tongue cling to the roof of my mouth—if I do not exalt Jerusalem above my chief joy" (Ps. 137:5-6, NKJV). When Jewish families around the world celebrate Passover, they conclude the meal with, "Next year in Jerusalem!"

The Jewish exiles wouldn't be happy with the three messages Ezekiel would bring them from the Lord, for he was going to announce the destruction of Jerusalem and the ravaging of the Promised Land. It was bad enough that the Jews were exiles in a pagan land, but to be told that they would have no city to return to was more than they could bear. No wonder they preferred the encouraging messages of the false prophets.

1. The sign messages: the siege of Jerusalem (Ezek. 4–5)

Most of the Jewish people had become so calloused they could no longer hear God's Word, so the Lord commanded Ezekiel to take a different approach. The prophet stayed home for the most part and didn't take part in the everyday conversation of the people. He remained silent at all times except when he had a message to deliver from the Lord. That made people want to listen. Furthermore, the prophet often "preached" his messages silently through "action sermons" that aroused the interest of the people. In this way, he was a visible sign to the "spiritually deaf" people (4:3; 12:6, 11; 24:24). Word got around that Ezekiel occasionally did strange things, and he soon became a curiosity and a celebrity among the exiles. People stood before his house and waited to see what he would do next (4:12). These two chapters record four "action sermons" that conveyed startling news to the Jewish people in Babylon.

The siege of Jerusalem (Ezek. 4:1-3). This "tile" was probably an unbaked brick or a soft clay tablet, both of which were commonplace in Babylon. On it, Ezekiel drew a sketch of the city of Jerusalem, which the people would easily recognize, and then he set it on the ground and began to "play soldier" as he acted out the siege of Jerusalem. Using earth and various objects, he set up fortifications around the city so nobody could get in or get out. He built a ramp to facilitate scaling the walls, and he provided battering rams for breaking down the gates and the walls. This, of course, was what would happen at Jerusalem in 588 B.C. when the Babylonian army began the siege of the city.

Imagine how shocked the spectators were when Ezekiel's face became hard and resolute and he placed a flat iron griddle between his face and the besieged city. It was the kind of utensil that the priests used in the temple for preparing some of the offerings (Lev. 2:5; 6:21; 7:9). The iron griddle symbolized the wall that stood between God and the sinful Jewish nation so that He could no longer look on them with approval and blessing. Ezekiel the priest could not pronounce on them the priestly blessing of Numbers 6:24-26, for God's face was not shining on them with blessing. God was *against* them (Ezek. 5:8; Isa. 59:1-3) and would permit the pagan Babylonians to destroy the city and the temple. Years later, Jeremiah would write, "You have covered yourself with a cloud, so that no prayer can get through" (Lam. 3:44, NIV, and see Ezek. 3:8-9).

During all this activity, Ezekiel didn't say a word, but the spectators surely got the message. It's possible for people to rebel against God such a long time that all God can do is allow them to reap the consequences of their own sins. The Jews were sinning against a flood of light. They knew the terms of the covenant, and they knew that God had sent prophet after prophet to rebuke their idolatry (2 Chron. 36:11-21), yet they had persisted in disobeying His will. Now it was too late. "Ephraim is joined to idols, let him alone" (Hosea 4:17, NKJV).

The judgment of Judah (Ezek. 4:4-8). At specified times each day (v. 10, NIV), Ezekiel was commanded to lie on the ground, facing the model he constructed of the siege of Jerusalem. He was to be bound (v. 8), his arm was to be bared, and he had to eat the meager food described in verses 9-17. He was to lie on his left side for 390 days and then on his right side for 40 days. This symbolic act told the Jewish exiles why the Lord was allowing their holy city to be ravaged and ruined: the nation had sinned and their sins had caught up with them. Of course, Ezekiel didn't "bear their sins" in the sense of atoning for them, for only the Son of God can do that (1 Peter 2:24). But "bearing the iniquity"[2] of the nation before God was one of the ministries of the priesthood, and Ezekiel was a priest (Ex. 28:36-38; Num. 18:1). The binding of the prophet and the baring of his arm spoke of the future binding of the prisoners and the baring of God's arm in judgment.

The Lord explained to Ezekiel that each day represented a year in the sinful history of the Jewish nation, and somehow he conveyed this fact to the people who watched him each day. But why did the Lord choose the numbers 390 and 40? Since one day was the equivalent of one year of Israel's rebellion, the Lord was undoubtedly looking back at the nation's past sins and not ahead at future disobedience. The forty years probably represented Israel's rebellion during their forty-year journey from Egypt to the Promised Land, but what is the starting point for the 390 years? The ministry of Ezekiel focused primarily on Jerusalem, the desecration of the temple by idolatry, and the departing of God's glory. It's likely that the 390-year period begins with Solomon's son Rehoboam who became king in 930 (1 Kings 14:21ff). When you add the years of the reigns of the kings of Judah from Rehoboam to Zedekiah, as recorded in 1 and 2 Kings, you have a total of 394 years. Since during three of the years of his reign Rehoboam walked with God (2 Chron. 11:16-17), we end up with a number very close to Ezekiel's 390 years.[3]

However we calculate the mathematics of this sign, the message is clear: God had been long-suffering toward the sinful people of Judah, warning them and chastening them, but they would not remain true to Him. Some of their kings were very godly men and sought to bring the people back to God, but no sooner did these kings die than the people returned to idolatry. Eventually, there came a time when their sins caught up with them and God's patience had come to an end. God would rather see His land devastated, the city of Jerusalem ruined, His temple destroyed, and His people killed and exiled, than to have them give such a false witness to the Gentile nations. Judgment begins with the people of God, not with the godless pagans (1 Peter 4:17-19), and it behooves believers and congregations today to walk in the fear of the Lord.

The famine in the city (Ezek. 4:9-17). In the first two "action sermons," Ezekiel showed the Jewish people the reality of the siege of Jerusalem and reason for it, and in the next two, he will display the horror of it, beginning with famine. The Lord commanded him to combine three grains (wheat, barley, and spelt) and two vegetables (beans and lentils) and grind them into flour and bake bread. This combination would produce the very poorest kind of bread and therefore represented the scarcity of food during the siege of Jerusalem. The people would eat almost anything, including one another (Deut. 28:49-57). God had warned them of this judgment in His covenant, so they shouldn't have been shocked.

The Jews sometimes cooked over fires made from cow dung mixed with straw, and this was not against the Law of Moses; but the use of human excrement was a sign of abject poverty and want. Of course, no priest would defile himself and his food by using human excrement for cooking his food (Deut. 14:3; 23:12-14), so the Lord allowed Ezekiel to use cow dung. His protest reminds us of that of Peter in Acts 10:14. Each day, the prophet would eat about eight ounces of bread and drink about two-thirds of a quart of water, reminding the spectators that the people within Jerusalem's walls would be starving and thirsting for water, but there would be no relief (see Lam. 1:11, 19; 2:11-12, 19). In His covenant, God had warned them about this judgment, but the people didn't listen (Lev. 26:26). Ezekiel was careful to obey the dietary laws, but the Jews scattered among the Gentile nations would be forced to eat defiled bread or else die of starvation.

God gave His chosen people a land of milk and honey and promised to bless their crops, their flocks and herds, and their families, if they obeyed His covenant. But they took their blessings for granted and turned away from the Lord and worshiped idols, so God cursed their blessings (Mal. 2:2). The land of milk and honey and the rich city of Jerusalem became places of scarcity and hunger, to the extent of parents eating their own children to stay alive during the siege (Ezek. 5:10; Deut. 29:22-28).

The destiny of the people (Ezek. 5:1-17). The Prophet Isaiah compared the invasion of an enemy to the shaving of a man's head and beard (Isa. 7:20), so Ezekiel used that image for his fourth "action sermon." Shaving could be a part of a purification ritual (Num. 6:5; 8:7), but the Jews had to be careful how they dressed their hair and their beards (Lev. 19:27; Deut. 14:1), and the priests had to be especially careful (Lev. 21:5-6). When Ezekiel, a priest, publicly shaved his head and his beard, the people must have been stunned; but it took extreme measures to get their attention so they would get the message. The shaving of the head and the beard would be a sign of humiliation and great sorrow and mourning, and that's the way the Lord felt about the impending destruction of Jerusalem and the holy temple. By using a sword and not a razor, Ezekiel made the message even more dramatic: an army was coming whose swords would "cut down" the people of the land.

The prophet was commanded to weigh the hair carefully and divide it into three parts. One part he burned on the "siege brick" to symbolize the people who died of famine or pestilence in Jerusalem. A second part was hacked to bits with the sword, symbolizing those slain by the Babylonian soldiers. The third part was thrown to the winds, picturing the Jews scattered among the Gentiles and the exiles taken to Babylon. However, before Ezekiel threw the hair to the winds, he took a small portion of it and hid it in the hem of his garment, a symbol of God's special care for a remnant of the people who would be spared to return to the land. The Lord in His covenant promised the sparing of a remnant (Lev. 26:36-39), for Israel still had a work to do in the world. But Ezekiel 5:4 indicates that anyone who was spared must not take his or her safety for granted, for more fire could come out from God's judgment of Jerusalem. This prophecy was fulfilled in the days after the siege of the city when innocent Jewish people were killed by scheming criminals (Jer. 40–44).

In Ezekiel 5:5-6, the Lord explained why He would permit His chosen people to suffer and die so shamefully at the hands of the Babylonians. As far as His eternal purposes were concerned, Jerusalem was His city and the center of the nations (38:12).[4] "Salvation is of the Jews" (John 4:22). Israel was a privileged people, but privilege involves responsibility and accountability. The day of reckoning had come and there was no escape. Israel was called to be a light to the Gentiles, to lead them to the true and living God (Isa. 42:6; 49:6); but instead, they adopted the wicked ways of the Gentiles and became greater sinners than their neighbors.

The Lord drew some telling conclusions or applications from this fact (Ezek. 5:7-11). God would punish Israel openly, in the sight of the nations whose evil practices they followed.[5] This would not only chasten Israel, but it would be a warning to the Gentiles that the God of Israel is a God of justice. Whereas before, God had been with and for His people, now He would be against them,[6] which reminds us of the iron skillet Ezekiel held between his face and the city of Jerusalem (4:3). The leaders had defiled the temple with their idols, a theme we'll hear more about later in Ezekiel's prophecy; the Lord responded by withdrawing His favor and refusing to pity His people in their great distress. "I will also diminish thee" in 5:11 can be translated

"I myself will shave you," taking us back to Ezekiel's fourth "action sermon."

In verses 12-17, the Lord explains again the awfulness of the judgment coming to the people left in the city and the land. Pestilence and famine will take one-third of them; another one-third will be killed by the Babylonian army; the remainder will be scattered. Why? Because God was "spending His wrath"[7] and "accomplishing His fury" upon His sinful people. God's anger against sin is a holy anger, not a temper tantrum, for He is a holy God. "Our God is a consuming fire" (Deut. 4:24; Heb. 12:29). There could be no doubt that these great judgments would come, because it was the Lord Himself who had spoken (Ezek. 5:13).[8] The whole land would be devastated and people would perish from famine and the pestilence that often accompanies famine, as well as bloodshed from enemy soldiers and hungry wild beasts. But as terrible as these judgments were, perhaps the greatest tragedy was that Israel would cease to bring glory to Jehovah God (v. 14) and would become a shameful reproach among the nations (Deut. 28:37; Jer. 18:15-17; 48:27; 2 Chron. 7:19-22).

Jesus Christ warned the church of Ephesus that they would lose their light if they refused to repent and obey His instructions (Rev. 2:6). What a tragedy it is when a local assembly openly disobeys God's Word and begins to act like the unsaved people of the world! Once a church has lost its witness for the Lord, is there anything left?

Throughout Old Testament history, the presence of a "faithful remnant" in Israel was important to the fulfillment of God's plan. The entire nation of Israel accepted God's covenant at Mount Sinai (Ex. 20:18-21) but most of them failed to obey the Lord and died in the wilderness. In the years that followed the nation's entrance into the Promised Land, the people gradually declined spiritually, and it was the remnant that prayed, obeyed God's Word, and remained faithful to the Lord. It is this remnant that will play an important role in the future of Israel (Isa. 1:9; 10:20-23; 11:11, 16; 37:31; Joel 2:32; Micah 2:12; 5:7; Zeph. 2:4-7; Zech. 8:1-8; Mal. 3:16; Rom. 9:27; 11:5). According to the letters to the seven churches of Asia Minor, there is a faithful remnant in the professing church today (Rev. 2:24; 3:4-6; and note our Lord's words to the "overcomers").

2. The first spoken message: the judgment of the land (Ezek. 6:1-14)

God had commanded His prophet to remain silent except for those times when He opened his mouth and commanded him to preach a special message. In these two chapters, there are two messages of judgment from the Lord. The first explains that the idolatry of the people had defiled the land and the temple, and the second describes the terrible disaster that would come with the arrival of the Babylonian army. Ezekiel the watchman was warning the people that an invasion was coming because God had seen their sins and was about to punish them.

God's judgment of the high places (Ezek. 6:1-7).[9] The land belonged to the Lord, and He allowed the Jewish people to use it as long as they didn't defile it with their sins (Lev. 25:23; 18:25, 27-28). If the Jews obeyed His law, God would bless them in their land (26:1-13). But if they failed to keep the terms of His covenant, the Lord would punish them by withholding blessing from the land He had given them or by "vomiting" them out of the land (Lev. 18:24-30; 26:14ff; Deut. 28:38-42, 49-52). This explains why Ezekiel "set his face"[10] against the mountains, hills, rivers (ravines), and valleys of the land, for they had been defiled by the idolatry of Israel. Of course, it wasn't the physical terrain that had sinned but the Jewish people who had polluted the Holy Land by erecting their "high places [idolatrous shrines] under every green tree" (Ezek. 6:13; see Deut. 12:2; 1 Kings 14:23; Jer. 2:20; 3:6, 13).

The Jewish prophets despised idolatry and spoke scornfully about the idols that the people valued so much. The prophets called the idols "nothings" or "vanity" (Isa. 66:3; 1 Chron. 16:26; Jer. 14:14), "abominations" (2 Chron. 15:8), and "terrors" (1 Kings 15:13); but the word Ezekiel used is even more derisive because it can mean "pellets of dung."[11] The people treated their false gods as the highest things in the land, but God saw them as the lowest and most defiling thing—dung.

The Babylonian army would come into the land and break down the shrines and altars and destroy the idols. But even more, the soldiers would kill the worshipers and leave their rotting corpses as "sacrifices" to the fallen idols. "I will bring a sword upon you" (v. 3)[12] and "you shall know that I am the Lord" (Ezek. 6:7). The enemy would stack the corpses around the shrines like so many logs and pieces of defiled flesh. In His covenant with Israel, God warned Israel that this would happen if they turned from Him and worshiped false gods. During Israel's history, godly kings would destroy these abominable places and evil kings would rebuild them (2 Kings 18:3-4; 21:1-6; 23:8-9).

God's grace to the Jewish remnant (Ezek. 6:8-10). Against the background of this nationwide slaughter, Ezekiel reminds the people of the grace of God in sparing a remnant, a topic that he had illustrated when he put some of the shaved hair in the hem of his garment (5:1-3). He will mention the remnant again in 7:16; 11:16-21; 12:15-16; 14:22-23; and 16:60-63. That a remnant of faithful people would be spared was part of the covenant promise (Lev. 26:40-46). It was this feeble remnant that returned to the land, rebuilt the temple, restored the worship of the Lord, and eventually made possible the coming of the Messiah (Luke 1–2).

Not only was the worship of idols an abomination and a participation in filth, but it was adultery (Ezek. 6:9).[13] The nation had been married to Jehovah at Sinai, and the worship of any other god was an act of adultery (Isa. 54:5; Jer. 2:1-8; 3:14; 31:32; Hosea 2:16). Here we see God's heart broken over the unfaithfulness of His people: "How I have been grieved by their adulterous hearts" (Ezek. 6:9, NIV). The jealousy of God over Israel, His adulterous wife, is often mentioned in Ezekiel's prophecy (8:3, 5; 16:38, 42; 23:25; 36:5; 38:19).

God's chaste love for Israel, His wife, is the major theme of the Prophet Hosea, whose wife became a prostitute and had to be bought back by her loving husband. This was an "action sermon" (and a costly one) that rebuked Israel for their unfaithfulness to God, but the prophet assured them that the Lord would forgive if they would repent and return. Ezekiel announced that the Jews scattered throughout the Gentile nations would realize their sins, remember their God, loathe themselves, and return to the Lord; and this remnant would become the future of the nation. In the midst of judgment, God would remember mercy (Hab. 3:2).

God's weapons of destruction (Ezek. 6:11-14). As he lamented the abominations that his people had committed, the prophet combined both speech and action (clapping, stamping his foot). In 21:14 and 17, these actions represented God's response to the invasion and assault of the Babylonians. From the context, when Ezekiel struck his hands together, it symbolized the marching of soldiers and the clashing of the swords as God's wrath was "spent" or "accomplished" against His disobedient people.[14] This wasn't something the Lord enjoyed doing, because He has no pleasure in the death of the wicked (18:23; 33:11). The Lord unleashed His three weapons against His people: the swords of the Babylonians, famine in the city, and the pestilence that usually accompanies famine (see 5:1-2).

Once again, Ezekiel described the unfaithful Jews being slaughtered at their idolatrous shrines and their corpses stacked up around the altars like so much dead wood (6:13; see vv. 3-5). When God "stretches out his hand" (v. 14), it means that judgment is coming (14:9, 13; 16:27; 25:7, 13, 16). The word "Diblah" might be a shortened form of Beth Diblathaim in Moab (Jer. 48:22), but if it is, the significance of the reference has been lost to us. Some Hebrew manuscripts read "Riblah," a city in Syria, and this seems to fit. God promised to devastate the land "from the desert to Riblah [Diblah]" (NIV), that is, from the south to the north. It's like saying "from Dan to Beersheba," from the north to the south.

At least sixty times, Ezekiel writes, "And they shall know that I am the Lord" (Ezek. 6:14). Whether in blessing or chastening, the Lord's purpose is to reveal Himself to us in His love and grace. If the people of Israel had truly known the character and ways of their God, they could never have rebelled against Him as they did. "Oh, that they had such a heart in them that they would fear Me and always keep all My commandments, that it might be well with them and with their children forever!" (Deut. 5:29, NKJV)

3. The second spoken message: the devastation of the land (Ezek. 7:1-27)

The nation of Israel was blessed with a gracious Lord to worship and love, a fruitful land to enjoy, and a holy law to obey. Their love for the Lord and their obedience to His law would determine how much blessing He could entrust to them in the land. These were the terms of the covenant and the Jewish people knew them well. The generation that first entered the land obeyed God's covenant, as did the succeeding generation, but the third generation provoked the Lord, broke their "marriage vows," and prostituted themselves to idols (Jud. 2:10-13). They disobeyed the law, defied their Lord, and defiled the land, and the Lord would not accept that kind of conduct. First, He punished them *in their land* by permitting seven enemy nations to occupy the land and oppress the people, as recorded in the Book of Judges. But each time God delivered Israel from their oppressors, the Jews eventually returned to the worship of idols; so He finally took them *away from the land*, some through death and others through exile in Babylon. It's a tragic story, but it reminds us that the Lord is serious about His covenant and our obedience.

Disaster announced (Ezek. 7:1-9). In this second spoken message, the key phrases are "the land," "an end," and "it is come." The land is personified in this message and Ezekiel speaks to it and announces that disaster is about to fall. The judgment was certain because the prophet announced "It is come!" at least nine times in verses 1-12. He was a faithful watchman, warning the people that the Babylonian army was coming from the north to invade the land, rob it, and ruin it. Babylon was God's weapon through which He would unleash His anger, judge Israel's abominable behavior, and repay them for their disobedience. In previous chastisements, the Lord had shown pity and spared His people, but this judgment would be different. They had defiled His land with their sins, and the only way the land could be cleansed was by punishing the people for their sins.

In verses 7 and 10, the KJV has the phrase "the morning is come," but both the NKJV and the NIV translate it "doom has come." The Hebrew word means "to plait, to braid," such as braiding a garland of flowers for the head, and it's translated "diadem" in Isaiah 28:5. How do the translators get either "morning" or "doom" out of this word? Probably from the image of "that which comes around," for a braided garland is the result of the weaving of flowers into a circle. "Morning" is that which comes around, day after day, and the doom of the Israelites had "come around." They had "woven" their own shameful crown of sin when they could have worn a diadem of glory to the Lord.

The disaster pictured (Ezek. 7:10-21). Always the master of vivid language to help the people "see" the truth, Ezekiel painted four word pictures to arouse their interest and perhaps reach their hearts. The first is *the budding rod* (vv. 10-11), an image from nature. God had been long-suffering as His people disobeyed His law and defied His prophets, but now their sins had "ripened" and the nation would have to reap what they sowed. In their pride, they had cultivated a false confidence that the Lord would never allow His people to be exiled or His temple destroyed, but their sin had now "matured" and both were now about to happen. Isaiah had used a similar image when describing the Assyrian invasion of the land (Isa. 10:5), only he saw the invaders as the "rod" in His hand. If that's the image Ezekiel had in mind, then the rod is Nebuchadnezzar and the "blossoming" means that the time was ripe for God to punish the people. Violence in the land had grown into a rod of wickedness, and the people's sins would find them out.

The second picture is taken from *the business world* (Ezek. 7:12-13), with the Jewish "Year of Jubilee" as the background (Lev. 25). Every seventh year was set apart as a Sabbatic Year, during which the land lay fallow and debts were cancelled (vv. 1-7; Deut. 15:1-6). After seven of these Sabbatic Years, the fiftieth year was set apart as a Year of Jubilee, when the land lay fallow, debts were cancelled, servants were set free, and the land was returned to the original owners. The price of a parcel of land was determined by the number of years until the Year of Jubilee and the amount of crops that could be harvested during that time. If a poor man sold his land or himself to be a servant, he knew the land would be returned to his family in the Year of Jubilee and he would be set free.

With the Babylonian invasion imminent, the price of land would certainly drop and wealthy people could quickly increase their holdings, but there was no guarantee that they would hold what they purchased. Furthermore, the seller couldn't be sure that he would get his land back when the Year of Jubilee arrived. Jeremiah had told the captives that they would be in Babylon for seventy years (Jer. 29:10), so they would spend their Sabbatic years and the next Year of Jubilee in captivity—if they were alive. The vision of coming judgment would "not be reversed" (Ezek. 7:13, NIV); instead, the whole economic pattern would be reversed. Had the Jews obeyed God's law, the slaves would have been freed and the ownership of the land would have been protected, but now the surviving Jews would be enslaved and their land taken from them. The people had not obeyed the laws concerning the Sabbaths for the land, so the Lord took the land from them until those Sabbaths were fulfilled (2 Chron. 36:14-21). What we selfishly keep for ourselves, we eventually lose; but what we give to the Lord, we keep forever.

The third picture is that of *the watchman* (Ezek. 7:14-15). God had made Ezekiel a watchman (3:17-21), and it was his responsibility to warn the people when danger was at hand. If an enemy army approached, the watchmen on the walls would blow their trumpets and summon the soldiers to man their posts and protect the city. But it was futile for the watchmen in Jerusalem to blow their trumpets because there was no Jewish army available and any resistance was futile. If the soldiers went outside the city into the country, they would be slain by the swords of the Babylonian army; and if the warriors stayed inside the city, they would die from famine and pestilence. Why risk your life in such a hopeless cause?

In his fourth picture, Ezekiel compares the fugitives who escape to *mourning doves* (7:16-18), frightened and alone in the mountains. It is from this group that the Lord would form His remnant, so they were important to Him. Instead of rejoicing at their escape, these people were mourning over their sins (Isa. 59:11), wearing sackcloth and shaving their heads in sorrow and repentance, a fulfillment of Ezekiel's prophecy in Ezekiel 6:9-10. They will be too weak and frightened to fight the enemy; all they can do is throw themselves on the mercy of the Lord.

People throwing away their valuables (Ezek. 7:19-21) is the fifth and final picture. During the final years of the kingdom of Judah, the rich were getting richer and the poor were getting poorer, with the rich robbing the poor without any interference from the courts. The prophets thundered against this evil, but the leaders would not listen. The refugees couldn't carry their wealth as they fled from Jerusalem, so they treated it like garbage and threw it into the streets. You can't eat money, and what good is money when there's no food to buy in the city? Furthermore, there wouldn't be any places to purchase supplies as the people fled to the mountains. Their gold and silver were only excess baggage that would slow them down, and their idols were even more worthless. In a time of crisis, we quickly learn what's valuable and important to life. The lust for wealth lured them into sin, and their sins brought about judgment. The Babylonian soldiers took the wealth of the Jews as loot, along with their expensive idols; this was God's payment to Babylon for their services in chastening Israel.

The disruption from the disaster (Ezek. 7:22-27). First, there would be no help from the religious leaders, neither the prophets nor the priests (v. 26); and the holy temple would be defiled and destroyed. The Jews had depended on the temple to save them, for surely God wouldn't permit His beautiful house to be ruined by pagan soldiers (Jer. 7:1-5). But the temple had become a den of thieves (v. 11), and the Lord was no longer pleased with the sacrifices the people offered there (Isa. 1:11-20). God would allow pagans to pollute His treasured place. The priests could give no encouragement from the Word of God because the people had broken the covenant and were outside the place of blessing. The false prophets could see no vision because they had rejected the truth.

Not only would there be religious chaos, but the political system would fall apart (Ezek. 7:27). In the eyes of Ezekiel, the king was Jehoiachin (1:2) and the prince was Zedekiah. Though Zedekiah was the last king of Judah, the prophet didn't recognize his reign but considered him only a prince (12:10, 12). The leadership in Judah began to collapse when the kings refused to listen to Jeremiah's messages from the Lord, admonishing them to surrender to Babylon and thus save the city and the temple. Whenever leaders of the Jewish nation depended on politics rather than the prophetic Word, they gradually moved into compromise and confusion (Isa. 8:20). Judah sought alliances with Egypt and tried to negotiate a way to peace (Ezek. 7:25), but the Lord had determined that His people should be chastened, and no political power can overrule the sovereign will of God.

"The Lord brings the counsel of the nations to nothing; He makes the plans of the peoples of no effect. The counsel of the Lord stands forever; the plans of His heart to all generations" (Ps. 33:10-11, NKJV).

CHAPTER THREE
THE GLORY HAS DEPARTED
Ezekiel 8–11

The Gentile nations had their temples, priests, religious laws, and sacrifices, but only the nation of Israel had the glory of the true and living God dwelling in their midst (Rom. 9:4). When Moses dedicated the tabernacle, God's glory moved in (Ex. 40:34-35), but the sins of the people caused the glory to depart (1 Sam. 4:19-22). When Solomon dedicated the temple, once again God's glory filled the sanctuary (1 Kings 8:11); but centuries later, the Prophet Ezekiel watched that glory leave the temple—and then come back again! Without the presence of the glory of the Lord, God's people are just another religious crowd, going through the motions. "If Your presence does not go with us," said Moses to the Lord, "do not bring us up from here" (Ex. 33:15, NKJV). The people of God are identified by the presence of God.

Recorded in these chapters is a remarkable vision that God gave Ezekiel, which he shared with the elders of the people of Israel (Ezek. 11:25). It wasn't an easy message to preach because it dealt with three great tragedies in the life of the Jewish nation: the temple was defiled (8:1-18), the people were doomed (9:1–10:22), and the leaders were deceived (11:1-25). The truths he shared in this message were opposite to what the false prophets were declaring both in Jerusalem and in Babylon. In their blind overconfidence, the false prophets and the officials who followed them all claimed that God would never permit His holy temple to fall into the hands of pagan Gentiles, but they proved to be wrong.

1. The temple is defiled (Ezek. 8:1-18)

Seeing dramatic visions and hearing God's voice were not everyday experiences for God's servants the prophets. As far as the record is concerned, fourteen months passed since Ezekiel was called and given his first visions. During that time he and his wife lived normal lives as Jeremiah had instructed (Jer. 29:4-9). Since the exiles in Babylon didn't have Jewish kings or princes to direct the affairs of the people, they chose elders to be their leaders; and some of these elders occasionally visited Ezekiel (see Ezek. 14:1; 20:1; 33:30-33). In this chapter, Ezekiel had two vivid experiences that led to a sad declaration: God would unleash His fury and judge His people without pity.

The glory of God was revealed (Ezek. 8:1-2). Above everything else, God's servants need to focus on the glory of God. It was seeing God's glory that kept Moses going when he was heavily burdened for the people (Ex. 33:18-23), and Ezekiel needed that same kind of encouragement. He saw the same glorious being and the same "chariot throne" that he had seen in the first vision (Ezek. 1). It's likely that this awesome being was Jesus Christ in a preincarnate appearance, and "the glory of God" in 8:4 was undoubtedly the spectacular vision of the wheels, cherubim, firmament, and throne which accompanied his prophetic call. God's servants may think that their greatest need is to see new visions and hear new voices, but the Lord doesn't always work that way. Instead, He often meets the need by giving us a fresh experience of the original call. The Lord reminded His servant that He was still on the throne and that His providential care for him and his people had never ceased. What more did Ezekiel need to know?

The idolatry of the people was exposed (Ezek. 8:3-16). Ezekiel was lifted from his house in Babylon and taken to the temple in Jerusalem! He wasn't transported bodily; he remained in his house and saw what was going on in the temple. (See 11:1, 24; 37:1; 43:5.) The first thing he saw in the temple was an idol! It's called "the image of jealousy" because idolatry provokes the Lord who is jealous over His people (Deut. 32:21). As the nation decayed spiritually, the religious leaders incorporated into the temple rituals the worship of other gods along with the worship of Jehovah. The stages in their idolatry were clear. First the Jewish people became curious about their neighbors' religion and then they investigated it. Its baser elements appealed to their fleshly appetites, and before long they were secretly participating in pagan worship. It was just a short step to start worshiping idols openly and then moving this false worship into the temple, as though Jehovah was just one of many gods (Deut. 7:1-11). Since the Lord and Israel were "married" in a covenant relationship, Israel's "religious prostitution" aroused the Lord's holy jealousy, just as a husband or wife would be jealous if a "lover" invaded their marriage (Ex. 20:5; Deut. 32:16).

King Hezekiah had removed idolatry from the land (2 Kings 18:1-5), but King Manasseh not only restored it but made it worse. It was he who put an idol into the Lord's temple (21:1-7), and Amon, his son and successor, continued his father's evil practices. But godly King Josiah purged the land of idolatry and burned that idol and crushed it to powder (23:4-20). But the idol had been replaced! The remarkable thing is that the glory of God was present in the same temple, but God was about to remove His glory and Ezekiel would watch it occur. Without the presence of God, the temple was just another building. It was the blasphemous sins of the religious leaders that drove God away from His holy house, and Ezekiel was about to see how wicked these leaders really were.

The Lord then led him to a place in the temple where there was a hole in the wall leading to a secret chamber. When Ezekiel entered the room, he saw seventy elders of the people (Ex. 24:9-10; Num. 11:16ff) burning incense before various idols whose images were painted on the wall, each man worshiping his own idol (see Ezek. 12, NASB). So gross was their appetite for false gods that they were even worshiping creeping things! (See Deut. 4:14-19; Rom. 1:18-25.) Ezekiel recognized Jaazaniah, one of the leading men in Jerusalem. (This is not the Jaazaniah of Ezek. 11:1.) It's possible that his father Shaphan was the same man who found the Book of the Law in the days of King Josiah and served the Lord so faithfully (2 Chron. 34). If so, he had at least three other sons: Ahikam, who protected Jeremiah from being killed (Jer. 26:24); Gemariah, who begged King Jehoiakim not to destroy Jeremiah's scroll (36:12ff); and Elasah, who delivered Jeremiah's scroll to the Jews in Babylon (29:1-3). Nebuchadnezzar appointed Shaphan's grandson Gedaliah to serve as governor of Judah after Jerusalem was destroyed (39:14). With this kind of godly heritage, it's difficult to believe that Jaazaniah became an idolater.

God knew what was in the hearts of these men and how they justified their sin: "The Lord does not see us, the Lord has forsaken the land" (Ezek. 8:12, NKJV). But the Lord isn't like the dead idols they worshiped which "have eyes but see not" (Ps. 115:5), and the people had forsaken the Lord long before He forsook them (2 Chron. 24:20; Jer. 1:16; 2:13, 17; 7:29, 15:6). Sad to say, the false thinking of these elders reached to the people, and they adopted it as their excuse for sin (Ezek. 9:9).

But there was more sin for Ezekiel to see in the temple. This time, it was the women at the gate of the temple who were openly taking part in a heathen ritual dedicated to Tammuz (8:13-14). While not all scholars agree, Tammuz is usually identified as a fertility god whom the Egyptians called Osiris and the Greeks called Adonis. According to their myths, Tammuz was killed by a wild boar and went to the underworld, and this tragedy brought winter each year. But his wife Ishtar (Astarte) would rescue him and bring the return of springtime and the rebirth of nature. It was nothing but superstition; the Jewish women had forsaken the truth of God for lies and were depending on gods that didn't exist. The rituals associated with the worship of Tammuz were unspeakably vile, as most fertility rituals were.

The fourth sight that would grieve Ezekiel's heart was that of twenty-five men at the door of the temple, between the porch (entry) and the brazen altar, openly bowing down to the sun (vv. 15-16). Since they were standing in an area by the altar of sacrifice available only to the priests, it's likely these men were priests, although in 9:6, these men are called elders. In worshiping the sun, they had to face the east, and this meant they turned their backs on the temple of God and the God of the temple. The idolatry of the seventy elders was hidden in the temple, but these men practiced their idolatry openly! It was contrary to God's law for the Jews to worship the heavenly bodies (Ex. 20:1-6; Deut. 17:3), but these men were worshiping the creation instead of the Creator (Rom. 1:25) and doing it openly in the temple precincts.

Idolatry was a besetting sin among the Jewish people. Abraham belonged to an idol-worshiping family before God called him (Josh. 24:2), and the Jews learned a great deal about idolatry when they sojourned in Egypt (Ezek. 20:7; Josh. 24:14). When they captured the Promised Land, they failed to destroy the idols and shrines of the residents of the land, and this idolatry became a snare to them (Jud. 2:10-15). While believers today may not bow before grotesque idols like those named in the Bible, we must still beware of idols, for an idol is anything that has our devotion and commands our will and takes the place of the true and living God. "Little children, keep yourselves from idols" (1 John 5:21) is an admonition that needs to be heeded by the church today.

The divine judgment is announced (Ezek. 8:17-18). Ezekiel had seen only a part of the evidence that the people in Jerusalem had abandoned themselves to idolatry. He had seen an idol in the temple, defiling its very precincts and yet being worshiped by people who also claimed to worship the Lord, as though Jehovah were one God among many, not the Lord of lords. Then he saw the leaders secretly worshiping false gods in the temple. After that, everything was out in the open: the women weeping for Tammuz, and the priests/elders bowing down to the sun. In God's sight, these things were abominable and detestable and they provoked Him to anger. Except for the faithful remnant, the Jewish people no longer feared God or cared about pleasing Him.

The strange phrase "put the branch to the nose" has no parallel in Scripture and may describe a part of an idolatrous ritual. Some see it as an insulting gesture, similar to our "sticking up the nose" at someone or something, while others suggest it should be translated "a stench in my nose." Whatever it means, the gesture was repulsive to God. He announced that the nation's idolatry was the cause of the violence in the land. Because the leaders despised God's law, they didn't care whether the courts were just toward everyone or partial toward the rich. When people lose their fear of God, they do as they please and don't worry about the consequences.

The Lord had presented the evidence and announced the verdict, and now He declared the sentence: He would obey His covenant and severely punish His people for their multiplied sins. "Unsparing fury" was the sentence, and no pity added. The guilty nation could cry out for mercy, but He would not listen to them,[1] and they couldn't appeal to a higher court. He had given them opportunity after opportunity to turn from their sins, but they refused to listen; and now He wouldn't listen to them.

2. The people are doomed (Ezek. 9:1–10:22)

This is the heart of Ezekiel's message, and it must have broken his heart to deliver it. Read the Book of Lamentations and see how thoroughly the Lord "dealt in fury" with His people. Jeremiah was an eyewitness of the destruction of Jerusalem, and what Ezekiel predicted, Jeremiah saw fulfilled.

The remnant spared (Ezek. 9:1-4). In his vision, Ezekiel was still in the temple in Jerusalem when he heard the Lord summon six "men" to prepare the way for the slaughter. These were probably angels who appeared as men, the angels assigned to the city of Jerusalem. Daniel learned that there were angels in charge of nations (Dan. 10:12-21), so it isn't unusual that Jerusalem should have six guardian angels. These angels were appointed to execute God's judgment in the city. But with the six angels was a seventh person bearing the equipment of a scribe, clothed in linen as though he were a priest. On the basis of his garment (Dan. 10:5; Rev. 1:13), some students have identified this man as the Lord Jesus Christ who came to preserve His faithful remnant, but this is only conjecture. On his belt or sash, the scribe wore a leather or metal container, about ten inches long and an inch and a half square, in which were reed pens and a container of ink. In ancient cities, the scribe would register the citizens and identify the aliens. These seven angels congregated at the altar of burnt offering, the place where the fire of God's holy judgment consumed the sacrifices.[2] The fire declared the holiness of God, but the blood sacrifice on the altar declared the grace of God.

At this point, the shekinah[3] glory that had been on the "chariot throne" (Ezek. 8:2, 4) moved from the throne to the threshold of the temple, in preparation for leaving the temple. It's interesting that the glory of God should be associated with the judgment of a polluted city, but it is for His glory that God judges sin.[4] It is also for His glory that that God graciously saves those who put their trust in Him (Eph. 1:6, 12, 14). The Jewish people who had God's glory dwelling among them didn't seek to glorify Him by obeying His will, so He received glory by punishing their sins.

The scribe-angel was commanded to go through the city and mark the people who lamented and grieved because of the sins of the city. No matter how dark the day, God has always had His faithful remnant who obeyed His will and trusted Him for deliverance, and Ezekiel was among them (Ezek. 6:11; 21:6). See Psalms 12:5; 119:53; 136; Isaiah 66:2; Jeremiah 13:17; Amos 6:6; and Malachi 3:16. The marking of people will also be a feature of the end times (Rev. 7:3; 9:4; 13:16-17; 20:4). Believers today are "marked" by the Spirit of God (Eph. 1:13-14) and should be "marked" by holy lives that glorify Christ.

The rebels judged (Ezek. 9:5–10:7). The other six angels were to follow the scribe-angel and kill everybody on whom he didn't put the mark, and nobody was to be spared because of sex or age. The word for "mark" in the Hebrew text is the last letter of the Hebrew alphabet (*taw* or *tau*), which in that day was written like a cross (X). The angels see to it that God's plans are fulfilled for individuals and nations, but they perform their duties invisibly, unseen by the people whose lives they affect. It was now the year 592 B.C. (8:1), and the city of Jerusalem wouldn't be taken until 586 B.C. Some of the inhabitants had already died of famine and pestilence, but when the Babylonian army broke through the walls, many more were to be slaughtered with the sword (5:8-13).

"Begin at my sanctuary" seems like a strange order, but it was the idolatry in the temple that had aroused the anger of the Lord. Often in Scripture you find God sending judgment, not because unbelievers have sinned, but because His own people have disobeyed His law! Twice Abraham brought judgment on innocent Gentiles because he lied about his wife (Gen. 12:10-20; 20:1-18). Aaron the high priest led Israel into idolatry and 3,000 people were slain (Ex. 32:1-6, 26-29). David committed adultery with Bathsheba and then murdered her husband, Uriah, and his sins brought years of trouble to his family and the nation. A crew of Gentile sailors almost drowned because of the disobedience of God's prophet Jonah. God's people are to be the salt of the earth and the light of the world (Matt. 5:13-16). If there were more salt in this world, there would be less decay, and more light would mean less darkness. Our good works glorify the Lord, but our sins invite His discipline. Peter warned believers in the first century that "judgment must begin at the house [household] of God" (1 Peter 4:17), a warning we need to heed today as our Lord's coming draws near.

A corpse was an unclean thing to a Jew, so corpses in the temple would defile the house of God. These people had defiled God's house by their wicked lives, and now they would defile it further in their terrible deaths. The idolaters would be as dead as the idols they worshiped (Ps. 115:8). When the Prophet Ezekiel saw this scene, he fell on his face to intercede for the remnant God had promised to protect. This attitude is the mark of a true shepherd (see Ezek. 4:14; 11:13). Abraham interceded for Lot in Sodom (Gen. 18:16ff), and Moses interceded for his brother Aaron and the idolatrous Jews (Ex. 32:11ff). The prophets asked God to spare the people of Israel, and Jesus prayed for the ignorant people who crucified Him (Luke 23:34). God informed Ezekiel that the land was defiled by innocent blood and the city was full of injustice, and the time had come for the people to reap what they had sown.

In response to Ezekiel's concern and prayer, the Lord revealed His glory once again, just as it had been revealed when Moses dedicated the tabernacle and Solomon dedicated the temple. The glory cloud left the chariot-throne and hovered over the threshold. The Lord commanded the scribe-angel to enter between the wheels and take coals from the fire that was there and to scatter the coals over the city of Jerusalem. Not only would the city be visited by famine, pestilence, and sword, but it would be burned by the Babylonian army. This was not a fire of purification, such as Isaiah experienced (Isa. 6:5-7), but a fire of condemnation (2 Kings 25:8-9).

The glory revealed (Ezek. 10:8-22). Ezekiel describes the vision of God's glory that he had seen on the day of his ordination (vv. 15, 20-22). One new feature is the fact that the living creatures were "full of eyes" even as the wheels were, which suggests God's omniscience (see 1:18). God's providential working in this world is not aimless or haphazard. Everything is done "according to the purpose of Him who works all things according to the counsel of His will" (Eph. 1:11, NKJV). Another new feature is the identifying of the wheels as "the whirling wheels" (Ezek. 10:13, NIV).

One problem that this new description presents relates to the description of the faces of the cherubim in verse 14. In 1:10, each cherub had the face of a man, a lion, an ox, and an eagle; while in 10:14, the face of the ox is apparently replaced by the face of "the cherub." The so-called contradiction is only apparent. From where Ezekiel was standing, he saw a different face of each of the cherubs. "The cherub" must have been the one that gave the coals of fire to the scribe-angel. We might paraphrase it, "The first face I saw was of the cherub and it was an ox, since the faces I saw of the other three cherubim were of a man, a lion, and an eagle." Each face was indeed the face of the cherub since each of the living creatures was a cherub.

God's glory departed from the threshold and stood over the throne-chariot which was on the right side of the house (v. 3), as though the Lord were calling His glory back to His throne. At the same time, the chariot-throne arose and stood at the door of the east gate of the temple. There Ezekiel would see some of the leaders of the nation engaged in worshiping the sun, and the Lord would judge one of them.

Ezekiel was learning that the most important part of the nation's life was to magnify the glory of God. The presence of God in the sanctuary was a great privilege for the people of Israel, but it was also a great responsibility. The glory of God cannot dwell with the sins of God's people, so it was necessary for the glory to leave, and the sanctuary and the people to be judged.

3. The leaders are deceived (Ezek. 11:1-25)

When you read the prophecy of Jeremiah, you discover that the civil and religious leaders of the kingdom of Judah, as well as the rulers of Jerusalem, were not interested in knowing and doing the will of God. When one of the kings inquired of Jeremiah, he did it secretly because he was afraid of what his advisers might do (Jer. 37:17). During Judah's last years, the people were ruled by weak men who promoted idolatry and would not call the people to repentance and prayer (2 Chron. 7:14). By publicly wearing a yoke, Jeremiah had made it clear that the only way to spare the city and the temple from destruction was for the Jewish leaders to surrender to the Babylonians (Jer. 27). Instead, the Jewish leaders secretly made an agreement with the Egyptians, asking them to rescue them from Babylon, but the Egyptians were helpless to do anything. God had decreed the fall of the nation, and He was using Nebuchadnezzar as His servant to accomplish His will (Jer. 25:9; 27:6; 43:10).

The city is like a cauldron (Ezek. 11:1-13). Ezekiel is still having his vision of Jerusalem and the temple, and the Lord showed him twenty-five men at the eastern door of the temple, worshiping the sun. (See 8:15-18.) Among them were the leaders of the people, Jaazaniah and Pelantiah. (This is not the Jaazaniah of v. 11.) These men were giving wicked advice to the king and other leaders in Jerusalem, but their counsel was not from the Lord. How could it be wise counsel when they were idolaters who worshiped the sun? At the same time, they were plotting evil so that they could benefit personally from the Babylonian attack on the city. In every crisis, you will find "opportunists" who seek to help themselves instead of helping their country, and they usually hide behind the mask of patriotism.

Not only were these leaders idolaters and wicked counselors, but they cultivated a philosophy that gave them and the other leaders a false confidence in their dangerous situation. "Is not the time near to build houses?" they asked. "This city is the pot and we are the flesh" (11:3, NASB). Jeremiah had told the exiles to build houses in Babylon and settle down and raise families, because they would live there for seventy years (Jer. 29:4ff). But it was foolish for the people in Jerusalem to build houses, for the Lord had ordained that the Babylonian army would destroy the city and slaughter most of the inhabitants. These evil leaders were sure that Jerusalem was as safe for them as a piece of meat in a cooking pot. The innuendo in this metaphor was that the people in Jerusalem were choice cuts of meat while the exiles in Babylon were just the scraps and rejected pieces. Of course, just the opposite was true! Had the leaders in Jerusalem listened to Jeremiah's message about the baskets of figs, they would have seen their philosophy completely reversed. The good figs were the exiles and the bad figs were the people left in Jerusalem (Jer. 24:1-7). God would preserve a remnant from among the exiles, but the idolaters in Jerusalem would be slain.

The Lord told Ezekiel to prophesy against those evil leaders and point out that they weren't the meat—they were the butchers! They had killed innocent people in Jerusalem and stolen their possessions, and even if the leaders weren't slain in Jerusalem, they would not escape judgment. They might flee the city, but the Babylonians would catch them at the border, pass sentence on them, and kill them; and that is exactly what happened (2 Kings 25:18-21; Jer. 39:1-7; 52:1-11, 24-27). Then the Jewish officials would learn too late that Jehovah alone is Lord of heaven and earth.

In his vision, Ezekiel preached this message and Petaliah fell down dead! The Lord gave the sun-worshipers a vivid proof that their evil thoughts and plans could only lead to disaster. Once again, Ezekiel revealed his shepherd's heart as he fell on his face before the Lord and prayed for the people. As in Ezekiel 9:8, he prayed that the Lord would spare a remnant of the people so Israel would have a future.

Jehovah the sanctuary of His people (Ezek. 11:14-21). This is God's word of encouragement to His servant that He would fulfill His promise and spare a remnant of the people. The people in Jerusalem were sure that God would deliver them and give back their land, because the exiles had left the land and were far from Jerusalem and the temple. In ancient days, people believed that each nation had its own gods, and when you left your home country, you left your gods behind.[5] Of course, Jehovah had revealed Himself to Abraham as "possessor of heaven and earth" (Gen. 14:22), so the Jewish leaders shouldn't have had such a narrow view of God. What they said was probably just an excuse for confiscating land that belonged to some of the exiles.

But the Lord made it clear that He had not forsaken the Jews in Babylon, for the "I will" statements in Ezekiel 11:16-20 declare His promises to the exiles. First, God Himself would be to them "a sanctuary for a little while" during their captivity. "Lord, You have been our dwelling place in all generations" (Ps. 90:1, NKJV). The self-confident Jews in Jerusalem thought they were secure as long as they had the temple, but the true temple was with the exiles in Babylon! Long before there ever was a tabernacle or a temple, the patriarchs had God as their refuge and strength, their sanctuary, and their abiding place. Wherever Abraham pitched his tent, he also built an altar to the Lord, because he knew that God was with him (Gen. 12:8; 13:1-4, 18). The New Testament equivalent of this experience is to abide in Christ (John 15:1-10).

His second promise is "I will even gather you" (Ezek. 11:17). A remnant of Jews would one day return to the land and rebuild the temple. No matter where the Jews had been scattered, the Lord would find them and bring them home. This promise goes far beyond the restoration after the Captivity, for the Lord has promised that in the end times He will gather His people back to their land (28:25-26; 34:11-16; 36:24-38; 37:11-28; Isa. 11:11-16; Jer. 24:4-7). His third promise is, "I will give you the land of Israel" (Ezek. 11:17). Since God had already given this land to Abraham and his descendants (Gen. 12:7; 13:14-17; 15:7), nobody else could successfully lay claim to it. When the exiles returned to their land, they would be cured of idolatry and would remove all the pagan worship.

The promises in Ezekiel 11:19-21 go beyond the return of the Jewish exiles after the Babylonian Captivity, for Scripture records no evidence of this kind of spiritual renewal in the post-exilic period. In fact, the account given in Ezra, Nehemiah, Haggai, and Malachi is just the opposite. The promises apply to the end times when God's people Israel will be regathered to their land, will repent of their sins and trust their Messiah (Zech. 12–14), and welcome Him as their King. They will experience a spiritual regeneration, a new birth. However, those who will not believe will be judged (Ezek. 11:21). Later in this book, Ezekiel will describe in greater detail the glorious blessings God has prepared for the Jewish nation (chaps. 33–48). Jeremiah had also announced a "New Covenant" for the people of Israel (Jer. 31:33; 32:38-39), a covenant not written on stones but engraved on the human mind and heart; and Christian believers today share in that covenant (2 Cor. 3; Heb. 9–10).

The glory departs (Ezek. 11:22-25). The chariot-throne had been lingering at the threshold of the east gate of the temple, with the glory of God above it (10:18-19). Now the glory of God departed and rested over the Mount of Olives, east of Jerusalem. Ezekiel could have written "Ichabod" over the east gate, for indeed, "the glory has departed" (1 Sam. 4:19-22). However, Ezekiel saw the glory return, this time to the new temple that will stand during the reign of Christ in His kingdom (Ezek. 43:1-5).

After the temple was destroyed in 586 B.C., the glory of God disappeared from the earth and didn't return until the birth of Christ in

Bethlehem (Luke 2:9, 32; John 1:14). Wicked men crucified the Lord of glory (1 Cor. 2:8), but He arose again and ascended back to heaven from Bethany (Luke 24:50-51; Acts 1:9-12) which is on the eastern slope of Mount Olivet. One day Jesus will return to the Mount of Olives (Zech. 14:4) to deliver His people and establish His kingdom. The glory will have returned!

When the vision ended, Ezekiel found himself back in his own house in Babylon, and he told the Jewish elders and the other exiles what the Lord had shown him. Some no doubt believed and prayed for the peace of Jerusalem, while others preferred to listen to the deadly soothing words of the false prophets. But four years later (Ezek. 24:1), Ezekiel would get the message that the siege of Jerusalem had begun. The date was January 15, 588 B.C. Three years later (January 8, 585 B.C.), a fugitive would arrive in Babylon with the news that the city had fallen (32:21).

God's Word never fails.

CHAPTER FOUR
THE TRUTH ABOUT THE FALSE
Ezekiel 12–14

In his *Notes on the State of Virginia*, Thomas Jefferson wrote, "It is error alone which needs the support of government. Truth can stand by itself."[1] During the siege of Jerusalem (606–586 b.c.), error had the support of government and religious leaders, and most of the Jewish exiles in Babylon agreed with them. "We will never give in to the Babylonian army!" was the cry of the Jewish people in Jerusalem. "The Lord will never allow the Gentiles to destroy His holy city or defile His holy temple!" One dissenting voice in Jerusalem was Jeremiah; in Babylon it was Ezekiel. Both in his "action sermons" and his oral messages, Ezekiel warned the people that they were trusting in illusions. No matter what the officials, the false prophets, and the people said, the city and the nation were doomed. In these chapters, Ezekiel exposes the errors that brought the nation to ruin.

1. False confidence (Ezek. 12:1-28)

When the Lord called Ezekiel, He warned him that he would be ministering to a rebellious people (2:3-8) who were spiritually blind and deaf (12:2). In order to understand God's truth, we must be obedient to God's will (John 7:17; Ps. 25:8-10), but Israel was far from being obedient. Years before, Isaiah spoke to people who were spiritually blind and deaf (Isa. 6:9-10), and that was the kind of people Jeremiah was preaching to in Jerusalem (Jer. 5:21). When our Lord was here on earth, many of the people were spiritually blind and deaf (Matt. 13:13-14) and so were the people who heard Paul (Acts 28:26-28). In order to get the attention of the exiles and excite their interest, Ezekiel performed two "action sermons" and after each one gave a message from the Lord.

The leaders cannot escape (Ezek. 12:1-16). The Lord instructed Ezekiel to play the part of a fugitive escaping from a besieged city. Part of his activity occurred in the daytime and part at twilight, and the curious but perplexed Jewish exiles watched his strange actions. First, Ezekiel prepared a knapsack with essentials for a journey and took it outside in the daylight and hid it somewhere away from his house. Then he returned to the house and that evening dug through one of its walls, probably from the outside since the people could see him work. Houses were constructed of sun-dried bricks, so digging through the wall wasn't a problem. After that, he retrieved his knapsack, went into the house, and climbed out through the hole, while his face was covered and his eyes were fixed on the ground. As the people watched, they asked, "What is he doing?"

Packing the knapsack and leaving it at a distance from his house conveyed the message that the leaders in Jerusalem were planning to flee for their lives. Digging through the wall from outside the house pictured the Babylonian army's assault on the walls of Jerusalem. That evening, when Ezekiel climbed out of the house through the hole, the knapsack on his back, he depicted the Jewish leaders secretly trying to flee from the city to save their lives. History tells us that King Zedekiah, his officers, and his army escaped from Jerusalem exactly that way, but they were pursued by the Babylonians and captured (2 Kings 25:1-7; Jer. 52:4-11). The Babylonians killed the king's sons and officers before his very eyes,[2] put out Zedekiah's eyes, and took him prisoner to Babylon, where he died.

The next morning, in the message that followed the "action sermon,"[3] Ezekiel predicted that these events would occur. He also announced that though Zedekiah would be taken to Babylon, he would not see it (Ezek. 12:13; Jer. 52:11). How could such a thing happen? It was very simple: the Babylonians gouged out his eyes and *Zedekiah couldn't see anything*! But it wasn't the Babylonian army that captured the king of Judah and his officers; it was God's "net" that caught them. Nebuchadnezzar and the Babylonian army didn't win because of their own skill; they were God's instruments to defeat the people of Judah and Jerusalem (Jer. 27:1-22). Jeremiah had admonished Zedekiah to surrender to the Babylonians (38:14ff), but the king didn't have the faith to trust God's Word and obey it. Had he humbled himself and surrendered, the people, the city, the temple, and the lives of the people would have been spared.

Not only would the Jewish officials be slain and their king humiliated, but the people in Jerusalem who survived the siege would be scattered abroad, and some of them would be taken to Babylon (Ezek. 12:14-16). Again, this would be the work of God—"I shall scatter them"—and not because these surviving Jews had been especially holy. Quite the opposite was true: the Lord allowed the survivors to go to Babylon as witnesses that their evil deeds deserved the punishment that God had sent to the nation. This will come up again in 14:22-23.

The people will live in terror (Ezek. 12:17-28). The prophet's second "action sermon" probably took place the next day when it was time for his meal. Perhaps some of the Jews were in the house with him, or what's more likely, he ate the meal outside and continued the fugitive image. He ate his bread and drank his water—a frugal meal—while shaking and trembling as if in fear. He was illustrating the tragic condition of the people in Jerusalem during the Babylonian siege. They would have very little food and would eat it with fear and trembling because it might well be their last meal. Their plight would be the fulfillment of the Lord's promise in 4:16-17. Anxiety, worry, fear, and consternation would grip the people as the fall of the city became more imminent.

The theme of Ezekiel's message (12:21-28) was the certainty and the nearness of God's judgment on Jerusalem and the land of Judah. The people were quoting a proverb that may have been devised by the false prophets to humiliate Ezekiel: "The days drag on and every vision comes to nothing and is not fulfilled" (v. 22, AMP). In other words, "Ezekiel tells us about all his visions, but nothing ever happens. Why worry? His prophecies will come to nothing!" The Jews had said a similar thing to Isaiah (Isa. 5:19), and people today say this about the return of Jesus Christ (2 Peter 3). People can predict the weather, but they don't discern "the signs of the times" (Matt. 16:3).

The Lord gave His servant a new proverb to share with the exiles: "The days are near when every vision will be fulfilled" (Ezek. 12:23, NIV). Because Ezekiel's prophecies had not been fulfilled immediately, the people were paying more attention to the false prophets than to the true Word of God. The visions of the false prophets were false and misleading, and they delivered only the soothing and encouraging words that the people wanted to hear (Jer. 28–29). The Lord made it clear that there would be no more "delays" and that His Word would be fulfilled. He had said to Jeremiah, "I am watching over My word to perform it" (1:12, NASB), and He told Isaiah that His Word always fulfilled the purposes for which it was sent (Isa. 55:8-11). God's Word has its appointed time and will never fail (Hab. 2:3).

Among the exiles, one part said that Ezekiel's words would never be fulfilled, but another group said, "Yes, they will be fulfilled, but not in our time. We don't have to worry about what will happen because it will take place a long time from now" (paraphrase of Ezek. 12:27). Their interpretation was wrong and so was their selfish attitude. Even if the Lord did delay His judgments, how could the Jewish people be content with the present knowing that a future generation would be wiped out and the holy city and temple destroyed? They were like King Hezekiah when Isaiah rebuked him for his pride and warned him that Babylon would conquer Judah: "At least there will peace and truth in my days" (Isa. 39:8, NKJV).

The Lord made it clear that Ezekiel's words would be fulfilled very soon. "The word which I have spoken shall be done" (Ezek.

12:28). Six years later, the Babylonian army breached the walls of Jerusalem and Ezekiel's predictions came true. How tragic it is when people deliberately ignore or reject the dependable Word of God and put their faith in the empty but soothing words of false religious leaders! It reminds me of a story that came out of World War II. A group of soldiers asked their new chaplain if he believed in hell, and he laughed and said that he didn't. The men said, "Well, sir, if there isn't a hell, then we don't need you. But if there is a hell, then you're leading us astray—and that's worse!" There is no substitute for God's Word.

2. False prophecy (Ezek. 13:1-23)

Ezekiel had answered the shallow selfish thinking of the exiles and the people in Jerusalem, but now he attacked the source of their blind optimism: the messages of the false prophets. Jeremiah in Jerusalem had to confront a similar group of men who claimed to have a word from the Lord. The false prophets claimed to speak in the name of the Lord, just as Jeremiah and Ezekiel did, but they didn't get their messages from the Lord. Ezekiel spoke against both false prophets (vv. 1-16) and false prophetesses (vv. 17-23) who were actually using the occult practices forbidden to the people of Israel (Deut. 18:9-14).

The lying prophets (Ezek. 13:1-16). Four times in this paragraph God declares that the false prophets saw vanity (nothingness) and spoke lies. God hadn't called them (Jer. 23:21-22) and God didn't give them their messages, yet they claimed to be His prophets. They spoke out of their own imaginations and their "inspiration" was self-induced. Ezekiel compared them to the foxes (jackals) that lived as scavengers in the deserted ruins of the land. They cared only for themselves, they did nothing to improve the situation, and they lived off the fears of the people. In times of crisis, there are always religious opportunists who prey on weak and ignorant people who are seeking cheap assurance and comfort.

Ezekiel also compared the false prophets to workmen who failed to build something that would last. The spiritual "wall" that had protected the Jewish people for centuries had fallen into ruin, and prophets like Ezekiel and Jeremiah were trying to rebuild and strengthen it by proclaiming the Word and calling the people back to God. But the false prophets ignored the Word of God and substituted their own lies ("untempered mortar," KJV = whitewash).[4] They were like workmen who whitewashed a weak wall to make it look sturdy, because they promised peace when God had promised destruction (Ezek. 13:10, 16; Jer. 6:14; 7:8; 8:11). Just as the storm would come, and the rain, hail, and wind knock down the wall, so God's wrath would come and destroy Jerusalem, the prophets, and their deceptive messages. A true prophet tells people what they *need* to hear, but a false prophet tells them what they *want* to hear (2 Tim. 4:1-5). A true servant of God builds carefully on a strong foundation and keeps the wall in good repair, but a hireling builds carelessly and whitewashes things to make them look better.

God explained how He would judge the false prophets (Ezek. 13:9). First, they would be exposed as counterfeits and no longer have an exalted reputation among the people. They would lose their prominent places in the councils of the nation. God would treat them like Jews who had also lost their citizenship (Ezra 2:59, 62) and therefore be deprived of the privilege of returning to their land. It appears that the false prophets in Jerusalem would be slain by the enemy and those in Babylon would be left there to die. The counterfeit prophets gave the people a false hope, so God gave them no hope at all.

It's a serious thing to be called of God and to speak His Word to His people. To assume a place of ministry without being called and gifted is arrogance, and to manufacture messages without receiving them from the Lord is impertinence. The false prophets in Ezekiel's day were guilty of both. Popularity is not a test of truth. History shows that those who spoke the truth were usually rejected by the majority, persecuted, and even killed. Jesus used the same image of a storm to warn us about false prophets (Matt. 7:15-27). It's easy for people to say, "Lord, Lord," but it's not easy to walk the narrow road and confront the crowd that's going in the opposite direction.

The lying sorceresses (Ezek. 13:17-23). The gift of prophecy wasn't given exclusively to men, for several prophetesses are named in Scripture: Miriam (Ex. 15:20), Deborah (Jud. 4:4-5), the wife of Isaiah (Isa. 8:3), Hulda (2 Kings 22:14), and the daughters of Philip the evangelist (Acts 21:8-9). Noadiah (Neh. 6:14) was apparently a self-styled prophetess and not a true servant of God.

The Jewish women Ezekiel was exposing were more like sorceresses who claimed to be prophetesses. They practiced the magical arts they had probably learned in Babylon, all of which were forbidden to the Jews (Deut. 18:9-14). They manufactured magic charms that people could wear on various parts of the body and thus ward off evil. They also told fortunes and enticed people to buy their services. Like the false prophets, they were using the crisis situation for personal gain and preying on the fears of the people. A Christian executive in Chicago told me that during the Depression, worried businessmen frequently visited a fortuneteller who sold her services from a fine restaurant.

But these women weren't helping people; they were hunting them and catching them like birds in a trap to take their money. They told the people lies, they didn't expose their sins, and they kept them from trusting the true and living God and depending on His Word alone. Instead of condemning the evil and rewarding the good, they were slaying the good and rewarding the evil! Through their divinations, they gave false hope to the wicked and condemned the just, and they were willing to do it for just a handful of barley and a scrap of bread![5] But their end would come. God would strip them of their charms and amulets and then take His people back to their land, leaving these evil women behind to die.

3. False piety (Ezek. 14:1-11)

Except when God told him to leave, Ezekiel was confined to his house (3:24) and was not allowed to speak unless he was declaring a message from the Lord. The elders of the exiled people came to visit him to see what he was doing and to hear what he had to say about their situation (8:1; 20:1). The prophet gave them two messages from the Lord.

He exposed their hidden sin (Ezek. 14:1-5). God told His servant that these elders were like some of the spiritual leaders Ezekiel had seen in his vision of the temple (chap. 8): outwardly they were serving the Lord, but secretly they were worshiping idols. Instead of having a love for God and His Word in their hearts, the elders had idols in their hearts. Yet they piously sat before God's prophet and acted spiritual, but to them, listening to Ezekiel speak was more like religious entertainment than receiving spiritual enlightenment (33:31). They were like the people in Isaiah's day who drew near to God with words but not with their hearts (Isa. 29:13). Jesus said that the Pharisees in His day were guilty of the same sin (Matt. 15:8-9), and so are some professed Christians today. Idolatry in the heart puts a stumbling block before the eyes (Ezek. 13:7; 7:19; 18:10; 44:12) and this leads to a tragic fall.

It's not likely that believers today would have a love in their hearts for actual images, but anything that replaces God in our affections and our obedience is certainly an idol. It might be wealth, as in the case of Achan (Josh. 7), Ananias and Sapphira (Acts 5), and the man we call "the rich young ruler" (Matt. 19:16-26). Jonah's idol was a selfish patriotism that made him turn his back on the Gentiles who needed to hear his message. Pilate's idol was holding the approval of the people and his status in the Roman Empire (Mark 15:15; John 19:12-16). What we have in our hearts affects what we see and how we live. If Christ is Lord in our hearts (1 Peter 3:15), then there will be no place for idols.

Loving and accepting the false prevents us from knowing and loving the true (2 Thes. 2:10) and results in our becoming estranged from the Lord (Ezek. 13:5). By worshiping false gods, Israel abandoned the Lord whom they had "married" at Sinai (Jer. 2:1-14), and they needed to turn back to the Lord. Like the believers in the church of Ephesus, they had "left their first love" (Rev. 2:4). God told Ezekiel that the Jewish people had deserted Him to follow after idols and that He would discipline them in order to "recapture" their hearts.

He called them to repent (Ezek. 14:6-11). Repentance is a change of mind; it means turning from sin and turning to the Lord. The Jewish exiles needed to change their minds about idols and the sin of worshiping idols, and then turn to the Lord who alone is worthy of worship. God would judge each sinner personally and deal with each one personally (v. 7), and some of them He would use as examples to warn the other exiles (v. 8).

A casual reading of verse 9 would give the impression that it was the Lord's fault that people were worshiping idols, but that isn't the case. Everybody in Israel knew the Ten Commandments and understood that it was a sin to make and worship idols (Ex. 20:1-6).

Even if someone very close to them enticed them to practice idolatry, they were not to yield (Deut. 13). God permitted these enticements to test the people to make sure they were loyal to Him. Of course, God knows what's in the human heart, but we don't know our own hearts, and these tests help us to stay humble before the Lord and walk in the fear of the Lord. An illustration of this truth is seen in 1 Kings 22. God permitted a lying spirit to work in the minds of the false prophets to convince Ahab to go into battle. Micaiah, the true prophet, told the assembly what would happen, but they rejected the truth and put their trust in lies. God spared the life of the king of Judah but took the life of wicked King Ahab.

When people will not receive "the love of the truth, that they might be saved," God may "send them strong delusion, that they should believe the lie, so that they all may be condemned" (2 Thes. 2:10-11, NKJV). It's the condition of the person's heart that determines the response to the Lord's test, for God deals with people according to their hearts (Ps. 18:26-27). The attitude of the lost world today is that there are no absolutes, and therefore there can be no "truth." Satan is the liar and the deceiver and he has blinded the minds of people so that they believe lies and reject the truth of God. We must do all we can to share the truth of the Word with a blind and deaf world, trusting the Holy Spirit to open their eyes and ears and save them by His grace.

4. False hope (Ezek. 14:12-23)

In this particular message, the Lord described once again the four judgments He would send on the people of Judah and Jerusalem, and He emphasized one compelling fact: there would be no escape. Perhaps some of the Jews remembered how their father Abraham interceded for Sodom and Gomorrah, and how the Lord promised to spare the city if He could locate in it ten righteous men (Gen. 18:16-33). God had told Jeremiah to stop praying for the people because they were beyond hope (Jer. 7:16; 11:14; 14:11), and now He would tell Ezekiel that the presence of three righteous men whom the Jews revered would not save the city of Jerusalem.

The judgments described (Ezek. 14:12-21). The first judgment is *famine* (vv. 12-14). God would break the staff of bread and cut off the lives of humans and animals. Both Jeremiah and Ezekiel mention this judgment (Jer. 14; Ezek. 5:12, 16-17; 6:11-12; 7:15; 12:16), and it came as promised. But God in His covenant with Israel had warned that famine would come if the people disobeyed His Word (Deut. 28:15-20, 38-40, 50-57). "But surely there are enough righteous men in Jerusalem to turn away God's anger," the leaders argued; but God silenced their lips. If Noah, Daniel, and Job were in the city, their righteousness would deliver only themselves and could not save the city.

Why did the Lord choose these three men? For one thing, all three of them are identified in the Old Testament Scripture as righteous men (Gen. 6:9; Job 1:1, 8; 2:3; Dan. 6:4-5, 22). All of them were tested and proved faithful, Noah by the Flood, Daniel in the lions' den, and Job by painful trials from Satan. They were all men of faith. Noah's faith helped to save his family and animal creation; Daniel's faith saved his own life and the lives of his friends (Dan. 2:24); and Job's faith saved his three friends from God's judgment (Job 42:7-8). However, the faith and righteousness of these three men could not be accredited to others. Noah's family had to trust God and enter the ark; Daniel's friends had to pray and trust God; and Job's friends had to repent and bring the proper sacrifices. There is no such thing as "borrowed faith."

The responsibility of each person before God is a key subject in the Book of Ezekiel, and he will deal with it in chapter 18. God doesn't punish people because of the sins of others, nor will God accept the righteousness of others to compensate for the wicked deeds of sinners. This principle is made clear in both the Law of Moses and the covenant God made with Israel. The only time God abandoned this principle was when Jesus Christ His Son died on the cross, for He suffered for the sins of the whole world. When we trust Jesus as Savior and Lord, we receive the gift of His righteousness and God accepts us because of His Son (Rom. 3:21–4:25; 2 Cor. 5:19-21).

The second judgment was *wild beasts in the land* (Ezek. 14:15-16). This judgment was also mentioned in the covenant: "I will also send wild beasts among you, which shall rob you of your children, and destroy your cattle, and make you few in number; and your highways shall be desolate" (Lev. 26:22). The Lord gave Israel victory in the Promised Land in about seven years, but the "mopping up" operation took a little longer. God gave the Jews victory over the residents "little by little" so that the land wouldn't revert to its natural state and the wild animals take over (Deut. 7:22). But now in a developed land, with many people, towns, and cities, the animals would still take over at the command of God! Unfortunately, it would be innocent children who would suffer most. But even if these three righteous men were living in the land, they couldn't deliver anybody other than themselves.

The third judgment was *the sword* (Ezek. 14:17-18), which means war. The word "sword" is used at least eighty-six times in Ezekiel. The Babylonian army would sweep through the land and show no mercy (Hab. 1:5-11). They would surround Jerusalem and besiege it until its food ran out and its fortifications failed. The presence of Noah, Daniel, and Job could not have saved the city.

The final judgment was *pestilence* (Ezek. 14:19-20), which usually accompanies famine and war (Rev. 6:3-8). Dying people and decaying corpses certainly don't make a besieged city a healthier place in which to live. Again, God gave the warning about the inability of the three righteous men to rescue the people. The fourfold repetition of this truth surely got the message across to the elders, but the Jewish people had a tendency to rest all their hopes on the righteousness of their "great men." Both John the Baptist and Jesus warned the Pharisees and Sadducees that they couldn't please God just because Abraham was their father (Matt. 3:7-9; John 8:33-47) or Moses was their leader (9:28).

God's judgments vindicated (Ezek. 14:21-23). The absence of even three righteous people in Jerusalem would make God's judgments of the city even worse, and when all four of His judgments converge, how terrible it will be! No doubt the false prophets and some of the other captives would debate with the Lord and argue that He was being too hard on Judah and Jerusalem. But in His grace, He would allow some of the people to escape the four judgments and be taken captive to Babylon (12:16). When the exiles who preceded them to Babylon see the wickedness of these people, they will have to agree that the Lord was righteous in His judgments (Jer. 22:8-9). The hearts of these survivors must have been incurably sinful if they could watch the siege, see thousands die, be spared themselves, and still not repent and turn to the Lord. Indeed, their eyes were blind, their ears were deaf, and they were a stubborn and rebellious people.

CHAPTER FIVE
PICTURES OF FAILURE
Ezekiel 15–17

The Prophet Ezekiel remained silent except when the word of the Lord came to him and God permitted him to speak (3:25-27). The three messages recorded in these chapters were given to the elders who were seated before him in his own house, men who outwardly appeared interested in hearing God's Word but inwardly were idolatrous (14:1-3). The Lord knew that neither the elders nor the people took Ezekiel's messages seriously because they saw him as a "religious entertainer" whose words were only "beautiful music" (33:30-33). Whenever God's people turn from His Word and become satisfied with substitutes, they are indeed headed for failure.

Because the people who heard him were spiritually blind and deaf, Ezekiel had to hold their attention, arouse their interest, and motivate them to think about God's truth. One way he did this was through his "action sermons," and another way was by means of sermons filled with vivid and arresting vocabulary and intriguing imagery. In these three messages, Ezekiel spoke about a vine, an unfaithful wife, and three shoots from a tree, and each of these images conveyed God's truth to those who really wanted to understand. These pictures and parables not only described the sins of the nation of Israel, but they also declared her terrible judgment. Ezekiel spoke to his people in the most vivid language found anywhere in Scripture, but the messages fell on deaf ears.

One more fact should be noted: these three "parables" answered the complaints of the people that God had rejected His people and was breaking His own covenant. False prophets in both Jerusalem and Babylon were building up the confidence of the people by telling them that the Lord would never allow Jerusalem and the temple to fall into the defiled hands of the Gentiles (Jer. 29:20-32). After all, Israel was Jehovah's special vine, planted by Him in the Promised Land. The nation was married to Jehovah in a divine covenant, and He would never divorce her. But even more, didn't the Lord promise David an endless dynasty? (2 Sam. 7) The Davidic dynasty was like a tall sturdy cedar tree that could never be felled by the Gentiles. Ezekiel used these same three images to teach the nation that the Lord was judging His people because He did have these special relationships to them! Privilege brings responsibility, and responsibility brings accountability.

1. The worthless vine (Ezek. 15:1-8)

The vine is an image found frequently in Scripture. Jesus compared Himself to a vine and His disciples to branches in the vine, because we depend wholly on Him for life and fruitfulness (John 15). Without Him, we can do nothing. Revelation 14:17-20 speaks of "the vine of the earth," a symbol of corrupt Gentile society at the end of the age, ripening for judgment in the winepress of God's wrath. But the image of the vine is often applied to the nation of Israel (Ps. 80; Isa. 5:1-7; Jer. 2:21; Matt. 21:28-46; Luke 20:9-19). In fact, Ezekiel will bring the image of the vine into his parable about the "shoots" (Ezek. 17:6-8).

When you study the references listed above, you learn that Israel was a lowly vine when God planted her in the Promised Land, but by His blessing she increased and prospered. During the reign of David and the early years of Solomon, the vine was fragrant and fruitful, a witness to the Gentile nations of the blessing of the God of Israel. However, Solomon introduced idolatry into the nation, the kingdom divided, and the Jewish people began to bear "wild grapes" (Isa. 5:2) instead of fruit for God's glory. Subsequent kings, both of Israel and Judah, worshiped idols and engaged in the evil practices of the neighboring nations. God allowed the Gentiles to invade the land and eventually destroy Jerusalem and the temple (Ps. 80:12-13). The holy vineyard was defiled and devastated.

Ezekiel's contribution to the "vineyard story" is to point out the worthlessness of the vine if it doesn't bear fruit. If a tree becomes useless, you can at least cut it down and make something useful out of the wood; but what can you make out of the wood of a vine? You can't even carve a tent peg or a wall peg out of it! It's good for only one thing, and that's fuel for the fire. If the wood was useless *before* it was thrown into the fire, it's even more worthless *after* it's been singed and marred by the flames.

Ezekiel saw the nation's first taste of the fire in 605 B.C. when Nebuchadnezzar took the temple treasures to Babylon along with some of the best of the young men, including Daniel. In 597 B.C., there was a second deportation of exiles, Ezekiel among them, so the fire was growing hotter. The siege of Jerusalem began in 588 B.C. and the fire began to blaze; and in 586 B.C., the Babylonians destroyed Jerusalem and the temple and took thousands of Jewish captives to Babylon. The vine was burned at both ends and in the middle! The inhabitants of the holy city certainly went from the "fire" of invasion and assault to the literal fire of destruction. "Then they [the Babylonians] burned the house of God, and broke down the wall of Jerusalem, burned all its palaces with fire, and destroyed all its precious possessions" (2 Chron. 36:19, NKJV).

Those of us who are branches in Jesus Christ, the true vine, need to take this lesson to heart. If we fail to abide in Christ, we lose our spiritual power, wither, and fail to bear fruit for His glory. The fruitless branch is tossed aside and eventually burned (John 15:6). I don't think this burning means condemnation in the lake of fire, for no true believer can be condemned for sins for which Jesus died (John 6:37; 10:27-29; Rom. 8:1).[1] The image of the burning branch is that of a worthless life, a life useless to God. John Wesley, the founder of the Methodist church, prayed, "Lord, let me not live to be useless!"

2. The unfaithful wife (Ezek. 16:1-63)

This long chapter contains some of the most vivid language found anywhere in Scripture. It is addressed to the city of Jerusalem but refers to the entire nation. The chapter traces the spiritual history of the Jews from "birth" (God's call of Abraham) through "marriage" (God's covenant with the people), and up to their "spiritual prostitution" (idolatry)[2] and the sad consequences that followed (ruin and exile). The Lord takes His "wife" to court and bears witness of her unfaithfulness to Him. At the same time, the

Lord is replying to the complaints of the people that He had not kept His promises when He allowed the Babylonians to invade the land. God did keep His covenant; it was Israel who broke her marriage vow and also broke the heart of her Lord and invited His chastening (Ezek. 6:9). But as we read the chapter, we must see not only the dark background of Israel's wickedness but also the bright light of God's love and grace. "But where sin abounded, grace abounded much more" (Rom. 5:20, NKJV).

Israel experienced a great love (Ezek. 16:1-14). Israel is pictured here as an unwanted child—exposed, abandoned, and left to die, but was then rescued by the Lord and became His wife. Many Jews were excessively proud of their heritage and called the Gentiles "dogs," but the Lord reminded them that they had descended from the Amorites and the Hittites (see Gen. 10:15-16; Deut. 20:17), and that their great city of Jerusalem was once inhabited by the Jebusites (Josh. 15:63). It wasn't until the time of David that Jerusalem belonged to the Jews and became the capital of the nation (Josh. 10:5; 2 Sam. 5:6-10). For that matter, their esteemed ancestor Abraham was an idol-worshiping pagan when God graciously called him! (Josh. 24:2-3) So much for national pride.

The parents of the newborn child didn't even given her the humane treatment that every baby deserves. They didn't cut the umbilical cord, wash the child, rub her skin with salt,[3] or even wrap her in cloths ("swaddled," KJV) for her protection and to keep her limbs straight. Without pity or compassion, they threw her out into the open field and exposed her to the elements. The Lord passed by, saw the helpless baby, took pity on her, and saved her. By the power of His Word He gave her life, and this was wholly an act of divine grace. "The God of glory appeared to our father Abraham" (Acts 7:2, nkjv), not because Abraham earned it or deserved it, but because of God's great love and grace.

The baby grew and became a young woman ready for marriage. The KJV phrase "come to excellent ornaments" in Ezekiel 16:7 means "come to full maturity." But would any suitor want a young woman who was forsaken by her own parents? By now, Israel was enslaved in the land of Egypt, so the Lord would have to redeem her. He wanted her for Himself so He "passed by" again (vv. 6, 8) and claimed her for His own bride. When a suitor spread his garment over a marriageable girl, that meant they were engaged (Ruth 3:9). He did deliver them from bondage, and at Sinai He entered into a "marriage covenant" with the people of Israel. (See Deut. 32:1-14.)

Once again, the Lord cleansed her and clothed her with beautiful, expensive garments, fit for a queen. During the reign of King David and during Solomon's early years, Jerusalem was indeed a queenly city and Israel a prosperous kingdom. As long as Israel, Jehovah's wife, obeyed His Word and kept His covenant, He blessed her abundantly just as He promised. He gave her healthy children, fruitful flocks and herds, abundant harvests, and protection from disease, disaster, and invasion. There wasn't one word of the covenant that the Lord failed to keep, and the reputation of Israel spread far and wide. During Solomon's day, foreign rulers came to listen to him (1 Kings 10:1-10, 24-25).

Israel committed a great sin (Ezek. 16:15-34). When Israel became prosperous and famous, she forgot the Lord who gave her such great wealth and began to use God's generous gifts for worshiping idols (Hosea 2:8, 13-14; Deut. 6:10-12; 8:10-20). Like the ignorant heathen nations around her, she worshiped the creation rather than the Creator (Rom. 1:21-25) and abandoned her "husband" for false gods. She didn't simply occasionally commit adultery, as wicked as that is. She became a professional prostitute, but unlike other prostitutes, she sought out her lovers and paid them to sin with her! She took the very treasures and blessings that God generously gave to her and devoted them to the making and worshiping of idols—her jewels and garments, her food, and even her children (Ezek. 16:20-21)![4] Idolatry was Israel's besetting sin, and it wasn't cured until the nation was exiled for seventy years in Babylon.

But the nation practiced another kind of idolatry when she trusted other nations to protect and defend her rather than trusting the Lord Jehovah, her "husband" (vv. 23-34).[5] She not only borrowed the gods of other nations and abandoned the true God, but she hired the armies of other nations instead of believing that the Lord could care for her. King Solomon made treaties with other countries by marrying the daughters of their rulers, and this is what led him into idolatry (1 Kings 11). The Jews were especially tempted to turn to Egypt for help instead of confessing their sins and turning to the Lord (2 Chron. 7:14). The Jewish leaders used every means possible to secure the help of Egypt, all the while acting like a common prostitute (Ezek. 16:23-26). They also went after the Philistines, the Assyrians, and even the Babylonians! But none of these alliances succeeded, and the Northern Kingdom (Israel) was taken captive by the Assyrians in 722 B.C., and the Southern Kingdom (Judah) was conquered by the Babylonians.

Israel's pride and ingratitude prepared the way for her idolatry. She forgot how good the Lord had been to her and became more concerned with the gifts than the Giver. Moses had warned about these sins (Deut. 6:10-15) but they didn't heed the warning. Believers today who live for the world and depend on the world are committing "adultery" in a similar way (James 4:4-6). The Lord desires and deserves our full and complete devotion (2 Cor. 11:1-4; Rev. 2:4).

Israel suffered a great discipline (Ezek. 16:35-42). The Lord was very patient with His people and warned them that their sins would bring them ruin, but they persisted in rejecting His Word, persecuting His prophets, and practicing the abominable sins of their neighbors. Many of the Jewish people were now exiled in Babylon and those left behind in Judah had either been slain by the Babylonians or were hopelessly imprisoned in Jerusalem and waiting for the siege to end. But the Jews shouldn't have complained to the Lord that He wasn't treating them fairly. They knew the terms of His covenant (Deut. 28–29) and He had already warned them many times that judgment was coming (32:22-43; 2 Chron. 36:14-21).

Their punishments are described as those of a prostitute, an adulteress, and an idolater, because the nation had committed those very sins. According to the law, prostitutes were to be burned (Lev. 21:9; see Gen. 38:24), adulterers and adulteresses stoned (Lev. 20:10), idolaters killed by the sword, and their possessions burned (Deut. 13:12-18). God used the Babylonian army to inflict these same judgments on the people of Israel (Ezek. 16:40-41). Many Jews were slain by the sword, and the city of Jerusalem and the temple were looted and burned.

Ezekiel gives a graphic description of the judgment of Israel, the prostitute. First the Lord would announce the crimes (vv. 35-36). She "poured out her lust" on the heathen idols[6] and exposed her nakedness in worshiping them. She disobeyed God's law, made idols of her own, and even sacrificed her children to them. Then the Lord announced the sentence (vv. 37-42). He would call her lovers (the heathen nations) to be her executioners, and they would gather around her and see her nakedness! She would be publicly exposed as an adulteress and a harlot. The enemy army would strip the city of Jerusalem, even as a convicted harlot is stripped, and then destroy the city (Deut. 22:23-24). Like adulterers and adulteresses, the people would be killed by stones; like idolaters, they would be slain by the sword; and like prostitutes, they would be burned in the fire. The Jews knew all these laws and their penalties, yet they flagrantly defied the Lord and persisted in their abominations.

Having described their sins, the Lord then *defended His sentence* (Ezek. 16:43-52). He not only knew what they had done, but He saw in their hearts why they had done it. In answer to the complaints of the people, the Lord proved that they deserved exactly what had happened to them. His judgment was not impulsive; He had waited a long time and they had refused to repent.

First, the nation had forgotten what the Lord had done for them (v. 43), and this was the very sin that Moses warned them to avoid (Deut. 6:10ff). God remembered the devotion they manifested in the early days of their commitment, like a young bride loving her husband (Jer. 2:2), but they didn't remember all that the Lord had done for them. When we forget to be thankful, we're in danger of taking credit for our blessings and failing to give God the glory He deserves.

Second, they failed to understand the enormity of their sins (Ezek. 16:44-52). The Jewish people excelled in quoting proverbs and ancient sayings, although such pithy statements usually don't go deep enough to answer the need. "As is the mother, so is her daughter" is the feminine version of "Like father, like son." Another version might be, "The apple doesn't fall too far from the tree." In other words, the children inherit their parents' nature, so don't be surprised if they repeat their parents' sins. The Jewish nation came from the Amorites and the Hittites—worshipers of idols. Immorality and idolatry ran in the family, for Israel's "sisters," Samaria (the Northern Kingdom) and Sodom,[7] were famous for their godlessness.

However, since the Jews possessed the revelation of God's law and had enjoyed the blessing of God's goodness, their sins were far more heinous than those of their "sisters." If God judged Sodom and Gomorrah by sending burning sulfur on them, and if He permitted the Northern Kingdom to be captured by the Assyrians, then surely He would have to judge the people of Judah and Jerusalem if they didn't repent. But Judah and her leaders didn't take these other judgments to heart. To paraphrase verse 47, "You not only walked after their ways and imitated their abominations, but you went beyond them and sinned ever more than they did!"[8]

God names the sins of Sodom (Ezek. 16:48-50). The people were proud and haughty, overfed, idle, unconcerned about the poor and needy, and guilty of detestable acts, which probably refers to their homosexual lifestyle (Gen. 19). These were abominable sins of attitude and action, commission and omission; *and yet the people of Jerusalem and Judah were far guiltier than were the people of Sodom*! When you read the other prophets, especially Isaiah, Jeremiah, and Amos, you hear them naming the sins of the people of Judah and warning them that judgment was coming. The people of Judah were twice the sinners as the people in Samaria, and by comparison, the people of Judah made the citizens of Samaria and Sodom look righteous! What a terrible indictment against God's chosen people!

But is the church today any less guilty? Members of local churches commit the same sins we read about in the newspapers, but the news doesn't always get to the headlines. Congregations are being torn apart because of professed Christians who are involved in lawsuits, divorces, immorality, family feuds, crooked business deals, financial scandals, and a host of other activities that belong to the world. Is it any wonder that lost sinners pay little attention to our public ministry or our personal witness?

Israel will experience a great restoration (Ezek. 16:53-63). The phrase "bring again their captivity" means "restore their fortunes." The captives in Babylon would be restored, return to the land, and rebuild the temple. God's goodness in allowing this to happen would bring them to shame and repentance (Rom. 2:4). When you read the prayers of Ezra (Ezra 9), Daniel (Dan. 9), and the Levites who labored with Nehemiah (Neh. 9), you see that there was still a godly remnant that humbly sought the face of the Lord and confessed their sins.

However, it's likely that this restoration is reserved for the end times when Israel will see their Messiah, weep over their sins, and enter into His kingdom (Zech. 12:9–13:1). History records no restoration for Sodom and the cities of the plain that God destroyed, nor for the kingdom of Samaria that was conquered by Assyria in 722 B.C. Ezekiel writes about an "everlasting covenant" (Ezek. 16:60), which indicates that this prophecy will be fulfilled in the end times. (See Jer. 31:31-34; Isa. 59:21; 61:8.) Later in his book (Ezek. 37:15-28), Ezekiel will predict a reunion of Samaria (the Northern Kingdom) and Judah (the Southern Kingdom) under the kingship of the Messiah. The Lord makes it clear that this restoration and reunion will not be on the basis of the covenant made at Sinai but wholly because of His grace. The Jewish people broke that covenant and suffered for their disobedience, but nobody can be saved by keeping the law (Gal. 2:16, 21; Rom. 4:5). It is only through the redemption provided in Christ Jesus that sinners can be forgiven and received into the family of God (Eph. 2:8-10; Rom. 3:24).

There will come a time when God's people Israel will remember their sins and recognize God's goodness and grace on their behalf. Their mouths will be shut because of conviction (Ezek. 16:63; Rom. 3:19) and they will be saved. How can a holy God forgive the sins of rebels, Jews or Gentiles? Because of the atonement that He made on the cross when He gave His Son as a sacrifice for the sins of the world. "The Father sent the Son to be the Savior of the world" (1 John 4:14), and that included Israel. Christ not only died for the church (Eph. 5:25) and for the sins of the world (John 3:16), but He died for His people Israel (Isa. 53:8). One day, that New Covenant will bring to them the cleansing and forgiveness that only the blood of Christ can give.

3. The two eagles and three shoots (Ezek. 17:1-24)

From the images of a vine and a marriage, Ezekiel turned to the image of a great tree, two eagles, and three shoots. This message is called a "parable" or "riddle," which means a story with a deeper meaning, an allegory in which various objects refer to people and what they do. The Jewish people were fond of discussing the wise sayings of the ancients and were always seeking to discover deeper meanings (Ps. 78:1-3). Ezekiel hoped that his allegory would awaken his dull hearers and give them something to think about. Perhaps the truth would grip their hearts and change their outlook on what God was doing.

This allegory is about three kings ("shoots"), because the cedar tree represents the royal dynasty of David.[9] David's dynasty was very important, because through it God had promised to bring a Savior to His people and to the world (2 Sam. 7:16; Luke 1:32-33, 69). It was essential that a descendant of David sit on the throne so that the blessing of God's covenant with David might rest on the land. At that time, the kingdom of Judah was a vassal state of Babylon and King Nebuchadnezzar was in charge. He is the first "great eagle" (Ezek. 17:3). The second eagle (v. 7) is the ruler of Egypt, probably Pharaoh Hophra who promised to help Judah in her fight against the Babylonians (v. 17). The eagle is used as a symbol of a strong ruler who invades a land (Jer. 48:40; 49:22). Now, let's consider the three kings, who are represented by three shoots.

King Jehoiachin (Ezek. 17:3-4, 11-12). When Nebuchadnezzar swooped down on Judah in 597 B.C., he deposed King Jehoiachin and took him and his family and staff to Babylon. He also took the temple treasures and 10,000 officers, artisans, and soldiers (2 Kings 24:8-17). This fulfilled the prophecy Isaiah had spoken to King Hezekiah after the king had shown all his wealth to the Babylonian visitors (Isa. 39; 2 Kings 20:17). Jehoiachin was the highest shoot or branch in David's family tree and he was "planted" in Babylon. Jehoiachin had reigned only three months and ten days (2 Chron. 36:9). He's the king that Jeremiah called "Coniah" (Jer. 22:24, 28; 37:1) and Jeconiah in Matthew's genealogy of Jesus (Matt. 1:11-12). In Ezekiel 19:5-9, Jehoiachin is compared to a lion who would be caught and taken to Babylon. During his three months on the throne, instead of leading the people back to faith in the Lord, Jehoiachin did evil in the sight of the Lord. He died in Babylon.

King Zedekiah (Ezek. 17:5-10, 13-21). After deposing Jehoiachin, Nebuchadnezzar made Jehoiachin's uncle Mattaniah the new king and changed his name to Zedekiah. He was the youngest son of good King Josiah and Nebuchadnezzar "planted" him in Judah where he "grew" for eleven years. But instead of producing a tree, King Zedekiah produced a humble vine. It was Zedekiah who asked Jeremiah to pray for him and the people and who hid him and cared for him (Jer. 37–38).

Nebuchadnezzar was kind to Zedekiah and the king took an oath to obey and serve him. Had he faithfully kept this treaty, Zedekiah would have saved the city and the temple; instead he chose to break the covenant and turn to Egypt for help. The second eagle represents Pharaoh who tried to rescue the kingdom of Judah but failed. This foolish decision on the part of Zedekiah resulted in the uprooting and withering of the vine, and this was the end of the kingdom of Judah. Nebuchadnezzar would not tolerate his treachery in seeking Egypt as an ally, so he captured Zedekiah, killed his sons before his eyes, blinded him, and took him captive to Babylon, where he died (Ezek. 17:16; 2 Kings 24:17–25:7).

But Ezekiel made it clear that it wasn't only Nebuchadnezzar's covenant that Zedekiah broke. He had broken God's covenant; and it was God who punished him through Nebuchadnezzar. Zedekiah had sworn his oath in the name of the Lord (2 Chron. 36:11-14); therefore he was obligated to keep it. In looking to Egypt for help, Zedekiah turned a deaf ear to the warnings of Jeremiah (Jer. 38), and Isaiah had preached the same message over a century before (Isa. 31:1; 36:9). It was the Lord who caught the king and his officers in His net and turned them over to the Babylonians (2 Kings 25:1-10; Jer. 52:1-11).

Messiah the King (Ezek. 17:22-24). Zedekiah had reigned for eleven years and was the twentieth and last king of Judah. His dethronement and death in Babylon seemed to mark the end of the Davidic line and therefore the failure of God's covenant with King David, but this was not the case. The Prophet Hosea predicted that the children of Israel would be "without a king, and without a prince" (Hosea 3:4), but the messianic line did not die out. After Babylon was conquered by the Medes and Persians, Cyrus allowed the Jews to return to their land, and one of their leaders was Zerubbabel, a great-great-grandson of godly King Josiah (1 Chron. 3:17-

19) and an ancestor of the Lord Jesus Christ (Matt. 1:11-16; Luke 3:27). Once again, a godly remnant stayed true to the Lord and the promised Messiah was born. The name "Zerubbabel" means "shoot of Babylon," but he helped to make possible the birth of the "shoot of David," Jesus Christ, the Savior of the world.

Jehoiachin had been a shoot plucked from the top of the cedar and taken to Babylon, but his descendants were rejected (Jer. 22:28-30), while Zedekiah was a shoot planted in Judah; but both of these men failed to please the Lord or do His will. Was there any hope left for the people of God? Yes. The Lord had promised to take a tender sprig "of the highest branch of the high cedar" (Ezek. 17:22) and plant it in the land of Israel where it would grow and become a great kingdom. This "shoot" is the Messiah, Jesus Christ, who came from the stem of Jesse and one day will establish His glorious kingdom on earth (Isa. 11:1-10; Jer. 23:5-6; 33:15-17; Zech. 6:12-13). The "high mountain" Ezekiel wrote about is probably Mount Zion, where Messiah will reign over His people. The small "shoot" will grow into a mighty tree and provide shelter (see Dan. 4:17, 32-37).

But in order for the "shoot" to be planted, take root, and grow, the other "trees" (kingdoms) will have to be removed. Some of them will be cut down and others will just wither. The kingdoms of men seem large and powerful today, and the kingdom of the Lord seems small and withering, but when Jesus returns to earth to reign, the tables will be turned. This is why we must never be afraid or discouraged when we survey the world scene. Jesus came as "a root out of a dry ground" (Isa. 53:1-2), an insignificant shoot from David's family tree, but one day His kingdom will fill the earth. Never stop praying, "Thy kingdom come" for that prayer will be answered. The fulfillment of God's kingdom promises to David (2 Sam. 7) is in Jesus Christ (Luke 1:26-55, 67-80), and He shall not fail.

It was a dark day for the people of Israel, but when the day is the darkest, the Lord's promises shine the brightest. God's people today need to take heed to this prophetic Word, which is a light that shines in our dark world (2 Peter 1:19). Just as Jesus fulfilled prophecy and came the first time to die for the sins of the world, so He will the second time and reign over His righteous kingdom. The tender "shoot" of David will be the mighty monarch, the King of kings and Lord of lords!

CHAPTER SIX
GOD IS JUST!
Ezekiel 18–21

Responsibility is one of the major themes of these four chapters. The Jewish exiles in Babylon were blaming their ancestors for the terrible judgment that had befallen them, so Ezekiel explained that God judges people individually for their own sins and not for somebody else's sins (chap. 18). He then pointed out that the Jewish leaders were responsible for the foolish decisions they had made (chap. 19), and that the nation itself had a long history of irresponsibility (chap. 20). Finally, the prophet reminded his listeners that the Lord Jehovah also had a responsibility to be faithful to Himself and His covenant with the Jews, and this was why He had chastened them (chap. 21). By dealing with the subject of personal and national responsibility, Ezekiel was able to answer the frequent complaints of the people that the Lord was treating them unfairly.

Responsibility and accountability are needed themes in our own day. Irresponsibility is rampant and very few people are willing to take the blame for wrongs committed or mistakes made. In his *Devil's Dictionary*, the cynical Ambrose Bierce defined responsibility as "a detachable burden easily shifted to the shoulders of God, Fate, Fortune, luck, or one's neighbor." After our first parents sinned, Adam blamed Eve and Eve blamed the serpent, but God still held Adam and Eve responsible for their disobedience and punished them accordingly. The Jews in Ezekiel's day were sure that God would deliver them and spare Jerusalem because Israel was God's chosen people, but they forgot that privilege always brings responsibility. They had the greatest law ever given to a nation, but they disobeyed it. The Lord gave them a wonderful land for their home, and they defiled it with idolatry. They violated the terms of the divine covenant and then were shocked when the Lord obeyed the covenant and chastened them.

1. Individual responsibility (Ezek. 18:1-32)

As you read this chapter, you find the prophet answering the erroneous statements the Jewish exiles were making about God and their difficult situation (vv. 2, 19, 25, 29). God knew what His people were saying and so did His prophet. Ignoring the inspired Word of God, the people were building their case on a popular proverb: "The fathers have eaten sour grapes, and the children's teeth are set on edge." In other words, "Our fathers have sinned and we, their children, are being punished for it." Their philosophy was a kind of irresponsible fatalism. "No matter what we do," they argued, "we still have to suffer because of what the older generation did." The Prophet Jeremiah quoted the same familiar proverb and preached the same truth that Ezekiel preached: God deals with us as individuals and punishes each of us justly for what we do (Jer. 31:29-30). He is a just and righteous God who shows no partiality (Deut. 10:17; 32:4). If He withholds punishment, it's only because of His grace and merciful long-suffering.

Where did Ezekiel's listeners get the idea that God punished the children for the sins of their fathers? This philosophy came from two sources: (1) a misinterpretation of what the Lord had said in His law, that He visited the sins of the fathers upon the children (Ex. 20:5; 34:6-7; Num. 14:18; Deut. 7:9-10), and (2) the Jewish idea of the oneness of the nation. According to the Law of Moses, innocent animals could suffer and die for guilty sinners, but nowhere was it taught that innocent people should be punished for sins committed by guilty people. In fact, Moses taught just the opposite: "The fathers shall not be put to death for their children, nor shall the children be put to death for their fathers; a person shall be put to death for his own sin" (Deut. 24:16, NKJV).[1] The warning in Exodus 20:5 and 34:6-7 implies that the Lord punishes the children *if they commit the sins their fathers committed.* Furthermore, God also promised to bless those children who followed godly examples and obeyed the Lord (20:6; Deut. 7:9-10), so He gave promises of blessing as well as warnings of chastening.

As for the solidarity of the nation, the Jewish people did consider themselves one people who descended from Abraham. Since each tribe descended from one of the sons of Jacob, Israel claimed both national and tribal solidarity. If only one Israelite disobeyed the Lord, it was as though all Israel had sinned, as in the case of Achan (Josh. 7:1, 11; and see Josh. 22, especially vv. 18-20). Knowing this fact, the Jewish people concluded that the Babylonian invasion and the nation's exile were the consequences of the sins of the previous generation.

Ezekiel answered the people's objections and explained the truth about God's judgment and justice by sharing some hypothetical situations and drawing some conclusions.

You cannot blame your ancestors (Ezek. 18:5-18). The prophet refutes the proverb by imagining a situation involving three men in a family, people with whom his listeners certainly could identify. He began with *a righteous father* (vv. 5-9), a hypothetical Jew who kept God's law and therefore was just and would not die because of sin (vv. 4, 9). Death is frequently mentioned in this chapter (vv. 4, 13, 17-18, 20-21, 23-24, 26, 28, 32) and refers to physical death and not necessarily eternal punishment, although any Jew who didn't exercise saving faith in the Lord would not be accepted by Him. Whether people lived under the Old Covenant or the New Covenant, before or since the cross, the way of salvation is the same: faith in the Lord that is evidenced by a new life of obedience (Heb. 11:6; Hab. 2:4; see Rom. 4).

In describing this man, Ezekiel named eight negative offenses along with eight positive virtues. The negative sins this man avoids are: attending idol feasts in the "high places" and worshiping idols in his own land, committing adultery, incurring ritual uncleanness (Ezek. 18:6), exploiting people and using violence to rob people (v. 7), lending money with interest and demanding a profit (v. 8). The eight positive virtues are: returning a debtor's pledge, feeding the hungry and clothing the naked (v. 7), living justly and promoting justice (v. 8), living by God's statutes and obeying His ordinances, and living with integrity (v. 9). These offenses and virtues are mentioned in the Law of Moses,[2] but the man acted as he did because he loved God and had "a new heart and a new spirit" within him (v. 31). He put God first in his life, treated people with kindness and mercy, and used his material wealth to honor God and serve others. As evidence of his faith in

Jehovah, he obeyed the two great commandments of the law, to love the Lord and to love his neighbor (Matt. 22:34-40)

This righteous father had an unrighteous son (Ezek. 18:10-13), about whom Ezekiel had nothing good to say. He listed ten offenses against God's law, three of them capital crimes: murder (vv. 12, 14), idolatry (vv. 11-12), and adultery (v. 11). This godless son exploited the poor and took interest from his debtors. He never returned the debtor's pledge (Ex. 22:26; Deut. 24:12-13) and did all he could to make a profit, even if it meant hurting people and defying God's laws. The verdict is clear: "he shall surely die."

The third character in this drama was a righteous grandson (Ezek. 18:14-18). How strange that the godly man of verses 5-9 should raise an ungodly son who himself had a godly son! The grandson followed the righteous example of his grandfather and not the evil example of his father. King Hezekiah was a godly father whose son Manasseh was evil, although late in life he did repent. Manasseh's son Amon was evil, but he fathered godly King Josiah! (See Matt. 1:10-11.) The ways of the Lord are sometimes strange, and "where sin abounded, grace abounded much more" (Rom. 5:20, NIV).

Twelve godly character traits are mentioned about this third man. The four that are lacking are ritual cleanness (Ezek. 18:6), living justly and promoting justice (vv. 12-13), and acting with integrity (v. 9). This doesn't mean that the man was actually guilty of these sins, because the first list doesn't mention every possible law in the Mosaic code. The point is that the third man, the grandson, resisted the bad influence in the home and obeyed the Lord in spite of his father's bad example. The Lord didn't kill the grandson because of his father's sins or even spare him because of his grandfather's righteousness, but dealt with the man on the basis his own faith and righteousness.

You can blame yourselves (Ezek. 18:19-24). In this part of his message, Ezekiel responded to the questions of his hearers given in verse 19, just as he had responded to their question in verse 2. He described a wicked man who repented, turned from his sins, and lived (vv. 19-23), and then described a righteous man who returned to his sins and died (v. 24). The lesson from these two examples is obvious and answered their questions: *people determine their own character and destiny by the decisions that they make.* Neither the exiles in Babylon nor the citizens in Jerusalem were the prisoners and victims of some cosmic determinism that forced them to act as they did. Their own unbelief (they rejected Jeremiah's message) and disobedience (they worshiped heathen idols and defiled the temple) brought the Babylonian army to their gates; and Zedekiah's breaking of the covenant with Nebuchadnezzar brought the army back to destroy Jerusalem.

Ezekiel was giving the Jewish nation a message of hope! If they would truly repent and turn to the Lord, He would work on their behalf as He promised (1 Kings 8:46-53; Jer. 29:10-14). However, if they persisted in sinning, the Lord would continue to deal with them as rebellious children. God has no delight in the death of the wicked (Ezek. 18:23, 32; see 1 Tim. 2:4; 2 Peter 3:9), but He isn't obligated to invade their minds and hearts and force them to obey Him.

In Ezekiel 18:24, Ezekiel isn't dealing with what theologians call "the security of the believer," because the issue is physical life or death, as stated in God's covenant (Deut. 30:15-20; Jer. 21:8). The righteous man who adopted a sinful lifestyle[3] in defiance of God's law would suffer for that decision. It wasn't possible for the Jews to "accumulate points" with God and then lose a few of them when they sinned. People have the idea that God measures our good works against our bad works, and deals with us according to whichever is the greater. But from Adam to the end of time, people are saved only by faith in what God revealed to them, and their faith is demonstrated in a consistently godly life.

You cannot blame the Lord (Ezek. 18:25-32). For the third time, Ezekiel quoted the words of the complaining exiles, "The way of the Lord is not equal" (v. 25, see vv. 2, 19). The word "equal" means "fair." They were saying that God wasn't "playing fair" with His people. But Ezekiel pointed out that it was the people who weren't being fair with God! When they obeyed the Lord, they wanted Him to keep the terms of the covenant that promised blessing, but when they disobeyed, they didn't want Him to keep the terms of the covenant that brought chastening. They wanted God to act contrary to His own Word and His own holy nature.

"God is light" (1 John 1:5), which means He is holy and just, and "God is love" (4:8, 16), and His love is a holy love. Nowhere does

Scripture say that we're saved from our sins by God's love, because salvation is by the grace of God (Eph. 2:8-10); and grace is love that pays a price. In His great love, God gave a gracious covenant to Israel, requiring only that they worship and serve Him alone with all their hearts. When sinners repented and sought the Lord, in His grace the Lord would forgive them; but when people deliberately rebelled against Him, in His holiness, God would punish them after bearing with them in His long-suffering. What could be fairer than that! For that matter, if God did what was fair, He would consign the whole world into hell!

The conclusion of this message was an invitation from the Lord for the people to repent (change their minds), turn from their sins, cast away their transgressions like filthy garments, and seek a new heart and a new spirit. God promised them a new heart if only they would seek Him by faith (Ezek. 11:19; see 36:26). This was one of the key themes in the letter Jeremiah had sent to the captives in Babylon (Jer. 29:10-14), but the people hadn't taken it to heart. God made it clear that He found no delight in the death of the wicked (Ezek. 18:23, 32), but if the wicked found delight in their sinful ways and would not repent, there was nothing the Lord could do but obey His own covenant and punish them. Ezekiel will develop this theme further in chapter 21.

2. Leadership responsibility (Ezek. 19:1-14)

Ezekiel had made it clear that individual Jews were responsible for their own sins, but it was also true that their leaders had led them astray because they had rebelled against God. Jeremiah had told the kings of Judah to surrender to Nebuchadnezzar because he was God's chosen servant to chasten Israel, but they had refused to obey. Zedekiah, Judah's last king, had agreed to a treaty with Nebuchadnezzar but then had broken it and sought help from Egypt. It was this foolish act that moved Nebuchadnezzar to send his army to Jerusalem and destroy the city and the temple.

Whether you read secular or sacred history, you soon discover that people become like their leaders. The same people who applauded Solomon when he built the temple also applauded Jeroboam when he set up the golden calves and instituted a new religion. One of the hardest tasks of Christian leaders today is to keep our churches true to the Word of God so that people don't follow every religious celebrity whose ideas run contrary to Scripture. It appears that being popular and being "successful" are more important today than being faithful.

In discussing the sins of the leaders, Ezekiel used two familiar images—the lion (vv. 1-9) and the vine (vv. 10-14)—and he couched his message in the form of a funeral dirge for "the princes of Israel." David's exalted dynasty had come to an end, but the men holding the scepter were nothing like David. Ezekiel wouldn't even call them "kings" but instead referred to them as "princes" (v. 1; see 7:27; 12:10, 12). Instead of lamenting their demise, the "funeral dirge" actually ridiculed the rulers of Israel; but later (21:27) Ezekiel would announce the coming of Messiah, the Son of David, who would be a worthy king.

Israel is like a lioness (Ezek. 19:1-9). The lioness represents the nation of Israel, or at least the royal tribe of Judah (Gen. 49:9; Num. 23:23; 24:9; 1 Kings 10:18-20; Micah 5:8). The first royal "whelp" was Jehoahaz, who reigned over Judah for only three months (Ezek. 19:2-4; 2 Kings 23:31-35). He was also known as "Shallum" (Jer. 22:10-12). Pharaoh Neco took him captive to Egypt where he died. The second royal "whelp" was Jehoiachin, who reigned three months and ten days (Ezek. 19:5-9; 2 Kings 24:8-16; 2 Chron. 36:9-10). Ezekiel describes him "strutting" and "roaring" (Ezek. 19:6-7) among the princes and the nations. Nebuchadnezzar took him to Babylon along with 10,000 captives and the temple treasures, and there he died. Jehoiachin turned a deaf ear to the preaching of Jeremiah, and the prophet didn't have anything good to say about him (Jer. 22:18-19). In this brief parable, the Lord made it clear that these two kings of Judah thought themselves to be great leaders, but they ignored the Word of God and He cut them down after their brief reigns.

Israel is like a vine (Ezek. 19:10-14). This is a familiar image in Scripture (Gen. 49:9-12;[4] Isa. 5; Ps. 80:8-13; Jer. 2:21) and in Ezekiel's prophecy (chap. 15; 17:1-10). The fruitful vine produced many kings who rebelled against God and was punished by being transplanted to Babylon, from "many waters" to a "desert" (Jer. 31:27-28). The last king of Judah, Zedekiah, broke his treaty with Babylon, rebelled against Nebuchadnezzar, and lost the scepter and the throne (2 Kings 24:17–25:7). With Zedekiah the Davidic dynasty ended, and he too died in captivity in Babylon (Jer. 52:11).

Had the nation of Israel obeyed the Lord, it would have become and remained a mighty lion and a fruitful vine that would have brought glory to the name of the Lord. Israel would have been a "light unto the Gentiles" (Isa. 42:6; 49:6) and many would have trusted in the true and living God. Israel didn't keep the terms of the covenant, but the Lord did; and that's why He chastened them and scattered them. God's chosen people have no temple, priesthood, sacrifice, or king (Hosea 3:4-5). Jesus Christ, Israel's Messiah, came as the lion of the tribe of Judah (Rev. 5:5) and the true vine (John 15:1), "a light to bring revelation to the Gentiles" (Luke 2:32), and the rightful heir to the throne of David (Luke 1:68-69), and His own people rejected Him. One day they shall see Him and receive Him, and God's gracious covenant with David will be completely fulfilled (2 Sam. 7) when Jesus reigns in His kingdom (Ezek. 34:23-24; 37:24-25; Matt. 1:1).

3. National responsibility (Ezek. 20:1-44)

Ezekiel delivered this message on August 14, 591 B.C., to some of the Jewish elders who came to his house to "inquire of the Lord." But the prophet knew that their hearts were not right with God and that they had no right to ask the Lord for instruction (vv. 30-32; see 14:1-3; 33:30-33).[5] A willingness to submit and obey is the mark of the person who can seek God's guidance and expect to receive it. Ezekiel's response to their request was to review the history of the nation of Israel and point out the repeated rebellion of the people and the gracious long-suffering of the Lord.

The American editor and writer Norman Cousins wrote in a *Saturday Review* editorial (April 15, 1978), "History is a vast early warning system." But some anonymous thinker has said, "The one thing we learn from history is that we don't learn from history"; or in the words of Dr. Laurence J. Peter, "History teaches us the mistakes we are going to make."[6] The Jewish historians, prophets, and psalmists were honest enough to declare the sins of the nation and write them down for future generations to read! Why? So that future generations wouldn't make the same mistakes that they made. But, alas, God's people haven't begun to learn the lessons, let alone obey them.

Scripture teaches that God is working out His plan for the nations (Acts 14:14-18; 17:22-31; Dan. 5:21; 7:27) and that His people Israel are at the heart of that plan. Other nations are mentioned in Scripture primarily as they relate to Israel, for Israel is the only nation with whom God has entered into covenant relationship. At Sinai, after Israel left Egypt, God gave them His law (Ex. 19–24); and before they entered the Promised Land, He reaffirmed that law and gave them the terms of the covenant they had to obey in order to possess and enjoy the land (Deut. 5–8; 27–30). It was because they violated the terms of the covenants that Israel suffered as she did.

Before we review the history of Israel and the lessons we can learn from it, we must deal with an important matter of interpretation. In chapter 18, Ezekiel taught that the children were not punished for the sins of the fathers, but in this chapter, he seems to say that the past sins of the nation (carefully documented) were the cause of Israel's failure and the Babylonian invasion. "Will you judge them, son of man, will you judge them? Then make known to them the abominations of their fathers" (20:4, NKJV). This statement from the Lord suggests that God was judging the Jews because of what their fathers had done.

But that wasn't what the Lord was saying to Ezekiel. By reviewing the history of the nation, God was judging that current generation *because they were guilty of the same sins of unbelief and rebellion.* Jeremiah said that his generation of Jews was *even worse than their fathers*! (Jer. 16:12) In this historical summary, God proved that He had been consistent in His dealings with the Jews. The exiles had complained that God had not treated Israel fairly (Ezek. 18:2, 19, 25, 29), but their national history proved that God was not only fair with them but also very long-suffering and merciful. God wasn't punishing the Jews in Ezekiel's day because of the sins their fathers committed centuries before but because Ezekiel's contemporaries had committed the very same sins! That's why God reviewed the history of Israel.

Israel in Egypt (Ezek. 20:5-8). God "chose" the nation of Israel when He called Abraham to leave Ur of the Chaldees and go to the land of Canaan (Gen. 12), but the nation didn't even exist at that time. God built the nation in the land of Egypt. When Jacob's family entered into Egypt, they numbered 66 people; Joseph's family was already in Egypt and they brought the total to 70 (Gen. 46). But when the Jews left Egypt at the Exodus, the fighting men alone numbered over 600,000 (Num. 1:46), so there may well have been over two million people in the nation. In Egypt, God revealed Himself to the Jews through the ministry of Moses and Aaron as well as through the terrible judgments He inflicted on the land of Egypt. He made it clear that the gods of the Gentile nations were only myths and had no power to do either good or evil. God reminded them how He had judged these false gods in Egypt and proved them to be helpless nothings. (See Ex. 12:12; Num. 33:4.)

However, while living in Egypt, the Jews began secretly to worship the gods of the Egyptians. After all, if the Egyptians were masters over the Jews, then the gods of Egypt must be stronger than the God of Israel! The Jews defiled themselves with the gods of Egypt and grieved the heart of God. When God opened the way for Israel to leave Egypt, some of the Jews took their Egyptian gods with them! God had sworn by an oath ("lifted up my hand")[7] that He was Israel's God (v. 5) and that He would set them free and give them the Promised Land (v. 6). The true God set them free, but they carried false gods with them! The nation rebelled against God even after He demonstrated His grace and power in delivering them!

Israel's exodus from Egypt (Ezek. 20:9-10). The Lord had every reason to pour out His wrath on Israel, but for His name's sake, He rescued His people. God often worked on Israel's behalf, not because they deserved it but for the glory of His own name (vv. 14, 22, 44; see Isa. 48:9; 66:5), just as He has saved His church today "to the praise of His glory" (Eph. 1:6, 12, 14). The account of the Exodus did go before the Jews as they marched toward the Promised Land (Josh. 2:10), and it did bring glory to God's name.

Israel at Sinai (Ezek. 20:11-12). Israel tarried about two years at Sinai where God revealed His glory and gave them His laws. While they tarried there, Moses directed the construction of the tabernacle and its furniture. But even after seeing God's glory and hearing His voice, Israel rebelled against Him by making and worshiping a golden calf (Ex. 32). God gave them the Sabbath day (the seventh day of the week) as a sign to remind them that they belonged to Him. By setting aside that one day each week to honor the Lord, Israel witnessed to the other peoples that they were a special nation, but they persisted in polluting the Sabbath and treating it like any other day (vv. 13, 16, 20).

The law that God gave Israel at Sinai consisted of statutes and ordinances governing every area of life: their civic responsibilities, the maintaining of courts and judges, the punishment of offenders, and the responsibilities of the people and their priests in the religious life of the nation. But because Israel was a theocracy and God was their King, every law had its religious implications. To break the law was to sin against the Lord, and the people did it frequently.

Those who obeyed God's law would "live" (Ezek. 19:11, 13, 21), an important word we considered in chapter 18 (vv. 9, 17, 19, 21, 28). It refers to physical life, not being subject to capital punishment because of deliberate disobedience to God's statutes. But for the Jew who loved the Lord, trusted Him, and obeyed Him, it included the spiritual life that comes to all who believe. Romans 10:5 and Galatians 3:12 make it clear that nobody is saved simply by obeying the law; but those who trust the Lord will prove their faith by their obedience. Religious people like the Pharisees have a "law righteousness," but those who trust Christ have a "faith righteousness" that enables them to obey God's will (Phil. 3:1-16; Rom. 10). Salvation is always by faith (Heb. 11:6) and this faith always issues in good works and obedience.

Israel in the wilderness (Ezek. 20:13-26). After leaving Sinai, the Jews marched to Kadesh Barnea where the Lord told them to enter Canaan and claim their promised inheritance (Num. 13–14). He had already searched out the land (Ezek. 19:6), but the people insisted on sending in a representative from each of the twelve tribes to scout out the land. They searched the land for forty days, and all of the men agreed that the land was exactly as God described it; but ten of the spies said that God wasn't great enough to enable Israel to conquer it! This led to God's judgment that the nation would wander in the wilderness for forty years and that everyone twenty years old and older would die during that time (Num. 14). You would have thought that the Jews had learned their lesson by now, but even during the wilderness wandering, they rebelled against God and He had to punish them. Once again, it was for the glory of His name that He didn't destroy them and start a new nation with Moses as the father (vv. 11-21). At the end of the forty years, Moses prepared the new generation to enter the land by reviewing the law and the covenants, as recorded in Deuteronomy.

Israel in the Promised Land (Ezek. 20:27-30). Joshua brought the people into Canaan and led them in the defeat of the enemy and the claiming of the land. Before he died, he directed the assigning of the land to the various tribes, and encouraged them to claim their land. Moses had commanded the people to wipe out the godless religion of the inhabitants of the land (Ex. 34:11-17; Deut. 7), and warned them that if they failed to obey, their children would become idolaters and lose the Promised Land. Of course, that's exactly what happened. The people lusted after the gods of the land and participated in the filthy rites of heathen worship in the high places (Ezek. 19:28-29; see Deut. 18:9-14; Lev. 18:26-30).[8] Instead of winning the Canaanites to faith in the true and living God, the Jewish people began to live like their enemies and worship their gods! They even offered their children as sacrifices to the pagan gods (Ezek. 19:26, 31), something that was expressly forbidden in the Law of Moses (2 Kings 21:6; 2 Chron. 28:3; Lev. 18:21; Deut. 12:31; 18:10). Children are a gift from God, and His precious gifts must not be used as heathen sacrifices!

Israel in exile in Babylon (Ezek. 20:31-32). This is the practical application of the message to the people of Ezekiel's generation: they were living just like their fathers! "Even unto this day" they were sinning against the Lord! Ignoring their privilege of being God's special people (Num. 23:9), their fathers wanted to be like the pagan nations in their worship and in their leadership (1 Sam. 8:5); and God let them have their way and then punished them. "When in Babylon, do as the Babylonians do" was the philosophy of the exiles, but they had been idolaters long before they went into exile.

Israel's future kingdom (Ezek. 20:33-44). Ezekiel had made it very clear to the elders why they weren't qualified to inquire of God, but he didn't end his message there. God in His grace gave him a message of hope for the people, though they certainly didn't deserve it. Ezekiel described a future "exodus" of the Jewish people from the nations of the world, a return to their own land which God swore to give them. He even used the same descriptive phrase Moses used when he spoke about the Exodus—"a mighty hand . . . an outstretched arm" (vv. 33-34; Deut. 4:34; 5:15; 7:19; 11:2). The "I will" statements of the Lord reveal both His mercy and His power.

"I will bring you out" (Ezek. 20:34) implies much more than the release of the exiles from Babylon. It speaks of a future regathering of Israel from the nations of the world to which they have been scattered (Deut. 30:1-8). God promises to bring them out, but He also says He will "bring them into the wilderness" (Ezek. 20:35-36) where He will deal with their sins and cleanse them of their rebellion (36:24-25; Hosea 2:14-15). His next promise is "I will bring you into the bond of the covenant" (Ezek. 20:37), teaching that Israel will be restored to her covenant relationship to the Lord and will experience the blessings of the New Covenant (18:31; 36:26-27). "I will purge out the rebels" (20:38) and they will not be allowed to enter the land of Israel and enjoy the blessings of the messianic kingdom.

As for the true believers who receive their Messiah, God declares, "I will accept them" (v. 40). God will establish a sanctified nation that will worship Him in holiness (v. 41). As the result of this New Covenant and new spiritual experience in their hearts, the people will come to know their God (v. 42) as well as know themselves and loathe themselves for the terrible sins they have committed (v. 43). No longer will they blame their fathers! They will come to know the grace of God, for all the blessing He showers on the nation will be for His name's sake and not because of any merit on their part (v. 44).

The experiences described in verses 33-44 cannot be applied to the return of the Jewish exiles to the land of Judah in 538 B.C. This was not an exodus from many countries nor did it result in the glorious restoration of the Jewish nation. We have to apply this paragraph to that time in the future that Ezekiel describes in chapters 33 to 48, when Christ will return and the promised kingdom will be established.

4. Divine responsibility (Ezek. 20:45–21:32)

In the Hebrew Scriptures, chapter 21 begins with 20:45, and this is the best arrangement, for 20:45-49 introduces the coming judgment on Judah and Jerusalem.[9] Ezekiel has explained the individual responsibility of the people and their leaders and the national responsibility of Israel. Now he focuses on the fact that God has a responsibility to punish His people when they rebel against Him. He must be true to His character and true to His covenant.

God identifies the target (Ezek. 20:45-49). Frequently in this book, God commanded His servant to "set his face" against something or someone (v. 46; 13:17; 21:2; 25:2; 28:21; 29:2; 35:2; 38:2). This was one way to point out the "target" at which His judgment would be hurled, in this case, Judah and Jerusalem (21:1-2). The prophet assumed a posture of stern judgment as he announced that threatened judgment was about to fall against "the south" (the Negev), and Judah and Jerusalem were in the territory south of Babylon. Using the image of a forest fire, he described the invasion of the Babylonians and the destruction of the Jewish nation. When you study chapter 21, you learn that the fire represents the deadly swords of the soldiers and that the "south" represents Judah and Jerusalem. According to Ezekiel 20:1, it was the year 591 B.C. when he gave these messages, so in five years, the Babylonians would set fire to the holy city and the temple. During Israel's wilderness wanderings, God didn't severely punish His people for their rebellion because He wanted to honor His name before the Gentiles (20:14, 22, 44); but now He would honor His name by burning their city and temple and sending them into exile.

God draws the sword (Ezek. 21:1-7). The word "sword" is used nineteen times in this chapter to represent the invasion and attack of the Babylonian army. God has His eye on three targets: the land of Judah, the city of Jerusalem, and the holy place of the temple. Unfortunately, some of the righteous would suffer along with the wicked, but this is often the case in times of war. Note that God declared that it was "My sword," because it was He who summoned the Babylonian army to punish His sinful people. If His own people won't obey Him, at least the pagan nations will!

At this point, God commanded Ezekiel to perform another "action sermon" by groaning like a man experiencing great pain and grief. When the people asked him why he was groaning so, he would tell them, "Because of the bad news that is coming," referring to the news of the fall of Jerusalem. The news didn't come until January 8, 585 B.C. (33:21-22), five months after the city had been burned, which was August 14, 586 B.C.; but the Lord told Ezekiel that the news was coming. The exiles nurtured the false hope that the Lord would spare the city and the temple, but everything the Lord had prophesied would come to pass.

God sharpens His sword (Ezek. 21:8-17). In this second "action sermon," Ezekiel not only cried and wailed (v. 12), but he smote his thigh and clapped his hands together (vv. 14, 17). It's possible that he was also brandishing a sword as he spoke, although the text doesn't state this. The Lord was preparing the Babylonian army to be effective and efficient in carrying out His plans. Despising the king of Judah (v. 13), the sword of Babylon would turn Judah's scepter into nothing but a stick! (v. 10) The invading soldiers would be so effective that one swordsman would do the work of three (v. 14), and for the Jews there would be no escape (v. 16). Even the Lord would applaud the soldiers as they executed the judgment that He had ordained (v. 17). Perhaps some of the Jews recalled Ezekiel's previous "action sermon" using the sword (5:1-4).

God directs the army (Ezek. 21:18-27). The pagan nations of that day used many forms of divination to discern the will of the gods, and Ezekiel pictured the Babylonian army at a fork in the road, trying to discover which way to go. Should they go to Rabbath, the capital of Ammon, and attack the Ammonites; or should they go to Jerusalem to attack the Jews? When the Lord told Ezekiel to "mark [appoint] two ways," he probably sketched on the ground a map of the roads looking like an inverted Y, and at the juncture stuck a "signpost" into the ground. (Remember his plan of Jerusalem drawn on a wet clay brick—4:1-8?) It was God's will that the army attack Jerusalem, so He overruled the soothsayers and diviners and made sure their decision was for Jerusalem. This doesn't mean that their system of divining was accurate or even proper, but that the Lord used it to accomplish His purposes.[10]

Nebuchadnezzar decided to attack Jerusalem, so he appointed his captains and made his plans. The people in Jerusalem were hoping he would attack the Ammonites, and when the word came that Jerusalem was his target, they hoped the diviners would say they had made a mistake. But God was in control and there had been no mistake. King Zedekiah had sworn an oath of allegiance to Nebuchadnezzar and had broken it (21:23; 2 Kings 24:20), and Nebuchadnezzar would not stand for this kind of rebellion from a weak vassal state. Zedekiah's sins had finally caught up with him (Ezek. 21:24).

Ezekiel paused to give a special message to Zedekiah, whom he refuses to call a king but refers to as a prince. He calls him profane and wicked, a man who has committed iniquity and will suffer because of it. He would lose his crown and his throne. The day had arrived when God would turn everything upside down. Those who were "great and mighty" would be humbled, and those who were humble would be exalted. The word translated "overturn" ("ruin," NIV) is *awwa*, and we can just hear Ezekiel lamenting: "Awwa—awwa—awwa!"

But once again, the Lord added a brief word of hope: the Messiah would one day come, the true Son of David and Israel's King, and would claim the Davidic crown and reign over His people (v. 27). The phrase "whose right it is" takes us back to Genesis 49:8-12, a messianic promise that we met in Ezekiel 19 when we studied the images of the lion and the vine.

God completes the task (Ezek. 21:28-32). But what about the Ammonites? When the Lord directed the Babylonian army to Jerusalem, did this mean He would not judge the Ammonites for their sins against Him and the Jewish people? They would rejoice to see Babylon ravage the land of Judah and set fire to Jerusalem and the temple. (See Ezek. 25.) Along with Judah and the other nations, Ammon had joined the alliance against Babylon (Jer. 27:1ff), so Ammon had to be punished. Their own false prophets and diviners would give them a false hope that they had been spared (Ezek. 21:29), but God hadn't told Nebuchadnezzar to put his sword in its sheath (v. 30). The message closed with another fire (see 20:47-48), but this time a furnace in which ore was smelted. God would "blow" against the furnace and make it hotter, and then He would pour out the molten metal on His enemies. The Ammonites would become fuel for the fire and the nation would disappear from the earth.

We come away from the study of chapters 18 to 21 with a fresh realization of the tragedy of rebellion against the Lord. Israel had a long history of rebellion, but the other nations weren't any better, except that Israel was sinning against the light of God's Word and His providential care over His people. If any people had the obligation to obey and serve the Lord, it was Israel, for the Lord had blessed them abundantly. Instead of becoming a holy nation to the glory of God, she became like all the other nations and failed to be God's light to the Gentiles.

And yet, woven throughout this series of messages is the theme of Israel's hope. The prophet reminded them that God had promised to regather them from the Gentile nations and give them their King and their kingdom. Historically speaking, weak King Zedekiah was the last ruler in the Davidic dynasty, but not prophetically speaking; for Jesus Christ, the Son of David (Matt. 1:1) will one day come and reign from David's throne. Ezekiel will discuss that theme in detail before he completes his book.

Under "Query 18" in his *Notes on the State of Virginia*, Thomas Jefferson wrote, "Indeed I tremble for my country when I reflect that God is just."[11] Ezekiel has defended the justice of God and magnified the mercy and grace of God. What more could he do?

CHAPTER SEVEN
SEE THE SINFUL CITY!
Ezekiel 22–24

If you refer to the suggested outline of the Book of Ezekiel, you will see that these three chapters complete the second section of the book "The Fall of Jerusalem." Ezekiel focuses on four final events: the end of the city (chap. 22), the end of the kingdom (chap. 23), the end of a delusion (24:1-14), and the end of a marriage (vv. 15-27). Chapter 24 records two heart-rending announcements from the Lord: the beginning of the siege of Jerusalem (vv. 1-2) and the death of the prophet's wife (vv. 15-17). What a sobering way to climax Ezekiel's many messages to the spiritually blind Jewish exiles in Babylon!

1. The end of the city (Ezek. 22:1-31)

"David took the stronghold of Zion" (2 Sam. 5:7) and made Jerusalem his capital. Not only was the royal throne there but also the holy altar, for it was in Zion that God put His sanctuary. "For the Lord has chosen Zion; He has desired it for His habitation" (Ps. 132:13, NKJV). The Jews were proud of Mount Zion (Ps. 48) and claimed that the Lord loved Zion more than any other place (Ps. 87). But now the city of Jerusalem and the temple would be invaded by "unclean Gentiles" *who were brought there by the Lord*! Why would the Lord destroy His own beloved city and temple? Because His people had sinned and broken the covenant and they were beyond remedy. Ezekiel described the true character of the "beautiful city" and named some of the sins that the people in Jerusalem were committing even while he spoke. Ezekiel had exposed the past sins of the nation, but now he brought Jerusalem into the courtroom and brought the record up-to-date.

A defiled people (Ezek. 22:1-12). The words "blood" or "bloody" are repeated seven times in this paragraph and speak of death and defilement. The prophet named two grievous sins: the shedding of innocent blood (injustice) and the worship of foreign gods (see 7:23; 9:9). The officials in Jerusalem were accepting bribes and condemning innocent people to death so that others could claim their property (Amos 5:11-17; see 1 Kings 21). These judges had no respect for God or for man made in the image of God, and yet they were supposed to be honest men who upheld the law of the Lord (Ex. 18:21-26; Deut. 16:18-20). So evil was the judicial system in Jerusalem that the Gentile nations heard about it (Ezek. 22:4-5) and reproached the name of the Lord. Jerusalem was a "city infamous [defiled] and much vexed [full of confusion]" (v. 5).[1] But the time of their judgment was fast approaching. God had already declared the sentence but He had not yet begun the punishment. The princes had abused their power, but God would display His power.

Idolatry, injustice, and the abuse of power are rampant in our world today, and God in His mercy is holding back His hand of judgment to give sinners opportunity to repent and be saved. Divine truth and human rights are being ignored, but "the day of the Lord will come" (2 Peter 3:10) and sinners will be judged righteously by the all-knowing Lord.

Ezekiel named some of the sins that the people were committing, and he began with the abuse of people—parents, strangers and aliens, and orphans and widows (Ezek. 22:7). The Jews were commanded to honor their fathers and mothers (Ex. 20:12), and so are believers today (Eph. 6:1-3). God even attached a special promise to this commandment—"that your days may be long upon the land"—and now the Jews were about to be exiled from their land. The law also gave special consideration to widows, orphans, and aliens (Ex. 22:21-24; 23:9-11; Lev. 19:33-34; Jer. 5:28), and this commandment contained a warning. If these needy people were abused, the Jewish wives would become widows and the Jewish children would become orphans. Disobedience is a serious thing! The church today has a ministry obligation to strangers (Matt. 25:35, 43; James 2:1-13), widows, and orphans (James 1:27; 1 Tim. 5).

After dealing with the inhumanity of the people in Jerusalem, God condemned their idolatry (Ezek. 22:8). They defiled the temple with their idols (8:5ff) and by "worshiping God" hypocritically, not worshiping with clean hands and obedient hearts (Isa. 1:10ff). Jeremiah told them that they had turned God's house into "a den of robbers" (Jer. 7:11), a place where thieves run to hide after they've broken the law. The Jews also polluted the Sabbath by treating it like any other day. The Sabbath was a special sign between God and Israel that they were His special people (Ezek. 20:12-13, 20; Ex. 31:13-17), and to violate this law was to defy the Lord's authority and deny Israel's calling and ministry in the world.

But how could the people persist in these sins and not be judged by the courts? Because the courts were run by wicked men who had no desire to acquit the innocent or punish the guilty. The rich were set free and the poor were exploited. People accepted bribes and agreed to slander innocent people (Ezek. 22:9, 12), forgetting that the law prohibited slander and false witness (Ex. 20:16; 23:1-3, 6-8; Deut. 16:19; 27:25). According to the law, if someone were accused of a capital crime, at least two witnesses had to testify, and these witnesses would be the first to cast stones at the convicted guilty party (Num. 35:30-31; Deut. 17:6-7; 19:15).

In my years of pastoral experience, I have seen local churches torn apart by slander and false witness, in spite of the clear teaching in the New Testament about integrity in bearing witness (1 Tim. 5:19; Matt. 18:16; 2 Cor. 13:1). It's a sobering thought that liars as well as murderers will have a place in the lake of fire and will not enter the heavenly city (Rev. 21:8, 27).

In Ezekiel 22:9b-11, God targeted the immorality of the Jewish people, starting with their participation in the unspeakably filthy "worship" at the pagan shrines. The tragedy is that these idolatrous men brought their immorality home with them! Sons had intercourse with their own mothers or stepmothers, fathers with daughters-in-law, and brothers with sisters or halfsisters! (See Lev. 18:6ff; 20:10ff.) Men were committing adultery with a neighbor's wife or with women having their monthly period (Ezek. 18:6; Lev. 18:19; 20:18).

How easy it is for us today to pass judgment on God's ancient people, but what about God's contemporary people? Sexual sins in the church and in so-called Christian homes have ripped churches and families apart, and many churches close their eyes to these offenses. Pornography—in print, on video, and on the Internet—is a common thing these days, and it's getting more and more daring on television. Unmarried people living together, "trial marriages," "gay marriages," and even "mate-swapping" have shown up in evangelical churches, and when faithful pastors have attempted to deal with such sin, they were told to mind their own business. The offenders simply left and starting attending other churches where they could live as they pleased. As Ruth Bell Graham said, "If God doesn't judge America, He will have to apologize to Sodom and Gomorrah."

"The love of money is a root of all kinds of evil" (1 Tim. 6:10, NKJV), so we aren't surprised that the business people in Jerusalem were charging exorbitant interest on loans and were practicing extortion rather than business (Ezek. 22:12). The Jews could charge interest to outsiders, but not to their own people (Ex. 22:25-27; Lev. 19:13; 25:35-38; Deut. 23:19-20), and they were to be fair in all their business dealings. The world's motto "Business is business" must never replace our Lord's commandment, "Give, and it will be given to you" (Luke 6:38, NIV).

Why were God's chosen people living such wicked lives? Because they had forgotten the Lord (Ezek. 22:12), a sin that Moses had commanded them to avoid (Deut. 4:9, 23; 6:10-12; 32:18). They were admonished to remember their slavery in Egypt and God's grace in redeeming them (5:15; 15:15; 16:12; 24:18), and also remember the Lord their God (8:18). People who forget God gradually become their own god and begin to disobey God's Word, mistreat other people, and take God's gifts for granted. The Prophet Jeremiah in Jerusalem was accusing the people of the same sin (Jer. 3:21).

A doomed people (Ezek. 22:13-22). God strikes His hands in angry response to the sins of His people (6:11; 21:14, 17),[2] and He announces that a day of reckoning is coming. The people of Jerusalem had the resolution to persist in their sins, in spite of God's warnings, but would they have the will and courage to endure God's day of judgment? His first act of judgment would be *dispersion* (22:13-16); the people would be exiled to Babylon and others scattered to the surrounding nations (vv. 15-16), some of which had already occurred. The people should have known this judgment was coming, because in His covenant, God had promised this kind of judgment (Lev. 26:27-39; Deut. 28:64-68). The Jewish people wanted to worship the gods of the Gentiles, so why not live with the Gentiles and learn how to do it? God would humiliate His people before the eyes of the Gentiles and through this experience bring His people back to Himself.

The second judgment would be *fire* (Ezek. 22:17-22), the destruction of their beloved city and temple. The prophet pictured a smelting furnace with different kinds of metals in it, and the dross (slag) being removed. That dross represented the people of Jerusalem who thought they were "the best" because they hadn't gone into exile. The image of the furnace is a familiar one in

Scripture. Israel's suffering in Egypt was a furnace experience that helped to form the nation and prepare them for the Exodus (Deut. 4:20; 1 Kings 8:31; Jer. 11:4). But now, God's furnace was Jerusalem, and the fire would be divine judgment for the sins of the people (Isa. 1:21-26; 31:9; Jer. 6:27-30). Two key words in this passage are "melt" and "gather." The people had gathered in Jerusalem for safety, but it was the Lord who gathered them so He could melt them in His furnace as He poured His fury upon them. This same image will be discussed in Ezekiel 24:1-14.

A debased people (Ezek. 22:23-27). Ezekiel pointed the finger of accusation at the princes (vv. 25, 27),[3] the priests (v. 26), the false prophets (v. 28), and the people of the land (v. 29), and each segment of society is found guilty. The princes were acting like animals, lions and wolves, hungry for their prey. Sin always debases people and turns them into beasts (Ps. 32:9; Prov. 7:21-23; 2 Peter 2:18-22), even into worse than beasts! These men abused their power and destroyed innocent people just to acquire more wealth. They manufactured poor widows by murdering innocent men and stealing their wealth.

You would think that the priests would have upheld the law and protested the evil deeds of the rulers, but instead they broke God's law (Jer. 32:32; Lam. 4:13). These men were given the sacred calling of explaining God's holy law (Mal. 2:6-8) so that the people could live holy lives and make a difference between holy things and common things (Ezek. 44:23; Lev. 10:10; 11:47; 20:25). But instead of teaching the law, the priests violated the law; and when others broke the law, the priests looked the other way. It was a situation not unlike that of Eli and his sons in the days of young Samuel (1 Sam. 2:12ff).

The people of the land (Ezek. 22:29) were the prominent land-owning citizens (12:19), often officers in the army, and they fell right in line with the princes and priests. They oppressed the poor when they should have aided them, and took advantage of the strangers instead of welcoming them and helping them. But everything they gained by their violence and abuse of power, they would lose when the day of judgment arrived.

A deceitful people (Ezek. 22:28). Along with the priests, the false prophets supported the evil political regime and encouraged the common people with lies. Instead of exposing sin, they whitewashed it! (See 13:10-16; Jer. 6:14; 8:11; 23:16-22.) They announced that God would never allow His holy city and temple to be trampled by the heathen, but that is exactly what the Lord planned to do. The false prophets manufactured lies and the people gladly believed them.

A disappointing people (Ezek. 22:30-31). God searched among His people for one person in authority who would stand in the gap so that the enemy wouldn't penetrate the wall and invade the city, but He found none. Of course, the Prophet Jeremiah was in Jerusalem, but he was a man with no authority who was rejected by the politicians, priests, and false prophets. Jeremiah himself had scoured the city, looking for a godly man (Jer. 5:1-6), but his quest was a failure. The Prophet Isaiah failed in a similar search (Isa. 51:18; 59:16). The Lord promised to spare Sodom and Gomorrah if He found ten righteous men in the city (Gen. 18:23-33), and He would have spared Jerusalem for one righteous man.

The Lord is still seeking men and women who will take their stand for the moral law of God, stand in the gap at the wall, and confront the enemy with God's help. As you read history, you meet godly men and women who had the courage to resist the popular evils of their day and dare to expose the breaks in the wall and seek to mend them. The Lord is looking for intercessors (Isa. 59:1-4, 16) who will cry out to God for mercy and for a return to holiness. Surely the Lord must be disappointed that His people have time for everything except intercessory prayer.

2. The end of the kingdom (Ezek. 23:1-49)

This chapter is a good deal like chapter 16 in that it depicts the history of the nation of Israel and its apostasy from the Lord. In both chapters, the image is that of prostitution, the nation breaking her "marriage vows" and like a harlot, turning to others for help.[4] However, in chapter 16, the sin is idolatry, trusting the false gods of the pagans, while in chapter 23, the sin is trusting other nations to protect her. In this chapter you will find both Israel (the Northern Kingdom) and Judah (the Southern Kingdom) playing the harlot and looking for help from Assyria, Babylon, and Egypt, instead of trusting Jehovah God to guide them and rescue them.

During the reign of Solomon's son

Rehoboam, the Jewish nation divided into two kingdoms, Israel and Judah. The Northern Kingdom of Israel (Samaria) almost immediately abandoned the true faith, started to worship idols, and eventually set up their own temple and priesthood; while the Southern Kingdom of Judah tried to remain true to the Law of Moses. Things got so bad in Samaria that in 722 B.C. God brought the Assyrians to conquer them and put an end to the nation. Judah had a few godly kings who sought to please the Lord, but the nation gradually disintegrated and was taken by the Babylonians (606–586 B.C.).

Oholah represents Israel whose capital was Samaria, while her sister Oholibah represents Judah whose capital was Jerusalem. Oholah means "her tent" while Oholibah means "my tent is in her." When hearing the word "tent," most Jews would immediately think of the tabernacle where God dwelt with His people. The Northern Kingdom of Israel had its own sanctuary and priesthood in Samaria, as well as idols and shrines throughout the land, but that was "her tent" and not "the Lord's tent." However, the Mosaic Law was still held in Judah, even though not always obeyed, and the levitical priests still served at the temple that Solomon built by God's direction and authority. Looking at Jerusalem, even with all of her sins, the Lord could still say, "My tent is in her." The glory had departed from the temple (9:3; 11:22-23), but the temple was still known as God's dwelling place.

With that background, we can now examine this parable and see how it applied to the Jews in Ezekiel's day as well as to God's people in our own day. The main message the Lord wanted Ezekiel to get across to the Jewish people was that He was perfectly just in punishing the kingdom of Judah because of the way they had behaved toward Him. The Lord made three declarations: Judah arrogantly ignored God's warning when He judged Samaria (23:5-13); Judah then went beyond the sins the Samaritans committed (vv. 14-21); therefore, the Lord had every right to judge Judah (vv. 22-35).

The people of Judah ignored God's warning (Ezek. 23:5-13). Both Israel and Judah were positioned in such a way geographically that the political tensions among the larger nations and empires (Egypt, Assyria, Babylon) affected them drastically. Israel and Judah were often the "bridges" over which these nations marched their armies, and it was impossible for the Jews not to take sides. In the days when the nation was united, King David trusted the Lord to help him defend and deliver his people, but King Solomon's policy was to make political treaties to guarantee peace. This is why he married numerous heathen princesses so that their fathers wouldn't attack the Jewish nation.

Samaria had no true faith in the living God, so she looked to the Assyrians to help her. The picture here is that of a prostitute seeking a lover to care for her and the language is quite graphic. Samaria not only welcomed Assyria's soldiers but also Assyria's idols, and the religion of the Northern Kingdom became a strange mixture of Mosaic Law and Assyrian idolatry (2 Kings 17:6-15). So, to punish her, the Lord used the Assyrians—her "lovers"—to conquer her and put an end to the Northern Kingdom. The ten tribes that comprised the Northern Kingdom were mixed with other conquered nations and the land became part of the Assyrian Empire.

The leaders of Judah knew what had happened to their sister kingdom and why it happened, but they didn't take the lesson to heart. Judah also made alliances with Assyria and "fell in love" with the handsome soldiers in their beautiful uniforms (Ezek. 23:11-13). Instead of looking to the Lord to protect them, the people of Judah looked to their powerful neighbors for help, but they proved to be broken reeds. Assyria invaded Judah during the days of King Hezekiah, ravaged the land, and were stopped in their tracks at Jerusalem and slain by God's angel (Isa. 36–37; 2 Kings 18–19). This was God's warning to Hezekiah not to let the people follow the sinful example of Samaria.

The people of Judah sinned even more than Samaria did (Ezek. 23:14-21). God's punishment of Samaria and His miraculous deliverance of Judah should have brought the people of Judah to their knees in gratitude and dedication, but it didn't happen that way. Hezekiah began to fraternize with the Babylonians (Isa. 39), a nation that was growing in power. As they had admired the Assyrian armies (2 Kings 16:1-9), so the rulers of Judah began to admire the power of Babylon. King Jehoiakim asked Babylon to help him break the power of Egypt (Ezek.

23:35–24:7), and this only made Judah a vassal state of Babylon. The kingdom of Judah became more and more idolatrous as one weak king after another took the throne, some of them for only three months. Judah was actually more corrupt than her sister Samaria! (23:11)

The people of Judah will suffer the wrath of God (Ezek. 23:22-35). The logic is obvious: if God punished Samaria for her sins, and if Judah sinned worse than Samaria, then Judah must be punished also. In this section of his message, Ezekiel delivered four oracles from the Lord. First, God would bring the Babylonians to punish Judah just as He brought the Assyrians to punish Samaria (vv. 22-27). Ezekiel described in detail the officers in the army and the equipment they would carry. Using the image of punishing a prostitute, he described how the invaders would strip the nation, expose her lewdness, and mutilate her body. It isn't a very beautiful picture.

The second oracle (vv. 28-31) repeats some of the facts in the first one and reminded the people that this judgment was perfectly just. At one time, Judah courted the friendship of Babylon, but now they hated the Babylonians; yet God would allow the people they hated to ravage their land and destroy Jerusalem and the temple. The third oracle (vv. 32-34) uses the image of the cup, a familiar image in Scripture for experiencing suffering (Isa. 51:17, 22; Jer. 25:15-29; 49:12; Lam. 4:21; Hab. 2:16; John 18:11; Rev. 14:10). The cup He hands them will be large and deep and filled with the wrath of the Lord, and they will have to drink it.

The final oracle (Ezek. 23:35) explained why God judged His people: they had forgotten Him (22:12) and had cast Him behind their backs—that is, rejected Him and left Him out of their thinking and living. "There is no fear of God before their eyes" (Rom. 3:18). God's "wife" had become a harlot and abandoned her Husband. Jeremiah used a similar image (Jer. 2:1-8) and was astonished that a nation should change its gods (vv. 9-11). He said that Judah had rejected the fountain of living water and turned to broken cisterns that could hold no water (v. 13).

The two accused sisters have been presented to the court and their crimes have been explained. All that remains is for the judge to sum up the case and describe the sentence, which Ezekiel does in 23:36-49. Neither Samaria nor Judah has any defense and they can't take their case to a higher court. God's verdict is true and final. Ezekiel includes Samaria in this summation so that Judah can't say that God's judgment of the Northern Kingdom was unjust. All the evidence was presented and there could be but one decision: guilty as charged.

What were their sins? Idolatry, injustice, unbelief (depending on the heathen nations for help), followed by blatant hypocrisy. They worshiped idols and killed innocent people, and then marched piously into the temple to worship Jehovah! They prostituted themselves to heathen nations when, if they had trusted the Lord, He would have taken care of them and delivered them. In their idolatry, they even sacrificed their own children, sons and daughters who really belonged to God ("whom they bore to Me").

When Judah should have remained a separated people, declaring their faith in Jehovah, their leaders participated in an international conference against Babylon and allied themselves with the enemies of the Lord (v. 40; Jer. 27). The prophet described how the Jewish leaders at the meeting behaved like harlots preparing to serve a customer, but he compared the meeting to a drunken brawl,[5] a "carefree crowd" that didn't want to face the fact that Babylon was going to win.

From God's point of view, Judah was nothing but a worn-out adulteress soliciting "lovers," and their sin was something His heart couldn't accept. As Samaria had sinned by patronizing Assyria, so Judah was playing the harlot by seeking the help of pagan nations instead of trusting the Lord. That being the case, Judah would be treated like an adulteress and even worse. The Law of Moses called for the adulteress to be stoned (Lev. 20:10; Deut. 20:20), prostitutes to be burned (Gen. 38:24; Lev. 21:9), and murderers to be put to death, probably by stoning (Ex. 21:12-14; Lev. 24:17). Judah would be punished for adultery, prostitution, and shedding innocent blood (Ezek. 23:47).[6] Her sins would find her out.

3. The end of a delusion (Ezek. 24:1-14)

This chapter closes the section of the book that focuses on the destruction of Jerusalem (chapters 4–24) and it is divided into two parts: a parable about a boiling pot (24:1-14) and an "action sermon" involving the sudden death of the prophet's wife (vv. 15-27). After that, Ezekiel deals with God's judgment on the Gentile nations (chaps. 25–32) and His glorious promises for the people of Israel (chaps. 33–48).

God's message came to Ezekiel on January 15, 588 B.C., the date of the beginning of the siege of Jerusalem. So critical is this date that it's mentioned in 2 Kings 25:1-3 as well as Jeremiah 39:1-3 and 52:4-6. During their years of exile, the Jews observed four annual fasts to remember the painful events of the destruction of Jerusalem (Zech. 7; 8:18-23). They marked when the siege began (tenth month), when the walls were breached (fourth month), when the temple was burned down (fifth month), and when Gedaliah the governor was assassinated (the seventh month, Jer. 41:1-2).

God called Judah a "rebellious house" not only because they broke His laws and violated His covenant, but also because Zedekiah had broken his treaty with Babylon and incited the displeasure of Nebuchadnezzar. The image of the cooking pot takes us back to Ezekiel 11:1-13 where the Jewish leaders boasted that the Jews left in Jerusalem were better than the Jews taken off to Babylon. The Jerusalem Jews were the best "cuts of meat," while the Jews in Babylon were only the scraps! Of course, God contradicted that idea and made it clear that the exiles in Babylon would form a remnant with which He could rebuild the nation and the temple. Jeremiah had written to the exiles and instructed them to settle down, build houses, and raise families so that the remnant could continue the ministry for which the Lord had chosen Israel. God warned the Jewish leaders in Jerusalem that they weren't the "meat"—they were the butchers! They were guilty of shedding innocent blood, and God would judge them for their sins. If they weren't "cooked" in the cauldron of Jerusalem, they would eventually be slain by the swords of the Babylonian soldiers. Even if they escaped the city, they would be caught and killed.

In his parable about the cooking pot, Ezekiel used the image and vocabulary of the Jerusalem leaders. Yes, God would put "the best cuts of meat" into His pot (Jerusalem) and boil the meat and the bones (the Babylonian siege). He wouldn't "cook" the flesh; He would consume it! (Ezek. 10) Then He would pour out the burned mess and *burn the pot itself*! Jerusalem was an evil city, filled with sin like a filthy pot encrusted with rust and scum. She had shed innocent blood and hadn't even been decent enough to cover the blood (Gen. 4:10; Lev. 17:13; Deut. 12:16, 24; 15:23). The murderers left the evidence for everyone to see and didn't worry about the consequences! But God would avenge the innocent victims and expose the blood of their murderers for all to see.

The Jerusalem leaders were confident of deliverance because they were depending on a lie: "Our God will never allow His chosen people to be killed, His holy city and temple to be destroyed." This was a delusion, and Ezekiel put an end to it. It was *because* the Jews were His chosen people that God was punishing them, and *because* Jerusalem was His holy city that He couldn't allow it to continue wallowing in wickedness. The only way to purge the city was to burn it and make it a great funeral pyre (Ezek. 24:9-10). He judged the people in the city (the "select pieces of meat in the pot") and then burned the pot as well!

Both Jeremiah and Ezekiel had to deal with the false confidence of the people, a confidence based on a false interpretation of theology. Jeremiah warned Judah, "Do not trust in these lying words, saying, 'The temple of the Lord, the temple of the Lord, the temple of the Lord are these'" (Jer. 7:4, NKJV). The presence of the temple in Jerusalem wasn't a guarantee that the city would be saved, especially when what was going on in the temple was contrary to the will of God. Any theology that makes sin easy and divine punishment unimportant is not biblical theology. God's judgment begins with His own people (2 Peter 4:17), and Hebrews 10:30 warns us that "the Lord will judge His people" (NKJV).

Our world today lives on delusions and myths because, like the Jews in Ezekiel's day, the world won't accept the authority of the Word of God. People still believe that might makes right, that money is the measure of worth and success, that the aim of life is to have fun and do what you want to do. You can believe whatever you please about God, yourself, and others, and everything will turn out fine because there are no consequences. But one day God will expose the stupidity of these delusions and the world will discover too late that there are consequences to what we believe and how we behave.

4. The end of a marriage (Ezek. 24:15-27)

It's interesting to study what is said in Scripture about the wives of the prophets. Abraham was a prophet (Gen. 20:7) who twice lied about his wife and got into trouble. Moses was criticized for the wife he chose (Num. 12:1), and Isaiah's wife was a prophetess (Isa. 8:3). She bore him at least two sons whose names were signs to the people of Judah. The Prophet Jeremiah wasn't allowed to have a wife (Jer. 16:1-4), and this was a sign to the Jews that judgment was coming and people would wish they had never married and brought children into the world. Hosea's wife became a prostitute and he had to buy her out of the slave market (Hosea 1–3). What a trial that must have been!

But Ezekiel paid a greater price than all these prophets. In order to give his message, Ezekiel had to see his wife die suddenly *and he was not to show great grief because of it*! God told him that she would suddenly die and that he was not to do what the Jews usually did in times of bereavement. He was allowed to groan quietly, but he was not permitted to weep or make the kind of lamentation that was typical of his people.

He gave his morning message to the elders, at evening his wife suddenly died, and the next morning he buried her. When the Jews came to console him, they were shocked to see that he wasn't weeping aloud and displaying the usual signs of bereavement. Nor was he to eat the food that people would bring to help him in his sorrow. As they had done in the past, the people asked him for an explanation (Ezek. 12:9; 21:7), and the Lord gave him the message and opened his mouth so he could speak.

The prophet's wife was the joy of his life and the desire of his eyes (24:16), but the Lord took her away. The temple in Jerusalem was the joy of the Jewish people, for no other nation had such a sanctuary, but now the Lord would take the temple away. On August 14, 586 B.C., the Babylonians set fire to the temple in Jerusalem. Nothing is said about Ezekiel's children and we don't know that he had any, but God announced that, along with the destruction of the temple, the relatives of the exiles still living in Jerusalem would lose their lives. Once again, Ezekiel was a sign to the exiles of what the Lord was doing, and this was the most painful and costly of all his "action sermons." In order to preach one sermon, Ezekiel had to lose his wife. But Ezekiel commanded the Jewish exiles to mourn over the loss of the temple just as he had mourned over the loss of his wife, without loud wailing, copious weeping, or any change in their dress or eating habits. The death of the prophet's dear wife was an act of God, and so was the destruction of the temple. The woman who had died was innocent of any gross sin, but the temple had become a den of thieves. God gave Ezekiel only one day's notice that he would become a widower, but He had been speaking to sinful Judah for many years and they had not listened. The destruction of the temple and the city should not be a surprise to anybody.

But how did the people know that the prophet was telling the truth? They didn't have instant news service as we have today, so perhaps the whole thing was only Ezekiel's way of dealing with his wife's death. But God said that a messenger would arrive in Babylon with the news of the fall of the city and the destruction of the temple, and this occurred five months later, on January 8, 585 B.C. (33:21-22).

The next day, God opened the prophet's mouth and removed the discipline He had imposed at the beginning of his ministry (3:25-27). From this point on, the prophet was free to speak as he felt led, and at the same time, the focus of his ministry shifted. He had exposed the nation's sins and announced her judgment. Now he would announce God's plans for the Gentile nations, including victorious Babylon; and then he would minister hope to the Jewish exiles and share with them visions of the kingdom yet to come.

Ezekiel has been a faithful servant of God, even to the point of sacrificing his beloved wife so he could declare the Word of God. What an example of dedication

!

CHAPTER EIGHT
GOD JUDGES THE NATIONS
Ezekiel 25–28

The destruction of Jerusalem was welcomed by the Gentile nations that were located in the vicinity of the kingdom of Judah. During the great days of their nation, the Jews had been a separated people, and this irritated their neighbors. The Jewish claim that Jehovah was the only true and living God meant that the other nations worshiped only dead idols. Both Saul and David had met many of these nations on the battlefield, and the Gentiles remembered and resented those humiliating defeats. But as the kingdom of Judah drifted from the Lord, the Jewish people adopted the gods and the practices of the Gentiles, and to their neighbors, this looked like pure hypocrisy. After all, if Jehovah is the true and living God, why do the Jews need other gods? And why would the kings of Judah look to human allies for protection if Jehovah is able to care for them? Nothing pleased the Gentiles more than to be able to laugh at the Jews in their day of humiliation and claim that the gods of the Babylonians were stronger than the God the Jews worshiped.

What the nations didn't realize was that the destruction of Jerusalem wasn't just a punishment of the Jews; it was also a warning to the Gentiles. "If the righteous will be recompensed on the earth, how much more the wicked and the sinner?" (Prov. 11:31, NKJV) For if God displays His wrath against His own people, "What shall the end be of them that obey not the gospel of God?" (1 Peter 4:17) There's a great difference between a loving parent chastening a child and a judge punishing a guilty criminal. Israel knew God's Word and therefore had sinned against a flood of light, but the Gentiles had the clear witness of creation (Rom. 1:18-32; Ps. 19) and conscience (Rom. 2:11-16) and were without excuse. But God was also judging the Gentiles for the way they had treated His people, because this was the covenant promise He had made with Abraham (Gen. 12:1-3).[1]

It's interesting that Ezekiel didn't have a message of judgment against the Babylonians; God used Isaiah (Isa. 13:1–14:23; 21:1-9) and especially Jeremiah (Jer. 31; 40; 50–51) for that job. God told Ezekiel to set his face against the nations (Ezek. 25:2; see 6:2; 13:17; 20:46; 21:2, 7) and declare that judgment was coming.

1. Judgment on nations related to Israel (Ezek. 25:1-14)

The Ammonites, Moabites, and Edomites were all blood relatives of the Jews. The Ammonites and Moabites were related to Israel through Lot, Abraham's nephew. Ammon and Moab were the two sons born out of the incestuous union of Lot and two of his daughters (Gen. 19:29-38). Edom is another name for Jacob's twin brother Esau (Ezek. 25:30; Edom means "red"), and Jacob fathered the twelve tribes of Israel. You would think that nations related by blood would be supportive of one another, but these three nations had a long-standing hatred against Israel and kept the feud going.

Note in these judgment messages that God gives the reason for the judgment ("because"—Ezek. 25:3, 6, 8, 12, 15; 26:2) and a description of the judgment ("therefore"—25:4, 7, 9, 13, 16; 26:3).

Ammon (Ezek. 25:1-7). When Israel was marching toward the Promised Land, defeating one nation after another, God commanded them not to attack the Ammonites because He had given them their land (Deut. 2:19). They were a fierce people (Jer. 40:14; 41:5-7), and both Saul and David had defeated them in battle (1 Sam. 11; 1 Chron. 19–20). Ammon had united with Moab in attacking Judah but both were soundly defeated (2 Chron. 20). The Ammonites rejoiced at the destruction of Jerusalem and the temple (Ezek. 25:3, 6), and when Nehemiah went to Jerusalem to rebuild the walls, the Ammonites joined with Sanballat in opposing him (Neh. 2:10-19).

The Lord announced that He would deliver Ammon into the hands of "the men of the east" (Ezek. 25:4), meaning the Babylonian army. In his march, Nebuchadnezzar had paused at the juncture of two roads, one of which led to Jerusalem and the other to Rabbah, the capital of Ammon (21:18-24). There he sought guidance from his diviners, and God saw to it that he marched to Jerusalem. The Ammonites had breathed a sigh of relief and had been joyful when they saw Jerusalem ruined and the temple desecrated, but now their time had come. God would destroy Ammon and the nation would perish from the earth forever.

Moab (Ezek. 25:8-11).[2] It was Balak, king of Moab, who hired Baalam to curse Israel as they camped on the plains of Moab (Num. 22–24), and it was Baalam who taught the Moabites how to seduce Israel into sinning against God (Num. 25:1-9; 31:16). The sin of Moab was slander against Israel, a refusal to see the Jews as God's special people. To the Moabites, the fall of Jerusalem proved that the Jews were just like any other people. "If you are such a special nation," they argued, "why have you experienced such a humiliating defeat?" Even Baalam had admitted that Israel was a special people set apart from every other nation (Num. 23:8-10).

The Moabites were a very proud people because they thought their nation was impregnable (Isa. 16:6). Moab was located in the high mountains, with the Dead Sea on the west and the desert on the east. God told them He would bring invaders through their "inaccessible" northwest border ("flank," Ezek. 25:9, NIV), even though it was made up of sheer cliffs; and He did. It was the Assyrians who invaded and destroyed Moab, and today Moab is no longer remembered among the nations.

Edom (Ezek. 25:12-14). Edom's hatred of the Jews began when Esau foolishly sold his birthright to his brother Jacob, and when their mother schemed to secure the patriarchal blessing for her favorite son Jacob (Gen. 25:29-34; 27).[3] Jacob went to Haran to live with his uncle primarily to escape the anger and murderous intent of his brother. Esau's descendants became powerful tribal chiefs (Gen. 36), but Jacob's sons became the founders of the twelve tribes of Israel, the people God chose to accomplish His great purposes on this earth.

The Prophet Obadiah wrote that God would destroy Edom because of the way they treated the Jews (Obad. 10-14). When Jerusalem was being attacked, the Edomites cheered for the Babylonians (Ps. 137:7) and gave no help to the Jewish refugees who were trying to escape. Instead, the Edomites helped the Babylonians capture the fleeing people and rejoiced over the terrible calamities that had come to the Jews. Along with the Babylonians, they looted the city and robbed their own blood relatives. Sins against humanity are sins against God, because humans are made in the image of God. The day came when Edom felt the heavy hand of God's judgment (Lam. 4:21-22).

God's message to Edom reminds us that family feuds are costly and often lead to pain and tragedy. The Edomites sustained their hatred for the Jews from generation to generation. "[Edom] stifled his compassion; his anger also tore continually, and he maintained his fury forever" (Amos 1:11, NASB). "Let no man pull you so low as to make you hate him," said Booker T. Washington, and Jesus said, "Love your enemies, bless them that curse you, do good to them that hate you, and pray for them which despitefully use you, and persecute you" (Matt. 5:44). Edom's hatred and lust for revenge finally led to their ruin (Obad. 1-14). Ezekiel will have more to say about Edom in chapter 35.

2. Judgment on neighboring nations (Ezek. 25:15–26:21)

Having dealt with the sins of the nations related to Israel, Ezekiel then set his face against Philistia (25:15-17) and Phoenicia, especially the Phoenician cities of Tyre (26:1–28:19) and Sidon (vv. 20-24). Once again, the themes of pride, hatred, and revenge come to the fore, sins that can motivate nations even today. It's very easy for arrogance to masquerade as patriotism, hatred as national zeal, and revenge as justice.

Philistia (Ezek. 25:15-17). After the Israelites entered and occupied the land of Canaan, the neighboring Philistines became serious enemies.[4] Among the judges, Shamgar (Jud. 3:31) and Samson (Jud. 13–16) attacked them, and both Samuel and Saul had to contend with them. It was David who finally defeated the Philistines, and they were kept under control throughout the reign of Solomon (2 Sam. 5:17-25; 21:15-22; 23:9-17). When the Jewish nation divided, the Philistines asserted their independence and became successful merchants and traders along with the Phoenicians.

The Philistines cultivated a national hatred for the Jews and seized every opportunity to harass and attack them. Ezekiel wasn't the only prophet who prophesied God's judgment on the Philistines (see Jer. 47; Amos 1:6-8; Zeph. 2:4-7). The Philistines allied with Egypt in an attempt to withstand Nebuchadnezzar; Babylon was too much for them and they were defeated and deported like the other vanquished nations (Jer. 25:15-32; 47).

Tyre (Ezek. 26:1-21). Ezekiel devoted four messages to the sins and the fate of the capital of Phoenicia (vv. 1-21; 27:1-36; 28:1-10, 11-19). During their reigns, both David and Solomon were friendly with Hiram, king of Tyre (2 Sam. 5:11; 1 Kings 5:1ff), and King Ahab's wife Jezebel was the daughter of Ethbaal, a later king of Tyre (1 Kings 16:31). The message in this chapter contains four parts, each beginning with a statement about the Word of the Lord (Ezek. 26:1-6, 7-14, 15-18, and 19-21).

Destruction announced (Ezek. 26:1-6). The image used here is that of a storm producing great destructive waves (vv. 3, 19). The city of Tyre was situated partly on the Mediterranean coast and partly on an island about half a mile from the coast, so Ezekiel's storm image was appropriate. God was angry at Tyre for rejoicing at Jerusalem's destruction and seeing it as an opportunity for Tyre to prosper even more. But the Lord announced that the nations would come like successive waves of the sea and bring Tyre to ultimate ruin. The name "Tyre" means "rock," so the statement "like the top of a rock" (vv. 4, 14) is significant. Tyre did become a bare rock and a place where fishermen dried their nets.

Tyre was able to survive the Assyrian conquest, but when Babylon came to power, Nebuchadnezzar besieged the coastal city for fifteen years (586–571 B.C.) and overcame it, but he did not conquer the island city. In 322 B.C., Alexander the Great besieged Tyre for seven months, built a causeway to the island, and was able to conquer the city.

Destruction accomplished (Ezek. 26:7-14). He gives a description of the Babylonian siege of the part of Tyre that was on the shore of the Mediterranean. Nebuchadnezzar began his siege in 587 B.C., after the siege of Jerusalem, and though the coastal city was a formidable fortress, he managed to persevere and conquer. The Babylonians threw the timbers and stones into the water and claimed the spoils for themselves. God didn't think Nebuchadnezzar was "paid enough" for his efforts, so He gave him Egypt as an extra bonus (29:18-20).

Destruction lamented (Ezek. 26:15-18). Since Tyre was at the center of all merchandising along the Mediterranean coast and did business with every known country, her fall was devastating to the economy. There wasn't a "ripple effect"; there was a tidal wave! Their partners in business—called "princes" (v. 16) and "kings" (27:35)—had lost everything and could only lament the great tragedy that had struck. In 26:17-18 we have a brief lamentation over the fall of the city. Keep in mind that in ancient days, the prophets sometimes used funeral lamentations in a satirical manner to poke fun at the enemies of God. We will have examples in chapters 27 and 32.

People along the coast trembled as they wondered what would happen to the economy now that the great mercantile network was destroyed. Our world today is united in a series of electronic networks that can transfer information, money, and orders for merchandise with such speed that it's scarcely possible to register them. Imagine what would happen in the world's economy if all these electronic business connections in New York City alone were dissolved. This reminds us that in the end times, when the Antichrist has organized his great world network called "Babylon," the Lord will destroy the whole thing and leave the business people desolate and in mourning (Rev. 18).

Destruction forever (Ezek. 26:19-21). The prophet gives us insight into the full extent of Tyre's destruction by describing the victims' descent into "the pit" (v. 20). The Hebrew word *bor* means "a well, a pit, a cistern," but it also refers to the pit of death (Pss. 28:1; 88:4, 6) and sometimes is an equivalent of *sheol*, the realm of departed spirits. There were tragic consequences to the pride of Tyre and their evil attitude toward the Jewish people. "I will make thee a terror" (26:21, KJV) should read, "I shall bring terrors on you" (NASB). Note the statements the Lord makes about His actions toward the city of Tyre: He would make them desolate, cover them with water, bring them down into the pit, bring them terrors, and remove them from the earth. On the other hand, He promised Israel, their enemies, future glory and blessing!

3. Lament over Tyre's destruction (Ezek. 27:1-36)

The Old Testament prophets occasionally used "funeral dirges" in a satirical manner to ridicule their enemies, and you find something of that spirit in this lament over the fall of Tyre. Neither the prophet nor the Jewish nation was grieved over Tyre's destruction, but the event gave Ezekiel opportunity to express spiritual truth in this song. Since Tyre was a maritime city, the chapter compares the city and its business to a beautiful ship that eventually sinks and brings great grief to merchants and customers alike. This image is what is called "an extended metaphor," not unlike our "ship of state." A nation or a city isn't really a ship, but there are many points of comparison that can help us better understand the nation and the city. The words "merchant" and "merchandise" are used twenty-one times in this chapter, because Tyre was a mercantile city. The ship metaphor included all that was a part of the city of Tyre, its agents and customers, its business, and all the network it had developed in the Mediterranean world.

Building the ship (Ezek. 27:1-7). This was not only a useful ship that brought wealth to the city, but it was a beautiful ship that the nations admired (vv. 3, 11; see 28:12). Tyre was proud of its beauty and its success but didn't give any praise to the Lord for His goodness. The very best materials went into the building of the ship, starting with great fir timbers from Mount Hermon for the hull and deck, and cedars of Lebanon for the masts. They made the oars of oak from Bashan and the deck from pinewood from Cyprus, inlaid with ivory (see NIV and NLT). A large Phoenician ship would have as many as 50 oarsmen in a crew of 200. Egypt provided embroidered linen for the sail and banner, and from Cyprus came the cloth to make the beautiful awnings for the decks.

I once heard a sincere but ill-informed TV preacher declare that the United States should quit doing business with nations that espouse wrong political beliefs and the denial of human rights. His motives were right but his comprehension limited. He couldn't hear me, but I said out loud, "If we did, you wouldn't have either a microphone or a television camera!" I'm told that the familiar telephone has material in it from at least twenty different countries! Tyre's "ship of state" reminds us that the world is growing smaller and that nations that disagree still depend on one another for what they need. "Internet" is short for "international network," that invisible electronic system that ties together millions of computers and the minds and hearts of the people using them.

Manning the ship (Ezek. 27:8-11). In describing the ship's crew, Ezekiel was actually naming some of the nations that made it possible for Tyre to become such a great success. Oarsmen came from Sidon and Arvad, two other cities in Phoenicia, but the skilled mariners, the people who really managed things, came from Tyre. Veteran shipwrights from Gebal, another coastal city, traveled on board to caulk the seams and keep the ship in good repair.

Briefly, the image shifts from the ship metaphor to the actual city itself (vv. 10-11). Tyre had a paid army, mercenary soldiers from Persia, Lydia (Asia Minor), Libia (North Africa), Arvad (Phoenicia), Cilicia, and Gammad. These mercenaries sold their services to protect the city and its shipping enterprise. It doesn't appear that the soldiers anticipated any danger because they hung up their helmets and shields on the walls as decorations to add to the city's beauty. The coastal city of Tyre was a strong fortress, so much so that Nebuchadnezzar needed thirteen years to break through the defenses.

We shouldn't carry a metaphor too far, but it is significant that Ezekiel brought in the army and navy as necessary parts of the business enterprise of Tyre. Certainly national defense is as important to the success of business as it is to the safety of the private citizen, and sometimes "national interest" and "business" become intertwined. "Big business" always appreciates a foreign policy that opens new markets and protects them.

Sailing the ship (Ezek. 27:12-25). The beautiful and impressive ship of state was made for the waters, not for the wharf, so Ezekiel described how the city of Tyre did business along the Mediterranean coast. The word "merchant," used thirteen times in the KJV, means "to do business, to trade." The nations named here bought merchandise from Tyre and sold products to Tyre. It was a business partnership that benefited all that were involved. Silver, iron, tin, and lead came from Tarshish, which was probably in Spain. Slaves[5] and bronze implements came from Greece and Turkey (Tubal). Also from Turkey came horses, chariot teams, and mules. But there were luxury items as well: ivory and ebony from Rhodes; and turquoise, coral, rubies, and fine fabrics from Jordan.

Tyre did business with the Jews and bought various foods from them. They also got wine and wool from Syria, and lambs, rams, and goats from Arabia. Also from Arabia came exotic spices, gold, and precious stones. Other nations supplied barks, perfumes, and manufactured products such as fabrics, wrought iron objects, and rugs. The people of Tyre would take the raw materials and manufacture various useful items and sell them to their agents and their customers. Along with bartering, money and credit were involved in these many transactions, so there were plenty of opportunities for moneylenders and brokers to make profits. Thanks to the business network of Tyre, luxuries and necessities, jobs and income were available to the nations of the known world.

Sinking the ship (Ezek. 27:26-36). Admiration turns to desolation. "But look! Your oarsmen are rowing your ship of state into a hurricane! Your mighty vessel flounders in the mighty eastern gale. You are shipwrecked in the heart of the sea!" (v. 26, NLT) The storm arrives that was promised in 26:3 and 19, and the great ship is shattered in the mighty waters. The "east wind" speaks of the invasion of the Babylonian army (17:10; 19:12). The valuable cargo, the beautiful ship, and the capable crew are all lost in the heart of the sea.

But that isn't all: Tyre's agents, brokers, traders, and customers will feel the repercussions of the sinking of the ship. People will stand on the shore and lament the end of the vast mercantile system that gave them jobs, income, and security. Some of the merchants will "whistle" or "hiss" when they hear the news (27:36), probably as a shocked response to the tragedy. However, the word can mean "to hiss in scorn or derision," suggesting that some of the leaders in the business network are happy to see Tyre fall. They cooperated in the system because they had to, but now perhaps they would have opportunity to build their own network and make a greater profit. This great lamentation is an advance demonstration of what the whole world will do when Satan's system, "Babylon the great," collapses before the Lord returns to establish His kingdom (Rev. 18:17-19).

No matter how efficient, rich, and beautiful the "ship of state" might be, when the Lord decides to sink it, nothing can stay His hand. When Queen Victoria celebrated her "Diamond Jubilee" in 1897, Rudyard Kipling published his poem "Recessional" which sounded a quiet word of warning to a great nation somewhat intoxicated by their vast empire. When people read the third verse, we wonder if any of them thought of Ezekiel's description of "the ship of state":

> Far-call'd our navies melt away—
> On dune and headland sinks the fire—
> Lo, all our pomp of yesterday
> Is one with Nineveh and Tyre!
> Judge of the nations, spare us yet,
> Lest we forget, lest we forget!

4. Judgment of Tyre's ruler (Ezek. 28:1-19)

It appears that two different persons are addressed in these verses: the prince of Tyre (vv. 1-10) and the king of Tyre (vv. 11-19). The first speech is a declaration of divine judgment, while the second is more of a lamentation. Both of these persons were guilty of great pride because of their wisdom and wealth, and both abused their privileges and offended the Lord. In fact, the prince of Tyre even claimed to be a god! However, foreign invaders would destroy the prince of Tyre (vv. 7-10), while the Lord Himself would judge the king of Tyre (vv. 16-19). The prince is called "a man" (v. 2), but the king is called "the anointed cherub" (v. 14). More than one student has identified the prince of Tyre as the ruler of the city when Nebuchadnezzar invaded, but they see the king of Tyre as Satan, the enemy of God and of the Jewish people, who energized the prince and used him to accomplish his own evil purposes.[6]

Judgment on the prince of Tyre (Ezek. 28:1-10). The issue here is pride, a sin which God hates (Prov. 6:16-17). This ruler was proud of his wisdom and his wealth (Ezek. 28:3-5), and because of this pride, he exalted himself as a god. However, God would demonstrate that he was but a man, for the prince of Tyre would be slain and die like any other man. When you read Scripture, you find occasions when God judged arrogant rulers, such as Pharaoh, whom the Egyptians treated as a god (Ex. 5:2), Nebuchadnezzar (Dan. 4), and Herod Agrippa (Acts 12). World leaders who ignore the Lord and act as if they are gods will all be exposed and judged.

Judgment on the king of Tyre (Ezek. 28:11-19). The previous declaration was one of Ezekiel's "because . . . therefore" (vv. 6-7) statements, such as you find in chapters 25 and 26, but this paragraph is simply a statement of God's intention to judge the king of Tyre and destroy him. As you read these verses, you get the impression that this "king" is much more than a human regent and that this could be a description of Satan. That Satan wants to control nations and their leaders is clear from 1 Chronicles 21 and Daniel 9, and Matthew 4:8-10 states that he has delegated authority to dispose of the nations.

The use of the word "cherub" (Ezek. 28:4, 16) suggests that we're dealing here with an angelic creature, also the fact that he had been "upon the holy mountain of God" (v. 14). This sounds a great deal like the description in Isaiah 14:12ff. Satan began as an obedient angel but rebelled against God and led a revolt to secure God's throne. The text describes his great beauty and names nine jewels that were a part of that beauty. All of these jewels were also found in the breastplate of the Jewish high priest (Ex. 28:17-20). This suggests that in "Eden, the garden of God" and upon "God's holy mountain," this person had special priestly functions to perform for the Lord. The settings and mountings for these jewels were of the finest gold. His pride and selfish ambitions led him into sin and God judged him by casting him out. While the original description refers to the ruler of Tyre, it certainly applies to the god of this age, Satan, the enemy of the Lord.

The prince of Tyre, motivated and energized by the devil, engaged in business and also in violence (Ezek. 28:16), for he considered himself a god (v. 2). His way of doing business was also dishonest, for verse 18 speaks of "dishonest trade" (NIV). Satan's boast was, "I will be like the Most High" (Isa. 14:14), and his promise to Eve was, "[Y]ou will be like God" (Gen. 3:5, NKJV). The prince of Tyre accepted Satan's offer and it led to his downfall, just as it led to Satan's downfall. But during the career of the prince of Tyre, he was used of Satan to defile and destroy. The nations would be appalled at the judgment of the prince of Tyre and his city, but they had no idea that Satan was behind the city's success and Jehovah was behind the city's destruction. It reminds us of the ministry of the apostles in Luke 10:1-24. God used the apostles to heal the sick, cast out demons, and proclaim the message of the kingdom; but Jesus saw in their victories the fall of Satan (vv. 18-19).

5. Promises to Israel (Ezek. 28:20-26)

After delivering a message of judgment, Ezekiel sometimes "dropped in" a message of hope for God's hurting people. Even though the Lord was chastising His own people by destroying Jerusalem and the temple, He was still their God and had a loving concern for them. "But where sin abounded, grace abounded much more" (Rom. 5:20, NKJV).

Judgment on Sidon (Ezek. 28:20-24). Sidon was a rival city located about twenty-five miles north of Tyre. Usually the two cities are mentioned together (Isa. 23:1-4; Jer. 47:4; Joel 3:4), but here Sidon is singled out for judgment by the Lord.[7] The people of Sidon despised the Jews and often caused trouble for them, but now that opposition would end. "They shall know that I am the Lord God" (Ezek. 28:24). Ezekiel makes the startling statement that God would be glorified in the destruction of the city (v. 22; see 39:12-13). How could the Lord be glorified by such carnage? Because it would demonstrate His holiness in rejecting false gods and punishing sin. The swords of the Babylonian soldiers would kill many of the people, and those that escaped would die of the plagues that often accompany wartime slaughter.

The regathering of Israel (Ezek. 28:25-26). One of the major themes of this book is the deliverance of the Jewish exiles from Babylon and the future regathering and reuniting of the nation.[8] After the seventy years of exile and the Persian conquest of Babylon, God did cause Cyrus to allow the Jewish people to return to their land and rebuild the temple (2 Chron. 36:22-23; Ezra 1). But the return of about 50,000 people (2:64-65) in 538–537 B.C. didn't completely fulfill the promises in Ezekiel, for they have an application in the end times. Certainly the Jewish remnant that returned with Zerubbabel didn't "dwell safely" (Ezek. 28:26) because they had all kinds of problems with the people in the land. Furthermore, Ezekiel mentioned "nations" (plural) and not just the one nation of Babylon where the Jews were in exile.

There is coming a time when God will call His chosen people together into their own land, judge them, cleanse them, and establish His glorious kingdom (Zech. 10:8-12; 12:9–13:1; Matt. 24:31). God gave the land of Palestine to Abraham and his descendants (Gen. 13:14-18; 15:7-17) and He renewed the promise to Jacob (28:10-15;

35:12; Ps. 105:8-11). The Jews owned the land because God gave it to them, but they possessed the land only when they obeyed the terms of the covenant God gave them. During the exile in Babylon, they were out of the land because they had rebelled against the Lord.

Ezekiel will have more to say about Israel's future in chapters 37–48, but this brief promise must have brought encouragement to the faithful remnant among the exiles, just as the sure promise of Christ's return brings encouragement to His people today.

CHAPTER NINE
EGYPT WILL FALL!
Ezekiel 29–32

Egypt is the seventh nation in Ezekiel's "judgment cycle" and receives more attention than any of the other nations the prophet addressed. Centuries before, Egypt had made the Jewish people suffer greatly as slaves, and even after the division of the Jewish kingdom, the Egyptians were a thorn in the flesh to the Jews and a most undependable ally. But the Jews were like their father Abraham (Gen. 12:10-20) and their ancestors (Ex. 14:10-12; 16:1-3; Num. 11:4-9, 18; 14:1-5) in that, whenever a crisis loomed, they were prone to look to Egypt for help. The longer the Jews were away from Egypt, the more they idealized their experiences there and forgot about the slavery and the toil. Of course, King Solomon had married an Egyptian princess and did a considerable amount of business with Egypt, but after he died, those bonds began to unravel. "Woe to those who go down to Egypt for help," warned Isaiah during an international crisis (Isa. 31:1, NKJV; see 30:1-2), and he would give the same warning to God's people today. Believers who look to the world for help, instead of trusting in the Lord, commit the same sin that the Jews often committed.

These four chapters are composed of seven messages (or oracles) that God gave to Ezekiel to deliver to the Egyptians and to the Jewish exiles. The phrase "the word of the Lord came," or a similar statement, marks off each message. Six of these seven messages are dated (the third one is not—30:1-19), so we are able to fit them into the chronology of the book. Each of the messages presents a picture—or metaphor—of the impending judgment of Egypt.

1. The monster slain (Ezek. 29:1-16)

The first message was given on January 7, 587 B.C., about seven months before Jerusalem was destroyed. The prophet set his face against Pharaoh Hophra, who ruled Egypt from 589 to 570 B.C. (See Jer. 44:30.) The picture here is of killing a sea monster.[1]

Pharaoh's sins (Ezek. 29:1-7). The Lord compared Hophra to a monster that dwelt in the waters of the river and claimed the river for himself. The Nile River was so essential to the life of Egypt that it was treated like a god; but Hophra claimed that he was the one who made the river and that it belonged to him. In this oracle, Pharaoh was compared to a ferocious crocodile, guarding the waters of the land—the Nile and all the canals—and attacking anybody who dared to challenge his claims. His major sin was pride (vv. 1-5), taking credit for what the Lord God had done. Whatever greatness belonged to Egypt, it was because of the gracious gifts of God and not because of what Pharaoh and his people had accomplished.

But the Lord wasn't impressed by the crocodile or afraid of him! He promised to catch him, put hooks in his mouth, and drag him and the fish clinging to him (the people of Egypt) out to the fields where they would be exposed to the sun and die. They would become food for the beasts of the field and the carrion-eating birds. The Egyptian pharaohs were diligent to prepare their burial places, but Hophra would be buried like an unwanted dead animal. What a humiliating way to bury a man who claimed to be a god!

Hophra's second sin was his disloyalty to Israel (vv. 6-7). Egypt was like a weak reed that couldn't be trusted. The Jews should never have turned to Egypt for help, but when they did, the Egyptians should at least have kept their word. The Egyptians had a reputation for making promises and not keeping them (2 Kings 18:20-21; Isa. 36:6). It was Egypt who encouraged Judah to break their agreement with Babylon, and this foolish act on King Zedekiah's part is what incited the Babylonian attack against Jerusalem. While Nebuchadnezzar was attacking Jerusalem, the Jews negotiated with Egypt to send their army to deliver Judah, and for a short time, the Babylonians turned away from Jerusalem so they could deal with Egypt. But the scheme didn't work. The people in Jerusalem rejoiced that the siege was ended, but God warned His people that the army would return to Jerusalem to finish the job. (See Jeremiah 34:21-22; 37:8.)

Nebuchadnezzar's invasion (Ezek. 29:8-12). This is a prophecy of the coming of the Babylonian army to Egypt where they would fulfill God's Word and destroy man and beast as well as ravage the land (Jer. 43:8-13; 46). The people would either be slain or scattered and the land would be left "utterly waste and desolate" (Ezek. 29:10). The phrase in verse 10, "From the tower of Seveneh even unto the border of Ethiopia" is the Egyptian equivalent of Israel's "from Dan to Beersheba" and signifies the whole land, from top to bottom. The NIV translates it "from Migdol [in the north] to Aswan [in the south]."[2] Nebuchadnezzar would make a clean sweep of the land, and the desolation would last forty years (vv. 11-13). Nebuchadnezzar attacked Egypt in 568-67 B.C. and fulfilled that prophecy.

Divine mercy (Ezek. 29:13-16). After forty years, the Lord would (1) regather the scattered Egyptians to their land and permit them to establish their kingdom, but (2) their kingdom would not regain its former power and glory. It would become a "base kingdom." The Jews would learn that Egypt couldn't be trusted and would not put their confidence in Egypt. (Compare 28:24 and 29:16.) Note that the statement "they shall know that I am the Lord" is repeated three times in this message (vv. 6, 9, and 16). This statement is one of the key affirmations in the Book of Ezekiel and is used some sixty times. The Lord reveals His attributes through His judgments just as much as He does through His blessings, and sometimes His judgments get our attention much more quickly.

2. The wages paid (Ezek. 29:17-21)

This second oracle was given April 26, 571 B.C., which is the latest date mentioned in the Book of Ezekiel. However, the prophet included it here because it related to Egypt. Since Nebuchadnezzar[3] was a servant of the Lord (Jer. 25:9; 27:6; and 43:19), he deserved his pay; but the spoils of war from the conquest of Tyre couldn't begin to compensate him for the time and work his army put into the siege. ("Great service" in Ezek. 29:18, NIV is "hard campaign.") They spent thirteen years building ramparts and attacking Tyre, but they couldn't prevent the city from using their large navy to transport their treasures elsewhere. Egypt had even assisted the people of Tyre in resisting the attack and relocating their wealth.

God determined that Egypt should provide the wages for the Babylonian army that had grown bald and bruised during the siege. God is sovereign over the nations and can accomplish His will without destroying either their freedom or their accountability to Him. In 568 B.C., Nebuchadnezzar did invade Egypt, sweeping through the country and leaving it desolate (see vv. 8-12). Thus God punished both Tyre and Egypt and rewarded Babylon.

But what does all this have to do with God's people Israel? The prophet added a word of promise for the Jews (v. 21), assuring them that there would come for them a time of restoration when He would give them new strength (the budding horn) for their new challenges. After the Medes and Persians conquered Babylon in 539 B.C. (Dan. 5), Cyrus issued the edict that permitted the Jews to return to their land and rebuild the temple (Ezra 1). Whatever the other nations may do, God sees to it that His people maintain their witness and accomplish their assigned work on earth.

The statement about opening Ezekiel's mouth doesn't refer to his enforced dumbness (Ezek. 3:26; 24:27), because that had been removed when the news arrived in Babylon that Jerusalem had been taken (33:21-22). That was on January 8, 585 B.C., but the prophecy in 29:17-21 was given on April 26, 571 B.C., which was fourteen years later. The promise to Ezekiel in verse 21 indicates that when his prophecy came true and the remnant returned to the land, they would respect Ezekiel's words and profit from them. The Jews in Babylon didn't take Ezekiel's ministry seriously (33:30-33), but the day would come when God would prove him right. "[T]hen at last your words will be respected" (29:21, NLT).

Ezekiel will return to the "monster" theme in 32:1-16.

3. The storm announced (Ezek. 30:1-19)

This third oracle isn't dated but was probably delivered about the same time as the previous one. It pictures the judgment of Egypt in terms of a great storm that shakes the very foundations of the land.

The storm is coming (Ezek. 30:1-5). "The day of the Lord" (v. 3) is a biblical phrase that describes any period of divine judgment, such as the judgment of Egypt. It particularly refers to the time of Tribulation in the last days when the Lord will punish the nations (Isa. 65:17-19; Joel 1–3; Zeph. 1–2; Rev. 6–19) before He returns to earth to establish His kingdom. Whether this judgment is local, as with Egypt, or global, as in the last days, it is the Lord's work and nobody can stop it or control it. It is "a day of clouds, a time of doom for the nations" (Ezek. 30:3, NIV). In the end times, all the nations will experience this time of wrath, but in Ezekiel's time, judgment would fall on Egypt and her neighboring allies. This would include Ethiopia (Cush, the upper Nile region; see vv. 5 and 9), Put (an African nation), Lud (Lydia), the Arabian nations, Cub (Libya), and "the people of the covenant" (v. 5, NIV), who are probably Jews serving as mercenaries in the Egyptian army (see 27:10).

Egypt will be desolate (Ezek. 30:6-9). When the Babylon sword invades the land, not only with Egypt fall, but so will their allies. Those areas were desolate enough before, but now they would be even worse as the land is devastated. God will crush Egypt's allies and light a fire that will destroy the land. The people of Cush will think they are secure, so the Lord will send them messengers to wake them up, but it will be too late.

Babylon will do God's work (Ezek. 30:10-12). When the Lord punished Egypt during the time of Israel's slavery, He did the work Himself; but now He would use Nebuchadnezzar as His appointed servant to punish the proud Egyptians. His army would be ruthless (28:7, "terrible," kjv; see 31:12; 32:12) and fill the land with corpses. But His judgments would also affect the rivers and make them dry, a great catastrophe for such an arid land.

Nothing shall escape God's wrath (Ezek. 30:13-19). Ezekiel has told us what would happen and how it would happen, and now he reveals the vast scope of God's wrath. Note the repetition of the phrase "I will" as the Lord describes His work of judgment in both Lower Egypt ("Noph" = "Memphis," v. 13) and Upper Egypt (Pathros). Instead of a land of pride, Egypt will be a land filled with fear. "Zoan" is "Rameses," "No" is "Thebes," and "Sin" is "Pelusium." The verbs used make it clear that the Lord will permit total devastation: destroy, make desolate, set fire, pour fury, cut off, the day darkened. The Jews were led out of Egypt by a bright cloud (Ex. 13:21), but the Egyptians who once enslaved them will be under a dark cloud. As a result of God's judgment, the power and pride of Egypt will be destroyed, and the nation would never rise to its former heights again. The young men would be slain and the young women taken into slavery, so the future generation would be given into the hands of the enemy.

Nations never seem to learn that God is serious about what happens to His people Israel. The devastating judgment that God sent to Egypt before the Exodus should have taught the Egyptians a lasting lesson, but apparently they forgot it. In opposing God's purposes for Israel, Egypt invited God's judgments on their own nation, for the Lord always keeps His covenant promises.

4. The bones broken (Ezek. 30:20-26)

This oracle was delivered on April 29, 587 B.C. and refers to God's crushing the Egyptian military power. The arm is a symbol of power, but God would break both of Pharaoh's arms and leave Egypt helpless. Nobody would apply splints or even bandage up the wounds to promote healing.

The first "breaking" took place at Carchemish in 605 B.C. when Nebuchadnezzar defeated Pharaoh Necho (2 Kings 24:7; Jer. 46:2). It was also at Carchemish that godly King Josiah was slain. The second "breaking" occurred when Pharaoh Hophra tried to help Judah when Nebuchadnezzar attacked Jerusalem (37:5ff). With both arms "broken," Egypt would not be able to wield a sword, and that would put an end to the battle. Pharaoh Hophra had a second title, "The Strong-Armed," but that title would not apply anymore.

While the Lord was permitting the Babylonians to break the arms of Egypt, He was also strengthening the arms of the Babylonians! He even put His own sword into the hand of Nebuchadnezzar! The Egyptians would be either slain or scattered and their land would be left desolate. "They shall know that I am the Lord" is repeated twice (Ezek. 30:25-26). During Israel's sojourn in Egypt, Pharaoh wouldn't recognize the Lord; but now the nation would learn that the Lord God of the Hebrews was indeed the only true and living God.

5. The tree felled (Ezek. 31:1-18)

The date of this message is June 21, 587 B.C., and the image in the message is that of a great tree that is cut down. In Scripture, a tree is sometimes used as the image of a nation or an empire (chap. 17; Dan. 4). The argument the prophet presented was simple. Egypt boasted in its greatness, yet Egypt wasn't as great as Assyria, and Assyria was conquered by Babylon. Conclusion: if Babylon can conquer Assyria, Babylon can conquer Egypt.

Assyria's greatness (vv. 1-9). Egypt boasted of its greatness, so the prophet asked Pharaoh to name a nation that compared with Egypt. "Who can be compared to Egypt?" Ezekiel asked, and then he answered his question: "Only Assyria!" The Egyptians would agree and be happy to have their country rated so high.

The cedars in Lebanon were widely known for their quality and their height. Assyria was like one of those cedars, impressive in height and expansive in growth. It was nurtured by many waters, which symbolize the nations under Assyria's control that contributed to her wealth. (These nations are also symbolized by the fowl and the beasts that had security because of the tree.) The Lord allowed Assyria to achieve greatness because He had a work for her to do. The Northern Kingdom of Israel had rebelled against the Lord, so He used the Assyrians to chastise them and conquer their land (722 B.C.). In the days of King Hezekiah, the Lord used the Assyrians to discipline the kingdom of Judah, but He didn't allow them to take Jerusalem (Isa. 37; 2 Kings 19; 2 Chron. 32). God is sovereign over the nations and is able to use even the pagan peoples to accomplish His purposes.

No other kingdom could compare with Assyria. In a burst of poetic exaggeration, Ezekiel said that even the cedars and other trees in the Garden of Eden paled into insignificance beside Assyria. But it was the Lord who made Assyria beautiful and great (v. 9), yet the Assyrians did not recognize or acknowledge this fact.

Assyria's fall (vv. 10-14). As we have seen before, God hates pride and judges it severely. He judged the pride of Judah and Samaria (chap. 16), Ammon, Moab, and Edom (chap. 25), and expecially Tyre (23:3; chaps. 26–28), and also Assyria, and He would eventually judge Egypt. The logic of this judgment, what hope was there for a lesser kingdom like Egypt? God would call "the mighty one of the nations" (v. 10) to humble Assyria, and this is, of course, King Nebuchadnezzar (30:11).

The tree was very tall and stately, but it would be cut down and left on the land to decay. The smaller nations would abandon Assyria ansd seek help elsewhere. From the highest heights, Assyria would end up in the deepest depths of the underworld (sheol). From a position of great strength, the kingdom would fall into utter weakness, and from sustaining the lives of others to experiencing death and decay. Whereas once Assyria was admired and praised, it would end up being mocked. God had to teach Assyria a lesson (v. 14), that those who exalt themselves will eventually be abased, a lesson nations and individuals need to learn today (Prov. 29:23; Isa. 2:12; Mal. 4:1; Matt. 23:11-12; 1 Peter 5:5-7).

Assyria's burial (vv. 15-18). As with Tyre in chapter 28 and Babylon in Isaiah 14, Assyria was brought down to the underworld along with all the other rulers and nations that rebelled against God. When Assyria fell, a shock wave went through the nations, but the king of Assyria had this comfort: he wasn't any different from the rulers who had preceded him. They were all in the same place. In verse 18 the prophet addressed the ruler of Egypt: "To which of the trees in Eden will you then be likened in glory and greatness? Yet you shall be brought down . . . to the depths of the earth . . ." (NKJV).

The Egyptians were very careful in their practice of circumcision, but their ruler would be lying in sheol with the dead from nations that didn't practice it at all. What humiliation! (See 28:10.) He thought he and his kingdom were as great as Assyria, so God humbled him by putting him with the Assyrians in the world of the dead.

6. The monster trapped (Ezek. 32:1-16)

The date of this oracle is March 5, 585 B.C.

two months after the exiles in Babylon received the news that Jerusalem had fallen (33:21-22). The "monster" theme was used in 29:1-16, but Ezekiel uses it again to bring out some additional spiritual truths.

The monster captured (vv. 1-10). This is an "official lamentation" for the king of Egypt who thought he was a great lion but in God's sight was only a crocodile.[4] Pharaoh thrashed about in the water and made a big scene, but all he did was muddy the waters and create problems by disobeying the Lord.

In chapter 29, God caught the Egyptian "crocodile" with a hook, but now Egypt is so weak, it can be easily caught with a net. (See 12:13; 17:20; 19:8.) God would take the crocodile to the land and leave him there to die, and the vultures would devour the carcass, reminding us of 29:3-5. But he adds two more images: the land drenched in blood and the heavens shrouded in darkness (vv. 6-8). These are reminders of the first and ninth plagues before Israel's exodus from Egypt, the turning of the water into blood and the darkness for three days (Ex. 7:20-24; 10:21-29). According to Revelation 8:8-9, a similar judgment will fall during the Great Tribulation.

The description of the signs in the heavens makes us think of the future day of the Lord described in Joel 3, Amos 5:18-20, and Matthew 24. It has well been said that past events cast their shadows before, and so it will be with the fall of Egypt. It was a dress rehearsal for the judgments of the last days. Once again, Ezekiel explained that just as the fall of Assyria caused a shock wave to go through the nations (30:16; see 27:35 and 28:19), so the fall of Egypt will frighten the nations (32:9-10). But will they learn from this experience and turn to the Lord? No, they will go right on sinning and rebelling against His truth.

The monster punished (vv. 11-15). Here the prophet repeated the prophecy that the sword of Babylon would leave Egypt desolate and that all of Egypt's pride and pomp would vanish. Even the animal life in the land would be destroyed as it was during the plagues of Egypt in Moses' time. With no people and animals available to work the land and draw the water, the streams and canals wouldn't be muddied and the water would "run like oil" with nothing to impede its flow. This is in contrast to Pharaoh's behavior described in verse 2. Ordinarily, the flowing of oil is a picture of peace and prosperity from God's blessings, but in this case, it speaks of peace because of God's judgment. No humans or animals are there to stir up the mud and defile the water. But the picture also reminds us that Egypt's defeat would help to bring peace to the "pool" of nations.

7. The corpse is buried (Ezek. 32:17-32)

This is the seventh oracle and since no other date is recorded, we assume it was given two weeks after the previous message—March 17, 585 B.C. It follows the style of 31:15-18 and describes the people of Egypt descending into sheol, the world of the dead. Ezekiel was instructed to wail because of the multitudes of people who would be slain by the swords of the Babylonians.

The picture is grim and almost macabre as the other nations welcome Pharaoh and his hosts and taunt them as they arrive in the underworld. We might paraphrase their words, "So you thought you were so beautiful and strong? Look at you now! You prided yourselves in being a circumcised people, but now you are lying down in death with the uncircumcised. Like us, you thought you were invincible, but now you have joined us in death and decay. You are no longer on a throne—you are in a grave! Your bed is a sepulchre."

Ezekiel named some of the nations, great and small, that welcomed Pharaoh and his people to sheol: Asshur (v. 22), which is Assyria; Elam (v. 24), an area in Iran; Meshach and Tubal (v. 26), probably located in Asia Minor; and Edom and the Sidonians, neighbors of Israel (vv. 29-30). Like the king of Assyria before him (31:16), Pharaoh would see all these princes and common people and be comforted that he wasn't the only one defeated and slain.

Death is the great leveler; and as John Donne reminded us, when the funeral bell tolls, "it tolls for thee." There are no "kings and commoners" in the land of the dead, and we can't enter that land in peace and safety without faith in Jesus Christ. "'O Death, where is your sting? O Hades, where is your victory?' The sting of death is sin, and the strength of sin is the law. But thanks be to God, who gives us the victory through our Lord Jesus Christ" (1 Cor. 15:55-57, NKJV).

INTERLUDE

Chapters 33 to 48 of Ezekiel focus on the hope of Israel as found in the promises God has made to His chosen people. In chapter 33, God reminds His prophet that he has been commissioned to be a watchman whose task it is to protect and inform the people by keeping his eyes open to what is happening and his ears open to what God is saying.

In the previous chapters, the Lord revealed His judgments on His own people and on the neighboring nations. Ezekiel told the exiles in Babylon that the city of Jerusalem would be taken by the Babylonians, the land would be ravaged, and the temple would be destroyed. But in this closing section of the book, he had the happy privilege of announcing a bright future for the people of God. The holy city and the Promised Land would be restored (chaps. 33–36), the divided kingdom would be united and protected (chaps. 37–39), and there would be a new temple in which the glory of the Lord would reside (chaps. 40–48). The glory that he had seen depart from the defiled temple (11:23) he saw return to the new temple (43:4-5; 44:4). The kingdom promised by the prophets would be established, and the Messiah, the Son of David, would reign from Jerusalem.

Some students prefer to interpret Ezekiel 33–48 idealistically or symbolically, applying these descriptions "spiritually" to the church today rather than literally to Israel in the future. But if we've been interpreting Ezekiel's prophetic word literally up to this point, what right do we have to change our approach and start interpreting his words symbolically? As Dr. David Cooper said, "When the plain sense of Scripture makes good sense, then we need no other sense." We must face the fact that both approaches—the symbolical and the literal—present problems to the interpreter, but taking Ezekiel's prophecies at face value seems to present fewer problems. Furthermore, seeing literal fulfillment of these prophecies accomplishes the purpose for which God gave them, the encouragement of the people of Israel. Few nations if any have suffered as Israel has suffered, and to rob God's chosen people of their hope is to make their suffering meaningless.

Our approach will be to assume that these prophecies will have a literal fulfillment and that Israel will one day see her Messiah and share in the glorious kingdom promised by Ezekiel and the other prophets. At the same time, we will seek to apply the basic spiritual lessons taught in these chapters, truths that apply to God's people in the church today.

CHAPTER TEN
WARNINGS AND PROMISES FROM THE WATCHMAN
Ezekiel 33–35

It has well been said that the most important thing about prophets is not that they have hindsight or foresight but that they also have *insight*. Prophetic hindsight is important because it helps us deal with the past and understand better what God did and why He did it. Foresight helps us avoid trouble and have hope for the future. But insight helps us better understand ourselves and those around us, and what we must do to become better men and women who do the will of God. In these chapters, Ezekiel exercises all three gifts as he exposes sin, analyzes history, and gives promises for the future. He deals with the sins of the Jewish people (chap. 33), the sins of their leaders (chap. 34), and the sins of the neighboring land of Edom (chap. 35).

1. The sins of the nation (Ezek. 33:1-33)

This chapter reaches back into some of Ezekiel's previous messages and brings together truths that were important to Israel's understanding of God, their situation, and what God wanted them to do. You will find here references to 3:15-27; chapters 5 and 6; 11:14-21; 18:1-32; 20:1-8; and 24:25-27. It's as though the Lord led His servant to combine these basic spiritual truths in one message so that nobody could say, "I didn't hear what the Lord said to us!" Ezekiel turned the light of God's Word on the nation as a whole (33:1-20), the people left in Judah and Jerusalem (vv. 23-29), and the exiles in Babylon (vv. 21-22, 30-33), and he revealed what was in their hearts and lives.

The entire nation (Ezek. 33:1-20). Every Jew who had ever lived in a walled city knew what Ezekiel was talking about when he referred to the watchmen on the wall, for these watchmen were important to the city's defense. Faithful watchmen kept their eyes focused on the horizon and gave the warning when they saw the enemy approaching. If the watchmen were alert and faithful and the people obedient, lives would be saved; if the watchmen were careless, or the people unconcerned, the city would be captured and people would die.

God had called Ezekiel to be His watchman (3:19-21) and it was his task to hear God's Word of warning and declare it to the people. The faithful watchman had clean hands, but the unfaithful watchman had hands that were stained by the blood of the victims who died because he didn't warn them. Isaiah compared unfaithful watchmen to blind men, dogs that can't bark, and people who can't stay awake (Isa. 56:10). Ezekiel was a faithful watchman who delivered God's message to the Jews in Babylon as well as those back in Judah, and that message was, "Repent—turn from your sins!" The word "turn" is used eight times in this chapter and it describes "repentance." The biblical words translated "repent" simply mean "to change your mind," but this change of mind also involves a change of life. If a thief truly repented, he or she would restore what had been stolen. The liars would confess their deception and ask for forgiveness, and the drunkards would stop their alcohol abuse.

The discussion in Ezekiel 33:10-20 reminds us of 18:1-32 where Ezekiel explained human responsibility before God. The Jews had blamed the older generation for what had happened to the nation, but Ezekiel made it clear that God didn't punish the children for the sins of their fathers. Each person was accountable for his or her own sins and couldn't blame somebody else. But 33:10 suggests that some of the Jews were now feeling the pain of their sins like a heavy weight on their shoulders, and day after day were "wearing away." However, this feeling of remorse fell far short of real repentance.

We must correctly distinguish regret, remorse, and true repentance. Regret is an activity of the mind; whenever we remember what we've done, we ask ourselves, "Why did I do that?" Remorse includes both the heart and the mind, and we feel disgust and pain, but we don't change our ways. But true repentance includes the mind, the heart, and the will. We change our mind about our sins and agree with what God says about them; we abhor ourselves because of what we have done; and we deliberately turn from our sin and turn to the Lord for His mercy.

When Peter remembered his sin of denying Christ, he repented and sought pardon; when Judas remembered his sin of betraying Christ, he experienced only remorse, and he went out and hanged himself. "For godly sorrow produces repentance to salvation, not to be regretted; but the sorrow of the world produces death" (2 Cor. 7:10, NKJV). If the sinner turns *from* his sins and turns *to* the Lord in faith, he will be forgiven. Paul's message was "repentance toward God, and faith toward our Lord Jesus Christ" (Acts 20:21), and that message is still valid today.

As they did previously (Ezek. 18:21-29), the Jews debated with Ezekiel and affirmed that God wasn't being fair and that His ways were unequal. This response in itself proved that they had not really repented, because repentant sinners don't argue with God's Word. The Jews were saying, "God isn't using standard weights on His scales! He's got the scales fixed!" But their accusation against the Lord was false. As Ezekiel had already told them (vv. 21-29), it wasn't *God's ways* that were false but *their own ways*! It wasn't their responsibility to prove God wrong but to admit that they were wrong!

The people of the land (Ezek. 33:23-29). The Babylonians had left some of the poor people to take care of the fields and the ruins (Jer. 52:16), while the rest who survived the siege were taken to Babylon. The Lord heard what these people were saying: "We have a right to this land because the Lord spared us to live here." After all, when Abraham was just one man,[1] God gave him the land; but the survivors were many and had lived on the land a long time. The very fact that they had survived proved that they were special to the Lord. Therefore, they could claim the land for themselves because the former owners were either dead or in exile.

They had forgotten that Jeremiah had already settled the question of which group was God's choice people, the exiles in Babylon or the survivors in Judah. As recorded in Jeremiah 24, God showed Jeremiah two baskets of figs, one filled with very good figs and the other with very bad figs. The very good figs represented the exiles in Babylon, the remnant God would use to rebuild the temple and restore the nation. The very bad figs were King Zedekiah and the leaders in Jerusalem who disobeyed the Lord by breaking the treaty with Babylon. It's obvious that the remnant in Judah was not considered "special" or "choice" by the Lord.[2]

But Abraham was a righteous man, and the people left in Judah had been living in defiance of God's law! In Ezekiel 33:25-26, Ezekiel listed some of the sins they were committing: eating meat with the blood still in it (Deut. 12:16, 23; Lev. 17:10); worshiping idols (Ex. 20:4-6); murder (v. 13); relying on violence ("stand upon your sword," KJV); and doing abominable things, like committing adultery (v. 14). No, instead of inheriting the land and becoming rich, the people would be slain by the sword, the beasts of the field, or the pestilence that often accompanies war (Ezek. 33:27; see 5:12; 7:15; 12:16; 14:12-21). Instead of the land becoming their prize possession, it would become desolate and enjoy its Sabbath rest (Lev. 26:32-35, 43; 2 Chron. 36:21).

The exiles in Babylon (Ezek. 33:21-22, 30-33). The Babylonian army set fire to Jerusalem on August 14, 586 B.C., and about five months later—January 8, 585 B.C.—a fugitive arrived in Babylon to announce the sad fact that Jerusalem and the temple had been destroyed. This validated the prophecies of Ezekiel and proved that he was indeed the prophet of God (Deut. 18:20-22). The night before he received this news, Ezekiel had been in a prophetic state with God's hand upon him, so he knew that something special was about to be revealed. The hearing of this news brought about the opening of Ezekiel's mouth so that he was no longer mute when he wasn't declaring the message of God (Ezek. 3:26-27). He was now able to converse with people and have a "pastoral" ministry among them apart from his prophetic preaching. For about seven and a half years, Ezekiel had been under this constraint, but now he was free to speak. Certainly the exiles noticed this and would be curious to know what had happened to him.

But Ezekiel knew that the people who came to his house to hear him speak didn't appreciate his ministry or obey what they heard. As the exiles met one another during the day, they would step out of the hot sunlight and discuss the prophet's ministry (v. 30). They even invited people to come with them to hear the preacher! But going to hear the Word of God wasn't a serious thing to them. "Come on, let's have some fun! Let's go hear the prophet tell us what the Lord is saying" (v. 30, NLT). But they weren't concerned about God's truth or their personal responsibility; all they wanted to do was get up-to-date information so they could make money! They listened to God's preacher but refused to obey what God told them to do (James 1:22-25; Ps. 78:36-37; 1 John 3:18). They saw Ezekiel as an entertainer who sang love songs, not as an exhorter who sought to convey God's love to them.

This information could have discouraged the prophet, but the Lord added a message of faith and hope: The day would come when the fulfillment of God's prophetic Word would convince careless people that a prophet had truly been among them. This would mean personal privilege (hearing the Word), personal responsibility (obeying the Word), and personal accountability (being judged by the Word that they had heard, John 12:48).

Believers today have the Word of God readily accessible not only in public meetings, but also in literature, on the Internet, over radio and television, as well as on video and audio tapes and CDs, and we will have much to answer for when we see the Lord. The important thing at the Judgment Seat of Christ won't be how much Bible we studied or learned, but how much we loved and obeyed.

2. The sins of the leaders (Ezek. 34:1-31)

Ezekiel had already exposed the sins of the nation's leaders (chap. 22), but he returned to this theme because it had a bearing on Israel's future. While this message applied to Israel's current situation in Ezekiel's day, it also had application in that future day when the Lord gathers His scattered people back to their land. This message certainly must have brought hope to the exiles as they realized the Lord has not forsaken them but would care for them as a shepherd for his sheep.

When the Lord spoke about "the flock," He

was referring to the nation of Israel (34:31). "We are His people, and the sheep of his pasture" (Ps. 100:3; see 77:20; 78:52; 80:1). Moses saw Israel as a flock (Num. 27:17; see 1 Kings 22:17) and so did Jeremiah (Jer. 13:17) and Zechariah (Zech. 10:3). Jesus spoke of "the lost sheep of the house of Israel" (Matt. 10:6; 15:24). Because Jesus called Himself "the Good Shepherd" and "the door of the sheep" (John 10:7, 11), the image of the flock carried over into the church (Acts 20:28-29; 1 Peter 5:2-3). Our English word "pastor" comes from the Latin and means "shepherd."

Exploiting and abusing the sheep (Ezek. 34:1-10). Kings and officers in government were referred to as "shepherds" (2 Sam. 7:7-8; Ps. 78:70-71; Isa. 56:10-11; 63:11; Jer. 23:9-11; 25:18-19). It was their responsibility to care for the people, protect them, and see to it that their needs were met. But the selfish leaders of the kingdom of Judah had abused and exploited the people because they thought only of themselves. They milked the sheep and ate the curds, fleeced the sheep and made garments of the wool, and butchered the sheep and enjoyed the meat, but they failed to care for the sheep and meet their needs. Whenever leaders take from their people but don't give them something in return, they are exploiting them. But true leaders don't exploit their people—they sacrifice for them. Jesus the Shepherd set the example by laying down His life for His flock (John 10:10).

The leaders not only exploited the sheep but they also abused them by neglecting to meet their needs. Sheep require constant care, but the leaders didn't manage the nation's affairs for the sake of the sheep but for their own profit. They didn't care for them at all. If the leaders' sins of commission were bad, their sins of omission were worse. They didn't minister to the sick and injured, nor did they seek for the lost and scattered sheep. They ruled only with force and cruelty. Three times Ezekiel accused them of allowing the sheep to be scattered, and a scattered flock without a shepherd is vulnerable and easily attacked by beasts of prey (Jer. 50:6). Because the leaders made selfish and unwise decisions, the nation fell apart and the flock was scattered.

Rescuing the flock (Ezek. 34:11-22). Was there any hope for God's scattered people? Yes, because the Lord would come to deliver His flock from their oppressors and gather them to Himself. In Ezekiel's time, the Lord brought His people back from Babylon; but the picture here is certainly much broader than that, for the Lord spoke about "countries" (v. 13). Ezekiel promises that in the end times, the Lord will gather His flock "from all places where they have been scattered" (v. 12) and bring them back to their own land where He will be their Shepherd (Matt. 24:31).

It's difficult to apply this prophecy to the return of the remnant after their exile in Babylon, and even more difficult to "spiritualize" it and apply it to the church today. The prophet is speaking about a literal future regathering of Israel, a topic that is mentioned frequently in Ezekiel's book (Ezek. 11:17; 20:34, 41-42; 28:25; 36:24; 37:21-25; 38:8). This promise of regathering is a part of God's covenant with the Jews (Deut. 30:1-10), and the Lord always keeps His promises. (See also Isa. 11:11-12; Jer. 23:3-8; and Micah 2:12; 4:6-8.) After He gathers His people, He will see to it that none of the "fat cattle" who preyed on the weaker ones will push them around, muddy their drinking water, or tramp down their pastures. The "fat [sleek] and strong" in Ezekiel 34:16 refer to the leaders who took advantage of the people. Don't read into "rams and he-goats" (v. 17) the New Testament image of "sheep and goats" as found in Matthew 25:31-46, because in Bible times, it was customary for shepherds to have both sheep and goats in the flocks.

Protecting the flock (Ezek. 34:23-31). This is definitely a prophecy of future events, because the returned remnant didn't have an august ruler caring for them, nor did "showers of blessing" come to the land. The economic situation at the beginning was difficult, the harvests were poor, and the peoples of the land were opposed to any Jewish presence there. But when Israel is regathered to her land in the end times, the Messiah will rule over them and be their Shepherd-King. The "prince" (v. 24) will not be King David, resurrected and enthroned, but the Lord Jesus Christ whom Israel will receive and trust when they see Him (Zech. 12:9–13:1; see Jer. 23:5; 30:8-10; Hosea 3:5). Ezekiel mentions "David the prince" in 37:24-25; 45:22; 46:4, and these references point to the Messiah.

Agriculture in the land of Israel depended on the early and latter rains from the Lord, and He promised to send the rain faithfully if the people honored His covenant (Lev. 26:1-5; Deut. 28:9-14). But if they disobeyed Him, the heavens would turn to brass and the ground to iron (Deut. 11:13-17; 28:23-24). If the people repented and sought His forgiveness, He would send the rain and heal the land (Deut. 30; 2 Chron. 7:12-14).

The Lord also promised that the people would be safe in the land and not be oppressed by the peoples around them. Except during the reigns of David and Solomon, the nation of Israel has been attacked, conquered, and ravaged by one nation after another, but this will cease when Messiah is on the throne. A "covenant of peace" would govern the land (Ezek. 34:25; see 37:26), which probably refers to the New Covenant that Jeremiah promised in Jeremiah 31:31-34. The law of God would be written on the hearts of the people and they all would know the Lord and obey His will.

Neither the pain of scarcity nor the shame of defeat will rob the Jewish people of the blessings the Lord has planned for them. In the past, their sins forced the Lord to turn His face against them; but in the future kingdom, He will smile upon them and dwell with them. Ezekiel had watched the glory of God leave the temple (Ezek. 11:22-23), but he would also see God's glory return (43:1-5). The name of the holy city would become "Jehovah Shammah—the Lord is there" (48:35).

3. The sins of Edom (Ezek. 35:1-15)

The Lord had already pronounced judgment on Edom through Isaiah (Isa. 34; 63:1-6), Jeremiah (Jer. 49:7-22), and Ezekiel (25:12-14), but now He did it again and added some details. Mount Seir is another name for Edom, the nation founded by Esau, Jacob's twin brother. "Edom" means "red" and was a nickname given to Esau (Gen. 25:30). Esau was a man of the world who had no spiritual desires and willingly sold his birthright to his brother Jacob. Esau fought with his brother even in their mother's womb (vv. 21-26) and hated his brother because the Lord had chosen Jacob to receive the blessings of the covenant. This hatred was passed on from generation to generation and the Edomites maintained what God called "a perpetual hatred" (v. 5; 25:15; Amos 1:11-12; Obadiah). This hatred was no doubt like some of the "ethnic wars" that the world has seen today.

Once again, the Lord reminded the Edomites of their great sin against their brethren when they assisted the Babylonians in attacking the Jews during the siege of Jerusalem. What their founder Esau vowed to do in his day, they accomplished in their day when they killed their own blood relatives (Gen. 47:41). In Ezekiel 35:6, the word "blood" in the KJV should read "bloodshed." The Edomites pursued the Jews to kill them, so bloodshed would pursue them. The Edomites carried on a perpetual hatred against Israel, so the land of Edom would receive a perpetual desolation. Edom would be no more.

Was this a just judgment? Yes, it was, and the prophet gave the reasons why the destruction of Edom was an act of righteous judgment. For one thing, the descendants of Esau were greedy and wanted to claim the conquered nations of Judah and Samaria for themselves, completely ignoring the will of the Lord. God had given the land of Canaan to Abraham and his descendants, and that meant Jacob and not Esau. During Israel's march to Canaan, they were warned not to meddle with the Edomites because God had assigned their land to them and they would not inherit any land in Canaan (Deut. 2:1-7). But the Edomites wanted to change God's plans and annul God's covenant and take the land for themselves. When the Babylonians invaded Judah in 606 B.C., the Lord was there fulfilling His own purposes (Ezek. 35:10) and He saw what the Edomites did.

The Lord also saw their anger (v. 11) and promised to repay them in kind, for nations as well as individuals reap what they sow. He heard their blasphemous words against their brothers the Jews, how they rejoiced because the land of Israel was being ravaged and plundered by the Babylonian invaders. But they weren't blaspheming men, they were blaspheming God and boasting in their pride as though they would escape judgment. In their arrogance, Edom rejoiced over the fall of Israel; but one day, the whole earth would rejoice over the fall of Edom!

God's promise to the Jews was that one day they would no longer be a prey to the other nations (34:28), and this chapter explains why: God will deal with their enemies and remove them from the face of the earth. "You will be desolate, O Mount Seir, you and all of Edom" (35:15, NIV).

CHAPTER ELEVEN
FROM RESTORATION TO REUNION
Ezekiel 36–37

"Our hope is lost!" That's what the Jewish exiles were saying to each other as they "pined away" in Babylon (37:11; 33:10), and from the human point of view, the statement was true. But if they had listened to their prophets, they would have had hope in the Lord and looked forward with anticipation. Jeremiah had written to them that they would be in Babylon for seventy years, and that God's thoughts toward them were of peace and not of evil (Jer. 29:10). Ezekiel had given them God's promise that He would gather His people and take them back to their land (Ezek. 11:17; 20:34, 41-42; 28:25). A Latin proverb says, "Where there is life, there is hope," but the reverse is also true: where there is hope, we find reason to live. Swiss theologian Emil Brunner wrote, "What oxygen is to the lungs, such is hope for the meaning of life."

In his previous messages, Ezekiel looked back and reproved the people because of their sins. Now he looks ahead and encourages the people by telling them what the Lord will do for Israel in the future. These promises go beyond the ending of the Babylonian Captivity and anticipate the end times. The Jewish people will be gathered to their land, the land will be cleansed and restored, and the nation will have a new temple and the presence of the glory of the Lord. The future of Israel can be summarized in four words: restoration, regeneration, resurrection, and reunion.

1. Restoration: the land healed (Ezek. 36:1-15)

God gave the land of Israel to the Jews as a part of the Abrahamic Covenant (Gen. 12:1-3; 13:14-18; 15:7-21). That settled their *ownership* of the land, but their *possession* and *enjoyment* of the land depended on their faith and obedience (Lev. 26). The Christian life is similar. We *enter* God's family by trusting Jesus Christ (John 3:16; Eph. 2:8-9), but we *enjoy* God's family by believing His promises and obeying His will (2 Cor. 6:18–7:1). Disobedient children have to be chastened (Heb. 12), and God often had to chasten the people of Israel because of their rebellion and disobedience.

Ezekiel had set his face against Mount Seir, which represented the land of Edom (Ezek. 35), but now he addressed "the mountains of Israel" as representative of the land of Israel. The Babylonians had ravaged and plundered the Promised Land and the neighboring nations (especially Edom) had tried to possess the land (36:10). Instead of assisting the Jews, the neighbors had ridiculed them and even helped the Babylonians loot the city of Jerusalem. Why? Because of their long-standing hatred of the Jews and a desire to possess the land of Israel. "Aha, even the ancient high places are ours in possession" (v. 2).

But the Lord knew what the enemy was saying and doing, and He determined that there would be serious consequences because of their decisions. That's why you find the word "therefore" six times in this section (vv. 3-7, 14). First, the fire of God's jealous love would burn against Israel's enemies because of the way they had treated His people and His land (vv. 4-6; Lev. 25:23). He even took an oath (Ezek. 36:7) that the nations would be repaid for the way they treated the Jews. They had taunted and ridiculed the Jews, but now they themselves would be put to shame.

Ezekiel described that future day when the land would be healed and once again produce abundant flocks, herds, and harvests (vv. 8-9). This was a part of God's covenant with Israel (Lev. 26:3-5). The land would not only be fruitful, but it also would be safe and secure (Ezek. 36:10-12). The combination of war, pestilence, and wild beasts had decreased the Jewish population (6:1-8; 7:15; 12:16), but God had promised they would be as numerous as the dust of the earth and the stars of the heavens (Gen. 13:16; 15:5). If the nation was to fulfill its divine purposes on earth, the people had to multiply.

God accused the mountains of Israel of depriving the Jews of their children (Ezek. 36:12-14, see NIV). This may refer to the fact that the pagan shrines were in the high places, and there some of the Jews offered their own children to the heathen gods. But that would end, because the exile in Babylon cured the Jews of their idolatry, and in the future kingdom, only the true and living God would be worshiped. In Ezekiel 40–48, Ezekiel will have more to say about the restored land of Israel when Messiah reigns on the throne of David in Jerusalem.

Since the founding of the nation of Israel in 1948, great progress has been made by the Jewish people in reclaiming the land. There has been a great deal of reforestation and irrigation, and the waste places are being transformed. As wonderful as this is, it is nothing compared with what the Lord will do when His people are gathered back to their land from the nations of the world. "Even the wilderness will rejoice in those days. The desert will blossom with flowers. Yes, there will be an abundance of flowers and singing and joy! The deserts will become as green as the mountains of Lebanon, as lovely as Mount Carmel's pastures and the plain of Sharon. There the Lord will display His glory, the splendor of our God" (Isa. 35:1-2, NLT).

2. Regeneration: the people cleansed (Ezek. 36:16-38)

The Jewish people forgot that the land belonged to the Lord, for He said, "The land is Mine" (Lev. 25:23). In fact, the whole earth belongs to the Lord (Ex. 19:5; Ps. 24:1), and we have no right to abuse the natural resources He shares with us.

God's indictment against His people (Ezek. 36:16-23). Israel was guilty of two great sins, the first of which was *polluting God's land* (vv. 16-19). Long before the Babylonians had swept through the kingdom of Judah, the sins of the leaders and the people had polluted the so-called "holy land." When God's people disobeyed God's law and behaved like the heathen nations around them, they defiled the land and broke the covenant (Lev. 18:26-30). Not only did they worship idols and sacrifice their children's innocent blood, but they also shed blood when they falsely accused the poor and needy in court and led them out to die. Each act of disobedience only polluted the land more, until the Lord was so grieved by their rebellion that He had the land vomit them out, and He sent them to Babylon. In our contemporary world, we wonder how much land is being polluted by the destruction of innocent babies, the murders of innocent people, including children in school, and the general disregard for both the laws of man and the law of God.

Their second sin was that of *profaning God's name before the Gentiles* (Ezek. 36:20-23). It was bad enough that they had polluted the land God allowed them to enjoy, but they also profaned God's holy name instead of being godly witnesses in the Gentile lands where He sent them (vv. 20-23). They had imitated the pagans for so long that they felt right at home among them and adopted more of their ways. During the exile, there was a godly remnant that remained true to the Lord, but in general, the Jews tended to forget their calling as the people of God. Five times in this paragraph we're told that the Jews profaned the name of God before the pagans before whom they had been sent to be a light (Isa. 42:6; 49:6). In spite of their disobedience, what an opportunity the Lord gave the Jews to introduce the Gentiles to the true and living God!

The Jews were separated from their temple, now destroyed, and from the things necessary for Jewish worship, but the Lord was still with them and could see their hearts. The Jews had profaned God's name by defiling the sanctuary (Ezek. 5:11; 22:26), but He had promised to be "a little sanctuary" for them there in Babylon (11:16). They had profaned the Sabbaths (22:8; 23:38), but they knew what day it was in Babylon and could still seek to obey God. The still had the Law and the Prophets and could meditate on the Word and praise the Lord. Instead of the Jews sanctifying God's name among the heathen, they profaned His name by their lack of separation and godly witness; but is the church today any different? Do we live in such commitment to Christ that the world sits up and takes notice and wants to hear what we have to say?

The Lord promises to change the people only because He desires to sanctify and glorify His great name (36:22). In the last days, when the Lord gathers His people back to their land, everything the Lord will do for them will be because of His grace and not because they deserve it. God didn't give them the land because of their righteousness (Deut. 9:6), and He won't restore the land because of anything good they have done. God in His grace gives us what we don't deserve, and in His mercy He doesn't give us what we do deserve! All that we have in Christ comes from God's grace

(Eph. 1:7; 2:8-10) and was designed for God's glory (1:6, 11, 14).

God's transformation of His people (Ezek. 36:24-38). In the last days, when God brings His chosen people back to the Promised Land (v. 24), He will change them spiritually; for, after all, only a transformed people can enjoy a transformed land. The spiritual experience described in this section illustrates what happens to every sinner who trusts Jesus Christ.

First, *God will cleanse them from their sins,* and this is pictured by "sprinkling" (vv. 25, 29; 37:23). According to the Mosaic Law, every Jew who became defiled[1] had to be cleansed before he or she could return to the camp and the blessings of the covenant community. This was accomplished either by bathing in running water or by being sprinkled with water prepared for that purpose (Lev. 14:1-9; Num. 19; 8:5-7; Heb. 10:22). Of course, water can never change the heart, but this is only a picture of the gracious forgiveness we have through faith. God forgives trusting sinners because of the death of Jesus on the cross (Eph. 1:7). When believers confess their sins to the Lord, they are cleansed because of Christ's blood (1 John 1:9).

Second, *the Lord will give them a new heart* (Ezek. 36:26). Ezekiel had already spoken about this inward change (11:18-20; 18:31), the kind of change that the Lord yearned for Israel to experience before they entered the Promised Land. "Oh, that they had such a heart in them that they would fear Me and always keep all My commandments" (Deut. 5:29, NKJV). The Prophet Jeremiah shared the same promise that Ezekiel gave: "Then I will give them a heart to know Me, that I am the Lord; and they shall be My people, and I will be their God" (Jer. 24:7, NKJV). Jeremiah spoke about the New Covenant God would make with the Jews, a covenant not written on stones but on their hearts and in their minds (31:31-33; 32:29; see Isa. 59:21; Heb. 8:8-13). A "stony heart" is a hard heart, one that doesn't receive God's Word and nurture spiritual growth (Ezek. 2:4; 3:7).

Third, *the Lord will give them the Holy Spirit within* (Ezek. 36:27). It is the Spirit who accomplishes these divine miracles in the hearts of those who trust the Lord for salvation. He gives us a new heart and a new spirit and also a new desire to love the Lord and obey Him. The Holy Spirit is given like refreshing water upon parched ground, and this produces the "fruit of the Spirit" in our lives (Isa. 44:3; Gal. 5:22-23). The witness of the Spirit in the heart is proof that the person has been born of God (Rom. 8:9, 14-17; Eph. 1:13-14). Because you have God's Spirit within, you share in the divine nature (2 Peter 1:1-4) and therefore want to obey the divine will. It is nature that determines conduct. Dogs act like dogs because they have a dog's nature, and God's people act like they belong to God because they have God's nature within (1 John 3:9). Ezekiel will deal again with this gift of the Spirit in Ezekiel 37:14 and 39:29.

Fourth, *the Lord will claim them again as His people* (Ezek. 36:28). It will be like a renewal of the covenant, for they will live in the land, He will be their God and they will be His people. This will be a permanent arrangement, for they will no longer rebel against the Lord and disobey His will.

Fifth, *the Lord will cause the land to flourish* (vv. 29-30, 33-35). Under the covenant God made with Israel before they entered Canaan, He agreed to bless them and meet their needs if they would obey Him (Lev. 26:1-13; Deut. 28:1-14). When you read these promises, you are amazed at what the Jews gave up when they turned from serving God to serving idols. But when Israel enters into the promised kingdom, God will bless them and make the land like the Garden of Eden (Ezek. 36:35). The land will yield its harvests and the people will be enriched by the blessing of the Lord. The cities will be rebuilt and the ruins removed. It will be a wonderful new land for the new people of God. The beauty and fruitfulness of the land will be a testimony to the nations (v. 36).

Sixth, *the people will abhor their sins* (Ezek. 36:31-32). When some people remember their sins, they enjoy them again in the dirty depths of their imagination. This is evidence that they really haven't judged them and repented. When true children of God remember their past disobedience, they're ashamed of themselves and abhor themselves because of what they have done to the Lord, themselves, and others. "You who love the Lord, hate evil" (Ps. 97:10, NKJV). "Abhor that which is evil; cleave to that which is good" (Rom. 12:9). One of the evidences of the Spirit's presence within is a growing sensitivity to sin and a strong desire to turn away from it.

A seventh blessing will be *fellowship with the Lord* (Ezek. 36:37). In Ezekiel's day, the people couldn't inquire of the Lord or pray and be heard because they had sin in their hearts (14:1-5; 20:1-3, 30-31). God even told the Prophet Jeremiah not to pray for the people (Jer. 7:16; 11:14; 14:11). But under the New Covenant, the people will have fellowship with the Lord and be able to pray to Him.

The eighth blessing will be *the multiplication of the population* (Ezek. 36:37-38). As in chapter 34, God pictures His people as a flock of sheep, and every shepherd wants to see his flock increase. The Jewish population was greatly reduced during the Babylonian invasion, but the Lord will bless His people and cause them to be fruitful and multiply (see 36:12-13). The picture here is of the men going to Jerusalem for the annual Passover feast, bringing animal sacrifices with them. The number of animals in Jerusalem would increase greatly, and that's the way the Jewish people will increase in their kingdom.

Finally, as the result of all these blessings, *the Lord will be glorified.* Israel didn't glorify God in their land or the temple, nor did they glorify Him in the countries to which they were scattered. But the day will come when God will be glorified by His people and the glory of the Lord will return to the land.

Every born-again believer sees a parallel here with his or her own experience of faith in Christ. The Lord has washed us (1 Cor. 6:9-11), given us new hearts and His Holy Spirit within, and because of this, we should have a holy hatred for sin. We have the privilege of communion with God and prayer for our needs, plus a desire within to do His will. God wants to make our lives abundantly fruitful so we will glorify His name. The Lord has made us a part of His New Covenant (Heb. 8; 10) so that our union with Him through Christ is eternal and unchanging. Hallelujah, what a Savior![2]

3. Resurrection: the nation reborn (Ezek. 37:1-14)

Ezekiel has told the people the Lord's promise to restore the land and regenerate His people. But what about the nation itself, a nation divided (Israel and Judah) and without a king or a temple? The remnant would return to the ravaged land and rebuild the temple and the city, but none of the blessings Ezekiel promised would come to them at that time. No, the Prophet Ezekiel was looking far down the corridor of time to the end of the age when Jesus the Messiah would return and claim His people. Ezekiel told the people that the dead nation would one day be raised to life, and the divided nation would be united![3]

The dry bones (Ezek. 37:1-3). At the beginning of Ezekiel's ministry, the Spirit transported him to sit among the discouraged exiles by the canal (3:14ff). Later, the Spirit took him in visions to Jerusalem (8:3ff), to the temple gate and then back to Babylon (11:1, 24). Now the Spirit brought him in a vision to a valley filled with many bleached bones, scattered on the ground, the skeletons of corpses long ago decomposed and devoured by carrion-eating birds and animals. These people were slain (37:9), and they may have been soldiers in the Jewish army (v. 10).

It was a humiliating thing for the body of a dead Jew not to be washed, wrapped, and buried with dignity in a grave or a tomb. These bodies were left on the battlefield to become food for the vultures to eat and objects for the sun to bleach. But the Lord had warned Israel in the covenant He made with them that their sins would lead to just that kind of shameful experience. "The Lord will cause you to be defeated before your enemies. . . . Your carcasses shall be food for all the birds of the air and the beasts of the earth, and no one shall frighten them away" (Deut. 28:25-26, NKJV). Jeremiah was preaching this same message in Jerusalem: "I [the Lord] will give them into the hand of their enemies and into the hand of those who seek their life. Their dead bodies shall be for meat for the birds of the heaven and the beasts of the earth" (Jer. 34:20, NKJV).

The Lord told Ezekiel to walk around among the bones so he could appreciate their vast number and see how dry they were. As a priest, Ezekiel was never to be defiled by the dead, but this was a vision and the bones were not toxic. The prophet must have been wondering why the Lord gave him this vision, but the Lord's question gave him the answer: "Can these bones live?" From the human point of view, the answer is no, but from the divine point of view, nothing is impossible. It is God who "gives life to the dead and calls those things which do not exist as though they did" (Rom. 4:17). Ezekiel's reply didn't question the power of God; it only expressed the prophet's conviction that God knew what He was going to do and was able to do it.

The dead army (Ezek. 37:4-8). Ezekiel had prophesied to the mountains (6:2; 36:1) and to the forests (20:47), and now he is commanded to prophesy to the dead bones. The Word of the Lord is "living and powerful" (Heb. 4:12); it not only *has* life but it *imparts* life (1 Peter 1:23). "The words that I speak to you, are spirit, and they are life" (John 6:63, NKJV). God's word of command in Ezekiel 37:4 is followed by His word of promise in verses 5 and 6. Ezekiel believed the promise and obeyed the command, and the bones came together. Then the skeletons were covered with flesh and skin so that what was lying there in the valley looked like a sleeping army. The bodies lacked only one thing: life.

The living army (Ezek. 37:9-14). God commanded Ezekiel to prophesy to the wind and told him what to say. In the Hebrew language, the word *ruah* can mean wind, breath, spirit, or Spirit. Jesus made use of this when He spoke to Nicodemus about the blowing of the wind and the new birth through the Spirit (John 3:5-8). There's also a reference here to the creation of Adam in Genesis 2. At his creation, Adam was complete physically, but he had no life until the breath of God entered into him (v. 7). When Ezekiel spoke the living Word of God, the breath from God entered the dead bodies and they lived and stood to their feet.

The Lord then explained the meaning of the vision. The dead dry bones represent the whole Jewish nation, both Israel and Judah, a divided nation and a dead nation, like bleached bones on a battlefield. Israel's situation seemed hopeless, but "with God, all things are possible" (Matt. 19:26). There will come a day when God's living Word of command will go forth and call His people from their "graves," the nations to which they have been scattered across the world (Ezek. 37:21; Jer. 31:8; Matt. 24:31). The Children of Israel will come together, but the nation will not have spiritual life until they see their Messiah, believe on Him, and receive the gift of the Holy Spirit of life (Ezek. 39:29; Zech. 12:9–13:1). The nation will be born—and born again—"in a day" (Isa. 66:7-9).[4]

Of course, there's a spiritual application in this vision for any individual or ministry that is in need of new life from God. Too often God's people are like that standing army, lifelike but not alive. How does the life come? Through the Holy Spirit using the faithful proclamation of the Word of God. Said Charles Spurgeon, "Decayed churches can most certainly be revived by the preaching of the Word, accompanied by the coming of the heavenly breath from the four winds."[5] From time to time, in response to His people's prayers, the Lord has seen fit to send a new "breath of life" to His church and His servants, and for that blessing we should be praying today.

4. Reunion: the kingdoms united (Ezek. 37:15-28)

The nation of Israel was a united people until after the death of Solomon. His son's unwise and arrogant policies divided the kingdom in 931 B.C., with ten tribes forming the Northern Kingdom of Israel (also called Ephraim or Samaria) and the tribes of Judah and Benjamin forming the Southern Kingdom of Judah. The Northern Kingdom soon went into idolatry and apostasy and in 722 B.C. was taken by Assyria, but Judah had some good kings and maintained the Davidic line and the ministry at the temple. However, toward the end of Israel's political history, some very weak kings reigned and the nation drifted into idolatry and unbelief. The Lord finally brought the Babylonians to chasten His people. There is a political Israel today, but the majority of the Jewish people are scattered around the world.

This is the last of Ezekiel's "action sermons." He took two sticks, each one to represent one of the divisions of the Jewish nation. One he labeled "For Judah" and the other "For Joseph." Like a performer before an audience, the prophet announced that the two sticks would become one in his hands—and they did! The people saw what he did but they didn't understand what he meant by it. He explained that the Lord would gather the people together to one place, their own land of Israel. He would make them one nation, obedient to one king, and (most important) worshiping one God. There would be no more idols or disobedience to the law of the Lord.

But what would maintain the unity of the people? For one thing, the Lord would cleanse them and renew spiritual life within them so that they no longer had any ambitions to compete with one another. Old jealousies and enmities would be gone (Isa.

11:13) and Israel and Judah would together humble themselves and seek the Lord (Jer. 50:4; Hosea 11:1). Another factor is that their one king would be the Messiah, and He would shepherd them with love and grace. He would be their "prince forever" (Ezek. 37:25) and serve as the Prince of Peace (Isa. 9:6).

Third, the Lord would so order and bless the land that the nation would be one (Ezek. 37:25). This will be further explained in chapter 45. The nation would be governed by a "covenant of peace" (37:26; 34:22-25), which is the "New Covenant" that Jeremiah wrote about in Jeremiah 31:31-34. But central to the nation's unity will be the new temple (Ezek. 37:26-28) where the glory of God will dwell. In their wilderness days, Israel had the tabernacle to unite the camp of Israel, with each tribe assigned a specific place to pitch their tents. The temple in Jerusalem was also a source of unity, for three times a year the men had to go to Jerusalem to celebrate feasts, and the people were allowed to offer sacrifices only at the temple.

In chapters 40–48, Ezekiel will go into detail describing this future temple and its ministries. God called it "my tabernacle" (37:27) because the Hebrew word means "a dwelling place."[6] God's presence with His people will sanctify the land, the temple, and the nation, just as He promised in His covenant (Lev. 26:11-12). The nations of the earth will come to worship the Lord with His people Israel (Isa. 2:1-5) and "the earth shall be filled with the knowledge of the glory of the Lord, as the waters cover the sea" (Hab. 2:14).

Whether it's the Children of Israel or the saints in the church today, the Lord wants His people to be united. "Behold, how good and how pleasant it is for brethren to dwell together in unity" (Ps. 133:1). Paul appealed to the believers in Corinth to cultivate unity in the church (1 Cor. 1:10), and he exhorted the Ephesian believers to "make every effort to keep the unity of the Spirit through the bond of peace" (Eph. 4:3, NIV). Sometimes it takes prayer, sacrifice, and patience to maintain the unity of God's people, but it's important that we do so. Jesus prayed that His people might be one and manifest to the lost world the living unity between Christ and His church and among believers and local churches (John 17:20-23). A divided church is not a strong church or a church bearing witness to the grace and glory of God. God's people today need the fresh wind of the Spirit to give us new life from God and new love for one another.

CHAPTER TWELVE
GOD PROTECTS THE NATION
Ezekiel 38–39

Many Bible scholars consider this section of Ezekiel to rank among the most difficult prophetic passages in Scripture and they don't all agree in their interpretations. Some have identified this invasion with the Battle of Armageddon, described in Revelation 16:13-16 and 19:11-21, but the contrasts between these two events are too obvious.[1] Others see Ezekiel 38–39 as a description of an "ideal battle" that assured the Jews in exile of God's power to protect His people. While the assurance is certainly there, this approach doesn't explain the many details recorded in these two chapters. We will approach these chapters assuming that they are describing actual events.

The reference to "Gog and Magog" in Revelation 20:7-9 has led some students to place this invasion *after* the Millennium, but this interpretation also has its problems. The army described in verse 8 will come from the four corners of the earth, while Gog's army will be comprised of men from six nations and will invade from the north. Also, if fire from heaven devours the army mentioned in verse 8, why would it be necessary to spend seven months burying the bodies and seven years (into eternity?) burning the weapons? The words "Gog and Magog" are probably used to relate the two prophetic events but not to equate them. Both Ezekiel and John describe attacks against Jerusalem and the Jews, and in both events, the Lord miraculously delivers His people.

A suggested scenario. Before we examine Ezekiel 38–39, we should review the "prophetic situation" prior to this invasion of the Holy Land. The next crisis event on God's prophetic calendar is the Rapture of the church, an event that can occur at any time (1 Thes. 4:13-18). Jesus Christ will come in the air and call His people to be with Him in heaven. According to Daniel 9:24-27,[2] the nation of Israel will make an agreement with the head of a ten-nation European coalition to protect them for seven years so they can rebuild their temple in Jerusalem. *We don't know how much time elapses between the Rapture of the church and the signing of this covenant.* It's the signing of the covenant that triggers the start of the seven-year Tribulation period described in Matthew 24:1-28 and Revelation 6–19.

After three and one-half years, this European leader will emerge as the Antichrist (the Beast). He will break the covenant with Israel, set up his own image in the Jewish temple, and try to force the world to worship and obey him (Dan. 9:27; 2 Thes. 2:1-12; Matt. 24:15; Rev. 13). During the last three and one-half years years of the Tribulation period, the world will experience "the wrath of God," and the period will climax with the return of Christ to the earth to defeat Satan and the Beast and establish His kingdom. That's when the Battle of Armageddon will be fought.

If this is the correct sequence of prophetic events, then during the first half of the Tribulation period, Israel will be in her land, protected by the strongest political leader in the world. It will be a time of peace and safety when the other nations won't threaten them (Ezek. 38:8, 11, 14). Since we don't know how much time will elapse between the Rapture of the church and the signing of the covenant, it's possible that the Jews and this powerful European leader will complete their negotiations very soon after the saints have been taken out. We don't know how long it will take for Israel to rebuild the temple, but it will be complete by the middle of this seven-year period. That's when this powerful European leader will break the covenant, reveal himself as the man of sin, and set up his own image in the temple.

With this suggested scenario in mind, perhaps we can better understand the invasion described in these two chapters.

1. Before the invasion (Ezek. 38:1-13)

The leader of this army is named Gog, ruler of "Magog," which means "the land of Gog." It was located between the Black Sea and the Caspian Sea. The title "chief prince" can be translated "prince of Rosh," a place that hasn't been determined yet. But if "prince of Rosh" is the correct translation, then this man will rule over Rosh, Meshech, and Tubal. The latter two places are located in eastern Asia Minor along with Gomer and Beth-Togarmah.[3] Prince Gog's allies will be Persia (Iran), Cush (ancient Ethiopia), Put (Libya), Gomer, and Beth-Togarmah, both located near the Black Sea.

Since all these nations except Put, Cush, and Persia are located north of Israel, it's tempting to identify Rosh with Russia and therefore Meschech with Moscow and Tubal with Tobolsk, both cities in Russia; but we would have a hard time defending this on linguistic grounds. This doesn't rule out the participation of modern Russia, since it is located in the north (vv. 6, 15; 39:2), but neither does it demand it.

The prophet encourages his listeners (and readers) by telling them the end of the story even before he begins: God will defeat this vast coalition army and rescue His people Israel in their land (38:3-4a). This invasion won't occur until "after many days . . . in the latter years" (v. 8), at a time when Israel is enjoying peace and security under the protection of the political leader who signed the covenant. Prince Gog and his allies will think that Israel is an easy target, but they forget the protection of the God of Jacob.

This raises the perplexing question: Why would Gog and his allies want to attack Israel at all, knowing that a powerful ten-nation European alliance had promised to defend the helpless Jews? The overt purpose stated in verses 12-13 is to seize the wealth in the land of Israel, a purpose that the other nations understood. But if our suggested scenario is correct, perhaps these nations also want to prevent the rebuilding of the Jewish temple. The nations named are identified with Islam, and they would want to protect the "Dome of the Rock," a revered Muslim monument[4] which has stood on the temple site for centuries.[5]

Whatever Prince Gog's thinking might be, it's clear that it is the Lord who brings this army out (v. 4, NASB; vv. 16-17). Prince Gog thinks he has worked out the whole scheme (vv. 10-11), but it is God who is in charge. The northern coalition comes into the land of Israel confident of victory, but they are walking into a trap.

2. During the invasion (Ezek. 38:14–39:8)

Enemies have frequently attacked Israel from the north, including Assyria, Babylon, and the Hittites. Prince Gog and his horde will swoop down from the north, "like a cloud to cover the land," totally ignorant that the God of Israel intended their destruction. The decisions made in the war room of Magog will conform to the will of the Lord who planned this invasion for His own purposes.[6] God in no way violated their own freedom to think and decide, but He overruled Gog's decisions for His own purposes, just as He did with Babylon (21:18-24). "The lot is cast into the lap, but its every decision is from the Lord" (Prov. 16:33, NKJV). "The king's heart is in the hand of the Lord, like the rivers of water; He turns it wherever He wishes" (Prov. 21:1, NKJV).

What does the leader of the European coalition think when this undeclared war begins? Surely a man of his intelligence would have known that these nations were mobilizing.[7] Having just entered into the seven-year covenant with Israel, he had to act to protect them; but he would also want to make the best use of the crisis to promote his own agenda. After all, he had agreed to protect Israel so that he might one day use their temple for his own evil purposes. Perhaps he could use Gog and his allies to hasten the day when he would become world dictator.

But before the European leader has time to act, God will intervene in His jealous wrath and wipe out the invading forces! First, He will cause an earthquake that will be felt around the world (Ezek. 38:19-20). This earthquake doesn't seem to fit any of the earthquakes mentioned in the Book of the Revelation (Rev. 6:12; 8:5; 11:13, 19; 16:18), but in some places on the earth, the damage will be terrible. The shaking of the land of Israel will throw the invading army into panic and the men will begin to slaughter one another. Then God will send rain, hailstones, and fire and brimstone (sulfur) from heaven as well as a plague on the army, and this will end the invasion, leaving so many corpses that it will take seven months to bury all of them (Ezek. 39:12).

The description of the defeat in chapter 38 focuses on the army, but in 39:1-8, the focus is on the leader of the army, Prince Gog of Magog. In the KJV, verse 2 gives the impression that one sixth of the invading army will be spared and sent home humiliated. However, the verse is stating that it is God who brings Prince Gog into the land and allows him to try to attack the people of Israel. "And I will turn you about, and will lead you on, and will cause you to come up from the uttermost parts of the north, and will lead you against the mountains of Israel" (AMP).

God not only leads the prince, but He also disarms him so that he is helpless before his enemy (v. 3). Instead of slaughtering the Jews, his soldiers will themselves be slaughtered and become food for the vultures and the beasts of the field. But the Lord won't stop with His judgment of the armies that invade Israel; He will also send a fiery judgment on the land of Magog! (v. 6)

In verse 23, the Lord gives three reasons for bringing Gog and his armies to Israel and then defeating them so dramatically. First, this victory will reveal the *greatness* of the Lord as He displays His power before the nations (v. 23). There is no evidence that the Israelite forces ever confronted the invading army. The Lord intervened and used weapons that no general on earth could use—rain, hailstones, and fire and brimstone from heaven! In fact, the invading army will get out of control and destroy itself! This victory will also reveal His *holiness* as He judges the sins of the leader from Magog and deals with his enmity against the Jews. The wealth of the Holy Land belongs to the Lord, and He has shared it with His people Israel, and the other nations have no right to exploit it.[8] Third, the victory will *make Jehovah known to the Gentile nations*, and the world will see that the God of Israel is the only true and living God.

But perhaps the most important reason is given in 39:7, that *Israel will recognize the holiness of God and be convicted of her own sins*. During their time of dispersion in the other nations, the Jews had profaned the name of the Lord (36:19-23). Now God has gathered them back into their own land, but they are still not a converted people; otherwise they would confess God's holiness and greatness. It will not be until they see their Messiah that they will loathe their sins, put their trust in Christ and become a regenerated people (37:25-38). But this great victory will be the beginning of their spiritual experience with the Lord. Both Israel and the nations will know that Jehovah is the Lord, the Holy One of Israel. During the difficult Tribulation period, did the Jewish people remember God's great victory over the invaders? Did it encourage their faith? Did any of the Gentiles remember and turn to God?

We're tempted to speculate on how the European leader responded to this remarkable series of events. No sooner did he guarantee his protection to Israel than a coalition of nations invaded Palestine and he couldn't do anything about it. Perhaps he said that the "forces of nature" were under his control! At least the Jews could build their temple without interference from the neighboring nations. The Lord will give Antichrist what he wants, but in the end, it will all combine to lead to his destruction.

3. After the invasion (Ezek. 39:9-29)

The sudden destruction of this great army will leave behind a multitude of corpses as well as a huge amount of military materiel. We aren't told how much other damage was done by the storm God sent, but it's clear that the land needed cleaning up.

The cleansing of the land (Ezek. 39:9-16). People from the cities of Israel will go out and gather and burn the weapons and supplies left by Gog's defeated army. The ancient military equipment listed here includes hand shields and body shields (bucklers), bows and arrows, and clubs and spears. These are not the weapons of a modern army, but Ezekiel used language the people could understand.[9] If he had written about jet planes and rockets, he would have been a poor communicator. So large will be the collection of unused equipment that the people will use it for fuel for seven years.

But supposing these were actually wooden weapons, would they last that long? Could that many people heat their homes, factories, and businesses for seven years by burning bows and arrows, clubs and spears and shields? And will the people in Israel at that future time be heating the buildings with fireplaces and wood-burning stoves? Wouldn't the dead soldiers ceremonially defile most of this equipment? The burning of the equipment simply says that the Jews didn't keep it to use themselves and they destroyed it so nobody else could use it. Gog and his army came to spoil Israel, but Israel spoiled them!

But the land also had to be cleansed of the corpses. The fact that the Jews show respect for their enemies and give the dead decent burial is a testimony to their kindness. Of course, exposed corpses defiled the land, so it was necessary to remove them as soon as possible; but it will take seven months to finish the job. And even then, a special crew of workers will continue searching for bodies or bones that may have been overlooked. It's likely that the city called Hamonah ("horde," referring to the "horde" of soldiers slain) will be established as a headquarters for this mopping-up operation. The nation of Israel will remember this great day of deliverance and perhaps make it an annual day of celebration to the glory of God (v. 13, NIV).

Where is the cemetery for this vast horde of dead soldiers? The graves are in Israel in a location where people travel (v. 11). In fact, there will be so many corpses that the burial operation will block the traffic.[10] Some students believe this burial place will be east of the Dead Sea in an area known as "The Valley of the Travelers." The new name will be "The Valley of Gog's Hordes."

The call to the feast (Ezek. 39:17-20). Not all the corpses can be buried immediately, so the carrion-eating birds and beasts will enjoy a feast at the invitation of the Lord. (The bones left behind will be buried; see v. 15.) This invitation to a feast is a frequent biblical image for the judgment of God and His victory over His enemies. Isaiah uses it for God's victory over Edom (Isa. 34:6), Jeremiah for God's victory over Egypt (Jer. 46:10), and Zephaniah for the Lord's dealing with Judah (Zeph. 1:7-8). A similar invitation will be given out after the great Battle of Armageddon (Rev. 19:17-21). So humiliating is this defeat of Gog and his allies that the Lord refers to their officers as rams, lambs, goats, and bullocks! They arrogantly entered Israel as proud soldiers but would be buried like slaughtered animals. Such is the fleeting greatness of man.

The compassion of the Lord (Ezek. 39:21-29). God destroyed the invading army not only for the protection of His people but also for the demonstration of His glory before the Gentiles. This miracle was also a reminder to the Jews, newly returned to their land (vv. 27-28), that Jehovah alone is the Lord. The fact that the Jews rebuild their temple is evidence they have faith in the ancient religious system, but that isn't the same as saving faith in their Messiah, Jesus Christ. This experience of deliverance will remind them of the many times their ancestors were miraculously delivered by the Lord, as recorded in their Scriptures.

But the victory over Gog and his hordes will say something to the Gentile nations about Israel (vv. 23-24). It will tell them that the Jews are indeed the people of God who were chastened by God in the past but now are destined for a kingdom. There will come a day when this rebellious nation will be cleansed and forgiven, and the Lord will pour out His Spirit on His people. That will happen when they see the Messiah, repent of their sins, and trust Him for their salvation.

The Gentile nations and the people of Israel will experience great suffering during the seven years of Tribulation. But the Lord in His mercy will seal 144,000 Jews to be the nucleus of the promised kingdom, and will also save a great multitude of Gentiles to share that kingdom with them (Rev. 7). The last temple the Jews ever build will be defiled by Antichrist and ultimately destroyed. But God has promised His people a new land and a new temple, and Ezekiel will describe these to us in the closing chapters of his book.

CHAPTER THIRTEEN
GLORY IN THE TEMPLE
Ezekiel 40–48

Ezekiel has described the return of the Jewish people to their land, the cleansing of the nation, and the restoring of the land to productivity and security. But for the picture to be complete, he must give them assurance that their beloved temple and its ministries will be restored, for the presence of God's glory in the temple was what set Israel apart from all the nations (Rom. 9:4). In the last nine chapters of his book, Ezekiel will describe in detail the new temple and its ministry, the new boundaries of the tribes in the land, and the return of the glory of God to Israel.

1. The interpretation of the new temple

For centuries, devout and scholarly Bible students, both Jewish and Christian, have struggled to interpret the vision described in these chapters, but they have by no means reached a satisfactory agreement. At least four views have emerged from these studies, and all of them have their strengths and weaknesses.

Ezekiel described "ideal worship" for God's people. Rejecting the idea that a literal temple will be built in Israel, this view spiritualizes the vision God gave Ezekiel and seeks to apply it to the church today. The temple represents the glorious presence of God among His people, and the gates speak of the open access the people have to the Lord. The river from the temple pictures the flowing forth of God's blessing from the church to the world, getting deeper and deeper and turning the desert into a garden. The arguments for this view center on the finished work of Christ and the end of the Old Covenant. Because of the death, resurrection, and present ministry of Christ our High Priest, we no longer need earthly temples, priests, or sacrifices. The New Covenant of grace has superseded the Old Covenant of law, and to go back to the Old Covenant is to reject the messages of Galatians and Hebrews. This interpretation is presented primarily by those of the amillennial school who also spiritualize the Old Testament promises to Israel. They believe there is no future for Israel as a nation, and this includes the establishing of an earthly kingdom.[1]

But this approach has its problems, not the least of which is the presence of so much detail in these chapters. If the Lord wanted Ezekiel simply to describe "ideal spiritual worship" for the church today, He didn't have to give us the measurements of the walls, gates, courts, and buildings. The prophet's use of temple imagery is no problem to us because he was a priest and the Jewish people understood this language; but why all the details? Do we ignore them or seek to understand and apply them? If so, what do they mean for spiritual worship today? Furthermore, why would Ezekiel leave out so many important elements from the Old Testament pattern of worship? Ezekiel's temple has no ark, golden altar of incense, lampstand, table of bread, veil, or high priest. He includes only three of the five levitical sacrifices, and two of the seven annual Jewish feasts, and yet none of these omissions is explained. (I will have more to say about the Old Covenant issue later in this chapter.)

When we start to spiritualize the Scriptures, every interpreter does that which is right in his own eyes and the results are confusing. We can't deny that the temple is used as an image of both the church universal (Eph. 2:19-22) and the local church (1 Cor. 3:9ff), but similarity of image is no proof that what the Bible says about a Jewish temple should be applied to the church. The idea that the river from the sanctuary pictures the worldwide blessings of the Gospel (or the church) is a bit hard to accept in the light of church history. Instead of the pure river of blessing flowing out from the church to the world, it appears that the dirty river of sin is flowing from the world into the church!

However, the "spiritual" approach does emphasize an important point. The Jewish people had defiled their temple and the glory of the Lord had departed, and Israel needed to return to holy worship and abandon their routine of empty religious activity. In fact, it's a lesson the church needs to recover today. Too much so-called worship is only a demonstration of man-centered religious activity that fails to bring glory to the Lord.

Ezekiel gave the plans for the post-captivity temple. If this is true, then the Jewish remnant didn't know it when they returned to their land, because they built the second temple according to the plans Moses gave in Exodus. The old men in the group wept, not because the second temple wasn't like Ezekiel's vision but because it was so unlike the magnificent temple Solomon built (Ezra 3:10-13). Perhaps the vision of the new temple may have encouraged the Jewish remnant in their difficult work, but that wasn't the reason God gave Ezekiel this glorious vision. The Jewish remnant had Joshua the high priest with them, but Ezekiel said nothing about a high priest, and nowhere is it recorded that the glory of the Lord filled the second temple. The "second temple" interpretation falls short of dealing honestly with the biblical text.

Ezekiel's vision anticipated John's vision in Revelation 21. Yes, there are some similarities. Both men were taken to high mountains (Ezek. 40:10) and both saw the glorious city of God. In both visions, a man was measuring the city (vv. 15-17), and both visions describe a life-giving river (Rev. 22:1). Ezekiel and John both emphasized the exclusion of defilement from the city (21:27). However, John's vision says nothing about worship; in fact, he states clearly that there will be no temple in the city he described (v. 22). Ezekiel's temple is designed in a square and is made from ordinary materials (stone abounds in Israel), while John's city appears to be a cube (v. 16) and is made out of precious metals and jewels. The heavenly city will be comprised of believers from the whole world (vv. 24-27), while Ezekiel's temple is emphatically Jewish, including the offering of levitical sacrifices.2 While this doesn't exclude believing Gentiles, it does mark the worship as Jewish. It doesn't appear that God had John's vision in mind when He showed Ezekiel the temple.

Ezekiel described a temple to be used during the millennial reign of Christ. This interpretation takes the prophetic Scriptures at face value and tries not to spiritualize them. Ezekiel described the design of a literal temple that will be the center for worship during the kingdom of Christ, a worship based on the levitical order in the Mosaic Law. According to Ezekiel 43:6-12, the Lord gave all the details in order to focus the Jews' attention on God's holiness and thus bring them to repentance. The Lord wanted them to treat His temple with respect and not like any other building in the neighborhood, and He especially wanted them to abandon their idolatry.

To this present day, Israel has had four different sanctuaries: the tabernacle of Moses, the temple of Solomon, the second temple after the Captivity, and Herod's temple in the time of Jesus. God's glory left the tabernacle (1 Sam. 4:19-22) which was eventually replaced by Solomon's temple. Before the temple was destroyed by the Babylonians, Ezekiel saw God's glory leave the temple (Ezek. 9:3; 10:4; 11:22-23). There is no evidence that the glory of God ever resided in either the second temple or Herod's temple. The Son of God ministered in Herod's temple and in that sense brought back the glory (John 1:14; Hag. 2:7). But Jesus abandoned the temple in a manner similar to the way the glory left Solomon's temple: He went to the Mount of Olives (Ezek. 11:22-23; Matt. 23:38; 24:3). When at His return, Jesus brings the glory to the millennial temple, He will come from the Mount of Olives (Ezek. 43:1-5; Acts 1:9-12; Zech. 14:4). The Jews have not had a temple since Herod's temple was destroyed by the Romans in A.D. 70.

There are two temples in Israel's future: the Tribulation temple, which will be taken over by the Antichrist (Dan. 9:24, 26-27; Matt. 24:15; 2 Thes. 2:1-4; Rev. 11:1; 15:5), and the millennial temple that Ezekiel described in these chapters. But Ezekiel isn't the only prophet who said there would be a holy temple during the Kingdom Age. You find a kingdom temple and kingdom worship mentioned in Isaiah 2:1-5, 60:7, 13; Jeremiah 33:18; Joel 3:18; Micah 4:2; Haggai 2:7-9; and Zechariah 6:12-15, 14:16, 20-21. Ezekiel 37:24-28 records God's promise to His people that He would put His sanctuary among them. "My tabernacle also shall be with them; indeed, I will be their God, and they shall be My people" (v. 27, NKJV).

God gave the plans for the tabernacle to Moses, a prophet (Ex. 25:8-9, 40), and the plans for Solomon's temple to David, a king (2 Chron. 28:11-19). Now He reveals the plans for the glorious millennial temple to Ezekiel who was a priest as well as a prophet. These plans had a direct bearing on the people to whom Ezekiel was ministering, discouraged Jews who in the Babylonian siege had lost their land, their holy city, their temple, and many of their loved ones. In these closing chapters of his prophecy, Ezekiel assured them that God would keep His covenant promises and one day dwell again with His chosen people.

As we study these difficult chapters, we will discover other reasons why the literal interpretation of this vision yields the best understanding and application of the Word that God gave Ezekiel.

2. The plan of the new temple (Ezek. 40:1–46:24)

It was on April 28, 573 B.C.—the first day of Passover—that God gave Ezekiel the vision recorded in chapters 40–48. The Jews had been captives in Babylon for twenty-five years, and Passover would only remind them of their deliverance from Egypt. Passover was also the beginning of the religious year for Israel (Ex. 12:2), and the Lord chose that significant day to tell His servant about the glory that Israel would share when Messiah established His kingdom.

In a vision, Ezekiel visited the land of Israel, but unlike his previous "visits," he didn't see sinful people, a devastated land, or a defiled temple. This time he saw a new land and a glorious new temple. Just as Moses received the tabernacle plans while on a mountain, so Ezekiel received the plans for the temple while on a mountain. Moses wasn't allowed to enter the Promised Land, but he saw it from a mountain (Deut. 34:1-4) and from a high mountain Ezekiel saw the land and its new tribal divisions.

It's unlikely that the new temple would be on any other site than Mount Zion, but critics of the literal interpretation of this vision point out that Zion is not really a "very high mountain." However, they may be overlooking the geographical changes that will occur in the land of Israel when the Lord returns to deliver His people and establish His kingdom (Zech. 14:4, 10). God promised that the Jews would worship and serve Him on a high mountain (Ezek. 20:40) and that Messiah would rule from a high mountain (17:22-23), and He will keep that promise. Both Isaiah and Micah speak of the high mountain (Isa. 2:1-2; Micah 4:1). Zion will not only be elevated physically, but it will become the center of the worship of the Lord for the whole earth.

In his vision, the prophet saw a man colored like bronze, which suggests he was an angelic visitor, standing just outside the eastern gate of the temple. He held a linen cord and a reed (rod), both of which were used for taking measurements, the line for long distances (Ezek. 47:3) and the rod for shorter measurements. The rod was probably a little over ten feet long (40:5).[3] To measure property is symbolic of claiming it for yourself. During those years when the Jewish remnant was trying to rebuild their temple, the Prophet Zechariah saw a man measuring the temple, and this was a sign that the temple and the city would one day be restored (Zech. 2). God commanded the Apostle John to measure the temple in Jerusalem before it was trampled down by the Gentiles (Rev. 11). This was evidence that no matter what happened, Jerusalem and the temple belonged to God and would one day be restored and sanctified.

The man would give Ezekiel a guided tour of the temple precincts, starting from the eastern gate and then returning there at the end of the tour. But before they walked up the seven steps that led through the eastern gate into the outer court, the guide gave Ezekiel some solemn counsel (Ezek. 40:4).

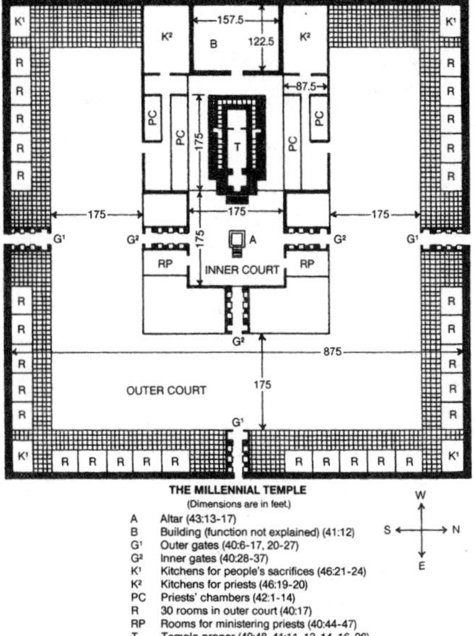

THE MILLENNIAL TEMPLE
(Dimensions are in feet.)

A Altar (43:13-17)
B Building (function not explained) (41:12)
G¹ Outer gates (40:6-17, 20-27)
G² Inner gates (40:28-37)
K¹ Kitchens for people's sacrifices (46:21-24)
K² Kitchens for priests (46:19-20)
PC Priests' chambers (42:1-14)
R 30 rooms in outer court (40:17)
RP Rooms for ministering priests (40:44-47)
T Temple proper (40:48–41:11, 13-14, 16-26)

The prophet was to pay close attention to what he saw and heard because he would have to tell everything he learned to the exiles in Babylon. Of course, through his book, he would tell generations of people what he learned from the Lord during his tour of the temple. This means that the facts recorded in these chapters contained truths that Jews in Ezekiel's day needed to know and believe. These truths are needed today by both Jews and Gentiles, if we are to understand God's plan for the future. If all God wanted to do was impress Ezekiel with "spiritual worship," the angel would have told him so.

The outer court (Ezek. 40:5-27). The entire sacred area was 875 feet square, including a wall 10 feet high and 10 feet thick (v. 5). The temple area itself was on the west side of the enclosure, 175 feet from the walls, and the back part reached to the edge of the sacred area. Behind the temple were two kitchens for preparing sacrificial meals, plus a third building whose purpose was not explained. At each corner of the walls, there was a kitchen; in the center of the east, north, and south walls there was a gate; and on either side of these three gates, built right into the walls, were five special rooms for the worshipers, making a total of thirty rooms. They were used for eating the meals associated with the sacrifices. As you walked through any of the three outer gates, you passed six rooms where the temple guards were stationed, and each of the chambers was about ten feet square and decorated with images of palm trees.

The outer court covers nearly 400,000 square feet, but it will not have a court of the Gentiles with the all-important separating wall (Eph. 2:14),[4] nor will it have a separate court of the women. In the millennial temple, our Lord's desire will be fulfilled that His house be a house of prayer for men and women of all nations (Mark 11:17; Isa. 56:7; Jer. 7:11). The size of the outer court and the accessibility of so many rooms suggest that the area will be a place for fellowship, where people can meet and enjoy sacrificial meals together.

The inner court (Ezek. 40:28-47; 43:13-17). Walking straight across the outer court from any of the three gates in the outer wall, you would come to one of the three gates leading into the inner court. Eight steps will take you through the gate (40:31), past the rooms for guards, and into the inner court. The walls containing these inner gates will contain chambers for the priests and for the preparation of offerings. The inner court is 175 feet square and the altar of sacrifice is placed in the center of the court (43:13-17).

The brazen altar in the Old Testament tabernacle was a "box" made of acacia wood covered with bronze. It was seven and one-half feet square and four and one-half feet high. About two and one-half feet from the top was a grating on which the sacrifices were laid and a fire was kept burning. The altar in Solomon's temple was thirty feet square and fifteen feet high and was approached on all four sides by steps (2 Chron. 4:1; 1 Kings 8:64).[5] The altar in the millennial temple will be about twenty feet tall, with a stairway on the east side. The altar will be tiered, with the base thirty-one and one-half feet square, the next level twenty-eight feet square, the third twenty-four and one-half feet square, and the top level (the "altar hearth") twenty-one feet square.

The sanctuary (Ezek. 40:48–43:12). Like the inner court where the altar will stand, the area containing the sanctuary will be 175 feet square. The portico leading to the sanctuary is quite elaborate with pillars on each side of the door. This reminds us of the two large pillars in Solomon's temple that stood before the entrance to the Holy Place (1 Kings 7:15-22). The angelic guide showed

Ezekiel the various rooms adjacent to the inner court and the temple proper, all of them set aside for the ministering priests (Ezek. 41:5–42:20).

Nothing is said about a veil between the Holy pPlace and the Holy of Holies, but since the Messiah will be present with His people, the veil is not necessary. He wants His glory to be revealed to all. There is also no mention of the ark of the covenant or the mercy seat on which the blood was sprinkled on the annual Day of Atonement. There is mention of a wooden altar or table that probably stood before the entrance to the Holy of Holies (41:21-22). Made completely of wood, it will stand about five and one-half feet high and be three and one-half feet square. Nothing could be burned on it, so perhaps it will be used to display the bread that formerly stood on the table in the tabernacle and the temple.

In the millennial temple, there is nothing said about a golden altar of incense or the seven-branched golden lampstand. The altar of incense symbolized the prayers of God's people ascending to the Lord (Ps. 141:2; Rev. 8:3), but since the Lord is present with them, there is no need for symbolic prayer. As for the lampstand, which symbolized the light of God's truth through the nation of Israel, the shekinah glory was present in the temple of the Lord.

Ezekiel had seen the glory depart from the temple, but now he saw the glory return (Ezek. 43:1-12). His guide took him back to the eastern gate in the outer court, and when the prophet looked out, he saw the glory approaching from the east. Along with the sight of the glory came the sound of the Lord's voice "like the noise [roar] of many waters" (v. 2; see 1:24; Rev. 1:15; 14:2; 19:6). The whole land of Israel was enlightened by the radiance of God's glory, and Ezekiel fell to the ground as he did when he saw the glory throne at the beginning of his ministry (Ezek. 1:28; 3:23; 9:8; 11:13). Then the temple was filled with God's glory, and the Spirit transported Ezekiel back into the inner court. When Moses dedicated the tabernacle (Ex. 40) and Solomon the temple (2 Chron. 5:11-14), the glory of God moved in, signifying that the Lord had accepted their worship and approved of their work.

In both the tabernacle and the temple, God's glory was "enthroned" on the mercy seat in the Holy of Holies (Ex. 25:22; Ps. 80:1; 99:1), but the millennial temple will have no ark and no mercy seat. However, the temple will still be God's throne (Ezek. 43:6-7) and the Messiah will reign as both King and Priest (Zech. 6:9-13). Today, Jesus Christ is enthroned in heaven as our "high priest after the order of Mechizedek" (Heb. 6:20; Ps. 110:1). It was the king-priest Melchizedek who met Abraham after the battle of the kings and blessed him with bread and wine (Gen. 14:17-24), and the spiritual significance of this event is explained in Hebrews 7. In Jewish history, prophets, priests, and kings were all anointed for their offices, but the offices were kept separate. Priests like Jeremiah, Ezekiel, and John the Baptist were called to be prophets, but no priest would dare to take the throne. The one king who tried to serve as a priest was smitten with leprosy (2 Chron. 26:16-23).

The presence of God's glory and God's throne will so sanctify the temple that the people will approach the sanctuary with awe and not treat it like any other building, nor will they repeat their heinous sin of defiling the temple with their idols. God spoke to the prophet and told him to tell the Jewish people what he saw and heard so they would be ashamed of their past sins and turn from them. He must describe the glory of the temple in detail and write it down so they will get the message and want to obey the Lord. You find a similar admonition in Ezekiel 44:4-8 when Ezekiel was at the north gate. This passage reminds us that people who frequent "holy places" ought to be "holy people." The Jewish remnant that returned to their land to rebuild the temple would need to take this message to heart, and we need to take it to heart today.

The altar and sacrifices (Ezek. 43:13-2; 45:13–46:24). We have already dealt with the brazen altar and we must now consider the perplexing problem of the sacrifices. The Lord instructs the priests in how the altar should be dedicated by the offering of a series of sacrifices during the week of consecration (43:18-27). In the dedication of the tabernacle (Ex. 40:29) and Solomon's temple (2 Chron. 7:1-10), sacrifices were offered and the blood applied to the altar.

When the millennial temple is discussed, the question is frequently asked, "Since Jesus has died for the sins of the world, fulfilled the law, and brought in the New Covenant, why would believing Jews want to return to the Old Covenant? What need is there to go back to animal sacrifices when Jesus has made one perfect offering for all time?" This is one of the major arguments used by some students against taking Ezekiel 40–48 literally. But if we understand the role of the sacrifices under the Old Covenant, it will help us see their significance in the millennial temple.

The sacrifices mentioned in this section of Ezekiel are: the burnt offering (40:38-39, 42; 43:18, 24, 27; 44:11; 45:15, 17, 23, 25; 46:2, 4, 12, 13, 15); the trespass or guilt offering (40:39; 42:13; 44:29; 46:20); the sin offering (40:39; 42:13; 43:19, 21, 22, 25; 44:27, 29; 45:17, 19, 22; 23, 25; 46:20); the peace or fellowship offering (43:27; 45:15, 17; 46:2, 12); the meal (grain) offering (42:13; 44:29; 45:15, 17, 24, 25; 46:5, 7, 11, 14, 15, 20); and the drink offering (45:17).[6] For the Mosaic regulations for these offerings, see Leviticus 1–7.

The burnt offering speaks of total dedication to the Lord, "all on the altar" (1:9; Rom. 12:1-2). The sin offering (Lev. 4; 6:21-30) and the tresspass or guilt offering (Lev. 5; 7:1-10) deal with the sinner's offenses against God and people. The sin offering was brought by those who sinned through ignorance, for there was no sacrifice available for high-handed deliberate sin (Num. 15:30-36; Ps. 51:1, 11, 16-17). The trespass offering dealt with offenses for which some kind of restitution should be made. The offerer was required to restore the amount of the property plus a fine of about 20 percent of its value. Sin is not a cheap thing—nor is God's forgiveness!

The peace or fellowship offering (Lev. 3; 7:11-38) was an expression of praise and thanksgiving or perhaps as the indication of the completion of a special vow to the Lord. Part of the meat from the sacrifice was given to the worshiper, who could cook it and enjoy a feast with family and friends. Except for weddings and other high occasions, the Jewish people rarely killed their animals just to have a meal. Meat was an occasional luxury. Thus the fellowship offering was an occasion for worshiping the Lord and enjoyment with His people. The grain or meal offering involved presenting sheaves, the roasted kernels of grain, fine flour, or various kinds of baked cakes. It was the acknowledgment that God is the source of the food that sustains life (1 Chron. 29:10-14). The drink offering was a portion of wine that was poured out along with another sacrifice. It symbolized life poured out wholly to the Lord (Phil. 2:17).

All of these offerings in some way pointed to Christ and His sacrifice of Himself for our sins (Heb. 10:1-18). God forgave the sins of the worshipers if they brought the sacrifice by faith and trusted the Lord, because the blood of animals can never remove the guilt of human sin (v. 4). God's forgiveness was declared (Lev. 4:20, 26, 31, 35; 5:10, 13, 16, 18; 6:7), but only because of the work of Jesus Christ which was pictured by the sacrifice. Old Testament believers weren't forgiven because animals died, but because they put their faith in the Lord (Heb. 11; Ps. 51:16-17; Hab. 2:4). Therefore, the use of animal sacrifices in the millennial temple no more minimizes or negates the finished work of Christ than these sacrifices did before Jesus died. It appears that the sacrifices will be offered in a memorial sense and as expressions of love and devotion to the Lord (Isa. 56:5-7; 60:7). They will also bring people together for fellowship and feasting to the glory of the Lord.

The temple will be a place of learning for both Jews and Gentiles (Isa. 2:1-3), and no doubt the worshipers will study the Old Testament law and learn more about Jesus. They will study the New Testament as well and see the deeper significance of the sacrifices and the feasts. The only "Bible" that the early church possessed was the Old Testament, and the Christians were able to lead sinners to faith in Christ without John 3:16 or "The Roman Road." Of the seven feasts that the Jews celebrated (Lev. 23), it appears that only Passover (Ezek. 45:21-24) and Tabernacles (v. 25; Zech. 14:16-19) will be observed in the Kingdom Age. Passover speaks of the Lamb of God and the deliverance of the Jews from bondage in Egypt, and Tabernacles was a joyous harvest feast that anticipated the coming kingdom and reminded the Jews of their wilderness journeys.[7] Ezekiel 44:24 indicates that the weekly Sabbath will also be observed.

Will the Lord's Supper also be observed in the Kingdom Age? The words of Jesus after He instituted the Lord's Supper seem to suggest so. "I say to you, I will not drink of this fruit of the vine from now on until that day when I drink it new with you in My Father's kingdom" (Matt. 26:29, NASB; see Mark 14:25; Luke 22:18). If the saints in the church can remember Christ by breaking bread and drinking the cup, why can't Jewish believers remember Him by bringing sacrifices?

Neither remembrance has any atoning value.

The priests (Ezek. 40:44-49; 42:1-14; 43:19-27; 44:9-31). God's desire was that the entire nation of Israel be "a kingdom of priests" (Ex. 19:6), but this was never fulfilled. Believers today are part of "a holy priesthood" and "a royal priesthood" (1 Peter 2:5, 9) through Jesus Christ their High Priest. In the millennial temple, the priests and Levites will minister to the people and to the Lord. There will be singers (Ezek. 40:44) to give a "sacrifice of praise" as well as priests to offer the sacrifices brought by the people. No high priest is mentioned because Jesus Christ, the King-Priest, is on the throne and reigning from the temple.

Three times we're told that the descendants of Zadok will be the priests (v. 46; 43:19; 44:15). Zadok was related to Aaron through Aaron's third son Eleazar (1 Chron. 6:1-8, 50-53) and served during David's reign along with Abiathar (2 Sam. 8:17; 1 Chron. 15:11). However, Abiathar defected

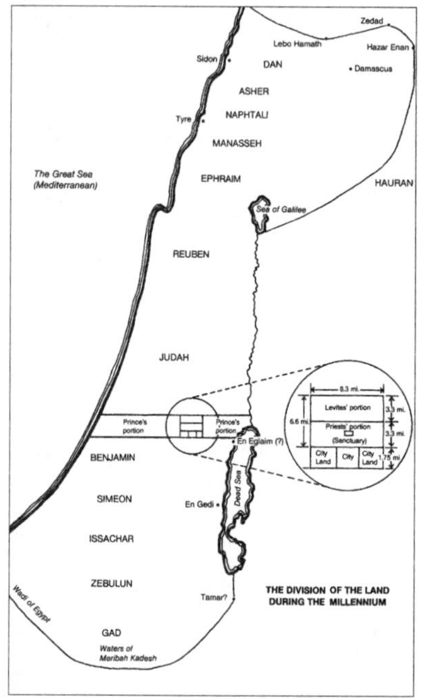

THE DIVISION OF THE LAND DURING THE MILLENNIUM

from David and joined the party that promoted Adonijah as David's successor to the throne (1 Kings 1), and this cost him and his descendants the priesthood (2:26-27). This act fulfilled the prophecy given concerning Eli the high priest and his wicked sons (1 Sam. 2:27-36). The name Zadok means "righteous," and in his book, the Prophet Ezekiel emphasizes separation and holiness.

We have already seen that special chambers will be set aside in the temple for the use of the priests (Ezek. 40:44-46; 42:1-14). Some will be residences while other rooms will be used for daily ministry, such as changing garments, preparing the sacrifices, and cooking the meat for the meals. (See verses 13-14.) When the temple is dedicated, the priests will offer the sacrifices (43:18-27), just as the priests did when the tabernacle and the temple were dedicated (Num. 7:2; 2 Chron. 7:1-11).

The Lord will be very particular about the way the sanctuary is used (Ezek. 44:5-9). He warns the future priests that they must teach the people to make a difference between the clean and the unclean (v. 23; see 22:26) and not to permit outsiders to defile the temple. Many of the Mosaic regulations for the priests are summarized in 44:10-31. The Levites will be disciplined because they didn't stand for what was holy and right in the years before the Captivity. They will be allowed to kill the sacrifices, assist the worshipers, serve as gatekeepers, and help in the temple, but they will not have priestly privileges.[8] The priests will be permitted to offer the sacrifices and draw near to table (44:16), which may refer to the altar or to the table standing before the Holy of Holies (41:22).

The Lord will also be particular about the conduct of the priests (44:17-31). He tells them what to wear (vv. 17-19), how to groom themselves (v. 20), not to drink wine while ministering (v. 21), who not to marry (v. 22), and at all times to show and teach the difference between clean and unclean (v. 23), even if a relative dies (vv. 25-27).[9] They will act as judges and see to it that the law was honored and obeyed (v. 24). Like the Old Testament priests, the kingdom priests will not have an inheritance of land but will have the Lord as their inheritance and be able to live from the temple offerings (vv. 28-31; see Num. 18:20; Deut. 18:1-2; Josh. 13:33).

3. The logistics of the new temple (Ezek. 45:1–48:35)

The closing chapters of Ezekiel's prophecy explain how the land of Israel will be divided during the Kingdom Age, with a section assigned to the Lord, another to the prince, and then one to each of the twelve tribes. The first assignments of the Promised Land were made after the conquest of Canaan, with Joshua, Eleazar the high priest, and the heads of the twelve tribes casting lots before the Lord to determine the boundaries (Num. 26:52-56; 34:16-29; Josh. 13–22). During his reign, King Solomon divided the land into twelve "royal districts," and required each district to provide food for the king and his household for one month (1 Kings 4:7-19), but no actual boundary lines were changed. However, the plan wasn't popular with the people (1 Kings 12:1-19).[10]

The Lord's portion (Ezek. 45:1-6; 48:8-9). Between the areas assigned to Judah and Benjamin will be a section reserved for the Lord and the prince. The Lord's section will be 8.3 miles square, which equals about 55 square miles. The area will be divided horizontally into three sections, each section 8.3 miles long. The top section (3.3 miles wide) will be the sacred area for the temple and the priests. The priests will not be permitted to own land but will be allowed to live there near the sanctuary (44:28). Like the Old Testament priests, the Lord will be the portion of their inheritance (Num. 18:20; Deut. 10:9; Josh. 13:14, 33). The center area will be the same size as the top area and will belong to the Levites. During the old dispensation, the Levites were allowed to own land but were scattered throughout Israel so they could minister to the people (Josh. 21). Genesis 49:5-7; 34:25-31 suggests that this scattering was also a form of discipline.

The bottom area (1.75 miles wide) will be assigned to "the city" and the free land around it. The city is first mentioned in Ezekiel 40:2 and is probably Jerusalem with a new name "Jehovah Shammah—the Lord is there" (48:35). The area assigned to the city will belong to the whole house of Israel (45:6) and will be at the center of the lower strip of land. The "common lands" on either side of that section will be available to all the people of Israel (48:15) and will also be used for growing food to feed the inhabitants of the city. The suggestion seems to be that a "staff" of people from the tribes will work this land so that the "staff" in the city can take care of civil affairs and host visitors who come to worship at the temple.

The prince's portion (Ezek. 45:7–46:18; 44:1-3; 48:21-22). Without explaining who he is, Ezekiel introduces "the prince" in 44:1-3 and mentions him at least sixteen times in the rest of the book. He is not to be confused with "David . . . their prince" (34:24; 37:24-25) whom some see as the Messiah, the heir to David's throne (Luke 1:30-32); nor should he be confused with the Messiah. The prince will be a married man and will have sons who can inherit his land (Ezek. 46:16-18), which is located on either side of the central sacred area. Nowhere is he identified as a member of the royal family, a priest, or a Levite. We aren't even told what tribe he will come from. Apparently he will be a civil ruler, a vice-regent under the authority of the Messiah, and yet most of his functions will be religious.

He will offer sacrifices for himself (44:3; 45:22)[11]—something Messiah would not have to do—and will receive gifts from the people to be used for the worship of the Lord (45:13-16). The prince will provide sacrifices for special occasions (vv. 17-25), including the dedication of the sanctuary, the Sabbaths, Passover, Tabernacles, and at new moon. On the Sabbath and at new moon, he will present his offerings before the people are permitted to worship (46:1-8). During the week, the eastern gate into the inner court will be closed, but it will be opened for the prince on the Sabbath and at new moon, or whenever he wants to present a voluntary burnt offering or peace offering (v. 12). He will be allowed to come as far as the eastern gate but not to the altar in the inner court. He will present his sacrifices, watch the priests prepare them, and when they are offered, will prostrate himself before the Lord (v. 2). After the sacrifice, he will leave the sanctuary just as he came in. When the people come in to worship on the special feast days, they must exit by the gate opposite the one by which they entered (v. 9). The prince will not isolate himself from the people on the feast days but be a part of the crowd (v. 10). The prince must see to it that the daily burnt offerings are presented on the altar, just as they were in the tabernacle and temple (Ex. 29:42; Num. 28:6).

The Year of Jubilee will be celebrated during the Millennial Age (Ezek. 48:16-18). This was the fiftieth year during which the land was not farmed, slaves were set free, and property reverted back to the original owners (see Lev. 25). During the 1,000-year reign of Christ, there will be time for twenty such celebrations. Ezekiel makes the special point that during the Kingdom Age, the prince would not oppress the people or confiscate their land as the rulers did during the last days of the kingdom of Judah. The people of Israel failed to obey the laws relating to the Sabbatic Year and the Year of Jubilee, so God had to send them into exile so that His land could enjoy the rest it needed (2 Chron. 36:14-21; Lev. 26:14ff; Jer. 25:9-12; 27:6-8; 29:10).

The river of life (Ezek. 47:1-12). After seeing the kitchens in the temple (46:19-24), the prophet noticed a trickle of water issuing from the Holy of Holies, past the altar on the south side. The guide led him out the north gate (the eastern gate was closed) and around the temple to the eastern gate where he saw the water coming out from under the building on the south side of the gate. (See Pss. 36:8; 46:4.) The guide measured the depth of the water four times and the river became so deep you could swim in it. Ezekiel learned that the river flowed to the Dead Sea where it brought new life to that forsaken area. The water from the temple would heal the Dead Sea as well as the rivers, and the water creatures would multiply wherever the waters came. The trees on the banks of the river would provide food each month and the leaves would be used for healing. Life comes from the temple of God, not from a palace or a government building!

Jerusalem is the only great city of the ancient world that wasn't located on a river, and in the east, a dependable water supply is essential for life and for defense. During the Kingdom Age, Jerusalem shall have a river such as no other nation ever had. But is this a literal river or merely a sacred symbol of the life-giving power of the Lord? Perhaps it is both. Joel 3:18 and Zechariah 13:1 and 14:8-9 speak of this river as a literal entity, so the river both illustrates and accomplishes the life-giving work of God. Jesus saw such a river as a symbol of the Holy Spirit (John 7:37-39), and the Apostle John saw a similar scene in the heavenly city of God (Rev. 22:1-2). A river played an important role in the Garden of Eden (Gen. 2:10-14).

The portions for the tribes (Ezek. 47:13–48:7, 23-29). In the millennial kingdom, the boundaries of the tribes will be altogether different from what they were before Israel fell to Assyria and Judah to Babylon. The boundaries of the land (47:13-23) will be about what Moses described in Numbers 34, but each tribe's allotment will cut straight across the land. From north to south, the tribes will be Dan, Asher, Naphtali, Manasseh, Ephraim, Reuben, and Judah. Next is the land assigned to the Lord, the prince, and the city, followed by the tribes of Benjamin, Simeon, Issachar, Zebulun, and Gad. It appears that all of the tribes will have access to the Mediterranean Sea except Zebulun and Gad. Judah, the royal tribe (Gen. 49:10) will be located adjacent to the temple area from which Jesus will reign. The tribes descended from sons born of Jacob's wives' maids, Zilpah and Bilhah—Dan, Asher, Naphtali, and Gad—are located the farthest north and south. We aren't told how much land each tribe is given, but only where they will be located. There will be peace among the tribes as they submit to the kingship of their Messiah, Jesus Christ.

The portion for the city (Ezek. 48:30-35). This will be a "kingdom Jerusalem," a new city for the new nation and the new era. Jerusalem's gates have always been significant (Neh. 3; Pss. 48; 87:2; 122:2), but now the city will have twelve gates, each one named after one of Jacob's twelve sons. Instead of "Ephraim" and "Manasseh" (two gates), there will be "Joseph" (one gate), and Levi will have a gate. Any Gentile coming to the city to learn about the Lord will have to enter the city through one of these gates and be reminded that "salvation is of the Jews" (John 4:22). The city will be about 1.6 miles square. These gates, of course, remind us of the gates to the holy city that John described in Revelation 22:10-13, 21.

But the most important thing about the new city will be the presence of the Lord among His united people (Ezek. 35:10). The new name will be "Jehovah Shammah—the Lord is there." This is one of seven compound names of Jehovah found in the Old Testament: Jehovah Jireh—"the Lord will provide" (Gen. 22:13-14); Jehovah Rapha—"the Lord who heals" (Ex. 15:26); Jehovah Shalom—"the Lord our peace" (Jud. 6:24); Jehovah Tsidkenu—"the Lord our righteousness" (Jer. 23:6); Jehovah Shammah—"the Lord is present" (Ezek. 48:35); Jehovah Nissi—"the Lord our banner" (Ex. 17:8-15); and Jehovah Ra'ah—"the Lord our shepherd" (Ps. 23:1).

4. The meaning of the new temple

In examining all the information Ezekiel recorded for us, we must be careful not to lose the major messages among these important details. There is a sense in which the messages of the entire book are wrapped up in one way or another in chapters 40 to 48. The spiritual lessons are as meaningful to us today as they were to Israel in Ezekiel's day, or as they will be to the Jewish people in Messiah's day.

Separation from sin. Ezekiel was a priest as well as a prophet, and it was the responsibility of the priests to teach the people the difference between the holy and the unholy and the clean and the unclean (Lev. 10:10-11; Ezek. 44:23). Israel drifted into sin because they began to erase these differences and became like the pagan nations around them. The temple in Jerusalem, with its special courts and holy chambers, reminded the people that God put a difference between the holy and the profane. For people to "call evil, good, and good, evil, [and] put darkness for light, and light for darkness" (Isa. 5:20) is to violate the basic principle of holy living. (See Ezek. 40:5; 42:14-20; 43:7.)

Worship. The temple was a place of worship, but the heart of the worshiper was far more important that his or her gifts. The Jews in the Southern Kingdom of Judah had defiled the holy temple of God and dared to worship Jehovah along with the idols of the nations around them! God's people don't decide how they are going to worship the Lord; they simple obey what He has told them in His Word.

Fulfillment. One of the purposes of the millennial kingdom is that God might fulfill His promises to His people, promises He couldn't fulfill because of their rebellion and unbelief. In His grace and mercy, God gave Israel a wonderful land, a perfect law, and a glorious Lord. They defiled the land by their terrible crimes; they disobeyed the law by adopting pagan practices; and they defied their Lord and tempted Him by resisting His calls to repentance. But during the kingdom, Israel will trust the Lord, obey His Word, worship in His temple as they should, and bring delight to the Lord who will rule from David's throne.

But there's a further fulfillment, for the Kingdom Age will "wrap up" all the previous ages in God's revelation of Himself and His purposes. The land will be like the Garden of Eden (36:35), complete with a river of life and trees of life. The promises made to Abraham will be fulfilled and his descendants will possess and enjoy their land. The Law of Moses will be obeyed from the heart, and the Lord will be worshiped and glorified. The Messiah that Israel rejected at His first coming will be received and honored and will reign over them (43:6-7). God will fulfill every kingdom promise found in the pages of the prophets![12]

God's glory and God's name. If the Book of Ezekiel teaches us anything, it teaches us that we must honor God's name and magnify His glory. The glory of God departed from Israel because they defiled the temple. The glory of God returned to the new temple because it was holy and a place where God could dwell. "They shall know that I am the Lord" is a statement found at least sixty times in Ezekiel's book. While God's glory doesn't dwell in our church buildings, God can be glorified or disgraced by what we do in those buildings we have dedicated to Him. As His people, we must be reverent and honor His name.

The sovereign rule of God. The first vision God gave Ezekiel was that of His glorious throne, moving quickly here and there so that His angelic creatures could accomplish His purposes in the world. Today, the church of Jesus Christ is left in this world not just to pray "Thy will be done on earth as it is in heaven," but to help accomplish that will in the power of the Holy Spirit. God is still on the throne and Jesus Christ has "all authority in heaven and on earth" (Matt. 28:18). Need we ask for more?

Endnotes

Chapter 1

1. Numbers 8:23 states that the priests began their work at age twenty-five, but during the first five years, they were "learning the ropes" in preparation for their twenty years of ministry (thirty to fifty). According to our calendar, Ezekiel was called on July 31, 593 B.C. He had spent his first five years as an exile in Babylon and was now ready for service.

2. Some students see some significant parallels between Ezekiel and Jeremiah: Ezekiel 2:8-9–Jeremiah 1:9; Ezekiel 3:3–Jeremiah 15:16; Ezekiel 3:8–Jeremiah 1:8, 17; 15:20; Ezekiel 3:14–Jeremiah 6:11; 15:17; Ezekiel 3:17–Jeremiah 6:17; Ezekiel 4:3–Jeremiah 15:12; Ezekiel 5:6–Jeremiah 2:10-13; Ezekiel 5:11–Jeremiah 13:14; Ezekiel 7:26–Jeremiah 4:20. There are numerous parallels between the Book of Ezekiel and the priestly code in the Pentateuch, as well as the Book of Revelation.

3. The Hebrew word *ruah* means spirit, Spirit, or wind, and in his book, Ezekiel uses the word in all three senses.

4. The theme of Israel's rebellion and hardness of heart is found often in the Book of Ezekiel: 2:3-7; 3:26-27; 5:6; 12:2-3, 9, 25; 17:12, 15; 20:8, 13, 21; 21:24; 24:3; 44:6.

5. The Lord used this image to describe the heathen people left in the land of Canaan (Num. 33:55). Once again, God classified His rebellious people with the pagan Gentiles.

6. Was this experience a vision or did God actually transport Ezekiel to Tel-Abib? The scholars are divided in their interpretation. That this was a literal moving of the prophet and not merely a vision seems to be the plain reading of the text. The fact that the prophet sat among the exiles for seven days suggests a physical move. (See 8:1; 11:1, 24; 43:5.)

7. The suggestion here is that Ezekiel was silent for those seven days. Under the levitical law, it took seven days for a priest to be ordained and installed into his ministry (Lev. 8:35). Ezekiel the priest spent seven days being ordained as a prophet.

8. The symbolic "action sermons" are found in 3:22-26; 4:1-3, 4-8, 9-11, 12-14; 5:1-3; 12:1-16, 17-20; 21:6-7, 18-24, 15-24; 37:15-28.

9. A.W. Tozer, *The Pursuit of God* (Tyndale House), 102.

Chapter 2

1. Samuel Heilman, *A Walker in Jerusalem* (Summit Books, 1986), 15.

2. The phrase "bear the iniquity" can mean to suffer for one's own sins (Lev. 17:15-16) or to take to oneself the sins of others (10:17; 16:22). Since the high priest represented the people before God, and the priests offered the sacrifices for sin, they were "bearing" the nation's sins in a symbolic sense. Without their ministry, there could be no forgiveness.

3. The subject of the length of the reigns of the Jewish kings is sometimes puzzling, so we shouldn't look for absolute figures. Fathers and sons were sometimes coregents, and at least two kings of Judah reigned for only three months each.

4. As far as the trade routes were concerned, there is a sense in which the land and the city were centrally located. The land was a "bridge" over which the nations trod as they attacked one another, and the Jews suffered the consequences.

5. In Ezekiel 25 and 26, God promised to punish the Ammonites and the people of Tyre because they laughed at the plight of Israel and took advantage of it. Indeed, the Jews were put to shame before the very people whose sins they practiced and thus brought judgment on themselves.

6. "Behold, I am against you" (v. 8) is a frequently repeated statement in the Book of Ezekiel: 13:8, 20; 21:3; 26:3; 28:22; 29:3, 10; 30:22; 34:10; 35:3; 36:9; 38:3; 39:1.

7. See 6:12; 7:8, 12, 14, 19; 9:8; 13:13, 15; 14:19; 16:38, 42; 20:8, 13, 21, 33-34; 21:17, 31; 22:20-24, 31; 24:8, 13-14, 17; 30:15; 36:6, 18-19. Ezekiel has much to say about the wrath of God.

8. This is another phrase found often in the Book of Ezekiel: 17:21; 21:17, 32; 23:34; 24:14; 26:5, 14; 28:10; 30:12; 34:24; 39:5. Ezekiel spoke by the authority of the Lord God.

9. Early in Israel's history, before worship was centralized at the tabernacle in Jerusalem, the "high places" were sometimes used for worshiping the Lord (1 Sam. 9:11-25; 10:5; 1 Kings 3:4). Then they were used to worship both the Lord and a false god, and finally they were dedicated totally to the idol. The Lord commanded all the high places and the idols to be destroyed when Israel entered the land (Deut. 12).

10. The phrase "set your face against" is found also in 13:17; 20:46; 21:2, 7; 25:2; 28:21; 29:2; 35:2; 38:2.

11. Some scholars translate this word (*gillulim*) to mean "logs" or "blocks of wood." No matter how the people decorated their idols, these false gods were still only "hunks of wood." But the word can mean "pellets of dung."

12. The word "sword" is used eighty-six times in the Book of Ezekiel:

13. Ezekiel will take up this theme of adultery again in chapters 16 and 23.

14. In 25:6, these same actions were Ammon's gleeful response to the destruction of the land of Israel, but the Lord certainly would be happy to see His people suffer and His land devastated.

15. Some expositors see here the image of a rope "woven" around the prisoners as they are led away to Babylon.

Chapter 3

1. It's interesting that the name Jaazaniah in verse 11 means "the Lord hears."

2. These angels remind us of the seven "trumpet angels" in Revelation 8–9.

3. The word "shekinah" comes from a Hebrew word that means "to dwell." God's glory had dwelt in the Holy of Holies in the temple, but now it would be taken away.

4. Before ushering in the great day of His wrath, God showed John the Holy of Holies in heaven and the ark of the covenant (Rev. 11:15-19). One reason the world resists the idea of divine judgment is because they divorce it from the holiness of God and the glory of God. God was "enthroned" on the mercy seat (1 Sam. 4:4; 2 Sam. 6:2; Pss. 80:1; 99:1, NIV). His throne is a holy throne.

5. Naaman took a load of soil from Israel to Syria so he could still be close to the Lord (2 Kings 5:17), and David complained that Saul had driven him away from his own land and therefore from the Lord (1 Sam. 26:17-20).

Chapter 4

1. *The Life and Selected Writings of Thomas Jefferson,* edited by Adrienne Koch and William Peden (The Modern Library, 1993), 255.

2. When the prophet covered his face and kept his eyes to the ground, it suggested the great humiliation God had brought upon the king. Had he obeyed God's message from Jeremiah, he and his family and staff would have been spared. The covering of the face also suggests the impending blindness of the king.

3. Whenever we use drama to convey God's truth to people, we still need the Word of God to make the message clear and authoritative. The spiritually "blind" and "deaf" will be attracted by drama and pantomime, but not everybody will accurately interpret what they see. Ezekiel preached a message after his "action sermons" because it's the Word of God that brings conviction and conveys faith (Rom. 10:17).

4. Ezekiel uses this image again in 22:28.

5. Some students think that the sorceresses used the barley and bread in their magical incantations to determine the future, and this is possible. It does seem like a small fee for their services.

Chapter 5

1. Parables and allegories are given primarily to elucidate one main truth, and it's dangerous to build one's theology on imagery that is supposed to illustrate theology. The major truth in John 15 is the believer's need to abide in Christ, through prayer, meditation in the Word, worship, and obedience. Our union with Christ never changes, because the Holy Spirit abides with us forever (John 14:16), but our communion with Him does change.

2. The Hebrew word for "professional prostitution" (*zana*) is used twenty-one times in this chapter. God considered Israel to be His wife, and her idolatry was the equivalent of adultery and harlotry (Hosea 2; Jer. 2:20-25; 3:1-13).

3. It was believed that the salt had an antiseptic power and would also help strengthen the skin.

4. On the practice of sacrificing children to idols, see 2 Kings 21:6; 23:10; Jeremiah 7:31; 19:5. The Law of Moses prohibited such an evil practice (Lev. 18:21; 20:2; Deut. 12:31; 18:10).

5. See Isaiah 20:5-6; 30:1-5; 31:1; Hosea 7:11; 12:1.

6. The Hebrew verb describes the changes in the woman's genital area when she is sexually aroused.

7. Sodom and Gomorrah are frequently named in Scripture as examples of the judgment of God against sin. See Genesis 18:16–19:29; Deuteronomy 29:23; 32:32; Isaiah 1:9-10; 3:9; 13:19; Jeremiah 23:14; Lamentations 4:6; Amos 4:11; Zephaniah 2:9; Matthew 10:15; 11:24; Mark 6:11; Luke 10:12; 2 Peter 2:6; Jude 7.

8. The word "daughters" (vv. 46, 48-49, 55) refers to smaller cities around a larger city, i.e., "daughter cities."

9. In Scripture, a tree can represent a ruler, a kingdom, or a dynasty (Jud. 9:8-15; Isa. 10:33; Ezek. 31:1-18; Dan. 4; Zech. 11:2).

Chapter 6

1. The guilt and condemnation for a parent's sin could not be passed on to the children, but the consequences of parental sin could bring suffering to the family. In Old Testament days, the Jewish people lived in extended families, and often four generations lived together. This meant that younger generations were influenced by the bad examples of their relatives as well as their good examples. Hereditary tendencies could be passed along as well as social diseases. But at the same time, a godly relative's example, teaching, and prayers could bring blessing to his or her descendants for years to come. Neither Ezekiel nor Jeremiah denied that innocent people were suffering because of the sins of the godless Jewish leaders (Lam. 5:7). The thing they opposed was that the people were using the proverb as an excuse for their own sins, claiming that their generation wasn't guilty of disobedience.

2. Idolatry and adultery were capital offenses (Deut. 13; 22:22; Lev. 18:20; 20:10). Offenses relating to material goods (stealing, exploiting, charging interest, etc.) were usually punished by restoration of an equal amount plus a fine.

3. The case described in verse 24 isn't that of a righteous man who commits one trespass, but it describes a righteous man who adopted a sinful lifestyle and repeatedly defied God's law. Certainly he could have repented and returned to God, even as King Manasseh did (2 Chron. 33:11-19); but the man Ezekiel described persisted in his sins. It's possible to have an outward behavior that appears righteous and still not have saving faith in the Lord.

4. It's interesting that the images of the lion and the vine are found in Genesis 49:8-12.

5. King Zedekiah tried the same approach with Jeremiah, but it didn't work (Jer. 37).

6. *Peter's Quotations: Ideas for Our Time*, 244. This is a version of George Santayana's famous saying, "Those who cannot remember the past are condemned to repeat it."

7. The phrase "lifted up my hand" means to make a solemn oath and is used seven times in chapter 20. God swore that He was their God (v. 5) and would deliver them and give them their land (v. 6). At Kadesh Barnea, He swore that the older generation would not enter the land (v. 15), and in verse 23, He swore to disperse them if they disobeyed Him (v. 23). He swore to give them the land of Israel (v. 28), and He swore to bring them back to the land after their dispersion (v. 42).

8. The word "Bamah" (v. 29) means "high place." In the question "What is the high place to which you go?" the word "go" is ba in Hebrew and "what" is ma.

9. Note the repetition of "the word of the Lord came" in 20:45 and 21:1, 8, and 18. This phrase introduces a new portion of God's message to the people.

10. Several kinds of divination are mentioned in verse 21: selecting an arrow from the quiver, as if drawing straws; consulting small images of the gods; and inspecting the entrails of an animal sacrifice. Perhaps verse 22 is describing the casting of lots (see NIV).

11. Adrienne Koch and William Peden, eds., *The Life and Selected Writings of Thomas Jefferson* (The Modern Library, 1993), 258.

Chapter 7

1. For a graphic description of what happens to society when officials break the law and are not punished for it, read Isaiah 59.

2. Of course, God is spirit and therefore doesn't have literal hands; but the Bible uses human terms to explain spiritual truths.

3. The KJV reads "prophets" in verse 25, but the word refers to the nobility in the city, the people with

authority.

4. You find a similar image and message in Jeremiah 3. The Book of Hosea is an exposition of the image of religious and political prostitution.

5. The word "Sabeans" in verse 42 could refer to the nomadic desert tribes who were invited to the conference, but the word may also mean "drunkards" (see NIV margin).

6. Who are the "righteous men" who sentence Judah? (v. 45, NIV) It probably refers to the people gathered at the conference, since "they" goes back to verse 40. The NASB translates it, "But they, righteous men . . ." referring to "they" (the delegates) in verse 44. But how could men from ungodly nations be called "righteous"? Ezekiel may have been using a bit of holy irony and saying, "These pagan Gentiles are more righteous than Judah who knows the true and living God but won't trust Him!" Of course, the prophets also passed judgment on Judah, and they were righteous men.

Chapter 8

1. In Amos 1:3–2:3, the prophet passed judgment on the Gentile nations on the basis of their inhumanity, their barbaric treatment of their enemies; but when Amos came to judging the Jewish people, it was on the basis of God's law and their covenant relationship to Him (Amos 2:4, 10; 3:1). See Romans 2:11-16.

2. See Isaiah 15–16; Jeremiah 48; and Amos 2:1-3. Note that "Seir" is another name for the land of Moab (Gen. 32:3; 36:20-21).

3. God had already told Isaac and Rebekah that both the blessing and the birthright were to be given to Jacob (Gen. 25:23), and He would have accomplished it apart from the scheming of Jacob and his mother. Both Jacob and Rebekah suffered for what they did, but God overruled their unbelief and fulfilled His plan (Rom. 9:10-16). When they finally met, Jacob's treatment of his brother was hardly honest and loving (Gen. 32–32). He tried to appease (bribe?) him with gifts, he refused to travel with him, and he lied when he said he would follow Esau. Instead, he went in a different direction! They met again at Isaac's funeral (35:28-29).

4. The word Palestine comes from Philistine.

5. Amos rebuked Tyre for selling slaves to other nations (Amos 1:9-10).

6. Isaiah 14:12-23 is a declaration of God's punishment of the king of Babylon, but there are certainly strong suggestions that the passage also involves Satan, the god of this age, who through his demonic forces is working in and through world leaders (Dan. 10).

7. For other prophetic denunciations on Sidon, see Isaiah 23; Jeremiah 25:22; 47:4. During our Lord's ministry, He visited the region of Sidon (Matt. 11:21-22; Mark 7:24-31), and people from Sidon came to see Him (3:8).

8. See Ezekiel 11:17; 20:34, 41-42; 29:13; 34:13; 36:24; 37:21; 38:8; 39:27.

Chapter 9

1. Many ancient peoples had myths concerning great sea monsters that fought one another to gain control of creation, and this imagery occasionally shows up in Scripture (Job 9:13; Ps. 74:13-14; Isa. 27:1). One of Egypt's names in Scripture is "Rahab" and Egypt is portrayed as a water monster (Pss. 87:4; 89:10; Isa. 51:9-10). Of course, the ancient mythology is not approved by the biblical writers but only used in an illustrative way.

2. When you look at a map of ancient Egypt, keep in mind that "lower Egypt" is at the top of the map (north) in the delta region, and "upper Egypt" is at the bottom of the map (south).

3. The alternate spelling of his name (Nebuchadrezzar) may be more correct than the spelling we're most accustomed to in Scripture. Both identify the same person.

Chapter 10

1. The Jews might have been thinking of Isaiah 51:2. Actually, Abraham didn't inherit the land during his lifetime (Acts 7:5). All he owned was a tomb where he had buried his wife (Gen. 23) and where he himself was buried (25:7-10).

2. Instead of following Abraham's example of faith, the Jews sometimes used their connection with Abraham as an excuse for disobeying the Lord. Because they were "children of Abraham," the religious leaders refused to submit to John's baptism, and they also argued with Jesus using the same excuse (John 8:33ff).

Chapter 11

1. "Defiled" means "ceremonially defiled" from coming in contact with someone or something unclean. See Leviticus 11–15.

2. The parallel between the present spiritual experience of the believer and the future spiritual experience of the Jewish nation shouldn't lead us to conclude that these Old Testament promises to the Jews should really be applied to the church. Whether in an Old Testament Jew, a New Testament Christian, or a future Jewish citizen in the Messianic Kingdom, regeneration is regeneration. It's the work of the Spirit in response to saving faith, and it's a miracle of God.

3. There is an interesting parallel between Ezekiel 37 and Ephesians 2, for both chapters deal with resurrection and reconciliation. Paul deals with the dead sinner raised to life (Eph. 2:1-10) and saved Jews and Gentiles reconciled in the one body, the church (vv. 11-22). It's clear, however, that Ezekiel's focus is on God's dealings with the nation of Israel and not the salvation of individual believers.

4. To interpret this vision as announcing the return of the remnant from Babylon or even the emergence of a nation of Israel in the world community is to misinterpret the message. Political Israel today is like the standing army without life, and there has been no great return of the Jews to their Holy Land. The fulfillment of the vision is yet to come.

5. *The Metropolitan Tabernacle Pulpit*, vol. 10, 426.

6. The Hebrew word shakan means "to dwell" and gives us the phrase "the Shekinah glory," the glory of God dwelling in His sanctuary.

Chapter 12

1. Ezekiel describes a six-nation coalition invading from the north (Ezek. 38:6, 15; 39:2), while the Battle of Armageddon involves all nations from the four quarters of the earth (Rev. 20:8). Before Gog and his hordes can do anything, God will attack them with pestilence, hailstones, and brimstone and the armies will fight each other (39:17-23), while the army at Armageddon will be destroyed by our Lord at His coming (Rev. 19:11-21). It will take seven months to bury the corpses from Gog's invasion (Ezek. 39:12), but the Armageddon army will be annihilated (Rev. 20:9). Gog will head the armies that invade Israel for wealth (Ezek. 38:7, 12), but the Beast will lead the armies at Armageddon (Rev. 19:19). Gog's army won't have a chance to do any damage, but the Armageddon army will do damage before the Lord descends to conquer them (Zech. 14:1-9).

2. For an exposition of the prophecies of Daniel, see my book *Be Resolute* (Chariot Victor).

3. These names are not symbolic but belong to actual people who founded nations bearing their names. See Genesis 10:1-7; 1 Chronicles 1:5-7; Ezekiel 27:13-24; 32:26.

4. Though it's frequently called "The Mosque of Omar," the building is technically not a mosque but a monument.

5. Even if archeologists discover that the Jewish temple stood on another site, it's likely that the Islamic nations would prefer that the temple not be rebuilt in Jerusalem.

6. Which of the prophets besides Ezekiel foretold the invasion of the land by these nations? (v. 17) Perhaps this isn't a reference to specific prophecies but to the fact that God has always promised to punish those nations that attacked Israel. This assurance from the Abrahamic Covenant (Gen. 12:1-3) is demonstrated frequently in Scripture.

7. Ezekiel described the invasion using language that the people in the ancient world would understand. If he had used modern military language, it would have conveyed nothing.

8. What this wealth is, the text doesn't say; but the mineral wealth in the Dead Sea area is immense. However, see Joel 2:1-8. At the same time, the claim of the Prince of Magog that he wants Israel's wealth may be a lie. What he may really want is control of the land for his Muslim allies, or perhaps he simply wants to keep the European leader from taking over.

9. Some writers suggest that world disarmament would make it necessary for Gog and his army to use ancient weapons and ride on horses. But ancient weapons and cavalries don't lend themselves to surprise attacks in a world equipped with satellites, the Internet, radar, and television reporters!

10. The KJV phrase "stop the noses of the travelers" gives the impression that it's the odor of the decaying bodies that creates problems, but it's the burial ground and the burial operation that get in the way of the travelers. The name of the cemetery will be "The Horde of Gog."

Chapter 13

1. For an excellent presentation of this view, see Patrick Fairbairn's *Commentary on Ezekiel* (Kregel, 1989), 439–58.

2. Of course, the Gentiles will be welcomed to the temple worship (Isa. 2:1-5).

3. The long cubit was twenty-one inches long. If the rod was six cubits long, that equals ten feet six inches. Some make the long cubit twenty-four inches, making the rod twelve feet long. As I follow Ezekiel and his guide touring the temple precincts, I will not convert each measurement into feet and inches, unless the number is important to the meaning of the text.

4. In Herod's temple, the inscription on this wall of separation reads: "No foreigner may enter within the barricade which surrounds the sanctuary and enclosure. Anyone who is caught so doing will have himself to blame for his ensuing death." This explains why the Jews wanted to kill Paul when they saw him in the temple, because they thought he had brought unclean Gentiles into the sacred courts (Acts 21:26ff).

5. The prohibition against approaching the altar by steps (Ex. 20:24-26) applied to altars of stones or earth erected elsewhere than the tabernacle or temple.

6. See Leviticus 1–7. For an exposition of these chapters, see my book *Be Holy* (Chariot Victor, 1994).

7. When, at the Transfiguration, Peter offered to build some booths for Jesus, Moses, and Elijah, his motive was right but his timing was wrong (Matt. 16:27–17:8). When Jesus comes in glory, the people will celebrate Tabernacles and live in booths.

8. We wonder if disciplining the descendants because of their ancestors' sins isn't a reversal of what Ezekiel taught in chapters 18 and 33:12-20, that the children are not punished for the sins of the fathers. But Ezekiel is speaking of the corporate apostasy of the Levites and not their individual sins.

9. The population of the millennial kingdom will include some people who will already have glorified bodies: the Old Testament saints who were resurrected (Dan. 12:2, 13), New Testament Christians (1 Thes. 4:13-18; 1 John 3:1-3), and Tribulation martyrs (Rev. 20:4). But believers who have survived the Tribulation, both Jews and Gentiles, will be in mortal bodies and subject to death. People will live long lives, but deaths will occur (Isa. 65:20). Children will be born and will be sinners needing salvation. One would think that the miraculously ideal conditions in the kingdom would motivate everyone to trust in the Lord, but at the end of the Millennium, Satan will be able to raise a large army to oppose the Lord (Rev. 20:7-10). During the thousand years, many people will feign obedience to the Lord and yet not trust Him. But can we be sure even today that everyone who belongs to a church is necessarily born again? (Matt. 7:21:29)

10. The KJV of 45:1 and 47:22 reads "divide by lot," but a better translation would be "to assign, to allot." It's clear from the text that the Lord partitioned the land and assigned it according to His own will. The places are already identified that mark the borders, although we aren't sure where some of these cities are located.

11. This eastern gate must not be equated with the one in present-day Jerusalem. The eastern gate in the millennial temple will be closed to the public because the glory of God entered through it (43:1-5).

12. In the promises to the "overcomers" in our Lord's letters to the seven churches (Rev. 2–3), you see a similar progression through the Old Testament periods, beginning with the Tree of Life in the Garden (Rev. 2:7) and concluding with reigning with Christ on His throne (3:21).

DANIEL

OUTLINE

Key theme: God is sovereign in history
Key verses: Daniel 4:34-35

I. DANIEL THE PRISONER (1:1-21)

II. DANIEL THE INTERPRETER (2:1–6:28)
1. Interpreting the image dream—(2)
2. The golden image (Daniel absent) —(3)
3. Interpreting the tree dream—(4)
4. Interpreting the handwriting on the wall— (5)
5. Daniel in the lions' den—(6)

III. DANIEL THE SEER (7:1–12:13)
1. The vision of the four beasts—(7)
2. The vision of the ram and he-goat —(8)
3. The seventy weeks appointed to Israel—(9)
4. The vision of Israel's future and the end—(10–12)

Six different kingdoms are presented in this book: Babylon—the head of gold (2:36-38) and the winged lion (7:4); Media-Persia—the arms and chest of silver (2:32, 39) and the bear (7:5); Greece—the thighs of brass (2:32, 39) and the leopard (7:6); Rome—the legs of iron (2:33, 40) and the "dreadful beast" (7:7); the kingdom of Antichrist—the ten toes (2:41-43) and the little horn (7:8); and the kingdom of Christ—the smiting stone that fills the earth (2:34-35, 44-45) and the Ancient of Days (7:9-14).

CONTENTS

CHAPTER ONE
GOD RULES AND OVERRULES
Daniel 1

From May to September 1787, the American Constitutional Convention met in Philadelphia to develop a system of government for the new nation. By June 28, progress had been so slow that Benjamin Franklin stood and addressed George Washington, president of the convention. Among other things, he said: "I have lived, Sir, a long time, and the longer I live, the more convincing proofs I see of this truth—that God governs in the affairs of men."[1] He then moved that they invite some of the local clergy to come to the assembly to lead them in prayer for divine guidance. The motion would have passed except that the convention had no budget for paying visiting chaplains.

Though not a professed evangelical believer, Franklin was a man who believed in a God who is the Architect and Governor of the universe, a conviction that agrees with the testimony of Scripture. Abraham called God "the Judge of all the earth" (Gen. 18:25), and King Hezekiah prayed, "Thou art the God, even thou alone, of all the kingdoms of the earth" (2 Kings 19:15). In Daniel's day, King Nebuchadnezzar learned the hard way that "the Most High is sovereign over the kingdoms of men" (Dan. 4:32, NIV).

The first chapter of Daniel's book[2] gives ample evidence of the sovereign hand of God in the affairs of both nations and individuals.

1. God gave Nebuchadnezzar victory (Dan. 1:1-2)[3]

For decades, the prophets had warned the rulers of Judah that their idolatry, immorality, and injustice toward the poor and needy would lead to the nation's ruin. The prophets saw the day coming when God would bring the Babylonian army to destroy Jerusalem and the temple and take the people captive to Babylon. A century before the fall of Jerusalem, the Prophet Isaiah had proclaimed this message (Isa. 13; 21; and 39), and Micah his contemporary shared the burden (Micah 4:10). The Prophet Habakkuk couldn't understand how Jehovah could use the godless Babylonians to chasten His own people (Hab. 1), and Jeremiah lived to see these prophecies, plus his own prophecies, all come true (Jer. 20; 25; 27). God would rather have His people living in shameful captivity in a pagan land than living like pagans in the Holy Land and disgracing His name.

The fall of Jerusalem looked like the triumph of the pagan gods over the true God of Israel. Nebuchadnezzar burned the temple of God and even took the sacred furnishings and put them into the temple of his own god in Babylon. Later, Belshazzar would use some of those holy vessels to praise his own gods at a pagan feast, and God would judge him (Dan. 5). No matter how you viewed the fall of Jerusalem, it looked like a victory for the idols; but it was actually a victory for the Lord! He kept His covenant with Israel and He fulfilled His promises. In fact, the same God who raised up the Babylonians to defeat Judah later raised up the Medes and Persians to conquer Babylon. The Lord also ordained that a pagan ruler decree that the Jews could return to their land and rebuild their temple. As missionary leader A.T. Pierson used to say, "History is His story."

God had made a covenant with the people of Israel, promising that He would care for them and bless them if they obeyed His statutes, but if they disobeyed, He would chasten them and scatter them among the Gentiles (Lev. 26; Deut. 27–30). He wanted Israel to be "a light to the Gentiles" (Isa. 42:6, NKJV) and reveal the glories of the true and living God; but instead, the Jews became like the Gentiles and worshiped their false gods. The nation's ungodly kings and civic leaders, the false prophets and the faithless priests were the cause of the moral decay and the ultimate destruction of the nation (Lam. 4:13; Jer. 23:9-16; 2 Chron. 6:14-21). How strange that God's own people didn't obey Him, but Nebuchadnezzar and the pagan Babylonian army did obey Him!

So wise and powerful is our God that He can permit men and women to make personal choices and still accomplish His purposes in this world. When He isn't permitted to rule, He will overrule, but His will shall ultimately be done and His name glorified. We worship and serve a sovereign God who is never caught by surprise. No matter what our circumstances may be, we can always say with confidence, "Alleluia! . . . The Lord God Omnipotent reigns!" (Rev. 19:6, NKJV)

2. God gave favor to Daniel and his friends (Dan. 1:3-16)

The king's policy was to train the best people of the conquered nations to serve in his government. He could benefit from their knowledge of their own people and could also use their skills to strengthen his own administration. There were several deportations of Jews to Babylon both before and after the fall of Jerusalem, and it appears that Daniel and his three friends were taken in 605 when they were probably fifteen or sixteen years old. The Prophet Ezekiel was sent to Babylon in 597, and in 586, the temple was destroyed.

A dedicated remnant (Dan. 1:3-4a). Even a cursory reading of the Old Testament reveals that the majority of God's people have not always followed the Lord and kept His commandments. It has always been the "faithful remnant" within the Jewish nation that has come through the trials and judgments to maintain the divine covenant and make a new beginning. The Prophet Isaiah named one of his sons "Shear-jashub," which means "a remnant shall return" (Isa. 7:3). The same principle applies to the church today, for not everybody who professes faith in Jesus Christ is truly a child of God (Matt. 7:21-23). In His messages to the seven churches of Asia Minor, our Lord always had a special word for "the overcomers," the faithful remnant in each congregation who sought to obey the Lord (Rev. 2:7, 11, 17, 24-28; 3:4-5, 12, 21). Daniel and his three friends were a part of the faithful Jewish remnant in Babylon, placed there by the Lord to accomplish His purposes.

These young men were superior in every way, "the brightest and the best," prepared by God for a strategic ministry far from home. They were handsome, healthy, intelligent, and talented.[4] They belonged to the tribe of Judah (Dan. 1:6) and were of royal birth (v. 3).[5] In every sense, they were the very best the Jews had to offer. Because Ashpenaz is called "master of the eunuchs," some have concluded that the four Jewish boys were made eunuchs; but that is probably an erroneous conclusion. Originally, the term "eunuch" (Heb., *saris*) referred to a servant who had been castrated so he could serve the royal harem; but the title gradually came to be applied to any important court official. The word is applied to Potiphar and he was married (Gen. 37:36). The Jewish law forbade castration (Deut. 23:1), so it's difficult to believe that these four faithful Hebrew men who resisted Babylonian customs in every other way would have submitted to it.

A difficult trial (Dan. 1:4b-7). It was an honor to be trained as officers in the king's palace, but it was also a trial; for these dedicated Jewish boys would have to adapt themselves to the ways and the thinking of the Babylonians. The purpose of the "course" was to transform Jews into Babylonians, and this meant not only a new land, but also new names, new customs, new ideas, and a new language. For three years, their Babylonian teachers would attempt to "brainwash" the four Jewish young men and teach them how to think and live like Babylonians.

The name Daniel means "God is my judge," but it was changed to Belteshazzar or "Bel protect his life." Hananiah means "the Lord shows grace," but his new name, Shadrach, means "command of Aku" (the moon-god). Mishael means "Who is like God?" and the new name, "Meshach," means "Who is as Aku is?" Azariah means "The Lord is my help," but "Abednego" means "Servant of Nebo (Nego)." The name of the true and living God was replaced by the names of the false gods of Babylon; but would we expect unbelievers to do anything else?

Learning a new language and even receiving new names didn't create much of a problem, but practicing customs contrary to the Law of Moses was a great problem. The Babylonians were great builders, calculators, and military strategists, but their religion was steeped in superstition and myth. Just as Christian students in secular schools today often have to study material that contradicts what they believe, so Daniel and his friends had to master Babylonian history and science. In fact, in the final examination, they excelled all the other students (v. 20), and later, God gave them opportunities to show that their Jewish faith was superior to the faith of their captives. But when their course of training required them to disobey the holy law, they had to draw the line.

Surely the king's food was the best in the land, so why should these four Hebrew students refuse it? Because it would defile them and make them ceremonially unclean before their God (v. 8). It was important to the Jews that they eat only animals approved by God and prepared in such a way that the blood was drained from the flesh, for eating blood was strictly prohibited (Lev. 11; 17:10-16). But even more, the king's food would first be offered to idols, and no faithful Jew would eat such defiled food. The early church faced this same problem.

A discerning test (Dan. 1:8-16). How can God's people resist the pressures that can "squeeze" them into conformity with the world? According to Romans 12:1-2, "conformers" are people whose lives are controlled by pressure from without, but "transformers" are people whose lives are controlled by power from within. Daniel and his three friends were transformers: instead of being changed, they did the changing! God used them to transform the minds of powerful rulers and to bring great glory to His name in a pagan land.

The first step in solving their problem and being transformers was giving themselves wholly to the Lord. Daniel's heart—the totality of his being—belonged to the Lord, as did the hearts of his friends (Dan. 1:8; Rom. 12:1-2). "Keep your heart with all diligence, for out of it spring the issues of life" (Prov. 4:23, NKJV). A heart that loves the Lord, trusts the Lord, and therefore obeys the Lord has no difficulty making the right choices and trusting God to take care of the consequences. It has well been said that faith is not believing in spite of evidence—that's superstition—but obeying in spite of consequences. When they had to choose between God's Word and the king's food, they chose the Word of God (Ps. 119:103; Deut. 8:3).

The second step was to be gracious toward those in authority. The four men noticed that Ashpenaz was especially friendly and kind to them and recognized that this was the working of the Lord. (Joseph had a similar experience when he was in prison. See Gen. 39–40.) "When a man's ways please the Lord, He makes even his enemies to be at peace with him" (Prov. 16:7, NKJV). Instead of expecting a pagan Gentile officer to obey the Law of Moses and get himself in trouble with the king, Daniel and his friends took a wise approach and asked for a ten-day experiment.

Throughout Scripture you will find courageous people who had to defy authority in order to obey God, and in every case, they took the wise and gentle approach. "If it is possible, as far as it depends on you, live at peace with everyone" (Rom. 12:18, NIV).

Along with Daniel and his friends, you have the examples of the Hebrew midwives (Ex. 1), the apostles (Acts 4), and even Jesus Himself (1 Peter 2:13-25). All of them had to resist the law in order to obey the Lord, and God gave them success. They were courteous and didn't try to get others into trouble. They had a meek and quiet spirit. They saw the challenge as an opportunity to prove God and glorify His name.

The four Jewish students didn't threaten anybody, stage a protest, or try to burn down a building. They simply excelled in their studies, acted like gentlemen, and asked Melzar to test them for ten days by feeding them only water and vegetables.[6] Christians have no right to ask others—especially the unsaved—to take risks that they won't take themselves. Unconsciously directed by the Lord, Melzar was willing to accept their suggestion, and God did the rest. In the end, the four Jewish boys were healthier in body and better looking than all the other students. This is a vivid illustration of the promise in Matthew 6:33 and the principle laid down in Colossians 4:5; 1 Thessalonians 4:12; and 1 Peter 3:15.

When it comes to solving the problems of life, we must ask God for the courage to face the problem humbly and honestly, the wisdom to understand it, the strength to do what He tells us to do, and the faith to trust Him to do the rest. Our motive must be the glory of God and not finding a way of escape. The important question isn't, "How can I get out of this?" but, "What can I get out of this?" The Lord used this private test to prepare Daniel and his friends for the public tests they would face in years to come. The best thing about this experience wasn't that they were delivered from compromise, as wonderful as that was, but that they were developed in character. No wonder God called Daniel "greatly beloved" (Dan. 9:23; 10:11, 19), for he was very much like His Beloved Son.

3. God gave ability and success to Daniel and his friends (Dan. 1:17-20)

If you want to make a living, you get training; and if you want to make a life, you add education. But if you want to have a ministry for God, you must have divine gifts and divine help. Training and education are very important, but they are not substitutes for the ability and wisdom that only God can give.

God's special blessing (Dan. 1:17). These four Hebrew youths had to study and apply themselves, but God gave them skill to learn the material, discernment to understand it, and wisdom to know how to apply it and relate it to God's truth. As students, all of us need to ask God for wisdom (James 1:5) and then work hard to do our very best. "Faith without works is dead" (2:26), and fervent prayer can never replace faithful study. Both are necessary.

What studies did these young men pursue? Surely they were taught the religion of Babylon as well as the system of astrology that formed the basis for both their religion and their science. The king's official counselors had to be able to interpret dreams and various omens, because understanding the times and knowing the future were both important to the king's success. The young men were given what we would call a "secular education" steeped in the superstition of that day.

But should the people of God learn "the wisdom of this world" when they have the inspired and infallible Word of God to instruct them? Some sincere believers think that all "worldly education" is sinful, while others, just as sincere, believe that God's people should understand the mind-set of the world but not be controlled by it. The great church father Tertullian (160–220) is an example of the first group, for he asked, "What indeed has Athens to do with Jerusalem? What concord is there between the Academy and the church?"[7] He also wrote, "So, then, where is there any likeness between the Christian and the philosopher? Between the disciple of Greece and of heaven? Between the man whose object is fame, and whose object is life?"[8]

On the other hand, Moses was "learned in all the wisdom of the Egyptians" (Acts 7:22), and the Apostle Paul read the classics and even quoted from them in his letters. In 1 Corinthians 15:33 he quoted the Greek poet Menander; in Acts 17:27 and 28, he quoted Epimenides, Aratus, and Cleanthes; and in Titus 1:12, he quoted Epimenides. In 2 Timothy 4:13, he asked Timothy to bring him his books and parchments, which were probably copies of some of the Old Testament Scriptures and possibly some of the classical writers. The point is that Paul knew the classics and sought to use what he knew to reach people with the truth of God's Word. "Beware of the atmosphere of the classics," Robert Murray M'Cheyne wrote in a letter to a friend. "True, we ought to know them; but only as chemists handle poison—to discover their qualities, not to infect their blood with them."[9]

By understanding the mind-set of the Babylonian people, especially the king's "magicians, enchanters, sorcerers and astrologers" (Dan. 2:2, NIV), Daniel and his three friends were better able to show them the superiority of God's wisdom. The Lord gave Daniel a special gift of understanding visions and dreams. In the first half of his book, Daniel interpreted the visions and dreams of others, but in the last half, he received visions of his own from the Lord.

The king's examination (Dan. 1:18-20). We don't know how many students went through the entire course of study, but it's interesting that Nebuchadnezzar himself took the time to examine them. Since the new graduates were to become his personal advisers, the king wanted to be sure he was getting the best. By adding exceptionally intelligent new men to the staff, the king would be assured of getting the best counsel available. He was familiar with the older advisers and possibly not too happy with all of them (see 2:5-13). Was he suspicious of a palace intrigue? As we shall see later, the addition and the promotion of these four Jewish boys created jealousy and resentment among the advisers and they tried to get rid of Daniel (chap. 6). As older men, they resented their youth; as Babylonians, they resented their race; and as experienced servants, they envied their great ability and knowledge.

"Magicians" were men who dealt in the occult, while "enchanters" used incantations to accomplish their purposes. "Sorcerers" specialized in casting spells, "astrologers" studied the movements of the stars and their influence on events, and "diviners" sought to see the future by using various methods. Of course, all of these were forbidden by the Law of Moses (Deut. 18:9-13). Daniel and his friends had to work alongside these men, yet they remained pure and gave a powerful testimony for the Lord.

The word "inquired" in Daniel 1:20 means "to examine and compare." The king not only questioned the graduates, but he also compared one with another, and in this way ended up with the very best. There's no reason why Christian students on secular campuses today shouldn't be among the finest students who win some of the highest awards to the glory of God. Tertullian didn't think that "Jerusalem" should have anything to do with "Athens," but if believers from "Jerusalem" don't witness to unbelievers in "Athens," how will these lost sinners ever hear about Jesus Christ? Going into "all the world" includes going to our pagan campuses and letting our lights shine.

4. God gave Daniel a long life and ministry (Dan. 1:21)

The first year of King Cyrus' reign was 539 B.C., but Daniel was still alive in 537 B.C., the third year of Cyrus (10:1). If Daniel was fifteen years old in the year 605 when he was taken to Babylon, then he was born in 620, and he would have been eighty-three years old when he received the revelations recorded in chapters 10–12. While reading the prophecy of Jeremiah (25:11; 29:10), Daniel understood God's plan for the Jews to return to their land and rebuild the temple and the city (Dan. 9:1-2); and he lived long enough to see this prophecy fulfilled! How long he lived after that nobody knows, nor is it important that we know. During Daniel's long life, he had opportunity to witness to Nebuchadnezzar, Darius, Belshazzar, and Cyrus, as well as to the many court officers who came and went. He was a faithful servant, and he could say with the Lord Jesus, "I have glorified You on the earth. I have finished the work which You have given me to do" (John 17:4, NKJV).

However, not every faithful servant of God is given the blessing of a long life. Stephen was probably a young man when he was martyred (Acts 7), and Paul was in his sixties when he was killed in Rome. The godly Scottish preacher Robert Murray M'Cheyne was two months short of being thirty years old when he died, yet his ministry still enriches us. William Whiting Borden ("Borden of Yale") was only twenty-five when he died in Egypt, and David Brainerd, missionary to the Native Americans, was only twenty-nine when God called him. "So teach us to number our days, that we may apply our hearts unto wisdom" (Ps. 90:12). We number our years, not our days, but everybody still has to live a day at a time, and we don't know when that final day will dawn.

In order to accomplish His plans for His people, the Lord providentially works to put some of His servants into places of special honor and responsibility. When He wanted to protect Jacob's family and the future of the nation of Israel, the Lord sent Joseph to Egypt and made him second ruler of the land. God had Esther and Mordecai in Persia, where they exposed a plot against the Jews and saved the people of Israel from being annihilated. Nehemiah was the king's cupbearer in Susa and was able to get royal assistance for restoring the walls of Jerusalem. I wonder if the men in high political office who assisted Paul were true believers in Jesus Christ? (Acts 19:30-31; Rom. 16:23) Even if they weren't, God placed them where they were and enabled them to accomplish His will.

The events recorded in this chapter should be a great encouragement to us when we experience trials and testings and become discouraged; for when God is not allowed to rule, He overrules. God is still on the throne and will never leave us nor forsake us.

Has the enemy destroyed the Holy City and the holy temple and taken God's people captive? Fear not, for there is still a godly remnant that worships the true God and serves Him. Does the enemy attempt to defile that godly remnant? Fear not, for the Lord will work on their behalf and keep them separated to Himself. Are godly believers needed in places of authority? Fear not, for the Lord will see to it that they are prepared and appointed. Does the Lord desire to communicate His prophetic truth to His people? Fear not, for He will keep His servants alive and alert until their work is done. Are you in a place of responsibility and wondering how long you can hold out? Fear not, for the same God who called you and equipped you is able to make you "continue" until you complete the tasks that He has assigned you. "He who calls you is faithful, who also will do it" (1 Thes. 5:24, NKJV).

Each believer is either a conformer or a transformer. We're either being squeezed into the world's mold or we're transforming things in the world into which God has put us. Transformers don't always have an easy life, but it's an exciting one, and it gives you great delight to know that God is using you to influence others.

CHAPTER TWO
THE GOD OF DREAMS AND DESTINIES
Daniel 2

As you turn from chapter 1 to chapter 2, the atmosphere in the king's palace changes radically. Chapter 1 closes with recognition and security, but chapter 2 introduces rejection and danger. Because they possessed almost unlimited power and authority, Oriental despots were notoriously temperamental and unpredictable, and here Nebuchadnezzar reveals this side of his character. (See also 3:19.) However, the hero and major actor in chapter 2 is not King Nebuchadnezzar but the Lord God "who reveals the deep and secret things" (v. 22, NKJV). As you read this chapter, you witness the God of Israel in complete control of every situation and accomplishing His purposes even through superstitious Gentile unbelievers. Note the divine activities that protected His servants and brought glory to His name.

1. God distresses a king (Dan. 2:1)

Nebuchadnezzar was in the second year of his reign and discovering the burdens of the kingdom as well as the far-reaching consequences of his decisions. Some of his concerns were causing him restless nights (Ecc. 5:12), and his mind was unsettled as he worried about the future of his kingdom (Dan. 2:29). How long would "Babylon the great" last? How long would he be the ruler? Shakespeare was right: "Uneasy lies the head that wears a crown."

The Lord gave Nebuchadnezzar a vivid dream that he couldn't understand, and it distressed him. That the Lord God Almighty would communicate truth to a pagan Gentile king is evidence of the grace of God. The phrase "dreamed dreams" may suggest that this one dream kept recurring. The Lord had given two dreams to Pharaoh (Gen. 41), another Gentile ruler, and Joseph had interpreted them; and He also gave a dream to the magi who came to worship Jesus (Matt. 2:12), and they were Gentiles. When God wanted to give a message to the Gentiles, He usually sent them a Jewish prophet (Amos 3:7)—Jonah to Nineveh, for example, or Amos to the neighboring nations (Amos 1–2). But here the Lord communicated directly to an unbelieving Gentile monarch. The Lord in His wisdom planned to use His faithful servant Daniel to describe and interpret the dream, and in this way, God's name would be glorified and Daniel and his friends would be honored and rewarded.

Does God still use dreams to communicate His will? Certainly He can do so if He pleases, but this isn't His usual approach. God guides His children today by His Holy Spirit as they pray, seek His face, meditate on His Word, and consult with their spiritual leaders. The danger is that our dreams may not come from the Lord. The human subconscious is capable of producing dreams, and Jeremiah 23:25-32 indicates that demonic forces can cause dreams that are Satan's lies and not God's truth. It's dangerous to accept dreams as messengers from the Lord.

2. God disgraces the "wise men" (Dan. 2:2-13)[1]

The king did what any ancient ruler would do: he summoned his special advisers to help him understand the significance of this dream that had interrupted his sleep and robbed him of peace. But this was no routine meeting, for the king not only commanded them to interpret the dream but also to reveal the dream to him! If they didn't do both, he would kill them without mercy and turn their houses into public latrines and garbage dumps. This, of course, was a new challenge for them and they knew they couldn't meet it.

Here we are confronted with a question that sincere Bible students don't answer the same way: Did King Nebudchadnezzar forget his dream, or was he using this approach to test his counselors to see if they were authentic? I hold to the second position, but let's consider both sides of the matter.

He forgot the dream. I find it difficult to believe that such a vivid dream would pass out of the mind of a great leader like Nebuchadnezzar, particularly if the dream occurred more than once. Of course, we do forget most of our dreams, but in this case, the Lord was seeking to communicate His truth to the king. Surely the same God who gave the dream could see to it that the king would remember it. After all, the dream was so agitating that the king lay awake wondering what it meant. Furthermore, if indeed the king had forgotten the dream, how would he be able to verify it even if the advisers could come up with the right answer?

The kjv and the Amplified Bible translate verses 5 and 8 "the thing is gone from me," which can be interpreted "the dream has left me." This is probably the strongest argument for the king having a bad memory. But the NASB translates that same phrase "the command from me is firm," and the NIV translates it "this is what I have firmly decided." The reference isn't to the dream but to the king's edict of judgment. If the counselors couldn't tell him the dream and interpret it, they would be publicly humiliated and mercilessly slain.

The king was testing his counselors. I believe that Nebuchadnezzar remembered the dream, pondered it, and realized that it contained a significant message concerning him and his kingdom. It must have brought fear and wonder to his heart when he beheld this massive metallic image smashed to atoms by a mysterious stone which then grew into a mountain. The interpretation of this dream was too important for the king to treat it as a routine matter. He wanted to be sure that his "wise men" would give him the correct meaning, for his future was involved in that dream. He didn't want to hear "misleading and wicked things" (v. 9, NIV) that they made up just to please the king. He wanted the truth.

Perhaps he recalled the difference between the counselors he inherited from his father and the four Jewish young men who had graduated at the top of the class (1:19-20). He had seen that these four boys were ten times better than his counselors and possessed a wisdom far beyond anything the "wise men" had ever shown. Perhaps he had concluded that his "wise men" had conspired to deceive him and that their interpretations and explanations weren't valid at all. If indeed they had the ability to interpret the dream, then surely they also had the ability to tell him the dream! It was a test of their ability and their veracity.

Regardless of which approach is correct, this much is true: the counselors were greatly humiliated because they couldn't tell Nebuchadnezzar the dream. This was a great opportunity for them to receive wealth, prestige, and promotion, and the fact that they stalled for time indicated that they were unable to meet the challenge. This in itself set the stage for Daniel to exalt the true and living God of Israel who alone can predict the future (Isa. 41:21-23). By issuing this impossible challenge, the king was unconsciously following the plan of God and opening the way for Daniel to do what the counselors could not do. As they pleaded their case, the "wise men" tried flattery and logic, but all their speeches only made Nebuchadnezzar more and more angry, until finally he issued an edict that all the "wise men" in the city of Babylon be slain.

Throughout Bible history, you find occasions when God exposed the foolishness of the world and the deceptiveness of Satan. Moses and Aaron defeated the magicians of Pharaoh and the gods of Egypt (Ex. 7–12), and Elijah on Mount Carmel exposed the deception of Baal worship (1 Kings 18). Jeremiah confronted the false prophet Hananiah and revealed his wickedness (Jer. 28), and Paul exposed the deception of Bar Jesus the sorcerer (Acts 13:1-12). But it was Jesus who by His life, teaching, and sacrificial death declared the wisdom of this world "foolishness" with God, and that includes all its myths and false religions (1 Cor. 1:18ff). The statement of the advisers in Daniel 2:10 wipes out astrology and other forms of human prophecy! Out of their own mouths they condemned their own practices!

3. God discloses the secret (Dan. 2:14-23)

The king's edict had to be obeyed, so Arioch, the captain of the king's guard and the chief executioner, set out to round up all the king's "wise men" and slay them. Satan had lost one battle but now he would try to pull victory out of defeat by having Daniel and his three friends killed. The Evil One is willing to sacrifice all his false prophets in the city of Babylon if he can destroy four of God's faithful servants. Satan's servants are expendable, but the Lord cares for His people. See how the Lord intervened and accomplished His purposes and blessed His people.

Remarkable Postponement (Dan. 2:14-16). When Arioch came to get Daniel and his friends, they were shocked to hear about the king's edict. As new "graduates" among the royal counselors, they hadn't been invited to the special session about the dream. Daniel spoke to Arioch "with wisdom and tact" (NIV), just as he had spoken to Ashpenaz and Melzar (1:9-14; see Col. 4:5-6), and the chief executioner explained how serious the matter was. By doing this and delaying his obedience, Arioch was risking his own life, but the officers in the palace had learned that the four Jewish men were trustworthy. Their gracious actions and words during their three years of training were now helping to save their lives.

Arioch allowed Daniel time to speak to Nebuchadnezzar, and the king must have been surprised to see him. Apparently his rage had subsided and he was willing to make some concessions. After all, Daniel hadn't been at the original meeting, so he deserved an opportunity to obey the king's orders. No doubt Nebuchadnezzar recalled that the four Hebrews had been exceptional students and were superior to the men whose lives were now in danger. Why kill your four best counselors just because of the incompetence of the others? By faith, Daniel promised to show the king his dream and the interpretation, for he knew that the Lord would answer prayer.

Believing prayer (Dan. 2:17-19). Throughout this book, Daniel and his friends are presented as men of faith and prayer (Dan. 6; 9). They were far from home, but by faith they could "look toward" Jerusalem and the temple and claim the promise of 1 Kings 8:44-45. The God of heaven[2] would hear their prayers and answer them for His own glory. The word "secret" (*raz*) is used eight times in this chapter and is the equivalent of the Greek word *mysterion* ("mystery") which is used twenty-eight times in the New Testament. It means "a hidden truth that is revealed only to the initiated." God had hidden prophetic truth in the dream and He enabled His servant to know both the dream and its interpretation and to understand God's future plans. "The effective, fervent prayer of a righteous man avails much" (James 5:16, NKJV).

Joyful praise (Dan. 2:20-23). Daniel's first response was to bless the Lord for hearing and answering their petitions. They asked for wisdom, and God gave it (James 1:5), and His mighty hand stopped the execution process and gave the four men time to pray. Little did the pagan "wise men" realize that the presence of the Hebrews in Babylon was making their deliverance possible.[3] The God of heaven is also the God of history, for He can set and change the times allotted to rulers and to nations, which was the very thing Nebuchadnezzar was worrying about. The dream was "darkness" to the king but light to Daniel, not unlike the glory cloud that stood between Israel and the Egyptian army (Ex. 14:19-20). Daniel included his three friends in his song of praise (Dan. 2:23) because they had shared the burden of prayer with him. Later he would share the honors with them and they would serve with him in the highest appointed office in the city of Babylon.

When God's people today face a crisis, they need to follow the example of Daniel and his friends and take the matter to the Lord in prayer. Faith is living without scheming, and faith brings glory to God. Daniel and his friends couldn't take credit for what happened because it came from the hand of God. "Call upon Me in the day of trouble; I will deliver you, and you shall glorify Me" (Ps. 50:15, NKJV). "Whatever God can do faith can do," said A.W. Tozer, "and whatever faith can do prayer can do when it is offered in faith. An invitation to prayer is, therefore, an invitation to omnipotence, for prayer engages the Omnipotent God and brings Him into our human affairs."[4]

4. God displays His wisdom and power (Dan. 2:24-45)

Once again we see the wisdom and tact of Daniel as he went immediately to Arioch and told him not to destroy the "wise men" because God had revealed to him both the dream and its interpretation. Daniel never heard the Sermon on the Mount, but he knew how to treat his enemies and was willing to rescue the pagan advisers. Since Arioch was in charge of executions, he could stop the process and save the lives of all the king's counselors in the city of Babylon. Daniel gave Arioch the privilege of taking him into the presence of the king and sharing some of the credit. The statement, "I have found a man" (v. 25) isn't exactly the truth, because it was Daniel who found Arioch; but Daniel wasn't the kind of person who worried about who got the credit so long as God got the glory.

In reply to the king's question, Daniel immediately gave all the glory to the God of heaven, and in this he reminds us of Joseph when he interpreted Pharaoh's dreams (Gen. 41:16). Nebuchadnezzar must have been shocked when Daniel even told him that he knew the king had been worrying about the future of his kingdom before he had this dream. The dream was God's answer to his concerns, for God revealed the future sequence of the Gentiles' kingdoms and how Gentile history would climax with the appearance of an eternal kingdom.

The phrase "latter days" ("last days," "last times") is found frequently in Scripture, beginning with Genesis 49:1 and ending with 2 Peter 3:3. Our Lord ushered in the "last days" with His death, resurrection, and ascension to heaven (Heb. 1:2; 1 Peter 1:20), so we are living now in that period of time when God is "wrapping things up." God has plans for the "latter days" of Israel (Gen. 49:1; Deut. 31:29; Dan. 2:28) which will climax with Messiah returning to earth and being received by His people (Hosea 3:5; Micah 4:1; Joel 2:28-29). The "last days" for the church include perilous times (2 Tim. 3:1), the apostasy of many, and the rise of scoffers and deniers of the truth (2 Peter 3:1ff); and this period will end when Christ takes His church to heaven (1 Thes. 4:13-18).

The image Nabuchadnezzar beheld in his dream depicted what Jesus called "the times of the Gentiles" (Luke 21:24), a period of time that began in 605 B.C. when Jerusalem was taken by Nebuchadnezzar and the Babylonian army. This period will end when Christ returns to establish His kingdom (Luke 21:25-28).[5] During the "times of the Gentiles," there will be four successive kingdoms, climaxed by a fifth kingdom that will destroy the other four and fill the earth. The fifth kingdom is the kingdom of the Lord Jesus Christ, King of Kings and Lord of Lords.

The dream (Dan. 2:31-35). First Daniel told the king what he had seen in his dream, and then he explained its meaning. He saw a large statue of a man, "an enormous dazzling statue, awesome in appearance" (v. 31, NIV), composed of five different materials: gold, silver, bronze, iron, and clay. Suddenly a stone appeared and smashed the feet of the statue so that the image was completely shattered and became like chaff that was blown away. Then the stone became a huge mountain that filled the earth. On hearing this accurate description, the king knew that Daniel was telling the truth and that what he said could be trusted. Only the God of heaven who sent the dream could have helped His servant know and interpret the dream.

The meaning of the dream (Dan. 2:36-45).[6] The large image represented four Gentile kingdoms:

- The head of gold—Nebuchadnezzar and the Babylonian kingdom (vv. 37-38). It lasted from 636 B.C. to 539 B.C. Jeremiah called Babylon "a gold cup in the Lord's hand" (Jer. 51:7).
- The breast and arms of silver—The Medo-Persian kingdom (539–330 B.C.). Darius the Mede conquered Babylon (Dan. 5:30-31).
- The belly and thighs of bronze—The Grecian kingdom (330–63 B.C.). Alexander the Great established what was probably the largest empire in ancient times. He died in 323 B.C.
- The legs of iron and feet of iron and clay—The Roman Empire (63 B.C.–ca. A.D. 475). Iron represents strength but clay represents weakness. Rome was strong in law, organization, and military might; but the empire included so many different peoples that this created weakness. "The people will be a mixture and will not remain united" (Dan. 2:43, NIV).
- The destruction of the image—The coming of Jesus Christ, the Stone, to judge His enemies and establish His universal kingdom.

As simple as this explanation appears, it carries with it some important and profound messages. First, it reveals that God is in control of history. He knows the future because He plans the future. This doesn't mean that God is to blame for the evil things that leaders and nations do, but that He can overrule even their wickedness to accomplish His divine purposes. The God of heaven gave Nebuchadnezzar his throne and enabled him to defeat his enemies and expand his empire (vv. 37-38; Jer. 27). But the God who gave him his authority could also take it away, and He did (Jer. 51–52). The king didn't know how long his empire would last, but he knew it would end some day. In fact, Babylon was conquered by what Daniel called an "inferior kingdom" (Dan. 2:39).

Second, the dream reveals that human enterprises decline as time goes on. The massive and awesome image not only changed in value from head to foot—from gold to clay—but it also changed in strength, finally ending in feet made of iron mixed with clay. Actually, the statue was top-heavy, for the atomic weight of gold is ten times that of clay, and silver is five times heavier than clay. From age to age, nations and kingdoms appear strong and durable, but they're always in danger of falling over and crashing. The image Nebuchadnezzar saw dazzled him with the brilliance of the gold, iron, and bronze, but it was standing on feet composed of iron and clay.

As we survey history, on one level we see progress and improvement; but when we go deeper, we see decay and decline. Thoreau said that America had "improved means to unimproved ends," and that can be said of any developing nation. We can speak easily to people in almost any part of the world, but do we have anything important to say? We can travel rapidly from one place to another, but we make little progress in solving the problems of war, violence, famine, and liberty. While we're grateful for the things that make modern life comfortable and enjoyable—good houses, cars and planes, powerful medicines, electronic devices—we have to admit that each of these brings with it new problems that have to be solved. It's easier to make a living but harder to make a life.

A third truth is that it will be difficult for things to hold together at the end of the age. The feet of the image were composed of a mixture of iron and clay. Iron is strong and durable but clay is weak and prone to crumble. The iron in the image gives the appearance of strength and endurance, but the clay announces just the opposite. In fact, the clay robs the iron of its ability to hold things together, for wherever the iron touches the clay, at those points there is weakness. Society today is held together by treaties that can be broken, promises that can be ignored, traditions that can be forgotten, organizations that can be disbanded, and money-making enterprises that can fail—all of it iron mixed with clay!

Man at his best is clay, for God made him out of the dust of the earth. Though man and woman are both made in the image of God, sin has robbed us of the dominion He gave us (Gen. 1:26). We are both creators and destroyers, and we seem bent on destroying one another and the world God has graciously given us. The heart of every problem is the problem in the human heart—rebellion against God.

The image gives us a fourth truth: Jesus Christ will return, destroy His enemies, and establish His kingdom. The stone is a frequent image of God in Scripture and especially of Messiah, Jesus Christ the Son of God (Ps. 118:22; Isa. 8:14; 28:16; Matt. 21:44; Acts 4:11; 1 Cor. 10:4; 1 Peter 2:4-8). The phrase "without hands" is used in Scripture to mean "not by human power" and refers to something only God can do (Col. 2:11; Heb. 9:11, 24). It appears that the Roman Empire will in some ways continue until the end of the age and culminate in the rule of ten kings (Dan. 2:44; 7:24-27; Rev. 17:3, 12-18). The world will be delivered from evil, not by a process, but by a crisis, the promised return of Jesus Christ. Whatever remains of the four Gentile kingdoms, passed from one kingdom to the next, will be destroyed and turned into chaff. Then Christ will establish His kingdom which will fill all the earth.

When we consider these truths, our response ought to be one of joyful confidence, knowing that the Lord has everything under control and will one day reign on this earth. While God's people should do everything they can to alleviate suffering and make this a safer and happier world, our hope is not in laws, political alliances, or moral crusades. Our hope is in the Lord. People's hearts need to be changed by the grace of God, and that means God's people must be witnesses to the ends of the earth. The only kingdom that will stand forever is Christ's kingdom (Dan. 2:44), and the only people who will be citizens of that kingdom are those who have trusted Him and been born again by the Spirit of God (John 3:1-18).

What would all of this have meant to King Nebuchadnezzar as he sat on his throne listening to a young Jewish lad explain God's mysteries? For one thing, the message of the image should have humbled him. It was not Nebuchadnezzar who conquered nations and kingdoms; it was God who enabled him to do it and who gave him his empire. "You, O king, are a king of kings," said Daniel. "For the God of heaven has given you a kingdom, power, strength, and glory" (Dan. 2:37, NKJV). Alas, the great king forgot this lesson and one day said, "Is not this great Babylon, that I have built for a royal dwelling by my mighty power and for the honor of my majesty?" (4:30, NKJV) God had to humble the king and make him live like an animal until he learned that God does according to His will (v. 35) and alone deserves glory.

In giving the dream and enabling Daniel to know the dream and explain it, God displayed His wisdom and power. God has the wisdom to plan the ages and the power to execute His plan. King Nebuchadnezzar ruled from 605 B.C. to 562 B.C., but Jesus Christ will reign forever and ever, and of His kingdom there shall be no end.

5. God distinguishes His servants (Dan. 2:46-49)

Being a pagan unbeliever, Nebuchadnezzar was so overwhelmed by what Daniel did that he treated him as though he were a god! Cornelius the Roman centurion treated Peter that way (Acts 10:25-26), and Paul and Barnabas were accepted as gods by the people of Lystra (14:8-18). Being a devout Jew, Daniel must have abhorred all this adulation, but he knew it was useless to protest the commands of the king. But in paying homage to Daniel, the king was actually acknowledging that the God of the Hebrews was greater than all other gods. Nebuchadnezzar hadn't yet come to the place where he believed in one true and living God, but this was the first step.

What the king did and said also announced to everyone in the court that Daniel was superior to the Babylonian advisers who could not describe the dream, let alone explain it. And yet what Daniel and his friends did saved the lives of those men!

The king kept his word and promoted Daniel with great honors, just as Pharaoh honored and promoted Joseph in Egypt (Gen. 41:39-43). He made Daniel ruler over the province of Babylon and, at Daniel's request, made his three friends helpers with him in that office. They were put in different offices in the province while Daniel remained at the court of the king and sat in the king's gate, a place of great authority (Dan. 2:49, NIV). What started out as possible tragedy—the slaughter of four godly men—was turned into great triumph; and the God of Daniel received great glory.

CHAPTER THREE
FAITH AND THE FIERY TRIAL
Daniel 3

The devil tempts us to destroy our faith, but God tests us to develop our faith, because a faith that can't be tested can't be trusted. False faith withers in times of trial, but true faith takes deeper root, grows, and brings glory to God. This explains why God permitted the three Hebrew men to be tested and then thrown into the fiery furnace. The Apostle Peter must have been well acquainted with the Book of Daniel because he used the metaphor of the "fiery trial" when he warned his readers of the persecutions about to come to the church (1 Peter 1:7; 4:12).[1]

The experience of these three men helps us examine our own faith and determine whether we have the kind of authentic faith that can be tested and bring glory to God.

1. True faith confronts the challenge (Dan. 3:1-12)

We don't know how much time elapsed between the night Nebuchadnezzar dreamed about the metallic image (Dan. 2) and the day he commanded the people to fall down before the golden image that he had made. Some students believe that the event described in Daniel 3 might have occurred twenty years after the promotion of Daniel and his friends, about the time Jerusalem was finally destroyed (586 B.C.).

The heart of the king (Dan. 3:1-3). When Daniel explained the meaning of the successive metals in the massive image, he identified Nebuchadnezzar as the head of gold (2:38), and perhaps this is what helped motivate the king to make an image of gold. Not content to be merely a head of gold, he and his kingdom would be symbolized by an entire image of gold! There was definitely an element of pride in this whole enterprise. Daniel had made it clear that no empire would last, including that of the great Nebuchadnezzar. The king's heart was filled with pride because of all his conquests, but along with that pride were fear and concern for himself and his vast kingdom. He wanted to make sure that his people were loyal to him and that there would be no rebellions.

There wasn't enough gold in his entire kingdom to make a solid image ninety feet high and nine feet wide, so the image was probably made of wood overlaid with gold (Isa. 40:19; 41:7; Jer. 10:3-9). But it must have been an awesome sight to see this golden image standing on the plain at Dura, a location perhaps six miles from the city of Babylon. ("Dura" simply means "a walled-in place," and there were several sites with that name in ancient Babylon.) Also in the area was a furnace into which people would be thrown if they refused to fall down before the image and acknowledge the sovereignty of King Nebuchadnezzar. Nebuchadnezzar planned to unify his kingdom by means of religion and fear. The alternatives were to fall down before the image and worship or be thrown into the furnace and be burned to death.

The king sent official messengers to all the provinces of his empire, commanding the officials to gather for the dedication of the great golden image. Eight different officers are especially named (Dan. 3:2-3) and they would represent the people left back home. Princes (satraps?) were the chief administrative officers in the provinces, while governors were probably their assistants (or perhaps military commanders). Captains ruled over the smaller districts in the provinces, and judges were their advisers. Treasurers served as do treasurers today, and counselors were experts in the law. Sheriffs were local judges and magistrates, and rulers were the miscellaneous officials in the province. Every level of authority was represented and all were expected to be present.

But this was more than a political assembly; it was a religious service, complete with music, and it called for total commitment on the part of the worshipers.[2] Note that the word "worship" is used at least eleven times in the chapter. Nebuchadnezzar was wise to use instrumental music because it could stir the people's emotions and make it easy for him to manipulate them and win their submission and obedience. Throughout history, music and song have played an important role in strengthening nationalism, motivating conquest, and inspiring people to act. Music has the power so to grip human thoughts and emotions that people are transformed from being free agents into becoming mere puppets. The English poet William Congreave wrote that "music has charms to soothe a savage breast," but music also has power to release the savage in the breast. Music can be used as a wonderful tool and treasure from the Lord or as a destructive weapon from Satan.

The hearts of the people (Dan. 3:4-7). The herald didn't ask for a vote. He simply told the people that what was about to happen was a matter of life or death. At the sound of the music, they would either fall down before the image or they would die. But the superstitious crowd was accustomed to worshiping many gods and goddesses, so the command was an easy one to obey, especially in light of the consequences. The difference between the true believer and the unbeliever isn't the presence of faith, because everybody lives by faith in something. The difference is in the object of that faith. The crowd believed the herald and the king, and therefore they obeyed. The three Hebrew men believed the commandment of God, so they disobeyed. The crowd had credulous faith, but the Jews had confident faith.

"Faith is one of the forces by which men live," said philosopher and psychologist William James, and he was right. People act by faith when they step into an elevator, order food in a restaurant, drive on the highway, or say their marriage vows. The Christian believer lives by faith in the living God and what He has revealed in His Word. The great multitude of Babylonians, exiles, and representatives from the provinces simply conformed to the edict of the king and did what everybody else was doing. "After all," they argued, "we all have to live!" There were thousands of Jewish exiles in Babylon, and they were represented by Shadrach, Meshach, and Abednego. If they bowed to the idol, all the Jews were involved!

This assembly of "worshipers" helps us better understand the plight of people in today's world who don't know our Lord Jesus Christ. They blindly follow the crowd and build their lives on the false and the futile. Concerned only with survival, they'll do almost anything to escape danger and death, even to the point of selling themselves into slavery to men and the empty myths that they promote. It's the philosophy of the devil: "Skin for skin! Yes, all that a man has he will give for his life" (Job 2:4, NKJV). It's quite the opposite of the outlook of the Christian believer who believes John 12:24-26.

The hearts of the three Jewish men (Dan. 3:8-12). But there were three men in that great crowd who stood tall when everybody else bowed low. Their faith was in the true and living God and in the Word that He had spoken to their people. Knowing the history of the Jewish people, they were confident that the Lord was in control and they had nothing to fear. The Prophet Isaiah had written, "Fear not, for I have redeemed you; I have called you by your name; you are Mine. When you pass through the waters, I will be with you; and through the rivers, they shall not overflow you. When you walk through the fire, you shall not be burned, nor shall the flame scorch you" (Isa. 43:1-2, NKJV). Faith means obeying God regardless of the feelings within us, the circumstances around us, or the consequences before us.

It's difficult to reconstruct the logistics of the event, but it seems that King Nebuchadnezzar and his advisers ("Chaldeans") were not together as they watched the event and that the king didn't require them to join with the crowd in their worship. They may have affirmed their loyalty privately and it would be an insult for them to join with "the rabble" in their worship. Since the three Hebrew men held offices in the province (Dan. 2:49), they had to be there; but we don't know where they were standing.[3] Apparently Nebuchadnezzar couldn't see them but the Chaldeans could; in fact, these evil men were no doubt watching and waiting for the opportunity to accuse these foreigners who had been promoted over the heads of the Babylonians. We don't know that this was the same group of advisers who was embarrassed when Daniel interpreted the king's dream, but if so, they quickly forgot that these "foreigners" had saved their lives.

True faith isn't frightened by threats, impressed by crowds, or swayed by superstitious ceremonies. True faith obeys the Lord and trusts Him to work out the consequences. These three Jewish men know the law of God—"You shall have no other gods before Me . . . . You shall not bow down to them nor serve them" (Ex. 20:3, 5, NKJV). Once the Lord has spoken on a matter, the matter is settled and there's no room for discussion or need for compromise. To bow before the image even once, no matter what excuse they might give, would have destroyed their witness and broken their fellowship with God. The tense of the Greek verb in Matthew 4:9 indicates that Satan asked Jesus to worship him only one time, and the Savior refused. Shadrach, Meshach, and Abednego would not bow down to the golden image even once because it would lead to serving Nebuchadnezzar's false gods for the rest of their lives.

2. True faith confesses the Lord (Dan. 3:13-18)

Once again we see the king in a fit of anger (v. 13; see v. 19 and 2:12). He had conquered many cities and nations, but he could not conquer himself. "Better a patient man than a warrior, a man who controls his temper than one who takes a city" (Prov. 16:32, NIV). Yet the three Hebrew officers were calm and respectful. "Always be ready to give a defense to everyone who asks you a reason for the hope that is in you, with meekness and fear" (1 Peter 3:15, NKJV).

The king must have had special respect for these men and the work they did in the empire because he gave them another opportunity to comply with his orders. He may have forgotten that he had called their God "the God of gods, the Lord of kings" (Dan. 2:47, NKJV), because he arrogantly asked, "And who is that God that shall deliver you out of my hands?" (3:15; and see Ex. 5:2) He was actually claiming to be a god himself! In a short time he would be humbled and have to confess that the God of the Hebrews is "the Most High God" and that nobody should blaspheme His name.

The three men could have compromised with the king and defended their disobedience by arguing, "Everybody else is doing it," or "Our office demands that we obey," or "We'll bow our knees but we won't bow our hearts." They might have said, "We can do our people more good by being officers in the king's service than by being ashes in the king's furnace." But true faith doesn't look for loopholes; it simply obeys God and knows that He will do what is best. Faith rests on commands and promises, not on arguments and explanations.

Times of adversity are usually times of opportunity, especially when God's people are being persecuted for their faith. "You will be brought before rulers and kings for My sake, for a testimony to them" (Mark 13:9). The three courageous Jews weren't concerned about themselves, nor were they afraid of the fury of the king. Their only concern was obeying the Lord and giving a faithful witness to all who were watching and listening. Their attitude was respectful and their words were few and carefully chosen.

"We are not careful to answer" (Dan. 3:16) means, "We don't need to defend ourselves or our God, for our God will defend both Himself and us." They weren't the least bit worried! It's a bit arrogant for God's people to think they have to defend God for God is perfectly capable of defending Himself and taking care of His people. Our task is to obey God and trust Him, and He will do the rest. "Behold, God is my salvation; I will trust, and not be afraid: for the Lord Jehovah is my strength and my song; he also is become my salvation" (Isa. 12:2).

Shadrach, Meshach, and Abednego were men of faith but not men of presumption. Had they affirmed that God would deliver them, that would have been presumption, because they didn't know what God had willed for their situation. Instead, they stated that their God was able to deliver them, but even if He didn't, they still wouldn't fall down before the king's golden image. There is such a thing as "commercial faith" that says, "We will obey God if He rewards us for doing it." Again, it's the devil's philosophy of worship: "All these things will I give You if You will fall down and worship me" (Matt. 4:9, NKJV; Job 1:9-12). In my pastoral ministry, I've heard people make promises to God so they can "persuade" Him to heal them or change their circumstances. But this isn't believing in God—it's bargaining with God. True faith confesses the Lord and obeys Him regardless of the consequences. From the very beginning of their time in Babylon, Daniel and his three friends determined that they would be different, and the Lord enabled them to maintain that determination.

Hebrews 11 lists the names and deeds of great men and women of faith, including these three Jewish men (Heb. 11:34), but at verse 36, the writer says "And others" and then lists people who seem to be failures in spite of their faith (vv. 36-40). The Greek word means "others of a different kind," that is, others who had faith but didn't see God do the miracles He did for those listed in the first thirty-five verses. God always rewards faith but He doesn't always step in and perform special miracles. Not everybody who prays is healed, but God always gives strength to bear with pain and grace to face death without fear. The three Hebrew men believed that God could deliver them, but they would trust Him even if He didn't. That is how faith is supposed to operate in our lives. See Habakkuk 3:17-19.

3. True faith confounds the enemy (Dan. 3:19-25)

The king's temper once more got the best of him—proud men don't like to be disobeyed—and he ordered the three Jewish believers to be thrown into the fiery furnace. They had turned down his generous offer, so they had to suffer the consequences. Whereas before, the king had been friendly with them and concerned to save them, now he was determined to destroy them. At last the court advisers would get their revenge on these Jewish exiles who had encroached on their territory and been promoted to the offices that belonged to the Chaldeans.

The furnace was used for smelting ore. It had a large opening at the top through which fuel and vessels full of ore could be placed into the fire, and there was a door at the bottom through which the metal was taken out. An opening in a wall enabled the smelters to check on the progress of their work, and through holes in the wall they could use bellows to make the fire blaze even more. The unit was large enough for at least four persons to walk around in it. It was into this furnace that Nebuchadnezzar cast the three faithful Jews, fully clothed and bound. It seemed like certain death for the men who refused to obey the king.

The king's anger must have affected his mind, for the best way to punish the men wasn't to increase the temperature but to decrease it. A hotter fire would kill them instantly and then burn them up, but a lower temperature would cause them to suffer intense pain before they died. However, it made no difference because the men weren't affected by the fire at all! When the king looked into the furnace, he saw that they were alive and not dead, loose and not bound, and that there was a fourth person with them! The king thought it was an angel who looked like "a son of the gods" (vv. 25, 28, NIV), but the fourth person in the furnace was Jesus Christ in one of His preincarnate appearances in the Old Testament (Isa. 43:2; Ps. 91:9-12). They were walking about as though they were in a palace and not in a furnace! The ropes with which the three men had been bound were the only things that had been affected by the fire. The God of Shadrach, Meshach, and Abednego was indeed able to deliver them!

The three men had refused to obey the king's order to fall down before the image, but when the king ordered them to come out of the furnace, they immediately obeyed. They were living miracles and they wanted everybody to know what their great God could do. Not only was each man's body whole and the hair unsinged, but their clothing didn't even smell like fire. The other officials at the dedication service witnessed this marvel (Dan. 3:27) and no doubt reported it when they arrived back home. What a story! The officers wouldn't dare speak up at that time, lest they offend their king. But King Nebuchadnezzar spoke out (v. 28)! He affirmed (1) the power of the God of Israel, (2) the effectiveness of faith in Him, and (3) the remarkable dedication of the three Jewish men who gave their bodies to the true God and not to the king's false god (Rom. 12:1-2). By one act of faith, the three Jewish men became witnesses of the true and living God to the entire Babylonian Empire!

4. True faith confirms the promises (Dan. 3:26-30)

Why did the Lord include this story in the Old Testament Scriptures? For the same reason He included stories about the "faith experiences" of Abraham, Moses, Joshua, David, and the prophets: to encourage God's people in their battle against the world, the flesh, and the devil. "For whatever things were written before were written for our learning, that we through the patience and comfort of the Scriptures might have hope" (Rom. 15:4, NKJV).

Encouragement in Daniel's day. Things couldn't have been worse for the Jewish people than they were during the period of the seventy years' captivity in Babylon. Their land was devastated, the temple and the city of Jerusalem were in ruins, and the people were either scattered among the Gentiles or in bondage in Babylon. The situation looked hopeless. The prophets foresaw the day when the Jews would return to their land and rebuild the city and the temple, but first they had to endure the shame and suffering of captivity.

The experience of Shadrach, Meshach, and Abednego must have greatly encouraged the faithful Jews and brought conviction to the Jews who were compromising with the enemy. These three men sent a strong message to their people: Jehovah God is still on the throne, He hasn't forsaken us, and He will one day fulfill His promises to His people. He promised to be with them in their furnace of affliction if they would trust Him and obey His will. Later, when the remnant returned to the land, the account of the fiery furnace must have helped to sustain them in those years of difficulty and delay.

Encouragement in our day. Life may be fairly safe and comfortable where you and I live, but in many parts of the world, God's people are paying a high price to maintain their testimony and their separation from the world. Day after day, they hear the herald shouting, "Fall down before the golden image! Everybody is doing it!" In his first epistle, Peter warned the church that the "fiery trial" was about to begin, and surely they remembered what happened to the three Hebrew men in the days of Nebuchadnezzar. We are told that there have been more martyrs for Christ during the twentieth century than during all the preceding centuries. Not every believer has been spared death in the furnace, but they have been spared compromising their witness for Christ and taking the easy way out. "Be faithful until death, and I will give you the crown of life" (Rev. 2:10, NKJV).

As we move toward the end of the age, the furnace of opposition will be heated seven times hotter and the pressure to conform will become stronger and stronger. It will take a great deal of grace, prayer, courage, and faith for God's people to stand tall for Christ while others are bowing the knee to the gods of this world. The Book of Daniel is a great source of encouragement, because it reminds us that God cares for His people and honors them when they are true to Him. "Them that honor me I will honor" (1 Sam. 2:30).

Encouragement for the future. The events in Daniel 3 remind us of prophecies found in the Book of the Revelation, especially chapters 13 and 14. There will one day arise a world leader like Nebuchadnezzar ("the Beast") who will have an image of himself constructed[4] and will force all the people of the world to worship him. The people who obey will be given a special mark on their forehead or their hand, and this mark will be the passport for staying alive and doing business. Those who refuse to obey will be persecuted and many of them slain (Rev. 13:4, 7, 12, 15). But the Lord will seal to Himself 144,000 Jews whom the Beast will not be able to touch, and they will come through the tribulation time to reign in Messiah's kingdom.

As our studies progress, we shall see that Daniel's book has a special bearing on "the time of the end" (Dan. 12:4) and that his prophecies will enlighten and encourage believers living in those difficult last days (Matt. 24:15). No matter how despotic the world's rulers become or how hot they stoke the furnace, God will be with His people in the furnace and will ultimately defeat their enemies and establish His kingdom.

> When through fiery trials thy pathway shall lie,
> My grace all sufficient shall be thy supply;
> The flame shall not hurt thee; I only design
> Thy dross to consume and thy gold to refine.
> (Author unknown)

CHAPTER FOUR
LEARNING THE HARD WAY
Daniel 4

This is a unique chapter in the Bible because it's an official autobiographical document, prepared by the king of Babylon and distributed throughout his vast kingdom.[1] That Nebuchadnezzar should openly admit his pride, his temporary insanity, and his beastly behavior, and then give glory to the God of Israel for his recovery, is indeed a remarkable thing. He learned an important lesson the hard way just as people are learning it the hard way today: "Pride goes before destruction, and a haughty spirit before a fall" (Prov. 16:18, NKJV).

There are five "acts" in this extraordinary drama.

1. Agitation: The king's dream (Dan. 4:4-18)[2]

Some students believe that twenty or thirty years may have elapsed between the episode of the fiery furnace described in chapter 3 and the events described in this chapter. Nebuchadnezzar was now enjoying a time of peace and security. After defeating all his enemies and completing several impressive building projects, he was able at last to rest at home and delight in what had been accomplished. Nebuchadnezzar thought that he was the builder of "Babylon the great" and the architect of its peace and prosperity, but he was soon to learn that all these things had been permitted by the will of the Most High God.

Once again God in His grace used a dream to communicate an important message to Nebuchadnezzar. In his first dream (Dan. 2), the king saw a great metallic image of which he was the head of gold, but in this dream he saw a huge flourishing[3] tree that fed and sheltered a host of animals and birds. He heard an angel command that the tree be chopped down, its branches and leaves cut off, its fruit scattered, and its stump banded with iron and bronze. Then a command from the angel announced that someone would live like a beast for "seven times" and then be restored. After the first dream—that of the great image—King Nebuchadnezzar was troubled (2:3), but after this second dream, he was terrified (4:5, NIV). He summoned his wise men and asked them for the interpretation of the dream, but they were baffled; so he called for Daniel. After the experience of the first dream, when the wise men failed so miserably, you would think Nebuchadnezzar would have bypassed his advisers and called Daniel immediately. But it seems that in the record of both of these dreams, Daniel is kept apart from the wise men, even though he was "master of the magicians" (v. 9). The Lord wants to remind us that the wisdom of this world is futile and that only He can give a true understanding of the future.

Nebuchadnezzar had changed Daniel's name to Belteshazzar which means "Bel protect his life" (vv. 8, 19; see 1:7). Bel (Marduk) was one of the king's favorite gods. The fact that Nebuchadnezzar used both the Hebrew name and the new name in this document suggests that he had grown fond of Daniel over the years and didn't treat him like the ordinary exile. The king recognized that "the spirit of the gods" was in Daniel and had give him remarkable wisdom and insight.4

The king described his dream to Daniel: the vastness of the tree (note the repetition of "all" in vv. 11-12), the terrifying words of the angel, the transformation of a man into a beast, and the affirmation of the angel that all of this was by the decree of the Most High God. The dream was sent to teach an important lesson: "the Most High is sovereign over the kingdoms of men and gives them to anyone he wishes and sets over them the lowliest of men" (v. 17, NIV). God saw the pride in Nebuchadnezzar's heart and was prepared to deal with it. The king could issue his decrees (2:13, 15; 3:10, 29; 6:7-10, 12-13, 15, 26), but it was the decrees from the throne of heaven that ruled events on earth (4:17, 24; 9:24-27). "The Lord has established his throne in heaven, and his kingdom rules over all" (Ps. 103:19, NIV).

2. Interpretation: The king's danger (Dan. 4:19-26)

After hearing the description of the dream, Daniel was stunned and troubled, and the king could see the perplexity on his face.[5] Daniel's thoughts were troubled because he saw what lay ahead of the successful monarch. He tactfully prepared the king for bad news by saying that he wished the dream applied to the king's enemies and not to the king. (See 2 Sam. 18:32.) We get the impression that Daniel had a great personal concern for the monarch, and as they had worked together in the affairs of Babylon, he had sought to introduce him to the true and living God.

Years before, Daniel had announced to Nebuchadnezzar, "You are this head of gold" (Dan. 2:38, NKJV); and now he announced, "It [the tree] is you, O king" (4:22, NKJV). Trees are often used in Scripture as symbols of political authority, such as kings, nations, and empires (Ezek. 17; 31; Hosea 14; Zech. 11:1-2; Luke 23:31). With the help of the Most High and by His decree, Nebuchadnezzar had built a vast empire that sheltered many nations and peoples. He ruled a great kingdom, a strong kingdom, and a kingdom whose dominion reached "to the end of the earth" (Dan. 4:22).

But the king was taking credit for these achievements and was in great danger because his heart was becoming proud. The king had learned from the first dream that the most High God ruled in the kingdom of men and no earthly throne was secure. The Babylonian kingdom would end one day and God would raise up another kingdom to take its place. In the episode of the fiery furnace, Nebuchadnezzar had witnessed the miracle of the preservation of the three faithful Hebrew men, and he had decreed that nobody speak against their great God (3:29). But now Nebuchadnezzar was about to meet this Most High God and receive severe discipline from His hand.

The cutting down and trimming of the tree symbolized Nebuchadnezzar's disgrace and removal from the throne, but the leaving of the stump was a promise that he would one day reign again.[6] The banding of the stump may suggest that he was marked by God and protected by Him until His purposes for him were fulfilled. For seven years ("seven times") the king would live like a beast, eating grass and feeling the forces of nature against his body. Years later, Daniel would tell Nebuchadnezzar's grandson Belshazzar that his grandfather had lived with the wild donkeys (5:21).[7]

The grand lesson God wanted the king to learn—and that we must learn today—is that God alone is sovereign and will not permit mortals to usurp His throne or take credit for His works. We are but creatures, and God is the Creator; we are only subjects, but He is the King of Kings. When men and women refuse to submit themselves to God as creatures made in His image, they are in grave danger of descending to the level of animals. It's worth noting that God used animals when He wanted to describe the great empires of history (Dan. 7), and that the last great world dictator is called "the beast" (Rev. 11:7; 13:1ff; 14:9, 11; etc.)

Men and women are made in the image of God, but when they leave God out of their lives and resist His will, they can descend to the level of animals. "Do not be like the horse or like the mule," warns King David, who was guilty of acting like both (Ps. 32:9, NKJV). Like the impulsive horse, he rushed into sin when he committed adultery with Bathsheba, and then like the stubborn mule, he delayed confessing his sins and repenting (2 Sam. 11–12). When the Lord arrested Saul of

Tarsus on the Damascus Road, He compared the pious rabbi to a stubborn ox when He said, "It is hard for you to kick against the goads" (Acts 9:5, NKJV).

3. Exhortation: The king's decision (Dan. 4:27)

Daniel concluded his explanation of prophecy with an exhortation to obedience and urged the king to turn from his sins and humble himself before the Lord (v. 27). Unlike some preachers, Daniel didn't divorce truth from responsibility. There was a "therefore" in his message. I have participated in numerous prophetic conferences and heard a great deal of interpretation and some speculation, but I haven't always heard personal and practical application. Some of the speakers talked a great deal about what God would do in the future, but they said very little about what He expected of His people in the present. An understanding of God's plan imposes on the hearer the responsibility to do God's will. To hear and understand the Word but not obey it is to deceive ourselves into thinking we have grown spiritually when we have actually moved backward (James 1:22-27).

"We can speak so glibly about the coming of our Lord and about the judgment seat of Christ," said William Culbertson, late president of Moody Bible Institute. "You do not truly hold the truth of the doctrine of the return of the Lord Jesus Christ until that doctrine holds you and influences your manner of living as the Bible says it should."[8] Peter's admonition in 2 Peter 3:11-18 explains how Christians behave when they really believe the Lord will return.

In ancient times, an Eastern monarch exercised supreme authority and was master of life and death. Daniel knew that the king had a violent temper (Dan. 2:12; 3:19) and that he was walking a dangerous path as he confronted him with his sins; and yet the faithful prophet must proclaim the Word and leave the consequences with the Lord. Moses learned that in the court of Pharaoh, and so did Nathan in the court of David when he told the king "You are the man!" (2 Sam. 12:7, NKJV) Elijah boldly confronted wicked King Ahab and Queen Jezebel (1 Kings 18:17ff), Isaiah rebuked Hezekiah (Isa. 39), and John the Baptist told King Herod to break off his evil relationship with Herodias (Mark 6:14-29). Preachers who tailor their messages to please people will never enjoy the blessing of God.

Unlike the Jewish rulers, who were supposed to be accessible to their people and serve them as shepherds, Eastern kings lived in splendid isolation and heard only the good news. Being a high official in the land, Daniel knew that Nebuchadnezzar had not been concerned about the poor or shown mercy to those in need. Daniel also knew how many times in the Law of Moses the Lord spoke of Himself as the protector and defender of the poor, the aliens, and the oppressed. Perhaps Nebuchadnezzar had exploited the people in pursuing his extensive building operations, and wealth that should have helped the poor had been used to gratify the selfish appetites of the proud king. "If a king judges the poor with fairness, his throne will always be secure" (Prov. 29:14, NIV), but Nebuchadnezzar was about to lose his throne.

Daniel was calling for repentance. He wanted the king to change his mind, acknowledge his sins, turn from them, and put his faith in the true and living God, the Most High God of the Hebrews. Nebuchadnezzar knew enough about Daniel's God to know that what Daniel spoke was the truth, but he did nothing about it.[9] The king was passing up a gracious opportunity to make a new beginning and submit to the will of the Most High God. He made the wrong decision.

4. Humiliation: The king's discipline (Dan. 4:28-33)

"All this came upon the king Nebuchadnezzar" (v. 28), because God's Word never fails to fulfill its purposes.[10] God graciously gave the king an entire year in which to heed His warning and repent of his sins, but the king refused to yield. Pride had so gripped his heart that he would not submit to the Most High God. "Because the sentence against an evil work is not executed speedily, therefore the heart of the sons of men is fully set in them to do evil" (Ecc. 8:11, NKJV). God waited patiently in the days of Noah and gave the inhabitants of the world 120 years to turn from their sins, but they refused (1 Peter 3:20; Gen. 6:3). He gave the city of Jerusalem almost forty years of grace after the religious leaders crucified their Messiah, and then the Romans came and destroyed the city and the temple. Just think of how longsuffering He has been with this present evil world! (2 Peter 3:9)

Nebuchadnezzar was probably walking on the flat roof of his palace, looking out over the great city when he spoke those fateful words recorded in Daniel 4:30.[11] One thing is sure: he was walking in pride (v. 37), and pride is one of the sins that God hates (Prov. 6:16ff). "When pride comes, then comes shame; but with the humble is wisdom" (11:2, NKJV). "God resists the proud but gives grace to the humble" (James 4:6, NKJV; Prov. 3:34; 1 Peter 5:5). It was pride that transformed the angel Lucifer into the devil (Isa. 14:12-15), and it was pride that brought about the downfall of King Uzziah (2 Chron. 26:16-21).

A solemn voice from heaven interrupted the king's egotistical meditations and announced that the time of probation had ended and judgment was about to fall. We never know when God's voice will speak or His hand touch our lives. Whether it's the call of Moses in Midian (Ex. 3), the drafting of Gideon to lead the army (Jud. 6), the opportunity of David to kill a giant (1 Sam. 17), the summons to the four fishermen to leave all and follow Christ (Matt. 4:18-22), or the warning that life has come to an end (Luke 12:16-21), God has every right to break into our lives and speak to us. What the king had learned from Daniel's interpretation of the dream, he now heard from heaven! "No man knows when his hour will come" (Ecc. 9:12, NIV).

God is long-suffering with sinners, but when the time comes for Him to act, there is no delay. The words were still on Nebuchadnezzar's lips when everything began to change. His heart became like that of an animal (Dan. 4:16) and he was driven from the royal palace to live in the fields with the beasts. Since the man was beastly at heart, God allowed his brutish nature to be revealed openly. It's likely that Daniel and the other officers managed the affairs of the kingdom during the king's seven years of discipline, so that when the king returned to the throne, he found everything in good order. That in itself was a strong witness to Nebuchadnezzar of God's grace and Daniel's faithfulness. How much the common people knew about this judgment isn't revealed in the record. It's been suggested that the court officials kept the king in the palace gardens and not in the public eye, but Daniel 5:21 states that he was driven from people and lived with wild donkeys. His mind and heart, and even his body, became beastly for seven years.[12]

God could have destroyed both the king and his kingdom, but He still had purposes to fulfill for His people and His Prophet Daniel. Furthermore, God wanted the king to tell the whole empire what He had done for him so that His name would be glorified among the nations. It was the privilege and responsibility of Israel to be a light to the Gentiles (Isa. 42:6; 49:6), but they failed miserably and started practicing the darkness of the pagan nations. So, God used a pagan king to give glory to His name!

5. Restoration: The king's deliverance (Dan. 4:34-37, 1-3)

The first-person narrative picks up again in verse 34, for at the end of the seven years, as God had promised, Nebuchadnezzar was delivered from his affliction and restored to sanity and normal human life. It began with the king lifting his eyes to God, which suggests both faith and submission. "I lift up my eyes to you, to you whose throne is in heaven" (Ps. 123:1, NIV). "Look to Me, and be saved, all you ends of the earth!" (Isa. 45:22, NKJV) Some students believe that Nebuchadnezzar experienced spiritual conversion, and his testimony in these verses would seem to back that up. We have no idea what the king had learned about the God of Israel as he had listened to Daniel over those many years, but now the seed was producing fruit.

The first thing the king did was to praise the Lord (Dan. 4:34-35). What a concise compendium of biblical theology this is, and what an exciting expression of worship! Theology and doxology belong together (Rom. 11:33-36), for spiritual experience that isn't based on truth is only superstition. The God of the Hebrews is the Most High God. Nebuchadnezzar's kingdom was limited, but God's kingdom includes everything in heaven and earth. Babylon would one day fall and give way to another empire, but God's kingdom will remain forever. Nothing can destroy His kingdom or defeat His purposes.

Seven years before, the king considered himself a great man and his kingdom a great kingdom, but now he had a different viewpoint. "All the peoples of the earth are regarded as nothing" (Dan. 4:35a, NIV)—and that would include the king! Perhaps Daniel had quoted the Prophet Isaiah to the king: "Behold, the nations are as a drop in a bucket, and are counted as the small dust on the scales . . . . It is He who sits above the circle of the earth, and its inhabitants are like grasshoppers" (Isa. 40:15, 22, NKJV).

The king acknowledged the sovereignty of God (Dan. 4:35b), which was the main lesson God wanted him to learn through this difficult experience (vv. 17, 25, 32). It's too bad that this wonderful Bible doctrine has been so maligned and misinterpreted by amateur Bible students, because an understanding of God's sovereignty brings the believer assurance, strength, comfort, and the kind of surrender that produces faith and freedom. The Bible teaches both divine sovereignty and human responsibility, and when you accept both, there is no contradiction or conflict. No person is more free than the believer who surrenders to the sovereign will of God. To ignore God's sovereignty is to exalt human responsibility and make man his own savior, but to deny responsibility is to make man a robot without accountability. The Bible preserves a beautiful balance that exalts God and enables His people to live joyously and victoriously no matter what the circumstances might be (Acts 4:23-31; Rom. 8:31-39).

Because God is sovereign, He can do as His pleases and nobody can hinder Him or call Him to account (Rom. 9:14-23). The heart of sinful man rebels at the very idea of a sovereign God, for the human heart wants to be "free" of all outside control (Ps. 2:1-6). Sinners think they are "free" and don't realize how much they are in bondage to their fallen nature and to the forces of Satan and the world. Charles Spurgeon was very balanced in his theology, and he said:

> Most men quarrel with this [the sovereignty of God]. But mark, the thing that you complain of in God is the very thing that you love in yourselves.
> Every man likes to feel that he has a right to do with his own as he pleases. We all like to be little sovereigns. Oh, for a spirit that bows always before
> the sovereignty of God.[13]

The Most High God is so wise and powerful that He can ordain that His creatures have the freedom to make decisions and even disobey His revealed will, and yet He can accomplish His divine purposes on this earth. "Man's will is free because God is sovereign," said A.W. Tozer, who was not a confessed Calvinist. "A God less than sovereign could not bestow moral freedom upon His creatures. He would be afraid to do so."[14] Submitting to God's sovereign will didn't make Nebuchadnezzar any less of a man; in fact, this commitment transformed him from living like a beast to living like a man!

Finally, Nebuchadnezzar gave joyful witness to all peoples of the marvelous grace of God (Dan. 4:1-3). In this preamble to the official account of his experience, the king extolled God's mighty wonders and His eternal kingdom, and he boldly announced that God had done great signs and wonders on his behalf. How different from Pharaoh's response to what the Lord did in Egypt! Instead of obeying the Word given by Moses, Pharaoh saw God's power demonstrated in the plagues and continued to resist the Lord. He arrogantly declared, "Who is the LORD, that I should obey his voice to let Israel go? I know not the Lord, neither will I let Israel go" (Ex. 5:2). As a result of his rebellion, his country was ruined, thousands of people died, and Israel was still delivered from his power! When God isn't permitted to rule, He overrules and accomplishes His divine purposes for His glory.

What was the result of this "conversion" experience? God not only restored the king's reason and removed the beastly heart and mind, but He also graciously restored the king's honor and splendor and gave him back his throne! He testified that he "became even greater than before" (Dan. 4:36). Where sin had abounded, grace abounded even more (Rom. 5:20). Instead of boasting about his own accomplishments, Nebuchadnezzar said, "Now I Nebuchadnezzar praise and extol and honor the King of heaven" (Dan. 4:37).

He closed his official statement with a word of warning based on the lessons the Lord had taught him: "Those that walk in pride, he [God] is able to abase" (v. 37). The world today doesn't think that pride is a wicked and dangerous sin, but instead practices flattery and exaggeration and exalts the words and the works of the "successful people" of the day. Some of them lack moral character, but as long as they are achievers, they get worldwide attention in the media. One day, the Lord will come in judgment, and His promise is this: "I will punish the world for its evil, the wicked for their sins. I will put an end to the arrogance of the haughty and will humble the pride of the ruthless" (Isa. 13:11, NIV).

Our Lord has the last word: "For whoever exalts himself will be humbled, and whoever humbles himself will be exalted" (Matt. 23:12, NIV).

CHAPTER FIVE NUMBERED, WEIGHED, AND REJECTED

Daniel 5

Many people who know little or nothing about the Babylonians, Belshazzar's feast, or Daniel's prophecies use the phrase "the handwriting on the wall." The phrase comes from this chapter (v. 5) and announces impending judgment. Belshazzar, his wives and concubines, and a thousand notable guests were feasting and drinking while the army of the Medes and Persians waited at the city gates, ready to invade. The city of Babylon boasted that it was impregnable and that there was enough food stored away to feed the population for twenty years! But the Lord said that Babylon's time had come. "The Lord brings the counsel of the nations to nothing; He makes the plans of the peoples of no effect. The counsel of the Lord stands forever, the plans of His heart to all generations" (Ps. 33:10-11, NKJV). The will of God shall be done, no matter what.

We shall look at the persons involved in this drama and see how they related to the plan of God.

1. Belshazzar—judgment defied (Dan. 5:1-4)

The great King Nebuchadnezzar died in 562 B.C. and was succeeded by his son Evil-Merodach, who reigned for only two years. His brother-in-law Neriglissar murdered him in 560, usurped the throne, and ruled for four years. Then a weak puppet ruler (Labashi-Marduk) held the throne for two months, and finally Nabonidus became king and reigned from 556 to 539. Historians believe Nabonidus was married to a daughter of Nebuchadnezzar and was the father of Belshazzar. Nabonidus ruled the Babylonian Empire but Belshazzar, his son, was coregent and ruled the city of Babylon.[1]

Indulgence (Dan. 5:1). Oriental despots took great pleasure in hosting great banquets and displaying their wealth and splendor (see Es. 1). Archeologists tell us that there were halls in the city of Babylon adequate for gatherings this large and larger. This feast was a microcosm of the world system and focused on "the lust of the flesh, and the lust of the eyes, and the pride of life" (1 John 2:16). "What shall we eat?" and "What shall we drink?" are the questions most people want answered as they go through life (Matt. 6:25-34), and they're willing to follow anybody who will entertain them and gratify their appetites. Why worry about the enemy when you have security and plenty to eat?

Indifference (Dan. 5:1). Belshazzar knew that the army of the Medes and Persians was encamped outside the city, but he was indifferent to the danger that they posed. After all, the city was surrounded by a complex series of walls, some of them over 300 feet high, and there were numerous defense towers on the walls. Could any army break through the fortified bronze gates? Wasn't there sufficient water for the people from the Euphrates River that flowed through the city from north to south, and wasn't there adequate food stored in the city? If ever a man was proud of his achievements and basked in self-confidence, it was Belshazzar. But it was a false confidence, not unlike what will happen to the people of this world before God declares war. "For when they say, 'Peace and safety!' then sudden destruction comes upon them" (1 Thes. 5:3, NKJV).

Belshazzar had been indifferent to the information God had given his grandfather Nebuchadnezzar in his famous dream (Dan. 2). It was decreed that the head of gold (Babylon) would be replaced by the breast and arms of silver (the Medo-Persian Empire). Daniel had seen this truth further verified in his vision recorded in Daniel 7, when he saw the Babylonian lion defeated by the Medo-Persian bear (vv. 1-5). This was in the first year of Belshazzar (v. 1). In his arrogant false confidence, Belshazzar was defying the will of God. "He says to himself, 'Nothing will shake me; I'll always be happy and never have trouble'" (Ps. 10:6, NIV).

Irreverence (Dan. 5:2-4). Was the king drunk when he ordered the servants to bring in the consecrated vessels that had been taken from the temple in Jerusalem? (See 1:2; 2 Chron. 36:9-10.) His grandfather[2] Nebuchadnezzar had decreed that all peoples were to give respect to the God of the Jews (Dan. 3:29), and he himself had praised the Lord for His sovereignty and greatness (4:34-37). But as the years passed, the great king's words were forgotten, and his grandson Belshazzar treated the God of Israel with arrogant disrespect. Both the men and the women at the feast impudently used these valuable consecrated vessels like common drinking cups, and while they were drinking, they praised the false gods of Babylon! After all, the gods of Babylon had defeated the God of the Hebrews, so what was there to fear? Belshazzar and his guests could not have behaved more blasphemously. But people can defy the will of God and blaspheme His name only so long, and then the hand of the Lord begins to move.

2. The Lord—judgment declared (Dan. 5:5-9)

"Do you not know this of old, since man was placed on earth, that the triumphing of the wicked is short, and the joy of the hypocrite is but for a moment? Though his haughtiness mounts up to the heavens, and his head reaches to the clouds, yet he will perish forever like his own refuse" (Job 20:4-7, NKJV). Zophar's words didn't apply to Job but they certainly applied to Belshazzar, and they apply today to anybody who defies the will of God.

Look at the wall (Dan. 5:5). Without warning, the fingers of a human hand appeared in an area of the plastered wall that was illuminated by a lampstand, and it must have been an awesome sight. The revelry gradually ceased and the banquet hall became deathly quiet as the king and his guests stared in amazement at words being written on the wall. Both Hebrew and Aramaic are read from right to left, and the vowels must be supplied by the reader; but we aren't told whether the four words were written in a line

N S R H P L K T N M N M

or in a square to be read from the top down

P T M M
R K N N
S L ' '3

Whether the message followed either pattern or a different one, the writing was a miracle from the God of Israel that the idols of Babylon could never accomplish. "They have hands, but they handle not" (Ps. 115:7). It was the finger of God that defeated the Egyptians when Pharaoh refused to let the people go (Ex. 8:19), and the finger of God that wrote the holy law for Israel on the tablets of stone (31:18). Jesus said that He cast out demons "by the finger of God" (Luke 11:20), referring to the power of the Spirit (Matt. 12:28). Now the finger of God was writing a warning to the Babylonian leaders that the hand of God would very soon execute judgment.

Look at the king (Dan. 5:6-7). Neither his exalted position nor his arrogant self-confidence could keep Belshazzar's face from turning pale, his heart from being overcome by terror, and his knees from knocking together. It must have been humiliating for the great ruler to be so out of control before so many important people. God had turned the banquet hall into a courtroom and the king was about to be declared guilty. If the king couldn't control the moving fingers, at least he could try to understand the message, so he called for his wise men and commanded them to explain the meaning of the message on the wall, offering royal honors and gifts to the one who explained the message. He would wear a royal robe and a golden chain, both of which denoted authority, and he would become third ruler under Nabonidus and Belshazzar.

Look at the wise men (Dan. 5:8-9). History repeats itself (2:10-13; 4:4-7) as the counselors confessed their inability to interpret the message on the wall. Even if they could have read the words, they didn't have the key to deciphering the meaning of the message. Mene could mean "mina," which was a measure of money, or the word "numbered." Tekel could mean "shekel" (another unit of money) or the word "weighed"; and peres (the plural is parsin) could mean "half-shekel," "half mina," or the word "divided." It could also refer to Persia!

The ignorance of the wise men made the king even more terrified, and his lords were perplexed and confused and could offer him no help. The time had come when political authority, wealth, power, and human wisdom could do nothing to solve the problem. Once again, the Lord had exposed the ignorance of the world and the futility of human power to discover and explain the mind and will of God.

3. The queen mother—judgment disregarded (Dan. 5:10-12)

The rest of the palace heard about the crisis in the banquet hall, and when the news came to the queen mother, she immediately went to her son to offer counsel and encouragement. He first words were, "Don't be alarmed! Don't look so pale!" (v. 10, NIV) Things aren't as bad as they appear to be! She was optimistic about the whole situation and certain that, once the handwriting was accurately interpreted, everything would be fine. The American humorist Kin Hubbard once defined an optimist as "a person who believes that what's going to happen will be postponed."

Her attitude didn't match the gravity of the situation, but her suggestion was a good one: summon Daniel, the king's greatest adviser. Her words reveal another characteristic of King Belshazzar—ignorance. It seems incredible that he didn't know Daniel, one of the highest officers in Babylon, and certainly the wisest counselor in the empire. Belshazzar had been told about his grandfather's dreams and Daniel's interpretations (v. 22), but too often younger leaders are so concerned about themselves and the present that they forget to catch up on the past. Had young King Rehoboam listened to the counsel of the elders of Israel, he would have avoided a great deal of trouble (1 Kings 12).

The queen mother's description of Daniel certainly shows what God can do in and through dedicated people. Daniel brought "light and understanding and wisdom" into every situation and was able to explain mysteries, solve riddles, and unravel hard problems. His interpretations always proved correct and his prophecies were always fulfilled. During my many years of ministry, I have known a few men and women who were especially gifted in "understanding the times" and determining what the Lord wanted us to do. And yet every believer can claim the promise of James 1:5 and seek the mind of the Lord about any perplexing problem.

4. Daniel—judgment described (Dan. 5:13-29)

If he was sixteen when he was taken to Babylon in 605 B.C., and Babylon fell to the Medes and Persians in 539, then Daniel was eighty-two years old when Belshazzar summoned him to the banquet hall, and perhaps he had been retired from royal service for many years. However, true servants of God never abandon their ministries even in retirement but are always available to respond to God's call "in season, out of season" (2 Tim. 4:2).

The king's offer (Dan. 5:13-17). To the king's shame, he knew Daniel only by name and reputation but did not know him personally. Yet Daniel had "done the king's business" in the third year of his reign (8:1, 27), which would have been 554 B.C. What a tragedy that the ruler of the mighty city of Babylon should ignore one of the greatest men in history and turn to him only in the last hours of his life when it was too late. Had the queen mother told her son about this remarkable Jewish exile and yet he paid no attention? What kept the king so busy that he had no time to sit at the feet of God's prophet and learn from him the things that really mattered in life? "The older I grow, the more I distrust the familiar doctrine that age brings wisdom," wrote newspaper editor H.L. Mencken. But Daniel possessed much more than the human wisdom that comes from experience; he had the kind of supernatural knowledge and wisdom that can come only from God. How much Belshazzar could have learned from him!

The scenario wasn't a new one for Daniel: a revelation from God, a fearful and frustrated ruler, incompetent counselors, and God's servant to the rescue. He paid little attention to the king's flattering speech, and he had no use for the king's generous offer. Even if he had been younger, Daniel would have had no interest in either personal wealth or political power. "Not greedy for money" is one of the qualifications of a servant of God (1 Tim. 3:3, NKJV; see 1 Peter 5:2). Along with Daniel, servants like Moses (Num. 16:15), Samuel (1 Sam. 12:3), and Paul (Acts 20:33) exemplify this unselfish attitude. They simply were not for sale.

The prophet's rebuke (Dan. 5:18-24). Daniel was respectful to the king but he was not afraid to tell him the truth. Even if we don't respect the officer and the way he or she lives, we must respect the office, for "the powers that be are ordained of God" (Rom. 13:1). From the very beginning of their lives in Babylon (Dan. 1), Daniel and his friends had always exercised humility and tact when dealing with the authorities, and because of this, God blessed them. "Sound speech, that cannot be condemned" (Titus 2:8) is standard equipment for the obedient servant of God.

The king didn't know Daniel personally, but Daniel certainly knew the personal life of the king! He knew of his pride and his knowledge of the history of his grandfather, but Daniel reviewed that history just the same. "Those who do not remember the past are condemned to relive it," wrote philosopher George Santayana, and Belshazzar qualified. The lesson that Nebuchadnezzar learned and that his grandson Belshazzar heard about but ignored was that "the Most High God ruled in the kingdom of men" (Dan. 5:21). The God of Israel alone is the true and living God and rules sovereignly in all the affairs of this world, including the affairs of the great empire of Babylon!

Nebuchadnezzar showed his pride by boasting about his achievements and taking credit for what God had helped him accomplish (4:29-30), but his grandson displayed his pride by desecrating the holy vessels from the temple of the Most High God and treating the Lord with contempt. By using the vessels of the true God to praise the idols of Babylon, the king was guilty of both blasphemy and idolatry; by ignoring what he knew of Babylonian royal history, he displayed his ignorance. Belshazzar acted as though he was in command and his life would go on for many more years, yet the very breath in his mouth was controlled by the hand of God (5:23). "For in him we live, and move, and have our being" (Acts 17:28). "This night your soul will be required of you" (Luke 12:20, NKJV).

Like King Belshazzar and his guests, many people in our world today are unmindful of the lessons of the past, unintelligent when it comes to interpreting the present, and totally unprepared for the consequences that lie in the future.

The Lord's warning (Dan. 5:25-29). Anyone who knew Aramaic could have read the words written on the wall, but Daniel was able to interpret their meaning and apply God's revelation to the people in the banquet hall, especially the king. Daniel didn't interpret the words to signify units of money (mina, shekel, half-mina or half-shekel) but to convey warning to the king. The word mina meant "numbered," and the repetition of the word indicated that God had determined and established the end of the kingdom and it would happen shortly (Gen. 41:32). Babylon's days were numbered! More than that, *tekel* indicated that the king himself had been weighed by God and found wanting; so the king's days were numbered. Who would bring an end to the kingdom and the king of Babylon? The answer was in the third word, *peres,* which carried a double meaning: "divided" and "Persia." Babylon would be divided between the Medes and the Persians whose armies were at the gates of the city that very night.

There are times when God gives warnings in order to bring sinners to repentance, such as when he sent Jonah to Nineveh (Jonah 3); but there are also times when His warnings are final and divine judgment is determined. When God warned Nebuchadnezzar about his pride and unconcern for the poor, He gave the king a year in which to repent and seek God's forgiveness (Dan. 4:28-33). The king refused to humble himself and judgment fell. But when Daniel confronted Belshazzar, he offered him no way of escape.

Even though Daniel didn't want the rewards, the king kept his promise and clothed him in royal purple, hung the golden chain around his neck, and declared that he was third ruler in the kingdom. Daniel didn't protest; he knew that the city would fall that very night and that the conquerors wouldn't care who was in office. They were now in command.

5. Darius—judgment delivered (Dan. 5:30-31)

The phrase "that very night" (v. 30, NIV) has an ominous ring to it. "He who is often reproved, and hardens his neck, will suddenly be destroyed, and that without remedy" (Prov. 29:1, NKJV). Belshazzar was slain that very night and the head of gold was replaced by the arms and chest of silver. According to historians, the date was October 12, 539 B.C.

The conquest of Babylon was engineered by Cyrus, king of Persia (1:21; 6:28; 10:1; and see 2 Chron. 36:22-23; Ezra 3–5, *passim*), who was God's chosen servant for the task (Isa. 44:28; 45:1-4). Who then was "Darius the Mede," mentioned in Daniel? (Dan. 5:31, 6:1, 9, 25, 28 and 9:1) Many students believe that Darius was Gubaru, an important officer in the army whom Cyrus made ruler of the province of Babylon. Darius the Mede must not be confused with Darius I who ruled from 522 to 486 and encouraged the Jewish remnant in the restoration of the temple (Ezra 1; 5–6).[4]

Because of the high walls, the guard towers, and the strong bronze gates, the people in the city of Babylon thought they were safe from the enemy; but the Medo-Persian army found a way to get into the city. The Euphrates River flowed through Babylon from north to south, and by diverting the stream, the army was able to go under the city gates and into the city. The conquest of Babylon and its ultimate destruction had been predicted by Isaiah (Isa. 13–14; 21; 47) and Jeremiah (Jer. 50–51). Babylon had been God's chosen instrument to chasten His people Israel, but the Babylonian army had carried things too far and mistreated the Jews (50:33-34). The conquest of Babylon was also God's punishment for what they had done to His temple (50:28; 51:11).

The prophecies were fulfilled and ancient Babylon is no more, but "mystery Babylon" is still with us (Rev. 17:5, 7; 18:2, 10). Throughout Scripture, Babylon (the rebel city) is contrasted to Jerusalem (the holy city). Babylon was founded by Nimrod, a rebel against the Lord (Gen. 10:8-10). It is seen in Scripture as the great city of this world, while Jerusalem symbolizes the eternal city of God. Revelation 17 and 18 describe the rise and fall of "mystery Babylon" in the end times, the satanic system that will seduce the world's peoples and entice them to reject the message of God and live for the sinful pleasures of this life. If you compare Jeremiah 50–51 with Revelation 18, you will see many similarities between the Babylon of ancient history and the Babylon of future prophecy. The future Babylonian world system will help Antichrist, the man of sin, rise to power in this world, but his kingdom will be destroyed by Jesus Christ when He returns to reign (19:11-21).

Years ago, Dr. Harry Rimmer published a book on prophecy called *Straight Ahead Lies Yesterday,* a title that could well be given to the Book of Daniel. The world has always had its great cities, its mighty empires, and its powerful dictators, but the Most High God still reigns in heaven and on the earth and accomplishes His purposes. No nation, leader, or individual citizen can long resist Almighty God and win the battle.

On the occasion of Queen Victoria's Diamond Jubilee in 1897, poet and novelist Rudyard Kipling wrote a poem entitled "Recessional." It wasn't received with great applause and approval because he warned the celebrating nation (and empire) that God was in charge and that pride eventually leads to defeat. One stanza reads:

> The tumult and the shouting dies;
> The captains and the kings depart—
> Still stands Thine ancient Sacrifice,
> An humble and a contrite heart.
> Lord God of Hosts, be with us yet,
> Lest we forget—lest we forget!

Belshazzar forgot the Word of God and the lessons of history and lost his kingdom and his life.

May we not make the same mistakes today!

CHAPTER SIX
LIARS, LAWS, AND LIONS
Daniel 6

Darius the Mede must not be confused with Darius I who ruled Persia from 522 to 486 and during whose reign the temple was restored by the Jewish remnant at Jerusalem. Darius the Mede was probably the name (or title) of the man King Cyrus appointed ruler of the city of Babylon (9:1) until he himself took charge; or it may have been the title Cyrus himself took when he came to reign.[1] King Cyrus ruled the Persian empire from 539 to 530 and was succeeded by Cambyses (530–522).

As is often the case after a conquest, the new ruler wants to reorganize the government of the conquered kingdom so as to establish his authority and make things conform to his own leadership goals. But when Darius began to reorganize Babylon, he brought to light a conflict between his officers and Daniel, a veteran administrator who was now in his eighties. Today, wherever you find dedicated believers living and working with unbelievers, you will often see the same forces at work that are described in this chapter, whether in families, churches, corporations, or governments.

1. Honesty versus corruption (Dan. 6:1-4)

Darius must have suspected that the officers he had inherited were not doing their work faithfully but were robbing him of wealth, and his suspicions were correct. It was impossible for Darius to keep his hands on everything in the empire, because that would have involved supervising every worker, auditing every account, and checking on every assignment. The king had to depend on his officers to see that the work was done well, and this meant he had to appoint officers he could trust. Darius was a man experienced in the ways of the world, and he knew that there was plenty of opportunity for graft in the Babylonian government (see Ecc. 5:8-9).

A wise leader first gathers information, and Darius soon learned about Daniel and the reputation he had for honesty and wisdom, what the KJV calls "an excellent spirit" (Dan. 6:3). It's likely that Daniel was in semiretirement at this time, but the king appointed him to be 1 of 3 key administrators over the kingdom. These 3 men were to manage the affairs of the 120 leaders who ruled over the provinces[2] and to report directly to the king. Daniel proved to be such a superior worker that Darius planned to make him his number-one administrator over the entire kingdom.

When the other leaders heard about this plan, it irritated them and they tried to find something wrong in his work, but nothing could be found. They opposed Daniel for several reasons, including just plain envy; but their main concern was financial. They knew that with Daniel in charge, they wouldn't be able to use their offices for personal profit and would lose their share of the graft that could go into their pockets. It's also likely that these younger men resented an older man—and a Jewish exile at that—telling them what to do and checking on their work. It was another case of anti-Semitism, a grievous sin that is found in Scripture from the days of Pharaoh to the end times (Rev. 12). Apparently these officers didn't know God's covenant with Abraham that promised to bless those who blessed the Jews and curse those who cursed them (Gen. 12:1-3). When these men started to attack Daniel, they were asking for God's judgment.

It isn't always the case that the honest employee gets the promotion while his enemies are judged. Joseph and Daniel were both promoted by pagan rulers, but I have a friend who was fired because he worked too hard! Apparently his Christian integrity and his diligent work showed up the laziness of the other workers, so the foreman found reason to dismiss him. However, it's better to maintain your integrity and testimony than to sacrifice them just to keep your job. If we put the Lord first, He'll care for us, even if we don't get the promotion (Matt. 6:33). Many a faithful Christian has been bypassed for promotion or a salary increase just because somebody higher up didn't like him, but the workers' rewards will one day come from the hand of the Lord.

2. Believing versus scheming (Dan. 6:5-11)

It's certainly a commendable thing when people possess character so impeccable that they can't be accused of doing wrong except in matters relating to their faith. The conniving officers could never tempt Daniel to do anything illegal, but they could attempt to make his faithful religious practices illegal. Daniel didn't hide the fact that he prayed in his home three times each day with his windows opened toward Jerusalem (v. 10), and his enemies knew this. If the king made prayer to other gods illegal, then Daniel was as good as in the lions' den!

The king's response (Dan. 6:5-9). King Darius must have been impressed when 122 government officials assembled in his throne room to have an audience with him. Of course, Daniel wasn't there, even though he was chief among the administrators; but the leaders had been careful not to include him. However, they deceptively included him in their speech, for they claimed that all the royal administrators had agreed on the plan presented to Darius. In fact, they included all the officers in the empire—"administrators, prefects, satraps, advisers, and governors" (v. 7, NIV)—to give the king the impression that his leaders were united behind him and desirous of magnifying him and his office. The men who hatched the plot probably had not consulted with the lesser officers throughout the empire, but these officers weren't likely to disagree with the plan. Anything that pleased the king would only strengthen their positions.

The administrators were very clever in the plot they conceived and the way they presented it. They knew that Darius wanted to unify the kingdom and as quickly as possible transform the defeated Babylonians into loyal Persians. What better way than to focus on the great king himself and make him not just the supreme leader but the only god for an entire month! To emphasize the importance of this law, the officers requested the ultimate sentence: anyone who didn't obey it would be thrown into a den of lions. Of course, their flattery fed the king's pride and he quickly agreed with them, had the law written out, and signed it. Once it was signed, the law could not be changed or nullified (vv. 8, 12, 15; Es. 1:19).

There's every evidence that Darius loved and appreciated Daniel, but in his haste, the king had put his friend in peril. It has well been said that flattery is manipulation, not communication, and in his pride, Darius succumbed to the flattery of evil men. "For there is no faithfulness in their mouth; their inward part is very wickedness; their throat is an open sepulcher; they flatter with their tongue" (Ps. 5:9).

Daniel's response (Dan. 6:10-11). The scheming officers lost no time in proclaiming the king's decree. Daniel probably prayed "evening and morning and at noon" (Ps. 55:17, NKJV),[3] and his enemies wanted to use the earliest opportunity to arrest him. The sooner Daniel was out of the way, the sooner they could start running the country for their own profit. When Daniel prayed toward the holy city and the temple, he was claiming the prayer promise that Solomon stated when he dedicated the temple (1 King 8:28-30, 38-39, 46-51). Jonah claimed this same promise when he was in the belly of the great fish (Jonah 2:4). The exiled Jews no longer had a temple or priesthood, but God was still on the throne and would hear their cries for help.

During the first year of Darius, Daniel had learned from the Book of Jeremiah that the Jewish captivity would end after seventy years, and he turned this great promise into prayer (Dan. 9:1ff). Daniel was interceding for his people and asking God to keep His promise and deliver them. Like the plot against the Jews recorded in the Book of Esther, the plot against Daniel the intercessor was an attack on the whole Jewish nation.

Had he not been a man of faith and courage, Daniel could have compromised and found excuses for not maintaining his faithful prayer life. He might have closed his windows and prayed silently three times a day until the month was over, or he could have left the city and prayed somewhere else. But that would have been unbelief and cowardice; he would have been scheming just like the enemy, and the Lord would have withheld His blessing. No, a man like Daniel feared only the Lord; and when you fear the Lord, you need not fear anyone else. "We ought to obey God rather than men" (Acts 5:29, NKJV). Some of the leaders spied on him, heard him pray, and brought the report to the king.

The most important part of a believer's life is the part that only God sees, our daily private time of meditation and prayer. "You pray as your face is set," said British theologian P.T. Forsythe, "towards Jerusalem or Babylon." Most of the world begins the day looking toward the world and hoping to get something from it, but the Christian believer looks to the Lord and His promises and enters each new day by faith. Outlook determines outcome, and when we look to the Lord for His guidance and help each day, we know that the outcome is in His hands and that we have nothing to fear. "Real true faith is man's weakness leaning on God's strength," said D.L. Moody, and we might add, man's weakness transformed into God's strength (Heb. 11:34).

3. God's power versus man's authority (Dan. 6:12-23)

Three times a day for many years, Daniel had prayed, given thanks, and made supplication (vv. 10-11), which is the same pattern Paul instructed us to follow (Phil. 4:6-7). No wonder Daniel had such peace and courage! Ernest Wadsworth, a champion of effective prayer, said, "Pray for a faith that will not shrink when washed in the waters of affliction." Daniel had that kind of faith. He had walked with the Lord for more than eighty years and knew that His God wouldn't fail him. Hadn't the Lord helped him stand true during his time of training? Didn't the Lord save his life by giving him the wisdom he needed to interpret the king's dream, and didn't the Lord deliver his three friends out of the fiery furnace? Daniel had a copy of the prophecy of Jeremiah (Dan. 9:2), so he must have read: "Behold, I am the Lord, the God of all flesh: is there anything too hard for me?" (Jer. 32:27) No doubt he responded with "there is nothing too hard for thee" (v. 17). A believer who knows how to kneel in prayer has no problem standing in the strength of the Lord.

Daniel accused (Dan. 6:12-13). The men who had spied on Daniel hurried to inform Darius that his favorite officer had disobeyed the law and shown disrespect to the king. It's remarkable how people can work together quickly to do evil but find it difficult to get together to do anything good. "Their feet are swift to shed blood" (Rom. 3:15). They showed no respect to Daniel who held a higher office than they did, but disdainfully called him "one of the exiles from Judah" (Dan. 6:13, NIV). These proud men didn't realize that God was with His exiled people and within the next twenty-four hours would vindicate His servant.

As they take their stand for what is right and what the Lord has commanded them to do, God's people in every age have been falsely accused, cruelly persecuted, and unjustly killed. "Yes, and all who desire to live godly in Christ Jesus will suffer persecution" (2 Tim. 3:12, NKJV). The Puritan preacher Henry Smith said, "God examines with trials, the devil with temptations and the world with persecutions." Another Puritan, Richard Baxter, said that God's people should be more concerned that they deserved the persecution than that they be delivered from it, because deserving it would be evidence of their faithfulness to the Lord.

The king distressed (Dan. 6:14-18). The king was distressed mainly because Daniel was both his friend and his greatest help in the governing of the empire, and he didn't want to sign his death warrant. But Darius was also distressed because of the way he had acted. His pride had gotten the best of him, he had believed the lies of the leaders, and had hastily signed the law. Had Darius taken time to consult with Daniel, he would have discovered the plot; but perhaps the Lord allowed events to proceed as they did so that Daniel's enemies could be exposed and judged. God works "all things after the counsel of his own will" (Eph. 1:11) and He knows what He is doing.

The king made it clear that he wanted to save Daniel from execution, but all his efforts failed. The situation is similar to the one described in the Book of Esther: once the law had been signed, nothing could change it. Since Darius was a "god" and the people were praying to him, how could he make any mistakes? And how could a "god" not punish someone who had broken one of his laws? Furthermore, the laws of the Medes and Persians couldn't be annulled or changed. For the entire day, Darius ignored all other matters concerning the kingdom and tried to free Daniel, but his attempts all failed. Of course, Daniel's enemies were on hand to remind the king that he had to enforce the law whether he liked it or not. At the end of the day, Darius had to call Daniel and have him put in the lions' den.

The lions' den was a large pit divided by a moveable wall that could be pulled up to allow the lions to go from one side to the other. The keeper would put food in the empty side and lift up the wall so the lions would cross over and eat. He would quickly lower the wall and clean the safe side of the pit. The animals weren't fed often or great amounts of food so that their appetites would be keen in case there was to be an execution. Living at the gnawing edge of hunger didn't make them too tame!

Before Daniel was lowered into the pit and the wall lifted up, the king offered a prayer that Daniel's God would deliver him because Daniel was faithful to serve Him continually (Dan. 6:16; see v. 20 and 3:17). He then had the pit covered and the rock sealed so that everything was done according to the law. Nobody would dare break the king's official seal, so that when the pit was opened, everybody would have to confess that God had performed a great miracle. It makes us think of the stone at our Lord's tomb that was sealed by the Roman authorities, and yet Jesus came forth alive!

The king had a bad night, not unlike the night Xerxes experienced in the story of Esther (Es. 6:1ff). Oriental kings were given all kinds of diversions to entertain them and help them relax and go to sleep, but Darius refused all of them. He spent a sleepless night and even fasted! He wondered if the Lord would deliver the old Jewish prophet from the lions' den.

The Lord victorious (Dan. 6:19-23). Darius arose with the first light of dawn and hastened to the lions' den. Even before he got to the pit and ordered the seals broken and the stone removed, he called out to Daniel in an anguished voice. In what he said, he confessed that Daniel's God was the living God, not a dead idol, and that He had the power to deliver His faithful servant. Daniel's faith brought him peace and assurance, but the king's faith was weak and wavering. "Is your God able to deliver you?"[4] When Darius heard Daniel's voice saying "O king, live forever," he knew that his friend and faithful officer and been delivered (Heb. 11:33).

Daniel was always quick to give God the glory (Dan. 6:22; see 2:27-28; 4:25; 5:21-23). God could have closed the lions' mouths by simply saying the word, but He chose to send an angel to do the job. The angel not only controlled the hungry beasts but also kept Daniel company, just as the Lord had come to walk with the three Jewish men whom Nebuchadnezzar had thrown into the fiery furnace (3:24-25). The Book of Daniel reveals a great deal about the work of angels in this world, not only their ministries to God's people but also their influence on nations (10:10-13, 20-21). When we think of an angel delivering Daniel, promises like Psalms 34:7 and 91:11 come to mind, and we remember the angels' ministry to Jesus (Mark 1:13; Luke 22:43). We don't know when angels are with us (Heb. 13:2), but we do know that they are present to serve us and sent by God to assist us (1:14). When Daniel was removed from the lions' den, he bore no wounds, just as the three Jewish men bore no evidence they had even been in the furnace (Dan. 3:27).

The Lord delivered Daniel because of his faith (6:23) and because he was innocent of any crime before the king or any sin before the Lord (v. 22). This means that the king's law about prayer was rejected in heaven and that Daniel was right in disobeying it. By suggesting such a law, the scheming officers disobeyed the true and living God (Ex. 20:1-6) and robbed Him of the glory He deserved. God saved Daniel because it brought great glory to His name and also because he still had more work to do. God's servants are immortal until their work is done.

However, it must be pointed out that not every faithful servant of the Lord is delivered from trial and death in some miraculous way. Hebrews 11:1-35 names some great men and women of faith and describes their achievements, but verses 36-40 describes the "others" who also had great faith and yet were persecuted and martyred. These unnamed "others" had just as much faith as the people in the first group but were not granted special deliverance. James the brother of John was martyred, but Peter was delivered from prison (Acts 12), yet both men were apostles and faithful servants of the Lord. It's unwise to draw conclusions from consequences lest we end up making wrong evaluations (Acts 14:8-20 and 28:1-6).[5]

4. God's glory versus man's disgrace (Dan. 6:24-28)

Daniel's night of confinement in the lions' den ended in a morning of glory and deliverance, with the king himself setting him free. Imagine the excitement in the city as the news spread that Daniel had spent the night in the lions' den and had come out unhurt. God could have prevented Daniel from going into the lions' den, but by allowing him to go in and bringing him out unhurt, the Lord received greater honor.

The traitors were judged (Dan. 6:24). Eastern monarchs had absolute power over their subjects (5:19) and no one dared to question their decisions, let alone try to change them. Darius didn't throw all 122 officers and their families into the den of lions but only those men and their families who had accused Daniel (6:11-13). "The righteous is delivered from trouble, but the wicked takes his place" (Prov. 11:8, NASB). The only exception to this law occurred when Jesus Christ the Righteous One took the place of guilty sinners when He died for them on the cross (1 Peter 3:18).

There is a law of compensation that says, "Whoever digs a pit will fall into it, and he who rolls a stone will have it roll back on him" (Prov. 26:27, NKJV). For example, Pharaoh ordered the Hebrew male babies destroyed in Egypt, and at Passover, all the Egyptian firstborn died. He commanded the newborn Jewish babies to be drowned in the Nile River, and his own army was drowned in the Red Sea (Ex. 14–15). Haman tried to destroy the Jewish nation and ended up being hanged on the gallows he had made for Mordecai (Es. 7:9-10; 9:25). Even if sinners aren't judged in this present life, they will be judged after they die (Heb. 9:27), and the judgment will be just.

It seems cruel to us that the families were destroyed along with the conspirators, but that was an official Persian law and the conspirators knew it. Jewish law prohibited punishing the children for the sins of the fathers (Deut. 24:16; Ezek. 18:20), but Eastern despots took a different view. They didn't want any remaining member of a traitor's family to conspire to kill the ruler who ordered the father's execution. It was much easier to bury corpses than to keep an eye on potential assassins, and besides, the example put fear into the hearts of potential troublemakers. Another important factor is God's covenant with Abraham. The Lord promised that those who blessed the people of Israel would themselves be blessed, but those who cursed them would be cursed (Gen. 12:1-3).[6] In allowing the families to be slain, God was only being faithful to His Word.

The Lord was glorified (Dan. 6:25-27). But Darius did more than execute the criminals. He also issued a decree to the whole empire, commanding his subjects to show fear and reverence to the God of Daniel, the God of the Hebrew exiles (vv. 25-27). Darius' first decree in this chapter declared that he was god (vv. 7-9), but this second decree declared that the God of the Hebrews was the true and living God! In doing this, Darius joined King Nebuchadnezzar by giving public testimony to the power and glory of the true and living God (2:47; 3:28-29; 4:1-3, 34-37). God could have kept Daniel out of the lions' den, but by rescuing him from the lions, God received greater glory.

The Jews had been humiliated by the destruction of Jerusalem and the temple because their defeat made it look as though the false gods of the Babylonians were stronger than the true God of Israel. The idolatry of the Jewish people, especially their kings and priests, had brought about the ruin of Judah, and the Lord used an idolatrous nation to defeat them. Jehovah hadn't been honored by His own people, but now He was receiving praise from pagan rulers whose decrees would be published throughout the Gentile world. These decrees were a witness to the Gentiles that there was but one true God, the God of the Jews; but the decrees were also a reminder to the Jews that Jehovah was the true and living God. The Jewish exiles were surrounded by idols and were constantly tempted to worship the gods of the conquerors. What a paradox that the Jews, who were supposed to be witnesses to the Gentiles of the true and living God, were being witnessed to by the Gentiles!

The theology expressed in the decree of Darius is as true as anything written by Moses, David, or Paul. Jehovah is the living and eternal God whose kingdom will never be destroyed (v. 26; see Deut. 5:26; Josh. 3:10; Ps. 42:2; Jer. 10:10; Ps. 145:13; Rev. 11:15). He is the God who saves people and rescues them from danger and death, and who performs signs and wonders (Dan. 6:27; see 3:28-29; 4:3; Deut. 6:22; Neh. 9:10; Pss. 74:9; 105:26-36; 135:9; Jer. 32:20-21).

God's servant prospered (Dan. 6:28). Since Darius the Mede is a "shadowy figure" in ancient history, we aren't sure how long he ruled Babylon and exactly when Cyrus took over the throne personally. It's been suggested that since Darius was sixty-two years old when he took Babylon (5:31), he may have died within a few years and then Cyrus ascended the throne. Regardless of what transpired, Daniel was respected by Darius and Cyrus and continued to be a witness for the Lord. He lived to see Cyrus issue the edict that permitted the Jews to return to their land and rebuild their temple (2 Chron. 36:22-23; Ezra 1:1-4) and may have been used of God to help bring about this fulfillment of Jeremiah's prophecy (Dan. 9:1-2; Jer. 25:11-12). Certainly his prayers for his people played an important role in the positive attitude Cyrus had toward the Jewish people.

Along with the account of the deliverance of the three men from the fiery furnace (Dan. 3), the report of Daniel's deliverance from the lions' den must have brought great encouragement to the Jews in exile. They knew about Jeremiah's prophecy and wondered if their God would really deliver them. But if He could deliver three men from a furnace and Daniel from the lions, surely He could deliver the exiles from Babylon and take them back to their own land.

But Daniel has a message for God's people today who are being attacked by the enemy and suffering because of their righteous stand for the Lord. Whether we face the fiery furnace (1 Peter 1:6-8; 4:12-19) or the roaring lion (5:8-10), we are in the Lord's care and He will work out His divine purposes for His glory. "Casting all your care upon Him, for He cares for you" (v. 7, NKJV).

CHAPTER SEVEN "THY KINGDOM COME" *Daniel 7*

King Nabonidus was monarch over the empire, but he made his son Belshazzar ruler over Babylon; and the first year of his reign was probably 553. This means that the events described in chapters 7 and 8 preceded those described in chapters 5 and 6, and Daniel was nearly seventy years old at the time these events occurred. Perhaps Daniel arranged the material in his book this way so that the records of his interpretations of the dreams and visions of others came before the visions that the Lord gave to him (7:1-2; 8:1; 9:20-27; 10:1ff). Except for Nebuchadnezzar's dream of the great image explained in chapter 2, the other visions in Daniel 2–6 don't have the wide sweep of application as do the visions granted to Daniel. The vision explained in this chapter parallels the vision God gave to Nebuchadnezzar in chapter 2.

In this vision, Daniel learned about six different kingdoms, four of them kingdoms of this world, one of them the kingdom of Satan, and the last one the kingdom of Messiah.

1. The kingdoms of this world (Dan. 7:1-7, 15-23)

God communicated with Daniel while he was asleep by giving him disturbing visions in a dream (vv. 1-2, 15). During this vision, Daniel was also a part of the event because he was able to approach an angel and ask for an interpretation (v. 16). Daniel doesn't explain how he could be asleep in his bed and yet be able to speak to an angel standing before the throne of God. Perhaps like Paul, he didn't know if he was in the body or out of the body (see 8:2; 2 Cor. 12:1-3).

The restless sea is a frequent biblical image for the nations of the world (Isa. 17:12-13; 57:20; 60:5; Ezek. 26:3; Rev. 13:1; 17:15). Just as the ocean is sometimes stormy, so the nations of the world are sometimes in confusion or even at war; and just as the waves and currents of the ocean are unpredictable, so the course of world history is beyond man's ability to chart or predict. Historians like Oswald Spengler and Arnold Toynbee have attempted to find a pattern to world history, but to no avail. From the human point of view, the nations seem to work out their own destinies, but the invisible winds of God blow over the surface of the water to accomplish His will in His time. If there's one message that is emphasized in the Book of Daniel it's that "the Most High rules in the kingdom of men" (Dan. 4:32, NKJV).

The angel told Daniel that the four beasts represented four kingdoms (7:17), the same sequence of empires that Nebuchadnezzar had seen in his dream (chap. 2). However, the king saw a great and impressive image, made of valuable metals, while Daniel saw dangerous beasts that ruthlessly devoured peoples and nations. To human eyes, the nations of the world are like Nebuchadnezzar's great image, impressive and important; but from God's viewpoint, the nations are only ferocious beasts that attack and seek to devour one another.

The lion with the wings of an eagle (Dan. 7:4) represented the empire of Babylon, which in Nebuchadnezzar's image was the head of gold (2:37-38). In Scripture, Babylon is identified with both the lion and the eagle (Jer. 4:7, 13; 48:40; 49:19-22; 50:17; Ezek. 17:3, 12; see also Hab. 1:6-8). The description of the lion being lifted up to stand like a man, and then given a man's heart, reminds us of how God humbled King Nebuchadnezzar, and made him live like a beast for seven years (Dan. 4:16, 28-34). God told Daniel that the Babylonian Empire would fall.

The bear with three ribs in its mouth (Dan. 7:5) symbolized the empire of the Medes and Persians who defeated Babylon (Dan. 5) and parallels the arms and chest of silver in the great image (2:39). The bear was raised up on one side because the Persians were stronger than the Medes. In the later vision of the ram with two horns (Dan. 8), the higher horn represented the Persians (vv. 3, 20). Interpreters aren't agreed on the meaning of the three ribs that the bear carried in its mouth. The best explanation is that they stand for Lydia, Egypt, and Babylon, nations that the Medes and Persians had conquered. The armies of the Medo-Persian Empire did indeed "devour much flesh" as they marched across the battlefields.

The leopard with four wings (Dan. 7:6) represented Alexander the Great and the swift conquests of his army, resulting in the incredible expansion of the kingdom of Greece. This beast is identified with the number four: four heads and four horns (see 8:8, 21-22). Alexander's untimely death in 323 left him without a successor and his kingdom was divided into four parts and assigned to his leaders. Palestine and Egypt went to Ptolemy I; Syria was ruled by Seleucus I; Thrace and Asia Minor were assigned to Lysimachus; and Macedon and Greece were governed by Antipater and Cassander.

The "dreadful and terrible" beast (Dan. 7:7) represented the Roman Empire, as strong and enduring as iron and as uncompromising as a beast on the rampage. The Roman armies swept across the ancient world and defeated one nation after another until the empire extended from the Atlantic Ocean east to the Caspian Sea and from North Africa north to the Rhine and Danube Rivers. Egypt, Palestine, and Syria were all under Roman domination.

This beast corresponds with the legs of iron on Nebuchadnezzar's image (2:40-43), but the ten toes (ten kings, vv. 43-44) are represented by ten horns (7:7, 24). Often in Scripture, a horn is a symbol of a ruler or of royal authority (1 Sam. 2:10; Ps. 132:17). Later in this study we will have more to say about the "little horn" of Daniel 7:8.

In the great movement of ancient history, one empire has replaced another, leading up to the establishing of the Roman Empire. The two visions (chaps. 2 and 7) make it clear that God knows the future and controls the rise and fall of nations and rulers. Daniel was then living in the Babylonian Empire, but he knew that Babylon would be taken by the Medes and Persians, and that Greece would conquer the Medo-Persian Empire, and Rome would eventually conquer all. Prophecy is history written beforehand.

2. The kingdom of Satan (Dan. 7:8, 11-12, 21-26)

The four kingdoms represented by the four beasts have already come and gone; however, verse 12 indicates that each kingdom continues to exist in some way within the succeeding kingdom that "devoured" it. But Daniel saw in his vision something that wasn't revealed to Nebuchadnezzar: the last human kingdom on earth would be a frightful kingdom, unlike any of the previous kingdoms, and it would even declare war on God! This is the kingdom of Antichrist, described in Revelation 13–19, an evil kingdom that will be destroyed when Jesus Christ returns to earth. This judgment was depicted in Nebuchadnezzar's vision as the "stone cut out without hands" that tumbled down the mountain and destroyed the image (Dan. 2:34-35, 44-45).

The ten horns (Dan. 7:7-8, 24; Rev. 13:1; 17:3, 7, 12, 16). These represent ten kings or kingdoms that will exist in the last days. Daniel wrote in language the people of his day could understand, and the concept of nations as we have them today would be foreign to the ancients. In Daniel's day countries were ruled by kings, but the "kingdoms" spoken of here will be nations as we know them. Some students of prophecy think that a ten-nation "United States of Europe" will emerge in the last days, and recent developments in Europe—the organization of the European Union and the use of the eurodollar—seem to point in that direction. However, there are more than ten nations in the E.U., so we had better not draw hasty conclusions.[1] It is out of this confederation of ten nations, which in some way is an extension of the Roman Empire, that the Antichrist will come and the final world kingdom will be organized and actively oppose God and His people.

The "little horn" (Dan. 7:8, 11, 24-26). This represents the last world ruler, the man called Antichrist. The Greek prefix *anti* can mean "against" and "instead of." The final world ruler will be both a counterfeit Christ and an enemy who is against Christ. John described the appearance of this "man of sin" (2 Thes. 2:3) in Revelation 13:1-10.[2] According to Daniel, the Antichrist has to overcome the power of three other rulers to be able to do what he wants to do and what Satan has planned for him to do (Dan. 7:24). The mention of his eyes suggests that he has remarkable knowledge and skill in planning his exploits. He will also be a man skilled in using words and able to promote himself so that people follow him (vv. 11, 25; Rev. 13:5-6). He will also blaspheme God and ultimately convince the unbelieving world that he is a god (2 Thes. 2:1-12). He will become the ruler of the world, and will control not only the economy and the religion, but also seek to change the times and the laws.

According to Daniel 7:25 and Revelation 13:5, his dictatorship will last for three and a half years, a significant period of time in the prophetic Scriptures. It's stated as "time, times and half a time" (Dan. 7:25, NIV; Rev. 12:14), "forty-two months" (11:2; 13:5) and "1,260 days" (11:3; 12:6). This period is half of seven years, another significant time span in prophecy. We shall learn from Daniel 9:24-27 that the Antichrist will make a covenant with the Jewish nation for seven years, but in the midst of that period will break the covenant and begin to persecute God's people.

The scenario seems to look like this. Antichrist will be leading one of ten confederated nations in Europe. He will overcome three other nations and, with the help of Satan, move into becoming a world dictator. At first he will appear to be friendly to the Jews and will sign a seven-year covenant to protect them (v. 27).[3] The signing of that covenant is the signal for the start of the last seven years of Daniel's seventy weeks outlined in verses 24-27. This period is generally known as "the Tribulation" and is described in Matthew 24:1-14; Mark 13:1-13; and Revelation 6–19.

After three and a half years, the Antichrist will break the covenant and set up his own image in the Jewish temple in Jerusalem, forcing the world to worship him and the devil, who is energizing him. Using the language of Daniel, Jesus called this "the abomination of desolation" (Dan. 11:31; Matt. 24:15; Mark 13:14; 2 Thes. 2:1-4). This signals the last half of the Tribulation, a period that is known as "the wrath of God" (Rev. 14:10, 19; 15:1, 7; and see Matt. 24:15-28; Mark 13:14-23). It will climax with the return of Jesus Christ to the earth and the defeat of Antichrist and his army (Matt. 24:29-44; Mark 13:24-27; Rev. 19:11-21). Jesus Christ will then establish His kingdom on earth (Dan. 7:13-14, 26-27; Rev. 20:1-6).[4]

Daniel doesn't go into all the details that John shares in the Book of Revelation, but he does assure us that the kingdom of Satan and his counterfeit Christ will be defeated and destroyed by Jesus Christ (Dan. 7:22, 26; see 2 Thes. 1:7–2:10).

War on the saints (Dan. 7:21-23, 25). The "saints" are mentioned in verses 18, 21-22, 25, and 27, and refer to the people of God living on the earth during the Tribulation period. The Apostle John makes it clear that there will be believing Jews and Gentiles on the earth during the seven years of the Tribulation (Rev. 7). If the church is raptured before the Tribulation, then these will be Jews and Gentiles who believe on Jesus Christ after the church departs. If the church goes through either part or all of the Tribulation, then they will be the "saints" mentioned by Daniel. In either case, some of them will die for their faith (14:9-13).

Three of the texts describe the saints as victorious over their enemies (Dan. 7:18, 22, 27), while two texts inform us that the Lord permits them to be defeated before their enemies (vv. 21, 25). The saints "receive" the kingdom (not "take" as in v. 18), "possess" the kingdom (v. 22), and the kingdom is "given" to them (v. 27). All of this is the work of the Most High God. He permits Antichrist to rise to power and rule the world, and even allows him to make war on the saints and temporarily win the victory (v. 21). The phrase "wear out the saints" (v. 25) describes Antichrist's continual oppression of God's people and his blasphemous words against the Lord and His people.

John wrote the Book of Revelation at a time when Rome was persecuting the church and trying to force Christians to worship the emperor. To confess "Jesus Christ is Lord" could mean imprisonment and even death. Both the Book of Daniel and the Book of Revelation brought encouragement and strength to the early church, just as they bring encouragement to suffering believers today.

3. The kingdom of Christ (Dan. 7:9-14, 27-28)

Daniel has seen the rise and fall of five kingdoms: the Babylonians, the Medes and Persians, the Greeks, the Romans, and the kingdom of Satan headed by the Antichrist. But the most important kingdom of all is the kingdom that Christ shall establish on earth to the glory of God, the kingdom that Christians long for each time they pray, "Thy kingdom come" (Matt. 6:10). Two aspects of the kingdom are seen in Scripture: "The kingdom of God," which is the spiritual reign of Christ over all who belong to Him (John 3:1-8; Col. 1:13) and the glorious kingdom on earth, prepared for God's people (Matt. 16:28; 25:34; 26:29; Luke 22:29).[5]

The heavenly throne of the Father (Dan. 7:9-12). The thrones were put into place and not "cast down" as in the King James Version. This event takes place before the kingdom of Antichrist is destroyed, so it probably parallels Revelation 4–5, where John describes the throne room of God. "Ancient of Days" (Dan. 7:9, 13, 22) is a name for God that emphasizes His eternality; He is the God who had existed from eternity past, has planned all things, and is working out His plan. The description of God must not be taken literally, because God doesn't have a body, wear clothes, or grow white hair. These things are symbolic of His nature and character: He is eternal, holy, and sovereign. In Revelation 1:12-20, these same characteristics are applied to Jesus Christ, thus proving that He is the eternal Son of God.

The vision of God's throne parallels Ezekiel 1:15-21, 26-27. The fire speaks of His holiness and judgment against sin and the wheels symbolize His providential working in the world in ways we can't understand. "Our God is a consuming fire" (Deut. 4:24; Heb. 12:29; see Ps. 97:1-4). He is praised by a multitude of saints and angels (Deut. 33:2; Rev. 5:11) as the books are opened and the Lord prepares to judge evil on the earth. No matter what Satan and the Antichrist do on earth, God is still on the throne and He executes judgment.

The earthly throne of the Son of God (Dan. 7:13-14, 27). "Son of Man" is a familiar title for our Lord Jesus Christ; it is used eighty-two times in the Gospels, frequently by Jesus Himself. (See also Rev. 1:13 and 14:14.) The phrase "clouds of heaven" reminds us of His promise to return in glory and reign on the earth (Matt. 24:30; 25:31; 26:64; Mark 13:26 and 14:62; Rev. 1:7).

The Son of Man is presented before the throne of the Father and given dominion over all nations, an everlasting dominion that will never pass away. This is the prelude to the stone being cut out of the mountain and coming down to destroy the kingdoms of the world (Dan. 2:34-35, 44-45), and it parallels Revelation 5:1-7. The Father promised the Son, "Ask of Me, and I will give You the nations for Your inheritance, and the ends of the earth for Your possession" (Ps. 2:8, NKJV). Unlike the previous four kingdoms, and the kingdom of Antichrist, the kingdom of Jesus Christ can never be removed or destroyed. This is the kingdom that God had in mind when he told David that his throne would never end (2 Sam. 7:13, 16). He will share this kingdom with His people (Dan. 7:27) and they shall reign with Him (Rev. 5:10; 11:15; 20:4).

The Kingdom Covenant that God made with David (2 Sam. 7) will one day be fulfilled in Jesus Christ. God's promise that David's seed would have a throne and a kingdom forever (2 Sam. 7:12-13) was certainly not fulfilled in Solomon or any of his successors, but it will be fulfilled in Jesus Christ (Luke 1:30-33, 68-79).[6]

In Revelation 20:1-8, we are told six times that the kingdom will last for a thousand years, which is why it is called "the Millennium," which is Latin for "thousand years." During that time, the Lord will fulfill the many kingdom promises made in the Old Testament Scriptures. Nature will be delivered from the bondage of sin and decay (Isa. 35; Rom. 8:18-25) and there will be peace in the world (Isa. 2:1-5; 9:1-7).

In this dramatic vision, Daniel had seen the vast sweep of history, beginning with the Babylonian Kingdom and closing with the thousand-year reign of Christ on earth. What comfort and strength it must have given to him and to his people in exile that the prophecies would one day be fulfilled and their Messiah would reign on the throne of David. The church of Jesus Christ today looks for the Savior to return, and then we will be caught up to meet him in the air (1 Thes. 4:13-18). We shall return with Him to earth, reign with Him, and serve Him. "Even so, come, Lord Jesus" (Rev. 22:20, NKJV).

How did Daniel respond to this great revelation? He was deeply troubled and his face turned pale (Dan. 7:28, NIV), but he didn't tell anyone what the Lord had shown him. We shall learn in later chapters that after he had received a vision from the Lord, Daniel often became ill and was unable to work. This is quite unlike some "prophetic students" today who, when they think they've discovered a great truth, go on radio or television and tell everybody what they think they know. It's a dangerous thing to study prophecy just to satisfy our curiosity or to give people the impression that we are "great Bible students." If divine truth doesn't touch our own hearts and affect our conduct, then our Bible study is only an intellectual exercise to inflate our own ego.

Said A.W. Tozer: "The Bible doesn't approve of this modern curiosity that plays with the Scriptures and which seeks only to impress credulous and gullible audiences with the 'amazing' prophetic knowledge possessed by the brother who is preaching or teaching!"[7]

To this, I say a hearty "Amen!"

CHAPTER EIGHT BEASTS, ANGELS, AND THE END TIMES
Daniel 8

From chapter 8 to the end of the Book of Daniel, the text is written in Hebrew, for the major emphasis of these chapters is God's plan for the nation of Israel in the end times. From 2:4–7:28, the book is written in Aramaic because the emphasis in those chapters is on the Gentile kingdoms in history and prophecy. It was the nation of Israel that God chose to be the vehicle of His revelation and redemption in the world. Through the Jewish people came the knowledge of the one true and living God, the written Scriptures and, most important of all, the Savior, Jesus Christ. "Salvation is of the Jews" (John 4:22). In this chapter, five persons move across the great stage of prophecy and history.

1. Daniel the prophet (Dan. 8:1-2, 15-19, 26-27)

King Belshazzar's third year was 551, so this vision came to Daniel before the fateful banquet described in chapter 5. This explains why the Babylonian Empire isn't mentioned, for within a dozen years Babylon would be taken by Cyrus who would usher in the rule of the Medes and Persians. In terms of Nebuchadnezzar's great image (Dan. 2), the era of the head of gold would end and the era of the silver arms and chest would begin. The lion with the eagle's wings would be defeated by the bear with the ribs in its mouth (7:4-5).

Receiving the vision (Dan. 8:1-2). Shushan (Susa) was a city about 200 miles southeast of Babylon and at that time wasn't too important to the Babylonians. Eventually it became the capital of the Persian Empire (Neh. 1:1; Es. 1:2). The River Ulai (Dan. 8:2, 16) was probably a canal that flowed through Susa.

It's unlikely that Daniel left Babylon and traveled to Susa to receive the vision.[1] It's more likely that God transported him to Susa just as He transported Ezekiel to Jerusalem (Ezek. 8; 40) and the Apostle John to the wilderness (Rev. 17:3) and to the high mountain (21:10). Since Daniel was about to describe the victory of the Medes and Persians over the Babylonians, God put him into the future capital of the Persian Empire.

Requesting the meaning of the vision (Dan. 8:5-19). In the earlier part of the book, Daniel was able to interpret and explain the dreams and visions of others; but here he had to ask an angel for the meaning of the ram defeating a goat and the little horn becoming a mighty kingdom. The voice that commanded Gabriel may have been the voice of the Lord. Gabriel means "man of God" and it was he who explained to Daniel the vision given in chapter 8 and well as the vision about the seventy weeks (9:21-22). Centuries later, Gabriel would be sent to Zechariah to announce the birth of John the Baptist (Luke 1:11-20), and to Mary to announce that she would give birth to the Messiah (vv. 26-38). The only other angel who is named in Scripture is Michael ("Who is like God?") who has been especially assigned to care for the nation of Israel (Dan. 10:13, 21; 12:1; Jude 9; Rev. 12:7).

When Gabriel moved closer to Daniel, the prophet became very frightened and fell into a faint and a deep sleep. (See Dan. 10:9, 15, 17 and Rev. 1:17.) Gabriel called him "son of man," which is a messianic title (Dan. 7:13); but here it was used to emphasize the weakness and humanness of the prophet. Gabriel's touch awakened Daniel (10:10-11, 16, 18) and the angel explained to him that the vision applied to the latter days of Jewish history. "The indignation" refers to God's displeasure with His people and the times of intense suffering Israel would endure before the coming of the end and the establishing of the promised kingdom.

2. Cyrus, King of Persia (Dan. 8:3-4, 20)

This is the man who conquered Babylon. Centuries before Cyrus appeared on the scene, the Prophet Isaiah called him by name and even called him God's "shepherd"[2] (Isa. 41:2, 25; 44:28–45:4). It was Cyrus whom God chose to defeat the Babylonians and permit the Jews to return to their land. Just as Babylon was identified with the lion and eagle, Persia was identified with the ram. The two horns symbolize the Medes and Persians, the Persians being the higher (stronger) of the two.

Cyrus and his armies did indeed "push

westward and northward and southward" and defeat their enemies, taking Libya, Egypt, all of Asia Minor and moving as far as India, creating the largest empire ever in the ancient east until the time of Alexander the Great. Once his conquests were consolidated, he attacked Babylon and took it in 539. Cyrus was kind to those he took captive and permitted the Jews to return to their land to rebuild the temple and restore the nation (Isa. 44:28; 2 Chron. 36:22-23; Ezra 1:1-3; 6:2-5). He also allowed them to take with them the sacred vessels that Nebuchadnezzar had taken from the temple (Ezra 1:5-11).

The imagery used in connection with Cyrus is fascinating. He is called "the righteous man" (Isa. 41:2), or as the NIV puts it, "calling him in righteousness." This means that he was called to fulfill God's righteous purposes in freeing Israel from their Babylonian yoke and allowing them to return to their land. Our sovereign Lord can use even a pagan king to accomplish His purposes! Isaiah 41:25 pictures his victorious conquest as a man walking on mortar or on soft clay, because these materials can't resist him. The Prophet Isaiah also called Cyrus the Lord's anointed (45:1) before whom He would go and open the way. Even the great gates of Babylon couldn't stand before his victorious march!

Why did God call Cyrus? "For the sake of Jacob my servant, of Israel my chosen" (v. 4, NIV). No matter how brutally the Gentile nations may treat the people of Israel, God uses the nations to accomplish His ordained purposes. His plans for Israel will be fulfilled no matter how much the Gentile nations may oppose His chosen people.

3. Alexander the Great of Greece (Dan. 8:5-8, 21-22)

In Nebuchadnezzar's image, Greece was depicted as the thigh of brass (2:32, 39), and in Daniel's vision described in chapter 7, Greece was a swift leopard with four heads. Now Daniel sees Greece as an angry goat who runs so swiftly his feet don't even touch the ground! The large protruding horn represents Alexander the Great who led the armies of Greece from victory to victory and extended his empire even beyond what Cyrus had done with the Persian army. But the horn was broken, for Alexander died in Babylon in June 323, at the age of thirty-three, and his vast kingdom was divided among four of his leaders, symbolized by the four horns that grew up (see 7:4-7; 11:4).

However, the remarkable conquests of Alexander were more than battle trophies, for they accomplished God's purposes in the world and helped to prepare the world for the coming of Christ and the spread of the Gospel. For one thing, Alexander put an end to the Oriental influence that threatened to take over the Western world. At the same time, he "shook the ancient world to its very foundations" and "compelled the old world to think afresh."[3] By extending Greek culture and language, he helped to bring peoples together; and eventually the common (*koine*) Greek became the language of the New Testament. Even though his empire divided four ways after his death, Alexander brought nations together so they could interact with each other. His policy of kindness toward conquered peoples introduced a powerful example of brotherhood into the world. He literally "wedded East to West" when 9,000 of his soldiers and officers (some historians say 10,000) married Eastern women in one mass wedding.

What Alexander and the Greeks began, the Romans completed, helping to prepare the ancient world for the coming of Christ. They are represented by the legs of iron (2:33, 40) and the "dreadful beast" (7:7). Roman roads and bridges enabled people to travel and share their ideas; Roman law kept nations under control; Roman legions enforced that law with an iron fist; and the Roman peace (Pax Romana) gave people the opportunity to experience more security than they had known before. All of this contributed to the taking of the Christian message throughout the Roman Empire, and sometimes, as in the case of Paul, Rome paid the bill for the missionaries to travel!

4. Antiochus IV Epiphanes (Dan. 8:9-14)[4]

As we have already seen, after the death of Alexander the Great (the "notable horn," v. 5), his empire was divided into four parts with four of his officers taking control (v. 8). Out of one of those horns a "little horn" appears who becomes a great leader, and this is Antiochus Epiphanes, the ruler of Syria from 175 to 163 B.C. and known as one of the cruelest tyrants in history.

Antiochus gave himself the name "Epiphanes," which means "illustrious, manifestation," for he claimed to be a revelation (epiphany) of the gods. He even had the word *theos* (god) put on the coins minted with his features on it, and his features on the coins came to look more and more like the Greek god Zeus. He had a passionate desire to turn the Jews into good Greeks. One of his first acts was to drive out the high priest Onias, an ardent Jew, and replace him with Jason, a patron of the Greeks. But Jason was replaced by Menelaus, who actually purchased the priesthood. Believing a rumor that the king was dead, Jason attacked Jerusalem only to learn that Antiochus was very much alive. The angry king attacked Jerusalem and plundered the temple. In 168 he sent an army of 20,000 men under Apollonius to level Jersualem. They entered the city on the Sabbath, murdered most of the men, and took the women and children as slaves. The remaining men fled to the army of the Jewish leader Judas Maccabeus.

But the king wasn't satisfied, so he issued an edict that there would be one religion in his realm and it wouldn't be the Jewish religion. He prohibited the Jews from honoring the Sabbath, practicing circumcision, and obeying the levitical dietary laws, and he climaxed his campaign on December 14, 168, by replacing the Jewish altar with an altar to Zeus—and sacrificing a pig on it! Any Jew found possessing a copy of the Law of Moses was slain. Jerusalem was eventually delivered by the courageous exploits of Judas Maccabeus and his followers, and on December 14, 165, the temple was purified, the altar of burnt offering restored, and Jewish worship once again restored. It is this event that the Jewish people celebrate as "The Feast of Lights" or Hanukkah (see John 10:22). Antiochus went mad while in Persia, where he died in 163.

Knowing these facts about Antiochus helps us better understand the text of Daniel's prophecy. Antiochus started in a small way but gradually accumulated power as he magnified himself and dealt ruthlessly with the Jewish people. He attacked the Jews in their "pleasant [beautiful]" land and put a stop to their religious practices. He even claimed that he was a god. In verse 10, the Jews are described as "the host of heaven" (i.e., "godly people") and "stars" (Gen. 15:5; 22:17). When Antiochus stopped the daily sacrifices in the temple and substituted pagan worship, this was called "the abomination that makes desolate" ("the transgression of desolation," Dan. 8:13). This concept is found in 9:27; 11:31; and 12:11, and is used by Jesus in Matthew 24:15 and Mark 13:14. What Antiochus did was a foreshadowing of what the Antichrist will do when he puts his image in the temple and commands the world to worship him (2 Thes. 2; Rev. 13). Daniel 8:13 and 11:31 refer to Antiochus, and the other references to Antichrist, of whom Antiochus is a picture.

The two angels (8:13-14; "saints") spoke together about this matter and from their conversation, Daniel learned the prophetic timetable. Between the desecration of the temple and its cleansing and restoration 2,300 days would pass. The Hebrew text reads "2,300 evenings and mornings," because burnt offerings were sacrificed at the temple each morning and each evening of every day. But does this mean 2,300 days or 1,150 days, 2,300 divided by two? And what date or event signals the beginning of the countdown? Some students opt for 2,300 days, that is, about six years, if you use 360 days for the year. Others prefer 1,150 days, which give us slightly over three years.

But what is the starting point for the countdown? The six-year advocates begin with 171 B.C., when Antiochus deposed the true high priest. Subtract six years and this takes you to 165 when Judas Maccabeus defeated the enemy and reconsecrated the temple. However, the three-year advocates begin with the establishment of the pagan altar in the temple on 25 Kislev, 168, and this takes us to 165. Either approach meets the requirements of the prophecy.

We'll meet Antiochus Epiphanes again before we complete our study of the Book of Daniel.

5. The Antichrist (Dan. 8:23-27)

The angel awakened Daniel from his deep sleep and told him there was yet more prophetic truth for him to hear, and it related to "the time of wrath" (v. 19, NIV) and the "time of the end" (vv. 17, 19, 23), which is the time of tribulation. The Old Testament prophets called this period "the time of Jacob's trouble" and "the day of the Lord," the period when God's wrath would be poured out on an evil world (Jer. 30:7; Isa. 2:11-12; 13:6, 9; Joel 2:1ff; Zeph. 1). In other words, what Daniel learns in Daniel 8:23-27 relates to the end times when Antichrist will oppose God and God's people.

The "king of fierce countenance" is the Antichrist, not Antiochus Epiphanes; but if you compare verses 23-27 with verses 9-14, you will see that the characteristics and career of Antiochus parallel those of Antichrist.

- Both begin modestly but increase in power and influence
- Both blaspheme God with mouths that speak great things
- Both persecute the Jewish people
- Both claim to be gods and put images in the temple
- Both impose their own religion on the people
- Both are opposed by a believing remnant that knows God
- Both are energized by the devil and are great deceivers
- Both appear to succeed marvelously and seem to be invincible
- Both are finally defeated by the coming of a redeemer (Judas Maccabeus and Jesus Christ)

Many other parallels exist which you will discover as you study the relevant Scriptures.

The "Prince of princes" (v. 25) is Jesus Christ, who is also the "God of gods" (11:36) and the "King of Kings" (Rev. 19:16). Antichrist opposes Jesus Christ and seeks to replace Him, but ultimately Jesus Christ defeats Antichrist and consigns him, his false prophet, and Satan to the lake of fire (20:1-3).

As a result of this experience of receiving the vision and communing with angels, Daniel became ill. One cause of his physical and emotional collapse was his inability to understand where this vision of the "king of fierce countenance," prefigured by "the little horn," fit into the prophetic scheme for Israel. He knew that the "little horn" would appear in the last days, but what would occur between his day and that day? He would learn from Jeremiah's prophecy that his people would be released from bondage and allowed to return to their land and rebuild their temple, but Daniel knew nothing about God's "mystery" concerning the church (Eph. 3:1-13) or the "mystery" concerning the partial blinding and hardening of Israel (Rom. 11:25-36). And who was the "king of fierce countenance" and why would he attack the Jewish people? Daniel felt the burden of the suffering his people would experience and he knew the awful consequences of truth being cast to the ground (Dan. 8:12; Isa. 59:14-15).

Daniel is a good example for students of prophecy to follow. He asked the Lord for the explanation (Dan. 8:15) and allowed the Lord to instruct him. But his investigation into God's prophetic program wasn't a matter of satisfying curiosity or trying to appear very knowledgeable before others. He was concerned about his people and the work they had to do on earth. He so identified with what he learned that it made him ill! Too many "prophetic students" don't wait before God for instruction and insight, nor do they feel burdened when they learn God's truth about the future. Instead, they try to display their "knowledge" and impress people with what they think they know. The whole exercise is purely academic; it's all in the head and never changes the hearts.

When he got over his weakness and sickness, the prophet went back to work for the king and didn't tell anybody what he had learned. But God still had more truth to teach him, and he was ready to receive it.

CHAPTER NINE
THE PROPHETIC CALENDAR
Daniel 9

When speaking at a press conference in Cairo on February 1, 1943 Sir Winston Churchill said, "I always avoid prophesying beforehand, because it is a much better policy to prophesy after the event has already taken place."

Among the Jewish people, that kind of "prophetic" activity could have resulted in the death of the so-called prophet (Deut. 18:20-22). Worshiping false gods and listening to false prophets had led to Israel's spiritual decay and ultimate collapse as a nation. The people hadn't obeyed what the prophets commanded, so Israel was exiled in Babylon; and there they learned to take the prophetic word very seriously, because it was the only hope they possessed. The church today needs to heed the word of prophecy because it's the light of certainty in a world of darkness and uncertainty (2 Peter 1:19-21).

Note three stages in Daniel's experience with the prophetic message that spoke concerning his people and the city of Jerusalem.

1. Insight: Learning God's plan (Dan. 9:1-2)

The first year of Darius was 539 B.C., the year that Babylon fell to the Medes and the Persians.[1] This great victory was no surprise to Daniel, because God had already told him that the Medo-Persian Empire would conquer Babylon. In Nebuchadnezzar's great "dream image," the head of gold would be replaced by the chest and arms of silver (chap. 2); and later visions revealed that the bear would conquer the lion (chap. 7). But long before Daniel's day, both Isaiah and Jeremiah had predicted the fall of Babylon, so it's no surprise that Daniel started studying afresh the scroll of the Prophet Jeremiah.

The Word of God. One of the beautiful things about the inspired Word of God is its constant freshness; no matter how often we read it, there is always something new to learn or something familiar to see in a new light. Had Jeremiah's scrolls of the Old Testament been organized like our modern Bibles, he would have read Jeremiah 24 and been reassured that the Lord would care for His people no matter what ruler was on the throne. From 25:1-14, he would learn the reason for the exile as well as the length of the exile—seventy years—and this would be corroborated in 29:10-14. The exile of the Jews in Babylon was no accident; it was a divine appointment, and they would not be released until the very time that God had ordained.

Daniel called Jeremiah's writings "the word of the Lord." King Jehoiakim had tried to burn up Jeremiah's prophecies, but the Lord preserved them because they were His very words (Jer. 36). "Heaven and earth will pass away, but my words will never pass away" (Matt. 24:35, NIV). "The grass withers and the flowers fall, but the word of our God stands forever" (Isa. 40:8, NIV). "Long ago I learned from your statutes that you established them to last forever" (Ps. 119:152, NIV). Over the centuries, people have ignored, denied, attacked, and sought to destroy the Holy Scriptures, but the Word of God is still here! God especially protected the scrolls written by Jeremiah because He wanted Daniel to have a copy to take with him to Babylon.

"All scripture is given by inspiration of God" (2 Tim. 3:16), the Old Testament as well as the New, and Holy Scripture is the only dependable source of truth about God, man, sin, salvation, and the future events God has in His great plan. In these days of rapidly changing ideas, events, and situations, the unchanging Word of God is our dependable light and unshakable foundation.

The God of the Word. This is the first time that Jehovah, the covenant name of God, is used in the Book of Daniel, and it is used only in this chapter (vv. 2-3, 10, 13-14, 20). But we must remember that, at that time, the Lord was calling the nation of Israel "Lo-Ruhama—not loved" and "Lo-Ammi—not my people" (Hosea 1) because Israel had broken His holy covenant. When you are outside the covenant, you can't sincerely use His covenant name and expect to receive covenant blessings.

However, Daniel came to God pleading for mercy and forgiveness for himself and his people, and that's the kind of praying the

Lord Jehovah wants to hear. In fact, the promise of God's forgiveness was written right into the covenant. "But if they confess their iniquity and the iniquity of their fathers, with their unfaithfulness in which they were unfaithful to Me, and that they also have walked contrary to Me . . . then I will remember My covenant with Jacob, and My covenant with Isaac and My covenant with Abraham I will remember; I will remember the land" (Lev. 26:40-42, NKJV). Certainly as Daniel studied the Scriptures and prayed to Jehovah, he had in his mind and heart both the holy covenant (Lev. 26; Deut. 27–28) and Solomon's prayer at the dedication of the temple (1 Kings 8:33-36).

God's plan for His people. God revealed to Jeremiah that the people of Israel would be taken to Babylon and be exiled from their land for seventy years (Jer. 25:11-12; 29:10). God had commanded His people to give the land a "sabbath rest" every seven years and a "year of jubilee" every fifty years (Lev. 25). Both the forty-ninth and the fiftieth years would be "sabbatic years" when the people were not allowed to sow seed or cultivate their orchards. They had to trust God to make the food grow to meet their daily needs. This law was not only good for the land, helping to restore its fertility, but it was also good for the spiritual life of the nation. However, it was not until the nation's captivity in Babylon that the land enjoyed its sabbath rests (2 Chron. 36:20-21).

From what date do we begin to count off the seventy years, and when did the captivity officially end? To answer these important questions, we must highlight the key dates in Jewish history at that time. Babylon began to attack the kingdom of Judah in 606 B.C., and Jerusalem and the temple were destroyed in 586. The first Jewish captives were taken to Babylon in 605, Daniel and his three friends being among them. In 538, Cyrus issued the decree that permitted the Jews to return to their land and rebuild the temple (Ezra 1:1-4), and in 537 about 50,000 Jews returned to Jerusalem under the leadership of Zerubbabel and Joshua the high priest (Ezra 1–2).

If we decide that the Captivity officially began in 606–05 with the attack on Jerusalem and the deporting of the first captives, then seventy years later would take us to 537–36, when the first exiles returned to their land and the foundations of the temple were laid. In other words, the first captives left Judah in 605 and the liberated exiles returned to the land in 537–36, a time period of roughly seventy years. However, some students feel that the destruction of Jerusalem and the temple should be the starting point (586), with the Captivity not officially ending until the second temple had been built and dedicated (515), another period of approximately seventy years. Since both interpretations make sense, it shouldn't be necessary to debate the issue.

We need to be aware of three important facts. First, in sending His people into captivity, the Lord was keeping His covenant promise, for He had warned them that they would be punished if they persisted in disobeying Him (Lev. 26). It appears that Israel's years of captivity in Babylon helped to cure the Jewish people of their detestable sin of idol worship.

Second, the Captivity brought blessing to the land, for the land had been abused by farmers who would not let the land enjoy its sabbatical rests. The land belonged to the Lord (25:23; see Deut. 11:12) and He would not permit His people to defile it by sin and idolatry and waste it by not giving it times of rest. For every sabbatical year the Jews failed to honor, they added one more year to their own bondage in Babylon.

Third, when Daniel made this discovery about the seventy years, the period of captivity was about to end! If Daniel was taken to Babylon in 605, and he discovered Jeremiah's prophecy in 539, then he had been in Babylon sixty-six or sixty-seven years. The next year (538), Cyrus would make his decree permitting the Jews to return to their land. The prophet was probably eighty-one years old at this time. He himself would not be able to return to the land, but he rejoiced that others could return.

2. Intercession: Praying for God's mercy (Dan. 9:3-19)

Daniel is a wonderful example of balance in the spiritual life, for he devoted himself to both the Word of God and prayer (Acts 6:4). Some believers are so wrapped up in prophetic studies that they have little concern for the practical outworking of God's will. All they want to do is satisfy their curiosity and then proudly share their "insights" with others. When Daniel learned God's truth, the experience humbled him and moved him to worship and to pray.

Preparing for prayer (Dan. 9:3). You don't have to read very far in the Book of Daniel before you discover that he was a man of prayer. Daniel and his three friends sought the face of God when Nebuchadnezzar threatened to slay all the magicians and counselors (2:16-23). It was Daniel's habit to pray to the Lord three times each day (6:10-11), a practice he continued even when it was illegal to pray to anyone except the king. When God showed Daniel visions of future events, the prophet wasn't satisfied until he had asked for an explanation (7:15ff; 8:15ff). Prayer was a vital part of Daniel's life.

Daniel prepared himself to pray, because he knew that his prayer would affect the future of the Jewish nation and the lives of the Jewish captives in Babylon. It would be his holy task to confess the sins of the Jewish nation, asking God to forgive His people and receive them back again. He humbled himself in sackcloth and ashes; he fasted; and he directed his heart and mind to the Lord. Preparation for prayer and worship is as important as prayer itself, for without a heart that is right with God, our prayers are just so many pious words. Daniel met the conditions for answered prayer set forth in Leviticus 26:40-45 and 2 Chronicles 7:14.

Worshiping the Lord (Dan. 9:4). Too often we rush into God's presence and ask for things, without first pausing to worship Him. Daniel prepared himself for prayer, as did Ezra (Ezra 9:3-5) and the Levites (Neh. 9:5-6). It's important that we focus on the character of God and not become too preoccupied with ourselves and our burdens. The "invocation" to Daniel's prayer is a primer of biblical theology. His words describe a God who is great and faithful to keep His promises, a God who loves His people and gives them His Word to obey so that He can bless them. He is a merciful God (Dan. 9:18) who forgives the sins of His people when they come to Him in contrition and confession.[2] This is also the way Nehemiah prayed when he sought God's will concerning rebuilding the walls of Jerusalem (Neh. 1:5ff).

It's one thing to pray to the Lord and quite something else to be a worshiping intercessor. When we see the greatness and glory of God, it helps to put our own burdens and needs in proper perspective. By exercising even little faith in a great God, we can move the hand of God to accomplish wonders that will glorify His name. Dr. Robert A. Cook used to say, "If you can explain what's going on in your ministry, God didn't do it."

Confessing sin (Dan. 9:5-15). Several times in Israel's ministry, the intercession of one person brought about the nation's deliverance from judgment. On two occasions, God was ready to wipe out the entire Jewish nation, but the intercession of Moses stayed His hand (Ex. 32:7-14; Num. 14:10-25). God answered Elijah's prayer and sent the rain that was so desperately needed (1 Kings 18), and He heard Jehoshaphat's prayer and gave Israel victory over the large invading army of Moabites and Ammonites (2 Chron. 20). King Hezekiah cried out to God when the Assyrian army surrounded Jerusalem, and the Lord sent His angel to slay 185,000 enemy soldiers (Isa. 37; 2 Kings 19). "The prayer of a righteous man is powerful and effective" (James 5:16, NIV). God doesn't have to wait for the entire nation to repent and cry out for mercy; He will start to work when He hears the believing prayers of one faithful intercessor.

While Daniel's prayer was certainly personal, he so identified with the people of Israel that his prayer involved national concerns. The pronoun he uses is we rather than they or I. He confessed that he and the people had sinned greatly against the Lord and broken the terms of His gracious covenant. According to Daniel 9:5-6, the Jews had sinned, rebelled, turned away from His law, disobeyed His commands, done wrong, and refused to listen to the messengers God had sent to them. "And the Lord God of their fathers sent warnings to them by His messengers, rising up early and sending them, because He had compassion on His people and on His dwelling place. But they mocked the messengers of God, despised His words, and scoffed at His prophets, until the wrath of the Lord arose against His people, till there was no remedy" (2 Chron. 36:15-16, NKJV). God had been long-suffering with His covenant people, but the time came when He had to act.

What were the consequences of the nation's rebellion? They became a sinful people, a people covered with shame ("confusion of face," Dan. 9:8), and a scattered people. Their land was overrun by enemy soldiers, their great city of Jerusalem was destroyed, and their holy temple was desecrated, robbed, and burned. No wonder the Jews were ashamed! But it was their own sins that had brought these disasters, because their kings, princes, and priests had disobeyed God's laws and refused to obey God's prophets.

The leaders and the people knew the terms of God's covenant, but they deliberately violated them. The Jews were unfaithful to God's covenant, but God was faithful to keep His Word. If the nation had obeyed, God would have been faithful to bless them (Ps. 81:11-16); but because they rebelled, He was faithful to chasten them. "You have fulfilled the words spoken against us and against our rulers by bringing upon us great disaster" (Dan. 9:12, NIV). Daniel didn't make excuses for the nation nor did he say that God's covenant was too demanding. Israel had enjoyed great blessings when they had obeyed the law, so why should they complain when they experienced great suffering because they disobeyed the law?

But there was something even worse than the sins that brought divine punishment to Israel. It was the refusal of the Jews to repent and confess their sins even after being taken captive! They spent their time praying for judgment against Babylon (Ps. 137) rather than seeking God's face and asking for His forgiveness. God's will for Israel in captivity was outlined in Jeremiah 29, but the Jews didn't always follow it. Daniel's approach was biblical: "For the Lord our God is righteous in everything He does" (Dan. 9:14, NIV). Why would He bring His people out of Egypt and then allow them to waste away in Babylon? Daniel knew that God had purposes for Israel to fulfill, and so he reminded God of His past mercies (v. 15).

Asking for mercy on Israel (Dan. 9:16-19). God in His grace gives us what we don't deserve, and God in His mercy doesn't give us what we do deserve. Daniel asked the Lord to turn away His anger from Jerusalem and the holy temple. He admits that the sins of Israel (including Daniel) were the cause of that great catastrophe, but that God had promised to forgive if His people would repent and confess their sins. "We do not make requests of you because we are righteous, but because of your great mercy" (v. 18, NIV). But even more, Daniel desired the nation to be restored that God might be glorified. After all, the Jews were God's chosen people, and Jerusalem was the place of His holy temple; the longer the people and the land were under God's wrath, the less glory the Lord would receive. "Your city and your people bear your Name" (v. 19, NIV).[3]

God answered Daniel's prayer. The next year, Cyrus issued a decree that permitted the Jews to return to their land, take the temple treasures with them, rebuild the temple, and restore the worship. What a remarkable ministry Daniel had in Babylon! He was counselor to four kings, intercessor for the people of Israel, a faithful witness to the true and living God, and the author of one of the basic books of prophecy in the Old Testament.

Daniel now knew God's immediate plans for the nation of Israel, but what about the distant future? He had already learned from the visions God gave him that difficult days lay ahead for God's people, with a kingdom to appear that would crush everything good and promote everything evil. Would God's people survive? Would the promised Messiah finally appear? Would the kingdom of God be established on the earth?

Daniel is about to receive the answers to those questions.

3. Instruction: Discovering God's timetable (Dan. 9:20-27)

We don't know at what time of day Daniel began to pray, but he was still praying at the time of the evening burnt offering, which was about 3 o'clock in the afternoon. He was living in Babylon but was still measuring time by Jewish religious practices! His body was in Babylon, but his mind and heart were in Jerusalem. Had the temple been standing and the priests still officiating, this would have been "the ninth hour" when the lamb was offered as a burnt offering (Ex. 29:38-41; Acts 3:1; 10:30). It was one of the three occasions during the day when Daniel set aside time to offer special prayer to the Lord (Dan. 6:10; Ps. 55:17). This was also the time when Ezra the scribe prayed for God to forgive the sins of the Jewish remnant that had returned to the land (Ezra 9:5). There is a sense in which prayer is seen by God as a spiritual sacrifice to Him (Ps. 141:1-2).

While Daniel was praying, the angel Gabriel came swiftly to him, interrupted his prayer, touched him, and spoke to him. Daniel had met Gabriel before after seeing the vision of the ram and the goat, and Gabriel had explained its meaning to him

(Dan. 8:15ff). Now the angel had come to explain to Daniel what God had planned for Jerusalem, the temple, and the Jewish people. The phrase "fly swiftly" (v. 21) has given rise to the idea that angels have wings and fly from place to place, but arrows, bullets, and missiles fly swiftly and don't have wings. Angels are spirits and therefore don't have bodies (Ps. 104:4; Heb. 1:7). When they appear to humans, they take on temporary human form. The angelic creatures seen by Isaiah (Isa. 6:2) and Ezekiel (Ezek. 1:6, 8, 11) did have wings, but they were special creatures performing a special ministries. The NIV translates the phrase "in swift flight"and makes no mention of wings.

The seventy "weeks" (Dan. 9:24). The word "weeks" means "sevens," so Gabriel was speaking about seventy periods of 7 years, or 490 years. Keep in mind that these years relate specifically to Daniel's people, the Jews, and their holy city, Jerusalem. In his prayer, Daniel's great concern was that his people be forgiven their sins against the Lord, the city be rebuilt, and the temple be restored (v. 16); and these are the matters that Gabriel will discuss. To apply this important prophecy to any other people or place is to rob it of its intended meaning.

Gabriel explained that during those 490 years, the Lord would accomplish six specific purposes for the Jewish people. The first three have to do with sin and the last three with righteousness. The Lord would "finish the transgression," that is, the transgression of the Jewish people, and "make an end of " Israel's national sins. This was one of the main burdens of Daniel's prayer. Israel was a scattered suffering nation because she was a sinful nation. How would the Lord accomplish this? By making "reconciliation for iniquity," that is, by offering a sacrifice that would atone for their sin. Here we come to the cross of Jesus Christ, Israel's Messiah.

When Jesus died on the cross, He died for the sins of the whole world (1 John 2:2; John 1:29), and therefore we can proclaim the good news of the Gospel to sinners everywhere. But He also died for the church (Eph. 5:25) and for the people of Israel. "For the transgression of my people was he stricken" (Isa. 53:8). Jesus died for sinners in every tribe and nation (Rev. 5:9; 7:9), but in a very special way, He died for His own people, the Jewish nation (John 11:44-52).

The last three divine purposes focus on righteousness and the future kingdom of Messiah. When Jesus returns, He will establish His righteous kingdom (Jer. 23:5-6; 31:31-34) and rule in righteousness (Isa. 4:2-6). In that day, the Old Testament prophecies of Israel's glorious kingdom will be fulfilled, and there will be no need for visions or prophets. "To anoint the most holy" refers to the sanctifying of the future temple that is described in Ezekiel 40–48.

These six purposes declare the answers to Daniel's prayer! Ultimately, Israel's sins will be forgiven (Zech. 12:10–13:1), the city of Jerusalem will be rebuilt, and the temple and its ministry will be restored, all because of the atoning death of Jesus Christ on the cross. All of these wonderful accomplishments will be fulfilled during the 490 years that Gabriel goes on to explain. He divides the seven sevens—490 years—into three significant periods: 49 years, 434 years and 7 years.[4]

Period #1—49 years (Dan. 9:25). During this period, the Jews will rebuild the city of Jerusalem in troubled times. The key issue here is the date of the decree. This is not the decree of Cyrus in 538 permitting the Jews to return to their land and rebuild their temple (Ezra 1; Isa. 44:28), because the emphasis of this decree is on the city of Jerusalem. While some students opt for the decree of Artaxerxes in 457, sending Ezra to Jerusalem (Ezra 7:12-26), that decree also emphasized the temple and its ministry. The decree of Daniel 9:25 is probably that of Artaxerxes in 445 authorizing Nehemiah to go to Jerusalem to rebuild the walls and restore the gates (Neh. 2:5-8).

Period #2—483 years (Dan. 9:26). Gabriel affirmed that 483 years are involved from the giving of the decree to the coming of "the Anointed One, the ruler" (7 x 7 = 49; 7 x 62 = 434; total = 483). When you count 483 solar years from the year 445, you end up with A.D. 29/30, which brings us to the time of Christ's ministry on earth.[5] But this Anointed One, the Christ, will not be permitted to rule; for His people cried out, "We have no king but Caesar" (John 19:15). "We will not have this man to reign over us" (Luke 19:14). The Messiah will be "cut off, but not for himself" ("and will have nothing," NIV). This speaks of His rejection by the Jewish nation (John 1:11; Luke 13:33-35) and His crucifixion as a criminal, turned over to the Roman authorities by His own people and one of His own disciples. But He died for the sins of the world, including the sins of the Jewish nation.

We know that Jesus arose from the dead and returned to heaven. He sent the Holy Spirit to empower His people to bear witness to the whole world (Acts 1:8), beginning in Jerusalem (Luke 24:46-53). But the same nation that allowed John the Baptist to be slain and asked for Jesus to be crucified went on to persecute the church and themselves kill Stephen (Acts 7). In A.D. 70, the prophecy in Daniel 9:26 was fulfilled when the Roman armies destroyed Jerusalem and the temple, and the Jewish nation was scattered. The Romans are "the people of the prince that shall come," and that prince is the future Antichrist that Daniel described as "the little horn" and the blasphemous king (7:8, 24-25; 8:23-27). This takes us to the third period.

Period #3—7 years (Dan. 9:27). The pronoun "he" refers to "the prince that shall come" (v. 26), this is, the Antichrist.[6] We are now in the final seven years of the prophetic calendar that Gabriel gave Daniel, the period that we know as "the Tribulation" or "the day of the Lord." While the world has always known wars and desolations (Matt. 24:3-24), the end of the age will introduce a time of terrible suffering that will climax with the return of Jesus Christ (Rev. 6–19; Matt. 24:15-35).

The event that triggers this last seven-year period is the signing of a covenant between the Antichrist and the Jewish nation. At this time, the Antichrist is a key political figure in Europe—one of the ten toes of the image in Daniel 2, and the "little horn" who emerges from the ten horns in 7:8, 24ff—and he has the authority and ability to end the "Middle East problem." He covenants to protect the Jews from their enemies, probably so they can build their temple and restore their sacrifices. The spiritually blind Jewish leaders, ignorant of their own Scriptures, will gladly enter into the covenant. "I have come in My Father's name, and you do not receive Me," Jesus told the Jewish leaders of His day; "if another comes in his own name, him you will receive" (John 5:43, NKJV).

After three and a half years, the Antichrist will break the covenant, seize the temple, and put his own image there, and will force the world to worship him (2 Thes. 2; Rev. 13). This is the "abomination of desolation" (Dan. 11:31; 12:11, NKJV) that Jesus spoke about that marks the midpoint of the Tribulation period (Matt. 24:15; Mark 13:14). The "man of sin" and "son of perdition" (2 Thes. 2:3) who up till now has deceived the world by playing a shrewd political game will now reveal himself as a tool of Satan and a cruel world dictator. Christ will defeat him when He returns to establish His kingdom (Rev. 19:11-21).

The strange parenthesis. Whether Daniel understood all that he heard is not revealed to us, but Gabriel's message assured him that the nation of Israel would be restored to their land, the city of Jerusalem and the temple would be rebuilt, and God would make provision for the cleansing of the nation. But Gabriel didn't tell Daniel what would happen between the sixty-ninth and the seventieth "weeks." Between Daniel 9:26-27 there is a strange parenthesis. Why?

Because this prophecy has to do with the Jews, the Jewish temple, and the city of Jerusalem (v. 24). But the period of time between the sixty-ninth and seventieth weeks has to do with the church, the body of Christ, which was a mystery God had hidden in Old Testament times and didn't reveal until the time of Christ and the apostles (Eph. 3:1-13).[7] Daniel wasn't told that the rejection and death of the Messiah would bring about a new thing, a spiritual body that would include Jews and Gentiles and in which all natural differences would be unimportant (Eph. 2:11-22; Gal. 3:22-29). One reason the Jewish legalists opposed Paul was because he put Jews and Gentiles on the same level in the church, and the traditionalists wanted to maintain the "superiority" of the Jews as revealed in the law and the kingdom prophecies.

Some of the prophecy in Daniel 9:24-27 has already been fulfilled, and the rest will be fulfilled in the end times. We are today living in the age of the church, when Israel has been partially blinded and temporarily set aside (Rom. 9–11). Like Paul, we must have a heart concern for the Jewish people, pray for them, and seek to share the Gospel with them. Gentile believers have a debt to the people of Israel (Rom. 15:24-27) because they gave us the knowledge of the true and living God, the inspired written Scriptures, and the Savior, Jesus Christ.

The Lord still has more to teach Daniel about the future of His people, and we will consider these prophecies in the chapters to come.

CHAPTER TEN
A REMARKABLE EXPERIENCE
Daniel 10

The third year of Cyrus would be 536 B.C., which is the latest date given in the Book of Daniel. This statement doesn't contradict 1:21, which tells us how long Daniel continued in the king's court. As we have seen, Daniel lived long enough to see Jeremiah's prophecy fulfilled and the first group of Jewish exiles return to their land and start to rebuild the temple. If he was fifteen when he was taken to Babylon, then he would be eighty-four or eighty-five at this time.

The fact that 10:1 speaks of Daniel in the third person suggests that the statement that opens this chapter may be an official "identification title" for the last three chapters of his book. In verse 2 and throughout the chapter, Daniel speaks in the first person. Also, the use of his Babylonian name, "Belteshazzar," indicates that this opening statement is probably an official "label" for the document. The vision God showed him was true, and Daniel understood the message of the vision and realized that it would be fulfilled many years later. The phrase "the time appointed was long" can also be translated "and of great conflict" (NIV, "and it concerned a great war"). Daniel would learn that his people would experience great suffering in the years ahead, but that the Lord would watch over them and ultimately establish the promised kingdom.

1. A concerned prophet (Dan. 10:1-3)

For three weeks, Daniel had fasted and prayed and used no ointments as he sought the face of the Lord. Why? One reason was probably his concern for the nearly 50,000 Jews who a year before had left Babylon and traveled to their native land to rebuild the temple. Since Daniel had access to official reports, he no doubt heard that the remnant had arrived safely in Jerusalem and that all of the tabernacle treasures were intact. He also would have heard that the men had laid the foundation of the temple but that the work had been opposed and finally stopped (Ezra 4). He knew that his people were suffering hardship in the ruined city of Jerusalem, and he wondered if God would fail to fulfill the promises He made to Jeremiah (Jer. 25:11-12; 29:10-14).

Daniel may not have understood that the prophecy of the seventy years had a dual application, first to the people and then to the temple. The first Jews were deported to Babylon in 605, and the first captives returned to their land in 536, a period of seventy years. The temple was destroyed in 586 by the Babylonian army, and the second temple was completed and dedicated in 515, another period of seventy years. Daniel was burdened that the house of God be rebuilt as quickly as possible, but he didn't realize that God was fulfilling His plans without a mistake. The work was stopped in 536, it resumed 520 and it was completed in 515. That sixteen-year delay kept everything right on schedule. This is a good reminder to us as we serve the Lord today, that our times are in His hands (Ps. 31:15) and He is never late in accomplishing His will.

But there may have been a second reason why Daniel was fasting and praying: he wanted to understand more about the visions and prophecies he had already received, and he longed for the Lord to reveal additional truth to him about the future of Israel. Daniel was an aged man, and before he went to his grave, he wanted to leave behind a prophetic message that would encourage and strengthen his people. Doubtless the prophecy of Daniel was a treasured book to the people of Israel in the centuries that followed. They knew they would experience great trials and persecutions, and yet they also knew that the Lord would be faithful and that they would one day enter into the promised kingdom.

When one day we gather in heaven, we will discover that what happened to God's people on earth depended a great deal on the prayers of burdened people like Daniel. "For who will have pity on you, O Jerusalem? Or who will bemoan you? Or who will turn aside to ask how you are doing?" (Jer. 15:5, NKJV) Nehemiah asked about the plight of Jerusalem and ended up being an answer to his own prayers! (Neh. 1–2) Jeremiah wept over Jerusalem and its people and wished that he could have wept more (Jer. 9:1-2; 8:21; 10:19; 23:9). Jesus also wept over the city (Matt. 23:37-39), and the Apostle Paul was willing to be condemned himself that his people might be saved (Rom. 9:1-3; 10:1). "Rivers of tears gush from my eyes because people disobey your law" (Ps. 119:136, NLT).

God laid a burden on Daniel's heart, and because Daniel fasted and prayed, we are studying his prophecies today. May the Lord help us to leave something behind in the journey of life so that those who come after us will be encouraged and helped!

2. An awesome vision (Dan. 10:4-9, 14)

Three days after the end of his fast, Daniel saw an awesome vision as he stood by the Tigris River. Why Daniel was there isn't explained in the text, but it was the place where God met with him and revealed Israel's future in the greatest prophecy God ever gave to His servant.

It was during the first month of the Hebrew year that the Jews celebrated Passover, the Feast of Unleavened Bread, and the Feast of Firstfruits (Lev. 23:1-14). Daniel couldn't celebrate these special events in Babylon, but certainly his heart was meditating on them. Passover spoke of Israel's release from Egyptian bondage, and now the Jews were being permitted to leave Babylon for their own land. During the week before Passover, the Jews had to remove every bit of leaven from their houses, a picture of sin being put out of their lives (Matt. 16:6-12; Mark 8:15; Luke 12:1; 1 Cor. 5:6-8; Gal. 5:9). Though he lived for eight decades in a pagan land, Daniel had kept his heart and life pure before God. He was praying that the Jewish remnant living in Jerusalem would be a holy people to the Lord so that He could bless them in their work.

Suddenly, without announcement, Daniel saw an awesome sight: a man wearing a linen garment and a golden girdle, with a body like chrysolite (topaz) and a face like lightning, his eyes like flaming torches, his arms and feet gleaming like polished brass, and his voice sounding like a great multitude. We aren't told what the man said when he spoke, but the combination of his appearance and his speech was overwhelming. The men with Daniel didn't see the vision but they felt the terror of a powerful presence and hid themselves.[1] Daniel was left alone, without strength, listening to the man's words but not able to respond. All he could do was stand there and stare at this great vision, and then he fell to the earth in a deep sleep.

Who was this man? Was he an angel sent to assure Daniel that God's heavenly armies would care for the Jewish people and see to it God's will was accomplished?[2] Was it Gabriel, who had already visited Daniel? Or was it a preincarnate appearance of Jesus Christ, the Son of God? Students of the Scriptures have ably defended each of these three views, and so it's unlikely we can be dogmatic. If we decide that this glorious man is the same being who touched Daniel and spoke to him (Dan. 10:10-15), then we will have to opt for Gabriel or another angel, because it's not likely that Jesus would need help from Michael to defeat an evil angel (v. 13). However, it appears that the being who touched Daniel and spoke to him is different from the glorious man that appeared in the vision (see NASB and NIV), and most students think it was Gabriel.

The description of the glorious man resembles the description of the glorified Christ given in Revelation 1:12-16—and John's response was the same as Daniel's! Daniel had already seen the Son of Man at the throne of God in heaven (Dan. 7:9-14), but this man was on the earth and very near to Daniel. I believe that this was a vision of the glorious Son of God and that the angel who spoke to Daniel was Gabriel. But why would the Son of God appear to Daniel at this time?

Frequently in the biblical account of salvation history, you find the Lord Jesus Christ appearing to His servants at special times, either to deliver a special message or to prepare them for a special ministry. He usually appeared in a fashion compatible with their circumstances or their calling. To Abraham, the pilgrim, Jesus came as a traveler (Gen. 18), but to Jacob the schemer, He came as a wrestler (Gen. 32). Before Joshua attacked Jericho, Jesus came as Captain of the Lord's armies (Josh. 5:13-15), and to Isaiah, He revealed Himself as the King on the throne (Isa. 6; John 12:37-41). But to the two Jewish exiles—Daniel in Babylon and the Apostle John on Patmos—Jesus appeared as the glorified King-Priest. After seeing the Son of

God, both men were given visions of future events that involved the people of God, events that would be difficult to accept and understand.

At the beginning of Daniel's prophetic ministry, he interpreted the meaning of the awesome image that King Nebuchadnezzar had seen in his dream (Dan. 2), and now at the end of his ministry, Daniel saw an even greater sight—the glorious King of Kings and Lord of Lords! When we know that Jesus is standing with us and fighting for us, we can accept any circumstance and accomplish any task He gives us.

Apart from the prophetic significance, there is a sense in which Daniel's experience by the Tigris River conveys a lesson to all Christian leaders. There is a price to pay if we're to see what God wants us to see and hear what He is saying to us. Daniel didn't have this great vision early in his ministry but at the end of a long and faithful life. "Blessed are the pure in heart, for they shall see God" (Matt. 5:8). Spiritual leaders often see what others can't see and hear what they fail to hear. They must stand when others flee, and they must receive God's message even if it makes them feel weak and helpless. By seeing the greatness and glory of God, Daniel was prepared to accept and record the prophetic message the angels brought.

The angel had come to give Daniel a special revelation concerning the Jewish people and what would happen to them in the latter days (Dan. 10:14). As we study this complex prophecy, we must focus on Israel and not on the church, even though all Scripture is profitable for all believers at all times. Parts of this prophecy have already been fulfilled, but much of it remains to be fulfilled in "the end times," that is, during the seventieth week of the "prophetic calendar" given in verses 24-27.

3. An invisible war (Dan. 10:10-21)

We get the impression that the glorious man clothed in linen vanished from the scene and one of the angels, perhaps Gabriel, touched Daniel. The old prophet was on his face on the ground, but the ministry of the angel enabled him to lift himself to his hands and knees. Then the angel spoke to him and this gave him the strength to stand upright. This reminds us that the angels ministered to our Lord after His temptation (Matt. 4:11; Mark 1:13) and in the garden when He prayed (Luke 22:41-43). This is the third time Daniel was touched by an angel (Dan. 8:18; 9:21; and see 10:16, 18-19).

This is the second time Daniel was addressed as "dearly beloved" (9:23, and see 10:19). We recall that our Lord Jesus Christ was spoken of this way by the Father (Matt. 3:17 and 17:5; Mark 1:11, 9:7; and 12:6; Luke 3:22 and 20:13; and cf. Isa. 42:1-4 with Matt. 12:15-21). Because we His children are "in Christ," we are "accepted in the beloved" (Eph. 1:6), and the Father loves us as He loves His Son (John 17:23, 26). It isn't enough for us to know that God loves us; we must so live in fellowship with Him that we "keep [ourselves] in the love of God" (Jude 21; John 14:19-24).

Daniel's conversation with the angel reveals to us the important fact that there is an "invisible war" going on in the heavenlies between the forces of evil and the forces of God. For three weeks, Daniel had been praying for wisdom to understand the visions he had already seen, but the answer to that prayer was delayed. Why would the Lord not immediately answer the petitions of His beloved prophet? Because "the prince of the kingdom of Persia"—an evil angel—had attacked the angel bearing the answer, probably Gabriel. This evil angel was assigned to see to it that the king of Persia did what Satan wanted him to do. Michael, the archangel assigned to minister to Israel (Dan. 12:1; Rev. 12:7; Jude 9), assisted Gabriel and together they won the battle.

Well-meaning people may scoff at the idea of demonic forces and good and evil angels, and they may caricature Satan, but the fact remains that this is biblical theology. When Lucifer rebelled against God and was judged, some of the angels fell with him and became the demonic evil angels that oppose Christ and obey Satan (Isa. 14:12-15; Rev. 12:7-12; Matt. 25:41). According to Ephesians 6:10-18, Satan has a well-organized army of evil spirits that obey his every command. Through His sacrificial work on the cross, Christ defeated Satan and his army (1:20-23; Col. 2:15; John 12:31; Rev. 12:11), and we can claim that victory by faith. The believer's responsibility is to put on the whole armor of God by faith and use the Word of God and believing prayer to oppose and defeat the wicked one.

It appears that there are specific evil angels assigned to various nations; some students of angelology call them "territorial spirits." That's why Paul told the Ephesian believers that the Christian's battle was not against flesh and blood but against demonic forces in the heavenlies that oppose the holy angels who always do God's will. The problems that the Jewish remnant were having in Jerusalem at that time weren't being caused by the local officials but by Satan's evil powers using those officials. Christians are never to worship angels (Col. 2:18-19; Rev. 19:10; 22:8-9) or pray to angels, for our worship and prayer belong to God alone. But when we pray, God directs the armies of heaven to fight on our behalf, even though we may know nothing about the battles that are being waged in this invisible war. (See 2 Kings 6:17.)

The Prophet Daniel realized the great significance of God's plans for Israel, and once again he fainted and was unable to speak. Here he had been involved in a cosmic spiritual conflict and didn't even know it, and the Lord was using some of His highest angels to answer his prayers! This certainly lifts prayer out of the level of a humdrum religious exercise and shows it to be one of our strongest and most important spiritual weapons. The neglect of prayer is the reason why many churches and individual believers are so weak and defeated. The late Peter Deyneka, missionary to the Slavic peoples, often reminded us, "Much prayer, much power; no prayer, no power!" Jesus taught His disciples that the demonic forces could not be defeated except by prayer and fasting, the very activities that Daniel had been involved in for three weeks (Matt. 17:14-21).

Our Lord Jesus took seriously the reality of Satan and his demonic forces, and so should we. This doesn't mean we should blame every headache and interruption on the demons, but it does mean we should respect Satan's power (like a roaring lion, 1 Peter 5:8) and his subtlety (like a serpent, 2 Cor. 11:3). One of Satan's chief traps is to get people to think he doesn't exist or, if he does exist, he's not worth worrying about.

Once again, the angel restored Daniel's strength so he could hear the prophetic message from the messenger and record for our learning. Twice the angels told him, "Fear not" (Dan. 10:12, 19). The angel also said, "Peace! Be strong now; be strong" (v. 19, NIV). Daniel needed strength to be able to hear the long message the angel brought to him.

Finally, the angel made it clear that the battle wasn't yet over. As soon as he finished instructing Daniel, Gabriel would return to assist Michael in battling the prince of Persia and the prince of Greece, two satanic evil angels who were opposing the plans of the Lord for these nations. The ruler of Persia had shown great kindness and mercy to the Jews in allowing them to return home, and Satan was against this decision. God also had plans for Greece (11:2-4) and Satan wanted to interfere there. One reason why God commands His people to pray for those in authority is so that God's will, not Satan's plans, might be fulfilled in their lives (1 Tim. 2:1-3). The destiny of more than one nation has been changed because God's people have fervently prayed.

"For the weapons of our warfare are not carnal but mighty in God for pulling down strongholds, casting down arguments and every high thing that exalts itself against the knowledge of God, bringing every thought into captivity to the obedience of Christ" (2 Cor. 10:4-5, NKJV).

INTERLUDE

The prophecy given in chapters 11 and 12 is long and complex. The first thirty-five verses of Daniel 11 were prophecy in Daniel's day but are now history. They deal with important but, for the most part, forgotten historical characters with difficult names and complicated relationships. The chapters may be outlined as follows:

1. Prophecies already fulfilled (11:1-35)
   a. About Persia —11:1-2
   b. About Greece—11:3-4
   c. About Egypt and Syria—11:5-20
   d. About Antiochus Epiphanes and Syria—11:21-35

2. Prophecies yet to be fulfilled (11:36–12:3)
   a. About the Tribulation and Antichrist —11:36–12:1
   b. About the promised kingdom—12:2-3
   c. Final instructions to Daniel (12:4-13)

These prophecies fill in the details of previous prophecies the Lord had given to Daniel and were the answer to his prayer for greater understanding of God's plans for Israel. The focus is on Israel in the last days.

CHAPTER ELEVEN
A REMARKABLE PROPHECY–PART 1
Daniel 11:1-35

Fulfilled prophecy is one of the proofs of the inspiration of the Bible, for only an omniscient God can know future events accurately and direct His servants to write them down. "He reveals deep and secret things; He knows what is in the darkness, and light dwells with Him" (Dan. 2:22, NKJV). It is no surprise, then, that the radical critics have attacked the Book of Daniel, and especially these chapters, because they claim that nobody could write in advance so many accurate details about so many people and events. Their "scientific conclusion" is that the Book of Daniel is a fraud; it was written centuries after these events, and therefore is not a book of prophecy at all. These critics can't deny the historicity of the events, because the records are in the annals of ancient history for all to read and cannot be denied. Therefore, to maintain their "scientific theories," they must deny the reality of prophecy.[1] Those of us who believe in a great God have no problem accepting "the word of prophecy" (2 Peter 1:19-21).

First, we will consider the verses that were prophecy in Daniel's day but have been fulfilled and are now ancient history. As we do, we will try to glean some practical spiritual lessons to help us in our Christian walk today.

1. Prophecies about Persia (Dan. 11:1-2)

It's likely that verse 1 should be at the end of the previous chapter since it deals with the holy angels' conflict with Satan's angels. The rulers of Persia had no idea that Satan was seeking to control their minds and lead them into making decisions that would hurt the people of God. The Persian rulers were much more considerate of the Jews than were the Babylonian rulers, and Satan didn't want this to happen. He hates the Jews and is the father of anti-Semitism wherever it is found (Rev. 12). However, Michael and Gabriel won that battle and Darius and Cyrus showed compassion for the Jewish exiles. In fact, it was Cyrus who issued the important edict that permitted the Jews to return to their land and rebuild their temple (Ezra 1:1-4).

The four kings that would rule in the future were Cambyses (529–522), Pseudo-Smerdis (522–521), Darius I Hystapes (521–486), and Xerxes (496–465), the Ahasuerus of the Book of Esther.

Cambyses was the son and successor of Cyrus the Great, and perhaps is the Ahasuerus of Ezra 4:6. His passionate ambition was to invade Egypt and regain the territory that Nebuchadnezzar had gained but that was later lost. Cambyses manufactured an excuse for the war, saying that he had asked for the hand in marriage of one of the Egyptian princesses but had been rejected by her father. He did conquer Egypt, but when he tried to take Ethiopia and Carthage, he failed miserably and had to retreat. He ruled Egypt with an iron hand and gave every evidence of being insane. He married two of his sisters, murdered his brother and heir Smerdis, and then murdered the sister who protested the murder of the brother. One of the leading Persian priests plotted an insurrection and seized the throne, taking the name of the dead prince. (Historians call him Pseudo-Smerdis.) Cambyses died while marching home to unseat the new king, who reigned for about a year.

But the most important of the four kings, and the wealthiest, was Xerxes I, the Ahasuerus of the Book of Esther. He ruled an empire that reached from Ethiopia to India and he had a great passion to conquer Greece. In 480 he tried to invade Greece, but his vast fleet was defeated at Salamis and Samos, and his army was defeated at Plataea. All of this occurred between chapters 1 and 2 of the Book of Esther. He came home a bitter and angry man and sought to find relief for his wounded pride by enjoying his harem. It was at this time that Esther entered the picture. Xerxes was assassinated in August 465.

2. Prophecies about Greece (Dan. 11:3-4)

From the previous visions, Daniel already knew the sequence of the great empires.

The image (chapter 2)	Vision (chapter 7)	Vision (chapter 8)
Babylon—head of gold	lion	
Medo-Persia—arms and chest of silver	bear	ram
Greece—belly and thigh of bronze	leopard	goat
Rome—legs of iron, feet of clay	terrible beast	

The mighty king of 11:3 is, of course, Alexander the Great, who was determined to punish the Persians for Xerxes' invasion. We have already met Alexander and know about his vast army and his lightning-like conquest of the nations. Indeed, he did what he pleased and nobody could stand in his way. In 332, Alexander defeated the Persians and in 323 he died and his kingdom was divided among four of his generals.

Once again, Alexander's incredible conquests were part of the sovereign plan of God. The spread of the Greek language and Greek culture assisted in the eventual spread of the Gospel and the Greek New Testament. Alexander's goal was not just to conquer territory but to bring people together in a "united empire." His soldiers married women from the conquered nations, and Alexander's empire became a "melting pot" for all peoples. This too assisted in the spread of the Gospel centuries later.

3. The kings of the north and the south (Dan. 11:5-20)

The nations here are Egypt (south) and Syria (north), and the rulers change regularly. The little nation of Israel was caught between these two great powers and was affected by their conflicts. All of these people and events may not be interesting to you, but the prophecies Daniel recorded tally with the record of history, thus proving that God's Word can be trusted. The Ptolemy line provided the rulers in Egypt, and the Seleucid line the rulers in the north (Syria). These paragraphs are merely summary statements, but if you read them in the light of the related verses, you will see how Daniel's prophecies were fulfilled. Along with reading your KJV, you may also want to read these verses in the NASB or the NIV.

V. 5—Ptolemy I Soter and Seleucus I Nicator. Seleucus was the stronger of the two and ruled over a large empire, but it was his alliance with Ptolemy that enabled him to seize the throne of Syria.

V. 6—Ptolemy II Philadelphus and Antiochus II Theos. As was often done in the days of monarchies, the rulers used marriage as a means of forming strong political alliances, a policy Solomon had followed (1 Kings 3:1; 11:1ff). However, Ptolemy demanded that Antiochus divorce his wife Laodice in order to marry his daughter Berenice. Ptolemy died after two years, so Seleucus took back his former wife, who then murdered both him and Berenice. It was one marriage where they all didn't live happily ever after. "She will not retain her power, and he and his power will not last" (Dan. 11:6, NIV).

Vv. 7-9—Ptolemy III Euergetes and Seleucus II Callinicus. The new king of Egypt was the brother of Berenice, and he was intent on defending his sister's honor and avenging her death. He attacked the northern power, won the victory, and collected a great deal of wealth. Then the two kings ignored each other for some years until Seleucus attacked Egypt in 240, was defeated, and had to return home in shame. He was killed by a fall from his horse and his son Seleucus III Soter took the throne, only to be assassinated four years later. Antiochus III the Great, who ruled from 223 to 187, succeeded him.

Vv. 10-19—Ptolemy IV Philopater and Antiochus III the Great.[2] The sons of Seleucus II were Seleucus III, who was a successful general but was killed in battle, and Antiochus III the Great, who carried out the Syrian military program with great skill. He regained lost territory from Egypt, but in 217 the Egyptian army defeated the Syrians. This didn't stop Antiochus, for he took his army east and got as far as India.

In 201, Antiochus mustered another large army, joined forces with Philip V of Macedon, and headed for Egypt (vv. 13-16), where he won a great victory against Ptolemy V Epiphanes. Contrary to God's law, but in fulfillment of the prophecies (vision), some of the Jews in Palestine joined with Antiochus, hoping to break free of Egyptian control; but their revolt was crushed (v. 14). Antiochus not only conquered Egypt and Sidon (v. 15), but also "the glorious land" of Palestine (v. 16).

Once again marriage enters the scene. Antiochus offered to negotiate with the Egyptian leaders and to marry his daughter Cleopatra I[3] to Ptolemy V, who was seven years old at the time! He hoped that his daughter would undermine the Egyptian government from within and use her position to help him take over. However, Cleopatra was loyal to her husband, so the marriage stratagem didn't succeed.

Antiochus decided to attack Greece but was defeated at Thermopylae (191) and Magnesia (189). The "prince on his own behalf" (v. 18) was the Roman consul and general Lucius Cornelius Scipio Asiaticus who led the Roman and Greek forces to victory over Antiochus. At an earlier meeting, Antiochus had insulted the Roman general, but the Romans had the last word. The Syrian leader died in 187 and his successor was his son Seleucus IV Philopator, who oppressed the Jewish people by raising taxes so he could pay tribute to Rome. Shortly after he sent his treasurer Heliodorus to plunder the Jewish temple, Seleucus Philopator suddenly died (probably poisoned), thus fulfilling verse 20. This opened the way for the wicked Antiochus Epiphanes to seize the throne.

As you review the history of the relationship between Egypt and Syria, and the family relationships among the Seleucids, you can't help but realize that human nature hasn't changed over these thousands of years. The ancient world had its share of intrigue, political deception, violence, greed, and war. The lust for power and wealth drove men and women to violate human rights and break divine laws, to go to any length to get what they wanted. They slaughtered thousands of innocent people, plundered the helpless, and even killed their own relatives, just to wear a crown or sit on a throne.

While God is not responsible for the evil that men and women have done in the name of government and religion, He is still the Lord of history and continues to work out His plans for mankind. Studying the evil deeds of past rulers could make us cynical, but we must remember that one day "the earth shall be filled with the knowledge of the glory of the Lord, as the waters cover the sea" (Hab. 2:14).

3. Prophecies about Antiochus Epiphanes and Syria (Dan. 11:21-35)

We have already met this wicked man (8:9-14) who in his character and activities is a picture of the future Antichrist. He gave himself the name "Epiphanes," which means "glorious one," but Gabriel calls him "a vile [contemptible] person." Antiochus wasn't the heir to the throne, but he obtained it by guile. The true heir was Demetrius Soter, who was very young, so Antiochus claimed to be his lawful protector and seized the throne.

He was very successful in his military endeavors and knew how to combine deceptive strategy with brute force. In his first campaign against Egypt (11:25-28), he won the battle even though he failed to take all of Egypt. He sat down at the bargaining table with the Egyptian leaders, never intending to keep any agreements. In spite of deception on both sides, the Lord was still in control and was watching the calendar. He has His appointed times and He is always on time.

On his return to Syria in 170, Antiochus turned his attention to Israel and the wealth in the temple (v. 28). He plundered and defiled the temple, abolished the daily sacrifices, killed a great many Jews, and left soldiers behind to keep things in control. Two years later (168) he again invaded Egypt, but this time the Romans (v. 30, "ships of Chittim") confronted him and told him to stop. He obeyed grudgingly and took out his anger on the Jews, with the help of Jewish traitors who forsook their own covenant to support him. He promised to reward them generously for their help.

On December 14, 168, Antiochus desecrated the temple by erecting an altar to Zeus and by offering a pig as a sacrifice. Gabriel calls this "the abomination that maketh desolate" (v. 31). The future Antichrist will put his own image in the Jewish temple when he breaks his covenant with the Jews in the middle of the seven-year tribulation period, Daniel's seventieth week (9:27; 11:31; 12:11; Matt. 24:15; Mark 13:14). Antiochus was doing his best not only to exterminate the Jewish people but also to eliminate their religion from the earth. He promised to reward the Jews who followed his orders, and there were those who forsook their holy covenant to obey him. This was a time of testing and refining for the Jewish people, when they had to decide to obey the God of their fathers and possibly be slain, or submit to the pagan Syrian leaders and live as traitors to their faith (Dan. 11:34-35).

According to verses 33-35, there was a small group of faithful Jews who opposed the godlessness of Antiochus and trusted God to enable them to fight back. A Jewish priest named Mattathias, with his five sons, gathered an army and were able to fight back. His son Judas, nicknamed Maccabeus ("the hammerer"), was one of the heroes of this revolt. Many Jews laid down their lives for their city, their temple, and their faith, and finally they won. On December 14, 165, the temple was purified and the altar dedicated. (See 8:9-14, 23-25.) The Jews celebrate this occasion annually as the Feast of Lights (Hanukkah). Their enemy Antiochus Epiphanes died in Persia in 163. He was judged insane, and it was no wonder people called him "Antiochus Epimanes—Antiochus the madman."

Gabriel closes this section about Antiochus by reminding Daniel that what he had related to him had implications for Israel in "the time of the end" (11:35). Although he had spoken about leaders who would appear after the fall of Persia, Daniel could see in those events some of the things that would happen to the Jews in the end times. This was especially true of Antiochus Epiphanes, a clear picture of the future Antichrist. Daniel knew that his people would endure great suffering for their faith, that some would apostasize and join the enemy, and that others would trust the Lord and "do exploits" (v. 32). No matter how difficult the times, God has always had His faithful remnant, and He will keep His covenant with His people to the very end.

Having mentioned "the time of the end," Gabriel will now speak about the future Antichrist and the terrible time of Jacob's trouble (11:36–12:1).

CHAPTER TWELVE
A REMARKABLE PROPHECY–PART II
Daniel 11: 36–12:13

At Daniel 11:36, the prophecy shifts from Antiochus Epiphanes to the man he foreshadowed, the Antichrist, the last world dictator.[1] We have moved to "the time of the end" (v. 35; see 12:4), when the following events are predicted to occur:

- The rise of Antichrist—11:36-39
- The Tribulation—12:1
- War and invasions—11:40-43
- The battle of Armageddon—11:44-45a
- The return of Christ to defeat Antichrist—11:45b
- The resurrection of the dead—12:2
- The glorious kingdom—12:3[2]

1. The time of tribulation (Dan. 11:36–12:1)

Both the Old Testament and the New Testament teach that a time of great tribulation will one day come to the world, and our interpretation of Daniel's seventy weeks (9:24-27) locates this period in the last "week" of his prophecy. The event that triggers the beginning of those last seven years is the signing of the covenant with Israel by the powerful leader in the ten-nation confederacy in Europe (see 7:7-28). The reason for the covenant seems to be the guarantee of his protection for Israel while the Jews rebuild their temple in Jerusalem. The Tribulation period will end with the return of Christ and the confinement of Antichrist and Satan in the lake of fire (Rev. 19:11-21).

The rise of Antichrist (Dan. 11:36-39). This evil ruler doesn't suddenly appear in his true character and assume leadership over the world. He begins his rise to power as a part of the ten-nation European coalition; he is the "little horn" that emerges from the ten horns (7:24ff). He begins as a man of peace who "solves" the Arab/Israeli problem and proves himself to be a master politician.3 Gradually his evil designs are revealed, and at the middle of the seven-year period, he will break that covenant, claim world control, and set himself up as god (9:27; 2 Thes. 2; Rev. 13).

Gabriel describes this evil ruler (king) as a selfish and willful person, a spellbinding orator who will arrogantly exalt himself. He is a man with no religious faith. He shall have a successful career until the Tribulation ends with the return of Jesus Christ to set up His kingdom.[4] "He [Antichrist] shall come to his end, and none shall help him" (Dan. 11:45). Since verse 37 uses the phrase "the God of his fathers," does this mean that this world ruler must be Jewish? Some hold that the answer is yes, arguing that the nation of Israel would not sign a pact with a Gentile, but no Scripture supports such a view. Over the centuries, the Jews have often negotiated with political leaders who were not Jewish. The phrase "God of our fathers" (or "Lord God of our fathers") does indeed refer to the God of Israel (Deut. 26:7; 1 Chron. 12:17; 2 Chron. 20:6; Ezra 7:27; Acts 3:13, 5:30, 22:14), but that may not be the meaning in Daniel 11:37. The phrase can be translated "the gods of his fathers" as is done by both the NIV and the NASB.[5] The Antichrist will be an atheist and reject all religions except the one he establishes when he declares himself "god."

Some have suggested that his rejection of "the desire of women" indicates that he has a homosexual orientation. But the phrase "desire of women" probably relates to Haggai 2:7, a title of the Messiah, for it was the desire of Jewish women to give birth to the promised Messiah. Not only will Antichrist reject all religion in general but he will oppose the Jewish religion in particular, especially the hope their Messiah will return and deliver them from their enemies. His god is the god of might and of military power. When the people of the world worship the man of sin, they are actually worshiping Satan, the one who empowers the Antichrist. Like Antiochus centuries before him, Antichrist will reward those who worship him and his manufactured god.

The Tribulation (Dan. 12:1). "At that time" means "during the time of the end," the time period the angel is describing in this part of the prophecy. We have now reached the middle of the Tribulation when Antichrist breaks his covenant with Israel, seizes the temple, and sets himself up as world dictator and god. This is the "abomination of desolation" that Daniel wrote about in 9:27; 11:31; and 12:11, and that Jesus referred to in His Olivet Discourse (Matt. 24:15; Mark 13:14). The last three and a half years of Daniel's seventieth week will usher in a time of terrible suffering. "For then shall be great tribulation, such as was not since the beginning of the world to this time, no, nor ever shall be," said Jesus (Matt. 24:21). See Revelation 13–19.

One of the features of this terrible time will be Antichrist's (Satan's) war against the Jewish people (Rev. 12), but Michael, the angel assigned to care for the Jewish people (Dan. 10:13, 21; Rev. 12:7), will come to their aid. God's elect people will be preserved (Matt. 24:22). This will include the 144,000 who are sealed by the Lord (Rev. 7:1-8). God will keep His covenant with Abraham and see to it that the Jewish remnant will enter into their promised kingdom.

Military invasion (Dan. 11:40-43). When Antichrist moves into the land of Israel and sets up his image in the Jewish temple and declares himself the ruler and god of the whole world, not everybody will bow down to his will. The kings of the north and the south will oppose him and bring their armies to Palestine. In previous prophecies in Daniel, the king of the south has been Egypt and the king of the north has been Syria, but those designations may not apply to the nations in the end times. Some students equate this invasion with the battle described in Ezekiel 38–39, and they see in it a northern confederacy headed by Russia and a southern confederacy headed by Egypt and its allies.[6] The Antichrist will overcome his enemies and acquire great wealth as a result.

Armageddon (Dan. 11:44-45). Throughout the last three and a half years of the Tribulation period, nations will submit to the rule of Antichrist, but there will be growing dissent and opposition, even though his work is energized by Satan. The news report in verse 44 refers to the growing army from the east that will meet the forces of Antichrist on the Plain of Esdraelon to fight what is called "the battle of Armageddon" (Rev. 9:13-21; 16:12-16; Joel 3:1-2, 12-14; Zech. 14:1-3). The word "Armageddon" means "mountain of Megiddo," and this battle ("campaign") occurs at the end of the Tribulation period.

The return of Christ. As the huge army from the east gets positioned to attack the forces of Antichrist in Israel, the sign of the returning Son of Man will appear in the heavens (Matt. 24:29-30), and the opposing armies will unite to fight Jesus Christ. But the Lord will descend from heaven with His armies, defeat both armies, and take captive Satan, Antichrist, and the false prophet and cast them into the lake of fire (Rev. 19:11-21; see also Zech. 12:1-9; 14:1-3). "He [Antichrist] shall come to his end, and no one shall help him" (Dan. 11:45).

Daniel doesn't reveal this truth, but the Prophet Zechariah promises that the nation of Israel will see their Messiah as He comes from heaven, recognize Him, repent of their sins, and trust Him, and the nation will be cleansed (Zech. 12:10–13:1). Jesus will stand on the Mount of Olives (14:4; Acts 1:11-12), "and the Lord shall be king over all the earth" (Zech. 14:9) and will establish His glorious kingdom for a thousand years (Rev. 20:1-7).

2. The kingdom (Dan. 12:2-3)

Six times in Revelation 20:1-7 you find the words "thousand years." The Latin for "thousand years" (*mille, annum*) gives us the English word "millennium," the word we use for the time when Christ will reign on earth. Those Christians who believe that the Old Testament prophecies of a kingdom on earth will be fulfilled literally are called "millennialists"; those who reject this view are called "amillennialists—not millennialists." They usually spiritualize the Old Testament prophecies of the Jewish kingdom and apply them to the church today. Certainly there are spiritual applications to the church from the Old Testament kingdom prophecies, but the basic interpretation seems to be that there will be a literal kingdom on earth with Jesus Christ as King and His people reigning with Him. (See Isa. 2:1-5; 4:1-6; 11:1-9; 12:1-6; 30:18-26; 35:1-10.)

The Father has promised a kingdom to His Son (Ps. 2; Luke 1:30-33), and He will keep His promise. One day Jesus will deliver that promised kingdom up to the Father (1 Cor. 15:24). Knowing the Father's promise, Satan tempted Jesus by offering Him all the kingdoms of the world in return for His worship (Matt. 4:8-10); and Jesus refused. Jesus affirmed the kingdom promise to His disciples (Luke 22:29-30), and when they asked Him when it would be fulfilled (Acts 1:6-8), He only told them not to speculate about the times but to get busy doing the work He left them to do. However, He didn't deny the fact that one day there would be a kingdom. Paul used the return of Christ and the establishment of the future kingdom to motivate Timothy in his ministry (2 Tim. 4:1ff), and this promise ought to be a motivating factor in our lives.

Resurrection (Dan. 12:2). The doctrine of the resurrection of the human body is hinted at in the Old Testament but isn't presented with the clarity found in the New Testament. When Abraham went to Mount Moriah to offer up Isaac, he believed that God could raise his son from the dead (Gen. 22; Heb. 11:19). Job expected to see God in his resurrection body (Job 19:25-27), and this anticipation was shared by the writers of the Psalms (17:15; 49:15; 71:20). The prophets believed in a future resurrection (Isa. 25:7; Hosea 13:14). Jesus brought "life and immortality to light" (2 Tim. 1:10) and clearly taught the fact of His own resurrection as well as what the resurrection meant to His followers (John 5:19-30; 11:17-44). First Corinthians 15 is the great resurrection chapter in the Bible.

Resurrection is not "reconstruction"; the Lord doesn't put back together the body that has turned to dust (Gen. 3:19), for that dust has become a part of other bodies as people eat food grown in the soil. The resurrection body is a new and glorious body. The relationship between the body that's buried and the body that's raised is like that of a seed to the mature plant (1 Cor. 15:35-53). There is continuity (the plant comes from the seed) but not identity (the plant is not identical to the seed). The burial of a body is like the planting of a seed, and the resurrection is the harvest.

When Jesus Christ returns in the air to call His church, the dead in Christ will be raised first, and then the living believers will be caught up with them to be with the Lord (1 Thes. 4:13-18). When Jesus returns to earth at the end of the Tribulation, He will bring His people with Him to share in the victory and the glory. At that time, the Old Testament saints and the Tribulation martyrs will be raised to enter into the kingdom. However, those who died without faith in Christ will not be raised until after the Kingdom Age, and they will be judged (Rev. 20:4-6, 11-15). As Daniel states it, some will awake to enjoy the glorious life with God, and some will awake (a thousand years later) to enter into shame and everlasting contempt—and everlasting judgment.[7] Hell is called "the second death" (Rev. 20:14). If you have been born only once, you can die twice; but if you have been born twice—born again through faith in Christ—you can die only once.

Reward (Dan. 12:3). How we have lived and served will determine the rewards the Lord will give us at the judgment seat of Christ (Rom. 14:9-12; 2 Cor. 5:6-10). Every cup will be full in heaven, but some cups will be larger than others. We will share in the glory of Christ, and those who have sought to win others to Christ will shine like the stars in the heavens. There is a special application here to those who have faithfully witnessed during the Tribulation period, when it will be a costly thing to identify with Christ and His people (Matt. 24:14; Rev. 7:9-17).

Our Lord emphasized the truth that faithfulness to Him today will lead to reward and ministry in the future kingdom (Matt. 13:43; 19:27-28; 25:14-30; Luke 19:12-27; Rev. 2:26-27; 5:9-10). During His reign on earth, we will share in whatever work He has for us to do, according to how we have lived for Him and served Him here on earth. Believers who have suffered in their service for Christ will be more than compensated as they share in His glory (Rom. 8:18; 2 Cor. 4:7-18).

3. Final instructions to Daniel (Dan. 12:4-13)

The servant of the Lord never has to fret over what to do next, for the Lord always has a word of encouragement and instruction for him at the right time. During all of his long life, Daniel prayed faithfully, studied the Scriptures, and sought to serve God, and the Lord always guided him, protected him, and used him for His glory. We today are able to study prophecy because Daniel was faithful in his day.

The book (Dan. 12:4). In the ancient world, official transactions were ratified with two documents, one that was sealed and kept in a safe place and one that was kept available (Jer. 32:1-12). God looked upon Daniel's book as the "deed" that guaranteed that He would faithfully keep His promises to the people of Israel. To close up the book and seal it didn't mean to hide it away, because God's message was given so His people would know the future. The book was to be treasured and protected and shared with the Jewish people. However, the book was "sealed" in this sense: the full meaning of what Daniel wrote would not be understood until "the time of the end" (see Matt. 24:15). Even Daniel didn't fully understand all that he saw, heard, and wrote! (Dan. 12:8)

When the Apostle John completed the Book of Revelation, he was told to keep the book unsealed because the time was at hand (Rev. 22:10). We need the Book of Daniel so we can better understand the Book of Revelation. At least seventy-one passages from Daniel are quoted or alluded to in sixteen New Testament books, most of them in the Book of Revelation. All of Daniel 6 is referred to in Hebrews 11:33.

"Many shall run to and fro, and knowledge shall be increased" is not a reference to automobiles and jet planes or the advancement of education. It has reference to the study of God's Word in the last days, especially the study of prophecy. Amos 8:11-12 warns us that the day will come when there will be a famine of God's Word and people will run here and there seeking for truth but won't find it. But God's promise to Daniel is that, in the last days, His people can increase in their knowledge of prophetic Scripture as they apply themselves to the Word of God. Some interpret "to and fro" to mean running one's eyes to and fro over the pages of Scripture.

The times (Dan. 12:5-7). Two more angels arrived on the scene, one on each side of the Tigris River. The man clothed in linen refers to the awesome person Daniel saw at the beginning (10:5-6), probably Jesus Christ. When one of the angels asked, "How long shall it be to the end of these wonders?" the Lord replied "for a time, times, and a half," that is, three and a half years (7:25). The last half of the Tribulation period is described in several ways: time, times and half a time (12:7, NKJV; Rev. 12:14); forty-two months (Rev. 11:2; 13:5); and 1,260 days (11:3). Once the treaty is signed between Antichrist and Israel, the clock starts ticking off seven years, and once Antichrist sets himself up as god in the temple, the last half of Daniel's seventieth week begins. The Lord Jesus spoke this under oath, raising both hands to heaven, so it is certain.

The key to God's timing is the purpose He fulfills for "the holy people," the nation of Israel. Throughout the Book of Daniel, the emphasis is on the nation of Israel, and the only reason other nations are mentioned is because of their relationship to the Jews. While the Tribulation period is a time for punishing the Gentile nations for the way they have sinned against the Jews (Joel 3:2-8), it's also a time for sifting and purging Israel and preparing the Jews for the return of their Messiah (Amos 9:9-12).

The end (Dan. 12:8-13). "How long?" and "How will it end?" are questions that we ask when the times are difficult and the future in doubt. "What's the purpose of it all?" Daniel did what all of us must do: he humbly asked God for the wisdom that he needed. But He may not tell us! (Deut. 29:29) He knows how much we need to know and how much we can take (John 16:12). He did promise that all these things would be clearer for those living in the end times, which is an encouragement for us to prayerfully study the prophetic Scriptures.

But the Lord did reveal that, in the end times, as trials come to the people on the earth, these trials will make the believers purer and wiser, but the wicked will only become more wicked. "But evil men and impostors will grow worse and worse, deceiving and being deceived" (2 Tim. 3:13, NKJV; see Rev. 22:11). The unbelievers will be ignorant of the truth but the believers will have their eyes opened to the truths of the Word. The Word of prophecy is our light when things get dark (2 Peter 1:19).

The significance of the 1,290 days and the 1,335 days isn't made clear, but there is a blessing attached to the second number. The starting point is the middle of the Tribulation, when the abomination of desolation is set up in the temple. Since there are 1,260 days (three and a half years) before the Tribulation ends, the 1,290 days would take us 30 days beyond the return of the Lord, and the 1,335 days 75 days beyond the end of the Tribulation. We aren't told why these days are important or how they will be used to bring blessing to God's people. Certainly there are activities that the Lord must direct and tasks to accomplish, all of which will take time. Perhaps the greatest task is the regathering of His people from the nations of the world (Ezek. 20:33-38; Isa. 1:24–2:5; 4:2-6; 11:1-16), their purging, and their preparation to enter the promised kingdom.

Though the Lord had taught Daniel many things and revealed to him many mysteries, it was not for him to know everything before he died. As the end of his life drew near, it was enough to know that he had been faithful to the Lord and would one day rest from his labors (Rev. 14:13). He will one day be raised from the dead and receive the reward the Lord has allotted for him (Matt. 25:21). "I shall be satisfied, when I awake, with thy likeness" (Ps. 17:15; 1 John 3:1-3; Rom. 8:29).

CHAPTER THIRTEEN
A RESOLUTE MAN GOD GREATLY LOVED
A Review of Daniel

It's important to study the prophecies that Daniel wrote, but it's also important to understand the life that Daniel lived. Knowing God's future plan and obeying God's present will should go together. "And everyone who has this hope in Him purifies himself, just as He is pure" (1 John 3:3, NKJV). "Therefore, since all these things will be dissolved, what manner of persons ought you to be in holy conduct and godliness?" (2 Peter 3:11, NKJV)

Both Daniel and Joseph were called of God to serve Him in difficult places at the center of authority in pagan empires. Both were cruelly taken from their homes and handed over to foreign masters. Both went through periods of testing, both were lied about and falsely accused, but both maintained godly character and conduct and became respected leaders in the nation. Most of all, both were able to minister to God's people and help preserve and encourage the nation of Israel when the days were difficult. What Daniel wrote gave the Jews courage in the centuries following their release from captivity, and it will encourage them in the end times when they again experience severe persecution from their enemies.

It's interesting to note that the Book of Daniel and Paul's letter to the Ephesians have much in common. Ephesians teaches us about the spiritual battle in the heavenlies (Eph. 6:10-18), and Daniel participated in such a battle (Dan. 10:10-21). Paul prays two prayers in Ephesians, the first for enlightenment (Eph. 1:15-23) and the second for enablement (3:14-21). Daniel and his friends also prayed that way, that they might understand God's plan and receive the power they needed to serve Him and remain true to the end.

Paul's epistle to the Ephesians emphasizes the spiritual posture of believers: we are seated with Christ (2:5-6), we walk with Him (4:1, 17; 5:1-2, 8, 15), we take our stand in Christ (6:11, 13-14), and we bow our knees to Christ (3:14). Daniel was a man who bowed his knees to the Lord, walked with Him, and was able to take his stand against Satan. He was given a place of authority in Babylon, but that was nothing compared to the authority God gave Him from the throne of heaven. Daniel was a pilgrim and stranger in Babylon because his home was in Israel, and we are pilgrims and strangers on this earth because our citizenship is in heaven (Phil. 3:20-21). Like Daniel and Joseph, we live in an alien culture with people whose thinking, values, actions, and goals are totally different from and opposed to that of God's people. And yet, just as Daniel and Joseph kept themselves pure and helped to transform people and circumstances, so we can become transformers in our world today.

The key to Daniel's successful life and ministry is given in Daniel 1:8—"But Daniel purposed in his heart that he would not defile himself." He was a resolute man. He wasn't intimidated by powerful people or frightened by difficult circumstances. Like Martin Luther at the Diet of Worms, he said, "Here I stand. I can do no other. God help me. Amen."

But what was the source of this man's courageous and resolute heart? For the answer to that important question, let's review the life of Daniel.

1. He believed in a sovereign God

"The Most High rules in the kingdom of men" (Dan. 4:25, 32, NKJV; 5:21) is one of the basic truths taught in the Book of Daniel. Dictators and petty politicians may have thought they were in control, but Daniel knew better. As a devoted Jew, Daniel knew that there was but one true God, the Lord Jehovah, and that He ruled all things with wisdom and power. The Babylonians changed Daniel's address, his name, and his education, and they tried to change his standards, but they couldn't change his theology! God was sovereign when He permitted Babylon to conquer Judah, and He was sovereign in sending Daniel and his friends to Babylon. In every aspect of Daniel's life and service, he depended totally on the God of heaven who is sovereign over all things.

Some people associate sovereignty with slavery, when actually our surrender to God's sovereign will is the first step toward freedom. "And I will walk at liberty, for I seek Your precepts" (Ps. 119:45, NKJV). We can yield ourselves to Him with great confidence because He is our Father, and He loves us too much to harm us and He is too wise to make a mistake.

Nor should divine sovereignty be confused with fatalism, "What will be will be." Fatalism is belief in an impersonal force that's working out its blind but inevitable purposes in this world, whether it's the economic forces of materialism and Communism or the "survival of the fittest" in Darwinian evolution. One is tempted to ask, "What established this force? What keeps it going? If it's inevitable, why can we resist it or choose not to accept it?" The Christian believer's faith is in a personal God, a loving God who plans for us the very best (Jer. 29:11). "The Lord is my shepherd; I shall not want" (Ps. 23:1).

2. He had a disciplined prayer life

Jewish people were accustomed to pray at nine o'clock in the morning, noon, and three o'clock in the afternoon, the third, sixth, and ninth hours of the day, and Daniel carried that discipline with him to Babylon. Those who set aside special times of prayer are more likely to "pray without ceasing" (1 Thes. 5:17), for the special times of prayer help to sanctify all times and keep us in touch with God.

When Daniel and his friends needed to know Nebuchadnezzar's dream and understand it, they gave themselves to prayer, and when the Lord gave them the answer, they prayed further and thanked Him (Dan. 2:14-23). When Daniel's life was in danger, he went to his home and prayed, and the Lord delivered him from the lions (6:10). Frequently Daniel asked the Lord or His messengers for wisdom to understand the visions the Lord gave to him. Daniel depended on prayer.

In the church today, it seems that many people turn to prayer only when everything else has failed. Their translation of Psalm 46:1 is, "God is our last refuge when our own strength is gone and we don't have anywhere else to turn." What a tragedy! A.W. Tozer used to say, "Whatever God can do, faith can do, and whatever faith can do prayer can do, when it is offered in faith."[1] Daniel not only prayed alone but he also prayed with his friends, because he knew the value of two or three believers assembling together to cry out to God. "I'd rather be able to pray than to be a great preacher," said evangelist D.L. Moody; "Jesus Christ never taught His disciples how to preach, but only how to pray."

3. He studied the Word of God and believed it

When Daniel and his friends left Jerusalem for Babylon, they carried with them some of the scrolls of the Old Testament Scriptures. We know that Daniel studied the prophecies of Jeremiah (Dan. 9:2) and we can assume that these godly young men had other portions of the Word as well.

Prayer and the Word of God go together (Acts 6:4). Someone asked an old saint, "Which is more important in my Christian life, praying or studying God's Word?" The saint replied, "Which wing on a bird is more important for his flight, the right one or the left one?" As we read the Word of God and study it, we must pray for wisdom to understand and power to obey. We should also turn the Word into prayer. As we pray, we must remember what we've learned from the Scriptures, for the Word increases our faith (Rom. 10:17) and helps us pray in God's will (John 15:7).

Daniel didn't study the Word to impress people; he studied it to ascertain the will of God and obey it. When God enlightened him concerning the seventy years of captivity, Daniel immediately began to pray that God would forgive His people and fulfill His promises, and He did. When you know the Word of God and walk in communion with the God of the Word, you will have a resolute heart and be able to withstand the attacks of the devil.

4. He had an understanding of spiritual warfare

Daniel 10 is a key chapter for prayer warriors, people who wrestle in prayer (Col. 4:12) and seek under God to tear down the strongholds that block God's truth from getting into the minds of unbelievers (2 Cor. 10:1-6). When I was pastoring the Moody Church in Chicago, I met regularly with three ministerial friends, and together we devoted ourselves to warfare praying. By faith, we sought to attack Satan's strongholds and open the way for the Word of God to change the lives of people in trouble. God gave us many wonderful victories in ways that we could never have imagined.

When by faith we put on the whole armor of God and depend on God's power, God gives us the ability to "stand" and to "withstand" (Eph. 6:10-14). We aren't just brave targets—we're energized combatants! We hold the ground God has given us and we move ahead to capture new ground.

I recognize the fact that the whole concept of spiritual warfare has been abused by some and ridiculed by others, but that shouldn't stop us from imitating great saints like Daniel and Paul who invaded Satan's territory and stood their ground when they were threatened. Isaac Watts said it perfectly:

> Are there no foes for me to face?
> Must I not stem the flood?
> Is this vile world a friend to grace,
> to help me on to God?
> Sure I must fight, if I would reign;
> increase my courage, Lord;
> I'll bear the toil, endure the pain,
> supported by Thy word.

5. He sought only to glorify God

"There is a God in heaven who reveals secrets," Daniel told the powerful monarch, giving all the glory to the Lord (Dan. 2:28, NKJV), and later Nebuchadnezzar himself was glorifying God (v. 47; 4:34-35). When the king rewarded Daniel for his service, Daniel asked him to include his three friends, for they were an important part of the praying that brought the answer. When Belshazzar tried to smother Daniel with compliments and influence him with gifts, the prophet brushed it all aside and courageously interpreted the bad news to the king (5:13-17).

Throughout his long life, Daniel was a great man in the kingdom, but he used his gifts, abilities, and opportunities to honor God and minister to others. It has well been said that true humility isn't thinking meanly of yourself, it's just not thinking of yourself at all! Jesus came as a servant (Phil. 2), and His example is the one we should follow. I see many leadership conferences for Christians advertised these days; perhaps we need to organize some "servanthood" conferences; for a true leader is always a humble servant. This was true of Joseph, Moses, Joshua, David, and Nehemiah, as well as our Lord and His apostles. Can we improve on what they teach us?

6. He realized that he had a work to do

Like Joseph in Egypt, Daniel didn't complain about his lot in life but tried with God's help to make the best use of it. He knew that the sovereign Lord whom he trusted had a special plan for his life and he sought to fulfill it. He didn't campaign for promotions; the Lord brought them to him. He did his work well, he was a faithful and dependable servant, and even his enemies couldn't find anything to criticize (Dan. 6:1-5). If anybody deserved the divine approval of Jesus found in Matthew 25:21, it was Daniel.

Daniel was both a government employee and a prophet of the Lord. God gave him his high position so he could use it to serve the Lord and the Lord's people. The record doesn't tell us, but there may have been many times when Daniel represented the Jewish captives before the king and helped to make life easier for them. He may have influenced the decision of Cyrus to allow the Jews to go back home. We need dedicated believers in places of authority, men and women who can be examples of godliness and instruments of righteousness.

7. He was tactful and considerate

Some people have the idea that the only way to change things in the political world is to blow up buildings, block traffic, or attack people they consider evil. Daniel exerted considerable influence during the reigns of four kings, and yet he never resorted to force, accusations, or threats. "And a servant of the Lord must not quarrel but be gentle to all" (2 Tim. 2:24, NKJV).

When Daniel and his friends wanted to eat clean food, not food dedicated to idols, they didn't stage a hunger strike or argue with those in charge. Daniel knew that any problems they created would reflect on the prince who was assigned to them and get him into trouble, so he took a different approach. He tactfully asked if they could be tested for ten days, knowing that the Lord would make the test successful. He won the respect and confidence of the prince in charge, and the word got out in the palace that the four Jewish boys in the training classes weren't troublemakers.

Certainly Daniel didn't agree with the theology or lifestyle of the people in charge, but even if he couldn't respect the officers, he respected their offices. (See Paul's teaching on this subject in Rom. 13.) He spoke respectfully to them and about them and cultivated "sound speech that cannot be condemned" (Titus 2:8, NKJV). Too often believers adopt a "holier than thou" attitude and fail to show proper respect for officials they disagree with, and this always hurts the cause of Christ.

8. He had insight into human history

Scholars have attempted to put together the pieces of the jigsaw puzzle that we call "history," but their best attempts have failed. Like the telephone book, the book of history has a huge cast of characters but no plot. Apart from knowledge of Scripture, we can't interpret history accurately.

At the center of history is the nation of Israel. Why? Because Israel is God's chosen vehicle to bring salvation to the world, for "salvation is of the Jews" (John 4:22). At the center of the Israel's history is God's covenant with Abraham (Gen. 12:1-3) as well as God's covenant with the Jews at Sinai (Ex. 20–24) and in the plains of Moab (Deut. 27–30). If Israel obeyed, God would bless them and make them a blessing to the Gentiles; if Israel disobeyed, God would discipline and use the Gentile nations to do it.

But the visions also taught Daniel that the nations of the world were beastly in character, like lions, bears, leopards, rams, and goats. Nebuchadnezzar's pride changed him into an animal (Dan. 4), and it is pride that turns leaders into worse than animals as they devour one another. In one sense, our world is improving, and we're grateful for every advancement in medicine, communications, transportation, security, and comfort. But in another sense, the nations of the world are becoming "cheaper and cheaper," as God revealed in the vision of the great image (Dan. 2). It goes from gold to silver, from silver to bronze, from bronze to iron, and from iron to clay! There's not only a decrease in value, but there's also a decrease in strength. By the time you get to the feet and toes of the image, there's nothing but clay to hold it together!

Daniel had no illusions about the future. He knew what the human heart was like and he knew what God had planned to do. No wonder his heart was resolute and nothing moved him or changed him! He could say as Paul did in the storm, "Therefore take heart, men, for I believe God that it will be just as it was told me" (Acts 27:25, NKJV).

9. He lived up to his name

Daniel means "God is my judge." Daniel lived his life before the all-seeing eyes of the Lord and did the things that pleased Him. He didn't worry about what the king thought of him or his interpretations; he simply delivered the message God gave him and left the results with the Lord. What difference did it make that the other counselors despised him and tried to have him killed? His life and reputation were in the hands of the Lord, and the will of the Lord was always best. Is it any wonder that the Lord greatly loved Daniel?

D.L. Moody often preached on Daniel, and here's an excerpt from the message:

> Daniel thought more of his principles than he did of earthly honor or the esteem of men. Right was right with him. He was going to do right today and let the morrows take care of themselves. That firmness of purpose, in the strength of God, was the secret of his success.[2]

One of Mr. Moody's associates, musician Philip P. Bliss, expressed this truth in a song that's not used much today, but the message is certainly needed. The chorus says:

> Dare to be a Daniel!
> Dare to stand alone!
> Dare to have a purpose firm!
> Dare to make it known!

Be resolute!

ENDNOTES

Chapter 1

1. Catherine Drinker Bowen, *Miracle at Philadelphia* (Boston: Little, Brown and Co., 1966), 125–127.

2. That Daniel wrote the book that bears his name is assumed from 8:1; 9:2, 20; 10:2. That he was an actual historical person is stated not only by his book but also by Ezekiel 14:14, 20; and 28:3, as well as by our Lord in Matthew 24:15 and Mark 13:14.

3. The Babylonians considered the first year of their king's reign "the year of accession" and the next full year his first year, while the Jews began to reckon from the time the king began to reign. That's why Jeremiah 25:1 calls this important year "the fourth year of Jehoiakim," for Jeremiah used Jewish reckoning.

4. This fact shouldn't discourage the rest of us who may not have such special gifts. God prepares and uses all kinds of people, but in the case of the four Hebrew men, excellence was a requirement they had to meet. Use the gifts God has given you and don't compare yourself with others. Each of us is unique.

5. Isaiah had promised that "the king's descendants" would become eunuchs in Babylon (Isa. 39:7).

6. The fact that God used a vegetarian diet to make these four young men succeed doesn't mean that we will succeed if we follow this example. The Bible makes it clear that all foods are permissible to believers (Col. 2:16; Rom. 14:17; Mark 7:1-23; 1 Tim. 4:1-5). The story encourages us to follow their faith, not their diet.

7. Tertullian, "On Prescription Against Heretics" in *The Ante-Nicene Fathers* (Eerdmans), vol. 3, 246.

8. Op. cit., 51.

9. Andrew Bonar, *Memoir and Remains of Robert Murray M'Cheyne* (Banner of Truth Trust), 29.

Chapter 2

1. From 2:4 to 7:28, the book is written in Aramaic, the language of Babylon, rather than in Hebrew. These prophecies deal primarily with the future of Gentile kingdoms, so Aramaic is more suitable. No doubt Daniel's writings were circulated among the Gentiles as well as the Jews.

2. This name for God is used six times in the Book of Daniel—2:18-19, 28, 37, 44; 5:23. It is first heard in Scripture from the lips of Abraham (Gen. 24:3, 7) and is found frequently in Ezra and Nehemiah. It appears to be the name of God used by His people during the years of their exile and dispersion. The God of heaven isn't limited to the land of Israel; He can work even in mighty Babylon!

3. Because Lot was in their city, the people of Zoar escaped the judgment that destroyed the cities of the plain (Gen. 19:18-25), and because Paul was on the ship, God saved all the passengers from drowning (Acts 27:21-26, 30-32, 42-44). The world opposes God's people, little realizing the blessing that come because of them.

4. A.W. Tozer, *The Set of the Sail* (Christian Publications), 33.

5. The "times of the Gentiles" must not be confused

with the "fullness of the Gentiles" (Rom. 11:25), when God has gathered into His church all who shall be saved during this present age. This period began at Pentecost and will climax at the rapture of the church. During this time, God is calling out from the Gentiles a people for His name (Acts 15:14). The church is composed of believing Jews and Gentiles, but it is predominantly a Gentile church.

6. Note the use of the pronoun "we" in verse 36. Daniel includes his three friends in the interpreting of the dream.

Chapter 3

1. The furnace is a metaphor for Israel's suffering in Egypt (Deut. 4:20; 1 Kings 8:51; Jer. 11:4); eternal judgment in hell (Matt. 13:42, 50; Rev. 9:2); the holy judgment of the Lord (Gen. 19:28; Ps. 21:9; Isa. 31:9; Mal. 4:1; Rev. 1:15); and times of testing for God's people (Job 23:10; Ps. 66:10; Prov. 17:3; Isa. 48:10; Jer. 6:27-30; 9:7; Mal. 3:3).

2. Six different instruments are named, two of them wind and the rest string, but the phrase "all kinds of music" (vv. 5 and 7) indicates that many more musical instruments were used, and possibly vocal music as well. The wind instruments were the trumpet and the pipes, and the string instruments were the five-string lyre (harp), the four-string harp (sackbut), the standard harp (psaltery), and the lute (dulcimer).

3. This raises the question, "Where was Daniel?" He was in charge of the province in which the ceremony was taking place, and we would expect the king to insist on his presence. Some suggest that Daniel was ill and couldn't attend, so the king excused him. Others believe he had been sent on a special mission by the king and was away from home. A third suggestion is that Daniel, being the ruler of the province, was "behind the scenes," making sure that everything was in order. But surely Daniel wouldn't want to participate in directing such an idolatrous activity. Since the Chaldeans were able to see the three Jewish men refusing to fall down to worship, they must have been on their feet and looking around. This may mean that the king didn't require his advisers to bow down, because he assumed they were loyal to the throne. Hence, if Daniel was absent, he wasn't committing a crime or rebelling against his king.

4. The "number" of this world ruler, the Beast, is 666 (Rev. 13:18), and Nebuchadnezzar's image was sixty cubits high and six cubits wide. Six different musical instruments are also named (Dan. 3:5, 7, 10).

Chapter 4

1. Verses 28-33 were written by another hand, but Nebuchadnezzar picks up the narrative in verse 34. Daniel himself may have written verses 28-33 and inserted them in the official royal document. Luke followed a similar approach in Acts 23:25-30. Neither the Babylonian king nor the Roman officer was inspired by the Spirit when they wrote, but Daniel and Luke were led by the Spirit to include their writings in what we know as Holy Scripture.

2. Since verses 1-3 were written after the king's recovery, we'll consider them when we study verses 34-37.

3. The Hebrew word translated "flourishing" (v. 4) and "prosperous" (NIV) means "growing green like a tree" (see Job 15:32; Ps. 92:14; Hosea 14:5). It describes luxurious growth.

4. The word "gods" in verses 9 and 18 is "Elohim" in the original and may be translated "God." But it's not likely that Nebuchadnezzar had the true God of Israel in mind.

5. The KJV translates it "astonished for one hour," but the text can be translated "for a moment, for a brief time." It's difficult to believe that the king would wait that long for one of his officers to reply or that the conversation recorded in verse 19 consumed that much time. The NASB reads "appalled for a while."

6. In Isaiah 10:33–11:5, a similar image is used with reference to Messiah. God permitted the "tree" of Israel to be cut down by their enemies, but out from the stump the Messiah would eventually come.

7. In Daniel 5, Belshazzar is called the son of Nebuchadnezzar (vv. 18-22), but it's likely that he was his grandson through his mother who was a daughter of Nebuchadnezzar. In Scripture, the words "son" and "father" are sometimes used in a general sense to mean "relative, descendant."

8. William Culbertson, *The Faith Once Delivered* (Moody Press, 1972), 54–55.

9. Did God know that the king would not repent that day? Of course He did, because He knows all things. Did that make His offer less than sincere? No, because neither Daniel nor the king knew what might happen when Daniel urged Nebuchadnezzar to repent. Had the king repented, the Lord would have relented and called off the judgment. The situation was similar to that of Jonah and Nineveh.

10. It's obvious that someone else wrote verses 28-33 since the first person "I" is replaced by the third person "the king." It was likely Daniel who added this to the official report.

11. The phrase "great Babylon" reappears in Revelation 17 and 18, but the city wasn't very great after God finished with it! See also Jeremiah 50–51.

12. While much that's written about werewolves is based on mythology, medical science has recorded the strange mental disease lycanthropy in which the victims think they are animals and they start to look and act like animals. What happened to Nebuchadnezzar was a direct judgment from the Lord that began immediately and ended when Daniel said it would end. This would not be true of a natural affliction.

13. Charles H. Spurgeon, *The New Park Street Pulpit* (Puritan Publications, 1981), vol. 4, 82.

14. A.W. Tozer, *The Knowledge of the Holy* (Harper, 1961), 118.

Chapter 5

1. At least twenty-three years elapsed between Daniel 4 and Daniel 5, and Daniel 7 and 8 occurred during those years, in the first and third years of Belshazzar's reign (7:1; 8:1). From the king's dream in chapter 2 and the vision in chapter 7, Daniel knew the succession of empires and that the Medes and Persians would conquer the city.

2. The word "father" in vv. 1, 11, 13, 18, and 22 sim-

ply means "relative," in this case, his grandfather.

3. The apostrophes represent the letter *aleph,* which is the "soundless" first letter of the Hebrew alphabet. The U in UPHARSIN represents the character for "and."

4. Some scholars think that "Darius" was the title of the Persian ruler just as "Pharaoh" was the title of the Egyptian ruler. This would mean that "Darius the Mede" could have been Cyrus himself.

Chapter 6

1. Daniel 6:28 can be translated, "Even in the reign of Cyrus, the Persian." This would make Darius and Cyrus the same person. However, most translators and Old Testament scholars avoid this approach and see Darius and Cyrus as two different persons.

2. Esther 1:1 and 8:9 state that there were 127 provinces in the Persian kingdom in the reign of Xerxes (486–465). No doubt the political boundaries changed from time to time.

3. In the time of Christ, pious Jews prayed at the third hour (9 A.M.), the ninth hour (3 P.M, the time of the sacrifice at the temple), and at sunset.

4. This question reminds us of the affirmation of faith given by the Daniel's three friends: "Our God whom we serve is able to deliver us" (3:17).

5. The Lord so worked that King Darius obeyed his own law and yet Daniel was still delivered from death. This reminds us that God has worked in a similar way in His great plan of salvation. "The wages of sin is death" (Rom. 6:23), so Jesus Christ died for the sins of the world and paid the debt we cannot pay. But He arose from the dead so that He might forgive all who will receive Him by faith. God obeyed His own law and is therefore "just and the justifier of the one who has faith in Jesus" (Rom. 3:26, NKJV).

6. Daniel's intervention in interpreting Nebuchadnezzar's dream saved the lives of the wise men (Dan. 2:24), and perhaps he would have saved these men and their families also; but it wasn't his decision.

Chapter 7

1. During the years between the two world wars, some prophetic students went out on a limb and named Mussolini as the Antichrist and began counting how many nations allied with Italy. Over the centuries, the chief candidate for Antichrist has been the Pope, and each time a new Pope is elected, prophecy addicts try to make his name fit in with the number 666 (Rev. 13:18). One man calculated that Napoleon Bonaparte was the Antichrist, but you had to write his name in Arabic and leave out two letters! All sorts of numerical gymnastics have been used to identify "the little horn" but they aren't very convincing.

2. First John 2:18-23 states that "many antichrists" were already in the world at the end of the first century, in the days of the Apostle John. These were false teachers who denied the deity and eternal sonship of Jesus Christ. These heretics were not taught by the Holy Spirit but by the spirit of Antichrist, which has its origin in Satan (4:1-4). Satan is a counterfeiter and his agents, posing as authentic Christian teachers, invaded the churches of the first century and attempted to change the apostolic doctrine (2 Peter 2; Jude).

3. It is possible that the covenant guarantees protection for Israel so they can rebuild their temple in Jerusalem and restore their worship. Of course, Antichrist plans to use the temple for the world to worship him.

4. In the traditional premillennial dispensational interpretation of prophetic Scripture, which is what I have outlined here, the church will be "raptured" and taken to heaven before the final week in Daniel's prophecy occurs (1 Thes. 4:13–5:11). How much time elapses between the rapture of the church and the signing of the covenant hasn't been revealed in Scripture. However, there are those of the dispensational persuasion who believe that the church will be raptured in the middle of the Tribulation (Rev. 11:3-19) or at the very end—caught up to be with Christ and then returning with Him in glory (Rev. 19:11-21). All three schools believe that at His glorious return, Christ will establish a literal kingdom on earth in fulfillment of the Old Testament prophecies.

5. There appears to be no distinction between "the kingdom of God" and "the kingdom of heaven." The Jews were afraid to use God's name lest they be guilty of blasphemy, so they substituted "heaven." Writing especially to the Jews, Matthew uses primarily "kingdom of heaven," while the other writers prefer "kingdom of God."

6. Those who believe that Christ will return before the Millennium are called "premillennialists." Those who think that man through the preaching of the Gospel will establish the kingdom on earth, and then Christ will return, are called "postmillennialists." Amillennialists are those who do not believe there will be a literal Jewish kingdom on earth, but that the Old Testament's prophecies given to the Jews should be applied spiritually to the church.

7. A.W. Tozer, *I Call It Heresy* (Christian Publications, 1974), 144-145.

Chapter 8

1. Some have suggested that Daniel was in Susa on a diplomatic mission when he received this vision, but Daniel 5:13 indicates that Belshazzar didn't know Daniel and therefore wasn't likely to send him anywhere.

2. "Shepherd" in the Old Testament was the title of a king or royal officer. In the New Testament, it referred to spiritual leaders in the church. The word "pastor" comes from the Latin word for "shepherd."

3. S. Angus in *The Environment of Early Christianity* (London: Duckworth and Co., 1914), 8. In this discussion, I have borrowed a number of helpful thoughts from this excellent book.

4. His name is pronounced "An-TY-i-cus E-PIPH-uh-nees."

Chapter 9

1. The Ahasuerus (Xerxes) named in verse 1 is not the same monarch found in the Book of Esther.

2. Note the repetition of the word "great": a great God

(v. 4), the great evil ("disaster," NIV) Israel had brought upon themselves (v. 12), and God's great mercies (v. 18). These three phrases summarize the prayer.

3. Note how often Daniel uses the pronouns "you" and "your" as he refers to the Lord: "your commands...your people . . . your Name . . . your truth . . . your holy hill." The prayer emphasizes the character of God and not the suffering of the people. This is God-centered praying.

4. The Jewish calendar is based on a series of sevens. The seventh day is the Sabbath day and the seventh year is a sabbatic year (Ex. 23:11-13). The fiftieth year (7 x 7 + 1) is the Year of Jubilee (Lev. 25). The Feast of Pentecost is seven weeks after Firstfruits (Lev. 23:15-22), and during the seventh month of the year, the Jews observed the Feast of Trumpets, the Day of Atonement, and the Feast of Tabernacles.

5. If you start with the 457 decree and use lunar years (360 days), you arrive at a similar figure.

6. To make "Messiah, the Prince" (v. 25) and "the prince that shall come" (v. 27) the same person is to confuse Daniel's words. Those who hold to an amillennial interpretation of prophecy take this approach and apply verses 24-27 to the earthly life and ministry of Christ. But His earthly ministry was three years long, not seven years, and the only covenant He established was the New Covenant in His blood, a covenant He did not break. While His death on the cross ended the Old Testament economy in the plan of God, the Jewish sacrifices continued for nearly forty years. Jesus did not bring any "abomination of desolation" into the temple; instead, He sought to purge it of its defilement. It takes a great deal of stretching the text to put it into the past tense.

7. It isn't unusual in Old Testament prophecy for the writer to move his outlook to the end times without warning. In Isaiah 9:6, after the word "given" you move from the birth of Messiah to His kingly reign. Isaiah 61:2 moves suddenly from the gracious ministry of Jesus into the "day of vengeance" (see Luke 4:18-20). Zechariah 9:9 predicts the entrance of Jesus into Jerusalem, but verse 10 moves ahead into the final victory of Christ and His reign of peace.

Chapter 10

1. This reminds us of the men who were with Saul of Tarsus when he had his vision of Christ. They could hear the Lord's voice but couldn't see the glorious vision that Saul beheld (Acts 9:1-7; 22:9).

2. For the description of another glorious angel, see Revelation 10.

Chapter 11

1. It doesn't seem very "scientific" for scholars to assume without proof that their theories are true and the Book of Daniel is false. A true scientist considers all the facts impartially and tries to avoid pretrial prejudice. Jesus called Daniel "the prophet" (Matt. 24:15; Mark 13:14), even though nowhere in the book is Daniel called a prophet.

2. This is not the infamous Antiochus Epiphanes whom we met in Daniel 8 and who will appear in 11:21-35.

3. This is not the Cleopatra that Hollywood has glamorized, who lived from 69 to 30 B.C. She was mistress to Julius Caesar and later to Mark Antony. She murdered her own brother (who was also her husband) and seized the throne, which she shared with her son Cesarion. Discovering that Octavianus planned to exhibit her in his "triumph celebration" in Rome, she committed suicide.

Chapter 12

1. Some expositors try to fit Antiochus into this section, but they have to twist and turn to do it. In his opposition to everything religious and Jewish, Antichrist will go far beyond anything Antiochus attempted or accomplished. Antiochus wasn't against religion in general, just the Jewish religion. He tried to make his subjects worship the Greek gods and he put a statue of Zeus in the Jewish temple. Antichrist will make himself a god and put his own image in the temple.

2. This outline follows the generally accepted premillennial position and seems to agree with the text.

3. Many students believe that Revelation 6:1-2 describes Antichrist as he begins his rise to power. He has a bow but no arrows; his crown is given to him; and he goes out to conquer. Since he is an "imitation Christ," we expect him to wear a crown and ride a white horse (Rev. 19:11ff). But Jesus uses the sword of the Word of God, and His crowns are His own.

4. The historic premillennial position teaches that the church will go through the Tribulation, be called up when Christ returns, and then come to earth with Him to reign in the kingdom. However, there are those who hold that the church will be raptured before the Tribulation (1 Thes. 4:13-18) and will therefore escape the predicted troubles.

5. The Hebrew word is *elohim*, which can mean God or gods. The context determines which you use.

6. Daniel's use of words like chariots, horsemen, and ships doesn't suggest that in the last days nations will revert to ancient methods of warfare. He used words that were meaningful to readers in his day, but we who read this text today will interpret them in modern terms. The same principle applies to the geographical names in the text, such as Moab, Edom, and Ammon. He is identifying the territories once occupied by those ancient peoples. One argument for making this the battle described in Ezekiel 38–39 is that it occurs at a time when Israel is at peace because of the protection of the man of sin (Ezek. 38:11). Note also that both invasions are like a storm or a whirlwind (Ezek. 38:9; Dan. 11:40).

7. It is the body, not the soul, that sleeps and that is "awakened" at the resurrection. Nowhere does the Bible teach "soul sleep." Death occurs when the spirit leaves the body (James 2:26; Luke 23:46). The spirit of the believer goes immediately to be with the Lord (2 Cor. 5:1-8; Phil. 1:20-24); the spirit of the unbeliever goes to a place of punishment, awaiting the final judgment (Luke 16:19-31). At the last judgment, death will give up the bodies of the unbelievers and hades will give up the spirits (Rev. 20:13).

Chapter 13

1. A.W. Tozer, *The Set of the Sail* (Christian Publications), 33.

2. D.L. Moody, *Bible Characters* (Fleming H. Revell, 1888), 9.

HOSEA

OUTLINE

Key theme: Devotion to the Lord is like faithfulness in marriage. Idolatry is like adultery.

Key verse: Hosea 2:20

I. ISRAEL'S UNFAITHFULNESS DESCRIBED. 1–3

God is gracious. 1:1–2:1
God is holy. 2:2-13
God is love. 2:14–3:5

II. ISRAEL'S SINS DENOUNCED. 4–7

Ignorance. 4:1-11
Idolatry. 4:12–5:15
Insincerity. 6:1–7:16

III. ISRAEL'S JUDGMENT DETERMINED. 8–10

The Assyrian invasion. 8
The nation scattered. 9
Reaping what they have sown. 10

IV. ISRAEL'S RESTORATION DECLARED. 11–14

God's past mercies. 11
God's present disciplines. 12–13
God's future promises. 14

CONTENTS

CHAPTER ONE
YOU MARRIED A WHAT?
HOSEA 1–3

Prophets sometimes do strange things. For three years, Isaiah embarrassed people by walking the streets dressed like a prisoner of war. For several months, Jeremiah carried a yoke on his shoulders. The prophet Ezekiel acted like a little boy and "played war," and once he used a haircut as a theological object lesson. When his wife suddenly died, Ezekiel even turned that painful experience into a sermon.[1]

Why did these men do these peculiar things?

"These peculiar things" were really acts of mercy. The people of God had become deaf to God's voice and were no longer paying attention to His covenant. The Lord called His servants to do these strange things—these "action sermons"—in hopes that the people would wake up and listen to what they had to say. Only then could the nation escape divine discipline and judgment.

But no prophet preached a more painful "action sermon" than Hosea. He was instructed to marry a prostitute named Gomer who subsequently bore him three children, and he wasn't even sure the last two children were fathered by him. Then Gomer left him for another man, and Hosea had the humiliating responsibility of buying back his own wife.

What was this all about? It was a vivid picture of what the people of Israel had done to their God by prostituting themselves to idols and committing "spiritual adultery." Since God's people today face the same temptation (James 4:4), we need to heed what Hosea wrote for his people. Each of the persons in this drama—Hosea, Gomer, and the three children—teach us important spiritual lessons about the God whom Israel was disobeying and grieving.

1. The Children: God Is Gracious (Hosea 1:1–2:1)

The times (Hosea 1:1). Hosea names four kings of Judah and only one king of Israel, Jeroboam II. The kings of Judah, of course, belonged to David's dynasty, the only dynasty the Lord accepted (1 Kings 11:36; 15:4). The kings of Israel were a wicked lot who followed the sins of Israel's first king, Jeroboam I, and refused to repent and turn to God (2 Kings 13:6)

After Jeroboam II died, his son Zechariah reigned only six months and was assassinated by his successor Shallum who himself was assassinated after reigning only one month. Menahem reigned for ten years; his son Pekahiah ruled two years before being killed by Pekah who was able to keep the throne for twenty years. He was slain by Hoshea, who reigned for ten years, the last of the kings of Israel. During his evil reign, the nation was conquered by Assyria, the Jews intermingled with the foreigners the Assyrians brought into the land, and the result was a mixed race known as the Samaritans.

What a time to be serving the Lord! Murder, idolatry, and immorality were rampant in the land, and nobody seemed to be interested in hearing the Word of the Lord! On top of that, God told His prophet to get married and raise a family!

The marriage (Hosea 1:2). Here we meet a bit of a problem because not every Bible student agrees on the kind of woman Hosea married. Hosea either married a pure woman who later became a prostitute, or he married a prostitute who bore him three children.[2]

In the Old Testament, prostitution is symbolic of idolatry and unfaithfulness to God (Jer. 2–3; Ezek. 16; 23). Since the Jews were idolatrous from the beginning (Josh. 24:2-3, 14), it seems likely that Gomer would have to be a prostitute when she married Hosea; for this would best symbolize Israel's relationship to the Lord. God called Israel in the idolatry; He "married" them at Mt. Sinai when they accepted His covenant (Ex. 19-21); and then He grieved over them when they forsook Him for the false gods of the land of Canaan. Like Gomer, Israel began as idolater, "married" Jehovah, and eventually returned to her idolatry.

If Hosea had married a pure woman who later became unfaithful, "wife of whoredoms" in 1:2 has to mean "a wife prone to harlotry who will commit it later" but this seems to be a strained reading of the verse.[3] But could God ask His faithful servant to marry a defiled woman? Why not? We might as well ask, "Could God permit Ezekiel's wife to die?" Though marrying a prostitute might not be the safest step to take, such marriages were forbidden only to priests (Lev. 21:7). Salmon married Rahab the harlot who became the great-grandmother of King David and an ancestress of Jesus Christ (Matt. 1:4-5).

The names (Hosea 1:3-9). As with Isaiah's two sons (Isa. 7:3 and 8:3), and numerous other people in Scripture, Gomer's three children were given meaningful names selected by the Lord.

The first child, a son, was called Jezreel (Hosea 1:4-5), which means "God sows" or "God scatters." Jezreel was a city in the tribe of Isaachar, near Mt. Gilboa, and is associated with the drastic judgment that Jehu executed on the family of Ahab (2 Kings 9–10; and see 1 Kings 21:21-24 and 2 Kings 9:6-10). So zealous was Jehu to purge the land of Ahab's evil descendants that he murdered far more people than the Lord commanded, including King Ahaziah of Judah and forty-two of his relatives (9:27-10:14).

Through the birth of Hosea's son, God announced that He would avenge the innocent blood shed by Jehu and put an end to Jehu's dynasty in Israel. This was fulfilled in 752 B.C. when Zechariah was assassinated, the great-great-grandson of Jehu and the last of his dynasty to reign. (See 2 Kings 10:30.) God also announced that the whole kingdom of Israel would come to an end with the defeat of her army, which occurred in 724.

The second child was a daughter named Lo-ruhamah (Hosea 1:6-7), which means "unpitied" or "not loved." God had loved His people and proved it in many ways, but now He would withdraw that love and no longer show them mercy. The expression of God's love is certainly unconditional, but our enjoyment of that love is conditional and depends on our faith and obedience. (See Deut. 7:6-12 and 2 Cor. 6:14–7:1.) God would allow the Assyrians to swallow up the Northern Kingdom, but He would protect the Southern Kingdom of Judah (Isa. 36–37; 2 Kings 19).

Lo-ammi (Hosea 1:8-9) was the third child, a son, and his name means "not My people." Not only would God remove His mercy from His people, but He would also renounce the covenant He had made with them. It was like a man divorcing his wife and turning his back on her, or like a father rejecting his own son (See Ex. 4:22 and Hosea 11:1).

The new names (Hosea 1:10–2:1). Here is where the grace of God comes in, for God will one day change these names.[4] "Not my people" will become "My people," "unloved" will become "My loved one." These new names reflect the nation's new relationship to God, for all of them will be "the sons of the living God."[5] Judah and Israel will unite as one nation and will submit to God's ruler, and the centuries' old division will be healed.

Instead of "Jezreel" being a place of slaughter and judgment, it will be a place of sowing where God will joyfully sow His people in their own land and cause them to prosper. Today, the Jews are sown throughout the Gentile world (Zech. 10:9), but one day God will plant them in their own land and restore to them their glory. As God promised to Abraham, Israel will become like the sand on the seashore. (Gen. 22:17).

When will these gracious promises be fulfilled for the Jews? When they recognize their Messiah at His return, trust Him, and experience His cleansing (Zech. 12:10–13:1). Then they will enter into their kingdom, and the promises of the prophets will be fulfilled (Isa. 11–12; 32; 35; Jer. 30–31; Ezek. 37; Amos 9:11-15).

The three children teach us about the grace of God. Now we'll consider the lesson that Gomer teaches us.

2. Gomer: God Is Holy (Hosea 2:2-13)

Hosea is preeminently the prophet of love, but unlike some teachers today, he doesn't minimize the holiness of God. We're told that "God is love" (1 John 4:8, 16), but we're also reminded that "God is light, and in Him is no darkness at all" (1:5). God's love is a holy love, not a sentimental feeling that condones sin and pampers sinners.

The prophet focuses on three particular sins: idolatry (spiritual adultery), ingratitude, and hypocrisy.

Idolatry (Hosea 2:2-5a). God speaks to the children and tells them to rebuke their mother for her unfaithfulness. Israel was guilty of worshiping the gods of the pagan nations around them, especially the Canaanite rain god, Baal. Whenever there was a drought or a famine in the land, the Jews repeatedly turned to Baal for help instead of turning to the Lord. (See 1 Kings 18–19.) Pagan worship involved sensual fertility rites; and for these rites, both male and female prostitutes were provided. In a literal as well as a symbolic sense, idolatry meant prostitution. [6]

Since the people were acting like prostitutes, God would treat them like prostitutes and shame them publicly. He would no longer claim the nation as His wife because she had broken the solemn marriage covenant and consorted with idols. According to Hebrew law, adultery was a capital crime, punishable by death, but God announced that He would discipline Israel and not destroy her.[7]

Unfaithfulness to the Lord is a serious sin, just as unfaithfulness to one's mate is a serious sin. The man who says he's 90 percent faithful to his wife isn't faithful at all. As Israel was tempted to forsake God for idols, the church is tempted to turn to the world system that hates God and wants nothing to do with God.

We must be careful not to love the world (1 John 2:15-17), be friendly with the world (James 4:4), become spotted by the world (1:27), or conform to the world (Rom. 12:2). Each believer and each local church must remain true to Jesus Christ the Bridegroom until He returns to take His bride to the heavenly wedding (2 Cor. 11:1-4; Eph. 5:22-33; Rev. 19:6-9).

Ingratitude (Hosea 2:5b-9). Instead of thanking the true God for His blessings of food, water, and clothing, the nation thanked the false gods and used those gifts to serve idols. What ingratitude! God provided rain for the land (Deut. 11:8-17), but the Israelites gave the credit to Baal, the rain god. Because it is God who gives us power to earn wealth (8:17-18) and enjoy the blessings of life (1 Tim. 6:17), we must thank Him and acknowledge His goodness. What wickedness it is to take the gifts of God and use them to worship false gods!

God had every right to abandon His people, but instead, He chose to discipline them. The nation would chase after false gods, but Jehovah would block their paths and confuse their plans so that they would stumble on the way. He would take back His gifts and leave the nation as naked as a newborn baby and as barren as a desert.

It's remarkable how many times God's people are admonished in Scripture to be thankful. I've noted at least fifteen places where we're commanded to "give thanks to the Lord," and Psalm 100:4 and Colossians 3:15 both admonish us to be thankful. Both Jesus and Paul set the example by giving thanks often to the Lord for His blessings. One of the first steps toward rebellion against God is a refusal to give God thanks for His mercies (Rom. 1:21). God will not allow us to enjoy His gifts and at the same time ignore the Giver, for this is the essence of idolatry.

Hypocrisy (Hosea 2:10-13). The people still enjoyed celebrating the Hebrew festivals, but in their hearts, they gave the glory to Baal and the other false gods that they worshiped. Unfortunately, the same sin was being committed by their brothers and sisters in the temple of Jerusalem (Isa. 1). How easy it is to attend divine services and go through the motions of worshiping God when our hearts are really far from Him (Matt. 15:7-9).

But the truth would eventually come out, for God would judge His people and expose their hypocrisy. He would take away their blessings and abandon them to their sins, for one of the greatest judgments God can inflict on any people is to let them have their own way. God is holy and will not permit His people to enjoy sin for long or to live on substitutes. Eight times in the Bible we read, "Be holy, for I am holy"; God means what He says.

3. Hosea: God Is Love (Hosea 2:14–3:5)

The three children have taught us about the grace of God, and Gomer has taught us about the holiness of God. Now Hosea will teach us about the love of God.

"Hosea takes his place among the greatest lovers of all the ages," wrote Kyle M. Yates. "His love was so strong that the vilest behavior could not dull it. . . . Gomer broke his heart but she made it possible for him to give to the world a picture of the heart of the divine Lover."[8]

God's love promised (Hosea 2:14-23). The repeated "I will" statements in these verses assure us that God has a wonderful future planned for the Jewish people. Let's note His promises.

He begins with *"I will allure"* (v. 14). God doesn't try to force His people to love him. Instead, He "allures" (woos) them as a lover woos his beloved, seeking her hand in marriage. Certainly God spoke tenderly to His people through His Word and through the manifold blessings He bestowed on them in their land. Just as He led her through the wilderness and "married" her at Sinai, so God will meet His beloved in the wilderness in the last days and lead her into her land and her glorious kingdom.

The next promise is *"I will give"* (v. 15) as the Lord guarantees a return to their land and a restoration of their prosperity. Once again, the Lord changes the meaning of a name, this time, "the Valley of Achor." To Israel, the Valley of Achor ("trouble") was the place where Achan stole from God and brought shameful defeat to Israel's army (Josh. 7), but that memory would be erased from their minds. The valley would become a "door of hope" through which Israel would enter into a new life. The experience would produce singing, as when Israel escaped from Egypt and saw her enemies defeated before their very eyes (Ex. 14–15). "And Sharon shall be a fold of flocks, and the valley of Achor a place for the herds to lie down in, for My people that have sought Me" (Isa. 65:10). This is an Old Testament version of Romans 8:28, for only the Lord can take defeat and shame and turn it into victory and glory.

God's third promise is *"I will take away"* (Hosea 2:16-17). God declares an end to idolatry among His people. They would have a new vocabulary and the "baals" would never be named again. "Ishi" means "my husband" in Hebrew and "Baali" means "my master." Both terms were used by Jewish wives when addressing their husbands, but in the future kingdom, every Jew will call God "my Husband," for the divine marriage relationship will be restored. Israel will no longer prostitute herself before idols, but will love and serve the true living God.

God's fourth promise is *"I will betroth"* (vv. 18-20). God's wooing of Israel will result in her yielding to Him and entering into a covenant relationship that would never end. This new covenant will include a restored creation (see Gen. 9:1-10; Rom. 8:18-22) and peace among the nations. Among the "wedding gifts" will be such blessings as righteousness, justice, love, compassion, and faithfulness—everything that Israel had lacked during her years of separation from her Husband, Jehovah God.

The fifth promise is *"I will respond"* (Hosea 2:21-22, NIV), (KJV, "I will hear"). These two verses describe a tremendous cosmic conversation in which the Lord speaks to the heavens and the earth and they respond to each other and bring blessings to God's people. The heavens send the rain, the earth brings forth the produce, and the Lord sends His rich blessings. It's the picture of a restored universe where sin and death no longer reign (Rom. 5:12-21).

The final promise in this text is *"I will plant"* (Hosea 2:23, NIV). The word "Jezreel" means "God sows." The image is that of God sowing His people in their land the way a farmer sows seed. He says to them, "You are My people!" They respond, "You are my God!" (NIV) This relates back to the names of the children that God in His grace had changed.

God's love pictured (Hosea 3:1-5). This is another "action sermon" as Hosea reclaims his estranged wife and brings her home to himself. Gomer had left Hosea and was living with a lover, another picture of the way Israel had treated the Lord. Hosea had to buy her back at a cost of fifteen pieces of silver (half the price of a slave, Ex. 21:32) and about ten bushels of barley. This was not an exorbitant price, but she had cheapened herself by her sins. We need to remember that God has purchased us at the tremendous cost of the precious blood of His only Son (1 Peter 1:18-19).

Hosea 3:3 suggests that Hosea didn't immediately enter into intimate relations with Gomer, but waited awhile to make sure she would be true to him. It's also possible that he wanted to make sure she wasn't pregnant with another man's child. But even this has a spiritual message attached to it: Israel today, though purchased by their Messiah (John 11:47-52; Isa. 53:8), has not yet returned to the Lord.

Israel today is without a king because she rejected her King and therefore has no kingdom. "We will not have this man to reign over us" (Luke 19:14). "We have no king but Caesar" (John 19:15). She has no prince because there is no reigning dynasty in Israel. All the records were destroyed when the Romans captured Jerusalem in A.D. 70, and nobody can prove to which tribe he or she belongs.

The Israelites have no sacrifice because they have no temple, altar, or priesthood. They don't have a pillar (image) or a household god (teraphim), because idolatry was purged from their culture during the Babylonian Captivity. (Like the Gentiles, they may have other kinds of idols in their hearts!) They lack an ephod (Ex. 28:1-14), because they have no high priest. The only High Priest God will acknowledge is the interceding Son of God in heaven.

But there is an "afterward"! Israel won't stay "without," for she will see her Messiah, repent of her sins, and say, "You are my God!" They will enter into that blessed relationship in which the Lord says, "You are My people!" This will occur in "the latter days" when the messianic King sits on David's throne and judges righteously (Matt. 19:28; Luke 1:32-33).

The key word is "return" (Hosea 3:5), a word that's used twenty-two times in Hosea's prophecy. When Israel repents and returns to the Lord, then the Lord will return to bless Israel (2:7-8). God has returned to His place and left Israel to herself (5:15) until she seeks Him and says, "Come, and let us return to the Lord" (6:1, NKJV).

This is Hosea's message: "O Israel, return to the Lord thy God. . . . Take with you words, and turn to the Lord: say unto Him, 'Take away all iniquity, and receive us graciously'" (14:1-2).

That prayer is good for any sinner, Jew or Gentile. To summarize:

God is gracious, and no matter what "name" our birth has given to us, He can change it and give us a new beginning. Even the "valley of trouble" can become a "door of hope."

God is holy and He must deal with sin. The essence of idolatry is enjoying the gifts but not honoring the Giver. To live for the world is to break God's heart and commit "spiritual adultery."

God is love and promises to forgive and restore all who repent and return to Him. He promises to bless all who trust him.

CHAPTER TWO
WHAT WILL I DO WITH YOU?
HOSEA 4–10

"Indeed I tremble for my country when I reflect that God is just."

Thomas Jefferson wrote those words about the United States of America, and as the Prophet Hosea surveyed the kingdom of Israel, he would have agreed. From his bitter experience with his wife, Hosea knew that sin not only breaks the heart of God, but also offends the holiness of God, for "righteousness and justice are the foundation of [His] throne" (Ps. 89:14, NKJV).

God wanted to forgive the sins of His people and restore their fellowship with Him, but they weren't ready. They not only would not repent, they wouldn't even admit that they had sinned! So God conducted a trial and brought them to the bar of justice. It's a basic spiritual principle that until people experience the guilt of conviction, they can't enjoy the glory of conversion.

1. God Convenes the Court (Hosea 4:1-5:15)

Just as Hosea had experienced a quarrel with his wife, so God had a quarrel with His estranged wife, the people of Israel. But it wasn't a personal quarrel; it was an official controversy: "The Lord has a charge to bring against you who live in the land" (4:1, NIV). The picture of God bringing men and nations to trial in His courtroom is a familiar one in Scripture (see Isa. 1:13; Jer. 2:9, 29; 25:31; Micah 6:2; Rom. 3:19). "Rise up, O Judge of the earth; pay back to the proud what they deserve" (Ps. 94:2, NIV).

The Judge read the charges to the accused as they stood before him.

The nation as a whole (Hosea 4:1b-3). The basis for judgment was the holy law of God, the covenant God made with Israel at Mt. Sinai. "All that the Lord has spoken we will do," was their promise (Ex. 19:8), but that promise was soon broken. Just as Gomer didn't take her marriage vows seriously but went to live with another man, so Israel reneged on her promises to God and turned to pagan idols. There was no faithfulness (truth) in the land, no loyal love to the Lord.

When people reject God's covenant, they begin to exploit each other, for the Ten Commandments deal with our relationship with our neighbor as well as with the Lord. If we love the Lord, we will also love our neighbor (Matt. 22:34-40; Rom. 13:8-10). But there was no mercy in the land, no love for one's neighbor, no compassion for the poor and needy. People were falsehearted toward God and hardhearted toward one another.

The basic sin was ignorance; there was "no knowledge of God in the land." "My people are destroyed for lack of knowledge" (Hosea 4:6).[1] This means much more than knowledge about God; it refers to a personal knowledge of God. The Hebrew word describes a husband's most intimate relationship with his wife (Gen. 4:1; 19:8). To know God is to have a personal relationship with Him through faith in Jesus Christ (John 17:3).

The Judge pointed to the Ten Commandments (Ex. 20:1-17) and reminded the people of how they had violated His law by pronouncing curses, telling lies, murdering, stealing, and committing adultery. As a result, they had brought suffering to themselves, to the land, and even to the animals. God's covenant promise was that He would bless the land if the people obeyed Him, but that He would punish the land if they disobeyed (Lev. 26; Deut. 27–28).

The land belonged to God (Lev. 25:23) and the sins of the people polluted the land (18:25-28; 26:32-33). Natural calamities like droughts, famines, and the devastations of war were sometimes sent by God to discipline His people. Whether to bless or to judge, God always keeps His covenant promises.[2]

The priests (Hosea 4:4-14). When Jeroboam I set up his own religious system in Israel, many of the true priests fled to Judah; so the king ordained priests of his own choosing (2 Chron. 11:13-15). Of course, these counterfeit priests knew neither the Lord nor His law. They were primarily interested in having an easy job that would provide them with food, clothing, and pleasure, especially opportunities to be with the shrine prostitutes. "Don't blame the people for what's happening," Hosea said to the corrupt priests, "because they're only following your bad example!"

When you obey God's word, you walk in the light and don't stumble (Prov. 3:21-26; 4:14-19), but when you reject the Word, you walk in the darkness and can't find your way (Isa. 8:20). Worldly and ignorant spiritual leaders produce worldly and ignorant people, and this brings destruction to the land. The phrase "your mother" in Hosea 4:5 refers to the nation of Israel (2:2, 5). As goes spiritual leadership, so goes the church; as goes the church, so goes morality; and as goes morality, so goes the nation. God's people are both salt and light in society (Matt. 5:13-16); when they are corrupt, society becomes corrupt.

God rejected Jeroboam's man-made religion[3] and warned the priests that their easy jobs would soon end in disaster. Instead of seeking God's will, they consulted their idols.[4] The more the people sinned, the more food the priests enjoyed. The more shrines the people built, the more they and the priests could indulge in lustful pleasures as they participated in the fertility rites. But the rites wouldn't accomplish anything, because God would cause the population and the produce to decrease instead of increase. Furthermore, the priests' own daughters and daughters-in-law would become shrine prostitutes and commit adultery![5] Their sins would bring judgment to their families and to the land.

The spectators in the court (Hosea 4:15-19). Now the prophet turns to the people of the Southern Kingdom of Judah who were carefully watching events in Israel. Hosea's warning is clear: don't meddle in the affairs of Israel because their doom is sure! "Ephraim is joined to idols: let him alone" (v. 17). The people of Judah were supposed to worship in Jerusalem and not go to the hill shrines in Israel or to the special shrines at Gilgal[6] and Bethel. (Hosea calls Bethel "Bethaven," which means "house of evil or deceit." Bethel means "house of God.") Israel was like a stubborn heifer, not a submissive lamb; and God's whirlwind of judgment would sweep the kingdom away.

Priests, rulers, and people (Hosea 5:1-7). This is a summation of the evidence that the Judge applied to all the accused. He condemned the leaders for trapping innocent people and exploiting them. There was no justice in the land. They were sinking deep in sin and lacked the power to repent and turn back to God, for their sins had paralyzed them.

What was the cause? They did not know the Lord (5:4; 6:3) and their arrogance only led them to stumble and fall (5:5; Prov. 16:18). Even if they came to the Lord with entire flocks and herds to sacrifice, God would not meet them; for He had withdrawn Himself from them. He rejected their illegitimate children,[7] and their monthly feasts would soon become funerals.

The sentence is pronounced (Hosea 5:8-15). There could be only one verdict: "Guilty!" A day of judgment was coming when the cites of Israel would be conquered by the invading Assyrian army and the citizens taken into capitivity. "Ephraim will be laid waste on the day of reckoning" (5:9, NIV).[8] The inner decay of the nation was like the slow hidden destruction caused by a moth (v. 12), but the coming of the Assyrians was like the sudden open attack of a lion (v. 14). Both were unavoidable and both brought ruin.

Israel and Judah were weak, sick nations (Isa. 1:5-6; Jer. 30:12-13), but instead of turning to the Lord for healing, both of them turned to the king of Assyria for help (Hosea 5:13).[9] They needed prayer and true repentance, but instead, they trusted politics and useless treaties. All the Lord could do was withdraw and wait for them to seek His face in truth and humility.

2. God Rejects the Appeal (Hosea 6:1–7:16)

It isn't unusual for the accused in a trial to express regret and remorse for what they've done and to ask for another chance. That's just what Israel did, but God anticipated their hypocritical subterfuge and exposed not only their duplicity but the sinful way they had treated their Lord.

The nation's false repentance (Hosea 6:1-3). When you read these words, you get the impression that the nation is sincerely repenting and seeking the Lord, but when you read what God says, you see how shallow their "confession" really was. "They do not return to the Lord their God, nor seek Him" (7:10). "They have spoken lies against Me" (v. 13). "They return, but not to the Most High" (v. 16). What went wrong with this "confession"?

To begin with, their concern was for healing and not for cleansing. They saw their nation in difficulty and wanted God to "make things right," but they did not come with broken hearts and surrendered wills. They wanted happiness, not holiness, a change of circumstances, but not a change in character. Many times in my own ministry I've met people in trouble who treated God like a celestial lifeguard who should rescue them from danger but not deliver them from their sins. They shed tears of remorse over their suffering, but not tears of repentance over their sin.

Furthermore, the people of Israel thought that the remedy would work quickly: "After two days will He revive us; in the third day He will raise us up" (6:2). What blind optimism! They were like the false prophets in Jeremiah's day who offered the nation superficial remedies but never got to the heart of the problem (Jer. 6:14; 8:11-16). They were like physicians putting suntan lotion on a cancerous tumor instead of calling for drastic surgery. Expecting a "quick fix" is one of the marks of an unrepentant heart that doesn't want to pay the price for deep cleansing (Ps. 51:6-7).

There is a third evidence of their shallowness: they saw forgiveness and restoration as a "mechanical" thing that was guaranteed and not as a relational matter that involved getting right with God. To paraphrase Hosea 6:3, "If we seek Him, His blessing is sure to come just as the dawn comes each morning and the rains come each spring and winter." This is formula religion, like getting a candy bar out of a vending machine: put in the money, push the button, and out comes the candy. The Christian life is a relationship with God, and the relationships aren't based on cut-and-dried formulas.

One more evidence of their shallowness is the fact that they depended on religious words rather than righteous deeds. When we truly repent, our words will come from broken hearts and they will cost us something. Hosea considered words to be like "spiritual sacrifices" brought to the Lord (14:2), and we must not give Him something cheap (2 Sam. 24:24). Words can reveal or conceal, depending on the honesty and humility of the sinner.[10] We must take to heart the warning in Ecclesiastes 5:1-2.

The nation's true condition (Hosea 6:4–7:16). In a series of vivid similes and metaphors, Hosea revealed the true character of the people of Israel.

Their love for the Lord was like a morning cloud and the dew (6:4-11). Early in the morning, the dew looks like sparkling jewels, but as soon as the sun comes up, the dew is gone. Israel's devotion to the Lord was temporary, lovely but not lasting. To give some substance to their faith, God sent them His prophets with the Word of God which is like a penetrating sword (Eph. 6:17) and a flash of lightning (Hosea 6:5), but the people turned a deaf ear.

God doesn't want our relationship with Him to be one of shallow, transient feelings and empty words and rituals, hearts that are enthusiastic one day and frigid the next. "For I desired mercy [loyal love], and not sacrifice, and the knowledge of God more than burnt offerings" (v. 6). A superficial ritual can never take the place of sincere love and faithful obedience (1 Sam. 15:22-23; Amos 5:21-24; Micah 6:6-8; Matt 9:13; 12:7).

"But like Adam they have transgressed the covenant" (Hosea 6:7, NASB).[11] God promised Adam His blessings if he obeyed His commands, but Adam deliberately destroyed and plunged the human race into sin and death (Rom. 5:12-21; 1 Cor. 15:21-22). God promised Israel the blessings of the Promised Land if they would obey Him (Deut. 28), but they broke the covenant and suffered the consequences. For both Israel and Judah, God had appointed a harvest, and they would reap just what they had sown (Gal. 6:7-8).

Their lust was like an overheated oven (Hosea 7:1-7). It's probable that the last statement in 6:11 should be joined with 7:1 to read, "When I would have returned the captivity of My people, when I would have healed Israel." What prevented God from helping His distressed people? They wanted Him to act on their terms and not according to the condition of His holy covenant. They thought they could get away with their many sins, but God saw them all and remembered them (v. 2; contrast Heb. 10:16-17).

Their passion for sin was like a fire in an oven: bank the fire at night, and it will be ready to blaze out in the morning. The oven was so hot that the baker could ignore it all night and know it would be ready for baking his bread in the morning. The "fuel" for the fire was wine, for alcohol and sin often go together.

Hosea describes a palace celebration during which the king and his officers get drunk, and this gives the king's enemies opportunity to overthrow him and even kill him. Remember, Israel had five kings in thirteen years, and four kings were assassinated in twenty years. From Jeroboam I, the first king of Israel, to Hoshea, the last king, there were nine different dynasties! Because the leaders were far from the Lord, the political situation was confused and corrupt.

The third simile is that of a half-baked cake (Hosea 7:8). The nomadic peoples of the East baked their bread on hot rocks. If the dough wasn't turned, one side of the loaf would be burned and the other side uncooked. Instead of remaining separate from the nations, Israel mixed with the nations and became like them. Because of her compromising political posture, the nation was "burned" by Assyria on the one hand and left uncooked on the other.

When it comes to our relationship with the Lord, we must be thorough and not "half-baked." His gracious work must permeate our whole being so that heart, mind, and strength are all devoted to Him. Compromise with the world leads to unbalanced conduct and immature character.

Continuing the theme of compromise, Hosea pictures Israel as a man getting gray and not knowing it (vv. 9-10). By mixing with the nations and ignoring the Lord, the nation was secretly losing her strength, like someone getting older and weaker but in her pride refusing to admit it. This is the tragedy of undetected losses that quietly lead to ultimate failures. Samson made this mistake (Jud. 16:20) and so did the church in Laodicea (Rev. 3:17). Israel saw her political strategy failing, but the leaders still refused to turn to the Lord. "The pride of Israel" (Hosea 7:10; see 5:5) refers to Israel's national glory which had greatly eroded since the days of David and Solomon. Selfish politicians and corrupt priests had brought the nation to ruin.

In their political policies, the Israelites were like a silly dove (7:11-12). First they turned to Egypt for help and then to Assyria, and both nations proved to be false allies (5:13; 8:8-10; 12:1). If the leaders had listened to the prophets, they would have known that Assyria would one day invade the land (9:3; 10:5-6; Isa. 7:18–8:10). God warned that Israel's "flying here and there" would come to an end when He caught them in His net and gave them to the King of Assyria. God is in control of the nations, but His people would not obey Him.

According to the covenant God had with His people, the Jews could trade with the other nations, but they were not to enter into political alliances that would compromise their obedience to the Lord. "I see a people who live apart and do not consider themselves one of the nations" (Num. 23:9, NIV). "You are to be holy to me because I, the Lord, am holy, and I have set you apart from the nations to be my own" (Lev. 20:26, NIV). Solomon used many wives to form alliances with other nations, and this was the beginning of the nation's downfall (1 Kings 11:1ff).

The final image is a faulty bow (Hosea 7:13-16), because God couldn't depend on Israel to be faithful. (This image is also used in Ps. 78:57.) God had called Israel and trained them, so they should have been able to "hit the target." But because they had strayed from the Lord, rebelled against Him, lied to Him (in their feigned repentance), and refused to call upon Him, so they could not win the battle.

As we review these images, we might take inventory of our own devotion to the Lord. How lasting is it? How deep is it? How strong is it? How serious is it? How dependable is it?

3. God Pronounces the Sentence (Hosea 8:1-10:15)

For the second time, Hosea calls for the trumpet to be blown (8:1; 5:8). According to Numbers 10, the Jews used trumpets to announce special occasions, to sound alarms, to gather the people for assemblies, and to proclaim war. This call was a trumpet of alarm because the enemy was coming and God was giving His people opportunity to repent. Hosea again used a number of familiar images to show the people what God would do to them because of their sin.

The eagle (Hosea 8:1-6). "The house of the Lord" refers to the nation of Israel, for the people were God's dwelling-place (9:15; Ex. 15:17; Num. 12:7). The Assyrian eagle was about to swoop down and destroy God's house because the nation was given over to idolatry, and the leaders were not seeking God's will in their decisions. They made kings and removed kings to satisfy their own desires, and they manufactured gods (especially the golden calves at Bethel and Dan) that could not help them.[12]

Sowing and reaping (Hosea 8:7). The concept of sowing and reaping as it relates to conduct is often used in Scripture (Job 4:8; Prov. 22:8; Jer. 12:13; Gal. 6:7-8), and Hosea used it twice (Hosea 8:7; 10:12-13). In their idolatry and political alliances, the Israelites were trying to sow seeds that would produce a good harvest, but they were only sowing the wind—vanity, nothing—and would reap the whirlwind. Nothing could stop the force of the Assyrian army. The harvest would be more powerful than the seed!

The sowing/reaping image continues with the picture of a blighted crop of grain. The rulers of Israel thought their worship of Baal and their foreign alliances would produce a good crop of peace and prosperity; but when the time came for the harvest, there was nothing to reap. And even where heads of grain did appear, the enemy reaped the harvest and Israel gained nothing. In the image of the wind, Hosea said, "You will reap far more than you sowed, and it will be destructive!" In the image of the grain, he said, "You will reap nothing at all, and your enemies will get the benefit of all the promises you made."

Worthless pottery (Hosea 8:8). There was no grain for Israel to swallow, but she herself would be "swallowed up" by Assyria. She was a useless vessel "in which no one delights" (NASB). Their compromise had so cheapened them that Israel was of no value to the community of nations. Nobody feared them, nobody courted them, nobody wanted them.

A stupid donkey (Hosea 8:9a) Israel wanted to be a part of the alliances that were forming to fight Assyria, but she was actually very much alone. She was like a dumb animal that had lost its way in the wilderness. Israel had forsaken her God, and she had been forsaken by her allies, so she was abandoned to face a terrible future alone.

A prostitute (Hosea 8:9b-10). In negotiating with the Gentile nations for protection, Ephraim (Israel) acted like a common prostitute selling herself for money. Israel's kings paid tribute to the king of Assyria and also sent gifts to Egypt (12:1). Instead of being faithful to her Husband, Jehovah God, Israel prostituted herself to the Gentile nations—and lost everything. God promised to gather them together for judgment and they would "waste away" (NIV) under the ruthless hand of the Assyrian king.

Egyptian bondage (Hosea 8:11-9:9). Hosea mentions Egypt thirteen times in his book, and these references fall into three distinct categories: past—the Exodus of the Jews from Egypt (2:15; 11:1; 12:9, 13; 13:4); present—Israel's unholy alliances with Egypt

(7:11, 16; 12:1); future—Egypt as a symbol of their impending bondage to Assyria (8:13; 9:3, 6; 11:5, 11). Three times in this section, the prophet announces, "They shall go to Egypt" (8:13; 9:3, 6); but 11:5 makes it clear that "Egypt" is a symbol for Assyrian bondage: "He shall not return to the land of Egypt; but the Assyrian shall be his king" (NKJV).

The prophet contrasts the past Exodus from the bondage of Egypt with the impending "exodus" into bondage of Assyria, the new "Egypt." When the Jews left Egypt, they had not yet received the Law nor did they have the tabernacle and its system of sacrifices. But now the Jews had heard the Law for centuries, and the temple had been standing since Solomon's time. Yet they ignored the Law, and the priesthood became corrupt. The NIV catches the irony in 8:11, "Though Ephraim built many altars for sin offerings, these have become altars for sinning."

Instead of trusting the Lord to protect her from Assyria, Israel fortified her towns and sought help from foreign nations, and from a spiritual point of view, this was like prostitution. (During the harvest season, prostitutes frequented the threshing floors where the men slept to guard the grain.) The harvest season was a time of great joy (Isa. 9:3), but there would be no joy in Israel. And when the people ended up in a foreign land, everything would be unclean to them, but they were an unclean people anyway, so what difference would it make?

Agriculture (Hosea 9:10-10:10). God reviews the history of His relationship with the Jews. You don't find grapes in the desert, but if you did, it would thrill you. That's how God felt when He called Israel. The early fruit of the fig tree is especially good, and Israel was special to the Lord. But this joyful experience didn't last, for King Balak gave Israel her first taste of Baal worship, and the nation indulged in idolatry and immorality with its neighbors (Num. 25).

God planted His people in a special land, but they polluted the land with their idols (Hosea 9:13). The more prosperous they became, the more they turned away from God. Now they must suffer a bitter harvest for their sins, they and their children.[13] The nation is blighted, having no roots and bearing no fruits. She was a "spreading vine" (10:1, niv), but now she is without fruit.[14] These agricultural images remind us that we reap what we sow.

There's an interesting agricultural image in 10:4, "Therefore lawsuits spring up like poisonous weeds in a plowed field" (NIV). People couldn't trust one another and few were keeping their promises; therefore, they had to sue one another to get what they deserved. The multiplying of laws and lawsuits is one evidence that integrity and credibility are vanishing from society.

The final agricultural image is in verse 8: the idolatrous shrines will become nothing but clumps and weeds, and the people will beg the Lord to destroy them quickly (v. 8; see Luke 23:30 and Rev. 6:16).

Twice in this passage, Hosea mentions "the days of Gibeah" (Hosea 9:9; 10:9). The reference is to the awful sins of the men of Gibeah and the tragic civil war that followed (Jud. 19-21). The men of Gibeah practiced unnatural lust and killed an innocent woman in a gang rape episode. The city would not punish the offenders, so the whole nation attacked Benjamin and almost destroyed the tribe. In Hosea's day, all the ten tribes of Israel were practicing these abominable things, but God would judge them and they would reap what they had sown.[15]

The chapter closes (Hosea 10:11-15) by comparing Israel to a young heifer that enjoys treading out the grain because she can eat and work at the same time. But then she is yoked to another beast and forced to do the hard work of plowing. Israel's "salad days' were over and she would feel the Assyrian yoke.

In verse 12, the prophet gives one more appeal to the nation to repent and seek the Lord. "Fallow ground" is land that has lain idle and become hard and full of weeds. This appeal sounds like the preaching of John the Baptist: "Repent! Bear fruits worthy of repentance!" (Matt. 3:1-12) The plow of conviction must first break up hard hearts before the seed of the Word can be planted and the gracious rain be sent from heaving.

The nation did not repent, and judgment fell. In 722 B.C., the Assyrian army invaded the land, and the ten tribes as a nation vanished from the pages of history.[16]

Righteousness exalts a nation, but sin is a reproach to any people" (Prov. 14:34, NKJV).

"Blessed is the nation whose God is the Lord" (Ps. 33:12, NKJV).

CHAPTER THREE
LOVE SO AMAZING
HOSEA 11–14

How could Hosea's unfaithful wife Gomer ever question her husband's love? Didn't he demonstrate it by seeking her out, pleading with her to come home, and paying the price to set her free?

How could Israel ever question God's love and refuse to respond to it? After all, the nation had not only broken the Law of God; they had broken the heart of God. In the closing chapters of this book, Hosea reminded them of God's compassion for His people, and he did it by presenting three clear evidences of God's love.

1. God's Mercies in the Past (Hosea 11:1-12)

At least fourteen times in the Book of Deuteronomy, Moses used the word *remember.* Deuteronomy is Moses' farewell address to the new generation of Israelites as they were preparing to enter the Promised Land. But why would Moses ask these young people to look back when they were getting ready to move forward? Because a correct understanding of God's dealings in the past is the best way to be certain of success in the future. Philosopher George Santayana expressed this truth succinctly: "Those who do not remember the past are condemned to relive it."[1]

God's love demonstrated at the Exodus (Hosea 11:1-2). God sent Joseph ahead into Egypt to prepare the way for Jacob and his sons. What Joseph's brothers did to their brother was meant for evil, but God used it for good (Gen. 50:20). Because of Joseph, the people of Israel were kept alive during the severe famine and were able to multiply in the ensuing years. From this humble beginning, God formed a nation; Moses led that nation out of Egypt in great power and triumph (Ex. 12–15).

Hosea pictures the God of the Exodus as a tender father who freed his son from bondage. The emphasis here is not on Israel, the unfaithful wife, but on Israel, the ungrateful son. (For God as "Father" and Israel as a "son," see Ex. 4:22-23; Isa. 1:2-4; and Deut. 32:5). After all God did for His son, he will refuse to return His love or obey His will.

God's love demonstrated in the wilderness (Hosea 11:3-4). The loving father not only carried His son out of bondage, but He taught him to walk and tenderly cared for him during the wilderness journey. When a child stumbles and gets bruised, mother and father are there to give healing and encouragement, and that's what God did for His people. He taught them, healed them, and led them; He was careful to lead them as you would a child and not as you would an animal. He bound Himself to them with cords of love, not with bit and bridle (Ps. 32:8-9) or a galling yoke.

Read Hosea 11:1-4 again, but instead of noting what God did for Israel, notice how Israel treated God. Like spoiled children, they rebelled against their Father and turned to idols. God spoke to them through His prophets, but the more God called to Israel, the more they strayed from Him! They were happy to enjoy His gifts, but they didn't want to obey the Giver. He sought to lead them with ties of love, but they said, "Let us break their bands asunder, and cast away their cords from us" (Ps. 2:3, KJV).

Throughout history, whether Jewish or Gentile, human nature is pretty much the same, and all of us are prone to do what Israel did: enjoy God's blessings, but take God for granted. "My people are determined to turn from me" (Hosea 11:7, NIV). "Also, sinful nation, a people laden with iniquity, a brood of evildoers, children who are corrupters!" (Isa. 1:4, NKJV) God set them free and guided them to their inheritance, but within one generation after the death of Joshua, the nation turned to idolatry and forsook the Lord (Jud. 2:7ff).

God's love demonstrated by His long-suffering (Hosea 11:5-7). On more than one occasion, God could have destroyed the nation and started over again (Ex. 32:10), but He chose to be long-suffering. When the journey became difficult, the Jews wanted to go back to Egypt; they complained when they should have been praying and giving thanks for God's mercies.

We have already seen that some of the references to Egypt in this book refer to the "new bondage" in Assyria (Hosea 11:5). Israel refused to repent, so the nation had to go into captivity. They made plans without consulting God, so their defenses would fall before the invaders. The only time they called on God was when they were in trouble, and God graciously helped them; but now the end had come.

God's love demonstrated by His faithfulness to His promises (Hosea 11:8-9). What a revelation we have in 11:8 of the compassionate heart of God! According to Jewish law, a rebellious son was supposed to be turned over to the elders of the city and stoned to death (Deut. 21:18-21), but how could God do this to His beloved son, Israel? (Centuries later, His innocent, only-begotten Son would suffer for the sins of the whole world.) God destroyed the cities of the plain because of their sins (Gen. 18:16–19:29), and those people didn't have the same privileges of learning about God that Israel had. What right did Israel have to expect God to spare them, especially since they were sinning against a flood of light.

What motivated God to spare Israel from total destruction? Not only His deep compassion, but also His faithfulness to His covenant. "For I am God, and not man" (Hosea 11:9, KJV). "God is not a man, that He should lie, nor a son of man that He should repent. Has He said, and will He not do it? Or has He spoken, and will he not make it good?" (Num. 23:19)

God's covenant with Abraham (Gen. 12:1-3) is unconditional and will not change; therefore, the nation of Israel is preserved. But His covenant with Israel at Sinai had conditions attached, and if the people failed to meet those conditions, God was obligated to withdraw His blessings. Israel's possession of the land and its blessings is based on the Abrahamic Covenant, but their enjoyment of the land and its blessings is based on the Mosaic Covenant. God was faithful to both covenants: He preserved the nation, but He disciplined them for their sins.

God's love demonstrated by the hope of future restoration (Hosea 11:10-12). Often in Scripture you will find a declaration of judgment immediately followed by a promise of hope, and that's the case here. Hosea looks ahead to the end times when Israel will be gathered together from all the nations, brought to their own land, cleansed of their sins, and established in their kingdom. In the past, God roared like a lion when He judged the nation (5:14; 13:7, but in the future, His "roar" will call His people to come back to their land. Like birds turned loose from their cages, the people of Israel will swiftly fly to their own land, and God will "settle them in their homes" (11:11, NIV).

Meanwhile, God is long-suffering with His people, as He is with all sinners (2 Peter 3:9), even though they lie to Him and rebel against Him (Hosea 11:12). What Jesus said to Jerusalem in His day, God was saying through Hosea to the people of that day: "How often I wanted to gather your children together, as a hen gathers her chicks under her wings, but you were not willing!" (Matt 23:37, NKJV)

God's mercies in the past certainly proved His love, but Hosea offered a second evidence that God loved His people.

2. God's Disciplines in the Present (Hosea 12:1-13:16)

"For whom the Lord loves He chastens, and scourges every son whom He receives" (Heb. 12:6; Prov. 3:11-12). Chastening isn't a judge inflicting punishment on a criminal in order to uphold the law. Rather, chastening is a loving parent disciplining his or her child in order to perfect his character and build his endurance.[2] Punishment has to do with law, which is important, but chastening has to do with love, which is also important.

The need for discipline (Hosea 12:1). The Jewish people were living for vanity—"the wind"—and receiving no nourishment. The word translated "feed" means "to graze"; but whoever saw hungry sheep ignoring the green grass and chewing on the wind? The very idea is ridiculous, but that's the way God's people were living.

Israel was committing two sins: First, they were worshiping idols which are nothing, even less than nothing, and turning from the true God to live on empty substitutes. They were feeding on the wind. Second, they were depending for protection on treaties with Egypt and Assyria instead of trusting their great God. This too was emptiness and chasing after the wind, and God had to discipline Israel to bring them back to Himself and His Word.

The example of discipline (Hosea 12:2-6, 12). Abraham is the father of the Jewish nation (Matt. 3:9), but it was Jacob who built the twelve tribes of Israel (Gen. 46:8-27).[3] Hosea used the name "Jacob" for the nation because Jacob is an illustration of God's loving discipline. Hosea cited several key events in Jacob's life.

Jacob struggled with his brother even before he and Esau were born (25:20-23), and at birth, Jacob tried to trip up his brother Esau even as they were coming from the womb (vv. 24-26). The name "Jacob" means "he grasps the heel," which is another way or saying, "He's a deceiver, a trickster."[4] During most of his life, Jacob struggled with himself, with others, and with the Lord, and until he surrendered to God at Jabbok, he never really walked by faith. God had to discipline him to bring him to that place of surrender.

In obedience to God's command, Jacob left Shechem and went to Bethel (Gen. 35), for it was at Bethel that he had first met the Lord years before (28:10-22). There God had revealed Himself and given Jacob promises for himself and his descendants, and there Jacob had made solemn vows to the Lord. Actually, the return to Bethel was a new spiritual beginning for his whole family; for Jacob commanded them to abandon their foreign gods and worship Jehovah alone. It does a family good to experience this kind of dedication. Alexander Whyte said that the victorious Christian life is a series of new beginnings, and he was right.

But the Bethel experience also included some pain, for it was on that journey that Jacob's beloved wife Rachel died in giving birth to Benjamin (35:16-22). She called the boy Ben-Oni, which means "son of my sorrow"; but by faith, Jacob renamed him Benjamin, "son of my right hand."5

The divine title "Lord God of hosts [armies]" (Hosea 12:5) reminds us of Jacob's experience at Mahanaim when he was about to meet his brother Esau (Gen. 32). Mahanaim means "the two camps," for Jacob saw an army of angels watching over his camp. He was afraid of Esau and tried to appease him with gifts instead of trusting the Lord to deliver him. After all, didn't God promise to care for Jacob and bring him safely back to Bethel? It was there that the angel of God wrestled with Jacob and "broke" him.

Jacob's experiences getting a wife and raising a family are examples of God's loving discipline (Gen. 29-30). In order to get the family blessing, Jacob had schemed and lied to his father Isaac, but now Laban would scheme and lie to Jacob in order to marry off two daughters in one week! Trying to please two wives, only one of whom he really loved, and trying to raise a large family, brought many burdens to Jacob, but he persisted, and God blessed him and made him a wealthy man. However, during those difficult years, Jacob suffered much (31:36-42), yet the Lord was working out His purposes.

The reasons for discipline (Hosea 12:7–13:6). Now Hosea names some of the sins that His people had committed. Some of these he has dealt with before, so there's no need to discuss them in detail.

He begins with dishonesty in business (12:7), defrauding people so as to make more money. Their prosperity led to pride (v.8), the kind of self-sufficiency that says, "We don't need God" (see Rev. 3:17). But the Lord warned that He would humble them. Instead of enjoying their houses, they would live in tents as they did during their wilderness journey. When the Assyrians were through with Israel, the Jews would be grateful even for the booths they lived in for a week during the Feast of Tabernacles.

The prophets God sent had warned the people, but the people wouldn't listen (Hosea 12:10). They turned from the Word of the living God and practiced idolatry (vv. 11-14). This provoked God to anger, and the way they shed innocent blood provoked Him even more. (On Gilead's wickedness, see 6:8-9).

Hosea singled out the arrogant attitude of the tribe of Ephraim (13:1-3). The name "Ephraim" is found thirty-seven times in Hosea's prophecy. Sometimes "Ephraim" is a synonym for the whole Northern Kingdom, but here the prophet was addressing the tribe of Ephraim in particular. Ephraim and Manasseh were the sons of Joseph whom Jacob "adopted and whose birth order he reversed (Gen. 48). Manasseh was the firstborn, but Jacob gave that honor to Ephraim.

The people of Ephraim felt they were an important tribe that deserved to be listened to and obeyed. After all, Joshua came from Ephraim (Num. 13:8) and so did the first king of the Northern Kingdom, Jeroboam I (1 Kings 11:26). The tabernacle of testimony was pitched in Shiloh which was in Ephraim (Josh. 18:1). In their arrogance, the tribe of Ephraim created problems for both Gideon (Jud. 7:24-25; 8:1-3) and Jephthah (12:1-6). After the death of King Saul, the Ephraimites refused to submit to David's rule (2 Sam. 2:8-11); in fact, they had a strong prejudice against the tribe of Judah, the ruling tribe (19:40-43). When the Northern Kingdom was established, so powerful were the Ephraimites that the kingdom was even called by their name.

But Ephraim abandoned Jehovah for Baal, and that brought spiritual death. They gladly participated in Jeroboam's man-made religion by sacrificing to the golden calves—even offering human sacrifices—and kissing the calves in worship. But idols are nothing, and those who worship them become like them—nothing (Ps. 115:8). Hosea compared the people to the "nothings" with which they were familiar: morning dew that the sun burns away; chaff that the wind blows away; smoke that disappears out the window and is seen no more.

One more sin that Hosea condemned was the nation's ingratitude (Hosea 13:4-6). It was the same old story: the Jews were glad for what God had done for their forefathers—the Exodus, God's provision and guidance in the wilderness, the abundant wealth in the Promised Land—but they didn't really show Him sincere appreciation. In their trials, they turned to God for help, but in their prosperity, they became proud and turned away from God to idols. Moses had warned them about this sin, but they committed it just the same (Deut. 8:10-20).

The name "Ephraim" means "fruitful," and this was a very fruitful tribe. Through Jacob, God had promised abundant blessings to Joseph and his sons (Gen. 48; 49:22-26), and that promise was fulfilled. It's too bad the people didn't use what God gave them for God's glory.

The kinds of discipline (Hosea 13:7-16). Once again, Hosea uses a number of similes and metaphors to describe the trials that God was sending on His disobedient people. Like a ferocious beast, He would suddenly attack them (vv. 7-8; see 5:14), a reference to the invasion of the Assyrian army. The rulers of Israel would be weak, temporary, and ineffective (13:9-11; see 8:4). Now the time had come for the nation to have no king (3:4), a situation that would last for centuries.

The woman in travail is used often in Scripture to picture extreme pain and sorrow (13:13; Isa. 13:8; Jer. 4:31; Matt. 24:8), but Hosea adds a new twist. He sees the woman too weak to deliver the child and the baby too stupid to come out of the womb! All the travail was wasted.

The invasion of the Assyrians will be like a hot, dry wind from the desert that will smother the people and dry up the watercourses. All the nation's treasures will be plundered, and their greatest treasure, their children, will be slain mercilessly. Why? Because the nation would not return to God.

Paul quotes Hosea 13:14 in 1 Corinthians 15:55 to emphasize the victory of Jesus Christ over death and the grave because of His resurrection, but Hosea's words in this context may have a different meaning.[6]

The next statement ("I will have no compassion") supports our interpretation that Hosea 13:14 refers to judgment and not victory over the enemy. This doesn't suggest that God no longer loved His people, because God's love for His people is the major theme of this book. But the time had come for God to discipline the nation, for they had rejected every other manifestation of His love. "For I will not relent!" is the way *The Living Bible* states it.

God revealed His love to Israel in His past mercies and now in His present disciplines. Hosea closes his book with a third evidence of God's love.

3. God's Promises for the Future (Hosea 14:1-9)

Though His people may turn away from Him, God will not abandon them, even though He disciplines them, for He is true to His covenant and His promises. "If we are faithless, He remains faithful; He cannot deny Himself" (2 Tim. 2:13, NKJV).

God pleads with His people to return to Him and forsake the sins that were causing their downfall (Hosea 14:1). He had already told them to plow up their hard hearts and seek the Lord (10:12) and to turn to God for mercy (12:6), but now He talks to them like little children and tells them just what to do. The Lord gives them promises to encourage them to repent.

He will receive us (Hosea 14:2-3). God had every reason to reject His sinful people, but He chose to offer them forgiveness. Instead of bringing sacrifices, they needed to bring sincere words of repentance and ask God for His gracious forgiveness. "For You do not desire sacrifice, or else I would give it; You do not delight in burnt offering. The sacrifices of God are a broken spirit, a broken and a contrite heart – these, O God, You will not despise" (Ps. 51:16-17, NKJV).

He will restore us (Hosea 14:4). God restores the penitent to spiritual health and heals their backsliding (Jer. 14:7). When a person collapses with sickness, it's usually the result of a process that's been working in the body for weeks or months. First an infection gets into the system and begins to grow. The person experiences weariness and loss of appetite, then weakness, and then the collapse occurs. When sin gets into the inner person and isn't dealt with, it acts like an insidious infection: it grows quietly; it brings loss of spiritual appetite; it creates weariness and weakness; then comes the collapse.

For example, when Peter denied his Lord three times, that sin didn't suddenly appear; it was the result of gradual spiritual deterioration. The denial began with Peter's pride, when he told the Lord he would never forsake Him and would even die for Him. The next stage was sleeping when he should have been praying, and then fighting when he should have put away his sword. Peter should have left the scene ("I will smite the shepherd, and the sheep of the flock shall be scattered abroad" [Matt. 26:31; Zech. 13:7]); but instead, he followed to see what would happen and walked right into temptation.

When we confess our sins to the Lord, He forgives us and the "germs of sin" are cleansed away (1 John 1:9) but, as with physical sickness, often there's a period of recuperation when we get back our strength and our appetite for spiritual food. "I will love them freely" describes that period, when we're back in fellowship with the Lord and enjoying His presence. We see the smile of His face, for His anger is turned away.

He will revive us (Hosea 14:5-8). Hosea pictures the restoration of the penitent as the emergence of new life in a dry field on which the refreshing dew has fallen.[7] In the summer and early autumn in the Holy Land, the dew is very heavy and greatly appreciated (Ps. 133:3; Isa. 18:4). That's what the word "revive" means: to bring new life. The rich vegetation appears, producing beauty and fragrance where once the farmer saw only ugliness and emptiness. The fallow ground becomes a fruitful garden!

The closing verse presents us with only two alternatives: rebel against the Lord and continue to stumble, or return to the Lord and walk securely in His ways. The first choice is foolish; the second choice is wise.

"I have set before you life and death, blessing and cursing; therefore, choose life" (Deut. 30:19).

Endnotes

Chapter 1

1. See Isaiah 20; Jeremiah 27-28; Ezekiel 4:1-8; 5:1ff; 12:1-16; 24:15ff.

2. When you study the commentaries, you discover a number of different views defended: (1) Gomer was a pure woman who later became a prostitute and bore Hosea three children; (2) Gomer was a pure woman who became a prostitute and bore Hosea a son, but also gave birth to a daughter and son who were not fathered by Hosea; (3) Gomer was a prostitute from the beginning and bore Hosea three children; (4) Gomer was a prostitute from the beginning and bore Hosea his own son, but also bore two children by another man; (5) Gomer was a prostitute who already had three children, but Hosea ultimately divorced her and married another woman who was an adulteress (3:1). It's easy to lose sight of the main message God wanted to get across: He loved His people and wanted them to return that love to Him. They were committing evil by worshiping idols, just like a woman who is unfaithful to her husband. They were not only sinning against God's law, but also sinning against God's love. As to the legitimacy of the children, the fact that 1:6 and 8 don't read "and bore him a daughter . . . a son" does not mean Hosea wasn't the father of these children. It seems natural to assume from the context that Hosea is the father. See Genesis 30:17-24 for a similar statement.

3. TLB reads, "Go and marry a girl who is a prostitute."

4. In Scripture, a change of names is often evidence of God's gracious working in people's lives. Abram became Abraham, and Sarai was renamed Sarah (Gen. 17). Simon became Peter (John 1:42), and Saul of Tarsus became Paul (Paulus = little).

5. Paul quotes Hosea 1:10 and 2:23 in Romans 9:25-26 to prove that the salvation of the Gentiles was always a part of God's plan. He applies "not My people" to the Gentiles as he did in Ephesians 2:11-22. In the early church, some of the more legalistic believers thought that the Gentiles had to first become Jews before they could be Christians (Acts 10–11; 15), but Paul defended the Gospel of the grace of God and proved that both Jews and Gentiles are saved by grace through faith in Jesus Christ.

6. The Hebrew words referring to prostitutes and prostitution (KJV, "whoredom," "harlotries") are used twenty-two times in Hosea's prophecy (1:2, 2:2, 4-4; 3:3, 4:10-15, 18; 5:3-4; 6:10; 9:1). Words connected with adultery are used six times (2:2; 3:1; 4:2, 13-14; 7:4). God looked upon His covenant relationship with His people as a marriage, and He saw their idolatry as marital unfaithfulness.

7. Hebrew law stated that a divorced woman could not return to her former husband and marry him again (Deut. 24:1-4). God gave unfaithful Israel a "divorce" in that He no longer shared His intimacy and His mercies with her (Isa. 50:1; Jer. 3:1-5). One day He will take her back and restore the broken relationship and heal their land (Isa. 54:4-8; 62:4).

8. Kyle M. Yates, *Preaching From the Prophets* (New York: Harper and Brothers, 1942), 53.

Chapter 2

1. See Hosea 2:8, 20; 5:4; 8:2; 11:3; 13:4-5.

2. Compare Hosea 4:3 with Genesis 9:8-11 and Revelation 4:7-11 and you will see that God takes seriously His covenant with creation. He will one day judge those who destroy the earth (Rev. 11:18). The basis for ecology is not politics or comfort but the holy law of God. We are stewards of God's creation.

3. Jesus said to the Samaritan woman at Jacob's well, "You worship what you do not know; we know what we worship, for salvation is of the Jews" (John 4:22, NKJV). So much for the Samaritan religion or for any other man-made system of worship!

4. "A stick of wood" (Hosea 4:12, NIV; KJV, "their staff") may refer to the idol or to the heathen practice called rhabdomancy. (The Greek word rhabdos means "a rod.") The priest drew a circle on the ground and divided it into sections, with each section assigned a meaning. A rod was held in the center and then allowed to fall, and where it fell revealed the future.

5. Hosea 4:14 is a clear statement that God expects sexual purity and marital faithfulness from both men and women. In Israel, the men often got away with their sexual sins while the women were punished. See Genesis 38 and John 8 for tragic examples of an unbiblical one-sided morality. Where was the man who assisted the woman in committing adultery? Wasn't he also supposed to be punished? See Leviticus 20:10 and Deuteronomy 22:22.

6. At one time, Gilgal was a sacred place where the Word of God was taught (2 Kings 2:1; 4:38). How quickly religious institutions can drift from their mooring and abandon the faith!

7. This may mean literal illegitimate children because of sexual promiscuity or children who were not a part of the covenant because of the sins of their parents during the pagan fertility rites. The sins of the fathers bring tragic consequences in the lives of the children.

8. Even Judah will be included in this discipline (Hosea 5:10). The Assyrians devastated Judah but were unable to capture Jerusalem, for God delivered King Hezekiah and his people in a miraculous way. See Isaiah 36–37. The sin of Judah, according to Hosea, was that of seizing territory that wasn't rightfully theirs, like people who moved the boundary markers in order to increase their holding (Deut. 19:14; Isa. 5:8; Micah 2:2).

9. The phrase "King Jareb" in Hosea 5:13 (KJV, NASB) is translated "the great king" in the NIV. The Hebrew word means "to contend, to strive." This could be a nickname for the king of Assyria, such as "King Contention." Israel and Judah turned to the King of Assyria for help and all he did was pick a fight!

10. This is made clear in 1 John 1, where the phrase "if we say" is repeated three times. See also King Saul's "religious lies" in 1 Samuel 15:10-35.

11. Since the Hebrew word translated "Adam" means "red earth," it's been suggested that verse 7 be translated, "They have treated the covenant like dirt." Adam also stands for mankind in general, so we might translate it, "Like mere humans, they have transgressed the covenant."

12. Dr. Leon Wood translates Hosea 8:5, "Your calf stinks!" *The Expositor's Bible Commentary*, Frank E. Gaebelein, gen. ed. (Grand Rapids: Zondervan, 1985), vol. 7, 201. J.B. Phillips isn't quite that blunt in his translation: "Samaria, I reject your calf with loathing!" *Four Prophets: A Translation Into Modern English* (New York: Macmillan, 1963), 41.

13. The adults sin and the children have to suffer: "Ephraim shall bring forth his children to the murderer" (9:13, KJV). When Hosea speaks in verse 14, he asks God to keep the women from having children so they won't be murdered. He is pleading for mercy for the innocent. See our Lord's words in Luke 23:29.

14. The vine as a symbol of the Jewish nation is also found in Deuteronomy 32:32; Psalm 80:8-11; Isaiah 5:1-7; and Jeremiah 2:21. The vine also pictures Christ and His church (John 15) and the Gentile world system ripening for judgment in the last days (Rev. 14:17-20).

15. The references to Israel's past history —Baal-Peor (Hosea 9:10) and Gibeah (9:9; 10:9)—show that "the only thing we learn from history is that we don't learn from history." Both of these events brought the judgment of God on the nation, yet later generations turned a blind eye to this fact. The sins of the fathers are committed by their children—and grandchildren.

16. Any group that calls itself "the lost tribes of Israel" is suspect, for only God knows where all the tribes are. See Acts 26:7; James 1:1; and Revelation 7:1-8.

Chapter 3

1. The prophet Hosea was very familiar with Jewish history, not only what happened but why it happened and how it related to the present and the future of his People. He refers to the Exodus (2:15; 11:11;12:9, 13; 13:4), the events surrounding Jehu and Jezreel (1:4, 11; 2:22), Achan and the Valley of Achor (2:15), the wickedness of Gibeah (9:9; 10:9), Israel's sins at Baal-Peor (9:10), the destruction of the cities of the plain (11:8), and events in the life of Jacob (12:3-4, 12).

2. Hebrews 12:11-17 is the classic passage in Scripture on chastening. The Greek word paideia means "the rearing of a child," because the purpose of discipline is maturity. Sometimes God disciplines us to correct our disobedience, but He may also discipline us when we're obedient in order to equip us to serve Him better. David is an example of correcting discipline (2 Sam. 12; Pss. 32; 51), while Joseph is an example of perfecting discipline (Gen. 39-42; Ps. 105:16-22). Note that the context of Hebrews 12 is that of athletics, running the race (12:1-3). Athletes must experience the pain of discipline (dieting, exercising, competing) if they ever hope to excel. Nobody ever mastered a sport simply by listening to a lecture or watching a video, as helpful as those encounters may be. At some point, the swimmer must dive into the water, the wrestler must hit the mat, and the runner must take his or her place on the track. Likewise, the children of God must experience the pain of discipline—correcting and perfecting—if they are to mature and become like Jesus Christ.

3. "Israel" is the new name God gave Jacob after struggling with him at Jabbok (Gen. 32:24-32), but scholars aren't agreed on its meaning. The generally accepted meaning is "prince with God," i.e., a "God-controlled person." Others suggest "he persists with

God," which certainly fits the account; for Jacob wrestled with the angel of the Lord and didn't want to give in. Though Jacob made some mistakes and sometimes trusted his own ingenuity too much, he did persist with God and seek God's help, and God used him to build the nation of Israel. Some people have been too hard on Jacob, forgetting that believers in that day didn't have the advantages we have today. God has deigned to call Himself "the God of Jacob," and that's a very high compliment to a great man.

4. All of us are Jacobs at heart according to Jeremiah 17:9, "The heart is deceitful above all things, and desperately wicked; who can know it?" The Hebrew word translated "deceitful" is the root word for the name "Jacob." It means "to take by the heel, to supplant." The English word "supplant" comes from a Latin word that means to "to overthrow by tripping up." Jacob tripped up his brother and took his place when it came to both the family birthright and the blessing (Gen. 27:36). Of course, God had given both to Jacob before his birth (25:23), but instead of trusting God, Jacob used his own devices to get what he wanted. Faith is living without scheming.

5. These two names suggest the two aspects of our Lord's life and ministry, a Man of Sorrows and the resurrected Son exalted to the Father's right hand.

6. When New Testament writers quoted Old Testament statements, the Holy Spirit directing them had every right to adapt those passages as He wished, since the Spirit is the author of Scripture. Surely God sees much more in His Word than we do! For example, Hosea 11:1 refers to Israel's Exodus from Egypt, but Matthew used it to point to Christ's coming out of Egypt when a child (Matt. 2:11-15).

7. Biblical images must be studied carefully and identified accurately, for the same image may be used with different meanings in different contexts. The dew is a case in point. In Hosea 6:4, it represents the fleeting religious devotion of the hypocrites, while in 13:3, it symbolizes the transiency of the people who think they're so secure. Both Jesus and Satan are represented by the lion (Rev. 5:5; 1 Peter 5:8).

JOEL

OUTLINE

Key theme: "the Day of the Lord" (1:15; 2:1, 11, 31; 3:14)
Key verse: Joel 2:12-13

I. THE IMMEDIATE DAY OF THE LORD. 1:1-20
1. Hear! (elders, citizens). 1:2-4
2. Wake up! (drunkards. 1:5-7
3. Mourn! (farmers). 1:8-12
4. Call a fast! (priests). 1:13-20

II. THE IMMINENT DAY OF THE LORD. 2:1-271
1. The invading army, like locusts. 2:1-11
2. The call to repent. 2:12-17
3. The promise of restoration. 2:18-27

III. THE ULTIMATE DAY OF THE LORD. 2:28–3:21
1. Before that day – Spirit poured out. 2:28-32
2. During that day – judgment poured out. 3:1-16
3. After that day – blessing poured out. 3:17-21

CONTENTS

Joel in His Time

Each prophet had his own unique approach to his own special message. Hosea's message was an application of his sad domestic trials, emphasizing God's jealous love; but Joel's message was an interpretation of a national calamity—a plague of locusts and a drought—and emphasized God's glorious kingdom.

Joel may well have been the first of the writing prophets; he probably ministered in Judah during the reign of King Joash (835-796 B.C.). You find the record in 2 Kings 11–12 and 2 Chronicles 22–24. Joash came to the throne at the age of seven, and Jehoiada the priest was his mentor. This may explain whey Joel says nothing about the king, since Joash was learning the job.

Joel's major theme is the "day of the Lord" and the need for God's people to be prepared. "day of the Lord" is used in Scripture to refer to different periods when God sent judgment to His people,[1] but the main emphasis is on the future "day of the Lord" when the nations will be judged and Christ shall return to set up His glorious kingdom.

Joel refers to three important events, each of which he calls a "day of the Lord." He sees the plague of locusts as an immediate day of the Lord (Joel 1:1-20, the invasion of Judah by Assyria as an imminent day of the Lord (21:27), and the final judgment of the world as the ultimate day of the Lord (2:27–3:21). In the first, the locusts are a metaphorical army; in the second, the locusts symbolize a real army; in the third, the locusts aren't seen at all and the armies are very real and very dangerous.

CHAPTER ONE
WATCHING THE DAY OF THE LORD
JOEL 1:1–2:27

If there had been newspapers in Joel's day, the headlines might have read:

LOCUSTS INVADE THE LAND!
NATION FACES SEVERE ECONOMIC CRISIS
No End to Drought in Sight

A wise preacher or teacher will get the people's attention by referring to something they're all concerned about. In this case, the people of Judah were talking about the economic crisis, so the Lord led Joel to use that event as a the background for his messages. The people didn't realize it, but they were watching the Day of the Lord unfold before their very eyes, and the Prophet Joel explained it to them.

The name "Joel" means "the Lord is God." Like all true prophets, Joel was commissioned to call the people back to the worship of the true God; and he did this by declaring "the word of the Lord" (1:1; see Jer. 1:2; Ezek. 1:3; and the first verses of Hosea, Micah, Zephaniah, Haggai, Zechariah, and Malachi). It was the task of the priests to teach the people the Law, and it was the responsibility of the prophets to call the people back to the Lord whenever they strayed from His Law. The prophets also interpreted historical events in the light of the Word of God to help the people understand God's will for their lives. They were "forth-tellers" as well as "foretellers."

Joel wanted the people of Judah to understand what God was saying to them through the plague and the drought. In our own times, the nations of the world are experiencing severe droughts and famines, frightening epidemics, unexpected earthquakes, devastating floods, and other "natural disasters," all of which have greatly affected national and global economy; yet very few people have asked, "What is God saying to us?" Joel wrote his book so the people would know what God was saying through these critical events.

As you can see from the suggested outline of Joel's book, the prophet announced "the Day of the Lord" and applied it to three events: the plague of locusts, the future invasion of the Assyrians, and the distant judgment that the Lord would send on the whole world. In this chapter, we want to focus on the first two applications of "the Day of the Lord."

1. The Immediate Day of the Lord (Joel 1:1-20)

When you're in a crisis, you'll hear all kinds of voices interpreting what's going on and telling you what to do. The optimists will say, "This crisis isn't going to last. Be brave!" The pessimists will sob, "It's going to get worse and there's no escape! We're done for!" The alarmists will see the enemy behind every tree, and the scoffers will question the news reports and shrug their shoulders saying, "What difference does it make anyway?"

But Joel was a realist who looked at life from the standpoint of the Word of the Lord. He addressed himself to five groups of citizens and gave them four admonitions from the Lord.

The elders and citizens in general: "Hear this!" (Joel 1:2-4) He addressed the old men[1] first for probably two reasons: they had long experience and could authenticate what he was saying, and they were respected citizens in the land. With their support, Joel wasn't just a voice crying in the wilderness. They agreed with the prophet that the nation faced a catastrophe of monumental proportion such as they had never seen before. It was something people would tell to their children and grandchildren for years to come.

Joel used four different words to describe the plague (v. 4; see 2:25), and it's been suggested that they represent four stages in the life cycle of the locusts. However, the words probably convey the idea of successive swarms of locusts invading the land, each swarm destroying what the others had left behind. A swarm of locusts can devastate the vegetation of a countryside with amazing rapidity and thoroughness, and nothing can stop them (Ex. 10:1-20).

To the drunkards: "Wake up and weep!" (Joel 1:5-7) Except for pointing out the insincerity of some of the worshipers (2:12-13), drunkenness is the only sin that Joel actually names in his book. However, this was a serious sin that the prophets often condemned (Hosea 7:5; Amos 4:1). Perhaps the drunkards represented all the careless people in the land whose only interest was sinful pleasure.

These people had good reason to weep because there was no wine and wouldn't be any more until the next season, if there was a next season. Because of the locusts and the drought, "the new wine is dried up . . . the vine is dried up" (Joel 1:10,12). Keep in mind that bread and wine were staples in the Jewish diet, so that even the people who didn't get drunk were affected by the loss.

Joel compared the locusts to an invading nation and to hungry lions with sharp teeth (v. 6; see 2:2, 11). They attacked the vines and the fig trees, two things essential to Jewish life. Having one's own vineyard and fig trees was a symbol of success and contentment in the East (2:22; Isa. 36:16; Amos 4:9; Ps. 105:33). Note how Joel uses the personal pronoun my as he speaks of the land and its vegetation, for all of it belonged to the Lord, and He had a right to do with it whatever He pleased.

To the farmers: "Despair and wail!" (Joel 1:8-12) Joel named some of the crops that had been ruined: the grain (wheat and barley), the new wine, the oil, and the fruit from the pomegranate, palm, and apple trees. From season to season, the locusts ate whatever was produced, and the drought kept the soil from producing anything more. In verses 18-20, Joel includes the flocks and herds and their pastures. All that the farmers could do was express their grief and lament like an engaged girl whose fiancé had died. It seemed a hopeless situation.

To the priests: "Call a fast!" (Joel 1:13-20) Not only were the people in need, but so was the temple. Nobody could bring the proper sacrifices because no meal, wine, or animals were available. Joel called the priests to lament and pray, including those who worked "the night shift" (Ps. 134:1).[2]

The Jews were required to observe only one fast, and that was on the annual Day of Atonement (Lev. 16:29, 31). But the religious leaders could call a fast whenever the people faced and emergency and needed to humble themselves and seek God's face (Jud. 20:26; 2 Chron. 20:3; Ezra 8:21; Neh. 9:1-3; Jer. 36:9). This was such an emergency. "Gird yourself" (Joel 1:13) means "Put on sackcloth!" (See Jer. 4:8 and 6:26). It was time for the people to humble themselves and pray (2 Chron. 7:14).

In Joel 1:15-18, we have the lament of the nation, and in verses 19-20, the prayer of the prophet as he interceded for the nation. The lament is a vivid description of the sad condition of the land, the crops, the flocks, and the herds; for "the Day of the Lord" had come to the nation. The immediate reference is to the assault of the locusts and the devastating effects of the drought, but later, Joel uses the phrase to describe the terrible "Day of the Lord" when the nations will be judged. God is the Lord of creation, and without His blessing, nature cannot produce what we need for sustaining life (Pss. 65; 104:10-18, 21; 145:15). We should never pray lightly, "Give us this day our daily bread," for only God can sustain life (Acts 17:25, 28).

"How the cattle moan!" (Joel 1:18, NIV) This reminds us that all creation "groans and labors" because of the bondage of sin in the world (Rom. 8:18-22; Gen. 3:17-19). Creation longs for that day when the Creator will return to earth and set it free from sin's shackles, and then "the wilderness and the solitary place shall be glad . . . and the desert shall rejoice, and blossom like the rose" (Isa. 35:1).

It wasn't enough for the people to humble themselves and lament; they also had to pray. This is what God required in His covenant with His people (2 Chron. 6:26-27; 7:12-15; see Deut. 28:23-24). Joel didn't ask God for anything; he simply told the Lord of the suffering of the land, the beasts, and the people, knowing that God would do what was right. "The fire" (Joel 1:20) refers to the drought, which left the land looking like it had been burned.

Too often we drift along from day to day, taking our blessings for granted, until God permits a natural calamity to occur and remind us of our total dependence on Him. When water is rationed and food is scarce, and when prices for necessities escalate, then we discover the poverty of our artificial civilization and our throwaway society. Suddenly, necessities become luxuries, and luxuries become burdens.

God didn't have to send great battalions to Judah to bring the people to their knees. All He needed was a swarm of little insects, and they did the job. Sometimes He uses bacteria or viruses so tiny that you need a special microscope to see them. He is the "Lord of hosts," the Lord of the armies of heaven and earth. He is "the Almighty" (v. 15) and none can stay His powerful hand.[3]

2. The Imminent Day of the Lord (Joel 2:1–27)

Now that he had their attention, Joel told the people to stop looking around at the locusts and to start looking ahead to the fulfillment of what the locust plague symbolized: the invasion of a fierce army from the north (v. 20). Unless Joel had some other attack in mind, about which we know nothing, he was probably referring to the Assyrian invasion, during the reign of King Hezekiah, which took place in 701 B.C. (Isa. 36–37). God allowed the Assyrians to ravage the land, but He miraculously delivered Jerusalem from being taken captive.[4] The prophet gave the people three timely instructions.

"Blow the trumphet!" (Joel 2:1-11) This was real war, so Joel commanded the watchmen to blow their trumpets and warn the people. The Jews used trumpets to call assemblies, announce special events, mark religious festivals, and warn the people that war had been declared (Num. 10; Jer. 4:5; 6:1; Hosea 5:8). In this case, they blew the trumpet to announce war and to call a fast (Joel 2:15). Their weapons against the invading enemy would be repentance and prayer; the Lord would fight for them.

Twice in this passage, Joel tells us that invasion is "the Day of the Lord" (vv. 1, 11), meaning a very special period that God had planned and would direct. "The Lord thunders at the head of His army" (v. 11, NIV). It was God who brought the locusts of the land and God would allow the Assyrians to invade the land (Isa. 7:17-25; 8:7). He would permit them to ravage Judah just as the locusts had done, only the Assyrians would also abuse and kill people. "Woe to Assyria, the rod of My anger and the staff in whose hand is My indignation. I will send him against an ungodly nation … to seize the spoil, to take the prey, and to tread them down like mire in the streets" (Isa. 10:5-6).

In his vivid account of the invading army, Joel sees them coming in great hordes, "like dawn spreading across the mountains" (Joel 2:2, NIV). Once again, he uses the locusts to describe the soldiers. Just as the locusts had destroyed everything edible before them, so the army would use a "scorched earth policy" and devastate the towns and the land (Isa. 36:10; 37:11-13, 18). The locusts looked like miniature horses, but the Assyrians would ride real horses and conquer the land.[5]

The prophet makes it clear that the Lord will be in charge of this invasion; this is His army fulfilling His Word (Joel 2:11). God can use even heathen nations to accomplish His purposes on this earth (Isa. 10:5-7; Jer. 25:9). The awesome cosmic disturbances described in Joel 2:10 are Joel's way of announcing that the Lord is in charge, for these signs accompany "the Day of the Lord" (3:15; see Zeph. 1:14).

"Rend your hearts!" (Joel 2:12-17) Once again, Joel called for a solemn assembly where God's people would repent of their sins and seek the Lord's help. The nation didn't know when this invasion would occur, so the important thing was for them to turn to the Lord now. But they must be sincere. It's easy to participate in a religious ceremony, tear your garments, and lament, but quite something else to humbly confess your sins and bring to God a repentant heart (Matt. 15:8-9). "The sacrifices of God are a broken spirit, a broken and a contrite heart—these, O God, You will not despise" (Ps. 51:17, NKJV).

The one thing that encourages us to repent and return to the Lord is the character of God. Knowing that He is indeed "gracious and compassionate, slow to anger and abounding in love (Joel 2:13, NIV) ought to motivate us to seek His face. This description of the attributes of God goes back to Moses' meeting with the Lord on Mt. Sinai, when he interceded for the sinful nation of Israel (Ex. 34:6-7). You find echoes of it in Numbers 14:18 (another scene of Moses' intercession); Nehemiah 9:17; Psalms 86:15, 103:8, and 145:8; and Jonah 4:2. Such a gracious God would "turn and have pity" (Joel 2:14, NIV).[6] Note that Joel's concern was that the people would once again have offerings to bring to the Lord, not just food on their tables.

But all the people must assemble and then turn to the Lord (vv. 15-17). This includes elders and children, nursing babies and priests, and even the newlyweds who were not supposed to be disturbed during their first year of marriage, not even because of war (Deut.

24:5). The prophet even gave them a prayer to use (Joel 2:17) that presents two reasons why God should deliver them: (1) Israel's covenant privileges as God's heritage and (2) the glory of God's name before the other nations. Moses used these same arguments when he pled for the people (Ex. 32:11-13; 33:12-23).

The Jews are indeed God's special treasure and heritage (Ex. 15:17; 19:5-6; Ps. 94:5; Jer. 2:7; 12:7-9). To Israel, He gave His laws, His covenants, the temple and priesthood, a special land, and the promise that they would bless the whole world (Gen. 12:1-3; Rom. 9:1-5). From Israel came the written Word of God and the gift of the Savior (John 4:22).

Israel was called to bear witness to the other nations that their God was the only true God. How could God be glorified if His people were destroyed and the pagans could gleefully ask, "Where is their God?" (See Pss. 79:10 and 115:2; also Micah 7:10.) The nation had to choose between revival (getting right with God) or reproach (robbing God of glory).

"Believe his promises!" (Joel 2:18-27) Joel now looks beyond the invasion to the time when God would heal His land and restore his blessings to His people. Just as He blew the locusts into the depths of the Dead Sea and the Mediterranean Sea (eastern and western seas), so He could drive the invading army out of the land. In one night, God killed 185,000 Assyrian soldiers, and Sennacherib went home a defeated king (Isa. 37:36-38). The corpses must have created quite a stench before they were buried.

Some Bible scholars believe that Psalm 126 grew out of this event, for it describes a sudden and surprising deliverance that startled the nation. (Judah's return from Babylonian Captivity was neither sudden or surprising.) "The Lord hath done great things for us; whereof we are glad" (v.3) is echoed in Joel 2:21, "Be glad and rejoice; for the Lord will do great things." Both Joel 2:23-27 and Psalm 126:5-6 describe the restoration of the ravaged earth and the return of the harvests. This fulfilled what Isaiah promised to King Hezekiah (Isa. 37:30).

Without the former rain (March-April) and the latter rain (October-November), the land could not bear its crops; and one way God disciplined His people was to shut off the rain (Deut. 11:13-17). But the Lord promised to give such bumper crops that the harvest would more than compensate for all the people lost during the locust plague and the drought. "I will repay you for the years the locusts have eaten" (Joel 2:25, NIV) is a word of promise to all who return to the Lord with sincere and broken hearts.

"You cannot have back your time," said Charles Spurgeon, "but there is a strange and wonderful way in which God can give back to you the wasted blessings, the unripened fruits of years over which you mourned. . . . It is a pity that they should have been locust-eaten by your folly and negligence; but if they have been so, be not hopeless concerning them."[7]

And why will God do this for His deserving people? So that they will praise His name and never again be shamed before the heathen. "Then you will know that I am in Israel, that I am the Lord your God, and that there is no other, never again will my people be shamed" (v. 27, NIV).[8]

As never before, our lands today need healing. They are polluted by the shedding of innocent blood and the exploiting of both resources and people. We can claim God's promise in 2 Chronicles 7:14 because we are "His people."

CHAPTER TWO
EXPECTING THE DAY OF THE LORD
JOEL 2:28–3:21

Joel's message to Judah (and to us) is reaching its conclusion. He has described the immediate "Day of the Lord," the terrible plague of the locusts. This led to a description of the imminent "Day of the Lord," the impending invasion of the northern army. All that remains is for him to describe the ultimate "Day of the Lord" when God will judge all the nations of the earth. "For the Day of the Lord is near upon all the heathen" (Obad. 15).

Joel describes a sequence of events relating to this "great and terrible Day of the Lord" (Joel 2:31), what will happen before that day, during that day, and after that day.

1. Before That Day: the Spirit Poured Out (Joel 2:28-32)

In the Hebrew Scriptures, these five verses form chapter 3 of Joel's prophecy; and chapter 4 in the Hebrew Scriptures is chapter 3 in the English Bible. The Jewish scholars who arranged the Old Testament Scriptures evidently thought that this paragraph was important enough to warrant a chapter by itself. However, now that we have a completed Bible, this important passage must be studied both in its Jewish context and in the context of the New Testament church.

The Jewish context. The "afterward" in 2:28 refers to the events described in 2:18-27 when the Lord heals the nation after the Assyrian invasion. However, it doesn't necessarily mean immediately afterward, for many centuries passed before the Spirit was poured out. When Peter quoted this verse in his sermon on the Day of Pentecost, the Holy Spirit led him to interpret "afterward" to mean "in the last days" (Acts 2:17).

"The last days" began with the ministry of Christ on earth (Heb. 1:2) and will conclude with "the Day of the Lord," that period of worldwide judgment that is also called "the Tribulation" (Matt. 24:21,29) and "the time of Jacob's trouble" (Jer. 30:7). Many students of prophecy think that this special time is detailed in Revelation 6–19, climaxing with the return of Christ to earth to deliver Israel and establish His kingdom (Isa. 2:2-5; Zech. 12–14; Rev. 19:11–20:6).[1]

Joel promised that before the "Day of the Lord" begins, there will be a remarkable outpouring of the Holy Spirit accompanied by signs in the heavens and on the earth. During the Old Testament era, the Holy Spirit was given only to special people who had special jobs to do, like Moses and the prophets (Num. 11:17), the judges (Jud. 3:10; 6:34; 11:29), and great men like David (1 Sam. 16:13). But the promise God gave through Joel declared that the Spirit will come upon "all flesh," which includes men and women, young and old, Jew and Gentile. "And it shall come to pass that whoever calls on the name of the Lord shall be saved" (Joel 2:32, NKJV; see Acts 2:39).

The church context. In Acts 2, Peter did not say that Joel's prophecy was being fulfilled. He said that the same Holy Spirit Joel wrote about ("this is that") had now come and was empowering the believers to praise God in various languages understood by the Jews who were assembled in Jerusalem from many parts of the Roman Empire (Act 2:5-12). In his prophecy, Joel promised "wonders in the heavens, and in the earth, blood, and fire, and pillars of smoke. . . . The sun . . . turned into darkness, and the moon into blood" (Joel 2:30-31), but there is no record that any of these things occurred at Pentecost. The miracle that fascinated the crowd was the miracle of the tongues, not remarkable signs of nature.[2]

Furthermore, Joel's promise included a much wider audience than the one Peter addressed at Pentecost. Peter's audience was made up of men (Acts 2:22, 29) who were either Jews or Gentile proselytes to Judaism (v. 11). The Gentiles didn't enter into the blessing of the Spirit until Cornelius and his family and friends were converted (Acts 10–11). Peter used Joel's prophecy to declare that the promised Spirit had come and this was why the believers, men and women (1:14), were praising God in such an ecstatic manner. Peter was answering the accusation that the believers were drunk (2:13-16) and backing up his defense from the Scriptures.[3]

When it comes to Israel, "the last days" (or "latter times") will involve both tribulation and exaltation (Isa. 2:1-5; Micah 4:1-5), a time of trouble followed by a time of triumph and glory. As far as the church is concerned, "the last days" involve "perilous times" of satanic opposition in the world and apostasy in the church (1 Tim. 4:1-5; 2 Tim. 3:1-8; 2 Peter 3:1-9; 1 John 2:18-23; Jude 18-19). Many Christians believe that during those trying "last days," the Lord will send a great moving of his Spirit, and many sinners will turn to the Savior before the awful "Day of the Lord" is ushered in.

Certainly the church today needs a new filling of the Spirit of God. Apart from the ministry of the Spirit, believers can't witness with power (Acts 1:8), understand the Scriptures (John 16:13), glorify Christ (v. 14), pray in the will of God (Rom. 8:26-27), or develop Christian character (Gal. 5:22-23). We need to be praying for revival, a deeper working of the Spirit in His people, leading to confession of sin, repentance, forgiveness, and unity.

2. During the Day: Judgment Poured Out (Joel 3:1-16)

The phrase "bring again the captivity" (3:1) means "reverse the fortunes" or "restore the fortunes" (NIV). Because of the judgments set during the "Day of the Lord," Israel's situation in the world will be dramatically changed, and God will deal justly with the nations of the world for the way they have treated His people Israel. Joel gives three important announcements.

"Nations, prepare for judgment!" (Joel 3:1-8) This great battle will take place in the Valley of Jehoshaphat (vv. 2, 12), a site mentioned nowhere else in Scripture. In verse 14, it's called "the valley of decision," referring to God's decision (decree) to punish the nations.[4] Since the name "Jehoshaphat" means "the Lord judges," the name "Valley of Jehoshaphat" might well be symbolic, but some students believe it refers to the Plain of Esdraelon where the "battle of Armageddon" will be fought (Rev. 16:16).

Joel lists some of the sins that the Gentiles have committed against the Jews: scattering them among the nations; selling them into slavery; treating them like cheap merchandise for which people cast lots; plundering the land of its wealth; and taking what belonged to the Lord and using it for their own gods. Of course, many of the tragic experiences that came to the Jewish people were disciplines from God because they had violated His covenant, but the Gentile nations went beyond discipline to exploitation. Jeremiah said to the Babylonians, "[Y]ou rejoice and are glad, you who pillage my inheritance, because you frolic like a heifer threshing grain and neigh like stallions" (Jer. 50:11, NIV).

It's worth noting that God refers to the Jews as "My people" and to the land as "My land." The wealth is "My silver and My gold." Even though the Jews have not obeyed the covenant or sought to please the Lord, He has not abandoned them. Even when they rejected their Messiah, God was merciful to them. He has preserved them as a nation and will one day come to their aid and defeat their enemies.

"Nations, prepare for war!" (Joel 3:9-15) This passage describes what is generally called "the battle of Armageddon," when the armies of the nations unite against the Lord and His Christ (Ps. 2:1-3) and gather to destroy Jerusalem (Joel 3:16; Zech. 12–14). Joel compares the battle to the harvesting of grain and grapes, when God will defeat the enemy as easily as a farmer wields a sickle or plucks grapes and crushes them to make wine (Joel 3:13). You will find a similar image in Revelation 14:14-20 when god reaps "the harvest of the earth" and "the vine of the earth" and crushes armies like clusters of grapes.

Frightening signs from the Lord will accompany this battle (Joel 3:15; see 2:10, 30-31), signs that Jesus mentioned in His prophetic discourse on the Mount of Olives (Matt. 24:29-31; Mark 13:19-27; Luke 21:25-28). Jesus taught that these signs would prepare the way for His personal coming to earth when He will defeat Israel's enemies, cleanse His people, and establish His kingdom (Zech. 12–14; Rev. 19:11ff).

Joel 3:10 commands the nations to arm for battle, even to the point of turning farm tools into weapons, but Isaiah 2:4 and Micah 4:3 describe a different scene: "they shall beat their swords into plowshares, and their spears into pruning hooks" (Isa. 2:4). But Isaiah and Micah are describing the future kingdom, when people will learn war no more and no longer need weapons; while Joel is describing the battle that ushers in that peaceful kingdom.

"Nations, prepare for defeat!" (Joel 3:16) The name "Armageddon" is found only in Revelation 16:16, referring to the Plain of Esdraelon where many major battles were fought in Old Testament times. Revelation 16:13-16 informs us that Satan, through his demonic powers, gathers the armies of the nations to fight against God at Jerusalem. But the invasion will fail, because Jesus will return in power and slaughter the enemy, turning the whole "battle" into a supper of flesh for the scavengers of the earth (19:17-19).

Like a fierce lion, God will "roar out of Zion" and conquer the enemy (see Amos 1:2, Hosea 11:10-11). When the Lamb becomes a Lion, the nations had better tremble (Rev. 5:5). The lost nations of the earth will perish when He utters His voice in judgment, but to His own people the Lord will be a refuge and a stronghold. "Come, My people, enter your chambers, and shut your doors behind you; hide yourself as it were, for a little moment, until the indignation is past. For behold, the Lord comes out of His place to punish the inhabitants of the earth for their iniquity"

(Isa. 26:20-21, NKJV).[5]

A Jewish proverb says, "No misfortune avoids a Jew." No people have suffered more at the hands of their fellow men than have the Jews. Pharaoh tried to drown the Jews, but instead, his own army was drowned by God (Ex. 14-15). Balaam tried to curse the Jews, but God turned the curse into a blessing (Num. 22:25; Deut. 23:5; Neh. 13:2). The Assyrians and Babylonians captured the Jews and put them in exile, but both of those great kingdoms are no more, while the Jews are still with us. Haman tried to exterminate the Jews, but he and his sons ended up hanging on the gallows (the Book of Esther). Nebuchadnezzar put three Jews into a fiery furnace, only to discover that their God was with them and was able to deliver them (Dan. 3).

My friend, the late Dr. Jacob Gartenhaus, gifted missionary to his own people, used to say, "We Jews are waterproof and fireproof; God has blessed us so that nobody can successfully curse us, and we shall be here long after our enemies have perished." God knows what the nations have done to the Jews, and He will one day settle accounts. Meanwhile, believers must pray for the peace of Jersusalem (Ps. 122:6) and lovingly witness to them in word and deed that Jesus is indeed their Messiah and Lord.

3. After That Day: Blessing Poured Out (Joel 3:17-21)

Everything will change when the King comes back and begins His reign! Joel promises a holy city, a restored land, a cleansed people, and a glorious King.

A holy city (Joel 3:17). When Solomon dedicated the temple, the glory of the Lord came down and filled the building (1 Kings 8:10-11; 2 Chron. 5:11-14). Mount Zion, on which Jerusalem was built and the temple stood, was a very special place to the Jews because it was the place God chose for His own dwelling (Pss. 48; 87; 132:13). When the Babylonians destroyed the temple, the Jews prayed for the time when their temple would be restored and God's glory would return. "For God will save Zion, and will build the cities of Judah: that they may dwell there, and have it in possession" (69:35).

Today, the Jewish people have no temple on Mount Zion; instead, a mosque stands there. But God promises that He will restore Zion and dwell there in all His glory. "For the Lord shall comfort Zion: He will comfort all her waste places; and He will make her wilderness like Eden, and her desert like the Garden of the Lord; joy and gladness shall be found therein, thanksgiving, and the voice of melody" (Isa. 51:3). The prophets anticipate that great day when "sorrow and mourning shall flee away" (v. 11) and God will once again dwell with His people (see Isa. 12; 33:20-24; 35; 52; Jer. 31; Micah 4; Zech. 1).

Jerusalem is called "the Holy City" at least eight times in Scripture (Neh. 11:1, 18; Isa. 48:2 and 52:1; Dan. 9:24; Matt. 4:5 and 27:53; Rev. 11:2), and we will call it "the Holy City" today. Like every other city in this world, Jerusalem is inhabited by sinners who do sinful things. But the day will come when Jerusalem shall be cleansed (Zech. 13:1) and truly become a holy city dedicated to the Lord. (Isa. 4:1-6).

A restored land (Joel 3:18-19). Over the centuries, the land of Israel had been ravaged by war, famines, droughts, and the invasions of marauding insects such as Joel wrote about in the first chapter of his book, but there is coming a day when the land will be like the Garden of Eden for beauty and fruitfulness. "He will make her deserts like Eden, her wastelands like the garden of the Lord" (Isa. 51:3, NIV).

In the first chapter of Joel's prophecy, the people were wailing because they had no food, but that will not happen when God restores His people and their land. It will not only be a "land of milk and honey," but it will have plenty of wine and water as well. The land of Israel has always depended on the early and latter rains for water, but God will give them fountains and a river to water the land.

Jerusalem is the only city of antiquity that wasn't built near a great river. Rome had the Tiber; Nineveh was built near the Tigris and Babylon on the Euphrates; and the great Egyptian cities were built near the Nile. But in the kingdom, Jerusalem will have a river that proceeds from the temple of God. "On that day living water will flow out from Jerusalem, half to the eastern sea [the Dead Sea] and half to the western sea [the Mediterranean], in summer and in winter" (Zech. 14:8, NIV). You find this river and its special blessings described in Ezekiel 47.

In contrast to the land of Israel, the lands of their enemies, Egypt and Edom, will be desolate as a punishment for the way they treated the Jewish people. This means that Egypt and Edom will have to depend on Israel for the basic things of life, such as food and water.

A cleansed people (Joel 3:20-21a). What good would it be to have a restored land if it were populated with a sinful people? God's people must be cleansed before they can enter into the promised kingdom. God promises to cleanse His people of their sins, forgive them, and restore them to Himself. "In that day there shall be a fountain opened to the house of David and to the inhabitants of Jerusalem for sin and for uncleanness" (Zech. 13:1).

The prophet Ezekiel describes this cleansing: "For I will take you from among the nations, gather you out of all countries, and bring you into your own land. Then I will sprinkle clean water on you, and you shall be clean; I will cleanse you from all your filthiness and from all your idols. I will give you a new heart and put a new spirit within you; I will take the heart of stone out of your flesh and give you a heart of flesh. I will put My Spirit within you and cause you to walk in My statutes, and you will keep My judgments and do them" (Ezek. 36:24-27, NKJV).

Under Old Testament Law, the Jews could cleanse that which was defiled by using water, fire, or blood. The priests were washed with water and sprinkled with blood when they were installed in office (Lev. 8–9), and the healed lepers were likewise washed with water and sprinkled with blood (Lev. 14). The priests had to wash their hands and feet and keep ceremonially clean as they served in the tabernacle (Ex. 30:17-21). If anything became defiled, it had to be purified with "the water of sprinkling" (Num. 19). Zechariah used this Old Testament truth to teach about the permanent internal cleansing that would come when the people saw their Messiah and trusted Him (Zech. 12:10). They would experience a new birth and become a new people for the Lord.

A glorious King (Joel 3:21b). What a wonderful way to close a book: "The Lord dwells in Zion!" (NIV) The Prophet Ezekiel watched as the glory of God departed from the temple that was about to be destroyed (Ezek. 8:4; 9:3; 10:4, 18; 11:23), and then he saw that glory return to the new temple in the restored nation (43:1-5). He saw a new Jerusalem that had been given a new name: "Jehovah Shammah—the Lord is there" (48:30-35).

The prophecy of Joel begins with tragedy, the invasion of the locusts, but it closes with triumph, the reign of the King of Kings and Lord of Lords. Jesus said to His disciples, "Assuredly I say to you, that in the regeneration [the future kingdom], when the Son of Man sits on the throne of His glory, you who have followed Me will also sit on twelve thrones, judging [ruling over] the twelve tribes of Israel" (Matt. 19:28, NKJV).

May we never lose the wonder of His glorious kingdom!

"The kingdom of this word has become the kingdom of our Lord and of His Christ, and He will reign for ever and ever" (Rev. 11:15, NIV).

"Thy kingdom come!" (Matt. 6:10)

"Even so, come, Lord Jesus!" (Rev. 22:20)

ENDNOTES

Joel in His Time

1. The term "Day of the Lord" is used to describe the fall of Israel in 722 B.C. (Amos 5), the fall of Judah in 586 B.C. (Ezek. 13:5), and the battle of Carchemish in 605 B.C. (Jer. 46:10). Each of these local calamities was a precursor of the worldwide judgment that is promised by the prophets and also by our Lord (Matt. 24; Mark 13).

Outline of the Book of Joel

1. The "imminent" Day of the Lord refers to the future invasion of Judah by the Assyrians, when the land would be devastated and Jerusalem surrounded by armies. (See Isa. 36–37; 2 Kings 18–19; and 2 Chron. 32.) This occurred during the reign of King Hezekiah (715-686 B.C.). Jerusalem was miraculously delivered from Assyria by the Angel of the Lord who killed 185,000 Assyrian soldiers in one night. However, not every Old Testament student sees a distinction between I and II. Some see II as an amplification of I. Regardless of how you outline the book, the message remains the same: each national calamity reminds us that the "Day of the Lord" is coming and we must be prepared.

Chapter 4

1. In the KJV, the Hebrew word is translated "old men" in 1:2 and 2:28, and "elders" in 1:14 and 2:16. The NIV uses "elders" everywhere except 2:28, where the contrast between "young men" and "old men" is quite obvious. It's possible that the "old men" were indeed the official elders of the land.

2. The phrase "your God" is used eight times in this book to remind the people of their personal relationship to Jehovah and their accountability to Him (1:13-14; 2:13-14, 23, 26-27; 3:17).

3. "Almighty" is a translation of the Hebrew word Shaddai, which is related to the Hebrew word for

"breast." He is the all-sufficient One, the bountiful One, the God who can do anything. The name is found forty-eight times in the Old Testament, thirty-one of them in the Book of Job, where the greatness of God is one of the major themes. "Almighty" is used eight times in the Book of Revelation.

4. Why should Joel call the people to repent in order to avoid an invasion that would take place a century later? But they didn't know when the invasion would come, and their brokenness before God was the means of postponing it. We look back and see that Isaiah 36–37 fulfilled what Joel wrote, but the people of Judah were looking ahead into an unknown future. It's always right to repent and submit to the will of God. That's the best way to secure the future.

5. The repeated use of the word "like" in 2:4-7 indicates that Joel is using a simile and not describing the actual army. The locusts looked and acted like an army, and the invading Assyrian army would be like them: numerous, ruthless, destructive, and invincible. When you get to 2:8-11, you are reading about real soldiers in a real battle: for locusts don't worry about swords.

6. God is said to "repent" when from man's point of view He changes His attitude and turns away His wrath. The word "relent" might be a better choice.

7. Charles H. Spurgeon, *Metropolitan Tabernacle Pulpit* (Pasadena, Texas: Pilgrim Publications), vol. 35, 217.

8. There may be a hint here that some of the people were involved in idolatry and needed to turn from heathen vanities and worship only the Lord (Ex. 20:1-6).

Chapter 5

1. Note that the phrase "a thousand years" is used six times in Revelation 20:1-7. The Latin word for "thousand years" is millennium; it is used to describe the kingdom Jesus Christ will establish on earth in fulfillment of the Old Testament promises to Israel. However, some students prefer to "spiritualize" these promises and apply them to the church today, and these people are called amillennialists, meaning "no millennium." Premillennialists are Christians who believe Jesus will return before the kingdom is established, for how can you have a kingdom without the King? There was a time when a postmillennial interpretation was popular: the church would "change the world" and "bring in the kingdom," and then Jesus would return to reign. The wars and atrocities of this past century and the spread of apostasy in the church have pretty well done away with this optimistic outlook.

2. Some say that the darkening of the sun from noon until three o'clock (Matt. 27:45) and the local earthquake (vv. 51-54) fulfilled Joel's promise, but Matthew doesn't say so. Invariably, when something happened that fulfilled Scripture, Matthew calls it to our attention (26:24, 56; 27:9, 35). At least twelve times in his Gospel, Matthew uses the word "fulfilled" to point to an Old Testament messianic prophecy, but he doesn't include Joel 2:28-32.

3. In Scripture, you sometimes find "near" and "distant" fulfillments of God's promises. The "near" fulfillment is partial, while the "distant" fulfillment is complete. In 2 Samuel 7, God promised to build David a house. The near fulfillment was the Davidic dynasty that ruled until Judah was exiled to Babylon. The distant fulfillment is found in Jesus Christ, the Son of David, whose reign shall never end (Luke 1:32-33).

4. To make the "valley of decision" a place where lost sinners decide to follow Christ is to twist the Scripture. It is God who makes the decision, and His decision (decree) is to judge and not save. The nations have had their opportunity; now it is too late.

5. Pretribulationists believe that the church will be taken to heaven (raptured) before the Day of the Lord breaks upon the world (1 Thes. 1:10; 5:9-10). This event is described in 1 Thessalonians 4:13-18. The saints will then return to the earth with Jesus when He returns in glory to defeat His enemies and establish His kingdom (Rev. 19:11ff; 2 Thes. 2). Prophetic students differ as to the details of the end-times scenario, but they agree that the world will grow hostile against God, the people of God will suffer persecution, and the Lord will return to conquer His enemies and rescue His people. This is what we are asking when we pray, "Thy kingdom come."

AMOS

OUTLINE

Key theme: A call for justice, a warning of judgments
Key verse: Amos 5:24

I. LOOK AROUND AND SEE GOD'S JUDGMENT. 1–2
Eight nations judged
1. Six Gentile nations condemned. 1:1–2:3
2. Judah condemned. 2:4-5
3. Israel condemned. 2:6-16

II. LOOK WITHIN AND SEE THE CORRUPTION. 3–6
Three sermons to the people of Israel
1. Message #1: Israel's judgment certain. 3:1-15
2. Message #2: Israel's sins denounced. 4:1-13
3. Message #3: Israel's doom lamented. 5:1–6:14

III. LOOK AHEAD AND SEE THE END COMING. 7–9
1. Five visions of judgment. 7:1–9:10
(1) The locusts. 7:13
(2) The fire. 7:4-6
(3) The plumb line. 7:7-9
Historical interlude: Amos at Bethel. 7:10-17
(4) The basket of summer fruit. 8:1-14
(5) The ruined temple. 9:1-10
2. A vision of the glorious kingdom. 9:11-15

CONTENTS

Amos in His Time

Amos ("burden bearer") was a herdsman and a cultivator of sycamore trees (Amos 1:1; 7:14) when the Lord called him to be a prophet. He lived in the village of Tekoa, about eleven miles from Jerusalem, during the reigns of Uzziah in Judah (790–740 B.C.) and Jeroboam II in the Northern Kingdom of Israel (793–753). Amos was a "layman," a humble farmer and shepherd who was not an official member of the Jewish religious or political establishment.

At this time, both Judah and Israel were enjoying prosperity and security. Luxury abounded (3:10–15; 5:1–6), and "religion" was popular. Israel flocked to the royal chapel at Bethel (4:4–5), and Judah celebrated the feasts enthusiastically (5:21–22), but the sins of both nations were eroding the religious and moral fiber of the people. Making money was more important than worshiping God (8:5); the rich exploited the poor, the judicial system was corrupt, and injustice flourished (5:11–15, 24; 8:4–6).

CHAPTER ONE
THE LION ROARS!
Amos 1:1–2:16

If the Prophet Amos were to come to our world today, he would probably feel very much at home; for he lived at a time such as ours when society was changing radically. Both Israel and Judah were at peace with their neighbors, which meant that their wealth and energy could be used for developing their nations instead of fighting their enemies. Both kingdoms were prosperous; their cities were expanding rapidly; and a new wealthy merchant class was developing in society. The two kingdoms were moving from an agricultural to a commercial society and experiencing both the benefits and problems that come with that change.

However, in spite of their material success, all was not well with God's chosen people. They were experiencing what the British poet Oliver Goldsmith wrote about back in 1770:

> Ill fares the land, to hast'ning ills a prey,
> Where wealth accumulates, and men decay ...[1]

There were ills aplenty in all the lands of that day, the Gentile nations as well as the Jewish kingdoms of Israel and Judah; and Amos wasn't afraid to name them. He opened his book with a denunciation of the sins of six Gentile nations, and no doubt the people of Israel and Judah applauded his words. Nothing would make the Jews happier than to see the Lord judge the surrounding nations. But when Amos denounced Judah and Israel, that was a different story; and his popularity began to suffer at that point.

1. Judgment on the Gentile nations (Amos 1:2–2:3)[2]

God wanted to get the nations' attention, but people weren't listening. You'd think they could hear a lion roar or the thunder roll and know that danger was at hand. God was speaking ("thundering") from Jerusalem, for judgment always begins at the house of the Lord (1 Peter 4:17). He had sent drought to the land so that even fruitful Carmel was withering, but it didn't bring the people to their knees. So God called a common farmer to preach to His people and warn them. "A lion has roared! Who will not fear? The Lord God has spoken! Who can but prophesy?" (Amos 3:8 NKJV)

Eight times Amos used the phrase "for three transgressions and for four," a Jewish idiom that means "an indefinite number that has finally come to the end." God is long-suffering with sinners (2 Peter 3:9), but He marks what they do and His patience eventually runs out. To try God's patience is to tempt the Lord; and when we tempt the Lord, we invite judgment.

Syria (Amos 1:3–15). Damascus was the capital of Syria, one of the Jews' persistent enemies. Amos denounced the Syrians for their inhuman treatment of the Israelites who lived in Gilead, east of the Jordan River. They cruelly "threshed them" as though they were nothing but stalks of grain. God had called the Syrians to punish Israel (2 Kings 10:32-33; 13:1-9), but the Syrians had carried it too far.

The man who began his prayer with "Lord, no doubt You saw in the morning newspaper ..." was stating a great truth in a clumsy way: God sees how the nations treat one another, and He responds appropriately. Benjamin Franklin said it well at the Constitutional Convention, "I have lived, Sir, a long time, and the longer I live, the more convincing proofs I see of this truth—that God governs in the affairs of men."[3]

The phrase "I will send a fire" (Amos 1:4, 7, 10, 12, 14; 2:2, 5) means "I will send judgment"; for fire represents the holiness and judgment of God (Deut. 4:11, 24, 36; Heb. 12:29). Indeed, the Lord did judge Syria: the dynasty of King Hazael ended; his son Ben-Hadad was defeated; Damascus lost its power (business was done at the city gate, Amos 1:5); and "the house of Eden" (delight, paradise) became a ruin. King Josiah defeated Ben-Hadad three times (2 Kings 13:25), but it was the Assyrians who finally subdued Syria and took them into captivity.

Philistia (Amos 1:6–8). Gaza, Ashdod, Ashkelon, Gath, and Ekron were the five key Philistine cities (Josh. 13:3), and Amos denounced all of them for trading in human lives.[4] They raided Jewish villages and captured people to be sold as slaves. To add insult to injury, the Philistines sold these slaves to Israel's ancient enemy, the Edomites. Since Edom was descended from Esau, Jacob's brother, it was a case of brother enslaving brother. (God had something to say to Edom in Amos 1:11-12.)

Throughout the history of ancient Israel, slavery was practiced, but the Law of Moses clearly governed how the slaves were treated. The law that permitted slavery at the same time protected the slaves. However, it was one thing to put a prisoner of war to work and quite something else to kidnap innocent people and sell them like cattle. Neither Jesus nor the apostles openly denounced slavery, but they made it clear that all people are sinners whom God loves and that all saved people are one and equal in Christ (Gal. 3:26–29). It took centuries for the light of the Gospel to dispel the darkness and make slavery illegal, although there are still places in our world where people are abused and exploited.

God's judgment on Philistia came in the days of King Uzziah (2 Kings 18:7-8) and the Assyrian invaders under Sargon and the Babylonians under Nubuchadnezzar. The slave masters were themselves taken into exile and slavery.

Tyre (Amos 1:9-10). Amos has moved from Damascus in the northeast to the Philistine cities in the southwest, and now he sets his sights straight north on Phoenicia and its major city, Tyre.

During the reigns of David and Solomon, Israel had a warm relationship with the people of Tyre (1 Kings 5:1ff). Amos called it "the brotherly covenant" ("treaty of brotherhood," NIV), suggesting that the "covenant" was more than a treaty but involved a friendly partnership that that went deeper than politics. Even if the peoples of different nations don't agree in their religious practices or their political structures, they can still treat one another like fellow human beings.

Tyre, however, committed the same sins as the Philistine cities by selling Jewish captives to the Edomites as slaves (Amos 1:6-8). When the Prophet Ezekiel gave his funeral dirge celebrating the fall of Tyre, he mentioned this grievous sin (Ezek. 27:13). But Tyre's sin was worse than that of Philistia because Tyre was violating a long-standing compact that was based on friendship and mutual respect for humanity. Tyre was selling its friends as slaves!

Judgment came in 332 B.C. when Alexander the Great wiped Tyre off the face of the earth and left it a place for drying nets (26:5, 14). "Though the mills of God grind slowly / yet they grind exceeding small."[5] When Rudyard Kipling published his poem "Recessional" during Queen Victoria's Diamond Jubilee in 1897, he used Tyre as a warning to any people who rebel against the will of God and mistreat men and women created in the image of God.

Far-called our navies melt away—
On dune and headland sinks the fire—
Lo, all our pomp of yesterday—
Are one with Nineveh and Tyre!

Edom (Amos 1:11-12). The Edomites nursed a long-standing grudge against the Jews, perpetuating the ancient rivalry between Jacob and Esau, which began before the twin boys were born (Gen. 25:21-26). In His sovereign will, God had chosen the younger brother, Jacob, to receive the blessings of the birthright and the Abrahamic Covenant (Mal. 1:2-3; Rom. 9:6-13). Esau despised his spiritual heritage and willingly sold his birthright to Jacob (Gen. 25:29-34; Heb. 12:14-17); but because Jacob cheated him out of the patriarchal blessing (Gen. 27), Esau vowed to kill Jacob. Later they were briefly reconciled, but the enmity continued (33:1-17). As far as the biblical record is concerned, their final meeting was at a funeral, where they buried their father but did not bury their bitterness (35:27-29).

The Edomites would not allow their Jewish cousins to pass through their land during Israel's march to Canaan (Num. 20:14-21). King Saul suppressed the Edomite army (1 Sam. 14:47), and David conquered them (2 Sam. 8:14), but in the days of King Jehoram, Edom revolted against Judah and won their freedom (2 Kings 8:16-22).

Amos condemned the Edomites for their persistent hatred of the Jews, ". . . because his anger raged continually and his fury flamed unchecked" (Amos 1:11 NIV). We don't know when the Edomites aided the enemy by pursuing the Jews with the sword. It could have been during any one of the numerous times when enemies invaded the land. When the Babylonians attacked and captured Jerusalem, the Edomites assisted the enemy and gave vent to their anger (Obad. 10-14; see Ps. 137:7). You would think that brother would help brother in a time of need, but the Edomites "cast off all pity" (Amos 1:11) and acted like beasts instead of humans. The phrase "his anger did tear" (v.11) uses a verb that describes ferocious beasts tearing their prey (Ps. 7:2; Gen. 37:33).

Temen and Bozrah were strong cities that today don't exist. The Edomites lived "in the clefts of the rock" and had their "nest among the stars" (Obad. 3-4), boasting that their fortresses were impregnable; but the Lord destroyed their nation so thoroughly that nothing is left today except ruins. When the Romans attacked Jerusalem in A.D. 70, they destroyed what was left of the Edomite (Idumean) people, and Edom was no more.

Ammon (Amos 1:13-15). The Ammonites and Moabites (2:1-3) were the descendants of Lot through his incestuous union with his daughters (Gen. 19:30-38). They were a ruthless people who were the avowed enemies of the Jews (Deut. 23:3-6; 1 Sam. 11:2; Neh. 2:10-19; Jer. 40:14; 41:5-7). In order to enlarge their land, they invaded Gilead; and not satisfied with attacking the men defending their homeland, the Ammonites killed women and unborn children (see 2 Kings 8:12; 15:16). To the Ammonites, land was more important than people, including defenseless women and innocent children. Such brutality shocks us, but is "modern warfare" any kinder?

Amos announced that a storm of judgment would come to the people of Ammon and that their capital city (Rabbah) would be destroyed. This took place when the Assyrians swept over the land in 734 B.C. Not only did Amos predict the destruction of their land, but so did Ezekiel (25:1-7). The chief god of Edom was Molech (Malcham, Milcom), which means "reigning one, king." Amos 1:15 could be translated, "Molech will go into exile," thus showing the inability of their god to save them.

Moab (Amos 2:1-3). Animosity between Moab and Israel began very early when the Moabites refused to give the Jews passage on the major highway (Deut. 23:3-4; Jud. 11:17). The king of Moab also hired Balaam to curse Israel (Num. 22–24), and then the Moabite women seduced the Jewish men to commit fornication and idolatry (Num. 25). During the period of the judges, Israel was subject to the Moabites for eighteen years (Jud. 3:12-30).

What was the sin of Moab? Disrespect for the dead and for royalty. We don't know which king's remains were subjected to this humiliation, but the deed disgraced the memory of the king and humiliated the people of Edom. How would Americans feel if somebody disinterred John F. Kennedy's body and mistreated it? Or what would the British people do if the body of a famous person were stolen from Westminster Abbey and publicly abused?

For the most part, society today shows respect for the dead, but ancient Eastern peoples protected their dead even more. Steeped in pagan superstition, they interred bodies carefully to insure the spirit's continued existence in the next world. Relatives of the deceased often inscribed frightful curses on the tombs, warning people to refrain from opening them.[6]

Amos announced that the king of Moab and his officials were all guilty and would be destroyed, along with their cities.[7] Moab was taken by the Assyrians, and the land eventually became the home of numerous nomadic tribes. The nation of Moab was no more. (For other prophecies of Moab's doom, see Isa. 15–16; Jer. 48; Ezek. 25:8-11; Zeph. 2:8-11.)

Before we listen to God's messages to Judah and Israel, we should pause to reflect on the messages we have just studied that were delivered to six Gentile nations. *God expected these Gentiles to listen to a Jewish prophet and heed what he said!* Though not under the Mosaic Law, these nations were responsible to God for what they did; and responsibility brings accountability. God sees what the nations do, and He judges them accordingly. World news from day to day may give the impression that evil leaders and violent subversive groups are getting away with terrible crimes, but God is still on the throne and will punish evildoers in His good time. It is God who controls the rise and fall of the nations (Acts 17:24-28), and His judgments are always just.

2. Judgment on the kingdom of Judah (Amos 2:4-5)

In his six messages, Amos had announced judgment to the nations surrounding Israel and Judah, starting with Syria in the northwest and ending with the trans-Jordanic nations of Ammon, Moab, and Edom. (There's probably a map of the divided kingdom in the back of your Bible.) As his fellow Jews heard these denunciations of the Gentiles, no doubt they applauded and wanted to hear more. But when Amos focused on Israel and Judah (his own land), that changed their attitude completely. The very idea of a Jewish prophet classifying God's chosen people with the Gentile "dogs"! "We know we aren't a perfect people," the people of Judah would argue, "but at least we worship the true and living God!"

Yes, the temple was filled with people bringing their sacrifices, but Judah was a nation given over to idolatry. "Their lies [idols] lead them astray, lies which their fathers followed" (2:4 NKJV). They were wandering like lost animals and like drunken men. The Gentiles had sinned against conscience and the laws of brotherhood and humanity, but the Jews had despised and rejected the very laws of God, given to them by Moses. Theirs was the greater sin, for greater privilege always brings greater responsibility (Rom. 2:17–3:9).

God had frequently punished His people *in their land* by allowing various nations to attack and subdue them, but now He would punish them *out of their land.* The Babylonian army would destroy Jerusalem and take thousands of captives to Babylon where they would live in the midst of gross idolatry for seventy years. However, unlike the six Gentile nations Amos had denounced, Judah would not be destroyed but would be spared. In His mercy, God would allow a remnant of Jews to return to establish the nation and rebuild the temple.

"I don't know why you preach about the sins of Christians," a church member said to the pastor. "After all, the sins of Christians are different from the sins of unsaved people."

"Yes," replied the pastor, *"they're worse!"*

3. Judgment on the kingdom of Israel (Amos 2:6-16)

Both Israel and Judah were enjoying peace and prosperity, and divine judgment was the furthest thing from their minds. Remember, Jewish theology equated prosperity with God's blessing;[8] and as long as the people were enjoying "the good life," they were sure God was pleased with them. They knew what the Law said about their sins, but they chose to ignore the warnings.

Amos first exposes *their sinful present* and names three flagrant sins. To begin with, the people of the Northern Kingdom were guilty of *injustice (Amos 2:6-7).* Supported by corrupt judges, the rich were suing the poor, who couldn't pay their bills, and forcing them into servitude and slavery. Even if they couldn't pay for a pair of shoes, the poor were neither forgiven nor assisted. Instead, they were trampled like the dust of the earth. As we shall see in our continued studies, the Prophet Amos has a great deal to say about caring for the poor (see 4:1; 5:11; 8:6; also Deut. 15:7-11; Ex. 23:6-9: Prov. 14:31; 17:15).

Their second gross sin was *immorality (Amos 2:7b),* with fathers and sons visiting the same prostitute! These may have been "cult prostitutes" who were a part of the heathen idolatrous worship. Thus there was a double sin involved: immorality and idolatry. Or the girl may have been a household servant or a common prostitute. You would think that a father would want to be a better example to his son by obeying the Law of Moses (Ex. 22:16; Deut. 22:28-29; 23:17-18). Perhaps what's described here is a form of incest, which was, of course, strictly forbidden by Moses (Lev. 18:7-8, 15; 20:11-12). Regardless of what the act of disobedience was, it was rebellion against God and defiled His holy name.

The third sin was *open idolatry (Amos 2:8).* Wealthy men took their debtors' garments as pledges but did not return them at sundown as the law commanded (Ex. 22:26-27; Deut. 24:10-13, 17). Instead, these rich sinners visited pagan altars, where they got drunk on wine purchased with the fines they exacted from the poor. Then, in their drunken stupor, they slept by the altars on other people's garments, defiling the garments and disobeying the law. The officials were getting rich by exploiting the people, and then were using their unjust gain for committing sin.

After describing their sinful present, Amos reminded them of *their glorious past (Amos 2:9-12).* God had led His people out of Egypt (v. 10a), cared for them in the wilderness (v. 10b), and destroyed other nations so the Jews could claim their inheritance in Canaan (vv. 9, 10c). He gave them His Word through chosen prophets (v. 11a), and He raised up dedicated people like the Nazirites (Num. 6) to be examples of devotion to God. What a glorious past they had! But instead of being humbled by these blessings, the people rebelled against the Lord by rejecting the messages of the prophets and forcing the Nazirites to break their holy vows. The Jews wanted neither the Word of God nor examples of godly living.

Amos closed his message with the announcement of *their terrible future (Amos 2:13-16).* Israel would be crushed by their own sins just as a loaded cart crushes whatever it rolls over. Judgment is coming, and nobody will be able to escape. The swift won't be able to run away; the strong won't be able to defend themselves; the armed will be as if unarmed; and even the horsemen will be unable to flee. The bravest soldiers will run away while shedding their equipment and clothing so they can run faster. Yes, Assyria would invade Israel (720 B.C.) and the nation would be no more.

Amos has looked around with eyes gifted with prophetic insight, and he has seen and announced what God would do to six Gentile nations and to the kingdoms of Judah and Israel. The lion has roared! Next, the prophet will look within and expose the corruption in the hearts of the Jewish people by explaining four divine calls.

But before we examine these four calls, we need to pause and ask ourselves whether we truly fear God and seek to obey His will. Just because we enjoy a measure of peace and prosperity, it doesn't mean God is pleased with us. For that matter, the goodness of God ought to lead us to repentance, as it did the Prodigal Son (Luke 15:17; Rom. 2:4).

" 'Vengeance is Mine, I will repay,' says the Lord. And again, 'The Lord will judge His people.' It is a fearful thing to fall into the hands of the living God" (Heb. 10:30-31 NKJV).

However, we can still claim the promises of 2 Chronicles 7:14 and 1 John 1:9 and experience the forgiveness of the Lord.

CHAPTER TWO
LISTEN TO WHAT GOD SAYS
Amos 3:1-15

Now that Amos had the attention of the people, he proceeded to deliver three messages, each of which begins with "Hear this word" (3:1; 4:1; 5:1). By using this phrase, he reminded them that they weren't listening to a mere man making a speech; they were listening to a prophet declaring the living Word of God.

It's indeed a great privilege to have God speak to us, but it's also a great responsibility. If we don't open our hearts to hear His Word and obey Him, we're in grave danger of hardening our hearts and incurring the wrath of God. "Today, if you will hear His voice, do not harden your hearts" (Heb. 3:7-8 NKJV; see Ps. 95:7-11).

The first message (Amos 3:1-15) was one of *explanation,* in which Amos clarified four divine calls and announced that Israel's judgment was certain. His second message (4:1-13) focused on *accusation* in which the prophet denounced Israel's sins. The final message (5:1–6:14) was a *lamentation* as the prophet felt the anguish of his nation's certain doom.

In this first message, Amos explains the significance of four divine calls.

1. God called Israel (Amos 3:1-2)

This message was delivered to "the whole family," that is, to both Israel and Judah; for both kingdoms were guilty of disobeying God's holy Law. Amos reminded them of their divine calling as the people of God, a calling that they were prone to despise and forget.

What kind of a calling did God give to the Jewish nation? To begin with, it was a *gracious call*; for the Lord had chosen them and no other nation to be the special recipients of His bountiful gifts. "For you are a holy people to the Lord your God; the Lord your God has chosen you to be a people for Himself, a special treasure above all the peoples on the face of the earth. The Lord did not set His love on you nor choose you because you were more in number than any other people, for you were the least of all peoples; but because the Lord loves you, and because He would keep the oath which He swore to your fathers" (Deut. 7:6-8 NKJV; see Ex. 19:1-5).

This principle of gracious election also applies to the church. Jesus said, "You did not choose me, but I chose you" (John 15:16 NIV); and Paul reminded the Corinthian believers that "not many wise men after the flesh, not many mighty, not many noble, are called"; but that God chose the foolish, the weak, the base, and the despised "that no flesh should glory in his presence" (1 Cor. 1:26, 29). God chose us in Christ before the foundation of the world (Eph. 1:4), and it was purely an act of grace.

God's call was also an *effective call* (Amos 3:1b), for the Lord had demonstrated His great power in delivering Israel from the bondage of Egypt. The blood of the Passover lamb protected the Jews from death, and they were taken through the Red Sea to be separated from Egypt forever. Christians today have been saved by the precious blood of Christ (1 Peter 1:18-19; 2:24) and separated from the world because of His mighty resurrection (Eph. 1:19-23).

Third, their calling was an *exclusive call* (Amos 3:2a). "You only have I chosen [known, KJV] of all the families of the earth" (NIV). The word "known" indicates an intimate relationship, such as that of husband and wife (Gen. 4:1). "To know" means "to choose" (see 18:19; Jer. 1:5; 2:2-3), a term Paul applies to Christian believers (Rom. 8:29). Because they were exclusively the Lord's, God did for Israel what He did for no other nation (9:4-5).

Finally, it was a calling that *involved responsibility* (Amos 3:2b). Because He had chosen them, called them, and blessed them, the people of Israel and Judah were responsible to love God and obey Him. If they didn't, God was responsible to chasten them in love and seek to bring them back to Himself.

The doctrine of divine election is not an excuse for sin; rather it is intended to motivate us to holy living. We should be so humbled by His grace and so amazed at His love (1 John 3:1-2) that our hearts would want to do nothing other than worship and serve Him. Privilege always brings with it responsibility (Eph. 1:3-5; John 15:16; 1 Peter 2:4-5, 9). "For everyone to whom much is given, from him much will be required" (Luke 12:48 NKJV).

As God's chosen people, we're to live worthy of our calling (Eph. 4:1) and not follow the practices of the unsaved world (v. 17). This means living in love (5:2), in wisdom (v. 15) and in the Spirit (v. 18). To do anything less is to live beneath our high calling and the privileges we have as the children of God.

2. God called Amos (Amos 3:3-8)

At this point, the people were probably saying, "Who is this rustic farmer that he should preach to us and claim to be God's prophet? What kind of authority does he think he has?" Amos even dared to preach uninvited at the king's chapel at Bethel, where King Jeroboam's chaplain told Amos to go home and preach in Judah (7:10-16).

No doubt when D. L. Moody began to preach, some people said, "What can this uneducated shoe salesman say to us?" And when Billy Sunday began to hold evangelistic campaigns, it's likely that the sophisticated religious crowd asked, "What can this former baseball player teach us?" But God used Moody and Sunday, not in spite of their humble background, but because of it; for He delights to bypass the "wise and prudent" and share His power with "babes" (Luke 10:21).

Amos replied to their ridicule by arguing from effect to cause. If two people want to walk together, they have to appoint a time and place to meet (Amos 3:3). If the lion roars, it's because he's caught his prey (v. 4). If a trap springs, it means the bird has been caught (v. 5); and if the people in a city are terrified, it's because the trumpet has blown, warning them of danger (v. 6). These are obvious facts of life that any thinking person would acknowledge.

Now for the final thrust: if an untrained rustic farmer is preaching God's Word, *it means God has called him.* This isn't a vocation Amos would have chosen for himself; it was chosen for him by the Lord. Amos said, "I was neither a prophet nor a prophet's son, but I was a shepherd, and I also took care of sycamore-fig trees. But the Lord took me from tending the flock and said to me, 'Go, prophesy to my people Israel' " (7:14-15 NIV).

When a prophet proclaims God's Word, it's because the Lord is about to do something important and wants to warn His people (3:7). Review the images Amos used in verses 3-6, and you will see what kind of work God called Amos to do. Because he was walking with God, he knew God's secrets. "The secret of the Lord is with them that fear him; and he will show them his covenant" (Ps. 25:14). The lion was roaring. "A lion has roared! Who will not fear? The Lord God has spoken! Who can but prophesy?" (Amos 3:8 NKJV) God was about to spring the trap: Israel would be wiped out by the Assyrians, and Judah would go into exile in Babylon. Amos was blowing the trumpet and preparing the people for the judgment to come.[1]

Amos clearly made his point. It was no accident of vocational choice that he was proclaiming God's message, for God had called him. And it was no accident of international diplomacy that Israel and Judah were facing judgment, for they had sinned against God. For every effect there is a cause. What caused Amos to preach God's Word? The call of God on his life.

Bible history and church history both reveal that God can and does use a variety of people to minister to His people. He used an educated man like Moses, and a humble shepherd like David, a priest like Jeremiah, and common fishermen like Peter, James, and John. Both Charles Finney and C. I. Scofield were trained to be lawyers, while John Bunyan was a mender of pots and pans, and D. Martyn Lloyd-Jones was a physician. Add to this the names of dedicated women God has greatly used—Catherine Booth, "mother" of the Salvation Army; Amy Carmichael, rescuer of abused children; Lina Sandell, Fanny Crosby, and Avis B. Christiansen, composers of beautiful hymns and Gospel songs—and you can see that God calls, equips, and uses all who will surrender to Him and let Him have His way.

Amos is an encouragement to all believers who feel they are inadequate to do the work of the Lord. He was a layman, not a graduate of a prophetic school. He learned spiritual truth as he communed with God while caring for the flocks and orchards. Self-taught? Yes, but he was God-taught; and he was willing to share with others what God had said to him. Robert Murray M'Cheyne wrote, "It is not great talents God blesses so much as great likeness to Jesus." This is not to minimize the importance of either talent or education, but to remind us that neither can be a substitute for heeding God's call and walking in communion with Him. Jesus said, "Apart from me you can do nothing" (John 15:5 NIV).

3. God calls witnesses (Amos 3:9-10)

In his day, the Prophet Isaiah called heaven and earth to witness against Judah (Isa. 1:2; see Deut. 30:19; 31:28); and Amos summoned the Gentile nations to witness against the Northern Kingdom of Israel whose capital was Samaria. The sin of Israel was so great that it even appalled the pagan nations; for, after all, Israel was sinning against a flood of light (1 Cor. 5:1).

It's tragic and humiliating when the unsaved world catches professed Christians in their sins. It happened to Abraham twice when he lied to heathen kings about his wife Sarah (Gen. 12:10-20; 20:1ff). Samson was shamed before the Philistines (Jud. 16), and David was embarrassed before the king of Gath (1 Sam. 21:10-15). David's adultery with Bathsheba gave "great occasion to the enemies of the Lord to blaspheme" (2 Sam. 12:14). In the late 1980s, the media ministry scandals brought great shame to the church; and whenever a prominent servant of God falls into sin, the news media seem to enjoy telling the story.

Amos called for the Philistines ("Ashdod," Amos 1:8) and the Egyptians to witness what was going on in Samaria (v. 9). The leaders of Israel weren't interested in obeying God's law and helping the less fortunate. Rather, they were eagerly and unjustly robbing the poor and amassing as much wealth as possible. They built costly houses, filled them with expensive furnishings, and lived in luxury while the poor of the land suffered (3:15; 4:1; 5:11; 6:4-6).

The Law of Moses made it clear that the nation was to care for the widows and orphans, the poor and the strangers in the land (see Ex. 22:25-27; 23:11; Lev. 19:9-15; 25:6; Deut. 14:28-29; 15:12-13; 16:11-14). Amos wasn't the only Hebrew prophet to accuse the rich of exploiting the poor and ignoring the needy, for you find similar messages in Isaiah (1:23; 10:1-2), Ezekiel (chap. 34), Micah (2:1-2), and Malachi (3:5).

What a terrible indictment: "They do not know how to do right" (Amos 3:10 NIV). They were so bound by their greed and idolatry that it was impossible for them to do what was right. Like many people today, they were addicted to affluence. They didn't care that others lacked the necessities of life so long as they themselves enjoyed luxuries. No wonder there was unrest in the land, for the possession of wealth never satisfied the hungers of the heart. "To pretend to satisfy one's desires by possessions," says a Chinese proverb, "is like using a straw to put out a fire."

Even more tragic than their greed was their arrogance. They lived in fortresses so they and their possessions were safe. Like the farmer in one of our Lord's parables (Luke 12:12-21), they thought they were safe and secure, but they discovered that their wealth couldn't stop death from coming. The attitude of the church of Laodicea is prevalent among God's people today: "I am rich, and increased with goods, and have need of nothing" (Rev. 3:17).

4. God calls for judgment (Amos 3:11-15)

Amos announced that the kingdom of Israel would fall to an enemy and the great city of Samaria would be plundered. This happened in 722 B.C. when the Assyrians invaded Israel. The people of Israel had plundered one another, but now a pagan Gentile nation would plunder them. We reap what we sow.

To illustrate what would happen to Israel, Amos borrowed from his experiences as a shepherd. According to Exodus 22:10-13, if a lion takes a sheep and tears it to pieces, the shepherd had to bring the remnants of the sheep to prove that it was truly dead (see Gen. 31:39). This would assure the owner of the flock that the shepherd wasn't stealing the sheep and lying to his employer. By the time Assyria was through with Israel, only a small remnant of the people would be left. The lion was about to roar! (Amos 1:2; 3:8)

According to 2 Kings 17:5ff, the Assyrians killed some Israelites, took others captive, and then brought into the land captives from other nations, thus producing a people with diverse racial and religious backgrounds. The surviving Jews in the ten tribes of the Northern Kingdom married people who were not Jews, and this produced the people we know as Samaritans. The "pure" Jews rejected this new "mongrel race" (John 4:9); so the Samaritans set up their own temple and priesthood and established their own religion, which the Lord rejected (vv. 19-24).

Amos made it clear that the invasion of the Assyrians was a work of God, for He was punishing Israel for her sins (Amos 3:14). Why? Because of their selfish luxury and their impudent idolatry. The people resting on their ivory beds in their expensive mansions would be stripped and led off as prisoners of war. The wealthy who had both summer and winter houses would have no houses.

When the Jewish kingdom was divided after the death of Solomon (1 Kings 12), King Jeroboam of Israel didn't want his people going to Jerusalem to worship, lest they go to Judah and never return to Israel. So he established shrines with golden calves at Dan and Bethel, set up his own priesthood, and encouraged the people to worship in Israel. Contrary to the Law of Moses, the kings also allowed the people to visit local shrines, where it was more convenient to worship whatever god they chose.

Amos announced that the Lord would destroy the royal chapel at Bethel (Amos 7:13); Israel's entire man-made religious system would be demolished. Nobody would be able to lay hold of the horns of the altar and claim protection (1 Kings 1:50-53), for the horns would be cut off.

For two centuries, God in His long-suffering had tolerated the people of the Northern Kingdom as they participated in their idolatrous rival religious system, but now it would come to an end. Instead of turning to God, however, the remnant in the land would set up another man-made religious system that the Lord would also reject. It would not be until the days of Christ (John 4) and the apostolic church (Acts 8) that the ancient division between Judah and Israel (Samaria) would be healed.

Like Israel of old, nations today measure themselves by their wealth; and the gross national product becomes the indicator of security and success. The rich get richer and the poor get poorer as people worship the golden calf of money and greedily exploit one another. But it doesn't take long for God to wipe out the idols that people worship and the unnecessary luxuries that control their lives. He hears the cries of the poor and eventually judges the guilty (see Pss. 10:14; 69:33; 82:3).

This isn't the end; Amos has two more messages to deliver.

CHAPTER THREE
SINS IN GOOD STANDING
Amos 4:1-13

I accompanied a pastor friend to hear a well-known preacher, who was visiting the United States. His message was powerful as he named the sins that he felt were destroying our nation.

As we were driving home after the meeting, my friend said, "Well, I must admit that he preached a great message, and it spoke to my heart. But I don't like it when visitors from other countries point out the sins of Americans. There's probably just as much sin back home in their own countries."

I disagree. After all, God has the right to use whatever servant He chooses to deliver His message wherever He pleases. But I'm sure the people in the kingdom of Israel must have felt the same way as my pastor friend when they heard Amos, a native of Judah, condemning the sins that were destroying Israel. No wonder Amaziah, the priest, told him to go home to Judah! (7:12-13)

In this second message, the Prophet Amos named three particular sins that were grieving the Lord and ruining the kingdom of Israel: luxury (4:1-3), hypocrisy (vv. 4-5), and obstinacy (vv. 6-13). They had the wrong values; their religious "revival" was a sham; and they had refused to listen to the warnings God had given them.

1. Luxury (Amos 4:1-3)

"Most of the luxuries and many of the so-called comforts of life are not only not indispensable, but positive hindrances to the elevation of mankind." So wrote Henry David Thoreau in his classic book Walden; and his friend Ralph Waldo Emerson wrote in his own journal, "Our expense is almost all for conformity. It is for cake that we all run in debt."[1] Let's seek to answer some questions about luxury.

What is luxury? The work "luxury" comes from a Latin word that means "excessive." It originally referred to plants that grow abundantly (our English word "luxurious"), but then it came to refer to people who have an abundance of money, time, and comfort, which they use for themselves as they live in aimless leisure. Whenever you are offered "deluxe service," that's the same Latin word: service above and beyond what you really need.

It isn't a sin to be rich or to have the comforts of life, if this is God's will for you. Abraham and David were wealthy men. Yet they used what they had for God's glory. In the eyes of people in the Third World, most of the citizens of the Western world, including the poor, are very wealthy. What the Western world considers necessities are luxuries to the citizens of other nations: things like thermostat-controlled heat and air conditioning, refrigerators, automobiles, adequate medical care, telephones, and abundantly available electricity and fuel.

Luxury doesn't mean owning abundant possessions so much as allowing possessions to own us. To live in luxury is to use what we have only for our own enjoyment and to ignore the needs of others. It means being irresponsible in the way we use our wealth, wasting it on futile pleasures instead of using it for the good of others and the glory of God. A sign in an exclusive clothing store read, "If you must ask the price of our garments, you can't afford them." People who live in luxury don't bother to ask the prices. They don't care how much they spend so long as they get what they want.

Who was committing this sin? "Hear this word, you cows of Bashan!"[2] (v. 1 NKJV). Amos addressed the wives of the wealthy leaders of the land, people who had gotten rich by ruthlessly and illegally robbing others. These "society women" lounged around all day, drinking wine and telling their husbands what to do. Any preacher today who called the women in the congregation "cows" would be looking for another church very soon.

Why did Amos, the farmer, use this image? Not because these women were overweight and looked like cows, but because by their sins they were fattening themselves up for the coming slaughter. Both they and their husbands were living in luxury while the poor of the land were suffering because these same men had exploited them and robbed them of money and land.

What will happen to them? What do farmers eventually do with cattle that have been fattened up? They lead them away to be killed and butchered. Amos described what would happen when the Assyrians invaded

Israel, how they would capture these women and treat them like cattle. The Assyrian practice was to put hooks in the noses or lower lips of their prisoners, attach ropes, and lead them away like animals, either to captivity or to death. This is what the enemy would do to the wealthy matrons Amos was addressing in his message.[3]

But note that their posterity would also be involved in this judgment (v. 2).[4] These wealthy women no doubt wanted "the best" for their children, but by their selfish priorities and their sinful example, they were giving their children the very worst. Their posterity had everything but a knowledge of the Lord; so they too would be led off like animals to the slaughter. The wealthy younger generation in Israel had everything money could buy, but they didn't have the things money can't buy, the things of the Lord that make life worthwhile.

While attending a banquet in Dearborn, Michigan, I found myself seated next to a wealthy gentleman whose name was famous in the business world. In our conversation, I discovered I had some information about a deceased preacher he greatly admired, and I offered to mail it to him. When I asked for an address, I thought he would hand me an expensive embossed calling card. Instead, he gave me a return label ripped off an envelope! I was told that he and his wife lived modestly in spite of their wealth. It's no wonder they were able to give so generously to Christian ministries and philanthropic causes.

Industrial magnate Andrew Carnegie said, "Surplus wealth is a sacred trust which its possessor is bound to administer in his lifetime for the good of the community." Paul wrote, "Command those who are rich in this present age not to be haughty, nor to trust in uncertain riches but in the living God, who gives us richly all things to enjoy. Let them do good, that they be rich in good works, ready to give, willing to share, storing up for themselves a good foundation for the time to come, that they may lay hold on eternal life" (1 Tim. 6:17-19 NKJV). Paul also quoted Jesus who said, "It is more blessed to give than to receive" (Acts 20:35).

2. Hypocrisy (Amos 4:4-5)

The prophet used "holy irony"[5] when he spoke these words, for he later instructed them to do just the opposite (5:5). It's as though a pastor today said to his congregation, "Sure, go ahead and attend church, but by attending, you're only sinning more. Go and visit the summer Bible conferences, but by doing so, you will be transgressing more. Your heart isn't serious about knowing God or doing His will. Since it's all just playacting. Since it's the popular thing to do, so you do it."

Bethel was a very special place to the Jewish people because of its associations with Abraham (Gen. 12:8; 13:3) and Jacob (28:10-22; 35:1-7). At one time, the ark was kept at Bethel (Jud. 20:18-28), but in Amos' day it was the site of "the king's chapel" where Amaziah, the priest, served (Amos 7:10ff). Gilgal was also important to Israel because that's where Joshua and the people camped when they first entered the Promised Land (Josh. 4:19-20; 5:2-9). Gilgal is also where Saul was made king of Israel (1 Sam. 11:15). Unfortunately, both of these places had become shrines, where the people worshiped pagan gods while claiming to worship the Lord.

On the surface, it looked as if Israel was experiencing a religious revival. Crowds of people were flocking to the "holy places" (Amos 5:5), bringing their sacrifices and tithes (4:4; 5:21-22)[6] and even singing songs of praise to the Lord (v. 23; 6:5; 8:3, 10). They offered sacrifices more frequently than the law required as if to prove how spiritual they were. But their gifts and songs didn't impress the Lord, for He saw what was in their hearts; and the sin in their hearts made their sacrifices unacceptable.

To begin with, their sacrifices were unclean, like offering leaven on the altar, which was forbidden by God (Lev. 2:11; 6:17). God doesn't want the sacrifices of bulls and goats; He wants the obedience of our hearts (1 Sam. 15:22-23; see Pss. 50:8-9; 51:16-17; Isa. 1:11-17; Hosea 6:6; Micah 6:6-8; Mark 12:28-34). If the heart isn't right with God, the sacrifice means nothing (Gen. 4:1-7).

Furthermore, they were proud of what they were doing and made sure everybody knew how generous they were to the Lord. They bragged about their freewill offerings, which were purely voluntary; and they boasted to one another of their sacrifices. It wasn't the Lord who got the glory! (See Matt. 6:1-4.) They were like people today who make sure their generosity is recognized from the pulpit and in the church bulletin. If it isn't, they stop giving.

The people of Israel "loved" going to religious meetings, but they didn't love the God they claimed to worship. Making a pilgrimage to Bethel or Gilgal was the popular thing to do in that day, and everybody wanted to keep up with the crowd. There was no confession of sin, no brokenness before the Lord, but only a religious event that made the participants feel good. The whole system was corrupt; the people were sinning when they thought they were serving the Lord.

The application to today's church is obvious. It's very easy for us to join a large, happy religious crowd, enthusiastically sing rousing songs, and put money in the offering plate, and yet not be changed in our hearts. The test of a spiritual experience is not "Do I feel good?" or "Did we have a big crowd and a good time?" The real test is "Do I know God better and am I more like Jesus Christ?"

The people in Amos' day didn't return home determined to help the poor, feed the hungry, and care for the widows and orphans. They went home with the same selfish hearts that they had when they left home, because their "worship" was only an empty ritual (Isa. 1:11-17). Any religious "revival" that doesn't alter the priorities of Christians and help solve the problems in society isn't a "revival" at all.

It's interesting that Amos mentioned music, because that's an important part of the church's worship. However, what the Jews thought was beautiful music, God considered nothing but "noise" (Amos 5:23). People today will pay high prices for tickets to "Christian concerts," yet they won't attend a free Bible study class or Bible conference in their own church. Christian music is big business today, but we wonder how much of it really glorifies the Lord. What we think is music may be nothing but noise to the Lord.

Whether it's evangelism, education, social action, world missions, or feeding the hungry, everything the church accomplishes for the Lord flows out of worship. If the fountainhead of worship is polluted, the church's entire ministry will be defiled. Like the Jews in Amos' day, we're only going to Bethel and sinning! Therefore, it behooves God's people to examine their hearts and make certain that their motives are right and that what they do in public meetings glorifies the Lord.

Amos has dealt with two of the three sins that the Lord told him to condemn—luxury and hypocrisy; and now he deals with the third, obstinacy. God's people were rebellious and hard-hearted, refusing to obey the Lord.

3. Obstinacy (Amos 4:6-13)

Five times in this passage, Amos says to the people, "Yet you have not returned to Me" (4:6, 8, 9, 10, 11 NKJV). The people of Israel experienced God's disciplines, but they wouldn't submit to His will; and yet they continued practicing their hypocritical religion! "Not everyone who says to Me, 'Lord, Lord,' shall enter the kingdom of heaven, but he who does the will of My Father in heaven" (Matt. 7:21 NKJV).

God's covenant with the Jews clearly stated that He would bless them if they obeyed His Law and would discipline them if they disobeyed (Deut. 27–29). God set before them life and death, blessing and cursing; and He urged them to choose life (30:19-20). Unfortunately, they spurned His love, rejected His warnings, and chose death.

Consider some of the disciplines that God sent to Israel to bring His people back to Himself.

Famine (Amos 4:6). "Cleanness of teeth" simply means the people had no food to eat. So their teeth didn't get dirty. (The NIV paraphrases it "empty stomachs.") God's covenant promised bumper crops if the people obeyed the Lord, but famine if they disobeyed (Lev. 26:27-31; Deut. 28:1-11). When farmers can't grow crops, food is scarce, food prices go up, and people suffer and die. You would think that this would move people to confess their sins and return to God, but Israel did not return to God.

Drought (Amos 4:7-8). Instead of sending a general drought over the entire kingdom, God withheld the rain in different places from time to time, thus proving that He was in control. This remarkable demonstration of God's sovereign power should have reminded the Jews of what the covenant said about the promised rains (Lev. 26:18-20; Deut. 11:16-17; 28:23-24), but they paid no heed.

Destruction of crops (Amos 4:9). Even when God did allow them to grow fruits and vegetables, they weren't grateful. So He destroyed the crops with blight, mildew, and locusts. Once again, God was being true to His covenant warnings (Deut. 28:38-42). So the nation should not have been surprised.

Sicknesses (Amos 4:10a). One of God's promises was that His people would not experience the dreadful diseases they saw in

Egypt if they were faithful to obey His Law (Ex. 15:26); but if they rebelled against Him, they would suffer all the diseases of Egypt (Lev. 26:23-26; Deut. 28:21-22, 27-29, 35, 59-62). As with the other disciplines, God kept His Word.

Defeat in war (Amos 4:10b). "The Lord will cause your enemies who rise against you to be defeated before your face; they shall come out against you one way and flee before you seven ways" (Deut. 28:7 NKJV; see Lev. 26:6-8). What a promise for a small nation surrounded by huge empires! But the promise would be fulfilled only if the people were faithful to the Lord. If they disobeyed, they would be humiliated and defeated before their enemies (Lev. 26:32-39; Deut. 28:49-58). So terrible would be their defeat that the dead bodies in the camps would not be given decent burial, but would lie there and rot. God kept His promise: the Assyrians conquered Israel and the Babylonians took Judah into captivity.

Catastrophe (Amos 4:11). We aren't sure just what this calamity was. Perhaps it was an earthquake (1:1), or it may have been the devastating invasion of an army (2 Kings 10:32-33; 13:7). Whatever it was, it had to be something terrible for the Lord to compare it to the destruction of Sodom and Gomorrah (Gen. 19:24-25; see Deut. 29:23; Isa. 1:9; 13:19). The image of a stick pulled out of the fire suggests that the Lord intervened and saved them at the last minute (Zech. 3:2). They had been burned but not consumed. If so, then their ingratitude and hardness of heart was even more wicked.

Ultimate judgment (Amos 4:12-13). The kingdom of Israel had experienced famine, drought, blight, plagues, wars, and devastating catastrophes as God had tried to speak to His people and bring them to repentance. No matter what discipline He sent, they would not return to Him. What more could He do? He could come Himself and deal with them! "Prepare to meet thy God, O Israel!" (v. 12) was not a call to repentance but an announcement that it was too late to repent. The Lord of Hosts (armies) Himself would come with the Assyrian hordes and take the people away like cattle being led to the slaughter (v. 2). "There will be wailing in all the vineyards, for I will pass through your midst" (5:17 NIV).

Amos ended his message with a doxology of praise to the Lord (4:13; see 5:8-9; 9:5-6). When a servant of God praises the Lord in the face of impending calamity, it shows he's a person of great faith (see Hab. 3:16-19). In this doxology, he reminds us that our God is the Creator who can do anything, including making the earth out of nothing. He can turn dawn into darkness; He can tread upon the mountains, and nobody can hinder Him. He is also the omniscient God who knows what we are thinking. Thus there's nothing we can hide from Him (Ps. 139:1-6). He is the Lord of Hosts, the God of the armies of heaven and earth!

But are God's people any more prepared today?

CHAPTER FOUR
HOW TO AVOID THE STORM
Amos 5:1-17

The prophet's third message (5:1–6:14) was a lamentation, a funeral dirge over the death of the nation of Israel. (Israel is mentioned four times in 5:1-4.) "There will be wailing in all the streets," he declares (v. 16 NIV), not just wailing in one or two houses where people have died. Since the people's grief will be so great that there won't be sufficient professional mourners available to express it, they'll call the farmers and workers in the vineyards to help them (vv. 16-17).

However, Amos weaves into his lamentation three pleas to the people, urging them to return to the Lord.

1. "Hear God's Word!" (Amos 5:1-3)

This is the third time Amos has called the people to give attention to God's Word (3:1; 4:1). The way we treat God's Word is the way we treat God, and the way we treat God's messengers is the way we treat the Lord Himself (John 15:18-21). "God . . . has in these last days spoken to us by His Son. . . . See that you do not refuse Him who speaks" (Heb. 1:1-2; 12:25 NKJV).

The listeners must have wondered why Amos was wailing a funeral dirge when nobody in his family or circle of acquaintances had died. They were perplexed as to why he was grieving over the death of his nation when the nation seemed to be prosperous and religious. But the prosperity and "revival" were only cosmetics to make the sick and dying nation look healthier. Amos looked at the vital signs, and they were almost gone. Israel's enthusiastic concerts would become funerals (5:23; 8:3, 10) and their sacred shrines ruins, for the Assyrians were destined to destroy the kingdom of Israel.

Amos compared the nation to a virgin daughter in the bloom of youth, ravaged and slain on the field of battle, her corpse left to rot.[1] All hope was gone, and nobody could help her get up. History records the fulfillment of Amos' words. After the Assyrian invasion, the kingdom of Israel ceased to exist and has never been restored. Some of the people were taken into exile, some were slain, and the rest were left to mingle with the Gentiles that were brought in to resettle the land. The result was a mixed race—the Samaritans—neither Jew nor Gentile.

Israel had a strong standing army, but it would be defeated, and the population decimated, just as the Lord had warned in His covenant (Lev. 26:7-8; Deut. 28:25; 32:28-30). There can be no victory when the Lord has abandoned you to your fate, because you have abandoned Him. Nations today depend on their wealth, their military establishment, and their political wisdom when they need to depend on the Lord. "Blessed is the nation whose God is the Lord" (Ps. 33:12).

Of course, what happened to the Northern Kingdom of Israel didn't end God's promises to the Jews or His purposes for them in the world. Groups who claim to be the "ten lost tribes of Israel" are suspect, because nowhere does Scripture say the ten tribes were "lost." The New Testament indicates that God knows where all twelve tribes are (Matt. 19:28; Luke 22:30; Acts 26:7; James 1:1; Rev. 7:4; 21:12), and the prophets speak of a time of reunion and glory (Ezek. 37:19-28; 33:23, 29; Jer. 3:18; 23:5-6; Hosea 1:11).

The first step toward revival and returning to the Lord is to hear what God has to say to us from His Word. "Will You not revive us again, that Your people may rejoice in You? Show us Your mercy, O Lord, and grant us Your salvation. I will hear what God the Lord will speak, for He will speak peace to His people and to His saints; but let them not turn back to folly" (Ps. 85:6-8 NKJV).

2. "Seek the Lord!" (Amos 5:4-6)

This phrase is found more than thirty times in Scripture. It applied to Israel in ancient days, and it applies to God's children today. Even if the whole nation (or church) doesn't respond to the message and return to the Lord, a remnant can return and receive the Lord's help and blessing. God was willing to save the evil city of Sodom if He had found ten righteous people in it (Gen. 18:32); and in Jeremiah's day, the Lord would have been happy to find even one righteous person in Jerusalem! God can work through the many or the few (1 Sam. 14:6), we should never despise the day of small things (Zech. 4:10).

What does it mean to "seek the Lord"? The Prophet Isaiah answers the question: "Seek the Lord while He may be found, call upon Him while He is near. Let the wicked forsake his way, and the unrighteous man his thoughts; let him return to the Lord, and He will have mercy on him; and to our God, for He will abundantly pardon" (Isa. 55:6-7 NKJV).

To seek the Lord means first of all to change our thinking and abandon the vain thoughts that are directing our wayward lives. Disobedient children of God are thinking wrongly about God, sin, and life. They think God will always be there for them to turn to, but they forget that sinners reap what they sow. To walk "in the counsel of the ungodly" is folly indeed (Ps. 1:1, NKJV), for it leads to a fruitless and joyless life.

When we return to the Lord, we also change directions: we "turn around" and start to move in the right direction. It means forsaking sin and turning to the Lord for mercy and pardon. Until we realize how heinous our sins are in the sight of God, we will never repent and cry out for mercy. To seek the Lord doesn't mean simply to run to God for help when our sins get us into trouble, although God will receive us if we're sincere. It means to loathe and despise the sin in our lives, turn from it, and seek the fellowship of God and His cleansing. "A broken and a contrite heart—these, O God, You will not despise" (Ps. 51:17 NKJV).

Why should we seek the Lord? The prophet gave three reasons, the first of which is that we might have life (Amos 5:4). The way of disobedience is the way of darkness and death. "Seek me and live" is God's invitation and admonition (v. 4 NIV). God disciplines His children in love so that they will repent and return; but if we don't change our ways, He may take our lives. "Moreover, we have all had human fathers who disciplined us and we respected them for it. How much more should we submit to the Father of our spirits and live!" (Heb. 12:9 NIV) The suggestion here is that if we don't submit, we may die; for "there is a sin unto death" (1 John 5:16).

The second reason we should seek God is because there is no other way to experience spiritual blessing (Amos 5:5). The people were going to the shrines in droves and coming home further from God than when they left. Emerson said that a change in geography never overcomes a flaw in character, and he was right.

During my years of ministry, I've been privileged to speak at many well-known conference grounds in the United States, Canada, and overseas. I've met people at some of these conferences who actually thought that their physical presence by that lake, in that tent or tabernacle, or on that mountain would change their hearts. They were depending on the "atmosphere" of the conference and their memories for them, but they usually went home disappointed. Why? Because they didn't seek God.

I'm reminded of a lady at one conference who, when she checked out to go home, asked if she could buy a carton of the soap used in the rooms. When asked why she wanted that particular kind of soap, she explained that it was so rich and lathery, much better than what she used at home. The conference director gave her a carton of the soap, but didn't have the heart to explain to her that it was the softness of the water, not the formula of the soap, that guaranteed the rich lather.

God doesn't franchise His blessings the way companies franchise their products to local dealers. You can't go to Bethel and Gilgal (see 4:4) or to Beersheba[2] and go home with a blessing in your baggage. Unless we personally meet the Lord, deal with our inner spiritual life, and seek His face, our hearts will never be transformed.

The "holy places" would all be destroyed. The people of Gilgal would go into captivity (5:27), the shrine would be abandoned, and Bethel, the "house of God," would become "Beth Aven," the "house of nothing" (see Hosea 4:15, 5:8; 10:5) and go up in smoke (Amos 5:6). Even if pilgrims traveled into Judah to visit Beersheba, that was no guarantee of blessing. Eventually Judah would fall to the Babylonians.

The third reason for seeking God is because judgment is coming (v. 6). The phrase, "lest he break out like fire" reminds us of God's repeated warning in chapters 1 and 2, "I will send a fire" (1:4, 7, 10, 12, 14; 2:2, 5). "For our God is a consuming fire" (Heb. 12:29; see Deut. 4:24). If the Gentiles, who never had the written Law of God, suffered fiery punishment for their sins, how much more would the Jews be punished who possessed God's holy Law! "The Lord shall judge His people" (Heb. 10:30; see Deut. 32:35-36; Ps. 135:14).

Fear of judgment may not be the highest motive for obeying God, but the Lord will accept it. Animals and little children understand rewards and punishments, but we hope that the children will eventually mature and develop higher motives for obedience than receiving some candy or escaping a spanking. God's people, Israel, never achieved that higher level of obedience, the kind of obedience that comes from a heart that loves God (Deut. 4:37; 6:4-6; 7:6-13; 10:12; 11:1; 30:6, 16, 20).

For Israel to repent and return to God was a reasonable thing to do. It would bring them life; it would produce spiritual reality; and it would save them from impending judgment. Those are good reasons for God's people to repent today.

3. "Seek the good!" (Amos 5:7-15)

To "seek the Lord" might appear difficult and distant for some people, an intangible experience they can't get their hands on. Thus Amos brought the challenge down to practical, everyday life. He spoke about justice, righteousness, and the importance of telling the truth. He named the sins the people needed to forsake: accepting bribes, charging the poor exorbitant rents, living in luxury while the poor starved, and sustaining a crooked legal system. True repentance begins with naming sins and dealing with them one by one.

We must notice that verses 8-9 are a parenthesis in the prophet's message, but a very important parenthesis as he reminded the people of the greatness of their God. Jehovah is the God who created the heavens and the earth, who controls the seasons and the daily motions of the earth, and who is Lord of the heavens, the sea, and the land.

The pagan Gentiles worshiped the heavenly bodies, but the Jews were privileged to worship the God who made the heavens and the earth (Jonah 1:9).

But this God of creation is also the God of judgment! "He flashes destruction on the stronghold and brings the fortified city to ruin" (Amos 5:9 NIV). J. B. Phillips graphically translated verse 9, "He it is who flings ruin in the face of the strong, and rains destruction upon the fortress."[3] In the light of the holiness of God and the terms of His holy covenant, the people of Israel should have been on their faces, calling out for mercy. Instead, they were complacently comfortable in their luxury and their sins. Amos named just a few of their sins.

Promoting injustice (Amos 5:7). God established human government because of the sinfulness of the human heart. Without the authority of government in society, everything would fall apart and the strong would enslave the weak and the rich would exploit the poor. Justice is supposed to be "a river ... a never-failing stream" (v. 24 NIV) that cleanses and refreshes society, but the leaders of Israel had turned that refreshing river into bitter poison (see 6:12).

Righteousness and justice should be the pillars that hold up society, but these selfish rulers had thrown the pillars to the ground. One of the evidences that the pillars of national justice are shaking and ready to fall is the increase in lawsuits. "They make many promises, take false oaths and make agreements; therefore lawsuits spring up like poisonous weeds in a plowed field" (Hosea 10:4 NIV). Israel was afflicted with poisonous weeds and poisonous water (Amos 5:7), and the Lord was displeased.

Instead of running to religious meetings, the people should have stayed home and seen to it that their leaders weren't poisoning the river of justice and knocking down the pillars of righteousness. Christians are the salt of the earth, and salt prevents corruption. They are the light of the world, and if there were more light, there would be less darkness (Matt. 5:13-16). The church must not abandon its marching orders and turn preachers into politicians, but it dare not ignore the problems of society—problems that can be solved by the application of the Gospel and the truth of the Word of God.

Rejecting rebuke (Amos 5:10, 13). The city gate was the place where the elders met and transacted city business (Ruth 4). When the dishonest leaders attempted to foist their lies on the people and manipulate the court, if somebody rebuked them, they turned on that person and tried to silence him or her. It got to the place where the righteous wouldn't say anything because their interference did no good (Amos 5:13). Leaders with integrity will gladly listen to counsel and even to rebuke, but leaders bent on evil will seek to destroy those who stand in their way. "Do not correct a scoffer, lest he hate you; rebuke a wise man, and he will love you" (Prov. 9:8 NKJV and see 1 Kings 22:5ff for an illustration of this principle).

For many years, American legal experts have called for an overhaul of the legal system. (Other nations probably have the same or worse problems.) So many cases are pending, and too many trials proceed at a snail's pace, with seemingly interminable appeals and delays, that very little justice results. Isaiah saw a similar situation in his day: "So justice is driven back, and the righteousness stands at a distance; truth has stumbled in the streets, honesty cannot enter. . . . The Lord looked and was displeased that there was no justice" (Isa. 59:14-15 NIV). A traffic jam!

Oppressing the poor (Amos 5:11-12). The Prophet Amos was the champion of the poor and oppressed (2:6-7; 4:1; 8:6) as he called for justice in the land.[4] He pictured the rich trampling the poor into the mud by claiming their crops for payment of the high rents they were charging. The rich were literally taking the food right out of the mouths of their tenants and their children. And if these hungry tenants appealed to the local judges for justice, the wealthy landowners bought off the judges.

So what did the rich do with this ill-gotten wealth? They used it to build mansions for themselves and to plant luxurious vineyards. They anticipated lounging in their big houses and drinking wine, but the Lord had other plans. He announced that they would neither live in their mansions nor drink their wine, because the Assyrians would destroy all their houses and vineyards. Like the selfish rich in the apostolic days, these powerful landowners were fattening their hearts for the day of slaughter (James 5:1-6).

God knew what these wealthy exploiters were doing, just as He knows what sinners are doing today; and though He appeared to be unconcerned, He would judge these evil people in due time. God had warned in His covenant with the Jewish people, "You shall build a house, but you shall not dwell in it; you shall plant a vineyard, but shall not gather its grapes" (Deut. 28:30 NKJV). God always keeps His promises, whether to bless when we've obeyed or to chasten when we've rebelled.

Arrogant self-confidence (Amos 5:14-15). The people were boasting, "The Lord God is with us!" After all, wasn't the nation enjoying great prosperity? Certainly that was a sign of God's blessing. And weren't the people active in religious activities, bringing their sacrifices and offerings to the shrines? And didn't the king have a special priest and a royal sanctuary in Bethel (7:10-17), where he consulted with Amaziah about the affairs of the kingdom?

Yes, these things were true, but they could not be used as evidence of the blessing of God. They were but a thin veneer of religious self-righteousness over the rotting corpse of the nation. The only proof that God is with us is that we love Him and do His will. Religion without righteousness and justice in the land is hypocrisy. No matter how many people attend religious meetings, if the result is not obedience to God and concern for our neighbor, the meetings are a failure.

How can we claim to love the good if we don't hate the evil? We claim to love the Lord, but God commands, "You who love the Lord, hate evil!" (Ps. 97:10 NKJV) We enjoy studying the Bible, but the psalmist said, "Through Your precepts I get understanding; therefore I hate every false way" (119:104 NKJV). Seeking the good means rejecting the evil and not being ashamed to take our stand against what's wrong.

Is there any hope for such a wicked society? Yes, as long as the grace of God is at work. "It may be that the Lord God of hosts will be gracious to the remnant of Joseph" (Amos 5:15 NKJV). Disaster was coming to Israel, but who knows what God would do if only a godly remnant turned to Him and sought His mercy?

"So I sought for a man among them who would make a wall, and stand in the gap before Me on behalf of the land, that I should not destroy it; but I found no one" (Ezek. 22:30 NKJV).

God is still seeking for wall-builders, for intercessors who will plead with God to send revival and renewal to His church. For it's only when God's Spirit is allowed to work among His people that the flood of evil can be stopped and righteousness and justice flourish in the land. The saints want God to judge the wicked, but "the time is come that judgment must begin at the house of God" (1 Peter 4:17).

If only a remnant will repent and turn to God, there is hope that He will send the revival that we desperately need.

"Hear God's Word!" *Are we listening?*

"Seek the Lord!" *Are we praying?*

"Seek the good!" *Do we hate that which is evil?*

There is no other way.

CHAPTER FIVE
"WOE TO THE SINNERS!"
Amos 5:18–6:14

Amos is still lamenting the impending doom of the nation of Israel. In this section, he pronounces "woe" upon four kinds of people in the kingdom: the ignorant (5:18-27), the indifferent (6:1-2), the indulgent (vv. 3-7), and the impudent (vv. 8-14). The circumstances are different, but we have these same people in the professing church today. Do you recognize them?

1. "Woe to the ignorant!" (Amos 5:18-27)

"The Day of the Lord" is a period of time during which God judges His enemies and establishes His kingdom on earth. It's the answer to our prayer, "Thy kingdom come" and is described in Revelation 6–20 and many passages in the books of the prophets.

The people Amos was addressing saw "the Day of the Lord" as a time of great deliverance for the Jews and terrible punishment for the Gentiles (Joel 2:28-32), but the prophets had a clearer vision of this momentous event. They realized that "the Day of the Lord" was also a time of testing and purifying for Israel (see Isa. 2:10-21; 13:6-13; Jer. 46:10; Joel 3:9-17; Zeph. 2:1-2), when God's people would go through tribulation before entering the kingdom of God.

Amos looked ahead and gave three descriptions of "the Day of the Lord." It would first of all be a day of despair and mourning (Amos 5:18a). "Woe to you who long for the day of the Lord!" (NIV) Good theology can lead to hope, but bad theology leads to false hopes. Since these hypocrites were sure that God would spare Israel but condemn their enemies, they longed for the Day of the Lord to come. They were like the editors of old editions of the Bible that I've seen: If the chapter was about judgment, the heading read, "God's judgment on the Jews"; but if the chapter was about blessing, the heading read, "God's blessing on the church." Heads we win, tails you lose!

Second, it would be a day of darkness (vv. 18b, 20). God had warned that He was about to pass through their midst (v. 17), but not "pass over" as He had in Egypt. This time He was coming to judge His own people; and as there was darkness for three days prior to that first Passover (Ex. 12:12), so "the Day of the Lord" would bring darkness. In addition, what Israel experienced at the hands of the Assyrians was a small sampling of what will happen in the end times when the whole world will see "the Day of the Lord."

Third, it would be a day of doom (Amos 5:19). There would be no escaping God's wrath because there were no hiding places! Run from the lion, and you meet the bear; run for safety into your house, and a serpent bites you. We would say, "Out of the frying pan, into the fire!" Remember, God's judgments are very thorough and accurate.

These Israelites were eagerly expecting "the Day of the Lord" without realizing what that day would bring to them. They were like some Christians today who want Jesus to come so they can escape painful situations and not because they "love His appearing" (2 Tim. 4:8). They forget that Christ's return means judgment as well as blessing. "For we must all appear before the judgment seat of Christ; that every one may receive the things done in his body, according to that he hath done, whether it be good or bad. Knowing therefore the terror of the Lord, we persuade men" (2 Cor. 5:10-11).

Next in his message, Amos looked around (Amos 5:21-24) and pointed out the sins of the people that made them totally unprepared to experience the Day of the Lord. He began with their hypocritical worship (vv. 21-22), something he had mentioned earlier (4:4-5). They honored special days on the Jewish calendar, called sacred assemblies, offered sacrifices, brought offerings, and sang songs of worship. Their meetings looked so beautiful and holy, yet God not only refused to accept their worship, He said He despised and hated it! (See Isa. 1:10-20.)

The prophet's second indictment was against their unconcern for others (Amos 5:24). This is a key verse in the Book of Amos, for it reveals God's concern that His people be righteous in their character and just in their conduct. We have already noted the emphasis on justice in Amos' messages and how the leaders of the land had turned the pure river of justice into a poisonous stream (5:7; see 6:12). No matter how much "religious activity" we participate in, if we don't love our brother and our neighbor, we can't honestly worship and serve the Lord.

Finally, Amos looked back (5:25-27) and reminded them of their relationship to Jehovah after He had delivered them from Egypt. God asked the Jews to give Him faith, obedience, and love; but at Mount Sinai, after vowing to serve God, the people worshiped a golden calf! (see Ex. 32) Their forefathers sinned further by offering sacrifices to false gods even while Jehovah was leading the nation through the wilderness! (Stephen quotes this in Acts 7:42-43.)[1]

After the Jews settled in the Promised Land, two generations of leaders guided them in the way of the Lord. But by the time the third generation came along, the people had turned to the idols of the nations around them (Jud. 2:10-15). God chastened them by allowing these nations to enslave Israel in their won land. But the message Amos had for the people was that they would have to leave their land and go into exile wherever the Assyrians sent them. It meant the end of the Northern Kingdom (2 Kings 17:6 ff).

"Where ignorance is bliss," wrote Thomas Gray, "'tis folly to be wise." But the poet was writing about the naive innocence of childhood, not to spoil the joys of children by telling them about the burdens of adulthood. However, in the Christian life, ignorance of God's truth keeps us in darkness (Isa. 8:20); so we must understand His "word of prophecy" that shines as a light in this world's darkness (2 Peter 1:19).

2. "Woe to the indifferent!" (Amos 6:1-2)

This "woe" was addressed to both Judah ("Zion") and Israel ("Samaria") because both kingdoms were indifferent toward God's Word and the judgment that hung over them. They called themselves "the foremost nation" (v. 1, NIV) and enjoyed an unwarranted false confidence for several reasons.

The first cause of their complacency was their geography. Situated on Mount Zion, Jerusalem was considered impregnable (Pss. 78:68-69; 132:13-18); and Samaria also had a seemingly secure position. But when God decided to deal with these cities, nothing could stop the enemy.

As for their prosperity, government, and military strength, Amos had already exposed the folly depending on them; for the heart of each nation was corrupt to the core. The notable men in Israel's government gave their opinion that the nation was safe and secure, and the people believed them, just as people today believe the political "experts" and the polls. False confidence that's based on expert advice, statistics, and material resources and that ignores the spiritual dimension of life is sure to lead to shameful defeat.

Amos mentioned areas in Syria and Philistia that had already fallen to the Assyrian army and then asked two questions: "Are you better than they? Is your territory bigger than theirs?" If the enemy had already destroyed places bigger and stronger than Samaria and Israel, what hope was there for the Jewish people, especially when the Jews were living like the Gentiles and were disobeying the Lord? God doesn't look at the talent of national leaders, the extent of a nation's army, or the prosperity of its economy. God looks at the heart, and the heart of the two Jewish kingdoms was far from the Lord.

Complacency is an insidious sin, because it's based on lies, motivated by pride, and leads to trusting something other than God (Zeph. 1:12). Like the people in the church of Laodicea, complacent people consider themselves "rich, and increased with goods" and in need of nothing (Rev. 3:17). In reality, however, they have lost everything that's important in the spiritual life. When the Lord sees His people becoming complacent and self-satisfied, He sometimes sends trials to wake them up.

3. "Woe to the indulgent!" (Amos 6:3-7)

"It can't happen here!" was the motto of the complacent leaders. "If a day of judgment is coming, it's surely a long way off." Whenever anybody mentioned the possibility of national disaster, the leaders laughed at the idea and disregarded it. But God had a different viewpoint. He said, "All the sinners of My people shall die by the sword, who say, 'The calamity shall not overtake us nor confront us' " (9:10 NKJV). Yet by their very indifference, they were bringing the day of judgment that much nearer.

Amos described their indulgent way of life—a way of life that left no place for the disciplines of the spiritual life. They were living for pleasure not for the glory of God. The common people usually slept on mats placed on the ground, but the wealthy enjoyed the luxury of beds of ivory and luxurious couches. They also used ivory to decorate their mansions (3:15). Excavations in Samaria have led to the discovery of the "Samaritan Ivories," fragments of beautiful ivory carvings that once adorned their houses and furniture.

The wealthy also enjoyed elegant feasts, eating lamb and veal, drinking wine in abundance, enjoying beautiful music, and wearing expensive perfumes. The poor people, whom they exploited, couldn't afford to kill tender lambs and calves, but had to settle for occasional mutton and beef, perhaps from a sacrifice. They would serve only cups of wine, not bowls; and their only "cosmetic" was olive oil.[2]

There's certainly nothing wrong with enjoying good food or good music, provided the things of the Lord are uppermost in your heart. David designed and made musical instruments, but he used them to praise the Lord. Abraham was able to prepare an elegant feast for his guests (Gen. 18:1-8), and the Lord didn't rebuke him. But the sin in Amos' day was that these luxuries distracted the people from the real problems of the nation, and "they [were] not grieved for the affliction of Joseph [Samaria]" (Amos 6:6). The NIV translates the Hebrew word sheber as "ruin," for it means the total collapse of the nation.

When nations get pleasure-mad, it's a sign that the end is near. Belshazzar and his leaders were enjoying a sumptuous feast when the city of Babylon fell to the Medes and Persians (Dan. 7). The Roman citizens enjoyed free "bread and circuses" as the empire decayed morally and politically and eventually fell to the enemy. One of the marks of the end days is the fact that people become "lovers of pleasures more than lovers of God" (2 Tim. 3:4). No wonder Jesus warned His followers, "But take heed to yourselves, lest your hearts be weighed down with carousing, drunkenness, and cares of this life, and that Day come on you unexpectedly" (Luke 21:34 NKJV).

It's difficult today to find people who are truly burdened about the sins of the nations and the sins of the church. Too many are like the rulers of Samaria or the members of the church of Laodicea, closing their eyes to reality and living on fantasy based on false theology. How many believers can honestly say, "Indignation has taken hold of me because of the wicked, who forsake Your law"? (Ps. 119:53 NKJV) Or, "Rivers of water run down from my eyes, because men do not keep Your law"? (v. 136 NKJV) Too many Christians are laughing when they should be weeping (James 4:8-10) and tolerating sin when they should be opposing it (1 Cor. 5:2).

Dr. Vance Havner told of having dinner in a dining room that was dimly lighted. At first, he could scarcely read the menu, but then he found he could see fairly well. He said to his friends, "Isn't it strange how easy it is to become accustomed to the dark?" That's one of the problems in the church today: we've gotten accustomed to the darkness, and our lights aren't shining bright enough.

Since these wealthy exploiters of the poor considered themselves to be the first in the land, God said they would be the first to go into captivity (Amos 6:7); for theirs was the greater responsibility. Certainly King Jeroboam and his priest Amaziah, the political and religious leaders of Israel, were among the first to be judged (7:10-17), but their self–indulgent followers eventually had to exchange their lounges for chains and their wine and expensive food for the meager fare of prisoners.

4. "Woe to the impudent!" (Amos 6:8-14)

"I abhor the pride of Jacob, and hate his palaces; therefore I will deliver up the city and all that is in it" (v. 8 NKJV). The Lord not only said this, but He also swore by Himself to fulfill it, which makes it a most solemn statement. The phrase "pride of Jacob" (KJV says "excellency of Jacob") is used in Psalm 47:4 to mean "the Promised Land."[3] God abhorred the very land of Israel, the land He had given to His people for their inheritance.

Jesus said, "That which is highly esteemed among men is abomination in the sight of God" (Luke 16:15). The people boasted of their fortresses, their mansions, and their elegant way of life, all of which God abhorred and would one day destroy. We're reminded of the destruction of the great Babylonian world system described in Revelation 17–18. People who live without God, whose god is really personal pleasure, will one day hear Him say, "Fool! This night your soul will be required of you; then whose will those things be which you have provided?" (Luke 12:20 NKJV).

These impudent people, who rejected God's warning, would one day face three judgments.

Death (Amos 6:9-10). Amos describes a hypothetical situation to emphasize the terrors that will come when the Assyrians invade Samaria. Ten men, perhaps the remnants of a hundred soldiers (5:3), would be hiding in a house, but pestilence would catch up with them, and they would die. If a relative came to burn the bodies (the safest thing to do in war when disease is rampant), anyone in the house guarding the bodies would deny there were others there who also might die in the plague. But the disposal of the dead bodies wouldn't be a "religious" occasion, for the people would be afraid to even mention the name of the Lord lest He become angry and send more judgment.

Destruction (Amos 6:11-13). Pride always goes before destruction (Prov. 16:18). The summer houses and winter houses that the wealthy enjoyed and boasted about would one day be nothing but ashes and fragments. The Babylonians would even burn Judah's beautiful temple. This would occur because the Lord commanded it, and His commands are always obeyed.

The prophet argues from the order of nature (Amos 6:12). Horses are too wise to gallop on slick rocks, where they might slip and fall. Farmers are too wise to try to plow the rocks or the sea,[4] because the plow won't accomplish anything on rocks or water. (Remember, Amos was a farmer.) Plain common sense convinces us of the truth of these statements. Then why would God's people poison their own judicial system? What they did just didn't make sense!

Their pride again came to the fore when they boasted of their military victories at Lo Debar and Karnaim (see NKJV or NIV). We aren't certain when Israel took these cities, and it's not important. What is important is that they were proud of their achievements and confident that nobody could defeat them. Lo Debar means "nothing," and that's what God thought of their victory! They boasted that the victory came because of their own strength, and their false confidence would lead to their destruction.

Disgrace and defeat (Amos 6:14). If a nation rehearses the victories of the past and gives the glory to God, that's one thing, but if they claim the victory for themselves, they are asking only for future defeat. Humble dependence on God is the only guarantee of His help and blessing.

Assyria's invasion of Israel wouldn't take place because of the accidents or incidents of international politics. God would bring the army into the land and give Assyria the responsibility of chastening His people. " 'Behold, I will bring a nation against you from afar, O house of Israel,' says the Lord" (Jer. 5:15 NKJV).

Hammath is in the north of Israel, and the river of the Arabah is in the south. Thus this means that Assyria would devastate the entire land. At the time Amos spoke those words, Assyria was a rather weak nation; and King Jeroboam was able to keep Assyria, Egypt, and Syria at bay. But that would change, and Assyria would become a threatening world empire. After all, it is God who controls the nations and assigns them their lands (Acts 17:26).

The Prophet Amos has finished preaching his three messages to the proud and complacent kingdom of Israel. He has looked within their hearts and exposed the corruption there. Now the Lord will give His servant six visions—five visions of judgment and one of the glorious kingdom that will be established after the Day of the Lord. With the record of these visions, Amos will close his book.

CHAPTER SIX STOP—LOOK—LISTEN!

Amos 7:1–9:15

The prophecy of Amos concludes with the record of five special visions of judgment that God gave to His servant: the locusts (7:1-3), the fire (vv. 4-6), the plumb line (vv. 7-9), the basket of fruit (8:1-14), and the ruined temple (9:1-10). However, the prophet closes his message on a positive note as he describes the future glorious kingdom that God has promised to His people (vv. 11-15).

But these visions center on three experiences of the prophet in which Amos struggles with God and man (chap. 7), declares that judgment is coming (chap. 8) and affirms that God is working out His perfect plan (chap. 9).

1. The prophet struggles (Amos 7:1-17)

The life of a prophet wasn't easy. On the one hand, he had to stay close to the Lord in order to hear His words and be able to share them with the people. But on the other hand, he also had to be with the people to whom he was ministering, and they didn't always want to accept his ministry. It's no wonder that some of the prophets wanted to resign, including Moses and Jeremiah. Amos had two struggles: one with the Lord and one with the authorities, especially the king and his priest. When you read the Book of Acts, you see that the apostles also faced struggles with the religious establishment and with the government.

Struggling with the Lord (Amos 7:1-9). Amos was a true patriot who loved God and loved his nation, and it grieved him that he had to tell Israel and Judah that judgment was coming. No doubt there were times when he wished he was back at Tekoa caring for the sycamore trees and the sheep. But the Sovereign Lord ("Lord God," used eleven times in these three chapters) was in control of history, and Amos knew that God's will was best. The prophet saw three visions of judgment and responded to them.

First, Amos saw the vision of the locusts (vv. 1-3) as they were poised to attack the second crop late in the summer, after the king had taken his share (1 Kings 4:7). This was the farmers' last chance for a harvest, and the harvest would be destroyed. The summer heat was on its way, and there would be no more chance for a crop. Being a man of the soil himself, Amos would sympathize with these farmers.

The strange thing is that it was God who prepared these insects and told them what to do! It was as though He turned against His own people and deliberately planned to strip their fields of food. But since the heart of Amos agonized for his people, he prayed that the Lord would call off the judgment; and He did. Amos joined that select group of intercessors, which included Abraham (Gen. 18), Moses (Ex. 32; Num. 14), Samuel (1 Sam. 12), Elijah (1 Kings 18), and Paul (Rom. 9:1-3; 10:1-2).

Amos argued that the nation was so small that they could never survive the plague of locusts. Amos didn't plead any of the covenant promises of God because he knew the people had violated God's covenant and were deserving of a plague (Deut. 28:38-42). But God heard the prophet's plea and relented (Joel 2:12-14).[1]

The second vision was that of the devouring fire (Amos 7:4-6) in which the fire dried up the water and burned the land. The image is that of a great drought, and Amos had mentioned a drought earlier (4:7-8). God's judgment so moved the prophet that he cried out to the Lord and begged Him to cease, and once more God relented.

The third vision was that of the plumb line (Amos 7:7-9), an instrument used to test whether a wall was straight and true. A man stood on top of the wall and dropped a line with a weight on it. By matching the line to the wall, the workers could tell if the wall was upright.

God's Law is His plumb line, and He measures His people to see how true they are to the pattern in His Word, and if they are of upright character and conduct. "Also I will make justice the measuring line, and righteousness the plummet" (Isa. 28:17 NKJV) Alas, in Amos' time, He found that Israel was "out of plumb" and therefore had to be destroyed. This would include Israel's high places and sanctuaries, where they worshiped contrary to God's law, for the only place the Jews were to bring their sacrifices was to the temple in Jerusalem (Lev. 17:1-7).

"I will spare them no longer" was certainly an ominous statement. The nation had gone too far, and now there was no hope. For this reason, Amos didn't intercede for the land as he had done twice before. Like Jeremiah, he did not pray for the people (Jer. 7:16; 11:14; 14:11).

Struggling with the authorities (Amos 7:10-17). Israel's main sanctuary was at Bethel; it was the king's chapel. God had told Amos that the sanctuary would be destroyed and that King Jeroboam II would be slain. This wasn't an easy message to proclaim, for Amos was attacking both the government and the religion of the nation. Yet he faithfully went to Bethel and preached the Word. Four different messages were involved in this event.

The first message was Amaziah's report to the king (vv. 10-11). Since the king had appointed Amaziah, he had an obligation to tell the king what the farmer preacher was saying to the people. The king didn't bother to go hear Amos himself, although it would have done him good to listen and obey. Jeroboam was very comfortable and complacent and wasn't about to have some visiting farmer tell him what to do.

The second message was Amaziah's message to Amos (vv. 12-13). Of course, Jeroboam II didn't want to hear that his chapel and shrines would be destroyed, that he would die, and that the Assyrians would exile his people. Such a pessimistic message had to be silenced. Thus the king told his priest to tell Amos to go home where he belonged.

Amaziah's words to Amos reveal the wicked attitudes in the priest's heart. He called Amos a "seer," which in this case means a "visionary." He claimed that there was no validity to Amos' message; he only dreamed it up. Then the priest suggested that Amos was also a coward, who would run away if the king began to deal with him. He hinted that Amos was interested only in earning bread. Finally, Amaziah told Amos to get out and stay out because the king's chapel was for the elite, and he was a prophet. It was a bitter speech that might have cut the prophet deeply.

It's not unusual to find conflicts between priests and prophets in the Old Testament. (Of course, Amaziah was a false priest and not a true servant of God.) Actually, both prophets and priests were needed in the land, because the priests "conserved" the ancient religious traditions, while the prophets applied the Word to the present situation and called people back to God. There were false prophets, who taught lies and sometimes worked with the priests to maintain the status quo, and the true prophets, who had to oppose both priests and false prophets. In Israel, there were false priests who had no valid connection with the levitical priesthood (see Isa. 1:12-15; Jer. 7:1-11; Ezek. 34:1ff; Hosea 4:4-9).

Now we listen to the prophet's message to the priest (Amos 7:14-16). First, Amos revealed the kind of man he was by not being intimidated or running away. Like Nehemiah, he could say, "Should such a man as I flee?" (Neh. 6:11). To run away would be to agree with all the accusations and insinuations the false priest had made. Then Amos told Amaziah what he was: a prophet called by God. In his native Judah, he did not work as a prophet but as a herdsman and a tender of sycamore trees. He didn't make himself a prophet, nor was he a "son of the prophets," that is, a student in one of the prophetic schools (1 Kings 2:35; 2 Kings 2:3, 5, 7, 15). God had called him, and he obeyed the call.

Amos then proclaimed the Word of the Lord to Amaziah and informed him of the judgment that God would send on him and his family. Amaziah would lose all his property, go into exile, and die far from his native land. The Assyrian soldiers would slay his sons. His wife would be left destitute and would become a prostitute. The nation of Israel would go into exile and be no more. It would be quite a change from serving as the king's chief religious leader at Bethel!

Amaziah had position, wealth, authority, and reputation, but Amos had the Word of the Lord. Amaziah served the king of Israel and depended on him for support, but Amos served the King of kings and had no fear of what men could do to him. Many times in the history of the church, God has called humble instruments like Amos to declare His Word; and we had better be prepared to listen and obey. It's not the approval of the "religious establishment" that counts, but the calling and blessing of the Lord.

2. The prophet declares (Amos 8:1-14)

After his painful encounter with Amaziah, Amos received further messages from the Lord; for it's just like the Master to encourage His servants after they've been through tough times (see Acts 18:9-11; 27:21-26; 2 Tim. 4:16).

The end is coming (Amos 8:1-3). God often used common objects to teach important spiritual truths, objects like pottery (Jer. 18-19), seed (Luke 8:11), yeast (Matt. 16:6, 11), and in this text, a basket of summer (ripe) fruit. Just as this fruit was ripe for eating, the nation of Israel was ripe for judgment. The Hebrew word translated "summer" or "ripe" in verse 1 (qayis) is similar to the word translated "end" in verse 2 (qes). It was the end of the harvest for the farmers, and it would be the end for Israel when the harvest judgment came (see Jer. 1:11-12 for a similar lesson). "The harvest is past, the summer is ended, and we are not saved" (Jer. 8:20).

There comes a time when God's long-suffering runs out (Isa. 55:6-7) and judgment is decreed. The songs at the temple[2] would become funeral dirges with weeping and wailing, and corpses would be thrown everywhere and not given proper burial. It would be a bitter harvest for Israel as the nation reaped what it sowed. People would be so overwhelmed that they would be unable to discuss the tragedy. Silence would reign in the land.

Why the end is coming (Amos 8:4-6). The reason was simple: Israel had broken God's law and failed to live by His covenant. The first table of the Law has to do with our relationship to God and the second table with our relationship to others, and Israel had rebelled against both. They did not love God, and they did not love their neighbors (Matt. 22:36-40).

They trampled on the poor and needy and robbed them of the little they possessed (Amos 8:4), an indictment that Amos had often brought against the people (2:6-7; 4:1; 5:11-12). When they did business, the merchants used inaccurate measurements so they could rob their customers. The Law demanded that they use accurate weights and measures (Lev. 19:35-36; Deut. 25:13-16), but they cared only for making as much money as possible.

Added to their deception was their desecration of the Sabbath and the religious holy days. The worship of God interrupted their business, and they didn't like it! You might expect Gentile merchants to ignore the holy days (Neh. 13:15-22), but certainly not the Jewish merchants. The poor were unable to pay for the necessities of life and had to go into servitude to care for their families, and the merchants would have them arrested for the least little offense, even their inability to pay for a pair of shoes.

These evil vendors would not only alter their weights and measures and inflate their prices, but they would also cheapen their products by mixing the sweepings of the threshing floor with the grain. You didn't get pure grain; you got the chaff as well. "For the love of money is a root of all kinds of evil" (1 Tim. 6:10 NIV).

How the end is coming (Amos 8:7-14). The prophet used four pictures to describe the terror of the coming judgment. The first was that of an earthquake (v. 8) with the land heaving like the rising waters of the Nile River. (The Nile rose about twenty-five feet during its annual flooding stage.) Even the land would shudder because of the people's sins. Earlier Amos referred to an earthquake (1:1), but we aren't sure whether it was the fulfillment of this prophecy.

God would also visit them with darkness (Amos 8:9), perhaps an eclipse. (There was one in 763 B.C.) The Day of the Lord will be a day of darkness (Isa. 13:9-10; Joel 2:30-31).

The third picture is that of a funeral (Amos 8:10), with all their joyful feasts turned into mourning and wailing. Instead of being dressed elegantly and going to banquets or concerts, the people would wear sackcloth and join in mourning. Parents would mourn greatly if an only son died because that would mean the end of the family name and line. But God's judgment would mean the end of a nation.

Finally, the judgment would be like a famine (vv. 11-14), not only of literal food but also of spiritual nourishment. "Man shall not live by bread alone, but by every word that proceeds from the mouth of God" (Matt. 4:4 NKJV; see Deut. 8:3). In times of crisis, people turn to the Lord for some word of guidance or encouragement; but for Israel, no word would come. "We are given no miraculous signs; no prophets are left, and none of us knows how long this will be" (Ps. 74:9 NIV).

What a tragedy to have plenty of "religion" but no Word from the Lord! That means no light in the darkness, no nourishment for the soul, no direction for making decisions, no protection from the lies of the Enemy. The people would stagger like drunks from place to place, always hoping to find food and drink for their bodies and spiritual sustenance for their souls.

3. The prophet affirms (Amos 9:1-15)

In this final chapter of the book, the Prophet Amos shares four affirmations from the heart of the Lord—three of which deal with judgment and the fourth with mercy.

"I will strike!" (Amos 9:1) In a vision, Amos saw the Lord standing by an altar and announcing that the worshipers would be slain because the building would be destroyed and fall upon them. This was probably not the temple in Jerusalem because Amos was sent to the Northern Kingdom of Israel; and when the Babylonians destroyed the temple in Jerusalem, it was by fire (Jer. 52:12-13). This may have been the king's royal chapel in Bethel, although we don't know what kind of building that was. God's warning in Amos 3:13-15 seems to parallel this vision, describing what the Assyrian army would do when it entered the land.

The altar was the place of sacrifice and the atonement, but God refused to accept their sacrifices and forgive their sins (5:21-23). Their man-made religion, carried on by unauthorized priests, was an abomination to the Lord; and He would now destroy it.

"I will search!" (Amos 9:2-4) Any idolatrous worshiper who tried to escape would be tracked down and slain. Though they run down into sheol, the realm of the dead, God would search them out; and if they could reach heaven, there would be no protection there. They couldn't hide from God on the highest mountain or in the depths of the sea (see Ps. 139:7-12). Even if they were taken captive to a foreign land, He would find them and judge them. His eye would be upon them for judgment, not for blessing (33:18; 34:15; Rev. 6:12-17).

"I will destroy!" (Amos 9:5-10) Nine times in the book, Amos calls God "the Lord of hosts," that is, "the Lord of the armies of heaven and earth." A. W. Tozer correctly says, "The essence of idolatry is the entertainment of thoughts about God that are unworthy of Him."[3] The people of Israel created their gods in their own image and held such a low view of Jehovah that they thought He would approve of their sinful ways.

Amos reminded them of the greatness of the God they thought they were worshiping. He is the God of creation, who can melt the earth with a touch and make the land rise and fall like the swelling of the Nile River. He controls the heavens, the earth, and the seas, and no one can stay His hand.

Jehovah is the God of history, who showed His great power by delivering the Jews from the bondage of Egypt (v. 7). He claimed them for His own people. Yet they turned against Him and went their own way. Therefore, He will have to treat the Jews (His special people) as He treats the Gentiles! The exodus from Egypt will be looked upon like any migration of a people from one place to another, for the people of Israel gave up their national distinctives when they abandoned the worship of the true God.

But He is always the God of mercy (vv. 8-10), who will keep His covenant with Abraham and his descendants and not destroy the nation. The nations would be sifted, and the sinners punished, but not one of His true worshipers would be lost. It's always the believing remnant that God watches over so that they might fulfill His will on the earth. The self-confident sinners, who don't expect to be punished, are the ones who will be slain by the sword (v. 10).

"I will restore!" (Amos 9:11-15) In contrast to God's destroying the Israelite house of false worship, God will raise up the "hut" of David, thereby assuring a bright future for the people of Israel and Judah. Like a rickety shack, David's dynasty was about to collapse. From the Babylonian Captivity to this present hour, there has been no Davidic king ruling over the Jews; and though a Jewish nation has been restored, they have no king, priest, temple, or sacrifice.

But one day, the Lord will restore, repair, and rebuild the dynasty of David and establish the kingdom He promised. When Jesus Christ comes again, the breach between Israel and Judah will be healed, and there will be one nation submitted to one king. God will bless the land and the people, and His people shall live in peace and security.[4] It will be a time of peace and prosperity to the glory of the Lord.

Amos ends his prophecy with the wonderful promise that Israel shall be planted, protected, and never again pulled up from her land "says the Lord your God." Your God! What a great encouragement for the Jews to know that, in spite of their unbelief, their God will be faithful to keep His covenant promises.

Endnotes

Chapter 1

1. "The Deserted Village" by Oliver Goldsmith, lines 51 and 52.

2. How could Amos rightfully announce judgment to the Gentile nations that had never been given the Law of God? On the basis of natural law and conscience (Rom. 1:18–2:16). When humans brutally sin against each other, they sin against God; for humans are made in the image of God. When Amos denounced the Jews, he appealed to the Law of God as well (Amos 2:4).

3. *See Miracle at Philadelphia* by Catherine Drinker Bowen (Boston: Little, Brown, 1966), 126. While there is no evidence that Franklin was an evangelical Christian, he was indeed a God-fearing man.

4. Amos did not mention Gath because by that time it had lost its prominence and had been subjected to Jewish authority (2 Chron. 26:6; see also Zeph. 2:4-5; Zech. 9:56).

5. Though the statement is anonymous, it is usually attributed to the German author Friedrich von Logau whose writings were translated into English by Henry Wadsworth Longfellow. Von Logau found it quoted in a book by the second-century Greek philosopher Sextus Empiricus.

6. Shakespeare had inscribed on his gravestone

Good friend, for Jesu's sake forbear
To dig the dust enclosed here.
Blest be the man that spares these stones,
And curst be he that moves my bones.

7. "Kerioth" (Amos 2:2) can also be translated "of her cities" (NIV margin), but it's likely Kerioth is the name of a Moabite city, possibly the capital city of the nation. Kerioth of Moab is mentioned in Jeremiah 48:24 and 41. There was also a Kerioth in Judah (Josh. 15:25), and it's possible that Judas Iscariot ("ish Kerioth" = man of Kerioth) came from there.

8. Under the Mosaic Covenant, God promised to bless His people if they obeyed His law but to remove His blessing if they disobeyed (Deut. 27–29). However, the people forgot that God often blessed them in spite of their sins so that He might be faithful to His promises to Abraham and David. In His love and long-suffering, God sent them messengers to call them back to obedience; but they refused to listen. "Because sentence against an evil work is not executed speedily, therefore the heart of the sons of men is fully set in them to do evil" (Ecc. 8:11).

Chapter 2

1. Note in Numbers 10 that trumpets were used to warn the people of danger, especially impending invasion.

Chapter 3

1. "Keeping Up with the Joneses" was the name of a popular newspaper comic strip that ran for twenty-eight years. It told the story of a man of limited means who tried to keep up with his neighbors.

2. Bashan was a fertile area east of the Sea of Galilee

in the tribe of Manasseh and was known for its fine livestock (Deut. 32:14; Ps. 22:12; Ezek. 39:18).

3. The end of verse 3 presents a problem. The KJV translates it "shall cast them out toward [or into] Harmon." Amos uses the Hebrew word twelve times; it's translated "palaces" in the KJV, and except for Amos 4:3, the NIV translates it "fortresses." The NIV text note gives "O mountain of oppression." If "Harmon" is a place, we don't know where it is. In his excellent commentary on Amos, Jeffrey Niehaus translates the sentence "and you will let go dominion" (*An Exegetical and Expository Commentary: The Minor Prophets*, edited by Thomas E. McComiskey [Grand Rapids, Mich.: Baker Book House, 1992], vol. 1, 391). These women who were accustomed to giving orders would find themselves taking orders!

4. Both the NASB and the NIV translate the Hebrew word "the last of you," meaning "nobody will escape," but the KJV and NKJV translate it "posterity." However, the NIV translates the same word as "descendants" in 1 Kings 21:21, Psalm 109:13, and Daniel 11:4.

5. The word "irony" comes from a Greek word (*eironeia*), which means "to speak deceptively, with dissimulation." What you say is to be interpreted just the opposite of what the words convey. (For other examples in Scripture, see Jud. 10:4; Ezek. 28:3).

6. Along with their annual tithes, the Jews were commanded to bring a special tithe every three years (Deut. 14:28; 26:12). The NIV renders it "every three years," but the Hebrew text reads "every three days" (NKJV, NASB) or "on the third day" (NIV margin), that is, "by the third day after you come to the sanctuary." It appears that Amos is again using "holy irony." "You are commanded to bring the special tithe every three years; but you are so spiritual, you bring tithes every three days!"

Chapter 4

1. "Virgin daughter of Israel" is a common phrase in the Old Testament (2 Kings 19:21; Isa. 37:22; Jer. 18:13; 31:4, 21: Lam. 2:13) and it is also applied to other nations, such as Egypt (Jer. 46:11) and Babylon (Isa. 47:1). It refers to an unmarried daughter still under protection of the father. Because the nation of Israel turned their back on their Heavenly Father, they got in trouble and were defiled and slain in their own land. Paul used a similar image in writing about the local church (2 Cor. 11:1-3).

2. The Jew associated Beersheba with God's appearing to Abraham (Gen. 21:31-33), Isaac (26:23-25), and Jacob (46:1-5).

3. J.B. Phillips, *Four Prophets: A Translation into Modern English* (New York: The Macmillan Col., 1963), 14.

4. The Hebrew word *mishpat* is translated "justice" in most modern translations and usually "judgment" in the KJV. The NIV uses "justice" in Amos 2:7; 5:7, 12, 15, 24; 6:12. The root word of *mishpat* is *shapat*, which means "to govern." The aim of the government is justice for all people. The Prophet Isaiah also pleaded for justice in the land.

Chapter 5

1. Amos 5:26 is a difficult verse to translate and interpret. Is it referring to Israel past or the nation during Amos' day, or both? Ezekiel 20:5-9 makes it clear that Israel learned idolatry in Egypt and ignored the fact that the plagues God sent were a judgment against these false gods (Ex. 12:12). Ezekiel 20:10-17 informs us that the Jewish people also practiced idolatry in the wilderness. The point Amos makes is that the people didn't learn from their past, a problem the church has today. "What experience and history teach us is this," wrote G. W. Hegel, "that nations and governments have never learned anything from history, or acted upon any lessons they might have drawn from it."

2. The Hebrew phrase translated "chief ointments" parallels Exodus 30:23, where the formula for the sacred anointing oil is given. Perhaps the careless Israelites were duplicating the holy oil for their own private use. If so, then we have an even greater sin—using the holy things of God for their own personal pleasure.

3. The phrase is used in Amos 8:7 to refer to God Himself, but that can't be the meaning here. The Jews prided themselves that their God was the true and living God, even though they often indulged in the worship of idols. They were also proud of the temple in Jerusalem (Ezek. 24:21). They might have been proud of God, but God certainly wasn't proud of them!

4. Some versions translate verse 12 "or plow the sea with oxen." However, to do so requires a slight change in the Hebrew text.

Chapter 6

1. The Bible often uses concepts to describe divine actions or emotions, such as God resting (Gen. 2:2), grieving (6:6), clapping His hands (Ezek. 21:17), laughing (Ps. 2:4), and writing (Ex. 31:18). When God "relents" ("repents" KJV), it doesn't mean that He made a mistake and has to change His mind. Rather, it means that He maintains His intentions but changes His way of working. A good illustration is found in Jeremiah 18:1-17.

2. Of course, the temple was in Jerusalem, but Amos is referring to the places of worship in Israel, such as the king's chapel. Since the word translated "temple" can also be translated "palace" (2 Kings 20:18), the prophet may have been referring to the banquets of the king.

3. A.W. Tozer, *The Knowledge of the Holy* (New York: Harper and Brothers, 1961), 11.

4. James quoted Amos 9:11 during the Jerusalem conference when the leaders discussed the matter of the place of the Gentiles in the church (Acts 15). The question was, "Must a Gentile become a Jew in order to become a Christian?" But note that James did not say that Amos 9:11 was fulfilled by the Gentiles' coming into the church, but that the prophets (plural) agreed with the Gentiles' being a part of the church (Acts 15:13-18). After all, if believing Gentiles are one day going to be a part of the Messianic Kingdom (David's dynasty restored), why can't they be a part of the church today? Why should they be forced to become Jewish proselytes in order to become Christians? However, some interpret Amos 9:11 and the words of James to mean that the church is the "tabernacle of David" so that the Old Testament prophecies about the

kingdom are now fulfilled in the church. How the church is like David's kingdom "as in the days of old" is difficult to understand, and the references to Edom (Amos 9:12) and the fruitfulness of the land (vv. 13-15) are also difficult to apply to the church.

OBADIAH

OUTLINE

Key theme: Nations and individuals reap what they sow
Key verse: Obadiah 15

I. GOD'S MESSAGE TO EDOM'S NEIGHBORS. 1

A call to arms against their old ally.

II. GOD'S MESSAGE TO EDOM. 2–16

1. Divine judgment declared. 2–9
   (1) Edom's pride brought down. 2–4
   (2) Edom's wealth plundered. 5–6
   (3) Edom's alliances broken. 7
   (4) Edom's wisdom destroyed. 8
   (5) Edom's army defeated. 9
2. Divine judgment defended. 10–16
   (1) Violence against the Jews. 10–11
   (2) Rejoicing at the Jews' plight. 12
   (3) Assisting the enemy. 13–14
   (4) Ignoring God's wrath. 15–16

III. GOD'S MESSAGE TO THE JEWISH PEOPLE. 17–21

1. God will deliver them. 17–18
2. God will defeat their enemies. 19–20
3. God will establish their kingdom. 21

Obadiah in His Time

We know very little about the Prophet Obadiah except that he wrote the prophecy bearing his name (the shortest book in the Old Testament) and that his name means "one who worships God." At least twelve other men in Scripture had this name, four of whom were connected in some way with the ministry at the temple (1 Chron. 9:16; 2 Chron. 34:12; Neh. 10:5, 12:25).

Students aren't even agreed as to when the events occurred that are described in Obadiah 10–14. The traditional view is that Obadiah was referring to the Babylonian invasion of Judah and the destruction of Jerusalem in 586 B.C. The psalmist states that the Edomites encouraged the Babylonians as the army razed the city (Ps. 137:7), but there is no evidence that the Edomites actually entered Jerusalem at that time or tried to stop the Jews from escaping.

Some Old Testament scholars think that Obadiah's reference is to an earlier invasion of Jerusalem by the Philistines and Arabians, at which time Edom assisted the invaders and broke free from Judah's control (2 Chron. 21:8–10, 16–17). This would have been during the reign of weak King Jehoram (853–841), who married King Ahab's daughter and led Judah into sin. God permitted the invasion of the land and the plundering of Jerusalem as a punishment for the king's disobedience.

Obadiah's themes are: (1) the evil of long-standing family feuds, (2) the certainty that people eventually suffer for the way they treat others, and (3) the assurance that Israel's enemies will be defeated and the kingdom established in the land.

A TALE OF TWO BROTHERS
Obadiah 1–21

Of all human conflict, the most painful and difficult to resolve are those between blood relatives. But if family feuds are tragic, national feuds are even worse. Almost every nation has experience a civil war, with brother killing brother in order to perpetuate a long-standing disagreement that nobody fully understands or wants to settle. History records that the roots of these disputes are bitter, long, and deep, and that every attempt to pull them up and destroy them usually meets with failure.

Esau and Jacob were twin brothers who had been competitors from before birth (Gen. 25:19–26). Unfortunately, their parents disagreed over the boys, with Isaac partial to Esau and Rebekah favoring Jacob. God had chosen Jacob, the younger son, to receive the blessing attached to the Abrahamic Covenant (Rom. 9:10–12), but Jacob and Rebekah decided to get this blessing by scheming instead of trusting God (Gen. 27).

When Esau learned that his clever brother had stolen the blessing, he resolved to kill him after their father was dead, and this led to Jacob's leaving home to find a wife among his mother's relatives (vv. 41–46). Years later, the two brothers experienced a brief time of reconciliation (Gen. 32), and they both faithfully attended the burial of Isaac (35:27–29), but the animosity was never removed. Esau established the nation of Edom (25:30; 35:1, 8; 36:1ff), and his descendants carried on the family feud that Esau had begun years before.[1]

The Law of Moses commanded the Jews treat the Edomites like brothers: "You shall not abhor an Edomite, for he is your brother" (Deut. 23:7 NKJV). In spite of this, the Edomites "harbored an ancient hostility" against Israel (Ezek. 35:5 NIV) and used every opportunity to display it.

In this brief book, Obadiah the prophet delivered three messages from the Lord.

1. God's message to Edom's neighbors (Obad. 1)

Like Isaiah (1:1), Micah (1:1), Nahum (1:1), and Habakkuk (1:1), the Prophet Obadiah received his message from the Lord by means of a vision. "Surely the Lord God does nothing unless He reveals His secret counsel to His servants the prophets" (Amos 3:7 NASB). Obadiah wrote the vision so it could be shared with others and eventually become a part of the Holy Scriptures.

The Lord enabled Obadiah to know what was going on among the nations that were allied with Edom against Judah. Thanks to today's international media coverage and the instant transmission of information, very little can happen in political and diplomatic arenas without the world knowing about it. But in Obadiah's day, the travels of national leaders and their political discussions were secret. There were no newspapers or press conferences.

God told His servant that an ambassador from a nation allied with Edom was visiting the other nations to convince their leader to join forces and attack Edom. Actually, it was the Lord who had ordained this change in policy, and what appeared to be just another diplomatic visit was actually the working out of the Lord's judgments against Edom. This was the beginning of the fulfillment of the prophecy in Obadiah 7, "All your allies will force you to the border" (NIV).

John Wesley is said to have remarked that he read the newspaper "to see how God was governing His world," and this is certainly a biblical approach. God rules over kingdoms and nations (2 Chron. 20:6; Dan. 5:21); and as A. T. Pierson used to say, "History is His story." This doesn't mean that God is to blame for the foolish or wicked decisions and deeds of government officials, but it does mean that He is on the throne and working out His perfect will.

The eminent British historian Herbert Butterfield said, "Perhaps history is a thing that would stop happening if God held His breath, or could be imagined as turning away to think of something else." The God who knows the number and the names of the stars (Ps. 147:4) and who sees when the tiniest bird falls dead to the ground (Matt. 10:29) is mindful of the plans and pursuits of the nations and is working out His divine purposes in human history.

Knowing that the Lord reigns over all things ought to encourage the people of God as we watch world events and grieve over the decay of people and nations. The sovereignty of God isn't an excuse for believers to be indifferent to evil in the world, nor is it an encouragement to slumber carelessly and do nothing. God's ways are hidden and mysterious, and we sometimes wonder why He permits certain things to happen, but we must still pray "Thy will be done" (Matt. 6:10) and then be available to obey whatever He tells us to do.

2. God's message to Edom (Obad. 2–16)

There are two parts to this message. First, the prophet declared that God would judge Edom and take away everything the nation boasted about and depended on for security (vv. 2–9). Second, Obadiah explained why God was judging Edom and named four ways in which the Edomites had sinned against the Jews and the Lord (vv. 10–16).

Divine judgment declared (Obad. 2–9).[2] What kind of judgment did God promise to send to the nation of Edom? To begin with, He said He would bring down their pride (vv. 2–4). Edom was a proud nation that considered itself impregnable and invulnerable because it was situated "in the clefts of the rock" (v. 3), a region of rugged mountains with high cliffs and narrow valleys that would dissuade any invader from attacking. Like the eagles, the Edomites lived on the rocks and looked down from the heights with disdain upon the nations around them. The Edomites thought they were a great people, but God said He would make them small, which means "paltry." "Pride goes before destruction, a haughty spirit before a fall" (Prov. 16:18 NIV).

The prophet also said that *their wealth would be plundered (Obad. 5–6).* Located on several major trade routes, Edom could amass the riches of other nations; and out of their mountains, they could dig copper and other minerals. Because of their isolation, they didn't have to worry about making treaties with the larger nations or helping to finance expensive wars. But their wealth would be no more. Unlike ordinary thieves, their plunderers would take everything they could find, and unlike grape harvesters, they would leave nothing behind for others. This would be the end of Edom and its boasted wealth.

Third, the Lord would work so that their alliances would be broken (v. 7). Though protected by their lofty heights, the Edomites were smart enough to know that they needed friends to help them stand against the great empires that frequently threatened the smaller eastern nations. Edom would also want allies to assist them in their constant feud with Israel (see Ps. 83:5–8). But God would turn these friends into enemies, and those who had eaten with them and made covenants of peace would break those covenants. While pretending to be friends, their allies would turn into traitors, set a trap, and catch Edom by surprise.

Nations today that boast of their political alliances and their formidable military establishments should take heed to what happened to Edom long ago, for that proud nation is no more. About 300 B.C., the Nabataean Arabs drove out the Edomites and occupied their key city Petra, the "rose red city" carved out of solid rock. The Romans took Petra in A.D. 105, but the decline in the caravan routes eventually led to the nation's demise.

God also warned that *Edom's wisdom would be destroyed (Obad. 8).* The people of the east were known for their wisdom (1 Kings 4:30), and this included the Edomites. Located as they were on the great trade routes, the leaders of Edom could get news and views from many nations. Job's friend Eliphaz was from Teman in Edom (Job 2:11; see Jer. 49:7). Without wisdom, the leaders of Edom couldn't make the right decisions, and the result would be confusion.

Finally, Obadiah announced that *Edom's army would be defeated (Obad. 9).* Without wisdom, the military leaders wouldn't know how to command their troops, and their mighty men would be defeated. This may have happened when the Babylonians took Jerusalem, or this promise may have been fulfilled when the Arabs invaded Edom and took over their cities, driving the Edomites to the west. The Greeks and Romans called these Edomites "Idumeans" (Mark 3:8), and from them came Herod the Great.

Having announced what God was going to do to Edom, Obadiah then proceeded to *defend God's judgment of the nation (Obad. 10–16).* The Edomites were guilty of at least four abominable sins, the first of which was using violence against their brothers, the Jews (vv. 10–11). When their founder Esau discovered he was deprived of his father's blessing, he determined to kill his brother Jacob (Gen. 27:41), and this malicious attitude was passed along to his descendants. If you had asked them, "Are you your brother's keeper?" they would have replied, "No! We're our brother's killer!"

Instead of assisting their brothers in their plight, the Edomites stood "on the other side" (see Luke 10:30–32) and watched the enemy soldiers cast lots for the spoils, including the captive Jews, who would become slaves. The Edomites acted like the enemy instead of behaving like blood brothers of the Jews.

A word from Solomon is appropriate here: "Deliver those who are drawn toward death, and hold back those stumbling to the slaughter. If you say, 'Surely we did not know this,' does not He who weighs the hearts consider it? He who keeps your soul, does He not know it?" (Prov. 24:11–12 NKJV) Also, a word from the Prophet Amos: "For three sins of Edom, even for four, I will not turn back my wrath. Because he pursued his brother with a sword, stifling all compassion, because his anger raged continually and his fury flamed unchecked" (Amos 1:11 NIV).

Not only did the Edomites ignore the plight of the Jews, but also *they rejoiced at what the enemy was doing (Obad. 12; see Ezek. 35:15; 36:5).* For the Jews, this was a day of destruction and distress; but for the Edomites, it was a day of delight and rejoicing. In their pride, Edom looked down on the Jews and gloated over their misfortune. Again, Solomon has counsel for us: "Do not gloat when your enemy falls; when he stumbles, do not let your heart rejoice, or the Lord will see and disapprove and turn his wrath away from him" (Prov. 24:17–18 NIV). God didn't spare the Jews but He did send judgment on Edom in due time.

Edom's third great sin was *assisting the enemy in attacking the Jews (Obad. 13–14).* It was bad enough for people to do nothing to help their brothers, and to stand and rejoice at their brothers' calamities, but when they gave aid to the enemy, that was carrying their ancient "family feud" too far. The Edomites entered the city and shared in dividing up the spoils, thus robbing their brothers of their wealth. (Later, Edom's wealth would be taken.) The Edomites also stood at the forks in the roads, ready to capture the fugitives who were trying to escape; and they turned them over to the enemy to be imprisoned or slain.

What the Prophet Jehu asked King Jehoshaphat is applicable here: "Should you help the wicked and love those who hate the Lord and so bring wrath on yourself from the Lord?" (2 Chron. 19:2 NASB). As God's people, we must love our enemies and pray for them (Matt. 5:44–48), but we certainly shouldn't assist sinners in opposing and persecuting believers. To do so is to turn traitor in the army of the Lord.

Edom's fourth sin was that of *ignoring the impending wrath of God (Obad. 15–16).* "For the day of the Lord draws near on all the nations" (v. 15 NASB), and that included Edom, but Edom was proud and didn't care about what the Lord might do to them. "The Day of the Lord" is a phrase that describes the time when God will pour His wrath out upon a wicked world, judge the nations, and then establish His kingdom, thus fulfilling the promises made to Israel.[3] However, the phrase was also used to describe God-ordained calamities sent to punish people at any time, and these judgments were foretastes of the future worldwide "Day of the Lord."

"Therefore, whatever you want men to do to you, do also to them, for this is the Law and the Prophets" (Matt. 7:12 NKJV). We call this statement "the Golden Rule," and it points out a positive approach to personal relationships. But Obadiah 15 gives the negative side: "As you have done, it will be done to you. Your dealings will return on your own head" (NASB). Or, as Paul expressed it, "Do not be deceived, God is not mocked; for whatever a man sows, that he will also reap" (Gal. 6:7 NKJV).

Edom had drunk in joyful celebration at Jerusalem's fall, but all the nations will one day drink of the cup of wrath that God will hand them—a cup they cannot refuse (see Isa. 51:17, 21–23; Jer. 25:15–33). No matter how discouraging the day may be for God's people, there is a just God in heaven who pays sinners back in kind: what they did to others is ultimately done to them. Since Pharaoh ordered all the Jewish boy babies drowned, God drowned the Egyptian army (Ex. 1; 14:26–31). The men who lied about Daniel in order to have Daniel thrown to the lions were themselves thrown to the lions (Dan. 6). The unbelievers on earth who shed the blood of God's servants will one day drink water turned into blood (Rev. 16:5–6). "The righteous is delivered from trouble, and it comes to the wicked instead" Prov. 11:8 NKJV). Indeed, God's judgments are true and righteous (Rev. 16:7).

3. God's message to the Jewish people (Obad. 17–21)

Now that the prophecy about Edom has been delivered, Obadiah turns to His own people and announces three divine promises.

God will deliver you (Obad. 17–18). God did deliver His people from Babylonian captivity, and He will again deliver them in the last days and establish His kingdom. Mount Zion will be consecrated to the Lord and all defilement removed. "Jacob" refers to the Southern Kingdom and "Joseph" the Northern Kingdom. They will be united into one nation and enter the Messianic Kingdom together, possessing the inheritance promised to them. It appears from Isaiah 11:10–16, a parallel passage, that Moab and Edom will be restored as nations in the last days, but the Jews will burn them as stubble (see Ex. 15:7; Isa. 10:17; Matt. 3:12 for parallels).

God will defeat your enemies (Obad. 19–20). Israel will reclaim the land formerly inhabited by the Edomites (the Negev), the Philistines (the Shephelah), and the Samaritans (Ephraim). The Jews have been struggling to possess their inheritance for centuries, but other powers have always stood in the way. The Jews will "possess their possessions" without the help of any nation, but only through the help of the Lord their God. Israel has returned to their land in unbelief, and the nation was established in 1948. However, one day they shall see their Messiah and believe on Him, and the nation will be "born in a day" (Isa. 66:8; Zech. 12:10–13:1; 14:1–9).

God will establish the kingdom (Obad. 21). The Lord will reign from Mount Zion, where His temple will stand, "and all the nations will stream to it" (Isa. 2:2 NASB). It's interesting to note that King Messiah will have "deliverers" ("saviors" KJV) assist Him in His rule over the nations. This fact should be studied with reference to our Lord's promises to His apostles (Matt. 19:27–30) and those who are faithful to Him today (24:42–51; 25:14–30; Luke 19:11–27). Jesus teaches that faithfulness to Him today will mean reigning with Him in the kingdom.

All of God's children look forward to the day when the kingdoms of this world will become the kingdom of our Lord, and He shall reign forever and ever (Rev. 11:15). Then every knee shall bow to Him and every tongue confess that He is Lord of all.

Meanwhile, God's people must do all they can to get the Gospel out to the billions of people in this world who have never had the opportunity to hear the name of Jesus or learn how to trust Him and be saved. When the great and terrible Day of the Lord dawns, the nations of the world will be judged for the way they have treated one another and the nation of Israel. Until that day dawns, God's church must keep praying "Thy kingdom come" and seek to obey His command to take the Gospel to the whole world.

Endnotes

1. Edom and the Edomites are found over one hundred times in the Old Testament. They are mentioned in the prophecies of Isaiah (chap. 34), Jeremiah (chap. 49; Lam. 4:21–22), Ezekiel (25:12–14; 35:1–15), Daniel (11:41), Joel (3:19), Amos (1:6–11; 2:1; 9:12) and Malachi (1:4), as well as Obadiah. King Saul overcame them (1 Sam. 14:47), and so did David (2 Sam. 8:13–14; 1 Kings 11:14–16), but Edom was a thorn in Israel's side for centuries. Consult a map of Bible lands for the location of Edom.

2. Compare Obadiah 1–6 with Jeremiah 49:7–22. The prophets often quoted from one another.

3. The Prophet Joel has a great deal to say about the Day of the Lord. See my book *Be Amazed*, which expounds Joel's prophecy.

JONAH

OUTLINE

Key theme: Obeying God's will brings blessings to us and to others through us; disobedience brings discipline.

Key verse: Jonah 2:9

I. GOD'S PATIENCE WITH JONAH. 1:1-17

1. Jonah's disobedience. 1:1-3
2. Jonah's indifference. 1:4-10
3. Jonah's impenitence. 1:11-17

II. GOD'S MERCY TOWARD JONAH. 2:1-10

1. He hears his prayer. 2:1-2
2. He disciplines him. 2:3
3. He honors his faith. 2:4-7
4. He accepts his confession. 2:8-9
5. He restores his ministry. 2:10

III. GOD'S POWER THROUGH JONAH. 3:1-10

1. The gracious Lord. 3:1-2
2. The obedient servant. 3:3-4
3. The repentant people. 3:5-9
4. The postponed judgment. 3:10

IV. GOD'S MINISTRY TO JONAH. 4:1-11

1. God hears him. 4:1-4
2. God comforts him. 4:5-8
3. God teaches him. 4:9-11

CONTENTS

Jonah in His Time

Those who consider the Book of Jonah an allegory or a parable should note that 2 Kings 14:25 identifies Jonah as a real person, a Jewish prophet from Gath Hepher in Zebulun who ministered in the Northern Kingdom of Israel during the reign of Jeroboam II (793-753 B.C.). They should also note that our Lord considered Jonah a historic person and pointed to him as a type of His own death, burial, and resurrection. (Matt. 12:42; Luke 11:32).

The reign of Jeroboam II was a time of great prosperity in Israel; the nation regained lost territory and expanded both its boundaries and influence. But it was a time of moral and spiritual decay as the nation rapidly moved away from God and into idolatry. Jonah's contemporaries Hosea and Amos both courageously denounced the wickedness of the rulers, priests, and people. It's worth noting that Hosea and Amos also showed God's concern for other nations, which is one of the major themes of Jonah.

While Jonah had a ministry to Nineveh, a leading city in Assyria, he also had a ministry to Israel through this little book. He discovered God's compassion for those outside Israel, even those who were their enemies. God had called His people to be a blessing to the Gentiles (Gen. 12:1-3), but, like Jonah, the Jews refused to obey. And, like Jonah, they had to be disciplined; for Assyria would conquer Israel and Babylon would take Judah into captivity. Jonah's book magnifies the sovereignty of God as well as the love and mercy of God. Jehovah is the "God of the second chance," even for rebellious prophets.

CHAPTER ONE
PATIENCE AND PARDON
JONAH 1–2

Most people are so familiar with the story of Jonah that nothing in it surprises them anymore, including the fact that it begins with the word "and."[1] If I opened one of my books with the word "and," the editor would probably wonder if something had been lost, including my ability to use the English language.

Jonah is one of fourteen Old Testament books that open with the little word "and." These books remind us of God's "continued story" of grace and mercy. Though the Bible is comprised of sixty-six different books, it tells only one story; and God keeps communicating that message to us, even though we don't always listen too attentively. How long-suffering He is toward us!

What is the Book of Jonah about? Well, it's not simply about a great fish (mentioned only four times), or a great city (named nine times), or even a disobedient prophet (mentioned eighteen times). It's about God! God is mentioned thirty-eight times in these four short chapters, and if you eliminated Him from the book, the story wouldn't make sense. The Book of Jonah is about the will of God and how we respond to it. It's also about the love of God and how we share it with others.

In these first two chapters, Jonah has three experiences.

1. Rebellion (Jonah 1:1-17)

Jonah must have been a popular man in Israel, because his prediction had been fulfilled that the nation would regain her lost territory from her enemies (2 Kings 14:25). Those were days of peace and prosperity for Israel, but they were autumn days just before the terrible winter of judgment.

Jonah the prophet disobeys God's call (Jonah 1:1-3). Jonah got into trouble because his attitudes were wrong. To begin with, he had a wrong attitude toward the will of God. Obeying the will of God is as important to God's servant as it is to the people His servants minister to. It's in obeying the will of God that we find our spiritual nourishment (John 4:34), enlightenment (7:17), and enablement (Heb. 13:21). To Jesus, the will of God was food that satisfied Him; to Jonah, the will of God was medicine that choked him.

Jonah's wrong attitude toward God's will stemmed from a feeling that the Lord was asking him to do an impossible thing. God commanded the prophet to go to Israel's enemy, Assyria, and give the city of Nineveh opportunity to repent, and Jonah would much rather see the city destroyed. The Assyrians were a cruel people who had often abused Israel and Jonah's narrow patriotism took precedence over his theology.[2] Jonah forgot that the will of God is the expression of the love of God (Ps. 33:11), and that God called him to Nineveh because He loved both Jonah and the Ninevites.

Jonah also had a wrong attitude toward the Word of God. When the Word of the Lord came to him, Jonah thought he could "take it or leave it." However, when God's Word commands us, we must listen and obey. Disobedience isn't an option. "But why do you call Me 'Lord, Lord,' and do not do the things which I say?" (Luke 6:46, (NKJV).

Jonah forgot that it was a great privilege to be a prophet, to hear God's Word, and know God's will. That's why he resigned his prophetic office and fled in the opposite direction from Nineveh.[3] Jonah knew that he couldn't run away from God's presence (Ps. 139:7-12), but he felt he had the right to turn in his resignation. He forgot that "God's gifts and His call are irrevocable" (Rom. 11:29, NIV). At one time or another during their ministries, Moses, Elijah, and Jeremiah felt like giving up, but God wouldn't let them. Jonah needed Nineveh as much as Nineveh needed Jonah. It's in doing the will of God that we grow in grace and become more like Christ.

Jonah had a wrong attitude toward circumstances; he thought they were working for him when they were really working against him. He fled to Joppa[4] and found just the right ship waiting for him! He had enough money to pay the fare for his long trip, and he was even able to go down into the ship and fall into a sleep so deep that the storm didn't wake him up. It's possible to be out of the will of God and still have circumstances appear to be working on your behalf. You can be rebelling against God and still have a false sense of security that includes a good night's sleep. God in His providence was preparing Jonah for a great fall.

Finally, Jonah had a wrong attitude toward the Gentiles. Instead of wanting to help them find the true and living God, he wanted to abandon them to their darkness and spiritual death. He not only hated their sins—and the Assyrians were ruthless enemies—but he hated the sinners who committed the sins. Better that Nineveh should be destroyed than that the Assyrians live and attack Israel.

Jonah the Jew becomes a curse instead of a blessing (Jonah 1:4-10). God called the Jews to be a blessing to all the nations of the earth (Gen. 12:1-3), but whenever the Jews were out of the will of God, they brought trouble instead of blessing.[5] Twice Abraham brought trouble to people because he lied (vv. 10-20; 20:1-18); Achan brought trouble to Israel's army because he robbed God (Josh. 7); and Jonah brought trouble to a boatload of pagan sailors because he fled. Consider all that Jonah lost because he wasn't a blessing to others.

First of all, he lost the voice of God (Jonah 1:4). We don't read that "the word of the Lord came to Jonah," but that a great storm broke loose over the waters. God was no longer speaking to Jonah through His word; He was speaking to him through His works: the sea, the wind, the rain, the thunder, and even the great fish. Everything in nature obeyed God except His servant! God even spoke to Jonah through the heathen sailors (vv. 6, 8, 10) who didn't know Jehovah. It's a sad thing when a servant of God is rebuked by pagans.

Jonah also lost his spiritual energy (v. 5b). He went to sleep during a fierce storm and was totally unconcerned about the safety of others. The sailors were throwing the ship's wares and cargo overboard, and Jonah was about to lose everything, but he still slept on. "A little sleep, a little slumber, a little folding of the hands to rest—and poverty will come on you like a bandit and scarcity like an armed man" (Prov. 24:33, NIV).

He lost his power in prayer (Jonah 1:5a, 6). The heathen sailors were calling on their gods for help while Jonah slept through the prayer meeting, the one man on board who knew the true God and could pray to Him. Of course, Jonah would first have had to confess his sins and determine to obey God, something he wasn't willing to do. "If I regard iniquity in my heart, the Lord will not hear me" (Ps. 66:18).[6] If Jonah did pray, his prayer wasn't answered. Loss of power in prayer is one of the first indications that we're far from the Lord and need to get right with Him.

Sad to say, Jonah lost his testimony (Jonah 1:7-10). He certainly wasn't living up to his name,[7] for Jonah means "dove," and the dove is a symbol of peace. Jonah's father's name was Ammitai, which means "faithful, truthful," something that Jonah was not. We've already seen that he wasn't living up to his high calling as a Jew, for he had brought everybody trouble instead of blessing, nor was he living up to his calling as a prophet, for he had no message for them from God. When the lot pointed to Jonah as the culprit, he could no longer avoid making a decision.

Jonah had already told the crew that he was running away from God, but now he told them he was God's prophet, the God who created the heaven, the earth, and the sea. This announcement made the sailors even more frightened. The God who created the sea was punishing His servant and that's why they were in danger!

Jonah the rebel suffers for his sins (Jonah 1:11-17). Charles Spurgeon said that God never allows His children to sin successfully, and Jonah is proof of the truth of that statement. "For whom the Lord loves He chastens, and scourges every son whom He receives" (Heb. 12:6, NKJV).

We must not make the mistake of calling Jonah a martyr, for the title would be undeserved. Martyrs die for the glory of God, but Jonah offered to die because selfishly he would rather die than obey the will of God![8] He shouldn't be classified with people like Moses (Ex. 32:30-35), Esther (Es. 4:13-17), and Paul (Rom. 9:1-3) who were willing to give their lives to God in order to rescue others. Jonah is to be commended for telling the truth but not for taking his life in his own hands. He should have surrendered his life to the Lord and let Him give the orders. Had he fallen to his knees and confessed his sins to God, Jonah might have seen the storm cease and the door open to a great opportunity for witness on the ship.

It's significant that the heathen sailors at first rejected Jonah's offer and began to work harder to save the ship. They did more for

Jonah than Jonah had been willing to do for them. When they saw that the cause was hopeless, they asked Jonah's God for His forgiveness for throwing Jonah into the stormy sea. Sometimes unsaved people put believers to shame by their honesty, sympathy, and sacrifice.

However, these pagan sailors knew some basic theology: the existence of Jonah's God, His judgment of sin, their own guilt before Him, and His sovereignty over creation. They confessed, "For you, O Lord, have done as You pleased" (Jonah 1:14, NIV). However, there's no evidence that they abandoned their old gods; they merely added Jehovah to their "god shelf." They threw themselves on God's mercy and then threw Jonah into the raging sea, and God stopped the storm.

When the storm ceased, the men feared God even more and made vows to Him. How they could offer an animal sacrifice to God on board ship is a puzzle to us, especially since the cargo had been jettisoned, but then we don't know what the sacrifice was or how it was offered. Perhaps the sense of verse 16 is that they offered the animal to Jehovah and vowed to sacrifice it to Him once they were safe on shore.

The seventeenth-century English preacher Jeremy Taylor said, "God threatens terrible things if we will not be happy." He was referring, of course, to being happy with God's will for our lives. For us to rebel against God's will, as Jonah did, is to invite the chastening hand of God. That's why the Westminster Catechism states that "the chief end of man is to glorify God and enjoy Him forever." We glorify God by enjoying His will and doing it from our hearts (Eph. 6:6), and that's where Jonah failed.

Jonah could say with the psalmist, "The Lord has chastened me severely, but He has not given me over to death" (Ps. 118:18, NKJV). God prepared a great fish to swallow Jonah and protect his life for three days and three nights.[9] We'll consider the significance of this later in this study.

2. Repentance (Jonah 2:1-9)

From an experience of rebellion and discipline, Jonah turns to an experience of repentance and dedication, and God graciously gives him a new beginning. Jonah no doubt expected to die in the waters of the sea,[10] but when he woke up inside the fish, he realized that God had graciously spared him. As with the Prodigal Son, whom Jonah in his rebellion greatly resembles (Luke 15:11-24), it was the goodness of God that brought him to repentance (Rom. 2:4). Notice the stages in Jonah's spiritual experience as described in his prayer.

He prayed for God's help (Jonah 2:1-2). "Then Jonah prayed" (2:1) suggests that it was at the end of the three days and three nights when Jonah turned to the Lord for help, but we probably shouldn't press the word "then" too far. The Hebrew text simply reads, "And Jonah prayed." Surely Jonah prayed as he went down into the depths of the sea, certain that he would drown. That would be the normal thing for any person to do, and that's the picture we get from verses 5 and 7.

His prayer was born out of affliction, not affection. He cried out to God because he was in danger, not because he delighted in the Lord. But better that he should pray compelled by any motive than not to pray at all. It's doubtful whether any believer always prays with pure and holy motives, for our desires and God's directions sometimes conflict.

However, in spite of the fact that he prayed, Jonah still wasn't happy with the will of God. In chapter 1, he was afraid of the will of God and rebelled against it, but now he wants God's will simply because it's the only way out of his dangerous plight. Like too many people today, Jonah saw the will of God as something to turn to in an emergency, not something to live by every day of one's life.

Jonah was now experiencing what the sailors experienced during the storm: he felt he was perishing (1:6, 14). It's good for God's people, and especially preachers, to remember what it's like to be lost and without hope. How easy it is for us to grow hardened toward sinners and lose our compassion for the lost. As He dropped Jonah into the depths, God was reminding him of what the people of Nineveh were going through in their sinful condition: they were helpless and hopeless.

God heard Jonah's cries for help. Prayer is one of the constant miracles of the Christian life. To think that our God is so great He can hear the cries of millions of people at the same time and deal with their needs personally! A parent with two or three children often finds it impossible to meet all their needs all the time, but God is able to provide for all His children, no matter where they are or what their needs may be. "He who has learned to pray," said William Law, "has learned the greatest secret of a holy and happy life."

He accepted God's discipline (Jonah 2:3). The sailors didn't cast Jonah into the stormy sea; God did. "You hurled me into the deep . . . all your waves and breakers swept over me" (v.3, NIV, italics mine). When Jonah said those words, he was acknowledging that God was disciplining him and that he deserved it.

How we respond to discipline determines how much benefit we receive from it. According to Hebrews 12:5-11, we have several options: we can despise God's discipline and fight (v. 5); we can be discouraged and faint (v. 5); we can resist discipline and invite stronger discipline, possibly even death (v. 9)[11]; or we can submit to the Father and mature in faith and love (v. 7). Discipline is to the believer what exercise and training are to the athlete (v. 11); it enables us to run the race with endurance and reach the assigned goal (vv. 1-2).

The fact that God chastened His servant is proof that Jonah was truly a child of God, for God disciplines only His own children. "But if you are without chastening, of which all have become partakers, then you are illegitimate and not sons" (v. 8). And the father chastens us in love so that "afterward" we might enjoy "the peaceable fruit of righteousness" (v.11).

He trusted God's promises (Jonah 2:4-7). Jonah was going in one direction only—down. In fact, he had been going in that direction since the hour he rebelled against God's plan for his life. He went "down to Joppa" and "down into the sides of the ship" (1:3, 5). Now he was going "down to the bottoms of the mountains" (2:6); and at some point, the great fish met him, and he went down into the fish's belly (1:17). When you turn your back on God, the only direction you can go is down.

What saved Jonah? His faith in God's promise. Which promise? The promise that involves "looking toward God's holy temple" (2:4, 7). When King Solomon dedicated the temple in Jerusalem, he asked God for this special favor (1 Kings 8:38-40, NKJV):

> Whatever prayer, whatever supplication is made by anyone, or by all Your people Israel, when each one knows the plague of his own heart, and spreads out his hands toward this temple: then hear in heaven Your dwelling place, and forgive, and act, and give to everyone according to all his ways, whose heart You know ... that they may fear You all the days that they live in the land which You gave to our fathers.

Jonah claimed that promise. By faith, he looked toward God's temple (the only way to look was up!) and asked God to deliver him; and God kept His promise and answered his call. "I remembered [the] Lord" (Jonah 2:7) means, "I acted on the basis of His commitment to me." Jonah knew God's covenant promises and he claimed them.

He yielded to God's will (Jonah 2:8-9). Now Jonah admits that there were idols in his life that robbed him of the blessing of God. An idol is anything that takes away from God the affection and obedience that rightfully belongs only to Him. One such idol was Jonah's intense patriotism. He was so concerned for the safety and prosperity of his own nation that he refused to be God's messenger to their enemies the Assyrians. We shall learn from chapter 4 that Jonah was also protecting his own reputation (4:2), for if God spared Nineveh, then Jonah would be branded a false prophet whose words of warning weren't fulfilled. For somebody who was famous for his prophecies (2 Kings 14:25), this would be devastating.

Jonah closes his prayer by uttering some solemn vows to the Lord, vows that he really intended to keep. Like the psalmist, he said: "I will go into Your house with burnt offerings; I will pay You my vows, which my lips have uttered and my mouth has spoken when I was in trouble" (Ps. 66:13-14, NKJV). Jonah promised to worship God in the temple with sacrifices and songs of thanksgiving. He doesn't tell us what other promises he made to the Lord, but one of them surely was, "I will go to Nineveh and declare Your message if You give me another chance."

Jonah couldn't save himself, and nobody on earth could save him, but the Lord could do it, for "salvation is of the Lord!" (Jonah

2:9b, NKJV) This is a quotation from Psalms 3:8 and 37:39 and it is the central declaration in the book. It is also the central theme of the Bible. How wise of Jonah to memorize the Word of God; because being able to quote the Scriptures, especially the Book of Psalms, gave him light in the darkness and hope in his seemingly hopeless situation.

3. Redemption (Jonah 2:10)

"And [the fish] vomited out Jonah upon the dry land." What an ignominious way for a distinguished prophet to arrive on shore! In chapter 1, the sailors treated Jonah like dangerous cargo to be thrown overboard, and now he's treated like a foreign substance to be disgorged from the fish's body. But when Jonah ceased to be an obedient prophet, he cheapened himself, so he's the one to blame. We can be sure that he was duly humbled as he once again stood on dry land.

The miracle. Few miracles in Scripture have been attacked as much as this one, and Christian scholars have gathered various kinds of evidence to prove that it could happen. Since the Bible doesn't tell us what kind of fish swallowed Jonah, we don't have to measure sharks and whales or comb history for similar incidents. It was a "prepared" fish (1:17), designed by God for the occasion, and therefore it was adequate for the task. Jesus didn't question the historicity of the miracle, so why should we?

The sign (Matt. 12:39; 16:4; Luke 11:29). The "sign of Jonah" is seen in his experience of "death," burial, and resurrection on the third day, and it was the only sign Jesus gave to the nation of Israel. At Pentecost, Peter preached the Resurrection (Acts 2:22-26) and so did Paul when he preached to the Jews in other nations (13:26-37). In fact, the emphasis in the Book of Acts is on the resurrection of Jesus Christ; for the apostles were "witnesses of the Resurrection" (2:32; 3:15; 5:32; 10:39).

Some students are troubled by the phrase "three days and three nights," especially since both Scripture and tradition indicate that Jesus was crucified on Friday. In order to protect the integrity of the Scripture, some have suggested that the Crucifixion be moved back to Thursday or even Wednesday. But to the Jews, a part of a day was treated as a whole day, and we need not interpret "three days and three nights" to mean seventy-two hours to the very second. For that matter, we can't prove that Jonah was in the fish exactly seventy-two hours. The important thing is that centuries after the event, Jonah became a "sign" to the Jewish people and pointed them to Jesus Christ.

Jonah was now free to obey the Lord and take God's message to Nineveh, but he still had lessons to learn.

CHAPTER TWO
PREACHING AND POUTING
JONAH 3–4

The question is usually asked in Old Testament survey classes, "Was the great fish more relieved to be rid of Jonah than Jonah was to get out of the great fish?" Maybe their sense of relief was mutual. At any rate, we hope that Jonah gave thanks to God for the divinely provided creature that rescued him from certain death.

In these two chapters, we are confronted with four marvels that we dare not take for granted:

1. The Marvel of an Undeserved Commission (Jonah 3:1-2)

Did anybody see Jonah emerge when the great fish disgorged him on the dry land? If so, the story must have spread rapidly and perhaps even preceded him to Nineveh, and that may help explain the reception the city gave him. Had Jonah been bleached by the fish's gastric juices? Did he look so peculiar that nobody could doubt who he was and what had happened to him? Since Jonah was a "sign" to the Ninevites (Matt. 12:38-41), perhaps this included the way he looked.

What the people saw or thought really wasn't important. The important thing was what God thought and what He would do next to His repentant prophet. "The life of Jonah cannot be written without God," said Charles Spurgeon; "take God out of the prophet's history, and there is no history to write."[1]

God met Jonah. We don't know where the

great fish deposited Jonah, but we do know that wherever Jonah was, the Lord was there. Remember, God is more concerned about His workers than He is about their work, for if the workers are what they ought to be, the work will be what it ought to be. Throughout Jonah's time of rebellion, God was displeased with His servant, but He never once deserted him. It was God who controlled the storm, prepared the great fish, and rescued Jonah from the deep. His promise is, "I will never leave you nor forsake you" (Heb. 13:5, NKJV; see Josh 1:5). "When you pass through the waters, I will be with you" (Isa. 43:2, NKJV).

God spoke to Jonah. After the way Jonah had stubbornly refused to obey God's voice, it's a marvel that the Lord spoke to him at all. Jonah had turned his back on God's word, so the Lord had been forced to speak to him through thunder and rain and a stormy sea. But now that Jonah had confessed his sins and turned back to the Lord, God could once again speak to him through His word. One of the tests of our relationship to God is, "Does God speak to me as I read and ponder His Word?" If we don't hear God speaking to us in our hearts, perhaps we have some unfinished business that needs to be settled with Him.

God commissioned Jonah. "The victorious Christian life, " said George H. Morrison, "is a series of new beginnings." When we fall, the enemy wants us to believe that our ministry is ended and there's no hope for recovery, but our God is the God of the second chance. "Then the word of the Lord came to Jonah a second time" (Jonah 3:1). "Do not rejoice over me, my enemy; when I fall, I will arise; when I sit in darkness, the Lord will be a Light to me" (Micah 7:8, NKJV).

You don't have to read very far in your Bible to discover that God forgives His servants and restores them to ministry. Abraham fled to Egypt, where he lied about his wife, but God gave him another chance (Gen. 12:10–13:4). Jacob lied to his father Isaac, but God restored him and used him to build the nation of Israel. Moses killed a man (probably in self-defense) and fled from Egypt, but God called him to be the leader of His people. Peter denied the Lord three times, but Jesus forgave him and said, "Follow Me" (John 21:19).

However encouraging these examples of restoration may be, they must never be used as excuses for sin. The person who says, "I can go ahead and sin, because I know the Lord will forgive me" has no understanding of the awfulness of sin or the holiness of God. "But there is forgiveness with You, that You may be feared" (Ps. 130:4, NKJV). God in His grace forgives our sins, but God in His government determines that we shall reap what we sow, and the harvest can be very costly. Jonah paid dearly for rebelling against the Lord.

God challenged Jonah. Four times in this book, Nineveh is called a "great city" (1:2; 3:2-3; 4:11),[2] and archeologists tell us that the adjective is well-deserved. It was great in history, having been founded in ancient times by Noah's great-grandson Nimrod (Gen. 10:8-10).[3] It was also great in size. The circumference of the city and its suburbs was sixty miles, and from the Lord's statement in Jonah 4:11, we could infer that there were probably over 600,000 people living there. One wall of the city had a circumference of eight miles and boasted 1,500 towers.

The city was great in splendor and influence, being one of the leading cities of the powerful Assyrian Empire. It was built near the Tigris River and had the Khoser River running through it. (This fact will prove to be important when we study the Book of Nahum.) Its merchants traveled the empire and brought great wealth into the city, and Assyria's armies were feared everywhere.

Nineveh was great in sin, for the Assyrians were known far and wide for their violence, showing no mercy to their enemies. They impaled live victims on sharp poles, leaving them to roast to death in the desert sun; they beheaded people by the thousands and stacked their skulls up in piles by the city gates; and they even skinned people alive. They respected neither age nor sex and followed a policy of killing babies and young children so they wouldn't have to care for them (Nahum 3:10).

It was to the wicked people of this great city that God sent His servant Jonah, assuring him that He would give him the message to speak. After making the necessary preparations, it would take Jonah at least a month to travel from his own land to the city of Nineveh, and during that trip, he had a lot of time available to meditate on what the Lord had taught him.

The will of God will never lead you where the grace of God can't keep you and the power of God can't use you. "And who is sufficient for these things? . . . Our sufficiency is of God" (2 Cor. 2:16 and 3:5).

2. The Marvel of an Unparalleled Awakening (Jonah 3:3-10)

From a human perspective, this entire enterprise appears ridiculous. How could one man, claiming to be God's prophet, confront thousands of people with this strange message, especially a message of judgment? How could a Jew, who worshiped the true God, ever get these idolatrous Gentiles to believe what he had to say? For all he knew, Jonah might end up impaled on a pole or skinned alive! But, in obedience to the Lord, Jonah went to Nineveh.

Jonah's message to Nineveh (Jonah 3:3-4). "Three days' journey" means either that it would take three days to get through the city and its suburbs or three days to go around them. The NIV translation of verse 3 suggests that it would take three days to visit all of the area. According to Genesis 10:11-12, four cities were involved in the "Nineveh metroplex": Nineveh, Rehoboth Ir, Calah, and Resen (NIV). However you interpret the "three days," one thing is clear: Nineveh was no insignificant place.

When Jonah was one day into the city, he began to declare his message: "Yet forty days, and Nineveh shall be overthrown." Throughout Scripture, the number forty seems to be identified with testing or judgment. During the time of Noah, it rained forty days and forty nights (Gen. 7:4, 12, 17). The Jewish spies explored Canaan forty days (Num. 14:34), and the nation of Israel was tested in the wilderness forty years (Deut. 2:7). The giant Goliath taunted the army of Israel forty days (1 Sam. 17:16), and the Lord gave the people of Nineveh forty days to repent and turn from their wickedness.

At this point, we must confess that we wish we knew more about Jonah's ministry to Nineveh. Was this the only message he proclaimed? Surely he spent time telling the people about the true and living God, for we're told, "The people of Nineveh believed God" (Jonah 3:5). They would have to know something about this God of Israel in order to exercise sincere faith (see Acts 17:22ff). Did Jonah expose the folly of their idolatry? Did he recount his own personal history to show them that his God was powerful and sovereign? We simply don't know. The important thing is that Jonah obeyed God, went to Nineveh, and declared the message God gave him. God did the rest.

Nineveh's message to God (Jonah 3:5-9). In the Hebrew text, there are only five words in Jonah's message; yet God used those five words to stir the entire population, from the king on the throne to the lowest peasant in the field. God gave the people forty days of grace, but they didn't need that long. We get the impression that from the very first time they saw Jonah and heard his warning, they paid attention to his message. Word spread quickly throughout the entire district and the people humbled themselves by fasting and wearing sackcloth.

When the message got to the king, he too put on sackcloth and sat in the dust. He also made the fast official by issuing an edict and ordering the people to humble themselves, cry out to God, and turn from their evil ways. Even the animals were included in the activities by wearing sackcloth and abstaining from food and drink. The people were to cry "mightily" ("urgently," NIV) to God, for this was a matter of life and death.

When Jonah was in dire straits, he recalled the promise concerning Solomon's temple (Jonah 2:4, 7; 1 Kings 8:38-39; 2 Chron. 6:36-39), looking toward the temple, and called out for help. Included in Solomon's temple prayer was a promise for people outside the nation of Israel, and that would include the Ninevites. "As for the foreigner who does not belong to your people Israel ... when he comes and prays toward this temple, then hear from heaven, Your dwelling place, and do whatever the foreigner asks of You, so that all the peoples of the earth may know Your name and fear You" (2 Chron. 6:32-33). Jonah certainly knew this promise, and perhaps it was the basis for the whole awakening.

Like the sailors in the storm, the Ninevites didn't want to perish (Jonah 3:9; 1:6, 14). That's what witnessing is all about, "that whoever believes in Him should not perish but have everlasting life' (John 3:16, NKJV). Their fasting and praying, and their humbling of themselves before God, sent a message to heaven, but the people of Nineveh had no assurance that they would be saved. They hoped that God's great compassion would move Him to change His plan and spare the city. Once again, how did they know that the God of the Hebrews was a merciful and compassionate God? No doubt Jonah told them, for this was a doctrine he himself believed (Jonah 4:2).

God's message (Jonah 3:10). At some point, God spoke to Jonah and told Him that He had accepted the people's repentance and would not destroy the city. The phrase "God repented" might better be translated "God relented," that is, changed His course. From the human point of view, it looked like repentance, but from the divine perspective, it was simply God's response to man's change of heart. God is utterly consistent with Himself; it only appears that he is changing His mind. The Bible uses human analogies to reveal the divine character of God (Jer. 18:1-10).

How deep was the spiritual experience of the people of Nineveh? If repentance and faith are the basic conditions of salvation (Acts 20:21), then we have reason to believe that they were accepted by God; for the people of Nineveh repented and had faith in God (Jonah 3:5). The fact that Jesus used the Ninevites to shame the unbelieving Jews of His day is further evidence that their response to Jonah's ministry was sincere (Matt. 12:38-41).

3. The Marvel of an Unhappy Servant (Jonah 4:1-11)

If this book had ended at the last verse of chapter 3, history would have portrayed Jonah as the greatest of the prophets. After all, preaching one message that motivated thousands of people to repent and turn to God was no mean accomplishment. But the Lord doesn't look on the outward things; He looks at the heart (1 Sam. 16:7) and weighs the motives (1 Cor. 4:5). That's why Chapter 4 was included in the book, for it reveals "the thoughts and intents" of Johah's heart and exposes his sins.

If in chapter 1 Jonah is like the Prodigal Son, insisting on doing his own thing and going his own way (Luke 15:11-32); then in chapter 4, he's like the Prodigal's Elder Brother—critical, selfish, sullen, angry, and unhappy with what was going on. It isn't enough for God's servants simply to do their Master's will; they must do "the will of God from the heart" (Eph. 6:6). The heart of every problem is the problem in the heart, and that's where Jonah's problems were to be found. "But it displeased Jonah exceedingly, and he was very angry" (Jonah 4:1).

The remarkable thing is that God tenderly dealt with His sulking servant and sought to bring him back to the place of joy and fellowship.

God listened to Jonah (Jonah 4:1-4). For the second time in this account, Jonah prays, but his second prayer was much different in content and intent. He prayed his best prayer in the worst place, the fish's belly, and he prayed his worst prayer in the best place, at Nineveh where God was working. His first prayer came from a broken heart, but his second prayer came from an angry heart. In his first prayer, he asked God to save him, but in his second prayer, he asked God to take his life! Once again, Jonah would rather die than not have his own way.

This petulant prayer lets us in on the secret of why Jonah tried to run away in the first place. Being a good theologian, Jonah knew the attributes of God, that He was "a gracious and compassionate God, slow to anger and abounding in love, a God who relents from sending calamity" (v. 2, NIV). Knowing this, Jonah was sure that if he announced judgment to the Ninevites and they repented, God would forgive them and not send His judgment, and then Jonah would be branded as a false prophet! Remember, Jonah's message merely announced the impending judgment; it didn't offer conditions for salvation.

Jonah was concerned about his reputation, not only before the Ninevites, but also before the Jews back home. His Jewish friends would want to see all of the Assyrians destroyed, not just the people of Nineveh. When Jonah's friends found out that he had been the means of saving Nineveh from God's wrath, they could have considered him a traitor to official Jewish foreign policy. Jonah was a narrow-minded patriot who saw Assyria only as a dangerous enemy to destroy, not as a company of repentant sinners to be brought to the Lord.

When reputation is more important than character, and pleasing ourselves and our friends is more important than pleasing God, then we're in danger of becoming like Jonah and living to defend our prejudices instead of fulfilling our spiritual responsibilities.[4] Jonah certainly had good theology, but it stayed in his head and never got to his heart, and he was so distraught that he wanted to die![5] God's tender response was to ask Jonah to examine his heart and see why he really was angry.

God comforted Jonah (Jonah 4:5-8). For the second time in this book, Jonah abandoned his place of ministry, left the city, and sat down in a place east of the city where he could see what would happen. Like the Elder Brother in the parable, he wouldn't go in and enjoy the feast (Luke 15:28). He could have taught the Ninevites so much about the true God of Israel, but he preferred to have his own way. What a tragedy it is when God's servants are a means of blessing to others but miss the blessing themselves!

God knew that Jonah was very uncomfortable sitting in that booth, so He graciously caused a vine (gourd) to grow whose large leaves would protect Jonah from the hot sun. This made Jonah happy, but the next morning, when God prepared a worm to kill the vine, Jonah was unhappy. The combination of the hot sun and the smothering desert wind made him want to die even more. As He had done in the depths of the sea, God was reminding Jonah of what it was like to be lost: helpless, hopeless, miserable. Jonah was experiencing a taste of hell as he sat and watched the city.

A simple test of character is to ask, "What makes me happy? What makes me angry? What makes me want to give up? Jonah was "a double-minded man, unstable in all his ways" (James 1:8, NKJV). One minute he's preaching God's Word, but the next minute he's disobeying it and fleeing his post of duty. While inside the great fish, he prayed to be delivered, but now he asks the Lord to kill him. He called the city to repentance, but he wouldn't repent himself! He was more concerned about creature comforts than he was about winning the lost. The Ninevites, the vine, the worm, and the wind have all obeyed God, but Jonah still refuses to obey, and he has the most to gain.

God instructed Jonah (Jonah 4:9-11). God is still speaking to Jonah and Jonah is still listening and answering, even though he's not giving the right answers. Unrighteous anger feeds the ego and produces the poison of selfishness in the heart. Jonah still had a problem with the will of God. In chapter 1, his mind understood God's will, but he refused to obey it and took his body in the opposite direction. In chapter 2, he cried out for help, God rescued him, and he gave his body back to the Lord. In chapter 3, he yielded his will to the Lord and went to Nineveh to preach, but his heart was not yet surrendered to the Lord. Jonah did the will of God, but not from his heart.

Jonah had one more lesson to learn, perhaps the most important one of all. In chapter 1, he learned the lesson of God's providence and patience, that you can't run away from God. In chapter 2, he learned the lesson of God's pardon, that God forgives those who call upon Him. In chapter 3, he learned the lesson of God's power as he saw a whole city humble itself before the Lord. Now he had to learn the lesson of God's pity, that God has compassion for lost sinners like the Ninevites; and his servants must also have compassion.[6] It seems incredible, but Jonah brought a whole city to faith in the Lord and yet he didn't love the people he was preaching to!

The people who could not "discern between their right hand and their left hand" (4:11) were immature little children (Deut. 1:39), and if there were 120,000 of them in Nineveh and its suburbs, the population was not small. God certainly has a special concern for the children (Mark 10:13-16); but whether children or adults, the Assyrians all needed to know the Lord. Jonah had pity on the vine that perished, but he didn't have compassion for the people who would perish and live eternally apart from God.

Jeremiah and Jesus looked on the city of Jerusalem and wept over it (Jer. 9:1, 10; 23:9; Luke 19:41), and Paul beheld the city of Athens and "was greatly distressed" (Acts 17:16, NIV), but Jonah looked on the city of Nineveh and seethed with anger. He needed to learn the lesson of God's pity and have a heart of compassion for lost souls.

4. The Marvel of an Unanswered Question (Jonah 4:11)

Jonah and Nahum are the only books in the Bible that end with questions, and both books have to do with the city of Nineveh. Nahum ends with a question about God's punishment of Nineveh (Nahum 3:19), while Jonah ends with a question about God's pity for Nineveh.

This is a strange way to end such a dramatic book as the Book of Jonah. God has the first word (Jonah 1:1-2) and God has the last word (4:11), and that's as it should be, but we aren't told how Jonah answered God's final question. It's like the ending of Frank Stockton's famous short story "The Lady or the Tiger?" When the handsome youth opened the door, what came out: the beautiful princess or the man-eating tiger?

We sincerely hope that Jonah yielded to God's loving entreaty and followed the example of the Ninevites by repenting and seeking the face of God. The famous Scottish preacher Alexander Whyte believed that Jonah did experience a change of heart. He wrote, "But Jonah came to himself again during those five-and-twenty days or so, from the east gate of Nineveh back to Gath Hepher, his father's house."[7] Spurgeon said, "Let us hope that, during the rest of his life, he so lived as to rejoice in the sparing mercy of God."[8] After all, hadn't Jonah himself been spared because of God's mercy?

God was willing to spare Nineveh, but in order to do that, He could not spare His own Son. Somebody had to die for their sins or they would die in their sins. "He that spared not His own Son, but delivered Him up for us all, how shall He not with Him also freely give us all things?" (Rom. 8:32). Jesus used Jonah's ministry to Nineveh to show the Jews how guilty they were in rejecting His witness. "The men of Nineveh shall rise in judgment with this generation, and shall condemn it; because they repented at the preaching of Jonah; and, behold, a greater than Jonah is here" (Matt. 12:41).

How is Jesus greater than Jonah? Certainly Jesus is greater than Jonah in His person, for though both were Jews and both were prophets, Jesus is the very Son of God. He is greater in His message, for Jonah preached a message of judgment, but Jesus preached a message of grace and salvation (John 3:16-17). Jonah almost died for his own sins, but Jesus willingly died for the sins of the world (1 John 2:2).

Jonah's ministry was to but one city, but Jesus is "the Savior of the world" (John 4:42; 1 John 4:14). Jonah's obedience was not from the heart, but Jesus always did whatever pleased His father (John 8:29). Jonah didn't love the people he came to save, but Jesus had compassion for sinners and proved His love by dying for them on the cross (Rom. 5:6-8). On the cross, outside the city, Jesus asked God to forgive those who killed Him (Luke 23:34), but Jonah waited outside the city to see if God would kill those he would not forgive.

Yes, Jesus is greater than Jonah, and because He is, we must give greater heed to what He says to us. Those who reject Him will face greater judgment because the greater the light, the greater the responsibility.

But the real issue isn't how Jonah answered God's question; the real issue is how you and I today are answering God's question. Do we agree with God that people without Christ are lost? Like God, do we have compassion for those who are lost? How do we show this compassion? Do we have a concern for those in our great cities where there is so much sin and so little witness? Do we pray that the Gospel will go to people in every part of the world, and are we helping to send it there? Do we rejoice when sinners repent and trust the Savior?

All of those questions and more are wrapped up in what God asked Jonah.

We can't answer for him, but we can answer for ourselves.

Let's give God the right answer.

Endnotes

Chapter 1

1. The KJV translates the Hebrew connective "now," while the NIV and NASB ignore it completely.

2. Jonah's hometown of Gath Hepher was on the border of Zebulun, one of the northernmost tribes, and therefore extremely vulnerable to the attacks of invaders. Perhaps he had seen what the Assyrians could do.

3. Tarshish was probably in Spain, over 1,000 miles west of Joppa. Jonah was supposed to travel east to Nineveh. The Jews weren't seafarers, but Jonah forgot his prejudices and fears in his attempt to escape doing God's will.

4. It was at Joppa that Peter got his divine call to go the Gentiles with the message of the Gospel (Acts 10). Though he protested somewhat at first, unlike Jonah, he obeyed God's call and opened the door of faith to the Gentiles. What a privilege!

5. One exception is when the fall of the Jews brought salvation to the Gentiles (Rom. 11:11ff). Israel was out of God's will when they rejected Christ and opposed the Gospel, but this opened the door of salvation to the Gentiles.

6. The word translated "regard" means "to look upon with knowledge and approval." It isn't only knowing that we've sinned that hinders prayer, but holding onto that sin, approving of it, and protecting it. (See 1 John 1:5-10.)

7. It appears that the sailors gave Jonah a nickname: "he who is responsible for causing all this trouble" (Jonah 1:8, NIV). Since the lot had already fallen on Jonah, the crew didn't need to ask him who was to blame. He was to blame, and they knew it; and that's why they gave him that embarrassing nickname. The KJV, NASB, and NIV all make the nickname into an unnecessary question.

8. The fact that Jonah wanted to die even after Nineveh was delivered (4:8-9) indicates that his heart was still bitter and unyielding with reference to God's will. A surrendered servant will say, "Not my will but Thy will be done."

9. Jonah 1:17 in the English versions is Jonah 2:1 in the Hebrew text.

10. Some expositors believe that Jonah actually died and was resurrected, and base their interpretation on statements in his prayer like "From the depths of the grave [Sheol-the realm of the dead] I called for help" (2:2, NIV) and "But You brought my life up from the pit" (v.6, NIV). But Jonah's prayer is composed of quotations from at least fifteen different psalms, and while some of these psalms describe near-death experiences, none describes a resurrection miracle. The reference to Sheol in verse 2 comes from Psalm 30:3 (and see 16:10 and 18:4-6), and the reference to "the pit" comes from 49:15, both of which were written by David. If these two psalms describe Jonah's resurrection, then they must also describe David's resurrection, but we have no evidence that David ever died and was raised to life. Instead, these psalms describe frightening experiences when God delivered His servants from the very gates of death. That seems to be what Jonah is describing as he quotes them in his prayer. Furthermore, if Jonah died and was resurrected, he could not be an accurate type of Christ (Matt. 12:39; 16:4; Luke 11:29); for types picture the antitype but don't duplicate it, for the antitype is always greater. It's a dangerous thing to build an interpretation on the poetic language of Scripture when we don't have a clear New Testament interpretation to lean on.

11. "There is a sin unto death" (1 John 5:17, KJV). "The Lord shall judge His people. It is a fearful thing to fall into the hands of the living God" (Heb. 10:30-31). Professed believers who play with sin and trifle with God's loving discipline are asking for trouble. Better that we should die than that we should resist His will and bring disgrace to the name of Christ.

Chapter 2

1. Charles H Spurgeon, *Metroplitan Tabernacle Pulpit*, vol. 42, 73.

2. "Great" is one of the key words in the Book of Jonah. Besides a "great city," the book mentions a great wind and tempest (1:4, 12); great fear (vv. 10, 16); a great fish (v. 17); great people, probably nobles (3:5, 7); and Jonah's great displeasure and great gladness (4:1-6).

3. Some date Nineveh's founding as early as 4500 B.C.

4. The early church faced this problem when Peter took the Gospel to the Gentiles (Acts 10–11; 15). According to Jewish theology, Gentiles had to become Jews (proselytes) before they could become Christians, but Cornelius and his family and friends were saved simply by believing on Jesus Christ. When Peter said "whoever believes in Him will receive remission of sins," the people present believed the promise, trusted Christ, and the Holy Spirit came upon them. Peter never got to finish his sermon (10:43-48). The legalistic Jews in the Jerusalem church argued late that Gentiles could not be saved apart from obeying the Law of Moses, and Paul had to debate with them to protect the truth of the Gospel (Acts 15; Gal. 1). Jonah would have sided with the legalists.

5. Both Moses (Num. 1) and Elijah (1 Kings 19) became so discouraged that they made the same request. We lose our perspective when we focus on ourselves and fail to look by faith to the Lord (Heb. 12:1-2).

6. The phrase in 4:11 "and also much cattle" reminds us of God's concern for animal life. God preserves both man and beast (Ps. 36:6), and the animals look to God for their provision (104:10-30). God has made a covenant with creation (Gen. 9:1-17); and even in the Law of Moses, He shows concern for His creation (Deut. 22:6-7; Lev. 22:26-28). An understanding of God is the basis for a true ecology.

7. Alexander Whyte, *Bible Characters from the Old and New Testaments* (Grand Rapids: Kregel Publications, 1990), 387.

8. Charles H. Spurgeon, 84.

MICAH

OUTLINE

Key theme: God judges sin and calls for justice

Key verse: Micah 6:8 Micah delivered three messages (Note "Hear" in 1:2; 3:1; 6:1)

I. A WARNING MESSAGE: JUDGMENT IS COMING. 1:1–2:13

1. The Judge appears. 1:1-5
2. The nations are judged. 1:6-16
   (1) Judgment on Samaria. 1:6-9
   (2) Judgment on Judah. 1:10-16
3. Why judgment is coming. 2:1-11
   (1) Because of covetousness. 2:1-5
   (2) Because of false prophets. 2:6-11
4. Hope for the remnant. 2:12-13

II. A PROMISE MESSAGE: A DELIVERER IS COMING. 3:1–5:15

1. The sins of the leaders. 3:1-12
2. The future of the nation. 4:1-13
3. The coming of Messiah. 5:1-5
4. The defeat of the enemy. 5:6-15

III. A CHALLENGE MESSAGE: TRUST THE LORD NOW. 6:1–7:20

1. In spite of the indictment. 6:1-8
2. In spite of the sentence. 6:9–7:6
3. Because of the Lord's mercies. 7:7-20

CONTENTS

Micah in his time

Micah's name is an abbreviated form of "Micaiah" and means "Who is like Jehovah?" (see 7:18). He was from the village of Moresheth near Gath, about twenty-five miles southwest of Jerusalem; he prophesied during the last half of the eighth century B.C., during the reigns of Jotham (750–735), Ahaz (735–715), and Hezekiah (715–686). He was a contemporary of Isaiah (1:1) in Judah and Amos and Hosea (1:1) in Israel.

During Jotham's reign, Assyria grew stronger. When Ahaz ascended the throne, both Syria and Israel tried to pressure him into joining a rebellion against Assyria (Isa. 7). Jeremiah 26:18 informs us that it was the ministry of Micah that encouraged the great reformation in Judah under the leadership of King Hezekiah (2 Kings 18–20).

Society in Judah was rapidly changing from rural to urban. In defiance of the Law of Moses, wealthy investors were buying up small family farms and developing huge land holdings, which created serious problems for the poor. Having come from a farming community, Micah championed the oppressed poor and rebuked the "robber barons" for their selfishness. Amos echoed his message.

Micah saw the coming judgment of the Israel under Assyria (722) as well as the fall of Jerusalem and Judah under the Babylonians (606–596). He sought to call the Jews back to faithful worship of Jehovah and sincere obedience to His covenant, but they refused to listen. He pled for social justice and a concern for the helpless, but the people would not repent.

CHAPTER ONE
JUDGMENT IS COMING!
Micah 1–2

King David had a great many talented men in his army, but the most valuable were perhaps the men of Issachar, who had "understanding of the times to know what Israel ought to do" (1 Chron. 12:32). Because they understood the times, the men of Issachar abandoned the ill-fated house of Saul and joined forces with David, God's chosen king. They saw which way God's hand was moving, and they obediently moved in that direction.

Micah of Moresheth was a man who had the same kind of discernment because God gave him insight into the changes taking place on the national and international scene. Micah received three messages from the Lord to deliver to the people in hopes they would abandon their idolatry and return to sincere faith in the Lord. (For the three messages, see the suggested outline of the Book of Micah.)

The first message (Micah 1:1–2:13) was a warning that divine judgment was coming on both Judah and Israel (Samaria). This message was fulfilled in 722 B.C. when Assyria defeated Israel, and in 606–586 when the Babylonians invaded Judah, destroyed Jerusalem and the temple, and took thousands of people captive to Babylon. When God's servant speaks, it pays to listen!

1. Declaration: God's wrath is coming (Micah 1:1-15)

When the Prophet Amos was about to indict Israel and Judah, he started by condemning the Gentile nations around them (Amos 1–2); but the Prophet Micah didn't take that approach. Without any formal introduction, he moved right into his message and sounded the alarm.

The court is convened (Micah 1:2). The image in verses 2-5 is that of a court of law, with God as the Judge and Judah and Samaria as the defendants. Micah addresses all the people of the earth because God is the Lord of the whole earth (4:2-3) and all the nations are accountable to Him. God is both judge and witness from His holy temple where His Law was kept in the ark of the covenant. A holy God must act in righteousness and judge sin.

The Judge arrives (Micah 1:3-4). Today when a judge enters a courtroom from his or her chamber, everybody in the courtroom rises—a symbol of the respect we have for the judge and the law that he or she represents. But no judge ever came to court in the manner described by Micah! The verb "to come forth" means "to come forth for battle." God opens the court and declares war!

A judge comes to court to see to it that justice is done, and he or she isn't allowed to take sides. But when God comes to judge the nations, He has all the evidence necessary and doesn't have to call any witnesses. God is angry at His people because of their sins. That's why His coming makes the earth split and the mountains melt so that the rock flows like melted wax or a waterfall.[1]

The Judge names the defendants (Micah 1:5). God points an accusing finger at His own people—Israel and Judah—as represented by their capital cities, Samaria and Jerusalem. After seeing what Assyria did to Israel in 722, the leaders of Judah should have repented and turned to the Lord, but they didn't. In fact, during the reign of Hezekiah, the Assyrians plundered Judah and would have taken Jerusalem had not the Lord miraculously intervened (Isa. 36–37).

Both Judah and Israel were guilty of idolatry, which is really rebellion against the Lord. When the nation was divided after Solomon's death, the Northern Kingdom established its own religious system in competition with the Mosaic worship in the temple at Jerusalem. But the people of Judah had secretly begun to worship the false gods of Canaan; and their hearts were not true to Jehovah, even when they stood in the temple courts and offered their sacrifices (Isa. 1). To God, the temple had become like one of the "high places" in the hills around Jerusalem, where the Jews secretly worshiped idols and offered their sacrifices.

2. Lamentation: the cities shall be ruined (Micah 1:6-16)

The prophet responded to God's message by acting like a grieving man at a funeral (v.

8; 2 Sam. 15:30). He was genuinely burdened because of what would happen to his people if they didn't heed God's Word and turn from their sin.

The ruin of Samaria (Micah 1:6-9). The capital city of the Northern Kingdom was situated on a hill that overlooked a fertile valley. The Prophet Isaiah called the city "the crown of pride" with "glorious beauty" (Isa. 28:1) and predicted that God's judgment would destroy the city (vv. 2-4). The Assyrians would turn the beautiful city into a heap of rubble, and her idols wouldn't be able to protect the city from its enemies.

God destroyed the city and nation of Samaria because the people rebelled against His Word, and He destroyed the Samaritan temple because it housed a false religion that was nothing but religious prostitution. (Throughout the Old Testament, idolatry is compared to prostitution.) But God destroyed the temple in Jerusalem because the leaders had turned the true religion into a false worship of Jehovah and the gods of the nations. Jehovah is a jealous God who will not share worship or glory with another (Ex. 20:5; 34:14; Deut. 4:24; 5:9; 6:15). The covenant God made with His people at Sinai was like a marriage contract, and their breaking that covenant was like committing adultery or engaging in prostitution.[2]

The destruction of the city of Samaria was begun in 722 under Sargon II, ruler of Assyria, who ordered many of the citizens to be taken captive or killed. Then he imported people into the land from various nations he had conquered; and as Jews and Gentiles intermarried, the result was a mixed race that the Jews despised. Even in our Lord's day, the Jews had no dealings with the Samaritans (John 4:1-9).

The ruin of Judah (Micah 1:9-16). The problem with Samaria was that she was toxic; her infection had spread to Judah. The prophet wept over his land, the way you would weep over an incurable patient in the hospital (v. 9). Isaiah used a similar image to describe the plight of Judah (Isa. 1:5-6), and Jeremiah wept because the spiritual leaders in his day didn't deal drastically with the sin sickness of the people (Jer. 6:14; 7:8; 8:11).

Micah describes the ruin of the southern part of Judah (the Shephelah) by the invading Assyrians in 701 B.C. (Micah 1:10-16; see 2 Kings 18:7ff).[3] They swept through the land and took forty-six cities, but they could not take Jerusalem because God protected it. Micah used a series of puns based on the names of the cities similar in sound to familiar Hebrew words. For example, "Gath" is similar to the Hebrew word for "tell." Thus he wrote "Tell it not in Gath." Beth Ophrah means "house of dust." Thus he wrote, "Roll in the dust." The people of Shaphir ("pleasant, beautiful") would look neither beautiful nor pleasant as they were herded off as naked prisoners of war.

The roll call of cities goes on. The citizens of Zaanan ("come out") would not be able to come out because of the danger. Beth Ezel means "house of taking away," and the city would be taken away. Maroth is related to "mara/myrrh" and means "bitterness," and the city would experience bitter calamity ("writhe in pain," NIV). Since Lachish sounds like the Hebrew word for "team of swift horses," he warned them to harness their horses to the chariots and try to escape.[4]

Micah came to his own city, Moresheth, which sounds like a Hebrew word meaning "betrothed"; and brides were given farewell gifts. In other words, the town would no longer belong to Judah but would "leave home" and belong to the invaders. Since Aczib means "deception," the connection is obvious; and Mareshah sounds like the word for "conqueror," and the town would be conquered by the enemy.

The tragedy of this invasion is that it need not have happened. Had the people of Israel and Judah turned to the Lord in repentance and faith, He would have given them victory. Instead, they believed the false prophets, held fast to their idols, and sinned their way right into defeat. Sad to say, even the little children suffered and went into exile (1:16), all because of the sins of the parents.

3. Accusation: the sins of the people (Micah 2:1-11)

How could the Lord Jehovah permit such suffering and shame to come to His covenant people? Were they not His special heritage? Was not the land His love gift to them? That was why He was punishing them! "You only have I chosen of all the families of the earth; therefore I will punish you for all your sins" (Amos 3:2 NIV). Privilege brings responsibility, and responsibility brings accountability. The prophet held them accountable for two particular sins: covetousness (Micah 2:1-5) and listening to false prophets (vv. 6-11).

Covetousness (Micah 2:1-5). The Mosaic Law required that the land remain with the families and within the tribes. The land actually belonged to the Lord (Lev. 25:2, 23, 38), and He "leased" it to the people in return for their obedience to His law. If they disobeyed Him, they defiled the land and invited His judgment (18:24-30; Num. 35:33-34). If anybody sold family property, it was only until the next Year of Jubilee, at which time all land reverted to the original owners (Lev. 25:13-17). This arrangement kept the rich from oppressing the poor and helped to stabilize the economy.

But the wealthy "robber barons" in Micah's day were bent on acquiring large estates on which they could enslave the poor and thus make huge profits with little investment. So intent were they on their pursuit of wealth that they made their ruthless plans in bed at night and then got up early the next morning to carry them out. Because of their wealth and their authority in the land, these men controlled the courts and the councils at the city gates. Thus they got what they wanted.

It mattered little to these proud men that they took away farms illegally and evicted families from their homes mercilessly. They practiced the world's version of the Golden Rule: "Whoever has the gold makes the rules." They forgot that the Lord owned the land, the Lord made the laws, and the Lord has compassion on the poor and oppressed (Ex. 23:11; Lev. 25:25; Ps. 82:3; Prov. 21:13; Jer. 22:16). But even if these thieves had no fear of God, they should have had concern for their fellow human beings and treated them like people made in the image of God.

The name for this sin is "materialism," and it's committed by people who are covetous and obsessed with acquiring more and more wealth and "things." But "robber barons" aren't the only people who commit these sins. Parents rob their children of time and companionship by working at several jobs so they can make more money to buy more "fun." People rob God of tithes and offerings that are rightfully His just so they can enjoy "the good life" (Mal. 3:7-12). People forget Matthew 6:33 and put everything else ahead of the kingdom of God.

However, ultimately the covetous sinners Micah addressed would reap what they sowed; and the dreadful harvest of their sins would one day appear (Micah 2:3-5). Their proud self–confidence would be taken from them, their authority would be gone, their crooked accomplices would turn against them and laugh at them, and their vast holdings would be snatched from their hands. They would see everything they lived for and sinned to acquire be taken over by the enemy and wasted. Many of them would go into exile and die away from the land they had coveted and stolen from innocent people.

False prophets (Micah 2:6-11). Just as the false prophets attacked Jeremiah (5:31) and Amos (7:10-17) for preaching God's truth, so the false prophets attacked Micah for faithfully declaring the message of God. These men espoused a shallow theology that had no place for either sin or repentance. "We are God's special people," they argued, "and He would never permit these judgments to happen in the land." As long as the people participated in religious services, they would incur the wrath of God, even if their hearts were not in their worship. The Jews were Abraham's children, and God would never break the promises He made to Abraham. Such were their false premises.

What these counterfeit religious leaders forgot was that God's covenants involve precepts as well as promises, obligations as well as blessings. Merely going through the motions of religion isn't the same as worshiping God "in spirit and in truth" (John 4:23). Anybody can join the crowd and be a part of some popular religious movement; but it takes devotion, prayer, obedience, and submission to worship God "with reverence and godly fear" (Heb. 12:28 NKJV). "Popular religion" is usually false religion, for the road to life is narrow and lonely (Matt. 7:13-20) and those who walk it are invariably persecuted (2 Tim. 3:12).

It is God who speaks in Micah 2:7b-13 as He defends His faithful servant. The fact that these religious leaders rejected Micah's message didn't mean that the message was wrong; it meant that the hearers were wrong. The way we respond to God's Word indicates our relationship to the Lord. "He who is of God hears God's words; therefore you do not hear, because you are not of God" (John 8:47 NKJV).

These false prophets were deceiving and robbing the people by giving them false assurance that everything was well in the land. God pictured their sinful deeds by describing two carefree men—a rich man walking confidently down the street and a victorious soldier returning home with the spoils of the battle—and both of them are robbed! Because of the evil rich leader, the confident mother and her family find themselves thrust from their homes and robbed of their land.

God originally gave the Jewish people the land of Canaan to be their "rest" from the trials of the wilderness wanderings (Deut. 12:9-10; Josh. 22:4; 23:1). After they had conquered the land and claimed their tribal inheritance, they should have enjoyed rest and blessing in the land, but instead they turned to the idols of the surrounding nations and rebelled against God. God punished them in their land by bringing in different nations that robbed and enslaved them (see the Book of Judges). But the nation didn't learn from its history; the people repeated the same sins as their ancestors *but thought they would avoid the same consequences.* Since they had defiled the land, God removed them from it.

Micah urged the people to get out of the land because no rest would be found there, in spite of what the false prophets promised. These men would preach any message the people wanted to hear, just so long as they were provided with their strong drink! The false prophets were using religion to make money and enjoy pleasure, and they had no concern for the future of the nation.

4. Consolation: hope for the future (Micah 2:12-13)

The faithful prophet must expose sin and announce judgment, but he must also provide consolation and hope for those who receive his message and turn to God. Consolation without true repentance is only giving false hope; it's saying "Peace, peace!" when there is no peace. But conviction without hope creates only hopelessness, like performing surgery without providing healing.

The Lord seems to be speaking here to the entire nation ("all of you, O Jacob . . . Israel," NIV), and His promise seems to reach ahead to the end times when Israel and Judah will be united and their King Messiah will reign over them. Micah describes a triumphant procession into the land, with King Messiah at the head and the Lord leading the people, just as He had led them out of Egypt (v. 13).

However, until that glorious day, God will deal with the "remnant" of His people. The "remnant" is a very important doctrine in the prophetic books, and there are many references to it.[5] Though the nation of Israel might rebel against God, there would always be a faithful remnant that would trust Him and seek to do His will and God would work because of the faith of this remnant. (This is also true of the professing church.) The hope of the nation lies with the remnant.

A remnant returned to Judah after the Babylonian Captivity, but it never became the great nation that the prophets promised. That will happen when the Lord returns, claims His chosen nation, and establishes His kingdom. The Messiah is described in verse 13 as "One who breaks open the way" (NIV), that is, who opens the doors that confine the Jews in the various nations so that He might bring them to their land. God certainly did this when the exiles left Babylon, but the promise here is for the last days when the Messiah shall come to overcome His enemies and redeem His chosen people.

Micah's first message aroused the opposition of the false prophets, but it didn't change the hearts of the people. Thus he gave a second message, announcing that "the Deliverer is coming."

But we today need to deal with our sins of covetousness, selfishness, and willingness to believe "religious lies." We must abandon "soft religion" that pampers our pride and makes it easy for us to sin. Why? Because "our God is a consuming fire" (Heb. 12:29), and "The Lord shall judge His people" (10:30). Remember, judgment begins in the house of the Lord (1 Peter 4:17).

CHAPTER TWO
A RULER IS COMING!
Micah 3–5

Micah's second message is at the heart of the book and focuses on Israel's future. First, Micah rebuked the leaders of the nation for their sinful conduct, which God would judge (3:1-12), and he outlined the events that would usher in the promised kingdom (4:1–5:15). Knowing that God has such a glorious future planned for their nation should have motivated the leaders to turn from their sins and obey the Lord. "Everyone who has this hope in him purifies himself, just as he is pure" (1 John 3:3 NIV). Alas, they didn't even pay attention to the sermon!

1. Rebuke: the sins of the leaders (Micah 3:1-12)

As with Micah's other two messages, this second message opens with a call for the people to "hear" what the Lord would say through His servant (1:2; 6:1). It's as though Micah had shouted, "Listen! God is speaking! This is important!" The statement reminds us of the Lord's repeated admonition, "Who has ears to hear, let him hear!" or the warning in Hebrews 12:25: "See that you do not refuse Him who speaks" (NKJV).

It's a dangerous thing to turn a deaf ear to the voice of God when He speaks through His Word. "Today, if you will hear His voice, do not harden your hearts" (3:7-8 NKJV). All creation responds to the voice of God and gladly obeys His will except man made in God's image! Yet the Father lovingly says to us, "Now therefore, listen to Me, My children; pay attention to the words of My mouth" (Prov. 7:24 NKJV).

Micah opened his message by rebuking the civil authorities (Micah 3:1-4), men who were not only permitting the wealthy to exploit the poor but were also doing it themselves! Leaders are supposed to love the good and hate the evil, but these men were just the opposite: they "hate the good, and love the evil" (v. 2). Ideal leaders are described as "able men, such as fear God, men of truth, hating covetousness" (Ex. 18:21 NKJV). Micah's contemporary Amos wrote, "Seek good and not evil, that you may live. . . . Hate evil, love good; establish justice in the gate" (Amos 5:14-15 NKJV; see Prov. 8:13). The city gate was the place where the elders met to settle disputes and make official decisions (Ruth 4:1ff). If there was no justice in the cities, there could be no justice in the land.

The description of these rulers' actions reminds you more of ravenous beasts than of human beings. Instead of being faithful shepherds who protected the flock (Micah 2:12; 7:14), they attacked the sheep, skinned them alive, butchered them, chopped them up, and made stew out of them! But the day would come when these wolves in shepherd's clothing would cry out for God's mercy, but no mercy would be given. "Then my anger shall be kindled against them in that day, and I will forsake them, and I will hide My face from them, and they shall be devoured" (Deut. 31:17).

Micah then turned to *rebuke the false prophets (Micah 3:5-8),* whose lies made it easy for the corrupt officials to carry on their evil deeds. "An astonishing and horrible thing has been committed in the land; the prophets prophesy falsely, and the priests bear rule by their means; and my people love to have it so" (Jer. 5:30-31 KJV). When God is left out of human government, it's easy for officials to use their authority selfishly to exploit the people.

As long as you gave them something to eat and drink (Micah 2:11), the prophets would declare whatever kind of message you wanted to hear. Like the false prophets in Jeremiah's day, they announced peace when war and desolation were just around the corner (Jer. 6:13-14; 8:10-11). But the time would come when these men who claimed to see the light would be shrouded in darkness, and everybody would know that they were counterfeits. They would cry out to the Lord, but He would not answer.

God's true prophet is described in Micah 3:8: this prophet is filled with the Spirit, faithfully proclaiming God's message and unafraid of what people might say or do. Micah fearlessly told the people their sins and warned them that judgment was coming, while the false prophets tickled the people's ears and told them what they wanted to hear.

Few men are as pitiable as those who claim to have a call from God yet tailor their sermons to please others. Their first rule is "Don't rock the boat"; their second is "Give people what they want." But a true servant of God declares God's message regardless of whether the people like it or not. He'd like to be a peacemaker, but sometimes he has to be a troublemaker. No wonder Jeremiah cried out, "Alas, my mother, that you gave me birth, a man with whom the whole land strives and contends!" (Jer. 15:10 NIV)

Micah also addressed all the leaders of the land (Micah 3:9-12)—the rulers, the priests, and the prophets—and accused them of numerous sins: committing injustice, distorting the truth, murdering innocent people, accepting bribes, and while doing these evil deeds, claiming to be serving the Lord! "We are depending on the Lord," they said, "Is He not among us? Then nothing evil can happen to us." It was hypocrisy of the worst kind.

Their ignorance of the Lord's character and the terms of His covenant gave them this false confidence. "Since we're Jews," they reasoned, "God's chosen people and sharers in His covenant, the Lord will never permit anything evil to happen to us. Even if we sin, He will never abandon us to the enemy." Their thinking was not unlike that of people today who "profess that they know God; but in works they deny Him" (Titus 1:16).

Any theology that makes it easy for us to sin is not biblical theology. Had the rulers, prophets, and priests read and pondered Leviticus 26 and Deuteronomy 28–30, they would have discovered that the God of the covenant is a holy God who will not countenance high-handed sin. They would also have learned that the blessings of the covenant depended on their obeying the conditions of the covenant, and that God punishes His people when they disobey.

What would be the result of the leaders' flouting God's law? Their holy city and temple would be destroyed, and thousands of Jewish people would be exiled to Babylon (Micah 4:10). God would rather destroy the city and the beautiful temple than allow His people to defile His property by their sins. The destruction of Jerusalem in 606–586 is a reminder to God's people that when God says, "Be holy, for I am holy,"[1] *He really means it!*

"For the sins of her prophets, and the iniquities of her priests" (Lam. 4:13) the nation was defeated and the city and temple were destroyed. That's why the prophet opened his message by rebuking the spiritual leaders of the land, not the unbelievers. If Micah were ministering among us today, he would probably visit denominational offices, pastors' conferences, Bible colleges, and seminaries to warn Christian leaders that privilege brings responsibility and responsibility brings accountability.

2. Hope: the promises of the Lord (Micah 4:1–5:5a)[2]

Micah moved from the destruction of Jerusalem (606–586) to "the last days" when there will be a new Jerusalem and a rebuilt temple at the heart of the righteous kingdom of Messiah. The period known as "the last days" began with the ministry of Christ (Heb. 1:1-2) and they climax with His return to establish His kingdom on earth. The Lord gave His people four wonderful promises.

A promised kingdom (Micah 4:1-8).[3] The situation of the two little Jewish kingdoms was hopeless when Micah delivered his messages. Assyria was about to pounce on Israel and put an end to that nation, and then the Assyrian army would ravage Judah and almost take Jerusalem. When the outlook is grim, try the uplook. Thus the prophet encouraged the people to look ahead to what God had promised for His chosen people.

God promised that the nation would be united and the people returned to their land. Jerusalem would become the world's most important city, the temple would be rebuilt, and the true worship of Jehovah would be restored[4] (see Ezek. 40–48). Instead of the Gentile nations fighting the Jews, they would "stream" to Jerusalem to worship God and hear His Word. There would be peace among the nations because they would obey God's truth, submit to the Messiah's rule, and destroy their instruments of war.[5]

Every Jewish family wanted to achieve what Micah described in 4:4: a pleasant home with a productive garden in a peaceful land (see 1 Kings 4:25; Isa. 36:16). But even more than peace and economic stability was the blessing of knowing the Lord and obeying Him (Micah 4:5). This verse doesn't refer to the future, because during the Kingdom Age all the nations will worship Jehovah. It was an affirmation of faith on the part of the true believers, the remnant in the land: "The other nations may now be serving their own gods, which are false gods; but we will walk in the name of Jehovah, the true God, and obey Him alone."

Though the remnant of Jews might be small, weak, and lame, God will gather them from all the nations and make a mighty army out of them (vv. 6-7a). Messiah will rule over them, and Jerusalem will become the glorious capital city for His kingdom. Jerusalem had once been David's capital city, the shepherd–king who cared for the flock (Ps. 78:67-72), but after the death of Josiah, not one of his four successors was a godly man. Messiah, the Son of David, will one day reign from Jerusalem and care for His flock as a faithful Shepherd–King.

A promised deliverance (Micah 4:9-10). The city of Jerusalem is called "daughter of Zion" (cities are usually classified as feminine), a term of endearment that assured the people of God's loving care no matter what might happen. But the city was in travail, like a woman with child, because the enemy had arrived and was capturing the people and taking them to Babylon. However, the exile wasn't the end; for God will redeem a remnant and bring them back to the land.

Had the leaders listened to the Prophet Jeremiah and peacefully surrendered to the Babylonians, they would have saved the city and the temple, but they resisted God's will, and their city and temple were ruined. However, Jeremiah promised that the exile would last only seventy years, and then the remnant could return and rebuild the city and the temple.

A promised conquest (Micah 4:11-13). Once again, the prophet looked down the centuries to the end times and saw his people being attacked by many Gentile nations, all of them gloating over Israel because they are so sure of defeating the Jews (see Zech. 12:1-9; 14:1-11). The nations are sure of victory because they ignore Scripture and don't know God's plans for His people (Jer. 29:11).

Israel will look weak and defenseless, but the Lord will make their soldiers sharp threshing instruments to "harvest" the nations (Rev. 14:14-20). God will give them "horns" (a symbol of power) and "hoofs" so that they will have both power and speed as they attack their enemies. This great battle is usually called "the Battle of Armageddon," although that phrase is not found in Scripture (Rev. 16:16; 19:17-21). When the battle is over, the victorious Jewish army will devote all the spoils to the service of the Lord.

A promised King (Micah 5:1-5a). Now Micah looks ahead to the Babylonian siege of Jerusalem. So many soldiers are encamped around Jerusalem that Micah calls her "the city [daughter] of troops." When King Zedekiah and his officers see that their situation is hopeless, they try to escape, but the Babylonians catch up with them and capture them (2 Kings 25:1-7). Of course, they humiliate the king by striking him with a rod across his face.[6] Then they kill his sons, put out his eyes, bind him, and take him to Babylon.

The fact that Micah 5:2 is in contrast to verse 1 ("But, thou, Bethlehem") is another proof that verse 1 is not speaking about Jesus; for verses 2-5 definitely refer to Messiah. God selected "the little town of Bethlehem" as the place where the King of the Jews was to be born. It was this prophecy that the priests shared with the magi who came to Jerusalem looking for the King (Matt. 2:1-12).

Bethlehem ("house of bread") has an interesting history. Jacob's favorite wife, Rachel, died near Bethlehem when she gave birth to Benjamin, and she was buried nearby (Gen. 35:16-20). Matthew cites this when he reports the slaying of the innocent children by Herod (Matt. 2:16-18; see Jer. 31:15). In her pain, Rachel named her son Ben-oni, which means "son of my sorrow"; but Jacob renamed the boy, calling him Benjamin, "son of my right hand." These two names remind us of our Lord's suffering and glory, the cross and the throne at the Father's right hand.

Ruth and Naomi came to Bethlehem; there Boaz fell in love with Ruth and married her. Ruth is an ancestor of the Messiah (Matt. 1:5). Of course, David was Bethlehem's greatest son; and it was through David's family that the promised Messiah would be born (2 Sam. 7; Matt. 1:1; Luke 1:26-27; Rom. 1:3). The Jews knew that their Messiah would come from Bethlehem (John 7:42).

In this prophecy, Micah reveals a number of important facts about the Messiah. To begin with, He is eternal God, for His "goings out are from old . . . from days of eternity" (see NIV margin). Jesus stepped out of eternity into human history, sent by the Father to die for the sins of the world (1 John 4:14). But He is also truly a man, for He is born as a human child. We have here the miracle of the Incarnation (John 1:14).

You would think that the very Son of God would come to a great city like Athens or Jerusalem, but He chose to be born in a humble stable (or cave) in Bethlehem. But the day would come when He would be glorified and take His throne in heaven; and one day, He shall return to be Ruler over His people.

However, before He can stand as a Shepherd and care for His flock, His own people must reject Him. Between the cross and the Kingdom Age, Israel will be "given up" by the Lord until the time when Jesus returns and the nation is "born" into her kingdom (see Isa. 66:8). This King will reign to the ends of the earth and will bring peace to all nations. Today, of course, Christ gives peace to all who will come to Him by faith (Matt. 11:28-30; Rom. 5:1).

Micah presented an encouraging scenario to the people, but they didn't seem to grasp the significance; for if they had, they would have turned to the Lord in gratitude and repentance. Whenever a prophet foretold the future, it was to awaken the people to their responsibilities in the present. Bible prophecy isn't entertainment for the curious; it's encouragement for the serious.

3. Victory: the purging of the nation (Micah 5:5b-15)

As he continued to view the distant scene, Micah announced that Israel's future enemies would be defeated (vv. 5b-6), the Jewish remnant would be blessed (vv. 7-9), and the nation would be purged of its sins (vv. 10–15).

The enemy defeated (Micah 5:5b-6). "The Assyrian" named in verse 5 isn't the Assyrian army of Micah's day, for the Jews in that day certainly didn't defeat Assyria and rule over her land. The Assyrians soundly defeated Israel, and the land of Israel was ruined. "The Assyrian" is another way of saying "the enemy," and here it refers to Israel's enemies in the last days when all nations will gather against her (Zech. 10:10-11; 12:9; 14:1-3).

The phrase "seven shepherds . . . eight leaders" is a way of saying "many shepherds, many leaders," and is similar to the repeated statement of Amos "for three transgressions . . . and for four" (Amos 1:3, 6, 9, etc.). When the enemy attacks in the last days, God will raise up leaders to face the enemy, just as He had raised up the judges and heroes like David. But Micah makes it clear that God is the Deliverer who will enable Israel to defeat her enemies and rule over their lands. The "he" of Micah 5:6 is the "ruler" of verse 2.

The remnant blessed (Micah 5:7-9). Though small in number the Jewish remnant of the last days will experience great help from the Lord as they face their enemies. Micah used two similes to illustrate this blessing: the refreshing dew from heaven and the conquering strength of the lion. God will enable His people to overcome like lions and then bring fruitfulness to the world like the dew that watered Israel's crops (Ps. 133:3). Israel will triumph over her enemies through the power of the Lord.

The nation purged (Micah 5:10-15). In Micah's day, both Israel and Judah were guilty of sins that violated God's law and grieved God's heart. Time after time, He had sent messengers to the people to denounce their sins and warn of impending judgment, but the people wouldn't listen (2 Chron. 36:14-21). In the last days, Israel will return to her land in unbelief and practice these same sins. But God will purge the land and prepare them for a new life in the kingdom. They will see their Messiah, trust Him, and be saved (Zech. 12:10–13:1).

God will destroy all their military defenses, the things that they trusted, instead of trusting the Lord. He will end their traffic with demonic powers and eliminate all idolatry from the land (Zech. 13:2). Israel will now seek to please God and obey His law and not imitate the sins of the nations on which God will "take vengeance."

God has not cast aside His people (Rom. 11:1); for today there is a believing remnant of Jews in the church. One day God will gather the unbelieving Jewish nation to their land, cause them to experience suffering, and then reveal Himself to them and give birth to a new nation. The prophets saw that day and tried to convey its message to the people of their day, but they wouldn't listen.

Christians today look for Jesus to return to gather His people to Himself (1 Thes. 4:13-18) and then establish His righteous kingdom. Peter assures us that "the day of the Lord will come as a thief in the night"; and then, in light of this fact, he asks, "Therefore . . . what manner of persons ought you to be in holy conduct and godliness?" (2 Peter 3:10, 11 NKJV) Future hope ought to produce present holiness.

Are we ready for His return?

CHAPTER THREE "THY KINGDOM COME"

Micah 6–7

The prophet had delivered two of his three messages: a message of warning (1–2) and a message of promise (3–5). His third message was a challenge for the Jews to trust the Lord and obey His will, for only then could the nation escape terrible punishment and fulfill God's purposes in this world.

As you read Old Testament history and prophecy, keep in mind how important it was for Israel to be obedient to the Lord. God had raised up the nation to bring blessing to the whole world (Gen. 12:1-3), for it was through Israel that the Savior would come. "Salvation is of the Jews" (John 4:22). When the Jews began to adopt the practices of the godless nations around them, it defiled them and made them less able to do the work God had called them to do. It was because they despised their high and holy calling that the nation had to be chastened so severely.

Micah's first message was presented as a courtroom drama, and so was this third message. The Judge declared the indictment (Micah 6:1-8), pronounced the sentence (6:9–7:7) *and then graciously promised mercy* (7:7-20)! Micah used these three factors—guilt, punishment, and mercy—as arguments to plead with his people to repent and return to the Lord. "Trust the Lord, not in spite of these things but *because of these things!*" is his closing message; and it's a message we need to hear today.

1. Because of great guilt, trust the Lord (Micah 6:1-8)

The sins of the people were hidden behind a veneer of religious activity—routine worship that didn't come from their hearts. Micah's contemporary, the Prophet Isaiah, told the people that the nation was sick from head to foot (Isa. 1:5-6) but wouldn't admit it, and that their "worship" was nothing more than "trampling" the temple courts (v. 12). They were like the patient who asked the doctor to retouch his X-rays so he wouldn't have to endure surgery! His deceit didn't cure him; it made him worse.

In this courtroom scene, *the Lord called the witnesses (Micah 6:1-2)* and told the people to be prepared to plead their case. The Lord opened the proceedings by telling His side of the controversy, emphasizing the gracious way He had dealt with the nation from the very beginning. He redeemed them from Egyptian slavery; He gave them leaders who guided them through the wilderness with His help; and He brought them to their promised inheritance. And throughout this journey, the Lord had put up with their unbelief, disobedience, and repeated complaints (Ps. 106).

On three occasions, Balak, king of Moab, commanded Balaam to curse Israel, but God turned the curse into blessing (Num. 22–24; Deut. 23:5; Neh. 13:2). The Israelites didn't even know that this spiritual battle was going on; yet God protected His people. What did the Jews do in return? They became friendly with the Moabites, attended their idolatrous religious rites, and committed fornication with their women! (see Num. 25). What Balaam couldn't do by means of his curses, the Jews themselves did with their sinful lusts.

The phrase "from Shittim unto Gilgal" (Micah 6:5) reminded the people of Israel's crossing of the Jordan River and entering the Promised Land (Josh. 3–4). The same God who opened and closed the Red Sea also opened and closed the Jordan River so His people might claim their inheritance. He did for them what they couldn't do for themselves, but they didn't remember.

It's good for God's people to know the past and remember with gratitude all that God had done for them. The word "remember" is found at least fourteen times in the Book of Deuteronomy, and frequently the Jews were instructed to teach their children the mighty deeds of the Lord (Ex. 10:2; 13:8, 14; Deut. 6:20ff; Josh. 22:24; Ps. 78:1-8).

While we don't live in the past, we must learn from the past or we'll commit the same mistakes. Philosopher George Santayana wrote, "Those who cannot remember the past are condemned to repeat it." Because Israel forgot God's mercies (Ps. 106:7), they also ignored God's commandments. The result was a hard heart that deliberately rebelled against God's will. God had every right to ask them, "What have I done to you that you should treat Me this way?"

Now the people replied to God (Micah 6:6-7). Instead of confessing their sins or standing mute because their mouths had been shut by their sense of guilt (Rom. 3:19), they asked what they could do to get rid of their sins. Their request shows how shallow their spiritual life really was and that they were ignorant of the enormity of their sin and the high cost of forgiveness. They were like the rich young ruler who didn't really see himself as a condemned sinner before God (Mark 10:17-27), but they were not like the people at Pentecost who were cut to the heart and cried out, "What shall we do?" (Acts 2:37)

We get the impression that these questioners were interested in bargaining with God and "buying Him off," for they kept raising the bid. "Shall we bring a few calves as burnt offerings? If that's not enough, maybe we could offer a thousand sacrifices, such as Solomon offered [1 Kings 3:4; 8:63]? Would rivers of oil please Him? How about the ultimate sacrifice: our own flesh and blood offered on the altar, as Abraham did with Isaac?" But God doesn't bargain with sinners, and none of the sacrifices they offered to bring could have cleansed them from their sins.

"Doing penance" without truly repenting and trusting God's mercy only multiplies the sin and deadens the conscience. Thinking they were good enough to please God, the people asked Jesus, "What shall we do, that we may work the works of God?" He replied, "This is the work of God, that you believe in Him whom He sent" (John 6:28-29 NKJV). True saving faith comes from a heart that's been broken in repentance and realizes that no amount of good works can atone for sin (Acts 20:21; 26:20; Eph. 2:8-9).

The prophet spoke to the people (Micah 6:8) and told them exactly what the Lord wanted each of them to do. It was a personal matter that each individual sinner had to consider. His reply emphasized moral and ethical conduct, not religious ceremonies.[1] Of course, we can't "do justly" unless we've been justified by faith and are right with God (Ps. 32:1-2; Rom. 4:1-8). And how can we "love mercy" if we've not personally experienced God's mercy? (Eph. 2:4; Titus 3:5). If we want to "walk humbly with [our] God," we must first bow humbly before Him, confess our sins, and claim His promise of forgiveness (Luke 14:11; James 4:10).

Our Lord's parable about the Pharisee and publican in the temple (Luke 18:9-14) illustrates all three points. The publican was justified by faith, not by doing the kind of good works that the Pharisee boasted about. Since the publican depended on God's mercy to save him, he humbled himself before the Lord. The Pharisee, on the other hand, informed God (and whoever was listening in the temple) how good he was and therefore how much he deserved eternal life.

To make Micah 6:8 a salvation text is to misunderstand what the prophet was saying to God's disobedient covenant people. None of us can do what God requires until first we come to God as broken sinners who need to be saved. Unsaved people who think they are doing justly, loving mercy, and walking humbly with God are only fooling themselves, no matter how moral their lives may be. "Not by works righteousness which we have done, but according to His mercy He saved us" (Titus 3:5).

The people to whom Micah ministered simply didn't get the point of his messages. The very fact that they were so guilty before God should have motivated them to turn from their shallow religion, humble themselves, and seek God's mercy. The only people God can save are lost people; the only people God can forgive are guilty people. If we see ourselves as God sees us, then we can by faith become what He wants us to become.

2. Because of impending judgment, trust the Lord (Micah 6:9–7:7)

For the second time in this message, Micah cried out to the people, "Listen!" (vv. 1, 9 NIV). Like the crowds that Jesus taught, these Jews had ears to hear His words, but they couldn't hear God's truth in those words (Matt. 13:9, 43). They lacked spiritual discernment.

God speaks about sin and its consequences (Micah 6:9-16). The Lord called to the people of Jerusalem to fear His name and heed what He had to say; for without the fear of the Lord, they could have neither knowledge nor wisdom (Prov. 1:7).[2] God specifically condemned the merchants of the city for being deceptive in their business practices (Micah 6:10-12). They used weights and measures that were dishonest so that customers didn't get full value for their money (see Lev. 19:35-36; Deut. 25:13-16).

Why did this sin grieve the Lord so much? Because by doing these illegal things, the businessmen were exploiting and abusing the poor and needy in the land for whom God has a special concern (Amos 8:4-10). The Mosaic economic system provided for the care of the poor and needy, but the wealthy merchants in Micah's time had abandoned the system. They robbed the poor of both justice and the necessities of life, a sin God could not overlook.

Moreover, along with making their own weights and measures and bribing the courts, the rich were openly violent (Micah 6:12; also see 2:2; 3:1-3). They forcibly evicted people from their houses and lands and left them helpless, without homes or any source of income. When the poor tried to protect themselves through the courts, the rich merchants lied about the situation and convinced the officials that their actions were right.

But God has ordained that people reap what they sow, whether good or evil (Hosea 8:7; Gal. 6:7-8). Therefore, judgment had to fall on the "robber barons" of the land. Indeed, God warned about two different kinds of judgments (Micah 6:13-16). The first (vv. 13-15) was already in progress, slow and secret, but very thorough. "Therefore, I have begun to destroy you, to ruin you because of your sins" (v. 13 NIV). This judgment was the collapse of their economic system, including their crops (stolen farms), their investments (stolen money), and even their enjoyment of all that they had accumulated. Everything these merchant thieves had amassed for their pleasure would disappear, and whatever they tried to enjoy would bring them no pleasure at all. (See God's covenant warnings in Deut. 28:15ff.)

The second judgment (Micah 6:16) would be sudden and open: the total ruin of the nation by the hand of Babylon. That Micah should point to Babylon as the aggressor (4:10) is remarkable, because Babylon wasn't a major power on the international scene at that time. It was Assyria that everybody feared, and Assyria did ruin the Northern Kingdom in 722 and did do great damage to Judah in 701. But by the time Babylon was finished with Judah and Jerusalem, the nation would be in ruin and the people in derision. The people's sins found them out.

The Lord tried to use the judgment on the Northern Kingdom to awaken and warn the people of Judah, the Southern Kingdom, but they wouldn't listen. Their defense was "It can't happen here. We have the temple!" But they weren't obeying God's law or honoring His house. Instead, they were following the godless ways of two kings of Israel, Omri and Ahab, both of whom "did evil in the eyes of the Lord, and did worse than all who were before [them]" (1 Kings 16:25; see v. 30 NKJV). They should have followed the godly ways of King David, because it was for David's sake that God held back His judgment for so long (11:13, 32, 34, 36; 15:4).

The prophet speaks of his sorrow (Micah 7:1-7). The prophets not only declared God's message with their lips, but they also felt the burden of the people on their hearts. Jeremiah wept over the sins of the nation in his day and wished he could weep even more (Jer. 9:1ff), and Micah lamented because there were no godly people left in the land. Looking for a godly person was as futile as looking for summer fruit after the harvest was over.[3]

Micah compared the evil officials to hunters who wove clever nets and threw them over the helpless and trapped them. These officials and judges were skilled at weaving their nets (perverting the law so they could rob the unweary), but they weren't skilled at obeying God's laws. They were like briars and thorns that hurt people, when they should have been like concerned shepherds who helped people.

"The day of your watchmen" refers to the day of judgment when the watchmen on the walls would see the enemy approaching and call out to warn the people. God's prophets were His watchmen (Ezek. 3:18-21), constantly warning the nation, but the leaders wouldn't listen. They preferred lies to truth and this brought about a "time of . . . confusion" (Micah 7:4 NIV).

This confusion reached into every level of society. Not only was Micah grieved at the corruption of the officials, but also he was grieved at the unfaithfulness of the common people of the land (vv. 5-6). You couldn't trust anybody! When truth is no longer the standard for society, then everything starts to fall apart; for faithfulness to our word is the cement that holds society together. It had come to the place where neighbor couldn't trust neighbor, friends couldn't trust each other. The basic unit of Jewish society, the family, was quickly falling apart. (In fact, Jesus quoted Micah 7:6 in Matt. 10:36.)

In the light of the terrible condition of the land and the judgment that was impending, wouldn't it have been a wise thing for the people to turn from their sin and trust the

Lord? Would it not have been a smart thing for them to claim 2 Chronicles 7:14 and seek God's face so that He might heal their land? But sinners don't do wise things, because their eyes are blinded as they walk in the darkness (John 3:19-21).

3. Because of God's great mercies, trust the Lord (Micah 7:7-20)

The prophet reached a turning point when he looked away from the sins of the people and meditated on the faithfulness of the Lord. "But as for me, I watch in hope for the Lord, I wait for God my Savior; my God will hear me" (v. 7 NIV). He would "watch and pray" and put his trust only in the Lord. This verse is the "bridge" that connects the sections on sin and judgment with this closing section on hope.

In this final section of Micah's third message, we must distinguish several voices: the nation (vv. 8-10), the prophet (vv. 11-13), the Lord (vv. 14-15), and the prophet again (vv. 16-20). We must also realize that Micah is looking down through the centuries with prophetic vision to the time when Israel will come through great tribulation to come, "dress rehearsals" as it were. But the future will bring victory to God's people, not defeat, when the Lord fulfills His promises and establishes the kingdom.

The voice of the nation (Micah 7:8-10). Perhaps the prophet is speaking on behalf of the remnant as he expresses their faith and courage. The enemy gloated over the defeated Jews and asked in derision, "Where is the Lord your God?" (v. 10 NIV; see Pss. 42:3, 10; 79:10; 115:2)[4] . But the people trust God and have confidence that, though they were in darkness, they would see light; and though they had been defeated, they would eventually conquer their enemies and trample them like mud in the streets.

Since these events did not occur after the Assyrian and Babylonian invasions, they must be assigned to a future time. According to Jesus, the Jewish nations will experience great tribulation and become the target of all the Gentile nations in the end times (Matt. 24:15-31). In the end, however, Christ will return and give His people great victory.

The voice of the prophet (Micah 7:11-14). Micah speaks to the city of Jerusalem and assures her that, though she had been attacked and destroyed, she would one day be rebuilt. The prophets speak in glowing terms of Israel having a new city and temple (Isa. 2:1-5; Ezek. 40–48). Not only that, but also the boundaries of the nation would be expanded to include more territory than she had before.

In the light of this great promise, the prophet lifted his heart to the Lord in prayer (Micah 7:14) and asked Him to be the faithful Shepherd of Israel and care for His people (see 5:4; Isa. 40:11; Ps. 80:1). Micah longed for "the good old days" when the land was fruitful and peaceful and the people were like obedient sheep who followed their Shepherd.

The voice of the Lord (Micah 7:15). God replied to His faithful servant and assured him that He would indeed watch over His flock and care for them, just as He had when they had departed from the land of Egypt. The "exodus" image is sometimes used in Scripture to point to the "exodus" of the Jews in the end times from the nations of the world to their own land (Isa. 11:15–12:6; 35:8-10; 43:14-20; 51:9-11). God will perform great wonders for His people at a time in their history when the nations are united against them.

The voice of the prophet (Micah 7:16-20). When Israel departed from Egypt and God opened the sea, the other nations heard about it and feared (Ex. 15:14-16; Josh. 2:8-11). But the wonders the Lord will do for Israel in the last days will startle the nations even more. The Gentiles will see the power of God and be ashamed and unable to act. They will come out of their hiding places to submit to the Lord. It will mean total victory for Israel.

But the most important event will not be Israel's victory over her enemies but God's victory over Israel. The prophet was confident of the unchanging character of God. "Who is a God like You?" (Micah 7:18 NIV) reminds us of the meaning of Micah's name, "Who is like the Lord?" He is a God who pardons sin, forgives transgressions, and delights in showing mercy. He shows compassion to His people and deals with their sins with finality. Some students see Israel's exodus experience illustrated in verse 19: The Egyptian army was buried in the depths of the Red Sea and ended up in the mire.

Micah knew that God would not go back on His promises or His covenant agreements with His people. The people weren't always true to Jehovah, but He will be true to His people (2 Tim. 2:12-13). What He promised to

Abraham, the father of the nation, He will fulfill in his many descendants. Micah could have sung

> How firm a foundation, ye saints of the Lord,
> Is laid for your faith in His excellent Word.

In the coming of Jesus Christ to this world, God fulfilled some of the promises He made to the Jews (Luke 1:72-73), and He will fulfill the rest of His promises as well. "For no matter how many promises God has made, they are 'Yes' in Christ" (2 Cor. 1:20 NIV).

Few passages in Scripture contain so much "distilled theology" as Micah 7:18-20. We see in them a reflection of what God told Moses on the mount (Ex. 34:5-7). The better we know the character of God, the more we can trust Him for the future. The better we know the promises and covenants of God, the more peace we will have in our hearts when things fall apart. When Micah wrote this confession of his faith, the future seemed hopeless; yet he had hope because he knew God and fully trusted Him.

No matter how dark the day, the light of God's promises is still shining. No matter how confusing and frightening our circumstances, the character of God remains the same.

You have every reason to trust Him!

Endnotes

Chapter 1

1. For other pictures of God coming like a warrior, see Exodus 15, Psalm 18, Isaiah 63, and Habakkuk 3.

2. The Prophet Hosea used the image of adultery to describe the sin of the nation in worshiping idols. In fact, Hosea's own wife was guilty of adultery and prostitution, and he had to buy her out of the slave market! See my book *Be Amazed* for an exposition of the Book of Hosea (Victor Books).

3. Several of these towns were located within a nine-mile radius of Micah's hometown, Moresheth Gath, and could easily be seen from there on a clear day. These were Micah's neighbors, and he had to tell them they were doomed to destruction!

4. How Lachish was "the beginning of sin" to Judah is not explained. Lachish was the most important and most powerful city-state in the Shephelah, and the Assyrians were very proud that they had conquered it. It was a highly fortified city, and the confidence of the people of Lachish and of Judah was in their military might, not in the Lord. This pride and self-assurance was the beginning of the nation's sin. The leaders depended on the outlying fortress cities to keep the enemy from invading, but these cities fell to the enemy.

5. See Isaiah 1:9; 7:3; 10:20-22; 11:11, 16; Jeremiah 6:9; 23:3; 31:7; 40:11; Ezek. 11:13, 14:22, Zephaniah 2:4-9; Haggai 1:12, 14; and Zechariah 8:1-8. Micah writes of the remnant in 2:12, 4:7, 5:3, 5:7-8, and 7:18. Paul uses the doctrine of the remnant to prove that God has not forsaken the Jewish people in the present age (Rom. 9; see also 11:1-6).

Chapter 2

1. This statement is found eight times in the Bible (Lev. 11:44-45; 19:2; 20:7, 26; 21:8, 15; 1 Peter 1:15-16).

2. The traditional verse division at 5:4-5 is unfortunate. "And this man shall be the peace" (or "their peace") belongs at the end of verse 4, not at the beginning of verse 5. The reference is to Jesus Christ the Messiah.

3. Isaiah painted the same picture (2:1-4). Some interpret these passages in a spiritual sense as describing the church today, but I prefer to see them as specific prophecies for the Jewish nation. The conditions on earth described by Isaiah and Micah haven't appeared, especially the elimination of war, anti-Semitism, and religious rivalry among nations.

4. Does the "exaltation of Jerusalem (v. 1) mean only that it will be honored and distinguished by the Lord, or that there will be actual changes in the topography of the land? The latter seems to be the case. The NIV translates verse 1, "It will be raised above the hills," which suggests the literal raising of Mount Zion to a place of special prominence. Zechariah 14:4-5 indicates that there will be changes in the topography when Christ returns.

5. Contrast with Joel 3:10, where the opposite picture is described.

6. It is unwise to make Micah 5:1 a prophecy of what happened to Jesus during His trial, although He was slapped in the face, beaten with a reed, and scourged (Matt. 27:30; Mark 15:19; John 19:3). The context of Micah 5:1 is definitely the siege of Jerusalem, not the trial of Jesus.

Chapter 3

1. However, Micah 6:8 must not be mistaken as a condemnation of the Mosaic sacrificial system. It was right for the Jews to bring their sacrifices to God if their hearts had been broken in repentance and confession of sin. God wants obedience, not sacrifice (1 Sam. 15:22), and the most important sacrifice is that of a broken and contrite heart (Ps. 51:16). See also Isaiah 1:11-15 and Hosea 6:6. Worship that doesn't produce a godly life is not true worship at all.

2. The phrase "hear ye the rod" (KJV) or "Heed the rod" (NIV) is a puzzle to translators and expositors. What or who is "the rod"? Does it refer to the punishment God sent to the nation or to the nation that brought the punishment? Or does it refer to the Lord Himself? According to Isaiah 10:5, God calls Assyria "the rod of My anger." In *The Minor Prophets: An Exegetical and Expository Commentary*, Dr. Bruce Waltke suggests an alternate translation: "Give heed, O tribe, and the assembly of the city" (Grand

Rapids, Mich.: Baker Book House), vol. 2, 736. When the officials met in assembly to consider business, each tribal leader would have his official staff symbolizing his authority (see Num. 17). God addresses not only the city of Jerusalem in general but also specifically the leaders who met to consider what to do.

3. We must be careful not to develop an "Elijah complex" and think we're the only godly people left (1 Kings 19:10). David felt that way (Ps. 12:1), and so did Isaiah (57:1). But in Micah's case, the godly remnant was so small that it seemed insignificant.

4. Micah 7:8-10 certainly expresses the feelings and hopes of the exiles from both Israel and Judah. Eventually both Assyria and Babylon were defeated and passed off the scene, but it wasn't the Jews who conquered them. The Jews' return from Babylonian exile was a small picture of the greater regathering of Israel that will take place in the last days (Isa. 11:11-16; Matt. 24:31).

NAHUM

OUTLINE

Key theme: The vengeance of God on His enemies

Key verses: Nahum 1:2, 7

I. GOD IS JEALOUS: NINEVEH WILL FALL. 1:1-15

1. God declares His anger. 1:1-8
2. God speaks to Nineveh . 1:9-11, 14
3. God encourages Judah. 1:12-13, 15

II. GOD IS JUDGE: HOW NINEVEH WILL FALL. 2:1-13

1. The invaders appear and advance. 2:1-4
2. The city is captured. 2:5-10
3. The conquerors taunt their captives. 2:11-13

III. GOD IS JUST: WHY NINEVEH WILL FALL. 3:1-19

1. Her ruthless bloodshed. 3:1-3
2. Her idolatry. 3:4-7
3. Her pride and self-confidence. 3:8-19

CONTENTS

Nahum in His Time

Little is known about Nahum except that he came from the town of Elkosh (whose location we can't identify with certainty) and that he was a prophet of God who announced the fall of Nineveh, capital city of the Assyrian empire. He mentions the capture of the Egyptian city of Thebes, which occurred in 663 B.C., and he predicted the fall of Nineveh, which took place in 612 B.C.; so these dates place him in Judah during the reigns of Manasseh (695-642) and Josiah (640-609). His contemporaries would have been Jeremiah, Zephaniah, and Habakkuk.

His name means "comfort" or "compassion," and his message of Assyrian's doom would certainly have comforted the people of Judah, who had suffered because of Assyria. The Assyrians had taken the Northern Kingdom of Israel in 722 and dispersed the people, and then they tried to take Judah in the days of Hezekiah (701), but they were defeated by the angel of the Lord (Isa. 37). Assyria was always looming over the tiny kingdom of Judah, and having these ruthless people out of the way would have greatly bettered Judah's situation.

Jonah had annouced Nineveh's doom over a century before, but God had relented because the people had repented. The Lord was certainly long-suffering to spare the city that long, especially since the Assyrians had returned to their evil ways. While Nahum's message was directed especially to the Assyrians, he was careful to encourage the people of Judah as well.

THE CITY IS NO MORE
NAHUM 1–3

Queen Victoria was celebrating sixty years on the British throne when Rudyard Kipling published his poem "Recessional." Not everybody in Great Britain liked the poem because it punctured national pride at a time when the empire was at its peak. "Recessional" was a warning that other empires had vanished from the stage of history and theirs might follow in their train. God was still the Judge of the nations. Kipling wrote:

> Far-called, our navies melt away;
> On dune and headland sinks the fire:
> Lo, all our pomp of yesterday
> Is one with Nineveh and Tyre!
> Judge of the Nations, spare us yet,
> Lest we forget—lest we forget!

The prophet Nahum would have applauded the poem, especially Kipling's reference to Nineveh, for it was Nahum who wrote the Old Testament book that vividly describes the destruction of Nineveh, the event that marked the beginning of the end for the Assyrian Empire.[1] Nahum made it clear that God is indeed the Judge of the nations, and that "[p]ride goes before destruction, and a haughty spirit before a fall" (Prov. 16:18, NKJV). In the seventh century B.C., the very mention of Nineveh brought fear to people's hearts, but today, Nineveh is mentioned primarily by Bible students, archeologists, and people interested in ancient history. *Sic transit gloria!*

In his brief book, Nahum makes three declarations about God and Nineveh.

1. God Is Jealous: Nineveh Will Fall (Nahum 1:1-15)

The prophet characterizes his inspired message as both a "burden" and a "vision," something he felt and something he saw. The word translated "burden" simply means "to lift up" and was often used to describe prophetic messages that announced judgment. Isaiah used the word ten times in his prophecy as he wrote about "the burden of Babylon" (Isa. 13:1), "the burden of Moab" (15:1), etc. These burdens came as a result of the visions God gave His prophets ("seers") of dreadful events determined for the nations. It wasn't easy to be a prophet and see what lay in the future, and they felt the burden of their messages. Nineveh isn't mentioned by name until Nahum 2:8, but its destruction is the theme of the book.

God speaks of Himself (Nahum 1:2-8). Three important words in this paragraph need to be understood because they all relate to the character of God: jealousy, vengeance, and anger.

Jealousy is a sin if it means being envious of what others have and wanting to possess it, but it's a virtue if it means cherishing what we have and wanting to protect it. A faithful husband and wife are jealous over one another and do everything they can to keep their relationship exclusive. "Jealous" and "zealous" come from the same root, for when you're jealous over someone, you're zealous to protect the relationship.

Since God made everything and owns everything, He is envious of no one, but since He is the only true God, He is jealous over His glory, His name, and the worship and honor that are due to Him alone. In the second commandment, God prohibited the worship of idols and backed up the prohibition with this reason: "for I, the Lord thy God, am a jealous God" (Ex. 20:5).

When we studied the Book of Hosea, we learned that the Lord was "married" to Israel in a covenant relationship, and any breach of that covenant aroused His jealous love. He will not share His people with false gods any more than a husband would share his wife with his neighbor. "For you shall worship no other god, for the Lord, whose name is Jealous, is a jealous God" (34:14, NKJV). "For the Lord your God is a consuming fire, a jealous God" (Deut. 4:24, NKJV; and see 6:15; 32:16, 21; 1 Kings 14:22). Nineveh was a city given over to iniquity, especially idolatry and cruelty, and God's jealous love burned against their pride and willful breaking of His law.

In Scripture, vengeance is usually presented as a sin. Both Jesus and Paul warned about it (Matt. 5:38-48; Rom. 12:17-21). But a just and holy God cannot see people flouting His law and do nothing about it. "It is mine to avenge; I will repay. . . . I will take vengeance on my adversaries and repay those who hate me" (Deut. 32:35, 41, NIV). The God's people prayed to God to avenge them when other nations attacked them. "O Lord God, to whom vengeance belongs—O God, to whom vengeance belongs, shine forth!" (Ps. 94:1, NKJV) When God takes vengeance by judging people, it's because He is a holy God and is jealous (zealous) for His holy law.

God's anger isn't like human anger, which can be selfish and out of control. His is a holy anger, a righteous indignation against all that defies His authority and disobeys His law. God's people ought to exercise a holy anger against sin (Eph. 4:26), for, as Henry Ward Beecher said, "A person that does not know how to be angry does not know how to be good." He was speaking, of course, about righteous anger that opposes evil. If we can stand by and do nothing while innocent, helpless people are mistreated and exploited, then something is wrong with us. "Anger is one of the sinews of the soul," wrote Thomas Fuller. "He who lacks it has a maimed mind."

In Nahum 1:2, Nahum wrote that God was "furious" ("filled with wrath," NIV); and in verse 6, he described God's "indignation" as so fierce and powerful that it is "poured out like fire" with the power to "shatter" the rocks (NIV). However, verse 3 assures us that God's wrath isn't a fit of rage or a temper tantrum; for "the Lord is slow to anger" (see Jonah 4:2; Ex. 34:6; Num. 14:18).

God is so powerful that if His anger were not a holy anger, and if He were not "slow to anger," He could easily destroy everything. He controls the forces of nature (Nahum 1:3); He opened the Red Sea for the people of Israel to march through, and he can turn off the rain and make the most fruitful areas of the land languish (v. 4).[2] At Sinai, He made the mountain shake (Ex. 19:18), and when He pleases, He can cause the people of the world to tremble (Heb. 12:18-21).

The God that Nahum introduces to us is a jealous God who is angry at sin (Nahum 1:2), but He is also a good God who cares for His people (v.7). Nahum invites us (as Paul put it) to "consider the goodness and severity of God" (Rom. 11:22, NKJV). "God is love" (1 John 4:8, 16), but He is also light (1:5), and His love is a holy love. He is a refuge for those who trust Him, but He is an "overwhelming flood" to those who are His enemies.

God speaks to Nineveh (Nahum 1:9-11, 14). He informs the leaders of Assyria that He knows their plots (vv. 9, 11) and will cause all of their plans to fail. When the proud nations plot against God, He laughs at them and turns their schemes into confusion (Ps. 2:1-4). The Assyrians had plotted against Judah in the days of King Hezekiah, and God thwarted their plans (Isa. 36–37), but the Lord wouldn't allow this to happen a second time. Instead of marching out triumphantly, the leaders would be like drunks entangled in thorn bushes, and stubble burned in a prairie fire (Nahum 1:10).

The plotter mentioned in verse 11 is the king of Assyria, and God addresses him in verse 14, making three declarations: (1) his dynasty will end, because he will have no descendants; (2) the help of his gods and goddesses will end, because they will be destroyed; and (3) his life will end, because God will prepare his grave. What a solemn message for a man who was sure his plans would succeed! Why would God do all these things? The answer is plain: "You are vile!"

God speaks to Judah (Nahum 1:12-13, 15). Although the Assyrian army outnumbered the army of Judah, and Assyria had more allies to help them fight, that didn't mean Assyria was bound to win, for God was fighting on behalf of Judah. Yes, the Lord had used Assyria to chasten Judah in the past, but that would not happen again.[3] This time, God would break the yoke and remove the shackles that Assyria had put on Judah, and Assyria would attack them no more.

In ancient days, news was carried by couriers, and the watchmen on the walls scanned the horizon hoping that messengers would bring good news. In this case, it was good news indeed: the courier would announce that Nineveh was fallen and the Assyrian army defeated and in disarray (v. 15).[4] Judah could now live in peace and enjoy her annual feasts and regular religious festivals.

You find this same statement in Isaiah 52:7, where the messenger announced the defeat of Babylon, and Paul quoted the verse in Romans 10:15 and applied it to the proclamation of the Gospel to lost sinners. We don't usually think of feet as being beautiful, but they certainly are beautiful when they enable a messenger to carry good news that God has defeated our enemies. To Judah, it meant that Assyria was completely destroyed and could never again invade her land. To us who trust Christ, it means that He has completed defeated sin, death, and Satan, and that we are now free to enjoy the blessings of salvation.

2. God Is Judge: How Nineveh Will Fall (Nahum 2:1-13)

In 612 B.C., the Medes and the Babylonians united to attack Nineveh, and the Lord used them to judge the evil city. This chapter is a vivid description of what happened as seen by Nahum in the vision God gave him.

The invaders appear (Nahum 2:1-4). The guards on the walls of the city see the army advancing and the officers issue orders and encourage their soldiers. You can almost hear the sharp commands: "Guard the fortress, watch the road, brace yourself, marshal all your strength!" (v. 1, NIV) Above all the noise, the voice of the Lord is heard as He speaks to Israel and Judah and assures them that they will be restored and reunited. (v.2).[5]

The invading army is formidable with its manpower, armor, weapons, and chariots (vv. 3-4). Already their shields are red with blood. The chariots look like flames of fire as they dash here and there in the streets of the city, and the soldiers find it easy to slaughter the defenseless people.

The city is captured (Nahum 2:5-10). "He" in verse 5 refers to the king of Assyria who had plotted against the Lord and His people (1:9). He gathers his best officers and gives them orders to protect the wall, but they are too late. They stumble like drunks instead of marching like heroes. The leaders were sure their fortress was impregnable, but their defenses proved to be their undoing.

The Khoser River flowed through the city, so the invaders damned it up and then released the water so that it destroyed part of the wall and some of the buildings. It was a simple matter for the Medes and Babylonians to enter the city and take control. But they can't take credit for the victory; it was decreed by God that the city be destroyed and the inhabitants be killed or taken captive (2:7). The invaders were but God's instruments to execute His will.

First, the soldiers line up the prisoners to march them off to their own lands where they'll become slaves. Nahum compares the exodus to water draining out of a pool. Then the soldiers begin looting this fabulously wealthy city, and the people watch with dismay. "Hearts melt, knees give way, bodies tremble, every face grows pale" (v. 10, NIV). Nineveh is being treated the way she treated others; her sins had found her out.

The captive leaders are taunted (Nahum 2:11-13). Speaking on behalf of God, the prophet has the last word. As the Assyrian captives are marched away, leaders and common citizens, and the city's treasures carried off by their captors, Nahum taunts the Ninevites by contrasting their present plight with their former glory.

The image of the lion was often used by the Assyrians in their art and architecture. Visit the Assyrian room in any large museum and you will see huge statues of lions. But even more, the Assyrians acted like lions as they stalked their prey and completely devoured their captives. "Where is the lions' den now?" Nahum asks as the city is destroyed. "Where is all your prey, the treasures you ruthlessly took from others?" Lions will normally take to their lair enough food for themselves and their cubs, but the Assyrians amassed wealth beyond measure, far more than they needed, and they did it at the cost of human lives.

No wonder the Lord announced, "I am against you" (v. 13). Over a century before, the Lord had sent Jonah to warn Nineveh, and when the city repented, He withdrew His hand of judgment. But now their time was up and the end had come. Assyria would be left with no weapons, no leaders, and no victories to be announced by their messengers. Instead, Assyria's enemies would hear the voice of couriers announcing peace because Assyria had been defeated (1:15).

3. God Is Just: Why Nineveh Will Fall (Nahum 3:1-19)

"Shall not the Judge of all the earth do right?" (Gen. 18:25) God is long-suffering, but there comes a time when His hand of judgment falls. "You have rebuked the nations, You have destroyed the wicked; you have blotted out their name forever and ever" (Ps. 9:5, NKJV). Nahum gives three reasons why Nineveh deserved to be judged.

Their ruthless bloodshed (Nahum 3:1-3). The Assyrians were clever diplomats who lied to other nations and then broke their promises and destroyed them. They slaughtered people without regard for age or sex, and they stacked up corpses like lumber as warning to anybody who would oppose them. The shedding of innocent blood is a serious sin that God notes, remember, and judges

(Deut. 19:11-13; 2 Kings 21:16; 24:4; Ps. 106:38; Prov. 6:16-17; Isa. 59:7). Depraved dictators who authorize the heartless slaying of innocent victims will someday answer to God for their crimes against Him and humanity.

Their idolatry (Nahum 3:4-7). Often in Scripture, idolatry is associated with prostitution, and when you consider that the chief deity of Nineveh was Ishtar, goddess of sexual passion, fertility, and war, you can understand why Nahum used this metaphor. Because of their spiritual blindness, the Assyrians were ensnared by this evil goddess and were under the control of lust, greed, and violence. People become like the god that they worship (Ps. 115:8), for what we believe determines how we behave. Assyria spread this evil influence to other nations and enslaved them by their sorcery. (See the description of the corrupt end-times religious system given in Rev. 17.)

In ancient times, prostitutes were often shamed by being publicly exposed, and this is what God promised to do to Nineveh. God would expose Assyria's nakedness before all the nations, and this would be the end of their evil influence. The magnificent wealthy city would become a heap of ruins.

Their pride and self-confidence (Nahum 3:8-19. In this closing paragraph, Nahum uses a number of images to show the Assyrians their weaknesses and assure them of their ultimate defeat.

He begins with a fact of history: the defeat of the Egyptian city of Thebes, or No-Ammon, by the Assyrians, in 663 (vv. 8-11). If you visit Karnak and Luxor in Upper Egypt, you will be at the site of ancient Thebes. This capital city of Upper Egypt was sure it was safe from any invader, yet it went down in defeat before Assyria. Like Nineveh, Thebes was situated by waters which were supposed to be their defense, but the city fell just the same. Thebes had many allies, but they couldn't protect her.

What Assyria did to the people of Thebes would in turn be done to them: their children would be dashed to pieces, the leaders would become slaves, and the people would become exiles. Now, argues Nahum, if this happened to Thebes, why couldn't it happen to Nineveh? Their pride and self-confidence would be totally destroyed as the Medes and Babylonians captured the city. Nineveh would drink the cup of God's wrath and become drunk (v. 11; see Ps. 75:8; Isa. 51:17; Jer. 25:14ff).

In fact, the conquest would be so easy, it would be like ripe figs dropping into a person's mouth (Nahum 3:12). Why? Because the ferocious Assyrian soldiers would be drained of their strength and be like women: weak, afraid, and unable to meet the enemy (vv. 13-14).[6] They wouldn't be able to bar the gates or stop the enemy from setting fire to them, nor would they be able to repair the walls or carry water to put out the fires.

The next image is that of insects (vv. 15-17). The invading soldiers would sweep through the land and the city like a plague of grasshoppers or locusts and wipe everything out. The Babylonian merchants were also like locusts as they collected all the treasures they could find. But the Assyrian leaders were like locusts that go to sleep on the wall on a cold day, but when the sun comes up, they feel the heat and fly away. The king and his council were overconfident, like locusts sleeping on the wall, but when the invasion occurred, they flew off to a safe place!

Assyria was like a scattered flock with sleeping shepherds (v. 18), or like a wounded body with no way to be healed (v. 19a). They had no allies to rescue them, for all the other nations would rejoice when they heard that the Assyrian Empire was no more (v. 19b).

Like the Book of Jonah, the Book of Nahum ends with a question: "for who has not felt you endless cruelty?" (v. 19, NIV) Nahum emphasizes the same truth that was declared by the Prophet Amos: God punishes cruel nations that follow inhumane policies and brutal practices (Amos 1–2). Whether it's practicing genocide, exploiting the poor, supporting slavery, or failing to provide people with the necessities of life, the sins of national leaders are known by God and He eventually judges.

If you question that fact, go and search for Nineveh.

ENDNOTES

1. Nineveh was destroyed by the Medes and Babylonians in 612 B.C., but the empire didn't collapse immediately. Remnants of the army and of political leadership struggled on until they were overpowered in 609 at the battle of Haran. But when Nineveh fell, it was the death knell for the empire.

2. Lebanon on the north, Carmel on the east, and Bashan on the west were known for their fruitfulness. See Isaiah 2:13; 33:9; and 35:2.

3. Isaiah 10:5-18 explains that Assyria was God's tool ("the rod of My anger") to chasten Judah because of her idolatry, but the Assyrians had gone too far and been too ruthless. In his pride, the king of Assyria had boasted of his past victories, so the Lord announced that He would humble him. This God did when His angel destroyed 185,000 Assyrian soldiers in one night (37:36-38; see 10:16).

4. Nahum 1:15 in our English versions is 2:1 in the Hebrew text. What a contrast between the announcement of peace in 1:15 and the declaration of war in 2:1!

5. "Jacob" probably refers to Judah, the Southern Kingdom, and Israel refers to the Northern Kingdom that was dispersed by Assyria in 722-721 B.C. Since this promise has not been fulfilled, its fulfillment awaits the return of Christ when He will establish His kingdom and restore the splendor of the Jewish nation.

6. This image is not meant to demean women in any way, whether civilians or in the armed forces, or to suggest that women lack strength and courage. The biblical examples of Rahab, Deborah, Jael, Ruth, and Esther prove that Scripture can magnify the courage and service of dedicated women. However, we must keep in mind that the ancient world was a masculine society; women were kept secluded and certainly wouldn't have been expected to participate in battles. Phrases like "weak as a woman" were current; both Isaiah (19:16) and Jeremiah (50:37; 51:30) used them.

HABAKKUK

OUTLINE

Key theme: The just shall live by faith
Key verse: Habakkuk 2:4

I. THE PROPHET WONDERING AND WORRYING. (CHAP. 1)
1. God is indifferent. 1:2-4
God's reply: I am working. 1:5-11
2. God is inconsistent. 1:12-17

II. THE PROPHET WATCHING AND WAITING. (CHAP. 2)
1. Write God's vision. 2:1-3
2. Trust God's world. 2:4-5
"The just shall live by faith." 2:41
3. Declare God's judgment. 2:6-20
(1) Woe to the selfish. 2:6-8
(2) Woe to the covetous. 2:9-11
(3) Woe to the exploiters. 2:12-14
"God's glory will fill the earth." 2:14
(4) Woe to the drunkards. 2:15-17
(5) Woe to the idolaters. 2:18-20
"God is still on His throne." 2:20

III. THE PROPHET WORSHIPING AND WITNESSING. (CHAP. 3)
1. He prays to God. 3:1-2
2. He ponders God's ways. 3:3-15
3. He praises God. 3:16-19

CONTENTS

Habakkuk in His Time

Habakkuk was a contemporary of Nahum, Zephaniah, and Jeremiah, during the reigns of Josiah (640-609 B.C.) and Jehoiakim (609-598). Assyria was off the scene; Babylon ("the Chaldeans") was in power. Nebuchadnezzar had defeated Egypt in 605 and was about to attack Judah. Jeremiah had announced that Babylon would invade Judah, destroy Jerusalem and the temple, and send the nation into exile. This happened in 606-586.

Habakkuk's little book indicates that he knew the Scriptures well, was a competent theologian, and had great faith in God. Because of the psalm in chapter 3, some scholars think he may have been a priest who led worship in the temple. If so, then like Jeremiah and Ezekiel, he was a priest called to be a prophet—a more difficult ministry.

His name means "to embrace" or "to wrestle," and in his book, he does both. He wrestles with God concerning the problem of how a holy God could use a wicked nation like Babylon to chasten the people of Judah, and then by faith, he embraces God and clings to His promises. Habakkuk also wrestles with the spiritual decline of the nation and why God wasn't doing something about it. Habakkuk wanted to see the people revived (3:2), but God wasn't answering his prayers.

The prophet's statement "The just shall live by his faith" (2:4) is quoted three times in the New Testament (Rom. 1:17; Gal. 3:11; Heb. 10:38). The emphasis in Romans is on the just, in Galatians on how they should live, and in Hebrews on faith. It takes three books to explain and apply this one verse!

CHAPTER ONE
THE PROPHET WORRYING
HABAKKUK 1

One of the modern "Christian myths" that ought to be silenced says that when you trust Jesus Christ, you get rid of all your problems. You don't.

It's true that your basic spiritual problem—your relationship with God—has been solved, but with that solution comes a whole new set of problems that you didn't face when you were an unbeliever, like: "Why do good people suffer and evil people prosper?" or "Why isn't God answering my prayer?" or "When I'm doing my best for the Lord, why do I experience the worst from others?"

Christians who claim to be without problems are either not telling the truth or not growing and experiencing real life. Perhaps they're just not thinking at all. They're living in a religious dream world that has blocked out reality and stifled honest feelings. Like Job's uncomfortable comforters, they mistake shallow optimism for the peace of God and "the good life" for the blessing of God. You never hear them ask what David and Jesus asked, "My God, My God, why hast Thou forsaken Me?" (Ps. 22:1; Matt. 27:46).

Habakkuk wasn't that kind of a believer. As he surveyed the land of Judah, and then watched the international scene, he found himself struggling with some serious problems. But he did the right thing: he took his problems to the Lord.

1. "Why Is God So Indifferent?" (Hab. 1:2-11)

Being a perceptive man, Habakkuk knew the kingdom of Judah was rapidly deteriorating. Ever since the death of King Josiah in 609 B.C., his religious reforms had been forgotten and his son and successor Jehoiakim had been leading the nation closer to disaster. (If you want to know what God thought about Jehoiakim, read Jer. 22:13-19.)

The prophet's concern (Hab. 1:2-3). Habakkuk's vocabulary in this chapter indicates that times were difficult and dangerous, for he uses words like violence, iniquity, grievance (misery), spoiling (destruction), strife, contention (disputes), and injustice. Habakkuk prayed that God would do something about the violence, strife, and injustice in the land, but God didn't seem to hear. In verse 2, the first word translated "cry" simply means "to call for help," but the second word means "to scream, to cry with a loud voice, to cry with a disturbed heart." As he prayed about the wickedness in the land, Habakkuk became more and more burdened and wondered why God seemed so indifferent.

The basic cause (Hab. 1:4). The nation's problems were caused by leaders who wouldn't obey the law. "Therefore the law is paralyzed, and justice never prevails. The wicked hem in the righteous, so that justice is perverted" (v. 4, NIV). The rich exploited the poor and escaped punishment by bribing the officials. The law was either ignored or twisted, and nobody seemed to care. The courts were crooked, officials were interested only in money, and the admonition in Exodus 23:6-8 was completely unheeded.

The Lord's counsel (Hab. 1:5-11). God answered His servant and assured him that He was at work among the nations even though Habakkuk couldn't see it.[1] God gave Habakkuk a revelation, not an explanation, for what we always need in times of doubt is a new view of God. The Lord doesn't owe us any explanations, but He does graciously reveal Himself and His work to those who seek Him.[2]

What God was doing was so amazing, incredible, and unheard of, that even His prophet would be shocked: God was planning to punish the Jews by using the godless Babylonians! They were a "ruthless and impetuous people" (v. 6, NIV), "a feared and dreaded people" who were a law unto themselves and afraid of nobody (v. 7, NIV). Their only purpose was to promote themselves and conquer and enslave other peoples.

The Lord then used a number of pictures from nature to describe the Babylonians and how they treated people. Their horses had the speed of leopards and the ferocity of wolves, and their troops swooped down on their prey like vultures. Their army swept across the desert like the wind and gathered and deported prisoners the way a man digs sand and ships it to a foreign land.

Could anything stop them? Certainly God could stop them, but He was the one who was enlisting their aid! Nothing human could hinder their progress. The Babylonians had no respect for authority, whether kings or generals. (One of their practices was to put captured kings in cages and exhibit them, like animals.) They laughed at gates and walls as they built their siege ramps and captured fortified cities. They worshiped the god of power and depended wholly on their own strength.

Habakkuk learned that God was not indifferent to the sins of the people of Judah. The Lord was planning to chasten Judah by allowing the Babylonians to invade the land and take them into exile.[3] This wasn't the answer Habakkuk was expecting. He was hoping God would send a revival to His people (see 3:2), judge the evil leaders, and establish righteousness in the land. Then the nation would escape punishment and the people and cities would be spared.

However, God had warned His people time and time again, but they wouldn't listen. Prophet after prophet had declared the Word (2 Chron. 36:14-21), only to be rejected, and He had sent natural calamities like droughts and plagues, and various military defeats, but the people wouldn't listen. Instead of repenting, the people hardened their hearts even more and turned for help to the gods of the nations around them. They had tried God's long-suffering long enough and it was time for God to act.

2. "How Could God Be So Inconsistent?" (Hab. 1:12-17)

As far as Habakkuk was concerned, God's first answer hadn't been an answer at all. In fact, it only created a new problem that was even more puzzling: inconsistency on the part of God. How could a holy God use a wicked nation to punish His own special people?

The holiness of God (Hab. 1:12-13). The prophet focused on the character of God, as Jonah had done when he disagreed with what God was doing (Jonah 4:2). "Men of faith are always the men who have to confront problems," wrote G. Campbell Morgan, for if you believe in God, you sometimes wonder why He allows certain things to happen. But keep in mind that there's a difference between doubt and unbelief. Like Habakkuk, the doubter questions God and may even debate with God, but the doubter doesn't abandon God. But unbelief is rebellion against God, a refusal to accept what He says and does. Unbelief is an act of the will, while doubt is born out of a troubled mind and a broken heart.

Habakkuk's argument with God is a short course in theology. He started with the fact of the holiness of God. The Babylonians were far more wicked sinners than the people in Judah, so how could God use evil, idolatrous Gentiles to punish His own chosen people? Yes, His people deserved punishment, but couldn't God find a better instrument? Would this mean the end of the nation? No, for "we shall not die" (Hab. 1:12). God had purposes to fulfill through the Jewish nation and He would preserve His people, but they would experience painful trials.

The prophet needed to remember two facts: (1) God had used other tools to chasten His people—war, natural calamities, the preaching of the prophets—and the people wouldn't listen; (2) the greater the light, the greater the responsibility. Yes, the Babylonians were wicked sinners, but they were idolaters who didn't know the true and living God. This didn't excuse their sins (Rom. 1:18ff), but it did explain their conduct. The Jews claimed to know the Lord and yet they were sinning against the very law they claimed to believe! Sin in the life of a believer is far worse than sin in the life of an unbeliever. When God's people deliberately disobey Him, they sin against a flood of light and an ocean of love.

Habakkuk reminded God that He was eternal, and therefore knew the end from the beginning and couldn't be caught by surprise. He was the Mighty God ("Rock," NIV) who had all power and never changed. So, what about His covenants with the Jews? What about His special promises? As a holy God, He couldn't look with approval on sin (Hab. 1:13); yet He was "tolerant" of sin in the land of Judah and "silent" as the Babylonians prepared to swallow up His people! Habakkuk wanted God to say something and do something, but God was silent and seemingly inactive.

Keep in mind that this wasn't simply a national problem to Habakkuk, or a theological problem; it was a personal problem as he cried out, "My God, my holy One" (v. 12, NIV). National and international events were affecting his personal walk with God, and this concerned him greatly. But wrestling with these challenges is the only way for our "faith muscles" to grow. To avoid tough questions, or to settle for half-truths and superficial pat answers it to remain immature, but to face questions honestly and talk them through with the Lord is to grow in grace and in the knowledge of Christ (2 Peter 3:18).[4]

The helplessness of the people (Hab. 1:14-15). After presenting his case on the basis of the holiness of God, Habakkuk argued from the viewpoint of the helplessness of the people (vv. 14-15). Judah could never survive an attack from the savage Babylonians. To the Babylonians, life was cheap, and prisoners of war were expendable. People were like fish to be hooked or sea creatures to be trapped.

How could God allow His weak people to be invaded by such a heartless and ruthless nation? Of course, the false prophets in Judah were saying, "It can't happen here" (see Jer. 6:14; 8:11; 14:13ff), but their blind optimism would soon be exposed as lies. For forty years, the Prophet Jeremiah warned the people of Judah and begged them to turn back to God, but they refused to listen. What Judah needed wasn't great military strength but obedient faith in God.

The haughtiness of the enemy (Hab. 1:16-17). The prophet's third approach was to point out the way the Babylonians lived and worshiped. Their god was power (see v.11) and they trusted in their mighty military machine ("their net," vv. 16-17) and worshiped the gods of power and violence. The Babylonians were "puffed up," (2:4, NIV) with arrogance and self-confidence. How could God honor them by giving them a victory over Judah? God was filling their net with victims, and the Chaldeans were emptying the net by destroying one nation after another (1:17, NIV).

Habakkuk could have said more about the abominable religion of the Babylonians. They believed in a multitude of gods and goddesses, with Bel as the head of their pantheon. Anu was the god of the sky, Nebo the god of literature and wisdom, and Nergal was the sun god. Sorcery was an important part of their religion, including honoring Ea, the god of magic. Their priests practiced divination and consulted omens, all of which was prohibited by the Law of Moses. It seemed unreasonable that the Lord would allow such spiritually ignorant people to conquer Judah, the land that housed His own temple.

Habakkuk finished his defense and waited for God to speak. Like a servant, he stood waiting and watching (2:1), wondering how God would respond to his "complaint." The answer God gave is recorded in chapter 2.

But before we listen to God's encouraging reply, we must pause to examine our own hearts. Are we fully yielded to God and willing for Him to have His way with us and with those whom we love? There's nothing wrong with wrestling with the problems of life and seeking a better understanding of God's will, but we must beware lest we start debating with God and trying to change His mind.

We admire Habakkuk for being an honest man and wanting God to spare the people he loved. We want to imitate him in his openness and sincerity and in his willingness to wait for God's answer. But we want to remember that Paul wrote to the believers in Rome:

> Oh, the depth of the riches both of the wisdom and knowledge of God! How unsearchable are His judgments and His ways past finding out! For who has known the mind of the Lord? Or who has become His counselor? Or who has first given to Him and it shall be repaid to him? For of Him and through Him and to Him are all things, to whom be glory forever. Amen.
>
> (Rom. 11:33-36, NKJV)

CHAPTER TWO
THE PROPHET WATCHING AND WAITING
HABAKKUK 2

This chapter reports an experience Habakkuk had that is similar to one recorded by Asaph the psalmist in Psalm 73. Like Habakkuk, Asaph was bewildered at the providential working of God in this world: he was disturbed because the wicked seemed to be prospering while the righteous were suffering. Like Habakkuk, he reasoned with God, and then, like Habakkuk, he gave God the opportunity to reply.

"When I thought to know this," he wrote, "it was too painful for me, until I went into the sanctuary of God" (Ps. 73:16-17). There in the sanctuary he found God's answer to his problem, and his sighing was turning into singing.

Let's join Habakkuk on the watchtower, which was his sanctuary, and listen to what the Lord said to him. When God did speak to His servant, He gave him three responsibilities to fulfill.

1. Write God's Vision (Hab. 2:1-3)

The prophet saw himself as a watchman on the walls of Jerusalem, waiting for a message from God that he could share with the people. In ancient days, the watchmen were responsible to warn the city of approaching danger, and if they weren't faithful, their hands would be stained with the blood of the people who died (Ezek. 3:17-21; 33:1-3). It was a serious responsibility.

The image of the watchman carries a spiritual lesson for us today. As God's people, we know that danger is approaching, and it's our responsibility to warn people to "flee from the wrath to come" (Matt. 3:7). If we don't share the Gospel with lost sinners, then their blood may be on our hands. We want to be able to say with Paul, "Therefore I testify to you this day that I am innocent of the blood of all men" (Acts 20:26, NKJV).

You get the impression that Habakkuk was fearful of what the Lord might say to him because of His servant's "complaint." But the Lord graciously answered Habakkuk and gave him the vision he needed to turn his worrying into worshiping. This vision included not only the words in Habakkuk 2, but also the revelation of God's glory recorded in 3:3-15. When you behold the glory of God and believe the Word of God, it gives you faith to accept the will of God.

We wouldn't be studying this book today had Habakkuk not obeyed God's orders and written down what God had told him and shown him. This writing was to be permanent so that generation after generation could read it. It was also to be plain, written so that anybody could read it, and it was to be public so that even somebody running past the tablets on display could get the message immediately.[1] Habakkuk wasn't the only person in Judah who needed this message, and it was his obligation to share it.

The revelation God gave was for a future time and about a future time. While the immediate application was to the end of the Babylonian Captivity, the writer of the Epistle to the Hebrews interpreted it to refer also to the return of Jesus Christ. Led by the Holy Spirit, he changed "it" to "He" and applied it to our Lord. "For yet a little while, and He that shall come will come, and will not tarry" (Heb. 10:37). Along with the scoffers Peter wrote about, some readers might ask, "Where is the promise of His coming? (2 Peter 3:3ff) and God's reply is, "Wait for it! It will surely come!" A discouraged Jew in Babylonian exile might ask, "Will the Lord come and deliver us?" and the answer is, "Yes! Wait for him!"

2. Trust God's Word (Hab. 2:4-5)

The contrast here is between people of faith and people who arrogantly trust themselves and leave God out of their lives. The immediate application was to the Babylonians.

The sinner. The Babylonians were "puffed up" with pride over their military might and their great achievements. They had built an impressive empire which they were sure was invincible. The words of Nebuchadnezzar express it perfectly: "Is not this great Babylon, that I have built for a royal dwelling by my mighty power for the honor of my majesty?" (Dan. 4:30, NKJV)

But Nebuchadnezzar and the Babylonians aren't the only ones puffed up with pride and self-sufficiency. This is the condition of most of the people in today's society who belong to the world and live for the world. The Apostle John warns us against "the pride [vain glory] of life" that belongs to this present evil world system which is against God and without God (1 John 2:15-17).

Besides puffing them up, what else does pride do to people? It twists them inwardly, for the soul of the unbeliever is "not upright," which means his inner appetites are crooked and sinful. He delights in the things that God abhors, the things God condemns in the five "woes" in this chapter. One of the chief causes of the corruption in this world is what Peter calls "lust" (2 Peter 1:4), which simply means "evil desires, passionate longing." Were it not for the base appetites of people, longing to be satisfied but never satisfied, the "sin industries" would never prosper.

Pride also makes people restless: they're never satisfied (Hab. 2:5). That's why they're given over to wine, never at rest, never satisfied. They're constantly seeking for some new experience to thrill them or some new achievement to make them important. Pride makes us greedy. The Babylonians weren't satisfied with what they had; they coveted even more land and wealth, and therefore set their course to conquer every nation that stood in their way. More than one king or dictator in history has followed this resolve, only to discover that it leads to disappointment, ruin, and death.

The just. Now for the contrast: "The just shall live by his faith" (v. 4b; see Rom. 1:17; Gal. 3:11; Heb. 10:38). This is the first of three wonderful assurances that God gives in this chapter to encourage His people. This one emphasizes God's grace, because grace and faith always go together. Habakkuk 2:14 emphasizes God's glory and assures us that, though this world is now filled with violence and corruption (Gen. 6:5, 11-13), it shall one day be filled with God's glory. The third assurance is in Habakkuk 2:20 and emphasizes God's government. Empires may rise and fall, but God is on His holy throne, and He is King of Kings and Lord of Lords.

"The just shall live by his faith" was the watchword of the Reformation, and they may well be the seven most important monosyllables in all of church history. It was verse 4, quoted in Romans 1:17, that helped to lead Martin Luther into the truth of justification by faith. "This text," said Luther, "was to me the true gate of Paradise."

Justification is the gracious act of God whereby He declares the believing sinner righteous and gives that believing sinner a perfect standing in Jesus Christ. The "just" person isn't someone who has met all of God's requirements by means of good works, "For by the works of the law shall no flesh be justified" (Gal. 2:19; see Rom. 4:5). "For if righteousness comes through the law, then Christ died in vain" (Gal. 2:21, NKJV).

Our Lord's parable of the Pharisee and the Publican makes it clear that no amount of religious effort can save a lost sinner (Luke 18:9-14). We can't justify ourselves before God because we stand with the whole world, guilty and condemned before His throne (Rom. 3:19). All we can do is put saving faith in Jesus Christ and His work on the cross, because that is the only way to be saved. "Therefore, being justified by faith, we have peace with God through our Lord Jesus Christ" (Rom. 5:1).

The victory. We are not only saved by faith (Eph. 2:8-9), but we are instructed to live by faith. "And this is the victory that has overcome the world – our faith" (1 John 5:4, NKJV). Faith is a lifestyle that is just the opposite of being "puffed up" and depending on your own resources. Habakkuk knew the difficult times were coming to the people of Judah, and their only resource was to trust God's Word and rest in His will.

Living by faith is the major them of the Book of Hebrews (Heb. 10:30), for in that book the phrase "by faith" is found over twenty times. To live by faith means to believe God's Word and obey it no matter how we feel, what we see, or what the consequences may be. This is illustrated in Hebrews 11, the famous "by faith" chapter of the Bible. The men and women mentioned in that chapter were ordinary people, but they accomplished extraordinary things because they trusted God and did what He told them to do. It has well been said that faith is not believing in spite of evidence; it's obeying in spite of consequence, resting on God's faithfulness.

3. Declare God's Judgment (Hab. 2:6-20)

To the faithful Jews in the land, God would be a refuge and strength (Naum 1:7; Ps. 46), but to the godless Babylonians invading the land, He would be a judge and eventually punish their sins and give them what they deserved. In this "taunt song," God pronounces "woe" upon five different sins, all of which are prevalent in the world today.

Selfish ambition (Hab. 2:6-8). Of itself, ambition can be a good thing, but if it motivates people to be greedy, selfish, and abusive, it's a bad thing. "It has always been my ambition to preach the Gospel where Christ was not known," wrote Paul (Rom. 15:20), and God honored that holy ambition. Paul also wrote, "Therefore also we have as our ambition . . . to be pleasing to him" (2 Cor. 5:9, NASB), an ambition we all should imitate.

The Babylonians were consumed by selfish ambition and they stopped at nothing to acquire wealth and expand their kingdom.

They had hoards of stolen goods, plundered from helpless people. God warned them that the owners of this wealth would one day rise up to condemn them and collect what was due.[2] Then the Babylonians will become the victims! This happened when the Medes and the Persians invaded Babylon and overthrew Belshazzar (Dan. 5). Babylon plundered other nations and she herself was plundered. Babylon had shed rivers of blood, and her blood was shed. It's a basic law of the universe that eventually we reap what we sow.

Covetousness (Heb. 2:9-11). According to Ephesians 4:28, there are three ways to get wealth: you can work for it, steal it, or receive it as a gift. Stealing is wrong because the eighth commandment says, "Thou shalt not steal" (Ex. 20:15). The Babylonians took land that wasn't theirs in order to build an empire that glorified them and assured them safety. Their goal was security, like the eagle's nest on the high mountain crags. Of course, this was a false security; because no individual or nation can build walls high enough to keep God out.

What will be the consequences of this covetousness? Instead of having houses and families that bring honor, they will have disgrace and shame and will eventually lose their lives. "For what shall it profit a man, if he shall gain the whole world, and lose his own soul?" (Mark 8:36) The very materials in their expensive houses would testify against them, for they were plundered from helpless people. James used a similar image when he warned the rich that the wages they owed their laborers would witness against them at the judgment (James 5:1-6).[3]

It's likely that some of the covetous Jews felt the sting of this rebuke, for they were amassing fortunes by exploiting the poor and using that money to build expensive houses. (See Amos 3:15 and 6:11). The prophets often rebuked the rich because they lived in luxury while the poor suffered. Jesus warned His disciples, "Take heed and beware of covetousness" (Luke 12:15), and that warning is valid today. "Thou shalt not covet" may be the last of the Ten Commandments (Ex. 20:17), but if we're guilty of covetousness, we're in danger of breaking the other nine!

Exploitation of people (Hab. 2:12-14). Babylon was built by bloodshed, the blood of innocent victims. It was built by prisoners of war, slave labor that was exploited to the fullest extent. Babylon was proud of what she had built, but God said it wouldn't last; it was only fuel for the fire. The city of Babylon was an architectural marvel, but their great projects were for nothing. It's all gone, and today, if you want to see what Babylon was like, you have to visit a museum.

When I was a seminary student in Chicago, one of our classes did just that: we visited a museum to see the exhibit on Babylon. I recall how impressed I was with the model of the city, marveling that such magnificent walls and gates and buildings could be constructed in those ancient days. But my wonder turned to disgust when I recalled that the city was built with slave labor and that the soul of one of those slaves meant more to God than all the buildings put together.

In contrast to the shame and infamy of Babylon, God promised that His glory would one day cover the earth (v. 14). The "glory" of Babylon didn't last, but the glory of the Lord will abide forever. Certainly, the Lord was glorified when Babylon fell before her enemies in 539 B.C. (see Jer. 50–51), and He will be glorified when the Babylon of the last days is destroyed, that final great world empire that opposes God (Rev. 17–18). When Jesus Christ returns and establishes His kingdom, then God's glory will indeed cover the whole earth (Isa. 11:1-9).[4]

The fall of "Babylon the great" is a reminder to us that what man builds without God can never last. The exploiter will eventually lose everything, and man's "utopias" will turn out to be disasters. We can't exploit people made in God's image and expect to escape God's judgment. It may take time, but eventually the judgment falls.

Drunkenness and violence (Hab. 2:15-17). This repulsive picture can be interpreted both personally and nationally. While the Bible doesn't demand total abstinence, it does warn against the evils of strong drink (Prov. 20:1; 21:17; 23:20-21, 29-35; Rom. 13:13; Gal. 5:21; 1 Thes. 5:7). Drunkenness and sensual behavior often go together (Gen. 9:20-27; 19:30-38; Rom. 13:11-14).

But the word "neighbor" could also refer to a neighboring nation that was "intoxicated" by Babylon's power and made naked before Babylon's invading armies. In Scripture, drinking a cup of wine can be a picture of judgment (Jer. 25:15ff), and nakedness sometimes speaks of the devastating effects of military invasion (Isa. 47:1-3).

However, what Babylon did to others, God would do to her. Babylon had been a golden cup in God's hands (Jer. 51:7), and He had used her to chasten the nations, but now God will give her a cup to drink that will bring her to ruin (see Rev. 16:19).[5] She will be ashamed as other nations look on her nakedness. Divine retribution will be hers: the violence she did to others will be done to her; as she shed the blood of others, her blood will be shed; and as she destroyed the lands of other nations, so her land will be devastated. The glory of God will cover the earth, but Babylon's "glory" will be covered with shame. The picture is that of a repulsive drunk, vomiting all over himself, and it isn't a very pretty picture.

It's worth noting that God mentions the way the Babylonians abused trees and animals (Hab. 2:17), suggesting that the soldiers wastefully chopped down trees and killed cattle to use both the wood and the meat for their war effort. God also mentions His concern for animals in Jonah 4:11, so check the references. You wonder how many birds and animals lost either their lives or their homes because of this policy. See Deuteronomy 20:19-20 for Israel's policy on war supplies.

Idolatry (Hab. 2:18-20). Sad to say, the people of Judah were also guilty of this sin, for during the declining years of the kingdom, they worshiped the gods of the other nations. All the prophets cried out against this flagrant violation of the second commandment (Ex. 20:4-6), but the people refused to repent.

What is idolatry? Romans 1:25 gives the best answer: worshiping and serving the creature instead of the Creator. It started with Lucifer who said, "I will be like the Most High" (Isa. 14:14), and it entered humanity when Satan tempted Eve with, "You will be like God" (Gen. 3:5, NKJV). It's the popular philosophy of the world that man is the highest thing in the universe and can pull himself up by his own bootstraps to any level he chooses. "Glory to man in the highest!"

Not only is idolatry disobedience to God's Word, but it's also foolish and useless. Of what value is a god made by a man? It's much more reasonable to worship the God who made the man! (See Rom. 1:18ff.) Not only is the idol useless (see Ps. 115), but it does definite evil by teaching lies (Hab. 2:18) and giving people false confidence that the dumb idol can help them. For a heartbreaking example of this kind of foolish reasoning, read Jeremiah 44.

Idols are dead substitutes for the living God (Ps. 115). Whatever people delight in other than God, whatever they are devoted to and sacrifice for, whatever they couldn't bear to be without, is an idol and therefore under the condemnation of God. Most people in civilized countries don't worship man-made images of things in nature, but if the above definition is correct, modern society has its idols just as the Babylonians did.

Famous people are the "idols" of millions, especially politicians, athletes, wealthy tycoons, and actors and actresses. Even dead entertainers like Marilyn Monroe, James Dean, and Elvis Presley still have their followers. People may also worship and serve man-made things like cars, houses, boats, jewelry, and art. While all of us appreciate beautiful and useful things, it's one thing to own them and quite something else to be owned by them. Albert Schweitzer said, "Anything you have that you cannot give away, you do not really own; it owns you." I've met people who so idolized their children and grandchildren that they refused to let them consider giving their lives for Christian service.

Social position can be an idol and so can vocation achievement. For some people, their god is their appetite (Phil. 3:19; Rom. 16:18); and they live only to experience carnal pleasures. Intellectual ability can be a terrible idol (2 Cor. 10:5) as people worship their IQ and refuse to submit to God's Word.

God ended His reply to Habakkuk by giving a third assurance: "But the Lord is in his holy temple; let all the earth keep silence before him" (Hab. 2:20; see Ps. 11:4). The first assurance focused on God's grace (Hab 2:4), and the second on God's glory (v. 14). This third assurance focuses on God's government; God is on the throne and has everything under control. Therefore, we shouldn't complain against God or question what He's doing. Like faithful servants, we must simply stand and listen for His commands. "Be still, and know that I am God" (Ps. 46:10).

Seeing the vision of God and hearing the voice of God made a tremendous difference in Habakkuk's life. As he grasped the significance of the three great assurances God gave him, he was transformed from being a worrier and a watcher to being a worshiper. In the closing chapter of this book, he will share with us the vision he had of God and the difference it made in his life.

CHAPTER THREE
THE PROPHET WORSHIPING
HABAKKUK 3

When Habakkuk started his book, he was "down in the valley," wrestling with the will of God. Then he climbed higher and stood on the watchtower, waiting for God to reply. After hearing God's Word and seeing God's glory, he became like a deer bounding confidently on the mountain heights! (3:19) His circumstances hadn't changed, but he had changed, and now he was walking by faith instead of sight. He was living by promises, not explanations.

It isn't easy to climb higher in the life of faith, but who wants to live in the valley? Like Habakkuk, we must honestly talk to God about our difficulties, we must pray, we must meditate on God's Word, and we must be willing to experience fear and trembling as the Lord reveals Himself to us (v. 16). But it will be worth it as we reach new summits of faith and discover new opportunities for growth and service.

What took Habakkuk from the valley to the summit? The same spiritual disciplines that can take us there: prayer, vision, and faith. Habakkuk interceded for God's work (vv. 1-2), pondered God's ways (vv. 3-15), and affirmed God's will (vv. 16-19).

1. Prayer: Pray for the Work of God (Hab. 3:1-2)

This chapter is a "prayer psalm" that may have been used in the temple worship in Jerusalem.[1] (For the other "prayer psalms," see Pss. 17; 86; 90; 102; and 142.) The prophet was now praying to the Lord and not arguing with the Lord, and his prayer soon became praise and worship.

He prayed because he had heard God speak. The word "speech" means "report" and refers to what God had told him earlier (Hab. 2:2-3). Knowing the will of God should motivate us to pray "Thy will be done." The same God who ordains the end also ordains the means to the end, and prayer is an important part of that means. "You do not have because you do not ask" (James 4:2, NKJV).

Also, hearing God's Word generates faith in the heart of the child of God (Rom. 10:17), and without faith, we can't pray effectively (Mark 11:22-24). The Word of God and prayer must always go together (Acts 6:4; John 15:7) lest our praying become zeal without knowledge. "I used to think I should close my Bible and pray for faith," said D.L. Moody, "but I came to see that it was in studying the Word that I was to get faith."

Habakkuk prayed because he was overwhelmed by God's splendor. "I stand in awe of Your deeds" (Hab. 3:2, NIV). He had seen a vision of the greatness of God, recorded for us in verses 3-15, and this vision left him weak and helpless (v. 16). All he could do was cry out to God.

Many people have the idea that it's always an enjoyable experience getting to know God in a deeper way, but that's not what the saints of God in the Bible would say. Moses trembled at Mt. Sinai when God gave the Law (Heb. 12:18-21). Joshua fell on his face before the Lord (Josh. 5:13-15), as did David (1 Chron. 21:16). Daniel became exhausted and ill after seeing the visions God gave him (Dan. 8:27; 10:11). The vision of Christ's glory on the Mount of Transfiguration left Peter, James, and John facedown on the ground and filled with terror (Matt. 17:6). When John saw the glorified Christ, he fell at His feet as though dead (Rev. 1:17).

A plaque hanging in my study carries this quotation from A.W. Tozer: "To know God is at once the easiest and the most difficult thing in the world." God certainly has the ability to reveal Himself to us, for He can do anything; but it's a problem for God to find somebody who is ready to meet Him. God doesn't reveal Himself to superficial saints who are only looking for "a new experience" they can brag about, or to curious Christians who want to "sample" deeper fellowship with God but not at too great a price.

We are the ones who make it difficult to get to know God better. "Draw near to God and He will draw near to you" (James 4:8, NKJV). "But on this one will I look," says the Lord, "on him who is poor and of a contrite spirit, and who trembles at My word" (Isa. 66:2, nkjv). "My flesh trembles in fear of you," wrote the psalmist; "I stand in awe of your laws" (Ps. 119:120).

Habakkuk prayed because he wanted God's work to succeed. God had told him that He was "working a work" in the world (Hab. 1:5), and now the prophet prayed that God would keep that work alive and cause it to prosper. What God was doing wasn't the work Habakkuk would have chosen, but he accepted God's plan and prayed, "Thy will be done." When God revealed that work to Habakkuk, he cried out, "We shall not die" (v. 12) Then in 2:4, God told him that the only way to live was by faith. So, when Habakkuk prayed for God's work to stay alive, he was also praying that his own faith might grow.[2]

Finally, Habakkuk prayed because He wanted God to show mercy. The prophet agreed that the people of Judah deserved to be chastened, and that God's chastening would work out for their good, but He asked that God's heart of love would reveal itself in mercy. He was like Moses when he interceded for the nation at Mt. Sinai (Ex. 32) and at Kadesh Barnea (Num. 14). Perhaps Habakkuk had the promise of Isaiah 54:7-8 in mind as he prayed, and see Jeremiah 10:23-24. Certainly the Lord did show mercy to the Jews, for He preserved them in Babylon and then permitted a remnant to return to their land and establish the nation.

If, like Habakkuk, you ever become discouraged about the condition of the church, the state of the world, or your own spiritual life, take time to pray and seek God's mercy. Charles Spurgeon said, "Whether we like it or not, asking is the rule of the kingdom." The greatest need today is for intercessors. "And He saw that there was no man, and wondered that there was no intercessor" (Isa. 59:16).

2. Vision: Ponder the Greatness of God (Hab. 3:3-15)

The Lord isn't likely to give us today a vision such as Habakkuk saw, but because it's recorded in the Word, we can ponder it and let the Spirit teach us from it.[3] God reveals His greatness in creation, in Scripture, and in history, and if we have eyes to see, we can behold His glory.[4]

God came in splendor (Hab. 3:3-5). According to some scholars, Mt. Paran is another name for the entire Sinai Peninsula, or for Mt. Sinai itself (Deut. 33:2). Teman is usually identified with Edom. In this song, Habakkuk seems to be retracing the march of Israel from Sinai to the Promised Land.

Everything about this stanza reveals the glory of God. He is called "the Holy One" (Hab. 3:3, and see 1:12), a name used in Isaiah at least thirty times. "His glory covered the heavens" (3:3) is an anticipation of the time when His glory will cover all the earth (2:14). God's appearance was like the lightning that plays across the heavens before the storm breaks. All of creation joined in praising Him as "the earth was full of His praise." God's brightness was like the sunrise only to a greater degree (see Matt. 17:2). "Horns" means "rays": "rays flashed from His hand (Hab. 3:4, NIV) where His power was hidden.

Verse 5 takes us to Egypt, where God revealed His power and glory in the plagues and pestilences that devastated the land and took the lives of the firstborn (Ex. 7–12). Those ten plagues were not only punishment because of Pharaoh's hardness of heart; they also revealed the vanity of Egypt's gods. "Against all the gods of Egypt will I execute judgment: I am the Lord" (Ex. 12:12; Ps. 78:50). But this verse might also include the various judgments God sent to Israel when they disobeyed Him from time to time during their wilderness march.

In Old Testament times, God often revealed His glory through such judgments, but in this present dispensation, He reveals His glory through Jesus Christ. "And the Word became flesh and dwelt among us, and we beheld His glory, the glory as of the only begotten of the Father, full of grace and truth" (John 1:14, NKJV). Pharaoh wouldn't acknowledge the truth, so he couldn't experience the grace. The first plague of Moses in Egypt was the turning of water into blood (Ex. 7:14-25), while our Lord's first recorded miracle was the turning of water into wine.

The Lord stood in power (Hab. 3:6-7). Invading generals either push forward to gain ground or they fall back in retreat, but the Lord simply stood and faced the enemy unafraid. In fact, He calmly measured the earth[5] as a sign that He possessed it. To measure something is an indication that it's yours and you can do with it what you please. It's also a preliminary step to action, as though the Lord were surveying the situation and estimating how much power it would take to execute His wrath on the nations. The Lord revealed His power when He shook the earth at Sinai before He delivered His Law to

Israel (Ex. 19:18; Heb. 12:18-21).

The nations that lay between Egypt and Canaan are typified by Cushan and Midian, two peoples living near Edom. As the news of the exodus from Egypt spread quickly through the nations, the people were terribly frightened and wondered what would happen to them when Israel arrived on the scene (Ex. 15:14-16; 23:27; Deut. 2:25; Josh. 2:8-11).

God marched in victory (Hab. 3:8-15). Habakkuk uses dynamic poetic imagery to describe Israel's march through the wilderness as they followed the Lord to the Promised Land and then claimed their inheritance. The Red Sea opened to let Israel out of Egypt, and the Jordan opened to let Israel into Canaan. The Egyptian chariots sank into the mud and their occupants were drowned, but God's chariots were chariots of salvation. Verse 9 pictures the various battles that the Israelites fought en route to Canaan, battles that the Lord won for them as they trusted Him and obeyed His commands.

In verse 10, we move into the Promised Land and see Israel conquering the enemy. God was in complete control of land and water and used His creation to defeat the Canaanites. Verse 10 describes the victory of Deborah and Barak over Sisera (Jud. 4-5), when a sudden rainstorm turned their battlefield into a swamp and left the enemy's chariots completely useless. In Habakkuk 3:11, we have the famous miracle of Joshua when the day was prolonged so Joshua would have more time for a total victory (Josh. 10:12-13). Leading His army, God marched through Canaan like a farmer threshing grain, and His people claimed their inheritance (Hab. 3:12).

Expositors aren't agreed as to what historical event is described in verses 13-15. This could be a picture of the nation's deliverance from Egypt, but if it is, Habakkuk should have mentioned it earlier. God's "anointed" would be the nation of Israel, for they were a holy people to the Lord (Ex. 19:5-8). Perhaps the prophet is referring to the various times God had to deliver His people, as recorded in the Book of Judges, and the "anointed one" would then be the judges He raised up and used to bring deliverance (Jud. 2:10-19).

However, perhaps Habakkuk was looking ahead and describing the deliverance of God's people from the Babylonian Captivity. God brought the Medes and Persians to crush Babylon and then to permit the Jews to return to their land (Ezra 1:1-4). The image of God stripping Babylon "from head to foot" (Hab. 3:13, NIV) parallels what Jeremiah prophesied in Jeremiah 50–51. Perhaps Habakkuk was looking both to the past (the Exodus) and to the future (deliverance from Babylon) and using the ancient victory to encourage the people to expect a new victory[6]

In this hymm, Habakkuk describes his God, the God of Abraham, Isaac, and Jacob, and the God and Father of our Lord Jesus Christ. He is the God of glory who reveals His glory in creation and in history. He is the living God who makes the dead idols of the nations look ridiculous. He is the God of power who can command land and sea, heaven, and earth, and therefore, He is the God of victory who leads His people in triumph.

There is no substitute for good theology, whether in our sermons or in our songs. The shallowness of some contemporary sermons, books, and songs may be the major contributing factor to the weakness of the church and the increase in "religious entertainment" in meetings where we ought to be praising God. The thing that lifted Habakkuk to the mountaintop was his understanding of the greatness of God. We need a return to the kind of worship that focuses on the glory of God and seeks to honor Him alone.[7]

3. Faith: Affirm the Will of God (Hab. 3:16-19)

This is one of the greatest confessions of faith found anywhere in Scripture. Habakkuk has faced the frightening fact that his nation will be invaded by a merciless enemy. The prophet knows that many of the people will go into exile and many will be slain. The land will be ruined, and Jerusalem and the temple will be destroyed. Yet he tells God that he will trust Him no matter what happens! Listen to his confession of faith.

"I will wait patiently on the Lord" (Hab. 3:16). If Habakkuk had depended on his feelings, he would never have made this great confession of faith. If Habakkuk looked ahead, he saw a nation heading for destruction, and that frightened him. When he looked within, he saw himself trembling with fear, and when he looked around, he saw everything in the economy about to fall apart. But when he looked up by faith, he saw God, and all his fears vanished. To walk by faith means to focus on the greatness and glory of God.

One of the marks of faith is a willingness to wait patiently for the Lord to work. "Whoever believes will not act hastily" (Isa. 28:16, NKJV). When we run ahead of God, we get into trouble. Abraham learned that lesson when he married Hagar and fathered Ishmael (Gen. 16), and so did Moses when he tried to deliver the Jews by his own hand (Ex. 2). "In quietness and confidence shall be your strength" (Isa. 3:15).

Habakkuk could wait quietly because he knew that God was at work in the world (Hab. 1:5), and he had prayed that God's work would be kept alive and strong (3:2). When you know that God is working in your life, you can afford to wait quietly and let Him have His way. Furthermore, God had commanded him to wait (2:3), and "God's commandments are God's enablements." No matter what we see and no matter how we feel, we must depend on God's promises and not allow ourselves to "fall apart." "Rest in the Lord, and wait patiently for him" (Ps. 37:7).

Over the years, I've often leaned on three verses that have helped me wait patiently on the Lord. "Stand still" (Ex. 14:13), "Sit still" (Ruth 3:18), and "Be still" (Ps. 46:10). Whenever we find ourselves getting "churned up" within, we can be sure that we need to stop, pray, and wait on the Lord before we do some stupid thing.

"I will rejoice in the Lord" (Hab. 3:17-18). By the time Babylon was through with the land of Judah, there wouldn't be much of value left (2:17). Buildings would be destroyed, treasures would be plundered, and farms and orchards would be devastated. The economy would fall apart and there would be little to sing about. But God would still be on His throne, working out His divine purposes for His people (Rom. 8:28). Habakkuk couldn't rejoice in his circumstances, but he could rejoice in his God!

The prophet's testimony here reminds us of Paul's admonitions to Christians today: "Rejoice always, pray without ceasing, in everything give thanks, for this is the will of God in Christ Jesus for you" (1 Thes. 5:16-18, NKJV). Habakkuk discovered that God was his strength (Hab. 3:19) and song as well as his salvation (see Isa. 12:1-2; Ex. 15:2; Ps. 118:14); and therefore he had nothing to fear.

It's one thing to "whistle in the dark" and try to bolster our courage, and quite something else to sing about the eternal God who never fails. Though his lips were trembling and his legs were shaking (Hab. 3:16, NIV), the prophet burst into song and worshiped his God. What an example for us to follow! It reminds us of our Lord before He went to the cross (Mark 14:26), and Paul and Silas in the Philippian dungeon (Acts 16:19-34). God can give us "songs in the night" (Pss. 42:8; 77:6; Job 35:10) if we'll trust Him and see His greatness.

"I will rely on the Lord" (Hab. 3:19). If my legs were shaking and my heart pounding, I'd find a safe place to sit down and relax, but Habakkuk began to bound up the mountain like a deer! Because of his faith in the Lord, he was able to stand and be as surefooted as a deer; he was able to run swiftly and go higher than he'd ever gone before. This is one reason why the Lord permits us to go through trials: they can draw us nearer to Him and lift us above the circumstances so that we walk on the heights with him.

God made us for the heights. If He allows us to go into the valley, it's so we might wait on Him and mount up with eagles' wings (Isa. 40:30-31). "He made him to ride on the high places of the earth" (Deut. 32:13). This is what David experienced when he was being chased by his enemies and by Saul: "It is God who arms me with strength, and makes my way perfect. He makes my feet like the feet of deer, and sets me on my high places" (Ps. 18:32-33).

The great British expositor G. Campbell Morgan said, "Our joy is in proportion to our trust. Our trust is in proportion to our knowledge of God."[8] As the hymn paraphrase of this passage puts it:

> Though vine nor fig-tree neither
> Their wonted fruit shall bear;
> Though all the fields should wither,
> Nor flocks nor herds be there;
> Yet God the same abiding,
> His praise shall tune my voice;
> For while in Him confiding,
> I cannot but rejoice.

Habakkuk teaches us to face our doubts and questions honestly, take them humbly to the Lord, wait for His Word to teach us, and then worship Him no matter how we feel or what we see.

God doesn't always change the circumstances, but He can change us to meet the circumstances. That's what it means to live by faith.

ENDNOTES

Outline

1. The statements in boldface type are the assurances God gave to Habakkuk in the midst of the "woes." They remind us that, no matter how difficult life may become, God's promises can be trusted (v. 4), His glory will one day prevail (v. 14) and He is on His holy throne in complete control of people and events (v. 20). When Habakkuk realized this, he broke out into singing (chap 3).

Chapter 1

1. Paul quoted this verse at the close of his message in the synagogue in Antioch of Pisidia (Acts 13:41; and see also Isa. 29:14). It was a warning to the people not to treat the Gospel lightly and thereby reject it. The original statement to Habakkuk referred to the coming of the Babylonians, but Paul applied it to the saving work of Jesus Christ and the offer of the Gospel. Both were incredible works of God.

2. What Habakkuk suffered in a small way, Job suffered in a great way, and God's answer to Job's many questions was simply to reveal Himself to Job. We don't live on explanations, we live on promises, and the promises of God are based on the character of God. The turning point in Job's experience came when he put his hand on his mouth, stopped arguing with the Lord, and began to worship the Lord (Job 40:1-5; 42:1-6). Habakkuk had a similar experience. There's nothing like a fresh view of the glory of God to give you strength for the journey!

3. Jeremiah would fill in the details and explain that the people would be in exile for seventy years. After that, a remnant would return to Judah, rebuild the temple, and establish the nation. See Jeremiah 25 and 29.

4. His question "Why are you silent?" (v. 13, NIV) has been asked by both saints and sinners for centuries. Of course, God is not silent, because He speaks through His Word to those who have ears to hear. He spoke the loudest at Calvary when His beloved Son died on the cross; for the atonement is God's final and complete answer to the sins of the world. Because of the cross, God is both "just and justifier" (Rom. 3:26). He has both upheld His holy law and manifested His loving heart. Sin has been judged and the way has been opened for sinners to become the children of God. Nobody can complain about such a wise and loving answer!

Chapter 2

1. Commentators and translators don't agree on what "that he may run that reads it" really means. The NIV translates it "so that a herald may run with it" and the NASB says "so that the one who reads it may run." The NRSV translates it "so that a runner may read it," and F.F. Bruce puts it "so that one who reads it may read with ease" (An *Exegetical and Expository Commentary on the Minor Prophets,* edited by Thomas E. McComiskey [Baker Book House, 1993], vol. 2, 858). Bruce explains the phrase to mean "not that the person who reads it will start running, but rather that the reader will be able to take it in at a glance, so large and legible is the writing; the eye will run over the text with ease." That seems to be what the Lord said to Habakkuk.

2. The KJV translation of 2:6b is a bit puzzling: "And to him that ladeth himself with thick clay!" The image seems to be that of a creditor giving a pledge to the banker (a clay tablet) and promising to pay his debt at a specific time. Habakkuk wrote, "The predator (Babylon) is really a creditor and his victims will one day rise up to collect what is due. It will be payday!" F.F. Bruce translates verse 6b: "Woe to him who multiplies what is not his own—but for how long? And loads himself with pledges" (F.F. Bruce, 864).

3. Jesus used the image of the stones crying out when He cleansed the temple and the children sang His praises (Luke 19:40). If people don't praise God, inanimate nature will do it! The idea of stones bearing witness goes back to Joshua 24:27.

4. Isaiah promised that "the earth shall be full of the knowledge of the Lord" (11:9), a phrase that relates to Numbers 14:21. When the seraphim before God's throne look upon the earth, they see it full of God's glory (Isa. 6:3), though it may not look glorious from our perspective. When we pray "Thy kingdom come," we are praying for Habakkuk 2:14 to be fulfilled. "Let the whole earth be filled with His glory" (Ps. 72:19).

5. Some see in this the picture of the conqueror giving the conquered rulers a cup of poison to drink. However, the emphasis seems to be on disgrace rather than death.

Chapter 3

1. We don't know what the Hebrew word "Shigionoth" means. Some scholars trace it to a root that means "to reel to and fro," so perhaps "Shigionoth" was a musical term that told the people how the psalm was to be sung. Three times in the psalm you find "Selah" (vv. 3, 9, 13), another Hebrew word whose meaning and significance are still a mystery. Some say it marks a pause in the psalm for the reader (or singer and listeners) to ponder what was said.

2. The phrase "in the midst of the years" probably refers to the period between Habakkuk's time and "the appointed time" when the vision would be fulfilled (2:3). Throughout the centuries, God's people have prayed for quickening power so that God's great work will prosper. While the word "revival" as we think of it wasn't in Habakkuk's mind, the concept is there. See Psalms 44 and 85.

3. Writing about his experience at the Transfiguration (2 Peter 1:15-21), the Apostle Peter points out that the written Word is superior to glorious experiences. Only a few people can have rapturous experiences, but any believer can ponder them in the Word with the Spirit's help. The people who had these great experiences have died, but the Word lives on. The memories of experiences will fade, but the Word remains the same. We now have a completed Bible, so the New Testament sheds light on the experiences of people like Moses, David, and the prophets; and we can see things that perhaps they didn't see. So, instead of saying, "I wish I could have that kind of experience," we should be asking, "Lord, what do You want to teach me from this experience?"

4. These mighty revelations of God in history are called "theophanies," from two Greek words meaning "an appearance of a God." For other examples, see Psalms 18; 68; and 77; and Exodus 15 and 19; and Deuteronomy 33.

5. The KJV has "measured" while the NIV has "shook." It all depends on what root you select, the Hebrew or the Arabic. Perhaps both ideas are included.

6. For other poetic descriptions of Israel's history, see Psalms 44; 68; 74; 78; 80; 83; 89; 105–106; 135; and 136.

7. William Cowper's hymn "God Moves in a Mysterious Way" is based partly on this hymn in Habakkuk 3.

8. G. Campbell Morgan, *The Westminster Pulpit* (London: Pickering and Inglis), vol. 6, 153.

ZEPHANIAH

OUTLINE

Key theme: The coming Day of the Lord
Key verse: 1:14 and 2:3

I. THE DAY OF THE LORD AND THE JEWS. 1:1–2:3
1. Pictures of that great day.
(1) Like a flood. 1:2–6
(2) Like a great sacrifice. 1:7–13
(3) Like a battle. 1:15–18
2. Plea to seek the Lord. 2:1–3

II. THE DAY OF THE LORD AND THE GENTILES. 2:4–15
1. Philistia. 2:4–7
2. Moab and Ammon. 2:8–11
3. Cush. 2:12
4. Assyria. 2:13–15

III. THE DAY OF THE LORD AND THE KINGDOM. 3:1–20
1. Jerusalem: God's jealous anger. 3:1–8
2. The Gentiles: graciousness and forgiveness. 3:11–20
3. The remnant: bounteous blessing. 3:11–20
(1) The sinners removed. 3:11–13
(2) The believers rejoicing. 3:14–17
(3) The land restored. 3:18–20

CONTENTS

Zephaniah in His Day

If the Hezekiah named in Zephaniah 1:1 is King Hezekiah (715–686), then the Prophet Zephaniah was his great-great-grandson. His name means "Jehovah hides" (i.e., "Jehovah protects") and describes God's ministry of protection for His faithful people when the day of His anger arrives (2:3).

Zephaniah's major theme is the Day of the Lord, that period of time when God will judge the nations and usher in His righteous kingdom.[1] This theme is found in almost all the prophets, but it is particularly evident in Joel and Zephaniah. "The great day of the Lord is near" (Zeph. 1:14 NIV).

The Scriptures reveal very little about Zephaniah's personal life. He ministered in Judah during the time of King Josiah (640–609), who led the nation in a religious reformation triggered by the finding of the Book of the Law in the temple in the year 622 (2 Chron. 34:14ff).[2] It's likely that Zephaniah preached prior to this reformation, or he would have said something about it in his book. Jeremiah and Zephaniah were contemporaries.

Politically, the times were in ferment. Assyria was losing its power, the Scythians were invading from the north, and Babylon had become the leading empire. King Manasseh (697–642) had led the people of Judah deeper and deeper into idolatry and the adoption of foreign ideas and customs, and Josiah had sought to reverse this trend. Alas, King Josiah died on the battlefield before his work was finished, and his successors on the throne allowed the people to return to their sinful ways.

CHAPTER ELEVEN
THERE'S A GREAT DAY COMING!
Zephaniah 1:1–2:15

When was the last time you sang a hymn about the future judgment of the world? Most modern hymnals don't contain songs about the Day of the Lord, and you certainly won't find the phrase in your daily newspaper or weekly news magazine. Even if they do believe in God, most people don't connect Him in any way with either current or future events. The closest we come to involving God in human events is when insurance policies mention "acts of God over which we have no control." But that's a far cry from Zephaniah's the Day of the Lord.

Thinking people used to take God's judgment of the world seriously and even sang hymns about it. A famous medieval Latin hymn was based on Zephaniah 1:15, "That day is a day of wrath, a day of trouble and distress. . . ." The first two verses read:

> Day of wrath! O day of mourning!
> See fulfilled the prophets warning,
> Heav'n and earth in ashes burning!
>
> O what fear man's bosom rendeth
> When from Heav'n the Judge descendeth
> On whose sentence all dependeth![3]

I wonder how popular a worship leader would be if he or she selected that particular hymn today?

The Day of the Lord is an important biblical concept that we must take seriously, because it tells us where things are going and how they're going to end. During the Day of the Lord, God will send tribulation to the world, judge the nations, save His people Israel, and then establish His righteous kingdom. God warns the world that judgment is coming, and it's foolish for anybody to be unprepared. The big question is "Where will you hide on that great day?" (see Zeph. 2:3).

In the first two chapters of his book, the Prophet Zephaniah relates the Day of the Lord to both the Jews and the Gentiles.

1. The Day of the Lord and the Jews (Zeph. 1:1–2:4)

You would expect the great-great-grandson of King Hezekiah to be living comfortably in Jerusalem, enjoying a life of ease. Instead, you find him ministering as God's prophet, which was a dangerous calling. His contemporary, Jeremiah, was arrested and put in a filthy cistern for admonishing the leaders of Judah to surrender to the Babylonians.

God had shown Zephaniah that judgment was coming upon Judah in the form of the Babylonian Captivity, and the prophet had to share this message with the people. However, Babylon's invasion of Judah was but a feeble example of what would occur on that final Day of the Lord, which would sweep over all the earth. Zephaniah opened his book by presenting *three graphic pictures of the Day of the Lord.*

The first picture is that of a *devastating universal flood (Zeph. 1:2–3).* The Hebrew word translated "consume" in the KJV means "to sweep away completely." The picture is that of total devastation of all that God created and is probably a reference to Noah's flood. (You find similar wording in Gen. 6:7; 7:4; 9:8–10.) God gave man dominion over the fish, the fowls, and the beasts (1:28; Ps. 8:7–8), but man lost that dominion when Adam disobeyed God. However, through Jesus Christ, man's lost dominion will one day be restored (Heb. 2:5–9).

God will not only destroy His creation, but He will also destroy the idols that people worship—the "stumbling blocks" that offend the Lord (Ezek. 14:1–8). In Zephaniah's day, idolatry was rife in Judah, thanks to the evil influence of King Manasseh. When God stretches out His hand, it means that judgment is coming (Isa. 9:12, 17, 21). The prophet names two of the false gods that had captured the hearts of the people: Baal, the rain god of the Canaanites (Zeph. 1:4), and Malcom (Milcom, Molech), the terrible god of the Ammonites (1 Kings 11:33; Amos 5:26). The people also worshiped the host of heaven (Deut. 4:19; Jer. 19:13; 32:29) and followed the godless example of the idolatrous priests ("Chemarim"[4] in Zeph. 1:4; see 2 Kings 23:5, 8; Hosea 10:5).

These idolaters may have claimed that

they were still faithfully worshiping Jehovah, the true and living God, but Jehovah will not share worship or glory with any other god. In turning to idols, the people had turned away from the Lord and were not seeking Him or His blessing (Zeph. 1:6). They were guilty of sins of commission (worshiping idols) and omission (ignoring the Lord).

During the Babylonian Captivity, the Jews were cured of their fascination with foreign gods. Their temple was destroyed, their priesthood was scattered, and for seventy years they could not worship the way Moses had commanded them. When they were finally allowed to return to their land, one of the first things the Jews did was rebuild their temple and restore the sacrifices.

The second picture is that of a *great sacrifice* (vv. 7–13). Since the Jewish people were accustomed to attending communal sacrifices (1 Sam. 9:11ff), this image was familiar to them. But this sacrifice would be different, for it was God who was hosting the sacrifice. His guests were the Babylonians; and the sacrifices to be offered were the people of Judah! No wonder the prophet called for silence as he contemplated such an awesome event![5] (See Amos 6:10; 8:3; Hab. 2:20.)

You would expect the royal family and the religious leaders[6] of the land to be the honored guests at God's feast, but they are the ones to be sacrificed! (Zeph. 1:8–9). God punishes them because they have abandoned His Word and adopted foreign practices, including wearing foreign clothes and worshiping foreign gods (see Num. 15:38; Deut. 22:11–12). After the death of King Josiah in 609, the last four kings of Judah were weak men, who yielded to the policies of the pro-Egyptian bloc in the government. Instead of trusting the Lord, they trusted their allies, and this led to disaster.

Zephaniah must have been a resident in Jerusalem, for he know the layout of the city (Zeph. 1:10–13). When the Babylonians, God's guests, would come to the sacrificial feast, they would enter the city, plunder it, and then destroy it. The Fish Gate was where the fisherman had their markets; the "second quarter" was where the rich people lived in their fashionable houses, built from the wages owed to poor laborers. "Maktesh" was the market and business district of the city where the merchants and bankers were located.[7]

But the city would be destroyed, and the merchants' wealth confiscated. So thoroughly would the Babylonians do their work that they would search the city carefully and find even the people who were hiding.

The tragedy is that the invasion could have been avoided if the people had not been so complacent and indifferent toward what God was saying through His prophets. Judah was certain that the Lord was on their side because they were God's covenant people. They were like wine that sits undisturbed for a long time (Jer. 48:11; Amos 6:1) and congeals because it isn't poured from vessel to vessel to get rid of the bitter dregs. The worship of false gods had polluted the nation and the pure wine had become bitter.

The prophet's third picture of the Day of the Lord is that of *a great battle (Zeph. 1:14–18).* The description is a vivid one: You can hear the cries of the captives and the shouts of the warriors; you can see thunderclouds of judgment and flashes of lightning; you behold the victims' blood poured out like cheap dust and their "entrails like filth" (v. 17 NIV). What a scene of destruction and carnage, and all because the nation refused to submit to the Word of the Lord. The fire of God's jealous zeal[8] would consume everything, and no one would escape. Even the wealthy would not be able to ransom their lives, and the enemy would take away their ill-gotten riches.

What Zephaniah describes here is but an illustration of what will happen in the end times when God's judgment falls on a wicked world, only that final Day of the Lord will be far more terrible (see Rev. 6–19). There will be cosmic disturbances that will affect the course of nature and cause people to cry out for a place to hide (Amos 5:18; 8:9; Joel 2:1–2, 10, 30–32; Rev. 6:12–17). Unless you know Jesus Christ as your own Savior, you will have no place to hide (Zeph. 2:3).

This explains why the prophet closed this message with a plea for the people to repent of their sins and turn to the Lord for His forgiveness (vv. 1–3). Like the Prophet Joel (2:16), he told them to call a solemn assembly and seek the Lord. Zephaniah especially called upon the godly remnant ("you meek of the earth") to pray and seek God's face, perhaps referring to the promise in 2 Chronicles 7:14. But even if the majority of the nation followed false gods and turned away from the Lord, God would still protect His own precious remnant when the Day of Judgment comes (Mal. 3:16–18).

Zephaniah and Jeremiah ministered during the same period in history, and both of them begged the rulers to trust God and turn from sin, but the kings, officials, and priests refused to obey. God would have rescued the nation at the last minute, but the leaders were insensitive to God's call and disobedient to His Word.

But the Lord did spare a godly remnant that stayed true to Him throughout the seventy years of captivity. They were a "company of the concerned," who became the nucleus of the restored nation when they returned to the land. In every period in history it is the godly remnant that keeps the light burning when it seems as if the darkness is about to cover the earth. Today, God needs a "company of the concerned," who will walk the narrow road regardless of what others may do, obey God's Word, and share His Gospel with the lost. God is keeping His "book of remembrance" (Mal. 3:16–17), and you and I want our names in that book.

2. The Day of the Lord and the Gentiles (Zeph. 2:4–15)

God's judgment begins in the house of the Lord (1 Peter 4:17), which explains why Zephaniah started with the people of Judah; but now he explains how the Day of the Lord will affect the Gentile nations surrounding Judah. Though they were never given God's Law as were the Jews (Ps. 147:19–20), the Gentiles are still responsible before God; for God has revealed Himself to them in creation and conscience (Rom. 1:18ff). Furthermore, these nations had not always treated the Jews kindly, and now the time had arrived for God to judge them.

The nations named may represent all the Gentiles, since these nations correspond to the four points of the compass: Assyria (north), Cush (south), Moab and Ammon (east), and Philistia (west). During the great Day of the Lord, all the nations of the earth will taste the judgment of God.

Philistia (Zeph. 2:4–7). The Philistines were ancient enemies of the Jews (Gen. 20–21, 26). According to Amos 1:6–8, they took Jewish people captive from cities in southern Judah and sold them to other nations as slaves. But the time would come when their populous cities would be empty and their land left desolate, a place for shepherds to feed their flocks. Their coastal cities, made wealthy by vast shipping enterprises, would be destroyed by the enemy and left in ruins. Nebuchadnezzar invaded Philistia and conquered it, and the only remnant of that great nation left today is the name "Palestine," which comes from "Philistine" (see Ezek. 25:15–28:26).

However, the Jews will inhabit the land of the Philistines when the kingdom is established, and the Lord will enable them to live in peace. Zephaniah will later have more to say about this when he describes the kingdom blessings (Zeph. 3:9–20).

Moab and Ammon (Zeph. 2:8–11). The Moabites and Ammonites originated from Lot's incestuous union with his two daughters (Gen. 19:30–38) and were hateful enemies of the Jews (Num. 22; Jud. 3, 10; 1 Sam. 11:1–5; 2 Sam. 12:26ff). But these two arrogant nations would end up like Sodom and Gomorrah, wiped off the face of the earth (Gen. 19; note the connection here with Lot). No more would they insult either the nation of Israel or the God of Israel. (See Amos 1:13–2:3 for further evidence of the wickedness and inhumanity of these two nations.) Once again, the prophet promised that the Jews would occupy the land of their enemies when the kingdom is established (see also Ezek. 25:1–11).

Cush (Zeph. 2:12). This nation was located in the upper Nile region. Some students think the reference includes Egypt, another long time enemy of the Jews. It was Nebuchadnezzar and the swords of the Babylonian soldiers that conquered this ancient nation (Ezek. 30:4–5).

Assyria (Zeph. 2:13–15). Until the rise of Babylon, Assyria had been the dominant power, a ruthless people who were notorious for their pride and their cruelty to their enemies. A century and a half before, God had sent the Prophet Jonah to Assyria's capital city of Nineveh to warn them of God's judgment, and the people had repented, but successive generations went back to the old pagan ways, and Nineveh was destroyed in 612. Within the next few years, the once great Assyrian Empire simply vanished from the face of the earth, and Zephaniah saw it coming.

Because Nineveh thought it was an impregnable city, her citizens were careless and carefree when Zephaniah made his prediction, but God brought both the people and their city down into the dust of defeat. (See the Book of Nahum and Isa. 45; 47:10)

Since the predictions about the destruction of these nations have all come true, isn't it reasonable to assume that Zephaniah's other predictions will also be fulfilled? Each of these local invasions and conquests was a precursor of the end times Day of the Lord, which will come upon the whole world. But when the Day of the Lord has run its course, Israel will be delivered, and the Lord will establish His glorious kingdom on the earth. In the last chapter of his prophecy, Zephaniah explains how the Day of the Lord will relate to this promised kingdom.

Before we leave Zephaniah 1 and 2, we must note some practical truths that apply to believers today. First, God judges His people when they deliberately disobey His law. His people are to be different from the other nations and not imitate their ways or worship their gods (Num. 23:9; Ex. 33:16; Deut. 32:8). "Be not conformed to this world" is an admonition for all believers today (Rom. 12:2; see 2 Cor. 6:14–7:1).

Second, God's promise to Abraham still stands: Those who bless Israel, God will bless; those who curse Israel, God will curse (Gen. 12:1–3). The nations that have sinned against God by mistreating the Jews can expect Him to judge them.

Finally, God's Word is true and will be fulfilled in its time. God's people can claim His promises and know that their God will be faithful, and God's enemies can be sure that His words of warning carry costly penalties. "It is a fearful thing to fall into the hands of the living God" (Heb. 10:31).

CHAPTER TWELVE
THE GLORY OF THE KINGDOM
Zephaniah 3:1–20

Why did the prophets consistently close their books with messages of hope? For at least three reasons. To begin with, hope is a great motivation for obedience, and the prophets wanted to encourage God's people to submit to God's will and do what He commanded. God's covenant blessings come to His people only when they obey His covenant conditions.

A second reason is the prophets' emphasis on the faithfulness of God. The Lord will keep His promises and one day establish the kingdom; and since God is faithful to keep His promises, we ought to be faithful obeying His Word. If we obey, God will be faithful to chasten; if we confess, He will be faithful to forgive.

Finally, the closing message of hope was an encouragement to the faithful remnant in the land, who were true to God and suffered because of their devotion to Him. It's difficult to belong to that "company of the committed" who stand true to the Lord and His Word no matter what others may do or say. Knowing that God would one day defeat their enemies and reign in righteousness would encourage the believers remnant to persist in their faithful walk with the Lord.

In this last chapter, God reveals His plans for Jerusalem, the Gentile nations, and the faithful remnant. At the same time, the Lord reveals Himself and His gracious working on behalf of His people in every age and in every place.

1. Jerusalem: God's jealous anger (Zeph. 3:1–8)

Jerusalem is commonly called "the holy city,"[1] but in Zephaniah's day, the city didn't manifest much holiness! Isaiah (1:21ff), Jeremiah (29:12ff), and Ezekiel (4–6, 9) gave the same assessment in their day. Even the Gentiles called Jerusalem "the rebellious and wicked city" (Ezra 4:12, 15), and they could cite proof for their statement.

A sinning people (Zeph. 3:1–2). Instead of being holy, the city was filthy and polluted because of shameful sin; and instead of bringing peace ("Jerusalem" means "city of peace"), the city was guilty of rebellion and oppression. God gave His people the revelation of Himself in His Word and His mighty acts, yet they didn't believe Him or seek Him. "Draw near to God and He will draw near to you. Cleanse your hands, you sinners; and purify your hearts, you double-minded" (James 4:8 NKJV).

A godless leadership (Zeph. 3:3–4). God expected the civil and religious leaders of the land to take His Word seriously and lead the people in the way of righteousness. Instead, the leaders acted like ravenous beasts in the way they oppressed the people and took what they wanted from them. The prophets were unfaithful to the Lord and His Word and dealt treacherously with the people. They didn't proclaim God's truth; they only preached what the people wanted to hear.

As for the priests, their very ministry was toxic and polluted the sanctuary! (Matt. 23:25–28 relates what Jesus said about the Pharisees in His day.) Instead of serving God for His glory, the priests twisted the Law to please themselves and gain what they wanted.

The tragedy is that God had spoken to His people and corrected them in discipline, and yet they wouldn't listen or obey (Zeph. 3:2). "If in spite of these things you do not accept my correction but continue to be hostile toward me, I myself will be hostile toward you and will afflict you for your sins seven times over" (Lev. 26:23–24 NIV). This was the message of Jeremiah to the city of Jerusalem even while Babylon was poised to attack (Jer. 2:30; 5:3; 7:8; 17:23; 32:33).

A righteous God (Zeph. 3:5–8). God's name was identified with the city and the temple (2 Sam. 7:13; 1 Kings 5:5; Neh. 1:9), and yet both were cesspools of iniquity. Therefore, He would have to act in judgment for His own name's sake. The wicked officials met at the city gate morning after morning to transact their evil business, and the Lord was there to behold their deeds. How patiently He waited, and yet they would not repent and turn to Him for cleansing!

Since the Lord reminded His people that He had judged the Gentiles and cut off nations (Zeph. 3:6), He was able to cut Judah off as well. In fact, the Jews were more guilty than were the Gentiles because the Lord had given Israel more truth and more blessing. The people were sinning against a flood of light. Surely God's judgment of the other nations should have awakened the Jews to their peril, but they paid no attention. After all, they were God's covenant people, and He would protect them from their enemies. They forgot that covenant privileges also involved covenant responsibilities.

The Lord concludes this message to Jerusalem by describing a courtroom scene in which He stands to testify against His people (v. 8). While the impending Babylonian Captivity is involved here, there is also an end-times application in the Battle of Armageddon, when the nations of the world converge against Jerusalem. God will pour out His wrath upon these nations, deliver His people, and establish His kingdom (Zech. 14:1–9). His jealous anger will burn like fire against all who resist His truth and disobey His Word. The terrible Day of the Lord will dawn and there will be no escape (see Zeph. 1:2ff).

2. The Gentiles: God's gracious forgiveness (Zeph. 3:9–10)

It's important to keep in mind that God's call of Abraham involved bringing God's blessing to the whole world (Gen. 12:1–3). God accomplished this by giving the Jews the knowledge of the true God, the written Word of God, and the Savior, Jesus Christ (Rom. 9:1–5). Therefore, they were to share these blessings with the Gentiles.

The Jews were supposed to magnify the Lord's name before the Gentiles. Instead, they imitated the pagan nations and disgraced God's name (Isa. 52:5; Rom. 2:24). The court of the Gentiles in the Jewish temple was supposed to be the place where Gentiles could talk with Jews about the true God and even pray to Him, but the religious leaders made that area into a market for selling sacrifices and exchanging money. What kind of testimony was that to the outsiders who were earnestly seeking the truth?

What blessings does God promise for the Gentiles in the last days? First, He promises that *the Gentiles shall be converted (Zeph. 3:9).* Instead of calling on their false gods, the Gentiles will call upon the true and living God and have their lips purified. Since what we say with our lips comes from the heart (Matt. 12:34–35), cleansed lips indicate forgiven sin and a cleansed heart (Isa. 6:1–8).

But the Gentiles will do much more than call on the Lord and receive His cleansing; they will also serve the Lord as one people and no longer be divided ("serve Him shoulder to shoulder," Zeph. 3:9 NIV). The prophets teach that during the Kingdom Age the Gentiles will go to Jerusalem to worship and serve the Lord (Isa. 2:1–5; 4:1–6; Ezek. 40–48; Zech. 14:9ff).2 The God of Israel will be the Lord of all the earth, and the Gentile nations will honor and serve Him. Along with the scattered Israelites who return to their land, the Gentiles will bring the Lord offerings and be called His "worshipers."

Before our Lord's death on the cross, there was a vast difference between the relationship of Jews and Gentiles to each other and to the Lord. But the middle wall that separated them has now been taken down (Eph. 2:11ff), and both can share in the spiritual blessings that come through faith in Christ. "For there is no distinction between Jew and Greek, for the same Lord over all is rich unto all who call upon Him. For *'whoever calls on the name of the Lord shall be saved'*" (Rom. 10:12-13 NKJV). This miracle of God's grace will be demonstrated in the Kingdom Age as the Gentile nations trust and worship the God of Israel.

3. The remnant: God's bounteous blessing (Zeph. 3:11–20)

When the terrible Day of the Lord is over, Israel will be a new nation. The Jews will look by faith upon the Messiah whom they crucified, believe in Him, and enter into a new life in the promised kingdom.

Sin will be removed (Zeph. 3:11–13). The Jews won't have to be "put to shame" because, when they see Christ, they will be ashamed of what they did to the Lord and will mourn over their transgressions (Zech. 12:10–13:1). It will be a time of deep repentance and confession that will lead to salvation. God will especially deal with the pride of Israel that for centuries had kept them from submitting humbly to the righteousness of God that comes only by faith in Christ (Rom. 9:30–10:13; Phil. 3:1–12). There will be no place on God's holy hill for proud sinners who think they can earn God's salvation by their good works. In contrast to the proud sinners will be the believing remnant, the "meek and humble, who trust in the name of the Lord" (Zeph. 3:12 NIV).

Faith in Christ will make everything new so that the people will no longer disobey God or practice deception. This suggests that all love of idolatry will be taken from their hearts, for idols are lies and to worship them is to practice deception. For the first time in centuries, the Jews will be able to enjoy their meals and their sleep, for all their enemies will have been defeated. During the years of their worldwide dispersion, in many places the Jews have been subjected to threats and intimidation, even fearing for their lives (Deut. 28:63–68), but that will end when God establishes the kingdom and Christ reigns over the nations.

God's people will rejoice (Zeph. 3:14–17). This is one of the most poignant passages in Scripture. It depicts the Lord as a loving mother, singing over her children and finding joy in their presence. The people of God sing and shout because of all that God has done for them. He has taken away their punishment, defeated their enemies, and come to dwell with them. Furthermore, He has guaranteed that the people of Israel will never again be afraid. Because the Lord is the King of Israel, His people have nothing to fear.

When Pilate presented a suffering Jesus to the Jewish leaders, they rejected Him and shouted, "We have no king but Caesar" (John 19:15). But now the Jewish people will joyfully acknowledge that Jesus Christ is King of kings and Lord of lords (Phil. 2:9–11). Instead of standing dejectedly like defeated prisoners of war, the Jews will enthusiastically shout God's praises.

What do they have to sing about? To begin with, they have God's presence with them and God's power working for them (Zeph. 3:17). Even more, their God holds them next to His heart like a loving mother holds a baby; He quiets them with His love,[3] and He even sings to them! This image of "the motherhood of God" assures forgiven sinners that God is with them, that He loves them, and that they have nothing to fear.[4]

Our God is a "singing" God. God the Father sings to the Jewish remnant entering the kingdom (v. 17). God the Son sang at the close of the Passover Feast, and then went to the garden to pray (Matt. 26:30). He also sang after His triumphant resurrection from the dead (Ps. 22:22; Heb. 2:12). God the Spirit sings today through the hearts and lips of Christians who praise God in the Spirit (Eph. 5:18–21).

The nation will be restored (Zeph. 3:18–20). During the seventy years of captivity in Babylon, and then during their worldwide dispersion among the Gentiles after A.D. 70, devout Jews were not able to celebrate their appointed feasts (Lev. 23). Since the destruction of the temple in A.D. 70, the Jewish people have had no temple, altar, priesthood, or sacrifice (Hosea 3:4–5). Of course, the types and symbols of the Old Testament Law have all been fulfilled in

Christ, including the feasts and sacrifices (Heb. 10), but Zephaniah intimates that these feasts will be restored in the Kingdom Age, and Zechariah 14:16–21 seems to support this interpretation.

Why would the Lord restore religious practices that have now been fulfilled? Possibly as a means of teaching Israel the meaning of the doctrine of salvation through Jesus Christ. The feasts described in Leviticus 23 picture "salvation history," from the slaying of the Passover lamb (John 1:29) to the Day of Atonement (the cleansing of Israel) and the Feat of Tabernacles (the Kingdom Age). The Prophet Ezekiel describes in great detail the structure and services of a great temple in Israel (Ezek. 40–48), and this includes the offering of the levitical sacrifices. Just as the Old Testament types looked forward to the coming of the Savior, perhaps during the Kingdom Age these rituals will look back to His finished work.

God's promise is that His scattered people will be gathered, His lame people will be rescued, and His sinful people will be forgiven and no longer bear the shame of their wicked deeds. "I will bring you home" (Zeph. 3:20 NIV) is God's gracious promise, and He will keep it. Where once the Jewish nation brought shame and disgrace to God's name and were poor witnesses to the Gentiles, now Israel will bring honor and praise to the Lord their God and reveal to the Gentile nations the glory of His name. Israel will receive honor from the Gentiles and give the glory to the Lord.

The state of Israel was "born" on May 14, 1948, but that event, significant as it is, was not the fulfillment of God's promise to regather His people and restore their fortunes. That promise will be fulfilled in the end times, after the Jews have experienced the Day of the Lord and been prepared to see their Messiah. But God's promises will be fulfilled, and God's people Israel will be restored and bring worldwide glory to the God of Abraham, Isaac, and Jacob, the God and Father of our Lord Jesus Christ.

But there is a present-day practical lesson here for any of God's people who have strayed from His will and have experienced His chastening. When you come to Him with a broken heart, confessing your sins, He will receive you the way a loving mother receives a disobedient child. He will love you and even sing to you! He will bring peace to your heart and "quiet you in His love." Yes, we suffer for our disobedience; and sometimes we carry the scars of that disobedience for the rest of our lives. But the Lord will forgive us (1John 1:9), forget our sins, and restore us into His loving fellowship.

Dr. William Culbertson, late president of Moody Bible Institute, sometimes ended his public prayers with, "And Lord, help us bear the consequence of forgiven sin and to end well." There are consequences to forgiven sin; for though God in His grace cleanses us, God in His government says, "You will reap what you have sown." After King David confessed his sin, the Prophet Nathan assured him that the Lord had put away his sin, but the rest of his days, David suffered the tragic consequences of what he had done (2 Sam. 12:1–15).

But when God establishes His kingdom on earth, He will restore His people, renew the land, and give His people a new beginning that will cause them to forget their past disobedience and focus on praising the Lord and glorifying His name.

Jehovah is "the God of hope." Therefore, He can fill us with "all joy and peace in believing" so that we can "abound in hope by the power of the Holy Spirit" (Rom. 15:13 NKJV).

Is that your experience today?

CHAPTER THREE YOU IN YOUR TIME

It does us little good to learn about the times of the Minor Prophets if we don't do something in our own times.

Situations vary from nation to nation, but the statistics for my own country aren't too encouraging.[1]

- Since 1960, the rate of births to unmarried teenagers has increased 200 percent.
- Since 1960, violent crime has increased by 560 percent.
- The fastest growing segment of the criminal population is children. Between 1982 and 1991, the arrest rate for juvenile murder increased 93 percent.
- The average child will watch up to 8,000

murders and 100,000 acts of violence on TV by the time he or she leaves grade school.

• Eight out of ten Americans can expect to be the victim of violent crime at least once in their lives.

• Since 1960, teen suicides have more than tripled. It is now the second leading cause of death among teens.

• The top problems in high schools are alcohol and drug abuse, pregnancy, suicide, rape, and robbery.

As go the homes, churches, and schools, so goes the nation. It's time to be concerned.

THE COMPANY OF THE CONCERNED

One of the key truths found in the Minor Prophets is the presence of a godly remnant in times of moral and spiritual decay. This remnant is a small group of people whose devotion to the Lord can make a difference in the nation. After all, if God had found as many as ten righteous people in Sodom, He would have spared the whole city! (Gen. 18:32).

Israel was at its lowest ebb during the period of the Judges. Yet God could always find a dedicated man or woman to lead His armies to deliver His people. Elijah thought he was the only faithful person left in the land, but God informed him that He had 7,000 who hadn't bowed the knee to Baal (1 Kings 19:18). The Prophet Isaiah wrote, "Unless the Lord of hosts had left to us a very small remnant, we would have become like Sodom, we would have been made like Gomorrah" (Isa. 1:9 NKJV).

I like to call this godly remnant "the company of the concerned." They are people who are truly concerned about the will of the Lord and the character of their country, people who are distressed by evil and want to do something about it. The Prophet Ezekiel had a vision of the remnant in his day: "Go through the midst of the city, through the midst of Jerusalem, and set a mark upon the foreheads of the men that sigh and that cry for all the abominations that be done in the midst thereof" (Ezek. 9:4). The NIV translates "sigh" and "cry" as "grieve" and "lament."

Whoever wrote Psalm 119 belonged to the "sighers and criers" of his day. "Indignation grips me," he wrote, "because of the wicked, who have forsaken your law" (v. 53 NIV); and he confessed, "I am a companion of all those who fear you, and of those who keep Your precepts" (v. 63 NKJV). He was an encouragement to others who belonged to the "company of the concerned," for he said, "Those who fear You will be glad when they see me, because I have hoped in Your word" (v. 74 NKJV). And he told the careless sinners in the land, "Depart from me, you evildoers, for I will keep the commandments of my God!" (v. 115, NKJV).

But I need to make one thing clear from the beginning: I'm not talking about people motivated by anger so much as by anguish. Certainly there's a place for righteous anger in the Christian life (Eph. 4:26), but anger alone may do more harm than good. "For the wrath of man does not produce the righteousness of God" (James 1:20 NKJV). When righteous anger is mingled with compassion, you have anguish; and anguish is what the "company of the concerned" feel as they behold the moral and spiritual decline of the nation. "Rivers of water run down from my eyes, because men do not keep Your law" (Ps. 119:136 NKJV). "Trouble and anguish have overtaken me, yet Your commandments are my delights" (v. 143 NKJV).

Each of the prophets whose writings we have studied belonged to the "company of the concerned," and they are good examples for us to follow.

First, they were totally committed to the Lord. Amos was an ordinary farmer and shepherd, untrained in the schools of the prophets; yet God called him to deliver His message at a strategic time in history. As I travel in ministry, I'm more and more impressed by the "laypeople" God has called to serve Him in significant places, people who have no professional ministerial training, yet who are doing great things for the glory of the Lord.[2] Robert Murray M'Cheyne wrote, "It is not great talents God blesses so much as great likeness to Jesus. A holy minister is an awful weapon in the hand of God."

The "company of the concerned" is made up of people who are separated from sin (Rom. 12:1–2; 2 Cor. 6:14–7:1), but who are not isolated from the real world. They aren't "holier than thou" in their attitude toward sinners. They have the courage to be different (but not odd) and to walk the narrow road no matter what it may cost them. They are people who pray consistently for those in authority (1 Tim. 2:1–4). It does no good to write letters and protest if we aren't praying for those leading our nation.

Second, the "company of the committed" is composed of people who have a proper fear of God in their hearts. The prophets certainly teach the love of God toward His people and toward lost sinners, but they also remind us that "our God is a consuming fire" (Heb. 12:29). They believed the Word of God and knew that judgment was coming to the land.

The only nation on earth that is in a special covenant relationship with God is the nation of Israel. While many of the founding fathers of the United States of America were God-fearing men, the people of the United States can't claim special privileges from God because of their citizenship. It's true that the Puritan forefathers felt called to build God's kingdom on American soil, but we have no biblical basis for their vision.

What do we have? The promises of God for those of His people who will obey 2 Chronicles 7:14 and intercede for their country. God works in response to believing prayer, and believing prayer must be based on the Word of God.

The fear of the Lord is the fear that conquers every fear. John Wesley said, "Give me one hundred preachers who fear nothing but sin and desire nothing but God, and I care not a straw whether they be clergymen or laymen, such alone will shake the gates of hell and set up the kingdom of God on earth." He was describing the "company of the concerned."

Third, the "company of the concerned" is indeed a company, composed of believers who realize that God wants His people to "flock together" and not try to do everything alone. The most dangerous believers are those who aren't accountable to anybody but do whatever they please and think they're serving God. They write angry letters to government officials, media people, and even local pastors, and often they don't sign their names. God has called them to set everything right in the world, even though they often don't really understand the problems they're trying to solve. Instead of belonging to the "company of the concerned," they're charter members of the "Company of the Confused".

Malachi 3:16 is a good description of the kind of "company" God is looking for: "Then those who feared the Lord spoke to one another, and the Lord listened and heard them; so a book of remembrance was written before Him for those who fear the Lord and who meditate in His name" (NKJV). "The more the truths by which we believe are contradicted," said Alexander Maclaren, "the more should we commune with fellow-believers." When you study the "one another" statements of the New Testament, you discover how much Christians need one another and need to minister to one another. It has well been said that you can't raise one Christian any more than you can raise one bee.

To be sure, every local church has its weaknesses and faults, but it's the family of God, and that's where we belong. Nobody was born into a perfect family. Yet we love our brothers and sisters and try to ignore the things that irritate us. When Jesus sent out the twelve apostles, He sent them out two-by-two, because "two are better than one" (Ecc. 4:9). People who are a part of the "company of the concerned" don't try to go it alone. They love one another, pray for one another, and seek to encourage one another.

Something else is true: They realize the importance of righteousness and justice in the land. "Righteousness exalts a nation, but sin is a reproach to any people" (Prov. 14:34 NKJV). The believers in the "company of the concerned" seek to be salt and light in the land (Matt. 5:13–16) and do all they can to prevent decay and dispel darkness. The influence of their character, conduct, and witness promotes righteousness, whether it's in their daily work, the way they vote or pay their taxes, their example, the way they raise their children, or how they invest their time and money.

Nehemiah is a person who exemplifies what it means to be in the "company of the concerned." When he heard about the tragic condition of Jerusalem, he sat down and wept, knelt down and prayed, and then stood up and worked to change things (Neh. 1–2). He could have excused himself by arguing, "It's not my fault that Jerusalem is in ruins," or "I have a job to do right here in the palace." Nehemiah never read the words of Edmund Burke, but he lived by them: "It is necessary only for the good man to do nothing for evil to triumph."

When you read the Book of Nehemiah, you

meet a man who enlisted the help of the Jewish leaders and rallied the common people to rebuild the wall of the city. He didn't try to do it alone. He was a man of prayer who trusted God to supply the needs and defeat the enemies around Jerusalem. In fifty-two days, the job was done, and the song of praise from Jerusalem could be heard for miles.

Much more can be said about the "company of the concerned," but let me close with this observation: these people know the importance of good leadership in the nation. "Everything rises and falls with leadership," claims Dr. Lee Roberson, and he's right. However, during the times of the prophets, the leaders of Israel and Judah were too often selfish, disobedient to God's Law, and unwilling to trust Him for the wisdom and help that they needed. The prophets warned the kings, princes, and priests that their sins would ruin the nation, but the men refused to listen. After Judah was ravaged and Jerusalem and the temple ruined, Jeremiah wrote that it had been caused by "the sins of her prophets, and the iniquities of her priests" (Lam. 4:13).

A democracy is not a theocracy, where the king is God's representative on earth; nor is a pluralistic society the same as the homogeneous society of the Jewish people, who were all governed by the same moral code. But leaders in a democracy should still be expected to be men and women of character, who practice honesty and integrity and who genuinely care for their people. Someone has said that a politician is concerned about his party and asks, "Is it popular?" The diplomat is concerned with policy and asks, "Is it safe?" But the statesman is concerned about the good of the nation and asks, "Is it right?"

Edward Everett Hale, author of *The Man without a Country*, wrote:

> I am only one, but still I am one. I cannot do every-
> thing, but still I can do something. And because I
> cannot do everything, I will not refuse to do the
> something that I can do.

That's a good motto for the "company of the concerned." But add to it the great words of Paul: "I can do all things through Christ who strengthens me . . . for it is God who works in you both to will and to do for His good pleasure" (Phil. 4:13; 2:13 NKJV).

It's time to be concerned.

Endnotes

Zephaniah in HIs Day, and Chapter 1

1. Strictly speaking, any time of divine judgment could be called the Day of the Lord. Local judgments were but examples of the final Day of the Lord to occur in the end times.

2. Some students call this "Josiah's revival," but it's doubtful that "revival" is the best word. Certainly the people put away their false gods and returned to the worship of Jehovah, but their motivation was not spiritual. Since the king commanded them to abandon the foreign gods, the people obeyed more from a fear of the king than a love for the Lord. The changes were only on the surface of the nation; the people's hearts were still devoted to the false gods. No sooner was Josiah dead than the nation reverted to their old ways. What they experienced was a surface reformation but not a deep revival.

3. The hymn is attributed to Thomas of Celano. This translation of "Dies Irae" ("day of wrath") is by William J. Irons.

4. The root of the Hebrew word means either "black," referring to the color of their robes (Jewish priests wore white), or "zealous," referring to the frenzy of their religious ceremonies as they prostrated themselves before their gods.

5. For other instances of judgment depicted as sacrifice, see Isaiah 34:5–7, Jeremiah 46:10, and Ezekiel 39:17–19; and note Revelation 19:17–21.

6. The phrase "leap on [over] the threshold" in verse 9 is usually related to the pagan practice described in 1 Samuel 5:1–5, but perhaps it describes the haste with which the covetous Jews left their houses to go out to exploit the poor and acquire wealth to devote to their false gods. The prophets condemned the rich for their brutal treatment of the poor in the land.

7. Maktesh means "mortar" in Hebrew, possibly because the district lay in a part of Jerusalem that was in a natural depression. But perhaps there is a double meaning here: God would deal with His people the way women pound grain in a mortar.

8. The Hebrew word translated "jealously" (1:18; 3:8) means "to be hot, to be inflamed." God's jealousy is not like human envy, for what could God envy when He has everything? He is jealous over His name and His glory, and His anger is aroused when His people worship other gods (Ex. 34:14; Pss. 78:58; 79:5). God is jealous over His people and wants their wholehearted love and devotion.

Chapter 2

1. See Nehemiah 11:1, 18; Isaiah 48:2; 52:1; Daniel 9:24; Matthew 4:5; 27:53; Revelation 11:2; 21:2; 22:19.

2. Interpreters are divided over whether the prophets are speaking literally (a real temple with real priests and sacrifices) or metaphorically (the temple as symbolic of worship and service in the new Kingdom Age). Certainly the prophets had to use language and

images that the people understood, but if these predictions are not to be take literally, it's difficult to understand why the prophets (especially Ezekiel) wrote in such great detail.

3. The Hebrew phrase has been variously explained: "He will quiet you with His love"; "He will be silent in His love" (i.e., not bring up your past sins); "He will renew you in His love"; "He will renew your love for Him"; "His love for you will make everything new." Perhaps it all means the same thing: A new and deeper relationship with God will bring peace and joy and make all things new.

4. Other passages that speak of the "motherhood of God" are Isaiah 49:14–16, 66:13; and Matthew 23:37–39. Psalm 131 might also be included, and see also 1 Thessalonians 2:7–8.

Chapter 3

1. Statistics taken from the *Index of Leading Cultural Indicators* by William J. Bennett (New York: Simon and Schuster, 1994).

2. This statement isn't a criticism of ministerial education. Since I teach for several evangelical Christian schools, I'm not anti-intellectual. But often God lays hold of "untrained" people and trains them in His own way to accomplish His work. There's a place in God's vineyard for a brilliant Jonathan Edwards and also for a D. L. Moody, who probably had the equivalent of a sixth-grade education.

HAGGAI

OUTLINE

Key theme: Complete the work you have begun

Key verse: Haggai 1:8

I. FIRST MESSAGE: CONVICTION — 1:1-15

1. Stop making excuses—1-4
2. Start considering your ways—5-11
3. Begin to serve the Lord—12-15

II. SECOND MESSAGE: COMPARISON —2:1-9

1. Discouragement—1-3
2. Encouragement—4-9
   (1) Be strong—4
   (2) Fear not—5
   (3) Glory will come—6-7
   (4) God will provide—8-9

III. THIRD MESSAGE: CONTAMINATION—2:10-19

1. The question of defilement—10-13
2. The assurance of blessing—14-19

IV. FOURTH MESSAGE: CORONATION—2:20-23

1. The coming judgment—20-22
2. The promised Messiah—23

CONTENTS

CHAPTER ONE
STIRRING UP GOD'S PEOPLE
Haggai 1

When the foundations of the temple were laid in Jerusalem in the year 536, the younger men shouted for joy while the older men wept (Ezra 3:8-13). Although Haggai probably had seen Solomon's temple in its glory (Hag. 2:3), he was undoubtedly among those who expressed joy, for the Lord was at work among His people.

But it doesn't take long for zeal to cool and God's people to grow apathetic, especially when opposition began an ominous growl that soon became a roar. The shout awakened the enemies of the Jews, aroused official opposition, and caused the work to stop (Ezra 4:1-6, 24); and the temple lay unfinished from 536 to 520, when Haggai and Zechariah brought God's message to Zerubbabel and Joshua.

In this first message, the prophet gave four admonitions to the leaders and to the people to encourage them to get back to work and finish rebuilding the temple.

1. "Put God first in your lives" (Hag. 1:1-4)

The first statement in the divine message went right to the heart of the problem and exposed the hypocrisy and unbelief of the people.

Excuses. "It isn't time to rebuild the house of the Lord" was their defense of their inactivity. Billy Sunday called an excuse "the skin of a reason stuffed with a lie," and Benjamin Franklin wrote, "I never knew a man who was good at making excuses who was good at anything else."

The first congregation I pastored met in a corrugated metal tabernacle that should have been replaced years before, but whenever somebody would suggest a building program, some of the fearful people would resurrect their excuses for maintaining the status quo. "The economy isn't good and there might be another strike," was the major excuse we heard, but in that part of the country, there were always strikes! And who can predict or control the economy? "Our pastors don't stay long," one member told me, "and it would be a tragedy to be in a building program without a leader." But the Lord led us to build a lovely sanctuary and He saw us through!

Evidence. What more evidence did the Jewish people need that God's time had come? How could they doubt that it was God's will for them to rebuild the temple and restore true worship in Jerusalem? Hadn't God moved King Cyrus to free the exiles and commission them to return to Jerusalem for that very purpose? (See 2 Chron. 36:22-23; Ezra 1:1-4.) Didn't the king generously give them the money and materials they needed, and didn't the Lord graciously protect the exiles carrying the temple treasures as they traveled from Babylon to Judah?

The Jews certainly knew the words that the Prophet Isaiah had recorded about Cyrus: "He is My shepherd, and he shall perform all My pleasure, even saying to Jerusalem, 'You shall be rebuilt,' and the temple, 'Your foundation shall be laid' "(Isa. 44:28, NKJV). Isaiah had also written, "I have raised him [Cyrus] up in righteousness, and I will direct all his ways; he shall build My city and let My exiles go free" (Isa. 45:13). By stopping their work, the Jews were admitting that they had no faith in God's Word or in God's power to perform it.

In the light of these facts, on what basis were the people refusing to obey God and build His house? For one thing, both Isaiah and Jeremiah had predicted a national restoration that would amaze the Gentile nations and bring glory to Israel, but that wonderful event had not yet occurred. (See Isa. 2:1-5; 11; 35; 60:1-5; Jer. 30–31.) The people failed to understand that some of these promises would be fulfilled in the end times ("the last days"); and when the situation in Judah became worse, the people questioned the dependability of the Word of God.

Perhaps some of the scribes studied Jeremiah's promise about the seventy years of captivity (25:1-14) and decided that the allotted time hadn't yet ended. Only fifty years had transpired since the temple had been destroyed in 586, said the experts, so the Jews would have to wait another twenty years for the prophecy to be fulfilled. God took them at their word, and the work stopped for sixteen years.[1] The temple was completed in 515, so the scholars got their seventy years accounted for!

Evasion. The people were terribly inconsistent: it wasn't time to build the house of God, but it was time to build their own houses! And some of the people had built, not just ordinary dwellings, but "paneled houses," the kind that kings built for themselves (1 Kings 7:3, 7; Jer. 22:14).

"But seek first the kingdom of God and His righteousness, and all these things [food, clothing, shelter] shall be added to you" (Matt. 6:33, NKJV). Haggai's congregation had never heard that great promise, but the principle behind Christ's words was written into their Law. "Honor the Lord with your possessions, and with the firstfruits of all your increase; so your barns will be filled with plenty, and your vats will overflow with new wine" (Prov. 3:9-10, NKJV; and see Lev. 26:3-13; Deut. 16:17; 28:1-14; 30:3-9).

It's obvious that the nation had its priorities confused, but are God's people today any different from those ancient Jews?

Local churches can't expand their budgets for world evangelism because the money isn't there, and yet many church members don't believe Matthew 6:33 and put God first in their giving. Measured by Third World standards, Christians in the Western world are living in luxury, yet their giving is low and their debts are high because their wealth is being used for things that really don't matter.

When we put God first and give Him what's rightfully His, we open the door to spiritual enrichment and the kind of stewardship that honors the Lord. A century after Haggai ministered, the Prophet Malachi accused the people of robbing God of tithes and offerings and thereby robbing themselves of blessing (Mal. 3:7-12); and his words need to be heeded today.

2. "Believe God's promises" (Hag. 1:5-6, 9-11)

Haggai's second admonition invited the people to examine their lifestyle and actions in the light of the covenant God made with them before the nation entered the land of Canaan (Lev. 26; Deut. 27–28). The word translated "consider" in the KJV is translated "give careful thought to" in the NIV (Hag. 1:5). It was time for the people to do some serious self-examination before the Lord.

God's covenant stated clearly that He would bless them if they obeyed His Law and discipline them if they disobeyed. "If you do not obey Me, then I will punish you seven times more for your sins. I will break the pride of your power; I will make your heavens like iron and your earth like bronze. And your strength shall be spent in vain; for your land shall not yield its produce, nor shall the trees of the land yield their fruit" (Lev. 26:18-20; see Deut. 28:38-40).

Indeed, their strength was spent in vain! They sowed abundantly but reaped a meager harvest. When they ate and drank, they weren't filled or satisfied. Their clothing didn't keep them warm and their income didn't cover their expenses. As supplies became scarcer, prices got higher, and a shopper might as well have carried his wealth in a wallet filled with holes!

While I don't believe that the Old Testament tithe is demanded of the New Testament believer (Acts 5:1-4), I think that tithing is a good place to start when it comes to systematic stewardship. After all, if an Old Covenant Jew under Law could gladly give tithes to the Lord, should a New Covenant believer under grace do less? But the tithe is only a start! The principles laid down in 2 Corinthians 8–9 encourage us to give offerings to the Lord and trust Him for all that we need (see 2 Cor. 8:9).

Because the Jews returned to the land in obedience to the Lord, they thought He would give them special blessings because of their sacrifices, but they were disappointed (Hag. 1:9). Instead, the Lord called for a drought and withheld both the dew and the rain. He took His blessing away from the men who labored in the fields, vineyards, and orchards. In verse 11, Haggai named the basic products that the people needed to survive: water, grain, wine, and oil (Deut. 7:13; 11:14).

Once more, the prophet revealed the source of their trouble: the people were busy building their own houses and had no time for the house of the Lord (Hag. 1:9). It's Matthew 6:33 all over again! Had the nation believed what God promised in His covenants, they would have obeyed Him and enjoyed His blessing.

However, we must be careful not to turn giving into a "business arrangement," for our obedience should be the evidence of our love and faith. Christian industrialist R.G.

LeTourneau used to say, "If you give because it pays, it won't pay!" He was right.

The Lord never made a "prosperity covenant" with the church as He did with Israel. In fact, our Lord's first statement in the Sermon on the Mount is, "Blessed are the poor in spirit, for theirs is the kingdom of heaven" (Matt. 5:3). "Blessed are you poor, for yours is the kingdom of God" (Luke 6:20). God has seen fit to bless some Christians with wealth, but it isn't a guarantee for every believer, in spite of what the contemporary "prosperity preachers" claim. If we help to meet the needs of others, God does promise to meet our needs (Phil. 4:10-20; 2 Cor. 9:6-1), but this isn't a pledge of material prosperity. No matter how much God gives us materially, we all must say with Paul, "as poor, yet making many rich" (2 Cor. 6:10).

3. "Honor God's name" (Hag. 1:7-8)

When the Babylonian army set fire to the temple, this destroyed the great timbers that helped to hold the massive stonework together. The stones were still usable, but the interior woodwork had been demolished and burned and had to be replaced.

According to Ezra 3:7, the Jews purchased wood from Tyre and Sidon, just as Solomon had done when he built the original temple (1 Kings 5:6-12). Now Haggai commanded the men to go into the forests on the mountains and cut down timber to be used for repairing and rebuilding the temple. What happened to that original supply of wood? Did the people use it for themselves? Did some clever entrepreneur profit by selling wood that had been bought with the king's grant? We don't know, but we wonder where the people got the wood for their paneled houses when no wood was available for God's house.

During nearly fifty years of ministry, I've noted that some professed Christians buy the best for themselves and give to the Lord whatever is left over. Worn-out furniture is given to the church and worn-out clothing is sent to the missionaries. Like the priests in Malachi's day, we bring to the Lord gifts we'd be embarrassed to give to our family and friends (Mal. 1:6-8). But when we do this, we commit two sins: (1) we displease the Lord, and (2) we disgrace His name. The Lord told the people through Haggai, "Build the house, so that I may take pleasure in it and be honored" (Hag. 1:7). God delights in the obedient service of His people, and His name is glorified when we sacrifice for Him and serve Him.[2]

"Hallowed be Thy name" is the first petition in the Lord's Prayer (Matt. 6:9), but it's often the last thing we think about as we seek to serve God. Jesus said, "I do always those things that please Him [the Father]" (John 8:29), and that's a good example for us to follow. "Let your light so shine before men, that they may see your good works, and glorify your Father, who is in heaven" (Matt. 5:16).

It certainly didn't please God or honor His name when the people neglected God's house and built elaborate houses for themselves. We know that God doesn't live in temples made by hands (Acts 7:48-50), and that our church buildings are not His holy habitation, but the way we care for these buildings reflects our spiritual priorities and our love for Him. Dr. G. Campbell Morgan said it best in a sermon he preached on Haggai 1:4 many years ago:

> Whereas the house of God today is no longer material but spiritual, the material is still a very real symbol of the spiritual. When the Church of God in any place in any locality is careless about the material place of assembly, the place of its worship and its work, it is a sign and evidence that its life is at a low ebb.[3]

4. "Obey His command" (Hag. 1:12-15)

When God speaks to us by His Word, there's only one acceptable response, and that's obedience. We don't weigh the options, we don't examine the alternatives, and we don't negotiate the terms. We simply do what God tells us to do and leave the rest with Him. "Faith is not believing in spite of evidence," said the British preacher Geoffrey Studdert-Kennedy; "it's obeying in spite of consequence."

The leaders and all the people united in obeying God's instructions, and they were motivated by a reverent fear of the Lord (v. 12). After all, He is the "Lord of hosts," a title used ten times in this little book (vv. 2, 9, 14; 2:4, 7, 8, 9, 23). It means "the Lord of the armies," the God who is in supreme command of the armies of heaven (stars and angels) and of earth.[4] Obedience always brings further truth (John 7:17), and the prophet assured them that God was with them in their endeavors (Hag. 1:13; see 2:4).

"The Lord of hosts is with us; the God of Jacob is our refuge" (Ps. 46:7, 11). The obedience of the leaders and people was the result of God working in their hearts, just as He had worked in the heart of King Cyrus and in the hearts of the exiles who had returned to Jerusalem with Zerubbabel (Ezra 1:5). "For it is God who works in you both to will and to do for His good pleasure" (Phil. 2:13, NKJV).

Haggai delivered this first message on August 29, 520, but it wasn't until September 21 that the people resumed their work on the temple. Why the three-week delay? For one thing, it was the month when figs and grapes were harvested, and the people didn't want to lose their crop. Also, before they could build, the Jews had to remove the debris from the temple site, take inventory of their supplies, and organize their work crews. It would have been foolish to rush ahead totally unprepared. It's also possible that they took time to confess their sins and purify themselves so that their work would be pleasing to the Lord (Ps. 51:16-19).

The church today can learn a lesson from the Jewish remnant of Haggai's day. Too often we make excuses when we ought to be making confessions and obeying the Lord. We say, "It's not time for an evangelistic crusade," "It's not time for the Spirit to bring revival," "It's not time to expand the ministry." We act as though we fully understand "the times and the seasons" that God has ordained for His people, but we don't understand them (Acts 1:6-7).

Any interpretation of the Bible that limits God and encourages His people to be lazy instead of busy in ministry is a false interpretation and must be abandoned. If the Lord is to be pleased with us and glorified before an unbelieving world, we must hear His Word, believe it, and act upon it, no matter what the circumstances may be. After all, God is with us, and "If God be for us, who can be against us?" (Rom. 8:31)

CHAPTER TWO
KEEPING THE WORK ALIVE
Haggai 2

It's one thing to get God's people back to work and quite another thing to keep them on the job. Dr. Bob Jones, Sr. often said that the greatest ability a person can possess is dependability but too often potential workers excuse themselves and say, "Here am I, Lord; send somebody else." God's pattern for His workers is stated in 1 Corinthians 15:52. "To work is to pray," said St. Augustine, and God's people can do any legitimate task to the glory of God (1 Cor. 10:31).

The rebuilding of the temple was a very special task, for it meant the restoring of true worship in Jerusalem; and completing the project would please the Lord and be a great testimony to the unbelieving nations who were watching the remnant in Jerusalem. Haggai delivered three more brief messages to encourage the laborers to complete their assignments. In each message, he asked them to look in a specific direction to learn what God wanted them to learn.

1. "Look up: God is with us" (Hag. 2:1-9)

When the foundation of the temple had been laid sixteen years before, some of the older men had looked back in sorrow as they remembered the glory and beauty of Solomon's temple (Ezra 3:8-13). It's likely that Haggai was a member of the older generation and had seen the temple before it was destroyed, but he certainly didn't weep with the rest of his peers. He rejoiced that the work had begun, and he wanted to see it completed.

Discouragement (Hag. 2:1-3). Rather than ignore the problem of discouragement that was sure to come when the people contrasted the two temples, the prophet faced the problem head-on. He picked an important day on which to deliver his message: October 17, the last day of the Feast of Tabernacles. This feast was devoted to praising God for the harvest and for remembering Israel's pilgrim days in the wilderness (Lev. 23:34-43).

But the important thing about the date was this: it was during the Feast of Tabernacles that King Solomon had dedicated the original temple (1 Kings 8:2), and Haggai wanted the people to think about that. The restored building had nothing of the splendor of Solomon's temple, but it was still God's house, built according to His plan and for His glory. The same ministry would be performed at its altars and the same worship presented to the Lord. Times change, but ministry goes on.

Encouragement: God's presence (Hag. 2:4-9). Haggai didn't deny that the new temple was "as nothing" in comparison to what Solomon had built, but that wasn't important. The important thing was that this was God's work and they could depend on Him to help them finish it. Haggai said "Be strong!" to the governor, the high priest, and the people working on the building, and those two words would be very significant to them.

During the Feast of Tabernacles, the Jews had the Book of Deuteronomy read to them (Deut. 31:9-13), so they heard the record of the three times Moses told Joshua and the people to be strong (Deut. 31:6-7, 23). No doubt they also remembered that three times the Lord told Joshua to be strong (Josh. 1:6-7, 9); and when King David charged Solomon with the task of building the original temple, three times he told his son to be strong (1 Chron. 22:13; 28:10, 20). "Be strong" wasn't an empty phrase; it was an important part of their own Jewish history.

It's one thing to tell people to be strong and work and quite something else to give them a solid foundation for those words of encouragement. Haggai told them why they should be strong and work, because the Lord was with them (Hag. 2:4; see 1:13).

The promise of God's presence was an encouragement to both Joshua (Josh. 1:5, 9; 3:7) and Solomon (1 Chron. 28:20). Believers today can claim the same promise as they serve the Lord, "For He Himself has said, 'I will never leave you nor forsake you'" (Heb. 13:5, NIV; and see Deut. 31:6, 8).

Encouragement: God's covenant (Hag. 2:5). The promise of God's presence with His people is guaranteed by His unchanging Word (v. 5). When the tabernacle was dedicated by Moses, God's presence moved in (Ex. 40:34-38), for the Lord had promised to dwell with His people. "Then I will dwell among the Israelites and be their God. They will know that I am the Lord their God, who brought them out of Egypt so that I might dwell among them" (Ex. 29:45-46, NIV). The same Holy Spirit who enabled Moses and the elders to lead the people (Num. 11:16-17, 25; Isa. 63:11) would enable the Jews to finish building the temple.

The Prophet Zechariah, who ministered with Haggai, also emphasized the importance of trusting the Holy Spirit for the enablement needed to do God's will: "Not by might, nor by power, but by my Spirit, saith the Lord of hosts" (Zech. 4:6). A.W. Tozer once said, "If God were to take the Holy Spirit out of this world, much of what we're doing in our churches would go right on, and nobody would know the difference." What an indictment!

Encouragement: God's promise (Hag. 2:6-7, 9). With prophetic insight, Haggai looked ahead to the time when the Son of God would minister in this temple and bring the glory of God into its precincts (John 1:14). Herod's temple replaced the temple Zerubbabel built, but the Jews still considered it "the second temple." Certainly the glory that Jesus brought into that temple was greater than the glory of the tabernacle or the temple Solomon built.

Then Haggai looked even farther into the future and saw the end of the ages, when God would shake the nations and Jesus would return (Hag. 2:7). This verse is quoted in Hebrews 12:26-27 and applied to the return of Christ at the end of the age. God had shaken Sinai when He gave the law (Heb. 12:18-21; Ex. 19:16-25), and He will shake the nations before He sends His Son (Matt. 24:29-30). But today, God's people belong to a kingdom which cannot be shaken (Heb. 12:28); and they will share the glory of Christ when He establishes that kingdom on earth.

In both Jewish and Christian tradition, the phrase "the desire of all nations" (Hag. 2:7) has been generally interpreted as a messianic title of Christ. The nations of the world inwardly desire what Christ alone can give, whether they recognize this spiritual yearning or not. Charles Wesley followed this interpretation when he wrote in his Christmas hymn "Hark! The Herald Angels Sing" —

Come, Desire of nations, come!
Fix in us Thy humble home . . .

In the Hebrew text, the verb "will come" is plural, while "desired" is singular; so some interpreters translate "desired" as a compound noun: "the desirable things of the nations," that is, their treasures. The remnant had no beautiful treasures with which to adorn their temple, but when Messiah comes to reign, the treasures of the nations will be brought to Him and will be used for His glory.

The glory referred to in Haggai 2:7 is the glory that Jesus brought to the temple in Jerusalem, but the glory in verse 9 refers to the glory of the millennial temple that will function during Christ's reign on earth (Ezek. 40–48; see 43:1-12). Isaiah 60:1-5 and Zechariah 14:14 teach that the nations will bring their wealth to the King when Israel is established in the promised kingdom.

God not only promised the coming of Messiah and the glory of God in the future temples, but He also promised peace (Hag. 2:9). "In this place" refers to the city of Jerusalem where the Messiah will reign as "Prince of peace" (Isa. 9:6). Those who believe on Jesus today have peace with God (Rom. 5:1) because of His atoning death and victorious resurrection (Col. 1:20; John 20:19-21). They may also enjoy the "peace of God" as they yield to Christ and trust wholly in Him (Phil. 4:6-9).

Encouragement: God's provision (Hag. 2:8). Finally, the Lord assured them that, in spite of the bad economy and their lack of wealth, He was able to provide all they needed. "The silver is mine, and the gold is mine" (v. 8). True, the remnant had promises of provision from the government (Ezra 1:4; 3:7; 6:4), but government grants are limited. God owns all the wealth, even the wealth stored in the king's treasury, and He can distribute it as He desires. God promises to supply all our needs according to His riches in glory (Phil. 4:19).

It's better to fail in an endeavor that you know will ultimately succeed than to succeed in an endeavor you know will ultimately fail. The humble temple the Jewish remnant was constructing would not last, and even Herod's ornate temple would be destroyed by the Romans, but there would one day be a glorious temple that nobody could destroy or defile. Knowing this, the discouraged remnant could take courage and finish their work.

2. Looking within: contamination (Hag. 2:10-19)

About two months later (Dec. 18), the Lord spoke to Haggai again and gave him a message about sin. God couldn't bless the people the way He wanted to because they were defiled, so it was important that they keep themselves clean before the Lord. "Clean" and "unclean" were very important concepts to the Jews living under the Old Covenant; in fact, this is one of the major themes of the Book of Leviticus.[1] If a Jew became defiled, perhaps by touching a dead body or an open sore, he was separated from the rest of the camp and required to bathe before being allowed to return. In some instances, he had to offer a proper sacrifice to restore fellowship with the Lord.

Haggai went to the priests, who were the authorities on this subject, and asked them two simple questions, not for his own education (he certainly knew the law) but for the benefit of the people who were present.

Question #1—holiness (Hag. 2:11-12). When an animal was presented on the altar as a sacrifice, the meat was considered holy; that is, it belonged to the Lord and was set apart to be used only as He instructed. The priests and their families were permitted to eat portions of some of the sacrifices, but they had to be careful how they ate it, where they ate it, and what they did with the leftovers (Lev. 6:8–7:38).

"If a garment containing a piece of consecrated meat touches food," Haggai asked, "does the garment make the food holy?" The priests replied, "No." Why? Because you can't transmit holiness in such a simple manner. Even though the garment is holy (set apart) because of the sanctified meat, this holiness can't be imparted to other objects by the garment.[2]

Question #2—defilement (Hag. 2:13). "Suppose somebody touched a dead body and became unclean," Haggai said. "Could that person touch another person and make him unclean?" The answer was obviously, "Yes." Haggai had made his point: you can transmit defilement from one thing or person to another, but you can't transmit sanctity. The same principle applies in the area of health: you can transmit your sickness to healthy people and make them sick, but you can't share your health with them.

The application (vv. 14-19). "What is Haggai driving at?" the people no doubt were asking, so he told them. The people working on the temple couldn't impart any holiness to it, but they could defile it by their sins. Not only was it important that they do God's work, but it was also important that they do His work from hearts that were pure and devoted to God. The prophet reviewed their recent history. During the years when they were selfish, they experienced the discipline of the Lord (1:1-11). The Jews weren't keeping the terms of the covenant, so God couldn't bless them as He promised, and their economy fell apart. When the grain was in the fields, God smote it with mildew and hail, and after the grain had been harvested, the supply didn't last (Deut. 28:22).

Why had God done this to His people? To get them to turn back to Him with all their hearts. "Yet you did not turn to Me" (Hag. 2:17, NIV). They were so concerned to build their own houses that they ignored the house of God, and yet the rebuilding of the temple was the task that had brought them to Jerusalem!

Haggai was issuing a call to repentance, and with that call came the assurance of God's blessing (vv. 18-19). He was reminding the people of the promise God gave Solomon after the dedication of the temple: "If My people, who are called by My name, shall humble themselves, and pray, and seek My face, and turn from their wicked ways, then will I hear from heaven, and will forgive their sin, and will heal their land" (2 Chron. 7:14).

Had the workers been devoted to the Lord when the foundation of the temple was laid, God's blessing would have followed immediately; but the people were sinful at heart, and their sin grieved the Lord and defiled their work. "Is the seed yet in the barn?" he asked his congregation (Hag. 2:19); and they would have had to answer, "No." It was late December and the men had just plowed the fields for the winter crops. Haggai was calling on them to trust God for the future harvest. It was another example of Matthew 6:33: put God's interests first and He'll take care of the rest. "From this day will I bless you" (Hag. 2:19).

Many local church constitutions assign to the elders the "spiritual direction" of the church, and to the deacons the responsibilities for the "material" aspects of the ministry. For organizational purposes, this may be convenient, but this separation of "material" and "spiritual" is not biblical. The construction of a new church sanctuary should be just as spiritual an endeavor as an evangelistic crusade or a missions conference. One of the best ways to show our spiritual devotion to the Lord is by using material things to His glory, including money and buildings. The managing of material blessings demands as much sanctity as the managing of the "spiritual" ministries of the church.

It must always be that sin hinders the work of God and robs us of the blessings of God. It was the sins of the people that brought about the destruction of Jerusalem and the captivity of the nation, and their sins could hinder the rebuilding of the temple and the renewing of the Jewish nation in their own land. "Righteousness exalts a nation, but sin is a reproach to any people" (Prov. 14:34).

Haggai has asked the people to look back and then to look within. They've learned about God's glory and God's holiness.

There is now a third look and a third lesson to learn.

3. Look ahead: coronation (Hag. 2:20-23)

Haggai has encouraged the Jewish people to stay on the job and finish God's house. Now he has a special word of encouragement for Zerubbabel the governor, and it was delivered on the same day as the third message, December 18. Being a faithful preacher of the Word, Haggai was always listening for God's voice and sensitive to whatever the Lord wanted him to say and do.

Zerubbabel was the grandson of King Jehoiachin (Jeconiah, Matt. 1:12; Coniah, Jer. 22:24, 28), and therefore of the royal line of David. But instead of wearing a crown and sitting on a throne, Zerubbabel was the humble governor of a struggling remnant of the Jewish nation, trying to complete the building of a rather inglorious temple. What a discouraging situation for a royal prince to be in!

So, God gave His servant Haggai a special word of encouragement for the governor. Were the nations around Jerusalem larger and stronger? Rest assured that the Lord will care for His people Israel as He has always done in the past. The same God who enabled Moses to defeat Egypt, and Joshua to conquer the nations in Canaan, would protect His people so that His purposes could be fulfilled through them. Israel will endure until the last days, and then the Lord will defeat her enemies and establish her in her kingdom.

The Lord called Zerubbabel "My servant," an exclusive title reserved for specially chosen people, and Zerubbabel was indeed chosen by the Lord. God compared him to a royal signet ring. The signet ring was used by kings to put their official "signature" on documents (Es. 3:10; 8:8, 10), the guarantee that the king would keep his promise and fulfill the terms of the document.

Zerubbabel's ancestor, King Jehoiachin (Coniah), had been rejected by God, but Zerubbabel was accepted by God. "'As I live,' says the Lord, 'though Coniah the son of Jehoiakim, king of Judah, were the signet on My right hand, yet would I pluck you off'" (Jer. 22:24, NKJV). God was reversing the judgment and renewing His promise that the Davidic line would not die out but would one day give the world a Savior. That's why we find Zerubbabel named in the genealogies of Jesus Christ (Matt. 1:12; Luke 3:27).

This message must have encouraged Zerubbabel to stay on the job and finish the work God gave him to do. He was special to God, chosen by God, the servant of God! He was as near and dear to God as a king's signet ring. The people of Israel would have many centuries of struggle and suffering before them, but the Messiah would come, and one day, Israel's enemies would be defeated and the glorious kingdom established.

As you read the Old Testament, you see how "salvation history" progressed from age to age, always moving toward the fulfillment of the messianic promise. Many people played different roles in the drama, but each of them was important. Abraham founded the nation, and Isaac and Jacob built it. Joseph protected it in Egypt and Moses redeemed the people from Egypt. Joshua gave them their promised inheritance, and David established the kingdom. In spite of sin, suffering, and failures, the Davidic line never ceased, and the day came when Jesus Christ, the Son of David, was born in Bethlehem.

When the Christian church celebrates the birth of Christ, people remember Mary and Joseph, the magi, the shepherds, and even wicked King Herod; but they rarely think about Zerubbabel, a humble player in the drama, but a faithful one.

We can't leave Haggai without noting some practical lessons for God's people today.

1. The work of God is begun, sustained, and encouraged by the Word of God. "So the elders of the Jews continued to build and prosper under the preaching of Haggai the prophet and Zechariah, a descendant of Iddo" (Ezra 6:14, NIV). When God's servants proclaim God's Word in the power of the Spirit, things begin to happen. "Is it not clear, as you take a bird's-eye view of church history," said Dr. D. Martyn Lloyd-Jones, "that the decadent periods and eras in the history of the church have always been those periods when preaching had declined? What is it that always heralds the dawn of a Reformation or of a revival? It is renewed preaching."[3]

2. God's servants must work together to build God's temple. Haggai and Zechariah, an older man and a younger man, both ministered the Word to the Jewish remnant, and God blessed their mutual efforts. It's tragic when preachers and churches compete with one another and even carry on public disputes that give the enemy ammunition to oppose the Gospel. "For we are laborers together with God" (1 Cor. 3:9).

3. When the outlook is bleak, try the uplook. Apart from God's promises, we have no hope. As Vance Havner used to say, "Faith sees the invisible, chooses the imperishable, and does the impossible." Our work today is a part of God's work in the future, and we want to do our best.

4. Putting God first is the guarantee of God's best blessing. Why should God's work suffer while we pursue pleasure and comfort for ourselves? An affluent generation of Christians that is wasting God's generous gifts on trivia and toys will have much to answer for when the Lord returns. Matthew 6:33 is still in the Bible, and so is Romans 14:12.

5. Apart from the power of the Holy Spirit, our labors are in vain. "For it is God who works in you both to will and to do for His good pleasure" (Phil. 2:13, NKJV). God still demonstrates His power and receives great glory through the weak things of this world (1 Cor. 1:26-31). If we're too strong in ourselves, the Lord can't use us. That's what ruined King Uzziah; "for he was greatly helped until he became powerful" (2 Chron. 26:15).

Now, we turn to Haggai's associate, the young prophet Zechariah, and study his striking prophecies and Jerusalem, the Jews and the Messiah.

Endnotes

Chapter 1

1. However, it's difficult to think that God's servants would wait for sixteen years before urging the people to get back to work rebuilding God's house. Did Haggai and Zechariah arrive in Judah much later, sent by God to get the work going again? Or do their books record only the success of their ministry? They may have been urging the people all along to return to the task for which they had been released from bondage. Ezra doesn't mention them in his book until 5:1. It's likely that God permitted His people to suffer sixteen years of discipline and disappointment to prepare them for the words of His prophets. It's a good illustration of the truth of Matthew 6:33.

2. One of the basic themes of Malachi is the honor of God's name. See my book *Be Amazed* (Victor) for an exposition of Malachi.

3. Morgan, G. Campbell. *The Westminster Pulpit* (London: Pickering and Inglis), vol. 8, 315.

4. Zechariah uses the title "Lord of hosts" thirty-seven times and Malachi twenty-three times. Why should the little Jewish remnant fear the Gentile armies around them when the Lord of Armies is their Savior and Commander? The Hebrew word for "hosts" [tsaba] is transliterated as "Sabaoth" in Romans 9:29 and James 5:4. Martin Luther used it in verse 2 of his hymn "A Mighty Fortress Is Our God."

Did we in our own strength confide,
our striving would be losing,
Were not the right man on our side,
the man of God's own choosing.

Dost ask who that may be? Christ Jesus, it is he;
Lord Sabaoth his name, from age to age the same,
And he must win the battle.

Chapter 2

1. In the Authorized Version of Leviticus, words relating to ceremonial cleanliness are used 71 times, and words relating to "uncleanness" 128 times. "Unclean" is used 31 times in Leviticus 11, the chapter that details what the Jews were allowed to eat. Of course, "unclean" refers only to ceremonial defilement and not the condition of the heart. No amount of washing or sacrificing could of itself make the inner person clean. For inner cleansing, there must be repentance, confession, and faith (Ps. 51).

2. Whatever touched the altar became holy (Ex. 29:37), as well as whatever touched the sanctified vessels of the tabernacle (30:28-29), but the "holiness" of the objects that touched the altar or the vessels couldn't be transmitted to anything else.

3. D. Martyn Lloyd-Jones. *Preaching and Preachers* (London: Hodder and Stoughton, 1971), 24.

ZECHARIAH

OUTLINE

Key theme: God's jealous concern for Jerusalem and the Jews
Key verse: Zechariah 1:14

I. GOD CALLS HIS PEOPLE TO REPENT —1:1-6

II. GOD ENCOURAGES HIS PEOPLE TO TRUST HIM—1:7–6:15

1. Eight night visions
   (1) The horsemen: God watches the nations—1:7-17
   (2) The horns and smiths: the nations judged—1:18-21
   (3) The measuring line: Jerusalem restored—2:1-13
   (4) The high priest: Israel cleansed—3:1-10
   (5) The olive trees: God empowers His people—4:1-14
   (6) The flying scroll: evil purged from the land—5:1-4
   (7) The ephah: evil taken to Babylon—5:5-11
   (8) The four chariots: the Gentiles judged—6:1-8
2. The crowning of Joshua: Messiah will reign—6:9-15

III. GOD INSTRUCTS HIS PEOPLE—7:1–8:23

1. About true fasting—7:1-7
2. About obedience to the Word—7:8-14
3. About Jerusalem's future—8:1-23

IV. GOD REDEEMS HIS PEOPLE—9:1–14:21

Two oracles

1. The rejection of Messiah—9:1–11:17
2. The return and reign of Messiah—12:1–14:21

The messages in chapters 1–8 were given to Zechariah during the building of the temple, and those in chapters 9–14 after the temple was completed.

CONTENTS

CHAPTER ONE
GOD AND HIS PEOPLE
Zechariah 1-2

A young preacher in his first pastorate phoned me for encouragement "Most of the people in the church are older than I am," he said. "I wonder if they pay any attention to me. I feel like I'm out of place preaching to them."

Since I had faced the same situation in my first church, I was able to give him the same answer a veteran pastor gave me when I asked for help. "As long as you're delivering God's message, don't worry about how old you are. When you open that Bible, you're over 2,000 years old!"

Zechariah[1] was a young man (Zech. 2:4) when God called him to minister to the struggling Jewish remnant trying to rebuild their temple in the ruined city of Jerusalem. The elder Prophet Haggai had delivered two of his messages before Zechariah joined him in ministry, and the two of them served God together for a short time. Haggai had gotten the building program going again after a sixteen-year hiatus, and now Zechariah would encourage the people to finish their work. God gave the young man "good and comforting words" (1:13, 17) to assure the people that, in spite of the hard times, God was with them and would see them through.

The prophet had two major emphases as he began his ministry to the remnant: God was calling them to repent, and God was assuring them of His personal concern. In a series of eight night visions, God explained His involvement with His people.

1. God calls His people to repent (Zech. 1:1-6)

A preacher's first sermon is usually difficult to deliver, but in Zechariah's case, his first message was doubly difficult because of the theme—repentance. God commanded His young servant to call the discouraged remnant to turn from their wicked ways and obey His Word. Zechariah boldly proclaimed what God told him to say, for, after all, the Lord couldn't bless His chosen people until they were clean in His sight. If Zechariah had wanted to quote a text for his sermon, it could well have been 2 Chronicles 7:14, a verse the Jewish people knew well.

Zechariah invited the people to look back and recall what their forefathers had done to provoke the Lord to anger and judgment (Zech. 1:2, 4). The Jewish people who had returned to the land knew their nation's history very well. They knew that God had sent prophet after prophet to plead with their forefathers to turn from idolatry and return to the Lord, but the nation had refused to listen.

Isaiah had warned the leaders that God would discipline the nation if they didn't change their ways (Isa. 2:6–3:26; 5:1-30; 29:1-14). Jeremiah wept as he warned Judah and Jerusalem that judgment was coming from the north (Babylon) and that the Jews would be exiled for seventy years (Jer. 1:13-16; 4:5-9; 6:22-26; 25:1-14). "And the Lord God of their fathers sent warnings to them by His messengers, rising up early and sending them, because He had compassion on His people and on His dwelling place. But they mocked the messengers of God, despised His words, and scoffed at His prophets, until the wrath of the Lord arose against His people, till there was no remedy" (2 Chron. 36:15-16, NKJV).

Then, Zechariah shared God's promise with them: "Return to Me...and I will return to you" (Zech. 1:3, NIV). God had left His people to their own ways, and that was why they were experiencing so much trouble. Haggai had already told them this in his first message (Hag. 1), but it was worth repeating. "Draw near to God and He will draw near to you" (James 4:8, NKJV). A.W. Tozer reminds us that "nearness is likeness,"[2] so, if we want to be close to God, we must be obedient and develop godly character. The remnant had not put God first, so He couldn't bless them as He desired to do.

At this point, Zechariah asked them two questions: "Your fathers, where are they? And the prophets, do they live forever?" (Zech. 1:5) Had the listeners answered honestly, they would have said, "Many of our fathers are dead because they were slain by the Babylonians, and some are still in exile in Babylon. Some of the prophets are dead because our ancestors killed them."

But the point Zechariah was making was that the death of the prophets indicated the loss of opportunity for the nation. God gave the Jews ample time to repent and escape punishment, but they wasted their opportunity, and now it was too late. However, the Word of God, spoken and written by the prophets, can never die, and that Word eventually "catches up with" rebellious sinners (v. 6; "take hold of"; "overtake," NIV). Once God's long-suffering runs out, His living words will track down the offenders and judge them.[3]

Some of their forefathers did repent (v. 6), but their repentance came too late to prevent the destruction of Jerusalem and the deportation of the people. Some Jews may have repented when Nebuchadnezzar and his army arrived at the gates of Jerusalem, while others turned to God while exiled in Babylon. They admitted that their punishment was deserved and that God was just (see Lam. 2:17).

By calling the people to repent, Zechariah was preparing them for the messages he would give them, for unless our hearts are right with God, we can't hear His Word with true spiritual comprehension. "Today, if you will hear His voice, do not harden your hearts" (Heb. 3:7, NKJV).

We occasionally hear evangelists calling lost sinners to repent, and this is good and biblical. But we rarely hear preachers calling God's people to repent, even though this was the message of the prophets, John the Baptist, and Jesus. "The last word of our Lord to the church is not the Great Commission," said Vance Havner. "The Great Commission is indeed our program to the end of the age, but our Lord's last word to the church is 'Repent.'"[4] It's one thing to ask God to bless us but quite another to be the kind of people He can bless!

2. God comforts His people (Zech. 1:7-17)

About three months later, during the night of February 15, 519, Zechariah had a series of eight visions that God gave to encourage the remnant and motivate them to finish rebuilding the temple. These visions focus primarily on God's ministry to Israel and His judgment on the Gentile nations that have afflicted Israel.

The army (vv. 7-11). In the first vision, the prophet saw a man on a red (bay) horse, leading an army astride red, brown, and white horses. This "man among the myrtle trees" was the Angel of the Lord (vv. 11-13), the second Person of the Godhead, who in Old Testament times made temporary preincarnate appearances on earth. As the Angel of the Lord, the Son of God appeared to Hagar (Gen. 16:7-14), Abraham (18; 22:11-18), Jacob (31:11, 13), Moses (Ex. 3), Gideon (Jud. 6:11-23), and Samson's parents (Jud. 13).

But there was also an "interpreting angel" there who explained various things to Zechariah (Zech. 1:9, 13-14, 19; 2:3; 4:1, 4-5; 5:10; 6:4-5). Ten times during these visions, Zechariah asked questions of this angel and received replies (1:9, 19, 21; 2:2; 4:4, 11-12; 5:5, 10; 6:6). "If any of you lacks wisdom, let him ask of God, who gives to all liberally and without reproach, and it will be given to him" (James 1:5, NKJV). "The secret of the Lord is with those who fear Him, and He will show them His covenant" (Ps. 25:14).

In this first vision, the Angel of the Lord taught Zechariah the meaning of the horsemen (Zech. 1:10): they are God's angelic army that patrols the earth and carries out the decrees of the Lord (v. 11, and see Deut. 33:2; 1 Kings 22:19; Job 1:6-7; 2:1-2; Dan. 7:10; Matt. 27:63). Jehovah is "Lord of Hosts," the Commander of the armies of heaven and earth.

The messengers reported that the Gentile nations were "at rest and in peace." After the upheaval of empires and Persia's conquest of Babylon and other nations, this would appear to be an encouraging report, but it really wasn't. The Jewish remnant was in distress while the Gentile powers were at ease. Haggai had promised that the Lord would shake the nations and redeem His people (Hag. 2:6-9, 20-23), but this important event hadn't occurred yet. The kingdom promised by the prophets seemed to be a dream that would never come true.

The appeal (Zech. 1:12). A remarkable thing happened: the Son of God interceded for the people of God who were in great affliction! For centuries, "How long?" has been the cry of suffering people, especially the people of Israel (Ps. 74:9-10; 79:5; 80:4; 89:46; Hab. 1:2). "How long?" is even the cry of the martyred saints in heaven (Rev. 6:10). That the Son of God should so identify Himself with the cries of His people reveals His compassion and concern. "In all their distress he too was distressed" (Isa. 63:9, NIV).

Jeremiah had promised that God's blessing

would come after the seventy years of captivity (Jer. 25:8-14; 29:10-11), but the nation was still suffering.[5] Why? Because they forgot that God had attached conditions to that blessing: the people had to repent, call upon God, and seek Him with all their heart, the very thing Zechariah had preached. Intercession for Israel should still be a part of our prayers. Moses (Ex. 32; Deut. 9:18), the prophets (1 Sam. 12:23; 1 Kings 18; Jer. 9:1; Hab. 3), Jesus (Luke 23:34), and Paul (Rom. 10:1) all prayed for Israel; good examples for us to follow. "You who call on the Lord, give yourselves no rest, and give Him no rest till He establishes Jerusalem and makes her the praise of the earth" (Isa. 62:6-7). "Pray for the peace of Jerusalem; they shall prosper who love thee" (Ps. 122:6).

The answer (Zech. 1:13-17). After interceding for Israel, the Lord gave "comforting words" to the angel to give to the prophet.[6] He affirmed His jealous love and concern for Jerusalem (see 8:2). God is jealous over His chosen people as a husband is jealous over his wife and as parents over their children (Ex. 20:5; Deut. 4:24; 5:9; 6:15). This explains why the Lord accused the Jews of adultery and unfaithfulness whenever they were guilty of worshiping heathen gods (Jer. 2:1-3; 3:14; 31:32; Hosea 1). Worldliness on the part of Christians is also pictured as "spiritual adultery" (James 4:4-10).

The Lord was angry with the Gentile nations because they had been unnecessarily brutal toward the Jews. True, God had called Assyria to punish the Northern Kingdom of Israel, and Babylon to chasten Judah; but these nations went beyond what God called them to do and tried to destroy the Jews. Other nations, like Moab, had also joined in the assault (see Pss. 83 and 137).

But the Lord's most heartening words had to do with Judah's future, not her enemies, for God promised to return to His people and prosper their nation. He would comfort Zion and prove to the enemy nations that Jerusalem was indeed His chosen city. This promise is repeated and expanded in the rest of Zechariah's prophecy.

When our situation appears to be hopeless, we must remind ourselves that God identifies with our sufferings and is in charge of the future. Our responsibility is to repent, confess our sins, and believe His "comforting words." His responsibility is to respond to our faith and work out His perfect will for us.

3. God vindicates His people (Zech. 1:18-21)

Over the centuries, the Jews have suffered repeatedly at the hands of many nations, and yet they have survived. But every nation that has sought to destroy the Jews has discovered the truth of God's promise to Abraham, "I will bless those who bless you, and I will curse him who curses you" (Gen. 12:3).

That's the message of the second vision that God gave to Zechariah: the nations that have scattered the Jews will be terrified and thrown down by God's agents of judgment. In a letter to President Ronald Reagan, Israeli Prime Minister Menachem Begin wrote, "My generation, dear Ron, swore on the altar of God that whoever proclaims the intent of destroying the Jewish state or the Jewish people, or both, seals his fate."[7] But it's the Lord who does the judging, not the armies of Israel, and His judgments are never wrong.

In Scripture, a horn is a symbol of power, especially the power of a nation or a ruler (Pss. 75:4-5; 89:17; 92:10; Jer. 48:25; Amos 6:13; Dan. 7:7-12; 8:1ff; Rev. 17). The four "smiths" (artisans, craftsmen) represent nations that God uses to defeat the enemies of the Jews. They would use their "tools" to cut off the horns and render them powerless.

The concept of four horns (nations) reminds us of Daniel's visions of the image (Dan. 2) and the beasts (Dan. 7), both of which speak of four empires: Babylon, Medo-Persia, Greece, and Rome.[8] In 722, Assyria devastated the Northern Kingdom of Israel, but God raised up Babylon to defeat Assyria (Jer. 25:9; 27:6) and eventually take Judah into captivity in 586. Babylon did indeed oppress the Jews, but then God raised up Cyrus to conquer Babylon in 539 (Isa. 44:28; 45:1); and in 538, he permitted the Jews to return to their land. The Persians were conquered by the Greeks, under Alexander the Great,[9] and Greece was conquered by Rome.

This scenario suggests that the "horns" also became "smiths" as each empire conquered the previous oppressors. It also reminds the Jews of God's providential care in the past and His promise of protection for the future, for God will not permit any nation to annihilate His chosen people. In the last days, when Antichrist, the "dreadful and terrible beast," establishes his kingdom (Dan.

7:7-8, 15-28) and persecutes the Jews, he and his kingdom will be destroyed by the return of Jesus Christ in glory and power. Zechariah will have more to say about this in the last part of his book.

4. God will restore His people (Zech. 2:1-13)

The remnant that had returned to Judah was concerned about rebuilding the temple and restoring the city and the nation, but their work was extremely difficult. In this vision, God assured His people that He planned future glory and honor for them and their city when He Himself would come to dwell with them.

Anticipation (vv. 1-3). If a total stranger came into my house and began to measure the windows for curtains and the floor for carpeting, I'd probably ask him to leave. After all, you measure property that belongs to you, over which you have authority. When the prophet saw a man measuring Jerusalem, it was evidence that Jerusalem was God's city and that one day He would claim it and restore it in glory.

The man with the measuring line is evidently the Angel of the Lord, Israel's Messiah. Leaders and diplomats may debate over who shall control Jerusalem, but the Lord Jesus Christ has the final word. By measuring the city, He declares that it is His and He will accomplish His divine purposes for the city no matter what leaders and international assemblies may decide.

But this symbolic act declares something else: Jerusalem will enjoy future expansion and glory such as the city has never experienced. The population will spill over the walls; in fact, there will be no need of walls because God will be a "wall of fire" around His people. (See Isa. 49:13-21 and 54:1-3.) The small remnant of Jews in ruined Jerusalem were helping to keep alive a city that would one day be greatly honored and blessed by Almighty God!

Admonition (Zech. 2:6-9). The Lord admonished the Jews yet in Babylon to leave the city and join the remnant in Jerusalem. Why remain in the comfort and security of a pagan society when they were desperately needed in their own land? The day would come when Babylon, now under Persian rule, would be judged for her sins and those who served her would plunder her. Get out while there is still opportunity!

This admonition didn't imply that every Jew who remained in Babylon was out of the will of God. Just as God sent Joseph to Egypt to prepare the way for his family, so He had people like Esther and Mordecai, Daniel and his friends, and Nehemiah, in places of authority in pagan cities where they could do the work He planned for them to do. The Lord was summoning the Jews who were putting comfort, vocation, and security ahead of doing God's work in their own sacred city. (See Isa. 48:20 and 52:11; Jer. 50:8 and 51:6, 9, 45; 2 Cor. 6:14-18; and Rev. 18:4.)

The Jews are very precious to God; He called them "the apple [pupil] of His eye" (Zech. 2:8; Deut. 32:10; Ps. 17:8). The pupil is the tiny opening in the iris that lets in the light, and this is a very delicate and important area of that vital organ. Hence, anything dear and precious is like the pupil of the eye.[10]

Messiah is still speaking when He says, "He [God the Father] sent Me after glory" (Zech. 2:8, NKJV), that is, "to bring Him glory." The whole purpose of Christ's life on earth, His ministry, and His death and resurrection was to bring glory to God (John 1:14; 12:23, 28; 17:4); and part of that glory will involve the future restoration of Israel in the kingdom when He reigns on earth (Isa. 61:3-11).

Acclamation (Zech. 2:10-13). Promises like these ought to make God's people "sing and rejoice" ("shout and be glad," NIV). Their Messiah will come and dwell with them, just as the glory of God had dwelt in the tabernacle and the temple. Ezekiel describes the new city and temple in Ezekiel 40–48, and closes his book by naming the glorious new city "Jehovah Shammah," which means "the Lord is there" (48:35). In that day, many Gentiles will trust in the Lord and be joined with Israel in the glorious kingdom over which Messiah will reign (Isa. 2:1-5; 19:23-25; 60:1-3; Zech. 8:20-23).

Zechariah 2:12 is the only place in Scripture where Palestine is called "the holy land." That designation is often used today, but it really doesn't apply. The land will not be holy until Messiah cleanses the people and the land when He returns to reign (3:9). A fountain will be opened to wash away sin and uncleanness (13:1), and then the Jews shall be called "the holy people" (Isa. 62:12). That's something to shout about!

But it's also something to make the nations of the world pause and consider in awesome silence (Zech. 2:13; Hab. 2:20; Zeph. 1:7). Why? Because before Messiah comes to reign, He will judge the nations of the earth during that period of time called "the time of Jacob's trouble" (Jer. 30:7), "the day of the Lord" (Isa. 2:12; 13:6, 9; Joel 1:15; 2:1ff; Zech. 14:1), and "the great tribulation" (Matt. 24:21; Rev. 6–19). It will be a time of intense suffering when the nations will receive their just sentence for their inhumanity and ungodliness. When the Lord has "roused Himself from His holy dwelling" (Zech. 2:13, NIV), the nations of the world will experience divine wrath; and there will be no escape.

As you review these three night visions, you learn that God watches the nations and knows what they are doing; that He judges the nations for their sins, especially for their mistreatment of Israel; and that there is a glorious future planned for Jerusalem and the Jewish nation, when Messiah will return to cleanse them and restore the glory of God in their midst.

No wonder we're taught to pray, "Thy kingdom come" (Matt. 6:10); for when we pray that prayer, we are praying for the peace of Jerusalem. And there can be no true peace in Jerusalem until the Prince of Peace reigns in glory.

CHAPTER TWO
GOD AND HIS LEADERS
Zechariah 3-4

According to management experts James M. Kouzes and Barry Z. Posner, one of the popular myths about leadership is that "leaders are prescient visionaries with Merlin-like powers."[1] In other words, leaders know everything and can do anything. But if that were true, leadership wouldn't be the difficult and demanding task that it is. Certainly successful leaders enjoy the "peaks" and "perks" that go with their positions, but they also have to deal with the valleys and sacrifices that are also a big part of the job. Real leadership isn't easy.

Zechariah 3 and 4 focus on Joshua and Zerubbabel, the two leaders of the Jewish remnant who knew how tough it is to lead. Joshua was high priest and had the concern for the spiritual life of the people, while Zerubbabel was governor and had the responsibility of managing the civil affairs of the nation. But their work wasn't easy. Zerubbabel was trying to motivate people who were discouraged and selfish, and Joshua was trying to educate people who were disobedient and sinful. Is there any hope for a defiled and discouraged nation, or a defiled and discouraged church or individual?

Yes, there is! God gave the Prophet Zechariah two visions that speak to us today and encourage us to keep serving the Lord no matter how difficult the people or circumstances may be.

1. God cleanses His people for service (Zech. 3:1-10)

Haggai's first message (Hag. 1:1-11) and Zechariah's call to repentance (Zech. 1:1-6) are evidence that the spiritual level of the Jewish remnant was very low.[2] Most of these people had been born in Babylon, where there wasn't much religious example or instruction to nourish their worship of Jehovah; and the difficult circumstances in their own land tested their faith greatly.

The accused (3:1a, 3). Joshua stood before the Lord as a representative of Israel, a people He had called to be a holy nation of priests (Ex. 19:5-6). He wore filthy clothes, not because he was sinful personally, but because the people had sinned and were unclean in God's sight. The emphasis here is on the nation collectively and not on Joshua individually, for both Joshua and Zerubbabel were "men symbolic of things to come" (v. 8, NIV). God had chosen Jerusalem and had plucked the Jews out of the fire of Babylonian Captivity (v. 2). What God did for Joshua symbolically He would do for Israel personally: the iniquity of the land would be removed in a day (v. 9).

To "stand before the Lord" means to be in a place of service (Gen. 41:46; Deut. 10:8; 1 Sam. 16:21), so the Jews became defiled while they were attempting to serve the Lord. If their service was unclean in God's sight, what must their deliberate sins have been like! The Hebrew word translated "filthy" denotes the worst kind of defilement possible for a Jew. According to Merrill Unger, the word can be translated "excrement-covered."[3]

Since the priests were commanded to keep themselves clean at all times, on penalty of death (Ex. 28:39-43; 30:17-21), Joshua's wearing filthy garments would be a terrible personal embarrassment and an offense against God's law. Those garments were "for glory and for beauty" (Ex. 28:2, 40), but the Lord saw neither glory nor beauty as He beheld His servant.

The accuser (Zech. 3:1b). Zechariah has described a courtroom scene, in which Joshua is the defendant, God is the Judge, Satan is the prosecuting attorney, and Jesus Christ is the defense attorney, the Advocate of God's people before the holy throne of God (1 John 2:1-2). The word "Satan" means "adversary" and refers to the enemy who resists God's work and God's people. Satan has access to the throne of God (Job 1–2) where he accuses God's people (Rev. 12:10). When Satan talks to us about God, he lies, but when he talks to God about us, he tells the truth!

God's throne is a throne of justice and God is a righteous Judge. Knowing this, Satan pointed out Joshua's defilement, which symbolized the defilement of the nation, and insisted that a holy God punish His sinful people. It seemed like an airtight case, except for one factor: the grace of God.

The Advocate (Zech. 3:2-5). Christ's present ministry in heaven is twofold. He's our High Priest, interceding for us and giving us the grace we need for life and service here on earth (Heb. 4:14-16; 13:20-21); and He's our Advocate, representing us before the throne of God when we do sin (1 John 2:1-2). Don't get the erroneous idea that the Father yearns to punish us and the Son pleads with Him to change His mind, because that isn't the picture at all. The Father and the Son both love us and want the best for us, but God can't ignore our sins and still be a holy God.

This explains why Jesus took His wounds back to heaven with Him (Luke 24:39-40; John 20:20, 25-27): they prove that He was "delivered over to death for our sins and was raised to life for our justification" (Rom. 3:25, NIV). Satan cannot accuse us, nor God condemn us, for sins for which Christ died! "There is therefore now no condemnation to them which are in Christ Jesus" (Rom. 8:1).

The Lord rebuked Satan on the basis of His own electing grace: He had chosen Jerusalem and the Jewish nation in His own love and grace (Deut. 7:7-11; Pss. 33:12; 132:13). He had not chosen them because of their good works, so how could He condemn them for their bad works? "Who shall bring a charge against God's elect? It is God who justifies. Who is he who condemns? It is Christ who died, and furthermore is also risen, who is even at the right hand of God, who also makes intercession for us" (Rom. 8:33-34, NKJV).

God proved His grace to Israel by rescuing them from Babylonian Captivity; the Jews were "a brand plucked out of the fire" (Zech. 3:2; see Amos 4:11). Scripture often compares Israel's sufferings to going through the fire. Their trials in Egypt were like being in a furnace (Deut. 4:20), and the exile in Babylon was compared to being refined in the fire (Isa. 48:10; see 43:1-6). When Israel goes through the Tribulation in the end times, it will be an experience of refining (Zech. 13:9; Jer. 30:7).

The answer (Zech. 3:4-5). The same Savior who died for our sins arose from the dead and now intercedes for His people at the throne of God (Heb. 7:23-28). "If we confess our sins, He is faithful and just to forgive us our sins, and to cleanse us from all unrighteousness" (1 John 1:9). God's reply to Satan's accusation was to say to the angels before His throne, "Take away the filthy garments from him." This is forgiveness.

He gave a word of assurance to Joshua: "See, I have taken away your sin" (Zech. 3:4, NIV). Believers today know they are forgiven when they confess their sins, because they have the assurance of His promise. According to 1 John 1:9, God is not only faithful [to His promise], but He is also just [toward His Son] and will not condemn His people for sins for which His own Son had already been condemned.

But God in His grace goes beyond forgiveness and clothes us in His own righteousness. "I will put rich garments on you" (Zech. 3:4, NIV). Adam and Eve tried to hide their guilt under garments of their own making (Gen. 3:7), but God killed animals and clothed them in skins (v. 21). Blood was shed that sin might be forgiven. "I will greatly rejoice in the Lord, my soul shall be joyful in my God; for He has clothed me with the garments of salvation, He has covered me with the robe of righteousness" (Isa. 61:10, NKJV; see Luke 15:22).

The climax of the cleansing (forgiveness) and robing (righteous in Christ, 2 Cor. 5:21) was the placing of the special turban on Joshua's head; for the golden plate at the front of the turban was inscribed: HOLINESS TO THE LORD (Ex. 28:36-38; 39:30-31). It was this that made him, the people, and their gifts acceptable to the Lord. We have no righteousness of our own, but we come in the righteousness and merits of Jesus Christ, our Savior (1 Peter 2:5).

The assurance (Zech. 3:6-7). The Lord Jesus Christ gave a charge to Joshua, because cleansing and restoration always involve responsibility. Joshua and his fellow priests weren't put on probation; they were cleansed and restored to service. But the continuation of their service depended on their faithfulness to the Lord and His Word. It's a privilege to serve the Lord, and we must never take it for granted.

"I will give you a place among these standing here" (v. 6, NIV) indicates that Joshua's service was in cooperation with the angels of God! (See v. 4, "those who stood before him.") The angels are God's servants, obeying His every command without fail, and God's earthly servants are united with them in accomplishing His will. "Your will be done on earth as it is in heaven" (Matt. 6:10, NKJV). God's invisible messengers play a vital part in His plans both for Israel (Dan. 10:10-21; Matt. 24:31) and the church (Heb. 1:13-14).

The announcement (Zech. 3:8-10). This remarkable announcement to Joshua and his fellow priests focuses on Jesus Christ and presents three different images of the coming Messiah: the Priest, the Branch, and the Stone. Zechariah will say more about the priest in 6:9-15, so we'll save our detailed study for that passage. In their priestly ministry, Joshua and his associates were "symbolic of things to come" (3:8, NIV).

"The Branch" is an image of Messiah frequently found in the prophets (Isa. 11:1-2). Here Messiah is called "my servant the Branch." He is also "the Branch of the Lord" (4:2), "the Branch of righteousness" raised up for David (Jer. 23:5; 33:15), and "the man whose name is the Branch" (Zech. 6:12-13). These four titles parallel four aspects of the person of Christ as seen in the four Gospels:

Branch of righteousness for David—Matthew, Gospel of the King

My servant the Branch—Mark, Gospel of the Servant

The man whose name is the Branch—Luke, Gospel of the Son of Man

The Branch of the Lord—John, Gospel of the Son of God

"The stone" is another image of Messiah found often in Scripture, revealing several aspects of His ministry. Messiah is the cornerstone (Ps. 118:22-23; Matt. 21:42; Eph. 2:19-22; 1 Peter 2:7; see Zech. 10:4, NIV), a stone of stumbling (Isa. 8:14; 1 Peter 2:8; Rom. 9:32-33), the rejected stone (Ps. 118:22-23; Matt. 21:42), the smitten stone (Ex. 17:6; 1 Cor. 10:4), and the smiting stone (Dan. 2:34-35). At His first advent, Jesus was a stumbling stone to Israel who rejected Him, but He became the foundation stone for the church. At His second advent, He will smite the kingdoms of the world and establish His glorious kingdom.

The seven "eyes" on the stone probably speak of our Lord's omniscience (Zech. 4:10, NIV; Rev. 5:6). The NIV margin translates it "seven facets," making this stone a precious and beautiful jewel because of the way it is engraved (cut). But the text refers to an inscription that God engraved on the stone, not a jewel, and it doesn't tell us what the inscription says. Some of the Church Fathers interpreted this engraving to mean the glorified wounds on Christ's body, but we have no indication from the text that this interpretation is warranted.

The key message of this difficult verse is the removal of Israel's sins in one day. This miracle of grace is described in Zechariah 5 and 12:10–13:1, and will be considered in later chapters. At the Second Advent, when Israel beholds the One whom they pierced (12:10), they will repent and be cleansed. "Who has ever heard of such a thing? Who has ever seen such things? Can a country be born in a day or a nation be brought forth in a moment?" (Isa. 66:8)

When that happens, God will fulfill the promises of peace that He has made to Israel through the prophets. Resting under one's vine and fig tree (Zech. 3:10) is an image of peace and security (1 Kings 4:25; 2 Kings 18:31; Micah 4:4), something that Israel has always longed for but has never found.

Knowing that God would forgive and cleanse His people and restore the ministry of His priests must have encouraged Joshua greatly. In the next vision, God will encourage His servant Zerubbabel.

2. God empowers His people for service (Zech. 4:1-14)

The young prophet had seen four wonderful visions, and the experience had exhausted him. He fell asleep and had to be awakened by the "interpreting angel" before God could reveal the fifth vision to him. Seeing divine visions and understanding their meanings made Daniel very weary and like a man who was dumb and without strength (Dan. 10:8, 15-19). The flippant jovial manner in which some of God's people speak of prophetic matters today makes us wonder if they have really seen what the Word of God communicates about the future.

The vision (Zech. 4:1-3, 11-14). In the holy place of the tabernacle, in front of the veil and to the left of the altar of incense, stood a golden candlestick with seven branches (Ex. 25:31-40).[4] At the end of each branch was a golden lamp, and it was the high priest's duty each morning and evening to trim the wicks and provide the oil needed to keep the lamp burning (Lev. 24:3). This candlestick provided light in the holy place so the priests could see to burn the incense on the golden altar each morning and evening (Ex. 30:7-8).

But the candlestick that Zechariah saw was totally unlike the one Moses had put into the tabernacle. Along with the seven branches and lamps, this candlestick had a bowl at the top into which olive oil dripped from two olive trees (Zech. 4:3), which symbolized Joshua and Zerubbabel (v. 14). The candlestick also had seven pipes going from the bowl to each lamp, making a total of forty-nine pipes. No priest had to provide the oil because it was always coming from the trees. Seven pipes to each lamp assured an ample supply of fuel to keep the lights burning.

The lampstand in the tabernacle was symbolic of Messiah, the light of the world (John 8:12), who one day would come and give the "light of life" to all who would trust Him. The light from the golden lampstand would shine on the table in the holy place (Ex. 26:35) and reveal the loaves of bread, Christ the bread of life (Ex. 25:30; John 6:33, 35, 48, 50-51).

The tabernacle candlestick also spoke of the nation of Israel, the nation God had chosen to be a light in a spiritually dark world (Isa. 60:1-3; 62:1). (The seven-branched candlestick, the menorah, is the official symbol of the modern State of Israel.) The light was burning very low when the remnant returned to the land to rebuild the temple, and Zerubbabel wasn't sure there was enough power to keep the work going.

Believers today must keep in mind that the church is a light in a dark world, and we must depend on the Holy Spirit to enable us to bear witness (Matt. 5:14-16; Phil. 2:14-16). In Revelation 1–3, local churches are symbolized by individual lampstands, and the purpose of a lampstand is to give light. If we don't do what Christ commands us to do, He may take away the lampstand (2:5).

God provides the power (Zech. 4:4-7a). When Solomon built the temple which the Babylonians destroyed, he had almost unlimited resources at his disposal. His father David had fought many battles and collected spoil to be used in building the temple (1 Chron. 26:20, 27-28), but the remnant didn't have an army. Solomon was monarch of a powerful kingdom that ruled over many Gentile nations and took tribute from them, but the Jews in Zechariah's day had no such authority.

That's why God said to them through His prophet, "Not by might nor by power, but by My Spirit" (Zech. 4:6). The word "might" refers to military might, what people can do together, but the remnant had no army. "Power" refers to the strength of the individual, but Zerubbabel's strength was no doubt waning. "Don't be discouraged!" was the prophet's message. "The Spirit of God will enable us to do what an army could never do!" Had they forgotten what Haggai said to them? "My Spirit remains among you. Do not fear" (Hag. 2:5, NIV).

There are three ways we can attempt to do the work of God: we can trust our own strength and wisdom; we can borrow the resources of the world; or we can depend on the power of God. The first two approaches may appear to succeed, but they'll fail in the end. Only work done through the power of the Spirit will glorify God and endure the fires of His judgment (1 Cor. 3:12-15).

With their limited resources, completing the temple must have looked to those Jews as impossible as moving a mountain, but God told Zerubbabel that he would, by God's power, level the mountain and make it a plain! Jesus told His disciples that exercising faith like a mustard seed (small but alive) could move mountains (Matt. 17:20; 21:21).

What "mountains" was Zerubbabel facing? Discouragement among the people, opposition from the enemies around them, poor crops, an unstable economy, people not obeying God's Law—problems not too different from those the people of God have faced throughout the centuries. The answer to these problems is prayer that releases the Holy Spirit's power. When the early Christians faced problems, they turned to God in prayer, and He answered by giving them a fresh filling of the Holy Spirit (Acts 4:23-31).

"We say we depend on the Holy Spirit," wrote Vance Havner, "but actually we are so wired up with our own devices that if the fire does not fall from heaven, we can turn on a switch and produce false fire of our own. If there is no sound of a rushing mighty wind, we have the furnace all set to blow hot air instead. God save us from a synthetic Pentecost!"[5]

God finishes His work (Zech. 4:7b-10). God assured Zerubbabel that he would complete the rebuilding of the temple and the people would rejoice at what God had done through them. Zerubbabel would "bring out the capstone [the last stone to be placed in the building] with shouts of 'God bless it! God bless it!'" (v. 7b, NIV) Another possible translation is "Beauty! Perfection!" That wasn't what some of the people were saying when the foundation of the temple was laid (Ezra 3:10-13) and while the temple was under construction (Hag. 2:3).

God gave a clear promise that Zerubbabel would complete the temple (Zech.4:9), which reminds us of God's promise in Philippians 1:6, "Being confident of this very thing, that He who has begun a good work in you will complete it until the day of Jesus Christ" (NKJV). It also echoes David's words to his son Solomon: "Be strong and of good courage, and do it; do not fear nor be dismayed, for the Lord God—my God—will be with you. He will not leave you nor forsake you, until you have finished all the work for the service of the house of the Lord" (1 Chron. 28:20, NKJV). That was the promise that sustained me during my first building program in my first pastorate, and I can assure you that—it works!

To some of the Jews, the project was but a "small thing" (Zech. 4:10) in comparison to Solomon's grand temple, but we must look at God's work through His eyes and not the eyes of the people of the world. Great oaks grow out of small acorns and great harvests from small seeds. When Messiah came to earth, He was but "a shoot...from the stump of Jesse" (Isa. 11:1, NIV) and was "despised and rejected of men" (Isa. 53:3). The church began with 120 people and today ministers around the world.

Bible history is the record of God using small things. When God wanted to set the plan of salvation in motion, He started with a little baby named Isaac (Gen. 21). When He wanted to overthrow Egypt and set His people free, He used a baby's tears (Ex. 2:1-10). He used a shepherd boy and a sling to defeat a giant (1 Sam. 17) and a little lad's lunch to feed a multitude (John 6). He delivered the Apostle Paul from death by using a basket and a rope (Acts 9:23-25). Never despise the day of small things, for God is glorified in small things and uses them to accomplish great things.

God and His servants must work together to accomplish His purposes. "For it is God who works in you both to will and to do for His good pleasure" (Phil. 2:13, NKJV). God supplies His servants with the Spirit, and the people are encouraged as they see Zerubbabel on the job with the plumb line in his hand, making sure the walls are straight. While Zerubbabel is working, the eyes of the Lord are watching over His people and monitoring the nations of the earth. (The phrase "those seven" in Zech. 4:10 refers back to 3:9, the eyes of the Lord, meaning His omniscience.)

The vision climaxes (4:14) with God calling Zerubbabel and Joshua "the two anointed ones, that stand by the Lord of the whole earth." What a noble title for His servants! As the two olive trees, Joshua and Zerubbabel received the empowering Spirit of God and kept the light of Israel's work and witness burning. Oil is a general symbol for the Holy Spirit in Scripture. Prophets, priests, and kings were anointed with oil, and the words "Messiah" and "Christ" mean "anointed one." The holy anointing oil was not to be prepared by anybody but the priests or be used for any other purpose than for anointing God's servants (Ex. 30:22-33). "The Spirit of the Lord God is upon Me, because the Lord has anointed Me" (Isa. 61:1; Luke 4:18-19).

If our God is "Lord of all the earth," what

have we to fear? If He promises us the power of His Spirit, why should we falter and fail? Let's remember Joshua and Zerubbabel, men who are encouragements to all who seek to serve the Lord in any way.

There are no "small places" or "small ministries," and there are no "big preachers." But we do have a great God who can empower and bless servants who are dedicated to Him. He can cleanse us and He can empower us, so let's trust Him and do His work!

CHAPTER THREE
GOD AND THE NATIONS
Zechariah 5-6

The previous vision ended with the interpreting angel calling Israel's God "the Lord of the whole earth" (4:14), a title that is also used in Psalm 95:7 and Isaiah 54:5. Zechariah's purpose in writing is to tell us about the future of the Jews and Jerusalem, but the future of the whole world is involved in the future of the Jews, for God called Israel to bring blessing or cursing to all the nations of the earth (Gen. 12:1-3).

The prophet describes three key events that give evidence that the God of Abraham, Isaac, and Jacob is indeed "the Lord of the whole earth."

1. The cleansing of the land (Zech. 5:1-11)

The vision of the flying scroll and the vision of the ephah focus primarily on the land of Israel.[1] In both of them, God performs a cleansing operation and deals with the sins of the nation.

God removes lawlessness (vv. 1-4). The prophet saw a large open scroll, fifteen feet by thirty feet, floating through the air, with writing on both sides. On one side he read the third commandment against taking God's name in vain (Ex. 20:7), and on the other side he read the eighth commandment against stealing (v. 15).

This scroll represented the Law of God that brings a curse on all who disobey it, and that includes all of us (Deut. 27:26; Gal. 3:10-12); because nobody can fully obey God's law. For that matter, the law was never given to save people (Gal. 2:16, 21; 3:21) but to reveal that people need to be saved; "for by the law is the knowledge of sin" (Rom. 3:20).

Out of Ten Commandments, why did the Lord select the two that forbid stealing and swearing falsely? Were these sins especially prevalent among the Jewish remnant at that time? It may be that many of the Jewish people were not faithful in their giving to the Lord, robbing Him of tithes and offerings and then lying about it. In their business dealings, they may have cheated one another. The Prophet Haggai rebuked them for putting their own interests ahead of the Lord's work (Hag. 1:1-11), and certainly robbing God was a grievous sin among the Jews a century later (Mal. 3:7-15).

But there is another reason. The third commandment is the central commandment on the first table of the Law, and the eighth commandment is the central commandment on the second table of the law, so these two commandments represent the whole law. "But whoever shall keep the whole law, yet offend in one point, he is guilty of all" (James 2:10).

If I'm suspended over a chasm by a chain of ten links, how many links have to break before I fall? If while driving down the highway, I'm pulled over by a policeman because I'm speeding, does it make any difference to him that I haven't broken the income tax laws or stolen anything from my neighbors? Obedience to one law doesn't negate disobedience to another law. To break one is to become a lawless person.

God announced that the scroll of His law would visit the individual homes in the land and judge those who were deliberately disobeying God. Whether "cut off" means killed or expelled from the covenant community isn't made clear. Like a thief or a plague, the curse would enter the houses unannounced and bring destruction.

The Jewish remnant was certainly familiar with the "blessings and curses" of the covenant recorded by Moses. They also knew that after Joshua had brought the people into the Promised Land, they gathered at Mount Ebal and Mount Gerizim and read the "blessings and curses" and promised to obey the Lord (Josh. 8:30-35).

Lawlessness abounds today and the only commandment many people worry about is

"Thou shalt not get caught!" Ethics is something studied in the classroom but not seriously practiced in the marketplace, and the Ten Commandments are only dusty artifacts in the museum of morality. No wonder Hosea wrote, "They make many promises, take false oaths and make agreements; therefore lawsuits spring up like poisonous weeds in a plowed field" (10:4, NIV). People break God's law and then try to use man's law to protect themselves, and often they win!

Ultimately, God will judge all sinners who have rebelled against His law (Jude 14-15); but He will start with Israel, the nation that gave us God's Law. It's a divine principle that judgment begins with God's people (1 Peter 4:17; Ezek. 9:6). This judgment will occur before our Lord establishes His kingdom on earth, and the "holy land" will truly become holy (Zech. 2:12). God will "remove the iniquity of the land in one day" (Zech. 3:9).

God removes wickedness (5:6-11). Not only will individual sins and sinners be judged, but wickedness itself will be removed from the land. In this vision, wickedness is personified by a woman, because the Hebrew word for "wickedness" is feminine. The ephah was a common measure in Israel, but no ephah would be large enough to house a person, so, like the huge scroll, this was a special ephah. The woman attempted to get out of the ephah, so a heavy lead cover was put on the ephah to keep her in. A talent of lead would weigh from seventy-five to one hundred pounds.

The prophet then saw two other women, but they had wings! With the help of the wind, they lifted up the basket and its contents, plus the heavy lead cover, and carried it in the air to Babylon. Although angels are actually sexless (Matt. 22:30), in Scripture they are generally depicted as male, so these two women were special agents of the Lord created just for this particular task. They took the ephah and the woman to Shinar (Babylon, Dan. 1:2) and put the ephah on a base in a special house.

In order to understand this vision, we must ask ourselves, "What did the Jews bring to their land from Babylon when they returned after their captivity?" It wasn't idolatry, for their years of exile cured them of that sin. The answer is—commercialism. The Jews were people of the land when they went to Babylon, but many of the Jews born in Babylon became people of the city and successful merchants. So it was the spirit of competitive commercialism that was represented by the woman in the ephah, for both the ephah and the talent are measures of commodities.

The ancient city of Babylon is first mentioned in Genesis 10:10 as a part of Nimrod's empire. Nimrod is called "a mighty one in the earth" and "a mighty hunter" (Gen. 10:8-9), which the NIV translates "a mighty warrior...a mighty hunter." This is the picture of a conquering despot, forging himself a kingdom at any cost and defying the Lord in the process. The famous Tower of Babel was built in Shinar as an attempt to exalt man and dethrone God (11:1-19).

Throughout Scripture, Babylon symbolizes the world's enmity against God, culminating in the vivid description in Revelation 17–18. (See also the parallel in Jer. 50–51.) The contrast in the Book of Revelation is between the Bride (the heavenly city) and the harlot (the earthly city of Babylon). When you read Revelation 18, you see that the emphasis is on the commercial success and the vast wealth of Babylon, the very "virus" that some of the Jews had caught during the Babylonian exile.

This doesn't imply that the people of Israel today are all guilty of bad business practices, or that it's wrong for anybody to earn money by engaging in business. Both believers and unbelievers, Jews or Gentiles, can be manufacturers and merchants and faithfully do their work. But if the worldly commercial spirit infects the child of God, it will result in twisted values, confused priorities, and a craving for wealth and position that grieves the Lord (1 Tim. 6). The best antidote is Matthew 6:33.

The two women with storklike wings placed the ephah on a base in a special house in Babylon, which suggests that "commercialism" was worshiped as one of the Babylonian gods. Unfortunately, money has become a god around the world and, like a god, money is trusted by people to give them help, to solve their problems, to provide happiness, and to empower them to accomplish their goals in life. The last of the Ten Commandments is "Thou shalt not covet" (Ex. 20:17), but coveting will cause people to break the other nine commandments. "For the love of money is a root of all kinds of evil" (1 Tim. 6:10, NKJV), everything from lying on one's income tax to murdering a helpless victim for a few dollars.

God has now cleansed the land. What is His next step in preparing His people for their promised kingdom?

2. God judges the nations (Zech. 6:1-8)

The images in this vision are similar to those described in 1:7-17, but the details are significantly different. The emphasis here is on the horses and chariots rather than the riders, and their ministry is that of accomplishing God's purposes rather than reporting on conditions in the Gentile world. In the first vision, there were many horses and riders but here, there are only four chariots, each with their horses.

The four chariots with their horses represented the "four spirits" from God, that is, four angels (Heb. 1:14) assigned to different parts of the world to do God's bidding. "The chariots of God are twenty thousand, even thousands of angels" (Ps. 68:17). The presence of chariots suggests battle, and this implies judgment. "For behold, the Lord will come with fire and with His chariots, like a whirlwind, to render [bring down, NIV] His anger with fury, and His rebuke with flames of fire" (Isa. 66:15, NKJV).

If the horses' colors are significant, then Revelation 6:1-8 can assist us. The red horses symbolize war; the black horses, famine; and the white horses, death. There are no dappled horses in the vision John had in Revelation 6, but they could well symbolize plagues. During the "Day of the Lord," God will use wars, famines, plagues, and death to punish the nations of the earth.

Since the two mountains (Zech. 6:1) were made of bronze, they are symbolic, for there are no bronze mountains in the Holy Land or anywhere else. In Scripture, bronze often symbolizes judgment. The altar of sacrifice in the tabernacle and the temple was made of wood covered with bronze, and that's where sin was judged when the sacrifices were burned. The serpent that Moses put on the pole was made of bronze (Num. 21:9), and when our Lord appeared to John and was about to judge the churches, His feet were compared to bronze "as if they burned in a furnace" (Rev. 1:15).

So, the cumulative effect of this vision is that God will judge the Gentile nations for their sins. This will occur during the period of time called "the Tribulation" or "the Day of the Lord" which precedes the return of Christ to the earth to set up His righteous kingdom. In the latter chapters of his book, Zechariah will describe many of the events that will occur during "the day of the Lord."

When Zechariah saw the horses, they were straining to go to their appointed destinations and do what God had ordered them to do. However, judgment is in the hands of God, reserved for the right time and place (see Rev. 9:15). The black horses were assigned to the north country (Babylon) and the white horses would follow them, while the dappled horses would go to the south (Egypt). Nothing is said about the red horses, so apparently the Lord was holding them back for another time.[2] God was angry with the nations in the north (Zech. 6:8; see 1:15), and His messengers would see to it that His holy purposes there were fulfilled. This would bring peace to God's heart as His justice was satisfied.

The ministry of angels among the nations and in dispensing God's judgments is clearly taught in other parts of Scripture (Dan. 4:4-18; 10; 12:1; Rev. 8; 14; 16). Zechariah's vision assures us that God is in control of the future and will judge the Gentile nations during "the Day of the Lord." God is long-suffering (2 Peter 3:9), but there comes a time when nations "fill up the measure of their sins" (Gen. 15:16; Matt. 23:32); and then God's judgment must fall.

3. God crowns His King-Priest (Zech. 6:9-15)

The eight visions came to an end, but there was yet another message from God to His servant. In the visions, God had assured His people that He would cleanse them and protect them from their enemies. But there was a message for the future as well. During the "Day of the Lord," the nations would be punished for their sins, but Israel would be delivered. At the climax of that day, Messiah would return, the Jews would see Him and trust Him, and the nation would be cleansed. Then Messiah would be crowned as King-Priest to reign over His righteous kingdom (Zech. 9–14).

Confrontation (6:9-11). We aren't told when God gave Zechariah these instructions, but it was probably shortly after he had seen the eight visions, for this event is really the climax of the revelations given in the visions.

God told Zechariah that three esteemed Jews would arrive from Babylon, bringing gold and silver offerings to the Lord for the building of the temple. They would stay at the home of Josiah, who had the wonderful nickname "Hen," which means "gracious one" (v. 14). After they arrived in Jerusalem, Zechariah went to see them.

We can only imagine what transpired when the prophet told the visitors what God had commanded him to do: take their silver and gold offerings and make an elaborate crown.[3] He was then to put this crown, not on the head of Zerubbabel the governor, who was of the royal line of David, but on the head of Joshua the high priest!

The visitors no doubt faced two problems: (1) the money from the Jews in Babylon was supposed to be used for the completion of the temple; and (2) there was no precedent in Scripture for a priest to be crowned king. Was Zechariah trying to oust the governor and make Joshua ruler of the struggling nation? How would this better the situation of the remnant and hasten the completion of the temple?

Coronation (vv. 12-13). Zechariah saved the explanation until he had fully obeyed the Lord. He made the crown and, taking the visitors with him, went to Joshua the high priest and conducted a coronation service. We don't know if all the elders of Israel were invited, but since the message this act conveyed was such an important one, it's likely that they were.

Then Zechariah explained God's message to the high priest and the witnesses. He must have told them that both Zerubbabel and Joshua were "men symbolic of things to come" (Zech. 3:8, NIV). Even though Zerubbabel was from David's line, he wasn't the one God chose to be crowned. God chose Joshua and for the first time in Jewish history, the Lord united the monarchy and the priesthood.

All of this refers, of course, to Jesus Christ; for He is "the man whose name is the Branch" (6:12; see 3:8).[4] Looking down to the time of the kingdom, God announced that Messiah would be both King and Priest: He would sit on the throne and reign, but He would also build the temple and serve as a priest. In fact, many Jews and Gentiles will come from afar off and help build the millennial temple (6:15; Isa. 60:5-12; Hag. 2:7-9).

No priest in Jewish history ever served as king; and the one king, Uzziah, who tried to become a priest, was severely judged by the Lord (2 Chron. 26:16-21). Only in Messiah does Jehovah unite both the throne and the altar. Today, Jesus Christ serves in heaven as both King and Priest, ministering "after the order of Melchizedek" (Heb. 7–8). This is in fulfillment of the Father's promise to the Son recorded in Psalm 110:4.

But during the reign of Christ on earth, there will be a restored temple and priesthood (Isa. 2:1-5; 27:13; Ezek. 40–48; Zech. 14:16), and Jesus Christ will sit on the throne of His father David as King and Priest (Luke 1:32-33).[5] This will be the fulfillment of God's covenant promise to David that he would always have an heir seated on his throne (2 Sam. 7).

The statement in Zechariah 6:13 that "the counsel of peace shall be between them both" is translated in the NIV, "And there will be harmony between the two." In the kingdom, there will be perfect peace and justice because all civil and religious authority will be harmonized in one Person, Messiah, the King and Priest.

Commemoration (vv.14-15). Zechariah then took the crown from off Joshua's head and gave him his priestly miter (3:5). Why? Because the symbolic act was over and the crown did not belong to Joshua. It belonged to the coming Messiah. Zechariah placed the crown somewhere in the temple as a memorial (reminder) of the Lord's promise of a King-Priest who would bring peace and holiness to His people.

God will be faithful to His promises even if His people are unfaithful (2 Tim. 2:12-13), but they will miss out on the blessings. He didn't put any conditions on the wonderful promise of a future King-Priest, but Zechariah 6:15 seems to limit God's working to the obedience of His people. "This will happen if you diligently obey the Lord your God" (NIV).

This statement is a reference to God's covenant recorded in Deuteronomy 28: "Now it shall come to pass, if you diligently obey the voice of the Lord your God" (v. 1). The remnant of Jews then in the Holy Land had to obey God's laws so that He might protect them and bless them as He promised, for the Messiah had to be born from this nation. Within a few centuries, the Angel Gabriel would visit Mary and tell her she had been chosen to bring the promised Messiah into the world (Luke 1:26-38). The faithfulness of one generation assured the blessing of the next generations and ultimately the blessing of the whole world.

The visions are ended. We have seen a vivid panorama of God's plans for Israel, culminating in the King-Priest on David's throne, ruling over Israel and the whole world.

Remember these prophecies the next time you pray, "Thy kingdom come."

CHAPTER FOUR
TRUTH, TRADITIONS, AND PROMISES
Zechariah 7-8

To what extent do the traditions of the past have authority over what the church does today? As times change, should customs also change? And who has the authority to change them? Are religious traditions to remain as they've always been, or can we drop the old ones and begin some new ones?

These are questions that are challenging churches today and even dividing churches, but these questions aren't new. Similar questions were asked centuries ago when Sharezer and Regemelech arrived in Jerusalem from Babylon. The Jews in Babylon had sent them to ask the Prophet Zechariah about the traditional Jewish fasts. Zechariah used the opportunity to teach the people about true spiritual worship, and then he turned their eyes away from the past to the promises of the future.

1. Problems concerning tradition (Zech. 7:1-14)

Tradition is a useful and necessary social practice. It helps to tie generations together and keep society moving in a united way. Whether the traditions involve the way we eat and dress, how we treat our parents and family, the way we move from childhood into maturity, or the way we choose a job or a mate, tradition helps to stabilize things and guide us in making acceptable choices. But sometimes tradition creates problems, especially when the times change radically and people don't want to change with the times.

The request (vv. 1-3). Almost two years had elapsed since the crowning of Joshua and the work of rebuilding the temple had gone on steadily. In another three years, the temple would be completed and dedicated. While we have no recorded messages from Zechariah during that time, certainly he was ministering to the people and encouraging the workers in their important task.

The Law of Moses required the Jews to observe only one national fast, and that was on the annual Day of Atonement (Lev. 23:16-32). Of course, individual Jews could fast from time to time as they felt led, but this wasn't required of the entire nation.

To commemorate events surrounding the destruction of Jerusalem and the temple, four new fasts had been added to the religious calendar by the Jewish exiles in Babylon (see Zech. 8:19): one in the tenth month, when the Babylonians had begun the siege of the city; another in the fourth month, when the city walls had been broken through; one in the fifth month, when the temple was burned; and the fourth in the seventh month, when the Jewish governor Gedaliah had been assassinated (see Jer. 41).

The significant question was: "Now that the temple was being rebuilt, was it necessary to continue the fast in the fifth month that commemorated the burning of the temple?"

The reply (Zech. 7:4-7). Zechariah didn't give them an immediate reply. In fact, the Lord didn't reveal His will in the matter until later (8:9). It was necessary first to deal with the heart attitudes of the people. After all, our relationship with the Lord isn't so much a matter of traditions and rules as it is faith, love, and a desire to please Him. Immature people require religious regulations to tell them what to do, and these regulations help them measure their "spiritual life." But God wants us to mature spiritually and grow from obeying rules to following principles and cultivating a vital personal relationship with Him.

In true rabbinical fashion, Zechariah answered their question by asking some questions! In fact, he asked these questions of all the people and priests, for they too had kept these fasts. "When you fasted," Zechariah asked, "did you do it for the Lord or for yourselves? And when you feasted, was it for the Lord or for yourselves? What was in your heart?"

The prophets who ministered prior to the fall of Jerusalem had taught the people that their religious observances had to come from the heart. To worship God any other way meant to practice hypocrisy. As far back as the ministry of Samuel, God told the people that He wanted their obedience and not their sacrifices (1 Sam. 15:22), and this truth was also taught in the Psalms (50:8-14; 51:16). Isaiah had proclaimed this message (Isa. 1:11-17; 58:1-14), and so did the Prophet Micah (6:6-8), but the people didn't listen. Life was peaceful and secure in those days, and it was much easier to maintain the traditions than to really meet with God and have a "heart experience" of worship.

Zechariah wasn't condemning traditions as such. He was emphasizing the fact that the true spiritual life can't be turned on and off at our convenience, so that we serve God one minute and forget Him the next. If we feast, we must do it to glorify God (1 Cor. 10:31); if we fast, we must do it to honor Him. The Lord must be the center of our lives and the reason for our actions. If we keep a fast (or any other religious tradition) just to please ourselves and win the admiration and approval of others, then God was not pleased and the activity was wasted.

God's final answer was given later (Zech. 8:19): all four fasts will one day be turned into feasts! This would take place during the Kingdom Age when Messiah will sit on the throne, judging with justice and truth. (Isaiah saw the same picture; Isa. 61:2-3; 65:19.) So, instead of living in the past tense and mourning over calamities, why not live in the future tense and rejoice over what God has promised to do for His people?

The rebuke (Zech. 7:8-14). Zechariah reminded the people of the way their forefathers routinely practiced their religion but failed to hear God's Word and obey it from their hearts. That was the reason Jerusalem and the temple had been destroyed. Their "religion" was just a part of their lives; it wasn't the very heart of their lives. They could go to the temple and piously present their prayers and sacrifices, but then leave the temple to break God's Law, worship idols, and abuse other people.

Through the prophets, the Lord had called the people to practice justice, but the leaders had continued to exploit the people for personal gain. The rulers of the nation had ignored the Law of Moses and refused to show compassion toward the poor, the widows and orphans, and the aliens in the land (Ex. 22:22-24; Deut. 10:18-22; Amos 2:6-8; 5:11-12, 21-24). God wasn't interested in their sacrifices and prayers so much as the obedience of their hearts.

The danger of tradition is that it can easily turn into traditionalism. "Tradition is the living faith of the dead," wrote theologian Jerislav Pelikan; "traditionalism is the dead faith of the living." Traditionalism means going through the outward motions instead of honoring the Lord from our heart; it means participating in a religious event but failing to have an inner spiritual experience.

Sometimes the only way the Lord can bring us back to reality is to force us to endure suffering. "Before I was afflicted I went astray, but now I have kept Thy word" (Ps. 119:67). When we find ourselves in the furnace of affliction, we turn to God and His promises, because that's the only hope we have. The Lord had to send the Jewish people into exile before they'd learn to turn from idols and appreciate all the blessings they had because of God's grace.

The word "tradition" simply means "that which is passed along." It comes from a Latin word that means "to hand over." The basic doctrines of the Christian faith must be handed from generation to generation (1 Tim. 2:2; 1 John 1:1-3; 1 Cor. 11:2; 1 Thes. 2:15; 3:6; Jude 3), but the customs and traditions of the early church don't carry the same authority as the inspired Word of God. In fact, as times change, some of these customs may be detrimental to the work of the Lord. To institute four fasts because of the tragedies that occurred in Jerusalem, and yet not repent because of the sins that caused these tragedies, was to miss the whole purpose of God's discipline.

Centuries ago, when the first missionaries went to Moravia, they weren't allowed to preach in the Slavic language! Why? Because the only "holy languages" the church approved were Hebrew, Greek, and Latin. Fortunately, the church leaders had sense enough to revoke this foolish edict; otherwise, evangelism would have been impossible. Believers today who insist that we sing only the Psalms in our public worship, accompanied only by an organ or a piano, are captive to traditions that have no biblical basis. City congregations that follow a Sunday time schedule that was tailored for the rural community may be losing opportunities to reach urbanites with the Gospel. Over the years, I've been privileged to minister in many churches of different denominations, and I've seen how dead traditions can become roadblocks to progress.

Churches are like families; each one has its own set of traditions, many of which may be good. The truths of God's Word don't change, but changing circumstances reveal new principles and new applications of that Word. The old Youth for Christ slogan said it perfectly: we must be "geared to the times, but anchored to the Rock."

Jesus dealt with the question of tradition when He was ministering here on earth (Matt. 15; Mark 7). He carefully distinguished between the inspired Word of God that never changes and man-made traditions that are always subject to review and revision. Final authority for faith and practice must rest in the Word of God. "Tradition is a guide and not a jailer," wrote novelist W. Somerset Maugham, but history reveals that it's a difficult thing for many people to break with tradition. It's easier to have a religion of habit than a religion of the heart. Churches, families, and individual believers need to examine their cherished traditions in the light of God's truth. Perhaps some of our fasts need to be turned into feasts! (Zech. 8:18)

2. Promises concerning Israel (Zech. 8:1-23)

God's people don't live on explanations; they live on promises. Faith and hope are nourished by the promises of God given to us in the Scriptures. That explains why Zechariah dropped the discussion of the traditions and delivered a new message from the Lord. In this message, he focused the people's eyes of faith on the future and shared some wonderful promises to encourage them. Note the repetition of the phrase, "Thus saith the Lord," which is used ten times in this chapter.

The city of Jerusalem will be rebuilt (vv. 1-6). God affirmed His jealous love and concern for Zion, just as He had done earlier (1:14). He promises that Jerusalem will be rebuilt and become a wholly different city, dedicated to truth and holi-ness. This promise will be fulfilled when Jesus Christ returns to earth to establish His kingdom (Isa. 1:26; 2:3; 60:14; 62:12).

But the compassionate Lord centers on people and not buildings, particularly the elderly and the children. He describes a city so safe and friendly that the elderly can leisurely sit in the streets and talk, and where the children can play in the streets and not be in danger. In today's man-made cities, the elderly and the children aren't safe in the streets or anywhere else! The children are killed before they have a chance to be born, and when the elderly are no longer "useful," we find legal ways to end their lives. But all of that will change when Jesus returns and righteousness reigns.[1]

The people of Israel will be regathered (Zech. 8:7). True to His covenant, God disciplined His disobedient people and dispersed them throughout the world (Deut. 28:63); but one day, He will regather them to their land and to their holy city (Isa. 11:11-12; 43:5-7; Jer. 30:7-11; 31:7-8). While groups of Jewish patriots have returned from time to time to their land, the kind of worldwide regathering described by the prophets has never yet occurred.

The relationship between Israel and Jehovah will be restored (Zech. 8:8). The promise "They will be My people" reminds us that God claimed the people of Israel as His own. When God delivered Israel from Egyptian bondage, He said to them, "Obey My voice, and do according to all that I command you; so shall you be My people, and I will be your God" (Jer. 11:4, NKJV; see Ex. 19:3-5). For a time, God abandoned His people because they abandoned Him, and He called them "Lo-ammi; for you are not My people, and I will not be your God" (Hosea 1:9, NKJV).

The nation of Israel was punished for her idolatry by being sent into Babylonian captivity. Then she was punished for rejecting her Messiah by being sent into worldwide dispersion. One day, God will summon His sons and daughters from afar and the streets of a restored Jerusalem will be crowded with His people. "At that time I will gather you; at that time I will bring you home. I will give you honor and praise among all the peoples of the earth when I restore your fortunes before your very eyes" (Zeph. 3:20).

The land of Israel will be refreshed (8:9-13). Haggai had rebuked the Jewish remnant because the people weren't faithful to the Lord in their stewardship (Hag. 1). Instead of honoring the Lord and building His house, they built their own houses first, and for this sin, God disciplined them. The weather turned bad, their crops failed, and the economy became worse and worse. God wasn't being unkind to His people; He was only being true to His covenant (Deut. 28:38-46).

But now the land would be refreshed by the Lord and the crops would grow abundantly. Laborers would get their wages and their money would be sufficient to pay their bills. The Lord would send the promised rain (Deut. 28:11-12) and the other nations would witness the blessing of the Lord on His people. Instead of being a reproach, Israel would become a witness to the glory of the Lord.

While this promise of material blessing was given primarily to the remnant in Zechariah's day, it has its application to the future regathered and restored nation. God promises that "the desert shall rejoice and blossom like the rose" (Isa. 35:1) in the kingdom of Messiah.

There are two facts about material blessings that we must always keep in mind. First, we don't obey God just to become wealthy and secure. We obey God because He is God and deserves our loving obedience. Obedience builds character, and when our character is what it ought to be, God can trust us with His blessings. Material blessings aren't bribes, nor are they rewards. They're God's way of saying, "You're maturing in godliness, and now I can give you more to use for My glory."

Second, God doesn't always respond with material blessings, and poverty is not a sign that God has forsaken His people. The experience of Job completely destroys this "commercial" idea of faith and obedience. Job's friends had a "commercial" view of faith, so they encouraged Job to confess his sins so God could again make him wealthy. Bargain with God! But Job refused to do that, though he didn't understand what the Lord was working out in his sufferings.

God's covenant with Israel declared that He would punish them physically and materially if they disobeyed Him, but bless them if they obeyed Him (Deut. 27–28; Lev. 26). However, He has no such covenant with Christian believers today. He promises to meet all our needs (Phil. 4:19) and direct in all our circumstances (Rom. 8:28), but our riches are of a heavenly nature (Eph. 1:3). If God chooses to make some of His people wealthy, it's that they might use what He gives them to help others (1 Tim. 6:17-19). He blesses us that we might be a blessing. However, riches are no proof of God's special love, nor is poverty evidence that He's forsaken us.

The covenant standards will be renewed (vv. 14-19). Whether God is dealing with His people in the Old Testament or the New Testament, His standards don't change. The church today doesn't live under Old Covenant law, but "the righteousness of the law" is still what God wants to develop in our lives (Rom. 8:1-4). "Be holy, for I am holy" is quoted from the Old Testament law for New Testament Christians (Lev. 11:44; 1 Peter 1:15-16).

God reminded His people of their obligations to speak the truth, to practice justice in the courts, to honor His name by not swearing falsely, and to love their neighbors. Of course, all the law is fulfilled in our conduct when we practice love (Rom. 13:8-10). The God of love hates sin! (See Prov. 6:16-19.) God's dispensations may change, and He can work in different ways at different times, but His character and standards never change. He wants His people to be "a holy nation" (Ex. 19:6; 1 Peter 2:9). "Therefore, love the truth and peace" (Zech. 8:19).

In verse 18, the prophet clearly answered the question about the fasts. The day would come when Messiah would reign and all Israel's fasts would become feasts! "And I will rejoice in Jerusalem, and joy in my people; and the voice of weeping shall be no more heard in her, nor the voice of crying" (Isa. 65:19). Zechariah and Isaiah were both saying, "Don't live in the past tense; live in the future tense! Rejoice at the promises God gives you for a joyful future!"[2]

The Gentiles will be redeemed (Zech. 8:20-23). God called Abraham and established the nation of Israel so His people would witness to the Gentiles and lead them to faith in the true God (Gen. 12:1-3). In setting apart one nation, God was seeking to reach a whole world. Many of the great events in Jewish history recorded in Scripture had behind them a witness to "the whole world": the plagues of Egypt (Ex. 9:16); the conquest of Canaan (Josh. 4:23-24); God's blessing of the nation (Deut. 28:9-11); and even the building of the temple (1 Kings 8:42-43). When David killed Goliath, he announced that God would give him victory so "that all the earth may know that there is a God in Israel" (1 Sam. 17:46).

But Israel failed in her mission to the Gentiles. Instead of the Gentile nations coming to worship the true God of Israel, the Jews forsook Jehovah and worshiped the false gods of the Gentile nations. The "court of the Gentiles" in Herod's temple became a market where Jews visiting Jerusalem from other countries could exchange their money and buy approved sacrifices. However, before we criticize the Jews too much, we had better examine the track record of the church when it comes to winning the lost at home and taking the Gospel to nations abroad.

When Messiah restores His people and establishes His kingdom, the Gentiles will trust the true and living God and come to Jerusalem to worship Him. Isaiah saw a river of Gentiles "flowing" into the city (Isa. 2:1-5) and Micah used the same figure (Micah 4:1-5). Zechariah describes a scene in which ten men (a Hebrew expression for "many men") will take hold of one Jew and beg to go with him to the temple!

It's a wonderful thing when God so blesses His people that others want what God's people have. "We have heard that God is with you" (Zech. 8:23). This sounds like what should happen in our local churches when an unbeliever beholds our worship of the Lord. "He will be convinced by all that he is a sinner and will be judged by all, and the secrets of his heart will be laid bare. So he will fall down and worship God, exclaiming, 'God is really among you!" (1 Cor. 14:24-25, NIV)

"I say then," wrote Paul, "has God cast away His people? Certainly not!" (Rom. 11:1, NKJV) There's a bright and blessed future for God's people Israel, even though the nation has been oppressed and persecuted by the Gentiles, some of whom claimed to be Christians. Our privilege is to love them, pray for them, and tell them that their Messiah, Jesus Christ, has come and will save them if they trust in Him.[3] The Gospel of Christ is still "the power of God for salvation to everyone who believes, for the Jew first and also for the Greek" (Rom. 1:16, NKJV).

CHAPTER FIVE
MESSIAH, THE SHEPHERD-KING
Zechariah 9-11

In the last half of his book, Zechariah presents two oracles ("burdens")[1] that focus on the first and second advents of the coming Messiah. These six chapters comprise one of the greatest concentrations of messianic truth found anywhere in Scripture, but the truth is always related to God's purposes for His people Israel. Zechariah reveals Messiah as the humble King, the loving Shepherd, the mighty Warrior, the gracious Savior, and the righteous Ruler who will reign on earth as King and Priest.

Bible students may not agree on the interpretation of each detail of these complex prophecies, but they do agree on the greatness of the Christ whose character and ministry are so vividly portrayed here. As we study these chapters, may our hearts burn within us (Luke 24:32) and may we love Him more.

1. Messiah's first advent (Zech. 9:1-9)

The coming of God's Son to this earth wasn't heaven's "Plan B" or a hasty decision by the Father after our first parents sinned. The plan of redemption was settled in eternity, before there ever was a creation. The coming of the Lamb of God was "foreordained before the foundation of the world" (1 Peter 1:20), for He was "the Lamb slain from the foundation of the world" (Rev. 13:8).

Preparation for the King (Zech. 9:1-8). These verses describe the march of Alexander the Great and his army through the area north and east of Palestine. Alexander defeated the Persians in 333 B.C. at the Battle of Issus and then turned to conquer the leading cities in Phoenicia. Daniel had predicted Alexander's success; he compared him to a winged leopard (Dan. 7:6) and a fighting he-goat (Dan. 8). It's been said that prophecy is history pre-written, and both Daniel and Zechariah wrote some of that history.

Hadrach was a region to the far north of Palestine, bordered by the Euphrates River, and Damascus was the capital of Syria. After defeating these nations, the Greek army then marched down the Phoenician coast, taking one city after another, from Tyre and Sidon in the north to Ashkelon and Gaza in the south. Indeed, God "cut off the pride of the Philistines" (Zech. 9:6) and put an end to their idolatrous worship (v. 7).[2]

The statement in verse 1 about "the eyes of men being toward the Lord" may mean that Alexander's victorious march caused people to look to God for help, but it could also mean that God's eyes were on the nations and especially on His people Israel. The NIV marginal translation says, "For the eye of the Lord is on all mankind, as well as on the tribes of Israel." Merrill Unger suggests that as the people were watching Alexander, they were actually watching God at work, for "history is His story."

After a two-month siege of Gaza, Alexander took the city and then went to Jerusalem.[3] He was unhappy with the Jews because they had refused to pay him the annual tribute that they usually gave to the Persians. The high priest in Jerusalem called for the people to fast and pray, and he presented sacrifices to the Lord to seek His special protection.

The night before Alexander and his army were to arrive at Jerusalem, the high priest had a dream in which God told him to adorn the city, tell the people to dress in white garments, and open the gates to their visitor. The high priest and the other priests would head the procession dressed in their holy robes. This they did, and Alexander was so impressed that he welcomed them in peace. The high priest told Alexander about Daniel's prophecies concerning him, and Alexander even offered sacrifices to Jehovah in the temple. Thus, the city and the people were spared.

But Zechariah had promised that Jerusalem and Judea would be spared. "I will camp around My house because of the army, because of him who passes by and him who returns" (v. 8, NKJV). Alexander had passed by Jerusalem en route to Gaza, but then he turned back to the Holy City. How much of Josephus' account is fact and how much is tradition, we can't tell, but we do know that God kept His promise and protected His people.

But why all this concern over the conquests of Alexander the Great? His conquests helped to prepare the world for the coming of Jesus Christ. By building Greek cities, encouraging his soldiers to marry women from conquered nations, and spreading Greek culture and the Greek language, he unified the known world, and when the Romans took over, they found an empire all prepared for them. Greek was the language of literature, and our New Testament is written in the common Greek language of the people of that day. The combination of Greek culture and Roman government, roads, and laws was just what the early church needed for the spread of the Gospel.

However, the promise in verse 8 goes far beyond the time of Alexander, for it states that God is always protecting His people and His house. No one can touch them without His permission. In the centuries since Alexander's conquest, the Jewish nation has suffered often because of invaders, and Jerusalem and the temple were destroyed by the Romans in A.D. 70. But the day will come when Messiah will reign and no invader will be able to threaten God's people let alone attack them.

Presentation of the King (v. 9). This prophecy was fulfilled when Jesus Christ rode into Jerusalem on what we traditionally call "Palm Sunday," and the event is recorded in all four Gospels (Matt. 21:1-11; Mark 11:1-11; Luke 19:29-44; and John 12:12-19). This is the only public demonstration Jesus allowed during His ministry, and He did it to fulfill Scripture.

When Zechariah put this prophecy about Jesus right after his prophecy concerning Alexander the Great, he was obviously inviting his readers to contrast the two conquerors. Alexander's arrival brought fear to people, but the Jews were commanded to rejoice and shout because their King had come. Jesus was righteous in all that He did, and His purpose in coming was to bring salvation to those who would trust Him. How different from Alexander!

Alexander rode a mighty steed and proudly led a great army from one victory to another, but Jesus rode a lowly donkey and came in humility.[4] The people who welcomed Him were common peasants who laid palm branches and garments before Him on the road. The great people of Jerusalem didn't welcome Him, but little children sang to Him in the temple. Jesus could have brought judgment, but instead He brought grace and forgiveness (John 3:17). Instead of making a grand oration, Jesus beheld the city and wept over it; instead of slaying His enemies, He went to a cross and died for them!

What a wonderful Conqueror! Let's move now to the future and examine His conquests.

2. Messiah's conquests at His second advent (Zech. 9:10–10:12)

The entire age of the church fits between Zechariah 9:9 and 9:10, just as it does between Isaiah 9:6 and 7 and after the comma in Isaiah 61:2. The prophet is now writing about what will happen when Jesus comes to earth to defeat His enemies and establish His kingdom. At His first advent, He rode a humble donkey; but at His second advent, He will ride a white horse and lead the armies of heaven (Rev. 19:11-21).

Messiah will proclaim peace (Zech. 9:10-13). At the beginning of World War I, British author H.G. Wells published a book called The War That Will End War. On November 11, 1918, at the end of the great war, Prime Minister David Lloyd George said to the British Parliament, "At eleven o'clock this morning came to an end the cruelest and most terrible war that has ever scourged mankind. I hope we may say that thus, this fateful morning, came to an end all wars." But Wells' title proved wrong and Lloyd George's wish was never fulfilled, for war is still with us.

However, when Jesus Christ comes again, He will "speak peace" (v. 10) which means "proclaim peace," for unlike authors and politicians, when Jesus speaks, His words carry authority and things happen (Ps. 33:9). His Word will go forth with power and there will be a general disarmament around the world. Chariots and war horses will be demobilized, every weapon will be destroyed, and "they shall beat their swords into plowshares, and their spears into pruning hooks; nation shall not lift up sword against nation, neither shall they learn war any more" (Isa. 2:4; see Micah 4:3). Our Lord's rule will be uNIVersal, from sea to sea and from the Euphrates River to the ends of the earth (see Ps. 72:8).

Zechariah 12:1-9 teaches that there will be one last battle before Jesus establishes His kingdom, as the Gentile armies attack Jerusalem. But the Lord will use Judah as His bow and Ephraim as His arrow and defeat all His enemies (9:13). He will call all His exiled people back from the many nations to which they've been scattered during this age, and they'll return to their "stronghold," which can mean both God their Refuge and the stronghold of Mount Zion. In their land, ruled over by their Messiah, the Jews will receive double blessing in return for all their suffering.

Messiah will march in triumph (9:14–10:1). The image here is that of a storm, not unlike what we read in Psalm 18:7-15 and Habakkuk 3:3-15. Messiah will march forth with a voice like thunder and arrows like lightning, and His army will march with Him. He'll shield them from danger and death and will enable them to defeat their enemies.

In Zechariah 9:15, the image changes from a storm to a feast and the prophet pictures the soldiers shouting like men who are drunk with wine. (See 10:7.) But instead of being drunk on wine, they're "drunk" with the blood of their enemies. Each man is "filled to the brim" like the bowls used at the temple to catch the blood of the sacrifices on the altar (Lev. 4:6-7).

Again, the image changes (Zech. 9:16–10:1) and the army is pictured as a flock of sheep which the Messiah saves by His power. Sheep are the last animals you would take to a war, but Israel has always been God's special flock (Ps. 100:3) and God "the Shepherd of Israel" (80:1). Zechariah will use the "flock" and "shepherd" images again in his prophecy (Zech. 10:2-3; 11:4-16; 13:7).

Once more, the image changes from sheep to precious stones (9:16). When the high priest Joshua was cleansed and clothed, he received the special holy turban that was his crown (3:5), and then he was crowned with a royal diadem that made him king as well as priest (6:9-12). But now it's God's people who are like beautiful precious jewels, sparkling in the land and revealing the beauty of their God.

This section ends with a brief description of the land and the changes God will make for the joy of His people (9:17–10:1). There will be plenty of grain in the fields and fruit in the vineyards because the Lord will provide the rain in its time. How often in their history the Jews turned for help to Baal, the god of storms, instead of turning to the Lord who alone can send the rain. (See 1 Kings 18.) During the Kingdom Age, the land of Palestine will be fruitful and beautiful as God provides the rain that is so necessary for anything to grow.

The promise of rain given in Zechariah 10:1 may have a spiritual meaning behind it, because the Holy Spirit is spoken of in terms of rain (Isa. 32:15; 44:3; Ezek. 29:39; Hosea 6:3; Joel 2:23-32). God promises to pour out His Spirit on Israel (Zech. 12:10) and bring them to repentance and faith in Christ.

Messiah will strengthen His people (10:2-12). Once again the prophet uses the image of the flock, this time a flock led by evil shepherds who cause them to wander and go astray (Matt. 9:36). The Jews were commanded to obey the priests, who would tell them God's will (Ex. 28:30; Lev. 8:8; Ezra 2:63), but too often the leaders turned to diviners and seers and used idolatrous divination devices which were forbidden by the law (Deut. 18:10-12). Israel in the latter days will be like wandering sheep because their leaders will follow lies instead of God's truth (see Ezek. 34).

But Messiah will turn the "sheep" into war-horses! (Zech. 10:3) He will punish the evil shepherds (leaders) and give victory to His people. Several striking images of Messiah are given in verse 4. The cornerstone speaks of Christ the foundation for His people, the keystone that joins the walls. (See 3:10 and references to the Stone.) The tent peg refers to Messiah as one on whom burdens may be placed with confidence (see Isa. 22:20-24), and as the battle bow, He is the victorious Warrior who never loses a battle (Ps. 45:5; Isa. 63:2-4). Note that Messiah comes "from Judah" (Zech. 10:4), for God gave the messianic promise to Judah in Genesis 49:10. Every ruler of the nation since David came from the tribe of Judah, for it was with David that God made His covenant (2 Sam. 7).

The emphasis in the rest of the paragraph is on "strength" and "mighty men" (Zech. 10:5-7, 12). Because the Lord will be with the Jews, they will trample their enemies down like mud in the streets, and they will go from victory to victory in the strength of the Lord. God will also call His scattered sheep back home from the many countries where they've been scattered. Just as a shepherd can whistle or play a tune on a pipe and call his flock together, so the Lord will gather His people. It will be like a second "exodus" when they pass through the "sea of affliction" to return to the Lord and to their land.

What a day of victory! God's people Israel will be regathered, redeemed, reunited as one nation, and rejoicing in the strength of the Lord! But this same God can give the same blessings to His church today. We're a scattered people, divided and sometimes distant from each other, but the Lord can unite us in Christ and bring us together. We're fighting battles against the enemy, but the Lord can strengthen us and turn His helpless sheep into victorious war-horses. How much He is willing to do for us, if only we would admit our failures and unbelief and turn to Him for help.

3. Messiah rejected by His people (Zech. 11:1-17)

The two chapters we've just surveyed indicate that Israel will be in trouble in the last days until their Messiah comes to rescue them, cleanse them, and give them a kingdom. How did they get into this trouble?

During the time of David and Solomon, Israel was the most powerful nation on earth, with wealth and resources beyond measure. After Solomon's death, the nation divided into two kingdoms, Israel and Judah. Israel, the Northern Kingdom, began to deteriorate, so God sent the Assyrians to conquer them and scatter them. Judah had a series of godless kings, so God sent the Babylonians to take Judah captive.

Seventy years later, a small band of Jews returned to their land to rebuild their temple. Life was difficult, and the nation had none of its former glory; but over the years they persisted and restored the temple and the city. Then their Messiah, Jesus Christ, came to them, and they rejected Him and asked their Roman rulers to have Him crucified. About forty years later, in A.D. 70, the Roman armies came and destroyed Jerusalem and the temple and scattered the Jews to the nations of the world. Because they didn't receive their own Messiah, they have been a scattered people ever since.

This chapter explains the nation's rejection of the true Messiah and how they will accept a false messiah, the Antichrist, who will appear at the end of the age and deceive the whole world. The key image in the chapter is that of the shepherd, and three different shepherds are presented.

The wailing shepherds (vv. 1-3). These brief verses describe the invasion of the Holy Land by the Romans. Key places like the Jordan, Lebanon, and Bashan are mentioned. The invading army is like a fire that burns the forests. The "wailing shepherds" are the rulers of the nation who have led the people astray and are now paying for their sins. In the East, leaders and rulers were called "shepherds" because they led the people, protected them, and provided for them. Jeremiah saw a similar scene: "Weep and wail, you shepherds; roll in the dust, you leaders of the flock. For your time to be slaughtered has come" (Jer. 25:34, NIV). Usually the shepherds gave the sheep for slaughter, but here the shepherds themselves are led to the slaughter!

The high priest Caiaphas thought that by killing Jesus, he would save the Jewish nation from destruction (John 11:47-53), but just the opposite occurred. By rejecting their Messiah, they opened the doors to judgment and dispersal. It was true that Jesus did die for the nation of Israel, for He died for the sins of the whole world (1 John 2:1-3), but their rejection of truth led to their acceptance of lies, and the result was the Roman invasion and the destruction of their temple and city.

The true Shepherd (Zech. 11:4-14). God commanded Zechariah to play the role of the true Shepherd. He became a type of the Messiah at the time when our Lord was ministering on earth. The flock of Israel was destined for slaughter because of their wicked rulers, but he was to do his best to rescue them. The Jewish leaders weren't concerned about the sheep; they were concerned only about their own position and power. Did Zechariah actually obtain a flock and become a shepherd, or was this only to be written in his book? Isaiah, Jeremiah, and especially Ezekiel used "action sermons" to get the attention of the careless people,[5] so perhaps that's what Zechariah did. He carried the two instruments of a faithful shepherd, a staff (crook) to guide the sheep and a rod to ward off enemies, and he paid special attention to the oppressed ("poor") in the flock, those who needed special attention. According to verse 11, some of the "poor of the flock" were watching him, so apparently this was an "action sermon."

He called the one staff "Beauty" (Favor, Grace) and the other one "Bands" (Union). He fed the flock and even got rid of three unfaithful shepherds.[6] Then one day he broke both of the staves! God's favor to His people had come to an end; the covenant union between God and His people was broken. But so also was the union between Judah (the Southern Kingdom) and Israel (v. 14).[7]

God is long-suffering and waits for sinners to repent and believe, but there comes a time when He has done all that He will do to reach them. This happened to Israel when Jesus was ministering on earth. "But although He had done so many signs before them, they did not believe in Him" (John 12:37, NKJV). Jesus Himself said, "How often I wanted to gather your children together, as a hen gathers her chicks under her wings, but you were not willing" (Matt. 23:37).

Actually, the people wanted Zechariah to quit! He asked for his wages and they gave him the price of a slave, thirty pieces of silver (Ex. 21:32), an amount that he sarcastically called "a lordly—handsome—price." So disgusted was he with his wages that he went to the temple and threw the money to the potter who was working there, perhaps supplying vessels for the priests.

According to Matthew 27:1-10, Zechariah's actions were prophetic, for Judas sold Jesus for thirty pieces of silver, brought the money back, and threw it into the temple. The priests took the money and used it to buy an abandoned potter's field as a cemetery for strangers. But verse 9 attributes the quotation to Jeremiah, not Zechariah, a fact that has puzzled Bible students for centuries.

If we have a high view of inspiration, we can't simply dismiss this statement as a mistake or a scribal error; nor can we escape by saying that Jeremiah spoke the prophecy, but Zechariah wrote it in his book. Wouldn't you expect to find it in Jeremiah's book? Perhaps the solution lies in understanding the way ancient authors used texts from other writers.

First of all, how does Jeremiah get into the picture? It appears that Matthew alludes to Jeremiah's actions recorded in Jeremiah 19, when he broke the jar and pronounced judgment on Judah and Jerusalem. He announced that the Valley of the Son of Hinnom, outside Jerusalem, would become a cemetery because of the sins of the people (Jer. 19:11). Note that this event took place near the entrance of the east gate, which was the Potter's Gate leading to a potter's field (vv. 1-2), and note also the phrase "innocent blood" in verse 4, a phrase that Judas used when he returned the silver to the priests (Matt. 27:4). So, from Jeremiah, Matthew borrowed the images of a potter's field, innocent blood, and a cemetery.

Matthew cited Zechariah 11:12-13 concerning the thirty pieces of silver which were thrown down to the potter in the temple. Why would a potter be in the temple? Since the priests used many different kinds of vessels, the services of a potter would certainly be necessary. So, from Zechariah, Matthew borrowed the temple, the thirty pieces of silver which were thrown down in the temple, and the potter to whom they were thrown.

Now, it's obvious that Zechariah's words don't perfectly parallel the events described in Matthew 27:1-10. In Zechariah, the money was given to the prophet while in Matthew, it was given to Judas the traitor. The prophet gave the money to the potter in the temple, but Judas gave his wages to the priests who then bought a potter's field. What Matthew did was unite (the technical word is "conflate") elements from both Jeremiah and Zechariah, but since Zechariah was a minor prophet, he named only Jeremiah, the major prophet.[8]

Whatever view you take of this matter, it's remarkable that Jesus was sold for thirty pieces of silver, that the silver was thrown down in the temple, and that the silver was used to buy a potter's field. And all of this happened because the Jewish people rejected Zechariah the shepherd and Jesus the Good Shepherd!

The false shepherd (Zech. 11:15-17). The prophet was then commanded to adopt the role of a "foolish shepherd." The word "foolish" doesn't mean "stupid" but "morally deficient, corrupt" because he doesn't receive God's truth. He's also called "a worthless (idle) shepherd," because he doesn't care for the sheep. Unlike the Good Shepherd, he doesn't seek the lost, care for the young, feed the flock, or heal the injured. All he does is slaughter the flock to feed himself! (See Ezek. 34.)

Because Israel rejected their true Shepherd, Jesus Christ, they will one day blindly accept and obey the false shepherd (Antichrist) who will lead them astray. Those who reject the light inevitably accept the darkness. "I have come in My Father's name," said Jesus, "and you do not receive Me; if another comes in his own name, him you will receive" (John 5:43, NKJV).

According to Daniel 9:27, the Antichrist will actually be able to make a covenant with the Jews for seven years. Probably this is for the purpose of protecting them so they can rebuild their temple and resume their sacrifices. But after three and a half years, he'll break the covenant, put his own image in the temple, and force the world to worship him (2 Thes. 2:1-12; Rev. 13).

That God's chosen people, who possess the inspired Scriptures, should reject Him who is "the truth" (John 14:6) and came from the Father, and follow one who is a liar and is energized by Satan, is incredible to comprehend, but it will happen just as the Scripture says. However, the Lord will judge this false shepherd by breaking his power (his right arm) and confusing his mind (right eye), and then Messiah will come from heaven and confine him to the lake of fire for a thousand years (Rev. 19:11-21).

During that thousand years, Christ will reign in His glorious kingdom, Israel will receive the blessings promised by the prophets, the church will reign with Him, and all creation will enter into "the glorious liberty of the children of God" (Rom. 8:21, NKJV).

Thy kingdom come!

CHAPTER SIX
REDEEMED, REFINED, AND RESTORED
Zechariah 12-14

In this second oracle, Zechariah takes us to the end times. He describes the Gentile nations attacking Jerusalem, the Jews experiencing severe trials ("the time of Jacob's trouble"), and then the Lord returning in power and great glory to deliver His people and establish the promised kingdom. What an exciting scenario it is! But it isn't fiction; it's God's own Word, and it will come to pass.

As you study these three chapters, note the repetition of the phrase "in that day," which is found sixteen times. "That day" is "the Day of the Lord," the day of wrath and judgment that the prophets wrote about (Joel 3:9-16; Zeph. 1), and that Jesus described in

Matthew 24:4-31 and John in Revelation 6–19.

Zechariah describes three key events.

1. The Lord will deliver Jerusalem (Zech. 12:1-9; 14:1-7)

Jerusalem is mentioned fifty-two times in the Book of Zechariah, and twenty-two of these references are in the final three chapters. In the first chapter of his prophecy, Zechariah told us that God was "jealous for Jerusalem and for Zion with a great jealousy" (1:14). This statement reveals the yearning heart of a loving Father for His firstborn (Ex. 4:22) and the desire of a faithful Husband for His unfaithful bride (Jer. 2:2; 3:2). God's timing isn't always what we would have planned, but He is wiser than we are and will keep His promises to Israel.

Jerusalem will be attacked (Zech. 12:1-3; 14:1-2). The oracle opens with an affirmation of God's sovereignty and power. If we look above us, we see the heavens He created; if we look beneath us, we see the earth that He founded; and if we look within, we find the spirit that He formed. The God of creation is the God who cares for us! "Great is our Lord and mighty in power; His understanding is infinite. The Lord lifts up the humble; He casts the wicked down to the ground" (Ps. 147:5-6, NKJV).

Note the emphasis on "all nations" and "all peoples" (Zech. 12:2-3, 6, 9; 14:2, 12, 14, 16), for this attack involves the armies of the whole world and is part of the famous "battle of Armageddon" described in Joel 3:9-16; Matthew 24:27-30; and Revelation 9:13-18; 16:12-16; and 19:17-21.1 Three forces are involved in the gathering of this great army: (1) the nations agree to cooperate in their fight against God and His people (Ps. 2:1-3); (2) Satan uses demonic powers to influence the nations to gather (Rev. 16:13-15); and (3) the Lord exercises His sovereign powers in gathering them (Zech. 14:2; Rev. 16:16).

To describe Jerusalem's situation "in that day," Zechariah used the images of a cup and a stone. A cup is a familiar biblical image for judgment (Ps. 75:8; Isa. 51:17, 21-23; Jer. 25:15-28; Ezek. 23:31-33; Hab. 2:16; Rev. 14:10; 16:19; 18:6). The nations plan to "swallow up" Jerusalem, but when they begin to "drink the cup," its contents makes them sick and drunk! History shows that every nation that has ever tried to destroy the Jews has itself been destroyed. It will be no different when the nations collectively attack God's chosen people.

Some of the enemy soldiers will enter the city, loot it, abuse the women, and take half of the inhabitants captive. But the Gentiles' hopes of destroying the city and the nation will be disappointed, for the Lord will make Jerusalem like an immovable rock that won't yield. This stone will eventually cut the invading armies to pieces.

The Lord will visibly appear (Zech. 14:3-7). Our Lord ascended to heaven from the Mount of Olives (Acts 1:9-12), and when He returns to earth, He will stand on the Mount of Olives and cause a great earthquake to change the terrain (Isa. 29:6; Rev. 16:18-19). This will create a new valley that will provide an escape route for many of the people. There will also be changes in the heavens so that the day will be neither light nor darkness, morning nor evening (see Isa. 60:19-20).

"The Lord is a man of war," sang the Jews after they were delivered from Egypt (Ex. 15:3), but this aspect of Christ's character and ministry is ignored, if not opposed, by people today. In their quest for world peace, some denominations have removed the "militant songs" from their hymnals, so that a new generation is growing up knowing nothing about "fighting the good fight of faith" or worshiping a Savior who will one day meet the nations of the world in battle (Rev. 19:11-21).

Before the nation entered the Promised Land, Moses promised them that the Lord would fight for them (Deut. 1:30; 3:22). "Who is the King of glory?" asked David; and his answer was, "The Lord strong and mighty, the Lord mighty in battle" (Ps. 24:8). Isaiah announced, "The Lord will march out like a mighty man, like a warrior He will stir up His zeal; with a shout He will raise the battle cry and will triumph over His enemies" (Isa. 42:13, NIV). Our God has been long-suffering toward the nations, but one day He will meet them in battle and triumph over them.

The Lord will defeat the enemy (Zech. 12:4-9; 14:12-15). Panic, a plague, and special power given to the Jewish warriors (12:8) are the means God will use to conquer the invading armies. The horses will panic in their blindness and the riders will be possessed by madness and end up fighting each other (14:13).2 God will watch over His people and see to it that they are delivered. He will make the Jews to be like fire and their enemies like dry stubble. Jesus Christ will demonstrate His great power as He defends His people and defeats His enemies.

While the inhabitants of Jerusalem are central in this account, special notice is given to the part Judah will play in the battle. For the invaders to get to Jerusalem, they must march through Judah (12:2); but the Lord will keep watch over the people of Judah and deliver them for David's sake (vv. 4, 7). The faith and courage of the people in Jerusalem will encourage Judah to wax valiant in the fight, and God will enable them to conquer (vv. 5-6). The weakest Jewish warrior will have the power of David, who slew tens of thousands of enemy soldiers (1 Sam. 18:7). The Jewish army will go forth like the Angel of the Lord who slew 185,000 Assyrian soldiers in one night (Isa. 37).

2. The Lord will cleanse Israel (Zech. 12:10–13:9)

In delivering Israel from her enemies, our Lord's ultimate goal is more than their national preservation, for their spiritual restoration is uppermost in His heart. He wants to reveal Himself to them and establish the kind of relationship that was impossible in previous centuries because of their unbelief.

The people will repent (12:10-14). Repentance isn't something we work up ourselves; it's a gift from God as we hear His Word and recognize His grace (Acts 5:31; 11:18; 2 Tim. 2:25). God will pour out the Spirit[3] upon Israel (Joel 2:28-29), and the people will realize their sins and call out to God for forgiveness. They will also see their Messiah whom the nation pierced (Ps. 22:16; Isa. 53:5; John 19:34, 37) and will put their faith in Him. Forgiveness comes to any believing sinner only through faith in the sacrifice of Christ on the cross.

The nation will go into mourning, the way parents would mourn over the loss of their only son, the way the nation mourned near Megiddo when their beloved King Josiah was slain in battle (2 Chron. 35:20-27). Zechariah mentions that all the families (clans) of Israel will mourn, the men and women separately, and this will include royalty (David's clan), the prophets (Nathan's clan; see 2 Sam. 7), and the priests (Levi's and Shimei's clans; Num. 3:17-18, 21). "All the families that remain" covers the rest of the nation. It will be a time of deep and sincere national repentance such as has not been seen before.

The nation will be cleansed (Zech. 13:1-7). Isaiah had admonished the nation, "Wash yourselves, make yourselves clean; put away the evil of your doings from before My eyes" (Isa. 1:16, NKJV), but they refused to listen. Jeremiah had pleaded with his people, "O Jerusalem, wash your heart from wickedness, that you may be saved" (Jer. 4:14, NKJV), but they wouldn't obey. But now, in response to Israel's repentance and faith, the Lord will wash them clean! This forgiveness is part of the new covenant that God promised to His people (Jer. 31:31-34): "For I will forgive their wickedness and will remember their sins no more" (v. 34).

William Cowper based his hymn "There Is a Fountain Filled with Blood" on Zechariah 13:1, for it's the sacrifice of Christ that atones for sin. The Jews could cleanse their external ceremonial uncleanness by washing in water, but for internal cleansing the sinful heart of men and women can be cleansed only by the blood of the Savior (Lev. 16:30; 17:11). "And He Himself is the propitiation for our sins, and not for ours only but also for the whole world" (1 John 2:2, NKJV).

But not only will their hearts be cleansed, but the land itself will be purged of all that is deceitful and defiling. The idols and the false prophets[4]—two of Israel's besetting sins—will be removed, as well as the very "unclean spirit" that caused people to turn from God. (See Zech. 5:5-11.)

According to the Law, false prophets were to be killed (Deut. 13); so the false prophets in that day will lie about their occupation in order to save their lives (13:2-6). They won't wear their special garments (v. 4; 2 Kings 1:8; Matt. 3:4), and they'll claim to be farmers rather than prophets. If asked about the scars on their bodies, actually caused by wounds inflicted while worshiping idols (1 Kings 18:28), they will lie and claim that their friends (or family) inflicted the wounds to discipline them.[5]

In contrast to the false prophets, the true Shepherd is presented in Zechariah 13:7. (Review Zech. 11 for the other "Shepherd" prophecies.) Jesus quoted part of this prophecy when He was on His way to Gethsemane with His disciples (Matt. 26:31), and He referred to it again when He was arrested in the garden (v. 56). Only Jesus the Messiah could the Father call "the man who is My fellow," that is, "the man who is My equal." (See John 10:30 and 14:9.)

But there is also a wider meaning of this text as it relates to the scattering of the nation in A.D. 70 when Jerusalem was taken by the Romans. The Jews had smitten their Shepherd on the cross (Isa. 53:10), and this act of rejection led to the nation being scattered (Deut. 28:64; 29:24-25). Israel today is a dispersed people, but one day they shall be gathered; they are a defiled people, but one day they shall be cleansed.

The nation will be refined (Zech. 13:8-9). This image reminds us of the value God puts on His people Israel: they are like gold and silver that need to be refined in the furnace of affliction. This had been their experience in Egypt (Deut. 4:20) and in Babylon (Isa. 48:10), but "the time of Jacob's trouble" will be their most difficult "furnace experience."

The goldsmith refines the gold or silver so that the dross may be removed, and that's what the Tribulation in the last days will accomplish for Israel. One third of the people will be spared, the true believing remnant, while the rest will be rejected and perish. That godly remnant who called on the Lord (Acts 2:21) will be saved and become the nucleus of the promised kingdom, for the Lord will acknowledge them as His own people (see Hosea 2:21-23).

Before we leave this section, we need to see the spiritual application for God's people today. Certainly the church is a defiled people who need to repent and be cleansed, and the promise of forgiveness is still valid (1 John 1:9). God often has to put us through the furnace of suffering before we'll call on Him and seek His face (Heb. 12:3-11; 1 Peter 4:12). If God's people will follow the instructions of 2 Chronicles 7:14, the Lord will cleanse and bless the church and bring healing to the land.

3. The Lord reigns over all the earth (Zech. 14:8-11, 16-21)

"And the Lord shall be king over all the earth; in that day shall there be one Lord, and His name one" (v. 9). After the nations have been punished and Israel has been purified, the Lord will establish His righteous kingdom and reign on David's throne (Luke 1:32-33; Rev. 17:14; 19:16). His reign will be uNIVersal ("over all the earth"), He will be the only God worshiped, and His name will be the only name honored. (See Ps. 72; Jer. 30:7-9.) What will happen when the King reigns supremely?

The land will be healed (Zech. 14:8). Jerusalem is the only great city of antiquity that wasn't built near a large river. But during the Kingdom Age,[6] a river of "living waters" will flow from Jerusalem and bring healing and fertility to the land. (See Ezek. 47:1-12 and Joel 3:18.) The river will divide so the waters can flow to the Dead Sea ("former sea," KJV, "eastern sea," NIV) and to the Mediterranean Sea ("hinder," KJV, "western," NIV). For centuries people have been wondering how the Dead Sea could be rescued, but it won't be accomplished until the kingdom. For a beautiful description of the land during the Kingdom Age, read Isaiah 35.

The topography will be changed (Zech. 14:10-11). Besides the changes caused by the earthquake at Christ's return (vv. 4-5), two other changes will occur: (1) the land around Jerusalem will be lowered and leveled and become a plain, and (2) Jerusalem itself will be raised above the land around it. These changes will be the fulfillment of Isaiah's prophecy, "Now it shall come to pass in the latter days that the mountain of the Lord's house shall be established on the top of the mountains, and shall be exalted above the hills; and all nations shall flow to it" (Isa. 2:2, NKJV; and see Zech. 8:1-3 and Micah 4:1-3).

If Messiah is to reign as King-Priest (Zech. 6:9-15), then there must be a temple and a priesthood during the Kingdom Age, and it is described in detail in Ezekiel 40–48. Jerusalem will be the most important city on earth and the temple area the most important part of that glorious new city.[7]

All dangers will be removed (Zech. 14:11). The mountains round about Jerusalem were for her protection (Pss. 48:1-8; 125:1-2); but now that Messiah is reigning, the city no longer faces danger from enemy invasion (Ezek. 34:22-31). "It will be inhabited" (NIV) reminds us that only 50,000 Jews were willing to leave the safe and comfortable city of Babylon to live in the ruins of Jerusalem, and even Nehemiah had trouble getting people to live in the city (Neh. 11). Zechariah has already told us that the children will play in the streets, and the old men and women will sit in the sun and talk together (Zech. 8:4-8).

The Gentiles will worship at Jerusalem (14:16). Israel will have a ministry to the Gentiles who will trust the true and living God and come to Jerusalem to worship at His temple (Isa. 2:2-5; Zech. 2:10-13). Of the seven annual feasts listed in Leviticus 23, the Feast of Tabernacles is the only one that will be celebrated during the Kingdom Age (Lev. 23:33-44). This feast commemorated the nation's wilderness wanderings, but it also was a time of rejoicing at the bountiful blessings of the Lord during the harvest (v. 40).

But why celebrate only the Feast of Tabernacles? Merrill Unger makes an excellent suggestion when he points out that the Feast of Tabernacles is the only one of the seven feasts of Leviticus 23 that will not have been fulfilled when the kingdom is established.

Passover was fulfilled in the death of Christ (1 Cor. 5:7; John 1:29), Firstfruits in His resurrection (15:23), and the week-long Feast of Unleavened Bread in the life of the church today as believers walk in holiness (5:6-8). Pentecost was fulfilled in Acts 2, and the Feast of Trumpets will be fulfilled before the kingdom begins when God regathers His people from the ends of the earth (Isa. 18:3, 7; Matt. 24:29-31). The Day of Atonement will be fulfilled when the nation sees her Messiah, repents, and is cleansed.

But the Feast of Tabernacles foreshadows the joyful and fruitful Kingdom Age, so it will be celebrated while the kingdom is in progress.[8] It will be an annual reminder to the Gentile nations that the bountiful blessings they enjoy come from a gracious and generous Lord. How easy it is to take our blessings for granted!

The Lord will exercise justice (Zech. 14:17-19). The nations that don't send their representatives to Jerusalem to worship will be disciplined by getting no rain for their land. This is the way God disciplined Israel when she refused to obey Him (Deut. 28:22-24). Remember, though the millennium is a time of peace and blessing, it is also a time when Jesus will reign over all the earth "with a rod of iron" and will judge disobedience (Ps. 2:9; Rev. 2:27; 12:5; 19:15). Not to celebrate the Feast of Tabernacles would be tantamount to despising the blessings of the Lord, and this is a serious transgression. (See Rom. 1:18.)

Egypt is mentioned specifically because that nation especially depended on the annual flooding of the Nile for irrigation, and without the rains, the river could not rise. During the time of Joseph, there were seven years of terrible famine in Egypt. Also, Egypt had been Israel's persecutor and enemy, and during the kingdom, she will enjoy blessing because of Israel's Messiah. Not to show gratitude would be a heinous sin.

Holiness will characterize all of life (Zech. 14:20-21). We might expect "holiness" to be written on the bells of the high priest's robe (Ex. 28:36-38), but certainly not on the bells worn by the horses! And why would the common utensils in the home be treated like vessels used in the temple?[9] These two images are God's way of saying, "In the Kingdom Age every aspect of life will be holy to the Lord." God had called Israel to be "a kingdom of priests" (Ex. 19:6), and now they would be just that by God's grace.

For the believer today, this is the Old Testament version of 1 Corinthains 10:31, "Therefore, whether you eat or drink, or whatever you do, do all to the glory of God" (NKJV). There is no "secular" or "sacred" in the Christian life, because everything comes from God and should be used for His glory.

The Hebrew word translated "Canaanite" in Zechariah 14:21 refers to merchants and traders or to any unclean person, both of whom would defile the temple of God. When Jesus began His ministry and ended it, He found "religious merchants" using God's house for personal gain (John 2:13-22; Matt. 21:12-13; Mark 11:15-17; Luke 19:45-46). The house of prayer for all nations had been turned into a den of thieves for the profit of the Jewish high priest and his family. But the millennial temple will be a holy temple, not defiled by those who neither know the Lord nor love Him, and in it a holy priesthood will serve the Lord.

Zechariah's book begins with a call to repentance, but it ends with a vision of a holy nation and a glorious kingdom. Zechariah was one of God's heroes who ministered at a difficult time and in a difficult place, but he encouraged God's people by showing them visions of what God has planned for their future. God is still jealous over Jerusalem and the Jewish people, and He will fulfill His promises.

"Pray for the peace of Jerusalem" (Ps. 122:6).

ENDNOTES

Chapter 1

1. Zechariah the postexilic prophet must not be confused with the Zechariah who was martyred in the days of King Joash (2 Chron. 24:20-22) and to whom Jesus referred (Matt. 23:35). Their fathers had the same first name, but this wasn't uncommon in Bible times. Since the Hebrew Bible ends with 2 Chronicles, Jesus was saying, "From the beginning of the Scriptures [Abel's murder in Genesis] to the very end of the Scriptures [Zechariah's murder in 2 Chron.], all the innocent blood that was shed will be held against you." We have no evidence that the Zechariah who ministered with Haggai was ever slain.

2. See chapter 29 of *Born After Midnight,* by A.W. Tozer (Christian Publications, 1959).

3. The Jews certainly knew the terms of God's covenant. If they obeyed, the blessing would overtake them (Deut. 28:2), but if they disobeyed, the curses would catch up with them. "But it shall come to pass, if you do not obey the voice of the Lord your God . . . that all these curses will come upon you and overtake you . . . Moreover all these curses shall come upon you and pursue you and overtake you until you are destroyed" (Deut. 28:15, 45, NKJV).

4. See Revelation 2:5, 16, 21-22; 3:3, 19. Five of the seven churches to which Jesus wrote were commanded to repent.

5. Students of prophecy aren't agreed as to the starting date for the Captivity. If you begin with 606–605, when the first prisoners were taken to Babylon, then the Captivity ended in 537 when the Jews returned to Judah, led by Zerubbabel and Joshua. If you count from the destruction of Jerusalem and the temple in 586, then the Captivity ended with the dedication of the second temple in 515. If the latter date is what the Lord had in mind, then the completing of the temple was indeed a key event. However, the question in Zechariah 1:12 implies that the seventy years were now over.

6. Jeremiah lamented that nobody had comforted Jerusalem after the city was destroyed (Lam. 1:2, 9, 16-17, 21).

7. The London Observer, 2 Jan. 1983. Quoted in *The Columbia Dictionary of Quotations,* compiled by Robert Andrews (New York: Columbia UNIversity Press, 1993), 477.

8. The neo-Roman Empire appears again at the end of the age under the control of the Beast (Dan. 7:8; Rev. 13). This empire will be destroyed by the return of Christ in power and great glory (Dan. 2:44-45 and 7:9ff).

9. Alexander's conquests are mentioned in Zechariah 9:1-8, 13.

10. The word "pupil" comes from the Latin pupilla, "a tiny doll," referring to the small reflection you see of yourself when you look into another's eyes. The Hebrew word for "apple" (pupil) in Deuteronomy 32:10 is literally "little man."

Chapter 2

1. Kouzes, James M., and Posner, Berry Z. *The Leadership Challenge* (San Francisco: Jossey-Bass Publishers, 1987), xvi.

2. It sunk even lower after the temple was completed. Read the prayer of Ezra (Ezra 9) and the Book of Malachi for proof. When our Lord came to earth, the flame of Jewish faith was flickering.

3. Unger, *Merrill F. Commentary on Zechariah* (Grand Rapids: Zondervan, 1963), p. 59.

4. In Solomon's temple, the one large candlestick was replaced with ten smaller ones (1 Kings 7:49; 1 Chron. 28:15).

5. Havner, Vance. *The Vance Havner Quote Book,* compiled by Dennis J. Hester (Grand Rapids: Baker Book House, 1986), 111.

Chapter 3

1. The Hebrew word eretz can mean either "land" or "earth" depending on the context, and sometimes it isn't easy to determine which is meant. In Zechariah 4:14, eretz is obviously "earth," for our God is "lord of the whole earth." The NIV translates eretz "land" in 5:3 and 6, meaning the land of Israel; while the KJV and NKJV use "earth," meaning the whole world. I prefer the NIV translation since these visions deal especially with the sins of the Jewish nation against the Law of God.

2. By making a minor change in the Hebrew text, the NIV translators have the white horses going to the west, but the received text has the white horses following the blackhorses.

3. The KJV translated it "crowns," but how could you put several crowns on one man's head? The Hebrew word is plural, but this refers to the elaborateness of the crown. It was a diadem (Rev. 19:12), one crown with several levels, one on top of the other.

4. The statement "Behold the man" (v. 12) reminds us of what Pilate said to the Jews in John 19:5 when he presented Christ to them. It reminds us of the Gospel of Luke, the Gospel of the Son of Man. "Behold my servant" (Isa. 42:1) reminds us of Mark, the Gospel of the Servant; "Behold your King" (Zech. 9:9) relates to Matthew, the Gospel of the King; and "Behold your God" (Isa. 40:9) reminds us of the Gospel of John, the Gospel of the Son of God.

5. Some people "spiritualize" these kingdom prophecies and relate them to the church today rather than to a restored Israel in the future. That there are present-day applications of Old Testament passages, no honest student would deny; for the only "Bible" the first-century church had was the Old Testament. But there's a difference between application and interpretation. Each passage has only one basic interpretation, even though there may be several applications.

Chapter 4

1. However, let's not wait until then to show compassion to the unborn and the elderly. If God's ideal is happy children playing together in the streets and elderly people chatting together, then why not aim for the ideal today? Jesus came that we might have abundant life as well as eternal life, but our modern cities are more and more becoming places of death.

2. For that matter, their fasts didn't accomplish anything because their hearts weren't right with God (Zech. 7:4-14). They only went through a religious ritual that did more harm than good. Better not to do it

at all than to do it and not mean it.

3. Contemporary opposition to Jewish evangelism is a subtle new form of anti-Semitism. The Christian church owes so much to Israel, and the best way to pay the debt is to share the Gospel with the Jewish people. If it's wrong to witness to Jews, then Jesus was wrong, and so were Peter and Paul. Jesus wept over Jerusalem and Paul was willing to go to hell for their conversion (Rom. 9:1-3). That ought to be motivation enough for us to lovingly witness to the people who gave us the Bible and the Savior.

Chapter 5

1. The Hebrew word means "to lift up," suggesting that the prophet lifted his voice to proclaim the Word of God. But there's also the idea of a heavy weight that the prophet carries because of the seriousness of the message.

2. The conquest of Philistia had also been predicted by Isaiah (23:1-18), Jeremiah (25:22; 47:4), Ezekiel (26:1-21 and 28:20-24), and Amos (1:9-10).

3. The account of Alexander's visit to the Holy City is recorded by the Jewish historian Josephus in his Antiquities of the Jews, book XI.8, sections 3–5.

4. The donkey was the animal used by royalty (2 Sam. 16:2; 18:9; 1 Kings 1:33).

5. Isaiah gave his two sons names that illustrated what he was preaching to the people, and he also dressed scantily, like a prisoner of war, for three years. Jeremiah wore a yoke, publicly broke pottery, and wore a dirty girdle. Ezekiel "played" at war, got a haircut and disposed of the cuttings in three unusual ways, and cut a hole in the wall so he could "escape."

6. Students have a tough time figuring out who these three shepherds were. They scour lists of the names of rulers, priests, and other important people who lived at that time, but we have to confess that we just don't know and it's useless to speculate.

7. History reveals that the Jews have had a tendency to break up into parties and sects rather than try to agree and work together for common goals. Over the centuries, they have produced many different groups, religious and political, and there will be no national unity until the "birth" of the new nation when Messiah comes.

8. In Mark 1:1-3, in the best Greek texts, Mark quotes Malachi 3:1 and Isaiah 40:3 and says, "As it is written in Isaiah the prophet." He names the greater prophet.

Chapter 6

1. The word "Armageddon" is used only in Revelation 16:16. Some students of prophecy prefer "the campaign of Armageddon" since the invasion and attack take place in several stages.

2. That the last great world battle will involve horses and riders is a puzzle to some. But the prophets wrote so that the people could understand, and horses and chariots were the strongest and best equipment an army could have in their day. However, the description of the results of the plague (14:12-15) resembles that of the victims of an atomic blast.

3. The NIV reads "a spirit of grace and supplication," that is, an attitude of heart, and gives "the Spirit" in the margin. But parallel passages suggest that it is the Holy Spirit of God who is referred to (Joel 2:28-29; Ezek. 29:39; and see Peter's reference to Joel's prophecy when the Spirit came at Pentecost (Acts 2:16-21).

4. Having rejected the truth, the Jewish nation fell prey to lies, especially false prophets. Jeremiah had to battle the false prophets in his day, and false prophets will abound in the end times (Matt. 24:4-5, 11, 23-24).

5. Some interpreters apply verse 6 to the Messiah, but the context prohibits this. In verses 2-6, it's clearly the false prophets who are being discussed.

6. The reign of Christ on earth is usually called "the Millennium" because it will last for 1,000 years. "Millennium" comes from the Latin: mille = thousand; annum = year. See Revelation 20:1-7.

7. Some students equate the millennial Jerusalem of Ezekiel 40–48 with the heavenly city described in Revelation 21–22, but to accept that view requires total disregard of several facts. There is no temple in the heavenly city (Rev. 21:22), but Jerusalem in the Kingdom Age will have a temple and a priesthood. Worshipers from all nations will celebrate the Jewish Feast of Tabernacles at the kingdom Jerusalem (Zech. 14:16-21), but surely there would be no such worship in the heavenly city. Furthermore, those who don't worship properly will be punished, something we can't begin to imagine happening in the heavenly city. During the Kingdom Age, Jesus will reign in Jerusalem from David's throne (Luke 1:32-33), but the throne in the heavenly city is "the throne of God and of the Lamb" (Rev. 22:3). The heavenly city is "the bride, the Lamb's wife" (Rev. 21:9), while the nucleus of the millennial Jerusalem is the refined Jewish remnant, "the wife of Jehovah" who is now cleansed and restored.

8. Unger, 265–66.

9. Zechariah 14:21 is another evidence that the temple and the priesthood will be important elements of life in the Kingdom Age.

MALACHI

OUTLINE[1]

Key theme: Honoring the name of God by living godly lives
Key verse: Malachi 1:11

I. DOUBTING GOD'S LOVE. 1:1-5
1. God's electing grace. 1:2
2. God's blessing on Israel. 1:3-5

II. DISHONORING GOD'S NAME. 1:6-2:9
1. Offering defiled sacrifices. 1:6-14
2. Despising divine privileges. 2:1-9

III. PROFANING GOD'S COVENANT. 2:10-16
1. Marrying heathen women. 2:10-12
2. Hypocritical repentance. 2:13
3. Divorcing their wives. 2:14-16

IV. QUESTIONING GOD'S JUSTICE. 2:17-3:6
1. Where are promised blessings? 2:17
2. The first messenger—John the Baptist. 3:1a
3. The second messenger—Messiah. 3:1b-6

V. ROBBING GOD'S HOUSE. 3:7-12
1. Robbing God. 3:7-8
2. Robbing themselves. 3:9-11
3. Robbing others. 3:12

VI. DESPISING GOD'S SERVICE. 3:13-4:6
1. The complainers. 3:13-15
2. The believers. 3:16-18
3. The evildoers. 4:1-3
4. The preachers. 4:4-6

Malachi in His Time[1]

The name Malachi means "My messenger" (3:1). He was the last of the writing prophets but wrote nothing about himself. We have no biblical information about his ancestry, call, or personal life. But the important thing about messengers is the message they bring, not who they are or where they came from.

In 538 B.C., Cyrus issued a decree that the Jews exiled in Babylon could return to their land and rebuild their temple (2 Chron. 36:22-23; Ezra 1). About 50,000 of them accepted the challenge, and in 515, after much delay, they completed the temple. Ezra visited them in 458, and in 445 Nehemiah became their governor and served for twelve years (Neh. 5:14).

While Nehemiah was back at his post in Shushan (Neh. 13:6-7), things began to fall apart in Jerusalem; and when he returned, he had to take some drastic steps to reform the nation. It's possible that the Prophet Malachi was called at that time to expose the sins of the people and call them back to God.

The conditions described in the Book of Nehemiah are the very things Malachi deals with in his book: poor crops and a faltering economy (Mal. 3:11), intermarriage with the heathen (2:11), defilement of the priesthood (1:6ff), oppression of the poor (3:5), lack of support for the temple (vv. 8-10), and a general disdain of religion (v. 13ff). It was a low time spiritually for Judah, and they needed to hear the Word of God.

Malachi was the last prophet Judah heard until John the Baptist came and the prophecy of 3:1 was fulfilled. His messages against "the sins of the saints" need to be heeded today.

THE SINS OF GOD'S PEOPLE: PART 1
MALACHI 1:1–2:16

A church member scolded her pastor for preaching a series of sermons on "The Sins of the Saints."

"After all," she argued, "the sins of Christians are different from the sins of other people."

"Yes," agreed her pastor, "they're worse."

They are worse, for when believers sin, they not only break the Law of God, but they break the heart of God. When a believer deliberately sins, it isn't just the disobedience of a servant to a master, or the rebellion of a subject against a king; it's the offense of a child against the loving Father. The sins we cherish and thing we get away with bring grief to the heart of God.

Malachi was called to perform a difficult and dangerous task. It was his responsibility to rebuke the people for the sins they were committing against God and against one another, and to call them to return to the Lord. Malachi took a wise approach: he anticipated the objections of the people and met them head-on. "This is what God says," declared the prophet, "but you say __" and then he would answer their complaints. The Old Testament prophets were often the only people in the community who had a grip on reality and saw things as they actually were, and that's what made them so unpopular. "Prophets were twice stoned," said Christopher Morley, paraphrasing Matthew 22:29-31, "first in anger, then, after their death, with a handsome slab in the graveyard."

In this chapter, we'll study what Malachi wrote concerning three of their sins, and then we'll consider the remaining three in the next chapter. But don't read Malachi as ancient history. Unfortunately, these sins are with us in the church today.

1. Doubting God's Love (Mal. 1:1-5)

Like Nahum (1:1) and Habakkuk (1:1), Malachi called his message a "burden." The prophets were men who personally felt "the burden of the Lord" as God gave them insight into the hearts of the people and the problems of society. It wasn't easy for Malachi to strip the veneer off the piety of the priests and expose their hypocrisy, or to repeat to the people the complaints they were secretly voicing against the Lord, but that's what God called him to do. "The task of a prophet," writes Eugene Peterson, "is not to smooth things over but to make things right."[1]

The first sin Malachi named was the people's lack of love for God. That was the first sin Jesus mentioned when He wrote to the seven churches of Asia Minor (Rev. 2:4), and perhaps it's listed first because lack of love for God is the source of all other sin. For centuries, the Jews have recited "The Shema"[2] as their daily prayer: "Hear, O Israel: The Lord our God, the Lord is one! You shall love the Lord your God with all your heart, with all your soul, and with all your might" (Deut. 6:4-5, NKJV). But the people Malachi preached to doubted that God even loved them, so why should they love Him?

The prophet presented several evidences of God's love for Israel, the first of which is God's clear statement of His love (Mal. 1:2a). Malachi was probably referring to what the Lord said through Moses in the Book of Deuteronomy, particularly 7:6-11. When God gave the Law at Sinai, the emphasis was, "Obey My Law because I am a holy God." But when Moses reviewed the Law for the new generation, the emphasis was, "Obey the Lord because He loves you and you love Him." Both motives are valid today.

The second evidence of God's love that Malachi presented was God's electing grace (Mal. 2b-3). As the firstborn in the family, Esau should have inherited both the blessing and the birthright, but the Lord gave them to his younger brother Jacob (Gen. 25:21-23).[3] The descendants of Esau had their land assigned to them, but God gave the Edomites no covenants of blessing as He did to Jacob's descendants.

The statement that God loved Jacob but hated Esau has troubled some people. Paul quoted it in Romans 9:10-13 to prove God's electing grace for both Israel and all who trust Jesus Christ for salvation. But the verb "hate" must not be defined as a positive expression of the wrath of God. God's love for Jacob was so great that, in comparison, His actions toward Esau looked like hatred. As an illustration, Jacob loved Rachel so much that his relationship to Leah seemed like hatred (Gen. 29:20, 30-31; see also Deut. 21:15-17). When Jesus called His disciples to "hate" their own family (Luke 14:26), He was using the word "hate" in a similar way. Our love for Christ may occasionally move us to do things that appear like hatred to those whom we love (see Matt. 12:46-50).

Someone said to Dr. Arno C. Gaebelein, the gifted Hebrew Christian leader of a generation ago, "I have a serious problem with Malachi 1:3, where God says, 'Esau I have hated.'" Dr. Gaebelein replied, "I have a greater problem with Malachi 1:2, where God says, 'Jacob, I have loved.'" We certainly can't explain the love and grace of God, nor do we have to, but we can experience God's grace and love as trust Christ and walk with Him. The Lord is even willing to be "the God of Jacob."

Malachi's third evidence for God's love is God's evident blessing on the people of Israel (v. 4). Like other nations in that area, Edom suffered during the Babylonian invasion of Israel, but the Lord didn't promise to restore their land as He promised the Jews. The proud Edomites boasted that they would quickly have their land in good shape, but God had other plans. He called Edom "The Wicked Land" (v. 4, NIV), but Israel He called "the holy land" (Zech. 2:12).[4] Keep in mind that the Edomites were indeed an evil people (see Obad. 8-14) who deserved every judgment God sent their way. To the Jews, the Babylonian invasion was a chastening, but to Edom, it was a judgment.

Think of how God showed His love to the Jewish people. First, He spared the Jews who were in exile in Babylon (see Jer. 29). Then, He moved Cyrus to issue the decree that enabled the Jews to return to Judah and rebuild the temple. He provided the leadership of Joshua the high priest, Zerubbabel, Nehemiah, and Ezra, as well as the prophetic ministry of Haggai, Zechariah, and Malachi. Had His people obeyed the terms of the covenant, the Lord would have blessed them even more. Yes, they were a weak remnant, but the Lord was with them and promised to bless them.

Note that the name God uses in Malachi 1:4 is "Lord of hosts" ("Lord Almighty" in the NIV), that is, "the Lord of the armies," a name used 24 times in Malachi and nearly 300 times in the Old Testament. This is the "military" name of God, for "hosts" comes from a Hebrew word which means "to wage war." The Lord is the Commander of the hosts and heaven: the stars (Isa. 40:26; Gen. 2:1), the angels (Ps. 103:20-21), the armies of Israel (Ex. 12:41), and all who trust in Him (Ps. 46:7, 11).

Finally, Malachi reminded the Jews of the great privilege God gave them to witness to the Gentiles (Mal. 1:5). During the reigns of David and Solomon, God manifested His glory through the nation of Israel so that the Gentiles came from distant lands to see what was happening in Israel. To a lesser degree, this also happened during the times of Josiah and Hezekiah. But the destruction of Jerusalem and the temple gave the Gentiles opportunity to ridicule Israel and laugh at their religion and their God (Pss. 74; 137; Jer. 18:13-17; Lam. 2:15-16).

When God brought His remnant back to the land, He wanted to bless them and once again manifest His glory through them, but they failed to trust Him and obey His law. Though they had been chastened by God and ruined by Babylon, and though they had lost the esteem of the Gentile nations around them, the Jews could have made a new beginning and witnessed to the Gentiles of the grace and mercy of God. Instead, they lapsed into the sins that Malachi attacks in his book, and they gave but a weak witness to the other nations. They missed their opportunity to glorify God.

But we need to remind ourselves that the trials we experience as individuals or congregations are also opportunities to glorify God before a watching world. That's how Paul viewed his imprisonment and possible death in Rome (Phil. 1:12-26), and that's the way we must look at the testings God sends our way. Every difficulty is an opportunity to demonstrate to others what the Lord can do for those who put their trust in Him.

2. Dishonoring God's Name (Mal. 1:6–2:9)

Now Malachi directs his message especially to the priests (1:6; 2:1, 7-8), who, instead of living exemplary lives, were guilty of breaking the very Law they were supposed to obey and teach. The way they were serving the Lord was a disgrace to His name.

Eight times in this section you find the phrase "My name" (1:6, 11, 14; 2:2, 5; see also 3:16 and 4:2), referring, of course, to God's character and reputation. The priests who were supposed to honor God's name were disgracing it before the people and the Lord. The priests were supposed to be God's children, yet they weren't honoring their Father; they were called to be God's servants, yet they showed no respect for their Master. When Malachi confronted them, the priests arrogantly asked, "In what way have we despised Your name?" (1:6, NKJV), so he told them.

To begin with, they were offering defiled sacrifices on the altar (vv. 6-14). The word "bread" means "food" and refers to the sacrifices provided in the Law of Moses (Lev. 1-7). These animals had to be perfect; nothing imperfect could be brought to the altar of God and accepted (Deut. 15:19-23; Lev. 22:17-33). After all, these sacrifices pointed to the Lamb of God who would one day die for the sins of the world (John 1:29; Heb. 10:1-14), and if they were imperfect, how could they typify the Perfect Sacrifice, the Son of God?

In short, the priests were permitting the people to bring God less than their best. If they had offered these defective beasts to their governor, he would have rejected them, but the animals were good enough for the Lord. These priests had forgotten what was written in their own Law: "Do not bring anything with a defect, because it will not be accepted on your behalf" (Lev. 22:20, NIV). What does this say to professed Christians who spend hundreds of dollars annually, perhaps thousands, on gifts for themselves, their family, and their friends, but give God a dollar a week when the offering plate is passed?

Our offerings to God are an indication of what's in our hearts, for "where your treasure is, there will your heart be also" (Matt. 6:21). People who claim to love the Lord and His work can easily prove it with their checkbooks! Giving is a grace (2 Cor. 8:1, 6-9), and if we've experienced the grace of God, we'll have no problem giving generously to the Lord who has given so much to us. How can we ask God to be gracious to us and answer prayer (Mal. 1:9) if we've not practiced "grace giving" ourselves?

Malachi told these disobedience priests that it would be better to close the doors of the temple and stop the sacrifices altogether than to continue practicing such hypocrisy. Better there were no religion at all than a religion that fails to give God the very best. If our concept of God is so low that we think He's pleased with cheap halfhearted worship, then we don't know the God of the Bible. In fact, a God who encourages us to do less than our best is a God who isn't worthy of worship.

The day will come when the Gentiles will worship God and magnify His great name (v. 11). Malachi looked ahead to the time when the message of salvation would be taken to all nations, and beyond that, he saw the establishing of the kingdom on earth when the Gentiles would "flow into it" (Isa. 2:2; see also 11:3-4, 9; 45:22-25; 49:5-7). God's call to Abraham involved the Jews becoming a blessing to the whole earth (Gen. 12:1-3), just as His call to the church involves taking the Gospel to all nations (Mark 16:15).

The priests even allowed the people to cheat on their vows (Mal. 1:13-14). If a man promised God a sacrifice but brought an animal that was sick or blemished, the priest would accept it, even though the man had a perfect animal back home. In the Mosaic Law, vows were purely voluntary, but once they were made, they were binding (Lev. 27; Num. 30; Deut. 23:21-23). If the governor wouldn't accept cheap offerings (Mal. 1:8), would a great king accept cheap substitutes? (v. 14) God is a great King and He deserves the best we can bring Him. What we promise, we must perform.

Why did the priests deliberately disobey their own law, pollute the altar of the Lord, and encourage the people to worship God in a cheap, careless manner? For one thing, the priests themselves weren't giving God their best, so why make greater demands on the people? "Like people, like priests" (Hosea 4:9; Jer. 5:30-31), for no ministry rises any higher than its leaders.

But there was another reason why blemished sacrifices were acceptable: the priests and their families were fed from the meat off the altar, and the priests wanted to be sure they had food on the table. After all, the economy was bad, taxes were high, and money was scarce, and only the most devoted Israelite would bring a perfect animal to the Lord. So the priests settled for less than the best and encouraged the people to bring whatever was available. A sick animal would die anyway, and crippled animals were useless, so the people might as well give them to the Lord! They forgot that "to obey is better than sacrifice, and to hearken than the fat of rams" (1 Sam. 15:22; Ps. 51:16-17; Micah 6:6-8; Mark 12:28-34).

The priests dishonored God's name in another way: they despised the very privilege of being priests (Mal. 2:1-5). They were taking for granted the high calling God had given them and treating the temple ministry with contempt. Serving at the altar was a job, not a ministry, and they did it to please themselves, not to please and glorify the Lord. Unfortunately, that same attitude is in the church today.

God warned them that He would "curse their [Israel's] blessings" if they didn't start "doing the will of God from the heart" (Eph. 6:6) and giving Him their best. In fact, their crops had already been ruined by devouring insects (Mal. 3:11; see Hag. 1:3-11), but things could get worse. God warned that He could curse the very seed that was planted so that it would never germinate and produce a harvest. Since the Law gave the priests and Levites a tithe of the produce, ruined crops would mean empty tables.

It's possible that the word "seed" in Malachi 2:3 may refer to their children. It was important that the Jews have children in order to perpetuate the nation, but God could prevent even the human seed from being productive. Another way of looking at it is that God would turn their children, who should be a blessing (Ps. 127), into a burden and a curse. It would be painful not to have children, but it would also be painful to have children who daily broke your heart and created grief in the home.

The refuse from the sacrifices was taken outside the camp and burned (Ex. 29:14), but God would humiliate the priests and "wipe their noses" in the dung of the sacrifices! This would make the priests unclean so that they would have to leave the camp. In short, God was saying, "You're treating Me with disrespect, so I'll treat you like garbage! You don't value the priestly ministry, so why should you be in office?"

The priests took their privileges for granted and forgot the gracious covenant God had made with them through Aaron (Mal. 2:4; Ex. 29) and Aaron's grandson Phinehas (Num. 25:1-13). It was a great privilege to be a priest, to serve at the altar, to minister in the temple, and to teach the Law to the people. But the priests had no fear of God; they treated the sacred things as if they were common things because their hearts weren't right with God (Ezek. 44:23). The Scottish novelist George Macdonald said, "Nothing is so deadening to the divine as an habitual dealing with the outside of spiritual things." What the priests were doing wasn't ministry; it was only ritual, empty religious formality that disgusted the Lord.

There was a third sin: they turned away from God's Law (Mal. 2:6-9). Verses 6-7 describe the perfect servants of God: truth on their lips, obedience in their walk, fellowship with God, a burden to bring others to the Lord, and a passion to share God's Word with those who need to hear it. But the priests weren't following this pattern; they were following their own ways. "They shall teach Jacob Your judgments, and Israel Your Law" (Deut. 33:10), but the priests weren't even obeying the Law themselves. "The prophets prophesy falsely, and the priests rule by their own power; and My people love to have it so. But what will you do in the end?" (Jer. 5:31, NKJV)

It was bad enough that the priests were disobeying the Law, but they were causing others to stumble as well (Mal. 2:8). Like the Pharisees Jesus described, the priests were "toxic" and defiled everything and everybody they touched (Matt. 23:15; 25-28). A false minister is an awful weapon in the hands of Satan. "One sinner destroys much good" (Eccl. 9:18, NIV). Because they showed partiality in the way they applied God's truth (Mal. 2:9), they disobeyed God and harmed His people. (See Lev. 19:15; Deut. 24:17; 1 Tim. 5:21.)

Over the years, I've participated in many ordination examinations, and I've looked for four characteristics in each candidate: a personal experience of salvation through faith in Jesus Christ; a sense of calling from the Lord; a love for and knowledge of the Word of God; and a high respect for the work of the ministry. Whenever we've examined a candidate who was flippant about ministry, who saw it as a job and not a divine calling, he didn't get my vote. Whether as a pastor, missionary, teacher, choir member, or usher, being a servant of God is a serious thing, and it deserves the very best that we can give.

God caused these hypocritical priests to be "despised and humiliated before all the people" (Matt. 2:9, NIV). The priests wanted to be popular, and even twisted the Law to gain friends, but the people had no respect for them. Leaders with integrity and character will have their enemies, but they will still gain the respect of the people. The recent religious television scandals in America have proved that unsaved people expect church leaders to practice what they preach.

3. Profaning God's Covenant (Mal. 2:10-16)

Having dealt with the sins of the priests, Malachi now turns to the nation as a whole and confronts the men who divorced their wives to marry pagan women.

Treachery (Mal. 2:10-11, 14). The men loving pagan women wasn't a new problem in the Jewish nation. When the Jews left Egypt, there was a "mixed multitude" that left with them (Ex. 12:38), which suggests that some Jews had married Egyptian spouses (Lev. 24:10; Num. 11:4). The Jews sinned greatly when they mixed with the women of Midian at Baal Peor (Num. 25), and God judged them severely. Ezra (Ezra 9:1-4) and Nehemiah (Neh. 13:23-31) had to contend with this problem, and it's not totally absent from the church today (2 Cor. 6:14-18).

In divorcing their Jewish wives and marrying pagan women, the men were committing several sins. To begin with, it was treachery as they broke their vows to God and to their wives. They were profaning God's covenant and treating it as nothing. Not only had the Lord given specific requirements for marriage in His Law (Ex. 34:11-16; Deut. 7:3-4), but the covenant of marriage was built into creation. "Have we not all one father?" (Mal. 2:10) refers to God as the Father of all humans, the Creator (Acts. 17:28). God made man and women for each other and established marriage for the good of the human family. So, what these men did was contrary to what God had written into nature and in His covenant.

Hypocrisy (Mal. 2:12-13). After committing these sins, the men then brought offerings to the Lord and wept at the altar (vv. 12-13), seeking His help and blessing. Perhaps they had the idea that they could sin blatantly with the intention of coming to God for forgiveness. But if they were truly repentant, they would have forsaken their heathen wives and taken their true wives back, which is what Ezra made them do (Ezra 9-10). These men were guilty of hypocritical worship that had nothing to do with a changed heart. Instead of forgiving them, God was ready to "cut them off."

In matters of ethics and morals, there are many things in society that are legal but are not biblical. Brides and grooms must remember that God is an unseen witness at every wedding (Mal. 2:14), and He also witnesses those who live together who aren't married. One day there will come a terrible harvest from the seeds being planted today by those who despise God's laws and the principles He has built into nature.

Purity (Mal. 2:15). In the entire Book of Malachi, this is recognized as the most difficult verse to translate and interpret. I think the best translation is given by Dr. Gleason Archer: "But no one has done so who has a residue of the Spirit. And what does that one seek for? A godly offspring! Therefore take heed to your spirit [as a true believer under the covenant] and let none of you deal faithlessly with the wife of his youth."[5]

Here Malachi commended the faithful husbands who obeyed the Spirit of God and the Word of God. Unlike the men who took pagan wives just to satisfy their sexual hunger, these faithful men wanted to father children who would be a godly seed, devoted Jews, and not idol worshipers. The basic issue was not race, for humans are humans whether they are Jews or Midianites. The basic issue was loyalty to the God of Israel and the maintaining of a godly home.

God called Israel to be the channel for bringing the Messiah into the world, and anything that corrupted that stream would work against His great plan of salvation. God commanded the Jews to be a separate people, not because they were better than any other nation, but because He had a very special task for them to perform. Anything that broke down that wall of separation would play into the hands of the evil one who did all he could to keep the Messiah from being born.

Hostility (Mal. 2:16). "I hate divorce!" (NIV) is about as clear a statement as God can make.[6] Those who want to please God certainly wouldn't want to do anything that God so abhors, but would do everything possible to heal the marriage. God gave Adam one wife, not many, and He declared that the two were one flesh (Gen. 2:21-25). Divorce pulls apart that which God put together, and Jesus warned us not to do that (Matt. 19:6).[7] It's like an act of violence in an area where there ought to be tenderness.

Why does Malachi mention a "garment" and "violence?" In modern Western society, a man puts an engagement ring on a woman's finger to propose marriage, but in ancient Israel, he placed a corner of his garment over her (Ezek. 16:8; Ruth 3:9).[8] If a man divorces his wife, instead of having a garment that symbolized love, he had a garment that symbolized violence. He wrenched apart that which God said is one; by his infidelity, he made the marriage bed a place of violence.

In spite of a difficult text and differing interpretations, the main lessons of this passage are clear. In marriage, a man and a woman become one flesh, and God is a partner in that union. Through marriage, the Lord is seeking a godly seed that will carry on His work on earth. Marriage is a physical union ("one flesh") and can be broken by physical causes: death (Rom. 7:1-3), sexual sin (Matt. 19:9), or desertion (1 Cor. 7:12-16). God's original intent was that one man and one woman be devoted to each other in marriage for one lifetime. Divorce for reasons other than those given in Scripture, even though legal, would grieve the heart of God.

In its "UNIversal Declaration of Human Rights," The United Nations describes the family as "the natural and fundamental unit of society." Historians Will and Ariel Durant call the family "the nucleus of civilization." Strong families begin with strong marriages, a man and a woman who love each other and want to live each for the other and both for the Lord. Anything less than that is less than God's will.

THE SINS OF GOD'S PEOPLE: PART 2

MALACHI 2:17–4:6

As Malachi continued his message, the people continued their resistance to God's truth. They had already argued with him about God's love (1:2), God's name (v. 6), and God's teaching about marriage and divorce (2:14), and now they would argue about three other matters: the justice of God, giving to God, and serving God. People who argue with God rarely receive blessings from God. It's when our mouth is stopped and we submit to His will that we can experience the grace of God (Rom. 3:19).

But Malachi didn't stop preaching; he went on to deal with these "sins of the saints."

1. Questioning God's Justice (Mal. 2:17–3:6)

"You have wearied the Lord with your words," the prophet said; and they replied, "How have we wearied Him?" (2:17, NIV) Of course, God never gets weary in a physical sense because God doesn't have a body (Isa. 40:28), but He does grow weary of some of the things His people say and do. The hypocritical people in Israel wearied God with their iniquities (43:24), and the Jewish remnant in Malachi's day wearied Him with their words.

Their words were cynical and skeptical. "We came back to the land, rebuilt the temple, and restored the worship," they said, "and look at the difficulties we're experiencing! Why isn't God keeping his promise? Where are all the blessings He promised through His prophets?" It was the age-old problem of "Why do the righteous suffer while the wicked prosper?" Job and his friends wrestled with it, and so did Asaph (Ps. 73), Jeremiah (Jer. 12), and Habakkuk.

But these skeptical Jews had forgotten the terms of the covenant and the conditions laid down by the prophets: if the people obeyed God's law, God would bless them with all they needed. But they were divorcing their wives, marrying pagan women, offering defiled sacrifices, robbing God of tithes and offerings, and complaining about having to serve the Lord! For God to bless people like that would mean approving of their sins. The Jews didn't need justice; they needed mercy!

Malachi answered their question "Where is the God of justice?" by speaking about two messengers.

"My messenger"—John the Baptist (Mal. 3:1a). As we've seen, the name Malachi means "my messenger"; and the messenger referred to in this statement we know as John the Baptist. Speaking of John the Baptist, Jesus said, "For this is he of whom it is written, 'Behold, I send My messenger before Your face who will prepare Your way before You'" (Matt. 11:10, NKJV; see Mark 1:2 and Luke 7:27).

While Malachi was the last of the writing prophets, John the Baptist was the last and the greatest of the Old Covenant prophets.[1] To John was given the unique privilege of ministering at the close of the old dispensation and the beginning of the new, and it was John who presented Jesus to Israel (John 1:29-31). Like Jeremiah and Ezekiel, John was born into a priestly family but was called of God to be a prophet. He was also a martyr, for he gave his life in the work God called him to do (Matt. 14:1-12).

The prophet Isaiah had also written about John's ministry (Isa. 40:3-5; Mark 1:3; Luke 3:4-6; John 1:23). The image is that of people preparing a way for the king to come, leveling the roads and removing the obstacles so that the king might enjoy an easy and comfortable trip. John prepared the way for the ministry of Jesus by preaching the Word to the crowds, urging them to repent of their sins, baptizing them, and then introducing them to Jesus.

But how does this answer the question, "Where is God's justice for His people?" When Jesus Christ came and died on the cross, He completely satisfied the justice of God. He paid the penalty for the sins of the world and vindicated the holiness of God. Nobody can ever truthfully say, "God isn't just!" The cross of Christ is proof that the same God who ordained "the law of sin and death" (Gen. 2:15-17; Rom. 6:23; 8:2-4) also "took His own medicine" (to quote Dorothy Sayers) and willingly died for sinners. Because of Calvary, God is both "just and justifier" of all who trust Jesus Christ (3:26).

The messenger of the covenant"—Jesus Christ (Mal. 3:1b-6). The first prophecy refers to our Lord's first coming in grace and mercy, but this prophecy speaks of His second coming in judgment. When He comes, He will prove that God is just by purifying His people and judging rebellious sinners. Jesus Christ is the "Messenger of the Covenant" in that He fulfilled all the demands of the covenant in His life, suffered the penalties in His death, and rose from the dead to usher in a New Covenant of grace (Jer. 31:31-40; Matt. 26:26-30; Heb. 8:6-13). All the covenants in Old Testament history unite in pointing to Jesus Christ and His marvelous work of redemption.

An unannounced coming (Mal. 3:3). Messiah's second coming will be sudden and unexpected, and its purpose will be the judging of sinners and the establishing of His kingdom on earth. "But of that day and hour, no one knows, no, not even the angels of heaven, but My Father only" (Matt. 24:36, NKJV). "For when they say, 'Peace and safety!' then sudden destruction comes upon them, as labor pains upon a pregnant woman" (1 Thes. 5:3).

An unprepared people (Mal. 3:1). The phrase "whom you delight in" suggests that the Jews in Malachi's day were hoping that "the Day of the Lord" would come soon, not realizing what a terrible day it would be for the whole earth. His listeners were like the people in the days of Amos the prophet who had the same false confidence that they were ready for the promised "Day of the Lord." Amos warned them, "Woe to you who long for the Day of the Lord! Why do you long for the Day of the Lord? That day will be darkness, not light" (see Amos 5:18-20).

When the Jewish remnant of that day read the prophets, they saw only the promises of blessing and not the warnings of judgment. They rejoiced in the prophecies of the coming King and His glorious kingdom, but they overlooked the prophecies that described worldwide terror when the wrath of God is poured out on sinners.[2] These Israelites were not unlike some Christians today who talk about the coming of the Lord as though seeing Him will be more like beholding a visiting celebrity and basking in his or her glory. Standing at the judgment seat of Christ will be an awesome experience, even though we know that we have a place reserved for us in heaven.

An unclean nation (Mal. 3:2b-4). Malachi asked, "But who may abide in the day of His coming?" and then described what Messiah would do when he came: He would purify the Jewish nation, especially the priests, and bring swift judgment to the sinners who arrogantly disobeyed His Law.

In the Law of Moses, God provided three ways for people and things to be cleansed and made acceptable to God: water, fire, and blood. There is no mention here of blood because Jesus Christ died for sinners at His first coming. But he would wash the unclean nation like a launderer washes dirty clothes. He would purify the tribe of Levi the way a jeweler purifies precious metal in his furnace. "In that day there shall be a fountain opened to the house of David and to the inhabitants of Jerusalem for sin and for uncleanness" (Zech. 13:1).

Once the nation is cleansed, and the priests are purified, then they can become an acceptable sacrifice to the Lord (Mal. 3:4), and He will be pleased with them. The priests in Malachi's time were offering sacrifices that were unacceptable (1:7-8), and the priests themselves were unacceptable, but in that great day, God's Messenger would make His people "living sacrifices" that would be acceptable to the Lord (Rom. 12:1).

An unsparing judgment (Mal. 3:5). This list of sinners gives us some idea of the kind of practices that were going on in Malachi's time and will be going on in the end times. All of them are contrary to God's Law. Sorcery is forbidden because it means trafficking with demons (Ex. 22:18; Lev. 20:27; Deut. 18:14). The "satanic revival" that's going on today indicates that many people aren't heeding God's warnings as they dabble in witchcraft and other demonic practices. In fact, witchcraft is a legal religion in many places.

"False swearers" describes people who commit perjury by lying while under oath. Perjury violates the third commandment, "Thou shalt not take the name of the Lord thy God in vain" (v. 7), and the ninth commandment, "Thou shalt not bear false witness against thy neighbor" (v. 16). Trust is the "cement" that holds society together, and when that cement crumbles, society falls apart. If we can't trust one another's words and promises, then how can we live and work together safely?

The oppressing of the poor and needy is a sin that the prophets condemned with vehemence, and it needs to be condemned today. God has a special concern for widows and orphans who are exploited and laborers who don't receive their wages (Ex. 22:22-24; Lev. 19:10; Deut. 10:17-19; 24:14-15, 19-32; 27:19; Ps. 68:5; Isa. 1:17, 23: Jer. 7:6; James 5:1-8).

An unchanging God (Mal 3:6). What was the reason for these social abuses? The people who committed them had no fear of the Lord. They thought that God was like themselves, that He would close His eyes to their sins and not judge them for breaking His law. "You thought that I was altogether like you, but I will reprove you" (Ps. 50:21, NKJV).

The Jews should have been grateful that God was unchanging in His nature, His purposes, and His promises, for if He were not, He would have consumed them for their sins. Twice Moses used this truth about God as his argument when he interceded for the nation (Ex. 33:12-23; Num. 14:11-21). The same principle applies to believers today, for 1 John 1:9 states that God is "faithful and just to forgive our sins." God is faithful to His promises and just toward His Son who died for our sins that we might be forgiven. (See also Num. 23:19; Deut. 4:31; and James 1:17.)

Malachi has proved that God is just. Now he discusses the fact that the people are unjust in the way they've robbed God of what rightfully belongs to Him.

2. Robbing God's Storehouse (Mal. 3:7-12)

If "like people, like priest" (Hosea 4:9) applied to the spiritual leaders of the nation, then "like father, like son" (or "like mother, like daughter") applied to everybody else. From the days of the patriarchs until Malachi's time, the nation frequently disobeyed God's Word, and God had to send prophets to call them to repent and return.

When the people heard Malachi call them to return to the Lord, instead of obeying that call, they began to argue with God's servant. They remind me of those people who evade the issue by saying, "Define your terms! What do you mean by 'return'?" But Malachi didn't hesitate to tell them how to start returning to God: "Bring God the tithes and offerings that are rightfully His!" Theirs was the sin of robbery in at least three different areas.

They were robbing God (Mal. 3:7-8). The needs of the priests and Levites were met from the sacrifices and also from the tithes and offerings brought to the temple by the people. The word "tithe" comes from a Hebrew word that means "ten." A tithe is 10 percent of one's grain, fruit, animals, or money (Lev. 27:30-34; Neh. 13:5). There were special storage rooms in the temple for keeping the grain, produce, and money that the people brought to the Lord in obedience to His Law. If people didn't want to carry heavy produce all the way to the temple, they could convert it into cash, but they had to add 20 percent to it just to make sure they weren't making a profit and robbing God (Lev. 27:31).

The annual tithe was given to the Levites (Num. 18:21-24), who in turn gave a tithe of that income to the priests (vv. 25-32). When a worshiper brought his tithe to the temple, he could use part of it to enjoy a special meal with his family and the Levites (Deut. 12:6-7, 17-19). Every third year a tithe was to be brought to the leaders locally to be used for the poor (14:28-29).

Tithing as an act of worship is as old as Abraham, who gave tithes to Melchizedek, acknowledging that Melchizedek was the representative of the Most High God (Gen. 14:20; Heb. 7). Jacob vowed to God that he would tithe (Gen. 28:22), so tithing antedates the Law of Moses. However, tithing was officially incorporated into the Law of Moses as a part of Israel's worship. In bringing the tithes and offerings, the people were not only supporting the ministry of the temple, but they were also giving thanks to God for His bountiful provision for their own needs.

Over the centuries, many of the Jews committed two errors with regard to the tithe: (1) the legalists obeyed the Law so scrupulously that, like the Pharisees, they even tithed the minute garden herbs (Matt. 23:23-24), all the while thinking that their obedience would earn them righteousness before God; (2) the irreligious neglected the tithe and by disobeying God deprived the temple ministry of what it needed to keep going. When Nehemiah returned to Jerusalem, the temple storerooms were empty of produce and many of the priests and Levites had abandoned their service to go back home and work their fields in order to care for their families (Neh. 13:10). The people had vowed to bring their tithes (10:34-39), but they hadn't kept their vow.

Since God made and owns everything, He doesn't need anything that we can bring Him (Acts 17:25). But when we obey His Word and bring our gifts as an act of worship with grateful hearts, it pleases him. While 1 Corinthians 16:1-2 suggests proportionate giving ("as God has prospered him"),[3] there is no express command to tithe given to the church in the New Testament. Paul teaches "grace giving" in 2 Corinthians 8–9, which is certainly beyond 10 percent. Many Christians feel that if believers under the Old Covenant brought their tithes, how could Christians under the New Covenant begin with anything less?

They were robbing themselves (Mal. 3:9-11). In robbing God, the people were not fulfilling the covenant they had made with the Lord; therefore, God couldn't fulfill His promise and bless them (Lev. 26:3ff). "The Lord will command the blessing on you in your storehouses and in all to which you set your hand, and He will bless you in the land" (Deut. 28:8). Insects had invaded the land ("the devourer," Mal. 3:11) and the grain and fruit were not maturing.

Whenever we rob God, we always rob ourselves. To begin with, we rob ourselves of the spiritual blessings that always accompany obedience and faithful giving (2 Cor. 9:6-15). But even more, the money that rightfully belongs to God that we keep for ourselves never stays with us. It ends up going to the doctor, the auto body shop, or the tax collector. "You have sown much, and bring in little . . . and he who earns wages, earns wages to put into a bag with holes" (Hag. 1:6, NKJV). If we don't trust God to care for us, whatever we do trust will prove futile. People who lovingly give tithes and offerings to God find that whatever is left over goes much farther and brings much greater blessing.

Yes, giving is an act of faith, but God rewards that faith in every way. That isn't the reason we give, because that kind of motivation would be selfish. "If you give because it pays, it won't pay!" said industrialist R.G. LeTourneau, and he was right. We give because we love God and want to obey Him, and because He's very generous to us. When we lay up treasures in heaven, they pay rich dividends for all eternity.

The promise in Malachi 3:10 was linked to the covenant the Israelites had made with the Lord (Deut. 28:1-14), so if they faithfully obeyed Him, He would faithfully keep His promises. But the spiritual principle behind this promise is echoed in Luke 6:38 and 2 Corinthians 9:6-8, so believers today can lay hold of it. For some Christians in America, a tithe would be much too small an amount, but each believer must be fully persuaded in his or her heart what the Lord wants him or her to do.[4]

They were robbing others (Mal. 3:12). The remnant that returned to Judah after the exile had a great opportunity to trust God and bear witness to the other nations that their God was the true and living God. Had the Jews trusted the Lord, He would have done great things for them and they would have been a testimony to others. As it was, they floundered in their faith and nobody could look at them and call them blessed.

God's promise was, "The Lord will establish you as a holy people to Himself, just as He has sworn to you, if you keep the commandments of the Lord your God and walk in

His ways. Then all the peoples of the earth shall see that you are called by the name of the Lord, and they shall be afraid of you" (Deut. 28:9-10). The Gentiles would have come to Jerusalem to learn about this great and wonderful God who could take a group of refugees and turn them into a blessed nation.

3. Despising God's Service (Mal. 3:13–4:6)

This is the sixth and last of Malachi's accusations: "'You have said harsh things against Me,' says the Lord" (3:13, NIV). As he closes his book, he points out four different groups of people and what they said and did.

The complainers (Mal. 3:13-15). These people were guilty of saying "harsh things" against the Lord. For one thing, they felt that serving the Lord was drudgery; it was "futile" to be His servants. The priests may have been the leaders in this complaining, but the common people were just as guilty. "We're not getting anything out of it!" was their grievance. "Things just keep getting worse."

I hear this complaint from some believers about their churches. "We're not getting anything out of it!" But a church is like a bank or a home: you don't get anything out of it unless you put something into it. We serve God because it's the right thing to do, not because we're rewarded for our service. (We shall be rewarded, but that's not our main motive.)

But they had a second complaint: the pagan peoples around them who didn't know the Lord were in better shape than the people of Judah! The wicked were prospering while the godly were suffering. Of course, it would have been difficult for the Jews to prove that they were "godly," because they were guilty of disobeying the Lord. God would have blessed them if they had yielded themselves to Him, but they preferred to have their own way and then complain about what didn't happen.

It's a serious thing to serve the Lord, and we're commanded to "serve the Lord with gladness" (Ps. 100:2). It's a sad thing when a servant of God is a drudge, merely doing a job because that's what he or she has to do or for what they get out of it. Philippians 2:1-12 is God's portrait of Christ, God's ideal Servant, and His example is the one that we should follow.

The believers (Mal. 3:16-18). There was a group of true believers in this remnant, and they remained faithful to the Lord. They feared the Lord, which means they held Him in awe and worshiped Him as the Lord Almighty. They met together, not to complain but to encourage and edify each other. They spoke about the Lord and they weren't afraid for Him to hear what they were saying!

Their assembly probably wasn't a large one, and they may have thought that very little was happening because they met and worshiped, but God was paying attention and keeping a record of their words. Their neighbors may have laughed at them, but God was pleased with them. They weren't wasting their time because they were investing in eternity.

God claimed them as His own, and God promised to spare them in the future judgment when everybody would see that there is a difference between the righteous and the wicked and that this difference is important.

One of the sins of the priests was that they failed to make the distinction between the way of holiness and the way of sin. To them, one sacrifice was just as good as another, yet they were supposed to teach the people "the difference between the holy and the common, and cause them to discern between the unclean and the clean" (Ezek. 44:23).

Many of God's faithful servants become discouraged because the times are difficult, the crowds are small, and their work seems to be unappreciated. People who aren't really walking with the Lord seem to be getting more attention than are the faithful servants. But the day will come when God will reveal "His jewels" ("treasured possession," NIV; see Ex. 19:5; Deut. 7:6), and then the faithful will receive their reward. Every discouraged servant of God needs to read and ponder 1 Corinthians 4:1-5.

The evildoers (Mal. 4:1-3). Once again, Malachi returns to the theme of the coming Day of the Lord when God will punish all evildoers. Sinners will be burned up the way fire eats up the stubble; they will become like ashes under the feet of the saints! But the true believers will see the dawning of a new day as the "Sun of righteousness" rises (Luke 1:78-79). Then Jesus will reign as King of Kings and His people will frolic like calves let out of their stalls!

The preachers (Mal. 4:4-6). Malachi has been faithful as God's messenger, and he closes his book by reminding the people of two other faithful prophets, Moses and Elijah. The Law of Moses was still God's rule of life for the Jews, and if they obeyed, God would bless them. Of course, believers today aren't under the Law (Rom. 6:15; Gal. 5:1-4), but they still practice the righteousness of the Law through the power of the indwelling Spirit of God (Rom. 8:1-4).

The promise in Malachi 4:5 was often discussed and debated by the Jewish rabbis who asked, "Who is the Elijah whom the Lord will send?" The Jewish leaders interrogated John the Baptist about it (John 1:19-21) and Peter, James, and John asked Jesus about it (Matt. 17:10).

The prophet Elijah is mentioned at least thirty times in the New Testament, and ten of those references relate him to John the Baptist. But John the Baptist said plainly that he was no Elijah (John 1:21, 25). He did come in the "spirit and power" of Elijah and turn the hearts of fathers and children (Luke 1:16-17). Like Elijah, John was a courageous man, a man of prayer empowered by the Spirit, a man who lived alone in the wilderness, and a servant who turned many people back to the Lord, but he was not Elijah returned to earth.

However, for those who believed on Christ during His earthly ministry, John the Baptist performed the work of Elijah in their lives: he prepared them to meet the Lord. "And if you are willing to accept it, he is the Elijah who was to come" (Matt. 11:14, NIV). "Elijah is come already," said Jesus, "and they know him not." The disciples understood Jesus to mean John the Baptist who came in the spirit and power of Elijah (17:10-13).

But Malachi 4:5 promises that Elijah himself will come, and that his coming is related to the "Day of the Lord" that will burn the wicked like stubble (v. 1). That's why Jesus said, "Elijah truly shall first come, and restore all things" (Matt. 17:11). Many students believe that Elijah is one of the two witnesses whose ministries are described in Revelation 11:3-12. (They believe the other is Moses.) It's worth noting that both Moses and Elijah appeared with Jesus on the Mount of Transfiguration (Matt. 17:3), which explains why the three apostles asked about Elijah.

Inasmuch as "the great and terrible Day of the Lord" did not occur in New Testament times, we have to believe that John the Baptist was not the promised Elijah, even though he ministered like Elijah. Therefore, this prophecy is yet to be fulfilled. It may well be that Elijah will return to earth as one of the two witnesses (Rev. 11:3-12), for the signs that these two men will perform remind us of the miracles of Elijah. After the ministry of the witnesses, the Lord will pour out His wrath upon the earth (v. 18; 16:1ff) and the Day of the Lord will burst upon the world in its fury.

It seems odd that the Old Testament Scriptures should end with the word "curse." When we get near the end of the New Testament, we read, "And there shall be no more curse" (Rev. 22:3). All of creation is eagerly awaiting the return of the Savior, expecting Him to deliver creation from the bondage of sin (Rom. 8:18-23). We too should be expecting Him and, while we're waiting, witness of Him to others. For when the Sun of righteousness arises, it will mean either burning or blessing (Mal. 4:1-2): blessing to those who have trusted Him, burning to those who have rejected Him.

Nobody can afford to argue with God the way the Israelites did when they heard Malachi, because God will always have the last word.

For you, will that last word be salvation or judgment?

Endnotes

Outline of the Book of Malachi

1. Note that the Book of Malachi is written as a dialogue between God and the people: God accuses and they answer to defend themselves. See 1:2, 6-7, 12-13; 2:14, 17; 3:7-8, 13-14. Note also Malachi's emphasis on the name of God (1:6, 11, 14; 2:2, 5; 3:16; 4:2) and his reminder that God wants His name to be known by the Gentiles (1:11; 3:12).

Part 1

1. Eugene Peterson, *Run with the Horses* (Downers Grove, Ill: InterVarsity Press, 1983), 69.

2. The word shema is Hebrew for "hear," the first word in the prayer.

3. In His sovereign grace, God often rearranged the birth order of children. Abel was older than Seth, but God chose Seth (Gen. 4:25-26). Ishmael was Abraham's firstborn son, but God bypassed him for Isaac (17:15-22). Manasseh was Joseph's firstborn, but God gave the blessing to Ephraim (48:13-22). This may be a reminder to us that in our first birth we are undone and without blessing, but because of the new birth, the second birth, we are "blessed with all spiritual blessings" in Christ (Eph. 1:3).

4. Zechariah 2:12 is the only place in Scripture where Palestine is called "the holy land." Malachi 3:12 calls it "a delightful land" (NIV); and it is also called a "beautiful land" (Dan. 11:41, NIV; "glorious"), "the

Lord's land" (Hosea 9:3), and "the pleasant land" (Zech. 7:14).

5. For a full discussion of the verse, see *The Encyclopedia of Bible Difficulties* by Gleason L. Archer (Grand Rapids: Zondervan Publishing, 1982), 305-6.

6. Some people are surprised that a God of love could hate anything, but see Proverbs 6:16-19, as well as Psalms 5:5 and 11:5; Amos 5:21; Zechariah 8:17; and Revelation 2:6 and 15. "You who love the Lord, hate evil!" (Ps. 97:10) and see 139:21-22.

7. If God hates divorce, then why did He allow it? God permitted the Jews to divorce their wives if the wives were given a certificate that protected their reputation so they could be married again. However, they could not return to their first husband (Deut. 24:1-4). Jesus made it clear that the permission of divorce was a concession and not a commandment (Matt. 19:1-12), but God, the Author of marriage, can do it. Good and godly people disagree on the interpretation and application of the New Testament teachings concerning divorce and remarriage, and few if any are consistent in the way they handle the matter. It would appear that sexual sin would be grounds for divorce, and so would desertion (1 Cor. 7:12-16).

8. Deuteronomy 22:30 reads literally, "A man should not marry his father's wife; he must not uncover the corner of his father's garment."

Part 2

1. Keep in mind that the Old Covenant was not ended by the birth of Jesus in the manger but by the death of Jesus on the cross. John's ministry took place at the close of the old dispensation, so strictly speaking, he was an Old Testament prophet.

2. Some of the old editions of the Bible made this same mistake in their chapter headings. If the chapter was about blessing, the caption read "God's blessing on the church," but if it was about judgment the heading said, "God's judgment on the Jews." Yet the Bible tells us that "judgment must begin at the house of God" (1 Peter 4:17).

3. The offering mentioned in 1 Corinthians 16:1-3 was not a regular weekly offering received at a meeting of God's people. It was a special "relief offering" Paul was receiving from the Gentile believers to give aid to the Jewish Christians in Jerusalem.

4. Multitudes of people have testified to the blessing of regular systematic proportionate giving. However, we must remember that even after we've given generously to the Lord, what remains is still His, for we are stewards of everything He gives us. Giving a tithe doesn't mean we have the right to use the remaining 90 percent for ourselves.